T0181705

Lecture Notes in Computer Science   **11730**

More information about this series at http://www.springer.com/series/7407

Igor V. Tetko · Věra Kůrková ·
Pavel Karpov · Fabian Theis (Eds.)

Artificial Neural Networks and Machine Learning – ICANN 2019

Text and Time Series

28th International Conference on Artificial Neural Networks
Munich, Germany, September 17–19, 2019
Proceedings, Part IV

 Springer

Editors
Igor V. Tetko 🆔
Helmholtz Zentrum München - Deutsches
Forschungszentrum für Gesundheit
und Umwelt (GmbH)
Neuherberg, Germany

Pavel Karpov 🆔
Helmholtz Zentrum München - Deutsches
Forschungszentrum für Gesundheit
und Umwelt (GmbH)
Neuherberg, Germany

Věra Kůrková 🆔
Institute of Computer Science
Czech Academy of Sciences
Prague 8, Czech Republic

Fabian Theis 🆔
Helmholtz Zentrum München - Deutsches
Forschungszentrum für Gesundheit
und Umwelt (GmbH)
Neuherberg, Germany

ISSN 0302-9743   ISSN 1611-3349   (electronic)
Lecture Notes in Computer Science
ISBN 978-3-030-30489-8   ISBN 978-3-030-30490-4   (eBook)
https://doi.org/10.1007/978-3-030-30490-4

LNCS Sublibrary: SL1 – Theoretical Computer Science and General Issues

This Springer imprint is published by the registered company Springer Nature Switzerland AG
The registered company address is: Gewerbestrasse 11, 6330 Cham, Switzerland

Preface

The fast development of machine learning methods is influencing all aspects of our life and reaching new horizons of what we have previously considered being Artificial Intelligence (AI). Examples include autonomous car driving, virtual assistants, automated customer support, clinical decision support, healthcare data analytics, financial forecast, and smart devices in the home, to name a few, which contribute to the dramatic improvement in the quality of our lives. These developments, however, also bring risks for significant hazards, which were not imaginable previously, e.g., falsification of voice, videos, or even manipulation of people's opinions during elections. Many such developments become possible due to the appearance of large volumes of data ("Big Data"). These proceedings include the theory and applications of algorithms behind these developments, many of which were inspired by the functioning of the brain.

The International Conference on Artificial Neural Networks (ICANN) is the annual flagship conference of the European Neural Network Society (ENNS). The 28th International Conference on Artificial Neural Networks (ICANN 2019) was co-organized with the final conference of the Marie Skłodowska-Curie Innovative Training Network European Industrial Doctorate "Big Data in Chemistry" (http://bigchem.eu) project coordinated by Helmholtz Zentrum München (GmbH) to promote the use of machine learning in Chemistry. The conference featured the main tracks "Brain-Inspired Computing" and "Machine Learning Research." Within the conference the First International Workshop on Reservoir Computing as well as five special sessions were organized, namely:

Artificial Intelligence in Medicine
Informed and Explainable Methods for Machine Learning
Deep Learning in Image Reconstruction
Machine Learning with Graphs: Algorithms and Applications
BIGCHEM: Big Data and AI in chemistry

A Challenge for Automatic Dog Age Estimation (DogAge) also took place as part of the conference. The conference covered all main research fields dealing with neural networks. ICANN 2019 was held during September 17–19, 2019, at Klinikum rechts der Isar der Technische Universität München, Munich, Germany.

Following a long-standing tradition, the proceedings of the conference were published as Springer volumes belonging to the *Lecture Notes in Computer Science* series. The conference had a historical record of 494 article submissions. The papers went through a two-step peer-review process by at least two and in majority of cases by three or four independent referees. In total, 503 Program Committee (PC) members and reviewers participated in this process. The majority of PC members had Doctoral degrees (88%) and 52% of them were also Professors. These reviewers were assigned 46 articles. The others were PhD students in the last years of their studies, who reviewed one to two articles each. In total, for the 323 accepted articles, 975 and 985 reports were submitted for the first and the second revision sessions. Thus, on average, each accepted article received 6.1 reports. A list of reviewers/PC Members, who agreed to publish their names, are included in these proceedings.

Based on the reviewers' comments, 202 articles were accepted and more than 100 articles were rejected after the first review. The remaining articles received an undecided status. The authors of the accepted articles as well as of those with undecided status were requested to address the reviewers' comments within two weeks. On the basis of second reviewers' feedback, another 121 articles were accepted and the authors were requested to include reviewers' remarks into the final upload. Based on these evaluations, diversity of topics, as well as recommendations of reviewers, special session organizers, and PC Chairs, 120 articles were selected for oral presentations. Out of the total number of 323 accepted articles (65% of initially submitted), 46 manuscripts were short articles with a length of five pages each, while the others were full articles with an average length of 13 pages.

The accepted papers of the 28th ICANN conference were published as five volumes:

Volume I Theoretical Neural Computation
Volume II Deep Learning
Volume III Image Processing
Volume IV Text and Time series analysis
Volume V Workshop and Special Sessions

The authors of accepted articles came from 50 different countries. While the majority of the articles were from academic researchers, the conference also attracted contributions from manifold industries including automobile (Volkswagen, BMW, Honda, Toyota), multinational conglomerates (Hitachi, Mitsubishi), electronics (Philips), electrical systems (Thales), mobile (Samsung, Huawei, Nokia, Orange), software (Microsoft), multinational (Amazon) and global travel technology (Expedia), information (IBM), large (AstraZeneca, Boehringer Ingelheim) and medium (Idorsia Pharmaceuticals Ltd.) pharma companies, fragrance and flavor (Firmenich), architectural (Shimizu), weather forecast (Beijing Giant Weather Co.), robotics (UBTECH Robotics Corp., SoftBank Robotics Group Corp.), contract research organization (Lead Discovery Center GmbH), private credit bureau (Schufa), as well as multiple startups. This wide involvement of companies reflects the increasing use of artificial neural networks by the industry. Five keynote speakers were invited to give lectures on the timely aspects of intelligent robot design (gentle robots), nonlinear dynamical analysis of brain activity, deep learning in biology and biomedicine, explainable AI, artificial curiosity, and meta-learning machines.

These proceedings provide a comprehensive and up-to-date coverage of the dynamically developing field of Artificial Neural Networks. They are of major interest both for theoreticians as well as for applied scientists who are looking for new innovative approaches to solve their practical problems. We sincerely thank the Program and Steering Committee and the reviewers for their invaluable work.

September 2019   Igor V. Tetko
                                                 Fabian Theis
                                                 Pavel Karpov
                                                 Věra Kůrková

Organization

General Chairs

Igor V. Tetko   Helmholtz Zentrum München (GmbH), Germany
Fabian Theis   Helmholtz Zentrum München (GmbH), Germany

Honorary Chair

Věra Kůrková   Czech Academy of Sciences, Czech Republic
  (ENNS President)

Publication Chair

Pavel Karpov   Helmholtz Zentrum München (GmbH), Germany

Local Organizing Committee Chairs

Monica Campillos   Helmholtz Zentrum München (GmbH), Germany
Alessandra Lintas   University of Lausanne, Switzerland

Communication Chair

Paolo Masulli   Technical University of Denmark, Denmark

Steering Committee

Erkki Oja   Aalto University, Finland
Wlodzislaw Duch   Nicolaus Copernicus University, Poland
Alessandro Villa   University of Lausanne, Switzerland
Cesare Alippi   Politecnico di Milano, Italy, and Università della
     Svizzera italiana, Switzerland
Jérémie Cabessa   Université Paris 2 Panthéon-Assas, France
Maxim Fedorov   Skoltech, Russia
Barbara Hammer   Bielefeld University, Germany
Lazaros Iliadis   Democritus University of Thrace, Greece
Petia Koprinkova-Hristova   Bulgarian Academy of Sciences, Bulgaria
Antonis Papaleonidas   Democritus University of Thrace, Greece
Jaakko Peltonen   University of Tampere, Finland
Antonio Javier Pons Rivero   Universitat Politècnica de Catalunya, Spain
Yifat Prut   The Hebrew University Jerusalem, Israel
Paul F. M. J. Verschure   Catalan Institute of Advanced Studies, Spain
Francisco Zamora-Martínez   Veridas Digital Authentication Solutions SL, Spain

Program Committee

Nesreen Ahmed	Intel Labs, USA
Narges Ahmidi	Helmholtz Zentrum München (GmbH), Germany
Tetiana Aksenova	Commissariat à l'énergie atomique et aux énergies alternatives, France
Elie Aljalbout	Technical University Munich, Germany
Piotr Antonik	CentraleSupélec, France
Juan Manuel Moreno-Arostegui	Universitat Politècnica de Catalunya, Spain
Michael Aupetit	Qatar Computing Research Institute, Qatar
Cristian Axenie	Huawei German Research Center Munich, Germany
Davide Bacciu	University of Pisa, Italy
Noa Barbiro	Booking.com, Israel
Igor Baskin	Moscow State University, Russia
Christian Bauckhage	Fraunhofer IAIS, Germany
Costas Bekas	IBM Research, Switzerland
Barry Bentley	The Open University, UK
Daniel Berrar	Tokyo Institute of Technology, Japan
Soma Bhattacharya	Expedia, USA
Monica Bianchini	Università degli Studi di Siena, Italy
François Blayo	NeoInstinct, Switzerland
Sander Bohte	Centrum Wiskunde & Informatica, The Netherlands
András P. Borosy	QualySense AG, Switzerland
Giosuè Lo Bosco	Universita' di Palermo, Italy
Farah Bouakrif	University of Jijel, Algeria
Larbi Boubchir	University Paris 8, France
Maria Paula Brito	University of Porto, Portugal
Evgeny Burnaev	Skoltech, Russia
Mikhail Burtsev	Moscow Institute of Physics and Technology, Russia
Jérémie Cabessa	Université Panthéon Assas (Paris II), France
Francisco de Assis Tenório de Carvalho	Universidade Federal de Pernambuco, Brazil
Wolfgang Graf zu Castell-Ruedenhausen	Helmholtz Zentrum München (GmbH), Germany
Stephan Chalup	University of Newcastle, Australia
Hongming Chen	AstraZeneca, Sweden
Artem Cherkasov	University of British Columbia, Canada
Sylvain Chevallier	Université de Versailles, France
Vladimir Chupakhin	Janssen Pharmaceutical Companies, USA
Djork-Arné Clevert	Bayer, Germany
Paulo Cortez	University of Minho, Portugal
Gennady Cymbalyuk	Georgia State University, USA
Maximilien Danisch	Pierre and Marie Curie University, France
Tirtharaj Dash	Birla Institute of Technology and Science Pilani, India
Tyler Derr	Michigan State University, USA

Sergey Dolenko	Moscow State University, Russia
Shirin Dora	University of Amsterdam, The Netherlands
Werner Dubitzky	Helmholtz Zentrum München (GmbH), Germany
Wlodzislaw Duch	Nicolaus Copernicus University, Poland
Ujjal Kr Dutta	Indian Institute of Technology Madras, India
Mohamed El-Sharkawy	Purdue School of Engineering and Technology, USA
Mohamed Elati	Université de Lille, France
Reda Elbasiony	Tanta University, Egypt
Mark Embrechts	Rensselaer Polytechnic Institute, USA
Sebastian Engelke	University of Geneva, Switzerland
Ola Engkvist	AstraZeneca, Sweden
Manfred Eppe	University of Hamburg, Germany
Peter Erdi	Kalamazoo College, USA
Peter Ertl	Novartis Institutes for BioMedical Research, Switzerland
Igor Farkaš	Comenius University in Bratislava, Slovakia
Maxim Fedorov	Skoltech, Russia
Maurizio Fiasché	F-engineering Consulting, Italy
Marco Frasca	University of Milan, Italy
Benoît Frénay	Université de Namur, Belgium
Claudio Gallicchio	Università di Pisa, Italy
Udayan Ganguly	Indian Institute of Technology at Bombay, India
Tiantian Gao	Stony Brook University, USA
Juantomás García	Sngular, Spain
José García-Rodríguez	University of Alicante, Spain
Erol Gelenbe	Institute of Theoretical and Applied Informatics, Poland
Petia Georgieva	University of Aveiro, Portugal
Sajjad Gharaghani	University of Tehran, Iran
Evgin Goceri	Akdeniz University, Turkey
Alexander Gorban	University of Leicester, UK
Marco Gori	Università degli Studi di Siena, Italy
Denise Gorse	University College London, UK
Lyudmila Grigoryeva	University of Konstanz, Germany
Xiaodong Gu	Fudan University, China
Michael Guckert	Technische Hochschule Mittelhessen, Germany
Benjamin Guedj	Inria, France, and UCL, UK
Tatiana Valentine Guy	Institute of Information Theory and Automation, Czech Republic
Fabian Hadiji	Goedle.io, Germany
Abir Hadriche	University of Sfax, Tunisia
Barbara Hammer	Bielefeld University, Germany
Stefan Haufe	ERC Research Group Leader at Charité, Germany
Dominik Heider	Philipps-University of Marburg, Germany
Matthias Heinig	Helmholtz Zentrum München (GmbH), Germany
Christoph Henkelmann	DIVISIO GmbH, Germany

Jean Benoit Héroux   IBM Research, Japan
Christian Hidber   bSquare AG, Switzerland
Martin Holeňa   Institute of Computer Science, Czech Republic
Adrian Horzyk   AGH University of Science and Technology, Poland
Jian Hou   Bohai University, China
Lynn Houthuys   Thomas More, Belgium
Brian Hyland   University of Otago, New Zealand
Nicolangelo Iannella   University of Oslo, Norway
Lazaros Iliadis   Democritus University of Thrace, Greece
Francesco Iorio   Wellcome Trust Sanger Institute, UK
Olexandr Isayev   University of North Carolina at Chapel Hill, USA
Keiichi Ito   Helmholtz Zentrum München (GmbH), Germany
Nils Jansen   Radboud University Nijmegen, The Netherlands
Noman Javed   Université d'Orléans, France
Wenbin Jiang   Huazhong University of Science and Technology,
                            China
Jan Kalina   Institute of Computer Science, Czech Republic
Argyris Kalogeratos   Université Paris-Saclay, France
Michael Kamp   Fraunhofer IAIS, Germany
Dmitry Karlov   Skoltech, Russia
Pavel Karpov   Helmholtz Zentrum München (GmbH), Germany
John Kelleher   Technological University Dublin, Ireland
Adil Mehmood Khan   Innopolis, Russia
Rainer Kiko   GEOMAR Helmholtz-Zentrum für Ozeanforschung,
                            Germany
Christina Klüver   Universität Duisburg-Essen, Germany
Taisuke Kobayashi   Nara Institute of Science and Technology, Japan
Ekaterina Komendantskaya   University of Dundee, UK
Petia Koprinkova-Hristova   Bulgarian Academy of Sciences, Bulgaria
Irena Koprinska   University of Sydney, Australia
Constantine Kotropoulos   Aristotle University of Thessaloniki, Greece
Ilias Kotsireas   Wilfrid Laurier University, Canada
Athanasios Koutras   University of Peloponnese, Greece
Piotr Kowalski   AGH University of Science and Technology, Poland
Valentin Kozlov   Karlsruher Institut für Technologie, Germany
Dean J. Krusienski   Virginia Commonwealth University, USA
Adam Krzyzak   Concordia University, Canada
Hanna Kujawska   University of Bergen, Norway
Věra Kůrková   Institute of Computer Science, Czech Republic
Sumit Kushwaha   Kamla Nehru Institute of Technology, India
Anna Ladi   Fraunhofer IAIS, Germany
Ward Van Laer   Ixor, Belgium
Oliver Lange   Google Inc., USA
Jiyi Li   University of Yamanashi, Japan
Lei Li   Beijing University of Posts and Telecommunications,
                            China

Spiros Likothanassis	University of Patras, Greece
Christian Limberg	Universität Bielefeld, Germany
Alessandra Lintas	University of Lausanne, Switzerland
Viktor Liviniuk	MIT, USA, and Skoltech, Russia
Doina Logofatu	Frankfurt University of Applied Sciences, Germany
Vincenzo Lomonaco	Università di Bologna, Italy
Sock Ching Low	Institute for Bioengineering of Catalonia, Spain
Abhijit Mahalunkar	Technological University Dublin, Ireland
Mufti Mahmud	Nottingham Trent University, UK
Alexander Makarenko	National Technical University of Ukraine - Kiev Polytechnic Institute, Ukraine
Kleanthis Malialis	University of Cyprus, Cyprus
Fragkiskos Malliaros	University of Paris-Saclay, France
Gilles Marcou	University of Strasbourg, France
Urszula Markowska-Kaczmar	Wroclaw University of Technology, Poland
Carsten Marr	Helmholtz Zentrum München (GmbH), Germany
Giuseppe Marra	University of Firenze, Italy
Paolo Masulli	Technical University of Denmark, Denmark
Siamak Mehrkanoon	Maastricht University, The Netherlands
Stefano Melacci	Università degli Studi di Siena, Italy
Michael Menden	Helmholtz Zentrum München (GmbH), Germany
Sebastian Mika	Comtravo, Germany
Nikolaos Mitianoudis	Democritus University of Thrace, Greece
Valeri Mladenov	Technical University of Sofia, Bulgaria
Hebatallah Mohamed	Università degli Studi Roma, Italy
Figlu Mohanty	International Institute of Information Technology at Bhubaneswar, India
Francesco Carlo Morabito	University of Reggio Calabria, Italy
Jerzy Mościński	Silesian University of Technology, Poland
Henning Müller	University of Applied Sciences Western Switzerland, Switzerland
Maria-Viorela Muntean	University of Alba-Iulia, Romania
Phivos Mylonas	Ionian University, Greece
Shinichi Nakajima	Technische Universität Berlin, Germany
Kohei Nakajima	University of Tokyo, Japan
Chi Nhan Nguyen	Itemis, Germany
Florian Nigsch	Novartis Institutes for BioMedical Research, Switzerland
Giannis Nikolentzos	École Polytechnique, France
Ikuko Nishikawa	Ritsumeikan University, Japan
Harri Niska	University of Eastern Finland
Hasna Njah	ISIM-Sfax, Tunisia
Dimitri Nowicki	Institute of Cybernetics of NASU, Ukraine
Alessandro Di Nuovo	Sheffield Hallam University, UK
Stefan Oehmcke	University of Copenhagen, Denmark

Erkki Oja	Aalto University, Finland
Luca Oneto	Università di Pisa, Italy
Silvia Ortin	Institute of Neurosciences (IN) Alicante, Spain
Ivan Oseledets	Skoltech, Russia
Dmitry Osolodkin	Chumakov FSC R&D IBP RAS, Russia
Sebastian Otte	University of Tübingen, Germany
Latifa Oukhellou	The French Institute of Science and Technology for Transport, France
Vladimir Palyulin	Moscow State University, Russia
George Panagopoulos	École Polytechnique, France
Massimo Panella	Università degli Studi di Roma La Sapienza, Italy
Antonis Papaleonidas	Democritus University of Thrace, Greece
Evangelos Papalexakis	University of California Riverside, USA
Daniel Paurat	Fraunhofer IAIS, Germany
Jaakko Peltonen	Tampere University, Finland
Tingying Peng	Technische Universität München, Germany
Alberto Guillén Perales	Universidad de Granada, Spain
Carlos Garcia Perez	Helmholtz Zentrum München (GmbH), Germany
Isabelle Perseil	INSERM, France
Vincenzo Piuri	University of Milan, Italy
Kathrin Plankensteiner	Fachhochschule Vorarlberg, Austria
Isabella Pozzi	Centrum Wiskunde & Informatica, The Netherlands
Mike Preuss	Leiden University, The Netherlands
Yifat Prut	The Hebrew University of Jerusalem, Israel
Eugene Radchenko	Moscow State University, Russia
Rajkumar Ramamurthy	Fraunhofer IAIS, Germany
Srikanth Ramaswamy	Swiss Federal Institute of Technology (EPFL), Switzerland
Beatriz Remeseiro	Universidad de Oviedo, Spain
Xingzhang Ren	Alibaba Group, China
Jean-Louis Reymond	University of Bern, Switzerland
Cristian Rodriguez Rivero	University of California, USA
Antonio Javier Pons Rivero	Universitat Politècnica de Catalunya, Spain
Andrea Emilio Rizzoli	IDSIA, SUPSI, Switzerland
Florian Röhrbein	Technical University Munich, Germany
Ryan Rossi	PARC - a Xerox Company, USA
Manuel Roveri	Politecnico di Milano, Italy
Vladimir Rybakov	WaveAccess, Russia
Maryam Sabzevari	Aalto University School of Science and Technology, Finland
Julio Saez-Rodriguez	Medizinische Fakultät Heidelberg, Germany
Yulia Sandamirskaya	NEUROTECH: Neuromorphic Computer Technology, Switzerland
Carlo Sansone	University of Naples Federico II, Italy
Sreela Sasi	Gannon University, USA
Burak Satar	Uludag University, Turkey

Axel Sauer	Munich School of Robotics and Machine Intelligence, Germany
Konstantin Savenkov	Intento, Inc., USA
Hanno Scharr	Forschungszentrum Jülich, Germany
Tjeerd olde Scheper	Oxford Brookes University, UK
Rafal Scherer	Czestochowa University of Technology, Poland
Maria Secrier	University College London, UK
Thomas Seidl	Ludwig-Maximilians-Universität München, Germany
Rafet Sifa	Fraunhofer IAIS, Germany
Pekka Siirtola	University of Oulu, Finland
Prashant Singh	Uppsala University, Sweden
Patrick van der Smagt	Volkswagen AG, Germany
Maximilian Soelch	Volkswagen Machine Learning Research Lab, Germany
Miguel Cornelles Soriano	Campus Universitat de les Illes Balears, Spain
Miguel Angelo Abreu Sousa	Institute of Education Science and Technology, Brazil
Michael Stiber	University of Washington Bothell, USA
Alessandro Sperduti	Università degli Studi di Padova, Italy
Ruxandra Stoean	University of Craiova, Romania
Nicola Strisciuglio	University of Groningen, The Netherlands
Irene Sturm	Deutsche Bahn AG, Germany
Jérémie Sublime	ISEP, France
Martin Swain	Aberystwyth University, UK
Zoltan Szabo	Ecole Polytechnique, France
Kazuhiko Takahashi	Doshisha University, Japan
Fabian Theis	Helmholtz Zentrum München (GmbH), Germany
Philippe Thomas	Universite de Lorraine, France
Matteo Tiezzi	University of Siena, Italy
Ruben Tikidji-Hamburyan	Louisiana State University, USA
Yancho Todorov	VTT, Finland
Andrei Tolstikov	Merck Group, Germany
Matthias Treder	Cardiff University, UK
Anton Tsitsulin	Rheinische Friedrich-Wilhelms-Universität Bonn, Germany
Yury Tsoy	Solidware Co. Ltd., South Korea
Antoni Valencia	Independent Consultant, Spain
Carlos Magno Valle	Technical University Munich, Germany
Marley Vellasco	Pontifícia Universidade Católica do Rio de Janeiro, Brazil
Sagar Verma	Université Paris-Saclay, France
Paul Verschure	Institute for Bioengineering of Catalonia, Spain
Varvara Vetrova	University of Canterbury, New Zealand
Ricardo Vigário	University Nova's School of Science and Technology, Portugal
Alessandro Villa	University of Lausanne, Switzerland
Bruno Villoutreix	Molecular informatics for Health, France

Paolo Viviani	Università degli Studi di Torino, Italy
George Vouros	University of Piraeus, Greece
Christian Wallraven	Korea University, South Korea
Tinghuai Wang	Nokia, Finland
Yu Wang	Leibniz Supercomputing Centre (LRZ), Germany
Roseli S. Wedemann	Universidade do Estado do Rio de Janeiro, Brazil
Thomas Wennekers	University of Plymouth, UK
Stefan Wermter	University of Hamburg, Germany
Heiko Wersing	Honda Research Institute and Bielefeld University, Germany
Tadeusz Wieczorek	Silesian University of Technology, Poland
Christoph Windheuser	ThoughtWorks Inc., Germany
Borys Wróbel	Adam Mickiewicz University in Poznan, Poland
Jianhong Wu	York University, Canada
Xia Xiao	University of Connecticut, USA
Takaharu Yaguchi	Kobe University, Japan
Seul-Ki Yeom	Technische Universität Berlin, Germany
Hujun Yin	University of Manchester, UK
Junichiro Yoshimoto	Nara Institute of Science and Technology, Japan
Qiang Yu	Tianjin University, China
Shigang Yue	University of Lincoln, UK
Wlodek Zadrozny	University of North Carolina Charlotte, USA
Danuta Zakrzewska	Technical University of Lodz, Poland
Francisco Zamora-Martínez	Veridas Digital Authentication Solutions SL, Spain
Gerson Zaverucha	Federal University of Rio de Janeiro, Brazil
Junge Zhang	Institute of Automation, China
Zhongnan Zhang	Xiamen University, China
Pengsheng Zheng	Daimler AG, Germany
Samson Zhou	Indiana University, USA
Riccardo Zucca	Institute for Bioengineering of Catalonia, Spain
Dietlind Zühlke	Horn & Company Data Analytics GmbH, Germany

Exclusive Platinum Sponsor for the Automotive Branch

∧RGMAX.ai

VOLKSWAGEN GROUP ML RESEARCH

Keynote Talks

Recurrent Patterns of Brain Activity Associated with Cognitive Tasks and Attractor Dynamics (John Taylor Memorial Lecture)

Alessandro E. P. Villa

NeuroHeuristic Research Group, University of Lausanne,
Quartier UNIL-Chamberonne, 1015 Lausanne, Switzerland
alessandro.villa@unil.ch
http://www.neuroheuristic.org

The simultaneous recording of the time series formed by the sequences of neuronal discharges reveals important features of the dynamics of information processing in the brain. Experimental evidence of firing sequences with a precision of a few milliseconds have been observed in the brain of behaving animals. We review some critical findings showing that this activity is likely to be associated with higher order neural (mental) processes, such as predictive guesses of a coming stimulus in a complex sensorimotor discrimination task, in primates as well as in rats. We discuss some models of evolvable neural networks and their nonlinear deterministic dynamics and how such complex spatiotemporal patterns of firing may emerge. The attractors of such networks correspond precisely to the cycles in the graphs of their corresponding automata, and can thus be computed explicitly and exhaustively. We investigate further the effects of network topology on the dynamical activity of hierarchically organized networks of simulated spiking neurons. We describe how the activation and the biologically-inspired processes of plasticity on the network shape its topology using invariants based on algebro-topological constructions. General features of a brain theory based on these results is presented for discussion.

Unsupervised Learning: Passive and Active

Jürgen Schmidhuber

Co-founder and Chief Scientist, NNAISENSE, Scientific Director,
Swiss AI Lab IDSIA and Professor of AI, USI & SUPSI, Lugano, Switzerland

I'll start with a concept of 1990 that has become popular: unsupervised learning without a teacher through two adversarial neural networks (NNs) that duel in a mini-max game, where one NN minimizes the objective function maximized by the other. The first NN generates data through its output actions while the second NN predicts the data. The second NN minimizes its error, thus becoming a better predictor. But it is a zero sum game: the first NN tries to find actions that maximize the error of the second NN. The system exhibits what I called "artificial curiosity" because the first NN is motivated to invent actions that yield data that the second NN still finds surprising, until the data becomes familiar and eventually boring. A similar adversarial zero sum game was used for another unsupervised method called "predictability minimization," where two NNs fight each other to discover a disentangled code of the incoming data (since 1991), remarkably similar to codes found in biological brains. I'll also discuss passive unsupervised learning through predictive coding of an agent's observation stream (since 1991) to overcome the fundamental deep learning problem through data compression. I'll offer thoughts as to why most current commercial applications don't use unsupervised learning, and whether that will change in the future.

Machine Learning and AI for the Sciences— Towards Understanding

Klaus-Robert Müller

Machine Learning Group, Technical University of Berlin, Germany

In recent years machine learning (ML) and Artificial Intelligence (AI) methods have begun to play a more and more enabling role in the sciences and in industry. In particular, the advent of large and/or complex data corpora has given rise to new technological challenges and possibilities.

The talk will connect two topics (1) explainable AI (XAI) and (2) ML applications in sciences (e.g. Medicine and Quantum Chemistry) for gaining new insight. Specifically I will first introduce XAI methods (such as LRP) that are now readily available and allow for an understanding of the inner workings of nonlinear ML methods ranging from kernel methods to deep learning methods including LSTMs. In particular XAI allows unmasking clever Hans predictors. Then, ML for Quantum Chemistry is discussed, showing that ML methods can lead to highly useful predictors of quantum mechanical properties of molecules (and materials) reaching quantum chemical accuracies both across chemical compound space and in molecular dynamics simulations. Notably, these ML models do not only speed up computation by several orders of magnitude but can give rise to novel chemical insight. Finally, I will analyze morphological and molecular data for cancer diagnosis, also here highly interesting novel insights can be obtained.

Note that while XAI is used for gaining a better understanding in the sciences, the introduced XAI techniques are readily useful in other application domains and industry as well.

Large-Scale Lineage and Latent-Space Learning in Single-Cell Genomic

Fabian Theis

Institute of Computational Biology, Helmholtz Zentrum München (GmbH),
Germany
http://comp.bio

Accurately modeling single cell state changes e.g. during differentiation or in response to perturbations is a central goal of computational biology. Single-cell technologies now give us easy and large-scale access to state observations on the transcriptomic and more recently also epigenomic level, separately for each single cell. In particular they allow resolving potential heterogeneities due to asynchronicity of differentiating or responding cells, and profiles across multiple conditions such as time points and replicates are being generated.

Typical questions asked to such data are how cells develop over time and after perturbation such as disease. The statistical tools to address these questions are techniques from pseudo-temporal ordering and lineage estimation, or more broadly latent space learning. In this talk I will give a short review of such approaches, in particular focusing on recent extensions towards large-scale data integration using single-cell graph mapping or neural networks, and finish with a perspective towards learning perturbations using variational autoencoders.

The Gentle Robot

Sami Haddadin

Technical University of Munich, Germany

Enabling robots for interaction with humans and unknown environments has been one of the primary goals of robotics research over decades. I will outline how human-centered robot design, nonlinear soft-robotics control inspired by human neuromechanics and physics grounded learning algorithms will let robots become a commodity in our near-future society. In particular, compliant and energy-controlled ultra-lightweight systems capable of complex collision handling enable high-performance human assistance over a wide variety of application domains. Together with novel methods for dynamics and skill learning, flexible and easy-to-use robotic power tools and systems can be designed. Recently, our work has led to the first next generation robot Franka Emika that has recently become commercially available. The system is able to safely interact with humans, execute and even learn sensitive manipulation skills, is affordable and designed as a distributed interconnected system.

Contents – Part IV

Text Understanding

Sentiment Classification

Human Reaction Prediction

Judgment Prediction

Text Generation

Sound Processing

Time Series and Forecasting

Clustering

Anomaly Detection of Sequential Data

Text Understanding

An Ensemble Model for Winning a Chinese Machine Reading Comprehension Competition

Jun He[1]([⊠]) [ID], Yongjing Cheng[1], Min Wang[1], Jingyu Xie[2], Wei Xie[1],
Rui Su[1], Shandong Yuan[1], and Yao Cui[3]

[1] College of Information and Communication,
National University of Defense Technology, Wuhan 430010, China
hejun_nudt@nudt.edu.cn
[2] Department of Electrical and Computer Engineering,
Technische Universität München, 80333 Munich, Germany
ge57quq@mytum.de
[3] Bureau of Public Security, Wuhan Police Headquarter, Wuhan 430010, China
94025708@qq.com

Abstract. To facilitate the application of machine reading comprehension, the
28th Research Institute of China Electronics Technology Group Corporation
organized a Chinese machine reading comprehension competition, namely the
LES Cup Challenge, in October 2018. The competition introduces a big dataset
of long articles and improperly labelled data, therefore challenges the state-of-
the-art methods in this area. We proposed an ensemble model of four novel
recurrent neural networks, which ranked on the top 2% over more than 250
teams (97 teams successfully submitted results) mainly from top universities and
AI companies of China, and won the third prize (3000 USD) of the competition.

Keywords: MRC · RNN · BIDAF · VNET · MwAN · Deep learning

1 Introduction

Machine reading comprehension (MRC), which aims to empower machine to answer
questions after reading articles, is an active research direction along the road towards
the goal of building general dialogue agents [16]. Recently, MRC has gained significant popularity in the natural language processing and machine learning communities
[1, 2, 4, 7], and near human performance has been achieved on some datasets
(e.g., SQuAD [11] and MS-MARCO [8]) by the state-of-the-art neural networks.

To facilitate the application of MRC, the 28th Research Institute of China Electronics Technology Group Corporation (CETC) organized a Chinese MRC competition, namely the LES Cup Challenge [5], in October 2018. The competition introduces
a dataset of 50,000 articles and 250,000 pairs of question and answer in Chinese. The
task is to train a model, so that it can predict the answer to a given question based on
information found in a given article. Performance is then evaluated on a hidden test
dataset of 10,000 articles and 50,000 questions using Rouge-L [6] and BLEU [9],
where Rouge-L is the main criterion and BLEU is only used for breaking a tier.

© Springer Nature Switzerland AG 2019
I. V. Tetko et al. (Eds.): ICANN 2019, LNCS 11730, pp. 3–8, 2019.
https://doi.org/10.1007/978-3-030-30490-4_1

The dataset is challenging mainly for two reasons: (1) Most of the articles are very long, and the longest one contains more than 40,000 Chinese words. While the state-of-the-art methods with deep neural networks hardly handle articles longer than 1000 words due to memory reasons. (2) The dataset is improperly labelled. Given an article and a question, a well labelled data should contain both of the answer and its location in the article. While the answer's location is missing in this dataset. We proposed an ensemble model of four novel neural networks, which ranked on the top 2% over more than 250 teams mainly from top universities and AI companies of China, and won the third prize (3000 USD). Our contributions can be summarized as follows:

- Given a long article and a question, we introduce a method of making the article much shorter by removing unrelated paragraphs from the article.
- Given an article, a question, and its answer, we introduce a method of finding the answer's location in the article, with a precision of 98% in the LES Cup dataset.
- We modify the state-of-the-art neural network MwAN [13], to make it memory efficient and suitable for this competition.
- We introduce a novel neural network, namely MwAN+VNET, by combining MwAN and VNET [15].
- We introduce an ensemble model of four novel neural networks, namely BIDAF [12], MwAN, VNET, and MwAN+VNET, for the competition. Our model achieves high accuracy (Rouge-L value of 89.89% and BLEU value of 81.19%).

2   Task Description

In the LES Cup Challenge, a training dataset of 40,000 articles and 200,000 pairs of question and human labelled answer (a simple example in its English translation is shown in Table 1) is given to all teams. After one month's offline training, a hidden test dataset of 10,000 articles and 50,000 questions (without answers) is given, and each team is required to submit their best results during one week's online competition, with a maximum of two submissions every day. Finally, the top ten teams are selected as the winning teams.

Table 1. An example from the LES Cup dataset.

Article	Question	Answer
… On July 25th, a Boeing 730 Jet was crashed over the Black Sea. A government officer claimed that the crash was caused either by a technical failure or an operational error, but not **a terrorist attack**. …	What didn't cause the crash of the Boeing 730 Jet over the Black Sea?	A terrorist attack

This task is not trivial. For example, to answer the question in Table 1, the model must first understand the question; then finds the related two sentences in the long article; finally locates the answer "a terrorist attack" after some logical reasoning.

3   Our Method

In the LES Cup dataset, more than 99% of the answers can be found as exact text spans in the articles. Hence, we choose to use the extraction method [12], as it is shown to work better than the synthesis method [14]. Our method follows the popular neural-network pipeline as in [12], which is shown in Fig. 1. Although all winning teams use similar architecture, we emphasize the difference of our method as follows.

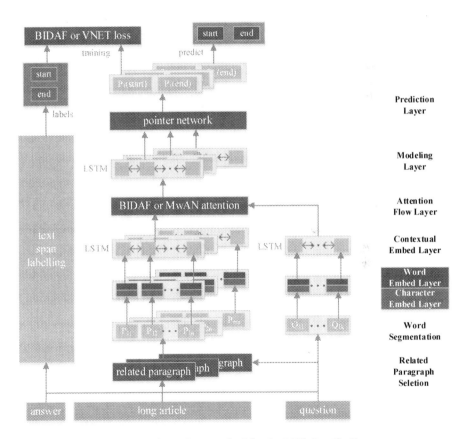

Fig. 1. Overview of our method for the LES Cup Challenge

3.1   Related Paragraph Selection

As argued in previous section, given a long article R and a question Q, we first shrink the article so that it contains at most 800 words by removing unrelated paragraphs. Given a paragraph $P \in R$, we define the related score rel_score(P, Q) as follows:

$$\text{rel\_score}(P, Q) = \sum_{i \in [1, |P|], j \in [1, |Q|]} sim(P_i, Q_j) / |P| \times |Q| \tag{1}$$

where $sim(P_i, Q_j)$ measures the similarity of words P_i and Q_j. We tried two different word similarity, the first (literal similarity) measures whether two words are the same, the second (semantic similarity) uses the cosine similarity of the word2vec embedding of two words, and found the first one has a better accuracy of 7%. Instead of choosing one most related paragraph of 800 words, we found that choosing 5 most related paragraphs with each one of at most 160 words, has a better accuracy of 9%, as the rel_score(P, Q) measurement has some problems with synonym and polyseme.

We also tried to use a neural network to rank the paragraphs, with the paragraphs chosen by rel_score(P, Q) as training label. However, this method is extremely time consuming, and has an accuracy drop of 4%. We guess there are two reasons causing this accuracy drop: first, the rel_score(P, Q) measurement is not perfect as it cannot handle synonym and polyseme properly; second, the neural network that ranks the paragraphs is not trained well.

3.2   Attention Flow Layer

In the attention flow layer, we use either the attention of BIDAF [12] or MwAN [13], as they are effective and efficient. The original MwAN costs too much memory for this task, and we have to use a small batch size of 16 for training, which causes a poor performance. To solve the problem, we use a revised version as in Eq. (3) instead of the Eq. (2) of the original MwAN.

$$h = \sum_{dim=1} \text{expand\_dims}(h, 1) \cdot \text{expand\_dims}(\text{softmax}(A), 2) \tag{2}$$

$$h = \sum_{dim=1} \text{expand\_dims}(h, 1) \cdot \text{expand\_dims}(\text{softmax}(A \times W), 2) \tag{3}$$

Where W is a low-dimension weight matrix to reduce the last dimension of the attention matrix A, symbols $\cdot$ and $\times$ denote dot and matrix multiplication respectively.

3.3   Ensemble Method

We use either the BIDAF [12] or VNET [15] loss function for training. Combing with the two options from the attention flow layer, we have four neural networks, namely BIDAF, VNET, MwAN, and MwAN+VNET (MwAN attention with VNET loss function), and the ensemble model that averages the results of the above four neural networks achieves a better accuracy of 1.5%. Compared with ours, the first prize winner trains their own word embedding using a corpus similar to the task dataset, uses the dynamic word embedding ELMo [10] to handle synonym and the more complicate neural network as in [3], hence gets a result that is 1.3% better than ours. The second prize winner's is 0.2% better than ours, and the last winner's is 2.1% worse than ours.

3.4 Training Data Labelling

In order to train the model, we must label the answer's start and end locations in a given article R. Considering an answer A might be a frequent string in the article R, we iterate all substrings S in the five most related instead of all paragraphs, and use the location of the particular S with maximum match to the answer string as the training label. Using this method, we get a labelling precision of 98%.

4 Conclusion and Future Work

In summary, we have shown an ensemble model that is competitive in a Chinese MRC competition. Future work includes further improving our model as follows: first, using TF-IDF to improve the related paragraph selection; second, our model uses the point network to predicate the start and end positions of the answer string, and uses the mismatch of the start and end positions as the training loss, which not necessarily reflects the error of the predicated answers. Hence, a better loss function is needed.

Acknowledgements. We are grateful to the anonymous referees for their comments that helped to improve the paper.

References

1. Cui, Y., Chen, Z., Wei, S., et al.: Attention-over-attention neural networks for reading comprehension. In: Proceedings of ACL 2017. https://doi.org/10.18653/v1/p17-1055
2. Hermann, K.M., Kocisky, T., Grefenstette, E., et al.: Teaching machines to read and comprehend. In: Proceedings of NIPS 2015. arxiv:1506.03340
3. Hu, M., Peng, Y., Huang, Z., et al.: Reinforced mnemonic reader for machine reading comprehension. In: Proceedings of AAAI 2018. https://doi.org/10.24963/ijcai.2018/570
4. Hu, M., Wei, F., Peng, Y., et al.: Read+verify: machine reading comprehension with unanswerable questions. In: Proceedings of AAAI 2019. arxiv:1808.05759
5. LES Cup Challenge (in Chinese: "莱斯杯"全国第一届"军事智能-机器阅读"挑战赛). http://47.96.153.138
6. Lin, C.Y.: Rouge: a package for automatic evaluation of summaries. In: Text Summarization Branches Out: Proceedings of ACL 2004
7. Min, S., Zhang, V., Socher, R., Xiong, C.: Efficient and robust question answering from minimal context over documents. In: Proceedings of ACL 2018. https://doi.org/10.18653/v1/p18-1160
8. Nguyen, T., Rosenberg, M., Song, X., et al.: MS MARCO: a human generated machine reading comprehension dataset. In: Proceedings of NIPS 2016. arxiv:1611.09268
9. Papineni, K., Roukos, S., Ward, T., Zhu, W.J.: Bleu: a method for automatic evaluation of machine translation. In: Proceedings of ACL 2002. 10.1.1.19.9416

10. Peters, M.E., Neumann, M., Iyyer, M.: Deep contextualized word representations. In: Proceedings of NAACL-HLT 2018. arxiv:1802.05365
11. Rajpurkar, P., Zhang, J., Lopyrev, K., Liang, P.: SQuAD: 100,000+ questions for machine comprehension of text. In: Proceedings of EMNLP 2016. arxiv:1606.05250
12. Seo, M., Kembhavi, A., Farhadi, A., Hajishirzi, H.: Bi-directional attention flow for machine comprehension. In: Proceedings of ICLR 2017. arxiv:1611.01603
13. Tan, C., Wei, F., Wang, W., et al.: Multiway attention networks for modeling sentence pairs. In: Proceedings of IJCAI 2018. https://doi.org/10.24963/ijcai.2018/613
14. Tan, C., Wei, F., Yang, N., et al.: S-Net: from answer extraction to answer generation for machine reading comprehension. In: Proceedings of AAAI 2018. arxiv:1706.04815
15. Wang, Y., Liu, K., Liu, J., et al.: Multi-passage machine reading comprehension with cross-passage answer verification. In: Proceedings of ACL 2018. https://doi.org/10.18653/v1/p18-1178
16. Weston, J., Bordes, A., Chopra, S., Mikolov, T.: Towards AI-complete question answering: a set of prerequisite toy tasks. In: Proceedings of ICLR 2016. arxiv:1052.05698

Dependent Multilevel Interaction Network for Natural Language Inference

Yun Li[1], Yan Yang[1(✉)], Yong Deng[1], Qinmin Vivian Hu[2], Chengcai Chen[3], Liang He[1], and Zhou Yu[4]

[1] East China Normal University, Shanghai, China
{hli,ydeng}@ica.stc.sh.cn, {yanyang,lhe}@cs.ecnu.edu.cn
[2] Ryerson University, Toronto, ON, Canada
vivian@ryerson.ca
[3] Xiaoi Research, Shanghai, China
arienecc@xiaoi.com
[4] University of California, Davis, USA
joyu@ucdavis.edu

Abstract. Neural networks have attracted great attention for natural language inference in recent years. Interactions between the premise and the hypothesis have been proved to be effective in improving the representations. Existing methods mainly focused on a single interaction, while multiple interactions have not been well studied. In this paper, we propose a dependent multilevel interaction (DMI) Network which models multiple interactions between the premise and the hypothesis to boost the performance of natural language inference. In specific, a single-interaction unit (SIU) structure with a novel combining attention mechanism is presented to capture features in an interaction. Then, we cascade a serial of SIUs in a multilevel interaction layer to obtain more comprehensive features. Experiments on two benchmark datasets, namely SciTail and SNLI, show the effectiveness of our proposed model. Our model outperforms the state-of-the-art approaches on the SciTail dataset without using any external resources. For the SNLI dataset, our model also achieves competitive results.

Keywords: Deep learning · Sentence interaction · Attention mechanism

1 Introduction

Natural language inference (NLI) is a challenging natural language processing (NLP) task which requires one to determine whether the logical relationship between two sentences is among *entailment* (the hypothesis must be true if the premise is true), *contradiction* (the hypothesis must be false if the premise is true) and *neutral* (neither entailment nor contradiction). In Table 1, three examples from the SNLI corpus show that the task requires to handle the full

© Springer Nature Switzerland AG 2019
I. V. Tetko et al. (Eds.): ICANN 2019, LNCS 11730, pp. 9–21, 2019.
https://doi.org/10.1007/978-3-030-30490-4_2

complexity of lexical and compositional semantics. Generally, NLI is also related to many other NLP tasks under the paradigm of semantic matching of two sentences, such as question answering [7], information retrieval [11], and so on. An essential challenge is to capture the semantic relevance of the two sentences.

Table 1. Samples from the SNLI dataset

Premise: A land rover is being driven across a river.
Hypothesis: A vehicle is across a river.
Label: entailment

Premise: During calf roping a cowboy calls off his horse.
Hypothesis: A first time roper falls off his horse.
Label: neutral

Premise: An older women tending to a garden.
Hypothesis: The lady is cooking dinner.
Label: contradiction

Recently, deep learning is raising a substantial interest in natural language inference and has achieved some great progress [5,7,14]. To model the complicated semantic relationship between two sentences, previous methods employed various kinds of interactions, such as Attention LSTM [17], Decomposable Att [14], BiMPM [21], etc. However, the above work was based on a single interaction.

In this paper, we propose a new interaction model, named Dependent Multilevel Interaction (DMI) network, which models multiple interactions between a premise and a hypothesis to capture more comprehensive information. In specific, we employ a single-interaction unit (SIU) to model an interaction between the sentences and cascade a serial of SIUs into a multilevel interaction layer. Each SIU utilizes a novel combining attention mechanism. In this mechanism, we map each sentence into different vector spaces to capture information from multiple aspects. Additionally, to reduce information redundancy, parameters between the adjacent SIUs are transferred. Finally, we aggregate all the information extracted from the multilevel interaction layer to make a prediction.

We conduct experiments over two datasets as SciTail and SNLI. On the SciTail dataset, our model achieves 85.5% accuracy on the test set, which is significantly better than the best-published result of 83.3% by Tay et al. [20]. We also provide an in-depth ablation study of our model and visualize the attention distribution to demonstrate that our model can extract more comprehensive features by multilevel interaction.

2   Related Work

The early exploration on NLI mainly relied on conventional methods and small scale datasets [12]. The relatively recent creation of 570K human annotated sentence pairs [1] have spurred on recent work that used neural networks for NLI.

The models trained on the NLI task can be divided into two categories: sentence-encoding method and interaction enhanced method. The sentence-encoding based methods encode sentences into independent sentence representations without any cross-interaction, then use a classifier such as a neural network to decide the relationship [8]. These methods are simple to extract sentence representation and are able to be used for transfer learning to other natural language tasks [4]. The interaction enhanced methods mainly focus on interactions by using attention mechanism to capture the word by word alignment information and achieve an impressive performance. Rocktäschel et al. [17] proposed a neural attention-based model which captured the attention information to predict the result. Wang et al. [21] proposed a bilateral perspective matching (BiMPM) model, which modeled the interaction between a premise and a hypothesis from both directions. Ghaeini et al. [5] proposed dependent reading strategies to model the dependency relationships explicitly during the encoding and inference.

However, to the best of our known, there is little work about multiple interactions. In this paper, we propose a dependent multilevel interaction model to focus on modeling multiple interactions between a premise and a hypothesis.

3   Our Proposed Model

In this section, we introduce the details of our proposed DMI including five layers: (1) word representation; (2) dependent multilevel interaction; (3) level fusion; (4) aggregation; and (5) prediction. The framework of the DMI network is presented in Fig. 1.

Mathematically, we note two sentences $P = (p_1, p_2, ..., p_m)$ with length m and $H = (h_1, h_2, ..., h_n)$ with length n, where P is a premise and H is a hypothesis. The goal is to predict a label y which indicates the logic relationship between P and H.

3.1   Word Representation Layer

This layer aims to represent each word with a d-dimensional vector. To learn feature-rich word representations, we construct the d-dimensional vector with three components: word embedding, character feature, and syntactical features. The word embedding is obtained by mapping the token to the high dimensional vector space by pre-trained word vector. Following KIM [10], we filter character embedding with 1D convolution kernel. The character convolutional feature maps are then max-pooled over time dimension for each token to obtain a vector. The character feature supplies extra information for some out-of-vocabulary

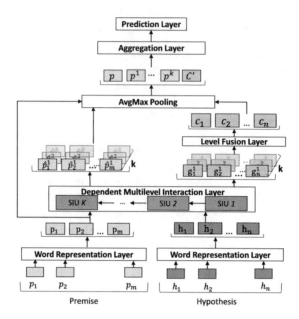

Fig. 1. Dependent multilevel interaction model

(OOV) words. Syntactical features include one-hot part-of-speech (POS) tagging feature and binary exact match (EM) feature. The EM value is activated if there are tokens with the same stem or lemma in the other sentence as the corresponding token. Finally, we sum the character feature with word embedding to get a new word embedding, and then concatenate the new word embedding and syntactical features to obtain a final representation for each word. Now we have the premise representation $\mathbf{P} \in \mathbb{R}^{m \times d}$ and the hypothesis representation $\mathbf{H} \in \mathbb{R}^{n \times d}$.

3.2   Dependent Multilevel Interaction Layer

As shown in Fig. 1, this layer provides multiple interactions by adopting a serial of single-interaction Units and cascading them together to capture comprehensive information.

Single-Interaction Unit. Single-interaction unit provides an interaction between a premise and a hypothesis, which combines the attention mechanism and the comparison module. The structure is shown in Fig. 2.

Combining Attention Mechanism. To better model the interaction between the premise P and the hypothesis H, we design the combining attention mechanism. Differing from the simple attention mechanism, we first map the sentence into different sub-spaces by convolution operations, then combine these spaces by

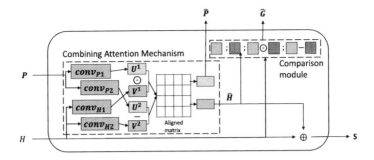

Fig. 2. The structure of single-interaction unit (SIU)

dot product and subtraction to compute the alignment matrix. The combining attention mechanism is defined as follows:

$$U^1, U^2, V^1, V^2 = [conv_{P1}(P), conv_{P2}(P), conv_{H1}(H), conv_{H2}(H)] \quad (1)$$

$$s[i;j] = F([U_i^1 \odot V_j^1; U_i^2 - V_j^2]), \quad i \in [1, m], j \in [1, n] \quad (2)$$

where $S \in \mathbb{R}^{m \times n}, U_i^1, U_i^2$ are the i-th elements in U^1 and U^2, and V_j^1, V_j^2 are the j-th elements in V^1 and V^2.

Then we have the hypothesis-aware representation of premise $\widehat{P}^I$ and premise-aware representation of hypothesis $\widehat{H}^I$ as follows:

$$\widehat{P}_i = \sum_j \frac{exp(s_{ij}^T))}{\sum_k exp(s_{ik}))} H_j \in \mathbb{R}^d, i \in [1, m] \quad (3)$$

$$\widehat{H}_i = \sum_j \frac{exp(s_{ij}))}{\sum_k exp(s_{ik}))} P_j \in \mathbb{R}^d, i \in [1, n] \quad (4)$$

where $\widehat{P}_i$ is the sub-phase in H that is softly aligned to P_i. Intuitively, $\widehat{P}_i$ is the weighted sum across $\{H_j\}_{j=1}^{l_H}$, with the most relevant part of H to represent $\widehat{P}_i$.

Comparison Module. In this module, we make a comparison between the input hypothesis and the interactive result of hypothesis, as an additional feature of the interaction. Specifically, we define this feature G as follows:

$$G = [H; \widehat{H}; H - \widehat{H}; H \odot \widehat{H}] \in \mathbb{R}^{4d} \quad (5)$$

Furthermore, we obtain a new representation of the hypothesis by adding the input H and the interactive result $\widehat{H}$ as follows:

$$S = H + \widehat{H} \quad (6)$$

Totally, we achieve three features from a SIU structure:

$$\widehat{P}, G, S = SIU(P, H) \quad (7)$$

Dependent Multilevel Interaction. Instead of performing a single interaction between a premise and a hypothesis, we find it beneficial to interact multiple times. We define the dependent multilevel interaction as follows:

$$Multilevel(P, H) = [level_1, level_2, ..., level_K] \tag{8}$$

$$where \quad level_i = SIU_i(P, H^i) \tag{9}$$

Levels Dependency. To reduce information redundancy and enhance the dependency between the adjacent interactions, we update the input H^i of SIU_i as follows:

$$H^i = \begin{cases} H & if \quad i = 1 \\ S^{i-1} & if \quad i > 1 \end{cases} \tag{10}$$

where H is the original representation of the hypothesis from the sentence encoder layer, and S^{i-1} is the output of the $level_{i-1}$.

Level Based Feature Collection. Suppose we set the number of levels as K, and we can obtain K hypothesis-aware representation vectors of premises and K cells feature representations. Then we concatenate these vectors as follows:

$$\widehat{P} = [\widehat{P}^1, \widehat{P}^2, ..., \widehat{P}^K] \in \mathbb{R}^{m \times K \times d} \tag{11}$$

$$G = [G^1, G^2, ..., G^K] \in \mathbb{R}^{n \times K \times d} \tag{12}$$

3.3   Level Based Fusion Layer

To extract more concise features from each level, we define a function on G, which contains the level-comparison information from different levels as follows:

$$G' = max(split(F(G))) \tag{13}$$

where $F(\cdot)$ is a standard projection layer with ReLU activation function, $split(\cdot)$ is a function that splits the input vector at the last axis, $max(\cdot)$ is to reduce dimensions of vectors by choosing the max numerical in each axis.

Now we use G' to replace G. Based on G', we use an attention mechanism to get a wide representation C:

$$A = softmax(ReLU(G'W_1)W_2) \in \mathbb{R}^{n \times k} \tag{14}$$

$$C = \sum_k A_{ik}G'_{ik} \tag{15}$$

where $W_1 \in \mathbb{R}^{d \times d}, W_2 \in \mathbb{R}^{d \times 1}, C \in \mathbb{R}^{n \times d}$.

We employ a BiGRU to encode C and then use an avg-max pooling to obtain a fixed vector of level-comparison:

$$C' = [avgPooling(BiGRU(C)); maxPooling(BiGRU(C))] \tag{16}$$

3.4   Aggregation Layer

In dependent multilevel interaction layer, we also get a set of hypothesis-aware representation vectors of premises $\widehat{P}$, we concatenate them with P which is the output of sentence encoder layer, and use an avg-max pooling at first axis to obtain a concise feature:

$$P^{'} = [P; \widehat{P}] \in \mathbb{R}^{m \times (K+1) \times d} \tag{17}$$

$$P^{''} = [avgPooing(P^{'}); maxPooling(P^{'})] \in \mathbb{R}^{(K+1) \times d} \tag{18}$$

To get a comprehensive representation vector of the total information, we concatenate $P^{''}$ with C^f:

$$Z = [P^{''}; C^{'}] \in \mathbb{R}^{(K+2) \times d} \tag{19}$$

Z can be seen as a unified representation of the given sentence pair. A convolution operation with the max pooling layer is employed to generate a fixed vector $Z^{'}$:

$$Z^{'} = maxPooling(Conv(Z)) \tag{20}$$

3.5   Prediction Layer

In order to make a final prediction, we feed $Z^{'}$ into a multi-layer perceptron classifier that includes a hidden layer with the ReLU activation function and a softmax output layer. The model is trained in an end-to-end manner.

$$Output = MLP(Z^{'}) \tag{21}$$

4   Experiments and Evaluation

4.1   Experimental Setup

We use the NLTK[1] to get syntactical features of all sentences in our datasets. We fix our word embeddings with pre-trained 300D GloVe 840B word vectors [15] while the out-of-vocabulary words are zeroed. The character embeddings are randomly initialized with 16D. We crop or pad each token to have 16 characters. We set the output channel size of the convolution operation to be 300 in character features extraction to obtain 300D vectors as character features which can be summed with the word embeddings. Dropout layers are applied for each fully-connected, recurrent or convolutional layer. The mini-batch size is set to 64. We use the Adamax optimizer with an initial learning rate of 5×10^{-4}, and decrease it by 0.5 after every 10 epoch. All the weights are constraint by L2 regularization and the L2 regularization factor is set to 10^{-6}.

---

[1] http://www.nltk.org/.

4.2 Experimental Results

We evaluate our model over the SicTail and SNLI datasets. SciTail is a new dataset which is derived from treating multiple-choice question-answering as an entailment problem. Premises are science questions, and the corresponding answer candidates are from relevant web sentences retrieved from a large corpus. The SNLI corpus has 570k human annotated sentence pairs. The premise data is drawn from the captions of the Flickr30k corpus, and the hypothesis data is manually composed. The labels provided in are "entailment", "neutral", "contradiction" and "-". "-" shows that annotators cannot reach consensus with each other, thus removed during training and testing as in other works. We use the same data split as in Bowman et al. [1].

Table 2. Performance for natural language inference on the SciTail dataset

Model	Dev acc	Test acc
1. Majority class [9]	63.3	60.3
2. Ngram [9]	65.0	70.6
3. ESIM [21]	70.5	70.6
4. Decomposable Att [14]	75.4	72.3
5. DGEM [9]	79.6	77.3
6. CAFE [20]	-	83.3
7. DMI (our model)	89.6	**85.5**

In Table 2, we compare our model with all other published models on the SciTail dataset. Here CAFE [20], the state-of-the-art model, introduced an architecture where alignment pairs were compared/compressed/propagated to the upper layers to enhance the interaction between the premise and the hypothesis. Without committing to complicate single interaction, our model employs multiple simple interactions to extract comprehensive features. The experiment shows that our model achieves the new state-of-the-art performance of 85.5%.

Table 3 reports our results on SNLI: (1) Experiments (2–5) are the sentence encoding based models; and (2) Experiments (6–14) are interaction-enhanced. We can see that KIM and ESIM+ELMO achieve the competitive scores, where KIM incorporates external knowledge to capture semantic features, and ESIM+ELMO integrates a language model into ESIM to enrich word representation. However, we find that the accuracy of ESIM will decrease to 88.0 if we remove the language model from ESIM+ELMO. Without adopting external resources (e.g. external knowledge and language models), our DMI model can still achieve a competitive score of 88.7%, which demonstrates its capability of semantic feature extraction.

5   Ablation and Configuration Study

We conduct ablation studies on the SciTail dataset to evaluate the individual contribution of each major component within our models, which is shown in Table 4. We first explore the utility of the character feature, and we find the score degrades to 88.56 after removing it. In the experiment 3–4, we respectively remove the POS feature and the EM feature. The performances all degrade, which confirms that these features have helped the model to better understand the sentences. After ablating the parameters transfer between interaction levels in experiment 5, we find the result drops about 1% on the accuracy, which demonstrates its importance in boosting performance. In experiment 6–8, we evaluate the effectiveness of the combining attention mechanism. We first remove the dot product, only keep the subtraction, and the accuracy degrades to 88.88%. We also remove the subtraction, only keep the dot product, and the accuracy degrades to 88.50%. The results demonstrate that both the dot product and subtraction are useful in comparing semantic information from different aspects. To further study how combining attention contributes to the model, we use simple dot-product attention to replace our combining attention, and then the performance degrades to 89.03%. In experiment 9, we remove the aggregation layer and the accuracy score drops to 87.65% on the development set. The result demonstrates the aggregation layer has a powerful capability to extract semantic features.

Table 3. Comparisons with the state-of-the-art models on the SNLI test sets.

Model	Dev acc	Test acc
1. Handcrafted features [1]	99.7	78.2
2. TBCNN [13]	83.3	82.1
3. Gated-Att BiLSTM [2]	90.5	85.5
4. DiSAN [18]	91.1	85.6
5. ReSAN [19]	92.6	86.3
6. Attention LSTM [17]	85.3	83.5
7. Decomposable Att [14]	89.5	86.3
8. BiMPM [21]	90.9	87.5
9. DIIN [6]	91.2	88.0
10. DR-BiLSTM [5]	94.1	88.5
11. CAFE [20]	89.8	88.5
12. KIM [3]	94.1	88.6
13. ESIM [16]	92.6	88.0
14. ESIM+ELMo [16]	91.6	**88.7**
15. DMI (our model)	94.7	**88.7**

We also study the influence of the number of interaction levels in our model, Fig. 3 shows the results. We can see that while multilevel interaction performs better than single interaction, performance will also drop off with too many levels.

Visualization analysis. We visualize the contributions of different interaction levels to the wide-perspective representation. The results of the 3 levels are shown in Fig. 4. We can see that in different levels of interaction, the attention distribution in the hypothesis H will change. For example in Fig. 4(a), the first level of interaction pays more attention to the words 'gas' and 'no', and in the second level, the words 'definite', 'volume' and 'shape' begin to get attention. In the third level, attention transfers to some irrelevant words. In this case, we can see that the second level of interaction has extracted useful information, which indeed gets more attention than the other two levels from our model. In example (Fig. 4(b)), the third level of interaction extracts useful features and finally get more attention. Thus we conclude that the multilevel interaction between the sentences is beneficial to extract useful information. In Fig. 5, we analyze the attention distributions within the multilevel interaction. We can see that the

Table 4. Ablation study results on the SciTail development set

Model	Dev acc
1. Full model	89.64
2. w/o character feature	88.56
3. w/o POS feature	89.14
4. w/o EM feature	88.74
5. w/o parameters transfer	88.60
6. w/o dot product in combining attention	88.88
7. w/o subtraction in combining attention	88.50
8. w/o combining attention	89.03
9. w/o aggregation layer	87.65

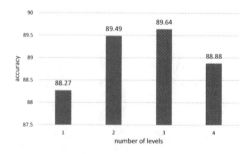

Fig. 3. Performance comparison across different number of interaction levels

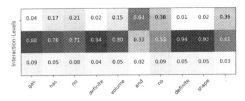

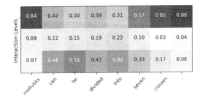

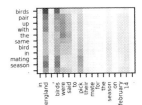

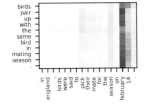

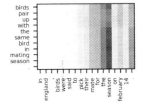

(a) **premise**: department of education gas does not have a definite shape and it does not have a definite volume. **hypothesis**: gas has no definite volume and no definite shape. **label**: entailment

(b) **premise**: divide the class into four teams of six or seven students. **hypothesis**: mollusks can be divided into seven classes. **label**: neutral

Fig. 4. Attention visualization in dependent multilevel interaction

(a) **premise**: in england , birds were said to pick their mate for the season on february 14. **hypothesis**: birds pair up with the same bird in mating season. **label**: neutral

Fig. 5. Attention visualization of combining attention within each interaction level

distribution in each level is different from the others, and each has its unique concerns. This is in line with our expectations to extract different features by multilevel interaction.

6 Conclusion and Future Work

In this work, we propose a dependent multilevel interaction model that provides multiple interactions by cascading a serial of single-interaction units (SIUs). Each SIU includes a novel attention mechanism and comparison module to model the interaction between the premise and the hypothesis. Experiments on two benchmark datasets demonstrate the efficacy of our model. In the future, we hope to improve the scalability of our model and apply it to other NLI tasks, such as machine reading comprehension and answer selection.

Acknowledgement. This research is funded by Xiaoi Research, the Science and Technology Commission of Shanghai Municipality (No. 18511105502) and the Key Teaching Reform Project for Undergraduates in Shanghai Universities.

References

1. Bowman, S.R., Angeli, G.: A large annotated corpus for learning natural language inference. In: EMNLP, pp. 632–642 (2015). https://doi.org/10.18653/v1/D15-1075
2. Chen, Q., Zhu, X.: Recurrent neural network-based sentence encoder with gated attention for natural language inference. In: Proceedings of the 2nd Workshop on Evaluating Vector Space Representations for NLP, RepEval@EMNLP, pp. 36–40 (2017). https://doi.org/10.18653/v1/W17-5307
3. Chen, Q., Zhu, X.: Neural natural language inference models enhanced with external knowledge. In: ACL, pp. 2406–2417 (2018). https://doi.org/10.18653/v1/P18-1224
4. Conneau, A., Kiela, D.: Supervised learning of universal sentence representations from natural language inference data. In: EMNLP, pp. 670–680 (2017). https://doi.org/10.18653/v1/D17-1070
5. Ghaeini, R., Hasan, S.A.: DR-BiLSTM: dependent reading bidirectional LSTM for natural language inference. In: NAACL-HLT, pp. 1460–1469 (2018). https://doi.org/10.18653/v1/N18-1132
6. Gong, Y., Luo, H., Zhang, J.: Natural language inference over interaction space. In: ICLR (2018)
7. Hu, B., Lu, Z.: Convolutional neural network architectures for matching natural language sentences. CoRR (2015)
8. Im, J., Cho, S.: Distance-based self-attention network for natural language inference. CoRR abs/1712.02047 (2017). arXiv:1712.02047v1
9. Khot, T., Sabharwal, A., Clark, P.: SciTail: a textual entailment dataset from science question answering. In: AAAI, pp. 5189–5197 (2018)
10. Kim, Y.: Convolutional neural networks for sentence classification. In: EMNLP, pp. 1746–1751 (2014). https://doi.org/10.3115/v1/D14-1181
11. Liu, X., Gao, J.: Representation learning using multi-task deep neural networks for semantic classification and information retrieval. In: NAACL, pp. 912–921 (2015). https://doi.org/10.3115/v1/N15-1092
12. Marelli, M., Menini, S.: A SICK cure for the evaluation of compositional distributional semantic models. In: LREC, pp. 216–223 (2014)
13. Mou, L., Men, R.: Natural language inference by tree-based convolution and heuristic matching. In: ACL (2016). arXiv:1512.08422v3
14. Parikh, A.P., Täckström, O.: A decomposable attention model for natural language inference. In: EMNLP, pp. 2249–2255 (2016). https://doi.org/10.18653/v1/D16-1244
15. Pennington, J., Socher, R., Manning, C.D.: Glove: global vectors for word representation. In: EMNLP, pp. 1532–1543 (2014). https://doi.org/10.3115/v1/D14-1162
16. Peters, M.E., Neumann, M.: Deep contextualized word representations. In: NAACL-HLT, pp. 2227–2237 (2018). arXiv:1802.05365v2
17. Rocktäschel, T., Grefenstette, E.: Reasoning about entailment with neural attention. In: ICLR (2016). arXiv:1509.06664v4
18. Shen, T., Zhou, T.: DiSAN: directional self-attention network for RNN/CNN-free language understanding. In: AAAI, pp. 5446–5455 (2018). arXiv:1709.04696v1
19. Shen, T., Zhou, T.: Reinforced self-attention network: a hybrid of hard and soft attention for sequence modeling. In: IJCAI, pp. 4345–4352 (2018). arXiv:1801.10296v2

20. Tay, Y., Luu, A.T., Hui, S.C.: Compare, compress and propagate: enhancing neural architectures with alignment factorization for natural language inference. In: EMNLP, pp. 1565–1575 (2018). https://doi.org/10.18653/v1/D18-1185
21. Wang, Z., Hamza, W.: Bilateral multi-perspective matching for natural language sentences. In: IJCAI, pp. 4144–4150 (2017). https://doi.org/10.24963/ijcai.2017/579

Learning to Explain Chinese Slang Words

Chuanrun Yi[1,2], Dong Wang[1,2], Chunyu He[1,2], and Ying Sha[1,2(✉)]

[1] Institute of Information Engineering, Chinese Academy of Sciences, Beijing, China
{yichuanrun,wangdong,hechunyu,shaying}@iie.ac.cn
[2] School of Cyber Security, University of Chinese Academy of Sciences,
Beijing, China

Abstract. The explosive development of social media has generated a
large number of slang words in Chinese social network. The appearance
of Chinese slang words has affected the accuracy of reading comprehension and word segmentation tasks. In this paper, we propose explaining
Chinese slang word automatically for the first time. Unlike matching
words in dictionary, we use a novel neural network called DCEAnn (a
Dual Character-level Encoder using Attention-based neural network) for
this specific task. One encodes slang word and its phonetics to learn
the word representation, the other encodes example sentence containing
slang word to enrich the semantic information of the slang word. Besides,
we propose a public dataset for the first time to deal with the absence
of parallel corpus for training model. Manual evaluation of experimental results shows that our model can generate reasonable explanations.
Furthermore, we find that our model has a better performance on the
network digital language which only contains numbers. To be specific,
we get the state-of-the-art result on Chinese slang words interpretation
whose BLEU score is 23.64, 3.59 higher than our baseline, and the state-
of-the-art result on network digital language interpretation whose BLEU
score is 54.23, 3.18 higher than our baseline.

Keywords: Chinese slang words · Attention · DCEAnn ·
Network digital language

1 Introduction

With the explosive development of social media, more and more Chinese slang
words have appeared. Chinese slang words or neologisms are words with new
forms, new meanings or new usages that are not found in basic vocabulary [1],
which are always generated and applied to the Internet in Chinese. Network
digital language is a special kind of Chinese slang, which uses the pronuncia-
tion of digits to express the meaning. People who don't usually use the Internet
are hard to understand them due to their metaphorical meanings. Besides, the
appearance of Chinese slang words has not only affected the accuracy of machine
reading comprehension task, but also has caused 60% of participle errors in word
segmentation as research shows [2]. Therefore, learning to explain the meaning

© Springer Nature Switzerland AG 2019
I. V. Tetko et al. (Eds.): ICANN 2019, LNCS 11730, pp. 22–33, 2019.
https://doi.org/10.1007/978-3-030-30490-4_3

of Chinese slang words automatically is very meaningful. Here are two examples. Figure 1(a) shows the explanation of Chinese slang word "高富帅 (tall, rich and handsome)" in Weibo. Figure 1(b) shows the explanation of network digital language "886 (phonetics: ba ba liu)" in WeChat.

(a) An example of Chinese slang word in Weibo. We aim at explaining "高富帅 (tall, rich and handsome)" as "形容财富、身材、相貌都比较好的男人 (describe a man who is wealthy, fit and good-looking)" automatically.

(b) An example of network digital language in WeChat record. We aim at explaining "886(phonetics: ba ba liu)" as "拜拜了 (bye bye)" automatically.

Fig. 1. Two examples of the non-standard expressions on Chinese social network.

The most common way to get an explanation of a slang word is to match the word in dictionary. Urban Dictionary is the largest slang dictionary in the world [3]. More than 2K entries are submitted daily to it. But there is no specific dictionary or parallel corpus for the explanation of Chinese slang words. Unlike matching words in dictionary, Ni et al. [4] is the first one to propose a data-driven combined neural network approach for interpretation of English slang. His method can generate plausible explanation for unseen non-standard words and phrases that are not involved in current dictionary. In the meantime, it can save the time and labor cost of maintaining the dictionary to some extent. However, the approach that Ni proposed is not applicable for Chinese slang words for two reasons. On the one hand, word formation is different in Chinese and English. On the other hand, a lot of Chinese slang words are homophones.

In our work, we propose a novel neural network called DCEAnn, which is especially designed for the explanation of Chinese slang words. It contains two character-level encoders. One encodes slang word which splices the phonetics to learn the word representation. The other one encodes example sentence containing slang word to enrich the semantic information of the slang word. Besides, in absence of parallel corpus for training, we manually label a parallel corpus as our dataset. Experimental results show that we get the state-of-the-art results and our model could generate a reasonable explanation for unseen Chinese slang word.

In summary, our main contributions are as follows:

(1) To the best of our knowledge, this is the first attempt to explain Chinese slang words automatically by machine, and use DCEAnn model for this specific task.
(2) Our novel DCEAnn model can generate reasonable explanations for Chinese slang words and get the state-of-the-art results.
(3) We constructs a parallel corpus for the explanation of Chinese slang words (continued growth), which can be applied to later academic research.

In next section, we will introduce the related work of slang words and sequence-to-sequence model. We will give details of our approaches in Sect. 3 and show the experimental results in Sect. 4. Finally, we will discuss the conclusion in Sect. 5.

2   Related Work

Researchers have done a lot of researches on non-standard language. Most of the researches focus on the detection of slang words, and only a small part of the researches focus on giving the definition of English slang. To the best of our knowledge, there is no researches on giving the definition of Chinese slang so far. Sequence-to-Sequence model is always used to solve text generation problems such as explaining slang words.

2.1   Slang Words

Zou et al. [1] gave a general definition of slang words and divided slang words into eight categories based on previous researches, which implies the difficulty of neologisms discovering and explaining in Chinese. Because slang words detection is the basis of slang words interpretation, most researchers are studying the approaches for neologisms discovery. At present, combining the rules with statistical machine learning is the most popular method to discover Chinese slang words [5–7]. Besides, Saha et al. [8] used semi-supervised learning models to detect abusive words in specific fields, which can also detect abbreviations and evaluate the probability that the detected words are slang. At the same time, the semi-supervised learning model is being used to discover new opinion words (slang) from QA communities [9].

As for slang interpretation, Hickman et al. [10] proposed that people must pay attention to the automatic generation of non-standard languages in 2013. Thanapon et al. [11] showed that it is possible to use word embedding to generate an explanation of a word. However, words have different meanings in different contexts. Then, Ni et al. [4] collected a total of 421K slang words and phrases from 1999 to 2014, and proposed a data-driven approach for automatically explaining new, non-standard English expressions in a given sentence. But there is no parallel corpus for Chinese slang words in this dataset, and its method is not applicable for the interpretation of Chinese slang words.

2.2 Sequence-to-Sequence Model

The sequence-to-sequence model was proposed in 2014 by the Google Brain team [12] and Yoshua Bengio et al. [13], who mainly focused on machine translation related issues. However, input information is markedly lost in the model. In order to solve this problem, Bahdanu et al. [14] proposed an attention mechanism based on Encoder and Decoder. The sequence-to-sequence model with attention mechanism has been widely used in various fields of NLP, especially for models incorporating multiple features. For instance, Serban et al. [16] incorporated contextual information with generative hierarchical Neural Network Models to build dialogue systems. And Zhao et al. [17] improved contents classification accuracy with phonetic feature.

In summary, because the Chinese words formation is different from English and many Chinese slang words are homophones, we propose a dual-encoder model which incorporates multiple features to explain Chinese slang words automatically. In addition, we propose a public dataset in the absence of parallel corpus for training model.

3 Our Approach

We define our task as learning to explain Chinese slang words in a given sentence automatically. The input is a sentence containing Chinese slang word, which is used to enrich the semantic information of the slang word. The output is the explanation of the slang word, which is also a sentence.

Our goal is to generate an explanation of Chinese slang word automatically. We select sequence-to-sequence model with attention mechanism as our fundamental framework. Because some words have different meanings in different contexts, we use one character-level BiGRU encoder of example sentence to help machine understand the slang word better. Besides, considering the particularity of Chinese and the fact that many network neologisms are homophones, we use another character-level BiGRU encoder of slang word and its phonetics to learn the representation of neologism. In general, our model is a dual character-level encoder using attention-based neural network, which we call it DCEAnn. An overview of our model is shown in Fig. 2.

3.1 GRU Network

GRU consists of an update gate and a reset gate. The update gate determines how much of the previous information should be passed, and the reset gate determines how much of the previous information should be discarded. At every

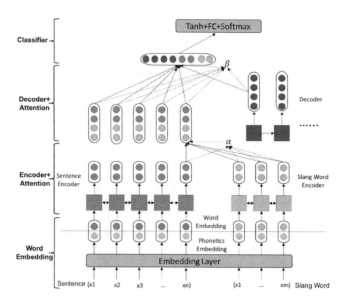

Fig. 2. The overview of our model. Two encoders encode the example sentence and Chinese slang word spliced phonetics respectively. Decoder generates the interpretation which relies on both hidden states of decoder and encoder. α and β indicate the attention sequence.

time step, GRU network will accept the output of the previous moment and the input of the current moment, generating the output of the current moment after passing through the two gate units. The calculation of information flow is as follows:

$$z_t = \sigma(\boldsymbol{W}_z \cdot [\boldsymbol{h}_{t-1}, \boldsymbol{x}_t]) \tag{1}$$

$$r_t = \sigma(\boldsymbol{W}_r \cdot [\boldsymbol{h}_{t-1}, \boldsymbol{x}_t]) \tag{2}$$

$$\widetilde{\boldsymbol{h}}_t = tanh(\boldsymbol{W} \cdot [r_t * \boldsymbol{h}_{t-1}, \boldsymbol{x}_t]) \tag{3}$$

$$\boldsymbol{h}_t = (1 - z_t) * \boldsymbol{h}_{t-1} + z_t * \widetilde{\boldsymbol{h}}_t \tag{4}$$

t is current time, while '·' represents vector multiplication, and '$*$' represents digital multiplication. $\boldsymbol{W}_z$, $\boldsymbol{W}_r$, and $\boldsymbol{W}$ are all weight matrices. σ represents sigmoid function. $\boldsymbol{x}_t$ represents the input, z_t represents update operation, deciding which previous information to pass by using a sigmoid function. r_t indicates reset operation, which will produce the value we wish to abandon from the previous time step. $\boldsymbol{h}_t$ represents the activation, and $\widetilde{\boldsymbol{h}}_t$ is the candidate activation.

In our work, GRU is the basis of the whole model. On the one hand, GRU is used to encode Chinese slang words, example sentences and other input information. On the other hand, GRU is used to decode the encoded information into label vectors.

3.2   DCEAnn Model

The DCEAnn Model includes three components: one is an encoder encodes the example sentence containing Chinese slang word, another is an encoder encodes the slang word with its spliced phonetics, the other is a decoder generates the explanation of Chinese slang word which is depended on the hidden state of encoders.

First, we map the inputs to word embedding vectors and splice the phonetic vector after neologisms vector.

$$\boldsymbol{x}_i^w = Emb(w_i) \quad i\epsilon[1,m] \tag{5}$$

$$\boldsymbol{x}_i^p = Emb(p_i) \quad i\epsilon[1,m] \tag{6}$$

$$\boldsymbol{x}_j^s = Emb(s_j) \quad j\epsilon[1,n] \tag{7}$$

$$\boldsymbol{x}^{wp} = concat[\boldsymbol{x}^w;\boldsymbol{x}^p] \tag{8}$$

m is the length of slang word and n is the length of example sentence. w_i is the i-th character in the slang word, whose vector is $\boldsymbol{x}_i^w$, and then the slang word vector is represented by $\boldsymbol{x}^w$. p_i is the i-th character's phonetics in the slang word, whose vector is $\boldsymbol{x}_i^p$, and then the phonetic vector of slang word is represented by $\boldsymbol{x}^p$. s_j is the j-th character in the example sentence, whose vector is $\boldsymbol{x}_j^s$. $\boldsymbol{x}^{wp}$ represents the slang word vector spliced with phonetic vector.

Second, we use GRU network to encode the sentence and slang word spliced phonetics.

$$[\boldsymbol{h}_1^{wp},\boldsymbol{h}_2^{wp},...,\boldsymbol{h}_i^{wp}] = GRU(\boldsymbol{x}_1^{wp},\boldsymbol{x}_2^{wp},...,\boldsymbol{x}_i^{wp}) \quad i\epsilon[1,l] \tag{9}$$

$$[\boldsymbol{h}_1^s,\boldsymbol{h}_2^s,...,\boldsymbol{h}_j^s] = GRU(\boldsymbol{x}_1^s,\boldsymbol{x}_2^s,...,\boldsymbol{x}_j^s) \quad j\epsilon[1,n] \tag{10}$$

l is the length of slang word with its spliced phonetics. While $\boldsymbol{h}_i^{wp}$ is the hidden state of the i-th slang word spliced phonetic vector, $\boldsymbol{h}_j^s$ is the hidden state of the j-th character.

Third, we calculate the attention of example sentence over every character of concat slang word.

$$att(\boldsymbol{h}_j^s,\boldsymbol{h}_i^{wp}) = \frac{exp(score(\boldsymbol{h}_j^s,\boldsymbol{h}_i^{wp}))}{\sum_i exp(score(\boldsymbol{h}_j^s,\boldsymbol{h}_i^{wp}))} \quad j\epsilon[1,m], i\epsilon[1,l] \tag{11}$$

Where the score calculating method is DOT, the calculation formula is as follows:

$$score(\boldsymbol{h}_j^s,\boldsymbol{h}_i^{wp}) = \boldsymbol{h}_j^s \cdot \boldsymbol{h}_i^{wp} \quad j\epsilon[1,m], i\epsilon[1,l] \tag{12}$$

Next, we calculate the weighted representation of slang words with the attention.

$$att(\boldsymbol{h}_j^s) = \boldsymbol{V}_j^{att} \cdot \boldsymbol{h}^{wp} \quad j\epsilon[1,m] \tag{13}$$

$\boldsymbol{V}_j^{att}$ represents the j-th character in example sentence which made attention over all characters of concat slang word, which is a vector. One of element in that vector can be calculated by (11). $\boldsymbol{h}^{wp}$ is the hidden state of slang word spliced phonetic vector.

Finally, we splice the weighted representation of slang word after the hidden state of example sentence. In this way, we get the final hidden state of each character in example sentence.

$$\widetilde{\boldsymbol{h}}_j^s = concat[\boldsymbol{h}_j^s; \boldsymbol{att}(\boldsymbol{h}_j^s)] \tag{14}$$

So far, this section has displayed a dual character-level attention-based encoder. As for decoder, we calculate the attention over hidden states sequence towards hidden state of decoder, to get the weighted representation of hidden states of encoder, then leverage both of them to predict the output at every time step. The process is similar to work from (10)–(14). At last, the hidden state will connect a Fully Connected layer and Softmax layer.

$$\boldsymbol{o}^t = FC(tanh(\widetilde{\boldsymbol{h}}_t^d)) \tag{15}$$

$$y^t = Softmax(\boldsymbol{o}^t) \tag{16}$$

$\widetilde{\boldsymbol{h}}_t^d$ represents the hidden state of decoder at the time step of t. y^t is the final output at the time step of t, a predicted character.

4   Experiment

We conducted four comparative experiments using our own manually labeled dataset, and we used BLEU scores as evaluation metrics. Because we are the first group to propose the task of Chinese slang words interpretation, we used a separate sequence-to-sequence model as baseline. Our proposed DCEAnn could generate appropriate interpretations of Chinese slang words and get 3.59 higher than the baseline on BLEU scores. We accidentally found that our model could explain the network digital language very well, so we did the interpretation experiment on the network digital language, using the dataset of network digital language alone.

4.1   Dataset

Dataset Construction. Due to the lack of parallel corpus for the explanation of Chinese slang words, we collected a large number of microblog corpus from Weibo through data crawler. In order to find neologisms in the corpus, we used slang words discovery algorithm combined with manual processing for data filtering and data cleaning. We use crowdsourcing to let three people mark the interpretation of the same word. According to the experiment, we choose one of the results in the combination of the two-two, which the BLEU score is higher than 80 and the meaning is accurate, then randomly choose one of the combination as the definition of the word. At last, we collected 2,831 Chinese slang words and 6,519 example sentences, among which 386 are network numbers. As shown in Fig. 3, the structure of each item is: Chinese slang word, example sentence and explanation. For example, network digital language-"520" in an example sentence can be "520, no matter what, I love you.", and the explanation of this slang word is "I love you".

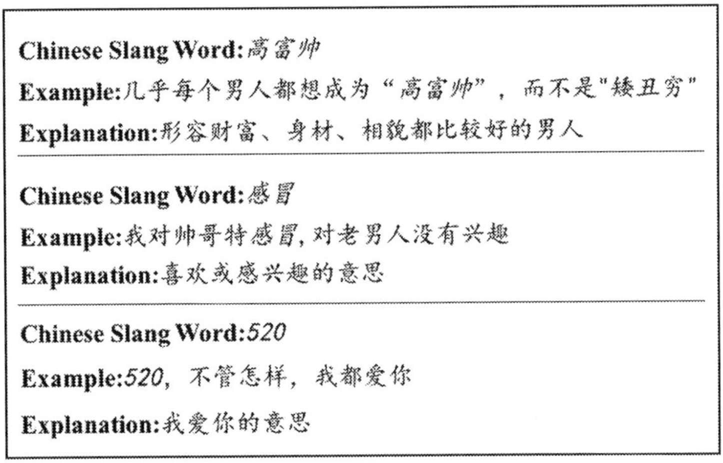

Chinese Slang Word:*高富帅*

Example:*几乎每个男人都想成为"高富帅"，而不是"矮丑穷"*

Explanation:*形容财富、身材、相貌都比较好的男人*

Chinese Slang Word:*感冒*

Example:*我对帅哥特感冒,对老男人没有兴趣*

Explanation:*喜欢或感兴趣的意思*

Chinese Slang Word:*520*

Example:*520, 不管怎样，我都爱你*

Explanation:*我爱你的意思*

Fig. 3. The example of parallel corpus for the explanation of Chinese slang words.

Dataset Settings. The training dataset and test dataset used in our experiments were all from the dataset we collected. The training dataset contains 2,531 Chinese slang words and 5,689 example sentences. The test dataset contains 300 Chinese slang words, which did not exist in the training dataset, and each test example corresponds to each slang word.

4.2 Experimental Settings

Our experiments were based on the pytorch framework. DCEAnn randomly initializes word embeddings, whose hidden size was set to 250, batch size was set to 32, dropout was set to 0.1, learning rate was set to 0.0001, and a total of 20,000 rounds of training iteration was set, which used the gradient descent algorithm to optimize our loss function. We used BLEU scores to evaluate the degree of polymerization, which are widely used in the evaluation for generating problems such as machine translation.

4.3 Experimental Results and Analysis

We conducted four sets of comparison experiments, the experimental results are showed in Table 1. The first set used a single character-level encoder model as baseline on the basic model of sequence-to-sequence with attention. The second set was added phonetic vector on baseline. The third set encoded both example sentence and slang item character. The forth set used the novel model we proposed, that is, a dual character-level encoder attention-based model with phonetic features.

As we can see from the Table 1, our novel dual encoder approach is superior to the other three methods. We could observe that dual-encoder models outperform single-encoder models, because contexts can enrich the semantic information of slang words. The machine can understand the meanings of slangs better due to the example sentences. We also can observe that once we added the phonetic features, our experimental results improved significantly, because that method solved the homophony that exists in Chinese slang words. Figure 4 shows two examples of the results that our models automatically generated. The first example is "死党", whose translation in Baidu and Google is "dead party". But its actual meaning is "good friends", whose reference interpretation in Chinese is "指关系特别好的朋友". The Chinese explanation generated by our dual encoder model is "好的朋友 (good friends)", which is a proper explanation. But the explanation generated by single encoder model is "各种利用或言众事物的人 (refers to people who make use of everything)", which is not an appropriate explanation. This is because without the context, the machine cannot fully understand the meanings of slang words. In the second example, the explanations generated by two models are all correct, except that words generation was different from the reference sentence.

Table 1. BLEU scores for the explanation of Chinese slang words on test dataset.

Seq-to-Seq (with attention)	BLEU-1	BLEU-2
Single character-level encoder	20.05	2.89
Single character-level encoder (phonetics)	22.25	3.13
Dual character-level encoder	21.62	3.12
Dual character-level encoder (phonetics)	**23.64**	**3.65**

In the test datasets, only 1% of the test datasets definitions coincided with the training datasets. According to experimental statistics, in all the interpretations generated by the model, less than 1% of the interpretations are exactly the same as the interpretations of the training datasets, so the generated contents are diverse but can guarantee a certain accuracy. Overall, our dual character-level encoder model could automatically generate reasonable explanations for Chinese slang words, especially when we added the phonetic features in model.

4.4   Network Digital Language Experiments

Network digital language is one kind of Chinese slang, which has special meanings in Chinese. In general, network digits are not the meanings of the digits literally.

Chinese Slang Word:死党

Example:死党是那群即便知道你傻还跟着你犯傻的人

Reference Explanation:指关系特别好的朋友

Generated Explanation(Dual):好的朋友

Generated Explanation(Single):指各种利用或言众事物的人

Chinese Slang Word:脱光计划

Example:我的脱光计划就是新年多赚钱暴富之后再脱单

Reference Explanation:脱离光棍的计划

Generated Explanation(Dual):脱离光棍的意思

Generated Explanation(Single):脱离单身

Fig. 4. Two examples of automatically generated explanations of Chinese slang words based on our experimental models.

For example, "520" usually refers to "我爱你 (I love you)" in Chinese. Since they often appear alone, we only use a single-encoder sequence-to-sequence model to generate the meaning of its allusion. The training dataset contains 300 pairs of parallel corpus of network digits, 86 network digits are used for test dataset, such as "520-我爱你". The results of the two groups of experiments are shown in Table 2. We can observe that the BLEU scores with phonetic features are better than none. This is because the phonetics of each digit in the network digital language is homophonic with some words in Chinese, and a number can represent a few characters similar to its phonetics. For example, "9 (phonetics: jiu)" can represent "就 (phonetics: jiu)", "久 (phonetics: jiu)", "求 (phonetics: qiu)" and so on. Therefore, phonetic features play a important role in our model.

Table 2. BLEU scores for the explanation of network digital language on test dataset.

Seq-to-Seq (with attention)	BLEU-1	BLEU-2
Single character-level encoder	50.05	35.34
Single character-level encoder (phonetics)	**54.23**	**38.17**

We can also observe that the BLEU score of the network digital language interpretation is much higher than other Chinese slang word interpretation. This is because different from the interpretation content of general slang word which is relatively long and unpredictable, the interpretation content of network digital language is relatively short, and the Chinese characters that can be implied by each number are limited.

There are several examples of model-generated explanations shown in Fig. 5. As we can see that the model with phonetic features could generate more reasonable explanations than the other three examples. For instance in Fig. 4, the reference explanation of "1314 (phonetics: yi san yi si)" is "一生一世 (phonetics: yi sheng yi shi)". The explanation generated by added the phonetic features model is exactly the same with the reference, but the explanation generated by single model without phonetic features is "要生一世 (phonetics: yao sheng yi shi)". This shows the importance of the phonetic features. After comparing the experimental results of network digital language with other Chinese slang words, we found that it is easier for machines to understand the meaning of network digital language than other Chinese slang words. From the above we can draw a conclusion that our model can automatically generate a reasonable explanation for the implied meaning of the network digital language, which can benefit machine translation, reading comprehension and social media analysis.

> **Network Digital Language:** *71345*
> **Reference Explanation:** 请你相信我
> **Generated Explanation(None):** 请你相信我
> **Generated Explanation(Pinyin):** 请你相信我
>
> **Network Digital Language:** *995*
> **Reference Explanation:** 救救我
> **Generated Explanation(None):** 救我
> **Generated Explanation(Pinyin):** 救救我
>
> **Network Digital Language:** *1314*
> **Reference Explanation:** 一生一世
> **Generated Explanation(None):** 要生一世
> **Generated Explanation(Pinyin):** 一生一世

Fig. 5. Examples of automatically generated explanations of network digital language based on our experimental models.

5   Conclusion

In this paper, we propose to explain Chinese slang words automatically for the first time. We use a novel dual character-level encoder using attention-based neural network to deal with this specific task. The experimental results show that our novel DCEAnn model can generate reasonable interpretations of Chinese slang words that have not appeared before, and perform better in the interpretation of network digital language. Also we construct a public dataset for training model. Now we are building an end-to-end system working from slang words discovery to slang words interpretation. In our future work, we will put the Chinese slang parallel corpus online and use transfer learning to optimize our model.

References

1. Zou, G., Yang, L., Liu, Q., et al.: Chinese slang word detection for Internet. J. Chin. Inf. Process. (2004). https://doi.org/10.3969/j.issn.1003-0077.2004.06.001
2. Huang, C., Zhao, H.: A review of Chinese word segmentation in the past ten years. J. Chin. Inf. Process. (2007)
3. Urban Homepage. https://www.urbandictionary.com/
4. Ni, K., Wang, W.Y.: Learning to explain non-standard English words and phrases. In: IJCNLP (2017)
5. Powers, D.M., Huang, J.H.: Chinese word segments based on contextual entropy. In: Proceedings of the 17th Asian Pacific Conference on Language, Information and Computation (2003)
6. Chen, F., Liu, Y.Q., Wei, C., et al.: The discovery of new words in open field based on conditional random field method. J. Softw. (2013)
7. Zhang, H.P., Shang, J.Y.: Neologism discovery in the open field of social media. Chin. J. Inf. Technol. (2017)
8. Pal, A.R., Saha, D.: Detection of Slang Words in e-Data using semi-Supervised Learning. IJAIA (2015). https://doi.org/10.5121/ijaia.2013.4504
9. Amiri, H., Chua, T.-S.: Mining slang and urban opinion words and phrases from cQA services: an optimization approach. In: WSDM 2012 Proceedings of the Fifth ACM International Conference on Web Search and Data Mining, pp. 193–202 (2012). https://doi.org/10.1145/2124295.2124319
10. Hickman, L.: Why IBM's Watson supercomputer can't speak slang. The Guardian (2013)
11. Noraset, T., Chen, L., Birnbaum, L., Downey, D.: Definition modeling: learning to define word embeddings in natural language. In: AAAI, pp. 3259–3266 (2016)
12. Cho et al.: Learning phrase representations using RNN encoder-decoder for statistical machine translation. arXiv preprint arXiv:1406.1078 (2014). https://doi.org/10.3115/v1/D14-1179
13. Sutskever, I., Vinyals, O., Le, Q.V.: Sequence to sequence learning with neural networks. In: Advances in Neural Information Processing Systems, pp. 3104–3112 (2014)
14. Bahdanau, D., Cho, K., Bengio, Y.: Neural machine translation by jointly learning to align and translate. arXiv preprint arXiv:1409.0473 (2014)
15. Chen, H., Sun, M., Tu, C., Lin, Y., Liu, Z.: Neural sentiment classification with user and product attention. In: Proceedings of the 2016 Conference on Empirical Methods in Natural Language Processing, EMNLP (2016). https://doi.org/10.18653/v1/D16-1171
16. Serban et al.: Building end-to-end dialogue systems using generative hierarchical neural network models. In: AAAI (2016)
17. Zhao, B.X., Fang, N., et al.: A deep learning model for text classification using phonetic features. Chin. High Technol. Lett. (2017). https://doi.org/10.3772/j.issn.1002-0470.2017.07.002

Attention-Based Improved BLSTM-CNN for Relation Classification

Qifeng Xiao⬤, Ming Gao⬤, Shaochun Wu⁽✉⁾⬤, and Xiaoqi Sun⬤

School of Computer Engineering and Science, Shanghai University,
Shanghai 200444, China
{hurricane,qywtgm950120,scwu,xiaoqisun}@shu.edu.cn

Abstract. Relation Classification as a foundational task with regard to many other natural language processing (NLP) tasks, has caught many attentions in recent years. In this paper, we propose a novel network architecture called Attention-Based Improved Bidirectional Long Short-Term Memory and Convolutional Neural Network (AI-BLSTM-CNN) for this task. To be specific, we take improved BLSTM that makes the utmost of sequential context information and word information in order to obtain temporal features and high-level contextual representation. Besides, attention mechanism is applied to improved BLSTM making it focus on the segments of a sentence related to the relation automatically. Finally, we take advantage of CNN to capture the local important features for relation classification. The experimental results on SemEval-2010 Task 8 and KBP37 benchmark datasets show that AI-BLSTM-CNN achieves better performance than the majority of existing methods.

Keywords: Relation classification · BLSTM-CNN ·
Attention mechanism

1 Introduction

The classification of semantic relation as a hot research topic in recent years has been becoming an essential task in many applications of the field of natural language processing (NLP), such as web searching, information extraction and the construction of knowledge base.

In this work, we focus on the relation between nominal pairs $<e1, e2>$ in the sentence S with the giving candidate relations [5]. For example, "He had chest pains and $<e1>$headaches$</e1>$ from $<e2>$mold$</e2>$ in the bedrooms.", Here, the marked entities "headaches" and "mold" are of the relation "Cause-Effect $(e2, e1)$". In this case, it's crucial for us to focus on the important parts of sentence in semantic relation classification.

Traditional methods based on machine learning (ML) have been applied to relation classification. As we all know, we need many human-designed features [8] or kernels [12] when we make use of machine learning (ML) methods to classify relation. Therefore, these methods lead to the propagation of the errors because

© Springer Nature Switzerland AG 2019
I. V. Tetko et al. (Eds.): ICANN 2019, LNCS 11730, pp. 34–43, 2019.
https://doi.org/10.1007/978-3-030-30490-4_4

of the use of pre-existing Natural Language Processing (NLP) tools. In addition, we need to spend a lot of time and effort on feature engineering.

Recently, neural networks has been applied to Natural Language Processing (NLP) tasks and overcome the problems of handcrafted features, which can acquire the text features automatically and reduce human interventions. Then, some researches also begin to pay attention to feature engineering of neural networks in the field of relation classification [15,18].

In this paper, we proposes a neural network attention-based Improved BLSTM-CNN (AI-BLSTM-CNN) for relation classification. On the one hand, convolutional neural networks (CNNs) is adept at learning local important features from raw data, nevertheless, it is weak in learning sequential information; On the other hand, recurrent neural networks (RNNs) has the capability to extract features from long sequence and can deal with the sequential information better compared with CNNs. So our model combines improved BLSTM and CNNs with attention mechanism for relation classification, which can obtain high-level word representation and the most important information of a sentence. This model doesn't need any features derived from lexical resources or NLP systems except for the information of word itself.

The contribution of this paper is that AI-BLSTM-CNN can not only acquire better words representation and important semantic information but also focus on the words between entities automatically without any extra lexical information. We carried out our experiments on SemEval-2010 Task 8 [5] and KBP37 [1] benchmark datasets. And, we achieved 84.8% and 63.7% F1-score respectively, higher than the most of the existing methods.

The rest of the paper is made up of as follows. We give the statement of related works of relation classification in Sect. 2. In Sect. 3, we expatiate our AI-BLSTM-CNN model for relation classification. Then, we describe details of experiments evaluation and the experimental result in Sect. 4. Finally, in Sect. 5, we give our conclusion.

2   Related Work

Over the years, there are so many methods proposed for relation classification. In the early days, a lot of methods utilize the human-designed features derived from existing NLP tools. The relevant work is presented by [7], which needs many features from external corpora for a Support Vector Machine(SVM) classifier.

In recent years, neural network models [9,13] is applied to relation classification and achieve better performance. Concretely, Zeng et al. utilized convolutional neural networks (CNNs) towards short text for relation classification [17]. Moreover, Zhang and Wang employed recurrent neural networks (RNNs) that achieves better performance towards long text for relation classification [18]. Besides, Xu applied long short term memory networks (LSTM) along shortest dependency paths (SDP) which focuses the words in the SDP for relation classification [16]. What's more, Peng et al. proposed attention-based bidirectional long short-term memory networks which gives weight to each word for relation classification [21]. In addition, Cai et al. came up with Bidirectional Recurrent Convolutional Neural Network which combines BLSTM and pooling of CNNs for relation classification [3]. Furthermore, Lei et al. put forward the BLSTM-CNN which combines the BLSTM and CNNs for relation classification [19].

In this paper, our model is related to BLSTM, CNNs, Recurrent Convolutional Neural Networks (RCNNs) and attention mechanism, achieving better performance than the most of existing methods. Specifically, inspired by RCNNs [10], we take full advantage of improved BLSTM and CNNs to gain the high-level word representation and local important semantic information respectively. On the side, attention mechanism is applied to our model in order to make the model focus on the words between entities.

3   Methodology

In this section we will elaborate AI-BLSTM-CNN model. As you can see in Fig. 1, the proposed model in this paper is made up of six components which will be presented in detail in this section.

(1) Input layer: input sentence with entities pairs to this model;
(2) Embedding layer: map each word and position information into a low dimension vector;
(3) Improved BLSTM layer: utilize Improved BLSTM to get high level features from step (2);
(4) Attention layer: give high weight to words between entities and low weight to words on both sides of entities;
(5) CNN layer: get the uppermost semantic information from step (4);
(6) Output layer: the sentence-level feature vector is utilized to match the most possible relation from candidate relations via fully connected layer.

The concise procedure is as follows.

Algorithm. Algorithm Procedure of Model

Forward propagation:
    Input Layer: input $S = [x_1, x_2, ..., x_N]$ where x_t is the t-th word in the sentence and N is the length of sentence;
    Embedding Layer: transform each word x_t into a vector ew_t by looking up the word embedding table and map the position of each word by relative distances to the two entities into d_{e_1} and d_{e_2} using a position embedding table, and get the word representation $e_t = [ew_t \oplus d_{e_1} \oplus d_{e_2}]$;
    Improved BLSTM layer: combine current word representation e_t, the forward state $\overrightarrow{h_{t-1}}$ and the backward state $\overleftarrow{h_{t-1}}$ as the word representation h_t;
    Attention layer: give high weight to these words between entities and low weight to these words on either side of entities. So, the final word representation is hw_t;
    CNN layer: extract the most important information of the sentence by feeding the hw_t into CNN layer and get $\hat{c}$ for classifying.

Backward propagation: update all parameters by loss function $J(\theta)$.

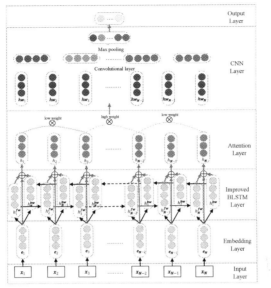

He had chest pains and <e1>headaches</e1> from <e2>mold</e2> in the bedrooms.

Fig. 1. AI-BLSTM-CNN model.

3.1 Embedding Layer

Given a sentence consisting of N words $S = [x_1, x_2, ..., x_N]$ where x_t is the t-th word in the sentence, we refer to each position indicator (PI) $<e1>, </e1>, <e2>, </e2>$ as a single word [18]. Besides, let the marked words x_{e_1} and x_{e_2} be the entities of our concern. Before entering the model, each word x_i is mapped into a vector ew_t by looking up the word embedding table $W^{word} \in \mathbb{R}^{d^w |V|}$, where V is number of the vocabulary, and d^w is the size of word embedding, which can be initialized either by a random process or by some pre-trained word embeddings [4]. Furthermore, we need to embed the position of each word by relative distances shown in Fig. 2 to the two entities. So, we transform the relative distances into real-value vectors d_{e_1} and d_{e_2} respectively with a position embedding table [17]. And then, we concatenate the word embedding ew_t and position embedding d_{e_1} and d_{e_2} into a vector $e_t = [ew_t \oplus d_{e_1} \oplus d_{e_2}]$ to represent the word x_t, where $\oplus$ denotes concatenate operation. Finally, the e_t is fed into the Improved BLSTM layer.

3.2 Improved BLSTM Layer

The second part of our model is the Improved BLSTM layer, the key component for modeling the sequential data, which not only captures the forward states and backward states of the word but also pays attention to the word itself. To be specific, Improved BLSTM layer combines current word representation e_t, the forward state $\overrightarrow{h_{t-1}}$ and the backward state $\overleftarrow{h_{t-1}}$ as the word representation.

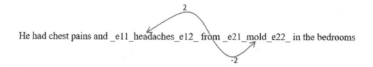

He had chest pains and _e11_headaches_e12_ from _e21_mold_e22_ in the bedrooms

Fig. 2. Relative distance and PI.

Concretely, the LSTM-based recurrent neural network is made up with four components: input gate i_t, forget gate f_t, output gate o_t, and a memory cell c_t. The three adaptive gates i_t, f_t, o_t depend on the previous state h_{t-1} and the current input e_t, and the candidate memory cell g_t is computed by Eq. 4. The more precise formula is as follows:

$$i_t = \sigma(W_i \cdot e_t + U_i \cdot h_{t-1} + b_i) \tag{1}$$

$$f_t = \sigma(W_f \cdot e_t + U_f \cdot h_{t-1} + b_f) \tag{2}$$

$$o_t = \sigma(W_o \cdot e_t + U_o \cdot h_{t-1} + b_o) \tag{3}$$

$$g_t = tanh(W_g \cdot e_t + U_g \cdot h_{t-1} + b_g) \tag{4}$$

where the various W or U, b are the weight matrices and bias vectors.

The current memory cell c_t is a combination of the previous cell content c_{t-1} and the candidate cell content g_t, weighted by the input gate i_t and forget gate f_t respectively.

$$c_t = i_t \otimes g_t + f_t \otimes c_{t-1} \tag{5}$$

The output of LSTM units is the recurrent network's hidden state, which is computed by Eq. 6 as follows:

$$h_t = o_t \otimes tanh(c_t) \tag{6}$$

In the formula above, σ denotes the sigmoid function; $\otimes$ denotes element-wise multiplication. Finally, we get the left-side context vector $\overrightarrow{h_t}$ and the right-side context vector $\overleftarrow{h_t}$. Subsequently, we regard the concatenation h_t of the left-side context vector, the word embedding and the right-side context vector as the representation of word. Therefore, we can make the model not only focus the context words but also focus word itself.

$$h_t = [\overrightarrow{h_t} \oplus x_t \oplus \overleftarrow{h_t}] \qquad t \in [1, N] \tag{7}$$

where $\oplus$ denotes concatenate operation.

3.3   Attention Layer

Attention mechanism first introduced into neural machine translation [2] has been successfully applied in various fields of natural language processing in recent years. In this paper, we introduce the attention mechanism for relation classification tasks. Inspired by the papers [14,20], we deem that these words between two marked entities play an important role for relation classification and words on either side of two entities have less effect on the result of relation classification than middle words. According to this idea, we give high weight to these words between entities and low weight to these words on either side of entities, called middle attention. So, the final word representation is calculated by the following formula:

$$hw_t = \begin{cases} h_t \times high\_w & word \in middle \\ h_t \times low\_w & word \notin middle \end{cases} \tag{8}$$

where middle denotes the words between two entities.

3.4   CNN Layer

In this layer, we will extract the most important information of the sentence by feeding the hw_t generated from attention layer into CNN layer. To be specific, the hw from attention layer is represented as $hw_{1:N} = hw_1 \oplus hw_2 \oplus ... \oplus hw_N$. In general, let $h_{i:i+j}$ refer to the concatenation of words $hw_i, hw_{i+1}, ...hw_{i+j}$. Firstly, the word representation hw is fed into the convolution layer in which a filter $\mathbf{W} \in \mathbb{R}^{hk}$ is applied to a window of h words to produce a new feature, where k is the dimensionality of hw. The detailed calculation process is as follows:

$$c_i = f(w \cdot hw_{i:i+h-1} + b) \tag{9}$$

Here $b \in \mathbb{R}$ is a bias term and f is a non-linear function. Furthermore, this filter is applied to whole sentence to produce a feature map $\mathbf{c} = [c_1, c_2, ..., c_{N-h+1}]$. Traditionally, we need to capture different features by employing multiple filters. After convolution, we can get a matrix $\mathbf{C} = [\mathbf{c}_1, \mathbf{c}_2, ..., \mathbf{c}_{fn}] \in \mathbb{R}^{fn \times (N-h+1)}$, where fn is number of filters. Then, in order to get the most important feature, we apply a max pooling operation [4] over the feature map and take the maximum value $\hat{\mathbf{c}} = max\{\mathbf{C}\}$ as the feature corresponding to the particular filter, where $\hat{\mathbf{c}}$ is the final sentence representation.

3.5   Classifying

The high-level sentence representation $\hat{\mathbf{c}}$ is used to predict label $\hat{y}$ from a discrete set of classes Y for sentence S by softmax classifier:

$$p(y|S) = softmax(W^{(S)}\hat{\mathbf{c}} + b^{(S)}) \tag{10}$$

The relation label with highest probability value is regard as final result:

$$\hat{y} = argmax P(y|S) \tag{11}$$

The negative log-likelihood is chosen as the cost function, however, we need to weigh each class because of the unbalanced data sets. So, the formula is as follows:

$$J(\theta) = -\frac{w_i}{m} \sum_{i=1}^{m} t_i log(y_i) + \lambda \parallel \theta \parallel_F^2 \tag{12}$$

where $t \in \mathbb{R}^m$ is the one-hot represented ground truth and $y \in \mathbb{R}^m$ is the estimated probability for each class by softmax (m is the number of target classes), and w_i is the weight of each class, and λ is an L2 regularization hyperparameter. In this paper we employ dropout [6] which proposed by Hinton et al. preventing co-adaption of hidden units by randomly omitting feature detectors from the network during forward propagation on the embedding and LSTM layer with L2 regularization to alleviate overfitting.

4   Experiments

In this section, we will expand on our experiments. Section 4.1 introduces the dataset and evaluation metrices; Sect. 4.2 presents the hyperparameter settings. In Sect. 4.3, we compare our model with other existing methods.

4.1   Dataset and Evaluation Metrics

We evaluate our model on two different datasets. The first one is the dataset provided by SemEval-2010 Task 8 [5]. The second dataset is KBP37, provided by Angeli et al. [1]. In the following, we will give a detailed introduction of them.

The SemEval-2010 Task 8 dataset [5] is an acknowledged benchmark for relation classification, which is made of 10717 sentences that 8000 sentences for training and 2717 sentences for testing. The dataset contains 10 relations which consists of 9 directed relations and an undirected "other" class. The directed relations covers 9 classes that "Cause-Effect", "Component-Whole", "Content-Container", "Entity-Destination", "Entity-Origin", "Message-Topic", "Member-Collection", "Instrument-Agency", "Product-Producer".

The KBP37 dataset consists of 19322 sentences that 15917 sentences for training and 3405 sentences for testing. The dataset is made up with 19 relations which contains 18 directed relations and an additional "no_relation" class. Detailedly, the directed relations includes 18 classes that "per:alternate_names", "per:origin", "per:spouse", "per:title", "per:employee_of", "per:countries_of_residence", "per:stateorprovinces_of_residence", "per:cities_of_residence", "per:country_of_birth", "org:alternate_names", "org:subsidiaries", "org:top_members/employees", "org:founded", "org:founded_by", "org:country_of_headquarters", "org:stateorprovince_of_headquarters", "org:city_of_headquarters", "o- rg:members".

In conclusion, the KBP37 dataset is larger than SemEval-2010 Task 8 dataset. Also, the average length of sentences in KBP37 is much longer than SemEval-2010 Task 8 dataset, which is shown in Table 1. In addition, the number of relations in KBP37 is much more than SemEval-2010 Task 8 dataset.

Table 1. The distribution of context lengths with two datasets

Dataset	Context length			Proportion of long context (≥ 11)
	≤ 10	11–15	≥ 16	
SemEval-2010	6658	3725	334	0.379
KBP37	6618	11647	15546	0.804

In our experiments, we don't distinguish the direction of relation. What's more, we use the macro-averaged F1-score to evaluate model performance (excluding the "Other" relation or "no_relation"). Also, we have no special treatment of "Other" or "no_relation" class in our experiments.

4.2   Parameter Settings

Table 2. Hyperparameter settings.

Hyperparameter	Value
Batch size	200
Learning rate	0.001
Word embedding size	100
Position embedding size	7
Hidden size	200
Word window size	3
Convolution size	1000
Dropout probability	0.5

In this part, we focus on the adjustment of parameter which consists of Batch size, Learning rate, Word embedding size, Position embedding size, Hidden size, Dropout probability. With regard to word embedding, we employ the pretrained word2vec vector [11] publicly available. On the other hand, for the other parameters, we take those hyperparameters shown in Table 2 achieving the best performance of proposed model.

4.3   Experimental Results

To prove the feasibility of our model, we conduct a series of experiments, comparing with other existing methods of relation classification. To be specific, the experimental results are shown in Table 3, where WV, PF, PI stand for word vectors, position features and position indicators respectively.

We can observe in Table 3 that, CNN achieves an F1-socre of 78.9% and 52.3% respectively in the condition of WV and PF features, and RNN achieves 77.4%

Table 3. Comparison of F1 scores with other models.

Model	SemEval-2010 Task 8	KBP37
CNN+WV+PF [17]	78.9%	52.3%
RNN+WV+PI [18]	77.4%	54.3%
SDP-LSTM+WV [16]	81.3%	55.7%
BLSTM+WV+PI [3]	82.7%	58.8%
Att-BLSTM+WV+PI [21]	84.0%	61.2%
BLSTM-CNN+WV+PF+PI [19]	83.2%	60.1%
I-BLSTM-CNN+WV+PF+PI	84.3%	63.4%
AI-BLSTM-CNN+WV+PF+PI	84.8%	63.7%

and 54.3% respectively by WV and PI features, and SDP-LSTM performs better than above two methods achieving 81.3% and 55.7% respectively with only WV feature, and BLSTM further improves the result to 82.7% and 58.8% respectively with WV feature and PI features, and Att-BLSTM raises the result to 84.0% and 61.2% respectively with WV and PI features, and BLSTM-CNN combines BLSTM and CNN to make the result reach 83.2% and 60.1% respectively with WV, PF and PI features.

Our proposed AI-BLSTM-CNN model yields an F1-score of 84.8% and 63.7%. It outperforms most of the existing methods in the same condition with simple attention mechanism.

5   Conclusion

In this paper, we propose a novel neural network model, named AI-BLSTM-CNN, for relation classification. Our model can make full use of Improved BLSTM-CNN with word embedding, position features and position indicators without any extra lexical information. Meanwhile, attention mechanism is applied to make the model pay more attention on the words between two marked entities. Experiments on the SemEval-2010 Task 8 and KBP37 benchmark dataset show that our model achieves better performances than other existing methods and demonstrate the feasibility of our model.

In the future, we will import better neural network structure for relation classification. Simultaneously, we will take attention mechanism based on class information into account for classifying the relation.

References

1. Angeli, G., Tibshirani, J., Wu, J., Manning, C.D.: Combining distant and partial supervision for relation extraction, pp. 1556–1567 (2014). https://doi.org/10.3115/v1/d14-1164

2. Bahdanau, D., Cho, K., Bengio, Y.: Neural machine translation by jointly learning to align and translate. arXiv preprint arXiv:1409.0473 (2014)
3. Cai, R., Zhang, X., Wang, H.: Bidirectional recurrent convolutional neural network for relation classification **1**, 756–765 (2016). https://doi.org/10.18653/v1/p16-1072
4. Collobert, R., Weston, J., Bottou, L., Karlen, M., Kavukcuoglu, K., Kuksa, P.: Natural language processing (almost) from scratch. J. Mach. Learn. Res. **12**, 2493–2537 (2011). https://doi.org/10.1016/j.chemolab.2011.03.009
5. Hendrickx, I., et al.: Semeval-2010 task 8: multi-way classification of semantic relations between pairs of nominals, pp. 94–99 (2009). https://doi.org/10.3115/1621969.1621986
6. Hinton, G.E., Srivastava, N., Krizhevsky, A., Sutskever, I., Salakhutdinov, R.R.: Improving neural networks by preventing co-adaptation of feature detectors. arXiv preprint arXiv:1207.0580 (2012)
7. Hong, G.: Relation extraction using support vector machine, pp. 366–377 (2005). https://doi.org/10.1007/11562214_33
8. Kambhatla, N.: Combining lexical, syntactic, and semantic features with maximum entropy models for extracting relations, p. 22 (2004). https://doi.org/10.3115/1219044.1219066
9. Kim, Y.: Convolutional neural networks for sentence classification. arXiv preprint arXiv:1408.5882 (2014). https://doi.org/10.3115/v1/d14-1181
10. Lai, S., Xu, L., Liu, K., Zhao, J.: Recurrent convolutional neural networks for text classification (2015)
11. Pennington, J., Socher, R., Manning, C.: Glove: global vectors for word representation, pp. 1532–1543 (2014). https://doi.org/10.3115/v1/d14-1162
12. Qian, L., Zhou, G., Kong, F., Zhu, Q., Qian, P.: Exploiting constituent dependencies for tree kernel-based semantic relation extraction, pp. 697–704 (2008). https://doi.org/10.3115/1599081.1599169
13. Sukhbaatar, S., Weston, J., Fergus, R., et al.: End-to-end memory networks, pp. 2440–2448 (2015)
14. Vu, N.T., Adel, H., Gupta, P., Schütze, H.: Combining recurrent and convolutional neural networks for relation classification. arXiv preprint arXiv:1605.07333 (2016). https://doi.org/10.18653/v1/n16-1065
15. Xu, K., Feng, Y., Huang, S., Zhao, D.: Semantic relation classification via convolutional neural networks with simple negative sampling. arXiv preprint arXiv:1506.07650 (2015). https://doi.org/10.18653/v1/d15-1062
16. Xu, Y., Mou, L., Li, G., Chen, Y., Peng, H., Jin, Z.: Classifying relations via long short term memory networks along shortest dependency paths, pp. 1785–1794 (2015). https://doi.org/10.18653/v1/d15-1206
17. Zeng, D., Liu, K., Lai, S., Zhou, G., Zhao, J., et al.: Relation classification via convolutional deep neural network
18. Zhang, D., Wang, D.: Relation classification via recurrent neural network. arXiv preprint arXiv:1508.01006 (2015)
19. Zhang, L., Xiang, F.: Relation classification via BiLSTM-CNN, pp. 373–382 (2018). https://doi.org/10.1007/978-3-319-93803-5_35
20. Zhang, S., Zheng, D., Hu, X., Yang, M.: Bidirectional long short-term memory networks for relation classification, pp. 73–78 (2015)
21. Zhou, P., et al.: Attention-based bidirectional long short-term memory networks for relation classification **2**, 207–212 (2016). https://doi.org/10.18653/v1/p16-2034

An Improved Method of Applying a Machine Translation Model to a Chinese Word Segmentation Task

Yuekun Wei, Binbin Qu$^{(\boxtimes)}$, Nan Hu, and Liu Han

Advanced Data Engineering and Real-time Computing Laboratory,
Huazhong University of Science and Technology, Wuhan, China
binbinqu_hust@163.com

Abstract. In recent years, a new approach of processing Chinese word segmentation (CWS) as a machine translation (MT) problem has emerged in CWS task research. However, directly applying the MT model to CWS task would introduce translation errors and result in poor word segmentation. In this paper, we propose a novel method named Translation Correcting to solve this problem. Based on the differences between CWS and MT, Translation Correcting eliminates translation errors by utilizing the information of a sentence that needs to be segmented during the translation process. Consequently, the performance of word segmentation is considerably improved. Additionally, We get a new model called CWSTransformer, which is obtained by improving the MT model Transformer using Translation Correcting. The experiment compares the performances of CWSTransformer, Transformer and the previous translation-based CWS model on the benchmark datasets, PKU and MSR. The experimental results show that CWSTransformer outperforms Transformer and the previous translation-based CWS model.

Keywords: Chinese word segmentation · Machine translation · CWSTransformer

1 Introduction

Since Chinese words have no clear boundaries, most Chinese natural language processing tasks, such as Chinese text classification and Chinese sentiment analysis, need to complete word segmentation first. The quality of Chinese word segmentation (CWS) greatly affects the results of subsequent tasks. Researchers have performed considerable work on CWS tasks. The most commonly used method is to treat CWS as a sequence labeling problem. Most works follow Xu [12]'s approach, which first use some tags to mark the relative position of the token in the word. Then, classical supervised learning methods such as maximum entropy [2] and conditional random field (CRF) [5] are used to construct a model for word segmentation.

© Springer Nature Switzerland AG 2019
I. V. Tetko et al. (Eds.): ICANN 2019, LNCS 11730, pp. 44–54, 2019.
https://doi.org/10.1007/978-3-030-30490-4_5

However, these methods require numerous artificial features. In recent years, deep neural networks have been widely used in CWS because they can automatically extract features. Chen et al. [3] use long short-term memory (LSTM) to capture dependencies between tokens in a sentence. Yao and Huang [13] uses bidirectional LSTM to capture previous and future context. Wang et al. [11] enhance bidirectional LSTM by adding a CRF layer upper bidirectional LSTM to constrain the relationship between outputs.

Most of the previous methods only consider the context within a fixed window [8]. To solve this problem, Shi et al. [8] put forward a new idea to treat CWS as a machine translation (MT) problem and utilize a MT model with post-editing method to solve CWS. This process is illustrated in Fig. 1.

Fig. 1. Chinese word segmentation using a MT model. The sentence on the left is before word segmentation, and the sentence on the right is after word segmentation. In this case, the space " " is considered as a segmentation character.

The translated sentences need to be generated by the model step by step. At each step, the model must output which character will be the next translated character. This process requires to calculate the probability distribution of the output character over the character dictionary, and select the character with the highest probability as the next translated character. However, the translation results of the model cannot be completely correct. During the process of generating a translated sentence, determination of the next character is unclear and the model occasionally predicts an incorrect character. This problem is inevitable in MT task. Therefore, using the MT model directly to solve CWS would introduce this error. Shi et al. [8] use an post-editing method to correct the error. This method can only correct some incorrect translated characters, but not incorrect segmentation results (This phenomenon will be seen in Sect. 5). In order to better eliminate this translation error, we propose a novel method to correct the translation results at each step. This method takes advantage of the difference between CWS and MT, which describes in Sect. 2.

The main contributions of this paper are summarized below:

1. We propose a novel method to eliminate the error in the translation process. It can prevent the current translation error from affecting the subsequent translation in time and improve the result of word segmentation.
2. By improving the MT model Transformer with this method, we obtain a novel CWS model CWSTransformer. The CWSTransformer works better on closed datasets than the translation-based CWS model proposed in previous work.

This paper is organized as follows. Section 2 describes our method Translation Correcting. Section 3 introduces the model architecture of CWSTransformer. Section 4 contains the translation process of CWSTranformer. Section 5 contains our experimental details and results analysis. We present our conclusion in Sect. 6.

2   Method

Most MT models are based on the encoder-decoder structure [7,9,10] shown in Fig. 2.

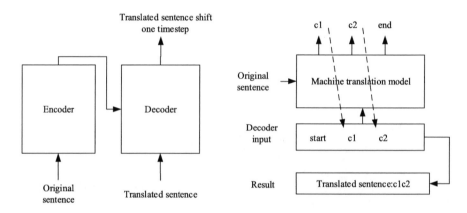

Fig. 2. Machine translation model architecture. The training process of model is shown on the left, and the translation process of model is shown on the right.

Suppose the original sentence is $X = \{x_1, x_2, ..., x_m\}$, where x_i is the character in the original sentence. In MT problem, the translated sentence is $Y = \{y_1, y_2, ..., y_n\}$, where y_i is the character in the translated sentence. The encoder converts the characters in original sentence into a vector representation $H = \{h_1, h_2, ..., h_m\}$. The goal of the decoder is to find a sequence Y that maximizes $P(Y|H)$:

$$P(Y|H) = P(y_1, y_2, ..., y_n|H)$$
$$= \prod_{i=1}^{n} P(y_i|H, y_0, y_1, y_2, ..., y_{i-1}) \tag{1}$$

y_0 is a start symbol. We do not know any information that helps us determine which character y_i is. y_i may be any character in the character dictionary. Thus, the model needs to calculate the probability distribution of y_i over the character dictionary at each step, and then select the character with the highest probability as the value of y_i. However, the translation result y_i may be wrong. In particular, when the training corpus is small and the model learning is insufficient, the translation error will be more obvious. To eliminate such error in translation and prevent it from being transmitted in translation process, we need to correct the translation result at each timestep during translation process.

When CWS is regarded as a machine translation problem, The input and output of the model have a fixed form: when the input is $X = \{x_1, x_2, ..., x_m\}$, the output is $Y = \{x_1, x_2, S, x_3, S, ..., x_m\}$, Where S represents the segmentation character. It can be seen that the input and output have the same characters (except for the segmentation character) and character order. Therefore, when the CWS problem is regarded as a MT problem, some information can be obtained from the sentence to be segmented to correct the translation result at each timestep. Translation Correcting corrects the result based on this fact. When the translation process needs to obtain the next translation character y_i according to $y_{0:i-1}$, y_i will be the segmentation character or the next position of last used character in X. Thus, the goal of the decoder in CWSTransformer is to find a sequence Y that maximizes $P(Y|H, X)$. The modified model and the specific details of the translation process are presented in Sects. 3 and 4.

3   Model Architecture

Using Translation Correcting to improve the MT model Transformer [10], we obtain a new CWS model, CWSTransformer. The architecture of the CWSTransformer is shown in Fig. 3. This model is based on an encoder-decoder framework, where both the encoder and decoder are composed of stacked blocks. Suppose the character sequence to be segmented is $S_{orig} = \{sc_1, sc_2, sc_3, ..., sc_m\}$, where sc_i is the i-th character in sequence, and the result of the word segmentation is $S_{seg} = \{y_0, y_1, y_2, ..., y_n\}$, where y_i is the i-th character in the segmented sequence, and y_0 is start symbol. By removing y_0 from S_{seg}, we get a sequence $Y = \{y_1, y_2, ..., y_n\}$. In the training process, S_{orig} and S_{seg} are used as inputs and Y as output to train the model.

3.1   Embedding

Before we input the character sequence into the encoder and decoder, we need to embed the character sequence to obtain the character representation including semantics and order information. Embedding consists of two parts: character embedding and position embedding. Character embedding represents each character in the input character sequence as a d_{emb} dimension vector. The semantic information of characters is preserved in the vector, which means that the characters with the similar meaning are closer in the vector space [6]. In addition to semantic information, character order information is equally important. Similar to Transformer [10], the CWSTransformer uses sine and cosine functions to achieve positional encoding. This approach is described as follows:

$$PE_{(pos, 2i)} = sin(pos/10000^{2i/d_{emb}}) \tag{2}$$

$$PE_{(pos, 2i+1)} = cos(pos/10000^{2i/d_{emb}}) \tag{3}$$

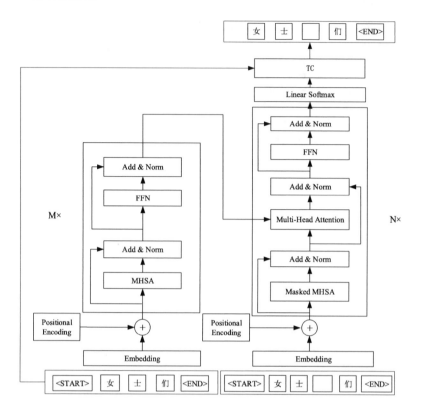

Fig. 3. CWSTransformer model architecture

where *pos* is the position and *i* is the dimension. Then, positional encoding is added to the character embedding. After embedding, We obtain matrices $L_{en}^0 \in \mathbb{R}^{m \times d_{emb}}$ and $L_{de}^0 \in \mathbb{R}^{(n+1) \times d_{emb}}$ in the encoder and decoder, respectively. Each row in a matrix represents a d_{emb}-dimensional representation of a character in the sequence.

3.2   Encoder

The encoder consists of stacked encoder blocks. Each encoder block contains a multi-head self-attention layer ($MHSA$) and a feed-forward layer (FFN). Each layer has a residual connection [4] and a layer normalization [1]. The input to each block is the output of the previous block. Assuming an input of $block_{en}^i$ is L_{en}^{i-1}, the processing results for $block_{en}^i$ are as follows:

$$M_{out} = Norm(L_{en}^{i-1} + MHSA(L_{en}^{i-1})) \tag{4}$$
$$L_{en}^i = Norm(M_{out} + FFN(M_{out})) \tag{5}$$

L_{en}^i is then passed as an input into the next block. The input of the bottom block is L_{en}^0.

MHSA. *MHSA* implements a multi-head self-attention operation, which assigns weights to indicate how much attention the current character pays to the other characters in the sequence, and obtains the representation containing character context information by weighted summation. Suppose we have h heads. The calculation of $MHSA$ is as follows.

$$MHSA(L) = Concat(head_1, ..., head_h)W^O \qquad (6)$$

$$where\, head_i = Attention(L_{en}W_i^Q, L_{en}W_i^K, L_{en}W_i^V) \qquad (7)$$

The attention operation calculation is:

$$Attention(Q, K, V) = softmax(\frac{QK^T}{\sqrt{d_k}})V \qquad (8)$$

where $L_{en} \in \mathbb{R}^{m \times d_{emb}}$ is the output of the previous block, and d_k is the column size of the K. For the bottom block, it is L_{en}^0. $W_i^Q \in \mathbb{R}^{d_{emb} \times d_{emb}/h}$, $W_i^K \in \mathbb{R}^{d_{emb} \times d_{emb}/h}$, $W_i^V \in \mathbb{R}^{d_{emb} \times d_{emb}/h}$, and $W_i^O \in \mathbb{R}^{d_{emb} \times d_{emb}}$ are weight matrices learned through training; they convert L_{en} into Q, K and V in each head. By using scaled dot-product attention [10] on Q, K and V, they obtain the context representation of characters. The results from all headers are connected, multiplying W^O to obtain the output. Then, a residual connection and a normalization operation are used to obtain the final output $M_{out} \in \mathbb{R}^{m \times d_{emb}}$.

FFN. After implementing the multi-head self-attention operation, we use a position-wise feed-forward network (FFN) to extract more useful features.

$$FFN(x) = max(0, M_{out}W_1 + b_1)W_2 + b_2 \qquad (9)$$

The inner transformation transforms the character representation into a high dimension representation for the construction of useful features. The outer transformation is used to limit the dimension of the output. A residual connection and a normalization operation are then used to obtain the block output $L_{en}^i \in \mathbb{R}^{m \times d_{emb}}$.

3.3   Decoder

The decoder consists of stacked decoder blocks. The structure of the decoder block is similar to the encoder block, with some differences. First, the decoder uses masked multi-head self-attention. The mask operation makes the current position character focus only on the information of the character in the previous position. Second, the decoder obtains the context information of the current character in the encode sequence by performing a multi-head attention operation on the current character representation and the output of the encoder. Finally, at the end of the decoder, a linear softmax layer is used to calculate the probability distribution of the output characters. Unlike Transformer, which chooses the character with the highest probability as the translation result of the current step, CWSTransformer has a TC module behind the decoder. This module uses Translation Correction to correct the translation result of decoder at each step, and it works in translation process. The specific process is introduced in the next section. When training the model, we use L_{de}^0 as an input to the decoder. When translating, we use translated sentences as input.

4   Translation Process

The translation (or inference) process of CWSTransformer is shown in Fig. 4. Translated sentence is generated step by step. The model uses the generated sentence to predict the next translated character at each step. The details of the translation process can be formalized into Algorithm 1. Before a sentence is translated, the sentence is transformed into a sequence composed of indexes in a character dictionary. Then, the index of the beginning character and the index of the ending character are added at the beginning and end of the sequence, respectively. Next, we start the translation process. In the step 1, we initialize an empty set S_{seg} to store the result of the translation process. Then, the index of the start symbol is added to S_{seg}. We initialize a position identifier pos in the step 3. Steps 4 to 10 show the translation process. We use S_{orig} and S_{seg} as input to predict the probability distribution of the output character. And we select the character with the highest probability as the result of translation $last\_token$. To correct the result, if the $last\_token$ is not segmentation character $index_{seg}$, we set the $last\_token$ to the character at pos in S_{orig} and move pos one step forward. After that, we append $last\_token$ to S_{seg}. We repeat the translation process until we encounter the end symbol. At this point, the remainder of the character index sequence S_{seg} except the start index and end index is the result of the word segmentation.

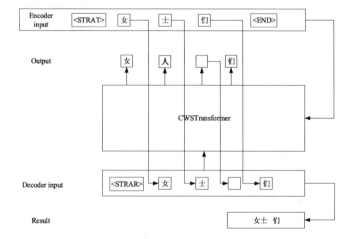

Fig. 4. Translation process. When the prediction result is not segmentation character, CWSTransformer takes the next character in the original sentence as the translated character. Otherwise, the segmentation character is used as the translated character. In the figure, CWSTransformer corrects the translation error of the second character.

5   Experiments and Analysis

5.1   Experiments Setting

The experiment compares the performance of CWSTransformer with Transformer and the previous translation-based CWS model [8]. We do all experiments on PKU and MSR datasets from SIGHAN Bakeoff-2005. They are benchmark of simplified CWS. These datasets contain a large number of sentences that are segmented according to their respective word segmentation criteria. We observe that these datasets contain various long sentences, which comprise several short sentences. Therefore, before training, we divide the long sentences into short ones by separating sentences using common symbols, such as commas and periods. We convert all full-width characters into half-width characters. Furthermore, we replace all numbers and English characters with single characters "0" and "X", respectively. We randomly select 10% of the data as the development set. Table 1 shows the size of datasets after partitioning.

Algorithm 1. Translation Correcting

    Input   : *model*: Machine translation model;

              S_{orig}: An original character sequence represented in index with a start and end symbol index;

              $index_{seg}$: Segmentation symbol index in dictionary;

              $index_s$: Start symbol index in dictionary;

              $index_e$: End symbol index in dictionary;

    Output : S_{seg}: Corresponding segmented character index sequence;

1 Initialize empty set S_{seg}

2 Append $index_s$ to S_{seg}

3 Initialize position $pos : pos \leftarrow 1$

4 **while** $S_{orig}^{pos} \neq index_e$ **do**

5   Predicting the probability distribution of the output character $predict \leftarrow model(S_{orig}, S_{seg})$

6      $last\_token \leftarrow argmax(predict)$

7   **if** $last\_token \neq index_{seg}$ **then**

8          $last\_token \leftarrow S_{orig}^{pos}$

9          $pos \leftarrow pos + 1$

10   Append $last\_token$ to S_{seg}

11 **return** S_{seg}

Table 1. The training and development samples in the PKU and MSR datasets

Dataset	Train	Development
PKU	132368	14708
MSR	282700	31412

To evaluate the performance of CWSTransformer, we use the performance of the CWS tool Jieba on the benchmark datasets as the baseline. Then we compare the performance of previous translation-based CWS model [8], Transformer-1 (1 encoder block, 1 decoder block), CWSTransformer-1 (1 encoder block, 1 decoder block), and CWSTransformer-3 (3 encoder blocks, 3 decoder blocks) on the PKU and MSR datasets. Our experiments are conducted with a single GeForce GTX 1080 GPU. We also apply word2vec [6] to each dataset to get pre-trained character embeddings. We use categorical cross-entropy loss function. The parameter settings of CWSTranformer and Transformer are shown in Table 2.

Table 3 show the results of the scoring. We use the standard scoring script to obtain the scoring results.

5.2   Results Analysis

The experimental results show that the performance of CWSTransformer is superior to Transformer and previous translation-based CWS model. By observing the correction results of post-editing [8] and Translation Correcting on PKU

Table 2. Hyperparameter settings

Parameter	Range
Embedding size	100
Max encoder input length	150
Max decoder input length	300
Encoder Block numbers	[1,3]
Decoder Block numbers	[1,3]
Head numbers	1
Feed forward hidden unit	512
Dropout rate	[0,0.2]
Batch size	[64,128]
Optimizer	Adam
Learning rate	0.001

Table 3. Score of each model (%)

Models	PKU			MSR		
	Recall	Precision	F-Score	Recall	Precision	F-Score
Baseline	78.7	85.3	81.8	81.2	81.7	81.5
Cheng et al. (2017)	88.6	87.0	87.8	93.2	95.1	94.1
Transformer-1	88.8	87.8	88.3	88.9	85.9	87.4
CWSTransformer-1	89.2	90.0	89.6	88.9	89.9	89.5
CWSTransformer-3	91.7	92.3	**92.0**	94.5	94.2	**94.4**

dataset, we find that Translation Correcting can not only correct the translation errors of characters, but also correct the segmentation errors. An example is shown in the Table 4. This verifies the validity of Translation Correcting.

Table 4. Comparison of error correction effects

Origin sentence	... 向多个国家领导人打电话求援, ...
Correct result	... 向 多 个 国家 领导人 打电话 求援 , ...
Transformer	... 向 多 个 国家 领导人 打电话 话 援援 , ...
Post-editing	... 向 多 个 国家 领导人 打电求援 , ...
Translation Correcting	... 向 多 个 国家 领导人 打电话 求援 , ...

Experiments also show that the increase in the number of encoder and decoder blocks improves the segmentation performance of CWSTransformer. Limited by resources, we could only evaluate a version of CWSTransformer containing 3 encoder and 3 decoder blocks. On the PKU dataset, CWSTransformer-3 exceeded the previous translation CWS model 4.2% points in the F-Score. On the MSR dataset, CWSTransformer-3 exceeded the previous translation CWS model 0.3% points in the F-Score.

6   Conclusion

This paper proposes an effective method for applying the MT model to a CWS task. This method can be applied to any MT model. Using this method, we improve the MT model Transformer and obtain a new CWS model, CWSTransformer. The experimental results show that CWSTransformer obtained by Translation Correcting corrects some translation errors in Transformer, thereby improving the word segmentation. CWSTransformer outperforms the CWS models proposed in previous studies. However, because of limited resources, we did not use a version of CWSTransformer containing more encoder and decoder blocks to conduct the experiments; thus, the performance of the model is limited in the experiment. In future works, we will try to improve CWSTransformer, which can use fewer resources to achieve better results.

References

1. Ba, J.L., Kiros, J.R., Hinton, G.E.: Layer normalization. arXiv preprint arXiv:1607.06450 (2016)
2. Berger, A.L., Pietra, V.J.D., Pietra, S.A.D.: A maximum entropy approach to natural language processing. Comput. Linguist. **22**(1), 39–71 (1996)

3. Chen, X., Qiu, X., Zhu, C., Liu, P., Huang, X.: Long short-term memory neural networks for Chinese word segmentation. In: Proceedings of the 2015 Conference on Empirical Methods in Natural Language Processing, pp. 1197–1206 (2015). https://doi.org/10.18653/v1/d15-1141

4. He, K., Zhang, X., Ren, S., Sun, J.: Deep residual learning for image recognition. In: Proceedings of the IEEE Conference on Computer Vision and Pattern Recognition, pp. 770–778 (2016). https://doi.org/10.1109/cvpr.2016.90

5. Lafferty, J., McCallum, A., Pereira, F.C.: Conditional random fields: probabilistic models for segmenting and labeling sequence data (2001)

6. Mikolov, T., Chen, K., Corrado, G., Dean, J.: Efficient estimation of word representations in vector space. arXiv preprint arXiv:1301.3781 (2013)

7. Neco, R.P., Forcada, M.L.: Asynchronous translations with recurrent neural nets. In: Proceedings of International Conference on Neural Networks (ICNN 1997), vol. 4, pp. 2535–2540. IEEE (1997). https://doi.org/10.1109/icnn.1997.614693

8. Shi, X., Huang, H., Ping, J., Guo, Y., Wei, X., Tang, Y.K.: Neural Chinese word segmentation as sequence to sequence translation. In: Chinese National Conference on Social Media Processing (2017). https://doi.org/10.1007/978-981-10-6805-8_8

9. Sutskever, I., Vinyals, O., Le, Q.V.: Sequence to sequence learning with neural networks. In: Advances in Neural Information Processing Systems, pp. 3104–3112 (2014)

10. Vaswani, A., et al.: Attention is all you need. In: Advances in Neural Information Processing Systems, pp. 5998–6008 (2017)

11. Wang, J., Zhou, J., Liu, G.: Multiple character embeddings for Chinese word segmentation. arXiv preprint arXiv:1808.04963 (2018)

12. Xu, N.: Chinese word segmentation as character tagging. IJCLCLP **8**(1) (2003). https://doi.org/10.3115/1119250.1119278. http://www.aclclp.org.tw/clclp/v8n1/v8n1a2.pdf

13. Yao, Y., Huang, Z.: Bi-directional LSTM recurrent neural network for Chinese word segmentation. In: Hirose, A., Ozawa, S., Doya, K., Ikeda, K., Lee, M., Liu, D. (eds.) ICONIP 2016. LNCS, vol. 9950, pp. 345–353. Springer, Cham (2016). https://doi.org/10.1007/978-3-319-46681-1_42

Interdependence Model for Multi-label Classification

Kosuke Yoshimura[1(✉)], Tomoaki Iwase[2], Yukino Baba[3],
and Hisashi Kashima[4,5]

[1] Sansan, Inc., Tokyo, Japan
yoshimura@sansan.com
[2] Yahoo Japan Corporation, Tokyo, Japan
tiwase@yahoo-corp.jp
[3] University of Tsukuba, Ibaraki, Japan
baba@cs.tsukuba.ac.jp
[4] Kyoto University, Kyoto, Japan
kashima@i.kyoto-u.ac.jp
[5] RIKEN Center for AIP, Tokyo, Japan

Abstract. The multi-label classification problem is a supervised learning problem that aims to predict multiple labels for each data instance. One of the key issues in designing multi-label learning approaches is how to incorporate dependencies among different labels. In this study, we propose a new approach called the *interdependence model*, which consists of a set of single-label predictors each of which predicts a particular label using the other labels. The proposed model can directly consider label interdependencies by reusing arbitrary conventional probabilistic models for single-label classification. We consider three prediction methods and one accelerated method for making predictions with the interdependence model. Experiments show the superior prediction performance of the proposed methods in several evaluation metrics, especially when there is a large number of candidate labels or when labels are partially given in the test phase.

Keywords: Multi-label classification · Supervised learning ·
Interdependence model

1 Introduction

The multi-label classification problem is a supervised learning problem that aims to predict multiple labels for each data instance, and it has various applications ranging from drug activation prediction to recommender systems. One of the significant features of the multi-label classification different from the standard (single-label) classification is the existence of dependencies among different labels. This introduces new important issues: how to incorporate such dependencies in the prediction models, and how to reduce the computational costs. Usually, there is a trade-off between these two objectives.

© Springer Nature Switzerland AG 2019
I. V. Tetko et al. (Eds.): ICANN 2019, LNCS 11730, pp. 55–68, 2019.
https://doi.org/10.1007/978-3-030-30490-4_6

One of the typical approaches to the multi-label classification problem is *problem transformation*, which boils down the problem to a (set of) single label classification problem(s). Binary Relevance (BR) and Label Powersets (LP) are the two (extreme) representative methods. BR is quite efficient, but cannot incorporate label dependencies. On the other hand, LP considers the problem as a single-label multi-class classification whose labels are the power set of all labels; however, LP suffers from its high computational costs and data inefficiency. There have also been proposed several intermediate methods, such as Classifier Chains (CC) [11], Meta Stacking (MS) [6], and Subset Mapping (SM) [12]; each of them assumes its own assumption on label dependencies to incorporate them with moderate computational cost.

In this paper, we propose a new multi-label classification method called *interdependence model*, which can directly consider label interdependencies. An interdependence model consists of a set of single-label classifiers, each of which predicts a particular label using the other labels. It can incorporate label interdependencies in an explicit and direct manner by reusing arbitrary existing probabilistic models for single-label classification. We propose a simple approximate method to train the interdependence model.

Since the prediction by each component model depends on the predictions by the other component models in the interdependence model, we need to solve an optimization problem to find a solution satisfying all of the component models. We consider three approximate prediction methods: Gibbs sampling (Gibbs), fixed-point iteration (FPI), and exhaustive search (ES). In addition, we propose an accelerated exhaustive search method ES$^+$, which is applicable when we use the logistic regression model as the component model.

Our experiments compare the proposed method with five existing problem transformation methods using seven datasets. The experiments also include the "partially-observed" situations where some of the labels for each test instance are given. The results indicate the proposed method is especially effective when there are a large number of candidate labels or when some of the labels for each instance are given in the test dataset.

Our contributions in this paper are three-fold:

1. a new multi-label classification model called *interdependence model* that can incorporate label interdependencies by considering a set of arbitrary single-label classifiers,
2. efficient prediction methods (Gibbs, FPI, and ES) and one accelerated method ES$^+$ for the logistic regression model, and
3. experimental comparisons to show the superior performance of the proposed method to existing methods especially when the "diverse-label" training situation and the "partially-observed" test situation.

2 Interdependence Model

2.1 Multi-label Classification Problem

We address the multi-label classification problem in this paper. Let us denote the training dataset by $\{(\boldsymbol{x}_i, \boldsymbol{y}_i)\}_{i=1}^{N}$, where $\boldsymbol{x}_i \in \mathbb{R}^m$ is the m-dimensional feature vector and $\boldsymbol{y}_i = (y_i^1, \ldots, y_i^k) \in \{0, 1\}^k$ is the label vector for the i-th sample. k is the number of the labels. Given the training data set, our goal is to obtain a multi-label classifier $h : \mathbb{R}^m \to \{0, 1\}^k$.

2.2 Model

We propose an *interdependence model* for multi-label classification, which directly models the dependency of a particular label on the other labels. Namely, the j-th label y^j is given by a probabilistic classifier h^j as:

$$y^j = h^j(\boldsymbol{x}, \boldsymbol{y}^{-j}; \boldsymbol{w}^j), \tag{1}$$

where $\boldsymbol{y}^{-j} = (y^1, \ldots, y^{j-1}, y^{j+1}, \ldots, y^k)$, and $\boldsymbol{w}^j$ is the model parameter. Given a feature vector $\boldsymbol{x}$, the prediction $\boldsymbol{y}$ is given as the solution of the following system of nonlinear equations:

$$
\begin{aligned}
y^1 &= h^1(\boldsymbol{x}, \boldsymbol{y}^{-1}; \boldsymbol{w}^1) \\
y^2 &= h^2(\boldsymbol{x}, \boldsymbol{y}^{-2}; \boldsymbol{w}^2) \\
&\cdots \\
y^k &= h^k(\boldsymbol{x}, \boldsymbol{y}^{-k}; \boldsymbol{w}^k),
\end{aligned}
\tag{2}
$$

which we denote by

$$\boldsymbol{y} = \boldsymbol{h}(\boldsymbol{x}, \boldsymbol{y}; \boldsymbol{W}), \tag{3}$$

where $\boldsymbol{W} = (\boldsymbol{w}^1, \boldsymbol{w}^2, \ldots, \boldsymbol{w}^k)$ is the model parameter matrix. Since labels are dependent of each other as Eq. (3), we call this the interdependence model. We can use arbitrary binary classifiers as the component models $\{h^j\}_{j=1}^{k}$, which gives great flexibility in modeling label interdependencies.

2.3 Training

Given a training dataset $\{(\boldsymbol{x}_i, \boldsymbol{y}_i)\}_{i=1}^{N}$, we minimize a loss function while satisfying the constraint (3). That is, we solve the following optimization problem:

$$\underset{\boldsymbol{W}, \{\boldsymbol{z}_i\}_{i=1}^{N}}{\text{minimize}} \quad \sum_{i=1}^{N} L(\boldsymbol{y}_i, \boldsymbol{z}_i) + \gamma \|\boldsymbol{W}\|_{\mathrm{F}}^2 \tag{4}$$

$$\text{subject to} \quad \boldsymbol{z}_i = \boldsymbol{h}(\boldsymbol{x}, \boldsymbol{z}_i; \boldsymbol{W}) \quad i = 1, \ldots, N, \tag{5}$$

where $\boldsymbol{z}_i$ is the predicted label vector for the i-th sample, $L(\boldsymbol{y}, \boldsymbol{z})$ is a loss function, $\gamma > 0$ is the regularization parameter, and $\|\cdot\|_{\mathrm{F}}$ is the Frobenius norm.

Because the solution of this optimization problem is intractable, we relax the problem by replacing z_i in the constraint (5) by the true label vector y_i; namely, the constraint is changed to $z_i = h(x, y_i; W)$. This relaxation allows us to remove the constraints and thus the new optimization problem is given as follows:

$$\underset{W}{\text{minimize}} \sum_{i=1}^{N} L\left(y_i, h\left(x, y_i; W\right)\right) + \gamma \|W\|_F^2. \tag{6}$$

Because we no longer have the interdependent constraints among $w^1, w^2, \ldots,$ w^k, we can fit the model parameter for each label independently. Our optimization problem for each label is finally formalized as follows:

$$\underset{w^j}{\text{minimize}} \sum_{i=1}^{N} L(y_i^j, h^j(x, y_i^{-j}; w^j)) + \gamma \|w_j\|_2^2. \tag{7}$$

Note that, even though each model is trained independently due to the above relaxation, the trained models still take label dependencies into account.

2.4 Prediction

Because the interdependence model requires the information of the other labels (i.e., y^{-j}) for predicting the target label y^j, it is not trivial to make a prediction. We use three prediction methods for the interdependence model.

Fixed Point Iteration (FPI). Fixed point iteration is a common solution for a non-linear system of equations such as Eq. (3). Given the initial solution $z^{(0)}$, the fixed point iteration iteratively updates the solution by

$$z^{(t+1)} = h(x, z^{(t)}; W), \tag{8}$$

until it converges or the maximum number of iterations is reached. Once the final solution $z^{(T)}$ is obtained, the prediction is made as $z^j = 1$ if $z^{j(T)} \geq \theta$ for each j, or $z^j = 0$ otherwise, where θ is a threshold.

Gibbs Sampling (Gibbs). The probabilistic classifier for each label, h^j, is considered as the conditional probability of j-th label y^j given the other labels y^{-j}. Gibbs sampling generates a sample z^j by sampling using the conditional distribution, that is,

$$z^j \sim h^j(x, z^{-j}; w^j). \tag{9}$$

The sequence of samples are then used to approximate the posterior distribution.

Exhaustive Search with Pruning (ES). Another prediction method is an exhaustive search method which finds the combination of the labels minimizing the cross entropy between z^j and $h^j\left(x, z^{-j}; w^j\right)$ for $j = 1, \ldots, k$. We need to solve an optimization problem to make a prediction:

$$\text{minimize} \atop z \quad -\sum_{j=1}^{k}\left\{z^j \ln h^j\left(\boldsymbol{x}, \boldsymbol{z}^{-j}\right) + \left(1 - z^j\right) \ln\left(1 - h^j\left(\boldsymbol{x}, \boldsymbol{z}^{-j}\right)\right)\right\} \quad (10)$$

$$\text{subject to } z^j \in \{0, 1\}, \quad j = 1, \ldots, k.$$

The worst-case running time of the exhaustive search is $O(2^k)$ and it is not feasible for large k; we use a pruning technique to shrink the search space.

Exhaustive Search with Pruning for Logistic Regression (ES$^+$). We present an accelerated exhaustive search method which is only applicable to a logistic regression classifier. The algorithm evaluates the upper and lower bounds of the probability of each label. If the upper bound is small enough or the lower bound is large enough, the current label is fixed. The algorithm repeats this evaluation process until the labels converge and then performs the exhaustive search for the unfixed labels.

In the prediction phase, the classifier $h^j\left(\boldsymbol{x}, \boldsymbol{z}^{-1}; \boldsymbol{w}^j\right)$ is considered as a function of z^j and it can be rewritten as $h^j\left(\boldsymbol{z}^{-1}\right)$. The model parameter $\boldsymbol{w}^j$ is a $(m + k)$-dimensional vector consisting of a bias, the m-dimensional weights for $\boldsymbol{x}$, and the $(k - 1)$-dimensional weights for $\boldsymbol{z}^{-1}$. The logistic regression classifier $h^j\left(\boldsymbol{z}^{-1}\right)$ is then represented as

$$h^j(\boldsymbol{z}^{-j}) = \frac{1}{1 + \exp(-(w_0^j + \boldsymbol{x}^\top \boldsymbol{w}_{[1:d]}^j + \boldsymbol{z}^{-j^\top} \boldsymbol{w}_{[d+1:d+k]\setminus d+j}^j))}, \quad (11)$$

where $\boldsymbol{w}_{[a:b]}^j = (w_a^j, w_{a+1}^j, \ldots, w_b^j)^\top$ and $\boldsymbol{w}_{[a:b]\setminus c}^j = (w_a^j, w_{a+1}^j, \ldots, w_{c-1}^j, w_{c+1}^j, \ldots, w_b^j)^\top$.

Because each of the elements in $\boldsymbol{z}^{-j}$ is either zero or one, by using the symbols of $\mathcal{S}_+^j = \{n \mid w_{d+n}^j > 0 \wedge z^n = \text{None}, n = 1, \ldots, j - 1, j + 1, \ldots, k\}$, $\mathcal{S}_-^j = \{n \mid w_{d+n}^j < 0 \wedge z^n = \text{None}, n = 1, \ldots, j - 1, j + 1, \ldots, k\}$, and $\mathcal{S}^j = \{n \mid n \notin \mathcal{S}_+^j \cup \mathcal{S}_-^j, n = 1, \ldots, j - 1, j + 1, \ldots, k\}$, the lower and upper limits of $h^j(\boldsymbol{z}^{-j})$ are given as follows:

$$ll = \frac{1}{1 + \exp(-(w_0^j + \boldsymbol{x}^\top \boldsymbol{w}_{[1:d]}^j + \sum_{n \in \mathcal{S}^j} z^n w_{d+n}^j + \sum_{n \in \mathcal{S}_-^j} w_{d+n}^j))}, \quad (12)$$

$$ul = \frac{1}{1 + \exp(-(w_0^j + \boldsymbol{x}^\top \boldsymbol{w}_{[1:d]}^j + \sum_{n \in \mathcal{S}^j} z^n w_{d+n}^j + \sum_{n \in \mathcal{S}_+^j} w_{d+n}^j))}. \quad (13)$$

Given a threshold θ, the algorithm determines $z^j = 0$ if $ul < \theta$, and $z^j = 1$ if $ll > \theta$. Algorithm 1 shows the procedure of the exhaustive search for logistic regression.

3 Experiments

3.1 Datasets

We use seven datasets: Emotions [16], Yeast [5], Flags [7], Birds [4], Enron [9], and Medical [10]. These datasets are open to the public on Mulan: A Java Library for Multi-Label Learning.[1] Table 1 shows their basic statistics. Cardinality$(\mathcal{D}) = \frac{1}{N} \sum_{i=1}^{N} \sum_{j=1}^{k} y_j^i$ of dataset $\mathcal{D}$ is the average number of given labels per instance in $\mathcal{D}$ [18]. Density$(\mathcal{D}) = \frac{1}{k}$Cardinality$(\mathcal{D})$ is the proportion of the cardinality to the number of candidate labels. Diversity is the number of label combinations that actually appear in the dataset.

Algorithm 1. Accelerated Exhaustive Search with Pruning (ES$^+$)

Input: $\boldsymbol{x}$, $\{h^j\}_{j=1}^{k}$, θ
Output: $\boldsymbol{z} = (z^1, \ldots, z^k)^\top$
1: Initialize each element of $\boldsymbol{z}$ by None
2: **while** True **do**
3:     $\boldsymbol{z}_{old} \leftarrow \boldsymbol{z}$
4:     **for** $j = 1, \ldots, k$ **do**
5:         $ll \leftarrow$ the right side of Eq. 12
6:         $ul \leftarrow$ the right side of Eq. 13
7:         **if** $ul < \theta$ **then**
8:             $z^j \leftarrow 0$
9:         **if** $ll > \theta$ **then**
10:             $z^j \leftarrow 1$
11:     **if** $\boldsymbol{z}_{old} = \boldsymbol{z}$ **then**
12:         **break**
13: Apply the exhaustive search to undetermined elements of $\boldsymbol{z}$
14: **return** $\boldsymbol{z}$

Table 1. Multi-label classification datasets and their basic statistics.

Dataset	Domain	#instances	#features	#labels	Cardinality	Density	Diversity
Scene [3]	Image	2407	294	6	1.074	0.179	15
Emotions [16]	Music	593	72	6	1.869	0.311	27
Yeast [5]	Biology	2417	103	14	4.237	0.303	198
Flags [7]	Image	194	19	7	3.392	0.485	54
Birds [4]	Audio	645	260	19	1.014	0.053	133
Enron [9]	Text	1702	1001	53	3.378	0.064	753
Medical [10]	Text	978	1449	45	1.245	0.029	94

3.2   Evaluation Metrics

We evaluate the performance of all methods using 10-fold cross-validation. We use four evaluation metrics as follows: Accuracy $= \frac{1}{n} \sum_{i=1}^{n} \frac{|Y_i \cap Z_i|}{|Y_i \cup Z_i|}$, F$_1$-measure $= \frac{1}{n} \sum_{i=1}^{n} \frac{2|Y_i \cap Z_i|}{|Y_i| + |Z_i|}$, 0/1-Loss $= \frac{1}{n} \sum_{i=1}^{n} I(\boldsymbol{y}_i \neq \boldsymbol{z}_i)$, and Hamming loss $= \frac{1}{nk} \sum_{i=1}^{n} \sum_{j=1}^{k} I(y_i^j \neq z_i^j)$, where n is the number of test instances, I is the indicator function, and $\boldsymbol{z}_i = (z_i^1, \ldots, z_i^k) \in \{0,1\}^k$ is the predicted label vector

---

[1] http://mulan.sourceforge.net.

for the i-th sample, $Y_i = \{j \mid y_i^j = 1, j = 1, \ldots, k\}$ and $Z_i = \{j \mid z_i^j = 1, j = 1, \ldots, k\}$. Note that the denominator of Accuracy and F_1-measure can be zero; we set the scores to one in such cases.

3.3   Baseline Methods

The following five methods are used as baselines: Binary relevance (BR) makes a prediction by using a single-label binary classifier for each label. Label power-sets (LP) uses a single-label multi-class classifier where classes correspond to the power set of all the labels. Meta stacking (MS) [6] is a two-step method based on BR. In the first step, MS predicts labels by using BR. In the second step, MS predicts final labels by using the predicted labels in the first step. Classifier chain (CC) [11] is a cascade method based on BR. For each $j = 2, \ldots, k$, CC uses the predicted labels, $z^1, \ldots, z^{j-1}$, to predict z^j. Following the original paper [11], we fix the order of labels to $j = 1, \ldots, k$. Subset mapping (SM) [12] is also based on BR. SM maps the predicted label vector to the closest label vector appeared in the training data.

3.4   Hyperparameter Settings

We use the logistic regression as the component model of the baseline methods and that of the proposed methods. We tune the regularization parameter, γ, in among $\{0.01, 0.1, 1, 10, 100\}$ with respect to each evaluation metric. We set $\theta = 0.5$ as a threshold in BR, MS, CC, SM, FPI, and Gibbs.

  We initialize each element of z in FPI and Gibbs to one. The maximum number of iterations is set to 10,000 for FPI. Gibbs sampling generates 10,000 samples for each label; we discard the initial 100 samples for each label from the posterior approximation.

3.5   Experimental Scenarios

We conduct experiments in two scenarios: the first one is the ordinary multi-label classification scenario where all of the labels for each test instance are unobserved. The second scenario assumes a "partially-observed" situation, where some of the labels for each test instance are already given and we predict the rest. Such situation is possible, for example, when some of the labels are given by human annotators.

  In the second scenario, we evaluate the prediction performance along with the number of observed labels per instance. The observed labels are randomly chosen for each instance. We evaluate the performance of each method by using Hamming Loss and 0/1 Loss.

3.6   Results

Table 2 shows the results in the ordinary multi-label classification setting. We set the maximum calculation time to 24 h; ES reached this limitation in Enron and Medical, and thus the results for these cases are not given.

Table 2. Performance of the baseline methods and the interdependence model with different prediction methods. A number in a bracket indicates the ranking of each method. Winners are bold-faced. ES and ES$^+$ outperform the baseline methods in most cases when the performance is evaluated by 0/1 loss. Our methods achieves higher accuracies and F$_1$ scores than the baseline methods in Birds, Enron, and Medical.

Accuracy (the larger the better):

Dataset	Baseline methods					Interdependence model			
	BR	LP	MS	SM	CC	Gibbs	FPI	ES	ES$^+$
Scene	.5985 (9)	**.7322** (1)	.6482 (5)	.6250 (7)	.6610 (4)	.6401 (6)	.6087 (8)	.7248 (2)	.7142 (3)
Emotions	.5175 (9)	.5582 (3)	.5346 (6)	.5376 (5)	.5216 (7)	.5206 (8)	.5620 (2)	**.5741** (1)	.5441 (4)
Yeast	.5019 (5)	**.5286** (1)	.5030 (3)	.5027 (4)	.5062 (2)	.5000 (6)	.3808 (9)	.4706 (8)	.4706 (7)
Flags	.5730 (6)	.5541 (8)	.5795 (4)	.5820 (3)	.5827 (2)	**.5842** (1)	.5751 (5)	.5565 (7)	.5509 (9)
Birds	.6024 (6)	.6045 (5)	.5989 (8)	.6014 (7)	.5927 (9)	.6080 (4)	**.6090** (1)	.6089 (2)	.6083 (3)
Enron	.4374 (6)	.4276 (8)	.4380 (5)	.4337 (7)	.4431 (3)	.4429 (4)	.4446 (2)	–(9)	**.4592** (1)
Medical	.7443 (7)	**.7756** (1)	.7438 (8)	.7448 (6)	.7684 (3)	.7675 (4)	.7602 (5)	–(9)	.7698 (2)
Avg. rank	6.857(9)	**3.857**(1)	5.571(7)	5.571(8)	4.286(3)	4.714(5)	4.571(4)	5.286(6)	4.143(2)

F$_1$-measure (the larger the better):

Dataset	Baseline methods					Interdependence model			
	BR	LP	MS	SM	CC	Gibbs	FPI	ES	ES$^+$
Scene	.6201 (9)	**.7432** (1)	.6670 (5)	.6405 (7)	.6791 (4)	.6520 (6)	.6226 (8)	.7363 (2)	.7254 (3)
Emotions	.5989 (9)	.6400 (3)	.6168 (6)	.6238 (4)	.6070 (7)	.5993 (8)	**.6631** (1)	.6547 (2)	.6170 (5)
Yeast	.6104 (5)	**.6208** (1)	.6099 (6)	.6106 (4)	.6117 (2)	.6109 (3)	.5305 (9)	.5760 (8)	.5760 (7)
Flags	.6898 (6)	.6708 (8)	.6928 (3)	.6969 (2)	**.6972** (1)	.6916 (4)	.6912 (5)	.6746 (7)	.6668 (9)
Birds	.6350 (6)	.6366 (5)	.6312 (8)	.6316 (7)	.6242 (9)	.6413 (4)	.6427 (2)	**.6440** (1)	.6424 (3)
Enron	.5457 (6)	.5258 (8)	.5460 (5)	.5415 (7)	.5507 (3)	.5504 (4)	.5527 (2)	–(9)	**.5597** (1)
Medical	.7729 (6)	**.8013** (1)	.7726 (7)	.7699 (8)	.7923 (4)	.7909 (5)	.7935 (2)	–(9)	.7932 (3)
Avg. rank	6.714(9)	**3.857** (1)	5.714(8)	5.571(7)	4.286(3)	4.857(5)	4.143(2)	5.286(6)	4.429(4)

Hamming loss (the smaller the better):

Dataset	Baseline					Interdependence model			
	BR	LP	MS	SM	CC	Gibbs	FPI	ES	ES$^+$
Scene	.0997 (8)	**.0904** (1)	.0931 (4)	.1296 (9)	.0935 (5)	.0945 (6)	.0978 (7)	.0928 (3)	.0920 (2)
Emotions	.2001 (2)	.2144 (6)	**.1965** (1)	.2010 (4)	.2041 (5)	.2007 (3)	.2257 (8)	.2147 (7)	.2268 (9)
Yeast	**.1996** (1)	.2085 (6)	.1998 (3)	.2044 (5)	.1996 (2)	.2025 (4)	.2218 (7)	.2360 (8)	.2360 (9)
Flags	.2708 (4)	.2978 (9)	.2702 (3)	.2709 (5)	.2666 (2)	**.2636** (1)	.2712 (6)	.2951 (7)	.2966 (8)
Birds	.0464 (3)	.0494 (9)	.0464 (2)	**.0459** (1)	.0466 (4)	.0472 (5)	.0473 (6)	.0483 (8)	.0482 (7)
Enron	**.0454** (1)	.0550 (8)	.0455 (2)	.0514 (7)	.0456 (3)	.0457 (5)	.0457 (4)	–(9)	.0462 (6)
Medical	.0099 (3)	.0110 (7)	.0099 (2)	.0123 (8)	**.0097** (1)	.0102 (5)	.0105 (6)	–(9)	.0101 (4)
Avg. Rank	3.143(2)	6.571(8)	**2.429** (1)	5.571(5)	3.143(3)	4.143(4)	6.286(6)	7.286(9)	6.286(6)

0/1 Loss (the smaller the better):

Dataset	Baseline					Interdependence model			
	BR	LP	MS	SM	CC	Gibbs	FPI	ES	ES$^+$
Scene	.4608 (9)	**.3008** (1)	.4042 (6)	.4209 (7)	.3827 (4)	.3918 (5)	.4317 (8)	.3095 (2)	.3187 (3)
Emotions	.7334 (8)	.6761 (3)	.7133 (4)	.7268 (7)	.7200 (5)	.7201 (6)	.7369 (9)	**.6627** (1)	.6728 (2)
Yeast	.8461 (8)	**.7410** (1)	.8378 (6)	.8296 (5)	.8275 (4)	.8432 (7)	.9843 (9)	.8134 (2)	.8134 (3)
Flags	.8408 (9)	.8145 (4)	.8250 (5)	.8303 (7)	.8350 (8)	.8042 (3)	.8300 (6)	**.7574** (1)	.7626 (2)
Birds	.4897 (6)	.4928 (7)	.4928 (8)	.4835 (3)	.4944 (9)	**.4835** (1)	.4835 (2)	.4882 (5)	.4851 (4)
Enron	.8654 (7)	**.8178** (1)	.8637 (6)	.8625 (4)	.8596 (3)	.8631 (5)	.8660 (8)	–(9)	.8314 (2)
Medical	.3364 (7)	.3007 (3)	.3364 (8)	.3283 (6)	.3006 (2)	.3027 (4)	.3221 (5)	–(9)	**.2996** (1)
Avg. Rank	7.714(9)	2.857(2)	6.143(7)	5.571(6)	5.000(5)	4.429(4)	6.714(8)	4.143(3)	**2.286** (1)

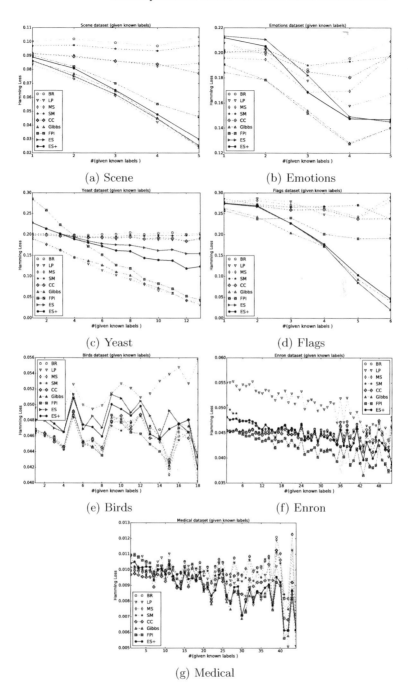

(a) Scene

(b) Emotions

(c) Yeast

(d) Flags

(e) Birds

(f) Enron

(g) Medical

Fig. 1. Performance comparison in the partially-observed cases. Hamming loss according to the number of the observed labels per instance is shown. Our approaches outperform the baselines in Emotions, Flags, and Enron, and achieve comparable performance to LP in Scene and Yeast datasets.

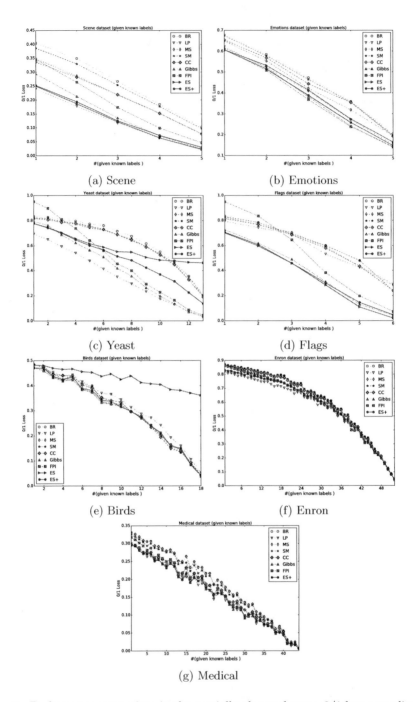

Fig. 2. Performance comparison in the partially-observed cases. 0/1 loss according to the number of the observed labels per instance is shown. Our approaches outperform the baselines in Scene, Emotions, and Flags datasets.

The proposed methods achieve the comparatively high performance in the experiments where we use 0/1 loss, accuracy, F_1-measure as the performance metrics for Birds, Enron, and Medical datasets, which have larger number of candidate labels than the others. On the other hand, the proposed methods perform rather poorly in Hamming loss.

We compare the performance of the four prediction methods. Gibbs method shows better performance in Flags dataset and moderate performance in the other datasets, which shows its overall stability. FPI method shows better performance in some datasets, but worse in the other datasets, which indicates the relative instability of FPI against Gibbs. ES achieves superior performance in 0/1 loss; however, it requires longer prediction time and sometimes does not complete the process within the maximum calculation time. ES^+ consistently shows high performance for all the datasets in 0/1 loss.

Figures 1 and 2 show the performance in the partially-observed situations in the Hamming loss and the 0/1 loss, respectively. The results of ES for the Enron dataset are not given because it reached the maximum calculation time. The proposed methods outperform the baseline methods in Emotions, Flags, and Enron, and achieve comparable performance to LP in Scene and Yeast in the Hamming loss. Our methods demonstrate higher performance than the baseline methods in Scene, Emotions and Flags in the 0/1 loss. The results show our proposed methods are especially effective when some of the labels are available in the test phase.

4   Related Work

One of the famous multi-label classification approaches is *Problem transformation approaches* [17]. Two representative methods of the problem transformation approaches are Binary Relevance (BR) and Label Powersets (LP). BR uses a set of binary classifiers each of which predict a particular label. Since the binary classifiers make predictions independently of each other, it is quite efficient; however, it does not consider dependencies among different labels. LP considers the power set of the labels, that is, all possible label combinations, and performs multi-class classification from the power set. LP is advantageous in that it directly handles arbitrary label dependencies. However, it suffers from two types of inefficiency; computational inefficiency, that is, the computational cost increases exponentially with respect to the number of labels, and data inefficiency, that is, two sets of labels are considered totally different power-set labels even if they are quite similar. Therefore, it is an important to consider "intermediate" methods between BR and LP that are two extremes of multi-label classification methods.

Meta Stacking (MS) [6], Classifier Chains (CC) [11], and Subset Mapping (SM) [12] are problem transformation methods that incorporate label dependencies without sacrificing their computational efficiency. MS makes two-stage predictions; it first applies BR that makes predictions only with input features, and then makes the second prediction using the first predictions as well as the input features. CC takes a similar approach; it orders labels and makes predictions in the order. Prediction of a particular label depends on the predictions of the previous labels. SM first applies BR to obtain the initial predictions, which are then mapped onto the closest label set among the labels sets that are actually observed in the training dataset. Another well-known transformation methods is RAndom k labELsets (RAkEL) [19]; it randomly generates label sets of size k, and then applies LP to each of them. The final predictions are made by ensembling the set of the first predictions.

More recently, embedding-based methods are also studied: the one applying compressed sensing [8], the one using matrix factorization and reconstruction [15], the two-stage method based on small label subsets [1], the error-correcting-output-coding method using canonical correlations [21], and the one using low-dimensional embeddings [20]. Extreme multi-label classification is also one of the recent trends, where the number of labels is extremely large, e.g., from 10^4 to 10^6. Several methods specialized to such situations are proposed [2,13,14].

5   Conclusion

We propose the interdependence model for multi-label classification. The optimization problem for training the interdependence model incorporates the interdependent constraints among the labels. We present a simple approximation method for training. Because the prediction by each single-label classifier in the interdependence model depends on the predictions by the other classifiers, we need to solve an optimization problem to find a solution satisfying all the component classifiers. We present the three prediction approaches and one acceleration method which is only applicable for the logistic regression model. The results of the experiments using real-world datasets show that the proposed methods are effective, especially for the datasets that have a large number of candidate labels. It is also observed that the proposed methods achieve higher performance in cases where the labels in the test instances are partially observed.

One of the possible future work would be to further speed up the prediction. The basic idea of the interdependence model is not limited to multi-label classification; extensions to other problems including multivariate regression and density estimation would be a promising future direction.

Acknowledgment. This work was supported by JSPS KAKENHI Grant Number 15H01704.

References

1. Balasubramanian, K., Lebanon, G.: The landmark selection method for multiple output prediction. In: Proceedings of the 29th International Conference on Machine Learning, pp. 283–290 (2012)
2. Bhatia, K., Jain, H., Kar, P., Varma, M., Jain, P.: Sparse local embeddings for extreme multi-label classification. In: Advances in Neural Information Processing Systems, vol. 28, pp. 730–738 (2015)

3. Boutell, M.R., Luo, J., Shen, X., Brown, C.M.: Learning multi-label scene classification. Pattern Recognit. **37**(9), 1757–1771 (2004). https://doi.org/10.1016/j.patcog.2004.03.009
4. Briggs, F., et al.: The 9th Annual MLSP Competition: New Methods for Acoustic Classification of Multiple Simultaneous Bird Species in a Noisy Environment (2013). https://doi.org/10.1109/MLSP.2013.6661934
5. Elisseeff, A., Weston, J.: A kernel method for multi-labelled classification. In: Advances in Neural Information Processing Systems, vol. 14, pp. 681–687 (2001)
6. Godbole, S., Sarawagi, S.: Discriminative methods for multi-labeled classification. In: Dai, H., Srikant, R., Zhang, C. (eds.) PAKDD 2004. LNCS (LNAI), vol. 3056, pp. 22–30. Springer, Heidelberg (2004). https://doi.org/10.1007/978-3-540-24775-3_5
7. Goncalves, E.C., Plastino, A., Freitas, A.A.: A genetic algorithm for optimizing the label ordering in multi-label classifier chains. In: Proceedings of the 25th International Conference on Tools with Artificial Intelligence, pp. 469–476 (2013). https://doi.org/10.1109/ICTAI.2013.76
8. Hsu, D., Kakade, S.M., Langford, J., Zhang, T.: Multi-label prediction via compressed sensing. In: Advances in Neural Information Processing Systems, vol. 22, pp. 772–780 (2009)
9. Klimt, B., Yang, Y.: The Enron corpus: a new dataset for email classification research. In: Boulicaut, J.-F., Esposito, F., Giannotti, F., Pedreschi, D. (eds.) ECML 2004. LNCS (LNAI), vol. 3201, pp. 217–226. Springer, Heidelberg (2004). https://doi.org/10.1007/978-3-540-30115-8_22
10. Pestian, J.P., et al.: A shared task involving multi-label classification of clinical free text. In: Proceedings of the Workshop on BioNLP 2007: Biological, Translational, and Clinical Language Processing, pp. 97–104 (2007)
11. Read, J., Pfahringer, B., Holmes, G., Frank, E.: Classifier chains for multi-label classification. In: Buntine, W., Grobelnik, M., Mladenić, D., Shawe-Taylor, J. (eds.) ECML PKDD 2009. LNCS (LNAI), vol. 5782, pp. 254–269. Springer, Heidelberg (2009). https://doi.org/10.1007/978-3-642-04174-7_17
12. Schapire, R.E., Singer, Y.: Improved boosting algorithms using confidence-rated predictions. Mach. Learn. **37**(3), 297–336 (1999). https://doi.org/10.1023/A:1007614523901
13. Tagami, Y.: AnnexML: approximate nearest neighbor search for extreme multi-label classification. In: Proceedings of the 23rd ACM SIGKDD International Conference on Knowledge Discovery and Data Mining, pp. 455–464 (2017). https://doi.org/10.1145/3097983.3097987
14. Tagami, Y.: Learning extreme multi-label tree-classifier via nearest neighbor graph partitioning. In: Proceedings of the 26th International Conference on World Wide Web, pp. 845–846 (2017). https://doi.org/10.1145/3041021.3054204
15. Tai, F., Lin, H.T.: Multilabel classification with principal label space transformation. Neural Comput. **24**(9), 2508–2542 (2012). https://doi.org/10.1162/NECO_a_00320
16. Trohidis, K., Tsoumakas, G., Kalliris, G., Vlahavas, I.P.: Multi-label classification of music into emotions. In: Proceedings of the 9th International Conference on Music Information Retrieval, vol. 8, pp. 325–330 (2008). https://doi.org/10.1186/1687-4722-2011-426793
17. Tsoumakas, G., Katakis, I.: Multi-label classification: an overview. Int. J. Data Warehous. Min. **2007**, 1–13 (2007). https://doi.org/10.4018/jdwm.2007070101

18. Tsoumakas, G., Katakis, I., Vlahavas, I.: Mining multi-label data. In: Maimon, O., Rokach, L. (eds.) Data Mining and Knowledge Discovery Handbook, pp. 667–685. Springer, Boston (2010). https://doi.org/10.1007/978-0-387-09823-4_34
19. Tsoumakas, G., Vlahavas, I.: Random k-labelsets: an ensemble method for multilabel classification. In: Kok, J.N., Koronacki, J., Mantaras, R.L., Matwin, S., Mladenič, D., Skowron, A. (eds.) ECML 2007. LNCS (LNAI), vol. 4701, pp. 406–417. Springer, Heidelberg (2007). https://doi.org/10.1007/978-3-540-74958-5_38
20. Zhou, W.-J., Yu, Y., Zhang, M.L.: Binary linear compression for multi-label classification. In: Proceedings of the 26th International Joint Conference on Artificial Intelligence, pp. 3546–3552 (2017). https://doi.org/10.24963/ijcai.2017/496
21. Zhang, Y., Schneider, J.: Multi-label output codes using canonical correlation analysis. In: Proceedings of the 14th International Conference on Artificial Intelligence and Statistics, vol. 15, pp. 873–882 (2011)

Combining Deep Learning and (Structural) Feature-Based Classification Methods for Copyright-Protected PDF Documents

Renato Garita Figueiredo$^{(\boxtimes)}$ (ID), Kai-Uwe Kühnberger(ID), Gordon Pipa(ID), and Tobias Thelen(ID)

University of Osnabrück, Osnabrück, Germany
{rgaritafigue,kkuehnbe,gpipa,tobias.thelen}@uni-osnabrueck.de

1 Introduction

This document describes the implementation of a copyright classification process for user-contributed Portable Document Format (PDF) documents. The implementation employs two ways to classify documents as copyright-protected or non-copyright-protected: first, using structural features extracted from the document metadata, content and underlying document structure; and second, by turning the documents into images and using their pixels to generate features for semi-supervised deep convolutional networks.

The implementation of an automatic classification procedure described here resulted from legal requirements in Germany. German copyright law permits the distribution of limited parts of copyrighted works for educational use without acquiring an individual licence. Typically, this limitation of copyright is relevant for uploaded documents in learning management systems.

In a pilot study conducted at Osnabrück university, an average of 37 documents per course was found in the learning management system. Approximately 20% of these documents contain unlicensed copyrighted works but instructors are not able to reliably classify the copyright status of the provided documents, as the Osnabrück study has shown [12]. In order to conduct negotiations to calculate remuneration from the universities a good estimation of the extent of usage of educational copyright material is needed from more universities in Germany.

Supervised [14] and semi-supervised machine learning (ML) [5] techniques will be used in this work. In this project a semi-supervised technique known as pseudo-labeling [17] was used.

2 Data

The PDF files were provided by Osnabrück University's e-learning center[1]. Close to 4000 files were extracted and labeled. The files were manually classified by

---

[1] https://www.virtuos.uni-osnabrueck.de/startseite.html.

© Springer Nature Switzerland AG 2019
I. V. Tetko et al. (Eds.): ICANN 2019, LNCS 11730, pp. 69–75, 2019.
https://doi.org/10.1007/978-3-030-30490-4_7

experts as part of a pilot study (cf. [12]) into different categories related to their copyright status. The following categories were considered as copyrighted material: Copyright-protected, published material, allowed by campus licence; published material, allowed by a free licence or no licence at all (author longer than 70 years dead); copyright-protected, published material, allowed by §52a UrhG (Text)[2]; copyright-protected, published material not covered by a known licence.

The files represent a big variety of material. The documents are all of different length and content.

In total, we used 3752 documents of which 3252 were used for training and 493 left for testing. In the case of the image data, a maximum of 3 pages were taken from each document for a total of 7997 data samples for training and 1248 data samples for testing. For the unlabeled data a total of 12802 PDF documents were available. Taking a maximum of 3 pages per document the total of available samples resulted in 31134.

3   Features

Different types of features were extracted from the PDF documents to train the classifiers.

3.1   Structural Features

Some of the features used for this work can describe the document's structure on a high level.

Text content from the documents was extracted using a *Bag-Of-Words* (BOW) approach [24] to generate a lexicon [21, pp. 22–32]. Each word of this lexicon is then linked to their frequency in the text and these frequencies are used in a feature vector as a multivariate sample of the contents of the document. This sample is then used as input for a classifier. The *vectorization* of the lexicon was tried using a count vectorizer and a *term-frequency inverse document-frequency (tfidf)* vectorizer [18]. Before processing the text content stop words were eliminated.

Metadata from the database of the university as well as extracted from the document itself was used and processed with a BOW approach similar to the one for text content. The metadata was also pre-processed to get rid of information like program versions.

Sixty-eight (68) features of the underlying structure of the documents were also generated.

3.2   Pixel-Based Features

In this project we used pre-trained convolutional neural networks (CNN [7]) to generate features from the pixels of the documents taken as images.

---

[2] Section of the German copyright law: https://www.gesetze-im-internet.de/urhg/__ 52a.html.

4   Classifiers

The structural features were divided in three main groups: the first group consists of the BOW features, the second group is comprised of those features related to the underlying structure of the document and the third type of features are the image-based pixel features generated by the DL models.

Classifiers were tested for each set of features using a grid search approach and 10-fold cross-validation. The classifiers were chosen based on a rule of thumb considering their general usage for similar types of data.

Classifiers tested on BOW features (text content, creator, producer, file name and folder name): Bernoulli Classifier [21, pp. 234–265], K-Nearest Neighbor Classifier [1], Linear Support Vector Classifier [9], Multinomial Naive Bayes Classifier [21, pp. 234–265], Nearest Centroid Classifier [23], Passive Aggressive Classifier [8], Perceptron/SGD Classifiers [11], Random Forest Classifier [2], Ridge Classifier[3].

Classifiers tested on underlying structure features: AdaBoost Classifier [10], Decision Tree Classifier [3], Gaussian Naive Bayes Classifier [4], Gaussian Process Classifier [19], K-Nearest Neighbor Classifier, Multilayer Perceptron Classifier [16], Quadratic Discriminant Analysis Classifier[4], Random Forest Classifier, Support Vector Classifier [13].

We also use three different image classification models. A Residual Network (ResNet) model [15] (*ResNet50*); the InceptionV3 module [22] and the Xception Module [6]. A small output network is then re-trained with the output from the models using our labels and then the process of pseudo-labeling is applied to finish adapting the model.

5   Results

The F1-score is calculated as a way to show that a larger proportion of one class was not biasing the accuracy of the predictions.

The best classifiers for each of the features after doing the grid search are summarized on Table 1.

The RFC was the best performing classifier for the majority of features but it takes a considerable amount of time for training and testing. When dealing with the text content of the documents it could be prohibitively slow in which case the use of Multinomial Naive Bayes can obtain similar results much faster.

For training the DL classifiers we took the documents and transformed them into images of 224×224 pixels. For each document we took a maximum of three random pages, the class of each document was decided by averaging the score of the pages.

---

[3] Source: https://scikit-learn.org/stable/modules/generated/sklearn.linear_model. Ridge.html.

[4] Source: https://scikit-learn.org/stable/modules/generated/sklearn.discriminant_ analysis.QuadraticDiscriminantAnalysis.html.

Table 1. Chosen classifiers and accuracy (All classifiers were taken from the scikit-learn python libraries).

Features	Chosen results		
	Best classifier	F1 score	Accuracy
Creator	Random Forest Classifier (RFC)	0.84	86%
Producer	RFC	0.81	81%
File name	Stochastic Gradient Descent (SGD)	0.765	77%
Folder name	Nearest Centroid (NC)	0.765	78%
Text content	RFC	0.89	88%
Underly. struc.	RFC	0.92	92%

After processing the images with the pre-defined networks, a small dense network is trained using the copyright and non-copyright labels. For this network, two different configuration models were tested using a grid search: *model 1* – A network with one dense layer with 0.5 dropout probability on the visible input layer and *sigmoid* activation function for the output layer. The loss is measured by *binary crossentropy*; *model 2* – A network with two dense layers. The input layer has dropout probability of 0.5 and the hidden layer has 512 neurons with 0.8 dropout probability and *Rectifier Linear Units (ReLU)* activation. The output layer uses a sigmoid activation function. The loss function is also *binary crossentropy*. The optimizers tested were: **sgd** – stochastic gradient descent, **rmsprop** – root mean square propagation and **nadan** – Nesterov-accelerated Adaptive Moment Estimation.

The rest of the hyperparameters were taken from a sequential optimization in the number of epochs with different combinations of dropout rates: no dropout, 0.5 and 0.8 in the different layers. Gradual learning rate reductions were tested from $1-e5$ to $1-e9$ after one third of the epochs. The hidden layer of the second model was kept at 512 neurons. After testing several configurations, the first model was trained for 60 epochs and the learning rate was reduced to $1-e5$, $1-e6$ and $1-e9$ at different stages of the training process. The second model was trained for just 6 epochs and the learning rate reduced to $1-e5$ and $1-e9$ during the process.

For the pseudo-labeling procedure a batch of 24 samples are taken from the training set that was already fed to the model while 8 or one third of that is taken from the newly labeled data to re-train the classifier. This is a rule of thumb for combining the properly labeled and the pseudo-labeled data during this training phase. The classification report for the best model (model 1) is on Table 2. The weighted average (WA) takes into account for class imbalances since the non-copyright-protected documents have more representation. The results were obtained by averaging the output value of each of the pages.

The best classifiers are then combined into an ensemble [20]. The output of the classifiers was combined using a RFC with 1000 estimators and using the

Table 2. Classification report for the first deep learning model with pseudo-labeling.

	Precision	Recall	F1-score
Copyright	0.91	0.77	0.83
Non-copyright	0.92	0.97	0.94
WA	0.92	0.92	0.91
Accuracy = 92%			

default hyperparameters[5]. The performance result of the classifier was of 93%. The classification report for this procedure can be seen in Table 3.

Table 3. Classification report for the random forest classification of the outputs of all classifiers.

	Precision	Recall	F1-score
Copyright	0.90	0.82	0.86
Non-copyright	0.94	0.97	0.95
Average	0.93	0.93	0.93
Accuracy = 93%			

6   Conclusions from the Results and Future Work

There are difficulties with comparing this work to others since we couldn't find other works that try to classify user contributed PDF documents in copyright-protected and non-copyright-protected classes using structural and pixel-based features or in general with other automated procedure. With that in mind we consider that the results are promising as a first approach of an automatic classification method for this type of data.

In future versions, more data from more universities in Germany will be used to improve and test the generalization of the results.

References

1. Altman, N.S.: An introduction to kernel and nearest-neighbor nonparametric regression. Am. Stat. **46**(3), 175–185 (1992). https://doi.org/10.1080/00031305.1992.10475879
2. Breiman, L.: Random forests. Mach. Learn. **45**(1), 5–32 (2001). https://doi.org/10.1023/A:1010933404324

---

[5] The rest of the default options can be found here: https://scikit-learn.org/stable/modules/generated/sklearn.ensemble.RandomForestClassifier.html.

3. Breiman, L.: Classification and Regression Trees. Routledge (2017). https://doi.org/10.1201/9781315139470
4. Chan, T.F., Golub, G.H., LeVeque, R.J.: Updating formulae and a pairwise algorithm for computing sample variances. In: Caussinus, H., Ettinger, P., Tomassone, R. (eds.) COMPSTAT 1982 5th Symposium held at Toulouse 1982, pp. 30–41. Springer, Heidelberg (1982). https://doi.org/10.1007/978-3-642-51461-6_3
5. Chapelle, O., Schölkopf, B., Zien, A.: Semi-Supervised Learning, 1st edn. The MIT Press (2010). https://doi.org/10.7551/mitpress/9780262033589.001.0001
6. Chollet, F.: Xception: deep learning with depthwise separable convolutions. In: Proceedings of the IEEE Conference on Computer Vision and Pattern Recognition, pp. 1251–1258 (2017). https://doi.org/10.1109/CVPR.2017.195
7. Cireşan, D., Meier, U., Schmidhuber, J.: Multi-column deep neural networks for image classification. In: Proceedings/CVPR. IEEE Computer Society Conference on Computer Vision and Pattern Recognition, February 2012. https://doi.org/10.1109/CVPR.2012.6248110
8. Crammer, K., Dekel, O., Keshet, J., Shalev-Shwartz, S., Singer, Y.: Online passive-aggressive algorithms. J. Mach. Learn. Res. **7**, 551–585 (2006). https://doi.org/10.1.1.385.8409
9. Fan, R.E., Chang, K.W., Hsieh, C.J., Wang, X.R., Lin, C.J.: Liblinear: a library for large linear classification. J. Mach. Learn. Res. **9**, 1871–1874 (2008). https://doi.org/10.1145/1390681.1442794
10. Freund, Y., Schapire, R.E.: A decision-theoretic generalization of on-line learning and an application to boosting. J. Comput. Syst. Sci. **55**(1), 119–139 (1997). https://doi.org/10.1006/jcss.1997.1504
11. Freund, Y., Schapire, R.E.: Large margin classification using the perceptron algorithm. Mach. Learn. **37**(3), 277–296 (1999). https://doi.org/10.1023/A:1007662407062
12. Fuhrmann-Siekmeyer, A., Thelen, T.: Einzelmeldungen urheberrechtlich geschützter sprachwerke gemäß §52 a urhg an die vg wort. Bibliothek Forschung und Praxis **39**(3), 394–400 (2015). https://doi.org/10.1515/bfp-2015-0045
13. Guyon, I., Boser, B., Vapnik, V.: Automatic capacity tuning of very large VC-dimension classifiers. In: Advances in Neural Information Processing Systems, pp. 147–155 (1993). https://doi.org/10.1.1.17.7215
14. Hastie, T., Tibshirani, R., Friedman, J.: Overview of Supervised learning. The Elements of Statistical Learning. SSS, pp. 9–41. Springer, New York (2009). https://doi.org/10.1007/978-0-387-84858-7_2
15. He, K., Zhang, X., Ren, S., Sun, J.: Deep residual learning for image recognition. In: Proceedings of the IEEE Conference on Computer Vision and Pattern Recognition, pp. 770–778 (2016). https://doi.org/10.1109/CVPR.2016.90
16. Hinton, G.E.: Connectionist learning procedures. In: Machine Learning, pp. 555–610. Elsevier (1990). https://doi.org/10.1016/B978-0-08-051055-2.50029-8
17. Lee, D.H.: Pseudo-label: the simple and efficient semi-supervised learning method for deep neural networks. In: ICML 2013 Workshop: Challenges in Representation Learning (WREPL), vol. 3, July 2013. https://doi.org/10.1.1.664.3543
18. Leskovec, J., Rajaraman, A., Ullman, J.D.: Mining of Massive Datasets. Cambridge University Press (2014). https://doi.org/10.1017/CBO9781139924801
19. Rasmussen, C.E.: Gaussian processes in machine learning. In: Bousquet, O., von Luxburg, U., Rätsch, G. (eds.) ML 2003. LNCS (LNAI), vol. 3176, pp. 63–71. Springer, Heidelberg (2004). https://doi.org/10.1007/978-3-540-28650-9_4
20. Rokach, L.: Ensemble-based classifiers. Artif. Intell. Rev. **33**(1–2), 1–39 (2010). https://doi.org/10.1007/s10462-009-9124-7

21. Schütze, H., Manning, C.D., Raghavan, P.: Introduction to Information Retrieval, vol. 39. Cambridge University Press, Cambridge (2008). https://doi.org/10.1017/CBO9780511809071
22. Szegedy, C., Vanhoucke, V., Ioffe, S., Shlens, J., Wojna, Z.: Rethinking the inception architecture for computer vision. In: Proceedings of the IEEE Conference on Computer Vision and Pattern Recognition, pp. 2818–2826 (2016). https://doi.org/10.1109/CVPR.2016.308
23. Tibshirani, R., Hastie, T., Narasimhan, B., Chu, G.: Diagnosis of multiple cancer types by shrunken centroids of gene expression. Proc. Natl. Acad. Sci. **99**(10), 6567–6572 (2002). https://doi.org/10.1073/pnas.082099299
24. Zhang, Y., Jin, R., Zhou, Z.H.: Understanding bag-of-words model: a statistical framework. Int. J. Mach. Learn. Cybern. **1**(1), 43–52 (2010). https://doi.org/10.1007/s13042-010-0001-0

Sentiment Classification

Collaborative Attention Network with Word and N-Gram Sequences Modeling for Sentiment Classification

Junwei Bao, Liang Zhang, and Bo Han$^{(\boxtimes)}$

School of Computer Science, Wuhan University,
Wuhan 430072, People's Republic of China
{lebronbao,liang.z}@whu.edu.cn, hanboemail@163.com

Abstract. Current state-of-the-art models for sentiment classification are CNN-RNN-based models. These models combine CNN and RNN in two ways: parallel models or serial models. Parallel models use CNN to capture n-grams and RNN to model word sequences, while serial models feed n-grams into RNN to model n-gram sequences. However, these models are different from the way humans read text. Intuitively, humans read text by capturing semantic elements that are made up of both words and n-grams. To tackle this problem, we propose a collaborative attention network with word and n-gram sequences modeling. Our model jointly processes sequences in both word granularity and n-gram granularity to form text embedding with collaborative attention. It utilizes a LSTM encoder to capture long-term dependencies among words and a CNN-LSTM component to capture long-term dependencies among n-grams on the same text. Next we incorporate these two parts via an attention mechanism to highlight keywords in sentences. Experimental results show our model effectively outperforms other state-of-the-art CNN-RNN-based models on several public datasets of sentiment classification.

Keywords: Sentiment classification · Sequence modeling ·
Attention mechanism

1 Introduction

Nowadays, most popular approaches for sentiment classification are based on deep neural networks. These methods can be divided into two categories. One category is based on convolutional neural networks (CNN) approaches [1–3], which leverage convolution filters to capture local features and pooling operation to extract influential n-grams in text. The other category is based on recurrent neural networks (RNN) approaches [4–6] that perform well in modeling sequential text. In recent years, some state-of-the-art hybrid models of CNN and RNN are proposed. And these CNN-RNN-based models combine CNN and RNN in two ways: parallel models or serial models. Parallel models [7–9] leverage CNN to capture n-grams and RNN to model word sequences, and incorporate them via an attention mechanism, while serial models [10, 11] feed n-grams into RNN to model n-gram sequences.

© Springer Nature Switzerland AG 2019
I. V. Tetko et al. (Eds.): ICANN 2019, LNCS 11730, pp. 79–92, 2019.
https://doi.org/10.1007/978-3-030-30490-4_8

Although these CNN-RNN-based models have achieved better performance than traditional methods, they are different from the way humans read text. It's intuitive that people read text by capturing semantic elements, and such semantic elements may consist of both words and n-grams. For example, in sentence *"Great phone but the description needed to be clearer"*, we can easily capture semantic elements *"great phone"*, *"description"* and *"to be clearer"*, which help us understand the meaning of the sentence. However, these methods model sequences only in either word granularity or n-gram granularity, and they don't conform to the way people read text.

In this paper, in order to alleviate the problem, we propose a collaborative attention network with both word and n-gram sequences modeling. Specially, we first apply a long short-term memory (LSTM) encoder to model input sentences in word granularity. Then, we introduce a CNN-LSTM component similar to the model in [12] to extract long-term dependencies among n-grams as attention weights. We calculate our attention weights as follows. First, we leverage convolution filters to extract n-gram features in original text. Second, we utilize LSTM to model these n-gram sequences to capture long-term dependencies from them. Finally, we combine outputs of the CNN-LSTM component and the LSTM encoder via element-wise multiplication. Experimental results demonstrate that our model outperforms most state-of-the-art models on three public sentiment classification datasets.

Our contributions can be summarized into following two aspects:

- Different from most CNN-RNN-based models processing sequences only in either word granularity or n-gram granularity, we propose a collaborative attention network to process sequences in two granularities and capture more contextual features. Specially, our model consists of a LSTM encoder to model word sequences and a CNN-LSTM component to model n-gram sequences. Thus, we consider long-term dependencies in both word granularity and n-gram granularity for the same text simultaneously.
- Different from most parallel CNN-RNN-based methods utilizing feature maps as attention and combining them with RNN directly, we introduce long-term dependencies among n-grams as attention weights, which not only contain local context but also semantic information among n-grams. Specially, we incorporate the outputs of the CNN-LSTM component and the LSTM encoder which capture features in two granularities, thus some keywords can be effectively highlighted in sentences.

2   Model

The proposed model consists of two parts in parallel as shown in Fig. 1. The first part is a bidirectional LSTM utilized to produce intermediate representation of sentences in word granularity, and the second part is a CNN-LSTM component for modeling sentences in n-gram granularity. In this section, we describe our model in detail as follows. First, we will describe word embedding layer which transforms words into vectors. Then, we will demonstrate the bidirectional LSTM and finally we will present the CNN-LSTM component and illustrate how to combine these two parts together via an attention mechanism.

2.1   Embedding Layer

In our model, embedding layer is the first layer and it is used to convert words from vocabulary into corresponding context-aware distributed representations. Specially, given a sentence containing n words $S = \{w_1, w_2, \ldots, w_n\}$ in order, we look up each word in an embedding matrix $\boldsymbol{E} \in \mathbb{R}^{d \times |V|}$, where d is the number of dimension of real-valued vectors and $|V|$ is the size of vocabulary, and all the real-valued vectors are pre-trained in a large amount of corpus. We map a word w_i into its corresponding vector e_i by matrix product as follows:

$$e_i = \boldsymbol{E}o_i, \tag{1}$$

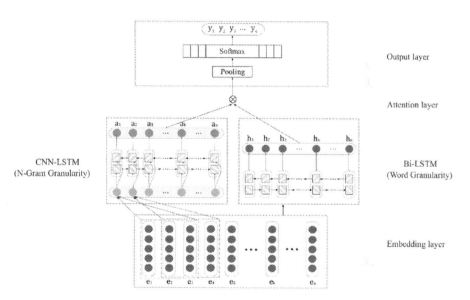

Fig. 1. The architecture of our collaborative attention network

in which o_i is a one-hot vector of the word w_i with the element corresponding to e_i set to 1 and other elements set to 0. In this way, the sentence S can be transformed into a word embedding matrix $\boldsymbol{W} \in \mathbb{R}^{d \times n}$, in which the i-th row is the distributed representation of the word w_i. Then the $\boldsymbol{W}$ will be fed into next layers, i.e., the bidirectional LSTM encoder and the CNN-LSTM component.

2.2   Bidirectional LSTM

RNN is good at modeling sequential data like reviews and comments in sentiment classification. However, the biggest problem that standard RNN suffers greatly from is vanishing gradient, which makes RNN incapable of memorizing long-term dependencies from text sequences. To alleviate the situation, LSTM [13] is proposed to control the update of information with three types of gates in each hidden cell. Each cell contains a forget gate f_t, an input gate i_t and an output gate o_t, which are defined by following equations:

$$f_t = \sigma\left(W_f \cdot [h_{t-1}, e_t] + b_f\right) \tag{2}$$

$$i_t = \sigma(W_i \cdot [h_{t-1}, e_t] + b_i) \tag{3}$$

$$o_t = \sigma(W_o \cdot [h_{t-1}, e_t] + b_o), \tag{4}$$

where h_{t-1} is the output of last hidden cell and e_t is current word embedding in the embedding matrix W to be processed. By means of these gates, cell internal state C_t is calculated to control the transmission of information between two adjacent hidden cells. The process is described by following equations:

$$C'_t = tanh(W_C \cdot [h_{t-1}, e_t] + b_C) \tag{5}$$

$$C_t = f_t \odot C_{t-1} + i_t \odot C'_t \tag{6}$$

$$h_t = o_t \odot \tanh(C_t). \tag{7}$$

In this way, we obtain the final output h_t and the internal state C_t of current cell and then put them into the next cell to continue the same calculations. Here we use two LSTMs working in opposite directions to model the sentence S forward and backward. And we define two hidden states $\overrightarrow{h_t}$ and $\overleftarrow{h_t}$ for corresponding word w_t. Then we concatenate $\overrightarrow{h_t}$ and $\overleftarrow{h_t}$, i.e., $h_t = \left[\overrightarrow{h_t}, \overleftarrow{h_t}\right]$. Therefore, the sentence S can be represented as $H = \{h_1, h_2, \ldots, h_n\}$ intermediately.

2.3   CNN-LSTM Component

In this subsection, we will describe our CNN-LSTM component in detail. The component consists of two layers of different neural networks: (i) a basic CNN layer without pooling operation and (ii) a bidirectional LSTM layer. These two layers are serially connected as shown in Fig. 1.

CNN is commonly used to capture window-based n-grams as meaningful representation of sentences. In the CNN layer, suppose we obtain the word embedding matrix W of the sentence S from the embedding layer in Sect. 2.1, we then adopt fixed-sized convolution filters through the matrix W. Each filter $F \in \mathbb{R}^{d \times k}$, where k is kernel size, is applied to each k embedding vectors $W[i : i+k-1]$ to produce a local feature c_i as follows:

$$c_i = f(F \cdot W[i : i+k-1] + b), \tag{8}$$

where f is a non-linear activation function such as tanh or RELU. The filter F slides in the word embedding matrix W to finish convolution operations for all possible k-size windows with stride 1 and generates a vector of feature map $c = \{c_1, c_2, \ldots, c_{n-k+1}\}$. In a similar way, we use m filters to generate m feature maps, which are stacked to construct a feature map matrix $M \in \mathbb{R}^{m \times n}$. In order to match the output of the bidirectional LSTM for sentences mentioned in Sect. 2.2, here we pad the embedding matrix before convolution operations so that the generated feature map matrix M has the same number of columns n as the embedding matrix W.

Afterwards we feed the feature map matrix M into a bidirectional LSTM layer to capture long-term dependencies among n-grams. Considering the feature map matrix M consists of n vectors and each vector can be regarded as the representation of corresponding n-gram in the sentence S. These vectors are put into the bidirectional LSTM step by step just like what we do for word embedding vectors in Sect. 2.2. Similarly, we concatenate forward and backward hidden states $\overrightarrow{a_t}$ and $\overleftarrow{a_t}$, i.e., $a_t = \left[\overrightarrow{a_t}, \overleftarrow{a_t}\right]$ for the t-th n-gram. Hence, the whole outputs of the bidirectional LSTM layer construct attention matrix $A = \{a_1, a_2, \ldots, a_n\}$ which has the same size as the intermediate representation of the sentence H.

2.4 Attention Combination Layer

Inspired by the way of designing attention in [8], we combine the attention matrix A and the intermediate representation H via element-wise multiplication as follows:

$$R = A \otimes H, \tag{9}$$

where R has the same size as both A and H. Considering the fact that the matrixes A and H are both hidden states of two LSTMs in two granularities based on the same sentence, that is, A and H extract dual-granularity (n-gram granularity and word granularity) long-term dependencies for the same sentence, respectively. We believe that coarse-grained hidden states not only contain a window-based context but also long-term dependencies in n-gram sequences, so that they are able to highlight key parts in the sentence by adjusting their corresponding fine-grained hidden states.

After that, pooling operation is applied to R then the final reduced representation is obtained and put into a softmax layer to get final predicted label y.

3 Experiments

In this section, we evaluate the performance of our model on three public review datasets of sentiment classification and compare it with several state-of-the-art models.

3.1 Datasets

We conduct experiments on three public online review datasets for sentiment classification task, and these datasets are described as follows:

Yelp Reviews. This dataset is released by the review website giant Yelp in America and the reviewed objects in the dataset consist of restaurants, home service, deliveries and so on. The number of review classes is five, i.e., 1–5. Bigger label number means people are more satisfied with what they comment on, and vice versa.

Amazon Food Reviews. The reviews in this dataset are only towards food sold on the online shopping platform Amazon. The number of the review classes is also five and the meaning of each class is the same as Yelp Reviews.

Amazon Electronic Products Reviews. The reviews in this dataset are about electronic products sold on Amazon such as phone, headset and so on. The number of the review classes is still five and the meaning of each class is the same as Yelp Reviews.

3.2 Baselines

We compare our model with several baseline models, which not only consists of traditional neural networks such as CNN and LSTM but also attention models combining CNN and RNN proposed in recent two years. In the following, we will summarize these contrastive models in brief.

Word-Based CNN. The model applies convolution filters on word embedding of text and then capture influential features to form final representation by pooling operation.

Bi-LSTM (Bidirectional Long Short-Term Memory). The model processes word embedding sequence of text with opposite directional LSTMs and use concatenation of last hidden states of LSTMs as representation for classification.

CRAN (CNN-RNN Attention-Based Model). A hybrid CNN-RNN attention-based model proposed in [7] uses CNN to extract context information as attention and combine the output of the CNN with hidden states from Bi-GRU as final representation of sentence.

CAM (Convolutional Attention Model). A convolutional attention model proposed in [8] utilizes convolution filters of different kernel sizes and average feature maps to construct attention weights, then the model combine the attention weights with output of LSTM via inner product to produce sentence embedding.

DAM (Double Attention Mechanism). A double attention mechanism proposed in [14] serially connects two kinds of attention mechanism for sentence embedding. The first is a self-attention similar to what was proposed in [15], and then the output of the first attention is combined with feature maps produced by CNN, which are regarded as the second attention, to form final sentence embedding.

CCG (Combination of CNN and Bidirectional GRU). The architecture of the combination of CNN and Bi-GRU proposed in [16] is similar to CRAN mentioned above. The main difference between CCG and CRAN is that CCG applies hidden states from Bi-GRU to feature maps from CNN to form attention weights.

3.3   Model Settings

Pre-trained word embedding is widely used in variety of natural language processing (NLP) tasks to initialize input words in text. In our experiments, we adopt global vectors for word representation (GloVe) [17] in the embedding layer of our model, which consists of 840 billion 300-dimension tokens trained on Common Crawl. We don't use fine-tuning strategy for these word vectors but keep them unchanged during training processes.

We select 47500 reviews as full set for each dataset and the numbers of reviews of different classes are shown in Table 1. Then we split training and testing set in a ratio of 18:1, which means there are 45000 reviews in training set and 2500 reviews in testing set. In order to do cross validation, we randomly split training and testing set for each training process. In addition, some of the key hyper-parameters that can help achieve the greatest performance are listed in Table 2.

Table 1. The number of reviews of different classes in three datasets

Dataset	Class 1	Class 2	Class 3	Class 4	Class 5
Yelp Reviews	9528	9455	9430	9539	9548
Amazon Food Reviews	9491	9515	9502	9497	9495
Amazon Electronic Product Reviews	9485	9513	9504	9486	9512

Table 2. Hyper-parameter settings of different datasets.

Dataset	Input length	Batch-size	Epoch	Kernel size
Yelp Reviews	120	64	10	2
Amazon Food Reviews	100	64	20	3
Amazon Electronic Product Reviews	80	64	30	5

As shown in Table 2, in order to avoid spending too much time training and extracting insufficient features, we set different input lengths for three datasets based on average length of all reviews in each dataset. Additionally, we choose 64 for batch size, which allows the model to converge as quickly as possible without compromising performance in contrast with other batch sizes such as 16, 32 and 128. As for epoch, we first set it to a random number by experience (for example 40) and train the model on three datasets. After that according to the trend of the model accuracy on these datasets, which is shown in Fig. 2, we can adjust the number of epoch to allow the model to achieve the greatest performance in the shortest possible time. For kernel size, we will discuss later in Sect. 3.5.

Moreover, the number of CNN filters is set to 300 so that we can obtain feature map matrix of the same size as the word embedding matrix. And the number of hidden units of bidirectional LSTM is the same as corresponding input length. We set dropout of 0.3 which helps achieve the best performance and we adopt cross-entropy as loss function and train our model using Adam [18] as optimizer.

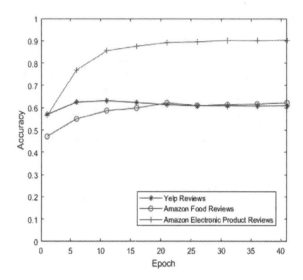

Fig. 2. Trend of model accuracy on three datasets. The accuracy on Yelp Reviews peaks at the 10th epoch and it begins to decline slightly after that. While the accuracy on Amazon Food Reviews and Amazon Electronic Product Reviews peaks at the 20th and 30th epoch respectively and then it remains roughly stable.

3.4   Experimental Results

The performance of our proposed model is compared with the baseline models mentioned in Sect. 3.2. For these baseline models, we train them from scratch on the three datasets and keep hyper-parameters consistent with those in Sect. 3.3. And we average the accuracy of five cross validation experiments for each model on each dataset. The accuracy of the whole models is shown in Table 3. We can conclude from the table that our model outperforms all the contrastive models on three public datasets, which indicates our collaborative attention network is effective and can achieve state-of-the-art performance in these sentiment classification tasks.

3.5   Effect of Kernel Size

In addition, in order to explore the effect of kernel size (size of granularity) in convolution operations, we select different kernel size in range from 2 to 6 to observe the trend of model accuracy on the three public datasets. Figure 3 shows the effects of the variation of the kernel size on the accuracy of our model. It's obvious that kernel size of 2 can achieve the greatest performance for both Yelp Reviews and Amazon Food Reviews while kernel size of 5 suits Amazon Electronic Product Reviews best.

Table 3. Classification accuracy of our model against other baseline models on three public datasets

Model	Yelp Reviews	Amazon Food Reviews	Amazon Electronic Product Reviews
Word-based CNN	0.5932	0.5635	0.8300
Bi-LSTM	0.6042	0.5685	0.8569
CRAN	0.6033	0.5993	0.9002
CAM	0.6046	0.5890	0.8970
DAM	0.6132	0.5938	0.8901
CCG	0.6201	0.5998	0.8929
Our model	**0.6274**	**0.6112**	**0.9062**

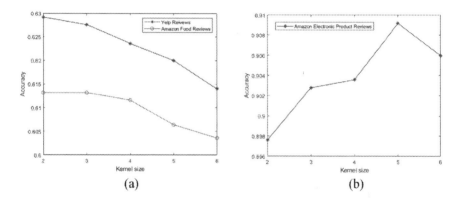

(a)   (b)

Fig. 3. Illustration of effects of kernel size on three datasets. We can notice kernel size of 2 can achieve the greatest performance for both Yelp Reviews and Amazon Food Reviews and with kernel size increasing, the accuracy goes down gradually in (a). For Amazon Electronic Product Reviews in (b), the accuracy peaks when kernel size is 5 and after that it begins to go down.

The most possible reason why different kernel sizes apply to different datasets is that each dataset contains more semantic n-grams of a specific size than other sizes. For examples in Yelp Reviews and Amazon Food Reviews, there are more informative 2-grams and 3-grams such as "*excellent food*", "*friendly service*", "*very delicious*", "*taste was great*" and "*easy to use*" than n-grams of other sizes. In a similar way, there are more informative 5-grams in Amazon Electronic Product Reviews such as "not easy to unlock it", "not capable of getting Wi-Fi", "ok phone for the price" and "very happy with my purchase". So convolution filters with corresponding kernel sizes can capture these semantic n-grams to help the model make correct predictions.

3.6 Visualization of Attention and Analysis

To further illustrate the effectiveness of our attention model, we select some positive and negative reviews from Amazon Electronic Product Reviews for visualization analysis. We visualize the results of element-wise multiplication of the LSTM encoder and the CNN-RNN component with different depth colors. Positive and negative examples are shown in Figs. 4 and 5, respectively. The darker the color is, the more contribution the words make to expression of emotion.

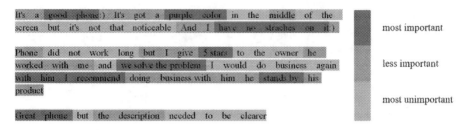

Fig. 4. Visualization of attention on positive reviews from Amazon Electronic Product Reviews. These reviews have label 5 and express satisfaction towards electronic products.

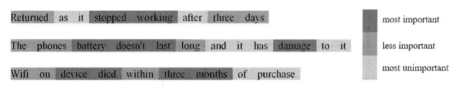

Fig. 5. Visualization of attention on negative reviews from Amazon Electronic Product Reviews. These reviews have label 1 and express complain about electronic products.

In Fig. 4, we can note that words "*good phone*" and "*have no starches on it*" contribute more to expressing positive sentiment in the first review than other parts of the sentence. In the second review, positive words "*5 stars*", "*solve the problem*" and "*recommend*" have great effect on the polarity of general sentiment, while some negative aspects are also mentioned in the same review. Similarly, in the third review, the former part that is positive is focused on while the latter part that is a little negative is paid less attention. In the same way in Fig. 5, we can easily observe words such as "stopped working", "battery doesn't last", "damage" and so on have a major impact on expression of negative emotion.

Furthermore, we analyze representations of reviews in Amazon Electronic Product Reviews via visualization of vectors and pick out some keywords and phrases, which make more contribution to expression of emotion than other common words. We list these keywords and phrases in Table 4.

Specially, we can make further analysis based on the keywords and key phrases above and divide them into three categories: (i) verb-based expressions, (ii) adjective-based expressions and (iii) degree-based expressions. Some examples of each category are shown in Table 5.

Table 4. Keywords and key phrases selected from both positive and negative reviews in Amazon Electronic Product Reviews. Positive keywords and key phrases are selected from reviews labeled 5 while negative keywords and key phrases are from reviews labeled 1.

Positive keywords and key phrases	Good phone, fast delivery, recommend, great phone, love it, love the phone, arrived on time, good service, so happy, no cosmetic issues, good condition
Negative keywords and key phrases	Wouldn't work, do not buy, did not function, awful, stopped working, damage, device died, phone died, not working, broke, not work

Table 5. Some examples of three types of common expressions. Verb-based and adjective-based expressions are often used in reviews to express emotion while degree-based expression are used to emphasize intensity of emotion. Such as *"I will give 5 stars to the product"* in which *"5 stars"* shows great satisfaction of reviewer, and *"The phone died within only two weeks"* in which *"two weeks"* emphasizes the time is short and intensify expression of disappointment indirectly.

	Verb-based	Adjective-based	Degree-based
Positive expressions	Love the phone, recommend, arrived on time, works fine,	Good phone, fast delivery, good condition	5 stars
Negative expressions	Wouldn't work, do not buy, did not function, not work, cannot return, came off	Not good, disappointed, terrible experience, false advertisement	Two weeks, three months

4 Related Work

As one of the hottest branch tasks in text classification, sentiment classification has appealed to plenty of researchers to explore and many outstanding progress have been made in this field. Traditional methods [19–22] adopted bag-of-words (BoW) or n-grams as sentence features to train a classifier like support vector machine (SVM). In [23, 24], topic-based methods were proposed to represent text with topic-related words. In addition, more complex lexical and syntactic features were also designed in [25, 26] to make use of as more structural information of sentences as possible. However, the main drawbacks of these traditional methods are not only lack of order of words in text but also troubles of selecting informative features.

Recent years have witnessed the booming of neural network in natural language processing (NLP), and a number of models have achieved great performance in sentiment classification. Convolution neural network (CNN) applies convolution filters to capture local window context and produce feature maps to represent text. [1] proposed CNN with two channels to classify sentences, while [2, 3] added character-level information in CNN to extract fine-grained semantic representation of sentences. However, it's challenging for CNN to capture long-term dependencies in text which have great impact on polarity of sentiment of text. Differently, recurrent neural network

(RNN) is effective on modeling sequential text and RNNs like long short-term memory (LSTM) and gated recurrent unit (GRU) are capable of memorizing long-term dependencies in text. [5] used gated RNN to encode semantics and their relations of sentences. And [4] proposed cached LSTM for document-level sentiment classification.

Moreover, in order to harness power of CNN and RNN, some hybrid models of CNN and RNN are proposed in these years. And these CNN-RNN-based models combine CNN and RNN in two ways: parallel models or serial models. Parallel models [7–9, 14, 16] commonly use CNN to capture local n-grams and RNN to model word sequences, and incorporate two parts via an attention mechanism. Serial models connect CNN and RNN serially. [10, 11] proposed models feeding feature maps from CNN into RNN, while [26, 27] applied convolution operations to hidden states from RNN.

Though the CNN-RNN-based models achieve better performance than traditional models, they are different from the way humans read text. It's intuitive that humans read text by capturing semantic elements which can help humans understand meaning of text. Different from all the studies above, in order to consider long-term dependencies among words and n-grams simultaneously, we propose a collaborative attention model consisting of a LSTM encoder to process word sequences and a CNN-LSTM component to process n-gram sequences. Then, we incorporate these two parts via an attention mechanism to highlight keywords in sentences.

5   Conclusion

In this paper, for the purpose of modeling long-term dependencies among words and n-grams at the same time, we elaborate a collaborative attention network with word and n-gram sequences modeling. Specially, we use a serial CNN-LSTM to model n-gram sequences and takes its output as attention weights, which is combined with the output of a parallel LSTM encoder for word sequences. Thus we can utilize coarse-grained semantics to adjust corresponding fine-grained semantics to highlight keywords in sentences. Experimental results show that our model can achieve state-of-the-art performance on three public datasets of sentiment classification in contrast with several baseline models. For future work, we will consider using more pre-trained models such as BERT [28] to reduce the amount of training set and the number of parameters.

Acknowledgements. This paper is funded by the National Key R&D Program of China under grant No. 2018YFB1702703, and also funded by the National Natural Science Foundation of China under grant No. U1531122, 71871170 and 61272272.

References

1. Kim, Y.: Convolutional neural networks for sentence classification. arXiv preprint arXiv: 1408.5882 (2014). https://doi.org/10.3115/v1/d14-1181
2. Zhang, X., Zhao, J., LeCun, Y.: Character-level convolutional networks for text classification. In: Advances in Neural Information Processing Systems, pp. 649–657 (2015)

3. Dos Santos, C., Gatti, M.: Deep convolutional neural networks for sentiment analysis of short texts. In: Proceedings of COLING 2014, The 25th International Conference on Computational Linguistics: Technical Papers, pp. 69–78 (2014)

4. Xu, J., Chen, D., Qiu, X., et al.: Cached long short-term memory neural networks for document-level sentiment classification. arXiv preprint arXiv:1610.04989 (2016). https://doi.org/10.18653/v1/d16-1172

5. Tang, D., Qin, B., Liu, T.: Document modeling with gated recurrent neural network for sentiment classification. In: Proceedings of the 2015 Conference on Empirical Methods in Natural Language Processing, pp. 1422–1432 (2015). https://doi.org/10.18653/v1/d15-1167

6. Tang, D., Qin, B., Feng, X., et al.: Effective LSTMs for target-dependent sentiment classification. arXiv preprint arXiv:1512.01100 (2015)

7. Guo, L., Zhang, D., Wang, L., Wang, H., Cui, B.: CRAN: a hybrid CNN-RNN attention-based model for text classification. In: Trujillo, J.C., et al. (eds.) ER 2018. LNCS, vol. 11157, pp. 571–585. Springer, Cham (2018). https://doi.org/10.1007/978-3-030-00847-5_42

8. Du, J., Gui, L., Xu, R., He, Y.: A convolutional attention model for text classification. In: Huang, X., Jiang, J., Zhao, D., Feng, Y., Hong, Yu. (eds.) NLPCC 2017. LNCS (LNAI), vol. 10619, pp. 183–195. Springer, Cham (2018). https://doi.org/10.1007/978-3-319-73618-1_16

9. Zhang, X., Huang, L., Qu, H.: AHNN: an attention-based hybrid neural network for sentence modeling. In: Huang, X., Jiang, J., Zhao, D., Feng, Y., Hong, Yu. (eds.) NLPCC 2017. LNCS (LNAI), vol. 10619, pp. 731–740. Springer, Cham (2018). https://doi.org/10.1007/978-3-319-73618-1_63

10. Zhou, C., Sun, C., Liu, Z., et al.: A C-LSTM neural network for text classification. arXiv preprint arXiv:1511.08630 (2015)

11. Wang, X., Jiang, W., Luo, Z.: Combination of convolutional and recurrent neural network for sentiment analysis of short texts. In: Proceedings of COLING 2016, the 26th International Conference on Computational Linguistics: Technical Papers, pp. 2428–2437 (2016)

12. Cai, R., Zhu, B., Ji, L., et al.: An CNN-LSTM attention approach to understanding user query intent from online health communities. In: 2017 IEEE International Conference on Data Mining Workshops (ICDMW), pp. 430–437. IEEE (2017). https://doi.org/10.1109/icdmw.2017.62

13. Hochreiter, S., Schmidhuber, J.: Long short-term memory. Neural Comput. 9(8), 1735–1780 (1997)

14. Kakanakou, M., Xie, H., Qiang, Y.: Double attention mechanism for sentence embedding. In: Meng, X., Li, R., Wang, K., Niu, B., Wang, X., Zhao, G. (eds.) WISA 2018. LNCS, vol. 11242, pp. 228–239. Springer, Cham (2018). https://doi.org/10.1007/978-3-030-02934-0_21

15. Lin, Z., Feng, M., Santos, C.N., et al.: A structured self-attentive sentence embedding. arXiv preprint arXiv:1703.03130 (2017)

16. Zhang, D., Tian, L., Hong, M., et al.: Combining convolution neural network and bidirectional gated recurrent unit for sentence semantic classification. IEEE Access. 6, 73750–73759 (2018). https://doi.org/10.1109/access.2018.2882878

17. Pennington, J., Socher, R., Manning, C.: Glove: global vectors for word representation. In: Proceedings of the 2014 Conference on Empirical Methods in Natural Language Processing (EMNLP), pp. 1532–1543 (2014). https://doi.org/10.3115/v1/d14-1162

18. Kingma, D.P., Ba, J.: Adam: a method for stochastic optimization. arXiv preprint arXiv:1412.6980 (2014)

19. Cavnar, W.B., Trenkle, J.M.: N-gram-based text categorization. In: Proceedings of SDAIR-94, 3rd Annual Symposium on Document Analysis and Information Retrieval, vol. 161175 (1994)

20. Joachims, T.: Text categorization with Support Vector Machines: learning with many relevant features. In: Nédellec, C., Rouveirol, C. (eds.) ECML 1998. LNCS, vol. 1398, pp. 137–142. Springer, Heidelberg (1998). https://doi.org/10.1007/BFb0026683
21. Pang, B., Lee, L., Vaithyanathan, S.: Thumbs up?: sentiment classification using machine learning techniques. In: Proceedings of the ACL-02 Conference on Empirical Methods in Natural Language Processing, vol. 10, pp. 79–86. Association for Computational Linguistics (2002). https://doi.org/10.3115/1118693.1118704
22. Lewis, D.D.: An evaluation of phrasal and clustered representations on a text categorization task. In: Proceedings of the 15th Annual International ACM SIGIR Conference on Research and Development in Information Retrieval, pp. 37–50. ACM (1992). https://doi.org/10.1145/133160.133172
23. Lin, C., He, Y.: Joint sentiment/topic model for sentiment analysis. In: Proceedings of the 18th ACM Conference on Information and Knowledge Management, pp. 375–384. ACM (2009). https://doi.org/10.1145/1645953.1646003
24. Li, F., Huang, M., Zhu, X.: Sentiment analysis with global topics and local dependency. In: Twenty-Fourth AAAI Conference on Artificial Intelligence (2010)
25. Post, M., Bergsma, S.: Explicit and implicit syntactic features for text classification. In: Proceedings of the 51st Annual Meeting of the Association for Computational Linguistics: Short Papers, vol. 2, pp. 866–872. Association for Computational Linguistics (2013)
26. Lai, S., Xu, L., Liu, K., et al.: Recurrent convolutional neural networks for text classification. In: Twenty-Ninth AAAI Conference on Artificial Intelligence (2015)
27. Zhou, P., Qi, Z., Zheng, S., et al.: Text classification improved by integrating bidirectional LSTM with two-dimensional max pooling. arXiv preprint arXiv:1611.06639 (2016)
28. Devlin, J., Chang, M.W., Lee, K., et al.: BERT: pre-training of deep bidirectional transformers for language understanding. arXiv preprint arXiv:1810.04805 (2018)

Targeted Sentiment Classification with Attentional Encoder Network

Youwei Song, Jiahai Wang[✉], Tao Jiang, Zhiyue Liu, and Yanghui Rao

School of Data and Computer Science, Sun Yat-sen University, Guangzhou, China
{songyw5,jiangt59,liuzy93}@mail2.sysu.edu.cn,
{wangjiah,raoyangh}@mail.sysu.edu.cn

Abstract. Targeted sentiment classification aims at determining the sentimental tendency towards specific targets. Most of the previous approaches model context and target words with RNN and attention. However, RNNs are difficult to parallelize and truncated backpropagation through time brings difficulty in remembering long-term patterns. To address this issue, this paper proposes an Attentional Encoder Network (AEN) which eschews recurrence and employs attention based encoders for the modeling between context and target. We raise the label unreliability issue and introduce label smoothing regularization. We also apply pre-trained BERT to this task and obtain new state-of-the-art results. Experiments and analysis demonstrate the effectiveness and lightweight of our model.

Keywords: Target-dependent sentiment classification ·
Sentiment classification · Sentiment analysis · Attention mechanism

1 Introduction

Targeted sentiment classification is a fine-grained sentiment analysis task, which aims at determining the sentiment polarities (e.g., negative, neutral, or positive) of a sentence over "opinion targets" that explicitly appear in the sentence. For example, given a sentence *"I hated their service, but their food was great"*, the sentiment polarities for the target *"service"* and *"food"* are negative and positive respectively. A target is usually an entity or an entity aspect.

In recent years, neural network models are designed to automatically learn useful low-dimensional representations from targets and contexts and obtain promising results [5,16]. However, these neural network models are still in infancy to deal with the fine-grained targeted sentiment classification task.

Attention mechanism, which has been successfully used in machine translation [1], is incorporated to enforce the model to pay more attention to context words with closer semantic relations with the target. There are already some studies use attention to generate target-specific sentence representations [2,11,19] or to transform sentence representations according to target words [10].

© Springer Nature Switzerland AG 2019
I. V. Tetko et al. (Eds.): ICANN 2019, LNCS 11730, pp. 93–103, 2019.
https://doi.org/10.1007/978-3-030-30490-4_9

However, these studies depend on complex recurrent neural networks (RNNs) as sequence encoder to compute hidden semantics of texts.

The first problem with previous works is that the modeling of text relies on RNNs. RNNs, such as LSTM, are very expressive, but they are hard to parallelize and backpropagation through time (BPTT) requires large amounts of memory and computation. Moreover, essentially every training algorithm of RNN is the truncated BPTT, which affects the model's ability to capture dependencies over longer time scales [20]. Although LSTM can alleviate the vanishing gradient problem to a certain extent and thus maintain long distance information, this usually requires a large amount of training data. Another problem that previous studies ignore is the label unreliability issue, since *neutral* sentiment is a fuzzy sentimental state and brings difficulty for model learning. As far as we know, we are the first to raise the label unreliability issue in the targeted sentiment classification task.

This paper propose an attention based model to solve the problems above. Specifically, our model eschews recurrence and employs attention as a competitive alternative to draw the introspective and interactive semantics between target and context words. To deal with the label unreliability issue, we employ a label smoothing regularization to encourage the model to be less confident with fuzzy labels. We also apply pre-trained BERT [3] to this task and show our model enhances the performance of basic BERT model. Experimental results on three benchmark datasets show that the proposed model achieves competitive performance and is a lightweight alternative of the best RNN based models.

The main contributions of this work are presented as follows:

1. We design an attentional encoder network to draw the hidden states and semantic interactions between target and context words.
2. We raise the label unreliability issue and add an effective label smoothing regularization term to the loss function for encouraging the model to be less confident with the training labels.
3. We apply pre-trained BERT to this task, our model enhances the performance of basic BERT model and obtains new state-of-the-art results.
4. We evaluate the model sizes of the compared models and show the lightweight of the proposed model.

2   Related Work

The research approach of the targeted sentiment classification task including traditional machine learning methods and neural networks methods.

Traditional machine learning methods, including rule-based methods [4] and statistic-based methods [7], mainly focus on extracting a set of features like sentiment lexicons features and bag-of-words features to train a sentiment classifier [14]. The performance of these methods highly depends on the effectiveness of the feature engineering works, which are labor intensive.

In recent years, neural network methods are getting more and more attention as they do not need handcrafted features and can encode sentences with low-dimensional word vectors where rich semantic information stained. In order to incorporate target words into a model, Tang et al. [16] propose TD-LSTM to extend LSTM by using two single-directional LSTM to model the left context and right context of the target word respectively. Tang et al. [17] design MemNet which consists of a multi-hop attention mechanism with an external memory to capture the importance of each context word concerning the given target. Multiple attention is paid to the memory represented by word embeddings to build higher semantic information. Wang et al. [19] propose ATAE-LSTM which concatenates target embeddings with word representations and let targets participate in computing attention weights. Chen et al. [2] propose RAM which adopts multiple-attention mechanism on the memory built with bidirectional LSTM and nonlinearly combines the attention results with gated recurrent units (GRUs). Ma et al. [11] propose IAN which learns the representations of the target and context with two attention networks interactively.

3   Proposed Methodology

Given a context sequence $\mathbf{w^c} = \{w_1^c, w_2^c, ..., w_n^c\}$ and a target sequence $\mathbf{w^t} = \{w_1^t, w_2^t, ..., w_m^t\}$, where $\mathbf{w^t}$ is a sub-sequence of $\mathbf{w^c}$. The goal of this model is to predict the sentiment polarity of the sentence $\mathbf{w^c}$ over the target $\mathbf{w^t}$.

Figure 1 illustrates the overall architecture of the proposed **A**ttentional **E**ncoder **N**etwork (AEN), which mainly consists of an embedding layer, an attentional encoder layer, a target-specific attention layer, and an output layer. Embedding layer has two types: GloVe embedding and BERT embedding. Accordingly, the models are named **AEN-GloVe** and **AEN-BERT**.

3.1   Embedding Layer

GloVe Embedding. Let $L \in \mathbb{R}^{d_{emb} \times |V|}$ to be the pre-trained GloVe [12] embedding matrix, where d_{emb} is the dimension of word vectors and $|V|$ is the vocabulary size. Then we map each word $w^i \in \mathbb{R}^{|V|}$ to its corresponding embedding vector $e_i \in \mathbb{R}^{d_{emb} \times 1}$, which is a column in the embedding matrix L.

BERT Embedding. BERT embedding uses the pre-trained BERT to generate word vectors of sequence. In order to facilitate the training and fine-tuning of BERT model, we transform the given context and target to "[CLS] + context + [SEP]" and "[CLS] + target + [SEP]" respectively.

3.2   Attentional Encoder Layer

The attentional encoder layer is a parallelizable and interactive alternative of LSTM and is applied to compute the hidden states of the input embeddings. This layer consists of two submodules: the **M**ulti-**H**ead **A**ttention (MHA) and the **P**oint-wise **C**onvolution **T**ransformation (PCT).

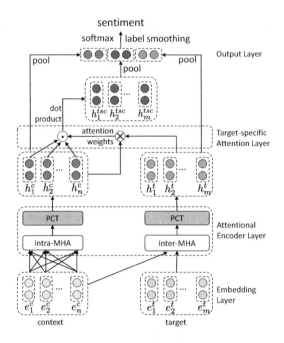

Fig. 1. Overall architecture of the proposed AEN.

Multi-Head Attention. Multi-**H**ead **A**ttention (MHA) is the attention that can perform multiple attention function in parallel. Different from Transformer [18], we use **Intra-MHA** for introspective context words modeling and **Inter-MHA** for context-perceptive target words modeling, which is more lightweight and target is modeled according to a given context.

An attention function maps a key sequence $\mathbf{k} = \{k_1, k_2, ..., k_n\}$ and a query sequence $\mathbf{q} = \{q_1, q_2, ..., q_m\}$ to an output sequence $\mathbf{o}$:

$$Attention(\mathbf{k}, \mathbf{q}) = softmax(f_s(\mathbf{k}, \mathbf{q}))\mathbf{k} \tag{1}$$

$$f_s(k_i, q_j) = tanh([k_i; q_j] \cdot W_{att}) \tag{2}$$

where f_s denotes the alignment function which learns the semantic relevance between q_j and k_i, and $W_{att} \in \mathbb{R}^{2d_{hid}}$ is learnable weight.

MHA can learn n_head different scores in parallel child spaces and is very powerful for alignments. The n_{head} outputs are concatenated and projected to the specified hidden dimension d_{hid}, namely,

$$MHA(\mathbf{k}, \mathbf{q}) = [\mathbf{o}^1; \mathbf{o}^2...; \mathbf{o}^{n_{head}}] \cdot W_{mh} \tag{3}$$

$$\mathbf{o}^h = Attention^h(\mathbf{k}, \mathbf{q}) \tag{4}$$

where ";" denotes vector concatenation, $W_{mh} \in \mathbb{R}^{d_{hid} \times d_{hid}}$, $\mathbf{o}^h = \{o_1^h, o_2^h, ..., o_m^h\}$ is the output of the h-th head attention and $h \in [1, n_{head}]$.

Intra-MHA, or multi-head self-attention, is a special situation for typical attention mechanism that $\mathbf{q} = \mathbf{k}$. Given a context embedding $\mathbf{e^c}$, we can get the introspective context representation $\mathbf{c^{intra}}$ by:

$$\mathbf{c^{intra}} = MHA(\mathbf{e^c}, \mathbf{e^c}) \tag{5}$$

The learned context representation $\mathbf{c^{intra}} = \{c_1^{intra}, c_2^{intra}, ..., c_n^{intra}\}$ is aware of long-term dependencies.

Inter-MHA is the generally used form of attention mechanism that $\mathbf{q}$ is different from $\mathbf{k}$. Given a context embedding $\mathbf{e^c}$ and a target embedding $\mathbf{e^t}$, we can get the context-perceptive target representation $\mathbf{t^{inter}}$ by:

$$\mathbf{t^{inter}} = MHA(\mathbf{e^c}, \mathbf{e^t}) \tag{6}$$

After this interactive procedure, each given target word e_j^t will have a composed representation selected from context embeddings $\mathbf{e^c}$. Then we get the context-perceptive target words modeling $\mathbf{t^{inter}} = \{t_1^{inter}, t_2^{inter}, ..., t_m^{inter}\}$.

Point-Wise Convolution Transformation. A **P**oint-wise **C**onvolution **T**ransformation (PCT) can transform contextual information gathered by the MHA. Point-wise means that the kernel sizes are 1 and the same transformation is applied to every single token belonging to the input. Formally, given a input sequence $\mathbf{h}$, PCT is defined as:

$$PCT(\mathbf{h}) = \sigma(\mathbf{h} * W_{pc}^1 + b_{pc}^1) * W_{pc}^2 + b_{pc}^2 \tag{7}$$

where σ stands for the ELU activation, $*$ is the convolution operator, $W_{pc}^1 \in \mathbb{R}^{d_{hid} \times d_{hid}}$ and $W_{pc}^2 \in \mathbb{R}^{d_{hid} \times d_{hid}}$ are the learnable weights of the two convolutional kernels, $b_{pc}^1 \in \mathbb{R}^{d_{hid}}$ and $b_{pc}^2 \in \mathbb{R}^{d_{hid}}$ are biases of the two convolutional kernels.

Given $\mathbf{c^{intra}}$ and $\mathbf{t^{inter}}$, PCTs are applied to get the output hidden states of the attentional encoder layer $\mathbf{h^c} = \{h_1^c, h_2^c, ..., h_n^c\}$ and $\mathbf{h^t} = \{h_1^t, h_2^t, ..., h_m^t\}$ by:

$$\mathbf{h^c} = PCT(\mathbf{c^{intra}}) \tag{8}$$

$$\mathbf{h^t} = PCT(\mathbf{t^{inter}}) \tag{9}$$

3.3   Target-Specific Attention Layer

After we obtain the introspective context representation $\mathbf{h^c}$ and the context-perceptive target representation $\mathbf{h^t}$, we employ another MHA to obtain the target-specific context representation $\mathbf{h^{tsc}} = \{h_1^{tsc}, h_2^{tsc}, ..., h_m^{tsc}\}$ by:

$$\mathbf{h^{tsc}} = MHA(\mathbf{h^c}, \mathbf{h^t}) \tag{10}$$

The multi-head attention function here also has its independent parameters.

3.4   Output Layer

We get the final representations of the previous outputs by average pooling, concatenate them as the final comprehensive representation $\tilde{o}$, and use a full connected layer to project the concatenated vector into the space of the targeted C classes.

$$\tilde{o} = [h^c_{avg}; h^t_{avg}; h^{tsc}_{avg}] \tag{11}$$

$$x = \tilde{W}_o^T \tilde{o} + \tilde{b}_o \tag{12}$$

$$y = softmax(x) \tag{13}$$

$$= \frac{exp(x)}{\sum_{k=1}^{C} exp(x)} \tag{14}$$

where $y \in \mathbb{R}^C$ is the predicted sentiment polarity distribution, $\tilde{W}_o \in \mathbb{R}^{1 \times C}$ and $\tilde{b}_o \in \mathbb{R}^C$ are learnable parameters.

3.5   Regularization and Model Training

Since *neutral* sentiment is a very fuzzy sentimental state, training samples which labeled *neutral* are unreliable. We employ a **L**abel **S**moothing **R**egularization (LSR) term in the loss function. Which penalizes low entropy output distributions [15]. LSR can reduce overfitting by preventing a network from assigning the full probability to each training example during training, replaces the 0 and 1 targets for a classifier with smoothed values like 0.1 or 0.9.

For a training sample x with the original ground-truth label distribution $q(k|x)$, we replace $q(k|x)$ with

$$q(k|x) = (1 - \epsilon)q(k|x) + \epsilon u(k) \tag{15}$$

where $u(k)$ is the prior distribution over labels, and ϵ is the smoothing parameter. In this paper, we set the prior label distribution to be uniform $u(k) = 1/C$.

LSR is equivalent to the KL divergence between the prior label distribution $u(k)$ and the network's predicted distribution p_θ. Formally, LSR term is defined as:

$$\mathcal{L}_{lsr} = -D_{KL}(u(k)\|p_\theta) \tag{16}$$

The objective function (loss function) to be optimized is the cross-entropy loss with $\mathcal{L}_{lsr}$ and $\mathcal{L}_2$ regularization, which is defined as:

$$\mathcal{L}(\theta) = -\sum_{i=1}^{C} \hat{y}^c log(y^c) + \mathcal{L}_{lsr} + \lambda \sum_{\theta \in \Theta} \theta^2 \tag{17}$$

where $\hat{y} \in \mathbb{R}^C$ is the ground truth represented as a one-hot vector, y is the predicted sentiment distribution vector given by the output layer, λ is the coefficient for $\mathcal{L}_2$ regularization term, and Θ is the parameter set.

Table 1. Statistics of the datasets.

Dataset	Positive		Neural		Negative	
	Train	Test	Train	Test	Train	Test
Twitter	1561	173	3127	346	1560	173
Restaurant	2164	728	637	196	807	196
Laptop	994	341	464	169	870	128

4   Experiments

4.1   Datasets and Experimental Settings

We conduct experiments on three datasets: SemEval 2014 Task 4^1 [13] dataset composed of *Restaurant* reviews and *Laptop* reviews, and ACL 14 *Twitter* dataset gathered by Dong et al. [5]. These datasets are labeled with three sentiment polarities: *positive*, *neutral* and *negative*. Table 1 shows the number of training and test instances in each category.

GloVe embeddings in AEN-GloVe do not get updated in the learning process, but we fine-tune pre-trained $BERT^2$ in AEN-BERT. Embedding dimension d_{dim} is 300 for GloVe and is 768 for pre-trained BERT. Dimension of hidden states d_{hid} is set to 300. The weights of our model are initialized with Glorot initialization [6]. During training, we set label smoothing parameter ϵ to 0.2 [15], the coefficient λ of $\mathcal{L}_2$ regularization item is 10^{-5} and dropout rate is 0.1. Adam optimizer [8] is applied to update all the parameters. We adopt the *Accuracy* and *Macro-F1* metrics to evaluate the performance of the model.

4.2   Model Comparisons

In order to comprehensively evaluate and analysis the performance of AEN-GloVe, we list 7 baseline models and design 4 ablations of AEN-GloVe. We also design a basic BERT-based model to evaluate the performance of AEN-BERT.

Non-RNN Based Baselines:
- **Feature-based SVM** [9] is a traditional support vector machine based model with extensive feature engineering.
- **Rec-NN** [5] firstly uses rules to transform the dependency tree and put the opinion target at the root, and then learns the sentence representation toward target via semantic composition using Recursive NNs.
- **MemNet** [17] uses multi-hops of attention layers on the context word embeddings for sentence representation to explicitly captures the importance of each context word.

---

[1] The detailed introduction of this task can be found at http://alt.qcri.org/semeval2014/task4.

[2] We use uncased BERT-base from https://github.com/google-research/bert.

RNN Based Baselines:

• **TD-LSTM** [16] extends LSTM by using two LSTM networks to model the left context with target and the right context with target respectively. The left and right target-dependent representations are concatenated for predicting the sentiment polarity of the target.

• **ATAE-LSTM** [19] strengthens the effect of target embeddings, which appends the target embeddings with each word embeddings and use LSTM with attention to get the final representation for classification.

• **IAN** [11] learns the representations of the target and context with two LSTMs and attentions interactively, which generates the representations for targets and contexts with respect to each other.

• **RAM** [2] strengthens MemNet by representing memory with bidirectional LSTM and using a gated recurrent unit network to combine the multiple attention outputs for sentence representation.

AEN-GloVe Ablations:

• **AEN-GloVe w/o PCT** ablates PCT module.

• **AEN-GloVe w/o MHA** ablates MHA module.

• **AEN-GloVe w/o LSR** ablates label smoothing regularization.

• **AEN-GloVe-BiLSTM** replaces the attentional encoder layer with two bidirectional LSTM.

Basic BERT-Based Model:

• **BERT-SPC** feeds sequence "[CLS] + context + [SEP] + target + [SEP]" into the basic BERT model for sentence pair classification task.

4.3   Main Results

Table 2 shows the performance comparison of AEN with other models. BERT-SPC and AEN-BERT obtain substantial accuracy improvements, which shows the power of pre-trained BERT on small-data task. The overall performance of AEN-BERT is better than BERT-SPC, which suggests that it is important to design a downstream network customized to a specific task. As the prior knowledge in the pre-trained BERT is not specific to any particular domain, further fine-tuning on the specific task is necessary for releasing the true power of BERT.

The overall performance of TD-LSTM is not good since it only makes a rough treatment of the target words. ATAE-LSTM, IAN and RAM are attention based models, they stably exceed the TD-LSTM method on *Restaurant* and *Laptop* datasets. RAM is better than other RNN based models, but it does not perform well on *Twitter* dataset, which might because bidirectional LSTM is not good at modeling small and ungrammatical text.

Feature-based SVM is still a competitive baseline, but relying on manually-designed features. Rec-NN gets the worst performances among all neural network baselines as dependency parsing is not guaranteed to work well on ungrammatical short texts such as tweets and comments. Like AEN, MemNet also eschews recurrence, but its overall performance is not good since it does not model the

Table 2. Main results. The results of baseline models are retrieved from published papers. "-" means not reported. Top 3 scores are in **bold**.

Models	Twitter		Restaurant		Laptop	
	Accuracy	Macro-F1	Accuracy	Macro-F1	Accuracy	Macro-F1
TD-LSTM	0.7080	0.6900	0.7563	-	0.6813	-
ATAE-LSTM	-	-	0.7720	-	0.6870	-
IAN	-	-	0.7860	-	0.7210	-
RAM	0.6936	0.6730	0.8023	0.7080	**0.7449**	**0.7135**
Feature-based SVM	0.6340	0.6330	0.8016	-	0.7049	-
Rec-NN	0.6630	0.6590	-	-	-	-
MemNet	0.6850	0.6691	0.7816	0.6583	0.7033	0.6409
AEN-GloVe w/o PCT	0.7066	0.6907	0.8017	0.7050	0.7272	0.6750
AEN-GloVe w/o MHA	0.7124	0.6953	0.7919	0.7028	0.7178	0.6650
AEN-GloVe w/o LSR	0.7080	0.6920	0.8000	0.7108	0.7288	0.6869
AEN-GloVe-BiLSTM	0.7210	**0.7042**	0.7973	0.7037	0.7312	0.6980
AEN-GloVe	**0.7283**	0.6981	**0.8098**	**0.7214**	0.7351	0.6904
BERT-SPC	**0.7355**	**0.7214**	**0.8446**	**0.7698**	**0.7899**	**0.7503**
AEN-BERT	**0.7471**	**0.7313**	**0.8312**	**0.7376**	**0.7993**	**0.7631**

hidden semantic of embeddings, and the result of the last attention is essentially a linear combination of word embeddings.

4.4 Model Analysis

As shown in Table 2, the performances of AEN-GloVe ablations are incomparable with AEN-GloVe in both accuracy and macro-F1 measure. This result shows that all of these discarded components are crucial for a good performance. Comparing the results of AEN-GloVe and AEN-GloVe w/o LSR, we observe that the accuracy of AEN-GloVe w/o LSR drops significantly on all three datasets. We could attribute this phenomenon to the unreliability of the training samples with *neutral* sentiment. The overall performance of AEN-GloVe and AEN-GloVe-BiLSTM is relatively close, AEN-GloVe performs better on the *Restaurant* dataset. More importantly, AEN-GloVe has fewer parameters and is easier to parallelize.

To figure out whether the proposed AEN-GloVe is a lightweight alternative of recurrent models, we study the model size of each model on the *Restaurant* dataset. Statistical results are reported in Table 3. We implement all the compared models base on the same source code infrastructure, use the same hyperparameters, and run them on the same GPU[3].

RNN-based and BERT-based models indeed have larger model size. ATAE-LSTM, IAN, RAM, and AEN-GloVe-BiLSTM are all attention based RNN models, memory optimization for these models will be more difficult. AEN-GloVe's lightweight level ranks second, since it takes some more parameters than

---

[3] NVIDIA GTX 1080ti.

MemNet in modeling hidden states of sequences. As a comparison, the model size of AEN-GloVe-BiLSTM is more than twice that of AEN-GloVe, but does not bring any performance improvements.

Table 3. Model sizes. Memory footprints are evaluated on the Restaurant dataset. Lowest 2 are in **bold**.

Models	Model size	
	Params $\times 10^6$	Memory (MB)
TD-LSTM	1.44	12.41
ATAE-LSTM	2.53	16.61
IAN	2.16	15.30
RAM	6.13	31.18
MemNet	**0.36**	**7.82**
AEN-BERT	112.93	451.84
AEN-GloVe-BiLSTM	3.97	22.52
AEN-GloVe	**1.16**	**11.04**

5   Conclusion

In this work, we propose an attentional encoder network for the targeted sentiment classification task. which employs attention based encoders for the modeling between context and target. We raise the label unreliability issue add a label smoothing regularization to encourage the model to be less confident with fuzzy labels. We also applies pre-trained BERT to this task and obtains new state-of-the-art results. Experiments and analysis demonstrate the effectiveness and lightweight of the proposed model.

Acknowledgement. This work is supported by the National Natural Science Foundation of China (61673403, U1611262).

References

1. Bahdanau, D., Cho, K., Bengio, Y.: Neural machine translation by jointly learning to align and translate. arXiv preprint arXiv:1409.0473 (2014)
2. Chen, P., Sun, Z., Bing, L., Yang, W.: Recurrent attention network on memory for aspect sentiment analysis. In: Proceedings of the 2017 Conference on Empirical Methods in Natural Language Processing, pp. 452–461 (2017)
3. Devlin, J., Chang, M.W., Lee, K., Toutanova, K.: BERT: pre-training of deep bidirectional transformers for language understanding. arXiv preprint arXiv:1810.04805 (2018)
4. Ding, X., Liu, B., Yu, P.S.: A holistic lexicon-based approach to opinion mining. In: Proceedings of the 2008 International Conference on Web Search and Data Mining, pp. 231–240. ACM (2008)

5. Dong, L., Wei, F., Tan, C., Tang, D., Zhou, M., Xu, K.: Adaptive recursive neural network for target-dependent twitter sentiment classification. In: Proceedings of the 52nd Annual Meeting of the Association for Computational Linguistics (Volume 2: Short Papers), vol. 2, pp. 49–54 (2014)

6. Glorot, X., Bengio, Y.: Understanding the difficulty of training deep feedforward neural networks. In: Proceedings of the Thirteenth International Conference on Artificial Intelligence and Statistics, pp. 249–256 (2010)

7. Jiang, L., Yu, M., Zhou, M., Liu, X., Zhao, T.: Target-dependent twitter sentiment classification. In: Proceedings of the 49th Annual Meeting of the Association for Computational Linguistics: Human Language Technologies-Volume 1, pp. 151–160. Association for Computational Linguistics (2011)

8. Kingma, D.P., Ba, J.: Adam: a method for stochastic optimization. arXiv preprint arXiv:1412.6980 (2014)

9. Kiritchenko, S., Zhu, X., Cherry, C., Mohammad, S.: NRC-Canada-2014: detecting aspects and sentiment in customer reviews. In: Proceedings of the 8th International Workshop on Semantic Evaluation (SemEval 2014), pp. 437–442 (2014)

10. Li, X., Bing, L., Lam, W., Shi, B.: Transformation networks for target-oriented sentiment classification. In: Proceedings of the 56th Annual Meeting of the Association for Computational Linguistics (Volume 1: Long Papers), vol. 1, pp. 946–956 (2018)

11. Ma, D., Li, S., Zhang, X., Wang, H.: Interactive attention networks for aspect-level sentiment classification. In: Proceedings of the 26th International Joint Conference on Artificial Intelligence, pp. 4068–4074. AAAI Press (2017)

12. Pennington, J., Socher, R., Manning, C.: GloVe: global vectors for word representation. In: Proceedings of the 2014 Conference on Empirical Methods in Natural Language Processing (EMNLP), pp. 1532–1543 (2014)

13. Pontiki, M., Galanis, D., Pavlopoulos, J., Papageorgiou, H., Androutsopoulos, I., Manandhar, S.: SemEval-2014 task 4: aspect based sentiment analysis. In: Proceedings of the 8th International Workshop on Semantic Evaluation (SemEval 2014), pp. 27–35 (2014)

14. Rao, D., Ravichandran, D.: Semi-supervised polarity lexicon induction. In: Proceedings of the 12th Conference of the European Chapter of the Association for Computational Linguistics, pp. 675–682. Association for Computational Linguistics (2009)

15. Szegedy, C., Vanhoucke, V., Ioffe, S., Shlens, J., Wojna, Z.: Rethinking the inception architecture for computer vision. In: Proceedings of the IEEE Conference on Computer Vision and Pattern Recognition, pp. 2818–2826 (2016)

16. Tang, D., Qin, B., Feng, X., Liu, T.: Effective LSTMs for target-dependent sentiment classification. In: Proceedings of COLING 2016, the 26th International Conference on Computational Linguistics: Technical Papers, pp. 3298–3307 (2016)

17. Tang, D., Qin, B., Liu, T.: Aspect level sentiment classification with deep memory network. In: Proceedings of the 2016 Conference on Empirical Methods in Natural Language Processing, pp. 214–224 (2016)

18. Vaswani, A., et al.: Attention is all you need. In: Advances in Neural Information Processing Systems, pp. 5998–6008 (2017)

19. Wang, Y., Huang, M., Zhao, L., et al.: Attention-based LSTM for aspect-level sentiment classification. In: Proceedings of the 2016 Conference on Empirical Methods in Natural Language Processing, pp. 606–615 (2016)

20. Werbos, P.J.: Backpropagation through time: what it does and how to do it. Proc. IEEE **78**(10), 1550–1560 (1990)

Capturing User and Product Information for Sentiment Classification via Hierarchical Separated Attention and Neural Collaborative Filtering

Minghui Yan[1,2], Changjian Wang[1,2], and Ying Sha[1,2(✉)]

[1] Institute of Information Engineering, Chinese Academy of Sciences, Beijing, China
{yanminghui,wangchangjian,shaying}@iie.ac.cn
[2] School of Cyber Security, University of Chinese Academy of Sciences,
Beijing, China

Abstract. Sentiment classification which aims to predict a user's sentiment about a product is becoming more and more useful and important. Some neural network methods achieved improvement by capturing user and product information. However, these methods fail to incorporate user preferences and product characteristics reasonably and effectively. What's more, these methods all only use the explicit influences observed in texts and ignore the implicit interaction influences between user and product which cannot be observed in texts. In this paper, we propose a novel neural network model HUPSA-NCF (Hierarchical User Product Separated Attention and Neural Collaborative Filtering Network) to address these issues. Firstly, our model uses hierarchical user and product separated attention on BiLSTM to incorporate user preferences and product characteristics into specific text representations respectively. Secondly, our model uses neural collaborative filtering to capture the implicit interaction influences between user and product. Lastly, our model makes full use of both explicit and implicit informations for final classification. Experimental results show that our model outperforms state-of-the-art methods on IMDB and Yelp datasets.

Keywords: Document-level sentiment classification ·
Attention mechanism · Neural collaborative filtering · BiLSTM

1 Introduction

Sentiment analysis aims to analyze and determine people's sentiments, opinions, emotions and attitudes towards entities (e.g., products, services, events or topics) according to their generated texts [1]. With the rapid growth of online shopping and review sites (e.g., Yelp, Amazon or IMDB), people have been used to write texts to express their sentiments. And these sentiments information in people's

© Springer Nature Switzerland AG 2019
I. V. Tetko et al. (Eds.): ICANN 2019, LNCS 11730, pp. 104–116, 2019.
https://doi.org/10.1007/978-3-030-30490-4_10

texts are greatly useful for many applications, e.g., financial prediction, recommendation system and political election. Therefore, sentiment analysis draws increasing attention of researchers and industries.

Sentiment analysis is studied at three levels of granularity mainly: document-level, sentence-level, and aspect-level. Our work focuses on the task of document-level sentiment classification which aims to predict the polarity intensities or ratings (e.g., 1–10 stars on the site IMDB) of a review written by a user for a product.

Most studies take sentiment classification as a special case of text classification and take the polarity intensities or ratings as the label of the text. So early methods usually apply machine learning to train sentiment classifiers with text features. However, the performance of these methods heavily depends on the quality of human-designed text features. With the maturity of word embeddings (e.g., Word2Vec [2]), some methods [3,4] begin use deep neural networks to learn text representations automatically and they perform better than machine learning methods. However, these methods all ignore the user and product information. It's a common sense that user preferences and product characteristics significantly effect the ratings. Because for different users or different products, same texts maybe express different emotional intensity and get different ratings.

To incorporate user and product information, Tang et al. [10] introduces a word-level preference matrix and a semantic-level vector for each user and product into CNN sentiment classifier. It gets some improvements but suffers from the high model complexity and only incorporates user and product information in word-level rather than in semantic level. Dou [12] trys to use deep memory network to capture user and product information, but it also suffers from the high model complexity. Chen et al. [11] uses user and product joint attention to incorporate user and product efficiently, and it has a good improvement. However, user and product joint attention has a little unreasonable, a more reasonable way of using attention mechanism is to use user attention and product attention separately, because the user and product have very different influences on reviews. The method is proposed by Wu et al. [13], but it separates user and product so heavily that it must maintain initialized word embeddings unchanged. What's more, all of above methods ignore the implicit interaction influences between user and product which cannot be observed in texts.

To address the issues, in this paper we propose a novel neural network model HUPSA-NCF. To incorporate user and product information into text representations reasonably and effectively, our model uses hierarchical user attention to generate user-specific text representation and uses hierarchical product attention to generate product-specific text representation. To capture implicit interaction influences between user and product, our model specifically uses a neural collaborative filtering to learn it. Then we combine both explicit and implicit informations for final classification. The experimental results show that our model performs better than state-of-the-art methods on Yelp and IMDB datasets.

In summary, our work has following three contributions:

(1) To incorporate user preferences and product characteristics into text representations reasonably and effectively, our model uses hierarchical user and product separated attention.
(2) To capture implicit interaction influences between user and product, our model specifically uses a neural collaborative filtering to learn it.
(3) We conduct experiments on Yelp and IMDB datasets and the results verify the effectiveness of our model and demonstrate that our model significantly outperforms state-of-the-art methods.

2   Related Work

Due to deep neural networks' powerful ability of learning high quality text representation without any feature engineering, almost all recent studies of document-level sentiment classification use deep neural network methods and they all achieve very competitive performances than traditional methods. So we will focus on deep neural network methods.

2.1   Deep Neural Network Methods

Glorot et al. [5] uses stacked denoising autoencoder in sentiment classification for the first time. Then Kim, Zhang et al. [3,6] use CNNs to learn text representation for sentiment classification. These CNN-based models achieve some performances. However, their ability of capturing word sequence information is so weak. To address this issue, Tang, Yang et al. [4,7] start use RNNs in sentiment classification. RNNs are very suitable for learning semantic representation from sequential texts because they learn text representation by feeding word embeddings one by one in order. And to deal with long-term dependencies Yang, Chen et al. [7,11] use long short-term memory (LSTM) [8] to learn text representation. Attention mechanism is proposed by Bahdanau et al. [9] and achieves significant performance in machine translation. So attention mechanism is also introduced to sentiment classification. Zichao et al. [7] propose HAN which uses hierarchical attention mechanism to select important words from sentences and select important sentences from document to enhance text representation.

2.2   Methods Incorporating User and Product Information

User preferences and product characteristics significantly influence the rating of reviews. So recently there are many proposed methods [10–13] incorporating users and products information in different ways. And they all achieve improvements in different degrees.

Tang et al. [10] introduce a word-level preference matrix and a semantic-level vector for each user and each product to capture user and product information. The word-level preference matrix of each user and each product is used to modify original word embeddings from user view and product view respectively, and the semantic-level vector of each user and each product is used to provide sentiment consistency which can not be observed in texts. The model gets some improvements but suffers from high model complexity because the parameters of matrix representations is much more than vector representations so that they can not be estimated easily. And it only considers word-level preference rather than semantic-level preference. Dou [12] trys to use deep memory network to capture user and product information, but it also suffers from the high model complexity because it consists of multiple computational layers and each of which contains an attention layer and a linear layer. In order to address these issues, Chen et al. [11] uses attention mechanism to incorporate user and product information. The work introduces user embedding to represent user preferences and product embedding to represent product characteristics. Then it uses hierarchical user and product joint attention to get user-product-specific text representation. However, user and product joint attention has a little unreasonable, because the user and product have very different influences on reviews. For example, for the review "The environment of this cafe is very quiet and sweet, I like this place.", "like" describes the user sentiments but "quiet" and "sweet" describe the product characteristics, mostly the texts about user are more subjective but the texts about product are more objective. So Wu et al. [13] propose a more reasonable way that uses user attention and product attention separately to incorporate user and product information, but it separates user and product so heavily that it must maintain initialized word embeddings unchanged which is very unreasonable and it also must train two word-level BiLSTM layers which makes the model complexity is large. And all these methods don't use implicit interaction influences between user and product which cannot be observed in review texts. For example, for a lenient user and a high quality product, the user has a high probability to give a high rating to the product even we don't know or don't use the review texts.

In a word, all of above methods fail to incorporate user and product information reasonably and effectively, and these methods all ignore the implicit interaction information between user and product. To address the issues, we propose HUPSA-NCF model which uses hierarchical separated attention to incorporate user and product explicit information and uses neural collaborative filtering to capture implicit interaction information between user and product.

3   The Proposed Model

3.1   Task Formalizations

We suppose U, P, D is the set of users, products and review documents respectively. A review $d \in D$ which written by $u \in U$ for $p \in P$ consists of n sentences $\{s_1, s_2, ...s_n\}$ and the $i-th$ sentence s_i consists of l_i words $\{w_1^i, w_2^i, ..., w_{l_i}^i\}$. Then our task can be formalized as follows: a user u writes a review d for p and give a rating r, we should predict the rating r based on the information of (d, u, p).

3.2   Model Architecture

The architecture of HUPSA-NCF model is shown in Fig. 1. The model consists of two components: hierarchical user product separated attention network (HUPSA) and neural collaborative filtering network (NCF).

(1) HUPSA is used to incorporate user preferences and product characteristics into text representations. HUPSA applies BiLSTM to encode the review in word-level and sentence-level. To incorporate user and product information, it uses hierarchical user attention and product attention separately to get user-specific text representation and product-specific text representation respectively.
(2) NCF applies a multilayer perception (three-layers perception in experiments) to capture and encode the implicit interaction representation between user and product.

Finally we concatenate user-specific text representation, product-specific text representation and implicit interaction representation to get the complete review semantic representation as the features of classification.

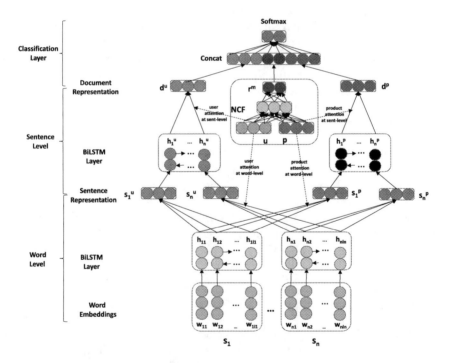

Fig. 1. The architecture of Hierarchical User Product Separated Attention and Neural Collaborative Filtering Network (HUPSA-NCF).

3.3   Using BiLSTM to Encode Reviews

We use LSTM to encode reviews because of its powerful ability on sequence modeling. In order to deal with the long-term dependency problem, LSTM introduces a memory cell that is able to preserve cell state over long periods of time. LSTM also introduces three kind gates to protect and control the cell state flow in LSTM unit. At each time step t, given an input vector x_t, the current cell state $\mathbf{c}_t$ and hidden state $\mathbf{h}_t$ can be updated by operated on previous cell state $\mathbf{c}_{t-1}$ and $\mathbf{h}_{t-1}$ as follows:

$$\begin{bmatrix} \mathbf{i}_t \\ \mathbf{f}_t \\ \mathbf{o}_t \end{bmatrix} = \begin{bmatrix} \sigma \\ \sigma \\ \sigma \end{bmatrix} (\mathbf{W}[\mathbf{h}_{t-1}; \mathbf{x}_t]\mathbf{b}), \tag{1}$$

$$\hat{\mathbf{c}}_t = \tanh(\mathbf{W}_c[\mathbf{h}_{t-1}; \mathbf{x}_t] + \mathbf{b}_c), \tag{2}$$

$$\mathbf{c}_t = \mathbf{f}_t \odot \mathbf{c}_{t-1} + \mathbf{i}_t \odot \hat{\mathbf{c}}_t, \tag{3}$$

$$\mathbf{h}_t = \mathbf{o}_t \odot \tanh(\mathbf{c}_t) \tag{4}$$

where $\mathbf{i}_t, \mathbf{f}_t$ and $\mathbf{o}_t$ are gate activations, σ is sigmoid activation function and $\odot$ means element-wise multiplication. The forget gate $\mathbf{f}_t$ decides what information we're going to throw away from the previous cell state, the input gate $\mathbf{i}_t$ decides what new information we're going to store in the cell state, and the output gate $\mathbf{o}_t$ decides what information we're going to expose from the current cell state. The hidden state $\mathbf{h}_t$ stands for the output information of LSTM unit's memory cell. For texts, a word of a sentence is not only effected by the previous words but also effected by the future words, so we adopt BiLSTM to encode reviews from forward and backward and get the complete hidden state: $\mathbf{h}_t = [\overrightarrow{\mathbf{h}_t}; \overleftarrow{\mathbf{h}_t}]$ which represents the information of the whole sequence centered around x_t.

In word-level, we feed the word sequence $[\mathbf{w}_1, \mathbf{w}_2, ..., \mathbf{w}_l]$ to BiLSTM and get the word-level hidden states, then we use attention mechanism to generate the sentence representation $\mathbf{s}$ based on the word-level hidden states. In sentence-level, we feed the sentence sequence $[\mathbf{s}_1, \mathbf{s}_2, ..., \mathbf{s}_n]$ to another BiLSTM and get the sentence-level hidden states, then we use attention mechanism to generate the document representation $\mathbf{d}$ based the sentence-level hidden states. The method of using attention mechanism will be illustrated in the next section.

3.4   Hierarchical User Product Separated Attention

User preferences and product characteristics have very different influences on reviews, so we use hierarchical user attention and product attention separately to incorporate user preferences and product characteristics into text representations respectively.

Hierarchical User Attention. For different users, it's obvious that each word of a sentence contributes to the sentence representation differently and each sentence of a document also contributes to the document representation differently. So we use user attention hierarchically.

In word-level, we use user attention to calculate the weight of each word to its sentence from user view and aggregate all words according to their weights to generate the sentence representation. Finally, The enhanced sentence representation is a weighted sum of word-level hidden states as:

$$\mathbf{s}_i^u = \sum_{j=1}^{l_i} \alpha_{ij}^u \mathbf{h}_{ij} \tag{5}$$

where $\mathbf{h}_{ij}^u$ is the hidden state of the $j-th$ word in the $i-th$ sentence, α_{ij}^u is the user attention weight of the $\mathbf{h}_{ij}^u$, and each user $u \in U$ will be mapped into a user embedding $\mathbf{u} \in \mathbb{R}^{d_u}$, where d_u is the dimension of the user embedding. The user attention weight α_{ij}^u for each word-level hidden state is defined as:

$$\alpha_{ij}^u = \frac{\exp(s(\mathbf{h}_{ij}, \mathbf{u}))}{\sum_{k=1}^{l_i} \exp(s(\mathbf{h}_{ik}, \mathbf{u}))} \tag{6}$$

where s is a score function which scores the importance of words for composing sentence representation from user view. The score function s is defined as:

$$s(\mathbf{h}_{ij}, \mathbf{u}) = (\mathbf{v}_w^u)^{\top} \tanh(\mathbf{W}_w^u [\mathbf{h}_{ij}; \mathbf{u}] + \mathbf{b}_w^u) \tag{7}$$

where $\mathbf{W}_w^u$ is the weight matrix and $\mathbf{v}_w^u$ is the weight vector in word-level for users.

In sentence-level, the way we use user attention is just like we use in word-level. The difference is that we calculate the weight of each sentence based on sentence-level hidden states. So the enhanced document representation from user view is calculated as:

$$\mathbf{d}_u = \sum_{j=1}^{n} \beta_i^u \mathbf{h}_i^u \tag{8}$$

where $\mathbf{h}_i^u$ is the hidden state of $i-th$ sentence and β_i^u is the user attention weight of $\mathbf{h}_i^u$.

Hierarchical Product Attention. For different products, each word of a sentence or each sentence of a document also contributes to the sentence representation or the document representation differently. So to incorporate product information, we use hierarchical product attention which is similar to hierarchical user attention. We generate sentence representation and document representation from product view as follows:

$$\mathbf{s}_i^p = \sum_{j=1}^{l_i} \alpha_{ij}^p \mathbf{h}_{ij}, \tag{9}$$

$$\mathbf{d}_p = \sum_{j=1}^{n} \beta_i^p \mathbf{h}_i^p \tag{10}$$

where α_{ij}^p is the product attention weight of word-level hidden state $\mathbf{h}_{ij}$ and β_i^p is the product attention weight of sentence hidden state $\mathbf{h}_i^p$.

HUPSA is different from HUAPA [13], because HUPSA shares word-level hidden states $\mathbf{h}_{ij}$ in user attention and product attention but HUAPA doesn't share.

3.5   Neural Collaborative Filtering

HUPSA only uses the explicit text representations which incorporate user and product information, but it ignores the implicit interaction information between user and product. So we use a neural collaborative filtering network which applies a multilayer perception to capture and encode the implicit interaction information as follows:

$$\mathbf{r}_1 = \phi(\mathbf{W}_1[\mathbf{u}; \mathbf{p}] + \mathbf{b}_1), \tag{11}$$
$$\mathbf{r}_2 = \phi(\mathbf{W}_2\mathbf{r}_1 + \mathbf{b}_2), \tag{12}$$
$$... \tag{13}$$
$$\mathbf{r}_m = \phi(\mathbf{W}_m\mathbf{r}_{m-1} + \mathbf{b}_m) \tag{14}$$

where $\mathbf{u}$ is the user embedding and $\mathbf{p}$ is the product embedding. Finally, we will get the implicit interaction representation $\mathbf{r}_m$.

3.6   Final Classification and Training Strategy

In the end, we concatenate the user-specific document representation $\mathbf{d}_u$, the product-specific document representation $\mathbf{d}_p$ and the implicit interaction representation $\mathbf{r}_m$ to get the final complete review representation as:

$$\mathbf{d} = [\mathbf{d}_u; \mathbf{d}_p; \mathbf{r}_m] \tag{15}$$

Then, we use a linear layer and softmax function to classify the review $\mathbf{d}$, and get the review sentiment distribution of C classes as:

$$p = softmax(\mathbf{W}\mathbf{d} + \mathbf{b}) \tag{16}$$

In our model, the cross-entropy error between the gold sentiment distribution p^g and the predicted sentiment distribution p is defined as the loss function L for optimizing during training:

$$L = -\sum_{d \in D} \sum_{c=1}^{C} p_c^g(d) \log(p_c(d)) \tag{17}$$

where D represents the training reviews, and p_c^g represents the gold probability of sentiment class c with ground truth being 1 and others being 0.

4   Experiments

In this section, we will introduce experimental settings and analysis experimental results to validate the effectiveness of our model.

4.1   Experimental Settings

We use three datasets which are derived from IMDB and Yelp Dataset Challenge in 2013 and 2014 [10]. Their statistical information are shown in Table 1, and they are split into three parts respectively: 80% for training, 10% for validating and 10% for testing. We use stanford CoreNLP [14] for sentence splitting and word tokenization. We pretrain 200-dimensional word embeddings with SkipGram [2] on the three datasets respectively and they will be fine-tune during training. User embedding dimension and product embedding dimension are set to 200 and are randomly initialized to a uniform distribution $U(-0.01, 0.01)$. We set the dimension of hidden state in LSTM unit to 100 and get 200 dimensional output hidden state because of bidirection. Hyper parameters are tuned on validation set and Adam [15] is used to update parameters during training. Finally, we select best configuration based on performance of validation set and evaluate the configuration on test set.

Table 1. Statistics of IMDB, Yelp2013 and Yelp2014 datasets.

Datasets	#classes	#docs	#users	#products	#docs/user	#docs/product	#sens/doc	#words/sen
IMDB	10	84,919	1,310	1,635	64.82	51.94	16.08	24.54
Yelp 2013	5	78,966	1,631	1,633	48.42	48.36	10.89	17.38
Yelp 2014	5	231,163	4,818	4,194	47.97	55.11	11.41	17.26

For metrics, we use standard *Accuracy* to measure the overall sentiment classification and *RMSE* to measure the divergences between predicted ratings and ground truth ratings. The two metrics are defined as:

$$Accuracy = \frac{T}{N}, \tag{18}$$

$$RMSE = \sqrt{\frac{\sum_{i=1}^{N}(r_i - \hat{r}_i)^2}{N}} \tag{19}$$

where T is the number of reviews with correct predicted ratings, N is the number of all reviews, r_i is the ground truth rating, and $\hat{r}_i$ is the predicted rating.

4.2   Baselines

We compare our model HUPSA-NCF with several baseline methods for document-level sentiment classification.

(1) **Trigram** trains an SVM classifier with unigrams, bigrams and trigrams.
(2) **TextFeature** trains an SVM classifier with richer text features (e.g. word and character ngrams, sentiment lexicon and cluster features).
(3) **UPF** extracts user-leniency and product features and then concatenates them with the features in **Trigram** and **TextFeature**.
(4) **AvgWordvec+SVM** averages word embeddings of a document to get the document representation which is used as features to train a SVM classifier.
(5) **SSWE+SVM** learns sentiment-specific word embeddings firstly, then use max/avg pooling to get document representation to train a SVM classifier.
(6) **Paragraph Vector** implements PVDM for document classification.
(7) **RNTN+RNN** uses recursive neural tensor network to get sentence representation, then uses recurrent neural network to get document representation for sentiment classification. The document representation is generated by averaging hidden state vectors.
(8) **JMARS** is a recommendation system that uses the information of users and aspects of a review with collaborative filtering and topic modeling.
(9) **UPNN** uses user and product information to capture user-product-specific word embeddings, then use CNNs to generate user-product-specific document representations for sentiment classification.
(10) **UPMNN** adopts deep memory networks to obtain users and products information, and generate document representation based on DMN, then feeds it to a softmax layer for sentiment classification.
(11) **NSC-UPA** applies hierarchical LSTM with user and product joint attention to generate document representation for sentiment classification.
(12) **HUAPA** models user attentions and item attentions separately in hierarchical BiLSTM.

4.3   Experimental Results and Analysis

The experimental results are shown in Table 2, and they are divided into two parts: the models only using text information and the models using both text information and user and product information. It's obvious that the second part models perform better than the first part models, and the first part models have been discussed a lot in studies [10–13]. So we will focus on the second part models' comparisons.

We have some important findings. Firstly, we find both NSC-UPA and HUAPA perform better that UPNN and UPDMN, and they both use attention mechanism. It indicates that attention mechanism is more effective in incorporating user and product information. Secondly, we find the way of using attention mechanism also effects the performance of models. HUAPA performs better than NSC-UPA because it separates user and product attention. Lastly, we find our model HUPSA-NCF achieves best performance, because HUPSA-NCF incorporates user and product information more reasonably and effectively by using user attention and product attention separately. What's more, HUPAS-NCF uses a

Table 2. Reviews sentiment classification results. Acc. (higher is better) and RMSE (lower is better) are the evaluation metrics. The best performances are in **bold**.

Models	IMDB		Yelp 2013		Yelp 2014	
	Acc.	RMSE	Acc.	RMSE	Acc.	RMSE
Models without user and product information						
Trigram	0.399	1.783	0.569	0.814	0.577	0.804
TextFeature	0.402	1.793	0.556	0.845	0.572	0.800
AvgWordvec+SVM	0.304	1.985	0.526	0.898	0.530	0.893
SSWE+SVM	0.312	1.973	0.549	0.849	0.557	0.851
Paragraph Vector	0.341	1.814	0.554	0.832	0.564	0.802
RNTN+RNN	0.400	1.764	0.574	0.804	0.582	0.821
Models with user and product information						
Trigram+UPF	0.404	1.764	0.570	0.803	0.576	0.789
TextFeature+UPF	0.402	1.774	0.561	0.822	0.579	0.791
JMARS	N/A	1.773	N/A	0.985	N/A	0.999
UPNN	0.435	1.602	0.596	0.784	0.608	0.764
UPDMN	0.465	1.351	0.639	0.662	0.613	0.720
NSC-UPA	0.533	1.281	0.650	0.692	0.667	0.654
HUAPA	0.550	1.185	0.683	0.628	0.686	0.626
HUPSA-NCF	**0.561**	**1.096**	**0.694**	**0.608**	**0.702**	**0.603**

multilayer perception as neural collaborative filtering to capture implicit interaction information between user and product.

Table 3 shows the effect of different ways of using attention mechanism. NSC-UPA (BiLSTM) uses user and product joint attention to incorporate user and product information simultaneously, but HUAPA separates user attention and product attention completely to incorporate user and product information respectively. According to experimental results, the second way of using attention is more reasonable because user and product have very different influences on reviews. HUPSA gets better performance than HUAPA, because HUAPA

Table 3. Effect of different ways of using attention mechanism on Acc. and RMSE.

Models	IMDB		Yelp 2013		Yelp 2014	
	Acc.	RMSE	Acc.	RMSE	Acc.	RMSE
NSC-UPA (BiLSTM)	0.529	1.247	0.655	0.672	0.669	0.654
HUAPA	0.550	1.185	0.683	0.628	0.686	0.626
HUPSA	0.554	1.124	0.688	0.612	0.691	0.621
HUPSA-NCF	**0.561**	**1.096**	**0.694**	**0.608**	**0.702**	**0.603**

can not fine-tune word embeddings during training while our HUPSA can fine-tune by sharing word-level hidden states in user attention and product attention. HUPSA-NCF achieves better performance than HUPSA, this comparison validates the effectiveness of neural collaborative filtering. According to comparisons among HUAPA, HUPSA and HUPSA-NCF, we find both the way of using attention mechanism in ouHUPSA-NCF and neural collaborative filtering are effective, and NCF is more effective.

5   Conclusion

In this paper, we propose a novel neural network model HUPSA-NCF for document-level sentiment classification. To incorporate user and product information into text representations reasonably and effectively, HUPSA-NCF uses user attention and product attention separately to BiLSTM layers. Then, HUPAS-NCF uses a multilayer perception as neural collaborative filtering to capture and encode implicit interaction representation between user and product. Finally, HUPSA-NCF concatenates explicit text representations and implicit interaction representation for final classification. Experimental results show that HUPSA-NCF outperforms other state-of-the-art methods on IMDB and Yelp datasets.

References

1. Liu, B.: Sentiment Analysis and Opinion Mining. Morgan & Claypool Publishers (2012). https://doi.org/10.2200/S00416ED1V01Y201204HLT016
2. Mikolov, T., et al.: Efficient estimation of word representations in vector space. arXiv preprint arXiv:1301.3781 (2013)
3. Kim, Y.: Convolutional neural networks for sentence classification. In: Proceedings of the 2014 Conference on Empirical Methods in Natural Language Processing, EMNLP (2014). https://doi.org/10.3115/v1/D14-1181
4. Tang, D., Qin, B., Liu, T.: Document modelling with gated recurrent neural network for sentiment classification. In: Proceedings of the Conference on Empirical Methods in Natural Language Processing, EMNLP (2015). https://doi.org/10.18653/v1/D15-1167
5. Glorot, X., Bordes, A., Bengio, Y.: Domain adaptation for large-scale sentiment classification: a deep learning approach. In: Proceedings of the 28th International Conference on Machine Learning, ICML (2011)
6. Zhang, X., et al.: Character-level convolutional networks for text classification. In: Advances in Neural Information Processing Systems, NIPS (2015)
7. Yang, Z., et al.: Hierarchical attention networks for document classification. In: Proceedings of the 2016 Conference of the North American Chapter of the Association for Computational Linguistics: Human Language Technologies (2016). https://doi.org/10.18653/v1/N16-1174
8. Hochreiter, et al.: Long short-term memory. Neural Comput. 9(8) (1997). https://doi.org/10.1162/neco.1997.9.8.1735
9. Bahdanau, D., et al.: Neural machine translation by jointly learning to align and translate. In: Proceedings of the International Conference on Learning Representations, ICLR (2015)

10. Tang, D., Qin, B., Liu, T.: Learning semantic representations of users and products for document level sentiment classification. In: Proceedings of the 53rd Annual Meeting of the Association for Computational Linguistics and the 7th International Joint Conference on Natural Language Processing, ACL&IJCNLP (2015). https:// doi.org/10.3115/v1/P15-1098

11. Chen, H., Sun, M., Tu, C., Lin, Y., Liu, Z.: Neural sentiment classification with user and product attention. In: Proceedings of the 2016 Conference on Empirical Methods in Natural Language Processing, EMNLP (2016). https://doi.org/10. 18653/v1/D16-1171

12. Dou, Z.-Y.: Capturing user and product information for document level sentiment analysis with deep memory network. In: Proceedings of the 2017 Conference on Empirical Methods in Natural Language Processing, EMNLP (2017). https://doi. org/10.18653/v1/D17-1054

13. Wu, Z., Dai, X.-Y., Yin, C., Huang, S., Chen, J.: Improving review representations with user attention and product attention for sentiment classification. In: Thirty-Second AAAI Conference on Artificial Intelligence, AAAI (2018)

14. Manning, C., et al.: The Stanford CoreNLP natural language processing toolkit. In: Proceedings of 52nd Annual Meeting of the Association for Computational Linguistics: System Demonstrations, ACL (2014). https://doi.org/10.3115/v1/P14-5010

15. Kingma, D.P., et al.: Adam: a method for stochastic optimization. In: Proceedings of the International Conference on Learning Representations, ICLR (2015)

Imbalanced Sentiment Classification Enhanced with Discourse Marker

Tao Zhang[1,2], Xing Wu[1,2], Meng Lin[1(✉)], Jizhong Han[1], and Songlin Hu[1,2]

[1] Institute of Information Engineering, Chinese Academy of Sciences, Beijing, China
{zhangtao,wuxing,linmeng,hanjizhong,husonglin}@iie.ac.cn
[2] School of Cyber Security, University of Chinese Academy of Sciences,
Beijing, China

Abstract. Imbalanced data commonly exists in real world, especially in sentiment-related corpus, making it difficult to train a classifier to distinguish latent sentiment in text data. We observe that humans often express transitional emotion between two adjacent discourses with discourse markers like "but", "though", "while", etc., and the head discourse and the tail discourse usually indicate opposite emotional tendencies. Based on this observation, we propose a novel plug-and-play method, which first samples discourses according to transitional discourse markers and then validates sentimental polarities with the help of a pre-trained attention-based model. Our method increases sample diversity in the first place, obtaining a expanded dataset with relatively low imbalanced-ratio, can serve as a upstream preprocessing part in data augmentation. We conduct experiments on three public sentiment datasets, with several frequently used algorithms. Results show that our method is found to be consistently effective, even in highly imbalanced scenario, and easily be integrated with oversampling method to boost the performance on imbalanced sentiment classification.

Keywords: Imbalanced sentiment classification · Discourse marker · Data augmentation

1 Introduction

Nowadays, people tend to express their feelings in online websites. Such information often contains sentiment and opinions towards specific target such as products, services and events. Analyzing these information can bring insights on what people need and can be helpful for both academic studies and industrial service. However, imbalanced data commonly exists in plenty of scenarios, making it hard to be utilized directly.

This phenomenon emerges frequently in sentiment-related area, where individuals tend to select and share content based on what the majority agrees with. In the review scenario, sentiment expressed by people is high imbalanced because they share similar evaluation standard on a relatively stable review object.

I. V. Tetko et al. (Eds.): ICANN 2019, LNCS 11730, pp. 117–129, 2019.
https://doi.org/10.1007/978-3-030-30490-4_11

For example, the service provided by the same restaurant is unlikely to change too much in a specific period, so the customer's reviews towards service are likely to be consistently good or bad except some extreme cases.

Supervised machine learning techniques are widely used for sentiment classification and achieve better results than traditional lexicon-based methods. Recently, deep learning models have shown promising results in this area. Nevertheless, the probability-based model is easily biased when the data distribution is highly imbalanced, which is often the case in sentiment classification task. As the imbalanced-ratio[1] increases, the performance of these models drops significantly [11].

A natural solution to this problem is utilizing data augmentation to balance the dataset. Existing work can be divided into three categories. Several studies on this matter have verified the effectiveness of re-sampling techniques, which either oversample data from the minority class [1] or undersample data from the majority class [11]. Generation-based methods employ deep generative models such as GAN or VAE to generate sentences from a continuous space with desired attributes of sentiment and tense. Replacement-based methods generate sentences with different polarities by replacing sentimental words with synonyms and antonyms. However, given a dataset which is highly imbalanced, all these methods are not good enough to achieve satisfying performance.

We observe that humans often express transitional emotion between two adjacent discourses with discourse marker like "but", "though", "while", etc., and the head discourse and the tail discourse[2] usually indicate opposite emotional tendencies. Specifically, given a positive sentence "We got some lazy service, but the food is delicious.", the head discourse clearly shows negative emotion towards service and the tail discourse expresses positive emotion towards food, together they constitute a sentence more inclined to a positive expression. This kind of transitional discourse marker generally emphasizes the meaning of the tail discourse. In sentimental scenario, the expressed sentiment of the whole sentence is inclined to that of the tail discourse, which can be used to generate discourse samples.

Based on the above observation, we propose a novel plug-and-play method. Firstly, we sample discourses connected by transitional discourse markers from original data. We annotate the head discourse with a opposite label and the tail discourse with original label from sampled sentence. Secondly, to prevent the problem of incorrect annotation, we introduce a pre-trained attention-based model to validate whether the semantics of generated samples are consistent with their label. Finally, we obtain a expanded dataset with relatively low imbalanced-ratio and we can further use other approaches like oversampling to rebalance the dataset. The whole process is illustrated in Fig. 1.

---

[1] We define imbalanced-ratio to be: number of samples in majority class/number of samples in minority class.

[2] In this paper, we use the term "head discourse" to denote the sentence before the discourse marker and "tail discourse" to denote the sentence after the discourse marker.

Our contributions are listed as follows:

1. We propose a novel method that can be easily integrated with existing work to tackle the problem of imbalanced sentiment classification.
2. To the best of our knowledge, this is the first work that apply discourse markers to data augmentation.
3. We conduct experiments on several public datasets and results show that our method can boost the performance enormously.

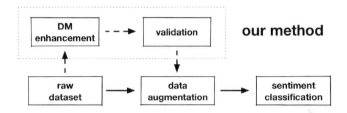

Fig. 1. Simple illustration of our data augmentation with our method. The dashed arrows show that our method is plug-and-play and easily serves as a upstream preprocessing part in data augmentation.

2   Related Work

2.1   Sentiment Classification

Recently, models such as the Convolutional Neural Network (CNN) [3], the Recurrent Neural Network (RNN) [18], memory network [19] have been introduced for sentiment classification tasks, outperforming traditional methods by a significant margin. These methods are endowed with powerful computation ability, capable of learning high-level features directly from low-level continuous representations. Apart from diverse models, language model pre-training has attracted wide attention and fine-tuning on pre-trained language model has shown to be effective for improving many downstream natural language processing tasks. BERT [2] obtained new state-of-the-art results on a broad range of diverse tasks by introducing deep masked language model. Such pre-trained model can be used as sentiment classifier, transferring pre-learned knowledge to current problem.

2.2   Data Augmentation

Sampling-based methods are the most common ones in data augmentation. Undersampling [13] randomly discards original samples from the majority class until the desired class distribution is obtained. Undersampling leads to data waste and suffers from the problem of information loss. On the contrary, oversampling repeatedly chooses samples from minority class, resulting in overfitting because of lacking data diversity. Some adaption of oversampling like SMOTE [1] generates new samples by interpolating between pairs of the closest minority neighbors on continuous space.

Some work solve this problem with generative models. Hu et al. [8] utilizes auto-encoder backbone to generate attribute controlled text. Jia et al. [9] creates adversarial examples by adding distracting sentences to the input paragraph. Generative methods can generate new samples. But limited by the model's capability, the quality of generated sentence can not be guaranteed.

Replacement-based methods can be seen as another paradigm, widely used in generation task. The replacement process contains two steps, where to replace and how to replace. Zhang et al. [21] extracts all replaceable words from the given text and randomly chose some of them to be replaced, then substitutes the replaceable words with synonyms from WordNet. Fadaee et al. [4] focuses on the rare word problem in machine translation, replacing words in a source sentence with only rare words.

Imbalanced sentiment classification was first discussed in [11], where several sampling techniques are applied. Their study demonstrates that imbalanced data distribution severely damages the performance of classifiers and sampling-based methods can significantly alleviate this situation. Liu et al. [12] proposes that the challenge is how to obtain useful information of minority class from a imbalanced dataset. Wu et al. [20] undersamples majority class to form several balanced subsets, then trains multiple classifiers which work together via an ensemble manner.

2.3   Discourse Marker

Discourse marker was first proposed in [14], indicating deep conceptual relations between sentences. Human writers naturally use a small set of very common words like "but", "and", to identify the relations between adjacent ideas. They propose a discourse marker prediction (DMP) task, leveraging a high-level relationship between sentences to learn a meaningful representations. The task aims to predict which discourse marker is used by the author to connect the two adjacent sentences. Dozens of discourse markers are in discussion, including most common ones such as *and, as, but, if, before* and less frequent ones. We observe that transitional discourse markers can be viewed as a sentiment transition signal, and adjacent discourses usually indicate opposite emotional feelings. Thus, the discourses connect by transitional discourse markers can be used to augment imbalanced datasets.

3   Method

In this section, we present our novel data augmentation method, most applicable to imbalanced sentiment classification. Firstly, we give a detailed discussion about different discourse markers and explain why transitional discourse markers work in such scenario. Then we introduce an attention-based method to validate

---

Algorithm 1. Detailed process of using our method for data augmentation.

1: Pretrain a sentiment classifier C
2: Given a imbalanced sentiment dataset D and a set of transitional discourse marker M
3: Choose sentences from D according to M, constituting D_m
4: Generate samples from D_m with **Swap** and **Crop** operations, constituting D_g
5: **for** each sample s with label l in D_g **do**
6:    Use C to get predicted sentiment l'
7:    **if** l is the same as l' **then**
8:        Add s to D
9:    **end if**
10: **end for**
11: Then, use other data augmentation methods like oversampling to get a balanced dataset D_b
12: Perform sentiment classification on D_b

---

generated samples, remedying for cases with false sentiment label. After filtering out inconsistent samples, we combine generated samples with original dataset to form a expanded dataset. Further operation like sampling-based method can be carried out, making it a balanced dataset for sentiment classification. The details of our method are shown in Algorithm 1.

3.1 Discourse Marker Enhancement

Words like *and, but, when, if*, etc., serving as connection between two adjacent discourses, are called conjunction originally. Nie et al. [14] introduces the term "discourse marker" to name them, indicating deep conceptual relations between discourses. A discourse can be one or several sentences, forming a relatively complete semantic sentence group. Different discourse markers serve as different roles in sentences. Based on their functions, we can divide them into fine-grained categories.

- Time: when, before, after, then
- Parallel: and, also
- Transition: but, though, although, still
- Other functions: ...

We can observe that some discourse markers show strong indication of semantic relationship between adjacent discourses, such as *and, but, because*, while some function in syntax aspect, such as *when, before*. Further observation leads to a interesting phenomenon that discourses linked by transitional discourse markers often indicate opposite sentiment tendencies when expressing emotion.

For example, in binary sentiment classification scenario, given a sentence "The actress is beautiful, but the plot is terrible."[3] with negative label, we can derive three sentences with clear sentiment inclination:

- Swap the discourses: "The plot is terrible, but the actress is beautiful." emphasizes the tail discourse, making it a positive sample.
- Crop the head discourse: "The actress is beautiful." is clearly a positive sample, contrary to original sentence.
- Crop the tail discourse: "The plot is terrible." is no doubt a negative sample, consistent with original sentence.

Based on this phenomenon, we can generate samples in both category and augment imbalanced datasets. Formally, given a compound sentence $< s_h, m, s_t >$ with label l, where s_h, s_t denote the head discourse and the tail discourse and m denotes a transitional discourse marker, we want to generate new sample s_h with label $\bar{l}$, s_t with label l and $< s_t, m, s_h >$ with label $\bar{l}$. l and $\bar{l}$ denote opposite sentiment.

One self-evident principle about data augmentation is that the new sample must agree with its label. For sampling-based methods, the principle is satisfied because we directly sample the data with its label. For our method, s_h/s_t can't be new samples if they are sentiment-irrelevant. For example, given a sentence "we have arrived here for half an hour, still no waiter comes to serve." the head discourse states an objective fact and can't be a new sample alone. And in few cases, traditional discourse markers may express gradation, like "A was bad, but B was even worse.", making $< s_t, m, s_h >$ likely to be falsely labeled. Thus, we need to validate whether generated samples are sentiment-irrelevant or falsely labeled before adding them to original dataset.

3.2 Attention-Based Validator

In this section, we present an attention-based validator to judge whether generated samples are sentiment-irrelevant or not. Our validator consists of two parts: a recurrent neural network (RNN) as backbone and an attention block. RNN is a class of neural networks, capable of processing sequential information like text. We use a bidirectional Long Short Term Memory network (LSTM) [6], an adaption of RNN, to model text from both directions.

Formally, given a input sentence $S = (w_1, w_2, ...w_T)$ of T words with label l, words are first embedded into continuous vectors: $x = (x_1, x_2, ..., x_T)$. Then word embeddings are then fed into LSTM. Each cell in LSTM can be computed as follows:

---

[3] In this paper, we only discuss relatively short sentences. The discourse structure in long sentences may be complex and we leave it for future work.

$$f_t = \sigma(W_f x_t + U_f h_{t-1} + b_f) \tag{1}$$
$$i_t = \sigma(W_i x_t + U_i h_{t-1} + b_i) \tag{2}$$
$$o_t = \sigma(W_o x_t + U_o h_{t-1} + b_o) \tag{3}$$
$$c_t = f_t \odot c_{t-1} + i_t \odot tanh(W_c x_t + U_c h_{t-1} + b_c) \tag{4}$$
$$h_t = o_t \odot tanh(c_t) \tag{5}$$

where all W, U are projection matrices and b is bias. σ is the sigmoid function and $\odot$ denotes element-wise multiplication. h_t stands for the hidden output of LSTM at timestep t corresponding to x_t. f, i, o are gates with different functions, spanning $[0, 1]$. For each word w_i, we obtain its hidden output by concatenating its forward state and backward state of LSTM of both directions $h_i = [\overrightarrow{h_i}^T; \overleftarrow{h_i}^T]^T$.

To better model long sentences and accurately catch their sentiments, we utilize the attention mechanism, which is inspired by the fact that human visual attention is able to focus on a certain region on an image with high resolution while perceiving the surrounding image in low resolution and then adjusting the focal point over time. In natural language processing, the attention mechanism works in a similar way and helps the model to learn which part of text should be paid more attention, resulting in more reasonable sentence representations. Formally, after obtaining hidden outputs, we align each hidden output h_i to the context vector v to get the attention weight:

$$f(h_i, v) = tanh(W_h h_i + W_v v + b) \tag{6}$$

where W_h, W_v, b are trainable parameters and f is to calculate how much attention we should pay to h_i. Then we calculate a normalized attention weights:

$$\alpha_i = \frac{exp(f(h_i, v))}{\sum_j exp(f(h_j, v))} \tag{7}$$

The attention weights evaluates the contribution of each word to sentiment classification. Thus we use the weighted sum of hidden outputs c to represent input sentence, and transform c into a probability distribution y on sentiment class labels:

$$c = \sum_{i=1}^{T} \alpha_i h_i \tag{8}$$

$$y = softmax(W_s c + b_s) \tag{9}$$

where W_s, b_s are also a projection parameter. After well pre-trained, an attention-based model can be used to filter generated samples whose semantics is not consistent with the label.

4   Experimental Settings

In this section, we introduce the detailed settings of our experiments. We present datasets in Sect. 4.1. The experiment design is introduced in Sect. 4.2. The experiment details are shown in Sect. 4.3.

4.1 Datasets

We conduct experiments on three public sentimental review datasets, most samples of which consist of one single sentence. In the last part of Sect. 3.1, we discuss the principle that data augmentation must agree with. For our method, s_h/s_t can't be new samples if they are sentiment-irrelevant. Thus, we hope that discourses in a transitional compound sentence are more likely to be sentiment-relevant in the first place.

The review datasets are able to fulfill our expectation. When people make comments, the review content is often about feelings towards specific targets. Moreover, in a transitional compound sentence, discourses in opposite emotions tend to express feelings about different aspects of review object, which makes the discourse alone more likely to be sentiment-relevant. Specifically, we choose three binary classification datasets:

- **MR** Movie Review Data (MR) proposed by Pang and Lee [15], consisting of 5,331 positive and 5,331 negative reviews. The reviews are generally in one sentence. We randomly choose 80% of them as training set and remain 20% as testing set.

- **SST2** Stanford Sentiment Treebank (binary version), an extension of the MR but with train/dev/test splits. T he split is 6,920 samples for training, 872 for validation, and 1,821 for testing [17].

- **CR** Customer reviews of various products with 2406 positive and 1367 negative samples [7]. We split the dataset following the same way as what we have done to **MR**.

Without loss of generality, we assume negative samples to be minority class and randomly sample sentences in negative class to construct imbalanced datasets.

4.2 Experiment Design

For one specific algorithm, we apply it to each dataset in two different settings to prove that our method can significantly boost performance when integrated with oversampling. Specifically:

- balanced dataset with oversampling.
- balanced dataset with our method and oversampling.

For algorithms, we consider three traditional machine learning methods: support vector machine (SVM), naive Bayes (NB), logistic regression (LR) and two basic deep neural networks: convolutional neural network (CNN), recurrent neural network (RNN).

4.3 Experiment Details

All traditional machine learning models, i.e. SVM, NB, LR are implemented with sklearn [16] in default settings, with unigram tf-idf vectors of the dataset as their inputs. For CNN model, we use filter size $[3, 4, 5]$, each with 100 filters. We use pre-trained word embeddings trained on Google News[4] and make them trainable. The dropout layer with dropout rate $= 0.5$ is appended to the convolutional module. For RNN model, we use a single layer bidirectional LSTM with 256 hidden units. Our attention-based validator is pre-trained on Yelp dataset [5], with LSTM hidden unit $= 32$ and Adam [10] optimizer. The transitional discourse markers we use are $M = [but, although, though, however, yet]$, the most common ones in language expression. Our evaluation metric is binary classification accuracy.

5   Experimental Results

5.1 Overall Effectiveness of Our Method

Following the experiment settings introduced in Sect. 4.2, we test the performance of listed methods. with imbalanced-ratio $\lambda = 5$. The results are shown in Table 1. Our method generates more samples and builds a more balanced dataset for further oversampling, consistently increasing the classification performance. It worthy to note that SVM performs unstable, even unchanged in CR dataset. We ascribe this to the special modeling process of SVM, which is not the focus of this paper. Since our propose is to verify the performance of our data augmentation method, we remove SVM in following experiments for comparison convenience.

5.2 Effectiveness of Validator

To verify the effectiveness of the attention-based validator, we conduct a group of ablation test in following settings:

– balanced dataset after discourse marker enhancement and oversampling, without attention-based validator.

Due to space limitations, we take CNN as a example and the details are shown in Table 2. We can observe that validator indeed contributes a lot to the total performance. As discussed in the last part of Sect. 3.1, the generated sample must agree with its label. In our method, the discourse sample may state a simple fact and be sentiment-irrelevant. Our attention-based model serves as a validator and filters out false labeled cases, significantly improving the quality of expanded dataset.

---

[4] https://github.com/mmihaltz/word2vec-GoogleNews-vectors.

Table 1. Experimental results of several methods in different settings. The evaluation metric is accuracy (%). "raw" denotes raw imbalanced sentiment datasets. "w/" represents "with". "os" denotes "oversampling". "our" denotes "our method".

Method	Setting	MR	SST2	CR	Avg improvement
NB	w/os	72.79	73.31	74.19	–
	w/our + os	71.90	76.99	76.20	1.60
LR	w/os	68.88	69.02	74.60	–
	w/our + os	67.95	71.14	76.20	0.93
SVM	w/os	66.34	49.91	50.00	–
	w/our + os	50.00	69.41	50.00	1.05
CNN	w/os	71.33	75.28	77.82	–
	w/our + os	74.14	79.95	81.45	3.70
RNN	w/os	71.80	74.30	75.60	–
	w/our + os	75.34	79.39	77.02	3.35

Table 2. Ablation test on attention-based validator. "wo/" represents "without". "val" denotes "validator". "full" denotes our full model.

Method	IR	Setting	MR	SST2	CR	Avg improvement
CNN	5	wo/val	72.84	74.84	79.43	–
		full	74.14	79.96	81.45	2.81
	20	wo/val	66.18	70.12	62.70	–
		full	70.95	74.74	68.75	5.15
	100	wo/val	61.65	65.01	60.28	–
		full	67.95	69.08	61.69	3.93

5.3 Highly Imbalanced Datasets

In this section, we test our method in highly imbalanced scenario, compared with only using oversampling method. We set the imbalanced-ratio λ as different values. The details can be seen in Table 3. Significant improvements are consistently obtained by integrating our method with oversampling. In extremely imbalanced scenario, i.e. $\lambda = 50, 100$, integrated method even shows more boost of performance. From the table illustration we can also observe that when dataset gets highly imbalanced, the oversample method does not help the classification[5].

Oversampling method is limited to the sample quality of minority class. When dataset gets extremely imbalanced, the problem of sample diversity deficiency becomes severe, which damages the model performance enormously. In comparison, our method is able to generate minority samples from both majority class and minority class. As long as the sample sentences contain transitional discourse

---

[5] In binary classification scenario, 50% accuracy means random guess.

Table 3. Experimental results on highly imbalanced datasets. "IR" denotes imbalanced-ratio.

IR	Method	Setting	MR	SST2	CR	Avg improvement
10	NB	w/os	68.15	68.86	69.75	–
		w/our + os	69.41	72.87	71.98	2.50
	LR	w/os	60.87	60.07	63.91	–
		w/our + os	63.74	65.24	70.96	5.33
	CNN	w/os	72.94	76.49	70.76	–
		w/our + os	74.51	79.74	75.40	3.15
	RNN	w/os	71.96	69.14	73.59	–
		w/our + os	71.90	77.05	76.01	3.42
20	NB	w/os	61.44	61.55	63.30	–
		w/our + os	63.21	67.55	68.75	4.41
	LR	w/os	53.85	54.31	54.43	–
		w/our + os	59.72	60.13	63.31	6.86
	CNN	w/os	68.26	67.87	53.42	–
		w/our + os	70.92	74.74	68.75	8.23
	RNN	w/os	60.93	70.84	60.69	–
		w/our + os	70.03	76.44	73.99	9.33
50	NB	w/os	55.10	56.12	55.84	–
		w/our + os	61.76	65.35	64.52	8.19
	LR	w/os	50.52	50.74	51.41	–
		w/our + os	56.24	56.01	57.46	5.61
	CNN	w/os	62.27	54.09	51.20	–
		w/our + os	67.69	68.97	67.14	12.08
	RNN	w/os	52.29	53.10	52.82	–
		w/our + os	67.48	71.06	63.91	14.75
100	NB	w/os	51.61	51.78	52.01	–
		w/our + os	61.76	65.34	64.51	12.07
	LR	w/os	50.15	49.97	50.40	–
		w/our + os	56.24	56.01	57.46	6.40
	CNN	w/os	53.74	50.74	50.60	–
		w/our + os	67.95	69.08	61.69	14.55
	RNN	w/os	50.62	50.85	50.60	–
		w/our + os	68.57	67.01	65.12	16.21

markers, they can be used to generate one sample with the same label and two samples with opposite label. It is worthy to note that transitional discourse markers is almost equally appearing in both positive and negative emotions, which means we can stably get a certain amount of minority samples through our method. In other words, the more skewed the data distribution is, the more minority samples we can obtain from transition sentences of majority class.

6   Discussion and Future Work

So far we have presented how to utilize the transition relation between two adjacent discourses to augment sentimental datasets. Sentiment is just one aspect of sentence semantics and what role traditional discourse markers play in general classification datasets is worth exploring. Moreover, different kinds of discourse markers may serve as different semantic indicator, which could certainly assist the research on a vast amount of NLP tasks, such as semantics compression and language inference. The chosen datasets have a relatively large number of sentiment-relevant discourses. So we will conduct experiments on non-review datasets and give a in-depth analysis of the attention-based validator. In the future, we plan to explore the functions of other discourse markers in other area. Additionally, we will conduct more complete experiments on integrating our method with other data augmentation approaches and give a detailed analysis.

7   Conclusions

In this paper, we focus on data augmentation technique in imbalanced sentiment classification. We propose a novel two-step method, which first generates new samples according to transitional discourse markers and then validates polarity correctness with a pre-trained attention-based model. The experimental results proves that the semantics conveyed by transitional discourse marker can be utilized to generate sentimental discourses. Our method is simple and plug-and-play, serving as a upstream part in data augmentation. Based on a expanded diverse dataset with a relatively low imbalanced-ratio, any other data augmentation methods can then rebalance it for further sentiment classification.

Acknowledgments. This work is supported by the National Key Research and Development Program of China (No. 2017YFB1010001). We also appreciate the valuable comments from anonymous reviewers.

References

1. Chawla, N.V., Bowyer, K.W., Hall, L.O., Kegelmeyer, W.P.: Smote: synthetic minority over-sampling technique. J. Artif. Intell. Res. **16**, 321–357 (2002)
2. Devlin, J., Chang, M., Lee, K., Toutanova, K.: BERT: pre-training of deep bidirectional transformers for language understanding. CoRR abs/1810.04805 (2018). http://arxiv.org/abs/1810.04805
3. Dos Santos, C., Gatti, M.: Deep convolutional neural networks for sentiment analysis of short texts. In: Proceedings of COLING 2014, the 25th International Conference on Computational Linguistics: Technical Papers, pp. 69–78 (2014)

4. Fadaee, M., Bisazza, A., Monz, C.: Data augmentation for low-resource neural machine translation. arXiv preprint arXiv:1705.00440 (2017)
5. He, R., McAuley, J.: Ups and downs: modeling the visual evolution of fashion trends with one-class collaborative filtering. In: Proceedings of the 25th International Conference on World Wide Web, pp. 507–517. International World Wide Web Conferences Steering Committee (2016)
6. Hochreiter, S., Schmidhuber, J.: Long short-term memory. Neural Comput. **9**(8), 1735–1780 (1997)
7. Hu, M., Liu, B.: Mining and summarizing customer reviews. In: Proceedings of the Tenth ACM SIGKDD International Conference on Knowledge Discovery and Data Mining, pp. 168–177. ACM (2004)
8. Hu, Z., Yang, Z., Liang, X., Salakhutdinov, R., Xing, E.P.: Toward controlled generation of text. In: Proceedings of the 34th International Conference on Machine Learning-Volume 70, pp. 1587–1596. JMLR. org (2017)
9. Jia, R., Liang, P.: Adversarial examples for evaluating reading comprehension systems. arXiv preprint arXiv:1707.07328 (2017)
10. Kingma, D.P., Ba, J.: Adam: a method for stochastic optimization. arXiv preprint arXiv:1412.6980 (2014)
11. Li, S., Zhou, G., Wang, Z., Lee, S.Y.M., Wang, R.: Imbalanced sentiment classification. In: Proceedings of the 20th ACM International Conference on Information and Knowledge Management, pp. 2469–2472. ACM (2011)
12. Liu, B., Zhang, M., Ma, W., Li, X., Liu, Y., Ma, S.: A two-step information accumulation strategy for learning from highly imbalanced data. In: Proceedings of the 2017 ACM on Conference on Information and Knowledge Management, pp. 1289–1298. ACM (2017)
13. Ng, W.W., Hu, J., Yeung, D.S., Yin, S., Roli, F.: Diversified sensitivity-based undersampling for imbalance classification problems. IEEE Trans. Cybern. **45**(11), 2402–2412 (2015)
14. Nie, A., Bennett, E.D., Goodman, N.D.: DisSent: sentence representation learning from explicit discourse relations. CoRR abs/1710.04334 (2017). http://arxiv.org/abs/1710.04334
15. Pang, B., Lee, L.: Seeing stars: exploiting class relationships for sentiment categorization with respect to rating scales. In: Proceedings of the 43rd Annual Meeting on Association for Computational Linguistics, pp. 115–124. Association for Computational Linguistics (2005)
16. Pedregosa, F., et al.: Scikit-learn: machine learning in python. J. Mach. Learn. Res. **12**, 2825–2830 (2011)
17. Socher, R., et al.: Recursive deep models for semantic compositionality over a sentiment treebank. In: Proceedings of the 2013 Conference on Empirical Methods in Natural Language Processing, pp. 1631–1642 (2013)
18. Tang, D., Qin, B., Feng, X., Liu, T.: Effective LSTMs for target-dependent sentiment classification. arXiv preprint arXiv:1512.01100 (2015)
19. Tang, D., Qin, B., Liu, T.: Aspect level sentiment classification with deep memory network. arXiv preprint arXiv:1605.08900 (2016)
20. Wu, F., Wu, C., Liu, J.: Imbalanced sentiment classification with multi-task learning. In: Proceedings of the 27th ACM International Conference on Information and Knowledge Management, pp. 1631–1634. ACM (2018)
21. Zhang, X., Zhao, J., LeCun, Y.: Character-level convolutional networks for text classification. In: Advances in Neural Information Processing Systems, pp. 649–657 (2015)

Revising Attention with Position for Aspect-Level Sentiment Classification

Dong Wang[1,2], Tingwen Liu[1,2(✉)], and Bin Wang[3]

[1] Institute of Information Engineering Chinese Academy of Sciences, Beijing, China
{wangdong,liutingwen}@iie.ac.cn
[2] School of Cyber Security, University of Chinese Academy of Sciences,
Beijing, China
[3] Xiaomi AI Lab, Beijing, China
wangbin11@xiaomi.com

Abstract. As a fine-grained classification task, aspect-level sentiment classification aims at determining the sentiment polarity given a particular target in a sentence. The key point of this task is to distinguish target-related words and target-unrelated words. To this end, attention mechanism is introduced into this task, which assigns high attention weights to target-related words and ignores target-unrelated words according to the semantic relationships between context words and target. However, existing work not explicitly take into account the position information of context words when calculating the attention weights. Actually, position information is very important for detecting the relevance of the word to target, where words that are closer to the target usually make a greater contribution for determining the sentiment polarity. In this work, we propose a novel approach to combine position information and attention mechanism. We get the position distribution according to the distances between context words and target, then leverage the position distribution to modify the attention weight distribution. In addition, considering that sentiment polarity is usually represented by a phrase, we use CNN for sentiment classification which can capture local n-gram features. We test our model on two public benchmark datasets from SemEval 2014, and the experimental results demonstrate the effectiveness of our approach.

Keywords: Aspect-level sentiment classification ·
Attention mechanism · Position information · CNN

1 Introduction

Recently, with the rise of the Internet, especially the e-commerce, aspect-level sentiment classification has attracted more and more attention. Unlike sentence-level sentiment classification [1], aspect-level sentiment classification [2] aiming at determine the sentiment polarity towards a particular target. For example, given a sentence *"The quality is good but the price is too high."*, the sentiment polarities for *"quality"* and *"price"* will be positive and negative respectively.

© Springer Nature Switzerland AG 2019
I. V. Tetko et al. (Eds.): ICANN 2019, LNCS 11730, pp. 130–142, 2019.
https://doi.org/10.1007/978-3-030-30490-4_12

Early works focus on using traditional machine learning approaches, such as SVM [3]. However, this type of methods require manually constructed features that can reflect the relationship between context words and target, which is time consuming and labor intensive.

Fig. 1. The illustration of how position distribution adjusts attention weight distribution. The green, yellow and blue represent original attention weight distribution, position distribution, and adjusted attention weight distribution respectively. The target is *"service"*. (Color figure online)

In recent years, neural networks have been widely used in natural language processing and show great power. Benefit from ability to model metanic relation, LSTM is particularly popular in aspect-level sentiment classification. Different from traditional machine learning methods, neural networks do not need manually constructed features.

The key point of aspect-level sentiment classification is to distinguish target-related words and target-unrelated words. For that, attention mechanism is introduced to assign different weights to words according to their semantic relationship with target. Existing work usually combine attention mechanism and LSTM, where LSTM encodes the sentence and the attention module assigns different weight to each word, then leverages the weighted representation of sentence to determine the sentiment polarity towards target, such as AE-LSTM [4], ATAE-LSTM [4], IAN [5] and EAM [6].

Intuitively, the closer a word is to target, the more important it is, and the higher its weight should be. For example, in sentence *"Great atmosphere, but the worst food."*, the sentiment polarity towards target *"food"* is negative and compared to words that are far away from target, the closer word *"worst"* play a more important role when determining the sentiment polarity, which is also in line with human cognition. However, the existing work either neglect the position information or don't explicitly model above phenomena. For example, PBAN [7] just appends position embedding after word embedding as input for model, EAM [6] just leverages the position information to select some keywords for attention module.

To this end, we propose a novel approach to explicitly model above phenomena. On one hand, we also use the standard attention mechanism to calculate the weight of each word and get the attention weight distribution. On the other hand, we use the distances between context words and target to get the position distribution. Then, we calculate the difference between attention weight distribution and position distribution, and add it to the classification loss as a penalty.

During the training process, model will adjust the original attention weight distribution to reduce the difference between it and the position distribution, and finally reaches a balance between classification error and distribution difference. The Fig. 1 shows the above process. Actually, we explore multiple ways to calculate the position distribution and the difference between position distribution and attention weight distribution, which will be detailed in the model section.

Considering that sentiment polarity is usually represented by a phrase, we used CNN to replace LSTM to capture local n-gram feature. Similar to textCNN [1], we also apply the CNN on word embeddings. The difference is that we will first adjust the word embeddings with the adjusted attention weights to eliminate the information of target-unrelated words, then use CNN to get the final sentiment polarity.

The main contributions of our work include: (1) We propose a novel approach to explicitly use position information: leverage the position distribution to adjust the attention weight distribution. (2) We explore a variety of ways to utilize position information and introduce CNN to replace LSTM for capturing local n-gram feature more effectively. (3) Our approach achieves comparable performance on two public benchmark datasets *Restaurants* and *Laptops* from SemEval 2014 [8].

2   Related Work

Early works focus on leveraging classification algorithms on manually built features that reflect some relationship between context words and target, such as SVM [3] and MaxEnt-LDA [9]. However, manually built features are based on heuristic rules or external resources, such as dependency tree and sentiment lexicon which focus on structural information of sentence but do not contain the deep semantic information.

Recently, neural networks have attracted more and more attention and benefit from ability to capture long distance dependencies of sentence, LSTM is widely used in aspect-level sentiment classification. TD-LSTM [10] leverage two LSTMs to code the left context and right context with respect to target for classification.

Later, attention mechanism was introduced to assign different weights to target-related words and target-unrelated words and the weighted hidden states of LSTM will be used for sentiment classification. Existing works focus on how to design effective attention mechanism. AE-LSTM and ATAE-LSTM [4] is the earlier work which just simply calculate the attention weights with standard attention mechanism. IAN [5] learn target-aware context representation and context-aware target representation with attention mechanism before final classification.

SA-LSTM-P [11] leverages CRF to make the calculation of attention no longer independent of each other. BILSTM-ATT-G [12] divides the sentence into two parts with respect to the target and determine how much information from each part should be preserved with attention mechanism. However, all above methods ignore the position information. EAM [6] and PBAN [7] take into account the position information where EAM leverages the position information to select keywords for calculating attention ignoring other words and PBAN appends position embedding after word embedding as the input of model. In addition, in relation extraction task, PaNSM [13] takes position embedding into the calculation formula of semantic attention. But, both of three approaches above do not explicitly model how position information guide the generation of attention weights.

Also, memory network, first proposed by Facebook in 2014 [14], is introduced to aspect-level sentiment classification, such as MemNet [15], which use the target-specific representation repeatedly to retrieve from memory, and then updates the target-specific representation with the retrieved information. Finally, the target-specific representation will be used for the sentiment classification. The memory of MemNet consists of word embeddings of context words, which will be adjusted according to the distances between context words and target.

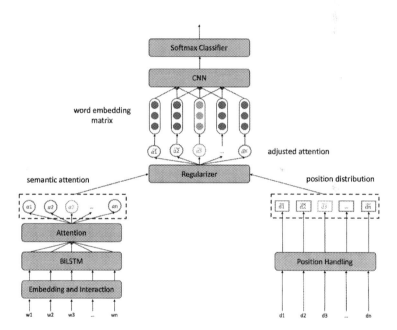

Fig. 2. An overview of our model. The lower left part is the module for calculating of attention, and the lower right part is the module for calculating of distance. The upper part is the classification module.

3   Our Method

In this section, we will introduce our model and give details about the internal structure and function of each module. Figure 2 is the overview of our model.

3.1 Problem Definition

Given a sentence s of length n, and a target t that appears in sentence s, aspect-level sentiment classification aims to assign sentiment polarity to target t.

We use w_i to indicate the i-th word, use x_i, x_t to indicate the embedding of i-th word and target respectively, h_i to indicate the hidden state of i-th word, h_t to indicate the hidden state of target, d_i to indicate the distance between w_i and target.

3.2 Embedding and Interaction

In this layer, we map each word to sparse vector representation for neural network. On one hand, we obtain the word embedding of each word by looking up the embedding table. On the other hand, we also use element-wise multiplication to get interaction between context word and target word [16] to capture richer information, then append it to word embedding vector:

$$x_i^c = [x_i; x_i \odot x_t], \quad i \in [1, n]. \tag{1}$$

The new representation x_i^c will be the input of BiLSTM.

3.3 BiLSTM

In this layer, we use BiLSTM to code the sentence which read the s from w_1 to w_n and w_n to w_1 at the same time so that the representation of each word can include both the past and future information:

$$\overrightarrow{h}_i = \overrightarrow{\mathrm{LSTM}}(x_i^c), \quad i \in [1, n], \tag{2}$$

$$\overleftarrow{h}_i = \overleftarrow{\mathrm{LSTM}}(x_i^c), \quad i \in [1, n]. \tag{3}$$

Then we concatenate the forward hidden state and backward hidden state at each time step to get the representation of every word:

$$h_i = [\overrightarrow{h}_i; \overleftarrow{h}_i]. \tag{4}$$

3.4 Attention

At this layer, we use attention mechanism to calculate the weights of context words towards target. We use hidden states from BiLSTM to represent each word and adopt the standard attention mechanism [17] to calculate the weight of each word:

$$att_i = \sigma(v^T \tanh(W_a[h_i; h_t])), \tag{5}$$

where W, v are trainable parameters, σ is sigmoid activate function which scales a scalar to 0-1, att is the attention weight vector.

3.5 CNN

In this layer, we use CNN to extract local n-gram features of sentence for sentiment classification. Firstly, we multiply word embeddings with attention weights obtained in the last layer, to erase the information of noise words:

$$\tilde{x}_i = x_i * att_i, \tag{6}$$

where x_i indicates the original word embedding.

After getting the weighted word embedding matrix, we use multi-sizes filters to get multiple features:

$$c_i = \text{ReLU}(W_c * \tilde{x}_{i:i+s} + b_c). \tag{7}$$

We use multiple kernels to capture as much as possible features and apply max pooling to capture the most crucial features:

$$z = [\max(c_1), \max(c_2), ..., \max(c_n)], \tag{8}$$

where z is the final representation of the sentence s given target t.

3.6 Softmax Classifier

In order to get the final sentiment polarity, we need to feed the sentence representation to a multi-classes classifier:

$$o = W_f * z + b_f. \tag{9}$$

The probability that a sentence's sentiment belongs to k-th class is calculated as follows, where C is the total number of classes:

$$p_k = \frac{exp(o_k)}{\sum_{i=1}^{C} exp(o_i)}. \tag{10}$$

The label with highest probability will be the predicated sentiment polarity of sentence given target t.

3.7 Position Handling and Regularizer

Although attention mechanism can distinguish the importance of words to a certain extent, it is semantic based which neglects the position information of words. In this layer, we will take into account position information and leverage the position distribution of context words to adjust the above attention weight distribution.

To this end, we explore two ways to compute the position distribution and three ways to measure the difference between the attention weight distribution and position distribution.

Calculating Position Distribution. In this part, we will introduce two ways to get position distributions of context words. Firstly, we calculate the distance d_i between i-th word and target t:

$$d_i = \begin{cases} |i - t_s|, & i < t_s, \\ 0, & t_s \leq i \leq t_e, \\ |i - t_e|, & i > t_e, \end{cases} \tag{11}$$

where t_s indicates the start index of target and t_e indicates the end index of target.

Normalized Position Distribution (N). We map d_i to between 0 and 1, in the same interval as attention weight:

$$\tilde{d}_i = 1 - \frac{d_i}{n}, \tag{12}$$

where the closer word is to target, the larger $\tilde{d}_i$.

Gaussian Position Distribution (G). We convert the original distance sequence into a gaussian distribution [18], where $\tilde{d}_i$ is also between 0 and 1:

$$\tilde{d}_i = exp(-\frac{d_i^2}{2\sigma^2}), \tag{13}$$

where σ is the standard deviation which is set as $\sigma = \frac{D}{2}$ and D is the window size.

Calculating Difference Between Position Distribution and Attention Weight Distribution. In this part, we will introduce three ways to calculate the difference between position distribution $\tilde{d}$ and attention weight distribution att.

Absolute Difference (AD). We use element-wise subtraction to get the absolute difference sequence between position distribution and attention weight distribution. Then we calculate the average of the sequence as the final absolute difference:

$$\text{AD}(\tilde{d}, att) = \frac{\sum_{i=1}^{n} |\tilde{d}_i - att_i|}{n}. \tag{14}$$

Kullback-Leibler Divergence (KL). Firstly, we use softmax function to convert $\tilde{d}$ and att into probability distribution with sum of 1, and then calculate the Kullback-Leibler divergence between them:

$$att^p = \text{softmax}(att), \tag{15}$$

$$\tilde{d}^p = \text{softmax}(\tilde{d}), \tag{16}$$

$$\text{KL}(att^p \parallel \tilde{d}^p) = \sum_{i=1}^{n} att_i^p * \log\frac{att_i^p}{\tilde{d}_i^p}. \tag{17}$$

Jensen-Shannon Divergence (JS). Just like the above method, except that we calculate the Jensen-Shannon divergence between position distribution and attention weight distribution:

$$\text{JS}(att^p \parallel \tilde{d^p}) = \frac{1}{2}\text{KL}(att^p \parallel \frac{att^p + \tilde{d^p}}{2}) + \frac{1}{2}\text{KL}(\tilde{d^p} \parallel \frac{att^p + \tilde{d^p}}{2}). \tag{18}$$

We use $\text{Diff}(\tilde{d}, att)$ to indicate the difference between position distribution and attention weight distribution which is calculated like above, and add it to classification loss as a regularizer. Our final loss is defined as follows:

$$loss = \frac{1}{N} [\sum_{i=1}^{N} -y_i \log p(y_i) + \beta \text{Diff}(\tilde{d}, att)], \tag{19}$$

where β is the coefficient of regularizer.

4 Experiments

4.1 Datasets

We perform experiments on SemEval 2014 [8] which includes two datasets: *Laptop* and *Restaurant*. Each sample in the datasets consists of a sentence, a target and the corresponding sentiment polarity. Table 1 shows the statistic results of the datasets.

Table 1. Statistic results of *Laptop* and *Restaurant*.

	Set	Total	Positive	Negative	Neutral
Laptop	Train	2328	994	870	464
	Test	638	341	128	169
Restaurant	Train	3608	2164	807	637
	Test	1120	728	196	196

4.2 Parameters Initializing

We use 300 dimensions pre-trained Glove vector [19] to initialize our word embedding, which will be tuned during training. The dimension of hidden state of BiL-STMs is set to 100 and learning rate is set to 0.0005. We use three convolutional kernel sizes 3, 4, 5 with 128 filters in each size. The weights of neural network are all uniformly initialized between -1 and 1 while the bias are set to 0. The coefficient of regularizer is tuned between 0 and 4, where we first find the maximum value and then fine-tune it from 0 to maximum. We set the dropout of input and output to 0.2 and 0.5 respectively by grid searching from 0 to 1. We use Adam [20] as our training method.

4.3   Model Comparisons

In order to inspect the performance of our model, we compare our model with some classical models, such as SVM, AE-LSTM, ATAE-LSTM, TD-LSTM, IAN, EAM, MemNet, PBAN. Also, we perform some ablation experiments to show the effect of individual modules. We report the accuracy and Macro-F1 on *Laptop* and *Restaurant* datasets.

- SVM [3]: This approach leverages traditional machine learning algorithm SVM with feature engineering to classify the sentiment polarity.
- AE-LSTM & ATAE-LSTM [4]: This approach employs two LSTMs to model the left and right contexts of the target separately, then performs predictions based on concatenated context representations.
- TD-LSTM [10]: This approach employs two LSTMs to model the left and right contexts of the target separately, then performs predictions based on concatenated context representations.
- IAN [5]: This approach leverages two LSTMs to model context and aspect target separately. Then both context and aspect target learn their representation from their interaction.
- EAM [6]: This approach models each aspect target as a mixture of K aspect embeddings and selectively focuses on a small subset of context words according to the position information on the dependency tree of sentence.

Table 2. Experimental results of our proposed model and compared baseline models. Models with * indicate that position information is taken into account.

	Models	Laptop		Restaurant	
		ACC	Macro-F1	ACC	Macro-F1
Baselines	SVM	70.49	–	80.16	–
	AE-LSTM	68.90	–	76.60	–
	ATAE-LSTM	68.70	–	77.20	–
	TD-LSTM	71.83	68.43	78.00	66.73
	IAN	72.10	–	78.60	–
	EAM*	71.94	69.23	80.63	71.32
	MemNet*	72.21	–	80.95	–
	PBAN*	74.12	–	81.16	–
LAC-Pos variants	LAC-Pos-N-AD	74.92	70.67	81.25	71.64
	LAC-Pos-N-KL	**75.08**	70.73	80.98	71.71
	LAC-Pos-N-JS	74.76	70.21	81.25	71.73
	LAC-Pos-G-AD	74.76	70.50	81.07	70.76
	LAC-Pos-G-KL	74.61	70.30	**81.34**	**71.91**
	LAC-Pos-G-JS	74.76	**70.76**	80.89	70.65

- MemNet [15]: This approach applies attention mechanism over the word embeddings multiple times and predicts sentiments based on the top-most sentence representations. And it also leverages the position information to adjust the word embeddings in memory.
- PBAN [7]: This approach append position embedding after word embedding and mutually models the relation between aspect term and sentence by employing bidirectional attention mechanism.

4.4   Experimental Results

Table 2 shows the experimental results of our proposed model and other baseline models. Since adding position information, we call our proposed basic model as LAC-Pos, which means LSTM-Attention-CNN-Position. According to the method of calculating the position distribution and calculating the difference between position distribution and attention weight distribution, we add suffix after LAC-Pos to represent our full model. For example, LAC-Pos-N-AD means basic LAC-Pos equipped with normalized position distribution and using absolute difference to calculate the difference between position distribution and attention weight distribution.

We explore a variety of methods to leverage position information which are called LAC-Pos Variants. From Table 2 we can observe that our approach outperforms all the compared approaches on both *Laptop* and *Restaurant*. And the performances among all the LAC-Pos variants are very close which demonstrates that our approach is robust, generalized and not limited to specific methods of calculating position distribution and calculating the difference. The reason that results of our full models vary in different distance measures may be that the calculating methods vary in different distance measures, which will give different results even given two same probability distributions.

Table 3. Experimental results of ablated LAC-Pos.

Ablated LAC-Pos	Laptops		Restaurants	
	ACC	Macro-F1	ACC	Macro-F1
LPC-N	72.26	67.26	79.73	69.50
LPC-G	71.79	67.36	79.73	69.59
LAC	73.35	68.53	80.54	71.24

IAN, EAM, MemNet and PBAN, with sophisticated attention modules, outperform than TD-LSTM on both *Laptop* and *Restaurant*, which shows the attention mechanism can figure out target-related words effectively. In addition, EAM, MemNet and PBAN all take into account the position information, although the methods of using position information are different, and they all outperform than IAN, which indicates the position information is helpful for this task.

Although PBAN has achieved good performance, it is still not as good as our model, especially on *Laptop*. The reason may be that position embedding does indicate the distance between context words and target, but it does not explicitly requires higher weights for words that are closer to target. In contrast, our model adds the difference between position distribution and attention weight distribution to final loss as penalty, which is a clear and strong signal: the closer the word is to the target, the higher the weight.

Furthermore, we observe that after adding the position information, the promotion on *Laptop* is greater than *Restaurant*. The reason may be the data in *Laptop* contain a large number of exclusive noun which are rare words, and it makes difficulties to calculate the accurate attention weights, so that the attention mechanism can not distinguish target-related words and target-unrelated words well, so the position information will be very helpful for adjusting attention weights.

4.5   Ablation Experiments

To demonstrate the effectiveness of our approach, we set up three ablated models which use either the attention weight or position information as features. LPC-N and LPC-G mean we abandon attention mechanism and only use normalized position distribution and gaussian position distribution to adjust word embeddings respectively. LAC means we use only attention weights to adjust word embedding.

We conduct the statistical t-test between our full models and LAC. From Table 3 we can observe that after abandoning the position information, the performance of LAC drops dramatically. And all of the produced p-values are less than 0.05, which indicates the improvements brought in by position information are significant. Further more, we can see that if we only use the position information without the attention module, the performances of LPC-N and LPC-G are worse than LAC, which proves the correctness of our strategy that combining the attention mechanism and position information.

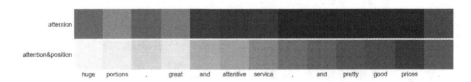

Fig. 3. Illustration of attention where horizontal axis is the sentence and the vertical axis is the method. The upper heat map is the attention distribution of LAC and the lower heat map is the attention distribution of LAC-Pos-N-AD, where the targets are *prices*.

Even if we abandon position information, LAC still outperforms than most compared models, which shows the power of CNN capturing local features. When we only use position information, LPC-N and LPC-G can still get pretty good results, which shows that position information is actually helpful to distinguish target-related words and target-unrelated words.

4.6   Case Study

In this part, we take a case to show the effectiveness of our method. Figure 3 shows two heat maps of attention weights from LAC and LAC-Pos-N-AD respectively. The attention weights are both transformed into between 0 and 1 which indicates how much information should be preserved for every word. The weight of each word is visualized by the color depth where the redder the color, the greater the attention weight.

As shown in the heat map of LAC, the attention-based model not only give high weights to the real target-related words *pretty good*, but also those target-unrelated words such as *huge, great* and *attentive*, which is also a common problem of the current attention mechanism.

However, after adding position information, our LAC-Pos-N-AD still pays attention to the target-related words but ignore those target-unrelated words according to the position information. Therefore, the position distribution can better guide the generation of attention weights.

5   Conclusions

In this paper, we analyze the importance of position information in aspect-level sentiment classification and propose a novel approach to combine position information and attention mechanism: leverage the position distribution to modify the attention weight distribution. Then we use the adjusted attention weights to adjust the word embeddings and apply CNN on the weighted embedding matrix to capture the local n-gram features for sentiment classification. We perform experiments on two datasets of SemEval 2014 and the experimental results show the effectiveness of our model.

References

1. Kim, Y.: Convolutional neural networks for sentence classification. arXiv preprint arXiv:1408.5882 (2014). https://doi.org/10.3115/v1/D14-1181
2. Liu, B.: Sentiment analysis and opinion mining. Synth. Lect. Hum. Lang. Technol. **5**(1), 1–167 (2012). https://doi.org/10.2200/S00416ED1V01Y201204HLT016
3. Jiang, L., Yu, M., Zhou, M., Liu, X., Zhao, T.: Target-dependent twitter sentiment classification. In: Proceedings of the 49th Annual Meeting of the Association for Computational Linguistics: Human Language Technologies-Volume 1, pp. 151–160. Association for Computational Linguistics (2011)
4. Wang, Y., Huang, M., Zhao, L., et al.: Attention-based LSTM for aspect-level sentiment classification. In: Proceedings of the 2016 Conference on Empirical Methods in Natural Language Processing, pp. 606–615 (2016). https://doi.org/10.18653/v1/D16-1058

5. Ma, D., Li, S., Zhang, X., Wang, H.: Interactive attention networks for aspect-level sentiment classification. arXiv preprint arXiv:1709.00893 (2017). https://doi.org/10.24963/ijcai.2017/568

6. He, R., Lee, W.S., Ng, H.T., Dahlmeier, D.: Effective attention modeling for aspect-level sentiment classification. In: Proceedings of the 27th International Conference on Computational Linguistics, pp. 1121–1131 (2018)

7. Gu, S., Zhang, L., Hou, Y., Song, Y.: A position-aware bidirectional attention network for aspect-level sentiment analysis. In: Proceedings of the 27th International Conference on Computational Linguistics, pp. 774–784 (2018)

8. Pontiki, M., Galanis, D., Pavlopoulos, J., Papageorgiou, H., Androutsopoulos, I., Manandhar, S.: Semeval-2014 task 4: aspect based sentiment analysis. In: Proceedings of the 8th International Workshop on Semantic Evaluation (SemEval 2014), pp. 27–35 (2014). https://doi.org/10.3115/v1/S14-2004

9. Zhao, W.X., Jiang, J., Yan, H., Li, X.: Jointly modeling aspects and opinions with a MaxEnt-LDA hybrid. In: Proceedings of the 2010 Conference on Empirical Methods in Natural Language Processing, pp. 56–65. Association for Computational Linguistics (2010)

10. Tang, D., Qin, B., Feng, X., Liu, T.: Effective LSTMs for target-dependent sentiment classification. arXiv preprint arXiv:1512.01100 (2015)

11. Wang, B., Lu, W.: Learning latent opinions for aspect-level sentiment classification. In: Thirty-Second AAAI Conference on Artificial Intelligence (2018)

12. Liu, J., Zhang, Y.: Attention modeling for targeted sentiment. In: Proceedings of the 15th Conference of the European Chapter of the Association for Computational Linguistics: Volume 2, Short Papers, vol. 2, pp. 572–577 (2017). https://doi.org/10.18653/v1/E17-2091

13. Zhang, Y., Zhong, V., Chen, D., Angeli, G., Manning, C.D.: Position-aware attention and supervised data improve slot filling. In: Proceedings of the 2017 Conference on Empirical Methods in Natural Language Processing (2017). https://doi.org/10.18653/v1/D17-1004

14. Weston, J., Chopra, S., Bordes, A.: Memory networks. arXiv preprint arXiv:1410.3916 (2014)

15. Tang, D., Qin, B., Liu, T.: Aspect level sentiment classification with deep memory network. arXiv preprint arXiv:1605.08900 (2016). https://doi.org/10.18653/v1/D16-1021

16. Yang, J., Yang, R., Wang, C., Xie, J.: Multi-entity aspect-based sentiment analysis with context, entity and aspect memory. In: Thirty-Second AAAI Conference on Artificial Intelligence (2018b). https://doi.org/10.1145/3321125

17. Luong, M.-T., Pham, H., Manning, C.D.: Effective approaches to attention-based neural machine translation. arXiv preprint arXiv:1508.04025 (2015). https://doi.org/10.18653/v1/D15-1166

18. Yang, B., Tu, Z., Wong, D.F., Meng, F., Chao, L.S., Zhang, T.: Modeling localness for self-attention networks. arXiv preprint arXiv:1810.10182 (2018a). https://doi.org/10.18653/v1/D18-1475

19. Pennington, J., Socher, R., Manning, C.: GloVe: global vectors for word representation. In: Proceedings of the 2014 Conference on Empirical Methods in Natural Language Processing (EMNLP), pp. 1532–1543 (2014). https://doi.org/10.3115/v1/D14-1162

20. Kingma, D.P., Ba, J.: Adam: a method for stochastic optimization. arXiv preprint arXiv:1412.6980 (2014)

Surrounding-Based Attention Networks for Aspect-Level Sentiment Classification

Yuheng Sun[1], Xianchen Wang[1], Hongtao Liu[1], Wenjun Wang[1], and Pengfei Jiao[2(✉)] ⓘ

[1] College of Intelligence and Computing, Tianjin University, Tianjin, China
{yhs,wangxc,htliu,wjwang}@tju.edu.cn
[2] Center for Biosafety Research and Strategy, Tianjin University, Tianjin, China
pjiao@tju.edu.cn

Abstract. Aspect-level sentiment classification aims to identify the polarity of a target word in a sentence. Studies on sentiment classification have found that a target's surrounding words have great impacts and global attention to the target. However, existing neural-network-based models either depend on expensive phrase-level annotation or do not fully exploit the association of the context words to the target. In this paper, we propose to model the influences of the target's surrounding words via two unidirectional long short-term memory neural networks, and introduce a target-based attention mechanism to discover the underlying relationship between the target and the context words. Empirical results on the SemEval 2014 Datasets show that our approach outperforms many competitive sentiment classification baseline methods. Detailed analysis demonstrates the effectiveness of the proposed surrounding-based long-short memory neural networks and the target-based attention mechanism.

Keywords: Aspect-level sentiment · Attention · Neural network

1 Introduction

Aspect-level sentiment classification (ASC) is a fundamental task in natural language processing (NLP). The goal of ASC is to identify the sentiment polarity of a specific target in a sentence [1]. It is an inevitable step to machine translation and understanding. For example, in the sentence *"the Italian food is magnificent, however, to our disappointment, the service is poor!"*, the target *"Italian food"* has a polarity of positive, while the polarity of the target *"service"* is negative. Aspect-level sentiment analysis is crucial to the exact understanding of user comments [1].

Existing studies in aspect-level sentiment classification can be categorized as either filter or wrapper approaches [21]. In a filter approach, features are pre-extracted before applied to training a classifier. For examples, in [1] and [17], context features, such as n-gram features, parse features and sentiment lexicon

ⓒ Springer Nature Switzerland AG 2019
I. V. Tetko et al. (Eds.): ICANN 2019, LNCS 11730, pp. 143–155, 2019.
https://doi.org/10.1007/978-3-030-30490-4_13

features, are first extracted/constructed, and then used to train a SVM classifier [4]. The performance of these approaches depends mainly on the quality of the extracted features. However, feature extraction is usually very tedious. Further, it has been found that the performance of this kind of approach has almost reached its limit [10,17].

The wrapper approach, on the other hand, incorporates feature extraction within the sentiment classification. Most wrapper approaches are built upon deep learning technologies in debt to their great capacity on learning context representation without the requirement of careful feature engineering. As such, deep learning approaches such as convolutional neural networks (CNN) [7], long short-term memory (LSTM) networks [18], and others, have been used extensively in sentiment analysis. In these neural network based models, only word-level features such as word embeddings [14] are used yet deeper sentence features can be automatically achieved.

Very recently, the effectiveness of attention mechanism has been explored in deep learning. This inspires the application of the attention mechanism for the aspect-level sentiment classification task. It has been found that the recognition of the importance of each context word to the target has achieved an obvious improvement by using attention mechanism [10]. Furthermore, by noticing a common sense in linguistics which states that words which are close to the target, such as adjectives, sentiment words, negation words, etc., tend to play more important roles in inferring the target sentiment, researchers have designed neural network based models in which the importances to contextual information (e.g. the target's surrounding words) are emphasized [18]. For examples, Tai et al. [18] proposed a tree-structured long short-term memory network for the learning of semantic sentence representation. In their work, sentence is parsed into a tree structure so that the correlation of a context word to the target is measured within the tree structure. In Tang et al. [19], they proposed a location attention mechanism to calculate each word's location attention weight to the target within a parsed tree structure.

Despite the success of these neural network based models, there are still some disadvantages. First, existing neural network models achieve this through sentence structure parsing which requires phrase-level annotation. Since annotation is expensive, these models can hardly be applied to large-scale datasets. Besides, the prediction accuracy depends highly on the accuracy of the sentence parsing results. A bad sentence parsing will deteriorate the prediction accuracy significantly. Second, most attention mechanisms proposed in existing neural network models [10] simply take the target information's embedding as an extra input to the attention layers. Such designs cannot fully explore the association between the target and each context word. To address this problem, Wang et al. [23] proposed to create an extra target embedding for each target and merge it with each context word embedding for the discovery of deep relationships. An additional target embedding list is kept for each target. However, this method is not quite realistic since the creation of extra comprehensive target embeddings in most aspect-level sentiment classification tasks is not always possible.

For example, their work cannot deal with the situation when complex targets (such as '*a pizza with the smell of Durian*') do not appear in training set but in test set. The additional target embedding list will not be updated for those complex targets during the training, thus make it impossible to predict on these targets. This phenomenon has been widely observed in most aspect-level sentiment classification tasks [12].

To address these shortcomings in existing approaches, in this paper, we propose a surrounding-based attention network (SBAN), in which two unidirectional LSTM neural networks and a new target-based attention mechanism are incorporated. The two LSTMs take the embeddings of the target's preceding and following words, respectively, as input, without requiring any sentence parsing. The surrounding-based model is able to explicitly reveal the deep relationships between the target and the surrounding words. On the other hand, the target-based attention mechanism combines the average target embedding with each context word's hidden state, so that the target information is able to be fully explored for producing an accurate attention weight for each word.

The proposed approach is evaluated on the restaurant and the laptop datasets from SemEval 2014 [12]. Empirical results indicate that SBAN outperforms nine baselines (including the state-of-the-art approaches) in terms of prediction accuracy. Detailed analysis is also carried out to demonstrate the effectiveness of the proposed surrounding-based network architecture and the new target-based attention mechanism. The main contributions of our work can be summarized as follows:

- A simple yet efficient surrounding-based architecture for ASC is proposed for the full exploration of the target's surrounding words.
- Only word-level features (i.e., word embeddings) are used as input in the proposed model. This makes it possible to apply the developed algorithm on large-scale datasets.
- A target-aware attention mechanism is proposed by combing the information of the target and each context word.

2   Related Work

2.1   Sentiment Analysis with Neural Networks

Neural network approaches have been extensively studied for sentiment analysis tasks. For examples, methods based on convolutional neural network [7], long shot-term memory [18], tree-structured LSTM [18], recursive neural networks [2], and others, have been developed and achieved great success. Compared with traditional machine learning methods, neural network approaches have the merits on learning text representation without any feature engineering. There are also some studies trying to combine linguistic features (e.g. sentiment words, negation words and intensity words) with neural network models [15].

2.2 Aspect-Level Sentiment Classification

Aspect-level sentiment classification is a fine-grained task in sentiment analysis. It aims to infer the sentiment polarity of a specific target in a sentence [13]. Since it is a target-dependent task, the target information should be taken into account when predicting [1]. In order to capture the relevant information of the target, Tang et al. [22] developed two target-dependent long short-term memory neural networks to model the left and right contexts of the target. Ma et al. [10] utilized the target and context to compute the attention vector and learn their representations respectively. Liu and Zhang [9] presented several target-separating attention neural networks and used three gates to control the output of the model. Recently, Ma et al. [11] proposed to introduce extra common sense knowledge in the model to infer the target sentiment polarity. Existing models either do not employ the target's contextual information properly, or the applied attention mechanism may be too simple to identify the target's sentiment polarity effectively.

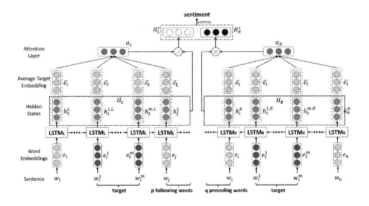

Fig. 1. The overall architecture of SBAN.

3 Methodology

Given a sentence $s = [w_1, w_2, \ldots, w_n]$ and a specific target $t = [w_t^1, w_t^2, \ldots, w_t^m]$ in s, aspect-level sentiment classification aims to infer the sentiment polarity (e.g., *positive, neutral, negative*) of t. Our model builds upon LSTM. It consists of five layers including a word encoder layer, two surrounding-based LSTM layers, a target-based attention layer and a sentence representation layer. The overall architecture of SBAN is shown in Fig. 1.

Given a sequence of words, SBAN first maps each word w into its embedding e by using methods such as in [3,5,14]. The collection of the sentence representation $s_r = [e_1, e_2, \ldots, e_n]$ and target representation $t_r = [e_t^1, e_t^2, \ldots, e_t^m]$ is used as the input to the LSTMs. Here, $e \in \mathcal{R}^V$ and V denotes the embedding dimension.

In NLP, recurrent neural network (RNN) [20,24] is widely used for its capacity of modeling the associations of words in context. Among a variety of RNNs, the long short-term memory (LSTM) [6,8] neural network is the most famous one. It is able to capture long-term dependencies, and overcome the gradient vanishing and expansion problems in training.

In our model, given the input word embedding e^t, previous cell state c^{t-1} and previous hidden state h^{t-1}, the LSTM cell updates the current cell state c^t and current hidden state h^t by

$$X = [h^{t-1}; e^t] \tag{1}$$
$$\mathbf{f}_t = \sigma(W_f \cdot X + b_f), \ \mathbf{i}_t = \sigma(W_i \cdot X + b_i), \ \mathbf{o}_t = \sigma(W_o \cdot X + b_o) \tag{2}$$
$$c^t = \mathbf{f}_t \odot c^{t-1} + \mathbf{i}_t \odot tanh(W_g \cdot X + b_g) \tag{3}$$
$$h^t = \mathbf{o}_t \odot tanh(c^t) \tag{4}$$

where $\mathbf{f}$, $\mathbf{i}$ and $\mathbf{o}$ represents the forget gate, input gate and output gate respectively, W's and b's denote the weight matrices and biases respectively, $\odot$ stands for the element-wise multiplication, σ is the sigmoid function.

To emphasize the impacts of the target's surrounding words, two unidirectional LSTMs, named as $LSTM_L$ and $LSTM_R$, are applied. $LSTM_L$ considers the context words from the start of the sentence to the target, and p following words of the target. Formally, the input $s_L = [e_1, e_2, \ldots, e_t^1, \ldots, e_t^m, e_j, \ldots, e_{j+p}]$ where $[e_j, \ldots, e_{j+p}]$ denotes the embeddings of the p following words. $LSTM_R$ accommodates the words from the target to the end, together with q preceding words of the target. That is, $s_R = [e_{i-q}, \ldots, e_i, e_t^1, \ldots, e_t^m, \ldots, e_{n-1}, e_n]$ where $[e_{i-q}, \ldots, e_i]$ denotes the embeddings of the q preceding words. p and q are hyperparameters taking integer values. The use of p following and q preceding words emphasizes the importance of the surrounding words to the target. To better utilize the target information, similarly to [22], the input for $LSTM_R$ starts from the end of the sentence.

For the sake of simplicity, assume that the length of s_L and S_R is l and r, respectively. In the sequel, we use $H_L \in \mathcal{R}^{l \times d}$ and $H_R \in \mathcal{R}^{r \times d}$ to represent the hidden states produced by the two LSTMs. Here d is the dimension of the hidden states.

An effective target-based attention mechanism is introduced upon the LSTM layer in SBAN to utilize the target information for recognizing the impact of each context word to the target. It can be summarized from Eqs. 5–9, see also Fig. 1. First, the average target embedding is calculated by averaging the target's constituting word vectors (cf. Eq. 5). Two non-linear layers are constructed to improve the network's capacity on learning (cf. Eqs. 6 and 7). Two softmax layers are then used to capture the importance of each context words (cf. Eq. 8). The hidden representations H_L^* and H_R^* are then obtained by multiplication with α_L and α_R.

$$\overline{e_t} = \frac{1}{m} \sum_{i=1}^{m} e_t^i \tag{5}$$

$$M_L = tanh(W_a \cdot [H_L; \overline{e_t} \otimes l] + b_a) \tag{6}$$

$$M_R = tanh(W_a \cdot [H_R; \overline{e_t} \otimes r] + b_a) \tag{7}$$

$$\alpha_L = softmax(W_u \cdot M_L), \ \alpha_R = softmax(W_u \cdot M_R) \tag{8}$$

$$H_L^* = \alpha_L \cdot H_L, \ H_R^* = \alpha_R \cdot H_R \tag{9}$$

where $\overline{e_t} \in \mathcal{R}^V, M_L \in \mathcal{R}^{2d \times l}, M_R \in \mathcal{R}^{2d \times r}, \alpha_L \in \mathcal{R}^l, \alpha_R \in \mathcal{R}^r, H_L^* \in \mathcal{R}^d, H_R^* \in \mathcal{R}^d$, and $W_a \in \mathcal{R}^{2d \times 2d}, b_a \in \mathcal{R}^{2d}, W_u \in \mathcal{R}^{2d}$ are the projection parameters. "$\otimes$" in Eqs. 6 and 7 is a concatenating operator $\overline{e_t} \otimes l = [\overline{e_t}, \overline{e_t}, \ldots, \overline{e_t}]$. In the attention layer, W_a, b_a and W_u are shared when calculating α_L and α_R.

It should be noted that the average target embedding $\overline{e_t}$ and each hidden state is combined as the input to the attention layer. This means to discover the deep relationship between the target and each context word. The attention mechanism results in two attention weights α_L, α_R and two weighted hidden representations H_L^* and H_R^*. They are concatenated to reach the final sentence representation $h^* = [H_L^*, H_R^*]$. A *softmax* layer is then used to get the conditional probability distribution

$$\hat{y} = softmax(W_s h^* + b_s). \tag{10}$$

To train the model, the cross-entropy with L_2 regularization is used as the loss function, that is

$$loss = -\sum_i y_i \log \hat{y_i} + \lambda ||\theta||^2 \tag{11}$$

where i is the index of sentence, y represents the gold sentiment distribution of sentence, $\hat{y}$ denotes the predicted sentiment distribution and λ is the weight for the L_2 regularization. SGD is used to optimize the parameters.

4   Experiments

4.1   Dataset

We conduct experiments on the datasets from SemEval 2014 Task 4[1] [12] to evaluate the performance of SBAN. The datasets consist of customer reviews from two domains: *Restaurant* and *Laptop*. All the targets are annotated. It is important to note that, similar to [10,19], we ignore the '*conflict*' category (relatively few records) to ensure consistency for comparing our model with other models. Thus, all the reviews are labeled with three sentiment polarities: *positive, neutral,* and *negative*. The datasets are split into the training sets and test sets. Statistics of the datasets are given in Table 1.

---

[1] Detailed information can be found at: http://alt.qcri.org/semeval2014/task4.

Table 1. Statistics of the datasets.

Dataset	Positive	Neutral	Negative
Laptop-Train	994	464	870
Laptop-Test	341	169	128
Restaurant-Train	2164	637	807
Restaurant-Test	728	196	196

4.2   Experiment Settings

In the experiments, we split 10% of the train dataset as validation dataset to tune the hyper parameters in our model. The dimensions of the word embeddings and LSTM hidden states are set to 300. We perform Glorot initialisation [16] for all the weight matrices, and all the biases are set to zeros. Standard stochastic gradient descent is applied to train the model with a learning rate of 0.1. The coefficient of the L_2 normalization in the loss function is set to 10^{-6}. Dropout is adopted with a probability of 0.5. All the word embeddings are initialized by GloVe[2] [14] while the out-of-vocabulary words are initialized with $Uniform(-0.25, 0.25)$.

4.3   Model Comparisons

We report the performance of our method and compare it to several competitive baseline methods to evaluate our model. The baseline methods include:

Majority: A basic baseline method, which assigns the majority sentiment polarity in the training set to each sample in the test set.

Feature+SVM: NRC-Canada proposed in [17]. It is a top system using n-gram features, parse features and lexicon features. This method achieves a rather great performance on the laptop and restaurant datasets.

LSTM/Bi-LSTM: A basic LSTM approach [6]. It produces a hidden state for each word and the last hidden state is regarded as the sentence representation, which is used to predict the target sentiment polarity. **Bi-LSTM** is a variant of **LSTM**. It exploits two parallel passes (forward and backward) and concatenates hidden states of the two LSTMs as the representation of each position. The last hidden state is regarded as the sentence representation and used for classification.

TD-LSTM/TC-LSTM: Target-dependent LSTM [22]. It uses a forward LSTM network and a backward LSTM network to process the left and right contexts with the target. Target-connection LSTM (**TC-LSTM**) extends **TD-LSTM** by incorporating an target connection component. It utilizes the connections between target word and each context word explicitly when composing the representation of a sentence. Note that **TD-LSTM** and **TC-LSTM** do not emphasize the impacts of the target's surrounding words. They simply split sentence into two parts (from the start to the target, and from the target to the end).

---

[2] Available at: https://nlp.stanford.edu/projects/glove/.

MemNet: Deep memory network [19]. This method consists of multiple computational layers, each of which is a context- and location- based attention model. This architecture can well utilize the target information and learn the impact of each context word for the target.

Table 2. Comparison results with the baselines in terms of the prediction accuracy of different methods on the laptop and restaurant datasets. All the results are based on the 3-classes classification task. Results marked with "*" are re-printed from [10,19]. Those with "∘" are obtained by our own implementations, and note that the difference of these baselines to the best result is statistically significant at 0.05 level. The best scores in each dataset are in bold. Specifically, for the best accuracy of SBAN in the Laptop dataset, $p = 2$ and $q = 3$. For the best accuracy of SBAN in the Restaurant dataset, $p = 3$ and $q = 1$.

Method	Laptop	Restaurant
Majority	0.534°	0.650°
Feature+SVM	0.721*	0.809*
LSTM	0.646°	0.739°
Bi-LSTM	0.656°	0.742°
TD-LSTM	0.691°	0.766°
TC-LSTM	0.672°	0.764°
MemNet	0.724*	0.810*
BILSTM-ATT-C	0.729°	0.801°
IAN	0.721*	0.786*
SBAN-Basic	0.735	0.808
SBAN	**0.754**	**0.824**

BILSTM-ATT-C: A contextualized attention model [9]. It uses a bidirectional LSTM with the left and right context-sensitive attention layers. The model combines the attention weights with the entire sentence, left contexts and right contexts to predict the target sentiment polarity.

IAN: Interactive Attention Network [10] It employs the LSTM networks to obtain the hidden states of words on the word level for a target and its context, respectively. The average values of the target's hidden states and the context's hidden states are then used to supervise the generation of the attention vectors. The IAN model can well represent a target and its collective context, which is helpful for target sentiment classification.

In particular, in order to evaluate the overall architecture of our model, especially the new target-based attention mechanism, we propose a model, dubbed as **SBAN-Basic**. It is the same as **SBAN** except that $p = 0$ and $q = 0$, which means the surrounding words are not considered in the model.

Table 2 summarizes the comparison results. We can conclude the following observations. (1) Feature+SVM performs quite well among all the baselines, even outperform some deep-learning based methods (e.g., LSTM, Bi-LSTM). This suggests that feature engineering can be very useful for ASC, however the feature engineering would be time-consuming. (2) Except Majority and Feature+SVM, all the other methods are based on LSTM. These models care less about features, but more on the architecture design. The basic LSTM and Bi-LSTM methods get poor scores since they treat different targets in a sentence equally and do not take full use of the target information, which is the key component in ASC task. (3) TD-LSTM performs better than basic LSTM and Bi-LSTM, which indicates that taking the target information into account is helpful. (4) MemNet, BILSTM-ATT-C and IAN adopt attention mechanisms to model the influence of each context word to the target. Their results show that the introduction of attention greatly improves the prediction accuracy on the two datasets.

Compared with the baselines, SBAN-Basic gets the highest scores on the laptop dataset and competitive scores on the restaurant dataset. The results indicate that the target-based attention mechanism, which combines the average target embedding with each hidden state to create attention weight for each word, can reveal a deep relationship between the target and each context word. Furthermore, after considering the target's surrounding words, our SBAN model achieves the best performance. The outperformance of SBAN against SBAN-Basic indicates the favor of the target's surrounding words.

The accuracy on the laptop dataset is 75.4%, which is 3.0% higher than the best scores obtained by the baselines. On the restaurant dataset, the accuracy reaches 82.4%, which is 1.4% higher than the best scores obtained by the baselines. Since it is well known that it is rather difficult to boost 1% of accuracy on aspect-level sentiment classification, especially on these benchmark datasets, we may conclude that our method is very promising.

4.4   Detailed Analysis of SBAN

Effects of the Target's Surrounding Words. In order to verify whether the target's surrounding words influence the prediction, we carry out experiments

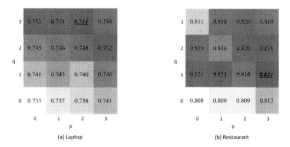

Fig. 2. The prediction accuracy of SBAN with different p and q. A deeper color depth indicates a higher accuracy. The best performance in each dataset is underlined. (Color figure online)

on different values of p and q, which are the number of the target's surrounding words considered in $LSTM_L$ and $LSTM_R$. The results are shown in Fig. 2. The color depth represents the classification accuracy. A deeper color implies a higher accuracy. In comparison with SBAN-Basic ($p = 0, q = 0$), Fig. 2 shows that SBAN with $p > 0, q > 0$ achieves an obvious improvement. We do not discuss how to set the hyper parameters p and q because it is problem-dependent. What attracts us more is the fact that taking the target's surrounding words into account is beneficial to capturing the target's surrounding information in aspect-level sentiment classification task. Furthermore, we explore how the target's surrounding words improve the performance. In Table 3, we list some examples from the restaurant test set whose polarity labels are inferred incorrectly by SBAN-Basic but correctly predicted by SBAN. We observe that adjectives (*fast*, *cheap*, *expensive*), intensity words (*very*) and negation words (*not*), which are the key words to describe the target, are usually close to the target. SBAN ($p = 3, q = 1$) can utilize this information to improve the classification accuracy.

Table 3. Examples drawn from the restaurant test set whose polarity labels are incorrectly inferred by SBAN-Basic but correctly predicted by SBAN ($p = 3, q = 1$). The target is typeset in bold. "SBAN-Basic" means the predicted sentiment label from the SBAN-Basic model. "−1" denotes negative, "0" denotes neutral and "1" denotes positive.

Example	Label	SBAN-Basic
tiny restaurant with very fast. **service**	1	−1
i thought the **food** *is not cheap at all compared to chinatown*	−1	0
the **food** *- not worth the price*	−1	1
meal *was very expensive for what you get*	−1	1

Attention Visualization. We select several sentences from the restaurant test set and visualize the weights of these sentences for a given target. The visualization results are shown in Fig. 3. We observe that the target-based attention can recognize important words for the target from the whole sentence dynamically. Different targets in a sentence share quite different attention weights. Given the sentence "*great food but the service was dreadful!*" and the target "*food*", the word "*great*" plays a rather positive effect on the sentiment judgement. While for the same sentence and different target "*service*", the adjective "*dreadful*" is more important for recognizing the target sentiment polarity. The similar phenomenon can be observed in the sentence "*the food is great and the milkshakes are even better!*". Besides, we can also observe that the target's surrounding information is well captured. This observation suggests that using two surrounding-based LSTM neural networks to consider the target's surrounding words is beneficial to sentiment classification.

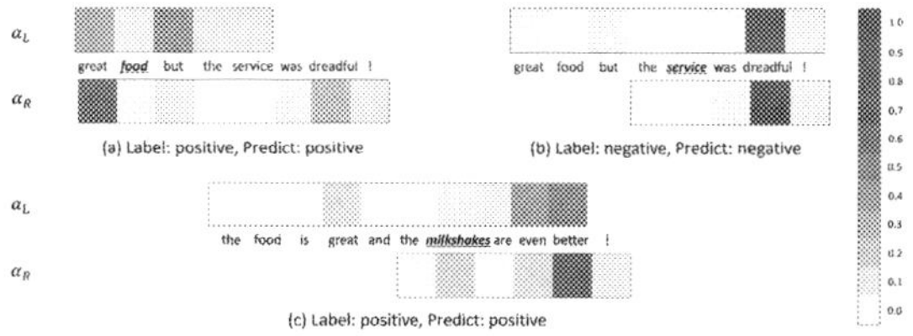

Fig. 3. Attention Visualizations. The target is underlined in the sentence.

4.5   Error Analysis

We carry out an error analysis to find out the weakness of our model. Firstly, linguistic resources such as intensity words and negation words are not fully employed. An example is that when given the sentence *"but dinner here is never disappointing, even if the prices are a bit over the top."* and the target *"dinner"*, our approach overlooks the impact of the word *"never"* and makes a predict of *negative* to *"dinner"*, which is the exact opposite of the label. Secondly, our model is not good at recognizing weak sentiment and neutral sentiment. When given the sentence *"when she complained, the waitress said, sorry."* and the target *"waitress"*, our model wrongly assumes the word *"sorry"* is important, which leads to a mistake.

5   Conclusion

In this paper, we proposed a surrounding-based attention network plus an effective attention mechanism for aspect-level sentiment classification. The proposed model was empirically compared with nine baselines (including some state-of-the-art models) on two commonly-used benchmarks. Experimental results suggested the proposed model performed the best on the benchmark datasets. Component analysis showed that the proposed surrounding-based attention network indeed contributes to the success of the proposed model.

Acknowledgments. This work is supported by the Humanities and Social Sciences Fund of Ministry of Education (13YJC870023) and the National Social Science Fund of China (15BTQ056).

References

1. Dinsoreanu, M., Bacu, A.: Unsupervised Twitter sentiment classification. In: KMIS, pp. 220–227 (2014). https://doi.org/10.5220/0005079002200227
2. Dong, L., Wei, F., Zhou, M., Xu, K.: Adaptive multi-compositionality for recursive neural models with applications to sentiment analysis. In: AAAI, pp. 1537–1543 (2014). https://doi.org/10.1109/TASLP.2015.2509257
3. Ganchev, T.D., Parsopoulos, K.E., Vrahatis, M.N., Fakotakis, N.D.: Partially connected locally recurrent probabilistic neural networks (2008). https://doi.org/10.5772/5552

4. Hearst, M.A., Dumais, S.T., Osuna, E., Platt, J., Scholkopf, B.: Support vector machines. IEEE Intell. Syst. Their Appl. **13**(4), 18–28 (1998). https://doi.org/10.1016/j.neunet.2010.01.002

5. Heeger, D.J., Gandhi, S.P., Huk, A.C., Boynton, G.M.: Neuronal correlates of attention in human visual cortex, pp. 25–47. The MIT Press, Cambridge (2001). https://doi.org/10.7551/mitpress/7125.003.0004

6. Hochreiter, S., Schmidhuber, J.: Long short-term memory. Neural Comput. **9**(8), 1735–1780 (1997). https://doi.org/10.4324/9781315174105-4

7. Kim, Y.: Convolutional neural networks for sentence classification. arXiv preprint arXiv:1408.5882 (2014). https://doi.org/10.3115/v1/d14-1181

8. Kurata, G., Ramabhadran, B., Saon, G., Sethy, A.: Language modeling with highway LSTM. In: ASRU, pp. 244–251. IEEE (2017). https://doi.org/10.1109/asru.2017.8268942

9. Liu, J., Zhang, Y.: Attention modeling for targeted sentiment. In: EACL, vol. 2, pp. 572–577 (2017). https://doi.org/10.18653/v1/e17-2091

10. Ma, D., Li, S., Zhang, X., Wang, H.: Interactive attention networks for aspect-level sentiment classification. arXiv preprint arXiv:1709.00893 (2017). https://doi.org/10.24963/ijcai.2017/568

11. Ma, Y., Peng, H., Cambria, E.: Targeted aspect-based sentiment analysis via embedding commonsense knowledge into an attentive LSTM. In: AAAI (2018). https://doi.org/10.1007/s12559-018-9549-x

12. Mubarok, M.S., Adiwijaya, Aldhi, M.D.: Aspect-based sentiment analysis to review products using Naïve Bayes. In: AIPC, vol. 1867, p. 020060. AIP Publishing (2017). https://doi.org/10.1063/1.4994463

13. Pang, B., Lee, L., et al.: Opinion mining and sentiment analysis. FTIR **2**(1–2), 1–135 (2008). https://doi.org/10.4000/books.oep.223

14. Pennington, J., Socher, R., Manning, C.: GloVe: global vectors for word representation. In: EMNLP, pp. 1532–1543 (2014). https://doi.org/10.3115/v1/d14-1162

15. Qian, Q., Huang, M., Lei, J., Zhu, X.: Linguistically regularized LSTMs for sentiment classification. arXiv preprint arXiv:1611.03949 (2016). https://doi.org/10.18653/v1/p17-1154

16. Shen, H.: Towards a mathematical understanding of the difficulty in learning with feedforward neural networks. In: CVPR, pp. 811–820 (2018). https://doi.org/10.1109/cvpr.2018.00091

17. Singla, Z., Randhawa, S., Jain, S.: Sentiment analysis of customer product reviews using machine learning. In: 2017 International Conference on Intelligent Computing and Control (I2C2), pp. 1–5. IEEE (2017). https://doi.org/10.1109/i2c2.2017.8321910

18. Tai, K.S., Socher, R., Manning, C.D.: Improved semantic representations from tree-structured long short-term memory networks. arXiv preprint arXiv:1503.00075 (2015). https://doi.org/10.3115/v1/p15-1150

19. Tang, D., Qin, B., Liu, T.: Aspect level sentiment classification with deep memory network. arXiv preprint arXiv:1605.08900 (2016). https://doi.org/10.18653/v1/d16-1021

20. Übeyli, E.D., Übeyli, M.: Case studies for applications of Elman recurrent neural networks (2008). https://doi.org/10.5772/5550

21. Wald, R., Khoshgoftaar, T.M., Napolitano, A.: Stability of filter-and wrapper-based feature subset selection. In: ICTAI, pp. 374–380. IEEE (2013). https://doi.org/10.1109/ictai.2013.63

22. Wang, H., Zhang, X., Liang, B., Zhou, Q., Xu, B.: Gated hierarchical LSTMs for target-based sentiment analysis. Int. J. Softw. Eng. Knowl. Eng. **28**(11n12), 1719–1737 (2018). https://doi.org/10.18293/seke2018-093
23. Wang, Y., Huang, M., Zhao, L., et al.: Attention-based LSTM for aspect-level sentiment classification. In: EMNLP, pp. 606–615 (2016). https://doi.org/10.18653/v1/d16-1058
24. Yang, T.H., Tseng, T.H., Chen, C.P.: Recurrent neural network-based language models with variation in net topology, language, and granularity. In: IALP, pp. 71–74. IEEE (2016). https://doi.org/10.1109/ialp.2016.7875937

Human Reaction Prediction

Mid Roll Advertisement Placement Using Multi Modal Emotion Analysis

Sumanu Rawat⬤, Aman Chopra⬤, Siddhartha Singh⬤,
and Shobhit Sinha(✉)⬤

Manipal Institute of Technology, Manipal 576104, Karnataka, India
sumanurawat12@gmail.com, amanchopra64@gmail.com,
singh.siddhartha23@gmail.com, shobhit.sinha19@gmail.com

Abstract. In recent years, owing to the ever-increasing consumer base of video content over the internet, promoting business via advertising between the videos has become a powerful strategy. Mid roll ads are the video ads that are played between the content of a video being watched by the user. While a lot of research has already been done in the field of analyzing the context of the video to suggest relevant ads, little has been done in the field of effective placement of the ads so that it does not deteriorate users' experience. In this paper, we are proposing a new model to suggest at which particular spot in a video, an advertisement should be placed such that most people will watch more of the ad. This is done using emotion, text, action, audio and video analysis of different scenes of a video under consideration.

Keywords: Advertisement placement · Audio analysis · Emotion analysis · Sentiment analysis · Video processing · LSTM · CNN · Artificial Neural Network

1 Introduction

Videos have an intuitive way of fostering attention. YouTube and Facebook are two famous platforms where video traffic is very high. While YouTube's mobile video consumption rises nearly by 100% every year, Facebook generates an average of 8 billion views every day. Considering the rate at which internet video traffic is increasing, mid roll advertisements are becoming a popular way to propagate business. Apart from the context and quality of the ad, it's placement also plays a crucial role in whether the user will watch and be interested in the ad's content. According to [5], mid roll ads could generate negative attitudinal responses and higher ad avoidance because consumers would likely find such ads more intrusive and irritating if they are not placed appropriately. Hence, the ad placement becomes very crucial.

Automatic mid roll ads might be placed in between scenes, or during a climax scene which severely deteriorates users' experience which in turn affects users' sentiments towards an ad or the brand. Generally, all videos consist of scenes

© Springer Nature Switzerland AG 2019
I. V. Tetko et al. (Eds.): ICANN 2019, LNCS 11730, pp. 159–171, 2019.
https://doi.org/10.1007/978-3-030-30490-4_14

which most of the users are particularly interested in watching. Placing ads near those scenes might increase the chances of that ad being watched by most of the users. It is also of extreme importance to place ads during scene transitions and not between a particular scene to not affect users' experience.

In this paper, we have predicted prospective points inside a video where an ad may be placed to increase the number of users that watch the ads without deteriorating their experience. This is done by analyzing underlying sentiments of different scenes of a video. In this paper, the classification models are trained on text sentiment, text emotion (extracted from speech), video emotion, audio, and the action of different scenes of a video to predict salient positions in an unseen video where a mid roll ad can be placed effectively to achieve the desired results. The paper has been laid out in the following manner. Section 2 deals with the primary objective of this paper. Section 3 talks about the key researches being already done in this field. Section 4 lays down the methodology the paper has followed to solve this problem. Section 5 discusses the case study. Sections 6 and 7 mention the results and conclusion.

2 Objective

This paper has proposed a design for a model which suggests effective markers in a video where an advertisement may be placed. Most of the times identifying where an advertisement should be placed turns out to be a difficult task as manual placement of an ad does not take into consideration the viewing patterns of the target audience. Placing an ad before a particular scene depends on a lot of factors like scene transition, emotion, and sentiment of the upcoming scene. Hence, analyzing these factors and training a model based on these extracted features can suggest places in the video where a suitable contextual ad can be placed without deteriorating the users' experience and encouraging maximum views.

3 Related Work

There have been studies related to object level and contextual Video Advertising. In work [12], the authors have proposed an approach to automatically detect objects that are continuously occurring and then select ads based on their relevance. According to the paper, the selected ads can be inserted at the time when the related objects appear. The drawback is that the related object might appear in between an engrossing scene and placing the ad between the scene might severely affect the users' experience. In work [7] the authors have identified the ads based on the contextual relevance of the video. For ad placement, they have identified insertion points which only depends on frame change and contextual relevance. While these two are significant factors, placing an ad does not just depend on these two factors, it also depends on the significance of the scene in a video which can be predicted using audio, text and frame analysis. In [11], the authors have proposed a dynamic framework to detect the climax of a

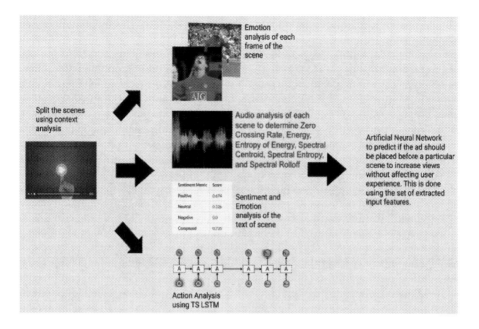

Fig. 1. Proposed methodology

scene for understanding the story in Video Advertisement. In [10], the authors have proposed a Computational effective Video-in-Video Advertising strategy where advertisements are inserted according to established psychological rules, by assessing the emotional impact of program content. This paper, apart from considering emotion analysis in the spatial domain, also considers action analysis in the temporal domain to better train the ANN model for improved results.

4   Methodology

Figure 1 shows the workflow diagram. The video is first divided into different scenes using content analysis. Multiple analysis like audio, video and text are done to generate data as these values play a major role in predicting the importance of each scene. They might indicate whether a scene carries high importance in the video or not. The individual scenes are then passed to an LSTM model for early action detection. All these extracted features are then fed to our classification model which suggests whether an ad should be placed before a particular scene or not.

4.1   Data Collection

A database of 56,435 scenes from 800 videos of different genres like 'Games', 'Art & Entertainment', 'Food & Drink', 'Business and Industrial' and 'Science' was created from the standard YouTube-8M Dataset [1].

4.2 Data Preprocessing

Machine learning datasets usually provide us with massive amounts of data scraped off the Internet. This data needs to be processed and constructed differently according to the needs of a case study. Multiple scenes were extracted from each video using standard python library *pyscenedetect* which splits the video into separate clips using Content-Aware detection. This paper experiments with its parameters like the threshold value to come up with fast, effective and relevant scene splitting. The optimal threshold value was 40. The start and end time of each scene in a video are saved. The start time values of different scenes are the prospective points where an advertisement may be inserted.

4.3 Model Generation

Each scene goes through a series of analysis, the output of which is fed to the classification model which decides ad placement before a particular scene.

Text Analysis. The video clip is first converted into an audio file using FFmpeg. The text is extracted from each audio clip using Google Cloud speech API. VADER (Valence Aware Dictionary and Sentiment Reasoner) is a lexicon and rule-based open source sentiment analysis tool [4]. Sentiment Analysis is a subfield of Natural Language Processing which classifies a sentence based on its emotional value. Each text phrase is given a sentiment score which ranges from [−1 to 1]. The negative sign in a sentiment score indicates a negative sentiment (sad, angry, gloomy), while the positive scores depict cheerful sentiments. The magnitude of this score measures the intensity of the given sentiment. To extract the context from text both sentiment analysis and text emotion analysis is necessary. While sentiment scores are just an indication of whether a phrase is positive, negative or neutral, the emotion analysis actually helps in categorizing the phrase into different categories of emotions. A CNN Model was trained on the dataset obtained from [8] to categorize the emotions of text in one of the four categories comprising of anger, joy, sadness, and fear. The CNN Model trained gives an accuracy of 93%. Figure 2 shows sentiment scores of some text extracted from an audio file.

Audio Analysis. A standard python library *pyaudioanalysis* is used to extract features from the audio files. We have used the short term feature extraction functionality of *pyaudioanalysis* for audio feature extraction. Short term feature extraction for an audio signal works by splitting each audio clip into frames of 50 ms with a 50% overlap of 25 ms. The library provides us with 6 audio features for each frame of an audio clip namely:

1. **Zero Crossing Rate** - The rate of sign-changes of the signal during the duration of a particular frame [3].
2. **Energy** - The sum of squares of the signal values, normalized by the respective frame length.

	Text	Sentiment score
0	My name is Aman	0.0000
1	Hundreds were killed in tribal violence last m...	-0.8625
2	Tonight's gonna be a good night	0.4404
3	Maria's level of happiness rose to ecstatic wh...	0.7845
4	The lakers lost the game	-0.3182

Fig. 2. Vader sentiment analysis

3. **Entropy of Energy** - The entropy of sub-frames' normalized energies. It can be interpreted as a measure of abrupt changes.
4. **Spectral Centroid** - The center of gravity of the spectrum.
5. **Spectral Entropy** - Entropy of the normalized spectral energies for a set of sub-frames.
6. **Spectral Rolloff** - The frequency below which 90% of the magnitude distribution of the spectrum is concentrated.

For each audio clip, we calculate the difference between the maximum value of a feature and the minimum value of a feature occurring in any of the 50 ms frames. The change in the energy level of a clip gives us a sense of high randomness or a 'burst' of excitement within a particular scene. The user experience would deteriorate if we would try to place an advertisement during this scene. This delta value is then scaled between 0 and 1 using the minmaxscaler of the scikit-learn preprocessing library. Scaling is done on per video basis as opposed to scaling on the whole dataset at once. Since the absolute value of these features may heavily vary with each video, our per video normalization provides a degree of evenness to the dataset. Every video contains scenes with a relatively high point and a relatively low point, which makes this a significant decision in our research and hence showed a good improvement in the results. Figure 3 shows Zero Crossing Rate (zcr) and Energy of different frames of a particular audio file.

Video Analysis. Emotion analysis of the video segment is an important attribute. To calculate the combined emotion of a scene extracted by *pyscenedetect*, we first split each scene into multiple frames which is essentially an image

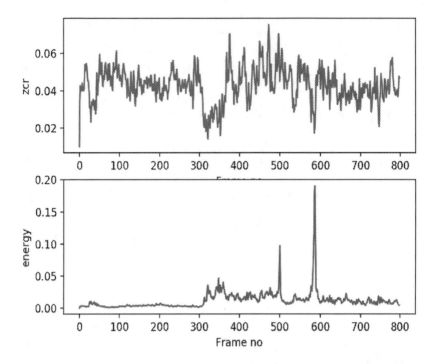

Fig. 3. ZCR, energy graph

using OpenCV. For emotion analysis, the paper has made use of Microsoft Azure cognitive emotion API. It identifies the face in the image and detects the emotion. The emotions detected are [anger, contempt, disgust, happiness, fear, neutral, sadness, and surprise]. These emotions are understood to be universally communicated with particular facial expressions. The emotion is neutral if the face is not detected in a particular frame. Now, to calculate the combined emotion of a particular scene, we take the emotion category with the highest confidence from each frame and label the scene with the category that occurred the most number of times in that scene. In case of a tie, our framework considers positive emotion. Since the interval of a particular scene is very small (7–12 s), one small scene will depict one emotion in most of the cases.

Action Analysis. The paper has taken a lot of spatial features into account using text, audio and image analysis. These features treat each scene as independent entities and have no relation to what happened before the scene took place. To detect the importance of a particular scene, features in the temporal domain are as important. Hence, the paper suggests action analysis which is used as an input attribute to the classification model. The extracted scenes are very small and therefore early detection of action is very important. The paper follows the methodology suggested in [2] to use a multi-stage LSTM Model for early action detection. This model gives an accuracy of 80.1% given only the first

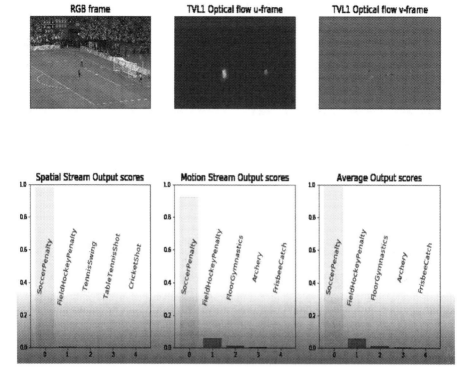

Fig. 4. LSTM Model detecting a soccer penalty

1% of the video. The LSTM model under consideration is trained over UCF101 action Recognition dataset which is a collection of 101 actions and it predicts one of these actions when the clip is fed into multi-stage recurrent architecture based on LSTMs. If the action is not present in the 101 actions on which the model is initially trained, it outputs the nearest action. These actions are then categorized into 5 categories comprising of [Human-Object Interaction, Body-Motion Only, Human-Human Interaction, Playing Musical Instruments, Sports] which are labeled from 1 to 5. This categorical numerical attribute of action is used as an input feature to the classification model.

Figure 4 shows the LSTM Model detecting a soccer penalty.

Min-Max Scaling. Before feeding the data into a classification algorithm, it is important to normalize the numeric features to prevent unnecessary imbalance in the data while training. The paper has used Min-max scaling as shown in Eq. 1, which scales a range of values down, such as their values vary from 0 to 1. The paper has applied min max scaling formula on the features namely text sentiment, Zero Crossing Rate, Energy, Entropy of Energy, Spectral Centroid, Spectral Entropy, Spectral Rolloff, Text_Emotion, Scene_Emotion, and Action.

$$z_i = \frac{x_i - min(x)}{max(x) - min(x)} \tag{1}$$

One Hot Encoding. Since the problem is a classification problem, the number of output columns should be equal to the desired number of output classes which is 2 as it is a binary classification problem. One hot encoding the output label column gives an array of 2 columns. Each of these columns denotes an output class. Whichever class a particular row belongs to, is assigned a value of 1 and the others are kept as 0.

Annotations. After extracting 56,435 scenes from the YouTube-8M dataset, it was necessary to annotate the videos with prospect ad insertion points to get the output in order to train and validate the classification model. Using *pyscenedetect*, we already got the start time of each clip of a video where an ad might be inserted, but to train the classification model, we had to find the points where the ads will not deteriorate the users' experience. We made use of the Amazon Mechanical Turk platform for this purpose. User psychology and their attitude towards advertisement are subjective and it also depends upon the background of the user, but using Amazon Mechanical Turk platform, we were able to give the task to annotators of different age groups and diverse location. We encouraged them to use VATIC (Video Annotation Tool from Irvine, California) [9]. We restricted participation on our tasks to annotators with at least 90% approval rate who submitted a minimum of 500 approved tasks in the past. We also added some special qualifications for the annotators, for instance, annotators should have some amount of knowledge and interest in the genre of the video they are annotating like 'Games', 'Science', 'Art & Entertainment' etc. We submitted each video for annotation to three workers satisfying the qualification. Using these qualifications, we tried to make sure that the model is generalized. A total of 56 annotators helped the study. Each was asked to watch the video and annotate the clips of the particular video where they won't mind the ad to be inserted. To ensure quality, annotators were also asked to describe what happens at the end of the video. We manually inspected a subset of them and found that the timestamps were reasonable.

Table 1 shows the accuracy of different algorithms used for model generation

The dataset was then shuffled with a random seed value and 25% of the dataset was used as the testing set. We split the remaining videos into one fifth (15%) for validation and four-fifths (60%) for training.

Table 1. Accuracy of algorithms

Algorithms	Accuracy
VADER Sentiment Analysis	96%
CNN Text Emotion Analysis	93%
Early Action detection using LSTM	80.1%

4.4 Classification Algorithms:

For this problem statement, the classification models predict whether an ad should be inserted before a scene of the video or not. The model is trained with 10 features i.e., Zero Crossing Rate, Energy, Entropy of Energy, Spectral Centroid, Spectral Entropy, Spectral Rolloff, Text_Sentiment, Text_Emotion, Scene_Emotion, Action and then the trained model is used for classification. We have used a comparative analysis of different classification models to come up with a model with the highest accuracy.

Logistic Regression. Logistic regression is used when the result expected is categorical in nature. In this paper, a special case of Logistic Regression, which is used to classify the result into two classes is used. This is called Binomial Logistic Regression. The main idea behind the Logistic Regression used is to establish a relationship between the attributes of the dataset and the probable outcome of the classes. In this paper, Binomial Logistic Regression uses a series of Bernoulli trials (pass, fail) to classify the start time of the clips as prospective ad insertion points. Our model of logistic regression makes use of L1 regularization in an attempt to introduce additional information that proves to be useful in the prevention of over-fitting to some extent. The equation to be solved by L1 regularized logistic regression is shown in Eq. 2.

The simplicity of logistic regression sets a bar, to begin with, and to compare the results of other classification algorithms used in the paper, namely, Support Vector Machine and Artificial Neural Networks.

$$\min_{w,c} \|w\|_1 + C \sum_{i=1}^{n} log(exp(-y_i(X_i^T w + c)) + 1) \tag{2}$$

Support Vector Machine. Due to a limited set of points in many dimensions, Support Vector Machine tends to be very good because it is able to find the linear separation that should exist. It also performs well with outliers as it will only use the most relevant points to find a linear separation (support vectors). In this project, we have used SVM with Radial Basis Function (RBF) kernel to find the prospect ad insertion points and compare its accuracy with baseline models like Logistic Regression and Complex models like Artificial Neural Networks.

Artificial Neural Networks. For this problem statement, the artificial neural network is predicting whether an ad should be inserted before a scene of the video or not. The artificial neural network is trained with 10 features i.e., Zero Crossing Rate, Energy, Entropy of Energy, Spectral Centroid, Spectral Entropy, Spectral Rolloff, Text_Sentiment, Text_Emotion, Scene_Emotion, Action and then the trained model is used for classification. Apart from the input and output layers, this model incorporates 2 hidden layers of 10 and 8 nodes respectively. The back-propagation algorithm is used to train the feedforward Multi-Layer Perceptrons to minimize the value of Categorical Cross Entropy loss function. As mentioned above, the dataset was divided into three sets. 60% of the data was used for training, 25% was used for testing and the remaining 15% was used for validation. After some experimentation, the number of iterations till convergence was found to be 47.

Transfer Function: Perceptrons perform the sigmoid function on output data as an activation function before passing the result on to the next layer. The Sigmoid function was chosen over the popularly used Rectified Linear Unit (ReLU) to maintain the relevance of negative sentiments. The output layer is subjected to the Softmax activation function because it strengthens the winning class and weighs down the losing one. It selects the output class with a higher probability.

Optimizing Algorithm: The optimization algorithm that showed promising results for the problem under consideration was the incorporation of Nesterov Momentum into Adam optimizing algorithm. The paper uses Keras's implementation of the 'nadam' optimizer for this purpose.

Regularization: It penalizes the weight matrices of the nodes of Artificial Neural Network. Here, we have used L1 Regularization to add a regularization term to update the general cost function. A drop out layer with $p = 0.45$ was also added. ANN are complex models and hence these steps become necessary to avoid over-fitting.

5   Case Study

The dataset used in this study consists of 56,435 scenes extracted from 800 videos of different genres from the standard YouTube-8M Dataset. The videos are split into scenes using *pyscenedetect* based on content analysis, fade in/out and fast cut detection of each shot. The Conditional attributes are extracted for each scene and are shown in Table 2. The Zero Crossing Rate, Energy, Entropy of Energy, Spectral Centroid, Spectral Entropy, Spectral Rolloff are calculated using audio analysis of each scene. The text sentiment analysis is done after extracting the text from speech and applying Vader sentiment analysis to get the sentiment score. The text emotion is calculated using a Convolution Neural Network model pre-trained on the dataset obtained from [8]. The action of the clip is identified using LSTM and the video emotion is categorized after splitting the scene into frames and passing each frame to Microsoft Azure's cognitive services to detect the emotion of a scene after combining the emotions of all the frames of that scene. Every scene also contains a video identifier from which it has been extracted along with start and end time of the scene. The advertisement will be placed at the start time of a particular scene predicted by the model.

Classification models are then trained on these features after feature normalization. After training, the model does a binary classification as to whether the advertisement should be placed before a particular scene or not with the aim of maximizing views without disturbing the users' experience.

Table 2. Dataset description

Conditional attributes	
Attributes	Description
Zero Crossing Rate	The rate of sign-changes of the signal during the duration of a particular frame
Energy	The sum of squares of the signal values, normalized by the respective frame length
Entropy of Energy	The entropy of sub-frames' normalized energies. It can be interpreted as a measure of abrupt changes
Spectral Centroid	The center of gravity of the spectrum
Spectral Entropy	Entropy of the normalized spectral energies for a set of sub-frames
Spectral Rolloff	The frequency below which 90% of the magnitude distribution of the spectrum is concentrated
Text_Sentiment	Vader sentiment score of the text of the scene
Text_Emotion	Classifies the text of the scene into four predefined emotions
Scene_Emotion	Classifies the frames of scene into eight predefined emotions
Action	Early Actions predicted by LSTM which are segregated into five categories

Table 3. Accuracy of classification algorithms

Algorithms	Accuracy (Rounded off to first decimal place)
Logistic Regression	72.8%
Support Vector Machine	82.2%
ANN	86.5%

6   Results

To evaluate the proposed model, the research collects 56,435 scenes from 800 videos of YouTube-8M Dataset. After training the models on 33,861 scenes from 480 videos of varied genres, the models were tested and validated. Table 3 shows the accuracy of different algorithms used for binary classification.

After comparative analysis, it was found that ANN with 2 hidden layers of 10 and 8 nodes respectively, sigmoid transfer function, 'nadam' optimizer, L1 regularisation and a dropout layer with $p = 0.45$ performed the best with an accuracy of 86.5%. Since it is a binary classification problem, to further validate our model, we also calculated the F1 score which is the harmonic mean of the precision and recall. The F1 score was calculated to be 0.885.

After carefully examining the insertion points suggested by the model on random videos, it was found that most of the points were after some climax positions and not towards the end of the videos which is in sync with a recent survey conducted by Facebook in which most people lose interest towards the end of the video, hence making it a not so effective position for ad insertion. Hence, the prospect ad insertion points to maintain a balance between ad completion rate and users' experience is after climatic positions (the highest dramatic tension or a major turning point in the video) near the middle of the videos.

In [10], the authors use CAVVA (Computational Affective Video-in-Video Advertising) to show a subjective user-study according to theories from marketing and consumer psychology and our results of prospect ad insertion points are in sync with the study. We also compared our results with the research done in the field of the Effectiveness of Video Ads [6] and our prospect insertion points in mid roll ads justify the result in that study. Most of the work done in this field is survey based and theoretical. We have proposed a new model to automatically place ads in a video which would not disturb users' experience as well as increase the ad completion rates.

7   Conclusion and Future Work

This paper has proposed a framework using audio, video and text processing along with early action analysis using LSTM, and Artificial Neural Network to automatically suggest mid roll advertisement insertion points. Considering the amount of traffic that online videos attract, this framework will help in establishing the right balance between video marketing and users' experience while watching the video. Inappropriate placement of ads can deteriorate a users' experience as well as their sentiments towards the ad even though the quality of the ad is up to the mark. Hence the placement of an ad is equally or even more important than the contextual relevance of an ad. This framework will hence promote automatic mid roll ad placement rather than manually analyzing and placing them.

In the future, the authors want to apply BiLSTM for early action detection and analysis as it might provide more accurate results. The research will try to incorporate more features from the temporal domain to increase the applicability of the model. Due to computational limitations, the amount of data is less but in future, an attempt will also be made to increase the dataset further and to validate the model on a larger dataset of videos with more varying genres.

References

1. Abu-El-Haija, S., et al.: YouTube-8M: a large-scale video classification benchmark. CoRR abs/1609.08675 (2016). http://arxiv.org/abs/1609.08675
2. Akbarian, M.S.A., Saleh, F., Salzmann, M., Fernando, B., Petersson, L., Andersson, L.: Encouraging LSTMs to anticipate actions very early. CoRR abs/1703.07023 (2017). http://arxiv.org/abs/1703.07023
3. Giannakopoulos, T.: pyAudioAnalysis: an open-source Python library for audio signal analysis. PLoS ONE **10**, e0144610 (2015). https://doi.org/10.1371/journal.pone.0144610

4. Hutto, C., Gilbert, E.: VADER: a parsimonious rule-based model for sentiment analysis of social media text (2014). https://www.aaai.org/ocs/index.php/ICWSM/ICWSM14/paper/view/8109
5. Kim, S.: Effects of ad-video similarity, ad location, and user control option on ad avoidance and advertiser-intended outcomes of online video ads (2015). http://hdl.handle.net/11299/175210
6. Krishnan, S.S., Sitaraman, R.K.: Understanding the effectiveness of video ads: a measurement study. In: Proceedings of the 2013 Conference on Internet Measurement Conference, IMC 2013, pp. 149–162. ACM, New York (2013). https://doi.org/10.1145/2504730.2504748
7. Madhok, R., Mujumdar, S., Gupta, N., Mehta, S: Semantic understanding for contextual in-video advertising, April 2018
8. Mohammad, S.M., Bravo-Marquez, F.: WASSA-2017 shared task on emotion intensity. CoRR abs/1708.03700 (2017). http://arxiv.org/abs/1708.03700
9. Vondrick, C., Patterson, D., Ramanan, D.: Efficiently scaling up crowdsourced video annotation. Int. J. Comput. Vis. 1–21. https://doi.org/10.1007/s11263-012-0564-1
10. Yadati, K., Katti, H., Kankanhalli, M.S.: CAVVA: computational affective video-in-video advertising. IEEE Trans. Multimedia 16, 15–23 (2014)
11. Ye, K., Buettner, K., Kovashka, A.: Story understanding in video advertisements, September 2018
12. Zhang, H., Cao, X., Ho, J.K.L., Chow, T.W.S.: Object-level video advertising: an optimization framework. IEEE Trans. Ind. Inform. 13(2), 520–531 (2017). https://doi.org/10.1109/TII.2016.2605629

DCAR: Deep Collaborative Autoencoder for Recommendation with Implicit Feedback

Jiong Wang[1,2(✉)], Neng Gao[1], Jia Peng[1], and Jingjie Mo[1,2]

[1] State Key of Laboratory of Information Security, Institute of Information Engineering, Chinese Academy of Sciences, Beijing, China
{wangjiong,gaoneng,pengjia,mojingjie}@iie.ac.cn
[2] School of Cyber Security, University of Chinese Academy of Sciences, Beijing, China

Abstract. In recent years, deep neural networks have been widely applied to recommender systems. Although there are extensive explorations of deep neural networks on the collaborative filtering problem in item recommendation, most of the existing methods employ a similar loss function, i.e., the prediction loss of user-item interactions, and only change the form of the input, which may limit the model's performance. To address this problem, we present a novel framework, named **DCAR**, short for **D**eep **C**ollaborative **A**utoencoder for **R**ecommendation. Specifically, with the implicit feedback matrix as the input, we employ the autoencoder module to obtain the latent representations of users and items respectively. Then, to predict the matching score of corresponding user-item pairs, an interaction prediction module is designed based on the neural network architecture. The two parts are coupled together and employ alternating training to learn. We conduct extensive experiments on several real-world datasets and the results empirically verify the superior performance of DCAR on item recommendation. The code related to this paper is available at: https://github.com/strange-jiong/DCAR.

Keywords: User-item autoencoder · Collaborative filtering · Matching function learning · Recommender system

1 Introduction

In the past few decades, with the development of the Internet, information overload is one of the dilemmas we confront with [15]. For example, there are sundry items in the e-commerce platforms, it is hard for individual consumers to quickly find what they want. Recommender system (RS) is an effective means to solve this problem as it can help select the appropriate data to satisfy the users' needs. RS is nowadays ubiquitous in various platforms and has become a hot research area [22].

The traditional recommendation methods are often based on Collaborative Filtering (CF), the key idea of which is to learn the user preferences on the

© Springer Nature Switzerland AG 2019
I. V. Tetko et al. (Eds.): ICANN 2019, LNCS 11730, pp. 172–184, 2019.
https://doi.org/10.1007/978-3-030-30490-4_15

items from user-item interactions. A representative method is matrix factorization (MF). By mapping users and items into a common latent space, it is convenient to calculate the matching score with the inner product operation. However, in MF learning, the mapping between the original representation space and the latent space is assumed to be linear, which can not always be guaranteed. Although much research effort has been devoted to enhancing MF, such as combining it with topic models of item content [18], extending it with social trust information [5], alleviating data sparsity with pseudo-implicit feedback [8], it is well known that their performance can be hindered by the simple measure of interaction. It is necessary to find other more effective metrics to adequately capture the complex interactions between user-item pairs.

Recently, due to the powerful representation learning abilities, deep learning methods have been widely explored and have shown promising results in recommendation task [12]. Restricted Boltzmann Machines [13] was first proposed to model users' explicit ratings on items. The vanilla autoencoder and its variants have also been applied to learn users and items representations, i.e., embeddings, in item recommendation [19]. The key idea of these methods is to reconstruct the users' rating vectors through multiple hidden layers. The recent work DMF [20] adopts a DSSM network structure to learn the latent factors of users and items. However, it still resorts to the dot product of cosine similarity when predicting the matching score.

Another research line based on deep learning adopts neural networks to directly learn the matching score function between the user and item pairs. Neural collaborative filtering (NCF) [6] was proposed to model the user-item interactions with a multi-layer feedforward neural network. DeepCF [2] proposed a general framework to combine the strengths of representation learning and matching function learning. Although DeepCF has explored the possibility of fusing these two methods, its loss function is still similar to the previous method, lacking direct restrictions on learning users' and items' representations.

According to the above discussion, we can see that it is necessary for us to utilize the representation learning and matching function learning based on deep neural network. More importantly, using different network structures can make better use of the advantages of these two types of methods. We incorporate them under our proposed model DCAR. Specifically, we design a user-item encoder module, which maps users and items into a latent representation space respectively. Next, inspired by the NeuMF, we adopt an MLP based interaction prediction module to model the complex user-item interactions sufficiently. These two components are connected with the latent representation layer of users and items, which captures the users' global preferences and items' profile as well as the corresponding matching information.

In sum, our main contributions are outlined as follows:

– We propose a novel deep collaborative filtering model named DCAR to model complex interactions between users and items. To be more specific, we design a user-item autoencoder module, which can project the users and items into a low-dimensional space. Connected with an interaction prediction module, it is flexible to learn the complex matching function.

- We conduct extensive experiments on four real-world datasets to demonstrate the effectiveness of our proposed DCAR model.

2   Related Work

Traditional recommender system approaches mainly focused on explicit feedback. However, it's often difficult to collect accurate explicit feedback. The quantity of implicit data, such as click, view, or purchase far outweighs the quantity of explicit data. Thus, it is of great importance to design recommendation algorithms that use implicit feedback. Most recently, the exploration of deep neural network on recommendation has attracted the attention of researchers. There are two main ways to learn from implicit feedback.

The autoencoder methods are usually used to learn lower-dimensional feature representations at the bottleneck layer [22]. AutoRec [14] takes user partial vector or item partial vector as input and aims to minimize the reconstruct loss in the output layer. CFN [16] is an extension of AutoRec. It deploys the denoising techniques, which makes CFN more robust and incorporates the side information, such as user profiles and item descriptions to alleviate data sparsity. [3] proposes a hybrid model which jointly performs deep users and items latent factors learning from side information and collaborative filtering from the rating matrix. In contrast to the aforementioned methods, CDNE [19] is principally used for ranking prediction. It additionally plugs a user node in the input layer to better reconstruct the user's ratings.

Another related work is the matching function learning based on neural networks. NeuMF [6] is a recently proposed framework to model latent features of users and items with the neural network architecture. It generalizes matrix factorization and leverages a multi-layer perceptron to capture the non-linearities between user-item interaction. Based on NeuMF, NNCF [1] integrates localized information with user and item neighbors as input. CoupledCF [21] proposes a neural user-item coupling learning for collaborative filtering. The work that is most relevant to our work is [2], which presents a deep collaborative filtering framework (DeepCF) with implicit feedback. It utilizes both representation learning-based and matching function learning-based collaborative filtering methods.

3   Problem Statement

Given a recommendation problem, assume there are M users $\mathcal{U} = \{u_1, u_2, ..., u_M\}$, N items $\mathcal{V} = \{v_1, v_2, ..., v_N\}$. The rating matrix $\mathbf{R} \in \mathbb{R}^{M \times N}$ denotes the interactions between users and items and $\mathbf{R}_{ij}$ is the explicit rating of user i on item j (such as 5-star ratings).

In this work, we focus on the user's implicit feedback on items, which is commonly formulated as the problem to predict whether there will be interactions between users and items. The implicit feedback matrix $\mathbf{Y}$ is defined as follows:

$$y_{ij} = \begin{cases} 1 & \text{user } i \text{ has interaction on item } j; \\ 0 & \text{otherwise.} \end{cases} \tag{1}$$

Here a value of 1 for y_{ij} indicates that there is an interaction between user i and item j. Unlike explicit feedback, implicit feedback is discrete and binary. Just treating it as a binary category problem cannot help us to further rank and recommend items. Previous work [6] employs a probabilistic treatment for interaction matrix $\mathbf{Y}$. Formally, the model-based approaches can be abstract as follows:

$$\hat{y}_{ij} = F(u_i, v_j | \Theta), \tag{2}$$

where $\hat{y}_{ij}$ denotes the predicted probability of interaction between user-item pairs, F denotes the function that maps the user-item pairs to the interaction scores and Θ denotes the model parameters.

4 Our Proposed Model

In this section, we mainly introduce the architecture of DCAR. Figure 1 illustrates the architecture of DCAR, which consists of two main components. We will elaborate their implements used in this paper and show how to learn the final model.

4.1 User-Item Encoder Module

As mentioned in Sect. 3, we construct an interaction matrix $\mathbf{Y}$ from original rating matrix $\mathbf{R}$. With the matrix $\mathbf{Y}$ as input, we employ the autoencoder to project users and items into a latent space. In Fig. 1, the green dashed rectangles on both sides illustrate the structure of user-item encoder module and we formulate it as follows:

$$\begin{aligned} \mathbf{h}_1 &= f(\mathbf{W}_1^T \mathbf{y}_{i*} + \mathbf{b}_1) \\ \mathbf{h}_i &= f(\mathbf{W}_i^T \mathbf{h}_{i-1} + \mathbf{b}_i), i = 2, 3, ..., K, \end{aligned} \tag{3}$$

where K denotes the number of layers for the user encoder and decoder. $f(.)$ represents the possible activation functions such as *sigmoid*, *ReLU* or *tanh*. In this paper, we use *ReLU* [4], i.e., $f(x) = max(0, x)$ as the activation function. $\mathbf{W}_i$ and $\mathbf{b}_i$ denote the weight matrix and bias vector in the ith layer respectively. To obtain representations of items, we utilize a similar network structure:

$$\begin{aligned} \mathbf{h}_1 &= g(\mathbf{W}_1^T \mathbf{y}_{*j} + \mathbf{b}_1) \\ \mathbf{h}_i &= g(\mathbf{W}_i^T \mathbf{h}_{i-1} + \mathbf{b}_i), i = 2, 3, ..., L, \end{aligned} \tag{4}$$

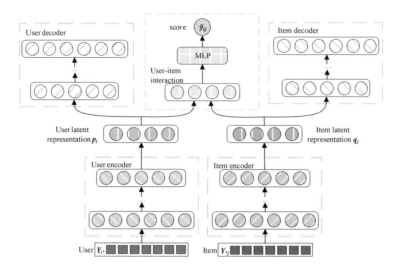

Fig. 1. The architecture of our proposed model DCAR. The green dashed rectangles on both sides denote the user-item encoder component and the yellow dashed rectangle is the interaction prediction module. These two components are connected with the user-item encoder layer. (Color figure online)

where L denotes the number of layers for item encoder part. $g(.)$ is the activation function. The goal of the standard autoencoder is to minimize the distance between original inputs and the reconstructed outputs. The reconstruction loss function is defined as follows:

$$
\begin{aligned}
\mathcal{L}_{ae} &= \mathcal{L}_{user\_ae} + \mathcal{L}_{item\_ae} \\
&= \sum_{i=1}^{M} \|\hat{\mathbf{u}}_i - \mathbf{u}_i\|_2^2 + \sum_{i=1}^{N} \|\hat{\mathbf{v}}_i - \mathbf{v}_i\|_2^2,
\end{aligned}
\tag{5}
$$

where $\hat{\mathbf{u}}_i$ and $\hat{\mathbf{v}}_i$ is the reconstruction of decoder. We adopt l_2-norm to measure the reconstruction distance.

However, due to the sparsity of the input vector, the number of zero elements in $\mathbf{y}_{i*}$ is much larger than that of non-zero elements. That means the autoencoder will tend to reconstruct the zero elements rather than non-zero ones, which is incompatible with our purpose [17]. Therefore, we set different weights to different elements, and re-defined the loss function in Eq. (5) as follows:

$$
\mathcal{L}_{ae} = \sum_{i=1}^{M} \|(\hat{\mathbf{u}}_i - \mathbf{u}_i) \odot \mathbf{x}_i\|_2^2 + \sum_{i=1}^{N} \|(\hat{\mathbf{v}}_i - \mathbf{v}_i) \odot \mathbf{z}_i\|_2^2,
\tag{6}
$$

where $\mathbf{x}_i$ is a weight matrix and $\odot$ means the Hadamard product. For $\mathbf{x}_i = \{x_i^t\}_{t=1}^{|\mathcal{V}|}$, $x_i^t = 1$ when $u_i^t = 0$ and $x_i^t = \beta > 1$ otherwise. Similar settings for $\mathbf{z}_i$.

In our user-item encoder module, the original input $\mathbf{Y}_{i*}$ and $\mathbf{Y}_{*j}$ represent a user's ratings across all items and an item's scores across all users. Utilizing autoencoder to learn latent representations for users and items with these rating vectors as input can to some extent preserve a user's global preference and an item's profile. It is useful for their final low-dimensional representations.

4.2 Interaction Prediction Module

Similar to [2], we construct a deep interaction prediction module to predict the probability of interaction between user-item pairs. To deeply model the interactions among users and items, we first construct interaction layer $\mathbf{r}$ to fuse the user and item latent representation. The interaction layer $\mathbf{r}$ can be defined as follows:

$$\mathbf{r} = \phi(\mathbf{p}_i, \mathbf{q}_j) = \begin{bmatrix} \mathbf{p}_i \odot \mathbf{q}_j \\ \mathbf{p}_i \\ \mathbf{q}_j \end{bmatrix}, \tag{7}$$

where $\mathbf{p}_i$ and $\mathbf{q}_j$ denote the user and item latent representation. $\odot$ represents the element-wise product operation.

In previous work, there exist two general ways of aggregating user and item embeddings: *(a)* using a simple concatenation operation [6]; *(b)* conducting the element-wise product [21]. Concatenation operation can directly retain the information in the original embeddings and element-wise product focuses on catching low-rank relations between corresponding user-item pairs. Therefore the interaction layer $\mathbf{r}$ employs these two aggregating methods simultaneously to combine the advantages of both. Then we adopt MLP to learn the matching score of the user-item pair. We formulate it as:

$$\begin{aligned} \mathbf{a}_0 &= \mathbf{r} \\ \mathbf{a}_1 &= \delta_1(\mathbf{W}_1^T \mathbf{a}_0 + \mathbf{b}_1) \\ &\cdots \\ \mathbf{a}_X &= \delta_X(\mathbf{W}_X^T \mathbf{a}_{X-1} + \mathbf{b}_{X-1}) \\ \hat{y}_{ij} &= \sigma(\mathbf{W}_{out}^T \mathbf{a}_X), \end{aligned} \tag{8}$$

where $\mathbf{r}$ is the interaction layer of corresponding user-item pair, $\mathbf{W}_{out}$ and $\sigma(.)$ denote the weight matrix and the *sigmoid* function respectively. The meanings of other notions are the same as the user-item encoder module.

Since the prediction score $\hat{y}_{uv}$ should reflect the user's preference for the item, it is natural to constrain the output $\hat{y}_{ij}$ in the range of $[0, 1]$. To endow such a probabilistic, NeuMF [6] employs a probabilistic function for the output layer. We follow it to use the binary cross-entropy loss, which is defined as:

$$\mathcal{L}_{prec} = - \sum_{(i,j)\in\mathcal{Y}^+\cup\mathcal{Y}^-} y_{ij} \log(\hat{y}_{ij}) + (1 - y_{ij}) \log(1 - \hat{y}_{ij}), \tag{9}$$

where the $\mathcal{Y}^+$ denotes all the observed interactions in $\mathbf{Y}$ and $\mathcal{Y}^-$ denotes the unobserved interactions.

4.3 Overall Architecture

To preserve the reconstruction ability of user and item representations, as well as the users' preference on items, we combine the objective in Eqs. (5) and (9), and propose a unified CF model DCAR. For each user-item pair (i, j) in $\mathcal{Y}^+ \bigcup \mathcal{Y}^-$, DCAR jointly optimizes the following objective function:

$$\mathcal{L} = \mathcal{L}_{prec} + \alpha[\mathcal{L}_{user\_ae} + \mathcal{L}_{item\_ae}] + \eta \mathcal{L}_{reg}. \tag{10}$$

Here, hyper-parameter α is used to balance the loss of autoencoder module and prediction module. Besides, to prevent overfitting, we employ $L2$-norm regularizer $\mathcal{L}_{reg}$ over all the model parameters Θ. To pick the best values of α and η, the grid search method is used.

4.4 Learning the Model

In order to optimize the model, we adopt Adam algorithm [10] to minimize the objective in Eq. (10). The batch size is fixed to 512 and the learning rate is 0.001. For parameter initialization, the weight matrixes are randomly initialized with a Gaussian distribution (the mean and standard deviation are 0 and 0.01 respectively). All biases in our model are initialized with zero. We sample the negative instances $\mathcal{Y}_{sampled}^-$ uniformly form unobserved interactions. We iteratively optimize these two coupled modules until the model converges. The detailed training method is described in Algorithm 1.

Algorithm 1. DCAR Training Algorithm

Input: original rating matrix: $\mathbf{Y}$, negative sampling ratio: neg, training iterations:
$\quad\quad\quad$ $Iters$, size of batch: $batch\_size$, learning ratio: ε
Output: user latent representation matrix $\mathbf{U}$,
$\quad\quad\quad\quad$ item latent representation matrix $\mathbf{V}$
1: Construct $\mathcal{Y}^+ \leftarrow$ all none zero interactions in $\mathbf{Y}$
2: Construct $\mathcal{Y}^- \leftarrow$ all zero interactions in $\mathbf{Y}$
3: Construct $\mathcal{Y}_{sampled}^- \leftarrow$ sample $neg * |\mathcal{Y}^+|$ interactions from $\mathcal{Y}^-$
4: Construct $\mathcal{T} \leftarrow \mathcal{Y}^+ \bigcup \mathcal{Y}_{sampled}^-$
5: Random initialization for all parameters set Θ
6: **while** not converged **do**
7: $\quad$ Sample a mini-batch of user-item pairs
8: $\quad$ Compute the gradient of $\nabla \mathcal{L}_{item\_ae}, \nabla \mathcal{L}_{user\_ae}$ based on Eq. (5)
9: $\quad$ Update the parameters of user-item autoencoder module
10: $\quad$ Compute the gradient of $\nabla \mathcal{L}_{prec}$ based on Eq. (9)
11: $\quad$ Update the parameters of match function learning module
12: Obtain user item latent representation $\mathbf{U}, \mathbf{V}$ based on Eq. (3) and Eq. (4)

Table 1. Statistics of the datasets.

Datasets	#Users	#Items	#Ratings	Rating sparsity
ML100k	944	1683	100000	0.9370
AMusic	1733	12489	46087	0.9978
AGrocery	2585	22941	84247	0.9985
AToys	3137	33953	84642	0.9992

5 Experiment and Evaluation

In this section, we conduct experiments to verify the effectiveness of our proposed model DCAR. We study the performance of the model under different values of top-K. Hypeparameter sensitivity analysis is discussed in the last part.

5.1 Experimental Settings

Datasets. We evaluate our models on several public available datasets: Movie-Lens dataset[1], Amazon dataset[2]. They are accessible on the internet website. Since MovieLens dataset was already processed, we don't do anything with it. For Amazon music and toys dataset, We filter it according to such rules [6,19]: *(a)* users with at least 20 interactions. *(b)* items with at least 5 interactions. The statistics of the datasets is summarized in Table 1.

Baselines. We compare the proposed model DCAR with the following methods.

- **ItemPop.** It is a non-personalized method and often used as the baseline to benchmark the recommendation performance. It simply rankes the items by their popularity judged by the number of interactions.
- **ItemKNN.** It is a standard item-based collaborative filtering method [11]. We utilized the same setting of [9] to adapt it for implicit data.
- **NeuMF.** Neural collaborative filtering (NCF) is a state-of-the-art neural method for recommendation. It concatenates latent factors learned from a generalized matrix factorization model and a multi-layered perceptron model and then utilizes the loss of cross entropy to train [6].
- **DMF.** Deep matrix factorization model (DMF) is another state-of-the-art method. It uses the matrix of explicit ratings and implicit feedback as the input. We followed the setting of [20] to adapt it for item recommendation.

Evaluation Metrics. To evaluate the performance of item recommendation, we use the widely-used leave-one-out evaluation [7]. More specifically, we hold out the latest interaction as the test item and remaining dataset with interactions as the training data. It is time-consuming to rank all items for every user, we

---

[1] https://grouplens.org/datasets/movielens/.
[2] http://jmcauley.ucsd.edu/data/amazon/.

randomly sample 99 items that are not interacted by the users as the negative items. We let the model get the ranking of these 100 items for each user and then evaluate the performance. We take the top-K hit ratio ($HR@K$) and Normalized Discounted Cumulative Gain ($NDCG$) [6] to evaluate the model performance.

5.2   Results and Analysis

Top-K Item Recommendation Results. We test the top-K (K= 1 to 10) item recommendations on AMusic dataset in Fig. 2. For simplicity, we only analyze the comparison with two other neural network methods. For AMusic dataset, DCAR outperforms other methods by a large margin, e.g., up to 5% improvement over NeuMF ($HR@8$) and averaged more than 10% over DMF ($NDCG@K$). This may be caused by the higher sparsity of AMusic dataset. Since our model employs a user-item autoencoder to represent users and items, it is helpful to deal with the sparsity problem.

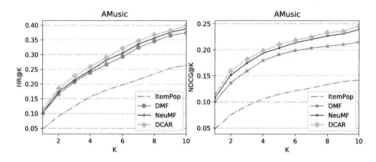

Fig. 2. Evaluation of top-K item recommendation where K ranges from 1 to 10 on AMusic dataset.

Comparison with Baselines. The performance of the DCAR model against all the baselines is reported in $HR@10$ and $NDCG@10$ in Table 2. The best scores are emphasized with bold fonts. According to the table, we summarize the following observations and analyses:

- DCAR achieves the best performance in general and obtains high improvements over the state-of-the-art methods in both metrics of HR and $NDCG$. Compared to the recent method NeuMF, DCAR obtain 2.4–2.9% and 2.3–6.2% relative improvements in HR and $NDCG$ metrics respectively (except ML100k dataset). More importantly, our model makes such improvement even on highly sparse data. This further justifies the effectiveness of DCAR model that combines the encoder and prediction components.
- Although DMF takes the user-item rating matrix as input, our proposed model DCAR consistently outperforms it. As its loss function is only related to the relationship between users and items which may lead to a lack of user's global preference and item's profile. This indicates that learning user and item representation with the autoencoder can effectively improve the performance.

Table 2. Comparisons of different methods in terms of *NDCG@10* and *HR@10*.

Datasets	Measures	Existing approaches				Our model	Improvement[a]
		Itempop	ItemKNN	DMF	NeuMF	DCAR	
ML100k	*HR*	0.4063	0.6010	0.6542	**0.6703**	0.6656	–
	NDCG	0.2308	0.3345	0.3712	**0.3950**	0.3864	–
AMusic	*HR*	0.2480	0.3510	0.3741	0.3891	**0.4003**	2.9%
	NDCG	0.1304	0.1989	0.2150	0.2391	**0.2460**	2.9%
AGrocery	*HR*	0.3512	0.3864	0.4497	0.4603	**0.4715**	2.4%
	NDCG	0.1967	0.2213	0.2850	0.2891	**0.2957**	2.3%
AToys	*HR*	0.2840	0.3143	0.3520	0.3643	**0.3745**	2.7%
	NDCG	0.1518	0.1756	0.2015	0.2145	**0.2280**	6.2%

[a]Improvement of DCAR vs. NeuMF.

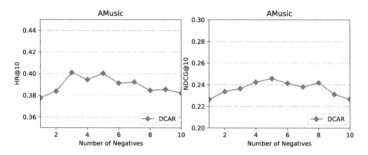

Fig. 3. The effect of different negative sampling ratios on performance on the AMusic dataset.

5.3 Sensitivity Anlaysis of Hyperparameters

Negative Sampling Ratio. To analyze the effect of negative sampling ratio, we apply different negative sampling ratios, i.e., the number of negative instances on the AMusic dataset. From the results shown in Fig. 3, we can find that few negative instances lead to poor results and more negative instances seem helpful to improve the performance. The best *HR@10* and *NDCG@10* are obtained when the negative sampling ratio is around 3 to 7 which is consistent with the results of previous work [6].

Dimensions of Latent Representations. In our proposed model, the user-item encoder component maps the users and items to a low-dimensional embedding space. The factors in each encoder layer is possibly another sensitive parameter. For simplicity, we just compare the performance with different number of factors on the final latent space. As shown in Table 3, our proposed model DCAR generates the best performance with 128 predictive factors on most of the datasets. It is clear that more predictive factors usually lead to better performance since it endows the model with larger ability of representation.

Table 3. Performance of DCAR with different number of predictive factors.

Datasets	Measures	Dimensions of predictive vector			
		16	32	64	128
ML100k	*HR*	0.6443	0.6578	0.6623	0.6670
	NDCG	0.3685	0.3812	0.3845	0.3810
AMusic	*HR*	0.3918	0.4003	0.3924	0.4059
	NDCG	0.2416	0.2460	0.2430	0.2522
AGrocery	*HR*	0.4601	0.4598	0.4702	0.4625
	NDCG	0.2878	0.2867	0.2943	0.2937
AToys	*HR*	0.3678	0.3656	0.3721	0.3745
	NDCG	0.2143	0.2139	0.2218	0.2280

6   Conclusion and Future Work

In this paper, we propose a novel collaborative filtering model DCAR to learn the complex interactions between users and items. The two main factors of the proposed model are the (i) exploit of maintaining user's global preference and item's profile; (ii) capture of the complicated non-linear correlations of user-item pairs. More specifically, through a user-item encoder component, users and items are projected into a low-dimensional space. Then, we design an interaction prediction module to learn the matching score between user-item pairs. These two parts are connected with the user and item latent representation layer. The experiments on several benchmark datasets demonstrate the effectiveness of our proposed model.

In the future work, we will consider incorporating more auxiliary information into our proposed model, such as the attribute information for users and items, sequence information for purchase behaviors, etc. Besides, using pairwise loss is also a feasible method in the field of top-N recommendation task.

Acknowledgments. This work is supported by National Key Research and Development Program of China, National Natural Science Foundation of China (No. U163620068).

References

1. Bai, T., Wen, J.R., Zhang, J., Zhao, W.X.: A neural collaborative filtering model with interaction-based neighborhood. In: Proceedings of the 2017 ACM on Conference on Information and Knowledge Management, pp. 1979–1982. ACM (2017). https://doi.org/10.1145/3132847.3133083
2. Deng, Z.H., Huang, L., Wang, C.D., Lai, J.H., Yu, P.S.: DeepCF: a unified framework of representation learning and matching function learning in recommender system. arXiv preprint arXiv:1901.04704 (2019)
3. Dong, X., Yu, L., Wu, Z., Sun, Y., Yuan, L., Zhang, F.: A hybrid collaborative filtering model with deep structure for recommender systems. In: Thirty-First AAAI Conference on Artificial Intelligence (2017)

4. Glorot, X., Bordes, A., Bengio, Y.: Deep sparse rectifier neural networks. In: Proceedings of the Fourteenth International Conference on Artificial Intelligence and Statistics, pp. 315–323 (2011)
5. Guo, G., Zhang, J., Yorke-Smith, N.: TrustSVD: collaborative filtering with both the explicit and implicit influence of user trust and of item ratings. In: Twenty-Ninth AAAI Conference on Artificial Intelligence (2015)
6. He, X., Liao, L., Zhang, H., Nie, L., Hu, X., Chua, T.S.: Neural collaborative filtering. In: Proceedings of the 26th International Conference on World Wide Web, pp. 173–182. International World Wide Web Conferences Steering Committee (2017). https://doi.org/10.1145/3038912.3052569
7. He, X., Zhang, H., Kan, M.Y., Chua, T.S.: Fast matrix factorization for online recommendation with implicit feedback. In: Proceedings of the 39th International ACM SIGIR conference on Research and Development in Information Retrieval, pp. 549–558. ACM (2016). https://doi.org/10.1145/2911451.2911489
8. He, Y., Chen, H., Zhu, Z., Caverlee, J.: Pseudo-implicit feedback for alleviating data sparsity in top-k recommendation. In: 2018 IEEE International Conference on Data Mining (ICDM), pp. 1025–1030. IEEE (2018). https://doi.org/10.1109/icdm.2018.00129
9. Hu, Y., Koren, Y., Volinsky, C.: Collaborative filtering for implicit feedback datasets. In: 2008 Eighth IEEE International Conference on Data Mining, pp. 263–272. IEEE (2008). https://doi.org/10.1109/ICDM.2008.22
10. Kingma, D.P., Ba, J.: Adam: a method for stochastic optimization. arXiv preprint arXiv:1412.6980 (2014)
11. Linden, G., Smith, B., York, J.: Amazon.com recommendations: item-to-item collaborative filtering. IEEE Internet Comput. (1), 76–80 (2003). https://doi.org/10.1109/MIC.2003.1167344
12. Van den Oord, A., Dieleman, S., Schrauwen, B.: Deep content-based music recommendation. In: Advances in Neural Information Processing Systems, pp. 2643–2651 (2013)
13. Salakhutdinov, R., Mnih, A., Hinton, G.: Restricted Boltzmann machines for collaborative filtering. In: Proceedings of the 24th International Conference on Machine Learning, pp. 791–798. ACM (2007). https://doi.org/10.1145/1273496.1273596
14. Sedhain, S., Menon, A.K., Sanner, S., Xie, L.: AutoRec: autoencoders meet collaborative filtering. In: Proceedings of the 24th International Conference on World Wide Web, pp. 111–112. ACM (2015). https://doi.org/10.1145/2740908.2742726
15. Srivastava, R., Palshikar, G.K., Chaurasia, S., Dixit, A.: What's next? A recommendation system for industrial training. Data Sci. Eng. 3(3), 232–247 (2018). https://doi.org/10.1109/icdmw.2017.35
16. Strub, F., Gaudel, R., Mary, J.: Hybrid recommender system based on autoencoders. In: Proceedings of the 1st Workshop on Deep Learning for Recommender Systems, pp. 11–16. ACM (2016). https://doi.org/10.1145/2988450.2988456
17. Tu, C., Zhang, Z., Liu, Z., Sun, M.: TransNet: translation-based network representation learning for social relation extraction. In: IJCAI, pp. 2864–2870 (2017). https://doi.org/10.24963/ijcai.2017/399
18. Wang, H., Wang, N., Yeung, D.Y.: Collaborative deep learning for recommender systems. In: Proceedings of the 21th ACM SIGKDD International Conference on Knowledge Discovery and Data Mining, pp. 1235–1244. ACM (2015). https://doi.org/10.1145/2783258.2783273

19. Wu, Y., DuBois, C., Zheng, A.X., Ester, M.: Collaborative denoising auto-encoders for top-N recommender systems. In: Proceedings of the Ninth ACM International Conference on Web Search and Data Mining, pp. 153–162. ACM (2016). https://doi.org/10.1145/2835776.2835837

20. Xue, H.J., Dai, X., Zhang, J., Huang, S., Chen, J.: Deep matrix factorization models for recommender systems. In: IJCAI, pp. 3203–3209 (2017). https://doi.org/10.24963/ijcai.2017/447

21. Zhang, Q., Cao, L., Zhu, C., Li, Z., Sun, J.: CoupledCF: learning explicit and implicit user-item couplings in recommendation for deep collaborative filtering. In: IJCAI, pp. 3662–3668 (2018). https://doi.org/10.24963/ijcai.2018/509

22. Zhang, S., Yao, L., Sun, A.: Deep learning based recommender system: a survey and new perspectives. arXiv preprint arXiv:1707.07435 (2017). https://doi.org/10.1145/3285029

Jointly Learning to Detect Emotions and Predict Facebook Reactions

Lisa Graziani[1]([⊠]) [ID], Stefano Melacci[2] [ID], and Marco Gori[2] [ID]

[1] DINFO, University of Florence, Florence, Italy
lisa.graziani@unifi.it
[2] DIISM, University of Siena, Siena, Italy
{mela,marco}@diism.unisi.it

Abstract. The growing ubiquity of Social Media data offers an attractive perspective for improving the quality of machine learning-based models in several fields, ranging from Computer Vision to Natural Language Processing. In this paper we focus on Facebook posts paired with "reactions" of multiple users, and we investigate their relationships with classes of emotions that are typically considered in the task of emotion detection. We are inspired by the idea of introducing a connection between reactions and emotions by means of First-Order Logic formulas, and we propose an end-to-end neural model that is able to jointly learn to detect emotions and predict Facebook reactions in a multi-task environment, where the logic formulas are converted into polynomial constraints. Our model is trained using a large collection of unsupervised texts together with data labeled with emotion classes and Facebook posts that include reactions. An extended experimental analysis that leverages a large collection of Facebook posts shows that the tasks of emotion classification and reaction prediction can both benefit from their interaction.

Keywords: Emotion detection from text · Facebook reactions ·
Learning from Constraints

1 Introduction

Social media have strongly changed the way we interact with each other and how we share contents. Many people exploit social networks to publish details of their daily lives, their opinions and their thoughts. These data represent a precious source of information for building large datasets of annotated multimedia contents, or for mining users' behaviours and other user-related information.

A valuable feature for every modern system that interacts with humans is understanding the emotional state of users. Conversational systems can adapt their language in function of the perceived user emotions, digital marketing platforms can customize recommendations, social media marketing strategies can be changed in function of the estimated emotions triggered when posting contents.

© Springer Nature Switzerland AG 2019
I. V. Tetko et al. (Eds.): ICANN 2019, LNCS 11730, pp. 185–197, 2019.
https://doi.org/10.1007/978-3-030-30490-4_16

If we restrict our attention to the case of text, emotion detection is a widely studied and still challenging task [1,8,10,12,19]. In the case of categorical emotion detection, sentences are usually classified into the six universal emotions defined by Ekman [4], namely *anger, disgust, fear, happiness, sadness*, and *surprise*.

This paper is rooted on the connections between the task of emotion detection and social media data. There is an intrinsic link between certain categories of tags attached to user posts and the emotional state of those users that participate in the tagging process. We focus on the case of Facebook, where users can express their feeling on a post through the so called "reactions", that are LOVE, HAHA, WOW, SAD, ANGRY, together with the widely known LIKE. While LIKE represents a universal and generic expression of a positive feedback, the other reactions are more fine-grained, and somewhat related to the aforementioned categories of emotions. However, this relationship is weak and distant, since some reactions can be loosely associated to emotional categories, sometimes with large ambiguity. For example, WOW expresses "surprise" but it can be also used to describe contents where the astonishment is accompanied by "fear". Moreover, Facebook reactions are the outcome of a tagging process where users might follow superficial and strongly subjective criteria to react.

Recently, Facebook reactions have been studied in the context of emotion detection. Some authors trained emotion classification models using Facebook reactions [13,15], while others tried to learn to predict Facebook reactions in a given domain, bootstrapping the system with the outcome of emotion mining [11]. Reactions are usually manually mapped to (a subset of) the aforementioned universal emotions, providing a form of distant supervision. Differently, the task of emotion detection from text has been the subject of a large number of studies, mostly distinguished into lexicon-based and machine learning-based approaches (or hybrid solutions). Lexicon-based approaches employ linguistic models or prior knowledge for the classification task, and they essentially give a score to a sentence using a predefined sentiment lexicon, without using labeled data [10,19]. In [1] the authors propose an unsupervised context-based emotion detection method that does not rely on any affect dictionaries or annotated training data. A constraint optimization framework based on lexicon is presented in [20]. Machine learning-based methods usually exploit supervised learning algorithms trained on annotated corpora. The approach of [14] focusses on Twitter data, while [3] uses a heterogeneous emotion-annotated dataset to recognize the six basic emotions. Finally, [8] focusses on an ensemble model, strongly exploiting pre-trained, dense word-embedding representations.

In this paper we propose a neural network-based model to jointly learn the task of emotion detection and the task of predicting Facebook reactions. Our model consists of a bidirectional Long Short-Term Memory (LSTM) recurrent neural network [9,17] to encode the input sentence, and two predictors associated with the considered tasks. Predictors are not independent, but are linked by prior knowledge on the relationships between the tasks. Such knowledge is represented by First-Order Logic (FOL) formulas, which allow us to naturally express how reactions are connected to emotion classes and vice-versa. Following the framework of Learning from Constraints [5], FOL formulas are converted into polynomial constraints and softly enforced into the learning problem, thus tolerating some violations. The system automatically learns "how" to fulfil the FOL formulas in function of the way the data are distributed. Our model is trained using a heterogeneous dataset composed of data labeled with emotion classes, Facebook posts that include user reactions, and a large collection of unsupervised posts. We do not use any external lexical resources, and an extended experimental analysis shows that the tasks of emotion classification and reaction prediction can both benefit from their interaction. The resulting emotion detector is competitive with some models that exploit lexical resources or ad-hoc features, and we also investigate the role of pre-trained word embeddings.

This paper is organized as follows. Section 2 describes the proposed model, while Sect. 3 focusses on the logic constraints. Experimental results are provided in Sect. 4 and, finally, Sect. 5 concludes the paper with our comments.

2   Model and Data Organization

We consider a multi-task setting where two predictors $p_r(x)$ and $p_e(x)$ operate on the same data x, that is a short input text. Such predictors are associated to the task of reaction classification (p_r) and emotion classification (p_e), respectively. In the context of this paper, both the tasks consist in predicting the most dominant reaction/emotion when processing a text x.[1] In detail, $p_r(x) \in [0,1]^R$ outputs a probability distribution over R reactions, and, analogously, $p_e(x) \in [0,1]^E$ outputs a probability distribution over E classes of emotions. We select the emotion-reaction pair associated to the largest probabilities.

Following the classical pipeline of several machine learning-based approaches in Natural Language Processing, the input text x is tokenized into words $x_0, \ldots, x_t$ belonging to a fixed-size vocabulary. Each word is embedded into a learnable latent dense representation, also known as "word embedding", and a Long Short-Term Memory (LSTM) recurrent neural network [9] processes the sequence of word embeddings in both directions (Bidirectional Recurrent Neural Network (BRNN) [17]). The forward and backward states are then concatenated, producing an embedded latent representation of x, that is provided as input to two Multi Layer Perceptrons (MLPs) with softmax activation functions in the output layers, thus implementing p_r and p_e, respectively. The choice of sharing the same latent representation of x with both predictors is due to the fact that the two prediction tasks are certainly correlated. Finally, during the training stage, the MLPs are connected by constraints that are devised from FOL rules, and that will be described in Sect. 3. The whole architecture is reported in Fig. 1.

Our model is trained using a heterogeneous collection of text $\mathcal{T}$ of partially labeled and unlabeled data, composed by the union of three disjoint sets, $\mathcal{T}_r$, $\mathcal{T}_e$, $\mathcal{T}_u$, that, in turn, consist of pairs (x, y), where y is either a reaction label,

---

[1] Some approaches consider these tasks as multi-label prediction problems [10,19], while other authors focus on the most dominant response [3], as we do in this paper. What we propose can be adapted to the case of multi-label prediction.

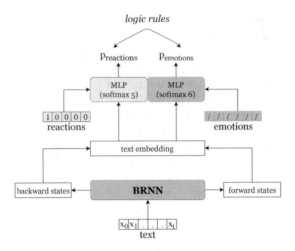

Fig. 1. The proposed model. Predictors p_r and p_e are reported with their expanded names: $p_{reactions}$ and $p_{emotions}$. When training the network, we feed it with text either labeled with emotions or reactions, and logic constraints bridge the two predictors.

an emotion label, or a dummy placeholder (i.e., unlabeled data), respectively. (*i*) The set $\mathcal{T}_r$ is a collection of Facebook posts, each of them labeled with one out of $R = 5$ reaction classes (listed in Sect. 1), encoded with a one-hot vector y_r of size R. We did not consider the class LIKE, since it is too generic, and we selected the most frequent reaction class in each post. Moreover, $\mathcal{T}_r$ is composed only by those posts with at least τ reaction hits in total ($\tau = 20$ in our experience), and where the most frequent reaction has a number of hits that is greater than the number of hits of all the other reactions scaled by a factor γ (we set $\gamma = 0.4$). (*ii*) The set $\mathcal{T}_e$ is a collection of sentences, each of them labeled with one of the $E = 6$ universal emotions (see Sect. 1), encoded with a one-hot vector y_e of size E.[2] We exploited existing databases to build $\mathcal{T}_e$ (see Sect. 4), keeping only the most dominant emotion in the case of multi-labeled data. (*iii*) Finally, the set $\mathcal{T}_u$ is a collection of unlabeled text, that in our experience, consists of a large collection of Facebook posts without reactions. Each sample is paired with a dummy label vector y_{none}. This set is exploited to enforce the logic constraints (Sect. 3) in space regions that are not covered by the labeled portion(s) of the training set. This allows the model to learn predictors that better generalize the information associated to the logic formulas. A sketch that summarizes the types of training data used in this paper is reported in Fig. 2.

---

[2] In our experience we did not consider the *neutral* class, that, however, could be easily introduced in the proposed model.

3   Multi-task Learning with Constraints

Before introducing the approach that we propose with this paper, we mention that the simplest way to bridge the tasks of emotion and reaction classification is to generate artificial labels, i.e., to define a fixed mapping between emotions and reactions and augment the training data with these new labels (see, for example [13], Table 1). Considering the emotion/reaction classes of Sect. 2, a reasonable mapping from reactions to emotions, represented with the notation "ground truth" → "new label", is the following one: LOVE → *happiness*, WOW → *surprise*, HAHA → *happiness*, SAD → *sadness*, ANGRY → *anger*. Similarly, we can map emotions to reactions: *anger* → ANGRY, *disgust* → ANGRY, *fear* → WOW, *happiness* → HAHA, *sadness* → SAD, *surprise* → WOW. However, this manual conversion is rigid and sometimes ambiguous. For example, no reactions are converted into labels of classes *fear* and *disgust*, and no emotions are mapped into the reaction LOVE.

We propose to describe the mappings between emotion and reaction classes using FOL formulas and to develop a multi-task system that learns from them, following the framework of Learning from Constraints [5–7]. Each class is associated to a predicate, whose truth degree is computed using a function that, for simplicity, we indicate with the name of the class itself. These predicates can be seen as the components of the vectorial functions $p_r(x)$ and $p_e(x)$, i.e., $p_r(x) = [\text{HAHA}(x), \text{SAD}(x), \text{ANGRY}(x), \text{LOVE}(x), \text{WOW}(x)]$, and $p_e(x) = [anger(x), disgust(x), fear(x), happiness(x), sadness(x), surprise(x)]$. We define the following rules,

$$\forall x \, \text{HAHA}(x) \Rightarrow happiness(x) \tag{1}$$
$$\forall x \, \text{SAD}(x) \Rightarrow sadness(x) \tag{2}$$
$$\forall x \, \text{ANGRY}(x) \Rightarrow anger(x) \vee disgust(x) \tag{3}$$
$$\forall x \, \text{LOVE}(x) \Rightarrow happiness(x) \tag{4}$$
$$\forall x \, \text{WOW}(x) \Rightarrow surprise(x) \vee fear(x) \tag{5}$$
$$\forall x \, anger(x) \Rightarrow \text{ANGRY}(x) \tag{6}$$
$$\forall x \, disgust(x) \Rightarrow \text{ANGRY}(x) \tag{7}$$
$$\forall x \, fear(x) \Rightarrow \text{WOW}(x) \tag{8}$$
$$\forall x \, happiness(x) \Rightarrow \text{HAHA}(x) \vee \text{LOVE}(x) \tag{9}$$
$$\forall x \, sadness(x) \Rightarrow \text{SAD}(x) \tag{10}$$
$$\forall x \, surprise(x) \Rightarrow \text{WOW}(x) \; . \tag{11}$$

Notice that these rules do not include negations, that is due to the probabilistic relationship (softmax) that we introduced in the output of the predictors (if a function goes toward 1, all the others will automatically go toward 0).[3]

We defined our FOL formulas after having analyzed the content of various Facebook posts and the associated reactions. Implications 3–5–9 include an ambiguous mapping, modeled with the ∨ operator (disjunction). The second predicate that we reported in each disjunction corresponds to a less trivial mapping that, at a first glance, might not always seem obvious. However, in our

---

[3] We did not write the rules in a more compact form using the double implication ⇔, since we will differently weigh the impact of some of them, as it will be clear shortly.

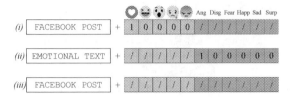

Fig. 2. Sample representatives of the types of data included in our heterogeneous training set. (*i*) A facebook post paired with the reaction label LOVE (encoded with the blue 1-hot vector) and no emotion labels. (*ii*) Text paired with the emotion class *anger* (orange 1-hot vector) and no reaction labels. (*iii*) An unlabeled Facebook post. (Color figure online)

experience, we found these cases to be more frequent than expected. We report an example for each of them: WOW could be *fear* instead of *surprise* (Eq. 5),

> *Snake on a plane: Frightening moment on an Aeromexico flight when a large snake fell from overhead mid-flight. The flight made a quick landing and animal control took the stowaway into custody.*

Emotion *happiness* could be converted into LOVE instead of HAHA (Eq. 9),

> *When I got a wedding ring of diamond from the boy I loved.*

The reaction ANGRY could be eventually mapped into *disgust* (Eq. 3),

> *The San Antonio police chief said that former officer Matthew Luckhurst committed a vile and disgusting act that violates our guiding principles.*

Our rules are converted into real-valued polynomials by means of T-Norms [5,6], that are functions modeling the logical AND whose output is in $[0, 1]$. We used the Product T-Norm, where the logical AND is simply the product of the involved arguments. In turn, this choice transforms $a \Rightarrow b$ into the polynomial $1 - a + a \cdot b$ (see [5,6] for further details). Constraining the FOL formula to hold true leads to enforcing the T-Norm-based polynomials to be 1, so we get equality constraints, e.g., $1 - a + a \cdot b = 1$ in the previous example. We introduce these constraints into the learning problem in a soft manner using penalty functions, so that the system might decide to violate some of them for some input x (in our implementation, we used the penalty $-\log(\cdot)$).

Formally, the multi-task function that we minimize to learn the model is

$$\sum_{(x,y_r)\in\mathcal{T}_r} L\left(p_r(x), y_r\right) + \sum_{(x,y_e)\in\mathcal{T}_e} L\left(p_e(x), y_e\right) + \sum_{j=1}^{11} \sum_{(x,y_{\text{none}})\in\mathcal{T}} w_j\phi_j\left(p_r(x), p_e(x)\right) \; , \quad (12)$$

where we avoided reporting the scaling factors in front of each term of the summation, to keep the notation simpler. The function L is the cross-entropy loss, while ϕ_j is the penalty term associated to the j-th FOL formula, weighed by the scalar $w_j > 0$.[4] Notice that FOL formulas are constrained to hold true on all the available training data, including the large collection of unlabeled text $\mathcal{T}_u$. This allows the system to learn predictors that fulfil the FOL rules in regions of the input space that might not be covered by the labeled data, thus increasing the information transfer between the two tasks (as typically done in the framework of Learning from Constraints [5,6]). Thanks to this formulation, we can differently weigh the impact of each constraint in function of the confidence we have on it, tuning the parameters w_j. For example, constraints associated to Formulas 4–7–8 are weaker that the other ones, and we decided to keep their weight small.

4   Experimental Results

In order to evaluate the proposed model, we created a heterogeneous data collection that follows the organization described in Sect. 2. In particular, we considered a large public dataset of *Facebook posts* that are scraped from Facebook pages of newspapers.[5] Data was filtered accordingly to what we described in Sect. 2, ending up with $\approx 200,000$ posts, out of which $100,000$ are left unlabeled. Then, we collected the most popular datasets containing text labeled with emotions, namely *AffectiveText*, *ISEAR*, and *Fairy Tales*. *AffectiveText* (SemEval-2007 [18]) contains 1,250 short newspaper headlines. Sentences are labeled with the six basic emotions, and each of them is scored in a range from 0 to 100. For the purpose of this experimentation, we took the emotion with the highest score. *ISEAR* (International Survey on Emotion Antecedents and Reactions [16]) contains 7,666 sentences from questionnaires about emotional experiences covering anger, disgust, fear, joy, sadness, shame, guilt. We discarded the last two classes since they are not part of the universal emotions, and mapped "joy" to "happiness" (the class "surprise" is missing). *Fairy Tales* [2] contains sentences belonging to short stories, annotated with multiple labels. We discarded the neutral class and we kept only sentences with four identical labels (three for the class "disgust", due to the small number of samples). In Table 1 we report the details of the data exploited in this paper.

We evenly divided our heterogeneous datasets into 3 splits, keeping the original data distribution among classes. Each split is further divided into training, validation and test sets, with special attention in preparing the test data. In particular, the test set is composed of 15% of the labeled Facebook posts, merged with one of ISEAR, Fairy Tales, Affective Text. As a matter of fact, each of such emotional datasets is small sized (considering the number of classes and the intrinsic difficulty of the learning task), and it has different properties w.r.t. the other two ones. We experienced that training and testing on subportions of the same emotional dataset leads to performances that do not reflect the concrete quality of the system when it is deployed and tested in a generic context. Differently, training and testing on different emotional datasets offers a more

---

[4] Each ϕ_j might only consider some of the output components of $p_r(x)$ and $p_e(x)$, depending on the FOL formula that it implements.

[5] https://data.world/martinchek/2012-2016-facebook-posts.

realistic perspective of the generalization quality of the resulting system. The training set includes 70% of the labeled Facebook posts and 80% of the two emotional datasets which are not present in the test set, plus the unlabeled Facebook posts. The validation set is composed of the remaining data, that is, 15% of labeled posts and 20% of the two emotional datasets which are not used as test set. We preprocessed all the data converting text to lowercase, removing URLs, standardizing numbers with a special token, removing brackets, separating punctuation and hashtags. Then, we created a vocabulary composed of the most frequent 10,000 words and we truncated sentences longer than 30 words, to make them more easily manageable by the BRNN.

Table 1. Number of Facebook posts for each reaction, and number of *unlabeled* posts (top). Number of texts for each emotion class, covering three public datasets (bottom).

	LOVE	WOW	HAHA	SAD	ANGRY	*Unlabeled*	TOTAL
Facebook Posts	31801	13807	17552	16689	15775	100000	195624
	Anger	*Disgust*	*Fear*	*Happiness*	*Sadness*	*Surprise*	TOTAL
Affective Text	91	42	194	441	265	217	1250
ISEAR	1087	1082	1089	1090	1083	0	5431
Fairy Tales	146	64	166	445	264	100	1185

We evaluated architectures with differently sized word embeddings (from 50 to 300 units each), states of the BRNN (in the range $[50, 200]$), hidden layers (and number of units) of the final MLPs (up to 2 hidden layers). After a first exploratory experimentation, we focussed on models with word embeddings of size 100, BRNN with a hidden state composed of 100 units and final predictors with no hidden layers, that were providing the best results in the validation data. Then, we kept validating in more detail all the other model parameters (learning rate, the possibility of introducing drop-out right after the BRNN, weight of the logic constraints w_j). We considered the (macro) F1 scores on each task to evaluate the quality of our models, and we early stopped the training procedure whenever the average F1 score on the validation data was not increased after 20 epochs (keeping the model associated to the best F1 score found so far).

We compared the following models:

PLAIN. The model of Fig. 1, without logic constraints ($w_j = 0, \forall j$).

CONSTR. The same as PLAIN, but including logic constraints ($w_j > 0, \forall j$).

ARTIFICIAL. The same as PLAIN, where the training data is augmented with artificially mapped classes as described at the beginning of Sect. 3.

+*Emb*. Variant of the models above, based on pre-trained word embeddings of size 300 (the popular Google word2vec model).[6]

---

[6] In this case, after our initial exploratory experimentation, we selected a BRNN with state size 200, and reaction predictor with a hidden layer of size 25.

We first evaluate the quality of the system in the task of reaction prediction. In Table 2, we can appreciate how introducing logic constraints constantly improves the quality of the predictor in all the reaction classes. Using artificial labels from emotional data is far from giving the same benefits of logic constraints, and we did not experience advantages in using pre-trained word embeddings, that might be due to the inherent noise in the reaction prediction task.

Table 2. F1 scores on Facebook reactions (test data, averaged over the 3 data splits - std dev. in bracket). Bold: cases in which constraints introduce improvements.

	LOVE	WOW	HAHA	SAD	ANGRY	Macro Avg
PLAIN	0.630 (0.009)	0.354 (0.008)	0.440 (0.009)	0.532 (0.014)	0.329 (0.012)	0.457 (0.007)
CONSTR	**0.639** (0.162)	**0.371** (0.013)	**0.443** (0.003)	**0.535** (0.005)	**0.347** (0.007)	**0.467** (0.007)
ARTIFICIAL	0.596 (0.051)	0.324 (0.015)	0.393 (0.028)	0.451 (0.077)	0.303 (0.030)	0.413 (0.038)
PLAIN+Emb	0.614 (0.019)	0.343 (0.014)	0.425 (0.012)	0.531 (0.007)	0.345 (0.013)	0.452 (0.006)
CONSTR+Emb	**0.638** (0.007)	**0.347** (0.003)	**0.437** (0.005)	**0.538** (0.012)	**0.356** (0.009)	**0.463** (0.003)
ARTIF.+Emb	0.608 (0.031)	0.323 (0.006)	0.375 (0.031)	0.446 (0.070)	0.311 (0.002)	0.412 (0.030)

Moving to the task of emotion classification, we report the results we obtained in the previously described test sets, that correspond to three different emotional datasets. In Table 3 we focus on testing in the ISEAR data. Logical rules always allow the model to improve the macro-averaged F1 scores. We notice that the F1 score on "disgust" and "fear" classes is largely better than when not using constraints. In fact, without exploiting the logical rules of Eqs. 3 and 5 there is no transfer of information from reaction data, and the supervised portion of the training set is not enough to learn good predictors. Interestingly, this consideration does not hold when using pre-trained embeddings, where the performances of the not-constrained model are already close to the constrained one. In this case, all the other classes are improved instead. Finally, artificial labels do not seem a promising solution.

Table 3. F1 scores on emotion classification (ISEAR). Bold: cases in which constraints introduce improvements.

	Anger	Disgust	Fear	Happiness	Sadness	Macro Avg
PLAIN	0.313	0.009	0.170	0.452	0.420	0.227
CONSTR	0.200	**0.185**	**0.272**	0.395	0.419	**0.245**
ARTIFICIAL	0.186	0.025	0.039	0.126	0.246	0.104
PLAIN+Emb	0.366	0.149	0.383	0.522	0.466	0.314
CONSTR+Emb	**0.383**	0.146	0.381	**0.551**	**0.486**	**0.324**
ARTIF.+Emb	0.160	0.002	0.039	0.128	0.262	0.098

The results on the Fairy Tales test data are shown in Table 4, still confirming the improvements introduced by constraints in the average case. Since "surprise" is poorly represented in the labeled portion of the training set (being it not included in ISEAR data), results in this class are pretty low. While artificial labels help in "surprise", they sometimes lead to very bad results. This is even more evident when using pre-trained embeddings, where the system constantly overfits the training data. Notice that the F1 scores on the validation splits were very promising when using such embeddings, but, as we mentioned when describing the experimental setting, the system badly generalizes to out-of-sample data that is related-but-not-fully-coherent with the training (validation) sets.

In the case of Affect Text test data (Table 5) constraints still increase the macro F1, but not when using pre-trained embeddings. We observe a less coherent behaviour with respect to the previous test sets, and this is due to the fact that Affective Text is composed of sentences that are significantly shorter than the ones of the other datasets, and they are evocative of multiple emotions in which it is harder to distinguish the most-dominant one.

In Fig. 3 we report precision and recall (averaged on the test splits, when needed) associated to the results of Tables 2, 3, 4 and 5. When predicting reactions and using constraints, we observe improvements in *both* precision and recall in the case of 3 out of 5 classes. When predicting emotions, improvements are usually either in terms of precisions *or* in terms of recall (we count a similar

Table 4. F1 scores on emotion classification (Fairy Tales). Bold: cases in which constraints introduce improvements.

	Anger	Disgust	Fear	Happiness	Sadness	Surprise	Macro Avg
PLAIN	0.238	0.151	0.397	0.533	0.410	0.018	0.291
CONSTR	**0.288**	**0.184**	0.362	0.533	0.400	0.038	**0.301**
ARTIFICIAL	0.261	0.029	0.079	0.598	0.471	0.101	0.256
PLAIN+*Emb*	0.365	0.137	0.451	0.546	0.365	0.037	0.317
CONSTR+*Emb*	**0.367**	0.127	0.424	0.521	**0.476**	**0.068**	**0.331**
ARTIF.+*Emb*	0.156	0.035	0.078	0.064	0.109	0.009	0.075

Table 5. F1 scores on emotion classification (Affective Text). Bold: cases in which constraints introduce improvements.

	Anger	Disgust	Fear	Happiness	Sadness	Surprise	Macro Avg
PLAIN	0.162	0.100	0.282	0.514	0.289	0	0.224
CONSTR	**0.187**	**0.111**	0.282	0.493	0.295	0	**0.228**
ARTIFICIAL	0.182	0	0.010	0.586	0.383	0.198	0.227
PLAIN+*Emb*	0.153	0.113	0.369	0.571	0.396	0.054	0.276
CONSTR+*Emb*	0.022	**0.117**	0.324	**0.577**	**0.447**	0	0.248
ARTIF.+*Emb*	0.126	0.047	0	0.059	0.093	0.045	0.062

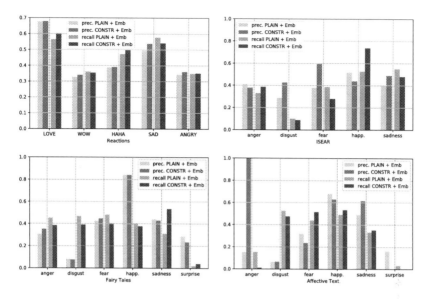

Fig. 3. Precision and recall associated to the results of Tables 2, 3, 4 and 5 (left-to-right, top-to-bottom), comparing PLAIN +*Emb* with CONSTR +*Emb*.

number of cases in which precision is improved and cases in which recall is improved).

Comparing our experimental analysis with existing literature that is about emotion detection is not straightforward. Existing approaches make use of lexical resources or focus on settings that are pretty different from the one we selected (they test on splits that are taken from the same emotional dataset, thus providing better results [12,20]). However, we found that, in some cases, our model is competitive with popular algorithms. Table 6 reports the F1 scores of existing models, emphasizing the cases in which our CONSTR +*Emb* outperforms them. In Affective Text, we compared with the WN-AFFECT system (based on WordNet Affect), and a model based on LSA to compute representations of emotion words [19] (even if they considered a multi-label learning problem). On the same data, as well as in ISEAR, we also considered the CNMF model from [10], based on non-negative matrix factorization, that was evaluated on a subset of the emotions we considered in this paper. Finally, we compared with (what we refer to as) the Wikipedia model from [1], that was trained on texts taken from Wikipedia and tested on the ISEAR data (and other datasets).[7]

---

[7] We did not consider Fairy Tales since existing approaches usually merge "anger" and "disgust", and also because the sentence truncation strongly affected this dataset.

Table 6. Results of existing approaches. We indicate with ∗ those cases in which our model (CONSTR+*Emb*) outperforms the result reported in this table.

	Anger	Disgust	Fear	Happiness	Sadness	Surprise	Macro Avg
ISEAR							
CNMF [10]	0.579	-	0.056*	0.010*	0.017*	-	-
WIKIPEDIA [1]	0.413	0.430	0.517	0.514*	0.396*	-	0.454
Affective Text							
WN-AFFECT [19]	0.061	-	0.033*	0.011*	0.066*	0.069	0.040*
LSA [19]	0.112	0.039*	0.219*	0.308*	0.206*	0.141	0.176*
CNMF [10]	0.278	-	0.618	0.648	0.475	-	-

5 Conclusions

In this paper we proposed to jointly learn the tasks of emotion classification and prediction of Facebook reactions, when processing raw text. While such tasks share several analogies, mapping emotion classes to Facebook reactions (and vice-versa) can easily become ambiguous. Our system exploits First Order-Logic formulas to model the task relationships, and it learns from such formulas, also exploiting large collections of unlabeled training data. The provided experimental analysis has shown that bridging these two tasks by means of FOL-based constraints leads to improvements in the prediction quality that clearly goes beyond more naive approaches in which artificial labels are generated in the data preprocessing stage. Our future work will focus on the introduction of lexical resources in our system.

Acknowledgements. This project has received funding from the European Union's Horizon 2020 research and innovation program under grant agreement No 825619.

References

1. Agrawal, A., An, A.: Unsupervised emotion detection from text using semantic and syntactic relations. In: Proceedings of the International Joint Conferences on Web Intelligence and Intelligent Agent Technology, pp. 346–353. IEEE (2012)
2. Alm, C.: Affect in text and speech. Ph.D. thesis, University of Illinois (2008)
3. Chaffar, S., Inkpen, D.: Using a heterogeneous dataset for emotion analysis in text. In: Butz, C., Lingras, P. (eds.) AI 2011. LNCS (LNAI), vol. 6657, pp. 62–67. Springer, Heidelberg (2011). https://doi.org/10.1007/978-3-642-21043-3_8
4. Ekman, P., Friesen, W.V.: Constants across cultures in the face and emotion. J. Pers. Soc. Psychol. **17**(2), 124 (1971)
5. Gnecco, G., Gori, M., Melacci, S., Sanguineti, M.: Foundations of support constraint machines. Neural Comput. **27**(2), 388–480 (2015)
6. Gori, M., Melacci, S.: Constraint verification with kernel machines. IEEE Trans. Neural Netw. Learn. Syst. **24**(5), 825–831 (2013)

7. Graziani, L., Melacci, S., Gori, M.: The role of coherence in facial expression recognition. In: Ghidini, C., Magnini, B., Passerini, A., Traverso, P. (eds.) AI*IA 2018. LNCS (LNAI), vol. 11298, pp. 320–333. Springer, Cham (2018). https://doi.org/10.1007/978-3-030-03840-3_24

8. Herzig, J., Shmueli-Scheuer, M., Konopnicki, D.: Emotion detection from text via ensemble classification using word embeddings. In: Proceedings of the International Conference on Theory of Information Retrieval, pp. 269–272. ACM (2017)

9. Hochreiter, S., Schmidhuber, J.: Long short-term memory. Neural Comput. 9(8), 1735–1780 (1997)

10. Kim, S.M., Valitutti, A., Calvo, R.A.: Evaluation of unsupervised emotion models to textual affect recognition. In: NAACL HLT Workshop on Computational Approaches to Analysis and Generation of Emotion in Text, pp. 62–70. ACL (2010)

11. Krebs, F., Lubascher, B., Moers, T., Schaap, P., Spanakis, G.: Social emotion mining techniques for Facebook posts reaction prediction. In: Proceedings of the 10th International Conference on Agents and Artificial Intelligence (2018)

12. Mohammad, S.: Portable features for classifying emotional text. In: Proceedings of the Conference of the NAACL HLT, pp. 587–591. ACL (2012)

13. Pool, C., Nissim, M.: Distant supervision for emotion detection using Facebook reactions. In: Proceedings of the Workshop on Computational Modeling of People's Opinions, Personality, and Emotions in Social Media, pp. 30–39 (2016)

14. Qadir, A., Riloff, E.: Learning emotion indicators from tweets: hashtags, hashtag patterns, and phrases. In: Proceedings of the 2014 Conference on Empirical Methods in Natural Language Processing (EMNLP), pp. 1203–1209 (2014)

15. Raad, B.T., Philipp, B., Patrick, H., Christoph, M.: ASEDS: towards automatic social emotion detection system using Facebook reactions. In: International Conference on High Performance Computing and Communications; on Smart City; on Data Science and Systems (HPCC/SmartCity/DSS), pp. 860–866. IEEE (2018)

16. Scherer, K.R., Wallbott, H.G.: Evidence for universality and cultural variation of differential emotion response patterning. J. Pers. Soc. Psychol. 66(2), 310 (1994)

17. Schuster, M., Paliwal, K.K.: Bidirectional recurrent neural networks. IEEE Trans. Signal Process. 45(11), 2673–2681 (1997)

18. Strapparava, C., Mihalcea, R.: SemEval-2007 task 14: affective text. In: Proceedings of the 4th International Workshop on Semantic Evaluations, pp. 70–74 (2007)

19. Strapparava, C., Mihalcea, R.: Learning to identify emotions in text. In: Proceedings of the ACM Symposium on Applied Computing, pp. 1556–1560. ACM (2008)

20. Wang, Y., Pal, A.: Detecting emotions in social media: a constrained optimization approach. In: IJCAI, pp. 996–1002 (2015)

Discriminative Feature Learning for Speech Emotion Recognition

Yuying Zhang[1] ⓘ, Yuexian Zou[1(✉)] ⓘ, Junyi Peng[1], Danqing Luo[1],
and Dongyan Huang[2]

[1] ADSPLAB, School of ECE, Peking University, Shenzhen, China
zouyx@pkusz.edu.cn
[2] UBTECH Robotics Corporate, Shenzhen, China

Abstract. It is encouraged to see that the deep neural networks based speech emotion recognition (DNN-SER) models have achieved the state-of-the-art on public datasets. However, the performance of DNN-SER models is limited due to the following reasons: insufficient training data, emotion ambiguity and class imbalance. Studies show that, without large-scale training data, it is hard for DNN-SER model with cross-entropy loss to learn discriminative features by mapping the speech segments to their category labels. In this study, we propose a deep metric learning based DNN-SER model to facilitate the discriminative feature learning by constraining the feature embeddings in the feature space. For the proof of the concept, we take a four-hidden layer DNN as our backbone for implementation simplicity. Specifically, an emotion identity matrix is formed using one-hot label vectors as supervision information while the emotion embedding matrix is formed using the embedding vectors generated by DNN. An affinity loss is designed based on the above two matrices to simultaneously maximize the inter-class separability and intra-class compactness of the embeddings. Moreover, to restrain the class imbalance problem, the focal loss is introduced to reduce the adverse effect of the majority well-classified samples and gain more focus on the minority misclassified ones. Our proposed DNN-SER model is jointly trained using affinity loss and focal loss. Extensive experiments have been conducted on two well-known emotional speech datasets, EMO-DB and IEMOCAP. Compared to DNN-SER baseline, the unweighted accuracy (UA) on EMO-DB and IEMOCAP increased relatively by 10.19% and 10% respectively. Besides, from the confusion matrix of the test results on Emo-DB, it is noted that the accuracy of the most confusing emotion category, 'Happiness', increased relatively by 33.17% and the accuracy of the emotion category with the fewest samples, 'Disgust', increased relatively by 13.62%. These results validate the effectiveness of our proposed DNN-SER model and give the evidence that affinity loss and focal loss help to learn better discriminative features.

Keywords: Deep neural network · Speech emotion recognition · Affinity loss · Focal loss · Deep metric learning

© Springer Nature Switzerland AG 2019
I. V. Tetko et al. (Eds.): ICANN 2019, LNCS 11730, pp. 198–210, 2019.
https://doi.org/10.1007/978-3-030-30490-4_17

Fig. 1. Illustration of emotion ambiguity and class imbalance problem. The picture (left) indicates the specific active nodes for Anger and Happiness [10]. As can be observed, the active nodes are similar for Anger and Happiness, reflecting the emotion ambiguity problem. The pie chart (right) shows the class imbalance problem on EMO-DB, i.e., different emotions account for different proportion.

1 Introduction

As one of the basic means for human communication, speech contains abundant emotional information. Recently, speech emotion recognition (SER) has gained increasing attention because of its various applications, especially in human-computer interaction, mental health analysis, remote education and so on. SER is a task of identifying human emotional state from the speech signal. When the emotional state is described as discrete labels, such as anger, happiness, neutral, etc., SER is essentially a multi-class classification problem.

Generally, SER systems derive emotion recognition decisions on the frame-level (short segment) or on the utterance-level. For frame-level approach, low-level descriptors (LLDs) are extracted from speech frame as input to the sequential classifier, which mainly uses Gaussian mixture model (GMM) [1] or hidden Markov model (HMM) [2] to model the distribution of the emotional state of speakers. For utterance-level approach, on the other hand, statistical functions are applied to the LLDs over all frames of an utterance to obtain global features, which are then used as input to discriminative classifiers such as support vector machines (SVM) [3]. In recent years, for SER task, deep neural networks (DNNs) have been employed to obtain high-level features (HFS) from low-level raw features. In the work of [4], DNN is trained to learn acoustic utterance-level features for SER. In [5], DNN is employed to extract short-term LLDs and the extreme learning machine (ELM) is used for final utterance level classification, which achieves the state-of-the-art for SER task.

Studies show that DNN-based SER (DNN-SER) methods have several limitations. Firstly, there is a lack of large-scale training datasets for SER tasks since it is extremely difficult to collect the speech emotion data [6]. Without large-scale training data, it is hard for DNN-SER models to learn discriminative features. Secondly, human emotions are naturally ambiguous [7]. Different types of emotions are easily confused with each other, which increases the difficulty of SER [8]. For example, previous studies have shown that 'Anger' and 'Happiness' have similar acoustic expression [9]. [10] shows the activations of different nodes for emotions at the recurrent neural network

(RNN) and observes that the active nodes are similar for 'Anger' and 'Happiness'. Thirdly, there is the class imbalance problem in the SER corpus, as illustrated in Fig. 1. Research outcomes of the visual object detection have shown that the class imbalance will cause performance degradation since the large well-classified samples affect the learning behavior of the deep model by dominating the gradient [11]. As discussed above, with insufficient training data, DNN-SER models ask for a very good discriminative feature learning mechanism. However, most of existing DNN-SER methods adopt the cross-entropy (CE) together with softmax as the supervision component, which cannot explicitly encourage the discriminative learning of features and has no advantage in handling the class imbalance problem because it assigns an equal weight of loss to the majority and minority examples.

In order to resolve the critical issue of discriminative feature learning, several approaches have been developed under the metric learning framework. Huang et al. [12] applied the triplet loss to a Long Short-Term Memory Neural Network (LSTM) SER model, which separates the positive pair from the negative one by a distance margin. Very recently, Lian et al. [13] applied the contrastive loss to Siamese neural network (SNN) SER model, which enables the model to learn more discriminative features. However, carefully examining the triplet loss and contrastive loss, it is noted that they require a carefully designed pair selection procedure, which results in the performance of SER heavily depending on the manual selection of training pairs. In addition, compared to the training samples, the number of training pairs or triplets dramatically grows even for a small dataset, which inevitably results in slow convergence and instability [14]. Moreover, we note that both of them neglect the class imbalance problem.

In this work, we propose a deep metric learning based DNN-SER method to promote the discriminative feature learning. For the proof of the concept, we take a four-hidden layer DNN as our backbone for implementation simplicity. Since the label information is given, the emotion identity matrix can be formed using the one-hot label vectors which are used as the supervision information. Correspondingly, the emotion embedding matrix is formed using the embedding vectors generated at the last hidden layer of the DNN. The affinity loss is designed based on the above two matrices to simultaneously maximize the inter-class separability and the intra-class compactness of the feature embeddings. It is noted that, compared to CE loss which measures the similarity of emotion posterior probability distribution, the affinity loss directly optimizes the similarities between emotion embeddings. In addition, compared to triplet loss and contrastive loss in [12, 13], the affinity loss eliminates the selection of the sample pairs by exploits the correlation information of all embedding pairs and avoids suffering from dramatic data expansion. Besides, to restrain the class imbalance problem, the focal loss [11] is introduced to down-weight the contribution of majority well-classified emotion class and gain more focus on minority misclassified ones. Specifically, the focal loss alleviates the adverse effect of class imbalance by preventing the vast number of well-classified examples from dominating the gradient during training. Our proposed DNN-SER model is jointly trained using affinity loss and focal loss. Extensive experiments have been conducted on two well-known emotional speech datasets, EMO-DB and IEMOCAP. Compared to the DNN-SER baseline, the unweighted accuracy (UA) on EMO-DB and IEMOCAP increased relatively by

10.19% and 10% respectively. Besides, from the confusion matrix of the test results on Emo-DB, it is encouraged to see that the accuracy of the most confusing emotion category, 'Happiness', increased relatively by 33.2% and the accuracy of the emotion category with the fewest samples, 'Disgust', increased relatively by 13.6%. These results validate the effectiveness of our proposed DNN-SER model and give the evidence for supporting our joint loss has the ability to learn better discriminative features.

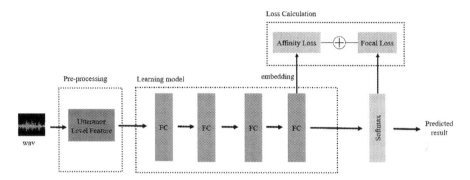

Fig. 2. An overview of DNN-SER system with proposed joint loss.

The rest of the paper is organized as follows. In Sect. 2, the proposed method is introduced. Section 3 presents the datasets and feature set. Section 4 explains the experimental settings and results. Conclusions and future work are given in Sect. 5.

2 Proposed Method

2.1 System Architecture

In this work, a four-hidden layer DNN-SER model is jointly trained using affinity loss and focal loss to address the emotion ambiguity problem and the class imbalance problem with insufficient training data, respectively. The architecture of the proposed SER system is shown in Fig. 2.

Our SER system essentially consists of three key ingredients: input data preparation (pre-processing), the learning model and learning criterion (loss calculation). In the pre-processing part, the utterance-level feature vector is extracted from the input training utterance. The training is carried out in batch size. In the learning model part, data flows through all the fully connected (FC) layers. The output of the last hidden layer is termed as the feature embeddings, which are used for computing the affinity loss specifically. The network is optimized with the joint supervision of the affinity loss and the focal loss using Stochastic Gradient Descent (SGD). Details of the loss design are given in Sect. 2.2.

2.2 Loss Function

In this subsection, we will introduce our proposed joint loss for training the DNN model. The proposed joint loss consists of two parts: the affinity loss and the focal loss, which will be addressed separately in the following subsequent paragraphs.

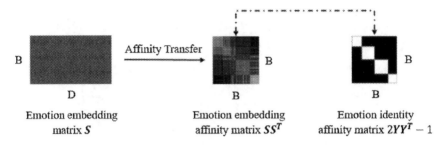

Fig. 3. The schematic diagram of affinity loss. B denotes the batch size of input data, D is the dimension of output emotion embedding, S is the emotion embedding matrix, and Y is the emotion identity matrix.

Affinity Loss. For this study, the affinity loss is adopted since it is able to mitigate the emotion ambiguity by reinforcing the discriminability of features and alleviate the data insufficiency problem by making full use of the correlation information and identity information.

The schematic diagram of affinity loss is shown in Fig. 3. In the following context, we will introduce our proposed method in formulating affinity loss for SER task.

Let's assume that the DNN-SER system designed (Fig. 2) is parameterized by θ and the training is conducted in a batch of size B (utterance-level). The DNN embedding extractor with four fully connected layers maps an utterance-level speech feature x to a D-dimensional unit-norm emotion embedding $s = f_\theta(x) \in \mathbb{R}^{1 \times D}$, i.e., $\|s\|_2 = 1$. While training in a batch, B utterance-level speech emotion features are randomly selected to form a set as $X = \{x_i\}$, $i \in \{1, \ldots, B\}$. Correspondingly, the output of the last fully connected layer is denoted as $S = \{s_i\}$, which is named as the emotion embedding matrix. Intuitively, the matrix $SS^T \in \mathbb{R}^{B \times B}$ is termed as the emotion embedding affinity matrix. In this study, one-hot label vector representation y_i is adopted which indicates the corresponding emotion identity of x_i. Therefore, the label matrix associated with X can be denoted as $Y = \{y_i\}$, which is termed as the emotion identity matrix and then $YY^T \in \mathbb{R}^{B \times B}$ is defined as the emotion identity affinity matrix.

Obviously, the matrix YY^T are available and can be taken as the supervision information. Our goal is to design a loss to fully make use of the limited training data by exploiting the correlation information of all emotion embeddings. Hence, affinity loss (AL) is defined as follows:

$$L_{AL} = \left\| SS^T - 2YY^T + 1 \right\|_F^2$$
$$= \sum_{i,j;y_i=y_j} \left(1 - \cos(s_i, s_j)\right)^2 + \sum_{i,j;y_i \neq y_j} \left(-1 - \cos(s_i, s_j)\right)^2 \qquad (1)$$

where $\|\cdot\|_F^2$ denotes the squared Frobenius norm. It is noted that $\left(SS^T\right)_{ij} = \left\{s_i \cdot s_j^T\right\}$ indicates the cosine similarity between s_i and s_j. When segment i and j belong to the same emotion class, the cosine similarity between s_i and s_j should be close to 1. By comparison, when i and j belong to different emotion class, the cosine similarity between s_i and s_j should be close to -1. Besides, it is clear that YY^T is a binary matrix. Therefore, if the segment i and j belong to the same emotion class (with the same one-hot label vector), we have $(YY^T)_{ij} = 1$. Otherwise, we have $(YY^T)_{ij} = 0$. Under a supervised learning framework, YY^T is known which can be calculated using the training data.

From the definition in (1), we can see that the affinity loss is composed of two parts. The first item promotes the similarity between the embeddings of the same emotion class while the second item promotes the discrimination between the embeddings from different emotion class. Two parts are optimized simultaneously during training. As analyzed above, the discriminability of features can be reinforced by increasing inter-class separability and intra-class compactness between feature embeddings.

Focal Loss. In this study, we introduce the focal loss (FL) to our DNN-SER model to mitigate the class imbalance problems and improve the ability of better discriminative feature learning.

The focal loss was first proposed by Lin et al. at Facebook AI Research (FAIR) in [11] to address the class imbalance problem for dense visual object detection. The estimated probability of the yi-th emotion sample is defined in (2) as follows:

$$p(y_i) = \frac{e^{W_{y_i}^T s_i + b_{y_i}}}{\sum_{j=1}^{N} e^{W_j^T s_i + b_j}} \qquad (2)$$

where $y_i \in \{1, \ldots, N\}$, N is the number of emotion class. $W_j \in \mathbb{R}^D$ is the j-th column of the weights $W \in \mathbb{R}^{D \times N}$ in the last fully connected layer and $b \in \mathbb{R}^N$ is the bias term.

Essentially, the focal loss is a simple extension to cross-entropy (CE) by adding a weighting factor α and a focusing parameter γ to the conventional CE loss, as formulated in (3):

$$L_{FL}(p(y_i)) = -\alpha_i (1 - p(y_i))^\gamma \log(p(y_i)) \qquad (3)$$

where $\alpha_i > 0$ and $\gamma \geq 0$ are two hyper-parameters, controlling the decaying extent of the loss. These two parameters can be fixed through the training process, or be changed according to the specific training condition (e.g. changing by the training epochs) [15]. It is noted that γ is a tunable focusing parameter, which is able to reduce the relative loss for large well-classified samples and gain more focus on the minority misclassified samples.

Joint Loss. Following the discussions above, to address the emotion ambiguity and class imbalance problems with insufficient training data simultaneously, the linear combination of the affinity loss and focal loss is taken as the joint loss for the training, which is given as:

$$L = L_{AL} + L_{FL} \qquad (4)$$

In this study, we only equally consider affinity loss and focal loss. However, a super-parameter can be introduced to assign different weight on the affinity loss and focal loss which will be further explored.

As shown in Fig. 2. the DNN model is trained in a supervision manner using the joint loss defined in (4) with the error back propagation method.

3   Dataset and Feature Set

3.1   Dataset

To evaluate the performance of our proposed SER system, experiments are conducted on the Berlin Emotional Database (EMO-DB) and Interactive Emotional Dyadic Motion Capture (IEMOCAP) database. EMO-DB consists of 535 utterances that displayed by ten professional actors, covering seven emotions (Anger, *Boredom, Neutral, Disgust, Fear,* Happiness *and* Sadness). IEMOCAP consists of 5531 utterances, including five sessions from 10 speakers. Each session is displayed by a pair of actors in scripted and improvised scenarios. At least three evaluators annotated each utterance in the database with the categorical emotion labels chosen from the set. In our experiments, we consider only the utterances with majority agreement (two out of three evaluators gave the same emotion label) over the emotion classes of Anger, Happiness, Neutral and Sadness, with "Excitement" considered as "Happiness", which is similar to prior studies [9, 12]. The distribution of EMO-DB and IEMOCAP database is shown in Tables 1 and 2.

Experiments are conducted in a speaker-independent manner. A 10-fold Leave-One-Speaker-Out (LOSO) cross-validation scheme was employed in all experiments. For each fold, the utterances from one speaker are used as the testing set, and the utterances from the other speakers are used as the training set. Such configuration is the same as that used in [9, 16–18], which makes the experimental results comparable between our work and others.

Table 1. The distribution of EMO-DB database.

Emotion	Anger	Boredom	Neutral	Disgust	Fear	Happiness	Sadness
Number	127	81	79	46	69	71	62

Table 2. The distribution of IEMOCAP database.

Emotion	Anger	Happiness	Neutral	Sadness
Number	1103	1636	1708	1084

3.2 Feature Set

Following [9, 17], the feature set designed for INTERSPEECH 2009 Emotion Challenge is adopted in our experiments. Specifically, the low-level descriptors (LLDs) include the zero-crossing rate (ZCR), root mean square (RMS), pitch frequency (normalized to 500 Hz), the harmonics-to-noise ratio (HNR), and 1–12 Mel-frequency cepstral coefficients (MFCC) [19]. Moreover, another 12 functionals are applied to all the frame-based features at utterance-level, such as mean, standard deviation, kurtosis, skewness and so on. The details are depicted in Table 3. Thus, the final feature vector for an utterance contains 384 attributes.

Table 3. Features set used in our experiment: low-level descriptors (LLD) and functionals [19].

LLD $(16 \cdot 2)$	Functionals (12)
(Δ) ZCR	Mean
(Δ) RMS Energy	Standard deviation
(Δ) F0	Kurtosisk, skewness
(Δ) HNR	Extremes: value, rel. position, range
(Δ) MFCC 1–12	Linear regression: offset, slope, MSE

4 Experiment Setup and Results

The raw waveform is segmented into frames with a sliding window of 25 ms at the step of 10 ms. Then LLDs are extracted from the frames and statistical functionals are computed for them. In this way, the 384-dim utterance-level feature vector is extracted for each utterance sample. In all experiments, the input data is pre-processed with z-score normalization to reduce the impact of data range variation and make the network easier to converge, where zero mean and unit deviation is set for the data distribution.

Regarding the proposed DNN-SER model, it contains four hidden layers, with 512, 256, 128 and 64 neurons respectively. We adopt a batch normalization after each fully connected layer and the activation function used is the Max Feature Map (MFM) [20]. In the training process, the batch size is set to 32 and the regular RMSprop is adopted as the optimizer, with an initial learning rate of 0.001. Learning rate is decayed if the validation loss has not decreased. The values of α and γ in Eq. 3 are set to 0.5 and 4, respectively.

As standard practice in SER research, results are reported using the weighted accuracy (WA) and the unweighted accuracy (UA) [19]. In this research, we focus on studying the effectiveness of the proposed joint loss when training on class-imbalanced data, so UA is taken as the primary evaluation metric.

4.1 Evaluation Results

Experiments are conducted with our proposed DNN-SER systems on EMO-DB and IEMOCAP database, where the joint loss in (4) is used for supervising the network training. To prove the effectiveness of our proposed method, a DNN of the same structure using the CE loss is used as the baseline model. Tables 4 and 5 compares the classification accuracy obtained using the proposed method to those obtained using other methods that have been tested on the same emotional speech database.

Firstly, from Tables 4 and 5, we can see that on both databases, the proposed DNN-SER system with joint loss outperforms other comparison methods.

It is noted that the works in [4, 5, 17, 21] all use DNN with CE loss, which does not strongly encourage the discriminative learning of features, leading to unsatisfactory performance. In addition, [12] uses triplet loss to reduce the intra-class distance and enlarge the inter-class distance which is also inferior to our model.

Table 4. Performance comparison on EMO-DB (%).

Model	WA	UA
GerDA [4]	81.9	79.1
Artificial Neural Network [16]	80.60	80.76
DNN-ELM [17]	–	84.09
SVM [18]	87.30	87.32
Baseline	83.33	81.82
DNN (AL+FL)	**89.34**	**90.09**

Table 5. Performance comparison on IEMOCAP database (%).

Model	WA	UA
DNN-ELM [5]	54.3	48.2
DNN-ELM [5] [21]	57.91	52.13
LSTM+SVM [12]	–	60.4
Naïve Bayes classifier [9]	57.85	62.54
Baseline	58.22	58.50
DNN (AL+FL)	**62.08**	**64.35**

For EMO-DB, our proposed DNN (AL+FL) SER system achieves WA of 89.34% and UA of 90.09%, which increased relatively by 7.21% and 10.19% respectively compared to the baseline. For IEMOCAP database, our proposed DNN (AL+FL) SER system achieves WA of 62.08% and UA of 64.35%, which relatively improved by 6.63% and 10% compared to the baseline.

4.2 Ablation Study

In order to understand the impact of individual loss functions, we conducted an ablation study on EMO-DB. Comparison of classification accuracy among different loss functions on EMO-DB is given in Table 6.

Table 6. Performance comparison among different loss functions on EMO-DB (%)

Methods	WA	UA
Baseline	83.33	81.82
DNN (FL)	84.90	86.55
DNN (AL)	88.16	88.93
DNN (AL+FL)	**89.34**	**90.09**

Experiment results show that, with the same DNN architecture, the WA and UA of using joint loss are highest among all the methods, and the WA and UA of using focal loss and affinity loss separately are better than the baseline.

To further investigate the capability of the CE loss, focal loss, affinity loss, and joint loss, Figs. 4, 5, 6 and 7 give the confusion matrices of the test results for four different loss settings. The AN, BO, NE, DI, FE, HA, and SA are short for Anger, *Boredom, Neutral, Disgust, Fear,* Happiness *and* Sadness, respectively.

From Fig. 1 and Table 1, we can see that the emotion category with the largest and fewest samples are 'Anger' and 'Disgust' respectively. It is noted that 'Anger' accounts for a significantly larger proportion (23.74%) than other categories and 'Disgust' accounts for a much smaller proportion (8.6%) than other categories.

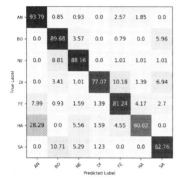

Fig. 4. Confusion matrix of test results on EMO-DB for baseline (%).

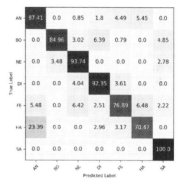

Fig. 5. Confusion matrix of test results on EMO-DB for DNN (FL) (%).

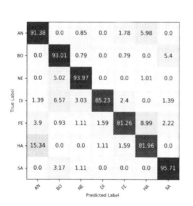

Fig. 6. Confusion matrix of test results on EMO-DB for DNN (AL) (%).

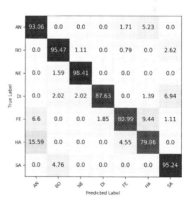

Fig. 7. Confusion matrix of test results on EMO-DB for DNN (AL + FL) (%).

As can be seen from Fig. 4, using the CE loss, the accuracy of 'Anger' is quite high and 'Disgust' is rather low. This phenomenon indicates that the majority category dominates the loss during training and the category with few examples cannot be trained adequately, which degrades the performance of SER. Besides, 28.29% of 'Happiness' is misclassified as 'Anger', reflecting that 'Happiness' is easily confused with 'Anger'.

In this study, we focus on improving the classification accuracy of the emotion category with the fewest samples, 'Disgust' and the most confusing emotion category, 'Happiness' to alleviate the problem of class imbalance and the emotion ambiguity, respectively.

As can be seen from Fig. 5, after using the focal loss, the accuracy of category 'Disgust' achieves 92.35%, which increased relatively by 19.84% compared to the baseline, indicating that focal loss helps to restrain class imbalance problem. As can be seen from Fig. 6, after using the affinity loss, the accuracy of 'Happiness' achieves 81.96%, which increased relatively by 36.55% compared to baseline. Besides, the ratio of "Happiness" misclassified as "Anger" decreased relatively by 45.74%. These results prove the capability of the affinity loss to deal with the ambiguity of emotions.

From Fig. 7, we observe that compared to the baseline, the accuracy of category 'Disgust' increased relatively by 13.62% after using the joint loss of affinity loss and focal loss. The accuracy of 'Happiness' increased relatively by 33.17% and the ratio of "Happiness" misclassified as "Anger" decreased relatively by 44.88%. These results demonstrate the effectiveness of the joint loss for both class imbalance and emotional ambiguity problems. Besides, the classification accuracy of 'Boredom', 'Neutral' and 'Sadness' are increased relatively by 6.46%, 11.63%, and 15.08%, respectively. The classification accuracy of the 'Anger' decreased relatively by 0.08%. The main reason is that the network reduces the focus on the large samples during training after applying the focal loss. As for the classification accuracy of 'Fear', which has a relatively decrease of 0.03%, we speculate that there may be some underlying factors undermine the system performance, and we will discuss it in our future work.

As discussed above, the experiment results validate the effectiveness of our proposed DNN-SER model and give the evidence that the proposed joint loss helps to learn discriminative features.

5   Conclusion

In this paper, we propose an effective SER system via learning discriminative emotion features with a DNN-SER model, which is supervised trained using our proposed joint loss consisting of affinity loss and focal loss. The affinity loss aims at simultaneously maximizing the inter-class separability and intra-class compactness of the embeddings while the focal loss targets at suppressing the contribution of majority well-classified samples and gaining more focus on the minority misclassified samples. Performance evaluation has been conducted on EMO-DB and IEMOCAP database. It is desired to observe that our proposed SER system outperforms the comparison methods, which illustrate the capability of the joint loss to deal with the emotion ambiguity problem as well as alleviating both the data insufficiency and class imbalance for SER task. More specifically, our proposed DNN-SER system achieves WA of 89.34% and UA of 90.09% on EMO-DB, which increased relatively by 7.21% and 10.19% respectively compared to the DNN-SER baseline model. For IEMOCAP, our proposed DNN-SER system achieves WA of 62.08% and UA of 64.35%, which increased relatively by 6.63% and 10% respectively compared to the baseline model. Besides, from the confusion matrix of the test results on EMO-DB, it is encouraged to see that the accuracy of the most confusing emotion category, 'Happiness', increased relatively by 33.17% and the accuracy of the emotion category with the fewest samples, 'Disgust', increased relatively by 13.62%. In our future work, we will evaluate our proposed joint loss with different deep models, such as LSTM and CRNN to further improve SER performance.

Acknowledgements. This work was partially supported by Shenzhen Science & Technology Fundamental Research Programs (No: JCYJ20170817160058246, JCYJ20170306165153653 & JCYJ20180507182908274). Special acknowledgements are given to AOTO-PKUSZ Joint Research Center for Artificial Intelligence on Scene Cognition & Technology Innovation for its support.

References

1. Neiberg, D., Elenius, K., Laskowski, K.: Emotion recognition in spontaneous speech using GMMs. In: Ninth International Conference on Spoken Language Processing (2006)
2. New, T.L., Foo, S.W., De Silva, L.C.: Speech emotion recognition using hidden Markov models. Speech Commun. **41**, 603–623 (2003)
3. Mower, E., Mataric, M.J., Narayanan, S.: A framework for automatic human emotion classification using emotion profiles. IEEE Trans. Audio Speech Lang. Process. **19**, 1057–1070 (2010)
4. Stuhlsatz, A., Meyer, C., Eyben, F., et al.: Deep neural networks for acoustic emotion recognition: raising the benchmarks. In: 2011 IEEE International Conference on Acoustics, Speech and Signal Processing (ICASSP), pp. 5688–5691 (2011)
5. Han, K., Yu, D., Tashev, I.: Speech emotion recognition using deep neural network and extreme learning machine. In: Fifteenth Annual Conference of the International Speech Communication Association (2014)
6. Huang, Y., Hu, M., Yu, X., Wang, T., Yang, C.: Transfer learning of deep neural network for speech emotion recognition. In: Tan, T., Li, X., Chen, X., Zhou, J., Yang, J., Cheng, H. (eds.) CCPR 2016. CCIS, vol. 663, pp. 721–729. Springer, Singapore (2016). https://doi.org/10.1007/978-981-10-3005-5_59
7. Mower, E., Metallinou, A., Lee, C.C., et al.: Interpreting ambiguous emotional expressions. In: 2009 3rd International Conference on Affective Computing and Intelligent Interaction and Workshops, pp. 1–8. IEEE (2009)
8. Chao, L., Tao, J., Yang, M., Li, Y., et al.: Long short term memory recurrent neural network based encoding method for emotion recognition in video. In: 2016 IEEE International Conference on Acoustics, Speech and Signal Processing (ICASSP), pp. 2752–2756 (2016)

9. Ma, X., Wu, Z., Jia, J., et al.: Speech emotion recognition with emotion-pair based framework considering emotion distribution information in dimensional emotion space. In: INTERSPEECH 2017, pp. 1238–1242 (2017)
10. Ma, X., Wu, Z., Jia, J., et al.: Emotion recognition from variable-length speech segments using deep learning on spectrograms. In: Proceedings of Interspeech 2018, pp. 3683–3687 (2018)
11. Lin, T.Y., Goyal, P., Girshick, R., He, K., Dollár, P.: Focal loss for dense object detection. In: Proceedings of the IEEE International Conference on Computer Vision (2018)
12. Huang, J., Li, Y., Tao, J., Lian, Z.: Speech emotion recognition from variable-length inputs with triplet loss function. In: Proceedings of Interspeech 2018, pp. 3673–3677 (2018)
13. Lian, Z., Li, Y., Tao, J., et al.: Speech emotion recognition via contrastive loss under siamese networks. In: Proceedings of the Joint Workshop of the 4th Workshop on Affective Social Multimedia Computing and First Multi-Modal Affective Computing of Large-Scale Multimedia Data, pp. 21–26. ACM (2018)
14. Li, N., Tuo, D., Su, D., et al.: Deep discriminative embeddings for duration robust speaker verification. In: Proceedings of Interspeech 2018, pp. 2262–2266 (2018)
15. Wang, S., Qian, Y., Yu, K.: Focal KL-divergence based dilated convolutional neural networks for co-channel speaker identification. In: 2018 IEEE International Conference on Acoustics, Speech and Signal Processing (ICASSP), pp. 5339–5343. IEEE (2018)
16. Bhargava, M., Polzehl, T.: Improving automatic emotion recognition from speech using rhythm and temporal feature. arXiv preprint arXiv:1303.1761 (2013)
17. Guo, L., Wang, L., Dang, J., Zhang, L., Guan, H.: A feature fusion method based on extreme learning machine for speech emotion recognition. In: 2018 IEEE International Conference on Acoustics, Speech and Signal Processing (ICASSP), pp. 2666–2670 (2018)
18. Gao, Y., Li, B., Wang, N., Zhu, T.: Speech emotion recognition using local and global features. In: Zeng, Y., He, Y., Kotaleski, J.H., Martone, M., Xu, B., Peng, H., Luo, Q. (eds.) BI 2017. LNCS (LNAI), vol. 10654, pp. 3–13. Springer, Cham (2017). https://doi.org/10.1007/978-3-319-70772-3_1
19. Schuller, B., Steidl, S., Batliner, A.: The interspeech 2009 emotion challenge. In: Tenth Annual Conference of the International Speech Communication Association (2009)
20. Wu, X., He, R., Sun, Z., Tan, T.: A light CNN for deep face representation with noisy labels. IEEE Trans. Inf. Forensics Secur. **13**, 2884–2896 (2018)
21. Lee, J., Tashev, I.: High-level feature representation using recurrent neural network for speech emotion recognition. In: Sixteenth Annual Conference of the International Speech Communication Association (2015)

Judgment Prediction

A Judicial Sentencing Method Based on Fused Deep Neural Networks

Yuhan Yin[✉] 🆔, Hongtian Yang, Zhihong Zhao, and Songyu Chen

Nanjing University, Nanjing, China
{yinyuhan,mgl632009}@smail.nju.edu.cn

Abstract. Nowadays, the judicial system has been hard to satisfy the growing judicial needs of the people. Therefore, the introduction of artificial intelligence into the judicial field is an inevitable trend. This paper incorporates deep learning into intelligent judicial sentencing and proposes a comprehensive network fusion model based on massive legal documents. The proposed method combines multiple networks, e.g., recurrent neural network and convolutional neural network, in the procedure of sentencing prediction. Specially, we use text classification and post-classification regression to predict the defendant's conviction, articles of law related to the case and prison term. Moreover, we use the simulated gradient descent method to build a fusion model. Experimental results on legal documents datasets justify the effectiveness of the proposed method in sentencing prediction. The fused network model outperforms each individual model in terms of higher accuracy and stability when predicting the conviction, law article and prison term.

Keywords: Intelligent judiciary · Text classification · Neural network

1 Introduction

With the development of society and the improvement of the judicial ability, the demands of people for judicial services are increasing, and the problems of traditional judicature are increasingly serious. First of all, knowledge reserves and business level of judicial official cannot satisfy social need because of a numerous number of laws and legal theories. In addition, the judicial standard fails to unify and get a fair state since judicial personals have uncertain knowledge reserves. For cumbersome legal provisions and case details, legal practitioners need to do a lot of repetitive work to judge sentencing. These problems have pushed artificial intelligence to the frontline in judicial field [1, 2]. In order to promote the intellectualization of the judicial field, we proposed a judicial sentencing method based on fused deep neural networks. In this method, the prediction of conviction and law article can be abstracted as text classification problems in natural language processing, while the defendant's prison term prediction can be formulated into a regression problem based on text classification. With the continuous improvement of neural network model, it is of great importance to develop a more effective model specifically for such issues to make the judiciary more intelligent.

© Springer Nature Switzerland AG 2019
I. V. Tetko et al. (Eds.): ICANN 2019, LNCS 11730, pp. 213–226, 2019.
https://doi.org/10.1007/978-3-030-30490-4_18

Current research directions include using intelligent lie detectors to assist trials, biotechnical suspect tracking and research on accessorial intelligent sentencing which is to be discussed in this paper. In [3] the authors mentioned that Britain proposed using an evidence-based accessorial system in the prosecution work of the Crown Prosecutor's Office. In 2005, Gao started to take professional research on intelligent sentencing with an emphasis on the crime of Larceny. Based on a massive number of cases, she used support vector machine (SVM) to predict the sentence of the defendant. Intelligent sentencing prediction can give out objective answers on sentencing rationally by using only legal knowledge and allow more people to conduct judicial supervision without understanding the criminal law, which is crucial for constructing a fair social environment.

Natural language processing (NLP) techniques are widely-used in intelligent sentencing prediction. In general, the processing of natural language text classification can be decomposed into four steps, including text preprocessing, text representation, text feature extraction, and text classification model construction. The purpose of text representation is to represent the pre-processed text in the way that computer can understand. The traditional approach is Bag of Words (BoW) [4]. The main shortcoming of this model is that it does not take text context into account. In recent years, Mikolov et al. [5] proposed the Word2Vec model for word embedding. Then, feature extraction mainly includes methods such as word frequency [6], document frequency and Information Gain [7]. In the subsequent step, we need to select the appropriate classifier to train the selected features. Traditional classifiers include SVM [8], nearest neighbor classification, Bayesian classification, decision tree, RBF neural networks, and random forest etc. With the emergence of neural networks, researchers have started to use recurrent neural networks (RNN) for text classification [9]. Kim [10] has applied word embedding to the simple CNN structure to construct a classic text classification model. Mikolov [11] proposed the FastText model, which is a simple and fast model based on BoW. Therefore, on the basis of deep learning, it is an inevitable trend to use the existing neural networks for intelligent judicial sentencing research.

Relying on multiple neural networks, this paper proposes a NLP-based judicial sentencing method. It fuses neural networks such as RNN, CNN, RCNN and FastText to perform sentencing prediction. Specifically, the technical contributions of this work can be summarized as follows: (1) In the issue of judicial sentencing, we compare the performance of a number of different neural networks in prediction. (2) Compared to the ordinary regression model, we proposed the idea of regression after classification can significantly improve the accuracy of regression. (3) We use the simulated gradient descent method to build a fusion model, and the model improves the performance of sentencing prediction. Experimental results show that the accuracies in predicting conviction, law article and prison term by the proposed method are 92%, 91% and 74%, respectively.

The rest of this paper is organized as follows. Section 2 introduces the preliminary knowledge relevant to this work. Section 3 details the model structure and explains the proposed method that combines multiple neural networks. Experimental results are demonstrated in Sect. 4. Finally, Sect. 5 concludes the whole paper and discusses future work directions.

2   Preliminaries

Deep learning is of great significance in natural language processing tasks. In recent years, neural network algorithms have also been frequently applied in text categorization. This section introduces TextCNN, TextRNN and TextRCNN, which will be used in this paper.

TextCNN is an algorithm for text categorization based on convolutional neural networks. It was proposed by Yoon Kim in 2014. Figure 1 shows the structure and mechanism for TextCNN. First of all, Kim convolves the text matrix with filters of different lengths, where the width of the filter is equal to the length of the word embedding. Then he use the max-pooling layer to operate on the vector generated by every filter so that each filter only produces a maximum value of the region. Next, the maximum values generated by different filters are spliced to compose an abstract vector that characterizes the sentence. Finally, the prediction is made relying on this vector. This model is one of the classic models in natural language processing.

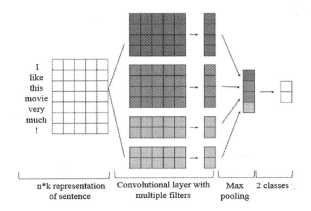

Fig. 1.   TextCNN structure. (adapted from [10])

However, a significant disadvantage of TextCNN is that the convolution and pooling operations lose the order and position information of the words in the text sequence, and it is difficult to capture the semantic information such as negation and antisense in the text sequence. In contrast, RNN can capture sequence information and RNN is a general-purpose model for modeling sequences [12]. Therefore, TextRNN is also one of the networks that NLP scholars are keen on.

In recent years, Bidirectional RNN (Bi-RNN) [13] is used more and more frequently due to its capability of taking more context information into account. The structure of the Bi-RNN is the combination of two unidirectional RNNs. At each moment, there are two RNNs in opposite directions in the input layer, and the output layer is determined by this two unidirectional RNNs. Figure 2 is a Bi-RNN structure expanding over time. In Bi-RNN, there are six unique weights being reused at each moment, including w1, w3 used from the input layer to the forward hidden layer and to the backward hidden layer, w2 and w5 used from one hidden layer to another hidden layer and w4, w6 used from the forward hidden layer and backward hidden layer to the output layer.

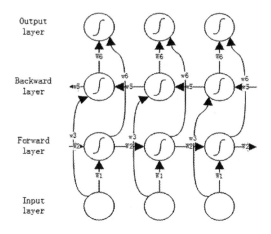

Fig. 2. Bi-RNN structure diagram. (adapted from [13])

There are two common variants of RNN: Gated Recurrent Unit (GRU) [14] and Long Short-Term Memory (LSTM) [15]. GRU has only two gates (update and reset), and it directly passes the hidden state to the next unit. Meanwhile, LSTM has three gates (forget, input, output), and the hidden state is wrapped with the memory cell. GRU and LSTM, either of which is a variant of RNN, have compatible performance in many tasks, and they both perform better than standard RNN. However, due to the difference in their structure, the GRU is less likely to converge because of its fewer parameters, which means the GRU is suitable for the case with less data volume, while the LSTM has better 'memory' effect and better performance when the training data set is large enough.

In 2015, the Chinese Academy of Sciences proposed a combined model of RNN and CNN [16], called RCNN. The RCNN model is one of the models commonly used in recent years. It is based on the two models above, and Fig. 3 shows its structure.

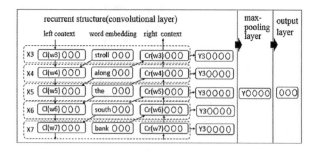

Fig. 3. RCNN structure diagram. (adapted from [16])

In this model, the word embedding of a word is not only the word embedding, but also the vector splicing of the word and its both side neighbors. Therefore, Bi-LSTM will be used for word vectorization before the CNN since it can remarkably improve the relevance of words and the accuracy of text vectors. Then, the constructed Bi-LSTM is connected to the TextCNN, the filter size of which is set as 1, and the rest of the parameters stay unchanged.

3 The Proposed Methods

Judicial sentencing prediction is the procedure of making predictions on the defendant's conviction of crime (task 1), articles of law concerned with the case (task 2) and prison term (task 3) via text analysis on legal documents including the case descriptions and factual statements.

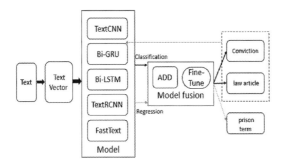

Fig. 4. The intelligent sentencing model structure diagram.

In this paper, the intelligent sentencing model based on fused neural networks is illustrated in Fig. 4. The proposed model aims to predict the conviction and the related law articles in the first place, and then predicts the prison term. For different model results, we propose a fusion method to make model weights adjustments. The final result can be obtained by weighted averaging.

3.1 Data Analysis and Preprocessing

In this section, we analyzes the text data of the legal documents in the training set, conducts targeted preprocessing work and then take these processed data as the input to the next stage in the model training.

Data Analysis
In this section, we analyzes the text data of the legal documents in the training set, conducts targeted preprocessing work and then take these processed data as the input to the next stage in the model training.

In this work, the contents of the legal documents and the input and output format of the model are shown in Fig. 5.

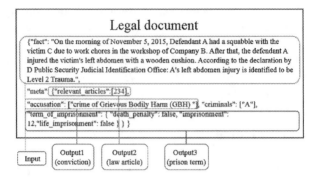

Fig. 5. An example of legal document structure and the Input/Output of the model.

Firstly, we observe the distribution of legal documents, two messages are conveyed on our research: (a) The distribution of convictions and law articles is not uniform, thus it is difficult to make predictions on rare samples. (b) There is an obvious co-occurrence phenomenon between convictions and articles of law.

Then, we analyze the two messages above. For message (a), since the sample data are extremely unbalanced in composition, resampling is necessary before data processing. For message (b), the co-occurrence phenomenon proves that convictions and law articles have the same rules and can be predicted in the same way. It is commonly known that prison term is closely related to the conviction and law articles. So, we prefer the following information topology among the three tasks (Fig. 6).

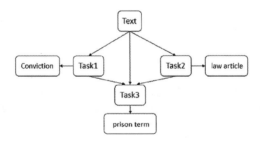

Fig. 6. Topology diagram among three tasks.

Data Processing

This section mainly describes the pre-processing procedure of legal document, and the main steps are as follows.

(a) Resampling. The data of rare samples are made multiple copies of so that model can achieve a more balanced composition of data.
(b) Data extraction. The description text, convictions, articles and prison terms which are the input and output of three tasks, are extracted from the legal documents. At the same time, convictions are converted into indexed values in the list of charges.

(c) Word segmentation [17]: We use Jieba (the Chinese word segmentation tool) for word segmentation. In this step, it is necessary to delete common punctuation symbols because legal documents are supposed to be objective and non-emotional.

(d) Word embedding training: In order to achieve semantic analysis, Word2vec is applied to train word vector and get the corresponding word features of the legal documents. Word2Vec model mainly includes the Continuous Bag-of-Words Mode (CBOW) and the Skip-Gram model. This article uses the Skip-Gram model to represent words as word embedding after word segmentation.

(e) Text truncation: In this experiment, text with different lengths needs to be converted into fixed-length text segment. That is to say, a text length N is set, and any text longer than N should be truncated while text shorted than N will be completed. We analyze the data and know that the length of legal documents mostly is between 200 and 500. Then, the experiments of N from 200 to 500 show that N is the best when it is 350. Because of the particularity of legal documents that the second half contains too much key information, in this experimental we will cut the text from back to front into 350 dimensions.

(f) Text data enhancement processing: In the construction of neural network models, the training data greatly affects the prediction results. In order to make the prediction results more accurate, data enhancement processing is necessary, including shuffle and dropping. This processing will reduce the over-fitting of the model and make the model training process more balanced. Data enhancement is applied as the final step before training to avoid the possible consequence that some deleted data details were not found in the previous steps.

3.2   Models

In this section, the pre-processed text vectors are trained by different deep neural networks that includes CNN, RCNN, Bi-LSTM and Bi-GRU respectively. By continuously adjusting the parameters of the neural network model, the three tasks obtained good experimental results. The parameters and structure are as follows (Fig. 7).

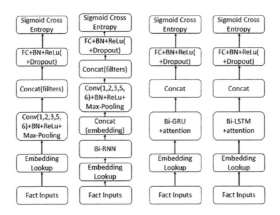

Fig. 7. The parameters and structure of the four neural network models

3.3 Model Fusion

Model fusion is one of the important steps in machine learning. Model fusion not only makes prediction results more accurate, but also can reduce the disadvantages of individual models. This experiment uses a weighted adjustment method that simulates the gradient descent method. Firstly, it is necessary to construct a prediction probability matrix of a singles model, in which the probability matrix in the single model i is P_i. Then the weight W_i is assigned according to the performance of the single model i. Finally, the model calculates the F1 value of the fusion verification set. Among them, score is a function to measure the performance of the model at this time.

In this experiment, CNN, LSTM, RCNN models with good experimental results and FastText with poor experimental results were selected for model fusion.

```
Algorithm 1: Model Fusion
  Input:
 weights, //Array of model weights
 label_list, //a list of output matrices
of different models
 label,   //Correct output matrix of
training set
 lr,    //Learning rate
 k  //The number of iterations
  Output:
 The highest model fusion accuracy F1,
 The weights of the highest accuracy
   (1) calculate the F1 of initial
weights;
   (2) for i = 0 to k do
   (3)  for j = 0 to len(weights) do
   (4)    weights[j] <- weights[j] + lr;
   (5)    calculate score(weights);
   (6)    if score(weights) > F1 then
   (7)       calculate weights[j];
   (8)    else weights[j] <- weights[j] -
lr;
   (9)       calculate score(weights);
   (10)      if score(weights) > F1 then
   (11)         calculate weights[j];
   (12)   endif
   (13) endfor
   (14) update weights;
   (15) if (score(new weights) > F1) then
   (16)    F1 <- score(new weights);
   (17)    record weights;
   (18) endfor
   (19) return F1,weights;
```

$$P = \sum_{1}^{k} w_i P_i \tag{1}$$

$$F1_{last} = score(P) \tag{2}$$

Algorithm 1 describes the algorithmic flow of the proposed network fusion model. Corresponding to lines 3–13, add and subtract the learning rate for the weight of each individual model, then update the weight if F1 is raised. In line 15–17, update the largest F1 and corresponding weight array after each round. After setting the different learning rate and the initial weight, the model fusion process ends with the F1 value stable through multiple iterations.

4 Experimental Results

4.1 Data Set

In this paper, the data set contains a set of legal documents, including 202 convictions, 183 law articles and prison term [18]. Prison term is divided into death penalty, life imprisonment and 0–300 months of imprisonment. This experiment selects 20,000 legal documents as test documents.

4.2 Performance Evaluation

This paper covers the evaluation on multiple classification problems and regression problems. For classification problems, performance evaluation is required through the confusion matrix. Specifically for the two classification problem, sample data can be classified into four categories according to the correct category and the category that predicted by classifier: true positive (TP), false positive (FP), false negative (FN), and true negative (TN). Precision (P), Recall (R) and F1 are used to test the classification accuracy [19].

$$P = \frac{TP}{TP+FP}, R = \frac{TP}{TP+FN}, F1 = \frac{2*P*R}{P+R} \tag{3}$$

Macro-averaging (Macro-P) and micro-averaging (Micro-P) [20] need to be introduced in the case of N classification.

$$Macro_P = \frac{1}{n}\sum_{i=1}^{n} P_i, Macro_R = \frac{1}{n}\sum_{i=1}^{n} R_i,$$
$$Macro_F = \frac{2*Macro_P * Macro_R}{Macro_P + Macro_R} \tag{4}$$

$$Micro_P = \frac{\sum_{i=1}^{n} TP_i}{\sum_{i=1}^{n} TP_i + \sum_{i=1}^{n} FP_i}, Micro_R = \frac{\sum_{i=1}^{n} TP_i}{\sum_{i=1}^{n} TP_i + \sum_{i=1}^{n} FN_i}$$
$$Micro_F = \frac{2*Micro_P * Micro_R}{Micro_P + Micro_R} \tag{5}$$

The evaluation methods of conviction prediction and law article prediction in this paper are as follows:

$$Score_{1,2} = \frac{Macro_F + Micro_F}{2} \tag{6}$$

In the prediction of prison term, if the result of the prediction is V1, the actual term is V2:

$$V = 1 - abs(\log(V1 + 1) - \log(V2 + 1)) \tag{7}$$

$$Score_3 = \frac{\sum_{i=1}^{n} V_i}{N} \tag{8}$$

Score1, 2, 3 represent the accuracy of task 1, 2, 3 respectively. The higher value of score means the classification performs better.

4.3   Experimental Results and Analysis

In this experiment, it is necessary to determine the length of text truncation input into the model before everything else. Taking CNN model as an example, the effects of different text lengths on the performance of the model are shown below. Therefore, 350 dimension is chosen as the most suitable truncation length in this paper (Fig. 8).

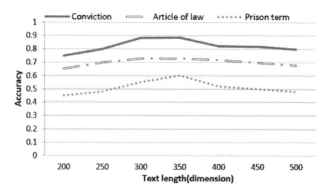

Fig. 8. The Relation of text length and prediction accuracy.

In the experiment, we use the deep neural networks LSTM, GRU, RCNN and CNN to predict the three tasks firstly. In addition, the comparative experiments of FastText and Support Vector Machine (SVM) are carried out. According to the experimental results in the Table 1, the performance based on deep neural networks CNN, RNN and RCNN is better than that of shallow networks like FastText and SVM. SVM has the worst prediction effect because of data imbalance and big data set. Finally, the fusion model can significantly improve the accuracy of sentencing prediction.

Each neural network model has its pros and cons. In order to improve the accuracy of prediction, this paper chooses several networks for model fusion. LSTM, GRU, RCNN and CNN are primary choices in this experiment. FastText tends to have a poor prediction result since its hidden layer is obtained by simply averaging the sum, but this shortcoming can be made up for by RCNN, whose focus on contextual connections. Therefore, FastText is also included in the fusion.

Table 1. Comparison of prediction accuracies.

Model	Conviction (Score1)	Law articles (Score2)	Prison term (Score3)
LSTM	0.90	0.89	0.71
GRU	0.89	0.88	0.70
RCNN	0.88	0.87	0.70
CNN	0.87	0.87	0.69
FastText	0.78	0.78	0.58
SVM	0.71	0.69	0.48
Fusion model	0.92	0.91	0.74

Since the model fusion adopts the simulated gradient descent method, it is possible for model to fall into local optimum. In order to handle this situation, multiple weight adjustments are needed to find the optimal results. After sufficient amounts of experiments, the optimal weights and performance evaluation are found out as follows.

Table 2. Weigh distribution and the score of conviction.

LSTM	GRU	RCNN	CNN	FastText	Score1
1.03	0.78	0.65	−0.53	−0.93	0.92

Table 3. Weigh distribution and the score of law article.

LSTM	GRU	RCNN	CNN	FastText	Score2
0.53	0.33	0.25	0.18	−0.29	0.91

Table 4. Weigh distribution and the score of prison term.

LSTM	GRU	RCNN	CNN	FastText	Score3
0.95	0.69	0.30	−0.06	−0.88	0.74

In Tables 2, 3 and 4, the weights of the fusion model and the experimental results justify that models with good performance should be assigned with large weights, while models with bad performance should be assigned with small weights. Furthermore, if the prediction result of a specific model has a positive impact on the final performance of the fusion model, this model should be assigned a positive weight. On the contrary, a model that has a negative impact should be assigned a negative weight.

Finally, the prediction performance can be improved by 2% to 3% through model fusion, and the global accuracy can reach 92%, 91% and 74%.

Table 5. The top three of the error rate in task 1

Conviction	Crime of scalping relics	Crime of ill-treatment of prisoner	Crime of hijacking a ship or car
Error rate	0.45	0.30	0.25

Having verified the prediction accuracy of the fusion model, it is necessary to further perform an error analysis on the frequency of large deviations. Take task 1 as an example, because the distribution of crimes is uneven, it is unreasonable to compare the error frequency of all categories. In this paper, we mainly analyze the error rate of a category which is the proportion of the number of category's prediction errors to the total quantity of the category. After summarizing the conviction categories of predicting the wrong result, there is a common regularity in convictions with higher error rates is the number of those in the training set does not exceed 500. Among them, the top three in the error rate ranking are crime of scalping relics, crime of ill-treatment of prisoner and crime of hijacking a ship or car. Table 5 lists the error rates of these three categories. We can conclude accordingly that, the categories with high prediction error rates are those categories that have an insufficient number of samples in the train set. It can be expected that the prediction accuracy can be significantly improved given sufficient number of samples.

5   Conclusions and Future Work

This paper introduces deep learning into the field of judicial sentencing, and abstracts intelligent sentencing into text classification in natural language processing and regression after classification. Through the training of CNN, RNN, RCNN, FastText and SVM, the performance of different models is compared in intelligent sentencing. Finally, it is meaningful to analyze and select the corresponding model for fusion to get a better prediction model. In our future research, the experiments will capture the main components in law documents, and then strengthen the useful text fragments while weakening the useless text fragments to highlight the text features. Moreover, we consider adding legal knowledge to further improve the prediction accuracy, making more significant contributions to the study of judicial sentencing based on deep learning. Last but not least, it is essential to improve the accuracy of categories that have an insufficient number of samples in the train set.

Acknowledgment. This paper is supported by the National Key Research and Development Program of China (Grant No. 2018YFC1801605), the Fund of State Key Laboratory for Novel Software Technology at Nanjing University (No. ZZKT2018B01).

References

1. Aletras, N., Tsarapatsanis, D., Preoţiuc-Pietro, D., Lampos, V.: Predicting judicial decisions of the European Court of Human Rights: a natural language processing perspective. PeerJ Comput. Sci. **24**(2), e93 (2016). https://doi.org/10.7717/peerj-cs.93
2. Schild, U.J.: Criminal sentencing and intelligent decision support. In: Sartor, G., Branting, K. (eds.) Judicial Applications of Artificial Intelligence, pp. 47–98. Springer, Dordrecht (1998). https://doi.org/10.1007/978-94-015-9010-5_3
3. Zong, B.: On the application of artificial intelligence in the judgment of criminal proof standard. Sci. Law (J. Northwest Univ. Polit. Sci. Law). https://doi.org/10.16290/j.cnki. 1674-5205.2019.01.004
4. Kantor, P.: Foundations of statistical natural language processing. Inf. Retrieval **4**(1), 80–81 (2001). https://doi.org/10.1023/A:1011424425034
5. Mikolov, T., Sutskever, I., Chen, K., Dean, J., Corrado, G.: Distributed representations of words and phrases and their compositionality. In: Advances in Neural Information Processing Systems (2013)
6. Eszter, B., István, C., Dániel, K., et al.: Race, religion and the city: twitter word frequency patterns reveal dominant demographic dimensions in the United States. Social Science Electronic Publishing (2016). https://doi.org/10.1057/palcomms.2016.10
7. Ahmed, A., Siraj, M.Md., Anazida, Z.: Feature selection using information gain for improved structural-based alert correlation. Plos One **11**(11) (2016). https://doi.org/10.1371/ journal.pone.0166017
8. Sun, A., Lim, E., Liu, Y.: On strategies for imbalanced text classification using SVM: a comparative study. Decis. Support Syst. **48**(1), 191–201 (2010). https://doi.org/10.1016/j. dss.2009.07.011
9. Arevian: Recurrent neural networks for robust real-world text classification. In: Proceedings of IEEE/WIC/ACM International Conference on Web Intelligence (2007). https://doi.org/10. 1109/wi.2007.126
10. Yoon, K.: Convolutional neural networks for sentence classification. Eprint arXiv (2014). https://doi.org/10.3115/v1/d14-1181
11. Armand, J., Edouard, G., Piotr, B., et al.: Bag of tricks for efficient text classification (2016). https://doi.org/10.18653/v1/e17-2068
12. Zhang, H., Xiao, L., Wang, Y., et al.: A generalized recurrent neural architecture for text classification with multi-task learning. In: Proceedings of the International Joint Conference on Artificial Intelligence (2017). https://doi.org/10.24963/ijcai.2017/473
13. Jagannatha, A., Yu, H.: Bidirectional RNN for medical event detection in electronic health records. In: Proceedings of the Conference of the North American Chapter of the Association for Computational Linguistics: Human Language Technologies (2016). https://doi.org/10. 18653/v1/n16-1056
14. Rahul, D., Salemt, F.M.: Gate-variants of Gated Recurrent Unit (GRU) neural networks. In: Proceedings of the IEEE International Midwest Symposium on Circuits and Systems (2017). https://doi.org/10.1109/mwscas.2017.8053243
15. Chen, J., Li, D., Mirella, L.: Long Short-Term Memory-Networks for machine reading (2016). https://doi.org/10.18653/v1/d16-1053
16. Lai, S., Xu, L., Liu, K., Zhao, J.: Recurrent convolutional neural networks for text classification. In: Proceedings of the Association for the Advancement of Artificial Intelligence (AAAI) (2015)
17. Huang, C., Zhao, H.: Chinese Word segmentation: a decade review. J. Chin. Inf. Process. **21** (3), 8–19 (2007). https://doi.org/10.3969/j.issn.1003-0077.2007.03.002

18. CAIL2018: A large-scale legal dataset for judgment prediction. arXiv preprint arXiv:1807. 02478 (2018)
19. Jake, L., Martin, K., Naomi, A.: Points of significance: classification evaluation. Nat. Methods **13**(8), 603–604 (2016). https://doi.org/10.1038/nmeth.3945
20. Yang, Y.: An evaluation of statistical approaches to MEDLINE indexing. In: Proceedings of the Conference of the American Medical Informatics Association (1996). https://doi.org/10. 1023/a:1009982220290

SECaps: A Sequence Enhanced Capsule Model for Charge Prediction

Congqing He[1], Li Peng[1(✉)], Yuquan Le[1], Jiawei He[1], and Xiangyu Zhu[2]

[1] College of Computer Science and Electroic Engineering, Hunan University,
Changsha, China
{hecongqing,rj_lpeng,leyuquan,hejiawei}@hnu.edu.cn
[2] JD Digits, Beijing, China
zhuxiangyu3@jd.com

Abstract. Automatic charge prediction aims to predict appropriate final charges according to the fact descriptions for a given criminal case. Automatic charge prediction plays a critical role in assisting judges and lawyers to improve the efficiency of legal decisions, and thus has received much attention. Nevertheless, most existing works on automatic charge prediction perform adequately on high-frequency charges but are not yet capable of predicting few-shot charges with limited cases. In this paper, we propose a **S**equence **E**nhanced **Caps**ule model, dubbed as SECaps model, to relieve this problem. Specifically, following the work of capsule networks, we propose the seq-caps layer, which considers sequence information and spatial information of legal texts simultaneously. Then we design an attention residual unit, which provides auxiliary information for charge prediction. In addition, SECaps model introduces focal loss, which relieves the problem of imbalanced charges. Comparing the state-of-the-art methods, SECaps model obtains 4.5% and 6.4% absolutely considerable improvements under Macro F1 in Criminal-S and Criminal-L respectively. The experimental results consistently demonstrate the superiorities and competitiveness of SECaps model.

Keywords: Charge prediction · Capsule networks · Few-shot · Focal loss

1 Introduction

The task of automatic charge prediction is to help lawyers or judges to determine appropriate charges (e.g., fraud, robbery or larceny) according to a given case. The automatic charge prediction plays a critical role in many legal intelligent scenarios (e.g., legal assistant systems or legal consulting). The legal assistant system can improve the efficiency of professionals. The legal consulting is benefit for people who are unfamiliar with legal terminology of their interested cases. Therefore, automatic charge prediction is an extremely beneficial topic for many legal intelligent scenarios.

© Springer Nature Switzerland AG 2019
I. V. Tetko et al. (Eds.): ICANN 2019, LNCS 11730, pp. 227–239, 2019.
https://doi.org/10.1007/978-3-030-30490-4_19

Most existing works of automatic charge prediction can be divided into three categories. The first categories are usually mathematical or quantitative [8,17], which are restricted to a small dataset with few labels. The second categories use a lot of manpower to design legal text features, and then the machine learning algorithms are applied. For example, Liu et al. [12] utilize word-level and phrase-level features and K-Nearest Neighbor (KNN) method to predict charges. Liu et al. [13] use Support Vector Machine (SVM) for preliminary article classification, and then re-rank the results by using word level features and co-occurence tendency among articles. Katz et al. [4] extract efficient features from case profiles (e.g., dates, locations, terms, and types). However, the shallow textual features of human designs require a lot of manpower and have limited ability to capture the semantic information of legal texts. Recently, owing to the success of deep neural networks on natural language processing tasks [9], some popular neural network methods apply on automatic charge prediction task [3,14], obtaining attractive performance. For example, Luo et al. [14] propose an attention-based neural network for charge prediction by incorporating the relevant law articles. This work is not yet capable of predicting few-shot charges with limited cases. Hu et al. [3] propose attribute-attentive model to alleviate few-shot charges problem. In the other hand, Zhao et al. [24] apply the capsule network [19] to the text classification scene and achieve attractive performance.

Inspired by the above observations, in this paper we propose a SECaps model. The SECaps model proposes the seq-caps layer, which can consider sequence information and spatial information of legal texts simultaneously. Then the model designs an attention residual unit, which can provide auxiliary information for charge prediction. In addition, the model introduces focal loss [10], which can relieve the problem of imbalanced charges.

To summarize, the main contributions of this paper are:

- We propose a SECaps model that not only considers sequence information and spatial information of legal texts simultaneously, but also has a competitive performance on the problem of few-shot charges.
- SECaps model introduces focal loss, which first appears on object detection problems and is able to alleviate the problem of imbalanced charges to some extent.
- Comparing the state-of-the-art methods, SECaps model achieves 4.5% and 6.4% absolutely considerable improvements under Macro F1 in Criminal-S and Criminal-L respectively. The experimental results consistently demonstrate the superiorities and competitiveness of SECaps model.

2   Model

2.1   Capsule Network

Capsule network proposed by Sabour et al. [19] has shown strong competitiveness in the field of images. Capsule network adopts dynamic routing mechanism, and routes the lower-level capsules to higher-level capsules.

Define lower-level capsules as $u = (u_1, u_2, \cdots, u_n)$ and higher-level capsules as $v = (v_1, v_2, \cdots, v_m)$, where $u_i \in R^d$ is the i-th capsule in lower-level and $v_j \in R^p$ is the j-th capsule in higher-level, d and p represent the dimension of lower-level capsules and the dimension of higher-level capsules respectively. The dynamic routing mechanism follows two steps:

- **Linear transformation.** In this step, an intermediate feature vector $u_{j|i}$ of u_i is produced by multiplying the output u_i by a weight matrix W_{ij}.

$$u_{j|i} = W_{ij}u_i. \tag{1}$$

where W_{ij} is a weight matrix which connects between lower-level u_i and higher-level v_j. There are $n \times m$ weight matrices W_{ij} between two capsule layers. However, the weight matrices W_{ij} produces a large amount of the parameters. In order to reduce parameters, we introduce share weight mechanism, which is similar to Zhao et al. [24]. In share weight mechanism, the connection between all the lower-level capsules and the j-th capsule in higher-level share a common weight matrix W_j, so the intermediate feature vector $u_{j|i}$ is computed as follows

$$u_{j|i} = W_j u_i. \tag{2}$$

- **Clustering for lower-level capsules.** In this step, the dynamic routing mechanism minimizes an agglomerative fuzzy k-means clustering-like loss function as follows:

$$\min_{C,S}\{loss(C, S) = -\sum_{i,j} c_{ij} \langle u_{j|i}, v_j \rangle + \alpha \sum_{i,j} c_{ij}\log c_{ij}\}$$
$$\text{s.t. } c_{ij} > 0, \sum_{j=1}^{n} c_{ij} = 1, \|v_j\| \leq 1 \tag{3}$$

where $C = [c_{ij}]$ is an n-by-m partition matrix, c_{ij} represents the association degree of i-th lower-level capsule $u_{j|i}$ to the j-th cluster s_j, $S = [s_1, s_2, \cdots, s_m]^T$ is m cluster centers. Then, similar to Hinton et al. [19], we use a non-linear "squashing" function to ensure that short vectors get shrunk to almost zero length and long vectors get shrunk to a length slightly below 1,

---

Algorithm 1. Dynamic Routing

Input: $u_{j|i}$, r
Output: v_j
1: for all capsule i in lower-level and capsule j in higher-level: $b_{ij} = 0$.
2: **for** r iterations **do**
3:     for all capsule i in lower-level and capsule j in higher-level:
4:         $c_{ij} = \frac{exp(b_{ij})}{\sum_k exp(b_{ik})}$.
5:     for all capsule j in higher-level capsule:
6:         $s_j = \sum_{i=1}^{m} c_{ij} \cdot u_{j|i}$, $v_j = \text{squash}(s_j)$,
7:         $b_{ij} = b_{ij} + u_{j|i} \cdot v_j$.
8: **end for**
9: **return** v_j

and thus get the higher-level capsule. The formula of "squashing" is described as follows:

$$\text{squash}(s_j) = \frac{\|s_j\|^2}{1 + \|s_j\|^2} \frac{s_j}{\|s_j\|}. \tag{4}$$

Deriving the coordinate descent updates of C and S, we obtain the updates in Algorithm 1 [23].

2.2   Seq-caps Layer

Capsule networks treat a feature as an activity vector, it can be used in many natural language processing (NLP) tasks [24]. Generally, the input of many NLP tasks is a sequence of words which represents a sentence or a text. Each word of the sequence is often transformed into the distributed representation of the word, due to the success of word embeddings [16]. The word distributed representation can be seen as an activity vector, and thus a sequence of words can be seen as a group of capsules. We can use capsule networks in these NLP tasks as long as we set the first layer of capsule networks to words distributed representation of words sequence.

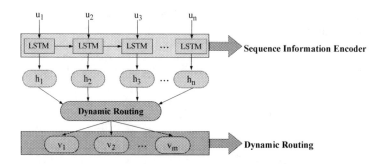

Fig. 1. The framework of seq-caps layer, the input capsules $u = \{u_1, u_2, \cdots, u_n\}$ is lower-level capsules and the output capsules of the seq-caps layer is $v = \{v_1, v_2, \cdots, v_m\}$.

However, the higher-level capsules capture the key information of lower-level capsules by making use of fuzzy clustering. This leads to the higher-level capsules loss the sequence information of the input word sequence. In fact, a word is often highly correlated with its context. Losing sequence information weakens the performance of capsule network in NLP tasks. Therefore, we propose a new basic structure, named seq-caps layer, to enhance the capsule layer by taking the sequence information into account.

Figure 1 shows the framework of seq-caps layer. Suppose the input capsules of the seq-caps layer is $u = \{u_1, u_2, \cdots, u_n\}$, seq-caps layer follows two component:

- **Sequence Information Encoder.** It uses a Long Short-Term Memory [2] (LSTM) encoder as a sublayer to restore sequence information of the input capsules. In this step, we get hidden layer $h_1, h_2, \cdots, h_n = LSTM(u_1, u_2, \cdots, u_n)$.
- **Dynamic Routing.** It transforms the hidden layer to higher-level capsules by using dynamic routing mechanism (Algorithm 1). In this step, we get higher-level capsules $\{v_1, v_2, \cdots, v_m\}$.

2.3   SECaps Model

In charge prediction task, the fact description of a case can also be seen as a sequence of words $x = \{x_1, x_2, \cdots, x_n\}$, where n is length of the fact description, x_i is a word. Given the fact description x, the charge prediction task aims to predict a charge $y \in Y$ from a charge set Y.

In real world, some charges (e.g., *"theft"*, *"intentional injury"*) have a large amount of cases, while others like *"scalping relics"*, *"disrupting the order of the court"* just have few cases. This is the so-called few-shot problem. Traditional models pay much attention to charges which have a large number of cases and thus ignore these few-shot charges. In order to mitigate the effect of few-shot problem, SECaps model combines seq-caps layer with the focal loss [10], in which, seq-caps layer captures the prominent features and the semantic information of legal texts in a better way and focal loss is able to alleviate category imbalances to some extent.

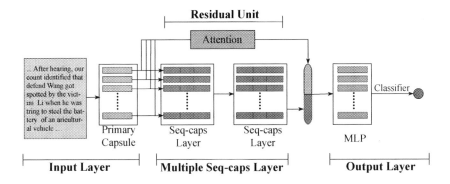

Fig. 2. The architecture of SECaps model, including Input layer, Multiple seq-caps layer, Attention, and Output layer.

SECaps model includes four parts: Input layer, Multiple seq-caps layer, Attention, Output layer. Figure 2 show the architecture of SECaps model.

Input layer: In this part, we treat the fact description of a case as a sequence of words $x = \{x_1, x_2, \cdots, x_n\}$, then, each word of the sequence is transformed to the primary capsule.

Multiple seq-caps layer: This part has two seq-caps layers. We treat the word embeddings as primary capsules, and then transfer primary capsules to higher-level capsules. The seq-caps layer outputs advanced semantic representation which is captured from fact description of a case. Meanwhile, seq-caps layer restores the sequence information of fact description, which is a key factor for charge prediction.

Attention: When the multiple seq-caps layer aggregates primary capsules into higher-level capsules, the model only focuses on the most important legal case's information. Similar to He et al. [1], we propose a novel residual unit to improve the generalization and provide auxiliary information for charge prediction. SECaps model introduces the attention mechanism as the residual unit, to encode the primary capsule which can capture the global context information. Suppose the primary capsules from the input part is $\{t_1, t_2, \cdots, t_n\}$, the residual unit's vector c is computed as follows:

$$e_i = tanh(Wt_i + b) \tag{5}$$

$$\alpha_i = \frac{exp(e_i)}{\sum_j exp(e_j)} \tag{6}$$

$$c = \sum_i \alpha_i t_i \tag{7}$$

where W is a weight matrix and b is the bias.

Output layer: In order to consider prominent features and the global context information together, we first flatten all the feature vectors from the Multiple seq-caps layer, and concatenate with the global context vector c. Then, we use a fully connected network and softmax function to generate the probability $y = (y_1, y_2, \cdots, y_k)$, where k is the number of charges. As for loss function, we apply focal loss to SECaps model. Focal loss is proposed for dense object detection initially, which address the few-shot problem by reshaping the standard cross entropy loss such that it down-weights the loss assigned to well-classified examples [10]. It can be calculate as follows:

$$FL(y_t) = \alpha_t(1 - y_t)^\gamma log(y_t) \tag{8}$$

where y_t is the t-th output of y, $\alpha_t \in [0, 1]$ is weighting factor and γ is the focusing parameter.

3   Experiments

3.1   Dataset and Evaluation Metrics

Datasets. We employ three public datasets[1] [3] for charge prediction, which were published by the Chinese government from China Judgments Online[2].

---

[1] https://thunlp.oss-cn-qingdao.aliyuncs.com/attribute_charge.zip.
[2] http://wenshu.court.gov.cn.

For each case in these datasets are constituted by several parts, such as fact, charges, and attributions. Three datasets contain the same number of charges but the different number of scales, named as Criminal-S (small), Criminal-M (medium) and Criminal-L (large). The statistics of our datasets are reported in Table 1.

Table 1. The statistics of different datasets

Datasets	Criminal-S	Criminal-M	Criminal-L
train	61,589	153,521	306,900
valid	7,755	19,250	38,429
test	7,702	19,189	38,368

Evaluation Metrics. Following previous works on charge prediction [3,14], we employ Accuracy (Acc.), Macro Precision (MP), Macro Recall (MR) and Macro F1 (MF) as our main evaluation metrics.

3.2 Baselines

The same as Hu et al. [3], we select several representative text classification models and two state-of-the-art methods for charge prediction as baselines.

TFIDF+ SVM is a simple machine learning model based on Support Vector Machine (SVM) [21] with linear kernel, extracting text features from term-frequency inverse document frequency (TFIDF) [20] as input. Then two based deep learning model are also to compare with SECaps model, the first is Convolutional Neural Network (CNN) [6] which is to encode fact descriptions with multiple filter widths, and the second employs a two-layer LSTM [2] with a max-pooling layer as the fact encoder.

Moreover, we compared SECaps model with two latest methods, Fact-Law Attention Model [14] and Attribute-attentive Model [3], to future illustrate the effectiveness of SECaps model. Fact-Law Attention Model is an attention-based neural network method for charge prediction, and Hu et al. [3] propose Attribute-attentive Model which can infer the attributes and charges simultaneously.

3.3 Experiment Settings

Since all the case documents have been employed THULAC[3] for word segmentation and set each document maximum length to 500. For the TFIDF+SVM, the experiment is established by extracting the feature size to 2,000 and using SVM with linear kernel for training. Moreover, to make a fair comparison, we establish a set of neural models. We employ word2vec [16] for word embedding

---

[3] https://github.com/thunlp/THULAC-Python.

with size to 100 before the experiment. For the CNN and the LSTM, by setting the filter widths to $\{2, 3, 4, 5\}$ with each filter size to 25 for consistency and the hidden state size to 100 of LSTM respectively. What's more, two recent models proposed by Luo et al. [14] and Hu et al. [3] respectively, the parameters remain the same as the original paper.

SECaps model uses the Adam [7] optimization method to minimize the focal loss [10] over the training data. For hyperparameters of Adam and focal loss, we keep it consistent with the original papers since better performance in their papers. The hyperparameters of two seq-caps layers are shown in Table 2. Then SECaps model utilizes two fully connected layers by setting to 1024×512.

Table 2. Hyperparameters for two seq-caps layers. CapsNums, CapsDims, Routing and Hidden units represent the number of capsules, the dimension of capsules, the number of dynamic routing and the hidden units of LSTM respectively.

Layer	CapsNums	CapsDims	Routing	Hidden units
seq-caps layer 1	10	16	5	200
seq-caps layer 2	5	10	5	128

4   Results and Analysis

4.1   Performance Comparison

Table 3 shows the results of SECaps model and baselines on three datasets. Overall, we find that SECaps model outperforms all previous baselines with a significant margin on three datasets. More specifically, compared to the previous state-of-the-art model [3], our model obtains 4.5%, 2.5%, and 6.4% absolutely considerable improvements across three datasets respectively under MF, which demonstrates that the effectiveness of SECaps model for charge prediction.

Table 3. Charge prediction results of three datasets

Datasets	Criminal-S				Criminal-M				Criminal-L			
Metrics	Acc	MP	MR	MF	Acc	MP	MR	MF	Acc	MP	MR	MF
TFIDF+SVM	85.8	49.7	41.9	43.5	89.6	58.8	50.1	52.1	91.8	67.5	54.1	57.5
CNN	91.9	50.5	44.9	46.1	93.5	57.6	48.1	50.5	93.9	66.0	50.3	54.7
CNN-200	92.6	51.1	46.3	47.3	92.8	56.2	50.0	50.8	94.1	61.9	50.0	53.1
LSTM	93.5	59.4	58.6	57.3	94.7	65.8	63.0	62.6	95.5	69.8	67.0	66.8
LSTM-200	92.7	60.0	58.4	57.0	94.4	66.5	62.4	62.7	95.1	72.8	66.7	67.9
Fact-Law Att. [14]	92.8	57.0	53.9	53.4	94.7	66.7	60.4	61.8	95.7	73.3	67.1	68.6
Attribute-att. [3]	93.4	66.7	69.2	64.9	94.4	68.3	69.2	67.1	95.8	75.8	73.7	73.1
SECaps model	**94.8**	**71.3**	**70.3**	**69.4**	**95.4**	**71.3**	**70.2**	**69.6**	**96.0**	**81.9**	**79.7**	**79.5**

This trend suggests that SECaps model is capable of capturing the advanced semantic representation of legal texts which are crucial for charge prediction.

We propose a novel layer, termed seq-caps, which considers sequence information and spatial information of legal texts simultaneously. Then SECaps model employs multiple seq-caps layer to capture sequence information and advanced semantic representation which has a significant impact for charge prediction. In addition, SECaps model introduces the residual unit and designs an attention mechanism to capture significant auxiliary information of the primary capsule for charge prediction. Consequently, SECaps model obtains state-of-the-art performance on three datasets without any additional ancillary information.

4.2   Few-Shot Charges Comparison

Table 4. Macro F1 values of various charges on Criminal-S

Charge type	Low-frequency	Medium-frequency	High-frequency
Charge number	49	51	49
LSTM-200	32.6	55.0	83.3
Attribute-att. [3]	49.7	60.0	85.2
SECaps model	**53.8**	**65.5**	**89.0**

Following Hu et al. [3], we run a set of experiments to split charges with different frequency to further illustrate the effectiveness of the SECaps model on handling few-shot charges. We divide the charges into three parts according to the frequencies (low-frequency, medium-frequency and high-frequency). Low-frequency is defined as the charges appears less than 10 times (includes 10 times) on Criminal-S, high-frequency is defined as the charges appears more than 100 times (excepts 100 times) on Criminal-S and otherwise belongs to medium-frequency.

Table 4 shows the performance of SECaps model with different frequency on Criminal-S, we report the low-frequency, the medium-frequency and the high-frequency results of MF. From the table, we see that the MF of low-frequency is 53.8% which achieves more than 65% improvements than LSTM-200 and obtains a considerable improvement by 4.1% over the state-of-the-art baseline [3]. SECaps model proposes a seq-caps layer, which can capture advanced semantic representation, and thus relieve the problem of insufficient features for few-shot charge prediction. Specifically, SECaps model has good power on vector representation and time series representation ability, the focal loss has a good performance in handling the problem of unbalanced classification, which can make up for lack of the unbalanced classification problem.

4.3   Ablation Studies

Table 5. Ablation studies comparing SECaps model with different residual units on Criminal-S.

Models	Acc	MP	MR	MF
SECaps model	**94.8**	**71.3**	**70.3**	**69.4**
SECaps$_{w/o\ Attention}$	94.7	67.7	68.1	66.4
SECaps$_{with\ Added\ Unit}$	94.6	66.1	65.3	64.0

In order to evaluate the residual unit for the influence of SECaps model, we conduct a series of ablation studies among various approaches. Table 5 shows the results of various variant approaches.

- **SECaps$_{w/o\ Attention}$** which employs only two seq-caps layers to encode the primary capsules provides less performance when compared to SECaps model. This signifies primary capsules aggregate higher-level capsules which only focuses on the most important legal case's information. It demonstrates that the residual unit is able to improve the generalization. Besides, it proves that the residual unit can provide auxiliary information for charge prediction.
- **SECaps$_{with\ Added\ Unit}$** which employ simply added primary capsule unit instead of attention unit. As can be seen in Table 5, SECaps$_{with\ Added\ Unit}$ model even worse than SECaps$_{w/o\ Attention}$ model. This phenomenon shows that the model brings some noise information if employ simply added primary capsules as the residual unit. Overall, attention unit can pay attention to the important information of primary capsules for charge prediction, which reinforces SECaps model for capturing critical evidence.

4.4   Impact of Hyperparameter

In this section, we first study how the number of capsules affects the performance on Criminal-S. SECaps model is set the number of capsules from 7 to 12 in the seq-caps layer 1 and retained the rest of parameters unchanged. As shown in Fig. 3(a), we find that SECaps model adds more capsules which can capture more vector representation. However, more capsules introduce noise which consequently decreases accuracy. We set the parameter $CapsNums = 10$ in seq-caps layer 1 to balance the ability of representation of higher-level capsules.

We also study how the dimension of capsules affect the performance on Criminal-S. As shown in Fig. 3(b), we find that SECaps model obtains the state-of-the-art performance when the dimension is set to 16. The results indicate larger dimension's capsule is contributing to improve the performance. However, when the dimension of capsules is too large, the model aggregates more information from primary capsules and brings noise information which is helpless for charge prediction. Therefore, the dimension of capsules should not be too large.

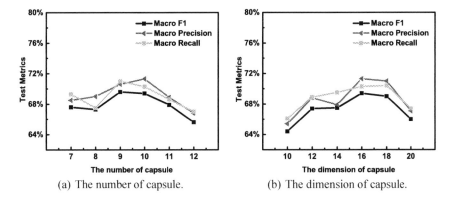

Fig. 3. (a) describes the relationship between MP, MR, MF and the number of capsules in seq-caps layer 1. (b) describes the relationship between MP, MR, MF and the dimension of capsules in seq-caps layer 1.

5   Related Works

Automatic charge prediction plays an important role in the legal area and thus has received much attention. Researchers have proposed many methods for implementing automatic charge prediction. In this paper, these methods are classified into three categories: (1) traditional methods, (2) machine learning methods, and (3) deep neural network methods.

Traditional methods are usually mathematical or quantitative. Kort [8] represents an attempt to apply quantitative methods to the prediction of human events. Nagel [17] applies correlation analysis to case prediction. Keown [5] introduces mathematical (e.g., linear models and the scheme of nearest neighbors) models, which is used for legal prediction. These traditional methods have achieved some effects in certain scenarios, but they are restricted to a small datasets with few labels.

Researchers begin to use machine learning methods to handle charge prediction because of its success in many areas. This type of work usually focuses on extracting features from case facts and then using machine learning algorithms to make predictions. Liu et al. [11,12] use K-Nearest Neighbor (KNN) method to classify criminal charges. Lin et al. [22] fetch 21 legal factor labels for case classification. Mackaay et al. [15] extract N-grams features which creates by clustering semantically similar N-grams. Sulea et al. [18] propose a SVM-based system, which uses the case description, time span and ruling as features. However, these methods only extract shallow text features or manual tags, which are difficult to collect on larger datasets. Therefore, when the amount of the data is large, they will not perform well.

Recently, owning to success of deep neural network in the natural language processing (NLP), computer vision (CV) and speech fields, some works begin to apply the deep neural network to the charge prediction tasks and show a huge performance boost. Luo et al. [14] propose an hierarchical attentional network method, which predicts charges and extracts relevant articles jointly. Hu et al. [3] propose an attention-based neural model by incorporating several discriminative legal attributes. The method proposed in this paper is classified into a deep neural network method.

Our work is also related to the task of text classification. Recently, various neural network (NN) architectures such as Convolutional Neural Networks (CNN) [6] and Recurrent Neural Networks (RNN) have been used for text classification. Zhao et al. [24] explore capsule network with dynamic routing for text classification. From the perspective of using the capsule network, our work is related to Zhao et al. [24].

Our model is loosely inspired from Hu et al. [3], they introduce several discriminative attributes of charges that provide additional information for few-shot charges. Compared with this line of works, although our work also handle the problem of few-shot charges, our work is different from their works, since (1) the strategy of SECaps model in dealing with the problem of few-shot charges is different from the above (2) as far as we know, we are the first to introduce capsule network for charge prediction and achieve the state-of-the-art performance in charge prediction task.

6   Conclusion

In this paper, we focus on the few-shot problem of charge prediction according to the fact descriptions of criminal cases. To alleviate the problem, we propose a SECaps model for charge prediction. In particular, SECaps model employs the seq-caps layer, which can capture characteristics of the sequence and abstract advanced semantic features simultaneously, and then combine with focal loss, which can handle the unbalanced problem of charges. Experiments on the real-world datasets show that SECaps model achieves 69.4%, 69.6%, 79.5% Macro F1 on three datasets respectively, surpassing existing state-of-the-art methods by a considerable margin.

References

1. He, K., Zhang, X., Ren, S., Sun, J.: Deep residual learning for image recognition. In: Proceedings of the IEEE Conference on Computer Vision and Pattern Recognition, pp. 770–778 (2016)
2. Hochreiter, S., Schmidhuber, J.: Long short-term memory. Neural Comput. **9**(8), 1735–1780 (1997)
3. Hu, Z., Li, X., Tu, C., Liu, Z., Sun, M.: Few-shot charge prediction with discriminative legal attributes. In: Proceedings of the 27th International Conference on Computational Linguistics, pp. 487–498 (2018)
4. Katz, D.M., Nd, B.M., Blackman, J.: A general approach for predicting the behavior of the supreme court of the united states. PloS One **12**(4), e0174698 (2014)
5. Keown, R.: Mathematical models for legal prediction. Computer/LJ **2**, 829 (1980)
6. Kim, Y.: Convolutional neural networks for sentence classification. Eprint arXiv (2014)

7. Kingma, D.P., Ba, J.: Adam: a method for stochastic optimization. arXiv preprint arXiv:1412.6980 (2014)
8. Kort, F.: Predicting supreme court decisions mathematically: a quantitative analysis of the "right to counsel" cases. Am. Polit. Sci. Rev. **51**(1), 1–12 (1957)
9. Le, Y., Wang, Z.J., Quan, Z., He, J., Yao, B.: ACV-tree: a new method for sentence similarity modeling. In: IJCAI, pp. 4137–4143 (2018)
10. Lin, T.Y., Goyal, P., Girshick, R., He, K., Dollár, P.: Focal loss for dense object detection. In: Proceedings of the IEEE international conference on computer vision, pp. 2980–2988 (2017)
11. Liu, C.L., Chang, C.T., Ho, J.H.: Case instance generation and refinement for case-based criminal summary judgments in Chinese*. J. Inf. Eng. **20**(4), 783–800 (2008)
12. Liu, C.L., Hsieh, C.D.: Exploring phrase-based classification of judicial documents for criminal charges in Chinese. In: International Conference on Foundations of Intelligent Systems, pp. 681–690 (2006)
13. Liu, Y.H., Chen, Y.L., Ho, W.L.: Predicting associated statutes for legal problems. Inf. Process. Manag. **51**(1), 194–211 (2015)
14. Luo, B., Feng, Y., Xu, J., Zhang, X., Zhao, D.: Learning to predict charges for criminal cases with legal basis, pp. 2727–2736 (2017)
15. Mackaay, E., Robillard, P.: Predicting judicial decisions: the nearest neighbour rule and visual representation of case patterns. Computer/l.J, v.3, pp. 302–331 (1974)
16. Mikolov, T., Sutskever, I., Chen, K., Corrado, G.S., Dean, J.: Distributed representations of words and phrases and their compositionality. In: Advances in Neural Information Processing Systems, pp. 3111–3119 (2013)
17. Nagel, S.S.: Applying correlation analysis to case prediction. Tex. L. Rev. **42**(7), 1006–1017 (1964)
18. Octavia Maria Sulea, Marcos Zampieri, M.V., Genabith, J.V.: Exploring the use of text classification in the legal domain. In: Proceedings of ASAIL Workshop (2017)
19. Sabour, S., Frosst, N., Hinton, G.E.: Dynamic routing between capsules. In: Advances in Neural Information Processing Systems, pp. 3856–3866 (2017)
20. Salton, G., Buckley, C.: Term-weighting approaches in automatic text retrieval. Inf. Process. Manag. **24**(5), 513–523 (1988)
21. Suykens, J.A., Vandewalle, J.: Least squares support vector machine classifiers. Neural Process. Lett. **9**(3), 293–300 (1999)
22. Lin, W.-C., Kuo, T.-T., Chang, T.J., Yen, C.A., Chen, C.J., Lin, S.D.., de Lin, S.: Exploiting machine learning models for Chinese legal documents labeling, case classification, and sentencing prediction. In: Proceedings of ROCLING (2014)
23. Wang, D., Liu, Q.: An optimization view on dynamic routing between capsules. In: 6th International Conference on Learning Representations 2018 (2018)
24. Zhao, W., Ye, J., Yang, M., Lei, Z., Zhang, S., Zhao, Z.: Investigating capsule networks with dynamic routing for text classification (2018)

Learning to Predict Charges
for Judgment with Legal Graph

Si Chen[1], Pengfei Wang[1(✉)], Wei Fang[1], Xingchen Deng[1], and Feng Zhang[2]

[1] Beijing University of Posts and Telecommunications, Beijing, China
chens_bupt@163.com, {wangpengfei,fang_wei,dengxc}@bupt.edu.cn
[2] Information Science Academy of China Electronics Technology Group Corporation,
Beijing, China
feng3982315@163.com

Abstract. The automatic charge prediction aims to predict the result of the judgment through fact descriptions in criminal cases, which is an important application of intelligent legal judgment system. Generally, this task can be formalized into a multi-label prediction task (i.e., we treat fact descriptions as inputs, and charges as labels). Most previous works on this task usually exploit informative features from fact descriptions for prediction while ignoring the charge space information (e.g., co-occurrence relation of charges or descriptions of charges). To better explore the charge space, in this paper, we propose to establish a Legal Graph Network (LGN for short) to solve this problem. Specifically, LGN fuses all the charge information (i.e., charge descriptions or correlations) into a unified legal graph. Based on the legal graph, four types of charge relations are designed to capture informative relations among charges. Then LGN embeds these relations to learn the robust charge representations. Finally both charge representations and fact representations are fed into an attention-based neural network for prediction. Experimental results on three datasets show that the model we proposed can significantly outperform state-of-the-art multi-label classification methods.

Keywords: Multi-label · Legal Graph Network · Charge prediction

1 Introduction

The task of automatic charge prediction aims to train a machine judge to determine the final charges (e.g., theft, robbery or traffic offence.) of the defendants in criminal cases which is an important application of intelligent legal judgment system. This capability, if developed, can either largely assist the tedious daily routine work performed by human judges, or give legal guidance and assistance to people without legal background knowledge. Significant progress has been made in recent years by the development of traditional machine learning methods, such as k-Nearest Neighbor (KNN) [19] and Support Vector Machine (SVM) [9]. Most existing works formalize this task under the text classification framework.

© Springer Nature Switzerland AG 2019
I. V. Tetko et al. (Eds.): ICANN 2019, LNCS 11730, pp. 240–252, 2019.
https://doi.org/10.1007/978-3-030-30490-4_20

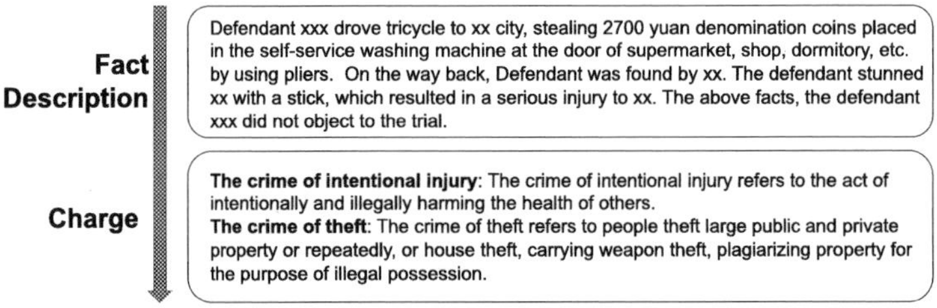

Fig. 1. An example of the judgment case, including the fact description, two charges violated and the charge description of each charge. Two charges have a co-occurrence relation.

For big successes of deep learning method in other areas, such as image [10] and text summarization [17], this method has been explored for charge prediction [15]. Practically, researchers found that charge descriptions (i.e. articles) have played an important role in the charge prediction. Specifically, for those countries with the civil law system (e.g., China, France, and Germany), each charge is defined in detail and accurately. For neural networks, articles are the same significant.

However, the information mining on charge space of existing models is not enough. Existing works always ignore the correlations of charges or the descriptions of charges. We give an example of the judgment case as shown in Fig. 1. People who commit theft in real life always commit the crime of intentional injury at the same time. Considering these co-occurrence of charges can well improve the prediction performance [20,21]. However, we can not learn these information only by existing models, which is a loss for the accuracy of the judgment prediction. On the other hand, the charges with similar descriptive information should have similar representations. The charge descriptions are of great importance to exploit charge space, so we employ the relations about words in charge descriptions.

Inspired by above motivations, we propose to establish a Legal Graph Network (LGN for short) to solve this problem. Specifically, LGN fuses all the charge information into a unified legal graph and defines four relations to construct a label structure. Then LGN embeds all entities relevant with charges to learn the robust charge representations. Finally both charge representations learned from legal graph and fact representations are fed into an attention-based neural network for prediction.

Overall, the major contributions of our work are as follows:

– To the best of our knowledge, this is the first work to fuse all information of charges into a legal graph and design four different types of relations to analysis the charge space for prediction.
– We propose a novel attention mechanism to learn the label-aware fact representation for charge prediction problem.

– We verify the proposed model with three benchmark datasets. The experiments show that our method beats the state-of-the-art multi-label classification methods.

The remainder of this paper is organized as follows: After reviewing the related works in Sect. 2, we present the framework of our method in Sect. 3. Experimental results are presented in Sect. 4 and we conclude this paper in Sect. 5.

2   Related Work

In this section we briefly review two research areas related to our work: legal judgment prediction and multi-label classification.

2.1   Legal Judgment Prediction

Employing automatic analysis techniques for legal judgment has drawn attention from researchers in the legal field for decades. With the development of machine learning, more researchers formalize this task under text classification frameworks. For example, Sulea et al. [11] utilized the fact, articles and time as input based on SVM. Inspired by the success of deep learning methods on classification tasks, researchers began to handle legal judgment prediction by incorporating neural models with legal knowledge. Most of the works encode the fact and use classification models to solve this problem [15]. Some other works handle the legal judgment prediction by reading comprehension models due to its ability to extract semantic [8]. There are many other novel ideas, for examples, Zhong et al. [22] explore and formalize the multiple subtasks of legal judgment under a joint learning framework, and Hu et al. [5] introduce legal attributes of charges into charge prediction task.

2.2   Multi-label Classification

Multi-label classification is fundamentally different from the traditional binary or multi-class classification problems which have been intensively studied in the machine learning literature. Binary classifiers treat class labels as independent target variables, which is clearly sub-optimal for multi-label classification as the dependencies among class labels cannot be leveraged. Multi-class classifiers rely on the mutually exclusive assumption about class labels, which is wrong in multi-label settings. For multi-label data, existing multi-label learning algorithms can be divided into two categories, namely problem transformation and algorithm adaption. The classical problem transformation algorithms include Binary Relevance (BR) [18], Multi-Class Classifications [14], Label Ranking [3] and so forth. On the other hand, algorithm adaption approaches improve traditional single-label classification algorithms, such as Lazy learning [19], Decision trees [12], Kernel learning [1], etc.

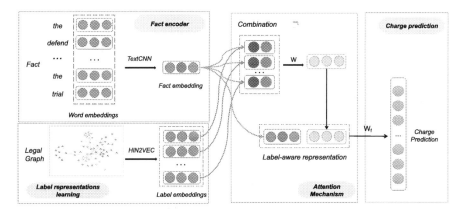

Fig. 2. The overall architecture of the proposed Legal Graph Network (LGN). It is divided into four parts: label representations learning, fact encoder, label-aware attention mechanism and charge prediction.

3   Our Approach

In this section, we first introduce the problem formalization of multi-label classification. We then describe the proposed model in detail. The overall architecture of LGN has been shown in Fig. 2.

3.1   Formalization

We use $X = \{x_1, x_2, ..., x_N\}$ to denote all the fact descriptions, and $y_j = \{y_{j1}, y_{j2}, ..., y_{jC}\}$ represents the charges owned by x_j, where C is the size of charge set and N is the number of instances. Each $y_{ji} \in \{0, 1\}$ indicates whether charge y_{ji} is violated or not. We denote the articles which describe charges by $L = \{l_1, l_2, ..., l_C\}$, where each y_{ji} is defined by l_i.

We assume that we have a set of fact descriptions, charges and articles, denoted as $D = \{(x_j, y_j)_{j=1}^{N}, L\}$. Our goal is to learn a classifier model to predict the optimal charges for each x_j. In the following sections, we will use "label" instead of charge for clarity.

3.2   Legal Graph Network

In the following parts, we first introduce how to establish graph structure. Afterward, we describe the neural encoder of fact description and label-aware attention mechanism. Finally, we show the charge prediction and the loss function of our model.

Label Representations Learning: Specially, we define two types of entities and four types of relations for the legal graph, where the entities include labels

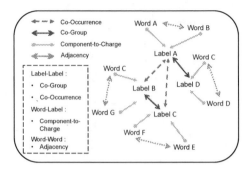

Fig. 3. The Structure of the Legal Graph. There are four relations we choose to reflect the label structure. They are co-occurrence, co-group, component-to-charge and adjacency.

and words. The word is the meaningful keyword extracted from the articles. A label is described by a clear article. Relations include:

- **Adjacency** (word-word): Adjacency describes the adjacency relation among words in the label description.
- **Co-Group** (label-label): Co-Group describes the relation among labels which have similar characteristics. The labels in the same criminal law section belong to the same group.
- **Co-Occurrence** (label-label): Co-Occurrence describes the co-occurrence relation among labels. For the same fact description, the label violated at the same time has this relationship.
- **Component-to-Charge** (word-label): Component-to-Charge describes the relation between word and label. The word in the label description has this relationship with its corresponding label.

The structure of the legal graph is shown in Fig. 3. Based on the generated legal graph, we exploit the local context information of the labels by exploiting the label node context information in the graph. There are many advanced methods for network representation learning or network embedding. In this paper, we adopt HIN2VEC same as [2] to tackle the representation learning problem by training a multi-label classifier whose function is to judge whether two nodes have a specific relationship.

We denote the label embeddings learned by legal graph, which is available on github[1], as $\mathbf{E} = \{e^{(1)}, e^{(2)}, ..., e^{(C)}\} \in R^{C \times D_e}$, where C is the size of label set and D_e is the dimension of the each label embedding. Each row $e^{(i)} \in R^{D_e}$ means the i-th label embedding. Next, our goal is to fix the label embeddings and improve the performance of the model by introducing these label embeddings.

---

[1] https://github.com/Angeliacs/label-embeddings.

Fact Encoder: In juridical field, each fact is described by a set of words. Here we take the bag-of-word representation as the input, and map each word to a vector in a continuous space. Then we aggregate all the word vectors using some operators to form the fact representations.

More formally, let $\mathbf{V} = \{w^{(j)} \in R^{D_w} \mid j = 1, .., N\}$ denote all the word vectors in a D_w -dimensional continuous space. For each fact x_k, we aggregate the word vectors to form the fact representation as follows:

$$v^{(k)} = g(w^{(j)}, j \in x_k) \tag{1}$$

where $g(\cdot)$ denotes the aggregation function to form our inputs same as the TextCNN [6] including a convolution layer, a max-pooling layer and a fully connected layer. $v^{(k)} \in R^{D_f}$ is a vector, where D_f is determined by the number of convolutional filters and parameters of fully connected layer.

Label-Aware Attention Mechanism: Next, given the fact representation $v^{(k)}$ and label embeddings $\mathbf{E} = \{e^{(1)}, e^{(2)}, ..., e^{(C)}\}$, we utilize an attention mechanism to generate label-aware fact representations.

Firstly, we connect $v^{(k)}$ with each label embedding as shown in Fig. 2.

$$\bar{v}^{(k,i)} = v^{(k)} \oplus e^{(i)} \tag{2}$$

where $\oplus$ means $v^{(k)}$ and $e^{(i)}$ are concatenated, $\bar{v}^{(k,i)} \in R^{D_f+D_e}$ is a vector generated by one label.

Then, we define a matrix $\mathbf{W} = \{w^{(1)}, w^{(2)}, ..., w^{(C)}\}$ to calculate the similar scores. $w^{(i)}$ is a vector which means the similar weight between the fact representation and the i-th label embedding. One similar score $a^{(i)}$ is calculated as

$$a_i = w^{(i)}(\bar{v}^{(k,i)})^T \tag{3}$$

where $w^{(i)}$ is a trainable parameter. We use a to represent the combination of all a_i.

$$a = a_1 \oplus a_2 \oplus ... \oplus a_C, \quad a \in R^C \tag{4}$$

As we can see, in our model, a can be regarded as attention scores to softly adjust which label is more likely to be hit for $v^{(k)}$.

Next, we introduce a for $v^{(k)}$ by combination.

$$A = a \oplus v^{(k)} \tag{5}$$

Until now, the label-aware fact representation A is generated.

Charge Prediction: After learning the label-aware fact representation, we put A into a fully connected layer. The predicted distribution $\hat{y}_k$ over all charges is calculated as follows:

$$\hat{y}_k = \mathbf{W}_f A^T + b_f \tag{6}$$

where $\mathbf{W}_f$ and b_f are weights and offsets respectively.

Table 1. Statistics of the datasets: Train and Test are the number of training and test instances respectively. C means the size of label type owned by the dataset. $\hat{L}$ is the average number of documents per label while $\hat{N}$ is the average number of labels per document.

Datasets	Train	Test	C	$\hat{L}$	$\hat{N}$
PKU	14915	3729	98	235.46	1.24
HLS	70726	17682	130	741.45	1.09
CAIL	2140860	535215	202	13705.86	1.03

Optimization: For charge prediction, we use the cross-entropy loss over the training data. The following formula is used in our experiment:

$$Loss = -\frac{1}{N} \sum_{i=1}^{N} \sum_{j=1}^{C} y_{ij} log\left(\sigma\left(\hat{y}_{ij}\right)\right) + \left(1 - y_{ij}\right) log\left(1 - \sigma\left(\hat{y}_{ij}\right)\right) \qquad (7)$$

where σ is sigmoid function. Our object is to minimize the cross-entropy between predicted charge distribution and the ground-truth distribution through Adam [7]. Then we fix the trained parameters to predict a new instance.

4   Experiments

In this part, we first introduce three datasets of criminal cases and strong baselines on classification used in our experiments. After that, we define the evaluation metrics which are suitable for charge prediction task. Finally, we verify the validity of our method through showing the experiment results and our analysis.

4.1   Datasets

We collect and construct three different charge prediction datasets for our experiments, including PKU, HLS, and CAIL. PKU contains criminal cases published by Peking University Law Online as a small dataset. HLS consists of more criminal cases published by the Chinese government from the Handle Case Online. We treat it as a medium dataset. CAIL whose more information can be found on[2] is a benchmark dataset with huge cases for charge prediction task released by the Supreme People's Court of China [16,22,23]. For our own datasets (PKU, HLS), the fact description, articles and charges are obtained by automatically extracting from the cases. Finally, We split all the datasets into two non-overlapping parts, the training set and testing set, with a ratio 8:2 similarly as [15] for several times to do experiments. The statistics of the datasets are shown in Table 1.

---

[2] http://cail.cipsc.org.cn/.

4.2   Baselines

We adopt the following five representative methods of text classification as baselines to compare with our model, including traditional learning methods and deep learning methods.

- SVM [1]: We employ TF-IDF to extract the word features. For implementation, we adopt the publicly available library from LibSVM[3].
- MLKNN [19]: For each new instance, the k instances closest to it can be obtained. The set of labels is determined by the maximum posterior probability. The code is available in sklearn[4].
- FastText [4]: FastText is defined as a lightweight model, which classify by simply adding the word vectors as the text feature.
- BiGRU-ML [13]: We implement a Bi-directional GRU with a max-pooling layer as the fact encoder.
- TextCNN-ML [6]: We implement the CNN with multiple filter widths as text classifier.

4.3   Evaluation Metrics

We employ macro-precision (MP), macro-recall (MR) and macro-F1 (MF) which are widely used in the classification task as evaluation metrics to evaluate the performance of the model on charge judgment prediction. The macro- precision/recall/F1 are calculated by averaging the precision/recall/F1 of each category same as [15].

4.4   Experiment Details

For traditional machine learning models (SVM, MLKNN), we use TF-IDF as the feature extraction method for fact representations and we limit the feature size to 5000 as [16]. Meanwhile, we set k to 7 when training for MLKNN.

For all other models, we adopt the pre-train word embeddings, with embedding size to 300 and frequency threshold set to 20, and we set the maximum document length to 500 words. Furthermore, for TextCNN, we set the filter widths to (3, 4, 5) with each filter size to 256 for consistency, and for BiGRU, we use 128 dimension hidden layers. In our model (LGN), we set the filter widths to (2, 4, 7) with each filter size to 256 for consistency. Meanwhile, when we use HIN2VEC to train the node embedding, we set the dimension of all embeddings to 300. Finally, the learning rate of Adam [7] optimizer is 10^{-3}, and the dropout probability is 0.5. The batch size is set to 128.

---

[3] http://www.csie.ntu.edu.tw/cjlin/libsvm/.
[4] http://scikit.ml/.

Table 2. Charge prediction results of three datasets. "−" means that the result can not be trained due to device memory limitations. Marked black denotes the best results on each dataset. Deviation means the difference of predicting charges performance for several times on each dataset.

Datasets	PKU			HLS			CAIL		
Metrics	MP	MR	MF	MP	MR	MF	MP	MR	MF
MLKNN	62.85	32.23	39.52	55.91	27.67	33.87	-	-	-
SVM	63.13	53.75	56.56	67.77	54.03	56.79	76.96	52.40	59.06
FastText	87.45	55.23	64.81	63.83	56.01	60.22	62.64	56.03	58.05
BiGRU-ML	87.45	59.25	68.01	82.39	52.15	60.62	84.29	56.23	64.87
TextCNN-ML	87.88	60.37	69.35	82.04	54.26	61.99	84.19	54.85	63.20
Our model	**89.14**	**63.57**	**72.28**	**84.31**	**57.38**	**65.31**	**85.55**	**58.60**	**66.99**
Improvement	1.26	3.2	2.93	1.92	1.37	3.32	1.26	2.57	2.12
Deviation	0.02	0.12	0.14	0.03	0.15	0.21	0.05	0.21	0.31

4.5   Result Analysis

As shown in the Table 2, we can see that our model significantly and consistently outperforms all the baselines and has a huge advantage over three datasets and achieves promising improvements (1.26% ∼ 1.92%, 1.37% ∼ 3.2%, and 2.12% ∼ 3.32% absolutely on three metrics respectively). We further compare our model to other baseline methods on charge prediction for the in-depth analysis. Compared against traditional models, manually defined feature extraction methods cause the extracted features limited. Hence, it is not surprising to see that traditional learning methods obtain the worst or the second worst performance in terms of all the evaluating indicator. Deep learning models are superior to the traditional learning methods in the charge prediction task. FastText has faster speed and smaller memory usage as the characteristics it has. However, its performance on various datasets is unstable. BiGRU and TextCNN ignore the representation information of labels, so they are not better than our model. Therefore, drawing conclusion from the above analysis, our method has its own unique advantages.

4.6   Ablation Test

Our method is characterized by the incorporation of various relations to explore the label space. Thus, we design an ablation test to investigate the effectiveness of these relations in the legal graph.

We first construct four graph structures. The latter graph structure considers one more relation than the former. For example, the first graph structure only considers co-occurrence relation, then we add one other kind of relation to the first graph to construct the second graph structure. After inputting both the label representations learned from the various graph structure and fact representations into our proposed model, we see the charge prediction results. If the

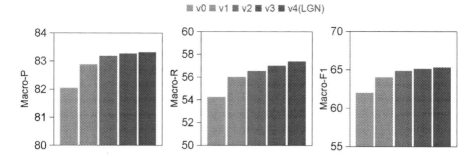

Fig. 4. Verification of the validity of each relation in the legal graph. v0 represents we just employ TextCNN without introducing label information, v1 represents we employ the graph consisting only of co-occurrence relation, v2 represents we employ the graph consisting of co-occurrence relation and component-to-charge relation, v3 represents we employ the graph consisting of co-occurrence relation, component-to-charge relation and adjacency relation, and v4 represents we employ the graph consisting of all relations.

prediction performance is better, we can prove the validity of the newly added relation for charge prediction. We employ the HLS dataset for experiment verification. The experiment results are shown in the Fig. 4. We conclude that for each newly added relation, there is a positive impact on the charge prediction. The improvement of performance is most obvious when the co-occurrence relation is added, increased by 0.8% ∼ 2%. Although the growth rate of other relations are not as obvious as the co-occurrence relation, the extent of the cooperation improvement of the three relations is obvious, increased by 0.5% ∼ 1.3%. We can believe that the co-occurrence relation makes the labels that are most likely to be violated together have a more similar label representations and the latter three relations make the labels with similar text descriptions have more similar representations. All the four kinds of information play a very important role for the charge prediction task.

4.7   Case Study

To better verify the performance of our method, we set up a case study experiment to compare the performance of the best three models (BiGRU [13], TextCNN [6], LGN). Taking HLS as an example, 130 labels are first sorted according to their frequency of occurrences, then we split the sorted labels into 6 groups, where the first five group contains 20 labels in each group and the last group contains 10 labels. In this way, the first group contains the most frequent 20 labels, while the sixth group contains the sparsest 10 labels. Given this, we compare the three models mentioned above on the first group, and we repeat the process five times. Each time we add the next label group into comparison. By this we want to test whether LGN can perform well when it faces with the label imbalance problem. The results are shown in Fig. 5.

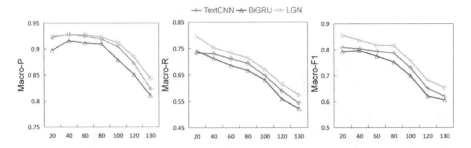

Fig. 5. Performance comparison among different label group size. The x-axis represents the label size modeled, y-axis represents the performance in terms of different evaluations metrics.

We have the following conclusions: (1) When the collection of labels is larger, the difficulty of charge prediction increases. The value of each evaluation indicator shows a downward trend. This is consistent with the expectation that feeding sparse labels will degrade the performance. (2) On the HLS dataset, TextCNN is more suitable than BiGRU, which can beat opponent on almost all indicators both on the small label prediction set and on the large label prediction set. (3) Although our model also conforms to the gradual decrease in the evaluation matrix as sparse labels are added to label predict set, our model achieves all the best results on various sizes of label sets.

5   Conclusion

For the charge prediction, this paper starts with modeling label space via a multi-relations legal graph. In contrast, existing methods ignore the various label space information. We are the first to focus on this problem and propose to fuse all charge space information into a unified legal graph to solve this problem in charge prediction. Moreover, we propose a novel attention mechanism to learn label-free and label-aware fact representation jointly for charge prediction. Finally, we conduct experiments on three real-world datasets, and verify that our approach can outperform many state-of-the-art baseline methods consistently under different evaluation metrics.

Acknowledgment. This research work was supported by the National Natural Science Foundation of China under Grant No. 61802029, and the fundamental Research for the Central Universities under Grant No. 500419741. We would like to thank the anonymous reviewers for their valuable comments.

References

1. Cao, P., Liu, X., Zhao, D., Zaiane, O.: Cost sensitive ranking support vector machine for multi-label data learning. In: Abraham, A., Haqiq, A., Alimi, A.M., Mezzour, G., Rokbani, N., Muda, A.K. (eds.) HIS 2016. AISC, vol. 552, pp. 244–255. Springer, Cham (2017). https://doi.org/10.1007/978-3-319-52941-7_25
2. Fu, T., Lee, W., Lei, Z.: HIN2Vec: explore meta-paths in heterogeneous information networks for representation learning. In: Proceedings of the 2017 ACM on Conference on Information and Knowledge Management, CIKM 2017, Singapore, 06–10 November 2017, pp. 1797–1806 (2017). https://doi.org/10.1145/3132847.3132953
3. Fürnkranz, J., Hüllermeier, E., Loza Menc'ia, E., Brinker, K.: Multilabel classification via calibrated label ranking. Mach. Learn. **73**(2), 133–153 (2008). https://doi.org/10.1007/s10994-008-5064-8
4. Grave, E., Mikolov, T., Joulin, A., Bojanowski, P.: Bag of tricks for efficient text classification. In: Proceedings of the 15th Conference of the European Chapter of the Association for Computational Linguistics, EACL 2017, Volume 2: Short Papers, Valencia, Spain, 3–7 April 2017, pp. 427–431 (2017). https://aclanthology.info/papers/E17-2068/e17-2068
5. Hu, Z., Li, X., Tu, C., Liu, Z., Sun, M.: Few-shot charge prediction with discriminative legal attributes. In: Proceedings of the 27th International Conference on Computational Linguistics, COLING 2018, Santa Fe, New Mexico, USA, 20–26 August 2018, pp. 487–498 (2018). https://aclanthology.info/papers/C18-1041/c18-1041
6. Kim, Y.: Convolutional neural networks for sentence classification. In: Proceedings of the 2014 Conference on Empirical Methods in Natural Language Processing, EMNLP 2014, A meeting of SIGDAT, a Special Interest Group of the ACL, Doha, Qatar, 25–29 October 2014, pp. 1746–1751 (2014). http://aclweb.org/anthology/D/D14/D14-1181.pdf
7. Kingma, D.P., Ba, J.: Adam: a method for stochastic optimization. In: 3rd International Conference on Learning Representations, ICLR 2015, San Diego, CA, USA, 7–9 May 2015. Conference Track Proceedings (2015). http://arxiv.org/abs/1412.6980
8. Long, S., Tu, C., Liu, Z., Sun, M.: Automatic judgment prediction via legal reading comprehension. CoRR abs/1809.06537 (2018). http://arxiv.org/abs/1809.06537
9. Manochandar, S., Punniyamoorthy, M.: Scaling feature selection method for enhancing the classification performance of support vector machines in text mining. Comput. Ind. Eng. **124**, 139–156 (2018). https://doi.org/10.1016/j.cie.2018.07.008
10. Sudharshan, P.J., Petitjean, C., Spanhol, F.A., de Oliveira, L.E.S., Heutte, L., Honeine, P.: Multiple instance learning for histopathological breast cancer image classification. Expert Syst. Appl. **117**, 103–111 (2019). https://doi.org/10.1016/j.eswa.2018.09.049
11. Sulea, O., Zampieri, M., Malmasi, S., Vela, M., Dinu, L.P., van Genabith, J.: Exploring the use of text classification in the legal domain. In: Proceedings of the Second Workshop on Automated Semantic Analysis of Information in Legal Texts co-located with the 16th International Conference on Artificial Intelligence and Law (ICAIL 2017), London, UK, 16 June 2017 (2017). http://ceur-ws.org/Vol-2143/paper5.pdf
12. Tanaka, E.A., Nozawa, S.R., Macedo, A.A., Baranauskas, J.A.: A multi-label approach using binary relevance and decision trees applied to functional genomics. J. Biomed. Inform. **54**, 85–95 (2015). https://doi.org/10.1016/j.jbi.2014.12.011

13. Tang, D., Qin, B., Liu, T.: Document modeling with gated recurrent neural network for sentiment classification. In: Proceedings of the 2015 Conference on Empirical Methods in Natural Language Processing, EMNLP 2015, Lisbon, Portugal, 17–21 September 2015, pp. 1422–1432 (2015). http://aclweb.org/anthology/D/D15/D15-1167.pdf

14. Tsoumakas, G., Vlahavas, I.P.: Random k -labelsets: an ensemble method for multi-label classification. In: Proceeding of 8th European Conference on Machine Learning, ECML 2007, Warsaw, Poland, 17–21 September 2007, pp. 406–417 (2007). https://doi.org/10.1007/978-3-540-74958-5_38

15. Wang, P., Yang, Z., Niu, S., Zhang, Y., Zhang, L., Niu, S.: Modeling dynamic pairwise attention for crime classification over legal articles. In: The 41st International ACM SIGIR Conference on Research and Development in Information Retrieval, SIGIR 2018, Ann Arbor, MI, USA, 08–12 July 2018, pp. 485–494 (2018). https://doi.org/10.1145/3209978.3210057

16. Xiao, C., et al.: CAIL2018: a large-scale legal dataset for judgment prediction. CoRR abs/1807.02478 (2018). http://arxiv.org/abs/1807.02478

17. Yadav, C.S., Sharan, A.: A new LSA and entropy-based approach for automatic text document summarization. Int. J. Semantic Web Inf. Syst. 14(4), 1–32 (2018). https://doi.org/10.4018/IJSWIS.2018100101

18. Zhang, M., Li, Y., Liu, X., Geng, X.: Binary relevance for multi-label learning: an overview. Front. Comput. Sci. 12(2), 191–202 (2018). https://doi.org/10.1007/s11704-017-7031-7

19. Zhang, M., Zhou, Z.: ML-KNN: a lazy learning approach to multi-label learning. Pattern Recogn. 40(7), 2038–2048 (2007). https://doi.org/10.1016/j.patcog.2006.12.019

20. Zhao, H., Rai, P., Du, L., Buntine, W.L.: Bayesian multi-label learning with sparse features and labels, and label co-occurrences. In: International Conference on Artificial Intelligence and Statistics, AISTATS 2018, Playa Blanca, Lanzarote, Canary Islands, Spain, 9–11 April 2018, pp. 1943–1951 (2018). http://proceedings.mlr.press/v84/zhao18b.html

21. Zhong, H., Squicciarini, A.C., Miller, D.J., Caragea, C.: A group-based personalized model for image privacy classification and labeling. In: Proceedings of the Twenty-Sixth International Joint Conference on Artificial Intelligence, IJCAI 2017, Melbourne, Australia, 19–25 August 2017, pp. 3952–3958 (2017). https://doi.org/10.24963/ijcai.2017/552

22. Zhong, H., Guo, Z., Tu, C., Xiao, C., Liu, Z., Sun, M.: Legal judgment prediction via topological learning. In: Proceedings of the 2018 Conference on Empirical Methods in Natural Language Processing, Brussels, Belgium, 31 October–4 November 2018, pp. 3540–3549 (2018). https://aclanthology.info/papers/D18-1390/d18-1390

23. Zhong, H., et al.: Overview of CAIL2018: legal judgment prediction competition. CoRR abs/1810.05851 (2018). http://arxiv.org/abs/1810.05851

A Recurrent Attention Network
for Judgment Prediction

Ze Yang[1], Pengfei Wang[1(✉)], Lei Zhang[1], Linjun Shou[2], and Wenwen Xu[3]

[1] School of Computer Science, Beijing University of Posts and Telecommunications,
Beijing, China
{yangze01,wangpengfe,zlei}@bupt.edu.cn
[2] STCA NLP Group, Microsoft, Beijing, China
lisho@microsoft.com
[3] Information Science Academy, China Electronics Technology Group Corporation,
Beijing, China
xuwenwenustb@163.com

Abstract. Judgment prediction is a critical technique in legal field.
Judges usually scan both of the fact descriptions and articles repeatedly to select valuables information for a correct match (i.e., determine
the correct articles for a given fact description). Previous works only analyze semantics to the corresponding articles, while the repeated semantic
interactions between fact descriptions and articles are ignored, thus the
performance may be limited. In this paper, we propose a novel Recurrent Attention Network (RAN for short) to address this issue. Specifically, RAN utilizes a LSTM to obtain both fact description and article
representations, then a recurrent process is designed to model the iterative interactions between fact descriptions and articles to make a correct
match. Experimental results on real-world datasets demonstrate that our
proposed model achieves significant improvements over the state-of-theart methods.

1 Introduction

Judgment prediction is a crucial and fundamental task in legal field. Given the
fact, one attempts to automatically determine the correct law articles violated,
which plays an important role in both professional and non-professional fields.
For one hand, it can provide a reference for judges to improve work efficiency,
on the other hand, it can provide legal advice to non-legal people.

Judgment prediction has been studied for decades [9,10,23], which is usually
formalized as a multi-label classification problem. Previous works on this task
usually exploit label correlations to improve the prediction performance. For
example, Classifier Chain converts the multi-label task into a chain to model the
correlation between labels [20]. Other methods such as BP-MLL [25], and kernel
method [6] also model the label correlations, however, these methods can only be
used to obtain low-dimensional relationships, and the high-order relationships
are not taken into account.

© Springer Nature Switzerland AG 2019
I. V. Tetko et al. (Eds.): ICANN 2019, LNCS 11730, pp. 253–266, 2019.
https://doi.org/10.1007/978-3-030-30490-4_21

Table 1. An example of the judgment case, including a fact and two articles, where article 263 is the one that the fact violated.

Fact	*At 0:00 on October 9, 2011, the defendant Shi Jiliang, after a prior negotiation, was driven by Wei Mouyi to drive a BYD car and the rest of the people saw the victim Chen took the money at the teller machine...*
Articles	***Article263: Anyone who robs public or private property*** *in a large amount or who has been robbed several times shall be sentenced to fixed-term imprisonment of not more than three years....* ***Article264: Anyone who robs public or private property*** *by violence, coercion or other means shall be sentenced to fixed-term imprisonment of not less than three years and not more than ten years...*

Generally, article semantics (i.e, definition of articles) provide informative properties for judges to make a correct decision. We give an example in Table 1. Specifically, given the fact, a natural approach for judges is that they first browse all articles to select some candidates that are relevant with this fact (e.g, article 263 and article 264 are selected as both of two articles are relevant with robbery, similar information is marked in bold). Then a detail analysis of semantics between fact and candidates are applied to choose correct article. This process repeats several times for judges to make final decision.

Previous works, however, usually ignore label semantics for prediction. In addition, the repeated iterative information between fact and label semantics are ignored, thus the performance may be limited.

In this paper, in order to address these issues, we propose a Recurrent Attention Network (RAN for short). Specially, the RAN utilizes LSTM and self-attention to embed both articles and facts into a low embedding space. After that, a recurrent block is designed to model the repeated interactions between facts and article semantics for a correct matching. To summarize, we make the following three main contributions:

- We formalize the judgment prediction task into a matching task to analyze the semantics matching between law articles and fact.
- We design a novel architecture of recurrent block to model the repeated semantic interactions between articles and facts.
- We conduct efficient experiments outperforms other baselines. Further analysis demonstrates the effectiveness of our proposed recurrent attention mechanism.

The rest of our paper is organized as follows. After a summary of related work in Sect. 2, we describe the problem formalization of judgment prediction and our proposed model in Sect. 3. We provide experiments and evaluations in Sect. 4. Section 5 concludes this paper and discusses future directions.

2   Related Work

In this section, we briefly review two research areas related to our work: judgment prediction and attention mechanism.

2.1   Judgment Classification

Judgment prediction has been studied for a long time. At the early time, the researchers model legal predictions via statistical analysis [13,19]. Recent attempts consider this task under text classification framework, the researchers usually extract efficient features from text and make use of machine learning methods [1,9,11] to learn a judgment prediction model. Inspired by the success of neural networks [3,12,17], researchers began to introduce neural network for modeling this task. Luo et al. proposed an attention-based neural network method to jointly model the judgment prediction task and the relevant article extraction task in a unified framework [15]. Hu et al. proposed an attribute-attentive charge prediction model to infer the articles and charges simultaneously [8].

As we can see, all of these works usually learn the mapping from fact to article, and ignore the semantic information of the article definition. Wang et al. introduced unified Dynamic Pairwise Attention Model for crime classification over articles [23]. In their work, a pairwise attention model based on article definitions was incorporated into the classification model to help alleviate the label imbalance problem, however, their work ignore the interactive information between fact and article definition.

In our work, we try to fuse both the repeated interactive information and the article semantic information into a unified model for judgment prediction.

2.2   Attention Mechanism

Attention mechanism is a technology widely used in neural networks. It is a method for automatically weighting a given input in order to extract important information. This mechanism was first used in the field of computer vision [18]. For instance, when we appreciate a painting, we first see the whole painting, then focus our attention on the part that attracts us and ignore the background information. The attention mechanism was first introduced into the field of NLP by machine translation [2], which method uses the attention mechanism between the source language and the target language to handle translation and alignment simultaneously. Luong et al. extended the previous work and proposed global and local attention [16]. Yin et al. performs the attention operation on the feature map for subsequent operations and achieved good results [24].

Many of the current works are based on a new attention mechanism called the self-attention mechanism [5,14]. In their works, the self-attention mechanism independently performed attention calculations on the original input and target input. Vaswani et al. replaced the RNN with the attention mechanism to build the entire model framework and proposed a multi-headed attention mechanism [22]. In their work, advanced results were achieved. Tan et al. proposed a deep attention neural network to model semantic role labeling with a self-attention sub-layer [21].

Our model is also related to the attention mechanism, but the main difference is that we utilize the article definition as external information, and we use a recurrent attention block to capture multiple repeated interaction attention information between fact and article to support the judgment prediction.

3   Our Approach

In this section, we first introduce the problem formalization of judgment prediction. After that, we then describe the proposed **RAN** model in detail. Finally, we present the learning and prediction procedure.

3.1   Formalization

We use $X = \{x^{(1)}, x^{(2)}, ..., x^{|X|}\}$ to denote all the facts, and $\mathcal{C} = \{y^{(1)}, y^{(2)}, ..., y^{(|C|)}\}$ for the set of all possible articles. $|X|$ and $|C|$ represent the total number of facts and labels. We use $\mathcal{L} = \{l^{(1)}, l^{(2)}, ..., l^{(|C|)}\}$ to represent the label description, $Y^{(i)}$ is a set of binary variables with $|C|$ elements, the j-th element is 1 or 0 to indicate whether the article is violated. In the following sections, we will use "label" instead of article for clarity.

Given all the facts X and label set $\mathcal{C}$, our task is to find an optimal $Y^{(i)}$ for a given fact $x^{(i)}$.

3.2   RAN

In this section, we present our **R**ecurrent **A**ttention **N**etwork (**RAN**) in details. Figure 1 shows the architecture of our model. Specifically, our model consists of three layers. Firstly, the encoder layer utilizes **LSTM** and self-attention to embed both label definitions and facts into a low-dimensional space. Secondly, the recurrent layer models the process by which judges repeatedly read the facts and label descriptions to obtain the repeated mutual information. Finally, the output layer gives the final prediction result of our model.

Encoder Layer. In juridical field, each fact and label is described by a set of words. We take the one-hot word representation as the input, and we map each word to a vector in continuous space.

More formally, let $x = \{w_1, w_2, w_3, \ldots, w_m\}$ be a fact with m words, $l = \{w_1, w_2, w_3, \ldots, w_n\}$ be a label definition with n words, and w_i is the bag-of-word representation of i-th word. Let $\mathbf{V}^I = \{\boldsymbol{v}_t^I \in \mathbb{R}^{D_v} | t = 1, \ldots, N\}$ denote all the word vectors in a continuous space.

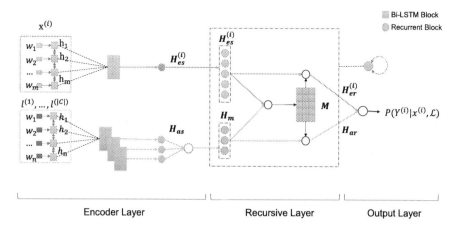

Fig. 1. The overall architecture of the proposed Recurrent Attention Model (RAN).

For each fact and label definition, we aggregate the word vectors to form the fact representation and label representation, a bidirectional **LSTM** (Bi-LSTM) is used to compute the hidden states for each word at step t as Eq. (1):

$$\overrightarrow{h_t} = \overrightarrow{\text{LSTM}}(\overrightarrow{h}_{t-1}, w_t)$$
$$\overleftarrow{h_t} = \overleftarrow{\text{LSTM}}(\overleftarrow{h}_{t-1}, w_t) \tag{1}$$

With the Bi-LSTM, we obtain the hidden representation of the i-th word by concatenating the hidden state of two directions, $h_t = [\overrightarrow{h_t}; \overleftarrow{h_t}]$, then the fact x and the label l are mapped into continuous representations $H_e = [h_1, h_2, \ldots, h_m]$, $H_a = [h_1, h_2, \ldots, h_n]$, respectively.

As we all known, different words have different importance in one sentence. Inspired by the idea of self-attention [22], we use self-attention to get the weighted fact and label representations H_{es} and H_{as}.

Recurrent Layer. In the judicial judgment, a judge carefully reads the fact to obtain the important information, and select relevant articles as candidates, then a detail analysis of semantics between fact and the candidate articles are applied to decide final result, this process is often repeated several times to make the final determination. Different from Cui et al. [4], instead of using a simple interactive attention between source and target text. We design a recurrent attention block to model the judge's repeated reading behavior.

Through encoder layer, we get the word-level representations of fact and label, H_{es} and H_{as} respectively. We use aggregation operation to get sentence-level representations of all labels as follow:

$$H_m = [c(H_{as}^{(1)}), c(H_{as}^{(2)}), \ldots, c(H_{as}^{(|C|)})] \tag{2}$$

Where c is a aggregation operation, which average the word-level representations to form the sentence-level representations of each label.

Then, we calculate the matching score matrix M between label representation and fact's word-level representations as follows:

$$\mathbf{M}(j,k) = H_m(j) \cdot H_{es}(k) \tag{3}$$

where $M \in \mathbb{R}^{|C|*|x|}$, each value represent interactive value between fact's word and each label.

After getting the matching score matrix $\mathbf{M}$, we apply a column-wise softmax function to get probability distributions in each column, where each column represents an independent attention, and we use $\alpha(t)$ represent the label-level attention of each fact word at each step t, which can be seen as a fact word to label attention:

$$\alpha(t) = softmax(\mathbf{M}(1,t), \mathbf{M}(2,t), \dots, \mathbf{M}(|C|,t))$$
$$\alpha = [\alpha(1), \alpha(2), \dots, \alpha(|x|)] \tag{4}$$

Then we average all the $\alpha(t)$ to get an averaged label-level attention $\alpha' \in \mathbb{R}^{|C|}$, where the averaging operation do not break the normalizing condition:

$$\alpha' = \frac{1}{|x|} \sum_{i=1}^{|x|} \alpha(t) \tag{5}$$

In the same way, we can use row-wise softmax to get label to fact word attention $\beta' \in \mathbb{R}^{|x|}$. So far, we have obtained both sides attention α' and β'. Our motivation is to simulate the behavior of judges reading article and fact alternately. We propose a recurrent structure. Intuitively, this operation is continuously looped to learn the important mutual semantic information. The calculation process is shown as follows:

$$H_{es} = H_{es} + H_{es} \mathbf{W}^{\alpha'} \alpha'$$
$$H_m = H_m + H_m \mathbf{W}^{\beta'} \beta' \tag{6}$$

Where $\mathbf{W}^{\alpha'}$ and $\mathbf{W}^{\beta'}$ is dimension transformation matrix. This process will be repeated several times as described above, after which we will get H_{er} and H_{ar}, representing H_{es} and H_m of the last circulation. They contain multi-level semantic interaction information for fact and label to support correct matching.

Output Layer. To integrate the fact and global label information, we use both fact side and label side feature to predict the final result for a given instance in the output layer. The probability distribution over all labels is calculated as follows:

$$\boldsymbol{v}_{er} = g(H_{er}) = \frac{1}{n} \sum_{t=1}^{n} \boldsymbol{v}_{er}(t)$$

$$\boldsymbol{v}_{ar} = g(H_{ar}) = \frac{1}{n} \sum_{t=1}^{n} \boldsymbol{v}_{ar}(t)$$

$$\boldsymbol{v}_f = \boldsymbol{v}_{er} \oplus \boldsymbol{v}_{ar}$$
$$\boldsymbol{v}_o = \mathbf{W}^o \boldsymbol{v}_f + b^o$$

Here, g is the operation of average, $\boldsymbol{v}_{er}$ represent the context representation of fact, $\boldsymbol{v}_{ar}$ is the averaged representation of all labels, which represent global label feature. $\oplus$ represent concatenate operation, $\mathbf{W}^o$ and $\mathbf{b}^o$ are learnable parameters.

3.3   Learning and Prediction

In order to learn parameters of **RAN** model, we use the stochastic gradient decent algorithm. We adopt binary cross-entropy loss in the training process as follows:

$$l = -\frac{1}{n}\sum_{i=1}^{n}\sum_{j=1}^{|\mathcal{C}|}[G^{(i)}(j)log(\sigma(\boldsymbol{v}_o^{(i)}(j))) + (1 - G^{(i)}(j))log(1 - \sigma(\boldsymbol{v}_o^{(i)}(j)))] \quad (7)$$

where σ is the sigmoid function $\sigma(x) = \frac{1}{1+e^{-x}}$, $G^{(i)}(j) \in \{1,0\}$ is a binary variable representing whether the label $y^{(j)}$ is violated by the instance $x^{(i)}$.

With the learned parameters, for each instance $x^{(i)}$, we can get the probability distribution of each label. With a threshold t, we can get the label set for the instance $x^{(i)}$, the calculation process is as follows:

$$Y^{(i)}(j) = \begin{cases} 1, & \text{if} \quad \mathbb{I}(\sigma(v_o^{(i)}(j))) > t \\ 0, & \text{else} \end{cases}$$

Where $\mathbb{I}$ is indication function, $Y^{(i)}(j)$ represent j-th element of $Y^{(i)}$, consider the label $y^{(j)}$ with output probability higher than t as the related label of $x^{(i)}$.

4   Experiment

In this section, we evaluate our proposed model on three real-world datasets. We first introduce the datasets, the experimental settings, then we compare our **RAN** with the baselines to demonstrate its effectiveness. Finally, we provide the analysis and discussion of experimental results.

4.1   Dataset

The experiments were evaluated on 3 real-world datasets:

- **CJO:** This dataset consists of 114576 samples, which dataset was collected by us from China Judge Online[1]. We removed the articles that appear less than 30 times because the data could not be used for training.
- **CAIL small:** This dataset is a criminal case dataset for competition released by the Supreme People's Court of China[2], and the dataset consists of fact, as well as the article involved in each instance, the charges of the defendants, and the term of penalty.

---

[1] https://wenshu.court.gov.cn/.
[2] http://cail.cipsc.org.cn/.

- **CAIL2018:** This dataset is the first large-scale Chinese legal dataset for judgment prediction [27]. CAIL2018 is a dataset, which is several times larger than other datasets in existing works.

The statistics of datasets is shown in Table 2. We split all the datasets into two non-overlapping parts, the training set and testing set, with a ratio 8:2.

Table 2. Basic statistics of the three datasets for experiments.

Dataset	Number of samples	Relevant articles	Average fact length	Average article size
CJO	114,576	137	825	1.17
CAIL small	204,231	183	263	1.27
CAIL 2018	1,710,856	183	279	1.04

4.2 Evaluation Metrics

Following the previous work, we use following evaluation metrics to evaluate the performance of models:

- **Jaccard similarity coefficients:** The Jaccard similarity coefficients is a widely used multi-label classification metric, it measures the similarity between two label sets, and it is defined as the size of the intersection divided by the size of the union of the label sets.
- **Macro-averaging:** macro-averaging is also a widely used metric in multi-label classification, which metric is calculated by counting the total true positives, false negatives, and false positives of each label, then calculate precision, recall, f1 for each label, and take their unweighted mean as macro-precision, macro-recall, macro-F_1.

4.3 Baselines

We adopt three types of baselines for comparison, including shallow model, nerual network based model, and attention based model.

- **KNN:** KNN [26] is a popular first-order multi-label method. Based on statistical information derived from the label sets of the neighboring instances of an unseen instance and use Bayesian inference to select assigned labels.
- **BR:** A first-order multi-label method [6]. In this model, transforms a multi-label classification with L labels into L single label classification, each classifier is a binary classifier by ignoring the correlations between labels, then unite all results of classifiers.
- **CC:** Classifier Chains [20] is a novel chaining method that can model label correlations while maintaining an acceptable computational complexity. This model train L classifiers with L labels, each next classifier is trained on the input space and all previous classifiers in the chain.

- **CNN:** A second-order multi-label method, which uses a convolution network for input representation [12], then inputted to linear layer followed by a sigmoid function to output the probabilities over the label space. The multi-label soft margin loss is optimized.
- **BiLSTM:** [7] which method is also a second-order method, and is a common way to model text and can get long-term associations.
- **DPAM:** DPAM [23] is a neural judgment prediction model by capture correlation between labels using a attention mechanism.

For all models, we set the maximum sentence length to 500 words. For shallow model, these model takes bag-of-words TF-IDF features as input, and uses chi-square to select top 5,000 features [15]. For other models, we set the evidence representation and article representation size to 256. The size of the vocabulary is 10,000 and out-of-vocabulary (OOV) words are replaced with unk. We use Adam optimization method to minimize the loss over the training data, we set the learning rate to be 0.001. Specially, Each LSTM in the **Bi-LSTM** is of size 128. For the CNN based models, we set the filter widths to $(3, 4, 5)$ with each filter size to 128 for consistency.

4.4   Comparison Against Baselines

We compare our model **SAN** with the state-of-the-art baseline methods on judgment classification. The performance results on three datasets are shown in Table 3, MP, MR, MF and JS represent macro-precision, macro-recall, macro-F_1 and Jaccard similarity coefficients, respectively (the percentage numbers with omitted). The best performance in each case is underlined.

Table 3. Comparison between our method and all baselines on three datasets.

Dataset	Metrics	Shallow model				Neural network based model		Attention based model	Our model
		KNN	BR	CC	SVM	CNN	BiLSTM	DPAM	RSAN
CJO	MP	59.49	74.28	72.33	67.68	78.53	78.81	79.39	**81.52**
	MR	32.14	50.84	53.22	51.37	54.16	54.96	55.60	**55.75**
	MF	38.85	57.41	58.60	55.77	61.40	62.17	62.79	**63.34**
	JS	53.25	79.40	82.02	83.55	80.25	80.40	80.76	**80.96**
CAIL small	MP	31.75	41.59	42.12	43.07	78.32	79.93	80.35	**81.23**
	MR	20.11	30.23	32.49	39.66	54.73	57.77	62.03	**64.90**
	MF	22.93	33.57	35.58	40.14	61.35	63.98	67.42	**69.49**
	JS	38.85	59.74	62.59	71.98	74.12	75.09	76.00	**77.42**
CAIL 2018	MP	28.88	40.42	38.91	40.82	80.83	82.94	82.78	**84.01**
	MR	16.59	26.95	28.86	31.53	56.66	56.08	57.15	**57.52**
	MF	19.68	30.65	31.59	34.01	63.51	63.36	64.44	**64.92**
	JS	70.28	88.34	90.57	90.92	94.61	94.61	94.39	**94.68**

From the result, we have the following observations:

- It is not surprising that **KNN** and **BR** obtain the worst performance in terms of all evaluation metrics, these two methods covert multi-label to single label classification, and ignore the label relation.
- **CC** approach perform better than **KNN** and **BR**, which verify that modeling the correlation among multiple labels can improve the performance. But with the error propagation, the improvement is limited.
- The Neural network based models perform significantly better than shallow models. We take **CNN** as an example, comparing with the best shallow model (**CC**), the improvement on CAIL small dataset over MP, MR, MF, and JS is around 36.2%, 22.24%, 25.77% and 11.53% respectively. It demonstrates that the neural network based model can effectively model text semantic information. This is also corresponding with the previous findings.
- Attention based Model (**DPAM**) achieve better performance than most text classification models (excluding **RAN**), which indicates that the article semantic information are integrated evidence.
- Our **RAN** obtains the best performance on all the evaluation metrics. Comparing with **DPAM**, **RAN** achieves significant improvement with the consideration of repeated interaction information between evidence and law articles. For example, compare with **DPAM** on CAIL Small, the relative performance improvement on MP, MR, MF, and JS is around 0.88%, 2.5%, 2.07%, 1.42%, respectively.

The experiments support our hypothesis, it's important to model the repeated mutual semantic information between evidence and article.

4.5   Analysis and Discussion

In this section, we first investigate the impact of the number of recurrent layer, then we utilize ablation test to explore the effectiveness of different layer.

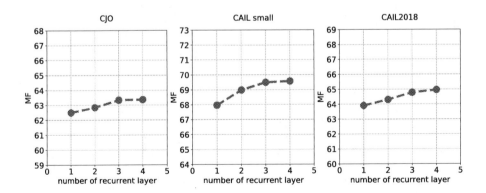

Fig. 2. The performance of different number of recurrent layers on three datasets.

The Impact of Recurrent Layer. We perform the performance of our model on three datasets when the number of recurrent layers $n \in \{1, 2, 3, 4\}$, and the results are shown in the Fig. 2.

From the results, we can get the following observations: (1) As the number of recurrent layer n increases, the performance increase too. (2) As the number of n increases, the performance gain between two consecutive trials decreases. (3) It also indicates that after 3 layers, we have obtained stable information, and if we continue to increase the number of recurrent layer, there will be less performance improvement.

Ablation Test. To further illustrate the significance of **RAN**, we evaluate the performance under difference scenario. We remove the recurrent layer (**R-r** for short), self-attention layer (**R-s** for short) to experiment separately. Result are shown in Table 4.

Table 4. The ablation experiment on CAIL small.

Dataset	Method	MP	MR	MF	JS
CJO	**DPAM**	79.39	55.60	62.79	80.76
	R-s	80.36	55.02	62.85	80.77
	R-r	78.78	54.56	61.97	80.35
	RAN	81.52	55.75	63.34	80.96
CAIL small	**DPAM**	80.35	62.03	67.42	76.00
	R-s	80.2	64.94	68.98	76.58
	R-r	79.37	62.08	66.75	76.93
	RAN	81.23	64.9	69.49	77.42
CAIL2018	**DPAM**	75.26	58.04	63.33	94.39
	R-s	75.3	58.06	63.9	94.64
	R-r	74.33	57.54	62.65	94.41
	RAN	77.69	58.69	64.88	94.68

We have the following findings: (1) Only the self-attention layer is retained, and the result is generally worse than **DPAM**. This is because the label that is confusing cannot be effectively distinguished due to the lack of associated information of the label. (2) Only keep the recurrent layer, the result is slightly better than **DPAM**, because the recurrent layer can effectively use the interactive attention mechanism. **DPAM** effectively utilizes the interaction information between the evidence and the label. (3) By combining the self-attention and recurrent attention mechanisms, **RAN** uses the important information obtained by self-attention for recurrent interaction, which enables the model to obtain more effective information.

This further testifies that the recurrent layer is capable of helping the model to acquire repeated semantic information for improving judgment prediction. f

5   Conclusion

In this paper, we propose an Recurrent Attention Network that can simulate the repeated reading behavior of judge, which method can utilize the semantic mutual information between evidence and article, Extensive experimental results show that the proposed model outperform the baselines. Further analysis demonstrates that our model not only obtain label correlation information, but also capture the multiple informative attention with the recurrent block.

In the future, we will seek to explore the following directions: (1) We will study how to improve the performance of the judgment prediction if more information is used as external knowledge. (2) Since judgment prediction has explicit logical reasoning properties, we will seek the interpret ability of the model to better understand what the model does.

Acknowledgement. This research work was supported by the National Natural Science Foundation of China under Grant No. 61802029, and the fundamental Research for the Central Universities under Grant No. 500419741. We would like to thank the anonymous reviewers for their valuable comments.

References

1. Aletras, N., Tsarapatsanis, D., Preotiuc-Pietro, D., Lampos, V.: Predicting judicial decisions of the european court of human rights: a natural language processing perspective. PeerJ Comput. Sci. **2**, e93 (2016). https://doi.org/10.7717/peerj-cs.93
2. Bahdanau, D., Cho, K., Bengio, Y.: Neural machine translation by jointly learning to align and translate. arXiv preprint arXiv:1409.0473 (2014)
3. Bordes, A., Glorot, X., Weston, J., Bengio, Y.: Joint learning of words and meaning representations for open-text semantic parsing. In: Proceedings of the Fifteenth International Conference on Artificial Intelligence and Statistics, AISTATS 2012, La Palma, Canary Islands, Spain, 21–23 April 2012, pp. 127–135 (2012)
4. Cui, Y., Chen, Z., Wei, S., Wang, S., Liu, T., Hu, G.: Attention-over-attention neural networks for reading comprehension. In: Proceedings of the 55th Annual Meeting of the Association for Computational Linguistics, ACL 2017, Volume 1: Long Papers, Vancouver, Canada, 30 July–4 August 2017, pp. 593–602 (2017). https://doi.org/10.18653/v1/P17-1055
5. Devlin, J., Chang, M., Lee, K., Toutanova, K.: BERT: pre-training of deep bidirectional transformers for language understanding, pp. 4171–4186 (2019)
6. Elisseeff, A., Weston, J.: A kernel method for multi-labelled classification. In: International Conference on Neural Information Processing Systems: Natural and Synthetic, pp. 681–687 (2001)
7. Graves, A., Schmidhuber, J.: Framewise phoneme classification with bidirectional lstm and other neural network architectures. Neural Netw. **18**(5–6), 602–610 (2005). https://doi.org/10.1016/j.neunet.2005.06.042
8. Hu, Z., Li, X., Tu, C., Liu, Z., Sun, M.: Few-shot charge prediction with discriminative legal attributes. In: Proceedings of the 27th International Conference on Computational Linguistics, COLING 2018, Santa Fe, New Mexico, USA, 20–26 August 2018, pp. 487–498 (2018)

9. Katz, D.M., II, M.J.B., Blackman, J.: Predicting the behavior of the supreme court of the united states: a general approach. CoRR abs/1407.6333 (2014)

10. Keown, R.: Mathematical models for legal prediction. John Marshall J. Inf. Technol. Priv. Law **2**(1), 29 (1980)

11. Kim, M.-Y., Xu, Y., Goebel, R.: Legal question answering using ranking SVM and syntactic/semantic similarity. In: Murata, T., Mineshima, K., Bekki, D. (eds.) JSAI-isAI 2014. LNCS (LNAI), vol. 9067, pp. 244–258. Springer, Heidelberg (2015). https://doi.org/10.1007/978-3-662-48119-6_18

12. Kim, Y.: Convolutional neural networks for sentence classification. In: Proceedings of the 2014 Conference on Empirical Methods in Natural Language Processing, EMNLP 2014, A meeting of SIGDAT, a Special Interest Group of the ACL, Doha, Qatar, 25–29 October 2014, pp. 1746–1751 (2014)

13. Kort, F.: Predicting supreme court decisions mathematically: a quantitative analysis of the "right to counsel" cases. Am. Polit. Sci. Rev. **51**(1), 1–12 (1957)

14. Lin, Z., et al.: A structured self-attentive sentence embedding (2017)

15. Luo, B., Feng, Y., Xu, J., Zhang, X., Zhao, D.: Learning to predict charges for criminal cases with legal basis. empirical methods in natural language processing, pp. 2727–2736 (2017)

16. Luong, T., Pham, H., Manning, C.D.: Effective approaches to attention-based neural machine translation. In: Proceedings of the 2015 Conference on Empirical Methods in Natural Language Processing, EMNLP 2015, Lisbon, Portugal, 17–21 September 2015, pp. 1412–1421 (2015)

17. Luong, T., Sutskever, I., Le, Q.V., Vinyals, O., Zaremba, W.: Addressing the rare word problem in neural machine translation. In: Proceedings of the 53rd Annual Meeting of the Association for Computational Linguistics and the 7th International Joint Conference on Natural Language Processing of the Asian Federation of Natural Language Processing, ACL 2015, Volume 1: Long Papers, Beijing, China, 26–31 July 2015, pp. 11–19 (2015)

18. Mnih, V., Heess, N., Graves, A., Kavukcuoglu, K.: Recurrent models of visual attention. In: Advances in Neural Information Processing Systems 27: Annual Conference on Neural Information Processing Systems 2014, Montreal, Quebec, Canada, 8–13 December 2014, pp. 2204–2212 (2014)

19. Nagel, S.S.: Applying correlation analysis to case prediction. Tex. L. Rev. **42**, 1006 (1963)

20. Read, J., Pfahringer, B., Holmes, G., Frank, E.: Classifier chains for multi-label classification. Mach. Learn. **85**(3), 333–359 (2011). https://doi.org/10.1007/s10994-011-5256-5

21. Tan, Z., Wang, M., Xie, J., Chen, Y., Shi, X.: Deep semantic role labeling with self-attention. In: Proceedings of the Thirty-Second AAAI Conference on Artificial Intelligence, (AAAI 2018), the 30th innovative Applications of Artificial Intelligence (IAAI 2018), and the 8th AAAI Symposium on Educational Advances in Artificial Intelligence (EAAI 2018), New Orleans, Louisiana, USA, 2–7 February 2018, pp. 4929–4936 (2018)

22. Vaswani, A., et al.: Attention is all you need. In: Advances in Neural Information Processing Systems 30: Annual Conference on Neural Information Processing Systems 2017, Long Beach, CA, USA, 4–9 December 2017, pp. 6000–6010 (2017)

23. Wang, P., Yang, Z., Niu, S., Zhang, Y., Zhang, L., Niu, S.: Modeling dynamic pairwise attention for crime classification over legal articles. In: The 41st International ACM SIGIR Conference on Research and Development in Information Retrieval, SIGIR 2018, Ann Arbor, MI, USA, 08–12 July 2018, pp. 485–494 (2018). https://doi.org/10.1145/3209978.3210057

24. Yin, W., Schütze, H., Xiang, B., Zhou, B.: ABCNN: attention-based convolutional neural network for modeling sentence pairs. TACL **4**, 259–272 (2016)
25. Zhang, M.L., Zhou, Z.H.: Multilabel neural networks with applications to functional genomics and text categorization. IEEE Trans. Knowl. Data Eng. **18**(10), 1338–1351 (2006)
26. Zhang, M.L., Zhou, Z.H.: ML-KNN: a lazy learning approach to multi-label learning. Pattern Recogn. **40**(7), 2038–2048 (2007). https://doi.org/10.1016/j.patcog.2006.12.019
27. Zhong, H., Zhipeng, G., Tu, C., Xiao, C., Liu, Z., Sun, M.: Legal judgment prediction via topological learning. In: Proceedings of the 2018 Conference on Empirical Methods in Natural Language Processing, pp. 3540–3549 (2018)

Text Generation

Symmetrical Adversarial Training Network: A Novel Model for Text Generation

Yongzhen Gao⬤ and ChongJun Wang$^{(\boxtimes)}$⬤

National Key Laboratory for Novel Software Technology,
Nanjing University, Nanjing 210046, China
gaoyz95@outlook.com, chjwang@nju.edu.cn

Abstract. Text generation has always been the core issue in the field of natural language processing. Over the past decades, Generative Adversarial network (GAN) has proven its great potential in generating realistic synthetic data, performing competitively in various domains like computer vision. However, the characteristics of text discretization limit the application of GANs in natural language processing. In this paper, we proposed a novel Symmetrical Adversarial Training Network (SATN) which employed symmetrical text comparison mechanism for the purpose of generating more realistic and coherent text samples. In the SATN, a Deep Attention Similarity Model (DASM) was designed to extract fine-grained original-synthetic sentence feature match loss for improving the performance of generative network. With DASM, the SATN can identify the difference between sentences in word level and pay attention to relevant meaningful words. Meanwhile, we utilize the DASM loss to compensate for the defect of the objective function in adversarial training. Our experiments demonstrated significant improvement in evaluation.

Keywords: Adversarial training · Attention mechanism · Symmetrical comparison

1 Introduction

With the widespread usage of social media, such as Facebook and Twitter, large amounts of text data is generated in people's daily lives. Automatically coherent text generation from real-world scenarios becomes a fundamental issue in many applications like dialogue generation [16] and machine translation [1]. However, previous works concentrated more on task-specific applications with supervised manner [23], which ignore text generation in common scenarios.

In the last decade, generating synthetic sentence by simulating the distribution over real-world data became a popular method [27,29,31]. In these papers, the most general approach to simulate data distribution is via Recurrent Neural Networks [6] (RNN) with neuron cells passing computation and weights. Besides, with the usage of embedding technique proposed by Mikolov et al. [19], we can

ⓒ Springer Nature Switzerland AG 2019
I. V. Tetko et al. (Eds.): ICANN 2019, LNCS 11730, pp. 269–280, 2019.
https://doi.org/10.1007/978-3-030-30490-4_22

handle text data more conveniently. Recently, RNNs with long short-term memory (LSTM) cells have shown excellent performance in text classification and text generation [9]. Apart from this, Convolutional Neural Network (CNN) proposed by Krizhevsky et al. [12] also showed great performance. The previous models trained CNN with Maximum Likelihood Expectation (MLE) [11] function to generate new sentences from given training sentence samples [25]. Other than this, some models reconstruct sentence features with an encoder-decoder model [5]. Besides, auto-encoder model [14] also lack the capability of extracting fine-grained sentence features. In practice, realistic statement space do not necessarily map to the generated statement space, which is always a key issue for text generation task.

Generative adversarial network (GAN) proposed by Goodfellow et al. [7] becomes a popular solution for generating synthetic data with a discriminative network, which can distinguish whether synthetic data is like original samples or not independently. However, inherent defects of text discretization hinder the development of GAN in the field of text generation. Recently, a method of short text generation was proposed by Lin et al. [17] and performed well. However, long text generation and discretized text processing are not well solved and still remain a problem.

Over the last two years, the attention model has been widely used in various types of machine learning tasks such as image recognition and speech recognition. For smoothing the generated text semantics, we extend the advantage of attention mechanism by matching sentence word-level features of original and synthetic sentences with the deep attention similarity model (DASM). In our work, the DASM is able to compute the similarity between the generated and original sentence fine-grained word-level feature. To evaluate the integrity of generated sentence, Papineni et al. [20] proposed a method to evaluate the integrity of synthesis data, which called bilingual evaluation understudy (BLEU) score.

In this paper, We proposed a framework called Symmetrical Adversarial Training Network (SATN) which used the idea of symmetrically sentence word-level feature match. And the feature match utilize information provided by real-world and synthetic sentence samples to calculate the similarity information match loss. The key contributions of this paper are summarized as following:

- We proposed a novel symmetrical adversarial training network model for text generation.
- We use sentence word-level feature relationship between original and synthetic sentence to smooth sentence semantics.
- We generate high quality and coherent sentences in a holistic way.

2   Related Work

Generating high quality sentences from existing text data is always not only challenging but important for many useful applications. In the last decade, many novel methods with great progress have been proposed in the direction of adversarial models [7] and sequence-to-sequence models [26].

On the one hand, generative adversarial network have drawn significant attention and showed vitality [8]. It turns out that GAN is very effective and successful and has been used in some fields in machine learning such as computer vision tasks of images generations [10,22,28]. GANs introduced a competition between a generator and a discriminator, where the discriminator can be considered as a judiciary which use the loss function to distinguish fed data is true or not. Zhang et al. [30] first tried to apply adversarial training in text generation and constructed a text-GAN model for convergent output with a smooth approximation. Yu et al. [27] adopted a different method which used text errors as a reward for enhanced learning, and trained the model in a feed-forward manner to update the generator network with an enhanced learning exploration. Kusner et al. [13] designed a new objective function which give an approximate output to deal with the discrete tokens in text generation. Pfau et al. [21] optimized previous GAN by combining policy-only and value function-only methods in a reinforcement learning model. MaliGAN proposed by Che et al. [4] changed the original objective function in GAN and put forward a set of training techniques to decrease the potential overfitting problems.

On the other side, feature match also became a new method used in data recognition and other fields. Brown et al. [3] provided an approach to automatically achieve panoramic image stitching by using feature match. And the model proposed by Zhang et al. [31] provided a different ideal model that alleviate the weak coherency and model collapse problems by matching the latent feature distribution of real and generated sentences.

3   Symmetrical Generative Adversarial Network

As shown in the Fig. 1, the proposed symmetrical adversarial training network (SATN) has two main components: the adversarial training model and deep attention similarity model (DASM). We will describe these two models in the following sections.

3.1   Generative Adversarial Network

Assume that we have a real-world sentence corpus $S = \{s_1, s_2 \cdots s_N\}$, where N is the number of sentences, and each sentence $s_i = \{w_{i,1}, w_{i,2}, \cdots, w_{i,j}\}$, $w_{i,j} \in W$, where W is the vocabulary of candidate tokens in raw sentences from corpus S. The goal of the model is to train a θ-parameterized generative model G_θ, which can generate coherent sentences $T = (t_1, t_2 \cdots t_N)$, where $t_i = \{w_{i,1}, w_{i,2}, \cdots, w_{i,j}\}$, and a ϕ-parameterized discriminator model D_ϕ to distinguish whether the sequences is original sentence or synthesized sentence.

As shown in Fig. 1, the proposed adversarial training network is composed of generator G, which takes the original sentence as input and outputs word-level features and synthetic sentence, and discriminator D. Generator mainly consists of two parts, feature extractor and encoder-decoder module. Feature extractor will act as text features extractor and data source of next stage in DASM.

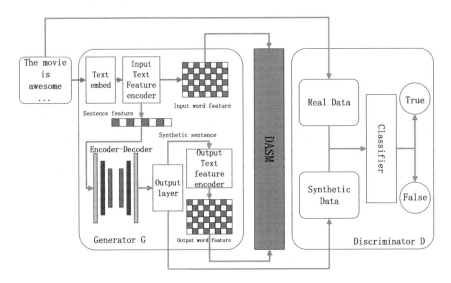

Fig. 1. The architecture of the proposed SATN. Green lines represent the flow of data. While the generator is responsible to generate the corresponding sentence, the discriminator judges where fed input sentence vector from. The module between these two components is the DASM, which was trained with the original and synthetic sentence word level feature. During the training stage, the DASM loss was put into the total loss function to improve the performance of the adversarial training network. (Color figure online)

We use LSTM network to implement this function. As a features extractor, it has two outputs: the word-level features $\hat{x} \in \mathrm{R}^{B*D*L}$ and the sentence-level features $x \in \mathrm{R}^{D*L}$, where L is the length of sequence length. Among these two kinds of features, the sentence-level features will be put into an encoder-decoder module. And then Sentence vector is computed in a sequence-to-sequence model. Above all, the dimension of word features will be reduced to $\hat{x} \in \mathrm{R}^{D*L}$ in DASM, and computed with the synthetic sentence word-level features $y \in \mathrm{R}^{D*L}$. At the end, the DASM loss will be added into total loss function and optimized by Adam-optimizer. Other than this, the adversarial training G-loss and D-loss are also part of total loss.

In order to generate coherent sentence in the proposed model, we replace the original objective function with a redefined one as

$$L = L_{AT} + \lambda L_{DASM} \tag{1}$$

Here, λ is a hyperparameter to balance different losses in (1). L_{AT} is the overall loss of adversarial training network, which is calculated as:

$$L_{AT} = -1/2E_{t \in P_G}[log(D(t))] - 1/2E_{s \in P_{true}}[log(D(s))] \tag{2}$$

The encoder-decoder module constitute the text generator by a sequence-to-sequence model. And we take its sequence generating loss as part of generator loss. Before fed into the sequence-to-sequence model, each word of real sentence will be embedded into a $k-$dimension word vector

$$x_{i,j} = W_e[w_{i,j}] \tag{3}$$

where $W_e \in R^{k,V}$ is a word embedding [19] matrix and V is the vocabulary size. This sequence-to-sequence model is composed of two LSTM network which transform a real sentence vector s_i into a synthetic sentence t_i. In the encoder-decoder module, the probability of jth word in a length T sentence $t_{i,j}$ given the real sentence word embedded vector $x_i = W_e * s_i$ is defined as

$$p(t_i|s_i) = p(t_{i,1}|s_i) \prod p(t_{i,j}|s, t_{i,1}, \cdots, t_{j-1}) \tag{4}$$

and each token in sequence can be rewritten in (5):

$$p(y_i|W_e[s_i]) = p(y_1|x_{1:L}) \prod_{t=2}^{T} p(y_l|y_{1:l-1}, x) \tag{5}$$

where y and L represent each token vector in each sentence t_i and the length of sentence generated in (5). By the previous definition, the probability of sentence can be calculated. Generally, the first token vector y^1 will be generated from x, and other words in the sentence followed are then generated sequentially by the LSTM network unless the following token is $<EOS>$ (the end token in sequence generation).

As defined in the above equation, we can rewrite the (5) as:

$$P(y_1, y_2, \cdots, y_L'|x_1, x_2, \cdots, x_L) = \prod_{l=1}^{L'} p(y_l|v, y_1, y_2, \cdots, y_{l-1}) \tag{6}$$

In the equation, L' represent the generated sentence length, and each probability p represents the distribution by a softmax function over all words in vocabulary.

Object Function: Given the sentence corpus S, our expectation is to generate coherent and meaningful sentence response T. Considering different requirements in our proposed model, different network structures are used in the two components. Among them, we use a CNN network, which constructed by blocks consisted of convolution layer and maxpooling layer, in discriminative model. So, the iterative objective function consists of following two aspects:

$$L_D = minimize(-E_{s \in S} log D_s - E_{t \in T} log[1 - D(t)]) \tag{7}$$

$$L_G = maximize(\prod_{i=1}^{L} p(y_i|x, y_{1:i-1})) \tag{8}$$

where L_G is the sequence generative probability given S, and L_D represent the expectation of discriminator. However, inconvenience will occur when we compute the maximize problem, so we rewrite (8) as:

$$L_G = minimize(-\sum_{i=1}^{L} \log p(y_i|x, y_{1:i-1}))$$

(9)

In the training procedure, the generator G an discriminator D are trained alternatively and accept adjustment from the DASM. And the DASM loss L_{DASM} will be introduced in Subsect. 3.2.

3.2 Deep Attention Similarity Model

The DASM model used in our method map features of generated and real sentence data into a common subregion semantic space and compute the fine-grained loss between their word-level similarities. The comparison of word-level feature between original sentence data and generated sentence data in DASM is symmetrical like a mirror, this is why we named it symmetrical adversarial training network. In this case, though text has a discrete nature, the similarity between original sentence and its synthetic coherent sentence output can still be found.

As mentioned above, the feature extractor has a function of text word-level features extraction. In the model, we designed two feature extractor with the same architecture, one is for input original sentence data and the other is for the output generated sentence data. Word-level features extracted from original sentence are computed with its synthetic sentence word-level features. As we can see in the Fig. 1, We design a output sentence feature extractor. The generated sentence feature matrix $\hat{y} \in R^{D*L}$ has the same shape as $\hat{x} \in R^{D*L}$. Its ith column is the word vector of the ith word in sentence. So we define the DASM-score to evaluate the coherence of generated and original sentence and calculate the features mapping pair based on a deep attention model.

The similarity matrix for pairs of word-level features is calculated by $c = \hat{y}^T \hat{x}$, where $c \in R^{D*T}$ and $c_{i,j}$ represent the word-word similarity between the i-th and j-th word of generated and real word. And in practice, we find that normalizing the similarity matrix makes result better. So the final score function is:

$$\hat{c} = \frac{exp(c_{i,j})}{\sum_{1}^{L} exp(c_{i,j})}$$

(10)

And then, the score matrix is fed into attention model to compute the match vector. f_{DASM} is the attention function used with weight matrix W_{DASM}, where $w_{i,j}$ in W_{DASM} is the attention factor that determines how much attention is paid to the features pair. And finally, we design the similarity matrix in a more suitable way as:

$$V(x_i, y_i) = \frac{f_{DASM}(\hat{y}^T \hat{x}}{||\hat{y}^T||||\hat{x}||})$$

(11)

The DASM loss was optimized in total loss function, in which the DASM parameters is trained with adversarial training networks parameters together. We took an approach like [24] and compute the probability of synthesis sentence data like

$$P(y|x) = \frac{exp(\gamma V(x_i, y_i))}{\sum_1^B (\gamma V(x_i, y_i))} \tag{12}$$

where B is batch-size of training batch, x, y is a batch-size tokens vector, and γ is a hyperparameter used for smoothing the matching process. Finally we define the DASM loss function with negative log posterior probability method and the DASM loss is computed as

$$L_{DASM} = -\sum_1^b logP(y|x) \tag{13}$$

In summary, we proposed a framework composed of adversarial training network and DASM. Among these two components, adversarial training network model works as a producer to generate qualified 'products' and accept the fine-grained guidance from the DASM. We applied our proposed model in text generation work and get a better performance.

Algorithm 1. SATN

Input: generator policy G_θ, discriminator policy D_ϕ, DASM policy M_ψ, sentence corpus S

Initialize G_θ, D_ϕ with random weight θ, ϕ

Pre-train G_θ using MLE on S

Generate samples using G_θ

Pre-train D_ϕ via minimize the cross entropy

repeat

    for train-epochs **do**

        Randomly choose sentences data $S_{part} \in S$, extract features in extractor

        Generate sequence $T_{1:T}$ with sentence feature $X_{i:N}$ by G_θ

        Update generator parameters in G_θ

        Distinguish generated sequence $T_{1:N}$ by (5)

        Update discriminator parameters in D_ϕ

        Calculate total loss by (1)

        Optimize total loss and update parameters

    end for

until SATN converges

---

4   Experiment

The experiment consists of three parts: training settings, synthesis data experiment, result and discussion. These three parts will be introduced in the following subsection.

4.1   Train Settings

Training Settings. To test the efficiency of our proposed model, we designed and implemented a simulation test on a Amazon book review data set, which consists of more than 8 million reviews text. We preprocess the data by eliminating sentences which are not clear or with too many errors. Finally we took about 2 million sentence text from the original corpus. What's more, we also had a test on IMDb movie review dataset, which consists of different kinds of movie review text.

In the generator of adversarial training network, we took a randomly initialized LSTM network as feature extractor and designed a LSTM-based encoder-decoder module. And a CNN network was designed as a discriminator. The generator was pre-trained with maximum likelihood estimation and the discriminator was pre-trained with cross entropy. In the adversarial training network, we can simulate the distribution of original sentence by minimizing the cross-entropy loss and make generated sentence more like artificial. During the training phase, we used generator G to synthesize about 50000 samples. However we still need a more accurate way to evaluate what we generate. We chose to evaluate the generated sentence quality with bilingual evaluation understudy score (BLEU) [20], a metric measuring algorithm scored by calculating similarity between the original and generated sequences. BLEU is an algorithm for evaluating the quality of sentence text which are generated from original natural language. This approach focus on compare the similarity between generated texts and references obtained from the original corpus. In our experiment, we mainly set the n-gram as 2 to 4 (BLEU-2, BLEU-3, BLEU-4), where in book reviews most comments composed of 2 to 4 words tokens or phrase, for review evaluation.

Three generative models are chosen as the baselines for SATN. The first model is the Policy Gradient with BLEU (PG-BLEU). In the PG-BLEU algorithm, policy gradient decrease by the score of BLEU. The second model we consider is variational autoencoder (VAE) [2]. In the training of the VAE model, we increased the KL divergence between the prior and approximated posterior. The third one is seqGAN [27]. We followed the author's guidelines of running experiments techniques. For BLEU score evaluation, we follow the strategy of using entire test set as reference. At the training stage, we use these models to generate sequence samples and calculate their BLEU score. And finally, we compare the differences in their effects. The result are shown in following tables.

4.2   Result and Discussion

Result. In order to verify the performance of our proposed model in the text generation scenarios, we applied the proposed SATN to generate coherent book and movie reviews from Amazon review dataset and IMDb dataset. While training with Amazon book review dataset, we chose 25% of up to 8 million sentence statement, about 2 million sentences, as a train corpus. In the Amazon review experiments, we used sentences of 60 words or less as corpus, and we did not give a prior special structure rule in order to avoid the influence of human factors. And when we tested SATN on IMDb dataset, we choose sentences of 120 to 200 words for the purpose of long text generation. We use BLEU [20] score as an evaluation method to score the similarity between the generated texts and the original texts in corpus.

The BLEU scores in the tables showed the performance of proposed SATN and compared methods. The performance of models on the Amazon book review dataset is shown in Table 1. In all measured metrics, SATN shows its significant performance compared to baseline models, the higher BLEU scores demonstrate that the sentence generated by SATN has high quality in imitating the details of real text. The result for SATN are presented in Table 4. The sentences generated by SATN are grammatically and semantically reasonable compared to those produced by baseline models. To evaluate the performance of SATN in longer text generation, we conduct our model in IMDb movie review dataset. We chose review text that satisfies a certain number of words. The experiments results are shown in Table 2. The result demonstrates that the proposed model also has a significant effect on long text generation. Long text generation has always been a difficult problem among text generation problems. The key to the issue is that errors will accumulate in the long-term dependency capture of sequences in long text generation as the length of the sentence grows. To solve this problem, we introduced a symmetrical comparison of word-level feature in DASM and experiment indicated our imagine. Since BLEU scores may not be sufficient for evaluating synthetic text generation quality, we also took some text judged by human on questionnaires as a supplement, with which we can figure out whether people can distinguish authenticity between original and generated sentences. In the questionnaires, each sentence will be judged by human, and if one sentence is regarded as a real one it gets 1 score, and 0 score otherwise. We conduct the test with text generated on Amazon review dataset. And finally the sum mean score for each model is calculated in total. For fairness, the test questionnaire was randomly distributed. Table 3 showed the result. The performance on two models indicates that sentences generated by SATN are of higher readability and conformity than those generated by SeqGAN, though still lower than ground truth. A few samples are illustrated in Table 4. As can be seen from the sentences in the table, the generated sentences are more advantageous in semantic connections.

Table 1. BLEU scores performance on Amazon book review dataset

Model	PG-BLEU	VAE	SeqGAN	SATN	p-value
BLEU-2	0.654	0.668	0.730	0.763	$<10^{-6}$
BLEU-3	0.504	0.517	0.549	0.574	$<10^{-6}$
BLEU-4	0.426	0.414	0.428	0.469	$<10^{-6}$

Discussion. In our experiments, we observed that the DASM loss in our approach has a significant impact on synthesis sentence data, so we tuned the hyperparameter λ lower. Probably the word features pair matching vector in the DASM model has the ability to pass the impact from original sentence to the synthetic sentence by word correlation, and in this situation the generated sentence can be trained in original way, which is not what we hope to happen in non-related text generation like dialogue generation. In such situation, what we can do now is tune the hyperparameter λ with a much more smaller value, and this will be the future work we continue to focus on. However, the characteristic of DASM model can be very useful in coherent sentence generation. A little bit higher value of the DASM loss hyperparameter in loss function can be helpful in coherent and meaningful sentence generation.

Table 2. BLEU scores performance on IMDb movie review dataset

Model	PG-BLEU	VAE	SeqGAN	SATN	p-value
BLEU-2	0.597	0.639	0.731	0.760	$<10^{-6}$
BLEU-3	0.467	0.483	0.610	0.622	$<10^{-6}$

Table 3. Human scores on the Amazon book review datasets

Dataset	VAE	SeqGAN	SATN	Ground truth
Amazon	0.380	0.452	0.483	0.625
IMDb	0.246	0.382	0.475	0.565

Table 4. Samples from different methods on Amazon book review dataset

Sentence	SeqGAN	SATN
a	Book got in time and the book is in good condition	We got the book in time and the book is in good condition
b	A woman found understanding topics that concerned me young	A young woman found understanding in topics that concerned me
c	If interfere with the nature, we overreacts in some way	If we interfere with nature, nature overreacts in some way
d	It is a unusual story very much and makes <UNK> reading a good satisfying	It is a very unusual story, and makes a good satisfying read
e	I was interested in at once the story plot and the characters	I was interested at once in the story plot and the characters

5 Conclusion

In this paper, we proposed a novel symmetrical adversarial training network framework named SATN for generating short and long text via symmetrical comparison of sentence features. By comparing the difference between the word-level features from original and synthetic sentence, SATN address the fine-grained word smooth problems of text generation. We demonstrate the proposed model with impressive performance and the sentence generated can be read like real ones. SATN showed its excellent potential in generating text token sequence and other kind of medium.

In the future work, we will attempt to apply SATN in more natural languages process applications and optimize the structure of the model to provide generator with more information from DASM. This model will be fine-tuned in the future work for better performance and we will take exhaustive quantitative comparison.

Acknowledgments. This paper is supported by the National Key Research and Development Program of China (Grant No. 2018YFB1403400), the National Natural Science Foundation of China (Grant No. 61876080), the Collaborative Innovation Center of Novel Software Technology and Industrialization at Nanjing University.

References

1. Bahdanau, D., Cho, K., Bengio, Y.: Neural machine translation by jointly learning to align and translate. arXiv preprint arXiv:1409.0473 (2014)
2. Bowman, S.R., Vilnis, L., Vinyals, O., Dai, A.M., Jozefowicz, R., Bengio, S.: Generating sentences from a continuous space. arXiv preprint arXiv:1511.06349 (2015)
3. Brown, M., Lowe, D.G.: Automatic panoramic image stitching using invariant features. Int. J. Comput. Vis. **74**(1), 59–73 (2007)
4. Che, T., et al.: Maximum-likelihood augmented discrete generative adversarial networks. arXiv preprint arXiv:1702.07983 (2017)
5. Cho, K., et al.: Learning phrase representations using RNN encoder-decoder for statistical machine translation. arXiv preprint arXiv:1406.1078 (2014)
6. Elman, J.L.: Finding structure in time. Cogn. Sci. **14**(2), 179–211 (1990)
7. Goodfellow, I., et al.: Generative adversarial nets. In: Advances in Neural Information Processing Systems, pp. 2672–2680 (2014)
8. Hinton, G.E., Osindero, S., Teh, Y.-W.: A fast learning algorithm for deep belief nets. Neural Comput. **18**(7), 1527–1554 (2006)
9. Hochreiter, S., Schmidhuber, J.: Long short-term memory. Neural Comput. **9**(8), 1735–1780 (1997)
10. Isola, P., Zhu, J.-Y., Zhou, T., Efros, A.A.: Image-to-image translation with conditional adversarial networks. In: Proceedings of the IEEE Conference on Computer Vision and Pattern Recognition, pp. 1125–1134 (2017)
11. Johansen, S., Juselius, K.: Maximum likelihood estimation and inference on cointegration-with applications to the demand for money. Oxf. Bull. Econ. Stat. **52**(2), 169–210 (1990)
12. Krizhevsky, A., Sutskever, I., Hinton, G.E.: ImageNet classification with deep convolutional neural networks. In: Advances in Neural Information Processing Systems, pp. 1097–1105 (2012)

13. Kusner, M.J., Hernández-Lobato, J.M.: GANs for sequences of discrete elements with the Gumbel-softmax distribution. arXiv preprint arXiv:1611.04051 (2016)
14. Lange, S., Riedmiller, M.: Deep auto-encoder neural networks in reinforcement learning. In: The 2010 International Joint Conference on Neural Networks (IJCNN), pp. 1–8. IEEE (2010)
15. Lavoie, B., Rainbow, O.: A fast and portable realizer for text generation systems. In: Fifth Conference on Applied Natural Language Processing (1997)
16. Li, J., Monroe, W., Shi, T., Jean, S., Ritter, A., Jurafsky, D.: Adversarial learning for neural dialogue generation. arXiv preprint arXiv:1701.06547 (2017)
17. Lin, K., Li, D., He, X., Zhang, Z., Sun, M.-T.: Adversarial ranking for language generation. In: Advances in Neural Information Processing Systems, pp. 3155–3165 (2017)
18. McKeown, K.: Text Generation. Cambridge University Press, Cambridge (1992)
19. Mikolov, T., Chen, K., Corrado, G., Dean, J.: Efficient estimation of word representations in vector space. arXiv preprint arXiv:1301.3781 (2013)
20. Papineni, K., Roukos, S., Ward, T., Zhu, W.-J.: BLEU: a method for automatic evaluation of machine translation. In: Proceedings of the 40th Annual Meeting on Association for Computational Linguistics, pp. 311–318. Association for Computational Linguistics (2002)
21. Pfau, D., Vinyals, O.: Connecting generative adversarial networks and actor-critic methods. arXiv preprint arXiv:1610.01945 (2016)
22. Reed, S., Akata, Z., Yan, X., Logeswaran, L., Schiele, B., Lee, H.: Generative adversarial text to image synthesis. arXiv preprint arXiv:1605.05396 (2016)
23. Roller, S., Speriosu, M., Rallapalli, S., Wing, B., Baldridge, J.: Supervised text-based geolocation using language models on an adaptive grid. In: Proceedings of the 2012 Joint Conference on Empirical Methods in Natural Language Processing and Computational Natural Language Learning, pp. 1500–1510. Association for Computational Linguistics (2012)
24. Ruder, S.: An overview of gradient descent optimization algorithms. arXiv preprint arXiv:1609.04747 (2016)
25. Salakhutdinov, R.: Learning deep generative models. Annu. Rev. Stat. Its Appl. **2**, 361–385 (2015)
26. Sutskever, I., Vinyals, O., Le, Q.V.: Sequence to sequence learning with neural networks. In: Advances in Neural Information Processing Systems, pp. 3104–3112 (2014)
27. Yu, L., Zhang, W., Wang, J., Yu, Y.: SeqGAN: sequence generative adversarial nets with policy gradient. In: Thirty-First AAAI Conference on Artificial Intelligence (2017)
28. Zhang, H., et al.: StackGAN: text to photo-realistic image synthesis with stacked generative adversarial networks. In: Proceedings of the IEEE International Conference on Computer Vision, pp. 5907–5915 (2017)
29. Zhang, X., LeCun, Y.: Text understanding from scratch. arXiv preprint arXiv:1502.01710 (2015)
30. Zhang, Y., Gan, Z., Carin, L.: Generating text via adversarial training. In: NIPS Workshop on Adversarial Training, vol. 21 (2016)
31. Zhang, Y., et al.: Adversarial feature matching for text generation. In: Proceedings of the 34th International Conference on Machine Learning-Volume 70, pp. 4006–4015. JMLR.org (2017)

A Novel Image Captioning Method Based on Generative Adversarial Networks

Yang Fan, Jungang Xu$^{(\boxtimes)}$, Yingfei Sun, and Yiyu Wang

University of Chinese Academy of Sciences, Beijing, China
fanyang16@mails.ucas.edu.cn, xujg@ucas.ac.cn

Abstract. Although the image captioning methods based on RNN has made great progress in recent years, these are often lacking in variability and ignore some minor information. In this paper, a novel image captioning method based on Generative Adversarial Networks is proposed, which improve the naturalness and diversity of image description. In the method, matcher is added to the generator to get the feature of the image that does not appear in the standard description, then to produce descriptions conditioned on image, and discriminator to access how well a description fits the visual content. It is noteworthy that training a sequence generator is nontrivial. Experiments on MSCOCO and Flickr30k show that it performed competitively against real people in our user study and outperformed other methods on various tasks.

Keywords: LSTM · GAN · Generator · Discriminator · Matcher

1 Introduction

Every day, we encounter a large number of images from various sources such as the internet, news articles, document diagrams and advertisements. Given an image, it is natural for a human to describe an immense amount of details about this image with a quick glance. However, machine needs to interpret some form of image captions if humans need automatic image captions from it. Making computers imitate humans' ability to interpret the visual world has been a long standing goal of researchers in the field of artificial intelligence.

Image captioning is a popular research area of Artificial Intelligence (AI) that deals with image understanding and a language description for that image. Although great progress has been made in various computer vision tasks, such as object recognition [1], attribute classification [2], action classification [3], image classification [4] and scene recognition [5], it is a relatively new task to let a computer use a human-like sentence to automatically describe an image that is forwarded to it.

Using a computer to automatically generate a natural language description for an image, is a challenging task. Because connecting both research communities of computer vision and natural language processing, image captioning not only requires a high level understanding of the contents of an image, but also needs to express the information in a human-like sentence. Image captioning needs to detect and recognize objects. It also needs to understand scene type or location, object properties and their

© Springer Nature Switzerland AG 2019
I. V. Tetko et al. (Eds.): ICANN 2019, LNCS 11730, pp. 281–292, 2019.
https://doi.org/10.1007/978-3-030-30490-4_23

interactions. Generating well-formed sentences requires both syntactic and semantic understanding of the language.

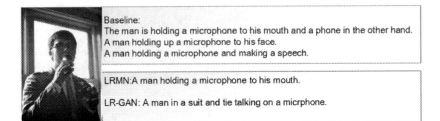

Fig. 1. The description statement for a given picture. Baseline from the dataset, the LRMN [11] is the model we proposed before and the LR-GAN is the model proposed in this paper.

As a challenging and meaningful research field in artificial intelligence, image captioning is attracting more and more attention and is becoming increasingly important.

Understanding an image largely depends on obtaining image features. Now, people often use the deep learning based techniques. In deep learning based techniques, features are learned automatically from training data and they can handle a large and diverse set of images and videos. For example, Convolutional Neural Networks (CNN) [6] are widely used for feature learning, and a classifier such as Softmax is used for classification. CNN is generally followed by Recurrent Neural Networks (RNN) in order to generate captions.

The advance in image captioning has been marked as a prominent success of AI. Like BLEU [7], METEOR [8], ROUGE-L [9] and CIDER [10], state-of-the-art techniques have already surpassed humans performance. But the problem of generating image descriptions has been solved? Figure 1 shows the results produced by the Encoder-Decoder model [11] (marked as LRMN) that a caption generator. The results of LRMN, though faithfully describing the content of the images, the sentence feel rigid, dry, lacking in vitality and very close to the baseline.

So, we hope to design a network model based on GAN, the mode jointly learns a generator (like Fig. 2) which we use the matcher to get the features that appear in the image that do not appear in the standard description that to produce descriptions conditioned on images, and discriminator (like Fig. 3) to access how well a description fits the visual content. Like Fig. 1, the results of LR-GAN model not only fit the image content, but also show the details (like suit and tie) in the image. Experiments on MSCOCO and Flickr30k show that the mode can generate a sentence with fidelity, naturalness and diversity. The image captioning can reflect the visual content faithfully, feel like the real people would say and also can produce different expressions given an image.

2 Related Work

Image captioning mainly discussed template based, retrieval based, and deep neural network based image caption generating models.

In early image captioning work, a type of methods that are commonly used is template based. In template based methods, image captions are generated through a syntactically and semantically constrained process. Typically, in order to use a template based method to generate a description for an image, a specified set of visual concepts need to be detected first. Then, the detected visual concepts are connected through sentence templates or specific language grammar rules or combinatorial optimization algorithms to compose a sentence.

Yang et al. [12] use a quadruplet (Nouns-Verbs-Scenes-Prepositions) as a sentence template for generating image captioning. Kulkarni et al. [13] employ Conditional Random Field to determine image contents to be rendered in the image caption. Li et al. [14] use visual models to perform detections in images for extracting semantic information including objects, attributes and spatial relationships. Then, they define a triplet of the format $\langle\langle adj1, obj1\rangle, prep, \langle adj2, obj2\rangle\rangle$ for encoding recognition results. Ushiku et al. [15] present a method called Common Subspace for Model and Similarity to learn phrase classifiers directly for image captioning.

Another type of image captioning methods that is retrieval based. Given a query image, retrieval based methods produce a caption for it through retrieving one or a set of sentences from a pre-specified sentence pool. The generated caption can either be a sentence that has already existed or a sentence composed from the retrieved ones.

Farhadi et al. [16] establish a object, action, scene meaning space to link images and sentences. Mason and Charniak [17] first use visual similarity to retrieve a set of captioned images for a query image. Kuznetsova et al. [18] propose a tree based method to compose image descriptions by making use of captioned web images.

Retrieval based and template based image captioning methods are adopted mainly in early work. Due to great progress made in the field of deep learning, recent work begins to rely on deep neural networks for automatic image captioning. Inspired by recent advances in neural machine translation [19, 20], the encoder-decoder framework is adopted to generate captions for images. The main framework for image captioning is encode-decoder. The framework is mainly designed for machine translation that to translate sentences from one language into another language.

The image captioning models follow the encoder-decoder pipeline, which use the pre-trained Convolutional Neural Network (CNN) to encode the image information, and use Recurrent Neural Networks (RNN) [9, 21] or Long Short Term Memory (LSTM) [22] networks as language models to generate image descriptions.

But, thought these models, we find the describing the content of images that feel rigid, dry and lacking in vitality. As reported in image generation [23, 24], they can produce natural images nearly indistinguishable from real photos. Based on GAN models for image caption have been proposed [25, 26], they can produce some different description results. Based on the encouragement of these methods, we hope that designing a model can also generate a description of diversity.

3   Based on Generative Adversarial Network of Image Captioning

The image captioning task can be formulated as follows: given an input image I, the generator G can produce a caption describing the content of the image. The standard approach to model G(I) is to use a recurrent language model conditioned on the input image I, and train it using a maximum likelihood (ML) loss considering every image-caption pair as an independent sample.

However, most image captioning architectures ignore the diversity during training. So, we want to use the adversarial framework [27] to produce diverse captions for an input image, which consists of a generator G, and a discriminator E. Input an image I, the generator G is for generating natural descriptions, while the discriminator E is for evaluating how well a sentence or paragraph describes I.

3.1   The Generator

We use the caption generator model shown in Fig. 2. It uses the encoder-decoder framework with two stages: (I) the encoder model which encode the image feature $F(I)$ from the input image, at the same time, the image features are input into the matcher D_1 and D_2 that output the image feature Z_1 and Z_2 are characterized by implicit information on the image. (II) We integrate the information Z_1, $F(I)$ and Z_2 together as input to the decoder, and the decoder which generate the description sentence.

In our model, given an image I, we integrate the information Z_1, $F(I)$ and Z_2 together as V_i input into the decoder. The image feature V_i contains derived from $F(I)$ of a convolutional neural network (CNN) and two related vectors Z_1 and Z_2 of image. The Z_1 and Z_2 express the details that represent the information in the image but do not appear in the standard description.

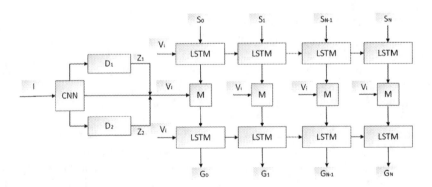

Fig. 2. The structure of LR-GAN. The matcher D_1 and D_2 generates implicit information Z_1 and Z_2 that shown in the image but not appear in the given description statement. V_i express the image information as input to the encoder. $(S_0, S_1, \ldots S_N)$ indicates the given description. $(G_0, G_1, \ldots G_N)$ indicates the description that we want to generate.

In particular, we adopting Resnet-101 [28] as the CNN architecture to generate the image feature $F(I)$. For generating some rich description, we adding vector Z_1 and Z_2. Then integrate the information Z_1, $F(I)$ and Z_2 together as initial conditions V_i input to the decoder, the decoder relies on the LRMN [11] net, which generates a sentence, word by word. We derive the input V_i through Eqs. 1–4.

$$x = CNN(I) \tag{1}$$

$$Z_1 = f_1(x) \tag{2}$$

$$Z_2 = f_2(x) \tag{3}$$

$$V_i = [Z_1, x, Z_2] \tag{4}$$

All recurrent connections are transformed to feed-forward connections in the unrolled version. In detail, I denotes the input image and $S = (S_0, S_1, \ldots, S_N)$ denotes a true sentence describing this image and $G = (G_0, G_1, \ldots, G_N)$ a sentence that we want to generate, the maximum probability of correct caption is defined as Eq. 5.

$$W^* = \arg\max_w \sum logp(G|V_i, W, S) \tag{5}$$

where W denotes the parameters of our model, the correct image caption sentence G which its length N is not fixed.

Our decoder uses the model based on the LRMN decoder we assign the structure to LR-GAN (Fig. 2). In Fig. 2, (S, I) is a training example pair, image information V_i which is input to the decoder, the unrolling procedure reads:

$$x_0 = V_i \tag{6}$$

$$x_i = (WS_t) \; t \in 1, \ldots, N - 1 \tag{7}$$

$$h_{t+1} = f_{recurrent}(h_t, x_t) \tag{8}$$

$$G_t = \arg\max_W Softmax(Wh_t) \tag{9}$$

Equation 4 is used to input image information and Eq. 7 is used to continuously input $(S_1, \ldots, S_N)$, then with Eqs. 8 and 9 we can obtain the final output $G = (G_1, \ldots, G_{N-1})$.

The memory is updated when a new input x_t arrives using a non-linear function $f_{recurrent}$, thereby continuously adjust the network parameters to optimize the network. When we use the LR-GAN to calculate $f_{recurrent}$, because the LRMN has shown state-of-the-art performance on image captioning. The non-linear function $f_{current}$ is defined as Eqs. 10, 11 and 12:

$$x_t^1, h_t^1 = f_{LSTM1}(x_{t-1}^1, h_{t-1}^1) \tag{10}$$

$$x_t^2 = (W_i V_i + W_h h_t^1) \tag{11}$$

$$x_t^2, h_t^2 = f_{LSTM2}(x_{t-1}^2, h_{t-1}^2) \tag{12}$$

3.2   The Discriminator

The primary purpose of E is to determine how well a description G describes a given image I. A good description needs to satisfy two criteria: natural and semantically relevant. To enforce both criteria, inspired to consider two types of descriptions for each training image I: (1) $S = (S_0, S_1, \ldots, S_N)$: the set of descriptions for I provided by human, (2) $G = (G_0, G_1, \ldots, G_N)$: those from the generator G.

The discriminator network E takes an image feature $F(I)$ that derived from the pre-trained convolutional neural network, and a set of real captioning $S = (S_0, S_1, \ldots, S_N)$ and generate captioning $G = (G_0, G_1, \ldots, G_N)$ as input. We want the discriminator classifies G can as either real or fake. And we want the discriminator E can discriminate that the generated description G is compatible with the picture, and it is also different from the input standard description statement S. The discriminator network as Fig. 3.

$$E_\theta = \log E(S, I) + \log(1 - E(G, I)) \tag{13}$$

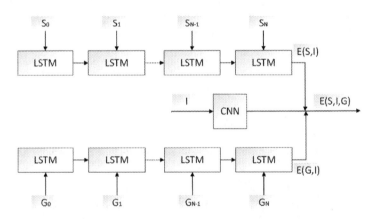

Fig. 3. The structure of captioning discriminator E. We obtain the results of the description of the network generated by $E(S, I, G)$.

$E(S, I)$ indicates the matching degree between the picture I and the real captioning S. $E(G, I)$ indicates the matching degree between the picture I and the description statement G. The first term, on the other hand, ensures the semantic relevance, by explicitly suppressing mismatched descriptions. The second term forces the evaluator to distinguish between the human descriptions and the generated ones, which would in turn provide useful feedbacks to G, pushing it to generate more natural descriptions.

For this framework, the learning objective of G is to generate descriptions that are natural from what humans would say when presented with the same image; while the objective of E is to distinguish between artificial descriptions (i.e. those from G) and the real ones (i.e. those from the training set). This can be formalized into a minimax problem as follows:

$$\min_{W} \max_{\theta} L(G_W, E_\theta) \tag{14}$$

Here, G_W and E_θ are a generator with parameter W and a discriminator with parameter θ.

The primary purpose of E is to determine how well a description G describes a given image I. A good description needs to satisfy two criteria: natural and semantically relevant. To enforce both criteria, inspired by [24] we consider two types of descriptions for each training image I: (1) S: the set of descriptions for I provided by human, (2) G: those from the generator G. To increase the scores for the descriptions in S while suppressing those in the others, we use a joint objective formulated as:

$$\max_{\theta} L_E(\theta) = \frac{1}{N} \sum_{i}^{N} \left(\max_{\theta} L_E(S, I), \min_{\theta} L_E(S, G) \right) \tag{15}$$

The Eq. (15) forces the discriminator to distinguish between the human descriptions and the generated ones, which would provide useful feedbacks in turn to G_W, pushing it to generate more natural descriptions.

4   Experiment

4.1   Datasets

In the experiment we selected the two most popular datasets in image captioning: MSCOCO [29] and Flickr30k [30]. The MSCOCO dataset contains 123,000 images and has five reference captions. We randomly choose 5,000 images for validation, 5,000 images for testing and the others for training. The Flickr30k dataset contains 31,000 images and has five reference captions, following the same principles as MSCOCO, we choose 1,000 images for validation, 1,000 images for testing and others for model training.

4.2   Evaluation Metrics

In order to evaluate the quality of the generated sentence, we consider multiple evaluation metrics, including BLEU [7], METEOR [8], ROUGE-L [9] and CIDER [10]. BLEU are the metrics that measure how many words are shared by the generated captions and ground truth captions. CIDER is a metric that measures consistency between n-gram occurrences in generated and reference sentences. METEOR is based on the explicit word to word matches between generated captions and ground-truth captions.

4.3   User Study and Qualitative Comparison

To fairly evaluate the quality of the generated sentences as well as how consistent the metrics are with humans perspective, we conducted a user study. Specifically, we invited 30 human evaluators to compare the outputs of different generators. Each time, a human evaluator would be presented an image with two sentences from different methods and asked to choose the better one. Totally, we collected about 3,000 responses. The comparative results are shown in Fig. 5: From humans views, LR-GAN is better than LRMN in 55% of all cases. In the comparison between human and models, LRMN only won in 11% of the cases, while LR-GAN won in over 27%. These results clearly suggest that the sentences produced by LR-GAN are of considerably higher quality, i.e. being more natural and semantically relevant.

The examples in Fig. 1 also confirm this assessment. Particularly, we can see when LRMN is presented with similar images, it tends to generate descriptions that are almost the same. On the contrary, LR-GAN describes them with more distinctive and diverse ones.

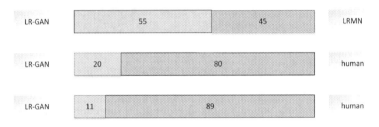

Fig. 4. The figure shows the human comparison results between each pair of generators. With names of the generators placed at each side of the comparison, the blue and orange areas respectively indicate percentages of the generator in the left and right being the better one. (Color figure online)

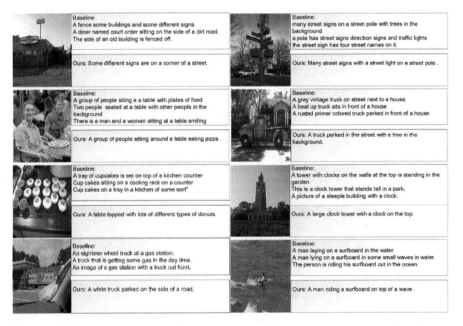

Fig. 5. Image captions generated by our LR-GAN model. We randomly choose eight images from the MSCOCO dataset and the Flickr30k dataset.

Table 1. Comparison of experimental results on the MSCOCO dataset. The high evaluation result of LRMN indicates that the generated description result is closer to the standard description, but the lower evaluation result of LR-GAN indicates that the generated description sentence is more diverse.

Approach	MSCOCO						
	BLEU-1	BLEU-2	BLEU-3	BLEU-4	METEOR	ROUGE-L	CIDER
LRMN	**72.0**	**54.7**	**40.0**	**29.0**	**24.3**	**52.6**	**91.7**
LR-GAN	70.5	52.1	38.4	27.6	23.2	51.3	90.4

Table 2. Comparison of experimental results on the Flickr30k dataset. The high evaluation result of LRMN indicates that the generated description result is closer to the standard description, but the lower evaluation result of LR-GAN indicates that the generated description sentence is more diverse.

Approach	Flickr30						
	BLEU-1	BLEU-2	BLEU-3	BLEU-4	METEOR	ROUGE-L	CIDER
LRMN	**62.7**	**43.5**	**29.6**	**20.5**	**19.3**	**44.2**	**91.7**
LR-GAN	59.5	41.1	27.4	18.6	17.7	41.9	89.2

4.4 Experimental Details

This experimental model uses python2 and open source machine learning framework TensorFlow. For the MSCOCO and Flickr30k datasets, we prune the vocabulary by dropping words with frequency less than 5, the final vocabulary includes special Begin-Of-Sentence (BOS) and End-Of-Sentence (EOS) tokens. In our captioner model, we first use pre-trained Resnet-101 to extract the image feature $F(I)$ and then the sentences are represented as one-hot encoding. Then the image features are input into the matcher D_1 and D_2 that output the image feature Z_1 and Z_2 are characterized by implicit information on the image features, Z_1 and Z_2 are a 128-dimensional vector. At last, we integrate the information Z_1, $F(I)$ and Z_2 together as input to the decoder, and the decoder which generate the description sentence.

We respectively pre-train G using standard MLE, for 12 epochs, and E with supervised training based on Eq. (15), for 3 epochs. Subsequently, G and E are jointly trained, where each iteration consists of one step of G-update followed by one step of E-update. We set the batch size to 64, use the ADAM optimizer [31] to set the learning rate to 0.0005 and we apply learning rate decay with a factor of 0.8 every three epochs to train the model with training datasets, and then evaluate the model with validation datasets, at last select the best model for test evaluation results with testing datasets.

4.5 LR-GAN Model Generate Caption and Analysis

Tables 1 and 2 lists the performances of different generators under these metrics. On both datasets, the sentences produced by LRMN receive considerably higher scores than the LR-GAN. This is not surprising. As discussed earlier, such metrics primarily focus on n-gram matching the references, while ignoring other important properties, e.g. naturalness and diversity. On the contrary, by the Fig. 4 the LR-GAN model generates the image description is different with the real sentence, but also very consistent with the image content.

We analyzed failure cases and found that a major kind of errors is the inclusion of incorrect details. e.g. colors (red/yellow), counts (two/three) and age (young and old). A possible cause is that there are only a few samples for each particular detail, and they are not enough to make the generator capture these details reliably. Also, the focus on diversity and overall quality may also encourage the generator to include more details, with the risk of some incorrect details.

5   Conclusions

In this paper, we proposed a novel image captioning method based on LR-GAN that jointly trains a generator G and a discriminator E. Results show that our adversarial model produces captions which are diverse and match the statistics of human generated captions significantly. On both MSCOCO and Flickr30k, the proposed method produced descriptions that are more natural, diverse, and semantically relevant as compared to the LRMN-based model.

Acknowledgment. This work is supported by the Beijing Natural Science Foundation Program under Grant No. 4162067 and the Beijing Science and Technology Plan Project Grant No. Z171100000117021.

References

1. Girshick, R., Donahue, J., Darrell, T., et al.: Rich feature hierarchies for accurate object detection and semantic segmentation. In: Proceedings of the IEEE Conference on Computer Vision and Pattern Recognition, pp. 580–587. IEEE (2014)
2. Gan, C., Yang, T., Gong, B.: Learning attributes equals multi-source domain generalization. In: Proceedings of the IEEE Conference on Computer Vision and Pattern Recognition, pp. 87–97. IEEE (2016)
3. Chao, Y.W., Wang, Z., Mihalcea, R., et al.: Mining semantic affordances of visual object categories. In: Proceedings of the IEEE Conference on Computer Vision and Pattern Recognition, pp. 4259–4267. IEEE (2015)
4. Krizhevsky, A., Sutskever, I., Hinton, G.E.: ImageNet classification with deep convolutional neural networks. In: Advances in Neural Information Processing Systems, pp. 1097–1105. Curran Associates (2012)
5. Zhou, B., Lapedriza, A., Xiao, J., et al.: Learning deep features for scene recognition using places database. In: Advances in Neural Information Processing Systems, pp. 487–495. Curran Associates (2014)
6. LeCun, Y., Bottou, L., Bengio, Y., et al.: Gradient-based learning applied to document recognition. Proc. IEEE **86**(11), 2278–2324 (1998)
7. Papineni, K., Roukos, S., Ward, T., et al.: BLEU: a method for automatic evaluation of machine translation. In: Proceedings of the 40th Annual Meeting on Association for Computational Linguistics, pp. 311–318. Association for Computational Linguistics (2002)

8. Banerjee, S., Lavie, A.: METEOR: an automatic metric for MT evaluation with improved correlation with human judgments. In: Proceedings of the ACL Workshop on Intrinsic and Extrinsic Evaluation Measures for Machine Translation and/or Summarization, pp. 65–72. ACL (2005)

9. Donahue, J., Anne Hendricks, L., Guadarrama, S., et al.: Long-term recurrent convolutional networks for visual recognition and description. In: Proceedings of the IEEE Conference on Computer Vision and Pattern Recognition, pp. 2625–2634. IEEE (2015)

10. Vedantam, R., Lawrence Zitnick, C., Parikh, D.: CIDEr: consensus-based image description evaluation. In: Proceedings of the IEEE Conference on Computer Vision and Pattern Recognition, pp. 4566–4575. IEEE (2015)

11. Fan, Y., Xu, J., Sun, Y., et al.: Long-term recurrent merge network model for image captioning. In: 2018 IEEE 30th International Conference on Tools with Artificial Intelligence (IC-TAI), pp. 254–259. IEEE (2018)

12. Yang, Y., Teo, C.L., Daum III, H., et al.: Corpus-guided sentence generation of natural images. In: Proceedings of the Conference on Empirical Methods in Natural Language Processing, pp. 444–454. Association for Computational Linguistics (2011)

13. Kulkarni, G., Premraj, V., Ordonez, V., et al.: BabyTalk: understanding and generating simple image descriptions. IEEE Trans. Pattern Anal. Mach. Intell. 35(12), 2891–2903 (2013)

14. Li, S., Kulkarni, G., Berg, T.L., et al.: Composing simple image descriptions using web-scale n-grams. In: Proceedings of the Fifteenth Conference on Computational Natural Language Learning, pp. 220–228. Association for Computational Linguistics (2011)

15. Ushiku, Y., Yamaguchi, M., Mukuta, Y., et al.: Common subspace for model and similarity: Phrase learning for caption generation from images. In: Proceedings of the IEEE International Conference on Computer Vision, pp. 2668–2676. IEEE (2015)

16. Farhadi, A., et al.: Every picture tells a story: generating sentences from images. In: Daniilidis, K., Maragos, P., Paragios, N. (eds.) ECCV 2010. LNCS, vol. 6314, pp. 15–29. Springer, Heidelberg (2010). https://doi.org/10.1007/978-3-642-15561-1_2

17. Mason, R., Charniak, E.: Nonparametric method for data-driven image captioning. In: Proceedings of the 52nd Annual Meeting of the Association for Computational Linguistics (Volume 2: Short Papers), vol. 2, pp. 592–598 (2014)

18. Kuznetsova, P., Ordonez, V., Berg, T.L., et al.: TreeTalk: composition and compression of trees for image descriptions. Trans. Assoc. Comput. Linguist. MIT Press. J. 2, 351–362 (2014)

19. Mnih, A., Hinton, G.: Three new graphical models for statistical language modelling. In: Proceedings of the 24th International Conference on Machine Learning, pp. 641–648. ACM (2007)

20. Och, F.J.: Minimum error rate training in statistical machine translation. In: Proceedings of the 41st Annual Meeting on Association for Computational Linguistics-Volume 1, pp. 160–167. Association for Computational Linguistics (2003)

21. Mao, J., Xu, W., Yang, Y., et al.: Deep captioning with multimodal recurrent neural networks (m-RNN). arXiv preprint arXiv:1412.6632 (2014)

22. Hochreiter, S., Schmidhuber, J.: Long short-term memory. Neural Comput. MIT Press J. 9 (8), 1735–1780 (1997)

23. Isola, P., Zhu, J.Y., Zhou, T., et al.: Image-to-image translation with conditional adversarial networks. In: Proceedings of the IEEE Conference on Computer Vision and Pattern Recognition, pp. 1125–1134. IEEE (2017)

24. Reed, S., Akata, Z., Yan, X., et al.: Generative adversarial text to image synthesis. arXiv preprint arXiv:1605.05396 (2016)

25. Dai, B., Fidler, S., Urtasun, R., et al.: Towards diverse and natural image descriptions via a conditional GAN. In: Proceedings of the IEEE International Conference on Computer Vision, pp. 2970–2979. IEEE (2017)

26. Laserson, K.F., Thorpe, L.E., Leimane, V., et al.: Speaking the same language: treatment outcome definitions for multidrug-resistant tuberculosis. Int. J. Tuberc. Lung Dis. 9(6), 640–645 (2005)

27. Goodfellow, I., Pouget-Abadie, J., Mirza, M., et al.: Generative adversarial nets. In: Advances in Neural Information Processing Systems, pp. 2672–2680. Curran Associates (2014)

28. He, K., Zhang, X., Ren, S., et al.: Deep residual learning for image recognition. In: Proceedings of the IEEE Conference on Computer Vision and Pattern Recognition, pp. 770–778. IEEE (2016)

29. Lin, T.-Y., et al.: Microsoft COCO: common objects in context. In: Fleet, D., Pajdla, T., Schiele, B., Tuytelaars, T. (eds.) ECCV 2014. LNCS, vol. 8693, pp. 740–755. Springer, Cham (2014). https://doi.org/10.1007/978-3-319-10602-1_48

30. Plummer, B.A., Wang, L., Cervantes, C.M., et al.: Flickr30k entities: collecting region-to-phrase correspondences for richer image-to-sentence models. In: Proceedings of the IEEE International Conference on Computer Vision, pp. 2641–2649. IEEE (2015)

31. Kingma, D.P., Ba, J.: Adam: a method for stochastic optimization. arXiv preprint arXiv:1412.6980 (2014)

Quality-Diversity Summarization
with Unsupervised Autoencoders

Lei Li[1], Zuying Huang[1(✉)], Natalia Vanetik[2], and Marina Litvak[2]

[1] Beijing University of Posts and Telecommunications, Beijing, China
zoehuang@bupt.edu.cn
[2] Sami Shamoon College of Engineering, Beer Sheva, Israel

Abstract. This paper introduces a novel perspective on unlabeled data driven technology for extractive summarization. Because unsupervised autoencoders, combined with neural network language models, help to capture deep semantic features for sentence quality, we propose to integrate autoencoders with sampling method based on Determinantal point processes (DPPs) [1] to extract diverse sentences with high qualities, and generate brief summaries. The unique fusion of unsupervised autoencoders and DPPs sampling has never been adopted before. We illustrate the advantages of this attempt against statistics based approaches through experiments in multilingual environment for single-document and multi-document summarization tasks. Our algorithms evaluated with ROUGE F-measure [2] obtain better scores in several varieties of languages on MMS-2015 dataset and MSS-2015 dataset.

Keywords: Summarization · DPPs · Autoencoders

1 Introduction

For extractive automatic summarization, the core procedure consists of two major tasks: document representation and sentence extraction. In 2017, Li and Zhang [3] put forward UIDS, a high-performing extensible framework for extractive summarization based on Deteminantal Point Processes (DPPs) sampling. Sentence quality and diversity are decisive factors for sampling algorithm in UIDS. However, deep semantic measurement for sentence quality and diversity requires appropriate document representation above all. Since the burst of Artificial Neural Networks, researchers tend not to keep satisfied with the mere statistical way to represent a sentence. BERT [4] and Sent2Vec [5] are widely used neural network language models in recent years. An unsupervised autoencoder is a neural network which is capable of automatically learning meaningful

This work was supported in part by the Beijing Municipal Commission of Science and Technology under Grant Z181100001018035; National Social Science Foundation of China under Grant 16ZDA055; National Natural Science Foundation of China under Grant 91546121; Engineering Research Center of Information Networks, Ministry of Education.

© Springer Nature Switzerland AG 2019
I. V. Tetko et al. (Eds.): ICANN 2019, LNCS 11730, pp. 293–299, 2019.
https://doi.org/10.1007/978-3-030-30490-4_24

representations by trying to reconstruct its input at the output layer. Chen et al. [6] introduce the k-competitive autoencoder for textual documents, which trains neurons to recognize specific patterns through the competition.

In this paper, we introduce a novel summarization approach, which combines unsupervised autoencoders and DPPs sampling. This approach has the following advantages over traditional systems: (1) it overcomes the semantic weakness of shallow statistical features and gains meaningful representation for sentences; (2) it is independent of labeled training corpus or prior knowledge for unfamiliar languages; and (3) it is suitable for multilingual environment. The experiments on MMS-2015 dataset and MSS-2015 dataset have shown its effectiveness for a variety of languages.

2   Quality-Diversity Automatic Summarization

2.1   Quality-Diversity Interpretation for DPPs

P is called a DPP if, when P on a ground set D is a probability measure over its subsets, where determinant offers some certain quantitatively analysis on this probability. Kulesza and Taskar [1] propose L-ensemble theory, which allows the kernel matrix to be indexed directly by items in the set D. The DPP kernel matrix L can be written as a Gram matrix:

$$L_{ij} = B_i^\top B_j = q_i \phi_i^\top \phi_j q_j \tag{1}$$

where B_i refers to sentence representation. We now write each B_i as the product of its norm q_i and a normalized vector ϕ_i. We call q_i the quality of a sentence x_i and assume $S_{ij} = \phi_i^\top \phi_j$ as a measure of the similarity between the two sentences x_i and x_j. In this way, we expect the decomposition of matrix L to guarantee both quality and diversity for sentence representation.

2.2   Quality-Diversity Automatic Summarization (QDAS)

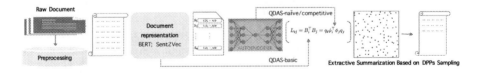

Fig. 1. QDAS-framework

Figure 1 shows the framework of our three types of QDAS systems. Our framework merely requires general preprocessing like sentence splitting and word segmentation, and then it can be applied in multilingual environment. When it comes to document representation, first we construct matrix L from holistic perspectives, through $L_{ij} = B_i^\top B_j$ from BERT and Sent2Vec directly, and call this framework as QDAS-basic. Furthermore, we build matrix L from partial perspectives, through $L_{ij} = q_i S_{ij} q_j$ concretely. QDAS-naïve and QDAS-competitive use autoencoder to extract quality q_i for a sentence, and calculate cosine similarity S_{ij} between every two sentences. The symmetric input and output layer units are corresponding to BERT and Sent2Vec representation for QDAS systems. QDAS-naïve is a Multi-Layer Perception with 3 hidden layers, while QDAS-competitive is s a shallow autoencoder with a single competitive hidden layer. The hidden layer structure is similar to KATE [6]. Algorithm 1[1] points out the training procedure for the autoencoders based on sentence vectors.

Algorithm 1. Quality-Diversity Autoencoder Based on Sentence Vectors

Input: Document $D = \{B^{(1)}, ..., B^{(N)}\}$ where each $B^{(i)}$ is a BERT/Sent2Vec representation of sentence i, *mode* of autoencoder
Output: Encoder f_ϕ, Decoder g_θ
1: Initialize parameters ϕ, θ randomly
2: **repeat**
3:     Calculate reconstruction error: $E = \sum_{i=1}^{N} \|B^{(i)} - g_\theta(f_\phi(B^{(i)}))\|$
4:     **if** *mode* $==$ naive $-$ autoencoder **then**
5:         Update parameters: Gradient Descent
6:     **else if** *mode* $==$ k $-$ competitive $-$ autoencoder **then**
7:         Update parameters: Apply k-competition on the output of the encoder layer
8:     **end if**
9: **until** Parameters ϕ, θ convergence

Given the matrix L, we encode every sentence with q_i through Encoder f_ϕ from Algorithm 1, and the sampling method based on DPPs displayed in Algorithm 2 $(O(N^2))$ can automatically choose diverse sentences with high quality. When constructing a semantic space using embedding expressions, quality refers to the length of a vector in the semantic space. Sentences that indicate strong semantic feature are called high quality and preferred for summarization. In the first loop, the cardinality $|Y|(=|V|)$ is determined[2]. A sample Y is produced during the second loop phase. Assume we have already selected the best B_i, then the V needs to be updated to an orthonormal basis for the subspace of the original V perpendicular to e_i for diversity. During each iteration, the first vector in V that contributes to the norm of B_i, which makes its quality the best, is eliminated.

3   Experiments

3.1   Datasets and Evaluation

The datasets come from Multilingual Multi-document Summarization Task (MMS-2015 dataset) and Multilingual Single-document Summarization Task

---

[1] Chen et al. [6] introduce the k-competitive autoencoder for textual documents.
[2] Kulesza and Taskar [1] provide mathematical proof in detail for DPPs sampling.

Algorithm 2. Summarization based on DPPs

Input: Document $D = \{B^{(1)}, ..., B^{(N)}\}$, encoded sentence representation $q_i = f_\phi(B^{(i)})$ and the ith standard basis N-vector e_i for all sentences $B^{(1)}, ..., B^{(N)}$

Output: Candidate sentence subset for summarization: Y

1: Quality and diversity: $quality\_i = \|q_i\|$, $sim_{i,j} = cosine(q_i, q_j)$, for all $i = 1...N$
2: matrix L for QDAS-basic: $L_{ij} = B_i^\top B_j$ for all $i, j = 1...N$
3: matrix L for QDAS-naïve/competitive: $L_{ij} = quality\_i * sim_{i,j} * quality\_j$, for all $i, j = 1...N$
4: $(\mathbf{v}_n, \lambda_n) = $ eigen_decompose(matrix L)
5: Initialize $J = \emptyset$, $V = \emptyset$, $Y = \emptyset$
6: **for** $i = 1, 2, ..., N$ **do**
7:     $J = J \cup \{i\}$ with prob. $\frac{\lambda_i}{\lambda_i + 1}$
8: **end for**
9: $V = \{\mathbf{v}_i\}_{i \in J}$
10: **while** $|V| > 0$ **do**
11:     Select sentence $B^{(i)} \in D$ with $prob(i) = \frac{1}{|V|} \sum_{v \in V} (v^\top e_i)^2$
12:     $Y = Y \cup B^{(i)}$
13:     $V = V_\perp$, an orthonormal basis for the subspace of V orthogonal to e_i
14: **end while**

(MSS-2015 dataset) [7]. MMS dataset is based on WikiNews in 10 languages for multi-document, while MSS dataset requires to generate a single document summary for all the given Wikipedia feature articles from 38 languages provided. We use ROUGE [2] package that measures skip n-gram overlap for evaluation; we provide F-measure results for n = 1, 2 and denote them by ROUGE1 and ROUGE2.

3.2 Results and Analysis

Tables 1 and 2 exhibit the results on MMS-2015 dataset utilizing BERT and Sent2Vec as the input for autoencoders respectively. Each table consists of QDAS systems, and UIDS introduced in [3] for comparison.

Slight differences exist between Tables 1 and 2. As we can see that the BERT-QDAS-basic doesn't perform so satisfied as Sent2Vec-QDAS-basic. We explain this phenomenon that the structures for Sent2Vec and autoencoders are both built on specific context environment of input text, while BERT is a pre-trained model from general public datasets. Nevertheless, in Table 1, BERT-QDAS-naïve still helps 9 out of 10 languages to get higher scores compared to the BERT-QDAS-basic. We believe that encoding in specific context of input text for summarization is beneficial for obtaining a deeper and more precise representation than just adopting language model trained from public datasets.

Displayed in Table 2, the Sent2Vec-QDAS-basic performs well especially on Czech, French and Greek. We also provide Sent2Vec-QDAS-naïve/competitive to enhance the algorithm. Surprisingly, when integrating unsupervised autoencoders with DPPs sampling, the result of Sent2Vec-QDAS-basic on Chinese

Table 1. BERT Performance on MMS-2015 dataset

LANGUAGE	UIDS		BERT-QDAS-basic		BERT-QDAS-naïve	
	ROUGE1	ROUGE2	ROUGE1	ROUGE2	ROUGE1	ROUGE2
Arabic	0.18224	0.05740	0.15039	0.03972	0.16048↑	0.03981↑
Chinese	0.12766	0.00808	0.11826	0.00422	0.12866↑	0.01201↑
Czech	0.18640	0.05495	0.22430	0.05916	0.23633↑	0.06424↑
English	0.36496	0.10615	0.35829	0.07800	0.33185	0.08267
French	0.12157	0.03044	0.20942	0.02728	0.22163↑	0.04322↑
Greek	0.29562	0.06838	0.30471	0.05803	0.34282↑	0.07395↑
Hebrew	0.18769	0.05639	0.13794	0.03653	0.16000↑	0.03900↑
Hindi	0.25615	0.07463	0.19971	0.04668	0.22187↑	0.06545↑
Romanian	0.28011	0.07309	0.15647	0.02860	0.20608↑	0.04356↑
Spanish	0.34502	0.09144	0.28320	0.06511	0.29022↑	0.07067↑

*↑ exhibits that BERT-QDAS-naïve (DPPs combined with Autoencoders) helps 9 out of 10 languages to get a higher score compared to the BERT-QDAS-basic (DPPs combined with neural network language model BERT).

Table 2. Sent2Vec Performance on MMS-2015 dataset

LANGUAGE	Sent2Vec-QDAS-basic		Sent2Vec-QDAS-naïve		Sent2Vec-QDAS-competitive	
	ROUGE1	ROUGE2	ROUGE1	ROUGE2	ROUGE1	ROUGE2
Arabic	**0.16367**	**0.04848**	0.11141	0.02703	0.16058	0.04084
Chinese	0.12890	0.00748	**0.34598↑**	**0.12283↑**	0.11632	0.00595
Czech	**0.26328↑**	**0.07659↑**	0.23920	0.09867	0.25368↑	0.07104↑
English	0.37903	0.10041	0.34449	0.07143	**0.38375↑**	**0.09303↑**
French	0.24088↑	0.04414↑	0.14903	0.02073	**0.24698↑**	**0.04710↑**
Greek	0.34277↑	0.07481↑	0.33507	0.08121	**0.34303↑**	**0.07159↑**
Hebrew	0.17438	0.04719	0.15843	0.04769	0.18069	0.05170
Hindi	0.24044	0.05717	0.18754	0.04437	0.23477	0.06123
Romanian	0.23178	0.04084	0.23585	0.04060	0.23476	0.04803
Spanish	0.32628	0.07961	0.34543	0.10122	0.32961	0.09018

*↑ suggests the cases that either QDAS-basic or QDAS-naïve/competitive performs better than UIDS system (Table 1). The results in bold are the best system among QDAS systems and UIDS system for each language.

improves obviously. Apart from the sustained advantages of Sent2Vec-QDAS-basic, the Sent2Vec-QDAS-competitive is clearly superior to its comparison UIDS on Czech, English, French and Greek. This demonstrates that through autoencoder neural networks, QDAS systems become capable of calculating better sentence qualities indeed rather than systems with trivial statistical features or language model trained from public datasets.

Also, given the superiority of Sent2Vec, we conduct experiment using Sent2Vec on MSS-2015-dataset, Table 3 shows the results partially (10/38 languages displayed). The results of QDAS systems have risen to varying degrees for these ten languages. For statistics marked in bold each line in these three tables,

Table 3. Sent2Vec Performance on MSS-2015 dataset

LANGUAGE	UIDS		Sent2Vec-QDAS-basic		Sent2Vec-QDAS-naïve	
	ROUGE1	ROUGE2	ROUGE1	ROUGE2	ROUGE1	ROUGE2
Afrikaans	0.32767	0.06756	**0.37797**↑	**0.07975**↑	0.37097↑	0.07962↑
Croatian	0.23344	0.02559	**0.23362**↑	**0.02616**↑	0.21468	0.01964
Japanese	0.38426	0.09298	0.39942↑	0.10926↑	**0.40072**↑	**0.11172**↑
Malayan	0.26570	0.05264	0.26768↑	0.05238↑	**0.27025**↑	**0.05877**↑
Dutch	0.36541	0.06748	**0.36691**↑	**0.06554**↑	0.36170	0.06614
Serbo-Croatian	0.22707	0.02455	**0.23003**↑	**0.02330**↑	0.22525	0.02330
Slovak	0.20360	0.02014	**0.22671**↑	**0.02617**↑	0.20281	0.02284
Slovenian	0.26273	0.04923	**0.26979**↑	**0.05935**↑	0.26744↑	0.05925↑
Serbian	0.27456	0.03692	**0.28073**↑	**0.04095**↑	0.26418	0.03993
Taibun	0.46316	0.16334	0.46977↑	0.17490↑	**0.47834**↑	**0.18219**↑

*↑ suggests the cases that either QDAS-basic or QDAS-naïve performs better than the UIDS system to some degree. The results in bold are the best system among QDAS systems and the UIDS system for each language.

according to the Wilcoxon statistical test [8], all QDAS systems significantly outperform UIDS (p-value < 0.05).

4   Conclusion

QDAS as a combination of both unsupervised autoencoders and DPPs sampling has never been adopted before. Our method is preferable in the multilingual domain because it automatically extracts features and adjusts itself to the different languages. It is robust because it does not require training data and rich morphological analysis for preprocessing. Thus, we believe the newly proposed system remains full of potential to be discovered. So far all the languages share a uniform set of parameters, important future work is to design for individuals to extract features that may not be captured by QDAS systems currently.

References

1. Kulesza, A., Taskar, B.: Determinantal point processes for machine learning. Found. Trends® Mach. Learn. **5**(2–3), 123–286 (2012). https://doi.org/10.1561/2200000044
2. Lin, C.-Y., Hovy, E.: Automatic evaluation of summaries using n-gram co-occurrence statistics, pp. 71–78 (2003). https://doi.org/10.3115/1073445.1073465
3. Li, L., Zhang, Y., Chi, J., Huang, Z.: UIDS: a multilingual document summarization framework based on summary diversity and hierarchical topics. In: Sun, M., Wang, X., Chang, B., Xiong, D. (eds.) CCL/NLP-NABD -2017. LNCS (LNAI), vol. 10565, pp. 343–354. Springer, Cham (2017). https://doi.org/10.1007/978-3-319-69005-6_29
4. Devlin, J., Chang, M.-W., Lee, K., Toutanova, K.: BERT: pre-training of deep bidirectional transformers for language understanding. CoRR abs/1810.04805 (2018)

5. Le, Q., Mikolov, T.: Proceedings of the 31st International Conference on Machine Learning. PMLR **32**(2), 1188–1196 (2014)
6. Chen, Y., Zaki, M.J.: KATE: K-competitive autoencoder for text. In: Proceedings of the 23rd ACM SIGKDD International Conference on Knowledge Discovery and Data Mining (KDD 2017), pp. 85–94. ACM, New York (2017). https://doi.org/10.1145/3097983.3098017
7. Giannakopoulos, G., et al.: Multiling 2015: multilingual summarization of single and multi-documents, on-line Fora, and call-center conversations. In: Proceedings of the SIGDIAL 2015 Conference, pp. 270–274 (2015)
8. Joosse, S.A.: In-Silico Online-Statistical tools. http://in-silico.online. Accessed May 2019

Conditional GANs for Image Captioning with Sentiments

Tushar Karayil[1,2(✉)], Asif Irfan[1], Federico Raue[2], Jörn Hees[2], and Andreas Dengel[1,2]

[1] TU Kaiserslautern, Kaiserslautern, Germany
[2] DFKI, Kaiserslautern, Germany
{tushar.karayi,asif.irfanl,federico.raue,jorn.hees,
andreas.dengel}@dfki.de

Abstract. The area of automatic image captioning has witnessed much progress recently. However, generating captions with sentiment, which is a common dimension in human generated captions, still remains a challenge. This work presents a generative approach that combines sentiment (positive/negative) and variation for caption generation. The presented approach consists of a Generative Adversarial Network which takes as input, an image and a binary vector indicating the sentiment of the caption to be generated. We evaluate our model quantitatively on the state-of-the-art image caption dataset and qualitatively using a crowdsourcing platform. Our results, along with human evaluation prove that we competitively succeed in the task of creating variations and sentiment in image captions.

Keywords: GAN · Sentiment · Caption · Policy Gradient

1 Introduction

A caption of an image is a short piece of text, provided by the user and describes the user's interpretation of the image. Automatic image captioning, where machines generate a short piece of text given an image, lies at the intersection of computer vision and natural language processing. In the last decade, there has been significant progress in generating descriptive image captions [16,17,19]. However, these image captioning approaches often only focus on describing the content of the image without any emotional or sentimental dimension. An analysis of the 3000 captions prevalent across the social media platforms (e.g. Flickr) reveal two characteristic dimensions of these textual descriptions [1]. First, sentiments are often prominently present in captions. These captions are more than mere *factual* descriptions of the image. Second, humans often use a wide variety of captions while describing images [3]. These aspects are often neglected in state-of-the-art image captioning models where the intention is to generate a caption which is often as close to the ground-truth as possible. Therefore,

---

T. Karayil and A. Irfan—Equal contribution from authors.

© Springer Nature Switzerland AG 2019
I. V. Tetko et al. (Eds.): ICANN 2019, LNCS 11730, pp. 300–312, 2019.
https://doi.org/10.1007/978-3-030-30490-4_25

in order for machines to generate effective captions for images it must at least include the above mentioned dimensions.

Our motivating question then becomes: *"Can a model generate captions with intended sentiment and variations?"*. The authors of [2] show that adjectives can be used to add sentiments and an adjective-noun pair can express the visual sentiment of an image. Therefore, we assume that incorporating adjectives into a caption enhances the sentiment component of the same. To combine sentiment and variability in a single model we use a generative approach.

Generative models have shown to be effective at approximating unknown distributions. The most successful among generative models, called Generative Adversarial Network, GAN [5] has proved to be highly efficient at tasks like image generation, image completion [10,21] etc. A typical GAN includes a generator network which, given a noise vector z, generates data items and a discriminator network which evaluates these items (if generated or real). Together, they perform a *min-max* game, where the generators objective is to generate data which can fool the discriminator and the discriminators objective is to accurately distinguish the generated data from real. A variant of GANs, called Conditional-GAN, CGAN [10] follows an architecture where generator and discriminators are conditioned on an external input. Our method takes inspiration from the CGAN architecture where sentiment acts as the external condition.

Training GANs for text generation is a challenging task, mainly due to two reasons: First, the process of generating language is a sequential-sampling procedure which is non-differentiable, making the direct application of backpropagation difficult; Second, the generator receives the feedback from the discriminator only after the entire sequence has been produced. This leads to several problems for training sequences like vanishing gradients. The authors of [3] have shown that reinforcement learning algorithms like Policy Gradients and Monte-Carlo rollouts can be used to mitigate these effects in order to train a GAN for caption generation. Our final model takes as input, an image and a binary variable (indicating the desired positive or negative sentiment of the caption) to generate captions accordingly. Figure 1 and Table 2 show the basic architecture of the model and few examples of generated captions respectively.

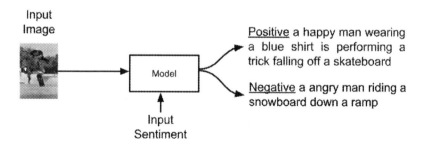

Fig. 1. Basic overview of our model. The input to the model is the image and a binary vector indicating the required sentiment (positive/negative) of the output captions. The model generates the caption which has the input sentiment and multiple variations.

In this regard, the contributions of this paper can be stated as follows:

- We design a generative sentiment-captioning model which is different from the regular encoder-decoder captioning models.
- The generative model can create captions with an input sentiment and variations. The required sentiment can be provided as an external input along with the image.
- We show that sentiment information can be embedded into a GAN with a two phase training approach. Our model outperforms the state-of-the-art for objective and sentiment captions.

The rest of the paper is organized as follows. Section 2 lists related work relevant to this paper. Section 3 gives a detailed description of the model architecture and training. Section 4 describes our experiments and discusses our findings, including the human evaluation. Section 5 concludes the paper and charts out the future direction.

2   Related Work

Image captioning frameworks generally follow an encoder-decoder architecture [16,17]. The input image is encoded into a n-dimensional space using a Convolutional Neural Network (CNN). The encoded image acts as the initial state for the decoder which is a Long Short Term Memory Network (LSTM) to generate a text sequence. The network is trained using a *maximum likelihood* loss (e.g. Cross Entropy Loss). Deviating from this convention, we can have a GAN architecture wherein the generator is an LSTM network and the discriminator, as second neural network, evaluates the caption. The generator given an image, generates a sequence which is evaluated by the discriminator.

To the best of our knowledge, there has been no previous work which combines sentiments and variability together in captioning. Therefore, this section lists out the related research in two directions: (a) captioning approaches for sentiment captions, (b) captioning approaches which use generative models (for variability) to generate captions.

2.1   Sentiment Captioning

The goal of these methods is to generate captions which have some sentiment information inside them. As mentioned previously, the addition of adjectives is one method to increase the sentiment of a caption. Therefore, the methods mentioned below have an extra module to inject sentiment into the caption.

In [14], authors use an additional CNN, along with the regular image captioning encoder-decoder model which learns sentiment features. The model keeps track of the noun with the highest probability in the generated caption to add a sentiment adjective to it. The additional CNN along with the encoder-decoder model means that the number parameters required are almost doubled. A parallel Recursive Neural Network (RNN) was used in [9] with the standard encode-decoder model which emphasizes on the descriptions with sentiments. The model is trained with a switching mechanism using a binary sentiment variable associated with each word. The parallel RNN architecture here is not truly end to end and needs to be trained first with the positive set of captions and again with a negative set of captions. The authors of [11] used a method which takes into account the current focus point inside the image (attention) to get the sentiments into the generated captions. A high-level as well as word level sentiment information with two different sentiment vectors are used here to capture the general sentiment of the image. Modified LSTM modules have also been proposed by [18] to inject sentiments.

The above mentioned approaches differ from our model in two ways: First, they are based on a variant of encoder decoder model. Second, they are trained on the *Maximum Likelihood* principle. This enforces the model to generate very rigid captions lacking the extra dimension of variability.

2.2 Generative Methods

The approaches listed here are based on generative models, specifically GANs. GAN training is often aided by the use of reinforcement learning algorithms. Here the discriminator acts as a reward agent and the objective of the generator is to create sequences which maximize the reward. The authors of [20] propose a framework to use GANs to train a captioning framework with the policy gradient algorithm. Policy gradient approaches try to find an optimal policy/rule through feedback from the discriminator. The work in [3] applies the aforementioned policy gradient based training to introduce variations in caption generation.

The above mentioned generative methods differ from our model in two ways: First, their focus is on generating neutral or objective captions and the sentiment dimension is found missing. Second, the z vector of the model is a random input whereas our model uses the z dimensions to encode input sentiment.

3 Proposed Method

We use an architecture similar to a CGAN [3] but with one generator and two discriminators. Our training also differs from the adversarial approach [5]. Briefly put, our training contains two phases. In the first phase, we train both the generator and discriminator. After the first phase, the discriminator weights are frozen and they now act as reward agents. In the second phase, the rewards produced by the discriminators (for the generated captions) act as a feedback to further train the generator. Training using this reinforcement technique is called policy gradients.

3.1 Architecture

Our model consists of a generator, G and two discriminator networks, D_r, D_s (Fig. 2 shows the detailed architecture of the model). G is a single layer LSTM network (hidden dimension h_g) which takes an image along with a noise vector

$z \in \mathbb{R}^m$ as input and generates a caption by sampling discretely from the output. The input image is first converted into a feature vector, $f \in \mathbb{R}^n$ using the last fully connected layer of a pretrained CNN. The objective of the generator is to generate captions which are relevant to the image and have a positive/negative sentiment based on the input noise vector z. The objective of D_r and D_s is to accurately judge the relevance and the sentiment of the generated caption respectively.

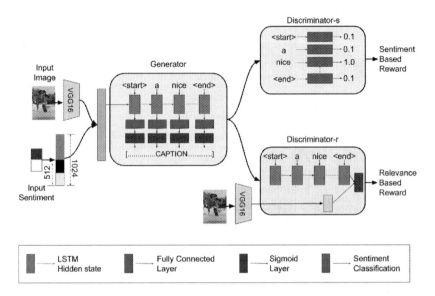

Fig. 2. Detailed architecture of our model. The Generator takes the image and a binary sentiment vector as input. Discriminator-r uses the same image to evaluate the quality of the generated caption. Discriminator-s uses the input sentiment vector and the generated caption while evaluating its reward.

The first discriminator D_r, is a LSTM network (hidden dimension h_d), which given an image and a caption, distinguishes between the captions generated by G from the ones present in the training set. D_r also takes into account the semantic relevance of the generated caption given the input image and the true caption of the input image. The objective function to train the discriminator is an extended version used by [3]. For D_r with parameters η, given an image I, the objective function (1) and reward (2) can be formulated as:

$$L_{D_r}(I; \eta) = \mathbb{E}_{S_r \sim S_T} \log R_{D_r}(I, S_r) + \alpha \cdot \mathbb{E}_{S_g \sim S_G} \log (1 - R_{D_r}(I, S_g))$$
$$+ \beta \cdot \mathbb{E}_{S_n \in S_N} \log (1 - R_{D_r}(I, S_n)) \tag{1}$$

$$R_{D_r} = \sigma(f_\theta(I) \cdot h_\eta(S)) \tag{2}$$

where η represents parameters of D_r, θ represents the parameters of the CNN, f and h are embedding functions of image and caption respectively, $<\cdot>$ is the dot product, S_T is the true caption for I from the training set, S_G is a generated caption from G for I and S_N is a "irrelevant-caption" from the training set that does not belong to I. α and β are balancing coefficients.

The second discriminator, D_s takes the generated caption from G, the input sentiment vector and assigns a reward for each of the tokens generated by the generator. Our experiments showed that a pre-trained sentiment classifier can also be used with our modified objective function[1]. D_s provides a high reward if the computed sentiment is the same as the expected sentiment and punishes G for deviations. Thus, the reward from D_s can be defined as follows:

$$R_{D_s}(S, \omega) = \mathbb{E}_{S \sim S_G}[\delta_{wp} \log f_p(S) + \delta_{wn} \log f_n(S)] \tag{3}$$

$$f_p(t) = \begin{cases} 1, & s(t) > 0.5, \\ 0.8, & 0 \le s(t) \le 0.5, \\ 0.1, & s(t) < 0 \end{cases} \qquad f_n(t) = \begin{cases} 1, & s(t) < -0.5, \\ 0.8, & -0.5 \le s(t) \le 0, \\ 0.1, & s(t) > 0 \end{cases}$$

where $\omega \in \{p, n\}$ is the input sentiment, $s(t)$ is sentiment value of token t assigned by D_s and δ is the kronecker delta. It should be noted that, after the discriminators are trained, their role is to provide a reward to each token in the caption generated by G.

3.2   Training

We divide the model training into two phases. In the first phase, the generator and discriminators are trained. After the first phase, the generator is able to generate words which are relevant to the image (without any specific language structure). For the second phase, the discriminators are frozen and the generator is further trained (via policy gradients) to incorporate sentiment and language variations in the caption. We found that this method of training increased the stability of the model and prevented the model from the "helvetica scenario" or mode collapse [5].

Phase 1. The generator G in this setup was pre-trained with maximum likelihood estimation technique for e_g epochs. This pre-training was done in order to stabilize the gradients. We reach a stage where the generator starts generating some relevant words related to the image. The discriminator D_r was then trained using this generator for e_r epochs (with the loss function in Eq. 1). Although, it can be argued that this is not truly an alternating adversarial training, we did not find any significant difference in variations of captions with alternating adversarial training. Moreover, with our approach it reduced the training time (in terms of number of required epochs) of Generator. The noise variable z was set to a 1024 sampling from $\mathcal{N}(0, 1)$.

---

[1] We used sentiment classifier provided by TextBlob (https://textblob.readthedocs. io/en/dev), which provides a sentiment value in $[-1, 1]$.

Phase 2. We used a policy gradient approach to further train G wherein the discriminators D_r and D_s act as reward agents. This means that G needs to generate captions through which it can maximize the rewards given by D_r and D_s. We also want to provide an input to G for the intended sentiment of the caption. To achieve this, we used the noise variable z. We split z into two parts: a 512-dimensional vector sampled from $\mathcal{N}(0, 1)$ and a 512-dimensional latent code vector which is assigned values based on the sentiment in the ground truth caption. If the ground truth caption was positive, the latent code is assigned values such that the first 256 dimensions are set to 1 and the rest to 0 and vice-versa (using smaller dimensions than 256 made the generator to ignore these values). We then used D_s in a way which forces the generator to use this information. This ensures that there is high correlation between G's distribution and the dimensions of z vector. Therefore, the Phase-2 loss of G can be formulated as follows:

$$L_G(I) = \mathbb{E}_{S_g \in S_G}[-\gamma_1 \cdot R_{D_r} - \gamma_2 \cdot R_{D_s} + \gamma_3 \cdot \Omega(S_g, S_t)] \tag{4}$$

where, $\gamma_1, \gamma_2, \gamma_3 \in (0, 1]$ are the balancing coefficients learned from the validation set and Ω is a regularizing term used to prevent the discriminator from collapsing to trivial patterns. We found that setting Ω to cross-entropy function (between generated caption S_g and true caption S_t of the image) gave the best results. During inference, to generate variations, the first 512-dimensions are sampled from $\mathcal{N}(0, 1)$ (the last 512 are set according to the required sentiment as mentioned above). Table 2 shows these variations where the first 512 dimension of z are changed to create three different captions for a given sentiment.

4   Experiments

In this section we describe the dataset, hyperparameters and the results from our experiments. We evaluate the results both quantitatively and qualitatively to get a better understanding of our performance. For these experiments we have chosen only the positive and negative emotions. This is because the state-of-the-art models in sentiment captioning have used only positive/negative emotion [9,11]. Therefore, choosing the same number of emotions for our experiments gave us a clear way to compare our results against the state-of-the-art.

4.1   Sentiment Enhanced MSCOCO

Microsoft-COCO (MSCOCO) [8] is an image-caption dataset containing 150,000 image-caption pairs in total (train, validation and test) and is also the preferred dataset for state-of-the-art image-captioning research [3,9,11,16,18,19]. Therefore, we chose to use MSCOCO as this gave us a clear way to compare our results against the state-of-the-art. Although MSCOCO is the benchmark dataset for captioning models, the captions provided are quite objective and clearly lack the sentiment dimension. A sentiment classification showed us that there were only 29,521 and 26,851 captions with a positive and negative sentiment respectively. The rest, 61,915 were neutral captions. The sentiment captions dataset from [9] (with 998 images) was found to be too small for our training task. To overcome these challenges, we decided to modify each of the nouns present in the MSCOCO dataset with a suitable positive or negative adjective. The intention was to enhance the sentiment value of the training set. Rather than randomly adding positive and negative adjectives, we used the work [6], to find the list of suitable adjectives for each noun. We used the 2017 train/val split of MSCOCO which consists of 118,287 training images and 5,000 validation images[2]. For each of these images, there are 5 captions in the dataset. Following the sentiment enhancement, we processed each of these captions similar to [3]: (a) remove all the non alphabetic characters apart from comma, (b) convert all the words to lower-case, (c) add a START (<start>) and END (<end>) token at the beginning and end of each caption, (d) remove all the words with the frequency of less than 5 in training and validation set combined. This gave us the vocabulary size of 10,496 words. All the words that were not in the vocabulary were replaced with a token <unk>. We used the maximum sequence length of 16 and thus truncated all captions up until this length and padded the shortened sequences with token <pad>. After the changes, the sentiment-enhanced MSCOCO contained 50,303 positive and 67,981 negative image-caption pairs.

4.2 Hyperparameters

In this section we describe the set of parameters which were empirically determined based on the validation set. The hidden dimensions of the generator and discriminator lstm networks, h_g, h_d were both set to 512. The VGG16 network was used as the feature extractor for images with the feature vector $f \in \mathbb{R}^{4096}$. The noise vector z was from R^{1024}. The coefficients for Eq. 1, α, β were set to 1. The coefficients for Eq. 4, $\gamma_1, \gamma_2, \gamma_3$ were set to $1, 1, 0.5$ respectively. For the first phase training, epochs e_g and e_r were $50, 30$ respectively. For the second phase, e_g was 100.

4.3 Results

Since our work addresses the dimensions of sentiment and variability, the results were evaluated both quantitatively as well as qualitatively. Quantitative evaluation usually involves reporting conventional scores of BLEU [12], METEOR [4], ROUGE [7] and CIDEr [15] against the ground truth. Qualitative evaluation uses human subjects to evaluate the generated captions for sentiment and grammar.

Quantitative Results. Classical score like BLEU, METEOR, ROGUE and CIDEr are generally evaluated by matching n-grams between target and the

---

[2] MSCOCO does not have ground-truth captions for the test set.

Table 1. Conventional metrics for Show n Tell (SnT), SentiCap (SCap) (for both positive and negative captions) and our model (with 1, 5 and 10 generated captions). Even though our objective is not to maximize conventional scores, we still outperform both objective and sentiment models in most of these scores as we increase the variations. SnT scores are the same for Positive and Negative captions because they generate a neutral caption.

	Metric	SnT [16]	SCap [9]	Ours		
				$c = 1$	$c = 5$	$c = 10$
Positive captions	BLEU-1	0.620	0.567	0.547	**0.621**	**0.656**
	BLEU-2	0.437	0.365	0.346	0.406	**0.439**
	BLEU-3	**0.306**	0.240	0.220	0.267	0.295
	BLEU-4	**0.218**	0.164	0.144	0.181	0.202
	METEOR	0.219	0.199	0.185	0.209	**0.221**
	ROUGE_L	0.473	0.443	0.418	0.469	**0.488**
	CIDEr	**0.752**	0.545	0.461	0.591	0.631
Negative captions	BLEU-1	0.620	0.572	0.570	**0.645**	**0.676**
	BLEU-2	0.437	0.367	0.362	0.428	**0.463**
	BLEU-3	0.306	0.246	0.234	0.287	**0.319**
	BLEU-4	0.218	0.164	0.151	0.191	**0.219**
	METEOR	0.219	0.200	0.199	**0.222**	**0.235**
	ROUGE_L	0.473	0.447	0.445	**0.483**	**0.504**
	CIDEr	**0.752**	0.516	0.509	0.627	0.688

generated captions. Therefore, a higher score would suggest that the generated caption is closer to the target sentence. Even though our models are not trained to emulate the ground truth (in turn maximize the benchmark scores), we would like to report these scores to show that we can still outperform the state-of-the-art, simply by increasing the variations for our captions. To compare against the state-of-the-art for objective captioning, we use the "Show n Tell" [16] model. For comparison against the state-of-the-art for sentiment captioning, we use "Senti-Cap" [9] model. We use the test set published by [9] which contains 433 positive and 433 negative image-caption pairs. The results show that even though we did not train the model according to the conventional criteria, we competitively outperform the state of art as shown in Table 1. As we increase our generated captions ($c = 1, 5, 10$), we also get some variations which are similar to the ground truth, thereby achieving high value for these scores. Furthermore, we have to use the same underlying vocabulary to generate variations. The nouns present in the ground truth caption, like park, kitchen, man etc. are present in the generated captions/variations as well (although their positions are different) providing a boost to these values.

In order to determine whether the z vector truly encodes the intended sentiment, we created 30,000 pairs (15,000 positive/negative each) of encoded z

vectors and calculated the sentiment of the generated caption. We then used t-SNE to visualize these vectors. Figure 3 (left) shows the distribution of these vectors. As can be seen, there are two clusters that represent two different sentiment encoded z vectors. The colors indicate the sentiment of the generated caption. Each of the two clusters are dominated by a single output sentiment (positive or negative) as indicated by their color coding. Figure 3 (right) shows the confusion matrix w.r.t the sentiment. As seen from the confusion matrix, the overall accuracy of the intended sentiment is 93.19%. The results (visual and confusion matrix) indicate that the encoding scheme is effective and achieves the intended sentiment in the generated caption.

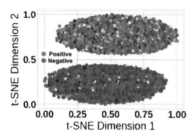

		Generated	
		Pos	Neg
Target	Pos	13,498	1,502
	Neg	541	14,459

Fig. 3. The plot (left) shows the t-SNE projection of the z vectors onto a 2-D space. Each of the two clusters formed by z vectors are dominated by a single sentiment (of generated caption). The right side shows the confusion matrix w.r.t the sentiment (expected vs generated sentiment).

Human Evaluation. As our task involves generating variable and sentiment captions, a fair evaluation is only possible through humans. The evaluation should include judgments about: (a) the validity of the caption (given the image), (b) the sentiment of the caption. In this regard, we randomly sampled 200 *held-out* images from the validation set of MSCOCO. We generated 3 positive and 3 negative captions per image. Each image-caption pair was evaluated by 3 subjects and a majority vote decided the final answer. Through the entire experiment, we collected 3600 responses from human subjects. Each subject was shown an image and 6 captions (3 positive, 3 negative) but in a random order. For each caption, given the image, subjects were then asked to answer the following questions:

1. Is this a valid caption for the given image?
2. What is the general sentiment of the caption: positive, neutral, negative?

We used the crowd sourcing platform, Amazon Mechanical Turk to conduct our human evaluation. To ensure quality, in addition to a validation set, only contributors with a minimum rating of 75% were allowed to participate. From the 3600 responses collected, 77.7% of the generated captions were voted valid and having the intended sentiment. This clearly indicates that the captions (and

Table 2. Positive and negative captions generated by our model. Positive/Negative captions are generated by providing the respective external input to the GAN along with the image. For each sentiment (+/−), there are three variations shown.

Image	Captions
	+ a proud woman walking down the street holding a colorful umbrella. + a attractive person walking across a street holding a umbrella. + a great person walking with a umbrella on top of a street. − a dangerous person walking down the street in the rain. − a evil person walking across with a umbrella. − a dangerous person walking holding a pink umbrella.
	+ a beautiful giraffe standing on top of a lush green field. + a beautiful giraffe standing near a tree in a field. + a wonderful giraffe in a field with a bird in the background. − a sad giraffe standing in a field next to a bush. − a sick giraffe standing in a lush green field. − a sick giraffe standing in a field next to a tree.
	+ a white and blue great plane is on a runway. + a popular passenger jet is parked on the runway. + a large white great airplane sitting on a runway. − a white and blue jet sitting on a wrong runway. − a expensive passenger jet is parked on the runway at an airport. − a fake airplane that is sitting on a runway.
	+ a professional tennis player returns a real shot. + a thoughtful woman plays a forehand. + a realistic tennis player returns a shot. − a crazy person plays a shot. − a unpredictable tennis player. − a angry woman on the ground.
	+ a adorable kitten is sitting on white couch. + a cute cat sleeps on a white sheet. + a proud group of cats resting on a couch. − a dramatic cat rests on a table. − lazy group of cats by the table. − a ridiculous cat laying on top of a piece of luggage.

the variations) from our model were of high quality (semantically relevant) and had the intended sentiment. Table 2 shows few examples that we used for this task. In 10.3% of the cases, the subjects voted for a "neutral" sentiment because of the generated adjective not being strong enough to convey the sentiment.

5 Conclusion and Future Work

The paper presented a generative approach to combine sentiments and variations for captions in a single model. To achieve this goal, we used an architecture similar to a GAN, training it with policy gradients. We trained the generator with two different discriminators to generate sentiment captions with a variability dimension. We showed that our model competitively outperforms the two state-of-the-art models (for objective and sentiment captions) for image captioning. To further evaluate the results, we also performed a human evaluation and showed that 77.7% of the generated captions are valid with intended sentiments. Our results imply that it is possible to generate variable-sentiment captions with good degree of accuracy. We plan to explore the control that one can have w.r.t the variations and sentiment. An interesting direction in this regard is to understand how each dimension of the $z - vector$ contribute to sentiments/variations. We also plan to extend this model with the newly introduced Google Conceptual Captions dataset [13] with 3.2 million images.

Acknowledgements. This work was supported by the BMBF project DeFuseNN (Grant 01IW17002) and the NVIDIA AI Lab (NVAIL) program.

References

1. Blandfort, P., Karayil, T., Borth, D., Dengel, A.: Image captioning in the wild: how people caption images on Flickr. In: Proceedings of the Workshop on Multimodal Understanding of Social, Affective and Subjective Attributes, pp. 21–29. ACM (2017), https://doi.org/10.1145/3132515.3132522
2. Borth, D., Ji, R., Chen, T., Breuel, T., Chang, S.F.: Large-scale visual sentiment ontology and detectors using adjective noun pairs. In: Proceedings of the 21st ACM International Conference on Multimedia, pp. 223–232. ACM (2013). https://doi.org/10.1145/2502081.2502282
3. Dai, B., Fidler, S., Urtasun, R., Lin, D.: Towards diverse and natural image descriptions via a conditional GAN. In: Proceedings of the IEEE International Conference on Computer Vision, pp. 2970–2979 (2017). https://doi.org/10.1109/ICCV.2017.323
4. Denkowski, M., Lavie, A.: Meteor universal: language specific translation evaluation for any target language. In: Proceedings of the Ninth Workshop on Statistical Machine Translation, pp. 376–380 (2014)
5. Goodfellow, I., et al.: Generative adversarial nets. In: Advances in Neural Information Processing Systems, pp. 2672–2680 (2014)
6. Karayil, T., Blandfort, P., Hees, J., Dengel, A.: The focus-aspect-value model for explainable prediction of subjective visual interpretation. In: International Conference of Multimedia Retrieval (2019). https://doi.org/10.1145/3323873.3325026

7. Lin, C.Y.: ROUGE: a package for automatic evaluation of summaries. Text Summarization Branches Out (2004)
8. Lin, T.-Y., et al.: Microsoft COCO: common objects in context. In: Fleet, D., Pajdla, T., Schiele, B., Tuytelaars, T. (eds.) ECCV 2014. LNCS, vol. 8693, pp. 740–755. Springer, Cham (2014). https://doi.org/10.1007/978-3-319-10602-1_48
9. Mathews, A.P., Xie, L., He, X.: SentiCap: generating image descriptions with sentiments. In: Thirtieth AAAI Conference on Artificial Intelligence (2016)
10. Mirza, M., Osindero, S.: Conditional generative adversarial nets. arXiv preprint (2014)
11. Nezami, O.M., Dras, M., Wan, S., Paris, C.: Senti-attend: image captioning using sentiment and attention. arXiv preprint arXiv:1811.09789 (2018)
12. Papineni, K., Roukos, S., Ward, T., Zhu, W.J.: BLEU: a method for automatic evaluation of machine translation. In: Proceedings of the 40th Annual Meeting on Association for Computational Linguistics, pp. 311–318. Association for Computational Linguistics (2002). https://doi.org/10.3115/1073083.1073135
13. Sharma, P., Ding, N., Goodman, S., Soricut, R.: Conceptual captions: a cleaned, hypernymed, image alt-text dataset for automatic image captioning. In: Proceedings of the 56th Annual Meeting of the Association for Computational Linguistics (Volume 1: Long Papers), vol. 1, pp. 2556–2565 (2018)
14. Shin, A., Ushiku, Y., Harada, T.: Image captioning with sentiment terms via weakly-supervised sentiment dataset. In: BMVC (2016)
15. Vedantam, R., Lawrence Zitnick, C., Parikh, D.: CIDEr: consensus-based image description evaluation. In: Proceedings of the IEEE Conference on Computer Vision and Pattern Recognition, pp. 4566–4575 (2015). https://doi.org/10.1109/CVPR.2015.729908
16. Vinyals, O., Toshev, A., Bengio, S., Erhan, D.: Show and tell: a neural image caption generator. In: Proceedings of the IEEE Conference on Computer Vision and Pattern Recognition, pp. 3156–3164 (2015). https://doi.org/10.1109/CVPR.2015.7298935
17. Xu, K., et al.: Show, attend and tell: neural image caption generation with visual attention. In: International Conference on Machine Learning, pp. 2048–2057 (2015)
18. You, Q., Jin, H., Luo, J.: Image captioning at will: a versatile scheme for effectively injecting sentiments into image descriptions. arXiv preprint arXiv:1801.10121 (2018)
19. You, Q., Jin, H., Wang, Z., Fang, C., Luo, J.: Image captioning with semantic attention. In: Proceedings of the IEEE Conference on Computer Vision and Pattern Recognition, pp. 4651–4659 (2016). https://doi.org/10.1109/CVPR.2016.503
20. Yu, L., Zhang, W., Wang, J., Yu, Y.: SeqGAN: sequence generative adversarial nets with policy gradient. In: Thirty-First AAAI Conference on Artificial Intelligence (2017)
21. Zhang, H., et al: StackGAN: text to photo-realistic image synthesis with stacked generative adversarial networks. In: Proceedings of the IEEE International Conference on Computer Vision, pp. 5907–5915 (2017). https://doi.org/10.1109/ICCV.2017.629

Neural Poetry: Learning to Generate Poems Using Syllables

Andrea Zugarini[1,2(✉)], Stefano Melacci[2], and Marco Maggini[2]

[1] DINFO, University of Florence, Florence, Italy
andrea.zugarini@unifi.it
[2] DIISM, University of Siena, Siena, Italy
{mela,maggini}@diism.unisi.it

Abstract. Motivated by the recent progresses on machine learning-based models that learn artistic styles, in this paper we focus on the problem of poem generation. This is a challenging task in which the machine has to capture the linguistic features that strongly characterize a certain poet, as well as the semantics of the poet's production, that are influenced by his personal experiences and by his literary background. Since poetry is constructed using syllables, that regulate the form and structure of poems, we propose a syllable-based neural language model, and we describe a poem generation mechanism that is designed around the poet style, automatically selecting the most representative generations. The poetic work of a target author is usually not enough to successfully train modern deep neural networks, so we propose a multi-stage procedure that exploits non-poetic works of the same author, and also other publicly available huge corpora to learn syntax and grammar of the target language. We focus on the Italian poet Dante Alighieri, widely famous for his Divine Comedy. A quantitative and qualitative experimental analysis of the generated tercets is reported, where we included expert judges with strong background in humanistic studies. The generated tercets are frequently considered to be real by a generic population of judges, with relative difference of 56.25% with respect to the ones really authored by Dante, and expert judges perceived Dante's style and rhymes in the generated text.

Keywords: Poem generation · Transfer learning · Language models · Recurrent neural networks · Natural Language Generation

1 Introduction

Natural Language Generation (NLG) is a challenging problem that has drawn a lot of attention in the Natural Language Processing (NLP) community [15,17]. NLG is crucial for multiple NLP applications and problems, such as dialogue systems [20], text summarization [4], and text paraphrasing [7]. Poem generation is an instance of NLG that is particularly fascinating for its peculiar features. Verses have precise structures, rhyme and meter that convey an aesthetic and

© Springer Nature Switzerland AG 2019
I. V. Tetko et al. (Eds.): ICANN 2019, LNCS 11730, pp. 313–325, 2019.
https://doi.org/10.1007/978-3-030-30490-4_26

rhythmic sound to the poetry. This expressive art of language is ancient and spread across all cultures in the world.

Automatically creating poems requires a strong attention to both the content and the form. The machine has to capture the linguistic features that strongly characterize a certain poet, as well as the semantics of the poet's production, that are influenced by their personal experiences and by their literary background. In the last few years, the machine learning community focussed on the problem of poem generation, proposing approaches that generate either English quatrains [5, 8, 10] or Chinese verses [21–24]. Most of them are based on neural architectures that combine several modules, post-processing the final results to generate well-formed verses (we postpone to Sect. 2 an in-depth description of related work). In order to cope with the lack of large scale data, these works usually do not try to mimic the style of a target poet, and they frequently consider the poetic production of several authors. Moreover, despite Italian poetry is one of the most significant and well known poetries, to the best of our knowledge it has not been the subject of studies in which neural approaches have been evaluated.

In this paper, we propose a simple and effective neural network-based model to generate verses. We focus on the Italian language and, in particular, on Dante Alighieri, the Italian poet that authored the Divine Comedy [2], the most important poem of the Middle Ages, widely considered as the greatest literary work in the Italian literature. Our model learns to generate tercets with Dante Alighieri's style by "reading" the Divide Comedy. The learning problem is tacked following Language Modeling tasks but, differently from what is commonly done by several authors, we consider syllables as input tokens (instead of words, generic n-grams, or characters, for example). This choice is motivated by the fact that poetry is constructed using syllables that regulate the form and structure of poems. For example, syllables play a crucial role in the context of meter and rhyme. Moreover, the use of sub-word information is even more useful in Italian that is a language with a rich morphology. Our model consists of a Recurrent Neural Network (LSTM [18]) that outputs one syllable at each time instant, conditioned to the previously generated text. The model is trained on Dante's tercets, that are composed of triples of hendecasyllables, with a precise structure of the rhymes. Due to its syllable-based nature, the proposed model can capture several properties of the input language, and it has a large flexibility in terms of what it can generate. The latter feature requires attention when using the language model to generate new text. We take into account the key properties of the Divine Comedy, automatically selecting the generations that are closer to Dante's style.

Training neural models on poems from a single target author can lead to low generalization quality, due to the small size of the training data. Moreover, the language used by poets from the middle ages can be significantly different from modern language, such as in the case of the Italian used by Dante Alighieri and nowadays Italian. We exploit the basic consideration that even if the form of some words have changed over time, there are a number of inherent regularities at the syllable level that have not changed that much. We propose to pre-train the system with a large modern Italian corpus (PAISA' [11]), and to perform transfer learning towards the poetry domain. The transfer of information is performed in multiple steps, exploiting Dante's prose and other Dante's poems (i.e. all the poet's production), and finally training the model with the Divine Comedy.

Our experimentation shows that exploiting Italian corpora and the poet's production improves the perplexity of the poetry-related language model, allowing the system to better capture the language and contents of the Divine Comedy. We performed a qualitative analysis of the generated tercets, based on human evaluation, where we also asked the collaboration of expert judges with strong background in humanistic studies. The generated tercets are frequently considered to be real by a generic population of judges, and expert judges perceived Dante's style and rhymes in the generated text. As expected, evaluators emphasized how the semantics behind the generated verses are sometimes hard to appreciate since they do not convey enough emotion, suggesting that more structured models that integrate additional information about the author could be an interesting topic for future work.

The paper is organized as follows. In Sect. 2 we describe related state-of-the-art approaches. Then, we introduce the proposed model and the generation mechanism in Sect. 3. Section 4 includes experiments and a discussion on the obtained results, while, finally, we draw our conclusions in Sect. 5.

2   Related Work

The scientific literature includes several works on machines that are either programmed to generate poems or that approach the problem of poem generation using machine learning algorithms. Early methods [5] rely on rule-based solutions, while more recent approaches focus on learnable language models. Language Modeling is the problem of predicting which word comes next, given a sequence of previous words. In the last few years, neural language models are the dominant class of algorithms applied to NLG. While Language Modeling was successfully addressed using feed-forward neural networks on a fixed window of words [3], in [13] a recurrent neural network approach proved to be preferable. As a matter of fact, several nowadays NLG approaches are based on recurrent nets [4,7,20].

Word-based language models usually require large vocabularies to store all the (most frequent) words in huge textual corpora, and, of course, they cannot generalize to never-seen-before words. Some other approaches tried to overcome this issue, exploiting sub-word information. A character-level solution was proposed in [9], while other authors [14] combine word embeddings with character-level representations. It has been shown [1,12] that character-based models can be adapted to produce powerful word and even context representations that capture both morphology and semantics. Sub-word information is very important in poetry, since it represents a crucial element to capture the "form" of a poem.

The first approach that proposes a deep learning-based solution to poem generation is described in [24], where the authors combined convolutional and recurrent networks to generate Chinese quatrains. Then, a number of approaches focussing on Chinese poetry were proposed. In particular, a sequence-to-sequence model with attention mechanisms was proposed in [21] and [19]. In [23] the authors extend Generative Adversarial Networks (GANs) [6] to the generation of sequences of symbols, exploiting Reinforcement Learning (RL). They consider the GAN discriminator to be the reward signal of a RL-based generator, and, among a variety of tasks, Chinese quatrains generation is also addressed. Another RL-based approach is proposed in [22], where two networks learn simultaneously from each other with a mutual RL scheme, to improve the quality of the generated poems.

In the context of English poem generation, transducers were exploited to generate poetic text [8]. Meter and rhyme are learned from characters by cascading a module that focusses on the content and a weighted state transducer that explicitly models the form of the generation. Differently, the more recent Deep-speare [10] combines three neural modules, sharing the same character-based representation, to generate English quatrains. These models consist in a word-level language model fed with both word and character representations, a network that learns the meter, and another net that identifies rhyming pairs. At the end, generations are selected after a post-processing step that picks the best quatrains combining the output of the three modules. We notice that the authors of [10] exploited a collection of poems from several authors in order to train the model.

Following the intuition of working with syllables, our solution is simpler and in the case of Italian poetry, as we will show in Sect. 4, it generates tercets not only with the proper form, but also resembling the style of the selected target author.

3   Model

The main module of the proposed model consists of a syllable-based Language Model, also referred to as SY-LM, that processes a sequence of syllables. In order to handle the input data, we have to convert the available text into a sequence of syllables, i.e., we have to segment the input text into words, and then to split words into syllables. Since we focus on the Italian language, we implemented a module that follows the most common Italian hyphenation rules that, apart from rare exceptions, correctly divides words into syllables (the same procedure could have been followed for other languages, English included).

We focus on data from Dante Alighieri's Divine Comedy, that is composed of a set of tercets (i.e., three verses). Each tercet is converted into a sequence of tokens (syllables) $x_1, \cdots, x_T$ belonging to the syllable dictionary V_{s_y}. We removed the punctuation and introduced some special tokens: word-separator <sep>, begin-of-tercet <go>, end-of-verse <eov>, end-of-tercet <eot>.

For each time instant t, SY-LM outputs the probability

$$\hat{y}_t = p(x_t | x_1, \cdots, x_{t-1})$$

for all $x_t \in V_{s_y}$. If we indicate with $\hat{\mathbf{y}}_t$ the vector with the probabilities associated to all the vocabulary elements, the model yields the syllable associated with the highest probability.

We follow the classic setting of neural network-based language models: each element of the vocabulary is encoded into a 1-hot representation of size $|V_{s_y}|$, and the system associates it to a latent dense representation that is learned jointly with the other model parameters. Such dense representations, also referred to as "syllable embeddings", are collected row-wise in matrix $W_{s_y} \in \mathbb{R}^{|V_{s_y}| \times d}$. Each token x_t of the input tercet is then mapped into its syllable embedding $\mathbf{e}_t \in \mathbb{R}^d$, that is the row of W_{s_y} associated to x_t. In detail, we have,

$$\mathbf{e}_t = W_{s_y} \cdot \mathbf{1}(x_t) \ ,$$

where $\mathbf{1}(\cdot)$ is a function returning the 1-hot column vector that has 1 in the position associated to the vocabulary index of its argument. It is important to notice that since V_{s_y} is the set of all syllables (and a few special tokens), its cardinality is smaller than traditional word-based vocabularies, therefore the embedding matrix W_{s_y} has a significantly smaller number of elements than what usually happens in the case of word-level representations.

The sequence of syllable embeddings of the input tercet is provided as input to a recurrent neural network, one element at each time step. The internal state of the recurrent network at time t is indicated with $\mathbf{h}_t$, and it is computed by updating the previous state using the current syllable embedding,

$$\mathbf{h}_t = r(\mathbf{e}_t, \mathbf{h}_{t-1}) \ , \tag{1}$$

where $r(\cdot, \cdot)$ is the state-update function of the network. We selected LSTMs as recurrent neural model, due to their good results in language modeling [18].

A projection layer (weights W, bias b, activation σ – that we set to the hyperbolic tangent) transforms $\mathbf{h}_t$ into a d-sized vector $\mathbf{z}_t$, and a dense layer followed by the softmax activation function computes the probability distribution $\hat{\mathbf{y}}_t$,

$$\mathbf{z}_t = \sigma(W\mathbf{h}_t + b) \tag{2}$$
$$\mathbf{o}_t = W'_{s_y} \mathbf{z}_t \tag{3}$$
$$\hat{\mathbf{y}}_t = \texttt{softmax}(\mathbf{o}_t) \ . \tag{4}$$

Notice that the dense layer of Eq. (3) shares its parameters with the syllable embedding matrix W_{s_y} (being $'$ the transpose operator), ulteriorly reducing the number of learnable parameters of the model.

We train the sy-LM by minimizing the cross-entropy between each $\hat{\mathbf{y}}_t$ and the ground truth from the Divine Comedy, thus pushing toward 1 the element of $\hat{\mathbf{y}}_t$ associated to the t-th syllable of the current tercet in the Divine Comedy. We measure the model performance in terms of perplexity (PPL), as commonly done in language modeling approaches [13]. An illustration of the entire model is presented in Fig. 1.

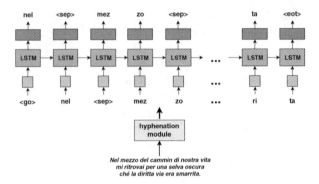

Fig. 1. Sketch of the Syllable LM. Input tercets are first pre-processed by a module that splits words into syllables and introduces some special tokens: word-separator <sep>, begin-of-tercet <go>, end-of-verse <eov>, end-of-tercet <eot>. Orange blocks are syllable embeddings, each blue block depicts the network of Eqs. (2–4). The system predicts the next syllable, i.e. the one associated to the largest probability in $\hat{\mathbf{y}}_t$. (Color figure online)

3.1   Multi-stage Transfer Learning

Learning from the Divine Comedy (or, more generally, from a single poem or from all the poems of a given target author) might not be enough to provide strong generalization skills to neural language models ($\approx 4,000$ tercets). For this reason, we follow a multi-stage training procedure that consists in sequentially pre-training our model with related data, before training it on the Divine Comedy. We want the model to deeply grasp most of the syntax and grammar of the Italian language, independently from the considered author, so that we pre-train the network using publicly available large Italian corpora (see Sect. 4). Dante Alighieri lived in the middle ages, and he wrote the Divine Comedy in Tuscan/Florentine Italian dialect of that time, giving a strong contribute in creating the currently standard language for Italy. His language is slightly different from modern Italian, including some old-fashioned words and forms not used anymore. Word-level models are likely to fail due to the unavoidable changes in the vocabulary when moving from modern Italian to Dante's Italian. Differently, our syllable-based vocabulary is flexible enough to be transferred to related data. The transition toward the Divine Comedy can be made smoother by performing a further pre-training step using all Dante's production (poems and prose), thus allowing the network to get more information on the main linguistic features of the author. Finally, we train the model on the Divine Comedy.

3.2   Poem Generation Procedure

Once SY-LM has been trained, it is directly exploited to generate new samples, i.e., new tercets. We start with $\mathbf{h}_0$ set to zeros, and we feed the system with the <go> input symbol, iteratively sampling the next token to generate. We follow a Monte Carlo sampling procedure as done in [23]. We keep sampling and generating tokens until the end-of-tercet symbol (<eot>) is generated or the number of syllables reaches a fixed maximum limit (75 in our experiments). Thanks to the randomness in the multinomial sampling, the system can generate multiple different sequences sampled from the distribution learned from the training data.

We generate a batch of tercets (2,000 in our experiments), and we assign a score $R(x) \in \mathbb{R}$ to each tercet x of the batch. Those tercets with highest scores are selected among all the generated ones (only the top-scored generation, if the goal is to generate a single tercet). $R(x)$ is the average of 4 different scores, $R_1(x), \ldots, R_4(x) \in \mathbb{R}$ that are based on known properties of the author of the Divine Comedy, in terms of form and language. In particular, tercets are composed of three hendecasyllables, with chained rhyming scheme ("ABA" – the first tercet is paired with the last one), and the words produced by the syllable-based generation must belong to the vocabulary used in the Divine Comedy. The first score penalizes non-tercet-like generations,

$$R_1(x) = -\mathsf{abs}(|x| - 3) + 1 \ , \tag{5}$$

where $|x|$ indicates the number of verses in the tercets and abs is the absolute value function. Differently, $R_2(x)$ promotes sequences with verses in x that follow an hendecasyllabic meter. Since our model is based on syllables, it is easy to count the number of syllables in a generated verse v, and we define R_2 as follows,

$$R_2(x) = -\sum_{v \in x}(\mathsf{abs}(|v| - 11)) + 1 \ . \tag{6}$$

The chained rhyming scheme is measured by $R_3(x)$,

$$R_3(x) = \begin{cases} 1, & \text{if } (v_1, v_3), v_1, v_3 \in x \text{ are in rhyme} \\ -1, & \text{otherwise} \end{cases}, \tag{7}$$

where a positive score is given when a tercet has first verse v_1 in rhyme with the third one v_3. Since the generated x is actually a sequence of syllables, words are identified by merging syllables until the word-separator token <sep> is predicted. In order to avoid the generation of words that are far from the poet's style – that is pretty unlikely in our experience –, we assign a small positive contribute a to words in x that belong to the vocabulary of the Divine Comedy. Formally,

$$R_4(x) = \sum_{w \in x} f_w(x), \quad f_w(x_i) = \begin{cases} a, & \text{if } w \in V \\ -b, & \text{otherwise} \end{cases} \tag{8}$$

where w indicates a word in tercet x. In the experiments a was set to 0.05 and b to 1 to strongly discourage not valid words.

4   Experiments

We performed several experiments to assess the quality of the SY-LM, reporting both quantitative and qualitative results. We considered multiple data sources (*i.*, *ii.*, *iii.* below), following the multi-stage learning procedure of Sect. 3.1. The core of this work is the Divine Comedy, the most important Dante Alighieri's contribution.

(*i.*) The Divine Comedy (**DC**). It is a poem composed of 100 "cantos" organized into three *cantiche*. Each canto is a poem with a variable number of tercets also known as "Dante's tercet". SY-LM was trained on 3768 tercets and evaluated on a test set of 472. We also kept a validation set of 471 to set the network hyper-parameters. Overall, there are about 180k syllables in the Divine Comedy.

(*ii.*) Modern Italian Dataset (**PAISA'**). We exploited PAISA',[1] a large corpus of Italian web texts. We considered a portion of 200k documents, consisting of about 836k sentences with more than 67M syllables.

(*iii.*) Dante's Production (**DP**). We collected most of Dante's known non-latin prose and poetry manuscripts. In particular, we gathered all the text from *Convivio*, *Le rime* and *La vita nuova*, collecting overall 1752 sentences (∼157k syllables) for prose and 2727 verses (∼48k syllables).

In order to select the hyper-parameters of the neural architecture we measured the perplexity (PPL) of several configurations on the validation set taken from the **DC** corpus. We found that the best performing size d for the syllable embeddings was 300, whereas the best size of the state of the LSTM was 1024. State neurons were dropped out [16] with probability 0.3. The size of V_{s_y} was set to 1884, including all the syllables in the Divine Comedy and the special tokens. When pre-training on **PAISA'** and then refining on **DP** (Sect. 3.1), we kept a small validation set to decide when to early stop the learning procedure, and different batch sizes and learning rates have been validated. Best results occurred with batch size 32 and learning rate of 0.001.

4.1   Results

We experimented the transfer learning procedure of Sect. 3.1, evaluating the impact of the different data sources. In Table 1 we report our results (PPL) on both validation and test set data. As expected, the model benefits from pre-training on additional data. In particular, the most significant improvement is given when pre-training on **PAISA'**, showing that there is a positive transfer of information from modern Italian to Dante's language. Moreover, despite the quantity of data in **DP** is still rather small, we can see further improvements when other Dante's productions are used to pre-train the model.

The quality of the generated tercets has been assessed by human judges in two different evaluations. In the first test, we involved 13 graduate and not graduated students, mostly from humanistic degrees. We refer to them as "non-expert" judges, since they were not specialized in Dante's production, but very

---

[1] http://www.corpusitaliano.it/en/contents/paisa.html.

Table 1. Perplexity on validation and test set data from the Divine Comedy, pre-training (or not) the model using multiple data. $A \to B$ means that we train on data A first, and then we train on data B.

Datasets	Val PPL	Test PPL
DC	12.45	12.39
PAISA' $\to$ DC	10.83	10.82
DP $\to$ DC	11.95	11.74
PAISA'$\to$ DP $\to$ DC	**10.63**	**10.55**

well aware of the author and of the Divine Comedy. They were asked to judge if a given tercet was authored by Dante Alighieri or not (i.e., generated by SY-LM). Each judge evaluated 10 tercets, 5 of which were from Dante and 5 generated by our model. In Table 2 we report the number of times (percentages) that tercets from a certain population were judged to be authored by Dante. It is clear that, given the humanistic background of the evaluators, judgements are rather thoughtful, however our generated tercets are considered as real almost half of the times of ones from Dante, with a relative difference of 56.25%.

Table 2. The number of times (percentages) that tercets from either SY-LM or Dante Alighieri (POET) are judged to be authored by Dante (i.e., they were marked as "real"). Our model is considered to be realistic almost half of the times of real Dante's production.

Generator	Real-Mark
SY-LM	28%
Poet	64%

We can further analyze this result by distinguishing between those judges that were less capable of identifying real Dante's tercets (marking them to be real less than 50% of the times) and the other ones. In Fig. 2 we can observe that the "less-capable judges" were even more attracted by SY-LM than by real Dante's tercets. Since these judges better represent the average population of users, this result suggests that SY-LM is very positively perceived. On the other hand, more capable evaluators are less frequently fooled by SY-LM with a relative difference of $\approx$67% from Dante.

In another experiment, we involved 4 expert judges with academic experiences on Dante Alighieri's production. Each expert evaluated 20 tercets, scoring (from 0 to 5) different properties of each of them: *emotion, meter, rhyme, readability* and adherence to the *author's style*. In particular, 10 tercets were generated by SY-LM and 10 were extracted from the Divine Comedy. Judges were not aware of how tercets were distributed. We report the test results in Table 3.

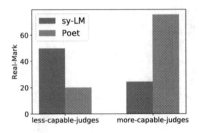

Fig. 2. Results of Table 2 further divided into two groups: judges that are less capable of recognizing real Dante's tercets and the other ones.

Dante's tercets are better scored, of course, however, we observe a good evaluation of the quality of the rhymes produced by SY-LM. Considering that judges know very well Dante Alighieri, it is interesting to see that they are experiencing some of the author's style in the generated tercets. Evaluators emphasized how the semantics behind the generated verses are sometimes hard to appreciate since they do not convey enough emotion, that is the motivation behind the lower scores on the first two columns of Table 3. Finally, judges applied very strict criteria in evaluating the meter, giving low scores whenever a small incoherence with Dante's meter was apparently detected, even if they reported that it was not far from the ideal case.

Table 3. Experts evaluations restricted to tercets generated by SY-LM. Votes vary from 0 to 5. The average rate is also reported. For comparisons, in the last line we also report the average rate in the case of Dante's real tercets (POET).

	Readability	Emotion	Meter	Rhyme	Style
Judge 1	1.57	1.21	1.57	3.36	2.29
Judge 2	1.64	1.45	1.73	3.00	2.27
Judge 3	2.83	2.33	2.00	4.17	2.92
Judge 4	2.17	2.00	2.33	2.92	2.50
Average	2.04	1.73	1.90	3.37	2.49
Poet (Average)	4.34	3.87	4.45	4.50	4.34

Finally, we report some examples of generated tercets in Table 4. The first three tercets were well rated by non-expert and also expert judges, while the last one was badly scored.

Table 4. Examples of generated tercets. The last one (bottom right) never fooled the judges, whereas the first three tercets were marked as real Dante's tercets by 88.00%, 55.56% and 45.45% of the evaluators, respectively.

e tenendo con li occhi e nel mondo	*per lo mondo che se ben mi trovi*
che sotto regal facevan mi novo	*con mia vista con acute parole*
che 'l s'apparve un dell'altro fondo	*e s'altri dicer fori come novi*
in questo imaginar lo 'ntelletto	*non pur rimosso pome dal sospetto*
vive sotto 'l mondo che sia fatto moto	*che 'l litigamento mia come si lece*
e per accorger palude è dritto stretto	*che per ammirazion di dio subietto*

5   Conclusions

We presented a syllable-based language model for poem generation, that was applied to generate tercets. The proposed model is general, and we studied it in the context of Italian language and, in particular, in Dante Alighieri's Divine Comedy. Despite its simplicity and the lack of large-scale collections of data from the target author, our model produces tercets that are considered real by evaluators with humanistic background roughly half of the times of Dante's verses. This is due to a scored generation mechanism that helps to keep Divine Comedy's meter and rhyme, and also due to a multi-stage training procedure that improves the quality of the content, exploiting all the poet's production and text in modern Italian. However, the outcome of the evaluation from expert judges clearly showed that, while the rhyme and style are positively captured by the model, the generations are still weak on meter and on conveying enough emotion. In future work we plan to exploit the scoring criteria that we used in generating text to setup a Reinforcement Learning strategy. We are also interested in exploring more structured models that include additional information about the author, to improve the emotional quality of the generations.

Acknowledgments. We thank Emmanuela Carbé and Elisabetta Bartoli for providing us Dante's data and for inviting several evaluators of our model. We would also like to thank Monica Marchi, Irene Tani, Maria Rita Traina and Simonetta Teucci, that helped us in evaluating the model. This research was partially supported by QuestIT s.r.l. in the framework of the joint laboratory SAINLab.

References

1. Akbik, A., Blythe, D., Vollgraf, R.: Contextual string embeddings for sequence labeling. In: Proceedings of the 27th International Conference on Computational Linguistics, pp. 1638–1649 (2018)
2. Alighieri, D., Sisson, C., Sisson, C., Higgins, D.: The Divine Comedy. Oxford University Press, New York (1998)
3. Bengio, Y., Ducharme, R., Vincent, P., Jauvin, C.: A neural probabilistic language model. J. Mach. Learn. Res. **3**, 1137–1155 (2003)

4. Chopra, S., Auli, M., Rush, A.M.: Abstractive sentence summarization with attentive recurrent neural networks. In: Proceedings of the 2016 Conference of the NAACL: Human Language Technologies, pp. 93–98 (2016)
5. Colton, S., Goodwin, J., Veale, T.: Full-face poetry generation. In: ICCC, pp. 95–102 (2012)
6. Goodfellow, I., et al.: Generative adversarial nets. In: Advances in Neural Information Processing Systems, pp. 2672–2680 (2014)
7. Hasan, S.A., et al.: Neural paraphrase generation with stacked residual LSTM networks. In: International Conference on Computational Linguistics: Technical Papers, pp. 2923–2934 (2016)
8. Hopkins, J., Kiela, D.: Automatically generating rhythmic verse with neural networks. In: Proceedings of the 55th Annual Meeting of the Association for Computational Linguistics (Volume 1: Long Papers), vol. 1, pp. 168–178 (2017)
9. Hwang, K., Sung, W.: Character-level language modeling with hierarchical recurrent neural networks. In: 2017 IEEE International Conference on Acoustics, Speech and Signal Processing (ICASSP), pp. 5720–5724. IEEE (2017)
10. Lau, J.H., Cohn, T., Baldwin, T., Brooke, J., Hammond, A.: Deep-speare: a joint neural model of poetic language, meter and rhyme (2018)
11. Lyding, V., et al.: The paisa' corpus of Italian web texts. In: 9th Web as Corpus Workshop (WaC-9)@ EACL 2014, pp. 36–43. EACL (2014)
12. Marra, G., Zugarini, A., Melacci, S., Maggini, M.: An unsupervised character-aware neural approach to word and context representation learning. In: Kůrková, V., Manolopoulos, Y., Hammer, B., Iliadis, L., Maglogiannis, I. (eds.) ICANN 2018. LNCS, vol. 11141, pp. 126–136. Springer, Cham (2018). https://doi.org/10.1007/978-3-030-01424-7_13
13. Mikolov, T., Karafiát, M., Burget, L., Černockỳ, J., Khudanpur, S.: Recurrent neural network based language model. In: Eleventh Annual Conference of the International Speech Communication Association (2010)
14. Miyamoto, Y., Cho, K.: Gated word-character recurrent language model. In: Proceedings of the 2016 Conference on Empirical Methods in Natural Language Processing, pp. 1992–1997 (2016)
15. Reiter, E., Dale, R.: Building Natural Language Generation Systems. Cambridge University Press, New York (2000)
16. Srivastava, N., Hinton, G., Krizhevsky, A., Sutskever, I., Salakhutdinov, R.: Dropout: a simple way to prevent neural networks from overfitting. J. Mach. Learn. Res. **15**(1), 1929–1958 (2014)
17. Subramanian, S., Rajeswar, S., Dutil, F., Pal, C., Courville, A.: Adversarial generation of natural language. In: Proceedings of the 2nd Workshop on Representation Learning for NLP, pp. 241–251 (2017)
18. Sundermeyer, M., Schlüter, R., Ney, H.: LSTM neural networks for language modeling. In: Thirteenth Annual Conference of the International Speech Communication Association (2012)
19. Wang, Q., Luo, T., Wang, D., Xing, C.: Chinese song iambics generation with neural attention-based model. In: Proceedings of the Twenty-Fifth International Joint Conference on Artificial Intelligence, pp. 2943–2949. AAAI Press (2016)
20. Wen, T.H., Gasic, M., Mrkšić, N., Su, P.H., Vandyke, D., Young, S.: Semantically conditioned LSTM-based natural language generation for spoken dialogue systems. In: Proceedings of the 2015 Conference on Empirical Methods in Natural Language Processing, pp. 1711–1721 (2015)

21. Yi, X., Li, R., Sun, M.: Generating Chinese classical poems with RNN encoder-decoder. In: Sun, M., Wang, X., Chang, B., Xiong, D. (eds.) CCL/NLP-NABD -2017. LNCS (LNAI), vol. 10565, pp. 211–223. Springer, Cham (2017). https://doi.org/10.1007/978-3-319-69005-6_18

22. Yi, X., Sun, M., Li, R., Li, W.: Automatic poetry generation with mutual reinforcement learning. In: Proceedings of the 2018 Conference on Empirical Methods in Natural Language Processing, pp. 3143–3153 (2018)

23. Yu, L., Zhang, W., Wang, J., Yu, Y.: SeqGAN: sequence generative adversarial nets with policy gradient. In: Thirty-First AAAI Conference on Artificial Intelligence (2017)

24. Zhang, X., Lapata, M.: Chinese poetry generation with recurrent neural networks. In: Proceedings of the 2014 Conference on Empirical Methods in Natural Language Processing (EMNLP), pp. 670–680 (2014)

Exploring the Advantages of Corpus in Neural Machine Translation of Agglutinative Language

Yatu Ji, Hongxu Hou[✉], Nier Wu, and Junjie Chen

Computer Science Department, Inner Mongolia University, Hohhot, China
jiyatu0@126.com, cshhx@imu.edu.cn, wunier04@126.com, chenjj@imau.edu.cn

Abstract. This study solves the problem of mismatch between rigid model and varied morphology in machine translation of agglutinative language in two ways. (1) a free granularity preprocessing strategy is proposed to construct a multi-granularity mixed input. (2) the value iteration network is further added into the reinforcement learning model, and the rewards of each granularity input are converted into decision values, so that the model training has higher target and efficiency. The experimental results show that our approach has achieved significant improvement in the two representative agglutinative language machine translation tasks, including low-resource Mongolian→Chinese, and common Japanese→English, and has greatly shortened the training time.

Keywords: Neural machine translation · Agglutinative language · Reinforcement learning · Free granularity

1 Introduction

The vocabulary of Neural machine translation (NMT) [1,4,15] models is typically limited, which is contrary to the open-vocabulary translation and especially for agglutinative languages with productive word formation processes such as affix agglutination and component-case compounding[1], translation models require mechanisms that go below the fixed level, such as character level, word level, stem-affix level and subword level. We note that such techniques make assumptions that often do not specific in practice. For instance, there is not always a fixed correspondence between source and target words because of variance in the degree of morphological synthesis between languages, especially the agglutinative language. As an example, a simple Mongolian sentence is used to illustrate that monotonous granularity can not perfectly adapt to the varied morphologies (Fig. 1).

---

[1] This study mainly focuses on the two most common morphological changes: affix and component-case. Affixes are mostly used as additional components to change part of speech or semantics in agglutinative language, component-case is a special affix used to determine its relationship to other words in a sentence.

© Springer Nature Switzerland AG 2019
I. V. Tetko et al. (Eds.): ICANN 2019, LNCS 11730, pp. 326–336, 2019.
https://doi.org/10.1007/978-3-030-30490-4_27

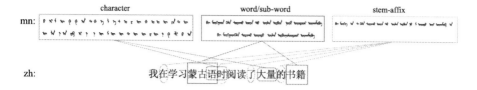

Fig. 1. Observing the distribution of the colored rectangles, we can find that different granularity encoding have unique advantages in decoding. Character level adapts to prepositions and individual words; Word level adapts to specific words; Subwords level adapts to common phrases; stem-affix level adapts to component-case and prepositions. (Color figure online)

In this study, we address a question on whether agglutinative language NMT can be done directly on a sequence of units without fixed level segmentation. To answer this question, we conduct the investigation on two aspects.

- we use the parallel corpus of multi-granularity (character, word, subword and stem-affix) as input samples without distinction.
- we adapt value iteration network (VIN) [16], a Markov decision algorithm [2], to the reinforcement learning (RL) [19] based translation model. The role of VIN is to transform the training reward of sequences into a decision value, so that the model pays attention to the sequences with higher value (suitable for the granularity of the current sequence). It also solves the problem of parameter updating and model training inefficiency in RL.

We construct the model on long short-term memory (LSTM) [5] and Transformer [18]. The temporal structure of LSTM enables it to capture dependency semantics in agglutination and low-resource language. Transformer has refreshed state-of-the-art performance on several languages pairs.

We evaluate the proposed model with a free-granularity input on two representative agglutinative language pairs to make our evaluation as convincing as possible. On the two language pairs: Mongolian-Chinese, Japanese-English, the models with the unfixed-level input and VIN-based model outperformed the ones with the fixed-level input baseline. We find these results to be a strong evidence that agglutinative language NMT can indeed learn to translate at the unfixed-level and that in fact, it benefits from doing so.

2   Related Work

There has been a recent line of work on the input of different granularity which achieves good results for NMT. [3] solve the modeling problem by a deep layers model at the character level, and prove that a standard sequence to sequence structure with sufficient depth is better than the same model which runs on word fragments. [10] propose an extension to the model at the character level and boost the decoder with target-side morphological information, they plugged an additional morphology table into the model and when decoder samples from a target vocabulary, the table will sends auxiliary signals from the most relevant affixes in order to enrich the decoder's current state and constrain it to provide better predictions. Byte Pair Encoding (BPE) is a data compression technique that iteratively replaces the most frequent pair of bytes in a sequence with byte. [21] extend the BPE style segmentation to a unsupervised framework with frequency, accessor variety and description length gain measures, they improve translation performance by weighting frequency. Except that, [17] propose a variant of BPE algorithm to perform effective subword segmentation of low-resource language and alleviate the out-of-vocabulary problem in NMT system. Phrase-based encoding method also plays an important role in NMT. [6] present phrase-based approach to explicitly model the phrase structures in output sequences which could perform local reordering of input sequences. In addition, [8] consider that the attention approaches are token-based and ignore the phrasal alignments, thus the quality of translation would be affected. So they propose a novel phrase-based attention approach, modeling n-grams of tokens as attention entities.

The training principle we propose is based on the spirit of [13] and [16]. Unlike the fixed-granularity input, we build representations for encoding from unfixed-granularity unit. In comparison with common translation model, our hybrid architecture is also hierarchical sequence-to-sequence model, but operates at a different granularity level.

3   Background and Our Models

3.1   RL in Machine Translation

Putting our problems into reinforcement framework [9, 14, 19] can clearly observe a group of correspondence between training processes and reinforcement learning, training model-agent $<S, A, P\{s,a\}, R>$, parameters of agent-policy whose execution results in the agent is selecting an action $a \epsilon A$ at a state $s \epsilon S$. The transition model predicts the next state s' based on the current state s and action a, denoted as $P\{s'|s,a\}$. Reward $R = R(s,a)$ represents an instant reward after an agent takes an action.

3.2   Model Description

The model can be clearly displayed when the training process is categorized into the following components (Fig. 2).

(1) *Unfixed level training*: (a) Optimal initial state. In order to improve efficiency, pre-training is necessary because it can provide a better initial search space. Among them, unlike the fixed level training, sampling: samples of different granularity are used as the input of the common input participation model; Prediction: the random and cyclic sampling mechanism provides various granularity inputs for hidden layer computing.

(2) *Reward observation*: The looping mechanism of the predictive computation continues until the end of the sequence, so as shown in Sect. 3.3, the reward of the sequence is generated.

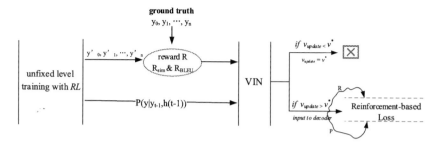

Fig. 2. Sequence-level training model based on VIN

(3) *Value Conversion (Fig. 3)*: This reward is received by a CNN that contains a convolutional layer and a linear activation function. The next iteration function layer is stacked with rewards, and the feedback of the loop is sent to the convolution layer for N times until the long-term value of a batch is generated, where N depends on the length of the sequence.

(4) *loss*: The mode of gradient propagation depends on the comparison between the obtained value and the optimal value. This strategy directly determines whether the current parameters should be adopted by the model and updated.

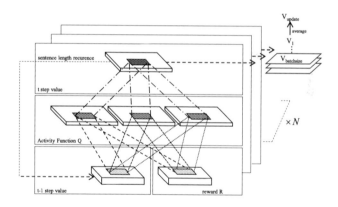

Fig. 3. VI algorithm represented by CNN

3.3 Reward Calculation

The reward for the sequence comes from its BLEU calculation with ground truth, which can be expressed as:

$$R_{BLEU} = bp \times exp(\sum_{n=1}^{n} w_n log p_n), \quad bp = \begin{cases} 1 & if\ c > l \\ e^{1-\frac{l}{c}} & if\ c \leq l \end{cases} \quad (1)$$

where p_n and w_n represent the precision calculation term and weight of the N-gram, bp is the standard term of length penalty, and c and l represent the sequence length of the translation and ground truth.

3.4 VIN

We combine VI with RL because its Markov characteristics are very similar to RL. An execution strategy $P\left\{s'|s,a\right\}$ of a sequence of length n is looped under state s, which produces an accumulated VI value V. We can formulate VI as

$$V_n(s) = max\ Q(s, a), \tag{2}$$

$$Q(s, a) = R(s, a) + \sum_{1}^{N} p(s'|s; a)V_{n+1}(s'). \tag{3}$$

The optimal value $V^*(n \to \infty)$ is obtained with the optimal policy argmax $Q_\infty(s, a)$. In this article, VIN is expressed by a simple CNN approximation. This allows us to easily train the model with popular end-to-end structure and error propagation. This form of VI can more naturally learn the parameters and reward functions of MDP, similar to a standard CNN, which is easy to understand and implement. The process is: the reward R generated by each iteration is cyclically calculated and transferred with the previous value V_n through the convolutional network. It should be noted that the convolution kernel here corresponds to the transition probability of the decoder. The value of the sequence is generated with N convolution operations, representing the decoding cost of the current state and the performance of the model. Therefore, we can determine the necessity of updating the current batch by comparing the current value with the optimal value, which enables the model to find the granularity that best fits the sequence.

3.5 Agent Update

The objective of training is to obtain the parameters of the agent with the highest expectation for reward: $-\sum_{y_t \sim p} r(y_t')$, $t\epsilon(1, 2, ..., n)$, therefore, we adopt the method of [12,22], ignoring the predicted probability of y_t', and y_t' is the word selected by the model at the t-th timestep. The model is dedicated to exploring how to obtain better rewards in decoding process. Therefore, gradient back-propagating can be expressed as:

$$\frac{\partial Loss}{\partial o_t} = \frac{\partial Loss(Reinforcement)}{\partial o_t}(r(y_t') - \bar{r}_{t+1})$$

$$= (p(y_{t+1}'|y_t', h_{t+1}, c_t) - y_{t+1}')(r(y_t') - \bar{r}_{t+1}), \quad t\epsilon(1, 2, ..., n), \tag{4}$$

where r is estimated by linear regression, and represents the average reward of $t + 1$ time step. o_t indicates the input of softmax, which needs to be passed carefully because incorrect controls will result in a high variance.

4   Experiments

4.1   Datasets

We validate the effectiveness of our approach on two typical agglutinative language NMT tasks, namely, low-resource task Mongolian-Chinese (Mo-Zh), and common task Japanese-English (Ja-En); we use data from CLDC, CWMT2017 (0.4M) and Wikipedia Kyoto Articles, OPUS in LREC2012[2] (2.2M), for the two tasks, respectively. In order to obtain input samples with unfixed granularity in two languages, we adopt independent-developed Mongolian affix segmenter, Japanese semantic word segmentation tool JUMAN++[3], BPE and joint BPE[4][13]. Finally, we divide the sample into four granularities: character level, word level, subword level and stem affix level. To avoid allocating excessive training time on long sentences, all sentence pairs longer than 50 words either on the source or target side are discarded.

We found and tried to get the best BPE operands in some effective studies [7,13]: Mo-Zh (Mongolian: 35000, Chinese: 15000) and Ja-En (Japanese: 60000, English: 30000). Due to the scarcity of corpus, we have removed the restrictions on the vocabulary.

4.2   Models

We select several NMT models that can capture context information effectively as baseline systems, seq2seq LSTM model, MIXER, Transformer, and Transformer+RL (We refer to this approach as TR). We stop the pre-training of initial model until the accuracy of dev achieves at δ which is set to 0.7 in the original Transformer_base and LSTM.

Following the studies [15] and [11], we set the dimension of embedding as 512 and beamsize 4. The Transformer_base configuration in [18] and [20] is an effective experience setting for our experiments. The difference is that according to the experience of [11] and [20], we set the number of hidden layer units to 256 and the size of beam search to 8.

4.3   Main Results and Analysis

We mainly analyze the experimental results in four aspects: BLEU evaluation, training efficiency, redundant and unknown word tokens in translations, translation examples.

---

[2] https://object.pouta.csc.fi/OPUS-MultiUN/v1/moses/ar-en.txt.zip.

[3] http://nlp.ist.i.kyoto-u.ac.jp.

[4] https://github.com/rsennrich/subword-nmt For the cases of transliteration or simple replication at source and target in NMT (e.g. Japanese-English), joint BPE has better preprocessing effect.

- *BLEU evaluation and training efficiency*

All experiments are performed on a single Titan-X GPU. The BLEU[5] score
for the 50 epochs of initial training and 30 epochs of reinforcement training
(including 10 epochs of RL training and 20 epochs of RL+VIN training) were
observed to illustrate the effect of our approach on the model (Fig. 4). When the
trained EPOCH exceeds the short straight line of orange and blue, RL and VIN
begin to affect the model. It can be clearly observed that the initial state begins
to decay after a small number of iterations, which is consistent with the falling
BLEU. Regaining the same state again requires the same number of epochs,
which is an intolerable computational cost. The free granularity mechanism can
fully exploit the advantages of each granularity through value iteration and keep
the model stable.

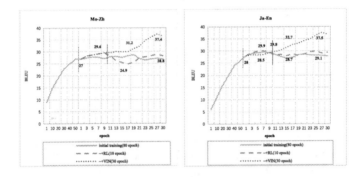

Fig. 4. Influences of training algorithms on different tasks.

From the results in Table 1, a single free granularity strategy (vertical *free
granularity*) or VIN (horizontal +*VIN*) can effectively improve the performance
of the model on BLEU, let alone an effective combination (VIN-based model
trained by free granularity strategy). In comparison with the baseline models,
our approach has achieved greater improvement in BLEU score and can converge
to optimal values faster. Table 1 shows the BLEU evaluation results.

In our experiments, monotonous BLEU enhancements not only did not bring
significant improvements, but even a considerable decline in Transformer. This
is attributed to the fact that the complex self-attention mechanism causes the
model to over-fitting, and an obvious phenomenon is a large number of repeated
translations. +*VIN* has an average of 2–5 BLEU score improvement on all the
two datasets at any fixed granularity level.

For samples with free granularity, we calculate the convergence time of each
system when the accuracy is not less than 0.8. The additional VIN's RL approach
can effectively reduce the convergence time of the model while achieving the
higher BLEU score, and saves approximately one-third of training time.

---

[5] https://github.com/moses-smt/mosesdecoder/blob/master/scripts/generic/multi-
bleu.perl.

Table 1. Performance of each training algorithm on BLEU-4

| | System | Fixed granularity | | | | Free granularity | Hours (for free granularity) |
		character	word	subword	stem-suffix		
Mo-Zh	LSTM [15]	29.5	24.2	28.7	31.3	*36.4*	31
	+RL [11]	31.1	29.7	30.9	30.1	*32.1*	44
	+VIN (our)	*33.2*	*32.4*	*33.7*	*34.1*	*★37.4*	*29*
	Transformer [18]	29	28.5	31.4	31.7	35.3	58
	+RL [20]	28.3	31.1	33.3	31.6	*34.1*	73
	+VIN (our)	*30.7*	*31.6*	*33.1*	*33.9*	*34.2*	*41*
Ja-En	LSTM [15]	31.9	29.7	31.2	33.6	*34*	54
	+RL [11]	30.3	27.4	31.4	31.1	*32.4*	70
	+VIN (our)	*34.8*	*29.5*	*34.2*	*35.6*	*★37.5*	*45*
	Transformer [18]	31.5	33.5	32.7	33.1	35.7	71
	+RL [20]	33.4	30.9	33.8	31.4	33.1	95
	+VIN (our)	*33.2*	*31.8*	*33.3*	*34.8*	36.6	*58*

- *translation examples*

Figure 5 shows examples of outputs of the translations. In Mo-Zh example, the word "靠左行驶" (*drive on the left*) is missing in the output of each baseline or replaced by <*unk*>, but "左行驶" (*driving on left*) is present in the output of free-granularity-based model. In Ja-En example, "*that*" (affix "と") are repeated or missing in the output of baselines, but they are accurate and appear only once in the output of our models.

		Mo–Zh	**Ja–En**
got	Source	ᠣᠯᠠᠨ ᠤ ᠬᠣᠭᠣᠷᠣᠨᠳᠣ ... ᠤ ᠠ ?	結婚後に太ると考えている人が多く。
	Reference	在英国，来往车辆都靠左行驶，对吗？	Many people think that they will gain weight after marriage.
	LSTM	在英国，车来回在左边，应该吗？	Many people think *" "* they will *grow fat* after marriage.
	+RL	在英国，车*来回在左边*<*unk*>，*应该*吗？	Many people think **that** *that* their *" "* weight *grow* after marriage.
	+VIN (our)	在英国，来*回*车辆都*在左*边行驶，对吗？	Many people think that they *" "* gain weight after marriage.
	Transformer	英国，*都跟刚在左边*<*unk*>，*应该跟刚*吗？	*There are* many people think *" "* they *" "* *become* weight after marriage.
	+RL	在英国，*车辆来往都在左*，对吗？	Many people think *" "* they will <*unk*> weight *when* marriage.
	+VIN (our)	在英国，车辆*在左*行驶，可以吗？	Many people think that they will *" " fat* after marriage.

Fig. 5. Performance of translation under different model

- *a discussion of free-granularity method for redundant and unknown tokens*

Free granularity strategy is mainly used to solve the negative impact of morphological noises on decoding process in agglutinative language. However, the free mechanism also causes the phenomenon of under-fitting or over-fitting of the model, which motivates us to alleviate the confusion of decoder on granularity selection through VIN. A clear explanation is the number of redundant words and unknown words in the translated. Table 2 shows a comparison of the number of word occurrences for each corpus and model. The columns show (i) the number of words that appear more frequently than the counterparts in the reference, and (ii) the number of words that appear more than once but are not included in the reference. Note that these numbers do not include unknown words, so (iii) shows the number of unknown words. In all the cases, the number of occurrence of redundant words is reduced in VIN-based models. Thus, we confirmed that VIN-based model achieves reduction of repeating and missing words while maintaining the quality of translation.

Table 2. Numbers of redundant and unknown word tokens.

System	Mo-Zh			Ja-En		
	i	ii	iii	i	ii	iii
LSTM	1887	725	1553	811	474	955
+RL	1592	707	1477	944	446	1028
+VIN (our)	*1250*	*663*	*1029*	*736*	*401*	*717*
Transformer	2228	554	1820	681	537	912
+RL	2039	478	1696	657	505	885
+VIN (our)	*1774*	*458*	*1331*	*614*	*442*	*794*

5   Conclusion

The main contribution of this paper is to show that NMT systems of agglutinative language are capable of free-granularity units translation by mixing samples of different granularity. This is both simpler and more effective than using a fixed granularity units.

Another contribution is that we assume that different granularity have unique contributions to decoding, which motives us to design a value-determining strategy that allows each granularity to be fully utilized and, on the basis of this, greatly enhances training efficiency.

The proposed approach has one limitation that exploration based on large-scale corpus will lead to out-of-vocabulary because of the restricted vocabulary (usually, the restriction of vocabulary is '<100000'). Constraints on sequence length, sentence frequency or other conditions can alleviate the confusion caused by vocabulary. However, we look forward to exploring strategies that do not depend on such constraints in future studies.

References

1. Bahdanau, D., Cho, K., Bengio, Y.: Neural machine translation by jointly learning to align and translate. arXiv preprint arXiv **1409**(0473) (2014)
2. Bennett, C.C., Hauser, K.: Artificial intelligence framework for simulating clinical decision-making: a Markov decision process approach. Artif. Intell. Med. **57**(1), 9–19 (2013). https://doi.org/10.1016/j.artmed.2012.12.003
3. Cherry, C., Foster, G., et al.: Revisiting character-based neural machine translation with capacity and compression. In: Conference on Empirical Methods in Natural Language Processing (EMNLP), pp. 4295–4305 (2018)
4. Gehring, J., Auli, M., et al.: Convolutional sequence to sequence learning. In: International Conference on Machine Learning (ICML), vol. 70, pp. 1243–1252 (2017)
5. Graves, A.: Supervised sequence labelling with recurrent neural networks. Neural Evol. Comput. **3**(1), 37–45 (2013). https://doi.org/10.1007/978-3-642-24797-2. arXiv
6. Huang, P.S., Wang, C., Huang, S., et al.: Towards neural phrase-based machine translation. In: International Conference on Learning Representations (ICLR), pp. 318–322 (2018)
7. Kunchukuttan, A., Bhattacharyya, P.: Learning variable length units for SMT between related languages via byte pair encoding. In: Association for Computational Linguistics (ACL), pp. 14–24 (2015)
8. Nguyen, P.X., Joty, S.: Phrase-based attentions. In: International conference on learning representations (ICLR) (2019)
9. Nogueira, R., Cho, K.: WebNav: a new large-scale task for natural language based sequential decision making. arXiv preprint arXiv **1602**(02261) (2016)
10. Peyman, P., Qun, L., Andy, W.: Improving character-based decoding using target-side morphological information for neural machine translation. In: The North American Chapter of the Association for Computational Linguistics (NAACL), pp. 58–68 (2018)
11. Ranzato, M., Chopra, S., Auli, M., Zaremba, W.: Sequence level training with recurrent neural networks. arXiv preprint arXiv **9**(06732) (2015)
12. Schwenker, F., Palm, G.: Artificial development by reinforcement learning can benefit from multiple motivations. Front. Robot. AI **6**(6) (2019). https://doi.org/10.3389/frobt.2019.00006
13. Sennrich, R., Haddow, B., Birch, A.: Neural machine translation of rare words with subword units. In: Association for Computational Linguistics (ACL), pp. 1715–1725 (2015)
14. Sunmola, F.T., Wyatt, J.L.: Model transfer for Markov decision tasks via parameter matching. In: Proceedings of the 25th Workshop of the UK Planning and Scheduling Special Interest Group (PlanSIG 2006), pp. 246–252 (2006)
15. Sutskever, I., Vinyals.: Sequence to sequence learning with neural networks. In: Conference and Workshop on Neural Information Processing Systems (NIPS), pp. 5998–6008 (2014)
16. Tamar, A., Wu, Y., Thomas, G., et al.: Value iteration networks. In: Advances in Neural Information Processing Systems (NIPS), pp. 2154–2162 (2016)
17. Thi-Vinh, N., Thanh-Le, H., Phuong-Thai, N., et al.: Combining advanced methods in japanese-vietnamese neural machine translation. In: International Conference on Knowledge and Systems Engineering (KSE), pp. 318–322 (2018)

18. Vaswani, A., et al.: Attention is all you need. In: Conference and Workshop on Neural Information Processing Systems (NIPS), pp. 5998–6008 (2017)
19. Volodymyr, M., Koray, K., et al.: Human-level control through deep reinforcement learning. Nature **518**(7540), 529 (2015). https://doi.org/10.1038/nature14236
20. Wu, L., Tian, F., Qin, T., et al.: A study of reinforcement learning for neural machine translation. In: EMNLP, pp. 3215–3222 (2018)
21. Wu, Y., Zhao, H.: Finding better subword segmentation for neural machine translation. In: Sun, M., Liu, T., Wang, X., Liu, Z., Liu, Y. (eds.) CCL/NLP-NABD -2018. LNCS (LNAI), vol. 11221, pp. 53–64. Springer, Cham (2018). https://doi.org/10.1007/978-3-030-01716-3_5
22. Zaremba, W., Sutskever, I.: Reinforcement learning neural turing machines-revised. arXiv preprint arXiv **1505**(00521) (2015)

RL Extraction of Syntax-Based Chunks for Sentence Compression

Hoa T. Le[1(✉)], Christophe Cerisara[1,2], and Claire Gardent[2]

[1] Laboratory LORIA Nancy, Villers-lès-Nancy, France
{hoa.le,christophe.cerisara}@loria.fr
[2] CNRS/LORIA Nancy, Villers-lès-Nancy, France
claire.gardent@loria.fr

Abstract. Sentence compression involves selecting key information present in the input and rewriting this information into a short, coherent text. While dependency parses have often been used for this purpose, we propose to exploit such syntactic information within a modern reinforcement learning-based extraction model. Furthermore, compared to other approaches that include syntactic features into deep learning models, we design a model that has better explainability properties and is flexible enough to support various shallow syntactic parsing modules. More specifically, we linearize the syntactic tree into the form of overlapping text segments, which are then selected with reinforcement learning and regenerated into a compressed form. Hence, despite relying on extractive components, our model is also able to handle abstractive summarization. We explore different ways of selecting subtrees from the dependency structure of the input sentence and compare the results of various models on the Gigaword corpus.

1 Introduction

While previous work on sentence compression has often focused on extractive compression i.e., compressions where most of the words occurring in the short sentence version are also present in the corresponding input [5,6], the Gigaword corpus can be viewed as a corpus containing both extractive and abstractive compressions (or sentence summarization).

Previous work on this dataset has used various ways of selecting key information in the input sentence. [3] uses dependency subtrees and information extraction triples to enrich the input of a encoder-decoder model. [1] investigates the use of linked entities to guide the decoder. [19] propose an encoding model which includes a gate network to select key information from the input sentence. [16] propose to enrich the encoder with information about the syntactic structure of the input sentence. [2] use target summaries as soft templates to guide the sequence-to-sequence model.

In this work, we propose a model that exploits syntactic parsing to extract coherent segments from the source document, then selects the best of these segments with reinforcement learning, and finally regenerates the summary with a

© Springer Nature Switzerland AG 2019
I. V. Tetko et al. (Eds.): ICANN 2019, LNCS 11730, pp. 337–347, 2019.
https://doi.org/10.1007/978-3-030-30490-4_28

recent sequence-to-sequence model. This model can thus transparently handles both types of extractive and abstractive summarizations. Furthermore, our approach departs from the recent end-to-end deep learning architectures by deterministically linearizing the syntactic tree into overlapping text segments to select with reinforcement learning. Although this method prevents a joint global optimization of the models, it also gives interesting adaptability and explainability properties. Adaptability, because it is easy to replace the syntactic parsing module with another shallow component, such as chunking, when full dependency parses are not available or not reliable. Explainability, because the segments that lead to the best summaries are clearly identified, which is not always the case with other deep learning approaches, for instance based on attention.

2   Related Work

Sequence-to-sequence models nowadays are a popular model used for summarization task but are still far from perfect. For instance, [1, 3, 10, 11, 16] observed that sequence models can produce incorrect, hallucinated and non-factual output. A common remedy often used consists to integrate additional structural bias to make sure that the attention of the model spreads over key information in the source. [1] observed that information around entities are related to the topic of the summary. They proposed to associate with linked entities a topic module to guide the decoding process. [3] used open information extraction and dependency parsing technique to infer actual facts from source text and force the generator to respect these descriptions. In the same spirit, [16] explored the use of syntactic relations from constituency parsing, [10] employed TextRank algorithm and [11] relied on entailment relations.

In parallel, another research path aims at directly learning to distill out important sentences from the source document. This is applied specifically on the CNN/Daily Mail dataset. [13] proposed to cast extraction as a ranking problem and used reinforcement learning to optimize the final objective. They argued that cross-entropy loss is not a suitable metric on this task. However, this framework lacks of a rewriting component. Mimicking how human summarizes text, [4] proposed both sentence extraction and rewriting components in a unified model and trained an agent to globally optimize them in an end-to-end manner.

Previous studies on summarization tasks, especially on the Gigaword dataset, have only used dependency parsing as additional structural bias to the models [3, 10, 16]. Subtrees from dependency structure are still not properly explored to help narrowing down input sentence into a short, concise and less ambiguous piece of information. We investigate different ways of selecting subtrees to help decoder to rewrite better.

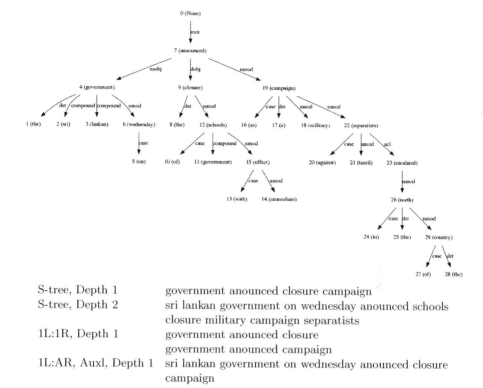

S-tree, Depth 1	government anounced closure campaign
S-tree, Depth 2	sri lankan government on wednesday anounced schools closure military campaign separatists
1L:1R, Depth 1	government anounced closure government anounced campaign
1L:AR, Auxl, Depth 1	sri lankan government on wednesday anounced closure campaign

Fig. 1. Dependency Tree and example subtrees extracted from the sentence *"The Sri-Lankan government on Wednesday anounced the closure of government schools with immediate effect as a military campaign against Tamil separatists escalated in the North of the country"*.

3   Extraction of Dependency Subtrees

We investigate different strategies for the extraction of the subtrees from the dependency structure of the input sentences. In all cases, we start from "sentence subtrees" i.e., subtrees which root node has an "nsubj" or an "nsubjpass" child node. Given such sentence trees, we then extract the following subtrees:

– **S-Tree**: All sentence trees.
– **1L:1R**: all subtrees of the sentence tree which contain one left- and one right-child. E.g., given the example in Fig. 1, *"government announced closure"* and *"government announced campaign"*
– **1L:AR (AL:1R)**: all subtrees of the sentence tree which contain one left- (right-) child and all right- (left-) children. E.g., *"government announced closure campaign"*
– **Auxl**: All subtrees below a subtree at depth 1 that contains "nsubj" or "nsubjpass".

We ignore all children nodes whose parent dependency relation is "punct" or "det". For each subtree type, we recursively extract subtrees of depth 1, 2 and 3. Figure 1 shows some examples of linearized extracted subtrees.

4 Model

Following [4], we use a two-steps model that combines an extractor agent to select dependency subtrees and an abstractor network to rewrite the extracted subtrees. Both networks are connected using reinforcement learning to overcome the non-differentiable behavior of the extractor and optimized with respect to the ROUGE evaluation, a standard metric used for sentence compression.

4.1 Extractor Network

Every linearized subtree from Sect. 3 is scored by the extractor network; this set of scored subtrees will later on be explored by the Reinforcement Learning agent to select the best candidates for summarization. In details, every subtree is passed to a temporal convolutional network [8] followed by a bidirectional LSTM [7] to produce a subtree embedding h_j. Assuming that h_j is selected, it is passed to an LSTM decoder for generation, which outputs z_t. A pointer network [17] computes a first attention e_t for z_t over all inputs $(h_j)_j$ with:

$$a_j^t = v_g^\top \tanh(W_{g1}h_j + W_{g2}z_t) \tag{1}$$
$$\alpha^t = \text{softmax}(a^t) \tag{2}$$
$$e_t = \sum_j \alpha_j^t W_{g1}h_j \tag{3}$$

It then computes the extraction probability of h_j with another attention:

$$u_j^t = v_p^\top \tanh(W_{p1}h_j + W_{p2}e_t)$$
$$P(j_t|j_1,\ldots,j_{t-1}) = \text{softmax}(u^t) \tag{4}$$

All the W's and v's are trainable parameters. Similarly to [4], we pretrain this extractor via a 'proxy' target label: for every ground-truth summary sentence, we find the most similar subtree via ROUGE-L_{recall} metric and minimize this classification cross-entropy loss.

4.2 Abstractor Network

To generate compression, we use state-of-the-art sequence-to-sequence model with copy mechanism [15]. We also pretrain abstractor by taking pair of each summary and its extracted subtree (in Sect. 4.1). The network is trained as usual on decoder language model $L(\theta_{abs}) = -\frac{1}{M}\sum_{m=1}^{M} \log P_{\theta_{abs}}(w_m|w_{1:m-1})$.

4.3 Reinforce Extraction

To make an extraction agent, we use vanilla policy gradient algorithm REIN-
FORCE [18]. At each extraction step t, the agent observes the current state
$c_t = (D, d_{j_{t-1}})$, where $d \in D$: set of document sentence input. It samples an
action $j_t \sim \pi_{\theta_a, \omega}(c_t, j) = P(j)$ from Eq. 4 to extract a subtree and receive a
reward. We denote trainable parameters of the extractor agent as $\theta = \{\theta_a, \omega\}$
(in Sect. 4.1). Then, because vanilla REINFORCE yields high variance, we maximize this following policy gradient objective:

$$\nabla_{\theta_a, \omega} J(\theta_a, \omega) = \mathbb{E}[\nabla_{\theta_a, \omega} \log \pi_\theta(c, j) A^{\pi_\theta}(c, j)] \tag{5}$$

where $A^{\pi_\theta}(c, j)$ is the *advantage function*, calculated as: $A^{\pi_\theta}(c, j) = Q^{\pi_{\theta_a, \omega}}(c, j) - b_{\theta_c, \omega}(c)$. As we can see here, the total return R_t could be used
as an estimate of action-value function $Q(c_t, j_t)$, a baseline $b_{\theta_c, \omega}(c)$ is needed to
reduce its variance. Finally, the baseline is then also updated by minimizing this
square loss: $L_c(\theta_c, \omega) = (b_{\theta_c, \omega}(c_t) - R_t)^2$.

5 Experiments

5.1 Data

We evaluate our approach on the Gigaword corpus [14], a corpus of 3.8M
sentence-headline pairs and where the average input sentence length is 31.4
words (in the training corpus) and the average sentence compression length is
8.3 words. The test set consists of 1951 sentence/compression pairs. Like [14],
we use 2000 sample pairs (among 189K pairs) as development set.

5.2 Extractive vs. Abstractive Compression

To better assess the impact of our approach on abstractive vs extractive compression, we divide the data (training, dev and test) into two parts: a part (extractive) where 80% of the tokens present in the sentence compression are present
in the input and another part (abstractive) which contains all other instances.
According to that criteria, out of the 1951 test instances, 207 are extractive and
1744 abstractive. We also report the ROUGE metrics over the whole corpus, to
allow for comparison with related works.

5.3 Evaluation Metric

We adopt ROUGE [12] for automatic evaluation. It measures the quality of summary by computing overlapping lexical units between the candidate summary
and actual summaries. We report ROUGE-1 (unigram), ROUGE-2 (bi-gram)
and ROUGE-L (LCS) F1 scores. ROUGE-1 and ROUGE-2 mainly represent
informativeness while ROUGE-L rather capture readability.

5.4   Hyperparameter Details

We use the Adam optimizer [9] with learning rate 0.001 for cross-entropy training of the extractor and abstractor. We use a learning rate of 0.0001 for extractor RL training. The vocabulary size is 30k, the batch size 32 samples, we use gradient clipping of 2.0 and early-stopping. We use 256 hidden units for all LSTM-RNNs. We truncate the maximum length of input sentences to 100 tokens and target sentences to 30 tokens. ROUGE-recall is used to create proxy label data as we want extracted sentences to contain as much information as possible for paraphrasing. However, ROUGE-F_1 is used as reward for reinforce agent as the generation should be as *concise* as the gold target sentence.

6   Results

6.1   Full Select-and-Paraphrase Model

Table 1 shows the results comparing the baseline model (a seq2seq model trained on input sentence/compression pairs) and our full Select-and-Paraphrase Reinforcement Learning (RL) model where the extractor is trained on all sentence trees (S-trees). The RL model under-performs because the extractor does not manage to handle the large number of candidate sub-trees (up to several hundreds). We thus explore next, using an oracle RL selector, which of the selection methods proposed in Sect. 3 help to reduce the set of candidate sub-trees while still preserving the relevant information from the input document.

We also report in Table 1 the performances obtained with state-of-the-art summarization systems. These figures come from [2], which appears to be the best system on the Gigaword corpus reported in http://nlpprogress.com/english/summarization.html, as of May 2019.

Table 1. Baseline (Seq2Seq trained on sentence/compression pairs) vs. RL select-and-paraphrase model (trained on S-Tree data).

Model	Extractive data			Abstractive data			Whole corpus		
	R-1	R-2	R-L	R-1	R-2	R-L	R-1	R-2	R-L
Baseline	59.57	31.28	57.87	27.55	10.16	25.94	30.95	12.40	29.33
S&P Model	54.38	28.13	52.42	24.48	8.49	23.15	27.65	10.57	26.26
[2]							37.04	19.03	34.46

6.2   Oracle Setting

In Table 2, we compare our model with an "oracle reinforcement learning" component that always chooses the best candidate subtree to pass to the abstractor. This allows us to study the impact of each sub-tree selection processes described in Sect. 3 and identify the ones that preserve relevant information to summarize.

We also apply our approach with another shallow syntactic process, by replacing the dependency parser by the CoreNLP OpenIE tool[1], which extracts a set of subject-predicate-object triples.

Table 2. Baseline vs. Oracle results. The last row S-tree+ includes Stree, 1L:1R, Auxl, 1L:AR, AL:1R, Auxl

Model	Extractive data			Abstractive data			Whole corpus		
	R-1	R-2	R-L	R-1	R-2	R-L	R-1	R-2	R-L
Baseline	59.57	31.28	57.87	27.55	10.16	25.94	30.95	12.40	29.33
Oracle									
OpenIE	51.21	24.1	48.7	27.35	9.24	25.68	29.88	10.82	28.12
S-Tree	60.52	31.21	57.29	30.61	10.69	28.77	33.78	12.88	31.80
1L:1R	46.33	19.15	43.6	22.63	5.84	21.03	25.14	7.25	23.43
1L:1R, Auxl	64.04	28.32	60.55	33.23	10.01	30.3	36.50	11.95	33.51
1L:AR, AL:1R	43.99	20.4	42	21.16	5.48	19.71	23.58	7.06	22.07
1L:AR, AL:1R, Auxl	62.57	32.02	58.98	30.61	10.69	28.77	34.00	12.95	31.98
S-Tree, 1L:1R, Auxl	68.95	36.34	65.49	38.95	13.9	35.54	42.13	16.28	38.72
S-Tree+	70.38	38.79	66.4	40	14.75	36.34	43.22	17.30	39.53

OpenIE Triples vs. Dependency Subtrees. We can first observe that scores are lower when taking as input OpenIE triples rather than Dependency subtrees. The results show that our specific S-tree heuristic rule outperforms OpenIE triples by +9, +7, +9 rouge-1,-2,-L respectively for extractive data, and +3, +1 and +3 points for abstractive data. OpenIE triples were in fact used by [3] on the same task and same dataset to improve faithfulness i.e., to favour output that is semantically correct with respect to the input sentence. Given that [3] achieved good scores on the Gigaword data and that S-trees outperform OpenIE triples, this suggests that S-Tree subtrees are potentially good alternatives to OpenIE triples.

Extractive vs. Abstractive. Unsurprisingly, the impact of the input dependency subtrees is much larger on extractive data. For extractive compressions, the scores increase by roughly a factor of two suggesting that the match between input dependency subtrees and summaries is much larger for extractive than abstractive data. This is in line with previous works [5,6], which show that extractive compression can be found by searching in the parse tree of the input sentence for a spanning tree linking the content words of the compression. It also indicates that further improvements on the Gigaword dataset will require a better modeling of the paraphrases and variations occurring in abstractive compressions.

---

[1] https://stanfordnlp.github.io/CoreNLP/openie.html.

Table 3. Example of oracle and full source generation.

Source

fred west told the **truth** – and should be believed – **when he exonerated his wife** in the **murders** of ## young women before killing himself , a jury heard wednesday .

Subtrees

...

12. fred west believed when exonerated wife heard wednesday
13. fred west believed when exonerated murders heard wednesday
14. fred west believed when exonerated killing heard wednesday
15. fred west believed he exonerated wife heard wednesday
16. fred west believed he exonerated murders heard wednesday
17. fred west believed he exonerated killing heard wednesday
18. fred west believed a jury heard wednesday

...

Abstract

fred west told truth when he exonerated his wife of murder defense by unk unk

Full source generation

jury hears west tells truth to be believed to be believed

Subtrees generation

...

12. fred west says he 's exonerated
13. fred west says west nile murders
14. fred west says it was exonerated in killing of ##
15. fred west says he exonerated wife
16. fred west says he exonerated murders
17. fred west says he exonerated killing of killing
18. fred west s west virginia jury hears

...

Oracle

fred west says he exonerated wife (from subtree 15)

Auxiliary Subtrees. We observe a large, significant improvement from (1L:1R) to (1L:1R, Auxl) and similarly, between (1L:AR, AL:1R) and (1L:AR, AL:1R, Auxl). In fact, this increase shows up systematically in all our experiments. This shows the importance of subtrees below the subject level, and that dependents and modifiers of these nodes often contain key information that is preserved in the compressed sentence.

Syntax Helps. The combination of subtrees shows substantial improvement. Among all possible setup, the (S-Tree, 1L:1R, Auxl, 1L:AR, AL:1R, Auxl) combination obtains the best performance. It is respectively +10, +7, +9 rouge-1,-2-L points higher than the first heuristic rule and the baseline seq2seq model on the extractive set. On the abstractive set, it is +13, +4, +11 rouge-1,-2,-L points higher respectively.

Qualitative Analysis. Table 3 shows examples of multiple subtrees retrieved from the input document as well as the summaries generated from them. We can see that normal sequence-to-sequence with attention and copy mechanism struggles to identify important information and produces loops and repetitions in the end. On the other hand, thanks to the dependency structure, the summaries generated from subtrees contain short and coherent sentences.

7   Conclusion

We have proposed a flexible select-and-paraphrase summarization model that decouples the syntactic analysis process from the generation component, hence enabling plugging-in and out various syntactic parsing modules. We have demonstrated this flexibility by seamlessly exploiting both a full-blown dependency parser and the shallow OpenIE triples extractor. The dependency parser giving better results, we have further proposed multiple heuristics to extract from the syntactic tree the most informative subtrees for the task of summarization and analyzed experimentally their potential. Compared to the state-of-the-art end-to-end deep learning systems, the proposed approach has another advantage, as it may more easily explain its generated summaries by presenting to the user the actual subtrees that have lead to the output sentence. Although this approach can theoretically handle both extractive and abstractive summarization, we show that it is particularly effective on extractive types of summaries, and that more work is still required to improve the generator component of this architecture.

References

1. Amplayo, R.K., Lim, S., Hwang, S.w.: Entity commonsense representation for neural abstractive summarization. In: Proceedings of the 2018 Conference ofthe North American Chapter of the Association for Computational Linguistics: Human Language Technologies, Volume 1 (Long Papers), pp. 697–707. Association for Computational Linguistics (2018). https://doi.org/10.18653/v1/N18-1064, http://aclweb.org/anthology/N18-1064
2. Cao, Z., Li, W., Li, S., Wei, F.: Retrieve, rerank and rewrite: soft template based neural summarization. In: Proceedings of the 56th Annual Meeting of the Association for Computational Linguistics (Volume 1: Long Papers), vol. 1, pp. 152–161 (2018). https://doi.org/10.18653/v1/p18-1015
3. Cao, Z., Wei, F., Li, W., Li, S.: Faithful to the original: Fact aware neural abstractive summarization. CoRR abs/1711.04434 (2017), http://arxiv.org/abs/1711.04434
4. Chen, Y.C., Bansal, M.: Fast abstractive summarization with reinforce-selected sentence rewriting. In: Proceedings of the 56th Annual Meeting of the Association for Computational Linguistics (Volume 1: Long Papers), pp. 675–686. Association for Computational Linguistics (2018). https://doi.org/10.18653/v1/p18-1061, http://aclweb.org/anthology/P18-1063

5. Filippova, K., Alfonseca, E., Colmenares, C.A., Kaiser, L., Vinyals, O.: Sentence compression by deletion with LSTMs. In: Proceedings of the 2015 Conference on Empirical Methods in Natural Language Processing, pp. 360–368. Association for Computational Linguistics (2015). https://doi.org/10.18653/v1/D15-1042, http://aclweb.org/anthology/D15-1042
6. Filippova, K., Altun, Y.: Overcoming the lack of parallel data in sentence compression. In: Proceedings of the 2013 Conference on Empirical Methods in Natural Language Processing, pp. 1481–1491. Association for Computational Linguistics (2013). http://aclweb.org/anthology/D13-1155
7. Hochreiter, S., Schmidhuber, J.: Long short-term memory. Neural Comput. **9**(8), 1735–1780 (1997)
8. Kim, Y.: Convolutional neural networks for sentence classification. In: Proceedings of the 2014 Conference on Empirical Methods in Natural Language Processing (EMNLP), pp. 1746–1751. Association for Computational Linguistics (2014). https://doi.org/10.3115/v1/D14-1181, http://aclweb.org/anthology/D14-1181
9. Kingma, D.P., Ba, J.: Adam: a method for stochastic optimization. arXiv preprint arXiv:1412.6980 (2014)
10. Li, C., Xu, W., Li, S., Gao, S.: Guiding generation for abstractive text summarization based on key information guide network. In: Proceedings of the 2018 Conference of the North American Chapter of the Association for Computational Linguistics: Human Language Technologies, Volume 2 (Short Papers), pp. 55–60. Association for Computational Linguistics (2018). https://doi.org/10.18653/v1/N18-2009, http://aclweb.org/anthology/N18-2009
11. Li, H., Zhu, J., Zhang, J., Zong, C.: Ensure the correctness of the summary: incorporate entailment knowledge into abstractive sentence summarization. In: Proceedings of the 27th International Conference on Computational Linguistics, pp. 1430–1441. Association for Computational Linguistics (2018). http://aclweb.org/anthology/C18-1121
12. Lin, C.Y.: Rouge: a package for automatic evaluation of summaries. In: Text Summarization Branches Out (2004)
13. Narayan, S., Cohen, S.B., Lapata, M.: Ranking sentences for extractive summarization with reinforcement learning. In: Proceedings of the 2018 Conference of the North American Chapter of the Association for Computational Linguistics: Human Language Technologies, Volume 1 (Long Papers), pp. 1747–1759. Association for Computational Linguistics (2018). https://doi.org/10.18653/v1/N18-1158, http://aclweb.org/anthology/N18-1158
14. Rush, A.M., Chopra, S., Weston, J.: A neural attention model for abstractive sentence summarization. In: Proceedings of the 2015 Conference on Empirical Methods in Natural Language Processing, pp. 379–389. Association for Computational Linguistics (2015). https://doi.org/10.18653/v1/D15-1044, http://aclweb.org/anthology/D15-1044
15. See, A., Liu, P.J., Manning, C.D.: Get to the point: Summarization with pointer-generator networks. In: Proceedings of the 55th Annual Meeting of the Association for Computational Linguistics (Volume 1: Long Papers), pp. 1073–1083. Association for Computational Linguistics (2017). https://doi.org/10.18653/v1/P17-1099, http://aclweb.org/anthology/P17-1099
16. Song, K., Zhao, L., Liu, F.: Structure-infused copy mechanisms for abstractive summarization. CoRR abs/1806.05658 (2018). http://arxiv.org/abs/1806.05658

17. Vinyals, O., Fortunato, M., Jaitly, N.: Pointer networks. In: Proceedings of the 28th International Conference on Neural Information Processing Systems - Volume 2, NIPS 2015, pp. 2692–2700. MIT Press, Cambridge (2015). http://dl.acm.org/citation.cfm?id=2969442.2969540

18. Williams, R.J.: Simple statistical gradient-following algorithms for connectionist reinforcement learning. Mach. Learn., 229–256 (1992). https://doi.org/10.1007/bf00992696

19. Zhou, Q., Yang, N., Wei, F., Zhou, M.: Selective encoding for abstractive sentence summarization. In: Proceedings of the 55th Annual Meeting of the Association for Computational Linguistics (Volume 1: Long Papers), pp. 1095–1104. Association for Computational Linguistics (2017). https://doi.org/10.18653/v1/P17-1101, http://aclweb.org/anthology/P17-1101

Sound Processing

Robust Sound Event Classification with Local Time-Frequency Information and Convolutional Neural Networks

Yanli Yao[1], Qiang Yu[1(✉)], Longbiao Wang[1(✉)], and Jianwu Dang[1,2]

[1] Tianjin Key Laboratory of Cognitive Computing and Application,
College of Intelligence and Computing, Tianjin University, Tianjin, China
{yaoyanli,yuqiang,longbiao_wang}@tju.edu.cn
[2] Japan Advanced Institute of Science and Technology, Nomi, Ishikawa, Japan
jdang@jaist.ac.jp

Abstract. How to effectively and accurately identify the sound event in a real-world noisy environment is still a challenging problem. Traditional methods for robust sound event classification generally perform well in clean conditions, but get worse in noisy situations. Biological evidence shows that local temporal and spectral information can be utilized for processing noise corrupted signals, motivating our novel approach for sound recognition by combining this with a convolutional neural network (CNN), one of the most popularly applied methods in acoustic processing. We use key-points (KPs) to construct a robust and sparse representation of the sound, followed by a CNN being trained as a classifier. RWCP database is used to evaluate the performance of our system. Our results show that the as-proposed KP-CNN system is effective and efficient for a robust sound event classification task in both mismatched and multi-condition environments.

Keywords: Key-point encoding · Robust sound event classification · Convolutional neural network

1 Introduction

Perception of complex environmental information, such as visual and auditory inputs, is an essential functionality to be considered in most artificial intelligent systems. Timely judgments can often be made based on auditory inputs, such as a specific sound, prior to other sensory information [6]. However, the important acoustic information is often embedded in a noisy environment, making the extraction challenging [14,22,23]. Considering the sound recognition task, the situation is even worse due to the unstructured complexity of environmental sounds. Therefore, how to effectively and reliably detect and classify sounds in a complex real-world environment demands more research efforts.

Similar to speech recognition, robust sound event classification depends primarily on the selection of different acoustic features and classifiers. Traditional

© Springer Nature Switzerland AG 2019
I. V. Tetko et al. (Eds.): ICANN 2019, LNCS 11730, pp. 351–361, 2019.
https://doi.org/10.1007/978-3-030-30490-4_29

sound event classification systems usually follow the common ones for speech recognition [2,17]. One of the most popular systems is to use frame-based Mel Frequency Cepstral Coeffieients (MFCCs) features allied with Hidden Markov Model (HMM) as the classifier. Traditional systems for robust sound event classification can provide high accuracy in clean conditions. However, their performance will severely drop when environmental noise increases. One of the major reasons is that MFCCs are extracted with a broad spectral range, making them vulnerable to noise.

Unlike speech signals, sound events usually present much shorter durations and much wider ranges of frequency and amplitude. These distinctive time-frequency characteristics of sound events are found to be utilized by the human auditory system to process acoustic information with low signal-to-noise ratios (SNRs) [1,16,19]. Based on these characteristics, various acoustic approaches have been proposed to represent sounds in a more robust and sparse way, such as the use of the spectrogram image feature (SIF) [4] and stabilized auditory images (SAI) [21]. With developments of advanced deep learning techniques [8], deep neural networks (DNNs) are applied with SAI and SIF features for the classification task [12]. Then convolutional neural networks (CNNs) are applied with SIF due to their advantage in image-related processing tasks [15,27], resulting in an approach of SIF-CNN. However, the above acoustic feature extraction methods are rather complicated. In addition, the image-based SIF method focuses on global image features, while experimental results suggests that sound information is characterized by local features that are uncoupled and distributed across frequency and time [1].

Our motivation is to overcome the limitations of current sophisticated feature representations for sound recognition by developing a more simple and biologically plausible approach. As is indicated by biological evidence, local time-frequency information plays an essential role in auditory processing [24], and thus it is utilized in our approach with the key-point (KP) based encoding. This encoding method is then combined with one of the most popular classifiers, i.e. CNNs, to evaluate the overall performance of the proposed system.

Therefore, we propose a novel KP-CNN approach for robust sound event classification in this study, based on key-point extraction from local temporal and spectral domains [3,5], using a convolutional neural network for classification. Our KP encoding is an improved approach over its alternatives by discarding extra steps where codebooks or self-organized mappings are used for further feature extraction [3,5]. We use the one-dimensional order filter [11] through either frequency or time of the sound spectrogram to detect the local maximum values (high energy peaks) as the key-points (KPs), which include the local temporal and spectral information. Then, two masking schemes are proposed to remove the unimportant KPs, resulting in a robust and sparse representation of the sound. To the best of our knowledge, our approach is the first one to combine the biologically plausible KP encoding and CNNs for robust sound recognition. The resulting system can gain advantages from both parts, leading to a better solution for the challenging sound recognition task.

The main contribution of this paper is that we propose a novel KP-CNN system for robust sound event classification task. Because of the effectiveness and robustness of the system, it can also perform remarkably well in processing tasks based on structured speech, such as speech recognition.

The rest of this paper is organized as follows. Section 2 introduces the detail of our proposed KP-CNN approach for robust sound event classification, including three major steps: data preprocessing, feature extraction and classification. Section 3 then describes the experiments used to evaluate our approach, followed by conclusions presented in the last section.

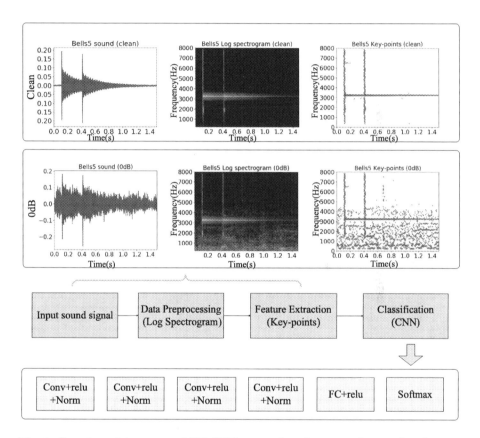

Fig. 1. Overview of the proposed KP-CNN system for robust sound event classification. The top two panels demonstrate a sample sound of 'bells5' in the clean and 0 dB noise level condition.

2   Proposed KP-CNN System for Sound Recognition

In this section, we describe the details of our proposed KP-CNN system. The system framework is demonstrated in Fig. 1 where three key parts are involved.

The first is the data preprocessing, followed by feature extraction and then classification. Details of these three parts are presented as follows.

2.1 Data Preprocessing

In the data preprocessing stage, the sound signal is firstly transformed into a spectrogram $S_{Abs}(f,t)$ with the Short-Time Fourier Transform (STFT). Then normalization and logarithm operations are used on the amplitude of the spectrogram to obtain a normalized and log-scaled representation $S_{log}(f,t)$. The logarithm operation applied is as follows:

$$S_{log}(f,t) = log(S_{Abs}(f,t) + \epsilon) - log(\epsilon) \tag{1}$$

where ϵ is set to 10^{-5}, $f = 1...F$ is the frequency scaling for the spectrogram, and t is the time frame. Since the sound signals in the database have different durations, the size of resulting spectrograms, $S_{log}(f,t)$, are not identical to each other. In order to prepare fixed dimensions of the inputs for CNNs, we adopt a padding scheme to extend the spectrogram of a smaller size to the largest one with zeros being added at the end. For convenience, the log-power spectrogram $S_{log}(f,t)$ is simply referred as spectrogram in the following.

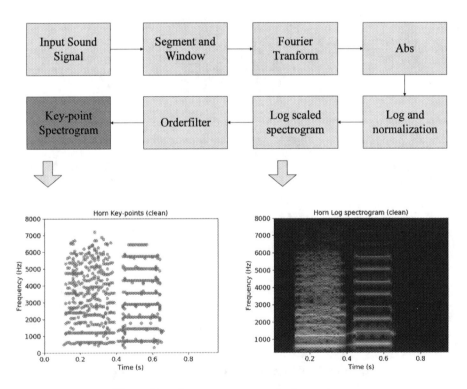

Fig. 2. Detail steps to extract the key-points.

2.2   Key-Point Encoding

KPs, extracted from both local temporal and spectral regions, localize the sparse high-energy peaks in the spectrogram. These peaks will remain prominent under noisy environments, making them robust in mismatched conditions. Therefore, key-point extraction used in our approach ensures a robust and sparse representation of the sound signal. The detail of our KP encoding approach is demonstrated in Fig. 2.

For each incoming spectrogram, $S_{log}(f, t)$, KPs are extracted from both local time and frequency domains. We use one-dimensional order filter to perform such extractions over the local regions in both domains. The local region is defined as follows:

$$Q_f(y) = S_{log}(f \pm d, t), \qquad d \in \{0, 1, ..., D\}$$
$$Q_t(y) = S_{log}(f, t \pm d) \tag{2}$$

where Q_f and Q_t are the local vertical spectral and local horizontal temporal vectors, respectively. $y \in [-D, D]$ represents the vector index. We set $D = 4$ as the local region size, which we found was small enough to extract significant sound information, but large enough to represent the sound features.

KPs are then detected from these local time and frequency regions, respectively. A key-point is determined according to the following criteria as:

$$S_{log}(f, t) \geq \begin{cases} Q_f(y), or & \forall y \in [-D, D] \\ Q_t(y) \end{cases} \tag{3}$$

The extracted keypoint information, K_i, is stored as:

$$K_i = \{f_i, t_i, s_i\} \tag{4}$$

where $s_i = S_{log}(f_i, t_i)$ is the spectral power corresponding to the key-point. f_i and t_i are the time and frequency coordinates, respectively.

Some of the extracted KPs do not represent significant information of the signal, and they are more likely to be part of the background noise. Therefore, we introduce two different masking schemes to further delete these less important KPs for a more spare representation. The first scheme is an absolute-value masking, while the other is a relative-background masking. In the absolute-value masking scheme, we use a macro filtering approach to reject those KPs that match the criteria of $s_i < \alpha_a$, where α_a is a hyper-parameter that controls the reduction level on the number of KPs. In the relative-background masking scheme, the contrast of each key-point and background mean value are examined to remove the unimportant KPs [25, 26]. We defined:

$$P(s_i) = \alpha_r \times s_i - mean\{S_{log}(f \pm d, t \pm d)\} \tag{5}$$

where α_r is another controlling hyper-parameter. If $P(s_i) > 0$, the corresponding KPs are kept, otherwise they will be regarded as background noise and then removed. In our experiments, we set α_a and α_r to 0.15 and 0.85, respectively.

Differing from [5], we only extract the KPs from spectrograms and then directly use these KPs as the input for post-processing, i.e. classification. This simplification with processing KPs only makes the operation easier and more efficient to extract important features from signals. Additionally, the introduced two masking schemes are proposed to further help suppress the remained less important information, making our representation more sparse and robust.

2.3 CNN-Based Classifier

Convolutional neural networks (CNNs) are multi-layer neural networks that are mainly composed of three different components: convolutional layers, pooling layers and fully connected layers. This hierarchical structure makes CNNs favorable and advantageous for image-based processing [9,10]. Our KP encoding provides an image-like representation of the sound, which can be combined with CNNs. Additionally, CNNs have several advantages such as location and scale invariant properties [7], making it more suitable for unstructured environmental sound recognition. Therefore, we use CNN as the classifier of our sound recognition system. CNN is used to process our KP-based spectrograms.

The CNN classifier architecture is set to $32C3@127 \times 211$-$64C3@63 \times 105$-$128C3@31 \times 52$-$256C3@15 \times 25$-$F64$-$F10$. It consists of four convolutional layers and a fully connected one, followed by a softmax classifier that is used as the output for sound event classification. All the layers except the input and output ones use non-linearly rectified linear units (ReLU) as the activation function, and a batch normalization is applied to avoid over-fitting. Additionally, we set 2×2 strides in all the learning layers except for the first convolutional layer. The CNN network is trained adopting the Adam optimizer with the learning rate of 0.0001.

3   Experiments and Results

3.1   Experimental Setup

In this section, experiments are conducted to examine the performance of our proposed KP-CNN system for a robust sound event classification task.

Sound Database: In our experiments, a total number of 10 sound categories are selected from the Real World Computing Partnership (RWCP) Sound Scene Database in Real Acoustical Environments [13], which are: bells5, bottle1, buzzer, cymbals, horn, kara, metal15, phone4, ring and whistle1. The isolated sound files are approximately 0.5–3 s with a high SNR. For each of the 10 categories, 40 files are randomly chosen as the training set and another 40 as the testing set. Therefore, a total number of 400 files are available for training and another 400 for testing. The performance is evaluated from the average 10 runs of the experiments.

Noise Conditions: To evaluate the robustness in mismatched conditions, babble noise from the NOISEX'92 database [20] is added from random beginning points to the sounds at levels of 20, 10, 0 and −5 dB SNRs, while using only clean samples for training. Then the average performance on different noise levels is reported. For multi-condition training, we impose random noise of the levels of clean, 20 and 10 dB to each sound signal during training, and then evaluate the performance on the different noise levels.

3.2   Experimental Methods

We compare our proposed KP-CNN system against several baseline systems. One is MFCC-HMM, which follows the traditional speech recognition method. Another one is the direct use of spectrograms as the inputs for DNN/CNN, the so-called SPEC-DNN/SPEC-CNN approach. The last one is logMel feature extraction with CNN, the so-called logMel-CNN method, which is currently the most standard technique used for sound event recognition.

Baseline MFCC-HMM [5]**.** Each state has five sub-states and five Gaussian mixtures. The frame-based MFCCs have 36-dimensions, with 12 cepstral coefficients excluding the zeroth component, plus deltas and accelerations.

Baseline SPEC-DNN [25]**.** Each sound signal is converted into a two-dimensional spectrogram with the size of 129 × 213. In other words, each spectrogram contains 213 frames with 129 attributes in each frame. These spectrograms are then fed directly to the DNNs. The DNN classifier structure is set to 256-180-64-32-10. In the output layer, a softmax classifier is used for classifying different sound categories. Apart from input and output layers, the ReLU activation function is used. In addition, the Adam optimizer is used to train the DNN model with the learning rate of 0.0001.

Baseline SPEC-CNN [25]**.** For the feature extraction, the spectrograms are extracted in the same way as in the baseline SPEC-DNN. Then the CNN classifier is used to classify the different sound categories in clean and noise conditions. The detail of CNN classifier structure is described in Sect. 2.3.

Baseline LogMel-CNN [18]**.** As the most currently standard method for sound recognition, the logMel spectrum features are extracted after obtaining the spectrograms. In this stage, 23 Mel-filterbank is used to extract the Mel spectrum features, which is followed by a logarithm operation. Then the obtained logMel spectrum features are used as the inputs of CNN to conduct the robust sound classification task.

Our Proposed KP-CNN. The spectrograms are also handled in the same way as in the baseline SPEC-DNN/SPEC-CNN. The main difference is that key-point extraction is added between the spectrogram and CNN to extract the sparse local temporal and spectral information.

The experiments are designed in both clean and multi-condition trainings, and then tests are evaluated with clean and different noise levels. In our experiments, spectrograms are firstly extracted from sound signals with STFT, where we select 256 FFT points, 256 window size and 96 overlap size. Additionally, a padding operation is used to obtain a fixed size of spectrogram. Then the KPs are extracted from the fixed spectrograms. Finally, the KPs are fed into the CNN classifier to classify different sound signals.

3.3   Results and Discussions

In this section, the classification accuracy of our proposed KP-CNN system for robust sound event classification is compared with the several baseline systems in both clean and multi-condition training scenarios.

Table 1. Classification accuracy in mismatched conditions.

Methods	MFCC-HMM [5]	SPEC-DNN [25]	SPEC-CNN [25]	logMel-CNN [18]	KP-CNN
Clean	99.0%	**100%**	99.83%	**100%**	99.88%
20 dB	62.1%	94.38%	**99.88%**	93.02%	99.85%
10 dB	34.4%	71.80%	98.93%	72.00%	**99.68%**
0 dB	21.8%	42.68%	83.65%	51.70%	**94.43%**
−5 dB	19.5%	34.85%	58.08%	39.92%	**84.80%**
Average	47.3%	68.74%	88.07%	71.33%	**95.73%**

Table 1 shows the classification results in the mismatched conditions under noise-free training. According to Table 1, we can find the following experimental results:

(1) For robust sound event classification task, traditional MFCC-HMM system can get an accuracy of 99.0% in the clean condition, while the performance decreased rapidly with the increasing noise, resulting in an average correct rate of 47.3%. Our proposed KP-CNN system performs better than the conventional MFCC-HMM system for both clean and noisy tests.

(2) As the noise increases, the classification accuracy of KP-CNN performs better than SPEC-DNN/CNN and logMel-CNN, indicating the robustness and effectiveness of our KP encoding. The main difference between these baseline systems is that the KP-CNN adopts a key-point extraction step to extract sparse local temporal and spectral information. Our proposed system gains a high average accuracy of 95.73%. Even if with strong noise of −5 dB, it still remains a relatively high accuracy of 84.80%. These classification results indicate that our KP extraction approach is robust and effective for noisy environments.

This result is because that the extracted significant KPs, as local peaks, are inherently resistant to noise. These key-points carry the most discriminative and robust information, while the spectrogram and logMel spectrum features are very sensitive to noise. The imposed noises are unlikely to destroy all the great KPs, leaving our proposed representation still effective to capture sufficient information for classification.

Table 2. Multi-condition Classification for several systems.

Methods	SPEC-DNN	SPEC-CNN	logMel-CNN	KP-CNN
Clean	99.90%	99.89%	99.87%	**99.93%**
20 dB	99.88%	99.89%	99.67%	**99.93%**
10 dB	99.50%	**99.89%**	99.22%	99.73%
0 dB	94.05%	**99.11%**	97.17%	98.13%
−5 dB	78.95%	91.17%	93.07%	**94.75%**
Average	94.46%	98.04%	97.80%	**98.49%**

In order to further increase the robustness of the sound event classification, a multi-condition training task is conducted. The purpose is to make the trained system less sensitive to background noise while improving its sensitivity to target sounds. Table 2 presents the classification results for the multi-condition case. As can be seen from the table, the multi-condition training can further improve the classification performance over the mismatched condition, with an average accuracy rate of 98.49%. Even in the −5 dB noise condition, it can obtain a high accuracy rate of 94.75%.

Overall, our proposed KP-CNN system is an efficient and brain-inspired one for the sound event classification task, which outperforms others in both clean and noisy conditions.

4   Conclusion

In this paper, we proposed a novel simple KP-CNN approach for the robust sound event classification task. To obtain the sparse local temporal and spectral information, the key-point encoding was used to extract local time-frequency information. Then, a CNN was used to classify sounds based on these KP representations. In the mismatched conditions, we achieved the mean accuracy of 95.73% over a variety of noise levels up to −5 dB. In addition, the system performance can be further improved with a multi-condition training scheme, and we obtained an average performance of 98.49%. To the author's knowledge, this paper contributes the first attempt by combining key-points extraction and CNN for the robust sound event classification task.

Acknowledgements. This work was supported by the Natural Science Foundation of China (No. 61806139, 61771333), and the Natural Science Foundation of Tianjin (No. 18JCYBJC41700).

References

1. Allen, J.B.: How do humans process and recognize speech? IEEE Trans. Speech Audio Process. **2**(4), 567–577 (1994). https://doi.org/10.1007/978-1-4615-2281-2_11

2. Cai, R., Lu, L., Hanjalic, A., Zhang, H.J., Cai, L.H.: A flexible framework for key audio effects detection and auditory context inference. IEEE Trans. Audio Speech Lang. Process. **14**(3), 1026–1039 (2006). https://doi.org/10.1109/TSA. 2005.857575

3. Dennis, J., Tran, H.D., Chng, E.S.: Overlapping sound event recognition using local spectrogram features and the generalised hough transform. Pattern Recognit. Lett. **34**(9), 1085–1093 (2013). https://doi.org/10.1016/j.patrec.2013.02.015

4. Dennis, J., Tran, H.D., Li, H.: Spectrogram image feature for sound event classification in mismatched conditions. IEEE Signal Process. Lett. **18**(2), 130–133 (2010). https://doi.org/10.1109/LSP.2010.2100380

5. Dennis, J., Yu, Q., Tang, H., Tran, H.D., Li, H.: Temporal coding of local spectrogram features for robust sound recognition. In: 2013 IEEE International Conference on Acoustics, Speech and Signal Processing, pp. 803–807. IEEE (2013). https:// doi.org/10.1109/ICASSP.2013.6637759

6. Ghiurcau, M.V., Rusu, C., Bilcu, R.C., Astola, J.: Audio based solutions for detecting intruders in wild areas. Signal Process. **92**(3), 829–840 (2012). https://doi.org/ 10.1016/j.sigpro.2011.10.001

7. Krizhevsky, A., Sutskever, I., Hinton, G.E.: ImageNet classification with deep convolutional neural networks. In: Advances in Neural Information Processing Systems, pp. 1097–1105 (2012). https://doi.org/10.1145/3065386

8. LeCun, Y., Bengio, Y., Hinton, G.: Deep learning. Nature **521**(7553), 436 (2015). https://doi.org/10.1038/nature14539

9. LeCun, Y., Bengio, Y., et al.: Convolutional networks for images, speech, and time series. In: The Handbook of Brain Theory and Neural Networks, vol. 3361, no. 10, p. 1995 (1995)

10. LeCun, Y., Bottou, L., Bengio, Y., Haffner, P., et al.: Gradient-based learning applied to document recognition. Proc. IEEE **86**(11), 2278–2324 (1998)

11. Lee, Y., Kassam, S.: Generalized median filtering and related nonlinear filtering techniques. IEEE Trans. Acoust. Speech Signal Process **33**(3), 672–683 (1985)

12. McLoughlin, I., Zhang, H., Xie, Z., Song, Y., Xiao, W.: Robust sound event classification using deep neural networks. IEEE/ACM Trans. Audio Speech Lang. Process. **23**(3), 540–552 (2015). https://doi.org/10.1109/TASLP.2015.2389618

13. Nakamura, S., Hiyane, K., Asano, F., Nishiura, T., Yamada, T.: Acoustical sound database in real environments for sound scene understanding and hands-free speech recognition (2000)

14. O'Shaughnessy, D.: Automatic speech recognition: history, methods and challenges. Pattern Recognit. **41**(10), 2965–2979 (2008)

15. Ozer, I., Ozer, Z., Findik, O.: Noise robust sound event classification with convolutional neural network. Neurocomputing **272**, 505–512 (2018). https://doi.org/10. 1016/j.neucom.2017.07.021

16. Paliwal, K.K.: Spectral subband centroid features for speech recognition. In: Proceedings of the 1998 IEEE International Conference on Acoustics, Speech and Signal Processing, ICASSP 1998, (Cat. No. 98CH36181), vol. 2, pp. 617–620. IEEE (1998). https://doi.org/10.1109/ICASSP.1998.675340

17. Phan, H., Hertel, L., Maass, M., Mazur, R., Mertins, A.: Learning representations for nonspeech audio events through their similarities to speech patterns. IEEE/ACM Trans. Audio Speech Lang. Process. **24**(4), 807–822 (2016). https:// doi.org/10.1109/TASLP.2016.2530401

18. Piczak, K.J.: Environmental sound classification with convolutional neural networks. In: 2015 IEEE 25th International Workshop on Machine Learning for Signal Processing (MLSP), pp. 1–6. IEEE (2015). https://doi.org/10.1109/MLSP.2015.7324337

19. Sharan, R.V., Moir, T.J.: Subband time-frequency image texture features for robust audio surveillance. IEEE Trans. Inf. Forensics Secur. **10**(12), 2605–2615 (2015). https://doi.org/10.1109/TIFS.2015.2469254

20. Varga, A., Steeneken, H.J.: Assessment for automatic speech recognition: Ii. noisex-92: a database and an experiment to study the effect of additive noise on speech recognition systems. Speech Commun. **12**(3), 247–251 (1993). https://doi.org/10.1016/0167-6393(93)90095-3

21. Walters, T.C.: Auditory-based processing of communication sounds. Ph.D. thesis, University of Cambridge (2011)

22. Wu, J., Chua, Y., Zhang, M., Li, H., Tan, K.C.: A spiking neural network framework for robust sound classification. Front. Neurosci. **12** (2018). https://doi.org/10.3389/fnins.2018.00836

23. Xiao, R., Tang, H., Gu, P., Xu, X.: Spike-based encoding and learning of spectrum features for robust sound recognition. Neurocomputing **313**, 65–73 (2018). https://doi.org/10.1016/j.neucom.2018.06.022

24. Yu, Q., Li, H., Tan, K.C.: Spike timing or rate? Neurons learn to make decisions for both through threshold-driven plasticity. IEEE Trans. Cybern. **49**(6), 2178–2189 (2018). https://doi.org/10.1109/TCYB.2018.2821692

25. Yu, Q., Yao, Y., Wang, L., Tang, H., Dang, J.: A multi-spike approach for robust sound recognition. In: ICASSP 2019-2019 IEEE International Conference on Acoustics, Speech and Signal Processing (ICASSP), pp. 890–894. IEEE (2019). https://doi.org/10.1109/ICASSP.2019.8682963

26. Yu, Q., Yao, Y., Wang, L., Tang, H., Dang, J., Tan, K.C.: Robust environmental sound recognition with sparse key-point encoding and efficient multi-spike learning. arXiv preprint arXiv:1902.01094 (2019)

27. Zhang, H., McLoughlin, I., Song, Y.: Robust sound event recognition using convolutional neural networks. In: 2015 IEEE International Conference on Acoustics, Speech and Signal Processing (ICASSP), pp. 559–563. IEEE (2015). https://doi.org/10.1109/ICASSP.2015.7178031

Neuro-Spectral Audio Synthesis: Exploiting Characteristics of the Discrete Fourier Transform in the Real-Time Simulation of Musical Instruments Using Parallel Neural Networks

Carlos Tarjano$^{(\boxtimes)}$ ⓘ and Valdecy Pereira ⓘ

Universidade Federal Fluminense, Niterói, RJ, Brazil
tesserato@hotmail.com, valdecypereira@yahoo.com.br

Abstract. Two main approaches are currently prevalent in the digital emulation of musical instruments: manipulation of pre-recorded samples and techniques of real-time synthesis, generally based on physical models with varying degrees of accuracy. Concerning the first, while the processing power of present-day computers enables their use in real-time, many restrictions arising from this sample-based design persist; the huge on disk space requirements and the stiffness of musical articulations being the most prominent. On the other side of the spectrum, pure synthesis approaches, while offering greater flexibility, fail to capture and reproduce certain nuances central to the verisimilitude of the generated sound, offering a dry, synthetic output, at a high computational cost. We propose a method where ensembles of lightweight neural networks working in parallel are learned, from crafted frequency-domain features of an instrument sound spectra, an arbitrary instrument's voice and articulations realistically and efficiently. We find that our method, while retaining perceptual sound quality on par with sampled approaches, exhibits 1/10 of latency times of industry standard real-time synthesis algorithms, and 1/100 of the disk space requirements of industry standard sample-based digital musical instruments. This method can, therefore, serve as a basis for more efficient implementations in dedicated devices, such as keyboards and electronic drumkits and in general purpose platforms, like desktops and tablets or open-source hardware like Arduino and Raspberry Pi. From a conceptual point of view, this work highlights the advantages of a closer integration of machine learning with other subjects, especially in the endeavor of new product development. Exploiting the synergy between neural networks, digital signal processing techniques and physical modelling, we illustrate the proposed method via the implementation of two virtual instruments: a conventional grand piano and a hibrid stringed instrument.

Keywords: Neural networks · Acoustic modeling ·
Digital musical instruments · Real-time audio synthesis

© Springer Nature Switzerland AG 2019
I. V. Tetko et al. (Eds.): ICANN 2019, LNCS 11730, pp. 362–375, 2019.
https://doi.org/10.1007/978-3-030-30490-4_30

1 Introduction

From industry's perspective, while the interest in digital musical instruments has grown significantly in the last decades [1, 2], cutting-edge virtual instruments used in professional studios still rely primarily on collections of pre-recorded sound samples [3], demanding a high amount of disk space and reasonable processing power of the hardware (in general personal computers) in which they are implemented.

For platforms where processing power and storage are limited, such as digital keyboards and electronic drumkits, it is common the use of libraries of a smaller size and quality, to accommodate hardware restrictions, designed primarily to enable the practice of the instrument; Production quality is achieved by connecting those devices to a computer and using them as controllers of a software implementation in order to access more elaborated libraries and algorithms.

The recent developments in neural networks theory and applications suggest their potential to mitigate those limitations. In the field of computer vision, for instance, one can observe a plethora of developments that regularly expand the frontiers of the field.

Most of the work related to the application of neural networks in an audio context, however, approaches the task from a higher level of abstraction than the direct representation of sounds: Those are usually based on the manipulation of human-readable musical representations, such as scores. The main reason for this is the high dimensionality of the data: in the case of CD quality audio, with a frame rate of 44100 samples per second, for example, the synthesis of a 10 s piece involves the creation of more than 4 million samples.

The work developed by the teams behind Google Brain [4] and DeepMind [5] is a notable exception: A neural architecture based on Wavenet [6] is used to directly generate sound after training using audio samples from various musical instruments. The results show that a multi-layered convolutional architecture is able to learn time-domain representations for several instrument types.

An experimental extension of this work, called Nsynth [7], further investigates latent representations for musical sequences in the time domain, from a probabilistic standpoint.

We can take advantage of the periodic character of the samples and represent them, instead, in the frequency domain. The Fourier transform provides an accurate and reversible representation of a wave in the frequency domain. Considering the fact that we are, in the present work, interested only in temporal representations in the real domain, the frequency-domain representations will consist of a vector of complex numbers, half the size of the original number of samples.

At first, such a domain transformation would not introduce a more compact wave representation, from a storage point of view, since complex numbers are represented by pairs of real numbers in most programming languages. Considering, however, that the human ear is not able to perceive frequencies outside the 20 Hz to 20 kHz band, we have identified one of the advantages of working in the frequency domain: we can truncate the FFT result to this interval (taking care to translate it in terms of the local frequencies of the transform).

Another advantage comes in the form of its independence from the duration of the signal, which allows the use of a dense architecture in the prediction of arbitrary length waves. Further advantages of this approach will be illustrated in next sections, taking into account the physical characteristics of the instrument to be emulated and the properties of the transform, and will provide de theoretical basis to the method introduced in this work.

To the best of our knowledge, frequency-domain representations of sound, a popular technique in the digital signal processing field, were seldom used in the context of neural sound synthesis, despite being common in neural-based sound classification tasks. This is unfortunate, as frequency-domain representations are far more well behaved than their time-domain counterparts when applied to harmonic sounds, as is exemplified in Fig. 1.

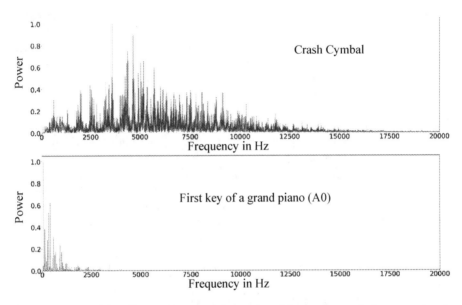

Fig. 1. Example of the difference between inharmonic and harmonic sounds frequency domain representations: audible frequency spectrum of a crash cymbal compared to key 1, note A0, of a grand piano.

It's clear that the change of domain, via an efficient implementation of the Fast Fourier Transform algorithm, greatly simplifies the representation of harmonic sounds. Insight from acoustic research can simplify those representations even further, alleviating the predictive burden of neural networks.

Considering the specific case of a standard grand piano, we can arrive at a basic model, to be extended later, that gives us a reasonable (albeit bland sounding) initial approximation. Observing that in equal-tempered instruments, as is the piano's case, the ratio of (theoretical) frequencies in adjacent notes is fixed at $2^{\frac{1}{12}}$, we can arrive at a formula of the form $f_0[k] = 440.2^{\frac{k-49}{12}}$ relating the 88 piano keys to their fundamental frequencies, where k stands for the piano key number, from 1 to 88, and 440 Hz is the standard frequency for key 49, with pitch A4, also known as concert pitch.

In practice, however, the fundamental frequencies deviate some cents from their theoretical value, due to a tuning technique named octave stretching that flattens the lowest octaves and sharpens the highest ones, with respect to their theoretical fundamental frequencies, in an attempt to attenuate the clash between partials from different keys [8]. This consistent behavior, arising from aural tuning techniques, was first exposed by Railsback in a 1938 paper published in The Journal of the Acoustical Society of America where the tuning of various pianos was compared. The data can be seen in the Fig. 2, with the smooth green line representing the average of deviations for various pianos.

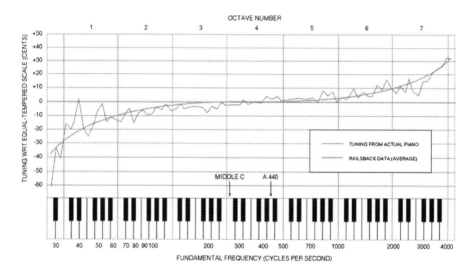

Fig. 2. Railsback curve [9]

This can be cheaply incorporated into the model before the neural network's treatment, via polynomial fitting. To account for the partials, one simple strategy consists in assuming the ideal string case, where partials are integer multiples of the system's fundamental frequency; we can thus write $f[p, k] = 440.2^{\frac{k-49}{12}}(p+1)$ to denote the frequency of the pth partial of the kth key.

While Fletcher [10], for example, proposes an equation that relates the fundamental frequency of a piano note with its pth partial, incorporating the inharmonicity present in piano strings, we can see from [8] that the inharmonicity coefficients per key aren't, in general, well behaved. That's also the case of partials' amplitudes; neural networks are, thus, in a better position to extract hidden features and learn the underlying associations needed to reproduce and generalize those quantities.

It is important to note that the base of peaks in the frequency domain is proportional to the decay of the corresponding frequency in the time domain: The extreme case of a perfectly periodic sinusoid, with zero decay, has a frequency spectrum of zero at all but one frequency. The Fig. 3 illustrates this relationship.

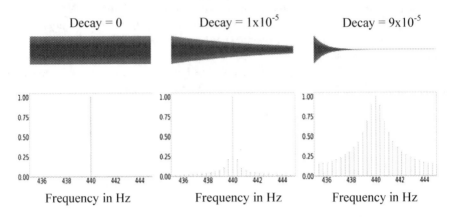

Fig. 3. Time (top row) and frequency (bottom row) domain representations of a 440 Hz sinusoid with 3 different exponential decay configurations.

One can observe that the decay introduces new frequencies around the nominal maximum frequency; it was empirically observed that the primordial effect of those additional frequencies is to reproduce the decay (or, more broadly, envelope) of the wave.

From this observation, two important intuitions can be drawn: the first is that, with a reasonable degree of approximation, we can describe a harmonic sound generated by an impulsive excitation as a function of the location of some of its frequencies (partials), their respective intensities, and their decays.

As partials envelopes are to be directly accounted for, original phase information can be discarded without significant perceptual effects, as is suggested empirically from the reconstruction of waves with their original phases zeroed or randomized.

In the Github repository dedicated to this work [11], on a folder named "RandomPhaseReconstructions/", reconstructions of the samples used to train the network can be found, where phase information was randomized for the first 100 partial frequencies. The original samples can be found at the same repository, at "00_samples/piano/".

Comparing the sounds, one can see that the reconstruction is quite accurate. Most of the perceptual difference between them originates in the number of partials considered, which does not include all the frequencies present in the transient phase of the wave in the lowest keys.

Noting, as we have, that harmonic instruments exhibit a well-behaved frequency domain distribution, consisting basically of peaks where the frequency of their partials are observed, and assuming exponential decays of the form e^{-dt}, with one value of d per partial and per key, one can elegantly account for the envelope of each one of the partials with knowledge of that partial's amplitude a and decay rate d.

2   Methods

Based on the theoretical discussion presented in the introduction, a neural network was created, using the Keras library on top of a Tensorflow backend. The architecture can be seen in Fig. 4. Receiving as inputs an array of the form [k, p], where k is the normalized piano key, in the range of 1 to 88, and p is the normalized partial frequency of interest, from 1 to 100, the network was trained to output, in parallel, the residual inharmonicity, the decay and the amplitude of each key-partial pair.

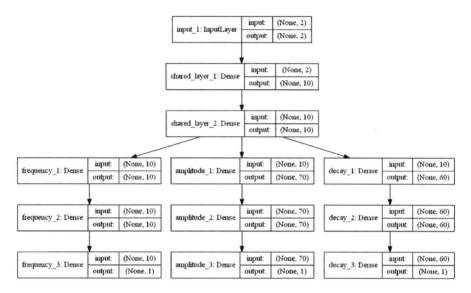

Fig. 4. Architecture of the neural network used in the model. Two dense layers serve as a common trunk, from which three branches with three dense layers each emerge in parallel.

The sound samples used to train the model were obtained at the website of the University of Iowa Electronic Music Studios [12]. The original library consists of a total of 260 samples recorded from a Steinway & Sons model B Grand Piano with a Neumann KM 84 microphone, and are encoded in stereo .aiff files, with 16-bit of depth and a framerate of 44.1 kHz.

From this sample library, we made use of the 88 (one per key) fortissimo articulations. Those were converted to mono .wav files with the same bitrate and framerate as the original .aiff format. Silences at the beginning of the files were removed and the audio intensity normalized. The processed samples are available at the Github repository prepared for this work [11].

Bearing in mind that, as discussed, the partial frequencies are approximately integer multiples of each key's fundamental frequency, one can search for the maximums in the frequency domain considering the appropriate intervals. Figure 5 compares this algorithm with the naïve enumeration of the highest intensity values, for a wave corresponding to the sound emitted by the key 35 of a piano, from which the first 30 partial frequencies are investigated.

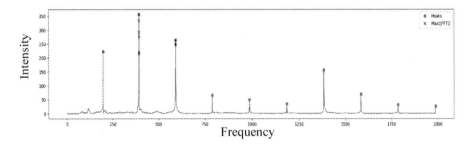

Fig. 5. Example of peak detection: peaks (red dot) x naïve maximum values (black "x") (Color figure online)

Figure 6, offers insight into the original tuning of the piano from which the samples were recorded; a polynomial of rank 3 offers a good compromise between simplicity and accuracy in the approximation of the stretched tuning, and was fitted using Numpy.

We can improve the theoretical fundamental frequencies $f_0(k) = 440.2^{\frac{k-49}{12}}$ with that term, in order to account for the octave stretching; As it was seen, this original equation disregards the inharmonicities present in the instruments, responsible for important characteristics of their timbres.

These equations present a very reasonable initial approximation that serves both to reinforce the basic harmonic characteristics in the final model and to alleviate the prediction effort of the network.

We can then write $f_0[k]$ as $440.2^{\frac{k-49}{12}}(c_1k^3 + c_2k^2 + c_3k + c_4)$. The effort is justified by the fact that improvements in f_0 are carried to all the theoretical partial frequencies, as they are multiples of f_0, greatly simplifying the neural architecture needed in the

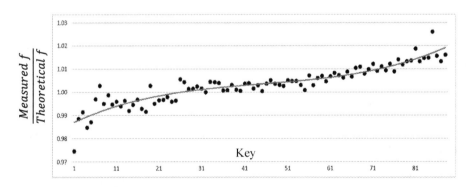

Fig. 6. Ratio between measured and theoretical fundamental frequencies as black dots and fitted polynomial as the red line. The effect of the tuning stretch can be observed (Color figure online)

model. The algorithm used to extract the fundamental frequencies, compare with the theoretical ones and proceed the fitting process can be found in the file "01_tuning_stretch.py", and Fig. 6 shows the polynomial along with the original ratios per key.

Thus, an arbitrary theoretical frequency, as a function of the piano key and the partial considered, will be represented in the model as follows: $f_0[k,p] = 440.2^{\frac{k-49}{12}}(c_1 k^3 + c_2 k^2 + c_3 k + c_4)(p+1)i[k,p]$, $k \in \{1, 2, \ldots, 88\}, p \in \{0, 1, 2, \ldots\}$, where $i[k,p]$ is the inharmonicity as given by the network.

Considering both fundamental and partial frequencies in the audible spectrum, the model would have to learn a range of frequencies from 27 Hz, the fundamental frequency of A0, to a little more than 20 kHz, corresponding, for example, to the fifth partial of C8, if it was to estimate directly the partial frequencies of a piano.

Working with inharmonicities, on the other hand, reduced the interval to the limit between 0.98 and 1.02. In addition, the behavior of inharmonicities is reasonably predictable, with a slightly exponential character, as illustrated in Fig. 7.

Despite being formulated and used in this work in the context of a piano, this framework is convenient for a wide range of instruments, since the 88 keys of a piano range from A0 to C8, covering the frequency spectrum of most instruments of interest; To train the network from any instrument, one has simply to label the samples of the relevant sounds with the equivalent key number of a piano, as will be shown in the creation of a hybrid stringed instrument.

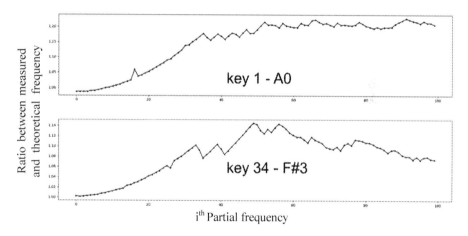

Fig. 7. Inharmonicities of two piano keys. The horizontal axis shows the number of the partial, while vertical axis shows the deviation from the theoretical value.

This same rationale is applied to the amplitudes, being predicted as a fraction of the maximum values found in each of the keys (or notes, more generally, in the case of an arbitrary instrument being trained), and residing in the closed interval between 0 and 1.

The decay curve can be estimated considering the difference in intensity of an arbitrary frequency in the first and second halves of the wave, using the formula

$d = \dfrac{2 \ln\left(\frac{a_1}{a_2}\right)}{l}$. Figure 8 illustrates the application of this procedure to a number of sound samples. Note that only in the first case in the left upper hand corner of the figure, the wave being a pure sinusoid, the extracted decay corresponds to the whole sample envelope.

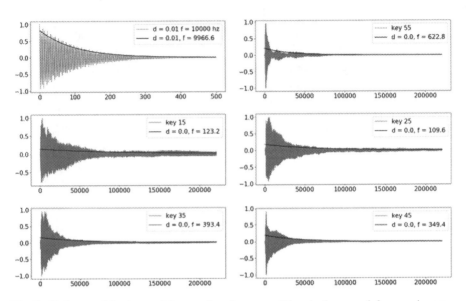

Fig. 8. Estimates of the decay of the prevalent frequency. Wave in the upper left corner is a pure sinusoid with 0.01 decay; the others are sounds of pianos keys, as specified.

As it was observed, with an estimate of the decays of the partial frequencies, the phase information has negligible impact on the sound of the reconstructed wave; we chose, thus, to randomize the phases: This approach has the advantage of imparting a more organic and varied character to the synthesized output of the final model, as no wave generated will be exactly the same as any other wave. Another option, less rich from the perceptual point of view, would be to give the phases an arbitrary value (zero, for example).

As activation function in each of the network layers, a modified version of the hyperbolic tangent, in the form $a(x) = \tanh(6x - 3)/2 + 1/2$, was used, so as to best cover the interval $[0, 1]$ in which the inputs and outputs reside.

The neural network used in the model has a total of 10,563 trainable parameters, with a size in disc of approximately 200 KB. The two initial layers, with 10 neurons each, are common to all the 3 predicted outputs, and provide a shared initial representation, to be extended later by each of the branches responsible for individual quantities.

This approach provides for less redundancy in the model while allowing for the number of neurons in the independent layers to be customized to account for the individual optimization of each of the outputs; It's worth noting that the fundamental frequency approximations made a priori allowed a small number of neurons in the branch responsible for the inharmonicities. Figure 9 compares the original targets and the behavior learned by the network.

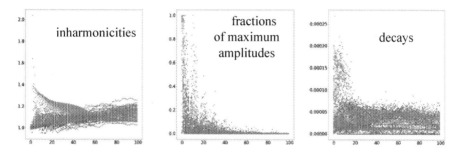

Fig. 9. Results of the model. Black dots are the original measured values and red dots are the values predicted by the network. (Color figure online)

Thus, we can define a new methodology for modeling of harmonic instruments, dubbed "Neuro-Spectral Synthesis", as summarized in Fig. 10.

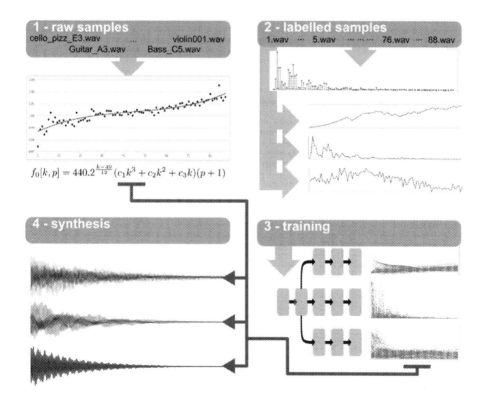

Fig. 10. Schematic view of the final model

As illustrated in step 1 of the representation in Fig. 10, the model starts with the selection of raw samples of an instrument, so that the behavior of their fundamental frequencies can be approximated by a polynomial; this generates an initial approximation for each of the n partials that are going to be used, since they are close to integer multiples of the fundamental frequency.

In step 2 the actual values of the partials are measured, and their deviations from the theoretical values calculated. This is done detecting the peaks in the frequency domain representation of each wave. The amplitude of each partial is also measured as a ratio of the amplitude of the fundamental frequency. Finally, the decay of each partial is estimated. This data will be used in the training process. For direct use of the model as it is implemented in "02_Info.py", samples should be renamed from 1 to 88, in order to mimic the keys of a standard grand piano.

In the third step the network architecture is built, and the training takes place. After training, the predicted values for each value are recorded and compared to the original values, to enable assessing the general behavior of the model. The trained neural network is saved. The implementation of this step can be seen in "03_train.py".

At this point all the data needed for the synthesis is already available. Here in the fourth and last step the polynomial approximation formulated in step 1 and the trained network created in step 3 are used to create sound in real time, as is demonstrated in "04_RealTime.py".

3   Results and Discussion

In order to assess the quality of the proposed model, we compare its results and behavior with implementations of the two most used approaches in sound synthesis, namely, digital waveguides [3] and the finite differences method [13]. For a comparison between those methods the reader is referred to [14].

On behalf of consistency, implementations of the two methods were prepared, in the Python programming language, and are available in the Github repository prepared for this work [11], under the name of "Digital_Waveguides.py" and "Finite_Differences.py". Some examples of outputs from those implementations can be heard at the folders "Demo Digital Waveguides" and "Demo Finite Differences", respectively.

The neural model presents more realistic results than the implementations based on either digital waveguides or finite difference methods, and is at least 10 times more efficient, in comparison with the aforementioned implementations.

Taking into account the generation of 5 1-s waves at 44,100 frames per second, the proposed method was, on average, 17 times faster than the digital waveguides-based method and 26 times faster than the finite differences. Table 1 summarizes the results.

Sounds generated by the proposed model can be heard, in a musical context, in the author's Soundcloud [15]. Some tracks make use of a drumkit generated with a similar approach as the one presented in this work.

In order to further investigate the flexibility of the model, a hibrid instrument was created, and is available in the Github repository dedicated to the project [11]. Being trained using samples of an acoustic bass, for the lowest notes, a violoncello and a

Table 1. Comparison of the latency in seconds for the 3 implementations

	Finite differences	Digital waveguides	Neuro-spectral synthesis
1	16.95213819	13.81114888	0.5896253586
2	19.62042928	13.02065825	0.8354649544
3	24.25646234	11.33273816	0.7555158138
4	17.89053726	12.3500874	0.7475204468
5	18.00246739	12.12223339	0.7735056877
Average	**19.34440689**	**12.52737322**	**0.7403264523**
Standard Deviation	**2.908692366**	**0.937300851**	**0.09102950916**

violin for the middle of the register, and samples from an acoustic guitar for the highest notes, this instrument presents a blend of its component's timbre and dynamics.

The on-disc size of the models, as can be seen in the Github repository, are far inferior to industry standard commercial piano synthesizers, of which Pianoteq 6 [16] is the slimmest, with approximately 30 Mb: both the hybrid and piano models occupy little less than 200 Kb.

The main limitation of the proposed methodology is that all the parameters to be manipulated in the final model must first have been incorporated into the training process. The two physical modeling paradigms used for comparison, both the finite difference method and the digital waveguides, allow some real-time manipulation of their parameters afterwards: in the examples presented, the excitation point can be changed from wave to wave and at any time, the pickup point can be changed, even during the simulation, reflecting on the timbre of the sound generated.

In addition, these models lend themselves to the reasonably trivial incorporation of a source, continuous or periodic, of excitation, and can be used for the simulation of continuous-sounding instruments, like bowed violins. That's not true for the model in its current state, as an assumption of strictly exponential decay is made. The authors are currently investigating more flexible ways of modelling the envelope of arbitrary frequencies in soundwaves, which would confer more generality to the model.

Another barrier is that the model learns sound characteristics from examples and does not lend itself, in a practical way, to direct sound exploration. The availability of reasonable representative sound libraries for each instrument one intends to emulate is another limitation: ideally, those libraries should contain at least a couple of different samples from each articulation present in the original instrument.

4 Conclusion

The present work, introducing a new method of acoustic instrument modeling, demonstrates one possibility of the use of neural networks to audio synthesis, establishing the potential of real-time applications based on this technique. The model generates more credible results than the most used and efficient real-time acoustic modeling algorithms found in the literature, at a lower computational cost.

Another advantage over models based on conventional physical simulation is that it can learn relevant sound characteristics that arise from parts of the system difficult to model, such as the influence of resonators of complex geometry.

The present work shows that dense architectures, given a suitable representation, are able to learn features that allow the reproduction and generalization of sound samples in a direct way; from the introduction of a compact, physically informed representation of harmonic sound waves, the work shows the synergetic potential between research developments on the acoustics of musical instruments and the use of neural networks to base models for the emulation of these instruments, or families of instruments.

Furthermore, through the use of specially designed activation functions to accommodate the pertinent representation parameters and appropriate initialization methods of weights and biases, these architectures can be simplified, and the required number of trainable parameters appreciably decreased, making them more effective for real-time sound synthesis.

The possibilities for future developments in this area of intersection between neural networks and acoustic modeling are numerous, given the scarcity of similar investigations: It would be interesting, for example, to use the outputs of a model based on the finite difference method, which can be formulated so as to simulate more sophisticated features of an instrument such as string stiffness, resonance and various terms of loss of a given acoustic system, at the cost of a high demand of computational resources, to train a model based on digital waveguides with a neural network at the point where losses and other calculations are concatenated.

Due to the high degree of recursion of the digital waveguides algorithm, direct training based on the expected outputs of the model is quite complex to be implemented; the output vectors of a simulation based on finite differences, however, are fully compatible with this approach, and the insertion of a neural network could lead to a model that retains at least part of the accuracy of the simulation by the finite difference method, with computational efficiency close to or even higher than that presented by the digital waveguides algorithm. In [17], for example, we find an example of this work, which explores the use of neural networks for the identification of relevant parameters to a simulation by digital waveguides of the human vocal tract.

Relaxing the simplification adopted during the work in relation to exponential decays is another future development with interesting potential: for some categories of sounds, like the human voice, for example, the envelope of the wave presents greater impact than the frequencies in perceptual characteristics of the sound, such as intelligibility.

Estimate the envelopes with the technique presented here, considering a larger number of points and use a neural network to learn the characteristics of that envelope for a set of samples from an arbitrary instrument, or even the human voice, is another interesting direction to be investigated.

Another development would be to implement the method in a more efficient programming language, such as C or C++, with the addition of a visual interface and compatibility with MIDI controllers. Those modifications can form the basis for a commercially viable product line, to be marketed in standalone and/or VST plugin format.

References

1. Medeiros, R., Calegario, F., Cabral, G., Ramalho, G.: Challenges in designing new interfaces for musical expression. In: Marcus, A. (ed.) DUXU 2014. LNCS, vol. 8517, pp. 643–652. Springer, Cham (2014). https://doi.org/10.1007/978-3-319-07668-3_62
2. Emerson, G., Egermann, H.: Exploring the motivations for building new digital musical instruments. Musicae Scientiae, p. 102986491880298 (2018). https://doi.org/10.1177/1029864918802983
3. Smith III, J.O.: Digital Waveguide Architectures for Virtual Musical Instruments. In: Havelock, D., Kuwano, S., Vorländer, M. (eds.) Handbook of Signal Processing in Acoustics, pp. 399–417. Springer, New York (2008). https://doi.org/10.1007/978-0-387-30441-0_25
4. Li, B., Zhang, Y., Sainath, T., Wu, Y., Chan, W.: Bytes are all you need: end-to-end multilingual speech recognition and synthesis with bytes. In: ICASSP 2019 - 2019 IEEE International Conference on Acoustics, Speech and Signal Processing (ICASSP) (2019). https://doi.org/10.1109/icassp.2019.8682674
5. Koster, R., et al.: Big-loop recurrence within the hippocampal system supports integration of information across episodes. Neuron **99**, 1342–1354.e6 (2018). https://doi.org/10.1016/j.neuron.2018.08.009
6. Tobing, P.L., Hayashi, T., Wu, Y.-C., Kobayashi, K., Toda, T.: An evaluation of deep spectral mappings and WaveNet vocoder for voice conversion. In: 2018 IEEE Spoken Language Technology Workshop (SLT) (2018). https://doi.org/10.1109/slt.2018.8639608
7. NSynth: Neural Audio Synthesis, Google Brain team and DeepMind, 6 April 2017. https://magenta.tensorflow.org/nsynth. Accessed 20 July 2019
8. Koenig, D.M.: Spectral Analysis of Musical Sounds with Emphasis on the Piano. Oxford University Press (2014). https://doi.org/10.1093/acprof:oso/9780198722908.001.0001
9. Tung, B.: The Railsback curve, indicating the deviation between normal piano tuning and an equal-tempered scale, 7 June 2006. https://en.wikipedia.org/wiki/Piano_acoustics#/media/File:Railsback2.png. Accessed 20 July 2019
10. Fletcher, H.: Normal vibration frequencies of a stiff piano string. J. Acoust. Soc. Am. **36**, 203–209 (1964). https://doi.org/10.1121/1.1918933
11. Tarjano, C.: Neurospectral Audio Synthesis Repository, Github, 15 July 2018. https://github.com/tesserato/neurospectral-audio-synthesis. Accessed 20 July 2019
12. University of Iowa: University of Iowa Electronic Music Studio (1997). http://theremin.music.uiowa.edu/MIS.html. Accessed 20 July 2019
13. Bilbao, S.: Numerical Sound Synthesis. Wiley, Chichester (2009). https://doi.org/10.1002/9780470749012
14. Karjalainen, M., Erkut, C.: Digital waveguides versus finite difference structures: equivalence and mixed modeling. EURASIP J. Adv. Signal Process. **2004**, 978–989 (2004). https://doi.org/10.1155/s1110865704401176
15. Tarjano, C.: Neuro-Spectral Audio Synthesis, SoundCloud, 12 June 2018. https://soundcloud.com/carlos-tarjano/sets/spectral-neural-synthesis. Accessed 20 July 2019
16. Pianoteq: Pianoteq, 04 July 2019. https://www.pianoteq.com/pianoteq6. Accessed 20 July 2019
17. Gully, A.J., Yoshimura, T., Murphy, D.T., Hashimoto, K., Nankaku, Y., Tokuda, K.: Articulatory text-to-speech synthesis using the digital waveguide mesh driven by a deep neural network. In: Proceedings of the Interspeech 2017 (2017). https://doi.org/10.21437/Interspeech.2017-900

Ensemble of Convolutional Neural Networks for P300 Speller in Brain Computer Interface

Hongchang Shan[1(✉)], Yu Liu[2], and Todor Stefanov[1]

[1] Leiden University, Leiden, The Netherlands
{h.shan,t.p.stefanov}@liacs.leidenuniv.nl
[2] KU Leuven, Leuven, Belgium
yu.liu@esat.kuleuven.be

Abstract. A Brain Computer Interface (BCI) speller allows human-beings to directly spell characters using eye-gazes, thereby building communication between the human brain and a computer. Convolutional Neural Networks (CNNs) have shown better ability than traditional machine learning methods to increase the character spelling accuracy for the BCI speller. Unfortunately, current CNNs can not learn well the features related to the target signal of the BCI speller. This issue limits these CNNs from further character spelling accuracy improvements. To address this issue, we propose a network, which combines our proposed two CNNs, with an existing CNN. These three CNNs of our network extract different features related to the target BCI signal. Our network uses the ensemble of the features extracted by these CNNs for BCI character spelling. Experimental results on three benchmark datasets show that our network outperforms other methods in most cases, with a significant spelling accuracy improvement up to 38.72%. In addition, the communication speed of the P300 speller based on our network is up to 2.56 times faster than the communication speed of the P300 speller based on other methods.

1 Introduction

A Brain Computer Interface (BCI) enables direct communication between the human brain and a computer by analyzing the human's neural activities. In this way, human-beings can use only the brain to express their thoughts without any real movement. Traditionally, BCIs are conceived as a pathway for people suffering from motor disabilities [10]. With the rapid development of BCIs, recent research is also focused on developing BCIs for healthy users to allow users' hands-free interaction with applications such as games [3], mental state monitoring [14], and IoT services [13]. Due to their non-invasiveness, easiness and safety, Electroencephalogram (EEG)-based BCIs attract most of the research. Among all kinds of EEG-based BCIs, the P300 speller is one of the most-commonly investigated applications because the P300 speller has a good performance on

© Springer Nature Switzerland AG 2019
I. V. Tetko et al. (Eds.): ICANN 2019, LNCS 11730, pp. 376–394, 2019.
https://doi.org/10.1007/978-3-030-30490-4_31

character spelling [10]. Therefore, this paper considers the P300 speller as our target BCI application.

Previously, traditional machine learning methods were used for character spelling in the P300 speller. These methods employ signal processing techniques for feature extraction and use classifiers such as Support Vector Machine (SVM) or Linear Discriminant Analysis (LDA) for the detection of P300 signals and the inference of characters. For example, Rivet [22] enhances the P300 potentials. Mennes [17] removes artifacts in the EEG recordings containing P300 signals. Bostanov [4] extracts useful features related to P300 signals. However, there are some problems with traditional machine learning methods. (1) they can only learn the features that researchers are focusing on but lose or remove other underlying features [23]; (2) brain signals have subject-to-subject variability, which makes it possible that methods performing well on certain subjects (with similar age or occupation) may not give a satisfactory performance on others. These problems prevent traditional machine learning methods from further increasing the character spelling accuracy for the P300 speller.

In recent years, deep learning, especially deep Convolutional Neural Networks (CNNs), has achieved significant success in the computer vision field. CNNs have the advantage of automatically learning features from raw data[1]. They can learn not only something we know but also something important and unknown to us [6,23]. Automatically learning from raw data has better ability to achieve good results which are invariant to different subjects. Thus, CNNs are able to boost the full potential of detecting BCI signals, overcoming the aforementioned shortcomings of traditional machine learning methods.

Therefore, in recent years, researchers have started to design (deep) CNNs for P300-based BCIs [6,15,16,23]. However, these CNNs have some limitations in increasing the P300 spelling accuracy. CNNs in [6,15,16] first use a spatial convolution layer to learn P300-related spatial features from raw signals. Then, they use several temporal convolution layers to learn P300-related temporal features from the abstract signals generated by the spatial convolution layer (the first layer). The abstraction of raw signals loses raw temporal information, which makes these CNNs not able to learn P300-related temporal features well. To solve the problem of [6,15,16], the CNN in [23] performs the spatial convolution and the temporal convolution at the same time (thereby performing the spatial-temporal convolution) in the first layer. The input to the first layer is raw signals. Thus, the CNN in [23] is able to learn temporal features from raw signals instead of abstract signals as in [6,15,16]. In this way, [23] learns better P300-related temporal features than [6,15,16]. Unfortunately, [23] extracts only P300-related joint spatial-temporal features through the spatial-temporal convolution. It does not extract P300-related separate temporal features and separate spatial features. These separate temporal features and separate spatial features have proven to be very important for the P300 speller [9,11,19,20]. Adding

---

[1] In this paper, we use "raw data, information, or signals" to denote the data which are only preprocessed (e.g., bandpass filtering and normalization) but not abstracted by a feature extraction method (e.g., a CNN).

several temporal or spatial convolution layers after the first spatial-temporal convolution layer enables [23] to learn P300-related separate spatial or temporal features. Nevertheless, this cannot make [23] learn these features well because the input to these added temporal or spatial convolution layers is the abstract signals generated by the first spatial-temporal convolution layer instead of raw signals. This leads to the loss of raw information related to the P300 signal. In order to solve this issue in [23], we propose a network which combines our proposed two CNNs, with the CNN in [23] for character spelling in the P300 speller. The novel contributions of this paper are the following:

- Each of our proposed two CNNs has only one convolution layer. One of the CNNs performs the temporal convolution in the convolution layer (the first layer) to extract P300-related separate temporal features. The other CNN performs the spatial convolution in the convolution layer (the first layer) to extract P300-related separate spatial features. These two CNNs are able to learn well P300-related separate temporal features and separate spatial features, respectively.
- Experimental results on three benchmark datasets show that our network, which is the ensemble of our two CNNs and OCLNN [23], outperforms other methods in most cases, with a significant spelling accuracy improvement up to 38.72%. In addition, the communication speed of the P300 speller based on our network is up to 2.56 times faster than the communication speed of the P300 speller based on other methods.

The rest of the paper is organized as follows: Sect. 2 describes the related work on P300 spelling. Section 3 introduces some background information about the P300 speller, and the datasets used in this paper. Section 4 presents our proposed network for P300 spelling. Section 5 compares the character spelling accuracy and the communication speed achieved by our network and other methods for the P300 speller. Section 6 analyses our proposed two CNNs on extracting P300-related features, performs an ablation study on our proposed network and discusses the importance of extracting P300-related features from raw signals. Section 7 ends the paper with conclusions.

2   Related Work

In [6,16], and [15], the authors propose CNNs for character spelling in the P300 speller. The CNN in [6,16], and [15] is called CCNN [6], CNN-R [16], and BN3 [15], respectively. CCNN, CNN-R, and BN3 first use a spatial convolution layer to learn P300-related spatial features. After this spatial convolution layer, they use several temporal convolution layers to learn P300-related temporal features. However, the problem of these CNNs is that they learn P300-related temporal features from abstract signals instead of raw signals, which makes these CNNs not able to learn P300-related temporal features well. P300-related temporal features are learned by the temporal convolution layers of these CNNs. The input to these temporal convolution layers is the feature maps generated by the spatial convolution layer (the first layer). These feature maps are abstract temporal signals instead of raw signals because this spatial convolution layer converts each receptive field of raw signals into an abstract datum in a feature map. These abstract temporal signals in the feature maps lose raw temporal information. Losing raw temporal information means losing important temporal features because the nature of P300 signals is the positive voltage potential in raw temporal information, see Fig. 1 explained in Sect. 3.1, as well as many important P300-related features are also embodied in raw information [20,23]. As a result, these CNNs can not learn temporal features well and can not further increase the spelling accuracy of the P300 speller.

In order to solve the problem of [6,16], and [15,23] proposes a CNN with one convolution layer, called OCLNN, for character spelling in the P300 speller. In contrast to CCNN [6], CNN-R [16], and BN3 [15], the network OCLNN [23] performs the spatial convolution and the temporal convolution at the same time, thereby performing the spatial-temporal convolution in the first layer instead of performing only the spatial convolution as in CCNN, CNN-R, and BN3. The input to this spatial-temporal convolution layer (the first layer) is raw signals. In this way, the data used to learn P300-related temporal features is raw signals instead of the abstract signals in CCNN, CNN-R, and BN3. Therefore, OCLNN is able to learn P300-related temporal features better than CCNN, CNN-R, and BN3. In addition, OCLNN can learn spatial features. As a result, OCLNN achieves higher spelling accuracy than CCNN, CNN-R, and BN3. Unfortunately, OCLNN loses other important P300-related features. OCLNN extracts P300-related spatial and temporal features at the same time in its single convolution layer, thereby extracting only P300-related joint spatial-temporal features through the spatial-temporal convolution. OCLNN does not extract P300-related separate temporal features and separate spatial features. These separate temporal features and separate spatial features have proven to be very important for the P300 speller [9,11,19,20]. Adding several temporal or spatial convolution layers after the first spatial-temporal convolution layer is a potential method to enable OCLNN to learn P300-related separate spatial or temporal features. Nevertheless, this method can not learn P300-related separate temporal or spatial features well due to the loss of raw information. The raw information loss happens because the input to these added temporal or spatial convolution layers for OCLNN is the abstract signals (generated by the first spatial-temporal convolution layer in OCLNN) instead of raw signals.

To address this issue of [23], we proposes a network which combines our proposed two CNNs with OCLNN in order to learn well the aforementioned P300-related separate spatial and temporal features, which are not extracted by OCLNN, as well as the spatial-temporal features. Each of these two CNNs has only one convolution layer. One of the CNNs performs the temporal convolution in the first layer to learn P300-related separate temporal features. The other CNN performs the spatial convolution in the first layer to learn P300-related separate spatial features. In this way, the input to each of the two CNNs is raw signals, thus these two CNNs are able to learn features from raw signals instead of the abstract signals in the aforementioned potential method for enabling OCLNN to learn more features. As a consequence, these two CNNs can learn well P300-related separate temporal features and separate spatial features, respectively. Our network uses the ensemble of these two CNNs and OCLNN, thereby extracting more useful P300-related features than OCLNN. As a result, our proposed network can achieve higher spelling accuracy than OCLNN.

3   Background

In this section, we provide some background information for the P300 speller and the benchmark datasets used in this paper.

3.1   P300 Speller

The P300 speller is one of the most investigated applications in BCI [10]. A target character is spelled using the property of the P300 signal. As shown in Fig. 1, a P300 signal, recorded in EEG, occurs as a positive deflection in voltage with a latency of about 300 ms after a rare stimulus is presented to a subject (person). The following experiment is used to evoke a P300 signal in a subject's brain and then the evoked P300 signal is used to spell characters. In this experiment, the subject is presented with a 6 by 6 character matrix (see Fig. 2) and he focuses his attention on a target character he wants to spell. The matrix performs random, separate, and successive row or column intensification. When the target row or column is intensified, it is a rare stimulus to the subject because there are only two target intensifications out of 12 intensifications. This rare stimulus evokes the subject's brain to generate a P300 signal. Then, with the detection of a P300 signal, the target row or column is inferred. By combining the target row position and the target column position, the target character position is inferred. Assume that one epoch includes 12 intensifications, in which there exist one target row intensification and one target column intensification. In practice, people use several consecutive epochs for the P300 speller to infer

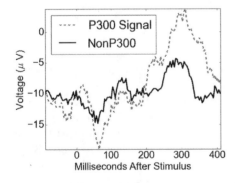

Fig. 1. P300 signal.   Fig. 2. P300 speller character matrix.

one target character, because it is hard to use only one epoch to correctly spell one target character [21, 23].

3.2 Datasets

We perform experiments on three benchmark datasets, i.e., BCI Competition II - Data set IIb [1] as well as BCI Competition III - Data set II Subject A and Subject B [2]. In this paper, we use II to represent BCI Competition II - Data set IIb, III-A to represent BCI Competition III - Data set II Subject A, and III-B to represent BCI Competition III - Data set II Subject B. These three benchmark datasets are commonly used to evaluate many methods for the P300 speller [4, 6, 15, 16, 21, 23]. Therefore, we are able to fairly compare the spelling accuracy achieved by our proposed network and other state-of-the-art methods for the P300 speller.

In Dataset II, III-A and III-B, the EEG signals are recorded from 64 sensors at a sampling frequency of 240 Hz when performing the P300 speller experiment described in Sect. 3.1. In this P300 speller experiment, one row or column is intensified for 100 ms. After each row/column intensification, the matrix is blank for 75 ms. In this experiment, 15 consecutive epochs are used for the spelling of one character. After every group of 15 epochs, the matrix is blank for 2.5 s to inform the subject to focus on the next character to spell.

In Dataset II, III-A and III-B, there are separate training and test datasets. In Dataset II, the training dataset has 42 characters and the test dataset has 31 characters. Since 15 epochs are used for the spelling of one character, the total number of epochs is 630 epochs and 465 epochs in the training dataset and test dataset, respectively. The training dataset in Dataset III-A and the training dataset in Dataset III-B have the same number of characters, i.e., 85 characters. The test dataset in Dataset III-A and the test dataset in Dataset III-B also have the same number of characters, i.e., 100 characters. Therefore, in Dataset III-A and Dataset III-B, the total number of epochs is 1275 epochs and 1500 epochs in each training dataset and each test dataset, respectively.

4   Proposed Network

This section introduces our proposed network for character spelling in the P300 speller. We call our network Ensemble of Convolutional Neural Networks (EoCNN). EoCNN uses our proposed two CNNs. We call these two CNNs One Spatial Layer Network (OSLN) and One Temporal Layer Network (OTLN).

4.1   Ensemble of Convolutional Neural Networks

The workflow of our EoCNN is shown in Fig. 3. First, the EEG signals are preprocessed to construct the input tensor. The construction of the input tensor is described in Sect. 4.2. Then, the input tensor is sent to three different CNNs, i.e., OSLN, OTLN, and OCLNN. OSLN and OTLN are described in

Sect. 4.3. OCLNN is the CNN proposed in [23]. OSLN extracts P300-related separate spatial features. OTLN extracts P300-related separate temporal features. OCLNN extracts P300-related joint spatial-temporal features. Our EoCNN uses the ensemble of the outputs from OSLN, OTLN, and OCLNN for character spelling in the P300 speller.

4.2   Input Tensor

The EEG signals are preprocessed to construct the input tensor $(Tem \times C)$, where C is the number of sensors used to acquire EEG signals. Tem is the number of signal samples in the time domain. In this tensor, in order to remove the high frequency noise, the temporal signal samples are bandpass filtered between 0.1 Hz and 20 Hz. Then, we normalize the temporal signal samples to make the signal samples to have zero mean and unit variance based on each individual pattern and for each sensor. Here an individual pattern denotes the Tem signal samples. The normalization is a common practice for preprocessing input data to CNNs. The normalization helps the CNN to perform well for the P300 spelling [6].

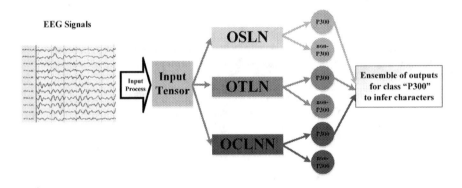

Fig. 3. Workflow of our EoCNN

4.3   Proposed OSLN and OTLN

The architectures of our proposed OSLN and OTLN are described in Tables 1 and 2, respectively. OSLN and OTLN are used in EoCNN (see Sect. 4.1), where OSLN is designed to learn P300-related separate spatial features and OTLN is designed to learn P300-related separate temporal features. Since only the convolution layer is different between OSLN and OTLN, below we describe the architectures of OSLN and OTLN together.

Layer 1 of OSLN (see Table 1) performs the spatial convolution operation with the kernel size $(1, C)$. This convolution operation converts each receptive field of the signal samples into an abstract datum in a feature map. The signal samples in each receptive field are from all C sensors in the space domain and

Table 1. OSLN architecture.

Layer	Operation	Kernel	Feature maps or neurons
1	Convolution	$(1, C)$	16
	Dropout	—	—
2	Fully-Connected	—	2

Table 2. OTLN architecture.

Layer	Operation	Kernel	Feature maps or neurons
1	Convolution	$(Tem/15, 1)$	16
	Dropout	—	—
2	Fully-Connected	—	2

sampled at only one time point in the time domain. Therefore, this convolution operation extracts P300-related separate spatial features. We use the kernel size $(1, C)$ in order to make this layer to learn the spatial features from EEG signals acquired using all sensors. The reason for using all sensors is that it is more helpful to increase the spelling accuracy than using part of all sensors [6,15,16, 23]. The input to this layer is the raw signals, so this layer learns P300-related separate spatial features from raw signals. This layer generates 16 feature maps, which are the input to Layer 2 of OSLN. The choice of 16 feature maps follows the suggestion in [23].

Layer 1 of OTLN (see Table 2) performs the temporal convolution operation with the kernel size $(Tem/15, 1)$. The temporal convolution operation converts each receptive field of the signal samples into an abstract datum in a feature map. The signal samples in each receptive field are sampled within a certain time period and are acquired from only one sensor. Therefore, this convolution operation extracts P300-related separate temporal features. We use the kernel size $(Tem/15, 1)$ because 1/15 of temporal signal samples is a proper receptive field for a CNN to learn P300-related temporal features [23]. The input to this layer is the raw signals, so this layer learns P300-related separate temporal features from raw signals. This layer generates also 16 feature maps, which are the input to Layer 2 of OTLN.

In both Layer 1 of OSLN and Layer 1 of OTLN, the activation function is the Rectified Linear Unit (ReLU) [18] function. We employ dropout [25], with a rate of 0.4, to prevent OSLN and OTLN from overfitting.

Layer 2 of OSLN (see Table 1) and Layer 2 of OTLN (see Table 2) are the same. This layer is a fully-connected layer with two neurons. These two neurons represent the class "P300" (the presence of a P300 signal) and the class "non-P300" (the absence of a P300 signal), respectively. The activation function used in this layer is the Softmax [12] function which outputs the predicted probability for the "P300" class and the "non-P300" class.

OSLN and OTLN each uses only one convolution layer. OSLN uses only one convolution layer because it does not make sense to add more spatial convolution layers for OSLN. This CNN is designed to learn P300-related spatial features from the EEG signals recorded with all C sensors in the first layer. If we add more spatial convolution layers after its first spatial convolution layer to learn P300-related spatial features, these added layers should learn spatial features from the abstract signals generated by the first spatial convolution layer. These abstract signals include only the time domain and do not have the space domain because the first convolution layer uses the receptive field including all C sensors. Thus, these abstract signals can not be used to extract spatial features. OTLN also uses only one convolution layer because one convolution layer is enough to extract useful P300-related separate temporal features (see Sect. 6.1).

4.4 Training

The training is carried out by minimizing the binary cross-entropy loss function [8]. It uses a Stochastic Gradient Descent [5] optimizer with momentum and weight decay. The momentum is 0.9 and the weight decay is 0.0005. The learning rate is fixed to 0.01. The batch size is 128. This setup of the training parameters follows the suggestion in [24].

4.5 Character Spelling Using EoCNN

The character spelling approach using EoCNN is performed by Eqs. (1), (2), (3), and (4).

$$P_{EoC}(i,j) = \frac{1}{3} \times (P_{OS}(i,j) + P_{OT}(i,j) + P_{OCL}(i,j)) \tag{1}$$

$$Sum_{(j)} = \sum_{i=1}^{k} P_{EoC}(i,j) \tag{2}$$

$$index_{col} = \underset{1 \le j \le 6}{argmax}\ Sum_{(j)} \tag{3}$$

$$index_{row} = \underset{7 \le j \le 12}{argmax}\ Sum_{(j)} \tag{4}$$

Equation (1) shows the ensemble processing of the outputs from OSLN, OTLN, and OCLNN. The output from a CNN used for character spelling is the predicted probability by this CNN for class "P300". In this equation, for epoch i and for intensification j, $P_{OS}(i,j)$ denotes the predicted probability by OSLN for class "P300", $P_{OT}(i,j)$ denotes the predicted probability by OTLN for class "P300", and $P_{OCL}(i,j)$ denotes the predicted probability by OCLNN for class "P300".

The calculation for the position of the target character when using the first k epochs is defined by Eqs. (2), (3) and (4), where $Sum_{(j)}$ denotes the sum of the predicted probabilities by EoCNN, $index_{col}$ denotes the index of the column position of the target character, and $index_{row}$ denotes the index of the row position of the target character. j denotes a column intensification when $j \in [1,6]$ and j denotes a row intensification when $j \in [7,12]$.

5   Experimental Evaluation

First, we introduce our experimental setup in Sect. 5.1. Then, we compare the spelling accuracy achieved by our EoCNN and other methods in Sect. 5.2. Finally, we compare the communication speed of the P300 speller based on our EoCNN and other methods in Sect. 5.3.

5.1   Experimental Setup

We use Keras with the Tensorflow backend [7] to implement our EoCNN.

We use every training dataset of Dataset II, III-A and III-B to train our EoCNN, separately. Therefore, for the input tensor to EoCNN (see Sect. 4.2), we have $C = 64$ because the number of sensors used to acquire EEG signals is 64. We have $Tem = 240$ because we take each individual pattern as the signals from the time period between 0 and 1000 ms posterior to the beginning of each intensification, and the signal sampling frequency is 240 Hz.

We evaluate every trained EoCNN on the corresponding test dataset of Dataset II, III-A and III-B, and calculate the spelling accuracy for every test dataset. The spelling accuracy is calculated using Eq. (5), where acc_k denotes the spelling accuracy when using the first k epochs for every character, R_k denotes the number of correctly inferred characters when using the first k epochs for every character, and A denotes the number of all characters.

$$acc_k = \frac{R_k}{A} \tag{5}$$

We compare our EoCNN with CCNN [6], BN3 [15], CNN-R [16], OCLNN [23], and Bostanov [4] on Dataset II. CCNN, BN3, CNN-R, and OCLNN are different CNNs used for the character spelling in the P300 speller. Bostanov is the method which won the championship on Dataset II in the BCI Competition II. We compare our EoCNN with CCNN, BN3, CNN-R, OCLNN, and ESVM [21] on Dataset III-A and Dataset III-B. ESVM is the method which won the championship on Dataset III-A and Dataset III-B in the BCI Competition III.

5.2   Character Spelling Accuracy

The spelling accuracy achieved by our EoCNN and other methods on Dataset II, Dataset III-A, and Dataset III-B is shown in Tables 3, 4, and 5, respectively. In these tables, the different methods, we compare, are shown in the first column. The spelling accuracy for different epoch numbers $k \in [1, 15]$ is shown in each row of the table. A number in bold indicates that the accuracy achieved by the corresponding method is the highest among all methods. "–" denotes that the corresponding paper, describing the method, does not provide this accuracy number. The accuracy in this table is shown in %. Overall, the spelling accuracy achieved by our EoCNN is higher than the spelling accuracy achieved by other methods in most cases. Our EoCNN increases the spelling accuracy achieved by other methods with up to 38.72%.

Table 3 shows that for Dataset II, for every epoch number $k \in [1, 15]$, the spelling accuracy achieved by our EoCNN is higher than the spelling accuracy achieved by all other methods. Our EoCNN can increase the spelling accuracy achieved by CCNN, CNN-R, BN3, OCLNN, and Bostanov with up to 38.72%, 12.90%, 19.36%, 6.45%, and 19.35%, respectively.

Table 4 shows that for Dataset III-A, in 14 out of 15 cases (epoch number $k \in [1, 8] \cup [10, 15]$), the spelling accuracy achieved by our EoCNN is higher than the spelling accuracy achieved by all other methods. Our EoCNN can increase

Table 3. Spelling accuracy achieved by different methods on Dataset II.

Method	Epochs														
	1	2	3	4	5	6	7	8	9	10	11	12	13	14	15
EoCNN	**83.87**	**93.55**	100	100	100	100	100	100	100	100	100	100	100	100	100
CCNN	58.06	54.83	77.41	93.54	93.54	93.54	93.54	96.77	96.77	100	100	100	100	100	100
CNN-R	70.97	83.87	93.55	96.77	100	100	100	100	100	100	100	100	100	100	100
BN3	77.42	74.19	80.65	83.87	93.55	96.77	96.77	96.77	100	100	100	100	100	100	100
OCLNN	77.42	90.32	100	100	100	100	100	100	100	100	100	100	100	100	100
Bostanov	64.52	83.87	93.55	96.77	96.77	100	100	100	100	100	100	100	100	100	100

Table 4. Spelling accuracy achieved by different methods on Dataset III-A.

Method	Epochs														
	1	2	3	4	5	6	7	8	9	10	11	12	13	14	15
EoCNN	**23**	**39**	**61**	**68**	**76**	**81**	**84**	**86**	88	**93**	**95**	**98**	**97**	**99**	**99**
CCNN	16	33	47	52	61	65	77	78	85	86	90	91	91	93	97
CNN-R	14	28	38	53	57	62	71	75	77	82	89	87	87	92	95
BN3	22	**39**	58	67	73	75	79	81	82	86	89	92	94	96	98
OCLNN	**23**	**39**	56	63	73	79	82	85	**90**	91	94	95	95	96	**99**
ESVM	16	32	52	60	72	–	–	–	–	83	–	–	94	–	97

Table 5. Spelling accuracy achieved by different methods on Dataset III-B.

Method	Epochs														
	1	2	3	4	5	6	7	8	9	10	11	12	13	14	15
EoCNN	**51**	**66**	**74**	**81**	**84**	**90**	**91**	92	**95**	**97**	**98**	**98**	**98**	98	**99**
CCNN	35	52	59	68	79	81	82	89	92	91	91	90	91	92	92
CNN-R	36	46	66	70	77	80	86	86	88	91	94	95	95	96	96
BN3	47	59	70	73	76	82	84	91	94	95	95	95	94	94	95
OCLNN	46	62	72	79	**84**	87	89	**93**	94	96	97	97	97	**98**	98
ESVM	35	53	62	68	75	–	–	–	–	91	–	–	96	–	96

the spelling accuracy achieved by CCNN, CNN-R, BN3, OCLNN, and ESVM with up to 16%, 23%, 7%, 5%, and 10%, respectively.

Table 5 shows that for Dataset III-B, in 14 out of 15 cases (epoch number $k \in [1,7] \cup [9,15]$), the spelling accuracy achieved by our EoCNN is higher than the spelling accuracy achieved by all other methods. Our EoCNN can increase the accuracy achieved by CCNN, CNN-R, BN3, OCLNN, and ESVM with up to 16%, 20%, 8%, 5%, and 16%, respectively.

Moreover, our method is robust across different subjects. Tables 3, 4, and 5 show that for all three subjects, our EoCNN achieves the highest spelling accuracy among all other methods in 43 out of 45 cases.

These experimental results also give some insights on how many epochs we should use for the spelling of one character in the P300 speller. The first insight is from the fact that, in Table 3, the spelling accuracy achieved by CCNN and BN3 on epoch number $k = 2$ is lower than the spelling accuracy achieved by CCNN and BN3 on epoch number $k = 1$. This shows that adding more epochs does not necessarily improve spelling accuracy for the P300 speller. This is also discussed in more details in [6]. The other insight is from the fact that in Dataset II, we need only 2 epochs to achieve the spelling accuracy which is higher than 90% while in Dataset III-A and Dataset III-B, in order to achieve the spelling accuracy higher than 90%, we need at least 10 epochs and 6 epochs, respectively. This indicates us that we can use different number of epochs for different subjects to spell characters using the P300 speller. In this way, we can use a small number of epochs for a subject when using the P300 speller such that we can significantly decrease the time needed for a subject to spell a character while keeping an acceptable spelling accuracy.

5.3   Information Transfer Rate

This section compares the Information Transfer Rate (ITR) of the P300 speller based on our EoCNN and other methods. ITR has been the most commonly applied metric to assess the communication speed of BCIs [26], combining the accuracy and the time needed for recognition. It is calculated by Eqs. (6) and (7) [27], where P denotes the probability to correctly spell a character, N denotes the number of classes, and T denotes the time needed to spell a character when using k epochs. For more detailed explanation about the ITR please refer to [27].

$$ITR = \frac{60(P \log_2(P) + (1 - P) \log_2 \frac{1-P}{N-1} + \log_2(N))}{T} \tag{6}$$

$$T = 2.5 + 2.1k \quad 1 \le k \le 15 \tag{7}$$

The ITR of the P300 speller based on our EoCNN and other methods for Dataset II, Dataset III-A and Dataset III-B is shown in Tables 6, 7, and 8, respectively. In these tables, the different methods, we compare, are shown in the first column. The ITR for different epoch numbers $k \in [1, 15]$ is shown in each row of the table. A number in bold denotes that the corresponding method achieves the highest ITR for the P300 speller, compared with all other methods. "–" in a table denotes that the ITR cannot be calculated because the corresponding method does not provide the spelling accuracy. The ITR is shown in bits/minute. Overall, in 43 out of 45 cases, the ITR of the P300 speller based on our EoCNN is higher than the ITR of the P300 spellers based on all other methods. The communication speed (i.e., ITR) of the P300 speller based on our EoCNN is up to 2.56 times faster than the communication speed of the P300 speller based on other methods.

Table 6. The ITR of the P300 speller based on different methods on Dataset II.

Method	Epochs														
	1	2	3	4	5	6	7	8	9	10	11	12	13	14	15
EoCNN	**88.92**	**58.62**	**46.28**	**35.24**	**28.45**	**23.85**	**20.53**	**18.03**	**16.07**	14.49	13.19	12.11	11.19	10.41	9.72
CCNN	48.9	24.26	29.02	30.63	24.73	20.74	17.85	16.74	14.92	**14.49**	**13.19**	**12.11**	**11.19**	**10.41**	**9.72**
CNN-R	67.48	48.33	40.25	32.72	**28.45**	**23.85**	**20.53**	**18.03**	**16.07**	**14.49**	**13.19**	**12.11**	**11.19**	**10.41**	**9.72**
BN3	77.79	39.42	31.06	25.26	24.74	22.15	19.07	16.74	**16.07**	**14.49**	**13.19**	**12.11**	**11.19**	**10.41**	**9.72**
OCLNN	77.79	54.97	**46.28**	**35.24**	**28.45**	**23.85**	**20.53**	**18.03**	**16.07**	**14.49**	**13.19**	**12.11**	**11.19**	**10.41**	**9.72**
Bostanov	57.88	48.33	40.25	32.72	26.41	**23.85**	**20.53**	**18.03**	**16.07**	**14.49**	**13.19**	**12.11**	**11.19**	**10.41**	**9.72**

Table 7. The ITR of the P300 speller based on different methods on Dataset III-A.

Method	Epochs														
	1	2	3	4	5	6	7	8	9	10	11	12	13	14	15
EoCNN	10.62	14.04	**19.74**	**17.89**	**17.31**	**16.13**	**14.76**	**13.49**	12.51	**12.46**	**11.81**	**11.55**	**10.44**	**10.14**	9.48
CCNN	5.45	10.67	13.02	11.65	12.14	11.26	12.76	11.45	11.78	10.84	10.69	10.01	9.25	8.95	9.07
CNN-R	4.19	8.11	9.24	12.01	10.89	10.44	11.18	10.73	9.99	10	10.48	9.25	8.55	8.77	8.7
BN3	9.81	**14.04**	18.22	17.47	16.2	14.2	13.32	12.19	11.09	10.84	10.48	10.21	9.82	9.51	9.27
OCLNN	10.62	14.04	17.22	15.83	16.2	15.47	14.17	13.22	**13.02**	11.98	11.58	10.84	10.02	9.51	**9.48**
ESVM	5.45	10.14	15.3	14.64	15.84	–	–	–	–	10.21	–	–	9.82	–	9.07

Table 8. The ITR of the P300 speller based on different methods on Dataset III-B.

Method	Epochs														
	1	2	3	4	5	6	7	8	9	10	11	12	13	14	15
EoCNN	**39.76**	**32.62**	**26.95**	**23.82**	**20.45**	**19.33**	**16.97**	15.2	**14.38**	**13.52**	**12.58**	**11.55**	**10.67**	9.92	**9.48**
CCNN	21.64	22.29	18.72	17.89	18.45	16.13	14.17	14.32	13.55	11.98	10.91	9.82	9.25	8.77	8.2
CNN-R	22.67	18.32	22.4	18.75	17.68	15.79	15.37	13.49	12.51	11.98	11.58	10.84	10.02	9.51	8.88
BN3	34.9	27.27	24.63	20.07	17.31	16.46	14.76	14.9	14.1	12.97	11.81	10.84	9.82	9.13	8.7
OCLNN	33.71	29.51	25.78	22.85	**20.45**	18.21	16.31	**15.51**	14.1	13.24	12.31	11.3	10.44	**9.92**	9.27
ESVM	21.64	22.98	20.26	17.89	16.93	–	–	–	–	11.98	–	–	10.23	–	8.88

Table 6 shows that the communication speed of the P300 speller based on our EoCNN is up to 2.42 times faster than the communication speed of the P300 speller based on other methods. The maximum increase of the communication speed occurs when comparing the ITR of the P300 speller based on our EoCNN with the ITR of the P300 speller based on CCNN for epoch number $k = 2$.

Table 7 shows that the communication speed of the P300 speller based on our EoCNN is up to 2.56 times faster than the communication speed of the P300 speller based on other methods. The maximum increase of the communication speed occurs when comparing the ITR of the P300 speller based on our EoCNN with the ITR of the P300 speller based on CNN-R for epoch number $k = 1$.

Table 8 shows that the communication speed of the P300 speller based on our EoCNN is up to 1.84 times faster than the communication speed of the P300 speller based on other methods. The maximum increase of the communication speed occurs when comparing the ITR of the P300 speller based on our EoCNN with the ITR of the P300 speller based on CCNN and ESVM for epoch number $k = 1$.

These experimental results show that by using our EoCNN, the communication speed of the P300 speller can be significantly increased for low epoch numbers.

6 Discussions

In this section, first, we analyse our proposed OTLN and OSLN in terms of spelling accuracy, and discuss the influence of the number of convolution layers on extracting useful P300-related separate temporal features. Then, we perform an ablation study on EoCNN. Finally, we explore the importance of extracting P300-related temporal features from raw signals.

In this section, all the experiments are performed by using the experimental setup described in Sect. 5.1. We have done experiments using all three datasets, which show the similar conclusions. Thus, we only present the experimental results on Dataset III-A.

6.1 Analysis on Our Proposed OTLN and OSLN

First, we perform experiments to show the spelling accuracy achieved by OTLN and OSLN, respectively. The experimental results are shown in Table 9. In this table, different CNNs, we compare, are shown in the first column. The spelling accuracy for different epoch numbers $k \in [1, 15]$ is shown in each row of the table. A number in bold indicates that the corresponding CNN achieves the highest accuracy compared to all other CNNs. The accuracy in this table is shown in %. Table 9 shows that OTLN and OSLN both have good ability to achieve high spelling accuracy when OTLN and OSLN are used independently for P300 spelling. Thus, OTLN and OSLN are able to extract very useful P300-related separate temporal features and P300-related separate spatial features, respectively.

Then, we analyse whether OTLN needs more convolution layers to extract P300-related separate temporal features. In order to analyse the influence of the number of convolution layers on OTLN, we perform experiments to compare the spelling accuracy achieved by OTLN and other two CNNs called OTLN-3l and OTLN-6l. OTLN-3l and OTLN-6l use 3 and 6 convolution layers, respectively.

Table 9. Spelling accuracy achieved by OTLN, OSLN and EoCNN on Dataset III-A.

Network	Epochs														
	1	2	3	4	5	6	7	8	9	10	11	12	13	14	15
OTLN	21	34	51	65	69	73	76	81	85	85	88	92	92	93	95
OSLN	**24**	35	55	63	69	75	78	79	80	82	89	92	94	95	96
EoCNN	23	**39**	**61**	**68**	**76**	**81**	**84**	**86**	**88**	**93**	**95**	**98**	**97**	**99**	**99**

These convolution layers use the same kernel size and generate the same number of feature maps as the convolution layer used in OTLN. The spelling accuracy achieved by OTLN, OTLN-3l and OTLN-6l is plotted in Fig. 4. This figure shows that the spelling accuracy achieved by OTLN-3l and OTLN is almost the same. The spelling accuracy achieved by OTLN-6l is lower than the spelling accuracy achieved by OTLN. These experimental results show that using one convolution layer is enough to extract useful P300-related separate temporal features for P300 spelling. Using more convolution layers for the extraction of the separate temporal features does not help increasing the spelling accuracy and may cause overfitting which decreases the spelling accuracy.

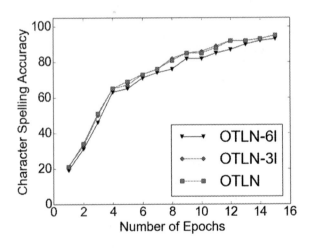

Fig. 4. Spelling accuracy achieved by OTLN, OTLN-3l and OTLN-6l on Dataset III-A.

6.2   Ablation Study on EoCNN

We perform an ablation study on EoCNN. We first remove a CNN from EoCNN. Then, we perform experiments to show the spelling accuracy achieved by the ensemble of the two CNNs left in EoCNN. In this way, we want to show the importance of each separate CNN in EoCNN for character spelling in the P300 speller. The experimental results are shown in Table 10. In this table, "-" indicates that we remove a given CNN from EoCNN. For example, "EoCNN-OSLN" indicates that we remove OSLN from EoCNN. The experimental results show that after removing any of the individual CNNs from EoCNN, the spelling accuracy achieved by the ensemble of the two CNNs left is lower, compared with the spelling accuracy achieved by EoCNN when none of the individual CNNs is removed. This shows that we need to combine all three CNNs (i.e., OSLN, OTLN, and OCLNN) in EoCNN in order to achieve high spelling accuracy.

Table 10. Spelling accuracy achieved by EoCNN after removing a separate CNN.

Network	Epochs														
	1	2	3	4	5	6	7	8	9	10	11	12	13	14	15
EoCNN-OTLN	**23**	**39**	58	67	75	**81**	82	**86**	86	91	93	96	96	97	**99**
EoCNN-OSLN	22	36	57	66	73	79	80	84	**89**	92	92	95	95	97	98
EoCNN-OCLNN	22	35	55	67	75	79	80	82	83	89	90	93	95	97	98
EoCNN	**23**	**39**	**61**	**68**	**76**	**81**	**84**	**86**	88	**93**	**95**	**98**	**97**	**99**	**99**

6.3 Exploration on the Importance of Extracting P300-Related Temporal Features from Raw Signals

We explore the importance of extracting P300-related temporal features from raw signals. We addressed this issue in Sect. 2. We build two sets of networks, called "RAW_networks" and "unRAW_networks", respectively. RAW_networks contains EoCNN, EoCNN-OSLN, EoCNN-OTLN, EoCNN-OCLNN and OCLNN. All the networks in RAW_networks extract P300-related temporal features from raw signals. unRAW_networks contains CCNN, CNN-R,

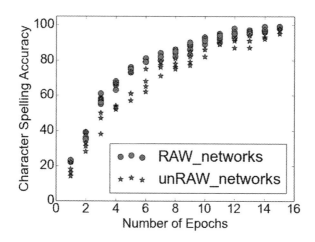

Fig. 5. Spelling accuracy achieved by networks in RAW_networks and networks in unRAW_networks on Dataset III-A.

and BN3. All the networks in unRAW_networks extract P300-related temporal features from abstract temporal signals (the feature maps generated by the spatial convolution layer). We perform experiments to show the spelling accuracy achieved by each network in RAW_networks and the spelling accuracy achieved by each network in unRAW_networks.

The experimental results are shown in Fig. 5. In this figure, the spelling accuracy achieved by the networks in RAW_networks and the spelling accuracy achieved by the networks in unRAW_networks are plotted in different shapes and colors. This figure shows that in most cases, the spelling accuracy achieved by the networks in RAW_networks is higher than the spelling accuracy achieved by the networks in unRAW_networks. This shows that extracting P300-related temporal features from raw signals is able to achieve higher spelling accuracy than extracting P300-related temporal features from abstract signals. These experimental results support our statement in Sect. 2.

7   Conclusions and Future Work

In this paper, we propose a novel and effective network, called EoCNN, for character spelling in the P300 speller. Our EoCNN uses an ensemble of three different CNNs for P300 spelling. These three CNNs extract different useful P300-related features. Experimental results on three datasets show that the spelling accuracy achieved by our network is higher than the spelling accuracy achieved by other methods. Also, the communication speed of the P300 speller based on our network is higher than the communication speed of the P300 speller based on other methods.

The future work includes two aspects. The first aspect is to evaluate the performance of our proposed network via an online P300 speller. The online P300 speller helps the BCI users spell characters in real time. Thus, the performance of the online P300 speller based on our proposed network is able to provide more accurate evaluation for the usage of this BCI system in people's real life. The second aspect of the future work is to evaluate our network with more subjects in terms of spelling accuracy and ITR. Evaluating our network using the EEG signals from more subjects is able to further prove that our network can solve the problem of the subject-to-subject variability in brain signals and achieve high spelling accuracy and ITR across subjects.

References

1. Blankertz, B.: BCI competition II (2003). http://www.bbci.de/competition/ii/
2. Blankertz, B.: BCI competition III (2008). http://www.bbci.de/competition/iii/
3. Bonnet, L., Lotte, F., Lécuyer, A.: Two brains, one game: design and evaluation of a multiuser bci video game based on motor imagery. IEEE Trans. Comput. Intell. AI Games **5**(2), 185–198 (2013)
4. Bostanov, V.: BCI competition 2003-data sets Ib and IIb: feature extraction from event-related brain potentials with the continuous wavelet transform and the t-value scalogram. IEEE Trans. Biomed. Eng. **51**(6), 1057–1061 (2004)

5. Bottou, L.: Large-scale machine learning with stochastic gradient descent. In: Lechevallier, Y., Saporta, G. (eds.) Proceedings of COMPSTAT 2010, pp. 177–186. Physica-Verlag, Heidelberg (2010). https://doi.org/10.1007/978-3-7908-2604-3_16

6. Cecotti, H., Graser, A.: Convolutional neural networks for P300 detection with application to brain-computer interfaces. IEEE Trans. Pattern Anal. Mach. Intell. **33**(3), 433–445 (2011)

7. Chollet, F., et al.: Keras (2015). https://github.com/keras-team/keras

8. De Boer, P.T., Kroese, D.P., Mannor, S., Rubinstein, R.Y.: A tutorial on the cross-entropy method. Ann. Oper. Res. **134**(1), 19–67 (2005)

9. Faux, S.F., Torello, M.W., McCarley, R.W., Shenton, M.E., Duffy, F.H.: P300 in schizophrenia: confirmation and statistical validation of temporal region deficit in P300 topography. Biol. Psychiatry **23**(8), 776–790 (1988)

10. Fazel-Rezai, R., Allison, B.Z., Guger, C., Sellers, E.W., Kleih, S.C., Kübler, A.: P300 brain computer interface: current challenges and emerging trends. Front. Neuroeng. **5**, 14 (2012)

11. Hoffmann, U., Vesin, J.M., Ebrahimi, T.: Spatial filters for the classification of event-related potentials, Technical report (2006)

12. Krizhevsky, A., Sutskever, I., Hinton, G.E.: ImageNet classification with deep convolutional neural networks. In: Advances in Neural Information Processing Systems, pp. 1097–1105 (2012)

13. Lin, C.T., Lin, B.S., et al.: Brain computer interface-based smart living environmental auto-adjustment control system in UPnP home networking. IEEE Syst. J. **8**(2), 363–370 (2014)

14. Lin, C.T., Tsai, S.F., Ko, L.W.: EEG-based learning system for online motion sickness level estimation in a dynamic vehicle environment. IEEE Trans. Neural Netw. Learn. Syst. **24**(10), 1689–1700 (2013)

15. Liu, M., Wu, W., Gu, Z., Yu, Z., Qi, F., Li, Y.: Deep learning based on batch normalization for P300 signal detection. Neurocomputing **275**, 288–297 (2018)

16. Manor, R., Geva, A.B.: Convolutional neural network for multi-category rapid serial visual presentation BCI. Front. Comput. Neurosci. **9**, 146 (2015)

17. Mennes, M., Wouters, H., Vanrumste, B., Lagae, L., Stiers, P.: Validation of ICA as a tool to remove eye movement artifacts from EEG/ERP. Psychophysiology **47**(6), 1142–1150 (2010)

18. Nair, V., Hinton, G.E.: Rectified linear units improve restricted boltzmann machines. In: Proceedings of the 27th International Conference on Machine Learning (ICML-10), pp. 807–814 (2010)

19. Pires, G., Nunes, U., Castelo-Branco, M.: Statistical spatial filtering for a P300-based BCI: tests in able-bodied, and patients with cerebral palsy and amyotrophic lateral sclerosis. J. Neurosci. Methods **195**(2), 270–281 (2011)

20. Polich, J.: Updating P300: an integrative theory of P3a and P3b. Clin. Neurophysiol. **118**(10), 2128–2148 (2007)

21. Rakotomamonjy, A., Guigue, V.: BCI competition III: dataset II-ensemble of SVMs for BCI P300 speller. IEEE Trans. Biomed. Eng. **55**(3), 1147–1154 (2008)

22. Rivet, B., Souloumiac, A., et al.: xDAWN algorithm to enhance evoked potentials: application to brain-computer interface. IEEE Trans. Biomed. Eng. **56**(8), 2035–2043 (2009)

23. Shan, H., Liu, Y., Stefanov, T.: A simple convolutional neural network for accurate P300 detection and character spelling in brain computer interface. In: 27th International Joint Conference on Artificial Intelligence (IJCAI), pp. 1604–1610 (2018)

24. Simonyan, K., Zisserman, A.: Very deep convolutional networks for large-scale image recognition. arXiv preprint arXiv:1409.1556 (2014)
25. Srivastava, N., Hinton, G., Krizhevsky, A., Sutskever, I., Salakhutdinov, R.: Dropout: a simple way to prevent neural networks from overfitting. J. Mach. Learn. Res. **15**(1), 1929–1958 (2014)
26. Wolpaw, J., Wolpaw, E.W.: Brain-Computer Interfaces: Principles and Practice. OUP, Oxford (2012)
27. Wolpaw, J.R., Ramoser, H., McFarland, D.J., Pfurtscheller, G.: EEG-based communication: improved accuracy by response verification. IEEE Trans. Rehabil. Eng. **6**(3), 326–333 (1998)

Time Series and Forecasting

Deep Recurrent Neural Networks with Nonlinear Masking Layers and Two-Level Estimation for Speech Separation

Jiantao Zhang$^{(\boxtimes)}$ and Pingjian Zhang

South China University of Technology, Guangzhou 510006, China
1277472231@qq.com, pjzhang@scut.edu.cn

Abstract. Over the past few decades, monaural speech separation has always been an interesting but challenging problem. The goal of speech separation is to separate a specific target speech from some background interferences and it has been treated as a signal processing problem traditionally. In recent years, with the rapid advances of deep learning techniques, deep learning has made a great breakthrough in speech separation. In this paper, recurrent neural networks (RNNs) which integrate multiple nonlinear masking layers (NMLs) to learn two-level estimation are proposed for speech separation. Experimental results show that our proposed model "RNN + SMMs + 3 NMLs" outperforms the baseline RNN without any mask in all the SDR, SIR and SAR indices, and it also obtains much better SDR and SIR than the RNN simply with original deterministic time-frequency masks.

Keywords: Speech separation · Deep learning · Deep neural network · Recurrent neural network · DNN · RNN · Time-frequency masking · Nonlinear masking layer · Two-level estimation

1 Introduction

Deep learning has demonstrated great power and potentials on automatic speech recognition (ASR) in recent years [2,14,29]. However, it is well known that ASR aims mainly to recognize what a single speaker says and even though there is some progress in multi-talker mixed speech recognition, the results are far from satisfactory [3,6,25]. Another topic related to ASR is speech separation, which is originated from the famous cocktail party problem studied by Cherry [4]. Over the past 6 decades, many classical approaches have been set forth to solve this problem. The computational auditory scene analysis (CASA) introduced in [1], for example, is based on perceptual principles of auditory scene analysis, and it makes use of grouping cues such as pitch and onset to estimate time-frequency masks that isolate the signal components belonging to different speakers. These masks are used to separate the source signals. The non-negative matrix factorization (NMF) [13,17], on the other hand, decomposes the spectrogram into

© Springer Nature Switzerland AG 2019
I. V. Tetko et al. (Eds.): ICANN 2019, LNCS 11730, pp. 397–411, 2019.
https://doi.org/10.1007/978-3-030-30490-4_32

two matrices $\mathbf{W}$ and $\mathbf{H}$, where $\mathbf{W}$ denotes spectral features and $\mathbf{H}$ denotes the importance of the features of each spectrum in the spectrogram. The basis in both two matrices is used to estimate mixing factors during evaluation.

Inspired by the success of deep learning in ASR, deep neural networks (DNNs) have played an increasingly important role in speech separation since 2010s [23]. Typically, some kinds of acoustic features from the waveform of the mixed speech are fed to a specific DNN, and then the DNN outputs several single-source signals from the mixture. In [20], the authors designed a DNN that stacks multiple hidden layers and made it a deep fully-connected neural network (FNN) for speech separation. Different from the FNN with a single output layer, this network contains two output layers and is able to predict both the target and the interference. In [10], an RNN with deterministic time-frequency masks was presented to perform speech separation. Similar to the previous neural network, this network contains two or more output layers, but the spectral features of the mixture are treated as sequential data in the input layer. Also, the discriminative training criterion is used for training the network to further enhance the separation performance. In [30], a novel deep learning training criterion called permutation invariant training was proposed to speed up the training procedure and deal with the label ambiguity (or permutation) problem of speech separation discussed in [25]. Alternatively, Hershey et al. developed the deep clustering approach in a neural network [8], which gives better generalized performance and provides some new views, i.e., clustering, for speech separation.

In this paper, deep RNNs with nonlinear masking layers and two-level estimation are proposed for speech separation. The whole model consists of two components: the first one is a regular stacked RNN which directly maps the spectral representation of the mixture to those of the sources. Usually, the output source spectral representations are used to recover the signals in time domain, however, in our new model, they are treated as the first level (level 1) estimation to build generic time-frequency masks [22,28], which are called original deterministic masks or original masks instead in this paper, and then one or more nonlinear masking layers are used to correct the original masks and generate the second level (level 2) estimation, i.e., the original masks are enhanced via the nonlinear masking layers to obtain more powerful nonlinear feature extraction. More specifically, the post-processed masks output by the nonlinear masking layers are applied to separate sources from the mixtures, and these separated sources are the second level estimation. The definition of the nonlinear masking layer and two-level estimation will be explained in detail in Sect. 3. Finally, evaluation of the proposed model is carried out on the TIMIT corpus [7], which is designed for speech related research. Experimental results show that the performance of the new model exceeds that of RNNs without any mask or simply with original masks according to the BSS-EVAL metrics.

2   Speech Separation

The goal of speech separation is to obtain several individual estimated source signals in a linearly mixed signal, which means that the mixture is a summation of all the source signals in time domain. Suppose that there are N source signals denoted as a set $\{\mathbf{y}^{(i)} | i = 1, 2, ..., N\}$, the linearly mixed signal can be expressed as $\mathbf{x} = \sum_{i=1}^{N} \mathbf{y}^{(i)}$. To make full use of the effective information in the mixed signals, a common method is to apply the short-time Fourier transform (STFT) on the signals in time domain to obtain the spectral representations of them. The spectral features of the signals are suitable to be handled by various DNNs. Let the STFT representation of the ith source signal be $\mathbf{Y}^{(i)}$ and the time-frequency bin at time index t and frequency index f be $\mathbf{Y}^{(i)}_{t,f}$, then a single time-frequency bin of the STFT representation of the linearly mixed signal can be given by $\mathbf{X}_{t,f} = \sum_{i=1}^{N} \mathbf{Y}^{(i)}_{t,f}$.

Generally, there are two groups of training targets used in deep speech separation. The first one adopts the mapping-based targets [23, 24, 31]. Typically, this approach usually treats spectral magnitudes as training targets and minimizes the loss between the output spectral magnitudes and the real spectral magnitudes. More precisely, let the deep learning model be $f(*)$ parameterized by $\boldsymbol{\theta}$, the model will minimize the loss to fit a function

$$|\mathbf{Y}^{(i)}| \approx f(|\mathbf{X}|; \boldsymbol{\theta}) \tag{1}$$

Here the operation $|*|$ obtains the spectral magnitude of a signal. The second one, by contrast, adopts the masking-based targets [23, 24, 31]. In this approach, the manually computed real time-frequency masks for different sources are treated as training targets. The loss between the output masks and the real masks is minimized during training. The output masks are used to recover the spectral magnitudes of the source signals from that of the mixture during evaluation. Let $\mathbf{M}^{(i)}$ represent the ith time-frequency mask to separate the ith source $\mathbf{Y}^{(i)}$ from the mixture $\mathbf{X}$, the model will minimize the loss to learn

$$\mathbf{M}^{(i)} \approx f(|\mathbf{X}|; \boldsymbol{\theta}) \tag{2}$$

Then $|\mathbf{Y}^{(i)}|$ is approximately given by

$$|\mathbf{Y}^{(i)}| \approx |\mathbf{X}| \odot \mathbf{M}^{(i)} \tag{3}$$

Here $\odot$ denotes the element-wise product. After that, we can simply apply the inverse short-time Fourier transform (ISTFT) on the ith estimated spectral magnitude and the phase of the mixture to obtain the ith source signal $\mathbf{y}^{(i)}$ in time domain approximately.

3   Proposed Model

3.1   Brief Introduction to the Model

For deep speech separation, designing a suitable neural network is crucial. Theoretically, FNNs, CNNs (convolutional neural networks) [12], RNNs, LSTMs (Long Short-Term Memory) [9] and GRUs (Gated Recurrent Neural Networks)

[5] may all work if the architecture and the hyper-parameter settings of the neural network are designed appropriately. By treating spectral features as sequential data, RNNs, LSTMs or GRUs are commonly considered to be better choices and hence are more suitable to be used as basic neural networks. By using the context window, continuous frames of the spectral feature matrix transformed through the STFT are concatenated together to construct one input feature vector at a single time step. These input feature vectors are called meta-frames hereafter. More specifically, suppose the input feature vector at time step t is a single frequency vector of the spectral magnitude of the mixture $\mathbf{X}$ at time index t, the activation of a single-layer RNN at time step t can be represented as

$$\mathbf{h}_t = \sigma(\mathbf{W}_h|\mathbf{X}_t| + \mathbf{U}_h\mathbf{h}_{t-1} + \mathbf{b}_h) \tag{4}$$

Here $\mathbf{W}_h$, $\mathbf{U}_h$ and $\mathbf{b}_h$ are the parameters of a single RNN hidden layer and $\sigma(*)$ is the activation function.

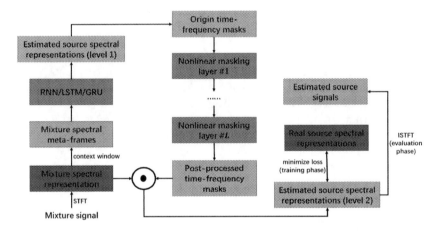

Fig. 1. The architecture of the RNN/LSTM/GRU with L nonlinear masking layers and two-level estimation, where L is the number of nonlinear masking layers.

Figure 1 illustrates the architecture of our proposed model. The output of the RNN, the LSTM or the GRU is considered as the level 1 estimation (intermediate estimation), which is used to construct original time-frequency masks for different sources

$$\tilde{\mathbf{M}}_{t,f}^{(i)} = \frac{|\tilde{\mathbf{Y}}_{t,f}^{(i)}|}{\sum_{j=1}^{N} |\tilde{\mathbf{Y}}_{t,f}^{(j)}|} \tag{5}$$

The Eq. (5) gives the mathematical expression of the spectral magnitude mask (SMM) [16,19,23], which is a kind of soft time-frequency mask that ignores the phase information. Here $\tilde{\mathbf{Y}}^{(i)}$ indicates the ith level 1 estimated source (level 1 estimation) and $\tilde{\mathbf{M}}^{(i)}$ is the ith corresponding estimated time-frequency mask for $\tilde{\mathbf{Y}}^{(i)}$. Another popular choice could be the ideal ratio mask (IRM) [16,23,24], a similar but more sophisticated mask

$$\tilde{\mathbf{M}}_{t,f}^{(i)} = \left(\frac{|\tilde{\mathbf{Y}}_{t,f}^{(i)}|^2}{\sum_{j=1}^{N} |\tilde{\mathbf{Y}}_{t,f}^{(j)}|^2} \right)^{\beta} \tag{6}$$

Here β is a hyper-parameter and commonly chosen to be 0.5 [23].

These masks are used as original time-frequency masks and nonlinear enhancement on these original masks is performed by multiple nonlinear masking layers to output post-processed masks. The nonlinear masking layer will be detailedly introduced in Sect. 3.2. After that, the element-wise product operation $\odot$ is applied between the spectral representation of the mixture and the post-processed masks, which forms the level 2 estimated sources (level 2 estimation). Finally, the level 2 estimation will be compared with the real sources, and the model tries to minimize the loss between them during the training phase or use the ISTFT to reconstruct source signals in time domain during the evaluation phase.

3.2   Nonlinear Masking Layers and Two-Level Estimation

Indeed, the SMMs or IRMs constructed from the level 1 estimated sources are treated as deterministic masking layers without any trainable parameter in [10]. The deterministic masking layers are simple but rough since there are not only source signals but also some other interferences such as background noise or reverberation in the mixture. Take the deterministic SMM layer as an example, it is more accurate to define it as

$$\tilde{\mathbf{M}}_{t,f}^{(i)} = \frac{|\tilde{\mathbf{Y}}_{t,f}^{(i)}|}{\sum_{j=1}^{N} |\tilde{\mathbf{Y}}_{t,f}^{(j)}| + \epsilon} \tag{7}$$

In the Eq. (7), ϵ indicates other interferences different from the sources. Although those interferences can still be learned by the DNNs, they will more or less end up in the isolated source signals during evaluation. In this paper, we propose the nonlinear masking layer which is applied on the original deterministic masks to correct the masks themselves. Here "nonlinear" means that there are one or more nonlinear functions which accept the time-frequency masks as input to output the post-processed masks that perform more powerful nonlinear feature extraction, i.e., these post-processed masks probably allow other interferences to be taken into account in the original masks in a more complex way. We believe that the post-processed masks perform nearly the same effect as the Eq. (7) in some form. Therefore, the nonlinear masking layer can help the model obtain better separation performance in the environment with various interferences but the model doesn't need to learn these interferences explicitly. Moreover, multiple nonlinear masking layers can be stacked together to construct much more powerful nonlinear time-frequency masks. In the following section, "masking layers" and "nonlinear masking layers" are treated as synonyms when there is no confusion. The simplest nonlinear masking layer which is applied on the SMMs can be given by the following equation

$$\hat{\mathbf{M}}^{(i)} = g(\mathbf{W}\tilde{\mathbf{M}}^{(i)} + \mathbf{b}) = g\left(\mathbf{W}\frac{|\tilde{\mathbf{Y}}^{(i)}|}{\sum_{j=1}^{N}|\tilde{\mathbf{Y}}^{(j)}|} + \mathbf{b}\right) \tag{8}$$

Formally, there is a little change on the Eq. (8), i.e., we add parameter $\alpha^{(i)}$, where $i = 1, 2, 3, ..., N$, to the corresponding ith level 1 estimated source signal $\tilde{\mathbf{Y}}^{(i)}$ to control how much the source contributes to the final nonlinear time-frequency masks. Note that $\alpha^{(i)}$ is a hyper-parameter which needs to be manually tuned and we empirically recommend setting the value of it between 1 and 2. By default, $\alpha^{(i)} = \alpha^{(j)}$, where $i \neq j$. This means that all sources are equally important for constructing the nonlinear masks.

$$\hat{\mathbf{M}}^{(i)} = g\left(\mathbf{W}\frac{\alpha^{(i)}|\tilde{\mathbf{Y}}^{(i)}|}{\sum_{j=1}^{N}\alpha^{(j)}|\tilde{\mathbf{Y}}^{(j)}|} + \mathbf{b}\right) \tag{9}$$

The Eq. (9) gives the full mathematical expression of a single nonlinear masking layer which is applied on the SMMs, where both $\mathbf{W}$ and $\mathbf{b}$ denote the trainable parameters of the nonlinear masking layer, $g(*)$ denotes the activation function and $\hat{\mathbf{M}}^{(i)}$ is the ith output post-processed mask corresponding to the ith source. In fact, the representation of a single nonlinear masking layer is similar to that of a single fully-connected layer. If multiple nonlinear masking layers are stacked together to correct the original time-frequency masks, it is just like training a FNN on the original masks to obtain masks with more powerful nonlinear feature extraction. Let L and the superscript l denote the number and the index of the nonlinear masking layer, respectively, where $l = 1, 2, 3, ..., L$, the ith output post-processed mask of the lth nonlinear masking layer can be represented as

$$\hat{\mathbf{M}}^{[l](i)} = \begin{cases} g\left(\mathbf{W}^{[l]}\frac{\alpha^{(i)}|\tilde{\mathbf{Y}}^{(i)}|}{\sum_{j=1}^{N}\alpha^{(j)}|\tilde{\mathbf{Y}}^{(j)}|} + \mathbf{b}^{[l]}\right) & l = 1 \\ g\left(\mathbf{W}^{[l]}\frac{\alpha^{(i)}|\hat{\mathbf{M}}^{[l-1](i)}|}{\sum_{j=1}^{N}\alpha^{(j)}|\hat{\mathbf{M}}^{[l-1](j)}|} + \mathbf{b}^{[l]}\right) & 1 < l \leq L \end{cases} \tag{10}$$

In the Eq. (10), the input features are the spectral magnitudes of the level 1 estimation if $l = 1$. By contrast, the input features are the hidden post-processed masks from the previous nonlinear masking layer if $1 < l \leq L$. In general, $L \geq 1$, but in particular, we say $L = 0$ means that there are no nonlinear masking layers, i.e., only the original masks (Eq. (5)) are kept in the model. Finally, the Eq. (3) is used to obtain estimated sources one more time. The estimated sources here are the level 2 estimation. Figure 2 shows the architecture of two nonlinear masking layers which are applied on the SMMs.

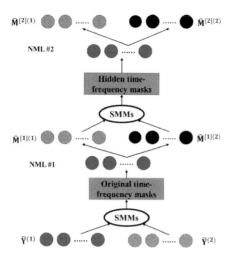

Fig. 2. The architecture of two nonlinear masking layers (NMLs) applied on the SMMs.

3.3 Objective Function

The supervised speech separation can be treated as a multi-class regression problem and the least squares error (LSE, also called L2-norm loss) is commonly used as an objective function to minimize the loss between the predictions and the targets (ground truth). Let $\hat{\mathbf{Y}}^{(i)}$ be the STFT representation of the ith level 2 estimated source, the objective function can be given by

$$\sum_{i=1}^{N} \left\| |\mathbf{Y}^{(i)}| - |\hat{\mathbf{Y}}^{(i)}| \right\|_{F}^{2} \tag{11}$$

Here the subscript F denotes the Frobenius norm, which is similar to the L2-norm. Moreover, taking the difference among sources into account leads to the discriminative objective function in [10], which would be helpful to increase Source to Interference Ratio

$$\sum_{i=1}^{N} \left(\left\| |\mathbf{Y}^{(i)}| - |\hat{\mathbf{Y}}^{(i)}| \right\|_{F}^{2} - \gamma \sum_{j=1, j \neq i}^{N} \left\| |\mathbf{Y}^{(i)}| - |\hat{\mathbf{Y}}^{(j)}| \right\|_{F}^{2} \right) \tag{12}$$

Here γ is a hyper-parameter commonly chosen between 0 and 0.2. When γ is set to 0, the objective function degenerates to the LSE. In practice, to suppress signals from other sources in the current source prediction, just increase γ.

4 Experimental Settings

4.1 Speech Data

The model proposed in this paper is evaluated on the TIMIT corpus, which is a collection of read speech designed for acoustic-phonetic study. Similar to the way of generating experimental data in [10], eight sentences from a male speaker and a female speaker are used for training, respectively. The circular shift algorithm [26] is used for data argumentation and carried out to generate more training signals in time domain. With the remaining sentences, one sentence from the male and one from the female are used as the validation set and the others are used as the test set. Still, the circular shift algorithm is used on both the validation set and the test set to increase the amount of the data. Also, test sentences are added up to form mixed signals at 0 dB SNR. Finally, we obtain about 36 h training data, 6 h validation data and 8 h test data.

4.2   Feature Preprocessing

In the experiments, the spectral magnitude is utilized as input to the proposed model and the phase information is ignored. The spectral representation is extracted using a 512-point STFT with hop size of 256, and the window size being the same as the number of Fast Fourier transform (FFT) points. Following the transformation, a spectral magnitude matrix is created for each signal with the shape of (513, 105), where 513 is the number of frequency bins and 105 is the number of time steps. Then, context windows of size 1, 3 and 5 are employed to construct meta-frames from the original frames of the spectral magnitude, respectively. A context window of size 1 means that there is no context, i.e., only the current frame is used. A context window of size 3 means concatenating one past frame, the current frame and one future frame to form a meta-frame of size 513 by 3, i.e., an input feature vector of size 1539 is constructed. A context window of size 5 can be interpreted analogously. The introduction of applying the context window is to capture more contextual information from the spectral magnitude.

4.3   Evaluation

Following the BSS-EVAL metrics mentioned in [21], the performance of blind source separation can be evaluated using three quantitative values: Source to Distortion Ratio (SDR), Source to Interference Ratio (SIR) and Source to Artifacts Ratio (SAR). SDR measures the overall separation quality, SIR measures the ability to reduce interferences from other sources and SAR measures the systematic error in the separation process.

5   Experimental Results

To begin with, a vanilla RNN, a LSTM and a GRU with two hidden layers of 150 hidden units (the hyper-parameter settings, i.e., the number of layers, the number of hidden units, etc., come from [10]) are set as baseline models. This means that they are simply mapping-based models without any time-frequency mask at all. In addition, no context windows are adopted for the baseline models and the RELU function [15] is taken to be the activation function in their hidden layers

$$y = \max(0, x) \tag{13}$$

The Adam algorithm [11] is chosen to perform gradient descent with the discriminative training loss function, and the training procedure of each model is kept for about 10 epochs. All experiments are repeated more than 10 times and the BSS-EVAL results are obtained by taking average. We also compare the performance of the bidirectional recurrent neural networks (BRNN, BLSTM or BGRU) [18] to that of the unidirectional recurrent neural networks (RNN, LSTM or GRU). The baseline experimental results on the test set have been listed in Table 1. From the vertical of Table 1, it turns out that the vanilla RNN obtains better SDR, SIR and SAR than both the LSTM and the GRU no matter γ is 0.0 or 0.1. Also, from the horizontal of Table 1, larger γ relatively maintains SDR and SAR but improve SIR, which helps reduce the interferences of one source to another. The vanilla RNN with $\gamma = 0.1$ obtains the best performance among all baseline models, which yields 6.18 dB SDR, 8.97 dB SIR, 8.02 dB SAR. Both the LSTM and the GRU are a little overfitting in the experiments. Furthermore, the bidirectional recurrent neural networks have not shown much effect because the separation procedure does not rely on the information of the long future frames to predict the current frame. The remaining experiments are all about the nonlinear masking layer, and we choose the vanilla RNN with $\gamma = 0.1$ as the basic neural network for the remaining experiments. In fact, the other variants of the RNN are all available for the experiments of the nonlinear masking layer since our main target is to figure out the powerful nonlinear feature extraction of the nonlinear masking layer but not just the effect of different RNNs. However, the selection of the neural network will essentially determine the upper bound of the performance of the model, and the nonlinear masking layer helps the network further reach that upper bound. Our basic experiments in Table 1 show that the performance limit of the LSTM and the GRU don't exceed the vanilla RNN (Though in many other deep learning applications, the LSTM/GRU may perform better than the RNN), so the architecture of "LSTM/GRU + NMLs" may not perform any better than that of "RNN + NMLs", where "NML" is short for the nonlinear masking layer.

Different from the activation function used in the hidden layers of the RNN, we use the leaky RELU function [27] as the activation function in the nonlinear masking layers

$$y = \max(\alpha x, x) \tag{14}$$

To explore the effect of the nonlinear masking layer, the output sources of the RNN are treated as the level 1 estimation, and the deterministic SMMs are constructed from the level 1 estimation to be used as original time-frequency masks. After that, we correct the deterministic SMMs by using 1, 2 and 3 nonlinear masking layers, respectively. In our experiments, when a single masking layer is used, all parameters $\alpha^{(i)}$'s are set to 1.0. Otherwise, $\alpha^{(i)}$'s of the first masking layer are set to 1.0 while those of the remaining masking layers are set to 1.5. Finally, we obtain the level 2 estimation. By contrast, we also train

Table 1. BSS-EVAL results (in dB) of different baseline recurrent neural networks with $\gamma = 0.0$ and $\gamma = 0.1$ on the test set.

Model	$\gamma = 0.0$			$\gamma = 0.1$		
	SDR	SIR	SAR	SDR	SIR	SAR
RNN	5.93	8.21	7.78	**6.18**	**8.97**	**8.02**
LSTM	5.24	8.08	7.53	5.35	8.19	7.51
GRU	4.96	8.23	7.12	4.88	8.73	7.46
BRNN	5.88	8.26	7.73	6.06	9.02	7.97
BLSTM	5.24	7.97	7.56	5.29	8.16	7.47
BGRU	4.94	8.28	7.15	4.81	8.66	7.39

a model which combines the RNN and the original SMMs, and compare this model to the models with multiple nonlinear masking layers.

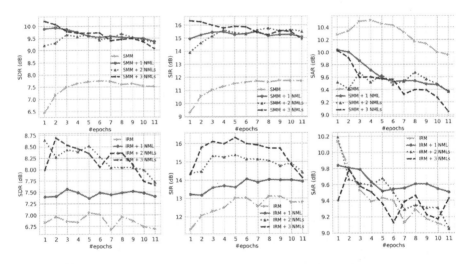

Fig. 3. The comparison of the evaluation performance on the validation set between models with original deterministic SMMs/IRMs and models with SMMs/IRMs followed by one or more nonlinear masking layers (NMLs) during the training procedure.

The evaluation performance of different models on the validation set during the training procedure is illustrated in Fig. 3. Both the SMM and the IRM are evaluated with the nonlinear masking layer, respectively. However, no matter which original mask is used, it turns out that SDRs and SIRs reach the maximum in about 1–5 epochs (and begin to decrease) on most of the models with one or more nonlinear masking layers. By contrast, if the original deterministic masks are not corrected at all, the models converge much more slowly on SDRs and SIRs since the values of them become stable nearly after 5–7 epochs. However, almost all models achieve best SARs in 1–4 epochs whether they integrate nonlinear masking layers or not. It demonstrates that the nonlinear masking layer is capable of accelerating the training procedure of the model especially for SDR and SIR. Also, the models with one or more nonlinear masking layers achieve much better SDRs and SIRs than those with original masks. By contrast, the effect of using the nonlinear masking layer is not necessarily better than that of not using the nonlinear masking layer for SAR. These results show that according to the evaluated values of SDRs, the nonlinear masking layer can improve the overall quality of speech separation. Moreover, according to the evaluated values of SIRs, the nonlinear masking layer can greatly reduce the interferences of one speech to another. However, the downside is, the evaluated values of SARs reflect that using the nonlinear masking layer is likely to increase the systematic error of the entire model, although this error is relatively small.

Table 2. BSS-EVAL results (in dB) of different numbers of nonlinear masking layers with either SMMs or IRMs as original masks on the test set. Here the basic neural network is the vanilla RNN with $\gamma = 0.1$. "OM" denotes the type of the original masks and "#NMLs" denotes the number of nonlinear masking layers for the current model. Note that $L = 0$ means that there are no nonlinear masking layers, and only the original masks are kept in the model.

OM	#NMLs	$\alpha^{[l](1)}$	$\alpha^{[l](2)}$	SDR	SIR	SAR
None	None	None	None	6.18	8.97	8.02
SMM	$L = 0$	None	None	7.76	11.75	**10.51**
SMM	$L = 1$	$\alpha^{[1](1)} = 1.0$	$\alpha^{[1](2)} = 1.0$	9.69	15.50	10.03
SMM	$L = 2$	$\alpha^{[1](1)} = 1.0$ $\alpha^{[2](1)} = 1.5$	$\alpha^{[1](2)} = 1.0$ $\alpha^{[2](2)} = 1.5$	9.94	15.75	9.68
SMM	$L = 3$	$\alpha^{[1](1)} = 1.0$ $\alpha^{[2,3](1)} = 1.5$	$\alpha^{[1](2)} = 1.0$ $\alpha^{[2,3](2)} = 1.5$	**10.20**	**16.33**	10.03
IRM	$L = 0$	None	None	7.05	13.12	10.13
IRM	$L = 1$	$\alpha^{[1](1)} = 1.0$	$\alpha^{[1](2)} = 1.0$	7.57	14.06	9.84
IRM	$L = 2$	$\alpha^{[1](1)} = 1.0$ $\alpha^{[2](1)} = 1.5$	$\alpha^{[1](2)} = 1.0$ $\alpha^{[2](2)} = 1.5$	8.64	15.38	10.19
IRM	$L = 3$	$\alpha^{[1](1)} = 1.0$ $\alpha^{[2,3](1)} = 1.5$	$\alpha^{[1](2)} = 1.0$ $\alpha^{[2,3](2)} = 1.5$	8.69	**16.33**	10.27

Table 2 shows the results of all experiments about the nonlinear masking layer on the test set. It is found that both SDRs and SIRs improve with the increasement of the number of nonlinear masking layers no matter what kind of original mask (SMM or IRM) is used. However, for both these two masks, SARs maintain relatively stable since they don't show obvious rising trends like SDRs and SIRs. When the original masks are chosen to be SMMs and 3 nonlinear masking layers are added, the model yields 10.20 dB SDR, 16.33 dB SIR and 10.03 dB SAR. It turns out that this model achieves better SDR and SIR than those with SMMs followed by 1 or 2 nonlinear masking layers. However, SAR obtained by this model doesn't improve but is relatively closed to best SAR obtained by the model with deterministic SMMs. By contrast, the model that uses IRMs followed by 3 nonlinear masking layers yields 8.69 dB SDR, 16.33 dB SIR and 10.27 dB SAR. Similarly, this model achieves better results than those with IRMs followed by 1 or 2 nonlinear masking layers. These experimental results demonstrate that the nonlinearity of multiple nonlinear masking layers is more obvious than a single nonlinear masking layer. Stacking multiple nonlinear masking layers within a certain number range can further enhance the nonlinear feature extraction of the original masks.

Moreover, the selection of the original deterministic mask will also affect the performance of a model. The model with SMMs followed by multiple nonlinear masking layers performs better than those with IRMs followed by the same number of nonlinear masking layers especially for SDR and SIR. It reflects that the choice of the original masks is related to the upper bound of the performance of the model, and the nonlinear masking layer helps the model reach that upper bound. This is similar to the effect of the basic neural network selection. The IRM emphasizes the ratio of the clean speech energy to the noisy speech energy, and the SMM can be viewed as a form of the IRM defined in the STFT domain [23]. The SMM is empirically better than the IRM since the STFT domain is similar to our auditory perception. Therefore, the model with SMMs followed by 3 nonlinear masking layers, which obtain both best SDR and SIR, is chosen to be fine-tuned in the remaining experiments.

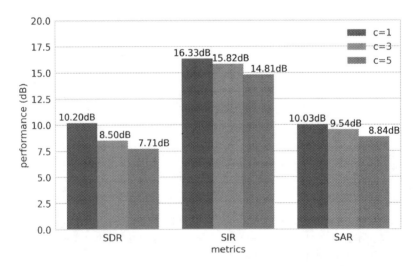

Fig. 4. The effects of different context windows on the model with SMMs followed by 3 nonlinear masking layers, where "c" denotes the size of the context window.

In addition, we evaluate the effect of the context window size to the performance of the model on the test set. The experimental results have been shown in Fig. 4. Surprisingly, it is found that increasing the size of the context window may harm the performance of the model. One possible reason is that the RNN is capable of extracting as much as contextual information from the mixture and increasing the size of the context window may cause overfitting.

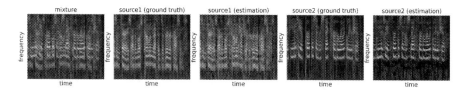

Fig. 5. An utterance example: the spectrograms of the real sources are compared to those of the estimated sources. Note that the estimated sources are output by the model "RNN + SMMs + 3 NMLs".

Finally, the spectrograms of an utterance example are illustrated in Fig. 5 (The estimated sources are output by the model "RNN + SMMs + 3 NMLs"). They are the spectrograms of the mixture, the first real source, the first estimated source, the second real source and the second estimated source from left to right, respectively. The model generates relatively good results since the spectral representations of the estimated sources are quite closed to those of the the real sources, and this demonstrates the ability of the nonlinear masking layer to form more powerful nonlinear time-frequency masks for speech separation.

6   Conclusion

In this paper, deep RNNs with nonlinear masking layers and two-level estimation are proposed for monaural speech separation. The output of the RNN is called the level 1 estimation which is used to construct original deterministic time-frequency masks (SMM, IRM, etc.). With the help of the additional nonlinear masking layers, original masks are enhanced and obtain more powerful nonlinear feature extraction. Finally, the element-wise product operation is applied between the mixtures and the nonlinear post-processed masks to output the level 2 estimation. Both deep RNNs without any mask and with original masks are used for comparison and taken to evaluate the effectiveness of the new models, respectively. The best results come from the RNN with SMMs followed by 3 nonlinear masking layers, giving an improvement of 4.02 dB SDR, 7.36 dB SIR and 2.01 dB SAR over the baseline RNN without any mask while that of 2.44 dB SDR and 4.58 dB SIR over the RNN with original masks (original SMMs). Future work on the design of appropriate and more complex integrated models on speech separation is a promising direction.

References

1. Brown, G.J., Cooke, M.: Computational auditory scene analysis. Comput. Speech Lang. **8**(4), 297–336 (1994). https://doi.org/10.1006/csla.1994.1016
2. Chan, W., Jaitly, N., Le, Q., Vinyals, O.: Listen, attend and spell: a neural network for large vocabulary conversational speech recognition. In: 2016 IEEE International Conference on Acoustics, Speech and Signal Processing (ICASSP), pp. 4960–4964. IEEE (2016). https://doi.org/10.1109/ICASSP.2016.7472621
3. Chang, X., Qian, Y., Yu, D.: Adaptive permutation invariant training with auxiliary information for monaural multi-talker speech recognition. In: 2018 IEEE International Conference on Acoustics, Speech and Signal Processing (ICASSP), pp. 5974–5978. IEEE (2018). https://doi.org/10.1109/ICASSP.2018.8461570
4. Cherry, E.: Some experiments on the recognition of speech, with one and with two ears. J. Acoust. Soc. Am. **25**(5), 975–979 (1953). https://doi.org/10.1121/1.1907229
5. Chung, J., Gulcehre, C., Cho, K., Bengio, Y.: Empirical evaluation of gated recurrent neural networks on sequence modeling. CoRR abs/1412.3555 (2014)
6. Cooke, M., Hershey, J.R., Rennie, S.J.: Monaural speech separation and recognition challenge. Comput. Speech Lang. **24**(1), 1–15 (2010). https://doi.org/10.1016/j.csl.2009.02.006
7. Garofolo, J.S., et al.: TIMIT corpus. Linguistic Data Consortium. https://catalog.ldc.upenn.edu/LDC93S1
8. Hershey, J.R., Chen, Z., Roux, J.L., Watanabe, S.: Deep clustering: discriminative embeddings for segmentation and separation. In: 2016 IEEE International Conference on Acoustics, Speech and Signal Processing (ICASSP), pp. 31–35. IEEE (2016). https://doi.org/10.1109/ICASSP.2016.7471631
9. Hochreiter, S., Schmidhuber, J.: Long short-term memory. Neural Comput. **9**(8), 1735–1780 (1997). https://doi.org/10.1162/neco.1997.9.8.1735
10. Huang, P.S., Kim, M., Hasegawa-Johnson, M., Smaragdis, P.: Deep learning for monaural speech separation. In: 2014 IEEE International Conference on Acoustics, Speech and Signal Processing (ICASSP), pp. 1562–1566. IEEE (2014). https://doi.org/10.1109/ICASSP.2014.6853860
11. Kingma, D.P., Ba, J.L.: Adam: a method for stochastic optimization. In: 3rd International Conference on Learning Representations, ICLR 2015 (2015)
12. Krizhevsky, A., Sutskever, I., Hinton, G.E.: ImageNet classification with deep convolutional neural networks. In: Advances in Neural Information Processing Systems, pp. 1097–1105 (2012). https://doi.org/10.1145/3065386
13. Lee, D.D., Seung, H.S.: Learning the parts of objects by non-negative matrix factorization. Nature **401**(6755), 788 (1999). https://doi.org/10.1038/44565
14. Maas, A.L., Le, Q.V., O'Neil, T.M., Vinyals, O., Nguyen, P., Ng, A.Y.: Recurrent neural networks for noise reduction in robust ASR. In: INTERSPEECH 2012, 13th Annual Conference of the International Speech, pp. 22–25 (2012)
15. Nair, V., Hinton, G.E.: Rectified linear units improve restricted boltzmann machines. In: Proceedings of the 27th International Conference on Machine Learning (ICML-10), pp. 807–814 (2010)
16. Pandey, A., Wang, D.: On adversarial training and loss functions for speech enhancement. In: 2018 IEEE International Conference on Acoustics, Speech and Signal Processing (ICASSP), pp. 5414–5418. IEEE (2018). https://doi.org/10.1109/ICASSP.2018.8462614

17. Schmidt, M.N., Olsson, R.K.: Single-channel speech separation using sparse non-negative matrix factorization. In: INTERSPEECH 2006 - ICSLP, Ninth International Conference on Spoken Language Processing (2006)
18. Schuster, M., Paliwal, K.K.: Bidirectional recurrent neural networks. IEEE Trans. Signal Process. **45**(11), 2673–2681 (1997). https://doi.org/10.1109/78.650093
19. Srinivasan, S., Roman, N., Wang, D.: Binary and ratio time-frequency masks for robust speech recognition. Speech Commun. **48**(11), 1486–1501 (2006). https://doi.org/10.1016/j.specom.2006.09.003
20. Tu, Y., Du, J., Xu, Y., Dai, L., Lee, C.H.: Speech separation based on improved deep neural networks with dual outputs of speech features for both target and interfering speakers. In: The 9th International Symposium on Chinese Spoken Language Processing, pp. 250–254. IEEE (2014). https://doi.org/10.1109/ISCSLP.2014.6936615
21. Vincent, E., Gribonval, R., Févotte, C.: Performance measurement in blind audio source separation. IEEE Trans. Audio Speech Lang. Process. **14**(4), 1462–1469 (2006). https://doi.org/10.1109/TSA.2005.858005
22. Wang, D.: Time-frequency masking for speech separation and its potential for hearing aid design. Trends Amplif. **12**(4), 332–353 (2008). https://doi.org/10.1177/1084713808326455
23. Wang, D., Chen, J.: Supervised speech separation based on deep learning: an overview. IEEE/ACM Trans. Audio Speech Lang. Process. **26**(10), 1702–1726 (2018). https://doi.org/10.1109/TASLP.2018.2842159
24. Wang, Y., Narayanan, A., Wang, D.: On training targets for supervised speech separation. IEEE/ACM Trans. Audio Speech Lang. Process. **22**(12), 1849–1858 (2014). https://doi.org/10.1109/TASLP.2014.2352935
25. Weng, C., Yu, D., Seltzer, M.L., Droppo, J.: Deep neural networks for single-channel multi-talker speech recognition. IEEE/ACM Trans. Audio Speech Lang. Process. (TASLP) **23**(10), 1670–1679 (2015). https://doi.org/10.1109/TASLP.2015.2444659
26. Wikipedia. https://en.wikipedia.org/wiki/Circular_shift. Circular Shift
27. Xu, B., Wang, N., Chen, T., Li, M.: Empirical evaluation of rectified activations in convolutional network. CoRR abs/1505.00853 (2015)
28. Yilmaz, O., Rickard, S.: Blind separation of speech mixtures via time-frequency masking. IEEE Trans. Signal Process. **52**(7), 1830–1847 (2004). https://doi.org/10.1109/TSP.2004.828896
29. Yu, D., Deng, L., Dahl, G.E.: Roles of pre-training and fine-tuning in context-dependent DBN-HMMs for real-world speech recognition. In: Proceedings of the NIPS Workshop on Deep Learning and Unsupervised Feature Learning (2010)
30. Yu, D., Kolbæk, M., Tan, Z.H., Jensen, J.: Permutation invariant training of deep models for speaker-independent multi-talker speech separation. In: 2017 IEEE International Conference on Acoustics, Speech and Signal Processing (ICASSP), pp. 241–245. IEEE (2017). https://doi.org/10.1109/ICASSP.2017.7952154
31. Zhang, H., Zhang, X., Gao, G.: Multi-target ensemble learning for monaural speech separation. In: INTERSPEECH, pp. 1958–1962 (2017). https://doi.org/10.21437/Interspeech.2017-240

Auto-Lag Networks for Real Valued Sequence to Sequence Prediction

Gilles Madi Wamba[✉][iD] and Nicolas Gaude[✉][iD]

Prevision.io, Paris, France
{gilles.madi,nicolas.gaude}@prevision.io

Abstract. Many machine learning problems involve predicting a sequence of future values of a target variable. State-of-the-art approaches for such use cases involve LSTM based sequence to sequence models. To improve they performances, those models generally use lagged values of the target variable as additional input features. Therefore, appropriate lag factor has to be chosen during feature engineering. This choice often requires business knowledge of the data. Furthermore, state-of-the-art sequence to sequence models are not designed to naturally handle hierarchical time series use cases. In this paper, we propose a novel architecture that naturally handles hierarchical time series. The contribution of this paper is thus two-folds. First we show the limitations of classical sequence to sequence models in the case of problems involving a real valued target variable, namely the error accumulation problem and we propose a novel LSTM based approach to overcome those limitations. Second, we highlight the limitations of manually selecting fixed lag values to improve the performance of a model. We then use an attention mechanism to introduce a dynamic and automatic lag factor selection that overcomes the former limitations, and requires no business knowledge of the data. We call this architecture Auto-Lag Network (AL-Net). We finally validate our Auto-Lag Net model against state-of-the-art results.

Keywords: Auto-Lag nets · Time series · LSTM · Sequence to sequence

1 Introduction and Related Work

Over the recent years problems involving time series [1], or sequence to sequence prediction have been of great interest. Several LSTM based approaches have been proposed in the case of text translation [2,3] and image captioning [4]. Those models rely on a discrete representation of the words using embeddings. In the case of real valued sequence prediction, the values are not discrete. We refer to those problems as real valued sequence to sequence prediction problems.

© Springer Nature Switzerland AG 2019
I. V. Tetko et al. (Eds.): ICANN 2019, LNCS 11730, pp. 412–425, 2019.
https://doi.org/10.1007/978-3-030-30490-4_33

1.1   Real Valued Time Series Forecasting

Time series forecasting involves observing values of a given measure over a period of time and predicting future values. They are well suited to model data such as weather, stock prices, retail sales or resources consumption [5].

A major application of real valued sequence to sequence prediction is the unit commitment problem. Unit commitment problem refers to a sets of problems where an energy supplier has to calibrate its production with respects to a set of constraints [6]. In this context, Bouktif et al. [7] propose an LSTM based real valued sequence to sequence prediction model. Their state-of-the-art model uses an orginal genetic algorithm for lag selection to forecast the next 30 min time step energy consumption value. However, in order to align the production of the energy with the demand, it is unrealistic to forecast only one 30 min time step ahead. In order to remain in realistic conditions, we evaluate our AL-Net model on the forecast of 48 time steps of 30 min each i.e we use our model to forecast a whole day of energy consumption at a granularity of 30 min. Although the promising results on this configuration, we also evaluate the AL-Net model against the state-of-the-art model in [7], for the case where one needs only one time step ahead forecast. Experimental results on a real-world data set shows that our AL-Net model outperforms theirs by up to 15%.

In some situations, one may wants to group several time series following some predefined criteria, we refer to them as grouped or hierarchical time series.

1.2   Hierarchical Time Series Forecasting

Hierarchical time series is a term that designates a set of time series that are hierarchically organized. The hierarchy is generally specified by geographical criteria or by product types (groups). There exists 3 main approaches that can be used to forecast hierarchical time series [8].

- **Bottom-up approach:** It consists in building several models to make low level predictions that can be aggregated into high level predictions. The need to build several models for each group is resource consuming as the number of group might be huge, and leads to error accumulation.
- **Top-down approach:** Here a single model makes high level predictions that are further disaggregated using another model like regression. The major issue is the loss of information relative to individual series dynamics [9].
- **Middle-out approach:** It is an hybridation of the Bottom-up and the Top-down approaches.

With AL-Net, we propose a novel **one-shot** approach. In the one-shot approach, a single model is built and is able to make prediction at each level of the time series hierarchy. In order to achieve this, non temporal data, i.e features specifying the group of each time series are used both at train and prediction time. We thus avoid all the issues inherent to Bottom-up and Top-down aproaches: no error is accumulated, no extra-resource is used to build and train several models, and finally, information relative to individual time series dynamics is preserved and taken into consideration. The evaluation of our one-shot approach on a real hierarchical time series use case [10] shows promising results.

The contribution of this paper is thus two-folds. First we show the limitations of classical sequence to sequence models in the case of problems involving a real valued target variable, and we propose a novel approach to overcome them. Second, we highlight the limitations of selecting fixed lag factors to improve the performance of a model. We then use an attention mechanism to introduce a dynamic lag factor selection that overcome the former limitations, and requires no business knowledge of the data. The proposed model also introduces a novel one shot-approach for hierarchical or grouped time series prediction. The rest of the paper is organized as follows: In Sect. 2, we give some background on machine learning concepts in the context of sequence prediction. Section 3 is dedicated to the presentation of our AL-Net model. The model is further validated both in realistic conditions and against a state-of-the-art model in Sect. 4. The work is finally concluded in Sect. 5.

2   Background on Time Series Forecasting

One of the most used method for time series forecasting is the auto-regressive integrated moving average (ARIMA) [11]. ARIMA model however suffers from the assumption of linear relationship between the predictors and the target variable. In order to overcome this limitation, deep machine learning approaches are more and more used for time series forecasting. In the following sections, we introduce classical deep learning models that are applied in this context.

2.1   Multilayer Perceptron

Multilayer perceptrons (MLP) [12] is a promising tool for most classification and regression problems. In the case of regression, a MLP is trained on a set of data of the form (X, y) where:

- X is a vector of features
- y is the target

The model approximates a function f such that $f(X) = y$.

There exists many types of MLPs, each of them having its own specificities. For sequence to sequence prediction use cases, one of the most promising MLP type is the Long Short Term Memory Network.

2.2   Long Short Term Memory Network

Long short term memory networks (LSTM) [13] were introduced to overcome the long term dependency issue encountered by traditional recurrent neural networks (RNN). LSTMs have a chain structure similar to the one we observe in a standard RNN. The main difference that provides LSTMs with the ability to handle long term dependencies lies within the modules. Each module comprises a four-layers network called gates. Those gates are shown in Fig. 1. Using this gates mechanism, an LSTM is able to select, edit, or delete persistent information in the long or short term.

In the following Section, we introduce our Auto-Lag Net model which embeds the contributions of this paper.

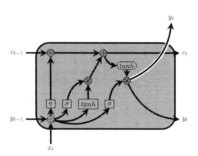

Fig. 1. Gates within an LSTM cell

3 Auto-Lag Net

In this section, we present how we iteratively construct our Auto-Lag Net architecture. The key difference between the first stage model and the final one is the dynamic lag factor selection through an attention mechanism. Auto-Lag Net uses an encoder-decoder architecture [14,15]. The key idea is that the model is made up of several stacked layers separated into two groups. The first one called encoder reads the input in and produces a fixed sized representation. The second group named decoder is responsible for reading the encoded representation of the input and produces the target output.

3.1 Encoder

The encoder is composed of 4 layers. The first two layers are convolutional layers. In order to preserve the temporal order within the data, those layers are padded. The third encoder layer is a max pooling layer whose main purpose is to reduce data dimensionality. Those layers ($conv1d\_1$, $conv1d\_2$, $max\_pooling\_1d\_1$) are shown in Fig. 2. Convolutions and max pooling layers are image oriented layers. Traditionally, they are applied to $2D$ image data with 3 channels (rgb). Nevertheless, for a stride length that is less than the time stamp, it is natural to apply a one dimensional convolution to a time series as it evolves with the time. The last encoder's layer is an LSTM layer (see $lstm\_1$ in Fig. 2).

3.2   Decoder

The decoder is made of a stack of 3 layers. The first is an LSTM layer identical to the encoder's last layer (*lstm_2* in Fig. 2). The second and the third decoder's layers are two identical time distributed dense layers.

Most sequence to sequence models are auto-regressive, i.e they consume the last generated symbol to produce the next one [16, 17]. We can see from Fig. 2 that our decoder takes two inputs in. The first input given by *lstm_1* is the encoder's output. The second one given by *input_2* is the previously generated symbol (it is the decoder hidden state denoted h_t), it is called the context.

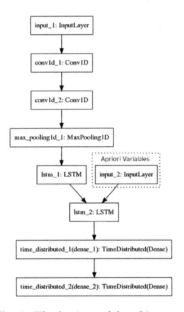

Fig. 2. The basic model architecture

3.3   Error Accumulation

Most auto-regressive machine learning models are trained with the *teacher forcing* method [18]. Teacher forcing uses the real output from the training data set at a time step t as input to produce the next output at time step $t + 1$. During the training, the model's loss is therefore evaluated on producing a single value at each time step. As noticed in [19], this presents two major issues:

1 **Exposure bias**. The *Exposure bias* is due to the fact that the model is trained to predict the future value of a time series given the previous ground truth value as input. The model is therefore never exposed to its errors during the training. At test time, the model iteratively produces a whole sequence from scratch by consuming at each step its own previous output to produce the next one. This causes the error to accumulate along the way.

2 **Train/Test metrics incoherence.** The *Train/Test metrics incoherence* issue is due to the fact that, the training loss is evaluated upon producing a single value at each time step whereas during testing, the model is evaluated on the whole produced sequence

As we will experimentally confirm in Sect. 4, the accuracy of the so constructed model suffers from error accumulation. To avoid the *Exposure bias* issue, some papers in the literature use the *beam search* heuristic [14,20,21]. Instead of using the model's output at a time step t to produce the output at time step $t + 1$, a *beam search decoder* keeps at each step t a list of k best candidate outputs. The beam search heuristic produces great results in text related tasks were the output dictionary is discrete and finite.

To overcome both the *Exposure bias* and the *Train/Test metrics incoherence* issues in the case of real valued sequence to sequence prediction, we proceed as follows:

1 **No teacher forcing and a priori variables.** The model's output is never fed back to produce the next time step output. Instead, we feed the decoder with additional variables that describe the prediction window. Examples of such variables include the weather forecast, day of the week, month, whether it is holiday or not. Values for those variables are known at prediction time, we call them *a priori variables*. In this work, we define *a priori variables* as exogeneous variables whose future values are always known in advance. By doing this, we avoid the *Exposure bias* issue.

2 **Multi-step-ahead direct forecasting.** In [22], the authors examine two alternative approaches to auto-regressive models: Independent value prediction and Parameter prediction. While the parameter prediction methods does not suffer from error accumulation, it doesn't take into consideration the time dependence between values of the sequence.

The AL-Net model uses a multiple input multiple output (MIMO) [23] strategy to produce the whole target sequence at once. As shown in [24], this strategy presents many advantages. This approach solves the *Train/Test metrics incoherence* issue as the model's loss is evaluated during training on the whole predicted sequence. By doing so, we also avoid error accumulation.

3.4   Dynamic Lags

A lagged value is a delayed variable. Many time series forecasting models [25] take into account lagged values of the target as input. The intuition is that, there might exist a natural number k such that the value of a time series at a given time step $t + n$ is correlated to its value at time step $t - k$.

While numerous papers introduce sophisticated lag selection algorithms [7,26], they all end up finding optimal observation windows. In this paper, we go a step further. We rely on the following intuition: All the values within an observation window do not account at the same time to produce every single value of the output sequence. As it is the case with problem involving neural image caption generation [4], a fixed representation of whole input observation window (the output of the encoder) is not optimal to produce every single value in the output sequence.

We therefore propose a dynamic lag selection mechanism. As illustrated in the heatmap of Fig. 6, we can see how the dynamic lag selection module makes use of the above intuition. Indeed, it learns to focus on different locations of the observation window to produce specific values of the output sequence. This relies on the attention mechanism.

Attention mechanism was first introduced in 2014 [3] to overcome the issue in neural machine translation were the decoder has to produce the whole translated sequence out of a summarized version of the input sequence.

There exists several implementations of the attention mechanism in the literature. They are classified into two categories: global and local attention [3]. Our dynamic lag selection mechanism relies on an original modification of a global attention mechanism.

A global attention model takes two arguments. A vector $\overline{y} = (\overline{y_1}, \ldots, \overline{y_n})$ and a context vector c of length n. It computes a vector of length n, that is interpreted as the relevant parts of $\overline{y}$ with respects to the context c.

Specifically, at each time step t, it does the following:

– Using the decoder intermediary states h_t, a context vector c_t is computed.
– A concatenation layer is used to produce an attentional layer $\overline{h}$ with the following equation:

$$\overline{h} = \tanh(W_c[c_t h_t]). \tag{1}$$

– $\overline{h}$ is then fed to a softmax layer to predict next values.

Using the attention model terminology, our dynamic lag selection mechanism is implemented as follows:

– Context vector c_t
   The context vector is computed as follows:
   1 Since we do not produce the target sequence in an iterative way (see Sect. 3.3) we can't access the decoder's intermediary states. We set h_t to be the output of the a priori variables fed to an LSTM (*lstm_2* of Fig. 3).
   2 c_t is obtained by taking a dot product over the encoder's output $\overline{y}$ and h_t (*dot_1* of Fig. 3).

$$c_t = \overline{y}.h_t.$$

– The attention a_t.
   At any time step t, the attention produces relevant parts of an input $\overline{y}$ with respects to a given context c_t. We proceed as follows: The context c_t is first fed to a softmax layer (*activation_1* of Fig. 3). Second, a dot product is taken over the output of that softmax layer and the output of the encoder (*dot_2* of Fig. 3).

$$c'_t = softmax(c_t),$$

$$a_t = \overline{y}.c'_t.$$

– The attentional vector $\overline{h}$.

We finally produce the attentional vector $\overline{h}$ with a concatenation layer (*concatenate_1* of Fig. 3) [3], following Eq. 1.

In Fig. 3, our dynamic lag module is made up of layers *dot_1*, *activation_1*, *dot_2* and *concatenate_1*.

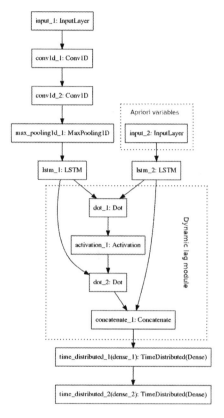

Fig. 3. The Auto-Lag net architecture with the dynamic lag selection module

4   Experiments

In this Section, we present the performance results of AL-Net on two real world data set. The first one is a simple time series use case while the second is a hierarchical time series one.

4.1   Electricity Consumption

We applied our AL-Net on an electricity consumption use case. It is a unit commitment problem where the electricity provider needs to adapt the energy production with energy consumption. The amount of produced energy needs to be carefully chosen in order to satisfy the demand without surpassing it. Surpassing the demands results in financial losses since it is complicated to store energy [27]. In order to remain in realistic conditions, we configure the AL-Net to predict a whole day of future energy consumption so that the energy provider can adapt the next day's production. Since the time step is 30 min, our prediction window is then made of 48 values i.e we want to predict the next 48 values of the energy consumption.

4.1.1   Dataset

We used the *Réseau de transport d'électricité (RTE) de France* data. This data set is the electricity consumption of France from January 1st 2012 to July 1st 2018 The time step is 30 min. We splitted the data into a sequential train test split in order to preserve data chronology. Train starts on January 1st 2012 and ends on September 30th 2016. The test set starts on October 1st 2016 and ends on July 1st 2018. Figure 4 shows the profile of the data set as well as the train/test split.

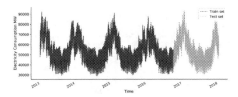

Fig. 4. RTE dataset splitted into train and test sets.

4.1.2   A Priori Variable Selection

As mentioned in Sect. 3.3, the AL-Net's output is never fed back as input to the model. We instead feed the encoder with explanatory variables called a priori variables. The purpose of those variables is to help the model to "understand" the target values. For example, a very high consumption value may be interpreted by the model as an outlier. However, an a priori weather variable might explain to the model that the encountered high value is due to a very low temperature at that time. The choice of the a priori variables is made by intuition. For example, Fig. 5a shows that, generally the energy consumption decreases as the temperature increases. Similar observation is shown in Fig. 5b with the type of the day. Therefore, we use the following a priori variables in our model: Week, Month, Temperature, Day type.

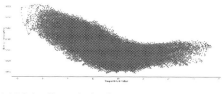

(a) Link effect relation between temperature and energy consumption.

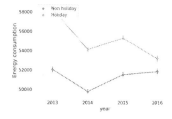

(b) Day type against energy consumption

Fig. 5. Intuitions on the choice of a priori variables

4.1.3   Results

In order to evaluate the AL-Net's performance, we used the root mean squared error (RMSE). This choice is justified by the fact that it penalizes high errors. This property is suitable as in our use case, large errors lead to huge mismatch between energy supply and demand. We used XGBoost with a priori input variables as baseline algorithm.

The results are presented in Table 1. The basic configuration of the model is the model without a priori variables and without dynamic lag selection. The fact that our base model is already more than 140% better than XGBoost shows that Al-Net is a good approach for time series forecasting problems. Iteratively adding day types and temperature as a priori variables takes the model performances from 2400 RMSE to 1247. This clearly shows the contribution of a priori variables to the model and thus validates our intuition. The last step further is the dynamic lag module. This again increases the performance of the model from 1247 RMSE to 991 i.e below 1000

Table 1. RMSE values for various configurations of the model

Configuration	RMSE
XGBoost	5890
Basic	2400
+Day types	1650
+Temperature	1247
+Dynamic lag	991

Figure 6 shows the heat-map of the dynamic lag selection module. The x-axis are the lagged values and the y-axis is the target 24-h prediction window. The heat-map shows how the model dynamically selects lag values to compute each of the 48 target values. A hotter color indicates a higher contribution of the corresponding lag. Specifically, we observe from the activation of the attention on a winter day and on a summer day (Fig. 6) how the selection of the lagged values dynamically changes. For example, to predict the energy consumption at $12PM$ on a winter day, the model focuses on lagged values around $12PM$ and $2PM$ of day-3 up til day-7. While on a summer day it instead focuses on lagged values around $10AM$ and $12PM$.

4.1.4   Model Validation on State-of-the-Art Results

In [7] the authors present an LSTM based sequence to sequence model to predict energy consumption with the RTE data set. Their model rely on feature selection and a genetic algorithm for lag selection. In order to evaluate our model against their state-of-the art performing model, we put ourselves in the unrealistic situation were the energy supplier needs only the next time step forecast of the consumption. We therefore set our prediction window to be a single time step. After feature selection and hyper-parameter tuning using their genetic algorithm, the RMSE score of their best model is 341.40. Using our AL-Net model, we surpass this score by up to **15%** without model tuning. More precisely, on that very same problem configuration, AL-Net obtains a **295.97** RMSE score.

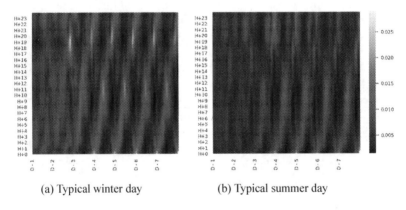

(a) Typical winter day   (b) Typical summer day

Fig. 6. Dynamic lag selection heat map

In order to compare AL-Net to [7]'s LSTM Metrics Optimal Time Lags Model (LMOTLM) on different time horizons, we train AL-Net to predict a whole day prediction window. Among the test set predictions, we randomly selected 100 single value predictions at various time horizons. The results are given in Table 2.

Overall, AL-Net is 17% better than [7]'s model. This results is impressive considering the fact that AL-Net was trained to predict a whole day. Further, we observe that these results are better than the 295.97 RMSE score achieved by AL-Net when trained to output a single target value. This observation definitely validates that, the architecture of AL-Net is well adapted to multi-step ahead direct forecasting. This is due to the fact that, by construction, the AL-Net gets more a priori informations (for the whole prediction windows) in multi-step ahead direct forecasting mode than in single-step ahead forecasting mode.

Table 2. Performance comparison on various time horizons

Time horizon	LMOTLM	AL-Net
2 weeks	339	221
2–4 weeks	258	245
2–3 months	294	240
3–4 months	275	290

4.2 Rossmann Store Sales

The Rossmann Store Sales is a hierarchical time series use case that was subject to a kaggle competition featuring more than 3000 participants [10]. We fitted the publicly available data set to the AL-Net to evaluate its performances on hierarchical time series.

4.2.1 Data Set and Results

The data set of this use case is the historical data of 1115 Rossman stores located across Germany, and the task is to predict 6 weeks of daily sales. Variables of the data set include *Store* and *StoreID*. We use those non temporal features to specify the group to which belong a time series. In this use case, AL-NET is used alone i.e not embedded in an ensemble method, and yet obtains a root mean squared percentage error (RMSPE) **0.13826**. When we exclude the aberrant RMSPE score of 2798997865347.38 obtained by a participant of the challenge, the remaining public leaderboad scores lies within the interval from 0.08932 to 1. AL-Net is thus by 35.39% worse than the best score, but more than 1000% better than the worst score in the public challenge leaderboard. Those satisfactory results show that the one-shot approach of AL-Net is competitive in hierarchical time series use cases.

5   Conclusion

In this paper, we presented a LSTM based sequence to sequence model in the context of real valued sequence prediction. The contribution of the paper is two-fold. First we propose a model architecture that overcomes the accumulating error problem encountered in classical sequence to sequence models. Second, we propose a dynamic lag selection mechanism. The proposed dynamic lag selection mechanism requires no knowledge of the data and can therefore be applied to any time series or hierarchical time series data set. Experimental results shows that our AL-Net model outperforms state-of-the-art models. Our model also shows promising performances on a realistic configuration and can therefore be deployed in real life.

Acknowledgement. We would like to thank the reviewers for their thoughtful comments towards improving our paper and our colleague Lucas Perret for the great production code quality.

References

1. Arafailova, E., et al.: Global constraint catalog, volume II, time-series constraints. arXiv preprint arXiv:1609.08925 (2016)
2. Luong, M.-T., Pham, H., Manning, C.D.: Effective approaches to attention-based neural machine translation. arXiv preprint arXiv:1508.04025 (2015)
3. Bahdanau, D., Cho, K., Bengio, Y.: Neural machine translation by jointly learning to align and translate. arXiv preprint arXiv:1409.0473 (2014)
4. Xu, K., et al.: Show, attend and tell: neural image caption generation with visual attention. In: International Conference on Machine Learning, pp. 2048–2057 (2015)
5. Wamba, G.M., Li, Y., Orgerie, A.-C., Beldiceanu, N., Menaud, J.-M.: Cloud workload prediction and generation models. In: SBAC-PAD, pp. 89–96. IEEE (2017)
6. Padhy, N.P.: Unit commitment-a bibliographical survey. IEEE Trans. Power Syst. **19**(2), 1196–1205 (2004)
7. Bouktif, S., Fiaz, A., Ouni, A., Serhani, M.: Optimal deep learning LSTM model for electric load forecasting using feature selection and genetic algorithm: comparison with machine learning approaches. Energies **11**(7), 1636 (2018)
8. Kosiorowski, D., Mielczarek, D., Rydlewski, J., et al.: Forecasting of a hierarchical functional time series on example of macromodel for day and night air pollution in silesia region: a critical overview. arXiv preprint arXiv:1712.03797 (2017)
9. Hyndman, R.J., Ahmed, R.A., Athanasopoulos, G., Shang, H.L.: Optimal combination forecasts for hierarchical time series. Comput. Stat. Data Anal. **55**(9), 2579–2589 (2011)
10. Rossmann store sales. https://www.kaggle.com/c/rossmann-store-sales/. Accessed 07 Jan 2019
11. Box, G.E.P., Jenkins, G.M., Reinsel, G.C., Ljung, G.M.: Time Series Analysis: Forecasting and Control. Wiley, Hoboken (2015)
12. Lippmann, R.: An introduction to computing with neural nets. IEEE ASSP Mag. **4**(2), 4–22 (1987)
13. Hochreiter, S., Schmidhuber, J.: Long short-term memory. Neural comput. **9**(8), 1735–1780 (1997)
14. Sutskever, I., Vinyals, O., Le, Q.V.: Sequence to sequence learning with neural networks. In: Advances in Neural Information Processing Systems, pp. 3104–3112 (2014)
15. Cho, K., et al.: Learning phrase representations using RNN encoder-decoder for statistical machine translation. arXiv preprint arXiv:1406.1078 (2014)
16. Graves, A.: Generating sequences with recurrent neural networks. arXiv preprint arXiv:1308.0850 (2013)
17. Vaswani, A., et al.: Attention is all you need. In: Advances in Neural Information Processing Systems, pp. 5998–6008 (2017)
18. Williams, R.J., Zipser, D.: A learning algorithm for continually running fully recurrent neural networks. Neural comput. **1**(2), 270–280 (1989)
19. Ranzato, M.A., Chopra, S., Auli, M., Zaremba, W.: Sequence level training with recurrent neural networks. arXiv preprint arXiv:1511.06732 (2015)
20. Freitag, M., Al-Onaizan, Y.: Beam search strategies for neural machine translation. arXiv preprint arXiv:1702.01806 (2017)

21. Wiseman, S., Rush, A.M.: Sequence-to-sequence learning as beam-search optimization. arXiv preprint arXiv:1606.02960 (2016)
22. Cheng, H., Tan, P.-N., Gao, J., Scripps, J.: Multistep-ahead time series prediction. In: Ng, W.-K., Kitsuregawa, M., Li, J., Chang, K. (eds.) PAKDD 2006. LNCS (LNAI), vol. 3918, pp. 765–774. Springer, Heidelberg (2006). https://doi.org/10.1007/11731139_89
23. Zamora-Martínez, F., Romeu, P., Botella-Rocamora, P., Pardo, J.: Towards energy efficiency: forecasting indoor temperature via multivariate analysis. Energies **6**(9), 4639–4659 (2013)
24. Taieb, S.B., Bontempi, G., Atiya, A.F., Sorjamaa, A.: A review and comparison of strategies for multi-step ahead time series forecasting based on the NN5 forecasting competition. Expert. Syst. Appl. **39**(8), 7067–7083 (2012)
25. Keele, L., Kelly, N.J.: Dynamic models for dynamic theories: the ins and outs of lagged dependent variables. Polit. Anal. **14**(2), 186–205 (2006)
26. Ribeiro, G.H.T., de Mattos Neto, P.S.G., Cavalcanti, G.D.C., Tsang, I.R.: Lag selection for time series forecasting using particle swarm optimization. In: IJCNN, pp. 2437–2444 (2011)
27. Poonpun, P., Jewell, W.T.: Analysis of the cost per kilowatt hour to store electricity. IEEE Trans. Energy Convers. **23**(2), 529–534 (2008)

LSTM Prediction on Sudden Occurrence of Maintenance Operation of Air-Conditioners in Real-Time Pricing Adaptive Control

Shun Matsukawa[1]($\boxtimes$), Chuzo Ninagawa[1], Junji Morikawa[2],
Takashi Inaba[2], and Seiji Kondo[2]

[1] Smart Grid Power Control Engineering Joint Research Laboratory,
Gifu University, Gifu, Japan
s_matsu@gifu-u.ac.jp
[2] Air-Conditioning Engineering Department, Mitsubishi Heavy Industries
Thermal Systems, Ltd., Kiyosu, Japan

Abstract. Predicting the occurrence of embedded maintenance operations in building multi-type air-conditioners is desirable during the Real-Time Pricing (RTP) scheme in the future smart grid. The maintenance operation is a kind of a high priority embedded control for complicated refrigerant circuit network in an office building. Since it suddenly operates and consumes large electric power, it becomes a big disturbance from the viewpoint of RTP control system in the cloud. In this research, we propose a model that forecasts the sudden occurrence of the maintenance operation. Since the occurrence of the operation depends on the refrigerant circuit operation history, the model is implemented as a Long Short Term Memory (LSTM) neural network. An accuracy of prediction was evaluated and then simulation experiments showed the improvement by 27% on RTP adaptive control result.

Keywords: LSTM · Air-conditioner · Real-Time Pricing

1 Introduction

Real-Time Pricing (RTP) [1, 2] is a scheme that changes the unit price of electricity fees in tens of minutes to adjust demand power consuming in the future smart grid. Several major loads for RTP are considered, and air-conditioners of office buildings are expected to become one of the important loads among them [3, 4]. The control system for RTP sends commands to many office buildings via the Internet, and provides the RTP adaptive control.

The RTP adaptive control algorithm in previous study is for power limitation of multi-type air-conditioner in office building and generates optimum power limitation command sequence according to RTP unit price [5–9]. However, it does not consider occasional maintenance operations that protects complicated refrigerant circuit network of multi-type air-conditioners. The maintenance operation is observed as a disturbance from the point of view of the RTP adaptive control system in the Internet cloud because the maintenance operation is performed by the embedded controller in the

© Springer Nature Switzerland AG 2019
I. V. Tetko et al. (Eds.): ICANN 2019, LNCS 11730, pp. 426–435, 2019.
https://doi.org/10.1007/978-3-030-30490-4_34

air-conditioner device. The top priority is given to the maintenance operation, ignoring the power limitation command from the adaptive control system on the cloud. The maintenance operation occurs stochastically and sometimes consumes high power, the RTP adaptive control algorithm cannot take the maintenance operation into account. As a result, the maintenance operation causes significant disturbances to the adaptive control system.

In order to avoid the influence of the disturbance as above, prediction models related to power consumption and room temperature change have been developed [6, 7]. However, the maintenance operation occurs stochastically and suddenly, and it depends strongly on the operation state history of the air-conditioner [9]. Therefore, an accurate and practical prediction model on occurrence of the maintenance operation has not been developed.

In this research, considering the time-history-dependence of maintenance operation, we have tried to construct this difficult prediction model using Long Short Term Memory (LSTM) neural network. In addition, we propose a new RTP adaptive control method that postpones the maintenance operation that consumes electric power within the time frame of expensive price by incorporating this prediction model. Our new RTP adaptive control algorithm postpones the maintenance operation by temporarily turning off the air-conditioner when the maintenance operation is forecasted in a time zone with a high price. In order to investigate the improvement effect by using the prediction model, an estimate calculation was made on the contribution to the RTP adaptive control score.

2 RTP Control with Maintenance Prediction

Figure 1 is a conceptual diagram of a change in power consumption of an air-conditioner during RTP adaptive control. In the figure, it changes to three kinds of unit price of ¥10 (cheap), ¥30 (medium degree), ¥100 (expensive), for example. In our RTP adaptive control system, an optimum power limitation command for the next time frame is searched by Simulated Annealing algorithm (SA) [10, 11] with a penalty function of electricity fee and room temperature.

In this example, the maintenance operation is occurred in the time frame from 15 to 20 min, where the unit price is most expensive (¥100). During that frame, the power limit command with the lowest level P_L was issued, but ignored to fail suppressing the power consumption because the maintenance operation suddenly occurred in the frame. However, if the maintenance operation is postponed to the cheaper time frame by the RTP adaptive control system using the prediction model, the electricity fee will be very cheap.

The new RTP adaptive control algorithm we propose makes decisions to temporarily turn off the air-conditioner during expensive time frames using maintenance prediction and RTP price schedule. Since a maintenance operation does not occur during the turn-off frame, the new algorithm will be executed so that the total electricity fee will be reduced by deferring the maintenance operation with high power consumption. Of course, the new algorithm does not defer the maintenance, depending on the trade-off between the room temperature and the total electricity fee.

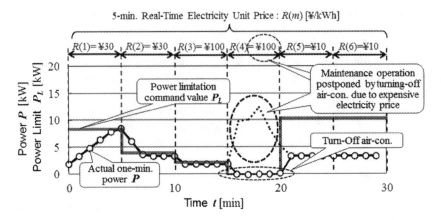

Fig. 1. The maintenance operation, if it occurs during the time frame with the lowest power limit, spoils the adaptive control.

The state vector $x(m)$ of air-conditioner in the five-minute time frame m is input to the adaptive control algorithm and the maintenance prediction model. The RTP unit price schedule $R(m) = \{R(1), R(2), \ldots\}$ is given by the smart grid organization. According to the combination of the RTP price and the room temperature condition, the prediction model calculates a maintenance occurrence forecast $F_O(m)$ for the next frame so that the Final Decision Switcher can decide whether to postpone the maintenance operation. In case that the maintenance occurrence forecast $F_O(m)$ is 0, the Final Decision Switcher keeps to operate the air-conditioner by sending power limitation command $P_L(m)$ at the next time frame $m + 1$. On the other hand, if $F_O(m)$ is 1 and the price $R(m)$ is expensive, the Final Decision Switcher send a turn-off command $T_{OFF}(m)$ to the air-conditioner to postpone the maintenance operation if the turn-off is effective at the expense of room temperature rise.

With the new RTP adaptive control algorithm, the prediction ability of the model for maintenance operation is very important. However, it is extremely difficult to construct a physical model that predicts the stochastic and sudden occurrence of maintenance operation. Therefore, using machine learning that learned time-series history data, we construct a statistical model for the maintenance operation. In this research, we used a Long Short-Term Memory neural network which is a kind of recurrent neural network.

3   Neural Network for Prediction of Maintenance

The LSTM neural network [12] is a kind of recurrent neural network (RNN) used in computational neuroscience and machine learning applications. In LSTM, nodes in the hidden layer are replaced with complicated units called memory units, so it is possible to overcome the vanishing gradient problem and hold long time series input data information.

The LSTM model constructed in this research is shown in Fig. 2. This model structure has vectors $x(m)$s composed of 40 dimensions as time series input to the upper layer, and has a vector $y(m+1)$ consisting of a 5 dimensional vector as an output. In this research, the following variables that are strongly related to the trigger of the automatic maintenance operations were used to represent the driving variables state in time t; $P(t)$ is the consumed instantaneous power [kW]. $S_O(t)$ is the actually observed 1-min state of the occurrence of maintenance operation. $C_{1hz}(t)$ and $C_{2hz}(t)$ are the revolution speeds [rps] of the compressors 1 and 2, respectively. $DA_{hz}(t)$ is the average of the rotational speed difference [rps] between compressor 1 and compressor 2. $C_{SV}(t)$ is the inverter current limit value [A]. $A_{Oh}(t)$ is the elapsed time after the proceeding maintenance operation [min]. The $x(m)$ contains these variables in the same 5-min frame m in accordance with the output vector contained 5-min frame prediction. Consequently, the $x(m)$ is composed of 40 elements, i.e., 8 [variables per minute] times 5 [min].

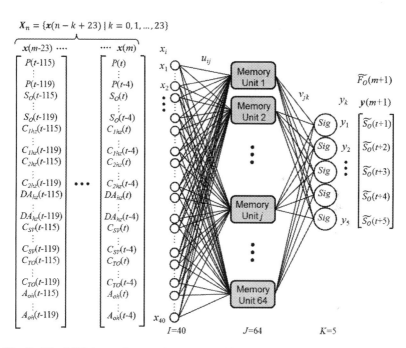

Fig. 2. The LSTM neural network structure with 24 series of input variable vectors.

In these data sets, $S_O(t)$ is expressed in binary variable vales, 0 for not-occurrence, 1 for occurrence, as follows;

$$S_O(t) = \{0, 1\} \tag{1}$$

These are input variables acquired from the built-in sensors of the multi air-conditioner via the Internet every minute.

The maintenance operation is carried out at intervals from 30 to 120 min, so the length of the time-series needs 120 min to make the LSTM learn the periodicity of the maintenance operation. The number of input frames of the time-series was determined to be 24, that is, an input time series X contains 24 of 5-min-state of vectors, $x(1), \ldots, x(m), \ldots, x(24)$, as indicated on the left in Fig. 2.

If 120-min time-series are input to the LSTM as 120 steps, the number of steps may be too large for the memory units to learn the relatively long time periodicity. After some trials, the 120-min time-series were decided to be divided into 24 steps of 5-min state vectors.

These time series data are input to the memory units on the hidden layer. A memory unit is constructed from five elements, i.e., an input gate, an input, a forget gate, an output gate and a memory cell. This architecture is suitable for time series data that abruptly changes pattern, like maintenance operation occurrence. The memory cell has self-regressive connections. Therefore, the outputs are fed back with a delay of one time step. The number of memory units in the hidden layer is 64; this was determined empirically.

The output vector y indicates the likelihood of occurrences of the maintenance operation between times $t+1$ and $t+5$. The closer the likelihood is to 1.0, the higher the possibility of an occurrence. The prediction model outputs five analog values of the occurrence probability $\widetilde{S}_O(t+t')(t' = 1, 2, \ldots, 5)$ of the time frame m in the next 5 min. For the next 5-min frame, "Maintenance operation forecast" $\widetilde{F}_O(m)$ is defined as follows;

$$
\widetilde{F}_O(m) = \begin{cases} 1 & \left(\text{if at least one } \widetilde{S}_O(t+t') \geq 0.5\right) \\ 0 & \left(\text{others, i.e., all } \widetilde{S}_O(t+t')s < 0.5\right) \end{cases} \tag{2}
$$

Using Eq. (2), if the analog value of the prediction result $\widetilde{S}_O(t+t')$ from the model within one frame exceeds 0.5, that frame is predicted as an occurrence of maintenance operation.

4 LSTM Neural Network Training

4.1 Processing Sequential Training Data Set

The LSTM network model was trained with the data taken in August 12, 2016 from the actual office building via the Internet under the name "Power Limited Modulation" [13] using the remote data collection system we developed. The data per day were acquired every minute for 10 h. Then 11 sets of $\{x(1), \ldots, x(m), \ldots, x(119)\}$ for each day were acquired. The n th training data set X_n within a day is represented as below:

$$
X_n = \{x(n-m+23) \mid m = 0, 1, \ldots, 23\} \tag{3}
$$

This formulation means that X_n contains the X_{n-1} shifted forward by one 5-min frames as the prediction interval.

Training data sets of $X_1, \ldots, X_n, \ldots, X_{96}$ were obtained from the actually measured data for 11 days and $X_1, \ldots, X_n, \ldots, X_{72}$ were obtained for one day due to malfunction of the measuring instrument. Consequently, the total of 1128 training data sets X_ns including 120 min long time series history of air-conditioner states, i.e., 24 of $x(m)$s, were obtained.

Training of the LSTM neural network was carried out as follows. First, all parameters of the LSTM model were initialized randomly. The weights of all memory units were set between -0.001 and 0.001 to be generated from a uniform distribution. Next, all memory cells were initialized as zero. After that, all X_ns were sequentially input to the LSTM neural network, and the training loss was calculated for each X_n. Then, the gradients were calculated from the training losses using the Back Propagation Through Time (BPTT) method [14] and these gradients were learned. The learning rate was optimized using the Adam method [15]. These training processes, from the initializing process of the memory unit to the loss-training process, are denoted by an epoch. In this research, the training was repeated until the number of the epochs reached 500. This number is decided by trial and error.

4.2 Evaluation on Performance of the Model

In order to evaluate the predicted performance of the model, we give the LSTM model a typical summer day dataset of August 1, 2016 of the same office building, and compare the success or failure of the maintenance forecast with actual occurrence. On this day, the operation load was high, the rotation speed of the inverter was fast and the operation time was long, so the occurrence of maintenance during the day was very high.

We evaluate the prediction performance of the LSTM model using "Accuracy" index;

$$AC = \frac{C_{TP} + C_{TN}}{C_{TP} + C_{TN} + C_{FP} + C_{FN}} \tag{4}$$

where the integers in (4), C_{TP}, C_{TN}, C_{FP} and C_{FN}, are the count numbers corresponding to each event category, TP (True Positive), TN (True Negative), FP (False Positive), and FN (False Negative), respectively. In this problem, TP is an event that the model predicted the occurrence of maintenance operation and truly it occurred. TN is an even that the model predicted the maintenance operation would not occur and truly it did not occur. FP and FN are a false prediction of occurrence and a false prediction of non-occurrence, respectively.

Using the predicted performance test data of Aug. 1, 2016, the count numbers were determined as $C_{TP} = 13$, $C_{TN} = 79$, $C_{FP} = 1$, and $C_{FN} = 3$. Consequently, the resultant values of the predicted performance index was obtained as $AC = 0.96$. Figure 3 is the line chart of the $S_O(t)$ plotted by black dots, and $\widetilde{S}_O(t)$ plotted by white dots. $S_O(t)$ represents only 1 or 0, and $\widetilde{S}_O(t)$ represents 0 to 1. The $\widetilde{F}_O(m)$ will be 1 if the $\widetilde{S}_O(t + t') \geq 0.5$ ($t' = 1, 2, \ldots, 5$), then the prediction and actual data is considered to be similar to each other.

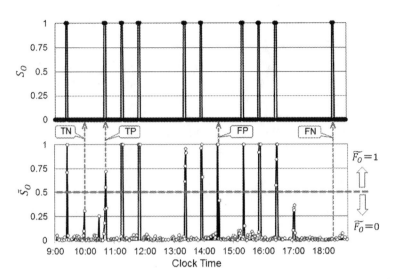

Fig. 3. Comparison between prediction and actual data of the occurrence of the maintenance operation.

5   Contribution to RTP Adaptive Control

5.1   A. Contribution Estimation Method

The maintenance operation postponement judgment shown in Sect. 2 was added to the base RTP control algorithm of the previous study [5]. That is, if the electricity unit price of the next frame is high and the occurrence of maintenance operation is forecasted when the price of the after next frame is cheap, the maintenance operation will be postponed by turn-off the air-conditioner while next frame.

The performance of this prediction model is described by improving the RTP control score. The RTP control score is calculated by the following formula J as a penalty score in consideration of a trade-off between the electricity fee by RTP control and room temperature amenity.

$$J = \alpha \sum_{m=1}^{m_{max}} R(m) \cdot W_5(m) + (1 - \alpha) \sum_{m=1}^{m_{max}} Z(m) \tag{5}$$

Here, α (from 0.0 to 1.0) is a trade-off coefficient between power consumption and comfort deterioration. $R(m)$ is the electricity unit price in frame $m \cdot W_5(m)$ is the power consumption amount for 5 min in frame m.

$$W_5(m) = \frac{1}{60} \sum_{t'=0}^{4} P(t + t') \tag{6}$$

The second term of $Z(m)$ is the comfort degradation penalty for room temperature in the frame m as defined in the previous study [5, 7] and is expressed as the square of the deviation between the set temperature and the control room temperature. We intend to extract only the difference due to the presence/absence of maintenance operation postponement judgment by the prediction model. However, when a case occurred, it cannot be reproduced the another case so that each case of the air conditioning operation cannot compare. Therefore, the RTP control evaluation score was calculated using the power consumption Air-conditioner Emulator "AE" of the air-conditioner developed in the previous research [16]. This AE model is a model statistically obtained from a large amount of measured time-series data of air-conditioners. This consists of the recurrence formula of the power consumption with respect to the power limitation command of the RTP control in 1 min and the recurrence formula of the room temperature change due to the heat balance of the building [7, 16].

5.2   Contribution Estimation Result

In this paper, an example conditions for the calculation of the RTP control evaluation score is as follows: the unit price permutation $R(m) = \{R(1), \ldots, R(6)\} = \{¥30, ¥30, ¥100, ¥100, ¥10, ¥10\}$. That is, in the RTP control time period of 30 min, it is assumed that it goes most expensive for the two middle frames ($m = 3, 4$) and becomes cheapest in the last two frames ($m = 5, 6$).

The timing of occurrence of maintenance operation is regarded as irrelevant to unit price permutation. In this example we calculated the effect of the case where an maintenance operation occurs in the last frame that switches from the most expensive to the cheapest one with the most predictable effect.

Here, the estimation calculation of the RTP control score J_{MEN} using the maintenance operation prediction model was calculated to match the performance index of the LSTM prediction model shown in the previous section. That is, the RTP performance score $J_{MEN} = 47.6$ was calculated using the occurrence rate of maintenance operations and its prediction success rate so that the performance index $AC = 0.96$ of the prediction model.

For comparison, the base RTP control score J_{BASE} without using the maintenance operation prediction model was calculated with the same estimation condition $J_{BASE} = 65.2$ pointed out in the previous section. Therefore, the contribution ratio was evaluated on the improvement rate $\Delta JRATE$ of the control score according to the following criteria.

$$\Delta J_{RATE} = \frac{J_{BASE} - J_{MEN}}{J_{BASE}} = 0.27 \tag{7}$$

That means the possible improvement of 27% will be obtained by using our LSTM prediction model as the current learning result of $AC = 0.96$.

6 Conclusion

To improve the RTP adaptive control system, we investigated a prediction model of maintenance operation for building multi-type air-conditioner. The model is implemented as a Long Short Term Memory (LSTM) neural network which was trained using 1128 time series data measured from actual air-conditioner operation. The training data is given as 24 state vectors representing the state of the air-conditioner in the past 120 min. Trained predictive models were able to predict the occurrence of maintenance operation with an accuracy of 0.96.

Calculating the RTP control goodness scores using our previous model of the power consumption and room temperature change, we showed that RTP adaptive control scores can be improved by postponing returns if the model predicts the occurrence of maintenance operations during the time frame with the most expensive power price. In result, 27% improvement in RTP control goodness score was obtained. From the above, our LSTM prediction model and postponement algorithm are effective for RTP adaptive power control.

References

1. Qian, L., Zhang, Y., Huang, J., Wu, Y.: Demand response management via real-time electricity price control in smart grids. IEEE J. Sel. Areas Commun. **31**(7), 1268–1280 (2013). https://doi.org/10.1109/JSAC.2013.130710
2. Ma, K., Hu, G., Spanos, C.: Distributed energy consumption control via real-time pricing feedback in smart grid. IEEE Trans. Control Syst. Technol. **22**(5), 1907–1914 (2014). https://doi.org/10.1109/TCST.2014.2299959
3. Kikuchi, H., Asano, H., Bando, S.: Load frequency control by commercial air-conditioners power consumption control with large penetration of renewable energy generation. IEEJ Trans. Power Energy **135**(4), 233–240 (2015). https://doi.org/10.1541/ieejpes.135.233. (in Japanese)
4. Noh, S., Yun, J., Kim, K.: An efficient building air-conditioning system control under real-time pricing. In: 2011 International Conference on Advanced Power System Automation and Protection, pp. 1283–1286 (2011). https://doi.org/10.1109/apap.2011.6180576
5. Morikawa, J., Ninagawa, C.: Fast real-time pricing optimization control of power consumption and room temperature for building multi type air-conditioning facilities. IEEJ Trans. Power Energy **136**(11), 817–823 (2016). https://doi.org/10.1541/ieejpes.136.817. (in Japanese)
6. Naramura, T., Morikawa, J., Ninagawa, C.: Prediction model on room temperature side-effect due to FastADR aggregation for a cluster of building air-conditioning facilities. IEEJ Trans. Power Energy **136**(4), 432–438 (2016). https://doi.org/10.1541/ieejpes.136.432. (in Japanese)
7. Aoki, Y., Ito, H., Ninagawa, C., Morikawa, J.: Smart grid real-time pricing optimization control with simulated annealing algorithm for office building air-conditioning facilities. In: IEEE International Conference on Industrial Technologies ICIT2018, pp. 1308–1313 (2017). https://doi.org/10.1109/icit.2018.8352367
8. Morikawa, J., Yamaguchi, T., Ninagawa, C.: Smart grid real-time pricing optimization management on power consumption of building multi-type air-conditioners. IEEJ Trans. Electr. Electron. Eng. **11**(6), 823–825 (2016). https://doi.org/10.1002/tee.22308

9. Nagata, Y., Ninagawa, C., Morikawa, J.: Prediction effect of oil-return protection operation on real-time pricing optimal control of building multi-type air-conditioning facilities. In: IEEJ Technical Meeting on Smart Facilities, SMF-17-004, pp. 19–24 (2017). https://doi.org/10.1109/tsg.2010.2055903. (in Japanese)

10. Kirkpatrick, S., Gelatt, C., Vecchi, M.: Optimization by simulated annealing. Science **220** (4598), 671–680 (1983). https://doi.org/10.1126/science.220.4598.671

11. Aarts, E., Korst, J.: Simulated Annealing and Boltzman Machines. Wiley, Chichester (1989). ISBN 0-471-92146-7

12. Hochreiter, S., Schmidhuber, J.: Long short-term memory. Neural Comput. **9**(8), 1735–1780 (1997). https://doi.org/10.1162/neco.1997.9.8.1735

13. Nakamura, A., Ninagawa, C., Morikawa, J.: Machine learning with training condition zone classification for neural network model of FastADR control of building air-conditioners.In: IEEJ Technical Meeting on Systems Technology, ST-16-047, pp. 29–34 (2016). Permalink: http://id.nii.ac.jp/1031/00093651/. (in Japanese)

14. Ismail, S., bin Ahmad, A.M.: Recurrent neural network with backpropagation through time algorithm for arabic recognition. In: Proceedings 18th European Simulation Multiconference 2004, Germany (2004). https://doi.org/10.1109/iscit.2004.1412458

15. Kingma, D.P., Ba, J.: Adam: a method for stochastic optimization. In: A Conference Paper at the 3rd International Conference for Learning Representations, San Diego (2015). arXiv: 1412.6980

16. Ito, H., Ninagawa, C., Morikawa, J.: Fast real-time pricing optimization control with dynamic prediction model for office building facilities. In: IEEJ Technical Meeting on Smart Facilities, SMF-16-049, pp. 79–84 (2016). Permalink: http://id.nii.ac.jp/1031/00093651/. (in Japanese)

Dynamic Ensemble Using Previous and Predicted Future Performance for Multi-step-ahead Solar Power Forecasting

Irena Koprinska[1](✉), Mashud Rana[2], and Ashfaqur Rahman[3]

[1] School of Computer Science, University of Sydney, Sydney, Australia
irena.koprinska@sydney.edu.au
[2] Data61, CSIRO, Eveleigh, Australia
mdmashud.rana@data61.csiro.au
[3] Data61, CSIRO, Sandy Bay, Australia
ashfaqur.rahman@data61.csiro.au

Abstract. We consider the task of predicting the solar power generated by a photovoltaic system, for multiple steps ahead, from previous solar power data. We propose DEN-PF, a dynamic heterogeneous ensemble of prediction models, which weights the individual predictions by considering two components – the ensemble member's error on recent data and its predicted error for the new time points. We compare the performance of DEN-PF with dynamic ensembles using only one of these components, a static ensemble, the single models comprising the ensemble and a baseline. The evaluation is conducted on data for two years, sampled every 5 min, for prediction horizons from 5 to 180 min ahead, under three prediction strategies: direct, iterative and direct-ds, which uses downsampling. The results show the effectiveness of DEN-PF and the benefit of considering both error components for the direct and direct-ds strategies. The most accurate prediction model was DEN-PF using the direct-ds strategy.

Keywords: Solar power · Dynamic ensembles · Neural networks · Meta-learning

1 Introduction

Solar energy is renewable, abundant and environmentally friendly. Solar energy produced by PhotoVoltaic (PV) panels is especially promising and its use is rapidly growing due to the reduced cost of PV panels and their improved efficiency. By 2020, the global solar capacity is expected to reach 700 GW, an increase of about 140 times compared to 2005 [1]. Compared to the traditional energy sources such as coal and oil, solar is more variable as it depends on the sunlight and other meteorological factors. This makes the large-scale integration of solar power into the power grid and electricity markets more challenging and motivates the need for accurate solar power forecasting.

In this paper we consider univariate, multi-step-ahead solar power forecasting. Specifically, given a time series of solar power outputs till time t, sampled every 5-min: $P_1, P_2, \ldots, P_t$, our goal is to forecast the next n values $P_{t+1}, P_{t+2}, \ldots, P_{t+n}$, for $n = 1$ to 36. While the solar power depends on weather conditions, this information is not

© Springer Nature Switzerland AG 2019
I. V. Tetko et al. (Eds.): ICANN 2019, LNCS 11730, pp. 436–449, 2019.
https://doi.org/10.1007/978-3-030-30490-4_35

always available for the location of the PV panels. On the other hand, historical PV power data with high frequency is easily available and recent studies [2–5] have shown promising prediction results using only previous PV data.

Different approaches for PV power forecasting have been proposed, e.g. using statistical methods such as Linear Regression (LR) and autoregressive moving average [2, 6, 7] or machine learning methods such as Neural Networks (NNs) [7–10], Support Vector Regression (SVR) [11, 12], k-Nearest Neighbors [2, 7, 8] and pattern sequence similarity [13]. While most of the previous work on time series forecasting has focused on using single prediction models, ensembles combining the predictions of several models, have also been investigated and shown to improve the accuracy [5, 14–16].

Ensembles for time series forecasting can be classified into static and dynamic. Static ensembles combine the predictions of the ensemble members in the same way for all new time points, regardless of the changes in the time series. Static ensembles for solar power forecasting have been proposed in [17, 18], demonstrating promising results. In contrast, dynamic ensembles calculate a separate prediction for each time point, by adapting the combination of ensemble members to the new time point and the changes in the time series. For example, this can be done by tracking the error on recent data and weighting the contribution of the ensemble members accordingly. Dynamic ensembles of NNs for solar power forecasting based on past errors [4] and predicted future errors [5] have been recently proposed showing competitive results. In this paper, we propose a dynamic ensemble that uses *both* the past errors and predicted future errors to determine the contribution of the ensemble members for the new time point. It also combines the predictions of different types of prediction models, not only NNs, to encourage diversity and complementary expertise by creating a heterogeneous ensemble.

Another difference with previous research is that we consider multi-step-ahead prediction (from 1 to 36 steps ahead) instead of single-step, and evaluate the proposed dynamic ensemble and the methods used for comparison under three different prediction strategies: direct, iterative and the recently proposed direct with downsampling (direct-ds) [19]. Our contribution can be summarized as follows:

- We propose DEN-PF, a new dynamic ensemble method for time series prediction, which weights the predictions of the ensemble members based on two components - the ensemble member's: (1) actual error on previous recent data, and (2) predicted error for the new time step. In our specific implementation DEN-PF is a heterogeneous ensemble, combining the predictions of LR, NN, SVR and Random Forest (RF).
- We compare the performance of DEN-PF with: (i) two dynamic ensemble versions which use only one of the two components, (ii) a static ensemble, (ii) the single models comprising the ensemble and (iv) a persistence baseline. The evaluation is done using 5-min Australian PV data for two years. Our results show the effectiveness of DEN-PF and the ability of dynamic ensembles using both past and predicted future errors to generate accurate forecasts.
- We evaluate the performance of DEN-PF and the other methods for multi-step-ahead prediction, from 1 to 36 steps ahead, using three prediction strategies: direct, iterative and the recently proposed direct-ds. Our results show that direct-ds was the most accurate strategy for all prediction methods, with DEN-PF using direct-ds obtaining the highest accuracy. We also analyse how the predictive performance changes as the forecasting horizon increases.

2 Dynamic Ensembles

Static ensembles combine the predictions of the individual ensemble members in the same pre-determined way for all time steps, without adapting the combination to the changes in the time series. For example, a static ensemble may always take the average of all individual predictions. In contrast, a dynamic ensemble adaptively weights the individual predictions for each new time step based a performance criterion. For example, higher weights can be assigned to ensemble members that were more accurate in the previous time steps.

The motivation behind using dynamic ensembles is that the different ensemble members have different areas of expertise and as the time series changes over time, some of them will be more accurate. By using a suitable criterion, e.g. tracking the error on recent data, we can select the most appropriate ensemble member or weighted combination of ensemble members for the new time step. Hence, dynamic ensembles try to match the expertise of the ensemble members to the characteristics of the new time points and the changes in the time series.

We consider three types of dynamic ensembles - based on: previous performance, expected future performance, and both previous and expected future performance. We denote them with DEN-P, DEN-F and DEN-PF, where DEN stands for Dynamic ENsemble, P for Previous performance and F for expected Future performance.

2.1 DEN-P - Dynamic Ensemble Based on Previous Performance

This ensemble method assumes that past performance on recent time lags is an indicator of the future performance. Figure 1 illustrates this method.

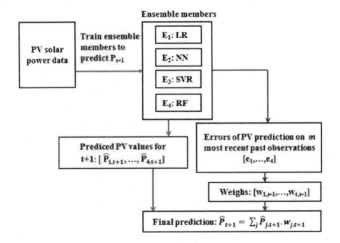

Fig. 1. Dynamic ensemble DEN-P

To predict a new time $t + 1$, each ensemble member E_i is assigned a weight $w_{j,t+1}$ calculated based on its most recent performance, i.e. its performance during the last D days. Higher weights are assigned to the more accurate ensemble members and lower to the less accurate ones. Thus, the weights of the ensemble members for time $t + 1$ depend on their performance on the previous m observations which makes the ensemble dynamic. We used $m = 360$ past observations ($D = 3$ days of past observations).

To calculate the weights, we apply the following strategy: the weight of an ensemble member E_i decreases exponentially as its error increases. Specifically, the weight of E_i for predicting time point $t + 1$ is calculated as a softmax function of the negative of its error e_i : $w_{i,t+1} = \frac{exp(-e_i)}{\sum_{j=1}^{S} exp(-e_j)}$, where e_i is the average MAE of E_i in the last m observations and j is over all S ensemble members. The weights $w_{i,t+1}$ sum to 1.

The final prediction of the dynamic ensemble is calculated by the weighted average of the predictions of the individual ensemble members: $\widehat{P}_{t+1} = \sum_{j=1}^{S} \widehat{P}_{j,t+1} \cdot w_{j,t+1}$.

2.2   DEN-F - Dynamic Ensemble Based on Predicted Future Performance

The main idea of DEN-F is to predict the error of the ensemble members for the new time points and use this predicted error to calculate the weights of the ensemble members in the final prediction. Ensemble members that are predicted to be more accurate will be assigned higher weights. In this way we again match the expertise of the ensemble members with the characteristics of the new time points, but take a more proactive approach, compared to DEN-P – instead of using previous performance, we use predicted future performance.

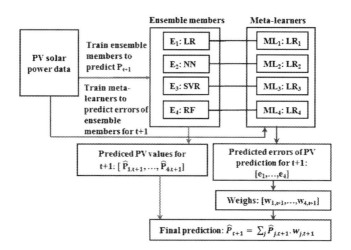

Fig. 2. Dynamic ensemble DEN-F

To predict the error of each ensemble member for the new time point, we utilized a meta-learning approach [5, 16]. As shown in Fig. 2, every ensemble member E_i has an associated meta-learner ML_i, which is trained to predict the error of E_i for the new time point. ML_i, takes as an input previous solar data from the forecasting window w (according to the prediction strategy) and predicts the error of E_i for time point $t + 1$. This error is then converted into a weight for E_i and used in the weighted average to combine the predictions of all ensemble members. Thus, E_i and ML_i take input data in the same format but predict different values - E_i predicts the solar power for $t + 1$, while ML_i predicts the error of E_i for this prediction.

To train a meta-learner ML_i for ensemble member E_i, we firstly need to create the training data for it. The key step is to obtain the target output. Using the trained ensemble member E_i, we obtain its prediction for all examples from the training set. The input and output depend on the prediction strategy and prediction step. For example, for the direct strategy (see Sect. 4.1), for 1-step-ahead prediction, the input consists of the previous w lags $P_{t-w+1}, \ldots, P_t$ and the output is the next lag P_{t+1}. We then calculate the error of this prediction, MAE_{t+1}. A training example for ML_i for 1-step-ahead prediction using the direct prediction strategy, will have the form: $([P_{t-w+1}, \ldots, P_t], MAE_{t+1})$, where the first component is the input vector and MAE_{t+1} is the target output.

As meta-learners we employed LR prediction models – they are easy to develop, accurate and fast to train. We also evaluated more complex models (RF) but there was no improvement in accuracy, so we chose LR. The weights of the ensemble members and the final prediction were calculated using the same methods as in DEN-P.

2.3 DEN-PF - Dynamic Ensemble Based on Both Previous and Predicted Future Performance

This ensemble method is a combination of the previous two. The key idea is to use both the previous performance on recent time lags and the predicted future performance for the new time lag to determine the weights of the ensemble members for the new time lag. The assumption is that both error components are important, and our hypothesis is that their combined use can improve the accuracy compared to using only one of them.

For each ensemble member, the weights for the two error components are calculated separately as in DEN-P and DEN-F, and then summed together. The new combined weights are then normalised over all ensemble members, so that they sum to 1. The final prediction is again the weighted average of the individual predictions.

2.4 Ensemble Members

Effective ensembles include diverse ensemble members. To introduce diversity we created a heterogeneous ensemble which combines four different types of prediction models representing different machine learning paradigms: LR, NN, SVR and RF. Heterogeneous ensembles have been shown to perform well in various applications [14, 16] by providing natural diversity and complementarity. The first three algorithms are also widely used in solar power forecasting, demonstrating good performance.

All prediction models were implemented in Python 3.5 using the *scikit-learn* library. For the direct and direct-ds prediction strategies, a separate prediction model is built for each step of the forecasting horizon, while for the iterative strategy, a single model is built. For parameter tuning, we used grid search with 10-fold cross validation on the data for the first year; the best model was selected and then evaluated on the data for the second year. Below we provide more details for the parameters included in the grid search and the final set of selected parameters for each model.

NN. The models were built using *MLPRegressor* with 1 hidden layer. The following parameters were used with the grid search: number of hidden neurons: from 2 to 30, activation function for the hidden layer: tanh, solver (weight optimization algorithm) = lbfgs, regularization parameter alpha = [0, 0.01, 0.1, 0.5], maximum number of epochs: 2000, with early stopping. The best models for each step (selected for evaluation on the test set) had different number of hidden neurons but alpha most often was 0.01 or 0.1.

SVR. The models were built using *epsilon-SVR*. The parameters used for the grid search: kernel: [linear, poly, rbf], C (penalty parameter of the error term) = [0.1, 0.5, 1], degree of the polynomial kernel: from 2 to 5, gamma (kernel coefficient for rbf and poly) = [0.001, 0.01, 0.1] and epsilon = [0.01, 0.01, 0.1, 0.2, 1]. For most of the prediction steps, SVR with the following parameters provided the highest accuracy and was chosen for evaluation on the testing set: C = 1, kernel = linear, epsilon = 0.1, gamma = 0.01.

RF. The models were built using *RandomForestRegressor*. The following parameters were used for the grid search: n_estimators (number of trees) = [10, 50, 100, 500, 1000, 1500, 2000], min_samples_split (minimum number of samples required to split an internal node) = [2, 5, 10, 20], min_samples_leaf (minimum number of samples required to be at a leaf node) = [1, 5, 10]. For most of the prediction steps, RF with n_estimators = 500, min_samples_split = 2 and min_samples_leaf = 1 provided the highest accuracy and was selected for evaluation on the testing set.

LR. The LR prediction models were built using *LinearRegression* and there were no tunable parameters.

3 Prediction Methods Used for Comparison

We compare the performance of the dynamic ensembles with three groups of methods: (1) a static ensemble, (2) the single prediction models comprising the ensembles (LR, NN, SVR and RF) and (3) a persistence model. Below we provide more details about (1) and (3); (2) were already described in the previous section.

Static Ensemble. The static ensemble (denoted with SEN from Static ENsemble) combines the predictions of the trained LR, NN, SVR and RF by taking the average of these predictions. Thus, it assigns equal weights to the contribution of each ensemble member. This equal weight combination is used consistently for all time lags, i.e. SEN doesn't adapt its predictions to the changes in the time series.

Persistence Model. As a baseline we developed a persistence model (Bplag) which uses the last observed value of the solar power output as the predicted value for all steps of the forecasting horizon, i.e. the predictions for all 36 values $P_{t+1}...P_{t+36}$ will be P_t.

4 Multi-step-ahead Prediction Strategies

All models output a single predicted value. To generate multi-step-ahead prediction for the next n future values, we consider three prediction strategies: *direct*, *iterative* and *direct-ds* which uses downsampling. The first two are commonly used, while the last one is a novel strategy recently proposed in [19].

4.1 Prediction Strategy *Direct*

To generate n-step-ahead predictions, the *direct* strategy builds n prediction models, one for each time steps. As shown in Fig. 3, each of the n models, uses the same previous data points as an input (a fixed window w of past observations, $w = 3$ in Fig. 3), while the output is different and corresponds to a different future time step.

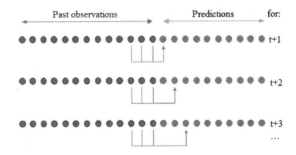

Fig. 3. Prediction strategy *direct*

4.2 Prediction Strategy *Iterative*

The *iterative* strategy develops only one forecasting model that is trained for 1-step-ahead prediction. As shown in Fig. 4, at time t, it makes prediction for time $t + 1$, and this prediction is then used to make the prediction for time t + 2 and so on. This means that the predicted data for time $t + 1$ is considered as actual data and appended to the end of the available data. The last w samples from the appended data are used to make a prediction for time $t + 2$, and this continues for all n time steps in the forecasting horizon. The main limitation of this approach is that the prediction errors in the previous steps are accumulated into the subsequent steps.

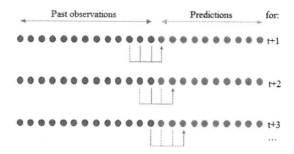

Fig. 4. Prediction strategy *iterative*

4.3   Prediction Strategy *Direct-DS*

This is a recently proposed variation of the direct strategy [19], illustrated in Fig. 5. It uses 1-step-ahead prediction on a set of sampled time-series generated from the original one. As shown in Fig. 5, for 1-step-ahead prediction, it uses the previous w values of the original time series: $P_{t-w+1}, \ldots, P_{t-2}, P_{t-1}, P_t$. However, for each of the n subsequent prediction steps, a new time series $P_{n,new}$ is created by downsampling the original time series. The downsampling process chooses every n sample from the original time series starting from t backward to construct the new time series of w observations.

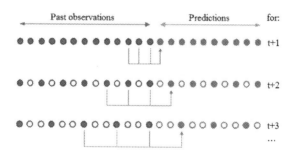

Fig. 5. Prediction strategy *direct-ds*

For example, for the second step ($n = 2$) the new time series is constructed by selecting every second observation: $P_{2,new} = P_{t-(w*n)+n}, \ldots, P_{t-4}, P_{t-2}, P_t$ and for the third step ($n = 3$) by selecting every third observation: $P_{3,new} = P_{t-(w*n)+n}, \ldots, P_{t-6}, P_{t-3}, P_t$. A forecasting model is then trained using the last w samples to make a 1-step-ahead prediction on the new time series $P_{n,new}$.

The motivation behind this strategy is that 1-step-ahead prediction on 1-step predictors (sampled time series) naturally incurs less error. Thus, our assumption is that the set of sampled time series, each using a different sampling rate but consisting of values that are 1-step apart, when combined with a 1-step-ahead prediction strategy, will capture better the pattern in the time series, compared to using the same w previous observations to make multi-step-ahead prediction as in the direct strategy.

5   Data and Experimental Setup

Data. We used solar power data for two years, from 1/1/2015 to 31/12/2016, collected from a rooftop PV plant located at the University of Queensland in Brisbane, Australia. For each day, we only selected data for 10 h during the daylight period between 7am and 5pm. The data is available from http://www.uq.edu.au/solarenergy/.

The original PV power data is measured at 1-min intervals and available for four buildings separately. We aggregated the data from all buildings together and changed the resolution from 1-min to 5-min by computing the average of the 5-min intervals. The data was also normalized to the range of [0, 1]. Hence, the dataset contains 2 years × 365 days × 120 5-min measurements = 87,600 data points.

Data Sets. The full dataset was divided into two subsets: training and validation (2015 data) and testing (2016 data). The first set was used to build the prediction models; the model parameters were tuned using grid search with 10-fold cross validation. The testing set was used to evaluate the accuracy of the prediction models.

Evaluation Measures. We use two standard performance measures: Mean Absolute Error (MAE) and Mean Relative Error (MRE): $\text{MAE} = \frac{1}{N} \sum_{i=1}^{N} \left| P^i - \widehat{P}^i \right|$, $\text{MRE} = \frac{1}{N \times R} \sum_{i=1}^{N} \left| P^i - \widehat{P}^i \right|$ (in %), where P^i and $\widehat{P}^i$ are the actual and predicted solar power values for the i-sample, N is the number of samples and R is the range of the target variable.

Task. Given the previous $w = 6$ lags of the time series P, we predict the next $n = 36$ lags. We experimented with extending w to 12 lags but this was not beneficial.

6   Results and Discussion

The following research questions guide our analysis:

Q1: How does the accuracy of the dynamic ensemble DEN-PF compare with DEN-P and DEN-F? In other words, is it beneficial to weight the contribution of the ensemble members by considering two components – the error on past time lags and the predicted error for the new time lag, compared to only either of them?

Q2: How does the performance of DEN-PF compare with the static ensemble, the single models comprising the ensemble and the baseline?

Q3: Which prediction strategy (direct-ds direct, direct or iterative) is the most accurate for multi-step-ahead prediction? How does the accuracy changes as the forecasting horizon increases?

Q1: Comparison of Dynamic Ensembles: DEN-PF vs DEN-P and DEN-F

Table 1 shows the accuracy results of all forecasting methods, for the three prediction strategies separately. To compare the performance of the dynamic ensembles, Fig. 6 presents the MAE results in sorted order, for each of the three prediction strategies (direct-ds, direct and iterative). The MRE results follow a similar trend as

MAE and are not shown in this and the subsequent figures. We can summarize the results as follows:

- *Overall best model:* DEN-PF using the direct-ds prediction strategy is the most accurate prediction model, achieving MAE = 110.03 kW and MRE = 10.48%.
- *Best dynamic ensemble:* DEN-PF is the most accurate dynamic ensemble for two of the prediction strategies: direct-ds and direct, and it is the second best model for the third strategy (iterative), after DEN-P. We note that iterative is the least accurate strategy due to accumulation of prediction error as discussed in Q3.
- *Comparison:* A detailed examination of the results shows that DEN-PF was better than DEN-P and DEN-F for all 36 points of the forecasting horizon for direct-ds and direct. For the iterative prediction, DEN-PF was the best method until step 12 (1/3 of the forecasting horizon) and after that DEN-P was more accurate. This can be explained with the accumulation of prediction error in the iterative strategy - DEN-P is less susceptible as it accumulates less error (e.g. it doesn't use predicted data to predict errors of ensemble members).

DEN-P is more accurate than DEN-F for all three prediction strategies, for all time points of the forecasting horizon. This shows that using actual previous performance than predicted future performance is more beneficial for our scenario. It is worthwhile exploring how this behaviour is affected by the size of w and n.

In summary, the results show that for the two direct prediction strategies (which were the most accurate) it was beneficial to consider both components in the dynamic ensemble

Table 1. Accuracy of all models (average over all steps) for the three prediction strategies

Method	direct-ds		direct		iterative	
	MAE [kW]	MRE [%]	MAE [kW]	MRE [%]	MAE [kW]	MRE [%]
DEN-PF	110.03	10.48	125.29	11.93	146.32	13.93
DEN-P	111.00	10.94	126.65	12.06	144.65	13.77
DEN-F	114.88	10.94	133.98	12.76	147.02	14.00
SEN	118.53	11.29	139.90	13.32	147.20	14.02
LR	126.21	12.02	151.27	14.40	152.26	14.50
NN	126.32	12.03	143.85	13.70	155.05	14.76
SVR	121.52	11.57	150.15	14.30	157.86	15.03
RF	110.46	10.52	124.66	11.87	167.08	15.91
Bplag	167.91	15.99	167.91	15.99	167.91	15.99

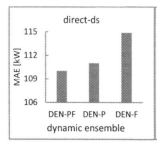
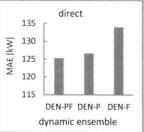
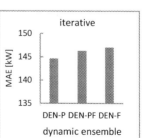

Fig. 6. Comparison of the dynamic ensembles for the three prediction strategies

- the error on previous time lags and the predicted error for the new time lag, when determining the contribution of the ensemble members, compared to only either of them.

Q2: Comparison of DEN-PF with Static Ensemble, Single Models and Baseline

Figure 7 compares the MAE results of the dynamic ensemble DEN-PF with the static ensemble (SEN), the models comprising the ensemble (LR, NN, SVR and RF) and the baseline (Blag), for the three prediction strategies. We can see that DEN-PF was the most accurate method for two of the prediction strategies (direct-ds and iterative), while RF was the best method for the direct strategy. For direct-ds and direct, DEN-PF performed similarly to RF and for iterative - similarly to SEN.

Q3: Comparison of Prediction Strategies: Direct-DS, Direct and Iterative

Figure 8 compares the overall performance of the three prediction strategies (MAE, averaged over all prediction steps), for all models. We can observe a consistent trend across all prediction models - the most successful prediction strategy is direct-ds, followed by direct and iterative. Note that the baseline Bplag doesn't depend on the prediction strategy and its accuracy is the same for all three strategies.

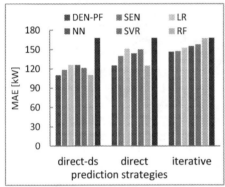
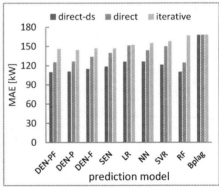

Fig. 7. Comparison of the dynamic ensemble DEN-PF with the static ensemble, single models and baseline (MAE)

Fig. 8. Comparison of the three prediction strategies for all prediction models (average MAE over all time steps)

To further understand the differences between the three strategies, we examined the evolution of the error for all steps in the forecasting horizon. Figure 9 shows some representative MAE graphs – for DEN-PF (representative of the dynamic ensembles), the static ensemble SEN, and the single models NN and SVR; LR and RF are similar to SVR and are not shown due to space limitation. We can make the following observations, which are consistent across all prediction methods.

As expected, the error of all three strategies increases with the increase in forecasting steps. Until step 11–13, all three strategies perform similarly. After that, the error of the incremental and direct strategies continues to increase at a similar rate. This increase is bigger for the incremental strategy due to the accumulation of error from the

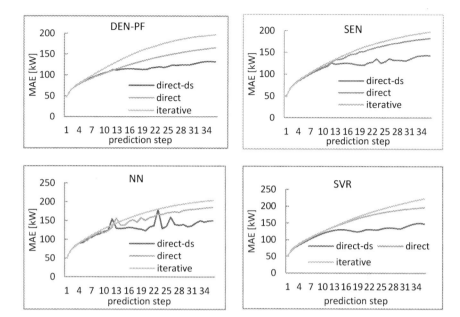

Fig. 9. Comparison of the prediction strategies - MAE for all steps of the forecasting horizon

predictions in the previous step. For the direct-ds strategy, the increase in error is much smaller and the difference with the other two strategies becomes more prominent as the forecasting step increases. This confirms that using 1-step prediction on 1-step predictors (sampled time series) incurs less error and is thus a promising strategy.

The performance of all prediction models except NN is stable. NN shows some error oscillations, e.g. at steps 11, 13 and 23, which deserve further investigation.

7   Conclusion

In this paper we considered univariate, multi-step-ahead prediction of PV solar power output. We proposed DEN-PF, a dynamic ensemble of prediction models which adapts the combination of ensemble members to the new time points and changes in the time series. It weights the individual predictions by considering two components – the ensemble member's error on previous data and its predicted error for the new time step.

We evaluated DEN-PF's performance under three prediction strategies – direct, iterative and the recently proposed direct-ds which uses downsampling, on 5-min Australian PV data for two years, for prediction horizons from 1 to 36 steps ahead. We compared DEN-PF with dynamic ensembles using only one of the error components, a static ensemble, the single models comprising the ensemble and a persistence baseline.

Our results showed that the direct-ds was the most accurate strategy, followed by the direct and iterative, for all prediction models. We believe that this is because it uses a combination of 1-step predictors (sampled time series) and 1-step prediction strategy. This captures better the pattern in the time series compared to the direct strategy (which uses the same input to make multi-step predictions) and the iterative strategy which accumulates the errors of the previous predictions. We found that DEN-PF was the most accurate dynamic ensemble for the direct-ds and direct strategies, demonstrating the benefit of using both error components for weighting the individual predictions. Overall, the most accurate prediction model was DEN-PF using the direct-ds strategy.

In future work, we plan to investigate: (i) if the addition of weather data can improve the results, (ii) how the performance varies for days with different weather type, e.g. consistently sunny vs others, (iii) the performance of DEN-PF for larger forecasting horizons, (iv) other methods for combining the two error components, and (v) applications of DEN-PF to other tasks such as electricity demand and wind power prediction.

References

1. Solar Power Europe: Global Market Outlook For Solar Power/2016–2020 (2016)
2. Pedro, H.T.C., Coimbra, C.F.M.: Assessment of forecasting techniques for solar power production with no exogenous inputs. Sol. Energy **86**, 2017–2028 (2012)
3. Rana, M., Koprinska, I., Agelidis, V.: Univariate and multivariate methods for very short-term solar photovoltaic power forecasting. Energy Convers. Manag. **121**, 380–390 (2016)
4. Wang, Z., Koprinska, I., Troncoso, A., Martinez-Alvarez, F.: Static and dynamic ensembles of neural networks for solar power forecasting. In: International Joint Conference on Neural Networks (IJCNN), pp. 528–537. IEEE (2018)
5. Wang, Z., Koprinska, I.: Solar power forecasting using dynamic meta-learning ensemble of neural networks. In: Kůrková, V., Manolopoulos, Y., Hammer, B., Iliadis, L., Maglogiannis, I. (eds.) ICANN 2018. LNCS, vol. 11139, pp. 528–537. Springer, Cham (2018). https://doi. org/10.1007/978-3-030-01418-6_52
6. Bacher, P., Madsen, H., Nielsen, H.A.: Online short-term solar power forecasting. Sol. Energy **83**, 1772–1783 (2009)
7. Chu, Y., Urquhart, B., Gohari, S.M.I., Pedro, H.T.C., Kleissl, J., Coimbra, C.F.M.: Short-term reforecasting of power output from a 48 MWe solar PV plant. Sol. Energy **112**, 68–77 (2015)
8. Long, H., Zhang, Z., Su, Y.: Analysis of daily solar power prediction with data-driven approaches. Appl. Energy **128**, 29–37 (2014)
9. Chen, C., Duan, S., Cai, T., Liu, B.: Online 24-h solar power forecasting based on weather type classification using artificial neural networks. Sol. Energy **85**, 2856–2870 (2011)
10. Chow, S.K., Lee, E.W., Li, D.H.: Short-term prediction of photovoltaic energy generation by intelligent approach. Energy Build. **55**, 660–667 (2012)
11. Rana, M., Koprinska, I., Agelidis, V.G.: 2D-interval forecasts for solar power production. Sol. Energy **122**, 191–203 (2015)
12. Shi, J., Lee, W.-J., Lin, Y., Yang, Y., Wang, P.: Forecasting power output of photovoltaic systems based on weather classification and support vector machines. IEEE Trans. Ind. Appl. **48**, 1064–1069 (2012)
13. Wang, Z., Koprinska, I., Rana, M.: solar power forecasting using pattern sequences. In: Lintas, A., Rovetta, S., Verschure, Paul F.M.J., Villa, Alessandro E.P. (eds.) ICANN 2017. LNCS, vol. 10614, pp. 486–494. Springer, Cham (2017). https://doi.org/10.1007/978-3-319-68612-7_55

14. Oliveira, M., Torgo, L.: Ensembles for time series forecasting. In: Sixth Asian Conference on Machine Learning, pp. 360–370 (2014)
15. Koprinska, I., Rana, M., Troncoso, A., Martínez-Álvarez, F.: Combining pattern sequence similarity with neural networks for forecasting electricity demand time series. In: International Joint Conference on Neural Networks (IJCNN). IEEE (2013)
16. Cerqueira, V., Torgo, L., Pinto, F., Soares, C.: Arbitrated ensemble for time series forecasting. In: Ceci, M., Hollmén, J., Todorovski, L., Vens, C., Džeroski, S. (eds.) ECML PKDD 2017. LNCS (LNAI), vol. 10535, pp. 478–494. Springer, Cham (2017). https://doi.org/10.1007/978-3-319-71246-8_29
17. Rana, M., Koprinska, I., Agelidis, V.G.: Forecasting solar power generated by grid connected PV systems using ensembles of neural networks. In: International Joint Conference on Neural Networks (IJCNN). IEEE (2015)
18. Rana, M., Koprinska, I., Agelidis, V.G.: Solar power forecasting using weather type clustering and ensembles of neural networks. In: International Joint Conference on Neural Networks (IJCNN). IEEE (2016)
19. Rana, M., Rahman, A.: Multiple steps ahead solar photovoltaic power prediction based on machine learning and data re-sampling, under review (2019)

Timage – A Robust Time Series Classification Pipeline

Marc Wenninger[1(✉)], Sebastian P. Bayerl[2(✉)] [iD], Jochen Schmidt[1] [iD],
and Korbinian Riedhammer[2] [iD]

[1] Department of Computer Science, Rosenheim Technical University
of Applied Sciences, Rosenheim, Germany
{marc.wenninger,jochen.schmidt}@th-rosenheim.de
[2] Department of Computer Science, Technische Hochschule Nürnberg
Georg Simon Ohm, Nuremberg, Germany
{sebastian.bayerl,korbinian.riedhammer}@th-nuernberg.de

Abstract. Time series are series of values ordered by time. This kind of
data can be found in many real world settings. Classifying time series is
a difficult task and an active area of research. This paper investigates the
use of transfer learning in Deep Neural Networks and a 2D representation
of time series known as Recurrence Plots. In order to utilize the research
done in the area of image classification, where Deep Neural Networks
have achieved very good results, we use a Residual Neural Networks
architecture known as ResNet. As preprocessing of time series is a major
part of every time series classification pipeline, the method proposed
simplifies this step and requires only few parameters. For the first time
we propose a method for multi time series classification: Training a single
network to classify all datasets in the archive with one network. We are
among the first to evaluate the method on the latest 2018 release of the
UCR archive, a well established time series classification benchmarking
dataset.

Keywords: Deep Neural Networks · Transfer learning ·
Time series classification

1 Introduction

Time series are N-dimensional signals ordered by time resulting in $N+1$ dimensions, hence all real world data recorded over time are a time series. The sequence
of data points allows one to identify higher features based on the combination
of multiple data points in respect to the order. All time series classification
approaches try to identify these higher features to separate the classes based on
them. Time series classification is a hard problem that is not yet fully understood and numerous attempts have been made in the past to create generic and
domain specific classification methods. Because of the diverse domains where
time series are present, the research and methods are diverse as well. Many proposed methods for time series classification are actually classification pipelines:
Multi-stage processes combining preprocessing steps and the actual classification

© Springer Nature Switzerland AG 2019
I. V. Tetko et al. (Eds.): ICANN 2019, LNCS 11730, pp. 450–461, 2019.
https://doi.org/10.1007/978-3-030-30490-4_36

method that separates the classes. Preprocessing is used to provide more easily separable features, e.g., by reducing dimensionality, identifying regions of interest, or simply reducing length, always with the goal to support the classification algorithm.

During preprocessing, domain specific knowledge plays a vital role, as domain knowledge allows for identifying and removing noisy features and boost class-unique features by transferring knowledge from related research. A generic classification pipeline needs to overcome the lack of domain knowledge. The authors of the UCR data set came to the conclusion that most probably there will never be one classification pipeline that rules them all, but every pipeline will have its advantages and disadvantages in the specific domain [3]. The reason for this lies within the differences of where higher features are located in the data. The importance of adaptable feature extraction is underlined by the success of classification pipelines that focus on feature extraction such as Weasel (Word ExtrAction for time SEriescLassification) [18] and BOSS (Bag-of-SFA-Symbols) [17], which are able to adapt the feature extraction to different domains. These methods preprocess the time series by encoding sliding windows into strings based on a similarity measure, followed by a classification using 1-nearest-neighbor. A nearly preprocess-less classification pipeline was proposed by [13] using a Convolutional Neural Network (CNN) with a Long Short-Term Memory (LSTM) path. [8] proposes a pipeline where time series are encoded as Recurrence Plot (RP) images, which are then classified using a CNN. Encoding the time series of a 1D signal into a 2D image introduces new texture features, that allows one to utilize research efforts from image classification on time series classification. RP in combination with a nearest neighbor classifier are used by [15]. The encoding of time series into images has also been used for sound classification, but instead of only using RP, [16] also evaluated the use of spectrogram images in combination with a CNN architecture that takes both image representations as the network input. [4] evaluate the use of Spectrogram, Mel-Frequency Cepstral Coefficients (MFCC), and RP for the classification of environmental sound recordings using the AlexNet and GoogLeNet image recognition networks. [10] presented results of an extensive experiment on feeding time series directly into 9 different well known neural network architectures such as MLP, FCN and ResNet. Their research shows that ResNet outperforms the others on the UCR archive. The same author also showed that CNNs can benefit from transfer learning by reusing network weights [11].

Our contribution is a robust time series classification pipeline using transfer learning on ResNet with RP called *timage*. The ResNet network architecture is kept unchanged apart from adapting the input and output size of the network to fit the dataset. As a starting point for transfer learning we reuse the network weights from the ImageNet challenge [9] and further experimented with different strategies to obtain better weights. We present a Single Classifier (SC) for each dataset in the UCR archive as done by all published models and are among the first to evaluate our method on the latest 2018 UCR release. For the first time we present an All Classifier (AC), a single classification model trained on all datasets in the archive at once.

2   Method

2.1   Approach

The main idea of this paper is to use existing knowledge in the form of pretrained image recognition networks to classify time series. In order to take advantage of these neural networks that were trained on huge amounts of image data, time series must be converted to images. This can be achieved by representations used for qualitative analysis like Recurrence Plots (RP), Spectrograms, Gramian Angular Summation/Difference Fields (GASF/GADF), and Markov Transition Fields (MTF) [2,14,19]. For our experiments we focus on RP for time series representation as proposed in [15,16].

Transfer Learning. One of the main concepts exploited in this paper is called transfer learning. The general assumption behind it is that something learned for one problem can be used to improve generalization for another problem. It is assumed that many factors which explain variations in the first problem are also relevant for a similar problem. Simply speaking, knowledge created by solving the first problem is used and applied to solve another problem [7]. This is especially useful when only a small amount of training data is available. In the case of the UCR archive, this means that even the sets with only very little training samples can be properly learned by a neural network which usually needs huge amounts of training data to converge.

As we wanted to explore the concept of transfer learning even further, we tried different strategies to obtain new weights. The first approach was ultimately the most successful one using the original weights obtained by training the networks on the ImageNet dataset and then use these weights for our networks. A second method to obtain better weights for transfer learning was to train an AC system and then use these weights in training SC systems. Another approach was training an AC not to separate all different classes but to separate datasets. For this, the UCR archive data was relabeled to only have one label per dataset. This means the network is trained to separate the datasets and not the classes within each dataset. This approach in itself worked reasonably well but using these weighs for training AC or SC systems did not improve overall accuracy. An interesting observation that could be made was that AC and SC systems trained on weights obtained by training with the RPs converged faster than systems using the original ResNet weights.

Recurrence Plots. The motivation for RP is that recurrence is a property of many natural and real world systems. Situations or states that have been observed once are often followed by similar states. RP can be used to visualize these recurrences [14]. RP plot the recurrence matrix that is formally defined by Eq. (1), where N is the number of measured points x_i, ϵ a threshold and Θ the Heaviside or step function where $\Theta(x) = 0$ if $x \leq 0$ and $\Theta(x) = 1$ otherwise. A proper distance measure has to be chosen for $||.||$, such as Euclidean distance or cosine distance.

$$R_{i,j}(\epsilon) = \Theta(\epsilon - ||\boldsymbol{x}_i - \boldsymbol{x}_j||), i, j = 1, ..., N \tag{1}$$

For states that are in an ϵ-neighborhood, the notion in (2) can be used:

$$\boldsymbol{x}_i \approx \boldsymbol{x}_j \iff R_{i,j} \equiv 1 \tag{2}$$

The RP is then generated by binarizing the recurrence matrix using a threshold [14]. These plots are particularly useful to humans in qualitative assessment because patterns can be quickly identified visually. For the use in image classification, more data in the form of more discriminable values in between might be desirable. This is the main reason for using a modification of recurrence plots where no thresholding is performed to get more information encoded into the image. Input data usually comes in the form of feature vectors, and the pairwise distances between those are computed, which creates the distance matrix $D_{i,j}$:

$$D_{i,j} = ||\boldsymbol{x} - \boldsymbol{y}||. \tag{3}$$

These pairwise distances are then plotted. This modification of the RP is also known as *unthresholded recurrence plot* or, maybe more appropriate, *distance plots* as described in (3) [14]. We chose to use Euclidean distance for our plots. After calculating the distances we apply some normalization by using a Min-Max scaler and a threshold cut-off at three times the standard deviation of all distances in the distance matrix. (4) represents the plots used in this paper best:

$$D_{i,j} = D_{i,j}(d \leq 3\sigma) = \begin{cases} 3\sigma & d \geq 3\sigma \\ d & d < 3\sigma \end{cases}. \tag{4}$$

The resulting plots show a gray-shaded pattern opposed to classical RP that have a simple black and white pattern. Two samples taken from UCR archives Adiac dataset can be found in Fig. 1.

Compared to methods like WEASEL or BOSS, our proposed method does not put much emphasis on extracting the best hyper-parameters for each dataset. The only parameter required in its configuration is the image size. By using the unthresholded RPs we got rid of the ϵ parameter used in traditional RPs which makes configuration easier and also leads to a plot that contains more information. By using Euclidean distance by default and not trying to determine the best distance measure for each dataset we reduce configuration even more. The individual datasets in the UCR archive are treated equally and no individual adaption is performed. Within every experiment, the dataset is preprocessed in the same way, and the same resolution is used for all images in order to be as generic as possible. It is reasonable to assume that this will lead to information loss, but through this inter-class normalization we gain more easily comparable images of equal size. To compensate for the in part heavily skewed datasets, we used class weights during training.

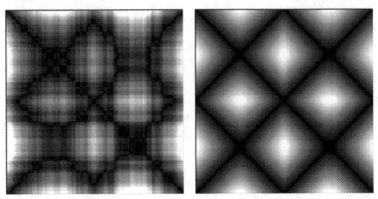

(a) Class *A* from the Adiac dataset   (b) Class *B* from the Adiac dataset

Fig. 1. Distance Plots of two classes from the Adiac dataset, where classes represent the outlines of unicellular algae taken from images.

2.2 Experimental Setup

Experiments were run on a HP Server with 1 TB of RAM, two Intel Xeon E5-2650 (28 cores @ 2.60 GHz), and NVIDIA Tesla V100 graphics cards. The server was running Ubuntu 16.04 LTS. To improve reproducibility, Docker containers were used during training. Docker encapsulates the runtime environment for the experiments. That way the environment is easy to recreate and version, as the runtime environment is simply described in structured text files.[1] All neural networks used in this paper were implemented using the Keras API with a TensorFlow back-end [1,5]. Keras also has a ready-to-go implementation of a Deep Residual Network (DSN) with 50 layers that will be referred to as ResNet-50 in this paper. Also a DSN with 152 layer was used.[2] Its implementation is based on code published on github.[3] It will be referred to as ResNet-152. The networks were trained with categorical cross entropy as the loss function, which is widely used for multi class problems, and used a Stochastic Gradient Descent (SGD) optimizer. The results were evaluated using the models' accuracy.

3   Data

The datasets used in this paper are all taken from the UCR Time Series Archive that was first introduced in 2002 and since then has been used in more than one thousand publications. The archive got an update in 2018, expanding it from 85 to 128 datasets. The new datasets on average have a higher number of training samples and also contain sets with variable length time series to represent many real-world problems [6], ranging from the movement of insect

---

[1] https://www.docker.com/.

[2] https://github.com/flyyufelix/cnn_finetune/blob/master/resnet_152.py.

[3] https://gist.github.com/previtus/c1a8604a4a07de680d5fb05cebfdf893.

wings to the energy consumption profile of electronic devices. Most datasets in the archive have already been Z-score normalized. For the sets that were not yet normalized, Z-score normalization was applied. The datasets are split in fixed train and test sets. The authors of the archive argue that the fixed train/test splits lead to more reproducible results and make publications and methods easier to compare. The sizes of the individual datasets vary significantly and in some of the sets, the class distribution is strongly skewed and class distributions of test and train set also differ. For example, the Chinatown train set consists of only 20 samples for 2 classes with 10 samples each, but the test set contains 95 samples of one class and 250 of the second class.

Another dataset that has at least indirectly been used in this paper is ImageNet, an image database containing millions of pictures[4]. The publishers of the dataset hold an annual competition, the Large Scale Visual Recognition Challenge (ILSVRC). The challenge was won with a Deep Residual network as proposed in [9]. The network together with weights obtained by training on the ImageNet dataset was published and is widely used in transfer learning applications.[5, 6, 7]

4   Experiments

To the best of our knowledge, there have been no publications using the complete UCR 2018 archive at the time of writing of this paper. Some results on the new dataset were only recently presented by [12]. Therefore, we present our results on the UCR 2018 archive separated into two tables. The datasets already contained in the 2015 archive are compared with results from relevant publications and the new datasets are compared to the Dynamic Time Warping (DTW) published on the archives website[8, 9].

In total we ran 3942 experiments during our work on this paper. Detailed results of all the experiments performed can not be properly presented nor discussed. We want to primarily present two methods. They will be referred to as All Classifier (AC) and Single Classifier (SC). The AC was trained on all images from the UCR archive at once with its 1118 overall classes, i.e. the AC network has 1118 targets using one-hot encoding. The SC is the classical approach to train one DNN per dataset. The AC was evaluated in the same way as the SC, using only one dataset at a time, resulting in individual accuracy for each dataset. Final results are presented for gray-scale images with a resolution of 224×224, the resolution used in the original ResNet publication. We experimented with different higher resolutions up to 512×512, but this did not improve classification accuracy significantly. For some data in the UCR archive

---

[4] http://image-net.org/.

[5] https://keras.io/applications/#resnet50.

[6] https://www.mathworks.com/help/deeplearning/ref/resnet50.html.

[7] https://pytorch.org/docs/0.4.0/_modules/torchvision/models/resnet.html.

[8] https://www.cs.ucr.edu/~eamonn/time_series_data_2018.

[9] Online results at https://github.com/patientzero/timage-icann2019.

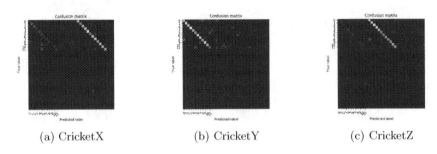

(a) CricketX   (b) CricketY   (c) CricketZ

Fig. 2. Confusion Matrix for AC on the Cricket datasets, which are accelerometer data taken from actors performing Cricket gestures.

this means length reduction, performed using average pooling after calculating the RP matrix. We also tried non gray-scale pictures with three colors channels by mapping the distance matrix to a color scheme, which lead to overall worse results. Detailed results on the 2015 datasets are shown in Table 2, results on 2018 datasets in Table 3.

The AC did exceed our expectations of it being nothing but an interesting idea by far. Results for some datasets are very good and come close to state of the art systems and results from the SC, but for some datasets it completely fails, being worse than the default rate. The default rate is defined by the accuracy a classifier would achieve by always predicting the most probable class. We need to keep in mind that using a single classifier for all datasets within the UCR archive increases the complexity dramatically since it requires separating the datasets as well. Maybe hyper-parameter tuning with special regard to the huge amount of classes might lead to better overall results.

Detailed results confirm some of the things we know about recurrence plots and the conclusions that can be drawn about a time series by looking at the plot. Patterns found in the images by the DNN will probably be too similar to be differentiated properly. An in-depth look at misclassifications revealed that some of the very poor results were almost completely misclassified within a single other dataset. An example of such a plot can be found in Fig. 2. The datasets are very similar in general. An accuracy of 64% could be reached with both AC classifiers, which is not particularly good but still better than the baseline (DTW) published by the authors. The AC completely fails to classify anything correctly within CricketX and CricketZ. Both datasets were almost exclusively classified as classes belonging to the CricketY dataset. A probable explanation for this can be found in shuffling and batching of training data. Shuffling the training data before feeding it in batches to the network may lead in case of very similar classes to over prioritizing earlier seen classes, thus failing to learn the classes later seen. In other random states or in a different order the (mis-)classification results might be reversed.

Table 1. Histograms of relative accuracy changes of SC models compared to Weasel and LSTM on (a) UCR 2015 and baseline (DTW) on (b) UCR 2018.

Rel. Diff. Accu		ResNet-50		ResNet-152	
Range		Weasel	LSTM	Weasel	LSTM
	< -0.80	0	0	0	0
>= -0.80	< -0.40	1	0	1	0
>= -0.40	< -0.20	2	0	2	1
>= -0.20	< -0.10	6	2	5	0
>= -0.10	< -0.05	7	1	8	0
>= -0.05	< -0.01	20	3	14	6
>= -0.01	< 0.00	5	1	7	1
0.00	0.00	5	7	5	4
> 0.00	<= 0.01	6	7	9	9
> 0.01	<= 0.05	12	23	13	19
> 0.05	<= 0.10	7	15	11	22
> 0.10	<= 0.20	7	14	5	16
> 0.20	<= 0.40	5	10	4	6
> 0.40	<= 0.80	2	2	1	1
> 0.80		0	0	0	0

(a)

Rel. Diff. Accu		ResNet-50	ResNet-152
Range		DTW	DTW
	< -0.80	2	3
>= -0.80	< -0.40	1	2
>= -0.40	< -0.20	8	5
>= -0.20	< -0.10	9	11
>= -0.10	< -0.05	3	4
>= -0.05	< -0.01	3	2
>= -0.01	< 0.00	0	0
0.00	0.00	0	0
> 0.00	<= 0.01	2	1
> 0.01	<= 0.05	3	2
> 0.05	<= 0.10	2	5
> 0.10	<= 0.20	4	0
> 0.20	<= 0.40	3	5
> 0.40	<= 0.80	3	3
> 0.80		0	0

(b)

Since there has been more research done on SC classifiers on the UCR archive we also present results in detail. Table 1 shows the relative accuracy differences of the SC timage compared to state of the art systems. Table 1(a) shows the differences for the UCR 2015 archive compared to LSTM and WEASLE [13,18] and Table 1(b) for the new datasets in the UCR 2018 archive compared to the baseline. For the UCR 2015 *timage* outperforms WEASEL using ResNet-50 for 41 datasets, and using ResNet-152 for 37 datasets. Same accuracy is achieved for 5 datasets for both ResNet-50 and ResNet-152. Compared to the LSTM, *timage* performs better for 7 datasets using ResNet-50 and for 8 datasets using ResNet-152. Equal results were achieved in 7 cases using ResNet-50 and 4 using ResNet-152. For 18 datasets relative classification accuracy was still comparable and only within a 5% relative difference using ResNet-50 compared to WEASEL and 22 for ResNet-152. Respectively for LSTM, 30 are within the 5% range using ResNet-50 and 28 using ResNet-152. For 8 datasets from the UCR 2015 archive, timage could achieve the best classification accuracy so far as shown in Table 2. Comparing the results for the UCR 2018 archive with the baseline, timage outperforms it in 26 out of 41 cases using ResNet-50 and 27 using ResNet-152. For 5 datasets results were within the 5% range using ResNet-50 and 3 using ResNet-152.

The results that can be achieved with the SC are comparable to state of the art systems as shown by Table 2. The method is able to classify all datasets well with the exception of ShapeletSim and TwoPatterns, where it is still better than the default rate.

Table 2. Accuracy of experiments on UCR 2015 archive. Best results are highlighted.

Dataset	WEASEL	F-t LSTM-FCN	SC ResNet50	SC ResNet152	AC ResNet50	AC ResNet152
Adiac	0.8312	**0.8849**	0.8440	0.8235	0.7238	0.6982
ArrowHead	0.8571	**0.9029**	0.8857	0.8629	0.8000	0.7486
Beef	0.7667	**0.9330**	0.7333	0.7667	0.8333	0.7000
BeetleFly	0.9500	**1.0000**	0.9000	0.9000	0.2000	0.2500
BirdChicken	0.8000	**1.0000**	0.9000	**1.0000**	0.1500	0.0500
Car	0.8667	**0.9670**	0.8833	0.9000	0.8500	0.8167
CBF	0.9833	**1.0000**	0.9044	0.9911	0.9478	0.9100
ChlorineConcentration	0.7526	**1.0000**	0.7844	0.7852	0.7237	0.7109
CinCECGTorso	**0.9935**	0.9094	0.8913	0.8580	0.9080	0.8971
Coffee	**1.0000**	**1.0000**	**1.0000**	**1.0000**	**1.0000**	**1.0000**
Computers	0.6560	**0.8600**	0.7400	0.6960	0.2960	0.2080
CricketX	0.7641	**0.8256**	0.7359	0.7333	0.1385	0.1564
CricketY	0.7897	**0.8256**	0.7359	0.7538	0.6462	0.6410
CricketZ	0.7872	**0.8257**	0.7282	0.7615	0.0897	0.0923
DiatomSizeReduction	0.8856	**0.9771**	0.9379	0.9346	0.8693	0.7941
DistalPhalanxOutlineAgeGroup	0.7698	**0.8600**	0.7842	0.7842	0.0216	0.0432
DistalPhalanxOutlineCorrect	0.7790	**0.8217**	0.8152	0.8080	0.2428	0.1014
DistalPhalanxTW	0.6763	**0.8100**	0.7194	0.6835	0.0432	0.0144
Earthquakes	0.7482	**0.8261**	0.7770	0.7986	0.6331	0.6475
ECG200	0.8500	0.9200	0.8700	**0.9400**	0.7900	0.7900
ECG5000	**0.9482**	0.9478	0.9458	0.9442	0.9358	0.9307
ECGFiveDays	**1.0000**	0.9942	0.8165	0.9024	0.9477	0.8269
ElectricDevices	0.7329	**0.7633**	0.7313	0.7297	0.6956	0.7181
FaceAll	0.7870	**0.9680**	0.7497	0.7828	0.7793	0.7704
FaceFour	**1.0000**	0.9772	0.7273	0.9091	0.8182	0.7273
FacesUCR	0.9522	**0.9898**	0.7771	0.8566	0.8371	0.8215
FiftyWords	**0.8110**	0.8066	0.7978	0.7868	0.7407	0.7253
Fish	0.9657	**0.9886**	0.9771	0.9771	0.9371	0.9257
FordA	0.9727	**0.9733**	0.9386	0.9235	0.6295	0.6667
FordB	0.8321	**0.9186**	0.8222	0.8074	0.5432	0.4926
GunPoint	**1.0000**	**1.0000**	**1.0000**	0.9933	0.9867	0.9867
Ham	0.6571	**0.8000**	0.7905	0.7429	0.7333	0.6952
HandOutlines	0.9487	0.8870	**0.9514**	0.9297	0.9162	0.9216
Haptics	0.3864	**0.5584**	0.5162	0.4968	0.4643	0.4351
Herring	0.6563	**0.7188**	0.6875	0.6563	0.5781	0.6094
InlineSkate	**0.6127**	0.5000	0.4036	0.4309	0.3055	0.3655
InsectWingbeatSound	0.6404	**0.6696**	0.6177	0.6212	0.5944	0.5894
ItalyPowerDemand	0.9514	**0.9699**	0.9602	0.9602	0.9475	0.9397
LargeKitchenAppliances	0.6827	**0.9200**	0.8080	0.7573	0.6267	0.4987
Lightning2	0.5574	0.8197	0.8525	**0.8525**	0.3279	0.2295
Lightning7	0.7123	**0.9178**	0.8493	0.7945	0.3014	0.3425
Mallat	0.9655	**0.9834**	0.9326	0.9441	0.9365	0.9032
Meat	0.9167	**1.0000**	**1.0000**	0.9833	0.8500	0.8833
MedicalImages	0.7408	**0.8066**	0.7868	0.7803	0.7276	0.7184
MiddlePhalanxOutlineAgeGroup	0.6039	**0.8150**	0.6364	0.6234	0.0000	0.0000
MiddlePhalanxOutlineCorrect	0.8076	0.8333	0.8522	**0.8591**	0.1959	0.1134
MiddlePhalanxTW	0.5390	**0.6466**	0.6234	0.5909	0.0195	0.0260
MoteStrain	0.9353	**0.9569**	0.8403	0.8866	0.4968	0.5719
NonInvasiveFetalECGThorax1	0.9288	**0.9657**	0.9405	0.9405	0.9196	0.9288
NonInvasiveFetalECGThorax2	0.9415	**0.9613**	0.9522	0.9547	0.9328	0.9405
OliveOil	**0.9333**	**0.9333**	**0.9333**	0.8667	0.5333	0.5000
OSULeaf	0.8967	**0.9959**	0.8678	0.8512	0.7355	0.6488
PhalangesOutlinesCorrect	0.8170	0.8392	0.8578	**0.8590**	0.1643	0.2960
Phoneme	0.3265	**0.3602**	0.2410	0.2416	0.2152	0.1930
Plane	**1.0000**	**1.0000**	**1.0000**	**1.0000**	**1.0000**	0.9810
ProximalPhalanxOutlineAgeGroup	0.8488	**0.8878**	**0.8878**	0.8732	0.0049	0.0000
ProximalPhalanxOutlineCorrect	0.8969	**0.9313**	0.9244	0.9278	0.3814	0.3883
ProximalPhalanxTW	0.8098	**0.8275**	0.8049	0.8195	0.0634	0.0293
RefrigerationDevices	0.5387	**0.5947**	0.5520	0.5440	0.4480	0.4267
ScreenType	0.5467	**0.7073**	0.4640	0.4720	0.2880	0.2853
ShapeletSim	**1.0000**	**1.0000**	0.5556	0.6333	0.4500	0.6667
ShapesAll	**0.9183**	0.9150	0.8850	0.8600	0.7600	0.7400
SmallKitchenAppliances	0.7893	**0.8133**	0.7333	0.6880	0.6587	0.6853
SonyAIBORobotSurface1	0.8236	**0.9967**	0.8802	0.9601	0.7953	0.7488
SonyAIBORobotSurface2	0.9349	**0.9822**	0.8143	0.8458	0.7650	0.7870
StarLightCurves	0.9773	0.9763	**0.9806**	**0.9806**	0.9709	0.9677
Strawberry	0.9757	**0.9864**	0.9811	0.9838	0.9676	0.9622
SwedishLeaf	0.9664	**0.9840**	0.9680	0.9616	0.9312	0.9232
Symbols	0.9618	**0.9849**	0.9719	0.9668	0.7739	0.8000
SyntheticControl	0.9933	**1.0000**	0.7133	0.6700	0.6767	0.6767
ToeSegmentation1	0.9474	**0.9912**	0.9167	0.9211	0.5570	0.5263
ToeSegmentation2	0.9077	**0.9462**	0.9385	0.8846	0.4077	0.4692
Trace	**1.0000**	**1.0000**	**1.0000**	**1.0000**	**1.0000**	**1.0000**
TwoLeadECG	0.9982	**1.0000**	0.9895	0.9956	0.9816	0.9974
TwoPatterns	0.9898	**0.9973**	0.5157	0.5145	0.5028	0.4903
UWaveGestureLibraryAll	0.9503	**0.9609**	0.9375	0.9436	0.9137	0.9112
UWaveGestureLibraryX	0.8096	**0.8498**	0.7074	0.7004	0.4738	0.4693
UWaveGestureLibraryY	0.7247	**0.7661**	0.7513	0.7133	0.5419	0.5034
UWaveGestureLibraryZ	0.7700	**0.7993**	0.7289	0.7052	0.4913	0.4740
Wafer	**1.0000**	**1.0000**	0.9977	0.9966	0.9971	0.9942
Wine	0.8519	**0.8890**	0.6667	0.8333	0.5000	0.6667
WordSynonyms	**0.7241**	0.6991	0.6850	0.6771	0.6348	0.6176
Worms	0.8052	0.6851	0.8182	**0.8442**	0.4156	0.3506
WormsTwoClass	0.8052	0.8066	**0.8961**	0.8442	0.2857	0.2727
Yoga	0.9090	**0.9163**	0.9000	0.8827	0.8730	0.8713

Table 3. Accuracy of experiments on UCR 2018 archive. Best results are highlighted.

Dataset	DTW	SC		AC	
		ResNet50	ResNet152	ResNet50	ResNet152
ACSF1	0.6400	0.7800	**0.7900**	0.5700	0.5300
AllGestureWiimoteX	**0.7157**	0.4943	0.5200	0.3757	0.3829
AllGestureWiimoteY	**0.7286**	0.6000	0.5629	0.4500	0.4586
AllGestureWiimoteZ	0.6429	**0.6514**	0.5871	0.5014	0.4943
BME	0.9000	**1.0000**	**1.0000**	0.9200	0.9533
Chinatown	**0.9565**	0.7246	0.7565	0.0058	0.0087
Crop	0.6652	**0.7559**	0.7532	0.7405	0.7377
DodgerLoopDay	0.5000	0.4875	**0.5125**	0.4000	0.3375
DodgerLoopGame	**0.8768**	0.6812	0.6812	0.0000	0.0870
DodgerLoopWeekend	0.9493	0.9420	**0.9710**	0.1667	0.0435
EOGHorizontalSignal	**0.5028**	0.2790	0.2652	0.1160	0.1326
EOGVerticalSignal	**0.4475**	0.2238	0.2569	0.1547	0.1215
EthanolLevel	0.2760	**0.8400**	0.7100	0.7100	0.7100
FreezerRegularTrain	0.8989	0.9961	**0.9975**	0.9221	0.9565
FreezerSmallTrain	0.7533	**0.9793**	0.9354	0.0667	0.0368
Fungi	0.8387	0.8871	**0.9194**	0.8763	0.8548
GestureMidAirD1	0.5692	0.5308	**0.6000**	0.4077	0.4231
GestureMidAirD2	0.6077	**0.6231**	0.5538	0.4923	0.4846
GestureMidAirD3	0.3231	0.4154	**0.4615**	0.3923	0.2231
GesturePebbleZ1	0.7907	**0.9186**	**0.9186**	0.4070	0.3547
GesturePebbleZ2	0.6709	**0.8544**	0.8354	0.0506	0.0949
GunPointAgeSpan	0.9177	**0.9873**	0.9842	0.1582	0.0886
GunPointMaleVersusFemale	**0.9968**	0.9937	0.9937	0.2247	0.2658
GunPointOldVersusYoung	0.8381	**0.9810**	**0.9810**	0.1873	0.2190
HouseTwenty	**0.9244**	0.8319	0.8403	0.6807	0.6218
InsectEPGRegularTrain	0.8715	**0.9719**	0.9639	0.8273	0.6988
InsectEPGSmallTrain	0.7349	**0.9438**	0.8795	0.1004	0.2088
MelbournePedestrian	**0.7906**	0.3604	0.3563	0.3298	0.3282
MixedShapesRegularTrain	0.8416	**0.9645**	0.9509	0.8470	0.8276
MixedShapesSmallTrain	0.7798	**0.9027**	0.8635	0.0247	0.0049
PickupGestureWiimoteZ	0.6600	0.7400	**0.8000**	0.4800	0.4800
PigAirwayPressure	0.1058	0.1442	**0.1683**	0.0913	0.1106
PigArtPressure	0.2452	0.3510	**0.5288**	0.1635	0.2548
PigCVP	0.1538	0.4279	**0.5288**	0.3462	0.3221
PLAID	**0.8399**	0.8231	0.8119	0.7877	0.7858
PowerCons	0.8778	0.9389	**0.9722**	0.9333	0.9000
Rock	0.6000	0.7800	**0.8400**	0.7400	0.6000
SemgHandGenderCh2	**0.8017**	0.7867	0.7767	0.1900	0.2117
SemgHandMovementCh2	**0.5844**	0.5244	0.5267	0.1422	0.1911
SemgHandSubjectCh2	**0.7267**	0.6644	0.6889	0.3133	0.2578
ShakeGestureWiimoteZ	0.8600	0.8800	**0.9400**	0.5400	0.6400
SmoothSubspace	0.8267	**0.9933**	0.9867	0.9800	0.9533
UMD	**0.9931**	0.8264	0.7847	0.6944	0.6528

5 Conclusion

Especially in the light of the huge diversity of datasets in the UCR archive, the robustness of using transfer learning on ResNet to classify time series by using RP is surprising. A number of changes in the preprocessing step like increasing the resolution or using a color scheme did not help the DNN to separate the classes more accurately compared to our initial experiments. Different strategies to obtain weights for transfer learning did not lead to significant improvements but had impact on the time networks needed to converge. The classification pipeline presented generally simplifies what needs to be done to detect patterns and correctly classify time series.

The analysis of confusion matrices for datasets that performed extremely bad with the AC show that some of them almost exclusively misclassified within one other dataset. They do not fail the task of separating classes within one dataset, but fail on the harder problem of an AC, that is separating not only classes within a dataset, but to separate very similar datasets as well. This supports some of the findings regarding RP for time series, and the conclusions regarding its properties, that can be drawn from looking at the respective RP: Similar time series produce very similar patterns [14].[10] Thus failing to always boost more easily separable features.

The nature of the UCR archive simplifies the classification task, because due to mostly fixed length and nearly perfect alignment of time series, some difficulties, like segmentation, faced in real world scenarios are removed. In the case of the UCR archive all data is pre-segmented, which in itself is a very hard task to begin with. Some of the harder tasks are included in the UCR 2018 archive where some datasets contain time series of different length and overall classification results are not as good as for the UCR 2015 archive. In the future it will be interesting to adapt and evaluate *timage* to real world scenarios where, for example, a sliding window is used.

Acknowledgement. This work is supported by a research grant of the Bayerisches Staatsministerium für Bildung und Kultus, Wissenschaft und Kunst and further by the Bayerische Wissenschaftsforum (BayWISS).

References

1. Abadi, M., Agarwal, A., Barham, P.: TensorFlow: large-scale machine learning on heterogeneous systems (2015). https://www.tensorflow.org/
2. Alessio, S.M.: Digital Signal Processing and Spectral Analysis for Scientists. Springer, Cham (2016). https://doi.org/10.1007/978-3-319-25468-5
3. Bagnall, A., Lines, J., Bostrom, A., Large, J., Keogh, E.: The great time series classification bake off: a review and experimental evaluation of recent algorithmic advances. Data Min. Knowl. Discov. **31**(3), 606–660 (2017). https://doi.org/10.1007/s10618-016-0483-9
4. Boddapati, V., Petef, A., Rasmusson, J., Lundberg, L.: Classifying environmental sounds using image recognition networks. Procedia Comput. Sci. **112**, 2048–2056 (2017). https://doi.org/10.1016/j.procs.2017.08.250
5. Chollet, F., et al.: Keras (2015). https://keras.io
6. Dau, H.A., et al.: The UCR time series classification archive, October 2018. https://www.cs.ucr.edu/~eamonn/time_series_data_2018/
7. Goodfellow, I., Bengio, Y., Courville, A.: Deep Learning. MIT Press, Cambridge (2016)
8. Hatami, N., Gavet, Y., Debayle, J.: Classification of time-series images using deep convolutional neural networks. In: Proceedings of SPIE 2018 (2017). https://doi.org/10.1117/12.2309486
9. He, K., Zhang, X., Ren, S., Sun, J.: Deep residual learning for image recognition. CoRR (2015). https://doi.org/10.1109/CVPR.2016.90
10. Ismail Fawaz, H., Forestier, G., Weber, J., Idoumghar, L., Muller, P.A.: Deep learning for time series classification: a review (2018). https://doi.org/10.1007/s10618-019-00619-1, https://arxiv.org/abs/1809.04356
11. Ismail Fawaz, H., Forestier, G., Weber, J., Idoumghar, L., Muller, P.A.: Transfer learning for time series classification. In: IEEE International Conference on Big Data, pp. 1367–1376 (2018). https://doi.org/10.1109/BigData.2018.8621990

---

[10] http://www.recurrence-plot.tk/.

12. Karim, F., Majumdar, S., Darabi, H.: Insights into LSTM fully convolutional networks for time series classification (2019). https://doi.org/10.1109/ACCESS.2019.2916828, https://arxiv.org/abs/1902.10756
13. Karim, F., Majumdar, S., Darabi, H., Chen, S.: LSTM fully convolutional networks for time series classification. IEEE Access **PP** (2017). https://doi.org/10.1109/ACCESS.2017.2779939
14. Marwan, N., Carmenromano, M., Thiel, M., Kurths, J.: Recurrence plots for the analysis of complex systems. Phys. Rep. **438**(5–6), 237–329 (2007). https://doi.org/10.1016/j.physrep.2006.11.001
15. Michael, T., Spiegel, S., Albayrak, S.: Time series classification using compressed recurrence plots, September 2015
16. Park, T., Lee, T.: Musical instrument sound classification with deep convolutional neural network using feature fusion approach. CoRR abs/1512.07370 (2015). https://arxiv.org/abs/1512.07370v1
17. Schäfer, P.: The boss is concerned with time series classification in the presence of noise. Data Min. Knowl. Discov. **29**(6), 1505–1530 (2015). https://doi.org/10.1007/s10618-014-0377-7
18. Schäfer, P., Leser, U.: Fast and accurate time series classification with WEASEL. CoRR abs/1701.07681 (2017). https://doi.org/10.1145/3132847.3132980, http://arxiv.org/abs/1701.07681
19. Wang, Z., Oates, T.: Imaging time-series to improve classification and imputation. CoRR abs/1506.00327 (2015). http://arxiv.org/abs/1506.00327

Prediction of the Next Sensor Event and Its Time of Occurrence in Smart Homes

Flávia Dias Casagrande[1(✉)], Jim Tørresen[2], and Evi Zouganeli[1]

[1] OsloMet – Oslo Metropolitan University, Pilestredet 35, 0166 Oslo, Norway
{flacas,evizou}@oslomet.no
[2] University of Oslo, Gaustadalléen 23B, 0373 Oslo, Norway
jimtoer@ifi.uio.no

Abstract. We present work on sequential sensor events in smart homes with results on the prediction of the next sensor event and its time of occurrence in the same model using Recurrent Neural Network with Long Short-Term Memory. We implement four configurations for converting binary sensor events and elapsed time between events into different input sequences. Our dataset has been collected from a real home with one resident over a period of 40 weeks and contains data from a set of fifteen sensors including motion, magnetic, and power sensors. When including the time information in the input data, the accuracy of predicting the next sensor event was 84%. In our best implementation, the model is able to predict both the next sensor event and the mean elapsed time to the next event with a peak average accuracy of 80%.

Keywords: Smart home · Sequence prediction · Time prediction · Binary sensors · Recurrent neural network

1   Introduction

Activity recognition and prediction can be performed by a number of algorithms. Most of the work reported in the literature uses data collected from scripted activities in a lab environment. Moreover, to the extent of our knowledge, there is no study that predicts both the next sensor event and the time it will occur in the same recurrent neural network (RNN). This is the focus of the current paper where we use sensor event data from a real home. The work has been carried out in an interdisciplinary project – the Assisted Living Project (ALP) – that involves experts in health, technology, and ethics [23]. The aim of the project is to develop assisted living technology (ALT) to support older adults with Mild Cognitive Impairment (MCI) or Dementia (D) live a safe and independent life at home. A fair amount of research on smart home functions has aimed at assisting older adults with MCI/D in their everyday life. Examples are

F. D. Casagrande—Financed by the Norwegian Research Council under the SAMANSVAR programme (247620/O70).

© Springer Nature Switzerland AG 2019
I. V. Tetko et al. (Eds.): ICANN 2019, LNCS 11730, pp. 462–473, 2019.
https://doi.org/10.1007/978-3-030-30490-4_37

functions such as prompting with reminders or encouragement, diagnosis tools, as well as prediction, anticipation and prevention of hazardous situations. These require quite robust and reliable activity recognition and prediction algorithms to perform well and be functional in real homes.

In a previous work we compared both probabilistic methods and neural networks for the prediction of the next sensor event only [5,7] with regard to a number of factors: the required number of preceding events to predict the next event (memory length), the necessary amount of data to achieve good accuracy and stability, the execution time for training/testing, and the number of sensors in the dataset. The best performing algorithm was shown to be the long short-term memory (LSTM) neural network with binary sensor events "on" and "off" converted to a text sequence. In this work, we further develop the LSTM network by including the time information and predicting the time of occurrence in addition to the next sensor event.

The paper is organized as follows. Section 2 gives an overview of algorithms used for sensor sequential prediction in the literature and work related to prediction of the time of occurrence. Section 3 gives an overview of our field trial and the sensor system in the apartment. Section 4 describes the data preprocessing and the LSTM configuration, followed by the results and discussion in Sect. 5. Finally, in Sect. 6 we discuss our findings and conclude the paper with some final remarks, ideas for improvement, and future work.

2   Related Work

Activity prediction includes mainly two tasks: sequence prediction and time prediction. A number of algorithms for sequence prediction have been studied in the past years [22]. These algorithms usually train a model based on a sequence of symbols to predict the next symbol. The Active LeZi (ALZ) uses Markov Models to predict the next symbol in a sequence [9]. Inspired by ALZ, the Sequence Prediction via Enhanced Episode Discovery (SPEED) algorithm predicts the next sensor in a sequence based on common patterns of sensor events [1]. Neural networks have also been used to predict the next sensor in a sequence with notable performance, typically recurrent neural networks (RNN) [6,14,21]. Other reported methods are Bayesian network, state prediction, and Markov predictor [19].

In addition to sequence prediction such algorithms should also be able to predict when the next symbol (representing either a sensor or an activity) will occur. The time of occurrence is important to enable a number of smart home functions, for example improved operation of automation features; prompting systems [12]; or anomaly detection in certain behaviour patterns [20].

The time series methods Autoregressive Moving Average (ARMA) and Autoregressive Integrated Moving Average (ARIMA) have been extensively applied in the literature [4]. However, they assume the time series to be linear, which is not applicable to activities in a home [17]. Rule-based algorithms have been developed for time forecasting as well [2,12]. They are simpler and useful, however do not account for more complex activities. Non-linear time series models would be more suitable to time prediction in smart homes, e.g. artificial neural networks. A Non-linear Autoregressive Network (NARX) was compared to an Elman network to predict a sensor activation's start and end time [15]. In this study, each sensor had its own network trained and tested on a twenty-day dataset with six binary sensors. The NARX performed better, with a RMSE ranging from 0.06 to 0.09, depending on the sensor. Decision trees have been used to predict the time a certain activity would happen [17]. This method relies on several features extracted from sensor event sequences. It was applied on a dataset with 51 binary and sampling sensors and achieved an average normalized RMSE of 0.01. Bayesian networks have been used to predict the next location, time of day and day of the week a person would execute an activity [18]. This algorithm was employed in two apartments with about 30 binary sensors each, where the next location was predicted with an accuracy of 47% and 61%. Poisson process has also been applied to predict the time an observed activity would occur [16]. An RMSE of 3.9431 s was achieved for the whole dataset.

Our dataset was collected from a real home, while most datasets from the cited works have been collected through scripted activities primarily in lab environments. It contains events from fifteen binary sensors, i.e. twice as many as used in [14,15], and less than one third of the number of sensors used in the Mavlab testbed [1,9,17] and half of [18]. The number of sensors is comparable to the work in [19] (16 rooms), however in that study the events were inserted by each user rather than being generated using sensors. In addition, we predict both the next sensor event and the time to the next event in the same model. From the works cited above, [18] is the closest to ours in the sense it predicts more than one feature in the same model. This work predicts the next location, time of day (slots of 3 h through the day), and day of the week using a Bayesian network with reported accuracies of 46–60%, 66–87% and 89–97%. Subsequently, the activity is predicted with an accuracy of 61–64% based on a combination of these features. They use data from testbeds collected over 6 and 4 months, and take into account 10 locations and 11 activities. Our work predicts the next sensor event and the time of occurrence for a set with 15 sensors with better overall accuracy.

3   Field Trial

Our field trial includes nine apartments in a community care facility with residents over 65 years old. In this work we use data from one of the apartments. The set of sensors has been chosen so that it can enable the realization of useful functions for older adults with MCI/D as these were indicated at dialogue cafes with the users [23]. Hence, our set of sensors contains motion, magnetic, and power sensors. These enable inference of occupancy patterns (movement around the apartment) and some daily activities – kitchen related activities, dressing, being in bed –, and leisure activities—reading, watching TV, listening to radio.

Figure 1 shows the schematic of the apartment we collected 40 weeks of data from 15 sensors in total. Seven motion sensors: one in each room and two over and by the bed to indicate whether the person is in bed. Four magnetic sensors: entrance and back doors, wardrobe, and cutlery drawer. Four power sensors on appliances: night stand lamp, coffee machine, TV, and living room/reading lamp. The sensors are connected wirelessly through Z-Wave and xComfort protocols to a Raspberry Pi 3, which transfers the data for storage in a secure server. The data comprise timestamp (date and time with precision of seconds), sensor ID, and sensor message (binary). Table 1 shows an example of data collected from the sensors.

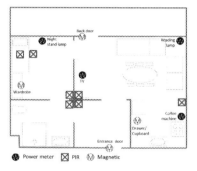

Fig. 1. Sensors system installed in the field trial apartment.

Table 1. Binary sensors data

Timestamp	Sensor ID	Sensor message
01.09.2017 07:58:40	4	1
01.09.2017 07:59:02	10	1
01.09.2017 08:03:05	10	0

4   Data Preprocessing and Prediction Method

4.1   Data Correction

The preparation of the data includes two steps: data correction and data conversion. The data correction is necessary because the data acquired from binary sensors often contain faulty events e.g. erroneous activation of motion sensors by sunlight, bouncing of contact sensors, or switch-off delays of motion sensors [8]. Such flawed data may substantially affect the performance of the models that will learn erroneous patterns. In our system, occasionally the motion sensors do not send an activation event when they should. Missing sensor events have been inserted to correct for this. For example, it is not possible to go to the bedroom directly from the kitchen without passing through the living room. When the living room activation event is missing, it is inserted. In the case where there are two possible sensor events (e.g. two possible paths in the apartment), the choice of the inserted sensor event is done such that the resulting distribution of events corresponds to the percentage distribution of the two options as observed in the data. The time of the inserted event is the mean between the previous and next event. This does not compromise the dataset accuracy because the faulty events are usually between relatively fast motions around the apartment, hence the elapsed time is short.

4.2   Data Conversion

Subsequently, the corrected data is converted to sequences of letters. This is inspired by the SPEED algorithm [1]. SPEED is a sequence prediction algorithm based on the frequency of occurrence of events in home environments. Upper- and lower- case letters represent a sensor's "on" and "off" events. For the sample data in Table 1, SPEED would generate the sequence "ABb", where sensors 4 and 10 are assigned the letters a/A and b/B, respectively. Subsequently, we include the time information. This is done in four ways as follows. In all cases the generated sensor events are treated as independent events, as presented also in the next section.

Sensor Event with Period of Day. Here we distinguish between four periods of the day: morning (from 7am to noon), afternoon (from noon to 6pm), evening (from 6pm to 10pm) and night (from 10pm to 7am).

Sensor Event with Elapsed Time Classes. Here we use two fixed sets of time intervals: [<1 min, 1–15 min, 15 min–1 h, >1 h] and [<1 min, 1–5 min, 5–15 min, 15–30 min, 30 min–1 h, 1–2 h, 2–5 h]. This results in a 4-class case and an 8-class case.

Sensor and Time-Cluster with Hour of the Day and Elapsed Time to the Next Event. We apply an unsupervised learning method to cluster the sensor samples, where the K-means algorithm clusters each sensor event according to the hour of the day occurrence and the time elapsed to the following sensor event. In the K-means algorithm the samples of each sensor are classified into K clusters such that the sum of square distances (SSD) within the clusters is minimized [3]. Each cluster contains a centroid, given by the mean value of each feature of the algorithm. We perform K-means for a number of clusters (K) between 1 and 8 and choose the best K manually according to the elbow method [13]. This method consists of plotting an SSD vs. K graph and choosing the K that resembles an "elbow" (the point of inflection on the curve), which is the best fit for that problem. Figure 2 shows an example of clustering the samples of the PIR sensor in the kitchen. This sensor results in four clusters.

Separate Dataset and Model for Each Period of the Day. Separate datasets are used for each period of the day (see above) and are modelled in separate neural networks.

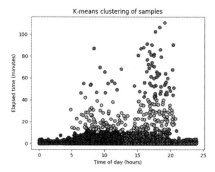

Fig. 2. K-means clustering of samples of PIR sensor events in the kitchen.

4.3 Long Short-Term Memory Network

RNN has been broadly applied to sequence prediction due to its property of keeping an internal memory. Hence, it attains a good performance for inputs that are sequential in time. The LSTM [11] is an RNN architecture designed to be better at storing and accessing information than the standard RNN [10].

We employ an LSTM network as this was the best performing algorithm for our data when compared to other methods [5, 7]. In this work the LSTM network is configured as a text generation network. The number of inputs is a certain number of symbols (sensor events with numbers indicating time) – equal to the memory length – and the output is the predicted next symbol in the sequence (Fig. 3). The input and output are one-hot encoded. In the one-hot encoding representation, each symbol is represented by a vector of bits of length equal to the number of symbols in a sequence. All values are zero, except for the one corresponding to that symbol (see Fig. 3). Hence, our input vector has as many values as the number of symbols in the sequence. In the case of 15 sensors, we have 30 inputs to represent the "on" and "off" states of each of these. E.g. when the time of day is taken into account, the number of inputs is multiplied by 4 (120 inputs in total) and similarly in the other cases.

A stateless LSTM network model was implemented in Python 3 using Keras open source library for neural networks. A number of parameters were tuned and the following optimal values were found. The optimum memory length (i.e. number of previous events used to predict the next event [6]) was 10. The model has one hidden layer with hyperbolic tangent activation and 64 neurons. Our batch size (i.e. number of samples used for training each iteration of the epoch) was 512. We used Adam as the optimization function with learning rate of 0.01 and categorical cross-entropy as loss function. The output layer was a softmax activation function. We used the early stopping method to avoid overfitting and unnecessary computations, allowing a maximum of 200 epochs for each model's training.

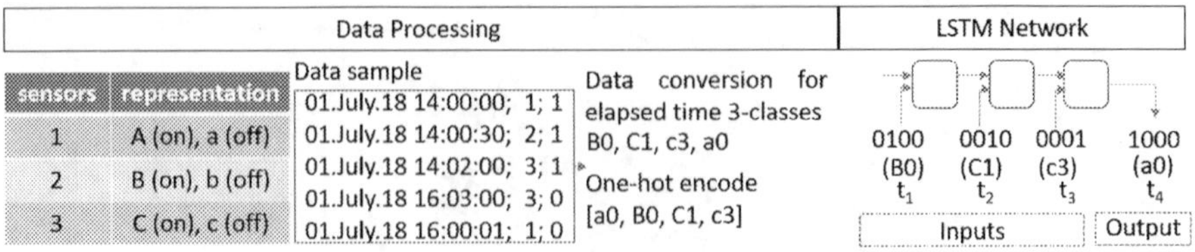

Data Processing			LSTM Network	

sensors	representation	Data sample	Data conversion for elapsed time 3-classes	
1	A (on), a (off)	01.July.18 14:00:00; 1; 1	B0, C1, c3, a0	
2	B (on), b (off)	01.July.18 14:00:30; 2; 1		
3	C (on), c (off)	01.July.18 14:02:00; 3; 1	One-hot encode	
		01.July.18 16:03:00; 3; 0	[a0, B0, C1, c3]	
		01.July.18 16:00:01; 1; 0		

0100 (B0) t_1	0010 (C1) t_2	0001 (c3) t_3	1000 (a0) t_4
Inputs			Output

Fig. 3. Configuration of LSTM network.

5   Results and Discussion

In all cases, the LSTM network was trained based on a 3-fold cross-validation. We have in total 40 weeks with recorded data from one apartment where we apply our algorithms, which accounts for 163347 events. Some accuracy curves do not show significant improvement after a certain number of events, and we therefore show the plots up to a certain point for better clarity on the lower range of the graph.

5.1   Prediction of Next Sensor Event

Firstly, we predict the next sensor event based on the four proposed input sequences with time information (Sect. 4.2). Figure 4 shows the performance of the prediction according to the amount of data in the dataset and Table 2 presents the top accuracies achieved for each method. In a previous work, we achieved an accuracy of 82.95% when predicting the next sensor event using previous sensor events as input (i.e. no time information) [5]. When we include the time information in the input the accuracy is improved by 1–1.4% for all methods, apart from the period of the day. The highest accuracy (84.39%) is achieved by the 4-class time-interval. The small improvement was initially somewhat surprising, as we had expected that the time information would increase accuracy significantly. However, on second thoughts, the apartments are quite small and there is a limited number of sensors. The standard deviation of the LSTM models is about 0.02–0.06%, hence the model is quite stable. The convergence to a stable behavior occurs at similar dataset sizes of about 3000 events for all methods apart from the period of day, that requires about 16000 events to reach stability. The choice of 4- or 8-class time-interval classes does not have a significant effect on the accuracy. This is presumably because most of the events have a short elapsed time to the next event, as indicated also in the example of sensors clustering in Fig. 2.

Next, we model four separate LSTM networks, one for each period of the day, using the best performing method in the previous analysis – the 4-class time-interval. We use the period's datasets with the sensor events and the elapsed time intervals for morning (57597 events), afternoon (32214 events), evening (28147 events), and night (45389 events). The accuracy plots for each period are shown in Fig. 5. The peak average accuracies for morning, afternoon, evening and night

are 83.69%, 82.74%, 82.05%, 83.29%, respectively. These are the peak results of
the model after reaching stability, which happens around 10000 events, except
for the night network that reaches stability with around 5000–10000 events,
depending on the period. The peak accuracy values are marginally worse from
having all the events together in one network. *However, the models converge
slower to stability. This is expected since information is lost when separating the
networks, and more data are therefore required to compensate for that. In addition, we have split the networks according to fixed hours, while an adjustment of
the algorithm to detect when is exactly morning, afternoon, evening and night
for this user would have been beneficial.

5.2   Prediction of Next Sensor Event and Time of Occurrence

In the following we examine the accuracy of predicting both the next sensor
event and time information. In this case, only the input sequences of 4- and
8-class time-intervals and K-means time-cluster are considered. Lower accuracies
are attained than when predicting only the next sensor event, as expected, since
now more information is being predicted with the same model – see Table 2. The
best accuracy was achieved by the K-means time-cluster (79.68%), 4% better
than the second best performing method. The required number of events in the
dataset is similar for the three methods, about 10000 events (Fig. 6).

Subsequently we investigate the performance of the input sequence of the
K-means time-cluster for four separate networks, one for each period of the
day – Fig. 7. The mean peak accuracies achieved are 77.99%, 78.13%, 74.84%
and 79.96% for morning, afternoon, evening and night, respectively. Most of the
periods converge to stability with about 10000 events, which is about the same
when all the data are used in the same network. It is interesting to note that
the morning period is the one that takes longer to converge when predicting the
time, whilst when predicting only the next sensor event the night period requires
longer time. This may indicate a bigger variety of elapsed time in the morning,
and a larger amount of data is required to learn patterns.

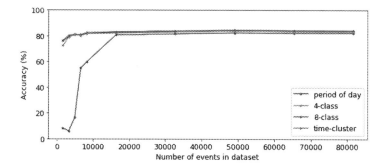

Fig. 4. Accuracy of prediction of next sensor event vs. the number of events in the
dataset.

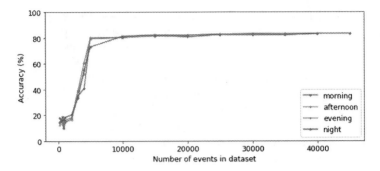

Fig. 5. Accuracy of prediction of the next sensor event vs. number of events, when using as input sensor events and 4-class method, for four separate models for each period of the day.

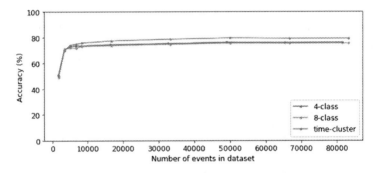

Fig. 6. Accuracy of prediction of next sensor event and time information vs. the number of events in the dataset.

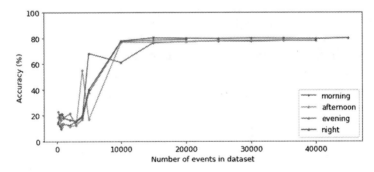

Fig. 7. Accuracy of prediction of the next sensor event and time information vs. number of events, when using as input sensor events and time-cluster, for four separate models for each period of the day.

We have also applied the same methods and models with the same input configurations for the 7 motion sensors only (Table 2). As in our previous work [5], the attained accuracy is about 3–4% higher with this smaller set of sensors

Table 2. Prediction accuracy

Algorithm	Accuracy (%)			
	Prediction of next sensor		Prediction of next sensor and time	
	15 sensors	7 sensors	15 sensors	7 sensors
Period of day	82.74	85.52	–	–
4 intervals	84.39	87.12	76.17	79.27
8 intervals	84.38	86.37	75.73	78.79
Time-cluster	83.59	86.37	79.68	83.40

compared with a set with all 15 sensors, i.e. a peak average accuracy of 83.40% is attained when predicting the next sensor and the time-cluster. This improvement is due to the fact that there is a smaller number of classes in the network to predict from. In addition, the sensors are all of the same type so that there are no concurrent events (i.e. no motion sensor events happening at the same time).

6 Conclusion and Future Work

We present results on the prediction of sequential sensor events and the time of occurrence in the same model using LSTM networks. The prediction is based on previous sensor events, combined with information on the time of occurrence. We incorporate the time information in several ways: period of the day (morning, afternoon, evening, night), time elapsed to the next sensor event, K-means cluster including information about the hour of the day and the time elapsed to the next sensor event. We also investigate the performance when using separate networks for the four periods of day.

Our best performing model for predicting the next sensor event included the time information in a 4-class time interval and attained a peak average accuracy of 84% for a set of fifteen sensors in total – motion, magnetic and power sensors. This is 1.4% better than without including the time information. Hence, the time elapsed between events contains some information that improves prediction, however, only marginally. Our best implementation for predicting both the next sensor event and the time of occurrence was obtained using K-means clustering of the hour of day combined with the mean time elapsed to the next sensor. This implementation attained an accuracy of 80% for a set of fifteen sensors for a dataset with 70000 events, which corresponds to approximately 20 weeks of data. The same method attained an accuracy of 83.4% for a set of seven motion sensors. Information on the time of occurrence of the next sensor event is an important cornerstone for improving automation functions in smart homes as they allow anticipation of the next event or activity. It also allows more accurate monitoring of any pattern changes that may indicate the onset or progress of a disease. There is quite limited work in the literature on the prediction of the time of occurrence of sequential sensor events in smart homes. In addition, the algorithms are still not accurate enough for implementation in real homes. To our knowledge, there is only one work in the literature predicting the next event and its time of occurrence in the same model. Bayesian networks are used in that work [18]. Our method attains better overall accuracy when predicting both the sensor event and its time of occurrence in the same LSTM network. In addition, our study sheds light to sensor event prediction methods, input configurations, predictability of such events in a home, and the number of sensors required for good accuracy.

Clearly, a higher prediction accuracy is required before such algorithms can be applicable to real homes. Future work will include activity recognition based on binary sensor events. Our hypothesis is that clustering sensors into activities and predicting these may improve the prediction accuracy. In addition, we will examine the variability of the performance of the models when used in different apartments as well as the applicability of transfer learning between apartments.

Acknowledgement. The authors would like to thank the residents and the housekeepers at the seniors' care unit Skøyen Omsorg+; Torhild Holthe and Dr. Anne Lund (OsloMet) for recruiting participants for the trial and communicating with the residents throughout the trial; Dejan Krunić and Øyvind Width (Sensio AS) for installations of the sensors; and the rest of the participants of the Assisted Living Project for a fruitful interdisciplinary collaboration.

References

1. Alam, M.R., Reaz, M.B., Mohd Ali, M.A.: SPEED: an inhabitant activity prediction algorithm for smart homes. IEEE Trans. Syst. Man Cybern. Part A Syst. Hum. **42**(4), 985–990 (2012). https://doi.org/10.1109/TSMCA.2011.2173568

2. Aztiria, A., Augusto, J.C., Izaguirre, A., Cook, D.: Learning accurate temporal relations from user actions in intelligent environments. Adv. Soft Comput. **51**, 274–283 (2009). https://doi.org/10.1007/978-3-540-85867-6_32

3. Bataineh, K.M., Najia, M., Saqera, M.: A comparison study between various fuzzy clustering algorithms. Jordan J. Mech. Ind. Eng. **5**, 335–343 (2011)

4. Box, G.E.P., Jenkins, G.: Time Series Analysis, Forecasting and Control. Holden-Day Inc., San Francisco (1990)

5. Casagrande, F.D., Tørresen, J., Zouganeli, E.: Comparison of probabilistic models and neural networks on prediction of home sensor events. In: Accepted at International Joint Conference on Neural Networks (2019)

6. Casagrande, F.D., Tørresen, J., Zouganeli, E.: Sensor event prediction using recurrent neural network in smart homes for older adults. In: 2018 International Conference on Intelligent Systems (IS) (2019). https://doi.org/10.1109/IS.2018.8710467

7. Casagrande, F.D., Zouganeli, E.: Occupancy and daily activity event modelling in smart homes for older adults with mild cognitive impairment or dementia. In: Proceedings of The 59th Conference on Simulation and Modelling (SIMS 59), pp. 236–242 (2018)

8. Elhady, N.E., Provost, J.: A systematic survey on sensor failure detection and fault-tolerance in ambient assisted living. Sensors **18**(1991), 19 (2018). https://doi.org/10.3390/s18071991

9. Gopalratnam, K., Cook, D.J.: Online sequential prediction via incremental parsing: the active LeZi algorithm. IEEE Intell. Syst. **22**(1) (2007). https://doi.org/10.1109/MIS.2007.15

10. Graves, A.: Generating sequences with recurrent neural networks. arXiv (2014). https://doi.org/10.1109/ICASSP.2013.6638947

11. Hochreiter, S., Schmidhuber, J.: Long short-term memory. Neural Comput. **9**(8), 1735–1780 (1997). https://doi.org/10.1162/neco.1997.9.8.1735

12. Holder, L.B., Cook, D.J.: Automated activity-aware prompting for activity initiation. Gerontechnology **11**(4), 534–544 (2013). https://doi.org/10.4017/gt.2013.11.4.005.00

13. Joshi, K.D., Nalwade, P.S.: Modified k-means for better initial cluster centres (2013)

14. Lotfi, A., Langensiepen, C., Mahmoud, S.M., Akhlaghinia, M.J.: Smart homes for the elderly dementia sufferers: identification and prediction of abnormal behaviour. J. Ambient. Intell. Hum. Comput. **3**(3), 205–218 (2012). https://doi.org/10.1007/s12652-010-0043-x

15. Mahmoud, S., Lotfi, A., Langensiepen, C.: Behavioural pattern identification and prediction in intelligent environments. Appl. Soft Comput. J. **13**(4), 1813–1822 (2013). https://doi.org/10.1016/j.asoc.2012.12.012

16. Mahmud, T., Hasan, M., Chakraborty, A., Roy-Chowdhury, A.K.: A poisson process model for activity forecasting. In: 2016 IEEE International Conference on Image Processing (ICIP), pp. 3339–3343, September 2016. https://doi.org/10.1016/j.asoc.2012.12.012

17. Minor, B., Cook, D.J.: Forecasting occurrences of activities. Pervasive Mob. Comput. (2016). https://doi.org/10.1016/j.pmcj.2016.09.010

18. Nazerfard, E., Cook, D.J.: CRAFFT: an activity prediction model based on Bayesian networks **33**(4), 395–401 (2015). https://doi.org/10.1038/nbt.3121.ChIP-nexus

19. Petzold, J., Bagci, F., Trumler, W., Ungerer, T.: Next location prediction within a smart office building. Cogn. Sci. Res. Pap. Univ. Sussex CSRP **577**, 69 (2005). https://doi.org/10.1.1.92.3723

20. Riboni, D., Bettini, C., Civitarese, G., Janjua, Z.H., Helaoui, R.: SmartFABER: recognizing fine-grained abnormal behaviors for early detection of mild cognitive impairment. Artif. Intell. Med. **67**, 57–74 (2016). https://doi.org/10.1016/j.artmed.2015.12.001

21. Vintan, L., Gellert, A., Petzold, J., Ungerer, T.: Person movement prediction using neural networks. Computer (2004). https://doi.org/10.1.1.142.9137

22. Wu, S., Rendall, J.B., Smith, M.J., Zhu, S., Xu, J., Wang, H., Yang, Q., Qin, P.: Survey on prediction algorithms in smart homes. IEEE Internet Things J. **4**(3), 636–644 (2017). https://doi.org/10.1109/JIOT.2017.2668061

23. Zouganeli, E., et al.: Responsible development of self-learning assisted living technology for older adults with mild cognitive impairment or dementia. In: ICT4AWE 2017 - Proceedings of the 3rd International Conference on Information and Communication Technologies for Ageing Well and e-Health (Ict4awe), pp. 204–209 (2017). https://doi.org/10.5220/0006367702040209

Multi-task Learning Method for Hierarchical Time Series Forecasting

Maoxin Yang, Qinghua Hu$^{(\boxtimes)}$, and Yun Wang

College of Intelligence and Computing, Tianjin University, Tianjin 300350, China
{yangmaoxin,huqinghua,wangyun15}@tju.edu.cn

Abstract. Hierarchical time series is a set of time series organized by aggregation constraints and it is widely used in many real-world applications. Usually, hierarchical time series forecasting can be realized with a two-step method, in which all time series are forecasted independently and then the forecasting results are reconciled to satisfy aggregation consistency. However, these two-step methods have a high computational complexity and are unable to ensure optimal forecasts for all time series. In this paper, we propose a novel hierarchical forecasting approach to solve the above problems. Based on multi-task learning, we construct an integrated model that combines features of the bottom level series and the hierarchical structure. Then forecasts of all time series are output simultaneously and they are aggregated consistently. The model has the advantage of utilizing the correlation between time series. And the forecasting results are overall optimal by optimizing a global loss function. In order to avoid the curse of dimensionality as the number of time series grows larger, we further learn a sparse model with group sparsity and element-wise sparsity constraints according to data characteristics. The experimental results on simulation data and tourism data demonstrate that our method has a better overall performance while simplifying forecasting process.

Keywords: Hierarchical time series forecasting · Multi-task learning

1 Introduction

In many applied fields like economics and statistics, time series forecasting plays an important role in management, decision-making and scheduling. However, there are often many related time series based on aggregation relations, which can form a tree-like hierarchical structure. The set of these time series is called hierarchical time series. Figure 1 shows a diagram of a three-level hierarchical time series where every node represents a time series. At any given moment, the observed value of a parent time series is equal to the sum of the observed value of its child time series. Hierarchical time series forecasting is widely used in many real-world applications, such as tourism [1,8], labour market [11], company revenue [14] and electricity demand forecasting [15,18,19].

© Springer Nature Switzerland AG 2019
I. V. Tetko et al. (Eds.): ICANN 2019, LNCS 11730, pp. 474–485, 2019.
https://doi.org/10.1007/978-3-030-30490-4_38

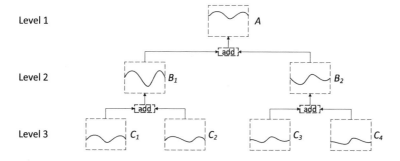

Fig. 1. A three-level hierarchical time series with seven series.

Compared to forecasting a time series, both aggregation consistency between levels and forecasting accuracy of every series are required in hierarchical forecasting. Aggregation consistency requires that the forecasts of all time series add up appropriately across the hierarchy, which is consistent with historical observations. These forecasts are called coherent forecasts. To get coherent forecasts, a two-step forecasting method is usually used. Firstly, all time series at each level of the hierarchy are forecasted independently. We call forecasts in this step base forecasts, but they are usually not aggregated consistently. Therefore, different reconciled strategies are adopted to get coherent forecasts in the second step. These will be introduced in detail in the next section.

However, there are two main disadvantages in these two-step methods. First, it is costly to fit the model separately for all time series especially when the number of series is large [11]. Second, the coherent forecasts have minimal errors with base forecasts rather than the true values, which are not optimal forecasts to some extent. To solve the above problems, we make hierarchical forecasting from a different view. We take full advantage of multi-task learning by regarding every bottom level time series forecasting as an independent task. In specific, we extract features of all time series at the bottom level into the overall input feature space, which utilizes similar information shared across them. What's more, the hierarchical structure can be easily incorporated into our multi-task learning model. Finally, by optimizing a global objective function, we can forecast all time series simultaneously and the forecasts are overall optimal. We call this method multi-task hierarchical forecasting model (**MHFM**).

As the number of the time series in the hierarchy increases, it's easy to fall into the curse of dimensionality. In such a high-dimensional context, it's expected to mine underlying structure in the data such as sparsity, low-rank structure, etc., which help improve the accuracy of the model and make it more robust. In hierarchical time series, many series tend to share some common features. For example, electricity demand forecasting is a specific application of hierarchical time series introduced in [15]. The author explored consumption patterns existing in bottom level electricity time series by clustering analysis. Furthermore, it's confirmed that many bottom level time series in Australia tourism data are highly similar. But at the same time, there are always exceptional time series which are unique.

According to [12], the data in hierarchical time series may not fall cleanly into block-sparse structure, i.e., they are *dirty* data. Therefore, a corresponding *dirty* model, which we call dirty multi-task hierarchical forecasting model (**DMHFM**), is further proposed. The model weights are divided into two components. One is the group sparsity component which achieves joint feature selection by imposing a $\ell_{1,\infty}$-norm regularization, and the other is the element-wise sparse component which keeps every series uniqueness by imposing a ℓ_1-norm regularization.

The main contributions of our work are summarized as follows.

- We propose a novel integrated hierarchical forecasting model based on multi-task strategy, which greatly simplifies the forecasting process. The forecasting results satisfy aggregation consistency and are overall optimal.
- We learn a sparse model by imposing different regularizations on two parts of the model, which can be solved effectively via the accelerated gradient methods (AGM)[13].
- We conduct our experiments on numerical simulations and real-world data. The results demonstrate that our models have a better overall performance than current methods.

2   Related Work

Base forecasting (BASE) [8] forecasted each time series independently. In other words, it is also the first step in two-step methods. Various algorithms are applied in BASE to get forecasts as accurate as possible. For example, exponential smoothing (ETS) [6] and autoregressive integrated moving average (ARIMA) models [3] are used most in hierarchical forecasting. However, the forecasts are usually not aggregated consistently. To get coherent forecasts, a simple approach called "bottom-up" (BU) forecasting [5,17,21] was first proposed. Forecasts of aggregated series are gotten by summing up base forecasts of the most disaggregated series according to the hierarchical structure. But the performance is poor when bottom series have a low signal-to-noise ratio.

Hyndman et al. [8] proposed to use ordinary least squares (OLS) to optimally reconcile base forecasts and followed by other researchers. All these works are based on proof that reconciled forecast errors are unidentified [20]. Therefore, different covariance matrices between base forecasts are estimated as alternative estimators. The covariance matrix is defined as an identity matrix based on assumption that all forecasts errors are independent and equal [8]. Weight least squares (WLS) [11] viewed covariance matrix as a diagonal matrix; i.e., only the variances between base forecasts are considered. HLS [2] is similar to WLS and it assumes that forecast errors of series only at the bottom level are equal. In recent work [20], the above methods were combined under the framework of minimum trace (MinT) reconciliation. A shrinkage estimator was proposed and performed better than other estimators.

3   Preliminaries

In order to facilitate the notation, we use a tree diagram to formalize the hierarchical time series. As presented in Fig. 1, a letter combined with a number labels a node where the letter identifies the level and the number identifies the individual time series. The top level is called the first level and level number increases from top to bottom. We use n_l to represent the number of time series at lth level. In Fig. 1, there are $n_1 = 1, n_2 = 2, n_3 = 4$.

Let $y_{i,t}$ be the observation of time series represented by node i at time t. Then at any time t, aggregation consistency requires the following equations: $y_{A,t} = y_{B_1,t} + y_{B_2,t}, y_{B_1,t} = y_{C_1,t} + y_{C_2,t}, y_{B_2,t} = y_{C_3,t} + y_{C_4,t}$.

To get a unified formulation, let $\boldsymbol{y}_t$ be a n-dimensional row vector containing observations of all time series at time t, $\boldsymbol{b}_t$ be a m-dimensional row vector containing observations of time series at bottom level and $\boldsymbol{a}_t$ be a l-dimensional row vector for the aggregated ones. Then $\boldsymbol{y}_t = (\boldsymbol{a}_t, \boldsymbol{b}_t)$ and $n = l + m$. In Fig. 1, we have $\boldsymbol{a}_t = (y_{A,t}, y_{B_1,t}, y_{B_2,t})$ and $\boldsymbol{b}_t = (y_{C_1,t}, y_{C_2,t}, y_{C_3,t}, y_{C_4,t})$. And above equations can be simplified to the following vector form:

$$\boldsymbol{y}_t = \boldsymbol{b}_t \boldsymbol{S}, \tag{1}$$

where $\boldsymbol{S} \in \{0,1\}^{m \times n}$ is named as the "summing matrix". In Fig. 1, the summing matrix $\boldsymbol{S}$ is given by:

$$\boldsymbol{S} = \begin{bmatrix} 1 & 1 & 0 & 1 & 0 & 0 & 0 \\ 1 & 1 & 0 & 0 & 1 & 0 & 0 \\ 1 & 0 & 1 & 0 & 0 & 1 & 0 \\ 1 & 0 & 1 & 0 & 0 & 0 & 1 \end{bmatrix}. \tag{2}$$

The same as $\boldsymbol{y}_t$ and $\boldsymbol{b}_t$, we use $\widehat{\boldsymbol{y}}_{T+h}$ to represent h-period-ahead predictions for all time series of the hierarchy and $\widehat{\boldsymbol{b}}_{T+h}$ to represent h-period-ahead predictions for bottom level series when we have T historical observations $\boldsymbol{y}_1, \boldsymbol{y}_2, \cdots, \boldsymbol{y}_T$. To keep the aggregation consistency, we have the following constraint:

$$\widehat{\boldsymbol{y}}_{T+h} = \widehat{\boldsymbol{b}}_{T+h} \boldsymbol{S}. \tag{3}$$

4   Proposed Method

4.1   Multi-task Hierarchical Forecasting Model

In hierarchical time series, each time series forecasting can be considered as a task. If we get s samples of d features for ith time series according to its historical observations, let $x_{i,j} \in \mathbb{R}^d$ be an input sample and $y_{i,j} \in \mathbb{R}$ be its corresponding target. Then $\boldsymbol{x}_i = [x_{i,1}, x_{i,2}, \cdots, x_{i,s}]^T \in \mathbb{R}^{s \times d}$ represents the input data matrix and $\boldsymbol{y}_i = [y_{i,1}, y_{i,2}, \cdots, y_{i,s}]^T \in \mathbb{R}^{s \times 1}$ is the target vector. In this paper, linear model is applied and we can get the forecasting model for ith time series as following:

$$\boldsymbol{y}_i = \boldsymbol{x}_i \boldsymbol{w}_i + \boldsymbol{e}_i, \tag{4}$$

where $\boldsymbol{w}_i \in \mathbb{R}^{d \times 1}$ is the weight vector and $\boldsymbol{e}_i \in \mathbb{R}^{s \times 1}$ represents error vector. According to ordinary least squares, its analytical solution is given by:

$$\boldsymbol{w}_i = (\boldsymbol{x}_i^T \boldsymbol{x}_i)^{-1} \boldsymbol{x}_i^T \boldsymbol{y}_i. \tag{5}$$

Now we consider a multi-task strategy. Let $i = 1, 2, \cdots, m$ represent m bottom level time series and $i = n - m + 1, n - m + 2, \cdots, n$ represent $n - m$ aggregated time series. Different from regular multi-task learning in which we may have n tasks, we make a m-task predication in the input feature space of bottom level series. By the summing matrix $\boldsymbol{S}$, we can obtain targets of all time series.

Similarly, let $\boldsymbol{X} = [\boldsymbol{x}_1, \boldsymbol{x}_2, \cdots, \boldsymbol{x}_m] \in \mathbb{R}^{s \times D}$ $(D = d \times m)$ be the input data matrix, $\boldsymbol{Y} = [\boldsymbol{y}_1, \boldsymbol{y}_2, \cdots, \boldsymbol{y}_n] \in \mathbb{R}^{s \times n}$ be corresponding target matrix and $\boldsymbol{W} = [\boldsymbol{w}_1, \boldsymbol{w}_2, \cdots, \boldsymbol{w}_m] \in \mathbb{R}^{D \times m}$ be the weight matrix. Then we can get a multi-task hierarchical forecasting model:

$$\boldsymbol{Y} = \boldsymbol{X}\boldsymbol{W}\boldsymbol{S} + \boldsymbol{E}, \tag{6}$$

where $\boldsymbol{E} \in \mathbb{R}^{s \times n}$ represents errors in the model. Because of the constraint of the summing matrix $\boldsymbol{S}$, the model satisfies aggregation consistency.

The objective of the model can be formulated as following:

$$\min_{\boldsymbol{W}} \|\boldsymbol{Y} - \boldsymbol{X}\boldsymbol{W}\boldsymbol{S}\|_F^2 + \lambda \|\boldsymbol{W}\|_F^2, \tag{7}$$

where $\|\cdot\|_F$ means the Frobenius norm of a matrix. In above formulation, the former is empirical loss on training sets and the latter is a regularizer to reduce model complexity. The coefficient $\lambda \geq 0$ is used to balance the two terms.

The analytical solution of optimization problem (7) can be obtained by following steps. Firstly, we take the derivative of (7) with respect to $\boldsymbol{W}$ and set it to zero:

$$\boldsymbol{X}^T \boldsymbol{X}\boldsymbol{W}\boldsymbol{S}\boldsymbol{S}^T + \lambda \boldsymbol{W} = \boldsymbol{X}^T \boldsymbol{Y}\boldsymbol{S}^T. \tag{8}$$

Because $\boldsymbol{S}\boldsymbol{S}^T$ is a full rank matrix, its inverse matrix exists. We can get

$$\boldsymbol{X}^T \boldsymbol{X}\boldsymbol{W} + \lambda \boldsymbol{W}(\boldsymbol{S}\boldsymbol{S}^T)^{-1} = \boldsymbol{X}^T \boldsymbol{Y}\boldsymbol{S}^T(\boldsymbol{S}\boldsymbol{S}^T)^{-1}. \tag{9}$$

Denote $\boldsymbol{A} = \boldsymbol{X}^T \boldsymbol{X}$, $\boldsymbol{B} = \lambda(\boldsymbol{S}\boldsymbol{S}^T)^{-1}$ and $\boldsymbol{C} = \boldsymbol{X}^T \boldsymbol{Y}\boldsymbol{S}^T(\boldsymbol{S}\boldsymbol{S}^T)^{-1}$, (9) becomes:

$$\boldsymbol{A}\boldsymbol{W} + \boldsymbol{W}\boldsymbol{B} = \boldsymbol{C}. \tag{10}$$

Then according to [16], $\boldsymbol{W}$ can be solved by

$$vec(\boldsymbol{W}) = (\boldsymbol{I} \otimes \boldsymbol{A} + \boldsymbol{B}^T \otimes \boldsymbol{I})^{-1} vec(\boldsymbol{C}), \tag{11}$$

where the operator vec stacks a matrix's column into a vector and the operator $\otimes$ means the Kronecker product of two matrixs.

We denote this method multi-task hierarchical forecasting model (**MHFM**). And it's used to verify the effectiveness of multi-task strategy.

4.2 Dirty Multi-task Hierarchical Forecasting Model

In the above multi-task hierarchical forecasting model, feature space X contains features of all bottom-level series. When the number of bottom-level time series m increases, the number of features D in X may be greater than the number of samples s. In such a high-dimensional setting, the complexity of the model is high and there are a lot of redundant features, which makes model perform worse. Therefore, it's necessary to learn a sparse model.

As is known to us, ℓ_1-norm (Lasso) regularization achieves an element-wise sparsity and ℓ_1/ℓ_q-norm regularization is used for group sparsity to select joint features. However, there exist both similarities and uniqueness in all time series. It's unreasonable to choose one of the above penalties. A solution is provided and proven valid in [12], where the model weights are decomposed into group sparse component and element-wise component. We call this model dirty multi-task hierarchical forecasting model (**DMHFM**).

Then the objective function of our dirty model becomes:

$$\min_{P,Q} \|Y - X(P+Q)S\|_F^2 + \lambda_1 \|P\|_{1,\infty} + \lambda_2 \|Q\|_{1,1},$$
$$s.t. \quad W = P + Q,$$

(12)

where $P \in \mathbb{R}^{D \times m}$ and $Q \in \mathbb{R}^{D \times m}$. And

$$\|P\|_{1,\infty} = \sum_i \|P_i\|_\infty = \sum_i \max_j |P_{i,j}|,$$

(13)

$$\|Q\|_{1,1} = \sum_i \|Q_i\|_1 = \sum_{i,j} |Q_{i,j}|.$$

(14)

The objective contains smooth part and non-smooth part, so no analytical solution is derived for it. Therefore, we use the accelerated gradient methods (AGM) [13] to optimize it and the DMHFM is formulated in Algorithm 1.

5 Experiments

In this section, we conducted experiments on a small hierarchical simulation data and a larger hierarchical tourism data. The data description, experimental setting, experimental results and analysis are presented in two subsections.

To demonstrate the effectiveness of the proposed models, we compare our methods with strong baselines and state-of-art methods. They are BASE [8], BU [21], OLS [8], WLS [11], HLS [2] and MinT [20]. For MinT, we choose shrink estimator, which performs best in most cases [20]. These compared methods are introduced in Sect. 2. We implement all reconciled methods with the help of *hts* package for R [9].

We use average root mean squared errors (ARMSE) [20] as a metric to evaluate the performance of each level. It's defined as

$$\boldsymbol{ARMSE} = \frac{1}{n_l} \sum_{i=1}^{n_l} \sqrt{\left(\frac{1}{N} \sum_{j=1}^{N} |y_{i,j} - \widetilde{y}_{i,j}|^2\right)},$$

(15)

Algorithm 1. Dirty Multi-task Hierarchical Forecasting Model (DMHFM)

Input: Input data matrix $X \in \mathbb{R}^{s \times D}$, targets matrix $Y \in \mathbb{R}^{s \times n}$ and the summing matrix $S \in \{0, 1\}^{m \times n}$. Regularization parameters λ_1 and λ_2. And maximum number of iterations K.

Output: Weight Matrix $W \in \mathbb{R}^{D \times m}$.

1: Initialize $P_1 \in \mathbb{R}^{D \times m}$ and $Q_1 \in \mathbb{R}^{D \times m}$ to be Zeros Matrices; set $t_1 = 1$, $P_n = P_1$ and $Q_n = Q_1$; denote $f(P + Q) = \|Y - X(P + Q)S\|_F^2$ and set γ to be small enough, s.t. $\gamma \leq (\|\nabla^2 f(P + Q)\|^{-1})$.

2: **for** $k = 1 : K$ **do**

3:     **repeat**

4:         Denote $C = P_n - \gamma \nabla f(P_n + Q_n)$, $\alpha_1 = \gamma \lambda_1$;

           $P_{k+1} = \arg\min_P 0.5 * \|P - C\|_F^2 + \alpha_1 \|Q\|_{1,\infty}$

           Denote $D = Q_n - \gamma \nabla f(P_n + Q_n)$, $\alpha_2 = \gamma \lambda_2$;

           $Q_{k+1} = \arg\min_Q 0.5 * \|Q - D\|_F^2 + \alpha_2 \|P\|_1$

           $t_{k+1} = \frac{1 + \sqrt{1 + 4t_k^2}}{2}$;

           Update $P_n = P_{t+1} + \frac{t_k - 1}{t_{k+1}}(P_{k+1} - P_k)$;

           Update $Q_n = Q_{t+1} + \frac{t_k - 1}{t_{k+1}}(Q_{k+1} - Q_k)$;

5:     **until** Convergence criterion satisfied.

6: **end for**

7: $W = P + Q$;

8: **return** W;

---

where n_l is the number of series at level l and N is the number of observations in test set. $y_{i,j}$ and $\widetilde{y}_{i,j}$ represent the true and predicted values, respectively. It represents the average error of all time series with similar magnitude at each level. Therefore, it is a general metric to measure the performance of different algorithms at each level and avoids presenting the results of all time series.

5.1 Numerical Simulations

We simulate a simple hierarchical time series as presented in Fig. 1. At first, all bottom-level time series are generated by ARIMA(p, d, q) processes, which are implemented via *arima.sim*() function in R language. The parameters p, d, q and the error covariance matrix are set according to [20]. Next, we sum up bottom-level time series to obtain aggregated time series across the hierarchy.

We generate 800 observations for every time series, where 600 are withheld as training sets, 200 are used as validation sets and 200 are used as test sets. We make 1- to 6-steps-ahead forecasts for every time series. This process is repeated 100 times and we get the average results. ETS models are used to produce base forecasts for all compared methods, and the purpose of fitting ETS models to series generated from ARIMA processes can be seen in the work [20]. We select an optimal ETS model [10] for every series by *forecast* package for R [7].

Table 1 presents the ARMSEs of each level for each forecast horizon. The last column is the average of the results for all forecast horizons. The bold

Table 1. Forecasting results on simulated hierarchical time series.

Method	$h = 1$	2	3	4	5	6	1–6
Level 1							
BASE	50.41	69.92	95.73	108.31	126.22	134.15	97.46
BU	50.35	69.87	95.45	108.09	125.84	133.84	97.24
OLS	50.37	69.89	95.61	108.22	126.08	134.03	97.37
WLS	50.35	69.88	95.52	108.15	125.95	133.93	97.29
HLS	50.36	69.88	95.55	108.17	125.99	133.97	97.32
MinT	50.35	69.87	95.49	108.11	125.91	133.88	97.27
MHFM	**45.25**	**60.23**	**79.23**	**86.85**	**96.12**	**100.62**	**78.05**
Level 2							
BASE	18.00	24.96	34.08	38.57	44.88	47.75	34.71
BU	17.98	24.94	34.05	38.53	44.83	47.70	34.67
OLS	17.99	24.95	34.10	38.57	44.89	47.76	34.71
WLS	17.98	24.94	34.07	38.55	44.86	47.73	34.69
HLS	17.99	24.94	34.08	38.56	44.87	47.74	34.70
MinT	17.98	24.94	34.06	38.54	44.85	47.72	34.68
MHFM	**16.13**	**21.45**	**28.12**	**30.81**	**33.99**	**35.51**	**27.67**
Level 3							
BASE	5.38	7.47	10.20	11.55	13.43	14.31	10.39
BU	5.38	7.47	10.20	11.55	13.43	14.31	10.39
OLS	5.38	7.48	10.21	11.56	13.45	14.32	10.40
WLS	5.38	7.47	10.20	11.55	13.44	14.31	10.39
HLS	5.38	7.47	10.20	11.56	13.44	14.32	10.40
MinT	5.38	7.47	10.20	11.55	13.44	14.31	10.39
MHFM	**4.85**	**6.47**	**8.47**	**9.28**	**10.23**	**10.69**	**8.33**

entries identify the smallest results for each level and each forecast horizon. We only present the results of MHFM, because these time series are generated from ARIMA process and features are confirmed by the parameters. DMHFM achieves similar performances.

From Table 1, it is observed that MHFM achieves the best performance at each level and each forecast horizon. The minor differences between compared methods may be due to the same covariance matrix in the simulation process, but it can still be seen that MinT performs better overall than other reconciled methods. However, compared to various reconciled methods, MHFM has a significant improvement in forecast accuracy over BASE method. What's more, MHFM slows down the rate of error expansion with the increase of forecast horizon. Compared with BASE method, 1-step-ahead forecast improved by 10.2% and 6-steps-ahead forecast improved by 25.0% at first level (Other levels have a similar performance) in MHFM.

5.2   Tourism Forecasting

In this subsection, we conduct experiment on Australian domestic tourism data [4], which are used in many works [1,2,8] for hierarchical forecasting. The data form a four-level hierarchical time series according to geographical division. Each level refers to the whole country, states, zones and regions from top to bottom. The number of time series at each level is 1, 7, 27 and 76, respectively. These time series are monthly data ranging from January 1998 to December 2016. In other words, there are 228 observations per time series. More detailed information on Australian tourism data can be found in the work [1].

We also split the data into training, validation and test sets. Observations for the first 132 months and 36 months are used as training set and validation set, and remaining months are used for testing. We choose 24 historical observations in each bottom level series as features and make 1- to 12-steps-ahead forecasts. The ARIMA model has a great advantage in seasonal time series forecasting, so we use it to generate base forecasts for all compared methods. The optimal ARIMA model is fitted using the default setting of automated algorithms [10].

The results are shown in Table 2. We can see that DMHFM has least forecasting errors in most cases and makes a significant improvement at the top level (Compared with BASE method, DMHFM improves by 23.7% while MinT improves by 6.8% for average result of all horizons). Furthermore, it can be also observed that MHFM has a good performance in some cases such as the first two levels. In terms of ARMSEs for all levels, DMHFM achieves the best performance except for the first forecast horizon, followed by MinT and MHFM. It demonstrates the effectiveness of multi-task learning strategy in real-world time series. At the same time, it shows that our sparse strategy works when data is high-dimensional.

From Tables 1 and 2, we can find that BASE method, i.e., forecasting all time series independently, usually has lager errors. Although in various reconciled methods, final forecasts are aggregated consistently and more accurate, they are still influenced by the bad performance of base forecasts. Therefore, it demonstrates that in our proposed models, the shared features between time series and a global loss function based on multi-task learning can help produce more accurate forecasts.

Table 2. Forecasting results on Australia tourism data.

Method	$h = 1$	2	3	6	12	1–6	1–12
Level 1: Australia (1 series)							
BASE	2259.48	2364.65	2395.18	2434.61	2621.77	2378.74	2466.87
BU	2211.17	2280.46	2320.79	2405.00	2638.88	2328.99	2449.46
OLS	2217.37	2321.14	2365.51	2408.63	2597.48	2347.51	2438.86
WLS	2102.83	2198.21	2258.95	2327.95	2547.48	2251.07	2363.93
HLS	2108.01	2200.72	2258.24	2318.72	2526.77	2247.38	2353.60
MinT	2016.79	2105.53	2186.84	2274.76	2480.59	2183.02	2298.21
MHFM	1787.02	1679.55	1688.42	1900.46	**2115.64**	1769.84	1945.55
DMHFM	**1662.16**	**1567.47**	**1611.21**	**1808.77**	2214.53	**1659.28**	**1882.33**
Level 2: states (7 series)							
BASE	442.94	455.14	464.96	471.49	490.76	461.95	472.02
BU	479.59	483.94	489.16	501.50	526.49	491.25	505.72
OLS	460.23	473.61	476.71	482.19	501.87	474.68	484.60
WLS	451.73	460.77	466.53	476.07	499.27	466.36	479.33
HLS	451.42	460.71	466.01	474.85	496.85	465.53	477.89
MinT	**442.35**	450.31	458.15	468.94	489.58	458.33	470.94
MHFM	472.32	453.35	453.84	468.09	**485.08**	461.65	471.79
DMHFM	465.01	**449.01**	**451.67**	**465.30**	493.69	**458.32**	**470.52**
Level 3: zones (27 series)							
BASE	194.50	197.20	197.69	197.22	200.90	196.61	197.91
BU	200.96	202.74	204.89	205.98	210.06	204.27	206.35
OLS	193.66	197.11	198.23	197.56	200.61	196.76	197.81
WLS	192.89	195.58	197.28	197.76	201.29	196.35	198.00
HLS	192.41	195.13	196.96	197.15	200.50	195.81	197.36
MinT	**189.54**	**191.82**	**193.89**	**194.58**	**197.67**	**193.06**	**194.61**
MHFM	205.47	201.19	202.32	202.51	206.80	202.70	203.84
DMHFM	196.36	193.76	194.97	196.38	201.97	195.36	197.27
Level 4: regions (76 series)							
BASE	100.29	100.25	100.84	101.41	102.91	100.86	101.56
BU	100.29	100.25	100.84	101.41	102.91	100.86	101.56
OLS	99.10	99.24	99.61	99.71	101.02	99.44	99.87
WLS	98.60	98.74	99.16	99.56	100.96	99.13	99.71
HLS	98.62	98.65	99.18	99.51	100.89	99.08	99.64
MinT	**97.42**	97.46	97.96	98.40	**99.77**	97.95	98.51
MHFM	101.67	100.27	100.64	101.34	103.17	100.96	101.60
DMHFM	97.88	**96.93**	**97.35**	**98.00**	100.56	**97.52**	**98.49**
All levels (111 series)							
BASE	164.26	166.61	168.03	169.07	173.90	167.44	169.66
BU	167.71	169.02	170.64	172.83	178.53	170.71	173.69
OLS	163.96	166.67	167.80	168.43	173.02	167.03	169.02
WLS	161.86	164.04	165.65	167.26	172.52	165.32	167.96
HLS	161.78	163.89	165.55	166.92	171.94	165.08	167.57
MinT	**158.87**	160.75	162.83	164.77	169.62	162.59	165.19
MHFM	165.48	161.32	161.95	165.29	170.59	163.49	166.42
DMHFM	159.08	**155.93**	**157.08**	**160.51**	**169.06**	**158.14**	**162.05**

6   Conclusions and Future Work

Hierarchical time series has been applied widely in many applications and aggregation consistency is an important point in hierarchical forecasting. In many previous works, a two-step strategy is adopted, but it has a high computational cost and the forecasts are not optimal overall. In this paper, we have proposed a novel integrated hierarchical forecasting method based on multi-task learning. By the advantage of utilizing correlation of time series, we achieve an integrated model, which greatly simplifies forecasting process and has a better prediction performance. What's more, we can learn a sparse model to avoid artificial feature selection. Both numerical simulations and tourism forecasting demonstrate the effectiveness of our approach.

This paper gives an easy start for hierarchical time series forecasting from the view of multi-task learning. Our method can be easily extended to non-linear and other regularized forms for solving more complicated time series. In the future work, we will consider applying it to more real-world applications.

Acknowledgments. This work is supported by the National Natural Science Foundation of China under Grants 61732011, 61432011, and U1435212.

References

1. Athanasopoulos, G., Ahmed, R.A., Hyndman, R.J.: Hierarchical forecasts for australian domestic tourism. Int. J. Forecast. **25**(1), 146–166 (2009). https://doi.org/10.1016/j.ijforecast.2008.07.004
2. Athanasopoulos, G., Hyndman, R.J., Kourentzes, N., Petropoulos, F.: Forecasting with temporal hierarchies. Eur. J. Oper. Res. **262**(1) (2017). https://doi.org/10.1016/j.ejor.2017.02.046
3. Box, G.E., Jenkins, G.M., Reinsel, G.C., Ljung, G.M.: Time Series Analysis: Forecasting and Control, 5nd edn. Wiley, New Jersey (2015). https://books.google.com/books?id=rNt5CgAAQBAJ
4. Canberra: Tourism forecasts. Technical report, Tourism Research Australia (2015). https://www.tra.gov.au/International/International-Tourism-Forecasts
5. Dunn, D.M., Williams, W.H., Dechaine, T.L.: Aggregate versus subaggregate models in local area forecasting. J. Am. Stat. Assoc. **71**(353), 68–71 (1976). https://doi.org/10.1080/01621459.1976.10481478
6. Holt, C.C.: Forecasting seasonals and trends by exponentially weighted moving averages. Int. J. Forecast. **20**(1), 5–10 (2004). https://doi.org/10.1016/j.ijforecast.2003.09.015
7. Hyndman, R.J.: forecast: Forecasting functions for time series and linear models (2019). http://pkg.robjhyndman.com/forecast
8. Hyndman, R.J., Ahmed, R.A., Athanasopoulos, G., Shang, H.L.: Optimal combination forecasts for hierarchical time series. Comput. Stat. Data Anal. **55**(9), 2579–2589 (2011). https://doi.org/10.1016/j.csda.2011.03.006
9. Hyndman, R.J., Athanasopoulos, G., Shang, H.L.: hts: An R package for forecasting hierarchical or grouped time series (2018). https://pkg.earo.me/hts

10. Hyndman, R.J., Khandakar, Y.: Automatic time series forecasting: the forecast package for R. J. Stat. Softw. **26**(3), 1–22 (2008). https://doi.org/10.18637/jss.v027.i03
11. Hyndman, R.J., Lee, A.J., Wang, E.: Fast computation of reconciled forecasts for hierarchical and grouped time series. Comput. Stat. Data Anal. **97**, 16–32 (2016). https://doi.org/10.1016/j.csda.2015.11.007
12. Jalali, A., Sanghavi, S., Ruan, C., Ravikumar, P.K.: A dirty model for multi-task learning. In: 24th Annual Conference on Neural Information Processing Systems, Vancouver, British Columbia, Canada, pp. 964–972. Curran Associates Inc. (2010). http://papers.nips.cc/paper/4125-a-dirty-model-for-multi-task-learning
13. Nesterov, Y.: Gradient methods for minimizing composite functions. Math. Program. **140**(1), 125–161 (2013). https://doi.org/10.1007/s10107-012-0629-5
14. Novak, J., Mcgarvie, S., Garcia, B.E.: A Bayesian model for forecasting hierarchically structured time series. arXiv preprint arXiv:1711.04738 (2017). https://arxiv.org/abs/1711.04738
15. Pang, Y., Yao, B., Zhou, X., Zhang, Y., Xu, Y., Tan, Z.: Hierarchical electricity time series forecasting for integrating consumption patterns analysis and aggregation consistency. In: 27th International Joint Conference on Artificial Intelligence, Stockholm, Sweden, pp. 3506–3512. ijcai.org (2018). https://doi.org/10.24963/ijcai.2018/487
16. Petersen, K.B., Pedersen, M.S.P.: The matrix cookbook. Technical University of Denmark **7**(15), 510 (2008). https://doi.org/10.1.1.113.6244
17. Shlifer, E., Wolff, R.W.: Aggregation and proration in forecasting. Manag. Sci. **25**(6), 594–603 (1979). https://doi.org/10.1287/mnsc.25.6.594
18. Taieb, S.B., Taylor, J.W., Hyndman, R.J.: Coherent probabilistic forecasts for hierarchical time series. In: 34th International Conference on Machine Learning, Sydney, NSW, Australia, pp. 3348–3357. PMLR (2017). http://dl.acm.org/citation.cfm?id=3305890.3306027
19. Taieb, S.B., Yu, J., Barreto, M.N., Rajagopal, R.: Regularization in hierarchical time series forecasting with application to electricity smart meter data. In: 31th AAAI Conference on Artificial Intelligence, San Francisco, California, USA, pp. 4474–4480. AAAI Press (2017). https://doi.org/10.1038/nature06229
20. Wickramasuriya, S.L., Athanasopoulos, G., Hyndman, R.J.: Optimal forecast reconciliation for hierarchical and grouped time series through trace minimization. J. Am. Stat. Assoc., 1–16 (2018). https://doi.org/10.1080/01621459.2018.1448825
21. Zellner, A., Tobias, J.: A note on aggregation, disaggregation and forecasting performance. J. Forecast. **19**(5), 457–465 (2000). https://doi.org/10.1002/1099-131X(200009)19:5⟨457::AID-FOR761⟩3.0.CO;2-6

Demand-Prediction Architecture for Distribution Businesses Based on Multiple RNNs with Alternative Weight Update

Yuya Okadome$^{(\boxtimes)}$, Wenpeng Wei, Ryo Sakai, and Toshiko Aizono

Intelligent Information Research Department, Hitachi, Ltd.,
1-280, Higashi-koigakubo, Kokubunji-shi, Tokyo 185-8601, Japan
{yuya.okadome.qj,wenpeng.wei.bo,toshiko.aizono.jn}@hitachi.com

Abstract. Predicting future demand is important for reducing costs, such as under- and over-stocking cost, in distribution business. To predict item demand, a prediction model such as an autoregressive model, directly uses order histories. It is difficult to manage models since the number of models equals that of items with in such an approach. It is not easy to apply of multi-step prediction. In this research, we propose an asynchronous-updating heterogeneous stacking model (AHSM) which is based on recurrent neural networks (RNNs). AHSM has three modules for prediction: feature extractor, predictor, and inner-state generator. By using the inner-state generator, the model enables stable learning and accurate prediction. We applied AHSM to demand prediction and compared it with other models, i.e., the auto-regressive, integral and moving average model and Prophet, and RNN-based model. The results indicate that AHSM enables the accurate demand prediction even in multi-step prediction.

Keywords: Recurrent neural network · Deep learning ·
Demand prediction · Industrial use

1 Introduction

Predicting future demand is important in supply chain management (SCM), e.g., in factories, warehouses and distribution businesses, as shown in Fig. 1. For example, short-term prediction (1–3 days) is useful for item ordering in warehouses to prevent over- and under-stocking, and long-term prediction (over 2 weeks) is useful for labor management. Since the number of orders, i.e., demand value, is differs significantly for each item and the life cycle of items is short in food warehouse/wholesales companies, it is difficult to achieve accurate demand prediction for food SCM. Losses of profit of over- and under-stocking due to the uncertainty of demand prediction becomes hundreds of million dollar for one company.

© Springer Nature Switzerland AG 2019
I. V. Tetko et al. (Eds.): ICANN 2019, LNCS 11730, pp. 486–496, 2019.
https://doi.org/10.1007/978-3-030-30490-4_39

With most of demand prediction models, a statistical model is created for each item based on demand history [1–3]. Since the number of models linearly increases along with the number of item, the maintenance cost of each model also increases. Each model also cannot predict newly launched items since it directly uses the previous demand, and it is difficult to use other demand-related information, e.g., temperature for ice-cream. Therefore, a recurrent neural network (RNN) model [4–7] as a single model predictor for all items is expected to be useful for demand prediction since it can handle multiple types of information and a large amount of data.

To enable accurate demand prediction in distribution businesses (especially, our targets are those for food warehouse/wholesales), we propose an asynchronous-updating heterogeneous stacking model (AHSM), which uses multiple RNNs. AHSM consists of three modules for prediction: feature extractor, predictor, and inner-state generator. The feature extractor extracts features from the input information via multiple RNNs, inner-state generator generates the inner state of the predictor's RNN, and the predictor predicts future demands with the initial inner state from the inner-state generator. The inner-state generator asynchronously updates from the entire network and learns to generate better inner states against the previous learning step by using the loss function with the previous prediction error.

We applied AHSM to demand-prediction task for 4,000 items and evaluated the prediction error. We compared it with the auto-regressive, integral and moving average (ARIMA) model, Prophet, and three other RNN-based models. AHSM enabled the accurate prediction; both short and long term.

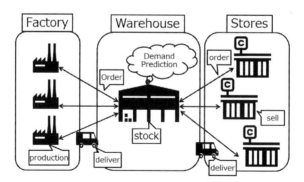

Fig. 1. Example of supply chain. To deliver ordered items to seller, wholesaler orders items from factory in advance.

2   Related Work

We briefly describe the types of demand-prediction models.

2.1 History-Based Prediction Models

Autoregressive (AR) models [1,8] are implemented in the many applications since they are easy to apply and enable accurate short-term prediction. The basic formulation of an AR model is: $\hat{x}_{t+1} = \sum_{i=n}^{t} a_i x_i$. a, x and $\hat{x}$ are weight, previous demand values, and predicted demand values, respectively. Demand values mean the number of orders for each item.

The AR models, ARMA and ARIMA are frequently used. These models combine moving averaging (MA), and integral (I). Since such a model is created for each item, the maintenance cost becomes high for distribution businesses with large numbers of items.

2.2 Modeling-Based Prediction Models

Prediction models that involve decomposing temporal demand data into multiple functions, such as trends and periodic changes, have been proposed [3,9]. If a large amount of data can be used for parameter estimation of each function, the computational cost becomes high. To overcome this problem, the Prophet model [3] was proposed. With this model, a model is also created for each item to predict demand.

2.3 Deep-learning-based Prediction Models

A demand-prediction model based on an RNN was recently proposed [10]. An RNN effectively handles temporal data and used for natural language tasks and signal processing [11–13]. This model can handle various types (e.g., image, numerical, and categorical) and large amounts of data as well as nonlinear regression tasks. Since it is not necessary to create a model for each item with this model, the maintenance cost is low.

3 Proposed Demand Prediction Model

To enable accurate demand prediction, an RNN-based model handles various scales and types of temporal data (e.g., weather, temperature, and item category sales). AHSM uses a normalized loss function, and stacked architecture to handle various scales and type of temporal data, respectively.

3.1 AHSM's Architecture

Figure 2 shows the architecture of AHSM. AHSM consists of three modules: 1. feature extractor, 2. inner-state generator, and 3. predictor. We give details of each bellow.

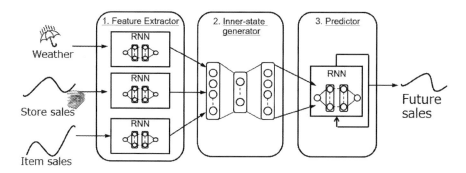

Fig. 2. AHSM's architecture. Number of RNN models in feature extractor changed based on amount of input temporal data. Architecture of inner-state generator is similar to that of auto-encoder.

Feature Extractor. RNNs are for different types of temporal sequences in the feature extractor (Fig. 2). The categorical information related to each temporal feature is encoded to the real numbers by an embedding layer [14] then encoded features and temporal feature are input to the RNNs. In the case of warehouse demand prediction, number of items are over a thousand, and item names (or item IDs) are encoded by an embedding layer. This module outputs the inner state h_t of each RNN. These states are used as the conditional information for the next module, i.e., inner-state generator.

Inner-State Generator. The inner-state generator generates the initial state of the predictor. This module is important for accurate prediction since the performance of a RNN is sensitive to its inner-state [15]. This module has an auto-encoder like architecture [16] to generate a state, and the input features are all the h_ts of the previous module. The equation of h_t generation based on each RNN state $h_t^e, e = 1, ..., M$ can be described as

$$h_t^{new} = g(f(\{h_t^e | e = 1, ..., M\})), \qquad (1)$$

where M is the number of RNNs in the feature extractor. $f(\cdot)$ is the encoding of the h_t into a low-dimensional space (e.g., from 1,240 to 128), and $g(\cdot)$ is the decoding architecture.

The purpose of this module is to generate a better h_t for demand prediction. To improve the quality of an h_t, the module is learned independently based on the prediction error as well as updating the entire network. When the module is independently updated, the weights of other modules are fixed and the previous prediction error p_e is used as the target value. The loss function for updating the module is defined as the sigmoid family function:

$$loss_g(\hat{p}_e, p_e) = \frac{\hat{p}_e - p_e}{1 + |\hat{p}_e - p_e|}, \qquad (2)$$

where $\hat{p}_e$ is the current prediction error. The objective of this function is to reduce $\hat{p}_e$ to enable accurate prediction.

Predictor. Predictor predicts future demands by using the generated inner-state h_t^{new}. To predict the demand of next time step, the current actual demand is necessary to input the model. For the multi-time step prediction, a predicted demand value is input. The error of multi-step prediction becomes large when the number of steps are large since input is estimated values. This procedure is same as the prediction with single RNN.

It is necessary to consider the long-term time dependency to predict the future demand, e.g., sales are affected by seasonal effect. Therefore, network architecture is not naive RNN but a long short-term memory (LSTM) [4] or a gated recurrent unit (GRU) [7,17]. We adopt GRU in all modules of AHSM as an RNN model. Details of architecture is described in the experiment section.

3.2 Loss Function

For estimating numerical data, the mean square error (MSE) is often used to learn parameter weights. Since value of MSE is proportional to the square of magnitude of data value, learned parameters of the network focus on items with large demand values by using this error even if the data are normalized by all the training data. In this research, we used MSE normalized based on each data value:

$$loss_w(\hat{x}_i, x) = \sum_{t=1}^{T} \frac{(x_t - \hat{x}_t)^2}{w^2}, \tag{3}$$

$$w = \frac{1}{T} \sum_{t=1}^{T} x_t \tag{4}$$

to cope with the various order of magnitude data, where w is the weight for each data scale and T is the length of test period.

The w is calculated as the mean of target demand values with T. This is to learn the sequence of newly launched items since such items do not have enough demand for the training period.

The negative binomial loss function was also proposed for demand prediction [10]. This loss function is expressed as the likelihood of probability distribution, and the prediction error is calculated by the maximum likelihood of the negative binomial distribution. A network learns the parameters of this loss function, such as the mean and variance, and the estimated demand values are obtained by sampling the estimated negative binomial distribution. By using this loss function, the prediction error rapidly increases for long-term prediction.

Learning Procedure. During the learning procedure, all parameters of a network are simultaneously updated in a general procedure of learning. During this procedure, learning tends to be unstable for AHSM since the h_t^{new} changes and affects the predictor, and the predictor learns weights based on such inner-state. To prevent this instability and enable more accurate prediction, we alternate between updating the entire network and inner-state generator.

With AHSM, Eq. (3) is adopted when all weights are updated, and when the weights of inner-state generator are updated, Eq. (2) is adopted. All parameters of the network are updated during a certain epoch ep_w and weights of the inner-state generator is during a certain epoch ep_i, and each learning phase is alternatively run. Note that, the prediction error after each ep_i is used as the p_e in Eq. (2).

4 Demand-Prediction Experiment

In this experiment, we conduct a demand-prediction task with an open dataset[1] containing actual demand data of grocery stores in Ethiopia. This dataset includes the demands of 4,000 items of 54 stores over 4 years. We summarized all store data with regard to the demand of each item, e.g., the demand for a certain type of chocolate in 54 stores was summarized and handled as one sequence, since our target is warehouse/wholesales management business.

4.1 Experimental Settings

The T was set to 16 days. We used mean absolute percentile error (MAPE) to evaluate the errors of short- and long-term prediction. To evaluate a demand prediction model for industrial use, we often adopt MAPE metrics since the metrics is often used in business field of warehouse/wholesales. For short-term prediction, today's demand was input to the predictor, which outputs tomorrow's demand, and the demand for the next 16 days was predicted for long-term prediction.

We created dataset to learn the RNN-based models by slicing of the item sales. The demand of 106 days was sliced for each item. We used 90 days of data as transition information and 16 days of data for estimation. The maximum number of the sliced demands was 100 for each of the 4,000 items.

We compared AHSM with five other models, i.e., ARIMA, Prophet, RNN-based model with negative binomial loss (NB-RNN), simple RNN-based model with loss function Eq. (3) (s-RNN), and AHSM with only whole weight learning (HSM). The order of ARIMA is defined by Akaike's Information Criterion. The parameters of Prophet model, such as the Fourier order, are optimized using Bayesian optimization [18,19]. If a parameter estimation is failed for ARIMA and Prophet model, MAPE is 100% since estimated demand values are defined 0 in such a case.

We adopted a GRU [7,17] as an RNN model since it requires low memory usage and can handle long-term dependency. The architectures of the RNN-based models are briefly described as below

- s-RNN: a 3-stacked-GRU with 1024 hidden units,
- NB-RNN: Seq-to-seq model of a 3-stacked-GRU with 1024 hidden units [10],

---

[1] Corporacion Favorita Grocery Sales Forecasting: https://www.kaggle.com/c/favorita-grocery-sales-forecasting/data.

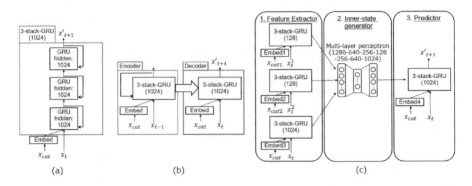

Fig. 3. Network architectures used in experiment. (a): an architecture of s-RNN. s-RNN is 3-stack-GRU with 1,024 hidden units, and this stacking model is shown as 3-stack-GRU (1024) in the figure. (b): an architecture of NB-RNN. (c): an architecture of AHSM. x_{cat} is the categorical features. x_{cat} in (a), (b) and (c) includes item ID, item category, and item family of target item of prediction, and corresponding embedding layer (Embed) is attached for each categorical feature. x_{cat1}, x_{cat2} in (c) are item category and item family. x_t^1 and x_t^2 in (c) are demands of item category and item family.

- HSM: Three 3-stacked-GRUs in the feature extractor and three multi-layer perceptrons (1,280-640-1,024) in the inner-state generator, and a 3-stacked-GRU in the predictor,
- AHSM: Three 3-stacked-GRUs in the feature extractor, seven multi-layer perceptrons (1,280-640-256-128-256-640-1,024) in the inner-state generator and a 3-stacked-GRU in the predictor.

Detailed architectures are shown in Fig. 3. The number of multi-layer perceptrons differs between HSM and AHSM because of the stability of learning. Number of learnable parameters of s-RNN, NB-RNN and AHSM is about 9.5, 19 and 21 million, respectively. The Adam optimizer [20] with a learning rate $1e^{-5}$ was used for all these models.

Categorical information, such as item category (e.g., snack, ice, grocery) and item family (defined by the data provider) was used for prediction with each RNN-based model. For HSM and AHSM, the related temporal sequence of item demand, such as total demand of item category and item family is also input via each feature extractor. This information was also sliced from the original demand data.

4.2   Experimental Results

Table 1 lists the MAPEs for short- and long-term prediction errors. With the RNN-based models (NB-RNN, s-RNN, HSM, AHSM), the errors of short- and long-term prediction decreased by 8 and 20% compared those with ARIMA and Prophet, respectively. The reduction in long-term prediction error was large

Table 1. Comparison of MAPEs for short- and long-term prediction

Method	MAPE: short-term prediction [%]	MAPE: long-term prediction [%]
ARIMA	32.8	63.1
Prophet	48.8	64.8
NB-RNN	24.9	43.2
s-RNN	24.7	38.1
HSM	24.6	35.7
AHSM	23.5	34.2

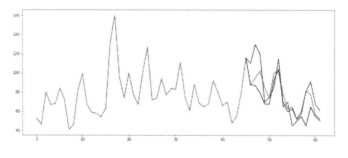

(a) typical item

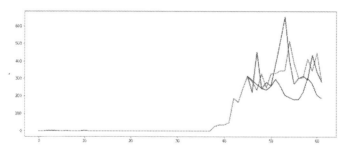

(b) newly launched item

Fig. 4. Prediction examples of typical and newly launched items by using AHSM. Vertical and horizontal axes are demand value and day. Red, blue, green, and black lines show demand history, target demand value of items, results of short-term prediction of demand values, and those of long-term prediction of demand values, respectively. The period of target and predicted demand values is 16 days. (Color figure online)

when the RNN-based models and ARIMA/Prophet model were compared. This is because the RNN-based models has high capacity and can handle non-linear data.

With s-RNN, the error of long-term prediction decreased by 5% compared those with NB-RNN. When predicting a long-term sequence, the error rapidly propagated since the input of NB-RNN is sampled data from the estimated distribution.

A comparison among s-RNN, HSM and AHSM shows the differences in their architecture. Models with complicated architecture, e.g., HSM and AHSM, were better than s-RNN with regard to the long-term prediction. From comparison of s-RNN and HSM and AHSM, an architecture of multiple s-RNNs improves the prediction error. Such complicated models use additional information of item demand, which is expected to decrease the prediction error.

AHSM was better than HSM with regard to prediction error since both errors of short-term and long-term prediction decreased by 1.1% and 1.5%, respectively. From the aspect of architecture differences, the structure of inner-state generator is different. It is expected that the appropriate inner-state is generated when asynchronous weight update and encoder-decoder inner state generator is adopted. Briefly estimated benefit of 1% improvement becomes about millions dollar for one wholesales company.

Figure 4 shows the prediction results of typical and newly launched items by using AHSM. Both types of items were predicted using AHSM. It could predict the newly launched item since the parameters of ARIMA and Prophet could not be estimated. Therefore, AHSM can handle a newly launched item for both short- and long-term prediction.

5   Conclusion

We proposed t demand-prediction model called AHSM for distribution businesses that involves multiple RNNs for accurate prediction. AHSM has as inner-state generator, and the weights of the generator and entire network are alternatively learned to stabilize learning and enable accurate prediction. This allows us to generate a more appropriate inner state for the predictor's RNN. We applied AHSM to a demand-prediction task and compared it with other demand-prediction models, i.e., ARIMA, Prophet, and other RNN-based models. The experimental results indicates that AHSM enables accurate demand prediction; both short and long term.

AHSM, specifically its inner-state generator, does not take into account the combination of past inner states. For more accurate prediction, it is necessary to add the weights for past states to current prediction, i.e., using attention architecture [21,22]. For future work, we plan to develop a prediction model with attention architecture.

To use AHSM for industrial use, e.g., an item ordering and a stock management system in warehouse, we should consider the amount of cost reduction from improving demand-prediction accuracy. By improving this, the over- and under-stocking and management costs decreases since it is necessary to decide the number of orders and order timing to maintain appropriate stocking. It is crucial to reveal the gap between the amount of cost reduction and accuracy improvement to evaluate models for determining the actual impact of warehouse management. For future work, we also plan to apply AHSM to the data of actual distribution businesses.

References

1. Melard, G., Pasteels, J.-M.: Automatic arima modeling including interventions, using time series expert software. Int. J. Forecast. **16**(4), 497–508 (2000)
2. Teräsvirta, T.: An introduction to univariate GARCH models. In: Mikosch, T., Kreiß, J.P., Davis, R., Andersen, T. (eds.) Handbook of Financial Time Series, pp. 17–42. Springer, Heidelberg (2009). https://doi.org/10.1007/978-3-540-71297-8_1
3. Taylor, S.J., Letham, B.: Forecasting at scale. Am. Stat. **72**(1), 37–45 (2018)
4. Hochreiter, S., Schmidhuber, J.: Long short-term memory. Neural comput. **9**(8), 1735–1780 (1997)
5. Liu, S., Yang, N., Li, M., Zhou, M.: A recursive recurrent neural network for statistical machine translation. In: Proceedings of the 52nd Annual Meeting of the Association for Computational Linguistics (Volume 1: Long Papers), vol. 1, pp. 1491–1500 (2014)
6. Graves, A., Schmidhuber, J.: Framewise phoneme classification with bidirectional LSTM and other neural network architectures. Neural Netw. **18**(5–6), 602–610 (2005)
7. Cho, K., et al.: Learning phrase representations using RNN encoder-decoder for statistical machine translation. arXiv preprint arXiv:1406.1078 (2014)
8. Williams, B.M., Hoel, L.A.: Modeling and forecasting vehicular traffic flow as a seasonal ARIMA process: theoretical basis and empirical results. J. Transp. Eng. **129**(6), 664–672 (2003)
9. Hyndman, R.J., Koehler, A.B., Snyder, R.D., Grose, S.: A state space framework for automatic forecasting using exponential smoothing methods. Int. J. Forecast. **18**(3), 439–454 (2002)
10. Flunkert, V., Salinas, D., Gasthaus, J.: DeepAR: probabilistic forecasting with autoregressive recurrent networks. arXiv preprint arXiv:1704.04110 (2017)
11. Graves, A., Mohamed, A., Hinton, G.: Speech recognition with deep recurrent neural networks. In: 2013 IEEE international Conference on Acoustics, Speech and Signal Processing (ICASSP), pp. 6645–6649. IEEE (2013)
12. Mikolov, T., Karafiát, M., Burget, L., Černocký, J., Khudanpur, S.: Recurrent neural network based language model. In: Eleventh Annual Conference of the International Speech Communication Association (2010)
13. Graves, A., Jaitly, N.: Towards end-to-end speech recognition with recurrent neural networks. In: International Conference on Machine Learning, pp. 1764–1772 (2014)
14. Mikolov, T., Sutskever, I., Chen, K., Corrado, G.S., Dean, J.: Distributed representations of words and phrases and their compositionality. In: Advances in Neural Information Processing Systems, pp. 3111–3119 (2013)
15. Sutskever, I., Vinyals, O., Le, Q.V.: Sequence to sequence learning with neural networks. In: Advances in Neural Information Processing Systems, pp. 3104–3112 (2014)

16. Masci, J., Meier, U., Cireşan, D., Schmidhuber, J.: Stacked convolutional auto-encoders for hierarchical feature extraction. In: Honkela, T., Duch, W., Girolami, M., Kaski, S. (eds.) ICANN 2011. LNCS, vol. 6791, pp. 52–59. Springer, Heidelberg (2011). https://doi.org/10.1007/978-3-642-21735-7_7

17. Chung, J., Gulcehre, C., Cho, K., Bengio, Y.: Empirical evaluation of gated recurrent neural networks on sequence modeling. arXiv preprint arXiv:1412.3555 (2014)

18. Snoek, J., Larochelle, H., Adams, R.P.: Practical Bayesian optimization of machine learning algorithms. In: Advances in Neural Information Processing Systems, pp. 2951–2959 (2012)

19. Contal, E., Perchet, V., Vayatis, N.: Gaussian process optimization with mutual information. In: International Conference on Machine Learning, pp. 253–261 (2014)

20. Kingma, D.P., Ba, J.: Adam: a method for stochastic optimization. arXiv preprint arXiv:1412.6980 (2014)

21. Luong, M.-T., Pham, H., Manning, C.D.: Effective approaches to attention-based neural machine translation. arXiv preprint arXiv:1508.04025 (2015)

22. Vaswani, A., et al.: Attention is all you need. In: Advances in Neural Information Processing Systems, pp. 5998–6008 (2017)

A Study of Deep Learning for Network Traffic Data Forecasting

Benedikt Pfülb[(✉)], Christoph Hardegen, Alexander Gepperth,
and Sebastian Rieger

University of Applied Sciences Fulda, Leipziger Straße 123, 36037 Fulda, Germany
{benedikt.pfuelb,christoph.hardegen,alexander.gepperth,
sebastian.rieger}@cs.hs-fulda.de
http://www.hs-fulda.de

Abstract. We present a study of deep learning applied to the domain
of network traffic data forecasting. This is a very important ingredient for network traffic engineering, e.g., intelligent routing, which can
optimize network performance, especially in large networks. In a nut-
shell, we wish to predict, in advance, the bit rate for a transmission,
based on low-dimensional connection metadata ("flows") that is available whenever a communication is initiated. Our study has several gen-
uinely new points: First, it is performed on a large dataset ($\approx$50 million
flows), which requires a new training scheme that operates on successive blocks of data since the whole dataset is too large for in-memory
processing. Additionally, we are the first to propose and perform a more
fine-grained prediction that distinguishes between low, medium and high
bit rates instead of just "mice" and "elephant" flows. Lastly, we apply
state-of-the-art visualization and clustering techniques to flow data and
show that visualizations are insightful despite the heterogeneous and
non-metric nature of the data. We developed a processing pipeline to
handle the highly non-trivial acquisition process and allow for proper
data preprocessing to be able to apply DNNs to network traffic data. We
conduct DNN hyper-parameter optimization as well as feature selection
experiments, which show that fine-grained network traffic forecasting
is feasible, and that domain-dependent data enrichment and augmentation strategies can improve results. An outlook about the fundamental challenges presented by network traffic analysis (data throughput,
unbalanced and dynamic classes, changing statistics, outlier detection)
concludes the article.

Keywords: DNN · Incremental learning · Network traffic engineering

© Springer Nature Switzerland AG 2019
I. V. Tetko et al. (Eds.): ICANN 2019, LNCS 11730, pp. 497–512, 2019.
https://doi.org/10.1007/978-3-030-30490-4_40

1   Introduction

This article is in the context of computer network traffic forecasting. We focus on using deep neural networks (DNNs). More precisely, we investigate how DNNs can predict, in advance, the approximate bit rate of a computer network communication. This is modeled as a classification task with three classes (low, medium and high). The key idea here is to take this decision based only on the metadata of the communication, which are represented, in their most basic form, as a 5-tuple: source and destination IP address, source and destination port as well as the transport protocol, e.g., TCP or UDP. An example of the flow metadata as well as the classification task is depicted in Fig. 1.

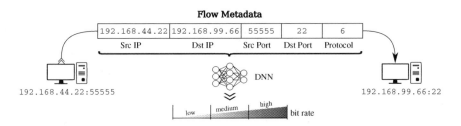

Fig. 1. Overview of the principal task of network traffic forecasting. Upon establishment of an IP-based network communication between two computers, the metadata (5-tuple) is supplied to a trained DNN that forecasts the bit rate (low, medium and high) for this communication. This is done before any data is exchanged. In order to train the DNN, target values have to be obtained after a communication is terminated.

The motivation for investigating this kind of classification problem stems from the field of software-defined networking (SDN). While traditional and still most prevalent network routing algorithms are primarily based on the destination address, SDN-like techniques enable dynamic determination of paths based on traffic characteristics. For example, routers can typically choose between several paths to forward network traffic to a specific destination. On the one hand, in the case of paths with unequal costs, using only the optimal path could cause congestion while alternative paths are underutilized. On the other hand, using the hash of a 5-tuple to decide between multiple equal-cost paths might lead to unequal load balancing because the amount of transmitted data cannot be considered in advance. Also, the path cannot easily be changed during the communication. Therefore, predicting the bit rate of a communication beforehand is of high value for the routing and load balancing process.

1.1   Problem Formulation and Approach of the Article

Challenges. The principal immediate challenges for machine learning in network traffic forecasting raised and addressed in this article are as follows:

- data acquisition: Here, one encounters difficulties creating the technical infrastructure (i.e., administrative access to network devices, handling large amounts of data resulting from capturing the network traffic) and the fact that metadata contain sensitive information, requiring an anonymization strategy that preserves information content and relations. Furthermore, the encoding of metadata into a form that is suitable for DNNs and the generation of target values is essential.
- regression problem: Network traffic forecasting is essentially a regression problem as a continuous and highly variable quantity (the bit rate) needs to be predicted, which is a challenging task that must be simplified suitably.
- class imbalance: Communications transmitting very few data are much more frequent than those transferring huge amounts of data [3]. The distribution regarding the bit rate as target value can be expected to change over time.
- concept drift: The statistics of the problem may be time-dependent, e.g., depending on the day of week, the time of day, the season, technical changes, etc. A DNN classifier trained on day X may therefore not be suited to classify metadata collected on day $Y \neq X$. We are therefore dealing with a problem where continual re-training must be conducted while retaining previous knowledge (see [4] for a recent review on this kind of training paradigm).
- big data setting: The amount of flows is so high, and their variability so significant, that DNN training on a representative training set can no longer be performed in-memory. In our scenario, the network devices we accessed to collect data delivered 57 million records in 8 h (about 15 GB of raw data respectively $\varnothing \approx 2\,000$ flows per second, including the 5-tuple).

Approach. In order to address these challenges, we first of all treat DNN training as a streaming problem by dividing all collected metadata into blocks of 100 000 flows each. Training and evaluation are then conduced in a semi-streaming fashion, starting with the first block and subsequently passing to following ones, with all relevant preprocessing operations being performed block-wise. Concept drift is thus incorporated into DNN training although it cannot be completely compensated. The class imbalance problem is currently fixed by different class balancing mechanisms, since the whole reference dataset[1] is known prior to DNN training. This will have to be replaced by more generic solutions in the future. Lastly, we transform the regression problem into a classification problem with three classes, thus balancing the need for precision and complexity of the problem.

1.2   Related Work

Network traffic forecasting with machine learning techniques is a field (see [3] for a review) that is receiving increased attention, probably due to the recent advances in machine learning techniques, notably deep learning models. From a machine learning point of view, many recent articles can be grouped according

---

[1] Our anonymized dataset is available upon request.

to whether they conduct online or offline learning on streaming network data, what machine learning models they employ in general, what dataset they operate on and whether they systematically investigate the effects of data enrichment. To the best of our knowledge, all related works operate on datasets of around 1 000 000 flows which is significantly smaller than the dataset we use in this study, and thereby avoid "big data" issues like the necessity to perform learning in blocks. Furthermore, related works reduce the network traffic forecasting problem to a binary classification into "mice" and "elephant" flows.

In [5], the authors apply online and offline learning methods (Multi-Layer Perceptron, Gaussian Process Regression and Online Bayesian Moment Matching). The problem is treated as a two-class classification problem using three different datasets, one self-created (not available) and the others from other authors [1]. No data enrichment is performed, however information about the first three exchanged packets is used in addition to a flow's 5-tuple as a basis for classification, which differs from our approach that does not consider such information. In [9], purely offline learning with two-class decision tree classifiers is performed on the "Wide" dataset and a self-created one (not available) coming from a data center, also without data enrichment. In [8], semi-supervised SVMs are trained in an offline fashion to solve a two-class problem using a simple form of data enrichment. Evaluations are conducted on a dataset of approximately 1 000 000 flows, "captured by the Broadband Communication Research Group in UPC, Barcelona, Spain" (no reference given, no data available). [6] use offline SVM training on two datasets captured on Chinese university campuses (no reference, not available), and experiment with feature selection schemes, however based only on the basic 5-tuple information. Another albeit not directly related application of machine learning is the routing of flows itself (see [7]).

1.3 Contribution of the Article

Overall, this study shows that fine-grained network traffic forecasting using three classes with DNNs is feasible, and that it can be performed in a "big data" setting, operating on separate data blocks sequentially. We furthermore investigate the effects of data enrichment beyond the basic 5-tuple information, while also dealing with anonymization and privacy issues. Lastly, we show that modern data visualization and clustering techniques can be readily applied to network traffic data in order to gain deeper insights into the structure of the problems and to "debug" machine learning solutions.

2 Flow Data Pipeline

We introduce a flow data pipeline (see Fig. 2) that is responsible for collecting the network traffic flows and producing a dataset consisting of flows describing communications. Data collection and the first parts of the data preparation (enrichment and anonymization) are entirely performed within our data center to ensure privacy (supported by the administration). The codebase of the pipeline is publicly available in our repository[2].

---

[2] https://gitlab.informatik.hs-fulda.de/flow-data-ml.

Fig. 2. Overview of the stages of the flow data pipeline: data collection, preparation and processing. At first, flow records are collected. Before IP addresses are anonymized, further related metadata is added during the enrichment phase. Afterwards, the fusion of individual *flow records* is applied to aggregate *flow entries*. Flow data is normalized and stored as a dataset that is used for DNN training in the data processing phase.

2.1   Data Collection

A flow is understood to be the history of a single transmission between two endpoints, from establishment to termination (only metadata). In particular, flows are partly characterized by the 5-tuple. Flows may include additional metadata, e.g., the duration or number of transferred bytes.

Flow data is collected from the networks at Fulda University of Applied Sciences. We export network flow data (57 million flow records) using the NetFlow standard from the two core network devices in our university data center during a continuous time interval of 8 h on a weekday (02/15/2019 9:00 AM to 5:00 PM). These core components connect multiple subnets from the data center, laboratory, WiFi and campus networks. Collecting data from these diverse networks ensures realistic traffic characteristics and patterns to be used for the subsequent data analysis and network flow prediction. For example, collected traffic patterns include internal and external flows originating from client-to-server as well as server-to-server communication.

2.2   Data Preparation

Due to the extremely large amount of collected flow records, these are partitioned into separate *blocks* of 100 000 records each (representing $\varnothing \approx 1$ min), and the operations given below are applied block-wise. We thus obtain the final dataset, which is used for all experiments in this article, containing about 53 million aggregated *flow entries* out of approximately 57 million captured *flow records*.

Enrichment. Based on the collected 5-tuples, additional context information is derived. For example, groups of internal and external addresses (e.g., IP subnets, VLANs and geographical regions) can be identified from the network addresses. These contexts deliver additional characteristics and patterns for the subsequent analysis and the prediction process.

Anonymization. To ensure that collected metadata cannot be traced back to individual network addresses and end users, while still keeping the syntax and semantic of the data intact to prevent distortion of contained characteristics for the subsequent analysis, an appropriate anonymization algorithm was developed. This mechanism anonymizes all address-related metadata, i.e., IP and network addresses. The data center that exports the traffic metadata defines a password, which is cryptographically hashed and used as a seed for randomized permutation tables. A seed ensures consistent anonymization for further data acquisitions. Each octet of an IP address is anonymized individually using these tables. This way, the semantics of an address, e.g., regarding the relevance and order of the octets forming a group of network addresses, will stay intact after the anonymization and can still be used as a characteristic feature for prediction. However, adjacency of addresses will not be preserved in favor of the anonymization due to the seeded randomization of the permutation tables.

Aggregation. Exported unidirectional *flow records* that potentially represent only a part of a communication (due to exporter timeouts or cache sizes) are aggregated to ensure coherent *flow entries*. The aggregation of records is based on the 5-tuple and additional traffic characteristics, e.g., flags and predefined time intervals. Duplicated flow records from both exporting network devices are filtered. During this phase, the number of records is reduced to, on average, 7.5% of the collected flow records. Afterwards, ports greater than 32 767 are replaced by zero because they are chosen randomly by common operating systems.

Normalization. We convert raw, heterogeneous features into a format suited for DNNs, e.g., a sequence of floating points, in three different ways: Bit patterns are converted by promoting each bit to a 0.0 or 1.0, float values are interpolated between 0.0 and 1.0 (min-max normalization) and categorical values are encoded as "one-hot" vectors, i.e., a single value of 1.0 put at an unique position, having a length of N, where N represents the number of distinct categories. An example is given in Table 1.

Table 1. Exemplary normalization of an IP address, a port and a protocol value using different data formats (bit pattern or float value). Each data type has a feature-dependent size specifying the number of individual float values that are used as input for the DNN. For example, next to its raw format, each octet of an IP address is represented in its original format as bit pattern or as float values.

Feature	Raw format	Bit pattern (size)	Float value(s) (size)
IP address	81.169.238.182	0,1,0,1,0,0,0,1,1,0,1,0,1,0,0,1, 1,1,1,0,1,1,1,0,1,0,1,1,0,1,1,0 (32)	0.3176, 0.6627, 0.9333, 0.7137 (4)
Port	80	0,0,0,0,0,0,0,0,0,1,0,1,0,0,0,0 (16)	0.0012 (1)
Protocol	6	0,0,0,0,0,1,1,0 (8)	0.0235 (1)

The output of the normalization and thus of the data preparation process is the actual dataset (about 2.3 GB). Next to the bit rate, there are other flow features that can be used as class labels and hence for a prediction, e.g., the number of transferred bytes or the duration of a flow. A combination of selected labels is conceivable as well. The datasets structure is summarized in Table 2.

Table 2. Overview of the dataset features and labels. For each raw flow feature, the supported respectively used (gray highlighting) data formats are shown, and the number of values is given, as well as the point in the flow data pipeline in which the information is added (Src). Features for both source and destination are marked with ⇄.

Feature		Data format			Src	Feature		Data format			Src
		Float	Bit	OH				Float	Bit	OH	
month		1	4	12		longitude	⇄	1	✗	✗	
day		1	5	31		latitude	⇄	1	✗	✗	
hour		1	5	24		country code	⇄	1	8	240	DE
minute		1	6	60	DC	vlan	⇄	1	12	✗	
second		1	6	60		locality	⇄	✗	1	2	
protocol		1	8	✗		flags		1	8	✗	
address	⇄	4	32	✗							
port	⇄	1	16	✗		Label		Data format			Src
network	⇄	4	32	✗		duration		✗	✗	✓	
prefix length	⇄	1	5	✗	DE	bytes		✗	✗	✓	DA
asn	⇄	1	16	✗		bit rate		✗	✗	✓	

DC = Data Collection; DE = Data Enrichment; DA = Data Aggregation; OH = One-Hot

2.3 Data Processing

In the data processing phase a fully-connected DNN is trained to predict the bit rate of a communication. During the processing of the created flow dataset, three steps are performed blockwise: At first, a sub-dataset can be extracted by feature selection. Afterwards, data samples are labeled based on predefined class boundaries, which are selected to fit an almost balanced data distribution (presented in Sect. 3.1). Finally, training and testing is done on each individual block sequentially. To evaluate different hyper-parameter setups, we do a parameter optimization. The detailed process and related results are presented in Sect. 4.

3 Exploratory Data Analysis and Visualization

To provide a better understanding of flow data, we explore the distribution of features used for labeling (see Sect. 3.1) and visualize the intrinsic structure of the data (see Sect. 3.2). The analysis is performed on the first 1000 flow entries (including all features) that are selected from the shuffled test data of the first block. Due to this, the same t-SNE output is used for all context-related taggings. No significant deviations were observed when performing this analysis on other blocks (every 50th block was compared). All comparisons of the tagged t-SNE outputs are done by visual inspection.

3.1 Label Distribution

We analyze the distribution of flow features that can be target values for traffic flow prediction, i.e., the transmitted bytes, the duration or the bit rate calculated from both. Results are shown in Fig. 3. As other authors noted previously [3], these features deviate strongly from a uniform distribution, which makes the determination of suitable class boundaries challenging. The principal conclusion we draw from this is that we must use class balancing (see Sect. 4). Although the data distribution justifies our class boundaries, their practical applicability, e.g., for intelligent routing, is questionable and considered as future work.

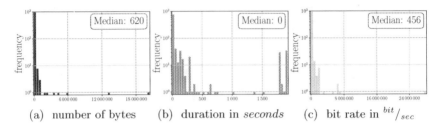

(a) number of bytes (b) duration in *seconds* (c) bit rate in $^{bit}/_{sec}$

Fig. 3. Histograms for three possible flow labels of the selected 1 000 elements in the first block. The majority of data samples have both a very small number of transferred bytes (a) and a short duration (b). Median values of 620 bytes respectively 0 s (<1000 ms) substantiate this fact. Hence, the bit rate values (c) are also very unevenly spread over the entire value range (median value is 456).

3.2 Structural Context

To discover structural relations and similarities between individual flow entries (see Figs. 4, 5), we use t-Distributed Stochastic Neighbor Embedding (t-SNE) [2], a state-of-the-art visualization method, which maps high-dimensional data samples to a low-dimensional space (2D or 3D). We use the t-SNE implementation of the scikit-learn framework, parameter values being an iteration counter of 500, a perplexity of 50 and a learning rate of 200.

Figure 4a illustrates feature similarities between flow entries that have a common transport protocol. Two symmetric accumulations indicate opposite directions of the same communication. Furthermore, there are examples that do not share the same transport protocol, but t-SNE points out similar feature data.

Tagging of each data sample according to its type of communication, which is the combination of the source and destination locality (either private or public), is shown in Fig. 4b. For each communication type symmetric accumulations can be identified, whereas coherent spots map to individual flow directions.

Additionally, we apply the k-means clustering algorithm on the sub-dataset and use the result for tagging the data samples in the t-SNE output. With k-means, high-dimensional data samples are grouped around a predefined number of iteratively relocated cluster centers. We use the implementation of tensorflow (v1.12) with 10 cluster centers, whereby the initial location of each center is determined randomly and the squared Euclidean distance is used as metric. The tagging of the t-SNE output based on k-means clustering for the data samples is shown in Fig. 4c. According to the t-SNE results, it can be observed that there are samples that belong to the same cluster but have certain feature differences

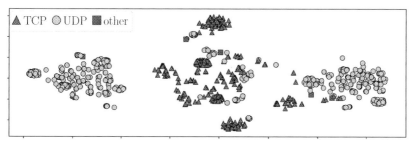

(a) Tagging is based on the transport protocol of each flow entry. While the proportion of TCP is ≈39 % (389 flows, ▲), the one for UDP is ≈60 % (604 flows, ◎). There are separate spots for traffic data using either TCP or UDP. Besides TCP and UDP data, about 1 % of the traffic data (7 flows, ■) is related to other protocols like ICMP.

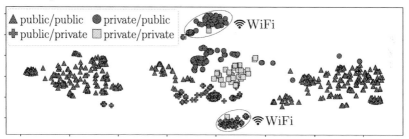

(b) Tagging is based on the localities of each flow entry. Four different types are distinguished based on the combined locality of the source and destination system. Both can be either private or public. About 92 % of the flows (922) describe traffic data where a public system is involved (▲, ●, ✤), while ≈8 % (78) belong to communications between two private systems (□). Additionally, wireless (≈13 %, 133 flows) and wired network traffic (≈87 %, 867 flows) are separately delineated. According to Fig. 4a and the shown locality, each part of the symmetric spots for WiFi traffic belongs to a specific transport protocol (TCP or UDP) and a separate communication direction.

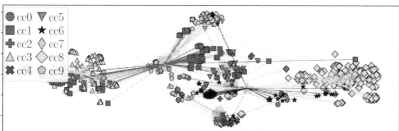

(c) Tagging is based on the output of k-means clustering. Positions of cluster centers (10) are visualized according to t-SNE output. Nearly uniform accumulations of samples can be identified (e.g., △, ◇), clusters are spread (e.g., ●, ⬠) and mixtures of samples of different clusters (e.g., ✤, ✖) are recognizable.

Fig. 4. Visualization of the selected 1 000 flow samples. All figures show the same t-SNE results but tagging is based on the transport protocol (a), locality (b) and clustering (c).

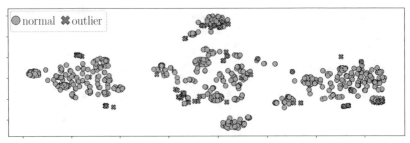

(a) Tagging is based on an outlier detection using k-means clustering with 20 cluster centers. About 11 % of the flow entries (108) are classified as outliers. Whereas outliers are marked with ✖, kept data samples are shown as ⊙.

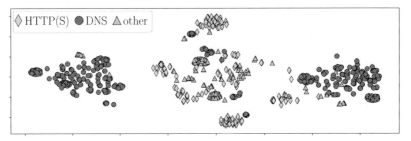

(b) Tagging is based on most frequent application protocols. Most samples belong to DNS communications (≈57 %, 571 flows, ⬤). Next to HTTP(S) (≈24 %, 241 flows, ◊), other application protocols are visualized (≈19 %, 188 flows, △). The latter include, for example, authentication, network monitoring and mail.

Fig. 5. Visualization of structures in the selected 1 000 flow samples. Tagging of the t-SNE result is based on an outlier detection (a) and the applications protocols (b).

and that there are samples of different clusters sharing feature properties. The actual results depend on the chosen number of cluster centers.

We also perform an outlier detection for each k-means cluster using different metric thresholds (average and median distance as well as both summed up with the standard deviation). See Fig. 5a for an exemplary presentation of detected outliers. With regard to our experiments described in the next section, the outlier detection has no significant influence on network flow prediction.

According to Fig. 5b DNS and HTTP(S) are the most used application protocols in the dataset. The huge proportion of DNS traffic states the rate of flow entries with a low bit rate respectively short duration.

The data analysis emphasizes relations and feature similarities between individual data samples. All visualizations use the same t-SNE output, but context-related tagging, e.g., regarding used protocols or communication directions, helps to clarify different structural patterns within network flow data.

4   Network Flow Prediction Experiments with DNNs

We employ a fully-connected DNN with L layers of identical sizes S, each hidden layer applying a ReLU transfer function whereas the output layer applies a softmax function. The batch size $bs = 100$ and the number of training epochs $\mathcal{E} = 10$ are fixed for all experiments. DNN training minimizes a standard cross-entropy loss by stochastic gradient descent by means of the Adam Optimizer. The last 10% of a chronologically ordered data block are completely used for testing every 50th iteration.

Choice of Evaluation Metrics. Since we are dealing with a three-class problem, the usual metrics for binary problems are not applicable, such as F1 score, precision, recall, etc. Instead, we present results in the more general form of a confusion matrix, from which we can derive classification accuracy by considering only the diagonal elements. Both of these measures are applicable for classification tasks with an arbitrary number of classes, which can be useful for comparison should we decide to introduce more classes at a later point. In order to allow a more in-depth comparison between the experimental conditions (using the 5-tuple information vs. using all features), we decided to additionally compute the standard binary performance metrics separately for each class.

Hyper-Parameters. Tunable parameters include the learning rate ϵ and the optional application of dropout to input d_i and hidden layers d_h, with different dropout probabilities. The assignment of labels is done based on a class boundary parameter $\mathcal{C}$. This list of boundary values is consistently used for all blocks before a training phase. In order to specify the class balancing method, the parameter $\mathcal{W}$ is introduced. Balancing for training and test data is achieved either by standard class weighting or under-sampling. Furthermore, a feature selector $\mathbb{F}$ provides support for the construction of sub-datasets. O_c specifies the number of cluster centers that are used for outlier detection using k-means clustering. All hyper-parameters mentioned here (L, S, ϵ, d_i, d_h, $\mathcal{C}$, $\mathcal{W}$, $\mathbb{F}$, O_c) are varied to perform a joint parameter optimization.

We train all DNN classifiers on the first 10 blocks sequentially and evaluate the achieved prediction accuracy on each block's test set. In order to obtain the best possible results, we conduct a combinatorial hyper-parameter optimization, leading to a total of 5400 DNN training and evaluation runs. The explored parameter ranges are summarized in Table 3. Depending on the hardware, the computation time of one experiment is between 8 and 15 min. Based on the complexity of the DNN and the chosen parameters, the GPU memory usage is between 140 and 264 MB and the RAM utilization varies from 762 to 1200 MB.

Labeling. Because of the unbalanced data distribution (see Sect. 3.1) that makes regression problematic (also addressed in [5]), we treat network flow prediction as a classification problem, using the three exemplary classes "low", "medium" and "high". The calculated bit rate of each flow is used for computing a class based on thresholding operation (with the two thresholds adapted such that the distribution of classes is approximately flat). Next to the used set of boundaries for class division, Table 4 presents related characteristics for each class.

Table 3. Overview of the variables and tested values for parameter optimization.

Parameter	Variable	Values
Dropout (input, hidden)	(d_i, d_h)	$\{(1.0, 1.0), (0.9, 0.6), (0.8, 0.5)\}$
Layers	L	$\{3, 4, 5\}$
Neurons per layer	S	$\{200, 400, 600, 800, 1\,000\}$
Learning Rate	ϵ	$\{0.01, 0.001, 0.0001\}$
Features	$\mathbb{F}$	$\{5\text{-tuple, all}\}$
Class boundaries (bit rate)	$\mathcal{C}$	$\{\{0, 500, 5\,000, \infty\}, \{0, 50, 8\,000, \infty\}\}$
Class balancing method	$\mathcal{W}$	$\{0 \text{ (under-sampling)}, 1 \text{ (class weighting)}\}$
Cluster centers (outlier detection)	O_c	$\{0, 20, 60, 100, 500\}$

Table 4. Exemplary class partitioning for the prediction of a flow's bit rate. Next to the related intervals, the median and mean value, the average number of elements using class balancing (class weighting or under-sampling) and the data distribution within each class for the first 10 blocks of the dataset are shown (log scale).

Class	Interval	Median/ Mean	Average elements		Data distribution
			class weighting	under-sampling	
0	$[0, 50)$	$0/$ 2	21 945		
1	$[50, 8\,000)$	$3\,904/$ $4\,004$	28 228	21 909	
2	$[8\,000, \infty]$	$16\,960/$ $131\,736$	24 459		

Figure 6 depicts the distribution of the true labels within the t-SNE output. Whereas some spots primarily have data samples belonging to the same class (c0), other spots are a mixture of different (c1, c2) or all classes. With regard to Fig. 4c, the results of k-means clustering cannot be used to classify the samples adequately. Respectively, it is not sufficient to predict the bit rate of a flow.

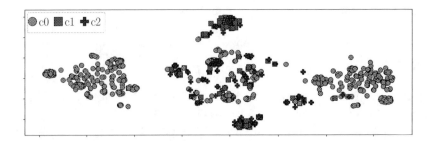

Fig. 6. Visualization of the t-SNE results based on the true labels for the 1000 samples. Tagging is based on the class labels ((c0≈ 65%, 652 flows, ●), (c1 ≈ 2%, 120 flows, ■), (c2 ≈ 23%, 228 flows, ✚)), whereby the exemplary boundaries are used.

The two experiments with the highest accuracy, determined by the parameter optimization, are shown in Fig. 7. In the first experiment, training is done on all available flow features (247 inputs), whereas in the second one only the 5-tuple (104 inputs) is used. Figure 7 depicts the trend of the prediction accuracy. At the beginning of a directly following block, the accuracy value can considerably vary compared to the rate for the previous block but generally stabilizes for each block after a few training iterations. This indicates a slight change in statistics (concept drift) between the individual blocks, which becomes clearer in Fig. 9. We achieve a maximum accuracy of ≈87% for the first respectively ≈85% for the second experiment. Regarding these maxima, the data enrichment leads to an accuracy increase of about 2%. Normalized confusion matrices for both experiments are

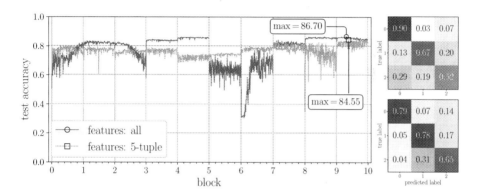

Fig. 7. Testing results for the best experiments determined by the parameter optimization: first ($\mathbb{F} = all$, blue, ○) and second experiment ($\mathbb{F} = 5\text{-}tuple$, orange, □). The trend of the accuracy for the first 10 blocks is depicted. Training and testing is done sequentially on each independent block for 10 epochs. Besides this, the normalized confusion matrices for the last iteration of block 0 in the first (top, blue) and second experiment (bottom, orange) are shown. Hyper-parameters $\mathbb{F} = all$: $\mathcal{C} = [0, 50, 8\,000], (d_i, d_h) = (1.0, 1.0), L = 3, S = 1000, \epsilon = 0.0001, \mathcal{W} = 1, C_k = 0$; parameters $\mathbb{F} = 5\text{-}tuple$: $\mathcal{C} = [0, 50, 8\,000], (d_i, d_h) = (0.9, 0.6), L = 5, S = 1000, \epsilon = 0.001, \mathcal{W} = 0, C_k = 0$. (Color figure online)

Table 5. Common binary classification measures, given separately for each of the three classes in a one-against-all setting. These measures are instructive, particularly when comparing performance between the two experiments (5-tuple against all features). The values can be computed from the unnormalized confusion matrices.

Experiment		Precision	Recall/Sensitivity	Specificity	Accuracy
$\mathbb{F} = all$	class 0	85.1	89.8	75.6	84.2
	class 1	50.0	66.7	92.0	89.3
	class 2	69.2	52.4	90.7	79.8
$\mathbb{F} = 5\text{-}tuple$	class 0	96.6	79.2	95.7	85.7
	class 1	38.8	78.0	85.3	84.5
	class 2	64.5	64.8	85.8	79.8

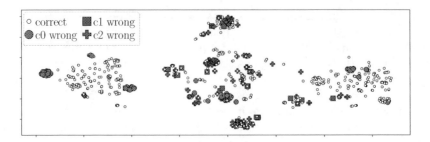

Fig. 8. Visualization of the t-SNE results based on the predicted labels for the selected 1000 flow samples. Correct classified samples are marked with ○ (correct ≈ 77%, 775 flows). For all false classified samples ((c0 wrong ≈ 9%, 86 flows, ◉), (c1 wrong ≈ 3%, 32 flows, ▣) and (c2 wrong ≈ 11%, 107 flows, ✚)) the true label is shown.

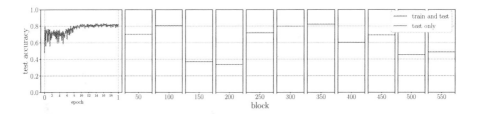

Fig. 9. Overview of the accuracy for different blocks of the dataset. A DNN is trained and tested for 20 epochs on the first block using all available flow features (blue line). Subsequently, only the accuracy is determined for each fiftieth block while measuring on test data for one epoch (red lines). Parameter setup: see first experiment in Fig. 7. (Color figure online)

also outlined in Fig. 7. Further evaluation metrics are outlined in Table 5. Figure 8 gives an overview of the false classified data samples. With regard to the false labels, prediction errors for coherent spots mainly belong to the same class.

5   Discussion and Principal Conclusions

The principal conclusions we can draw from the presented experiments are: First of all, DNNs are a feasible tool for performing fine-grained network traffic flow prediction in a "big data" setting, achieving an accuracy of roughly 87% even though performed in a streaming fashion on successive and independent blocks of flow data. Previous studies reached accuracies over 90% but grouped network flows in only two classes ("mice" and "elephant" flows), which is considerably less useful for fine-grained network traffic engineering, and, above all, processed all training data in a single block. Secondly, we find that data enrichment can be useful, as it improves classification accuracy by roughly 2% at manageable computational cost. Thirdly, our visualization and clustering studies show that there is no simple way to improve results by outlier detection, presumably because the data samples do not lend themselves to clustering using Euclidean distance, and a custom distance metric would have to be used here. We establish nevertheless that t-SNE is a useful tool to visualize structures and relations in network flow data. Lastly, we confirm by experiments that there is moderate to strong concept drift in flow data, and that appropriate measures will have to be taken in future works to address this issue.

Comparability and Validity of Results. We may ask how generalizable our results are, and the answer is of course complex. In a university campus scenario such as ours, there are numerous factors that may affect the results, like the day of week, the season, the proximity of tests, etc. For example, the WiFi network – including thousands of connected students – represents a dynamic setup that probably cannot be solved easily for a DNN because connections are unique and non-recurring (in contrast to, e.g., communications between servers). Identifying and excluding such "difficult" flows could conceivably improve prediction accuracy and generalizability of our results. As stated in Sect. 1.2, publicly available datasets are relatively small. Larger datasets are not accessible, probably due to privacy issues. Even though our campus network is unique in its structure and thus results on our data do not guarantee in any way that the approach will work in other networks, the same can be said for any of the previous studies on the subject. The only way to show generality would be to have access to several datasets of network flows of comparable size, and to perform the same experiments on all of them. Comparing our results to other studies on the subject is further complicated by the fact that we perform three-class classification whereas previous studies were concerned with two-class scenarios only.

Discussion of the Three-Class Scenario To show that our architecture can replicate previous results, we trained our DNNs on a two-class task with a threshold value of 500 bits per second between "mice" and "elephant" flows and obtain a test accuracy of over 90%, which is comparable to the results of other studies while taking the abovementioned caveats into consideration. Obviously, introducing an additional class degrades the classification accuracy, simply because guessing has a lower chance of success with one more class to choose from. Whether this lower prediction accuracy is compensated by the benefit of a more fine-grained prediction would have to be tested in simulation, which is what we are currently working on. For this study, we wished to establish that more than two classes can be successfully integrated into a prediction scheme, all the more since the computational cost of predicting more classes is negligible at inference time. When also considering that we perform learning in a streaming setting, which in general degrades performance w.r.t. settings where all data are simultaneously available for training, our results must be considered very competitive.

Justification of Using DNNs. The principal reason for using DNNs as opposed to other methods proposed in the literature, e.g., Gaussian Process Regression (GPR) [5], is the fact that in future we want to train our classifiers in a streaming fashion: As soon as a new data block has been collected, model re-training is conducted automatically, and the trained model is immediately deployed and used for flow classification. This puts a strong focus on the scalability of the training process w.r.t. the number of data samples. In [5], a training complexity of $\mathcal{O}(n \cdot m^2)$ is reported for GPR, where concrete values for m, or how they are chosen, are unclear. Naively, GPR has a training complexity of $\mathcal{O}(n^3)$, and it is unclear whether the optimizations discussed in [5] can be tuned without human intervention (no code is provided). In contrast, DNNs have a natural training complexity of $\mathcal{O}(n)$ without any optimizations, so they do seem a more natural choice in the "big data" context. We will investigate the performance of other learning algorithms in future work, and compare them to our approach.

Acknowledgements. We thank Sven Reißmann from the university data center for assistance with data collection and preparation. We gratefully acknowledge the support of NVIDIA Corporation with the donation of the Titan Xp GPU.

References

1. Benson, T., Akella, A., Maltz, D.A.: Network traffic characteristics of data centers in the wild. In: 10th ACM SIGCOMM Conference on Internet Measurement (2010)
2. van der Maaten, L., Hinton, G.: Visualizing data using t-SNE. J. Mach. Learn. Res. **9**(Nov), 2579–2605 (2008)
3. Nguyen, T.T., Armitage, G.J.: A survey of techniques for internet traffic classification using machine learning. IEEE Commun. Surv. **10**, 56–76 (2008)
4. Pfülb, B., Gepperth, A.: A comprehensive, application-oriented study of catastrophic forgetting in DNNs. In: International Conference on Learning Representations (ICLR) (2019)
5. Poupart, P., et al.: Online flow size prediction for improved network routing. In: IEEE 24th International Conference on Network Protocols (ICNP) (2016)
6. Shi, H., Li, H., Zhang, D., Cheng, C., Wu, W.: Efficient and robust feature extraction and selection for traffic classification. Comput. Netw. **119**, 1–16 (2017)
7. Valadarsky, A., Schapira, M., Shahaf, D., Tamar, A.: Learning to route. In: 16th ACM Workshop on Hot Topics in Networks (2017)
8. Wang, P., Lin, S.C., Luo, M.: A framework for QoS-aware traffic classification using semi-supervised machine learning in SDNs. In: IEEE International Conference on Services Computing (SCC) (2016)
9. Xiao, P., Qu, W., Qi, H., Xu, Y., Li, Z.: An efficient elephant flow detection with cost-sensitive in SDN. In: 1st International Conference on Industrial Networks and Intelligent Systems (INISCom) (2015)

Composite Quantile Regression Long Short-Term Memory Network

Zongxia Xie and Hao Wen[✉]

College of Intelligence and Computing, Tianjin University, Tianjin 300350, China
caddiexie@hotmail.com, wenhao@tju.edu.cn

Abstract. Based on quantile long short-term memory (Q-LSTM), we consider the comprehensive utilization of multiple quantiles, proposing a simultaneous estimation version of Q-LSTM, composite quantile regression LSTM (CQR-LSTM). The method simultaneously estimates multiple quantile functions instead of estimating them separately. It makes sense that simultaneous estimation allows multiple quantiles to share strength among them to get better predictions. Furthermore, we also propose a novel approach, noncrossing composite quantile regression LSTM (NCQR-LSTM), to solve the quantile crossing problem. This method uses an indirect way as follows. Instead of estimating multiple quantiles directly, we estimate the intervals between adjacent quantiles. Since the intervals are guaranteed to be positive by using exponential functions, this completely avoids the problem of quantile crossing. Compared with the commonly used constraint methods for solving the quantile crossing problem, this indirect method makes model optimization easier and more suitable for deep learning. Experiments on a real wind speed dataset show that our methods improve the probabilistic prediction performance and reduce the training cost. In addition, our methods are simple to implement and highly scalable.

Keywords: Quantile regression · Long short-term memory network · Noncrossing

1 Introduction

Long short-term memory (LSTM) [8] network has shown excellent performance in analyzing sequence data [7,9,13]. Due to the presence of high uncertainties in various applications [5,10,17], it is natural to introduce probabilistic output to LSTM to maximize the sharpness of the predictive distribution and mitigate the impact of uncertainties.

Quantile LSTM (Q-LSTM) [6] is a successful method that enables LSTM to generate probabilistic prediction results. It extends LSTM with quantile regression [11], which is a commonly used method for introducing probabilistic output [3,14]. By setting a suitable set of quantile probabilities, such as $\tau = (\tau_1, \tau_2, \cdots, \tau_K)$, where $0 < \tau < 1$ and K is the number of τ, Q-LSTM

© Springer Nature Switzerland AG 2019
I. V. Tetko et al. (Eds.): ICANN 2019, LNCS 11730, pp. 513–524, 2019.
https://doi.org/10.1007/978-3-030-30490-4_41

can focus on the different positions (middle or tail) of the dependent variable distribution and output the desired confidence intervals.

However, multiple quantiles are estimated separately in Q-LSTM. For $\tau = (\tau_1, \tau_2, \cdots, \tau_K)$, this requires training K models to complete the prediction. We consider a better way called simultaneous estimation. This method can train all parameters at the same time and output multiple quantiles. Our method uses a composite optimization function based on quantile loss, which allows for the comprehensive use of multiple quantiles. Two main advantages of simultaneous estimation have been pointed out by Liu and Wu [12]. One is that multiple quantiles can share strength in simultaneous estimation to gain a better estimation accuracy. Many models based on simultaneous estimation, such as SNQR [12] and CQRNN [16], show that simultaneous estimation does improve the robustness and accuracy of the prediction compared with individual estimation. The other advantage is that joint estimation allows incorporating simultaneous noncrossing constraints to avoid quantile crossing.

Quantile crossing [2] is a longstanding practical problem in the process of estimating quantiles. It is caused by individually estimating each quantile curve without any restriction. As Cannon states [4], "quantile crossing violates the property that the conditional quantile function should be strictly monotonic". Fortunately, by adding appropriate constraints [1,12,14], simultaneous estimation is a good choice for solving the problem of quantile crossing. But a serious problem is that these constraints are not easy to optimize in deep learning. The optimizations of most deep-learning networks are implemented by backpropagation (BP) algorithm which cannot directly handle the constraints of the objective function. For this reason, we propose an indirect method to solve the quantile crossing problem. In a forward process, we first estimate the most intermediate quantile and the intervals between adjacent quantiles. Then all quantiles can be obtained by relational calculations. The quantile crossing can be completely avoided as long as we ensure that these intervals are positive real numbers. Since there is no constraint on objective function, our method is simple to implement in deep learning.

The monotone composite quantile regression neural network (MCQRNN) [4] proposed in 2018 is the first neural network-based QR model without crossing. It takes the quantile probabilities τ as a feature of the input, resolving the quantile crossing problem by ensuring that all parameters relating to τ are positive. Obviously, since most of the parameters are limited to nonnegative values, this greatly reduces the learning ability of the network. In comparison, our method only uses exponential functions for the intervals, so it does not reduce the learning ability of the model.

Based on the above, two models are proposed in this paper. The first one is a composite quantile regression LSTM (CQR-LSTM) as the simultaneous estimation version of Q-LSTM. Compared with the separately estimated Q-LSTM, the model speeds up training and brings performance improvements. The second model is proposed to solve the problem of quantile crossing. It is a novel indirect method based on CQR-LSTM, called noncrossing composite quantile regression LSTM (NCQR-LSTM). This method not only inherits the advantages of CQR-LSTM, but also does not need to consider complex constraint calculations. Further, the proposed methods are simple to implement and have strong scalability. Experiments on a real wind speed dataset show the advantages of our approaches.

2   Preliminaries

2.1   Quantile Regression

Given a set of data samples: (x_t, y_t) for $t = 1, 2, \cdots, N$ and $x_t = (x_1, x_2, \cdots, x_p)$, where N, p are the number of samples and features, respectively. Defining the conditional τ-quantile function $f_\tau(x_t)$

$$P(\boldsymbol{Y} \leq f_\tau(x_t)) = \tau, \tag{1}$$

where τ is the quantile probability $(0 < \tau < 1)$. In QR, using the pinball loss function which is defined as

$$\rho_\tau(\mu) = \begin{cases} \tau\mu & \text{if } \mu \geq 0 \\ (\tau - 1)\mu & \text{if } \mu < 0 \end{cases}. \tag{2}$$

This is an asymmetric loss function that enables QR to estimate the sample distribution of different locations. For a particular τ-quantile, the parameters are estimated by minimizing the optimization function

$$E_\tau = \frac{1}{N} \sum_{t=1}^{N} \rho_\tau(f_\tau(x_t) - y_t). \tag{3}$$

2.2   Quantile Long Short-Term Memory

LSTM is a commonly used RNN architecture. It uses gate units to control the saving and dropping of information. The gates are actually vectors with changeable elements. These elements are normalized to $(0, 1)$ by the sigmoid function σ. As shown in (4), LSTM has three gate units, the forget gate f_t, the input gate i_t and the output gate o_t as follows,

$$\begin{aligned} f_t &= \sigma(W_f \cdot [h_{t-1}, x_t] + b_f), \\ i_t &= \sigma(W_i \cdot [h_{t-1}, x_t] + b_i), \\ o_t &= \sigma(W_o \cdot [h_{t-1}, x_t] + b_o). \end{aligned} \tag{4}$$

In LSTM unit, $\tilde{C}_t$ is the candidate cell state which includes the new input information,

$$\tilde{C}_t = tanh(W_c \cdot [h_{t-1}, x_t] + b_c). \tag{5}$$

The update of cell state C_t is given in (6)

$$C_t = f_t \odot C_{t-1} + i_t \odot \tilde{C}_t. \tag{6}$$

It should be noted that the working mechanism of the gates is an element-wise multiplication. The new cell state C_t makes use of the last cell state information and the new input information from the candidate cell state. It can be seen that f_t controls the use of old information while i_t controls the use of new information. Finally, the LSTM unit needs to use o_t to determine how much information can be output,

$$h_t = o_t \odot tanh(C_t). \tag{7}$$

It usually requires a fully connected part to convert h_t into the desired output size. We use a two-layer fully connection in experiments. The final output $f(x_t)$ is

$$\begin{aligned} z_t &= \sigma(W_h \cdot h_t + b_h), \\ f(x_t) &= W_z \cdot z_t + b_z. \end{aligned} \tag{8}$$

For Q-LSTM, $f_\tau(x_t)$ is used to replace $f(x_t)$ under a given τ. The model is trained by minimizing (3). It is obvious that it requires retraining a new model for a new τ, which means multiple Q-LSTM models are needed to estimate multiple quantiles when $\tau = \{\tau_1, \tau_2, \cdots, \tau_K\}$ in real applications.

3   Methods

3.1   Composite Quantile Regression Long Short-Term Memory Network

Defining $F_\tau(x_t) = \{f_{\tau_1}(x_t), f_{\tau_2}(x_t), \cdots, f_{\tau_K}(x_t)\}$ are the quantiles estimated at time t. To get $F_\tau(x_t)$ at the same time instead of repeatedly building multiple independent models, we propose CQR-LSTM. Its framework is presented in Fig. 1.

For each τ_i, there is a $LSTM_i + FC_i$ submodel to predict f_{τ_i}. Each submodel is the same as (4)–(8), and finally f_{τ_i} is

$$f_{\tau_i}(x_t) = W_{iz} \cdot z_{iz} + b_{iz}, \tag{9}$$

where W_{iz}, z_{iz}, b_{iz} are partial parameters of the i-th submodel. Then, the corresponding sub-loss ρ_{τ_i} is computed by using quantile loss

$$\rho_{\tau_i}(\mu) = \begin{cases} \tau_i \mu & \text{if } \mu \geq 0 \\ (\tau_i - 1)\mu & \text{if } \mu < 0 \end{cases}, \tag{10}$$

where $\mu = y_t - f_{\tau_i}$ and $i = 1, 2, \cdots, K$. Like CQRNN, we combine the strength of all regression quantiles to estimate $F_\tau(t)$ simultaneously by constructing a composite objective function

$$E_{CQR} = \frac{1}{KN} \sum_{i=1}^{K} \sum_{t=1}^{N} \rho_\tau(y_t - f_{\tau_i}(x_t)). \tag{11}$$

CQR-LSTM synthetically utilizes multiple quantiles modeled by the Q-LSTM submodel. It is trained by minimizing (11).

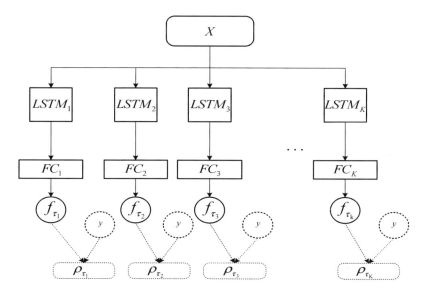

Fig. 1. The framework of CQR-LSTM.

3.2 Noncrossing Composite Quantile Regression Long Short-Term Memory Network

Obviously, CQR-LSTM cannot solve the quantile crossing problem. Considering the complexity of constraint calculations, we use an indirect method to avoid quantile crossing, building NCQR-LSTM. The main ideas of NCQR-LSTM are presented as follows.

- We first choose one quantile and estimate it directly through a $LSTM_f + FC_f$ submodel to get f_{τ_f}, we call it the starting quantile.
- To get $f_{\tau_{f+1}}$, we use the $LSTM_{f+1} + FC_{f+1}$ submodel to estimate the interval δ_{f+1} between $f_{\tau_{f+1}}$ and f_{τ_f} instead of directly estimating $f_{\tau_{f+1}}$. Then, the τ_{f+1}-quantile is obtained by $f_{\tau_{f+1}} = f_{\tau_f} + \delta_{f+1}$. For $f_{\tau_{f+2}}$, we can estimate the interval δ_{f+2} between $f_{\tau_{f+1}}$ and $f_{\tau_{f+2}}$ through the $LSTM_{f+2} + FC_{f+2}$ submodel, then $f_{\tau_{f+2}} = f_{\tau_f} + \delta_{f+1} + \delta_{f+2}$. For the subsequent quantiles, they can be analogized.
- The conditions are similar in another direction. For $f_{\tau_{f-1}}$, we estimate the interval δ_{f-1} between f_{τ_f} and $f_{\tau_{f-1}}$ by the $LSTM_{f-1} + FC_{f-1}$ submodel. Then $f_{\tau_{f-1}} = f_{\tau_f} - \delta_{f-1}$. For $f_{\tau_{f-2}}$, we need to estimate δ_{f-2} by using the $LSTM_{f-2} + FC_{f-2}$ submodel, then $f_{\tau_{f-2}} = f_{\tau_f} - \delta_{f-1} - \delta_{f-2}$ and so on.

During the above process, exponential functions are added to guarantee all δ_i are positive,

$$\delta_i = \exp(W_{iz} \cdot z_{iz} + b_{iz}). \tag{12}$$

Since all intervals are non-negative, this completely avoids the problem of quantile crossing.

There is an important issue about how to choose the starting quantile f_{τ_f}. Depending on different directions, there are three main ways.

– Left to right. Select f_{τ_1} as the starting quantile, then the subsequent quantiles can be obtained by

$$f_{\tau_i} = f_{\tau_1} + \sum_{j=2}^{i} \delta_j \quad 2 \leq i \leq K. \tag{13}$$

– Right to left. Select f_{τ_K} as the starting quantile, then the other quantiles can be obtained by

$$f_{\tau_i} = f_{\tau_K} - \sum_{j=i}^{K-1} \delta_j \quad 1 \leq i \leq K - 1. \tag{14}$$

– Middle to sides. Select f_{τ_m} as the starting quantile, where $1 < m < K$, then other quantiles can be obtained by

$$f_{\tau_i} = \begin{cases} f_{\tau_m} - \sum\limits_{j=i}^{m-1} \delta_j & \text{if } 1 \leq i < m \\ f_{\tau_m} + \sum\limits_{j=m+1}^{i} \delta_j & \text{if } m < i \leq K \end{cases}. \tag{15}$$

We finally choose the most intermediate quantile as the starting quantile. In our model, by (13)–(15), except for the starting quantile, each quantile depends on the starting quantile and the intervals between them. Assume that the dependencies between any two adjacent quantiles are the same. When the most intermediate quantile is selected as the starting quantile, the total number of dependencies among quantiles is minimized, which reduces the training difficulty of the model and indirectly improves the predictive ability of the model. We define the most intermediate quantile as f_{τ_S}. The framework of NCQR-LSTM is shown in Fig. 2, where

$$\delta_i = \begin{cases} f_{\tau_{i+1}} - f_{\tau_i} & \text{if } 1 \leq i < S \\ f_{\tau_i} - f_{\tau_{i-1}} & \text{if } S < i \leq K \end{cases}. \tag{16}$$

The loss calculation and optimization process of NCQR-LSTM are the same as CQR-LSTM, which are shown in (10) and (11).

The above models are optimized by the RMSprop algorithm [15] which is a common method in deep learning.

4   Experiments

In order to validate the proposed methods, experiments are performed on a real wind speed dataset. The evaluation criteria, data description, experimental setting and result analysis are shown below.

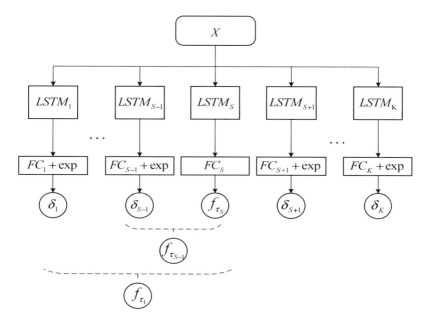

Fig. 2. The framework of NCQR-LSTM.

4.1   Evaluation Criteria

For probabilistic prediction, it is very important to measure the reliability, resolution and sharpness of the forecasting results. Therefore, the average quantile score (AQS), average coverage error (ACE) and interval sharpness (IS) are employed in this paper.

As a performance evaluation criterion, AQS considers the contributions of all estimated quantiles. It is designed to describe the overall performance of probabilistic prediction and is defined by

$$AQS = \frac{1}{KN} \sum_{i=1}^{K} \sum_{t=1}^{N} \rho_\tau(y_t - f_{\tau_i}(x_t)). \tag{17}$$

AQS is the same as the objective function (11) of our models. So it also illustrates the rationality of simultaneous estimation.

ACE measures the degree of how well the estimated quantiles match the observed values, and IS is used to evaluate the sharpness of prediction interval (PI) through applying punishment into the wider PI. They are expressed as

$$ACE = \frac{1}{N} \sum_{t=1}^{N} r_t \times 100\% - PINC, \tag{18}$$

$$r_t = \begin{cases} 1 & \text{if } y_t \in PI \\ 0 & \text{else} \end{cases}, \tag{19}$$

$$IS = \frac{1}{N} \sum_{t=1}^{N} \begin{cases} -2\alpha\delta_t^\alpha - 4[L_t^\alpha - y_t] & \text{if } y_t < L_t^\alpha \\ -2\alpha\delta_t^\alpha & \text{if } y_t \in PI \\ -2\alpha\delta_t^\alpha - 4[y_t - U_t^\alpha] & \text{if } y_t > U_t^\alpha \end{cases} , \tag{20}$$

where PINC represents the prediction interval nominal confidence. U_t^α and L_t^α are the upper bound and lower bound of PI, respectively. δ_t^α represents the width between U_t^α and L_t^α. α is confidence level parameter and $PINC = (1 - \alpha) \times 100\%$. For QR-based models, the appropriate two quantiles can be selected as the boundary of the PI.

A best performance is obtained with a small value of AQS and ACE as well as a value of IS closed to 0.

4.2   Data Description

The wind speed dataset used in this paper was collected from the wind farm in Saihanba, China. They were recorded at 5 s intervals, from January to December, 2013. A one-hour historical sequence is used as features to predict the wind speed value after five seconds. As a result, there are 720 features per sample. We use 4-fold cross-validation to improve the credibility of these experiments. Considering the accuracy and time, we set the timestep to 30, hence the input shape of these LSTM-based models is (30×24). Before training, data are standardized by the StandardScaler of sklearn.

4.3   Experimental Setting

The experiments are implemented on a computer with 16G RAM and an i7-7700 CPU, using the Tensorflow 1.7.0 framework, which is very popular in deep learning.

Probabilistic prediction performance is compared in four QR-based models, including QRNN, Q-LSTM, CQR-LSTM and NCQR-LSTM. Firstly, we compare the overall performance of quantile predictions over different ranges of τ by AQS. These ranges are artificially set to represent different locations and scales. Secondly, we set up a series of typical intervals, using ACE to compare how well the prediction distributions of these models match the real wind speed distribution and observe their sharpness by IS. Thirdly, for quantile crossing, we determine whether crossover occurs by counting the number of negative intervals between adjacent quantiles. Only when the number of negative intervals is 0, the model completely solves the quantile crossing.

For convenience, we specify that each LSTM+FC submodel has the same structure. By observing the validation set, we use a layer of LSTM and a 2-layer fully connection in the experiments. Q-LSTM also uses the same structure. In addition, an early stop mechanism is used to prevent overfitting. Specifically, when the loss of the validation set is not optimal for 10 consecutive times, the training will stop.

4.4   Result Analysis

The AQS experiment involves the whole, the lower half and the upper half of the wind speed distribution, each with three different scales. These results are shown in Table 1. Clearly, the LSTM-based QR models are more accurate than QRNN in overall quantile prediction. This shows that the combination of QR and LSTM is very effective. Comparing Q-LSTM and CQR-LSTM, CQR-LSTM shows better performance clearly, which demonstrates that the collaborative training of multiple Q-LSTM submodels is indeed better than training them separately. In addition, we can see that only the NCQR-LSTM model solves the quantile crossing problem. However, in order to ensure that the quantiles do not cross, the total quantile loss of NCQR-LSTM is increased compared with CQR-LSTM. But the noncrossing guarantees the rationality of the quantile prediction and the increase is slight, hence this is acceptable. As for time, our models cost less.

Table 1. AQS and time comparison with different scales and locations.

Range of τ	Model			
	QRNN	Q-LSTM	CQR-LSTM	NCQR-LSTM
(0.1, 0.3, 0.5, 0.7, 0.9)	0.3320	0.2594	0.2598	**0.2569**
(0.1, 0.2, 0.3, $\cdots$, 0.9)	0.3694	0.2745	**0.2744**	0.2753
(0.05, 0.1, 0.15, $\cdots$, 0.95)	0.3612	0.2639	**0.2629**	0.2667
(0.1, 0.2, 0.3, 0.4, 0.5)	0.3641	0.2831	**0.2791**	0.2837
(0.05, 0.1, 0.15, $\cdots$, 0.45)	0.3375	**0.2587**	0.2588	0.2625
(0.025, 0.05, 0.075, $\cdots$, 0.475)	0.3337	0.2533	**0.2527**	0.2622
(0.5, 0.6, 0.7, 0.8, 0.9)	0.4129	0.2825	**0.2810**	0.2838
(0.55, 0.6, 0.65, $\cdots$, 0.95)	0.3828	0.2603	**0.2594**	0.2611
(0.525, 0.55, 0.575, $\cdots$, 0.975)	0.3465	0.2581	**0.2561**	0.2583
Average AQS	0.3600	0.2663	**0.2649**	0.2678
Total time (s)	-	5705 s	**4187s**	4758 s
Crossing	yes	yes	yes	**no**

Based on ACE and IS, Tables 2 and 3 show the interval prediction results of the four QR models under different target intervals. There is no doubt that NCQR-LSTM has demonstrated the best performance on both ACE and IS. ACE measures the consistency of the predicted distribution with the target distribution. Its results show that the prediction distribution of NCQR-LSTM is more realistic and reasonable under real wind speed. From the results of IS, the models of simultaneous estimation are more confident about determining interval widths. In addition, compared with NCQR-LSTM, CQR-LSTM has little

Table 2. ACE comparison with different intervals.

PINC	Interval selection	ACE			
		QRNN	Q-LSTM	CQR-LSTM	NCQR-LSTM
99%	(0.005, 0.995)	−0.0363	−0.0191	−0.0266	**−0.0164**
95%	(0.025, 0.975)	−0.1119	−0.0524	−0.0516	**−0.0330**
90%	(0.05, 0.95)	−0.1180	−0.0562	**−0.0423**	−0.0437
85%	(0.075, 0.925)	−0.1812	−0.0907	−0.0709	**−0.0464**
50%	(0.25, 0.75)	−0.1035	0.0467	0.0335	**−0.0076**
49%	(0.005, 0.495)	−0.0197	−0.0179	**−0.0148**	0.0478
45%	(0.025, 0.475)	−0.0733	−0.0197	−0.0488	**0.0188**
40%	(0.05, 0.45)	−0.0496	−0.0544	−0.0563	**0.0346**
49%	(0.5005, 0.995)	−0.0772	−0.0173	**0.0001**	0.0177
45%	(0.525, 0.975)	−0.0566	−0.0284	−0.0222	**0.0166**
40%	(0.55, 0.95)	−0.0342	**0.0086**	−0.0643	0.0120
Absolute average		0.0783	0.0366	0.0387	**0.0245**

Table 3. IS comparison with different intervals.

PINC	Interval selection	IS			
		QRNN	Q-LSTM	CQR-LSTM	NCQR-LSTM
99%	(0.005, 0.995)	−0.2290	**−0.1479**	−0.1597	−0.1496
95%	(0.025, 0.975)	−0.7194	−0.5336	−0.5316	**−0.4987**
90%	(0.05, 0.95)	−1.1385	−0.8708	−0.8493	**−0.8310**
85%	(0.075, 0.925)	−1.6972	−1.1636	−1.1497	**−1.1033**
50%	(0.25, 0.75)	−3.1644	−2.2479	**−2.2402**	−2.2641
49%	(0.005, 0.495)	−4.4939	−4.2265	−3.9715	**−3.5519**
45%	(0.025, 0.475)	−3.6411	−3.4977	−3.3847	**−3.3579**
40%	(0.05, 0.45)	−3.5239	−3.2895	−3.2997	**−3.1559**
49%	(0.5005, 0.995)	−4.9737	−3.8187	**−3.6545**	−3.7943
45%	(0.525, 0.975)	−3.9711	**−3.1323**	−3.2606	−3.1587
40%	(0.55, 0.95)	−3.9462	−3.1415	**−3.0295**	−3.0600
Absolute average		2.8635	2.3700	2.3210	**2.2659**

improvement in interval prediction, which indicates that solving the quantile crossing problem is of great significance for the reasonable prediction of probability distribution.

Finally, as shown in Fig. 3, we extracted a section of wind speed prediction results for display. Overall, both models accurately characterize the wind speed curve. By zooming in on the details, we can see that NCQR-LSTM does solve the problem of quantile crossing.

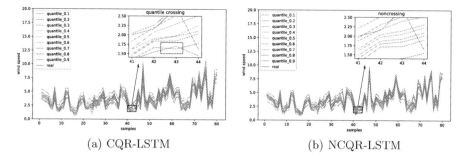

(a) CQR-LSTM   (b) NCQR-LSTM

Fig. 3. Wind speed forecasting demonstration.

5   Conclusions and Future Work

In this paper, we proposed two models, CQR-LSTM and NCQR-LSTM. CQR-LSTM simultaneously estimates multiple regression quantiles by using a composite objective function. This not only saves time, but also improves the overall prediction accuracy. NCQR-LSTM solves the problem of quantile crossing. It is based on CQR-LSTM hence has the advantage of simultaneous estimation. Since an indirect method is used to avoid constraint calculations, the model can be used directly for deep learning.

Though we use the same submodels for predicting different quantiles in the experiments. In future, it is worth studying the methods to measure the complexity of each submodel and adaptively use different structures of submodels to coordinate training.

Acknowledgments. This work is supported by the National Natural Science Foundation of China under Grants 61432011, U1435212, 61105054, and Open Research Program of Key Laboratory of Solar Activity.

References

1. Bang, S., Cho, H., Jhun, M.: Simultaneous estimation for non-crossing multiple quantile regression with right censored data. Stat. Comput. **26**(1–2), 131–147 (2016). https://doi.org/10.1007/s11222-014-9482-0
2. Bassett Jr., G., Koenker, R.: An empirical quantile function for linear models with IID errors. J. Am. Stat. Assoc. **77**(378), 407–415 (1982). https://doi.org/10.1080/01621459.1982.10477826
3. Cannon, A.J.: Quantile regression neural networks: implementation in R and application to precipitation downscaling. Comput. Geosci. **37**(9), 1277–1284 (2011). https://doi.org/10.1016/j.cageo.2010.07.005
4. Cannon, A.J.: Non-crossing nonlinear regression quantiles by monotone composite quantile regression neural network, with application to rainfall extremes. Stochast. Environ. Res. Risk Assess. **32**(11), 3207–3225 (2018). https://doi.org/10.31223/osf.io/wg7sn

5. Constante-Flores, G.E., Illindala, M.S.: Data-driven probabilistic power flow analysis for a distribution system with renewable energy sources using monte carlo simulation. IEEE Trans. Ind. Appl. **55**(1), 174–181 (2019). https://doi.org/10.1109/icps.2017.7945118
6. Gan, D., Wang, Y., Zhang, N., Zhu, W.: Enhancing short-term probabilistic residential load forecasting with quantile long-short-term memory. J. Eng. **2017**(14), 2622–2627 (2017). https://doi.org/10.1049/joe.2017.0833
7. Gers, F.A., Eck, D., Schmidhuber, J.: Applying LSTM to time series predictable through time-window approaches. In: Tagliaferri, R., Marinaro, M. (eds.) Neural Nets WIRN Vietri-01, pp. 193–200. Springer, London (2002). https://doi.org/10.1007/978-1-4471-0219-9_20
8. Hochreiter, S., Schmidhuber, J.: Long short-term memory. Neural Comput. **9**(8), 1735–1780 (1997). https://doi.org/10.1162/neco.1997.9.8.1735
9. Huang, Z., Xu, W., Yu, K.: Bidirectional lstm-crf models for sequence tagging. arXiv preprint arXiv:1508.01991 (2015)
10. Jeong, M.C., Lee, S.J., Cha, K., Zi, G., Kong, J.S.: Probabilistic model forecasting for rail wear in seoul metro based on bayesian theory. Eng. Fail. Anal. **96**, 202–210 (2019). https://doi.org/10.1016/j.engfailanal.2018.10.001
11. Koenker, R., Hallock, K.F.: Quantile regression. J. Econ. Perspect. **15**(4), 143–156 (2001). https://doi.org/10.1257/jep.15.4.143
12. Liu, Y., Wu, Y.: Simultaneous multiple non-crossing quantile regression estimation using kernel constraints. J. Nonparametric Stat. **23**(2), 415–437 (2011). https://doi.org/10.1080/10485252.2010.537336
13. Malhotra, P., Vig, L., Shroff, G., Agarwal, P.: Long short term memory networks for anomaly detection in time series. In: Proceedings, p. 89. Presses universitaires de Louvain (2015)
14. Takeuchi, I., Le, Q.V., Sears, T.D., Smola, A.J.: Nonparametric quantile estimation. J. Mach. Learn. Res. **7**(Jul), 1231–1264 (2006)
15. Tieleman, T., Hinton, G.: Lecture 6.5-rmsprop: divide the gradient by a running average of its recent magnitude. COURSERA: Neural Netw. Mach. Learn. **4**(2), 26–31 (2012)
16. Xu, Q., Deng, K., Jiang, C., Sun, F., Huang, X.: Composite quantile regression neural network with applications. Expert Syst. Appl. **76**, 129–139 (2017). https://doi.org/10.1016/j.eswa.2017.01.054
17. Zongxia, X., Yong, X., Qinghua, H.: Uncertain data classification with additive kernel support vector machine. Data Knowl. Eng. https://doi.org/10.1016/j.datak.2018.07.004

Short-Term Temperature Forecasting on a Several Hours Horizon

Louis Desportes[1]([✉]), Pierre Andry[1], Inbar Fijalkow[1][iD], and Jérôme David[2]

[1] ETIS, Univ Paris Seine, Univ Cergy-Pontoise, ENSEA, CNRS,
95000 Cergy-Pontoise, France
{louis.desportes,pierre.andry,inbar.fijalkow}@ensea.fr
[2] ZenT, 95000 Neuville sur Oise, France
jerome.david@zent-eco.com

Abstract. Outside temperature is an important quantity in building control. It enables improvement in inhabitant energy consumption forecast or heating requirement prediction. However most previous works on outside temperature forecasting require either a lot of computation or a lot of different sensors. In this paper we try to forecast outside temperature at a multiple hour horizon knowing only the last 24 h of temperature and computed clear-sky irradiance up to the prediction horizon. We propose the use different neural networks to predict directly at each hour of the horizon instead of using forecast of one hour to predict the next. We show that the most precise one is using one dimensional convolutions, and that the error is distributed across the year. The biggest error factor we found being unknown cloudiness at the beginning of the day. Our findings suggest that the precision improvement seen is not due to trend accuracy improvement but only due to an improvement in precision.

Keywords: Forecast · Temperature · Smart building · CNN

1 Introduction

1.1 Motivation: EcobioH2 Building

Today's buildings energy consumption is decreasing due to progress in used materials and appliances energy management, so that in the near future we could envision positive energy buildings, i.e. buildings that produce more energy than they consume. This implies using a local source of energy, like solar panels on the rooftop or a windmill, rather than power from the grid. However, local energy sources are usually intermittent. Therefore, a storage of the energy is required for the low-to-no-production periods, like batteries, and a way to control storage/usage periods. This implies knowing in advance the energy production

The research reported in this publication is part of the EcobioH2 project supported by EcoBio and ADEME, the french agency for environnement and energy. This project is funded by the PIA, the french national investment plan for innovation.

and demand. Both being highly influenced by external climate, ourstudy focuses on temperature forecast.

The EcobioH2 project [3,4] intends to be the first low footprint building in France using hydrogen fuel cells for energy storage and a neural network for its control. The 6-storey building of approximately 10 000 squared meters will host retail, cultural, lodging, offices and digital activities. It will have solar panels on its rooftop to produce energy, hybrid hydrogen energy storage to store it. EcobioH2 project requires temperature forecast to design an energy control and monitoring system balancing local energy needs and energy production.

1.2 Temperature Forecast

Temperature forecast is required to refine electricity load forecast [9]. The influence of heat is important on appliances consumption and need for cooling/heating. Moreover the weather fluctuations cause behavior shifts of inhabitants.

Knowing what the outside temperature will be in the next 6 to 24 h, we can predict, and take into account, how much energy will be needed for heating or cooling the building. The aim of this paper is to investigate the temperature forecast on a several hours horizon with a limited amount of sensors. In particular neither wind speed nor wet-bulb thermometers will be available. The exploitation of our predictor should also not require a too large amount of data.

1.3 Related Works

Different methods have been proposed for short-term temperature forecasting. [6] uses Abductive networks, a method that links multiple Volterra series together in order to ease network interpretation. However this method uses a network for each prediction hour which induces a huge complexity. Better methods have since been found. Those methods are outlined below.

Based upon a physical model of temperature, [15] uses Volterra series to propose probabilistics forecasts. The authors propose to use hidden Markov models and the Viterbi algorithm to account for the cloudiness variation. They predict at short terms of 15 min and 30 min and still have a lot of parameters to learn (2 Volterra series, 2 HMM, 1 Autoregressive filter).

[9] is using Echo-State networks hidden state to account for cloudiness. This implies a long and complex convergence for the network. Furthermore the authors only predict at an hour horizon, when we want to have a several hours horizon, or a day horizon using one completely different network depending on the hour the forecast is made.

Simpler Artificial Neural Networks forecasting methods have also been proposed, such as [11]. The authors use many different sensors (wet temperature, wind speed, humidity, pressure, ...) that we don't have on site. [7] needs the last 10 years of values of a given day as an input of their network and only predicts the values of the next day while we need a forecast for several hours of the current day.

The closest work to ours is [16] detailed in [17]. After training it predicts temperature using only the last 24 h of temperature measures and computed irradiance data. This prediction happens only at the next hour. The authors then use the prediction in 1 h of the network to predict the temperature in 2 h yielding to a propagation error that increases with the forecast horizon. Moreover this prediction method preprocess the data before feeding it to the network. This preprocessing might limit the network learning capacity.

In the sequel, we will investigate different neural networks architectures to improve the several hours horizon forecast.

2   Model and Problem Setting

We want to forecast the outside temperature T_{out} for each hour up to an horizon of $H = 6$ h or $H = 24$ h. At the trained network input, we use only the $N = 24$ last hours of temperature values $\mathbf{T_{out}}(t - N + 1 : t)$ and the computed irradiance I_{th} between $t - N + 1$ and $t + H$, where t is the current instant. In other words, we want to find the function f such that the H hours temperature forecast $\widehat{\mathbf{T}}_{out}(t + 1 : t + H)$ is given by: $\widehat{\mathbf{T}}_{out}(t + 1 : t + H) = f(\mathbf{T_{out}}(t - N + 1 : t); \mathbf{I_{th}}(t - N + 1 : t + H))$, where MSE: $\sum_{t=1}^{T} \sum_{h=1}^{H} \left(T_{out}(t + h) - \widehat{T}_{out}(t + h) \right)^2$ is minimal. This problem is shown in Fig. 1.

We denote $\mathbf{X}(t + 1 : t + H) = (X(t + 1), X(t + 2), \ldots, X(t + H))$ the vector containing the H values of X between hours $t + 1$ and $t + H$ with a time step of 1 h. Identically for $X(t - N + 1 : t)$. The computed irradiance I_{th} is the clear-sky irradiance. It is the power received if the sky does not have any cloud. I_{th} can be computed using the equations found in [12]. T_{out} is given in K, and I_{th} in W/m^2.

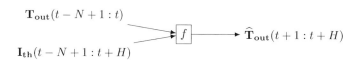

Fig. 1. Temperature forecast scheme

3   Temperature Forecasting Using Neural Networks

In the sequel, we will use neural networks to learn the function f as defined in Fig. 1, from the sole T_{out} and I_{th}.

Our work is based upon [17]. This method preprocesses the input data as

$$\mathbf{y_1} = \left[I_{th}(t + 1); \overline{T_{out}}(t); \max(\mathbf{T_{out}}(t - N + 1 : t)); \min(\mathbf{T_{out}}(t - N + 1 : t)); T_{out}(t); T_{out}(t - 1) \right]$$

where $\overline{T_{out}}(t)$ is the mean of $\mathbf{T_{out}}(t - N + 1 : t)$. This preprocessed input y_1 is then fed to an hidden neural network layer with bias $\mathbf{b_2}$ and a $tanh$ activation function such that $\mathbf{y_2} = tanh(\mathbf{y_1} \times W_2 + \mathbf{b_2})$. The hidden layer output is then fed to the output layer $Dense(1)$ with bias $\mathbf{b_2}$ and no activation function giving the one value output $\widehat{T}_{out}(t + 1) = \mathbf{y_2} \times \mathbf{w_3} + b_3$. This method is displayed in Fig. 2. We suspect that using $\widehat{T}_{out}(t + 1)$ as an input of the neural network to predict $T_{out}(t + 2)$ may induce error propagation.

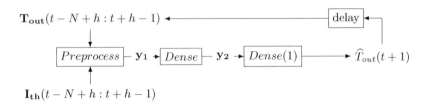

Fig. 2. [17] network structure

3.1 Multi-horizon

In order to avoid error propagation, we propose to adapt the network proposed in [17] to directly forecast up to $t + H$ horizons with each $t + n$, $n \in [1, H]$ as an output of the network.

We preprocess the data in the same way as [17]. However to ensure our network has the same input information as their when run over H horizons we add $I_{th}(t + 2 : t + H)$ to the output of the preprocessing: $\mathbf{y_1} = \big[\mathbf{I_{th}}(t + 1 : t + H); \overline{T_{out}}(t); \max(\mathbf{T_{out}}(t - N + 1 : t)); \min(\mathbf{T_{out}}(t - N + 1 : t)); T_{out}(t); T_{out}(t - 1)\big]$. In the contrary of [9], we don't want to train as many networks as the number of outputs. This means that our network's $Dense$ layer is common to all prediction horizons. The formula for this layer is the same, only the dimension changes; the output is made of H values, one for each of the horizon time-step. This yields to: $\widehat{\mathbf{T}}_{out}(t + 1 : t + H) = \mathbf{y_2} \times W_3 + \mathbf{b_3}$ This network named preprocess_multih is shown in Fig. 3.

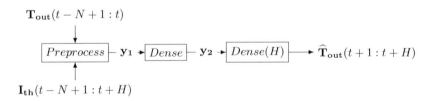

Fig. 3. preprocess_multih network structure

3.2   Raw Input

In order to understand if the preprocessing proposed by [17] limits the method performance, we propose to remove the inputs preprocessing and to feed the network with the raw inputs: in $\mathbf{y_r} = (\mathbf{I_{th}}(t - N + 1 : t + H); \mathbf{T_{out}}(t - N + 1 : t))$. These raw inputs are sent to $Dense$ and $Dense(H)$ layers using the same formulas as the previous network preprocess_multih with different dimension. Figure 4 show this network named raw_multih.

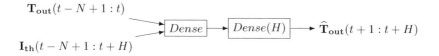

Fig. 4. raw_multih structure

3.3   Convolutions

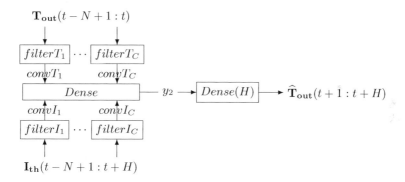

Fig. 5. conv_multih structure

Next, we investigate the usage of a convolutional layer enabling the network to do a better analysis of the inputs [14] because convolutions enable the network to factor for local temporal convolutions. Doing so, we adopt a similar approach as in audio processing [13]. In our case a 1D convolution should be sufficient since our signal seems has a slow frequency evolution. To our knowledge, it is the first attempt to apply such solution to temperature forecasting.

Each raw input is fed to a separate convolutional layer with bias, no activation and no padding. For each convolution c in C, the number of convolutions, the formula is $convI_c = \mathbf{I_{th}}(t - N + 1 : t + H) * filterI_c + bI_c$ and $convT_c = \mathbf{T_{out}}(t - N + 1 : t) * filtersT_c + bT_c$. With $*$ the convolution operator. The output of those two convolutional layer is flattened and concatenated in a 1 dimension vector y_1 to be sent to the hidden layer. The hidden layer *Dense* and the output layer *Dense(H)* use the same formulas as raw_multih and preprocess_multih. This method depicted in Fig. 5 is named conv_multih.

3.4 Linear Predictor

For the sake of comparison, we want to measure the benefit of the neural networks in regards to linear forecasts. We will call the linear method linear_raw_multih. In this case, the same raw inputs, $\mathbf{I_{th}}(t-N+1:t+H)$ and $\mathbf{T_{out}}(t-N+1:t)$, are fed to the output layer with bias $\mathbf{b}$ and no activation function:

$$\widehat{\mathbf{T}}_{\mathbf{out}}(t+1:t+H) = \mathbf{y_r} \times W + \mathbf{b}$$

4 Available Datasets

There are many datasets available that take their data from weather stations around the world. The World Meteorological Organization (WMO) has its own set of weather stations. Composed of an aggregation of weather stations from country specific meteorological organizations. Information about the current weather status is broadcasted using synoptic code, also known as "code synop" [1]. Each station has its own diffusion schedule from each hour to every 6 h.

The aeronautic industry also has its own weather records called Metar (METeorological Aerodrome Report) [2]. Each airport makes its own report and broadcasts it every half hour.

The US National Radiation Research Laboratory built some weather stations to study solar radiations. Their data [8] is freely available on each project website and include the local temperature.

Other datasets take their sources from satellite observations. They only use weather stations to calibrate the interpretation of their imagery. Satellite imagery has the benefit of having data for more locations instead of a few discrete measure points.

In this work, we use the NASA Merra-2 [10] data. Those data are composed of an aggregation of different, wordwide, observations with a 1 h frequency. The dataset is packed with clear-sky irradiance and available freely for specific locations and the years 2005–2006.

In the following experiments we used the Merra-2 dataset on the town of Avignon (43.95°, 4.817°) in France, the location of the EcobioH2 building, obtained through SoDa HelioClim-3 Archives for free [5]. Using the data of 2005 as the train set and of 2006 as the validation and test set. Using the same data for test and validation can be made since we did not reach overfitting in any of our training. And therefore, could not optimize the number of epochs for the validation dataset.

5   Used Metrics

We pose $T = T_{out}(t+1 : t+H)$ to improve readability and N the sample size. Next, we recall the equations of different metrics.

$$RMSE = \sqrt{\frac{1}{N} \sum_{i=0}^{N} (T_i - \widehat{T}_i)^2} \tag{1}$$

$RMSE$ is our primary metric. It lends itself easily to interpretation as an error interval since it is expressed in the same metric as the output variable.

$$R^2 = 1 - \frac{\sum_{i=0}^{N}(T_i - \widehat{T}_i)^2}{\sum_{i=0}^{N}(T_i - \overline{T}_i)^2} \tag{2}$$

R^2 allows us to know how much of the signal is predicted. Giving us an idea of our room for improvement.

$$MAE = \frac{1}{N} \sum_{i=0}^{N} |T_i - \widehat{T}_i| \tag{3}$$

MAE is used in many works. It can be interpreted as an error interval but does not penalize far-off predictions.

6   Results

Using the training data, we perform a stochastic gradient descent algorithm in order to find the different parameters W_i and b_i for the different networks and hyperparmeters combination. Then we evaluate each hyperparmeter combination on the train set and select the best one. The result is displayed in Table 1.

Table 1. Best hyper-parameters found for each network

Algorithms	Epochs	Learning rate	Batch size	Number of neurons in hidden layer	Conv sizes	Number of conv
[17]	50 k	0.001	8	5		
preprocess_multih	50 k	0.001	8	50		
linear_raw_multih	150 k	0.001	32			
raw_multih	150 k	0.001	32	14		
conv_multih	50 k	0.001	8	60	3	24

Then we predict on the test set to obtain RMSE and MAE and R^2. While the error values of RMSE and MAE are in Kelvin, they are equal to the error values in degree Celsius.

In Table 2 we see that [17] error increases way more the further the horizon. It suggests that indeed using $\widehat{T}_{out}(t+1)$ as an input of the neural network to predict $T_{out}(t+2)$ induce error propagation. Therefore our approch to multiple horizon forecast is the right one.

Table 2. RMSE (K) for each horizon and network

Algorithms	$t+1$	$t+2$	$t+3$	$t+4$	$t+5$	$t+6$
[17]	0.475	0.996	1.433	1.753	1.962	2.084
preprocess_multih	0.412	0.715	0.962	1.171	1.354	1.515
linear_raw_multih	0.409	0.756	1.030	1.256	1.413	1.540
raw_multih	0.375	0.644	0.882	1.098	1.289	1.428
conv_multih	**0.340**	**0.602**	**0.846**	**1.053**	**1.236**	**1.380**

The same Table exhibits that, according to the RMSE metric, the best precision for all given metrics is achieved with the conv_multih network. We explain this result by the ability of convolution to characterize the sky cloudiness. Table 3 is available to enable comparison with other works who uses this metric.

Table 3. MAE (K) for each horizon and network

Algorithms	$t+1$	$t+2$	$t+3$	$t+4$	$t+5$	$t+6$
[17]	0.342	0.761	1.125	1.396	1.568	1.665
preprocess_multih	0.293	0.531	0.729	0.895	1.038	1.169
linear_raw_multih	0.294	0.565	0.785	0.964	1.089	1.182
raw_multih	0.277	0.481	0.660	0.832	0.982	1.091
conv_multih	**0.2413**	**0.440**	**0.629**	**0.792**	**0.936**	**1.048**

Table 4 indicates that we predict most of the signal. The fact that even the most basic predictor, linear_raw_multih, gives excellent results validate the way

Table 4. R^2 in percentage for each horizon and network

Algorithms	$t+1$	$t+2$	$t+3$	$t+4$	$t+5$	$t+6$
[17]	99.72	98.77	97.44	96.17	95.20	94.59
preprocess_multih	99.79	99.36	98.85	98.29	97.72	97.14
linear_raw_multih	99.79	99.29	98.68	98.03	97.51	97.05
raw_multih	99.82	99.48	99.03	98.50	97.93	97.46
conv_multih	**99.86**	**99.55**	**99.11**	**98.62**	**98.10**	**97.63**

we stated the problem of temperature forecast. However even small forecasting improvement can be useful since they can be leveraged by other predictors.

7   Analysis

We analyze in more details the results of the proposed conv_multih, because it is the most precise one, to understand its weaknesses. In Fig. 6, we plot the RMSEagainst the prediction hour. We see that there is a spike in error at the beginning of the day, from 5 am to 8 am. Since cloudiness is defined as $c = 1 - \frac{I_{real}}{I_{expected}} = 1 - \frac{I_{local}}{I_{clear\,sky}}$, and since the clear sky irradiance is zero before sunrise, we can't have a cloudiness information before the sunrise. Hence, this spike is due to the insufficient information regarding the upcoming cloudiness of the day.

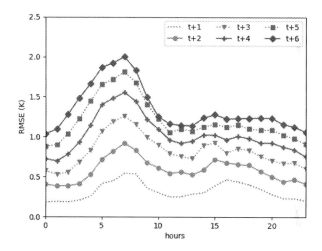

Fig. 6. RMSE in Kelvin, depending on the forecast hour for the best network

We did the same analysis regarding the month of the instant t (Fig. 8) and the evolution of error (RMSE) during the year (Fig. 7). No other spike can be seen, the error is evenly shared across the year.

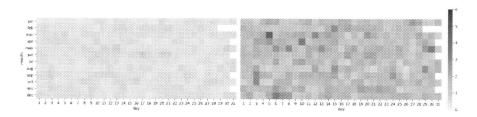

Fig. 7. RMSE in Kelvin, versus the day of the year for $t+1$ and $t+6$

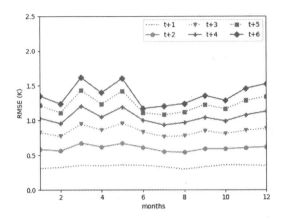

Fig. 8. RMSE in Kelvin, versus the month for the best network

The location of prediction has a great influence on the prediction error. We see in Table 5 that Nice, a city by the sea in the south of Avignon, has better results than Avignon. This is due to the climatic conditions of the city, Nice having way less clouds than Avignon. We used Nice as a comparison point since it is the location [17] used.

Table 5. RMSE (K) of conv_multih for the cities of Nice and Avignon

Location	$t + 1$	$t + 2$	$t + 3$	$t + 4$	$t + 5$	$t + 6$
Nice	**0.2171**	**0.4006**	**0.5635**	**0.7004**	**0.8049**	**0.8916**
Avignon	0.3397	0.6021	0.8460	1.0527	1.2355	1.3800

The goal of forecasting is to be precise (RMSE). It should be noted that this precision can be slightly improved by letting the training continue even when the gradient is small. This can be seen when using a logarithmic scale as in Fig. 9. Still this improvement cost a lot more computations per error unit.

We also want to know if the prediction is reliable. For this reason, we introduce the trend accuracy:

$$
trend_k(x) = \begin{cases} 0 & \text{if } |x'| \leq k \\ sign(x') & \text{otherwise} \end{cases}
$$

$$
trend\_accuracy_k = \frac{count(trend_k(\widehat{T}_i) = trend(T_i))}{N}
$$

(4)

That is the accuracy of the network to forecast if the temperature will rise, fall or stay constant. We choose $k = 0.3$ as the interval for the constant class. From our results, Table 2, this value seems to be lowest standard deviation we could have. Thus values in this interval could be seen as a stable trend.

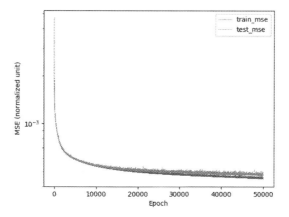

Fig. 9. Normalized MSE of the best network throughout learning

In Table 6 we see that if the conv_multih is always very close from the best accuracy. It is rarely the best one. When preprocessing is removed accuracy values are in a very small interval. This show the improvement seen in RMSE is not due to an improvement in accuracy but solely in an improvement in precision. Keep in mind that the categorization of trends been a bit arbitrary, variation is to be expected, so the difference seen may not be significant.

Table 6. Trend accuracy (.3) for each horizon and network

Algorithms	$t+1$	$t+2$	$t+3$	$t+4$	$t+5$	$t+6$
[17]	0.834	0.710	0.659	0.665	0.683	0.695
preprocess_multih	0.835	0.735	0.690	0.694	0.683	0.689
linear_raw_multih	0.809	0.724	0.704	**0.704**	**0.699**	**0.705**
raw_multih	0.811	0.729	**0.714**	0.697	0.699	0.697
conv_multih	**0.848**	**0.756**	0.713	0.698	0.696	0.695

8 Conclusion

In this paper, we proposed several neural networks for temperature forecast based on the sole previous 24 h temperature and computed irradiance. We showed that convolutional neural networks are a good tool for temperature forecasting. The proposed networks display precision improvement over linear predictors and non-linear ones. However progress should be made to account for cloudiness at sunrise and improve prediction accuracy. Our solution has the main advantage of not propagating forecasting error through time, and to have the best precision of forecast.

References

1. International Codes, Volume I.1, Annex II to the WMO Technical Regulations: part A- Alphanumeric Codes (2011–2018). https://library.wmo.int/doc_num.php? explnum_id=5708
2. Meteorological Service for International Air Navigation (Annex 3) (2013). https://www.icao.int/Meetings/METDIV14/Documents/an03_cons_secured.pdf
3. ECOBIO H2 – ADEME, March 2019. https://www.ademe.fr/ecobio-h2
4. Ecobioh2 - etis, February 2019. https://ecobioh2.ensea.fr
5. HelioClim-3 Archives for Free - www.soda-pro.com. March 2019. http://www.soda-pro.com/web-services/radiation/helioclim-3-archives-for-free. Accessed 11 Mar 2019
6. Abdel-Aal, R.: Hourly temperature forecasting using abductive networks. Eng. Appl. Artif. Intell. **17**(5), 543–556 (2004). https://doi.org/10.1016/j.engappai.2004.04.002
7. Abhishek, K., Singh, M., Ghosh, S., Anand, A.: Weather forecasting model using artificial neural network. Procedia Technol. **4**, 311–318 (2012). https://doi.org/10.1016/j.protcy.2012.05.047. 2012 C3IT
8. Andreas, A.M.: NREL: Measurement and Instrumentation Data Center (MIDC), March 2019. https://midcdmz.nrel.gov. Accessed 2 Apr 2019
9. Deihimi, A., Orang, O., Showkati, H.: Short-term electric load and temperature forecasting using wavelet echo state networks with neural reconstruction. Energy **57**, 382–401 (2013). https://doi.org/10.1016/j.energy.2013.06.007
10. Gelaro, R., McCarty, W., Suárez, M.J., Todling, R., et al.: The Modern-Era Retrospective Analysis for Research and Applications, Version 2 (MERRA-2). J. Clim., June 2017. https://doi.org/10.1175/JCLI-D-16-0758.1
11. Hayati, M., Mohebi, Z.: Application of artificial neural networks for temperature forecasting. Int. J. Elect. Comput. Energ. Electron. Commun. Eng. **1**(4), 662–666 (2007). https://doi.org/10.5281/zenodo.1070987
12. Ineichen, P.: Quatre années de mesures d'ensoleillement à Genève. Ph.D. thesis 19 July 1983. https://doi.org/10.13097/archive-ouverte/unige:17467
13. Korzeniowski, F., Widmer, G.: A fully convolutional deep auditory model for musical chord recognition. In: 2016 IEEE 26th International Workshop on Machine Learning for Signal Processing (MLSP), pp. 1–6, Septembe 2016. https://doi.org/10.1109/MLSP.2016.7738895
14. LeCun, Y., Bengio, Y., et al.: Convolutional networks for images, speech, and time series. Handb. Brain Theor. Neural Netw. **3361**(10) (1995)
15. Ramakrishna, R., Bernstein, A., Dall'Anese, E., Scaglione, A.: Joint probabilistic forecasts of temperature and solar irradiance. In: IEEE ICASSP 2018. https://doi.org/10.1109/ICASSP.2018.8462496
16. Salque, T., Marchio, D., Riederer, P.: Neural predictive control for single-speed ground source heat pumps connected to a floor heating system for typical french dwelling. Building Serv. Eng. Res. Technol. **35**(2), 182–197 (2014). https://doi.org/10.1177/0143624413480370
17. Salque, T.: Méthode d'évaluation des performances annuelles d'un régulateur prédictif de PAC géothermiques sur banc d'essai semi-virtuel. Ph.D. thesis (2013), http://www.theses.fr/2013ENMP0095, eNMP 2013

Using Long Short-Term Memory for Wavefront Prediction in Adaptive Optics

Xuewen Liu[✉], Tim Morris, and Chris Saunter

Centre for Advanced Instrumentation, Department of Physics,
Durham University, South Road, Durham DH1 3LE, UK
xuewen.liu@durham.ac.uk

Abstract. Time lag between wavefront detection and correction in Adaptive Optics (AO) systems can sometimes severely degrade its targeted performance. We propose a nonlinear predictor based on long short-term memory (LSTM) to predict open-loop wavefronts in the next time step based on a time series of past measurements. Compared with linear predictive control technique, this approach is inherently model free. Incorporation of LSTMs offer additional benefit of self tuning, which is especially favourable in terms of evolving turbulence. Numerical simulations based on a low-order single-conjugate AO (SCAO) system demonstrate over 50% reduction in bandwidth error in a relatively wide range of application scenarios. Agility and robustness against non-stationary turbulence is also demonstrated using time-variant wind profile.

Keywords: Long short-term memory · Time series forecasting · Adaptive Optics

1 Introduction

Adaptive Optics (AO) technology is nowadays widely adopted on major ground-based telescopes to alleviate distortions induced by atmospheric turbulence on astronomical images. The classical AO scheme, single-conjugate AO (SCAO), is composed of a wavefront sensor (WFS) for detecting incoming distortions, a real time controller/reconstructor which converts WFS signals to deformable mirror (DM) commands, and a DM which adjusts its shape in real time for phase compensation and to deliver ideally flat wavefronts for science imaging. It can either work in open loop (WFS sees distortions before DM correction) or closed loop (WFS sees residual distortion corrected by DM).

However, because of finite integration and readout time of WFS detector, there is an inevitable time lag between wavefront sensing and correction, during which time the atmosphere constantly evolves. This induces bandwidth error in AO error budget. For Extreme Adaptive Optics (ExAO) systems, the target of which is to detect exoplanets through high-contrast imaging, this error term severely degrades contrast, especially at small star separations [5].

© Springer Nature Switzerland AG 2019
I. V. Tetko et al. (Eds.): ICANN 2019, LNCS 11730, pp. 537–542, 2019.
https://doi.org/10.1007/978-3-030-30490-4_43

Predictive control is a linear solution to this problem. One most popular framework is Kalman filter based Linear Quadratic Gaussian (LQG) control [9, 10], which requires incorporation of a physical model (such of autoregressive models) of turbulence temporal evolution for deriving control law. As a result, estimation and update of a subset of turbulence parameters is unavoidable to cope with ever-evolving turbulence. In this paper, we propose a nonlinear, model-free artificial neural network (ANN) predictor based on long short-term memory (LSTM) [3] to predict open-loop wavefront measurements one frame ahead based on a time sequence of past noisy measurements.

2 Methodology

A 7×7 subaperture open-loop SCAO system operating at 150 Hz is simulated using Soapy [11]. Data flow between modules can be seen in Fig. 1. To simulate turbulence and its temporal evolution, a large phase screen with certain statistics is generated before each loop starts. It is then translated over telescope aperture with given speed to simulate pure frozen flow driven by wind [12]. At each time step, a smaller portion of the phase screen over telescope is interpolated and passed to relevant modules. The system then performs wavefront corrections based on input distortions and outputs residual wavefront error (WFE) as performance metric.

The simulated SCAO system serves two purposes. Its wavefront sensing subsystem is used to generate a series of time sequences of wavefront slopes as training data, with the last frame of slopes in each sequence being the training target and the remaining being training input. After training, the predictor is fed back into the SCAO system, the performance of which is then used for model evaluation and optimisation. There is an inherent frame of delay between wavefront sensing and correction in Soapy (blue in Fig. 1), which can be artificially compensated in simulation by applying wavefront measurements immediately to correction (green). Performance of our predictor (orange) is expected to be between these two situations.

Training. ANN training and optimisation is implemented using Keras [1]. Overall 200,000 training samples each of length 30 (#time steps) $\times$ 72 (#measurements) are generated to balance between model fitting and generalisation. Each sample is from a different phase screen with the same turbulence statistics. The last frame in each sample is used as training target. The ANN predictor is structured as stacked LSTM cells and a final fully-connected output layer. The optimal number of LSTM cells and their neurons are explored in a later process. 10% of overall training samples are split to form a validation set, the performance of which during training is monitored for learning rate scheduling. The training metric is mean squared error (MSE) between targeted and actual outputs evaluated on the remaining 90% of data. The optimisation algorithm used is Adam [6] featuring adaptive learning rate. Dropout is deployed for each LSTM

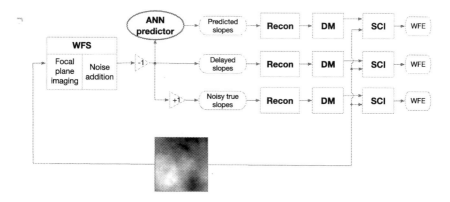

Fig. 1. Data flow in Soapy. Residual wavefront error (the upper loop) from predicted correction is expected to lay between delayed (the central loop) and delay-compensated (the lower loop) correction. (Color figure online)

cell [2], the ratio of which is adjusted to maintain balance between MSE evaluated on training set and on validation set during training. Batch size is set to 128. Training is terminated when overall 40 epochs are reached, by when both training and validation metrics have stagnated.

Evaluation and Optimisation. The predictor is further evaluated by feeding it back into the SCAO system after training (see Fig. 1). We define a statistical bandwidth error,

$$\overline{\sigma}^2_{BW, \text{ delay or pred}} = \overline{\sigma}^2_{\text{delay or pred}} - \overline{\sigma}^2_{\text{noisy true}}, \tag{1}$$

where σ_{delay}, σ_{pred} and $\sigma_{\text{noisy true}}$ are WFEs after correction calculated from delayed $\mathbf{S}_{29}$, predicted $\tilde{\mathbf{S}}_{30}$ and delay-compensated $\mathbf{S}_{30}$ respectively. Overlines in Eq. 1 denote mean value averaged over another 1,000 samples of length 30 frames. Those samples have the same statistics as training data and are used for model evaluation only.

Overall three types of hyperparameters that typically have most impact on performance are tuned to deliver an optimised model that achieves minimal $\overline{\sigma}^2_{BW, \text{ pred}}$: number of stacked LSTM cells (up to 4), neurons of each LSTM cell (between 50 and 250) and initial learning rate. The resulting model has two LSTM cells with 235 and 242 neurons respectively as a trade-off between performance and computing time. No significant improvement is achieved during tuning learning rate so the default value is kept (1e-3). Overall number of trainable parameters is 769,720. Computational load corresponding to an AO system of frequency 150 Hz is then 2.3×10^8 FLOPS.

3   Simulation Results

Reduction in bandwidth error within its training regime is about 70% evaluated on a separate test set of 1,000 samples, each of length 100 frames (Liu *et al.*, in prep.).

To demonstrate efficacy of our predictor out of its training regime, we generate 7 test sets each comprising 1,000 samples, each sample of length 100 time steps. While the predictor is trained with low signal-to-noise ratio (SNR) of wavefront sensing and in mild turbulence condition (turbulence strength $r_0 = 0.16$ m), we now test it in much higher SNR regime to alleviate interaction of noise error with bandwidth error. Turbulence strength is also varied among those test sets, each set representing a different turbulence level. Both noise profile and turbulence strength affect temporal statistics of ANN input sequence. Figure 2 shows bandwidth error calculated using Eq. 1 vs. r_0. Here the statistical mean is averaged over all samples and all time steps after the predictor stabilises (after 20th frame). Although optimised for prediction of the 30th frame, the predictor manages to build internal states in a shorter period of time and remain stable after that. Reduction in bandwidth error is over 50% when r_0 is between 10 and 18 cm.

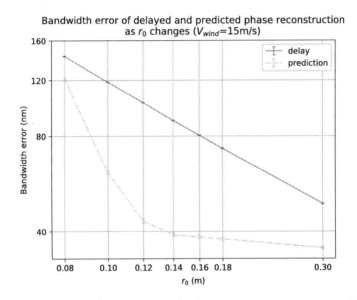

Fig. 2. Bandwidth error (in nanometers) before (solid blue line) and after (dashed orange line) prediction vs. turbulence strength. (Color figure online)

Effect of non-stationary turbulence is also considered by using time-variant wind profile (see dash-dotted line in Fig. 3). Another 1,000 samples of length 100 frames are used with a higher SNR as in the above test and mild turbulence ($r_0 = 0.16$ m). Although trained in conditions where wind speed is constant within each sequence (although different among sequences), our predictor adapts quickly to varying statistics and maintains relative stability in terms of small wind speed fluctuations (<5 m/s @ 15 Hz), showing better agility and robustness compared to a low-order linear predictor [7].

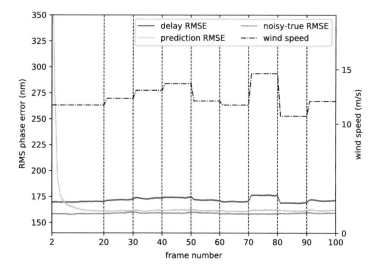

Fig. 3. Residual wavefront error in condition where wind speed changes every 10 frames after the predictor stabilises. The ANN predictor is insensitive to such mild wind speed variations, demonstrating both agility and robustness brought by flexible context-based control of data flow within LSTMs.

4 Conclusion and Future Work

We have demonstrated efficacy of ANNs as a framework for wavefront prediction. Compared with existing linear predictive control technique, this approach is inherently model-free and can potentially explore any linear and nonlinear relationships within input statistics, thus removing the need of model fitting and parameter identification. Use of a dynamic model as LSTM further enables predictor to self update conditioned on input features without any user tuning. It can also benefit from features of variable instead of fixed time scales. Although computational load can be expensive compared with a linear Fourier predictor [10], potential compression technique such as weight tuning can be incorporated into current scheme when applying it to higher-order AO systems such as ExAO systems [4].

Our next step will be to test our predictor using CANARY on-sky telemetry [8]. Much work will also be devoted to exploiting sparsity of our model and extending such framework to higher-order AO system simulations.

References

1. Chollet, F., et al.: Keras (2015). https://keras.io
2. Gal, Y., Ghahramani, Z.: A theoretically grounded application of dropout in recurrent neural networks. In: Proceedings of the 30th International Conference on Neural Information Processing Systems, pp. 1027–1035. NIPS 2016 (2016). https://arxiv.org/abs/1512.05287

3. Gers, F.A., Schmidhuber, J., Cummins, F.: Learning to forget: continual prediction with LSTM. In: 1999 Ninth International Conference on Artificial Neural Networks ICANN 99. (Conf. Publ. No. 470), vol. 2, pp. 850–855 (1999). https://doi.org/10.1162/089976600300015015

4. Han, S., Pool, J., Tran, J., Dally, W.: Learning both weights and connections for efficient neural network. Adv. Neural Inf. Process. Syst. **28**, 1135–1143 (2015). https://arxiv.org/abs/1506.02626

5. Kasper, M.: Adaptive optics for high contrast imaging. In: Proceedings of SPIE 8447. vol. 8447, p. 84470B (2012). https://doi.org/10.1117/12.924877

6. Kingma, D., Ba, J.: Adam: a method for stochastic optimization. In: Proceedings of the 3rd International Conference on Learning Representations (2014). https://arxiv.org/abs/1412.6980

7. van Kooten, M., Doelman, N., Kenworthy, M.: Impact of time-variant turbulence behavior on prediction for adaptive optics systems. J. Opt. Soc. Am. A **36**(5), 731–740 (2019). https://doi.org/10.1364/JOSAA.36.000731

8. Morris, T.J., et al.: Canary: the NGS/LGS moao demonstrator for eagle. In: 1st International Conference on Adaptive Optics for Extremely Large Telescopes (AO4ELT) (2009). https://doi.org/10.1051/ao4elt/201008003

9. Petit, C., et al.: Sphere extreme AO control scheme: final performance assessment and on sky validation of the first auto-tuned LQG based operational system. In: Proceedings of SPIE 9148. vol. 9148, p. 91480O (2014). https://doi.org/10.1117/12.2052847

10. Poyneer, L.A., Macintosh, B.A., Véran, J.P.: Fourier transform wavefront control with adaptive prediction of the atmosphere. J. Opt. Soc. Am. A **24**(9), 2645–2660 (2007). https://doi.org/10.1364/JOSAA.24.002645

11. Reeves, A.: Soapy: an adaptive optics simulation written purely in python for rapid concept development. In: Proceedings of SPIE 9909, vol. 9909, p. 99097F. International Society for Optics and Photonics (2016). https://doi.org/10.1117/12.2232438

12. Taylor, G.I.: The spectrum of turbulence. Proc. Roy. Soc. A **164**(919), 476–490 (1938). https://doi.org/10.1098/rspa.1938.0032

Incorporating Adaptive RNN-Based Action Inference and Sensory Perception

Sebastian Otte[(✉)], Jakob Stoll, and Martin V. Butz

Cognitive Modeling Group, University of Tübingen, Sand 14,
72076 Tübingen, Germany
sebastian.otte@uni-tuebingen.de

Abstract. In this paper we investigate how directional distance signals can be incorporated in RNN-based adaptive goal-direction behavior inference mechanisms, which is closely related to formalizations of active inference. It was shown previously that RNNs can be used to effectively infer goal-directed action control policies online. This is achieved by projecting hypothetical environmental interactions dependent on anticipated motor neural activities into the future, back-projecting the discrepancies between predicted and desired future states onto the motor neural activities. Here, we integrate distance signals surrounding a simulated robot flying in a 2D space into this active motor inference process. As a result, local obstacle avoidance emerges in a natural manner. We demonstrate in several experiments with static as well as dynamic obstacle constellations that a simulated flying robot controlled by our RNN-based procedure automatically avoids collisions, while pursuing goal-directed behavior. Moreover, we show that the flight direction dependent regulation of the sensory sensitivity facilitates fast and smooth traversals through tight maze-like environments. In conclusion, it appears that local and global objectives can be integrated seamlessly into RNN-based, model-predictive active inference processes, as long as the objectives do not yield competing gradients.

Keywords: Temporal gradients · Collision avoidance ·
Sensor integration · Active inference · Recurrent neural networks ·
Anticipatory behavioral control

1 Introduction

Model-predictive control [7] formalizes goal-directed control by assuming the existence of a forward model, which is used to minimize anticipated system states to goal states. Recently, we have shown that similar mechanisms can be applied in artificial recurrent neural networks (RNNs). For example, in [15] we have controlled a rocket-like object in 2D by learning a sensorimotor forward model with a long short-term memory RNN (LSTM, [10]). Similar methodological approaches also work when learning to predict the kinematic forward model

© Springer Nature Switzerland AG 2019
I. V. Tetko et al. (Eds.): ICANN 2019, LNCS 11730, pp. 543–555, 2019.
https://doi.org/10.1007/978-3-030-30490-4_44

of a many joint robot arm, yielding very natural behavioral patterns when inverting this model for reaching particular end-point postures [16,17]. Such control methodology is even applicable when the system faces a dual optimization task, where both goal-states need to be reached and the controlled system needs to be identified [4].

The typically observable rather natural behavior suggests a rather close relation to cognitive control processes that are unfolding in biological organisms. In fact, the goal-directed inference process is closely related to active inference as formalized by the free-energy principle for cognition [8,9,15]. While the RNN-based predictive models are not probabilistic, their differentiability allows gradient-based active inference, approximating model-predictive control.

In [14] we have integrated local directional gradients based on simulated distance sensors into a many joint robot arm, showing that the unfolding, kinematic active inference process can be modified based on local gradient information. As a result, the arm, controlled by kinematic active inference, was able to smoothly pursue goal locations and postures of its end-point, while avoiding local collisions with its trunk-like arm. Here, we investigated if a similar mechanism can be integrated into temporal active inferences processes, as employed in the rocket-like object. That is, we were interested in developing a model-based path planning mechanisms that avoids obstacles in a local manner. Accordingly, we equipped the rocket with simulated local distance sensors that indicate the presence of obstacles in the vicinity. Obstacles signals are then converted into directional gradient information away from the obstacle. As a result, the rocket flies around the obstacle as long as the obstacle is not overly large or hollow.

The results confirm that global, anticipated temporal gradient information can seamlessly be combined with local gradients, yielding goal-directed behavior that avoids local obstacles. Similar approaches have been applied in robotics, where, for example, wall following is combined with a global directional goal. Our contribution is to show how such multiple objectives can be effectively integrated and pursued by means of active inference techniques that are integrated into a learned predictive RNN-based sensorimotor model.

2   RNN-Based Action Inference

In the first part of this section we briefly recapitulate how prospective action inference can be accomplished with recurrent neural forward models [4,5,15]. Afterwards we define a simple sensory model adapted and show how this can be integrated within the continuous inference process adequately.

Establishing RNN-based action inference involves essentially two aspects. First, training the forward model, that is, learning a neural approximation of the dynamical system of interest. Second, inferring dynamic action sequences in order to generate adaptive goal-directed behavior in a continuous, dynamic control scenario.

2.1   Neural Forward Model

The forward model assumes a controllable discrete-time dynamical system, with the states depending on time step t. The model furthermore assumes a *partially observable Markov decision process* (POMDP) [18], such that the states are basically separated into perceivable states $\mathbf{s}^t \in \mathbb{R}^n$ and unobservable (hidden) states $\boldsymbol{\sigma}^t \in \mathbb{R}^m$. Additionally, the system can be influenced via k control commands denoted by $\mathbf{x}^t \in \mathbb{R}^k$. The next system state $(\mathbf{s}^{t+1}, \boldsymbol{\sigma}^{t+1})$ is determined by the mapping

$$(\mathbf{s}^t, \boldsymbol{\sigma}^t, \mathbf{x}^t) \overset{\varPhi}{\longmapsto} (\mathbf{s}^{t+1}, \boldsymbol{\sigma}^{t+1}), \tag{1}$$

which models the forward dynamics of the system. As this process unfolds recursively over time, the next system state depends not only on the current control inputs, but also, in principle, on the entire state history. It is the learning task of the RNN to approximate the forward model $\varPhi$ given the current state $\mathbf{s}^t$ and current control commands $\mathbf{x}^t$, as well as an internal memory encoding derived from the previous state information $\{\mathbf{s}^0, \mathbf{s}^1, \ldots, \mathbf{s}^{t-1}\}$ and motor commands $\{\mathbf{x}^0, \mathbf{x}^1, \ldots, \mathbf{x}^{t-1}\}$. Of course the RNN does not know the unobservable states of the system. The assumption is, however, that it is able to deduce the unobservable information approximately such that it can predict the observable state progression sufficiently reliably.

The learning of $\varPhi$ proceeds simply by dynamically processing current state information and predicting the next state information. LSTM-like RNNs [10] have been proven to be particularly suitable for this task [15], as they can predict accurately and can associate even temporally dispersed input events, which is essential when learning forward models in POMDP. Another advantage is that they provide stable gradients over long time periods, which is relevant when complex control trajectories are required.

2.2   Action Inference

Based on a certain action sequence (at first arbitrarily initialized) and an initial state, the learned recurrent forward model can predict a state progression—it executes the given motor sequence and prospectively generates an imagination of the future. In order to control the system of interest, the inverse mapping is required. Specifically, an action sequence needs to be inferred to approach a desired goal-state (or follow a sequence of goal-states) from the original state.

This can be achieved with the active inference-like procedure introduced in [15], which is sketched-out in Fig. 1. This procedure unfolds with the recurrent forward model. At a certain point time step t, the RNN has a corresponding internal neural activity encoding the dynamical system's state, which the RNN recurrently updates given the current state and motor command signals. The RNN maintains a preinitialized anticipated action sequence and anticipated gradient statistics. At each time step one or multiple optimization cycles are performed in which the policy is (further) refined taking the actually encountered experiences into account. We assume that the anticipated action sequence has

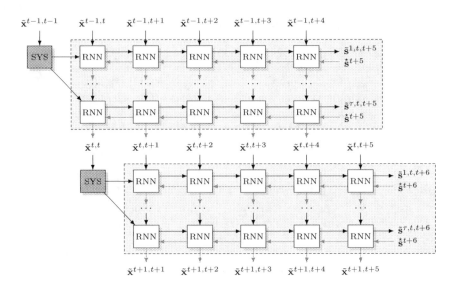

Fig. 1. The continuous action inference procedure [15]. In each iteration, an optimization cycle (gray boxes) is performed, refining the anticipated actions. Within an optimization cycle the progression of the dynamical system is projected into the future (here $T = 5$ time steps ahead) and the discrepancy between the predicted state and the desired goal-state is back-projected via BPTT onto the individual motor commands of the policy. The black lines indicate context and information forward flow. The blue lines indicate gradient flow. $\tilde{\mathbf{x}}^{t',t''}$ refers to the action vector for time step t'' based on the context of world time step t'. Note that the gradient updates the action vectors additively. Within the optimization cycle, $\tilde{\mathbf{s}}^{\tau,t',t''}$ refers to the state prediction for time step t'' based on the context of world time step t' in the τ-th optimization iteration, whereas $\overset{\star}{\mathbf{s}}^{t''}$ refers to the desired system state for time step t''.

a fixed length, which corresponds to the actual temporal planning horizon T. Based on the previous system state as well as the previous forward RNN hidden activation (the recurrent context) the action policy is adapted by generating a sequence of error gradients. This is accomplished by unrolling the predicted state progression into the future given the current action policy and back-projecting the discrepancy (quantified by the loss $\mathcal{L}$) between the predicted state and the desired goal-state (or sequence of goal states) in time using back-propagation through time (BPTT) [19]. During the forward-projection, the RNN is driven with its own state prediction. After back-projecting the error (backward pass over the unrolled planning horizon), the input gradient is computed by

$$\frac{\partial \mathcal{L}}{\partial x_i^{t'}} = \sum_{h=1}^{H} \left[\frac{\partial net_h^{t'}}{\partial x_i^{t'}} \frac{\partial \mathcal{L}}{\partial net_h^{t'}} \right] \sum_{h=1}^{H} w_{ih} \delta_h^{t'}, \tag{2}$$

where h indicates the hidden units after the input layer, $net_h^{t'}$ refers to the weighted sum of inputs for unit h at time t', and t' with $t \leq t' \leq t + T$ is the running time index over the unrolled future sequence. Each gradient signal $\delta_h^{t'}$ recursively depends on the future $\delta_{h'}^{t'+1}$, $\delta_{h'}^{t'+2}$, ..., $\delta_{h'}^{t+T}$ signals, which carry the gradient information back through time.

The above outlined procedure is repeated several times at each time step and embedded in a higher level optimization process, for which we use Adam [11].

After a certain number of optimization cycles, the first action of the refined sequence is executed (including both system and RNN update) and the anticipated action sequence begins with its successor, whereas the new last action is initialized with the previous last or a neutral motor command.

As a result, the procedure can be applied seamlessly and a continuous, active inference-like process unfolds, generating goal-directed interactions with the environment while continuing to plan the next steps [15].

2.3 Sensor Integration

Recently, the effectiveness of sensor integration for collision avoidance in an robot-arm controlling scenario has been demonstrated in [14]. Here we adapt the proposed sensor model for action inference with a dynamical system. Moreover, we will incorporate sensory information within the dynamic forward model, which was not done in [14].

In this work we focus on a in simple, simulated 2D flying vehicle, which we refer to as *rocket ball*. This multi-copter-like object is positioned in a rectangular, bounded environment with gravity. The vehicle has two propulsion units spread at a 45° angle from the vertical axis to both sides, inducing thrust forces in the respective direction. Each unit can be throttled within the interval $[0, 1]$.

We attached this vehicle with a ring-like apparatus of distance sensors, equally distributed around the vehicle's surface. Each sensor (indexed by k) casts a ray along its current orientation axis $\mathbf{a}_k^t$. The sensory input is simulated by intersecting the ray with surround polygons. Specifically, the closest intersection point with possibly surrounding geometry is computed (see Fig. 2) Based on this closest intersection point $\mathbf{q}_k^t$ at system time step t the sensory value of the k-th sensor is calculated by

$$v_k^t = \begin{cases} \max\left\{0, \ 1 - \dfrac{|\mathbf{q}_k^t - \mathbf{o}_k^t|}{d_k}\right\} & \text{if } \mathbf{q}_k^t \text{ exists} \\ 0 & \text{otherwise} \end{cases} \tag{3}$$

Thus, v_k^t effectively represents the strength of a particular sensory signal. It is 0 when no obstacle is detected in the sensor's range, while it converges towards 1 when an obstacle is right in front of the sensor.

2.4 Sensory Gradient Injection

Our goal is to enable active obstacle avoidance with our vehicle. To achieve this we integrated the sensory information into the active inference process as

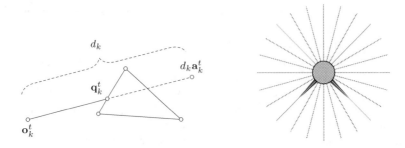

Fig. 2. Illustration of the simple ray-based sensor model (left) and the entire sensory apparatus of the dynamic vehicle (right).

outlined in the following: for each sensor k the respective sensory signal is projected onto the sensor's main axis in negative direction, which is referred to as *sensory-induced counter vector* (SCV) $\check{\mathbf{c}}_k^t = -[v_k^t]^{\omega_k} \mathbf{a}_k^t$, where ω_k (we use $\omega = 3$ throughout this paper) is an exponential scaling factor. The resulting SCVs are summed up per time step and additionally smoothed over time:

$$\check{\mathbf{c}}^t = \lambda \check{\mathbf{c}}^{t-1} + (1 - \lambda)\gamma \sum_k \gamma_k^t \check{\mathbf{c}}_k \qquad (4)$$

where $\gamma_k \in [0, 1]$ is the (variable) individual sensor sensitivity, which weights the influence of each sensor to the SCV. Additionally, the constant γ scales the entire SCV and regulates in turn its influence to the inference gradient. $\lambda \in [0, 1]$ is another smoothing factor. This slight sensor smoothing is very effective to support more soft initiations of collision avoiding maneuvers.

For all planning time steps $t \leq t' \leq T$ the $\check{\mathbf{c}}^t$ are added to the respective goal states (e.g. the target velocities). In order to prevent the current sensory influence to dominate the action inference procedure, we propose to exponentially decay the goal state adaptation in the future using

$$\overset{\star}{\mathbf{s}}^{t'} \leftarrow \overset{\star}{\mathbf{s}}^{t'} + \frac{1}{4^{(t'-t)}} \check{\mathbf{c}}^t \qquad (5)$$

2.5   Adaptive Sensor Regulation

We found in preliminary experiments that when obstacle constellations are tight and the rocket ball maneuvers within, weighting of all involved sensors can be counterproductive. This can, for instance, prevent the vehicle to pass gaps, which are in principle wide enough.

One simple solution to overcome this issue is to establish an adaptive sensor regulation based on the current vehicle's flight direction, referred to as $\mathbf{u}^t$, and the particular sensor axes $\mathbf{a}_k^t$. We propose to use the *cosine similiarity*:

$$\cos(\varphi_k) = \frac{\mathbf{u}^t \cdot \mathbf{a}_k^t}{|\mathbf{u}^t| \cdot |\mathbf{a}_k^t|} \qquad (6)$$

We then dynamically adapt the respective sensor sensitivity via

$$\gamma_k^t = \frac{1}{2}\left(\cos(\varphi_k + 1)\right) \tag{7}$$

As result the less the sensor axis corresponds with the current flight direction the more this sensors contribution to the SCV is suppressed and vice versa.

3 Experiments

For this first experiment we compared two different forward RNNs. The first model receives the current velocity $\mathbf{v}^t$ of the rocket ball as well as the current motor command $\mathbf{x}^t$, and predicts the velocity in the next time step $\mathbf{v}^{t+1}$ (but also the acceleration, which is, however, only used to improve the recurrent forward model and not for inference purposes). The second model additionally receives the current sensor stimuli.

Both RNN models consisted of 16 LSTM units with one fully connected recurrent hidden layer. We trained the RNNs with 2 000 sequences each consisting of 200 time steps using stochastic sampling (no mini-batches) and Adam with default parameters (learning rate $\eta = 0.001$, first and second moment smoothing factors $\beta_1 = 0.9$, $\beta_2 = 0.999$). The training sequences were generated based on continuously randomly adjusted thrust values within an environment without additional obstacles except for the boundaries. All experiments were implemented using Tensorflow at version 1.8.0.

For motor command inference the planning horizon was set to $T = 8$, thus the RNN unfolds eight time steps into the future. This action sequence is initialized with zero. For optimizing the action sequences we 30 refinement cycles per time step using Adam with $\eta = 0.01$ and $\beta_1, \beta_2 = 0.9$. The goal state at each future time step is a velocity vector pointing towards the target, whereas its length is clipped at the value of 0.03. Note that previously these parameters have been shown to produce a stable control behavior [4,5,15].

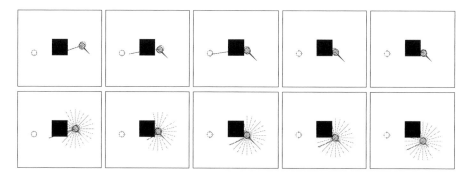

Fig. 3. Behavior comparison of the model without sensor inputs (top row) and the model with sensor input (bottom row).

3.1   Results

The first comparison demonstrates that already just incorporating the sensory information has a positive effect on the resulting goal-directed behavior (see Fig. 3). In this comparison the sensor information is not used to adapt the goal. While the model with sensor information plans right through the obstacle. The sensor-aware model can already incorporate the obstacle's presence in the inference procedure as its tends to circumvent the obstacle autonomously.

Hence, for the remaining experiments we focused on the sensor-aware forward model. Additionally, from now on sensor-based target goal adaption is performed (using $\omega = 3$, $\gamma = 2$, and $\lambda = 0.5$). Preliminary experiments indicated that

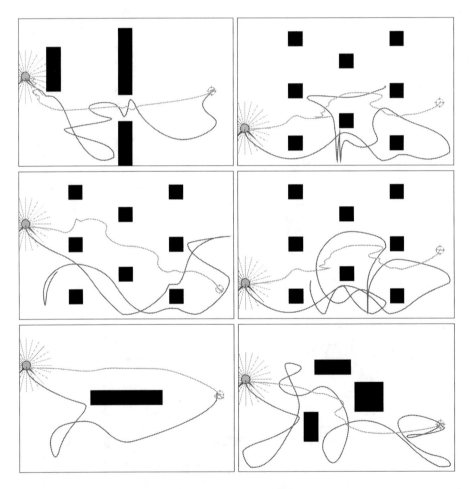

Fig. 4. Several examples demonstrating the effectiveness of adaptive sensor regulation. With adaptive sensor regulation (green trajectories) the vehicle can pass the environment more quickly and smoothly as without regulation (red trajectories). (Color figure online)

these parameters work well for the presented scenarios. The choice of $\omega = 3$ in combination with a general SCV scale of $\gamma = 2$ caused a smooth reaction onset with a significant increase of reaction intensity with decreasing distance. The choice of $\lambda = 0.5$ is a trade-off between reaction onset smoothness and latency.

As motivated earlier, equally weighted sensors can cause unwanted side effects. As a result maneuvering through smaller gaps between obstacles becomes unnecessarily difficult. Figure 4 compares the effect of the adaptive sensor regulation, which we proposed to overcome this problem. As can be seen it significantly stabilized the behavior of the vehicle in complex obstacle constellations—the rocket ball can quickly and smoothly pass even tight passages. Moreover, Fig. 5 shows a quantitative analysis, indicating that the desired behavior can be generated reproducible.

Finally, the last experiment presented in this paper involves a dynamic environment. The image sequence in Fig. 6 gives an impression how the behavior

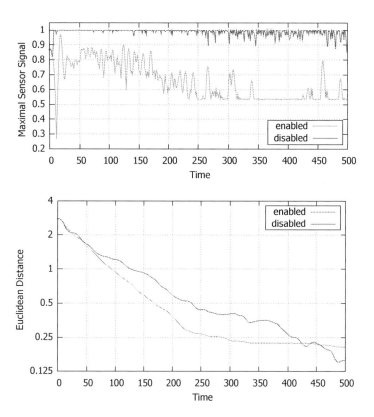

Fig. 5. Quantitative evaluation of vehicles' behavior in complex obstacle constellations (8 obstacles), averaged over 100 random flights. The upper graph shows the maximum sensor signal (1 = contact). The lower graphs show the euclidean distance to the target. The green line corresponds to adaptive sensor sensitivity, whereas the red line corresponds to equal sensor sensitivity. (Color figure online)

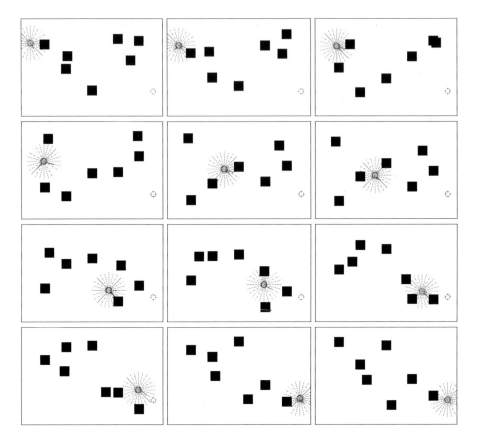

Fig. 6. An exemplary flight of the vehicle through an environment with moving objects in which any collision is avoided.

unfolds in the presence of moving objects. The rocket ball manages to reach the goal position reliably and without any collision with the obstacles. When, for instance, an obstacle suddenly appears in front the vehicle it immediately stops its flight and smoothly navigates around it.

Quantitative analyzes showed (cf. Fig. 5 for comparison) that there are no collisions as long as the dynamic obstacles move towards the rocket ball from the front or the sides. Objects approaching the rocket ball from the back can cause collisions when the vehicle moves slowly. This is due to the fact that with the current flight direction dependent sensor sensitivity the sensors in the back are mostly deactivated and thus cannot contribute to the SCV sufficiently. Investigating alternative sensor regulation schemes (e.g. based on changes over time) is a major future research task.

4   Summary and Conclusion

Goal-directed motor control requires per definition the presence of goals before actual motor behavior unfolds. However, in many RNN-based deep ANN approaches nowadays, full faith is often given to model-free, deep Q-learning and related approaches combining policy-based actor and critics [13]. From a computational cognitive science perspective, however, it is quite clear that such approaches will always lack versatility and adaptability in complex scenarios, where model-based planning and behavioral adaptations are necessary [6,12]. Here, we integrated model-based behavioral optimization in a RNN-based senso-rimotor predictive model, which is learned from self-supervised data. The optimization procedure is closely linked to neuro-computational theories of active inference, which can be derived from the free energy minimization principle [8,9]. With respect to reinforcement learning, the implemented mechanism essentially approximates model-based reinforcement learning [18]. With respect to control theory, our approach approximates model-predictive control approaches by means of learning and prospective (active) inference mechanisms in a RNN-based predictive model.

In this work we have shown that additional optimization criteria can be added into the active inference process. By converting sensory distance signals into repulsive forces—essentially modifying the active inference-inducing loss function with the additional objective to avoid large distance sensor signals, that is, small distances to walls and other obstacles—the RNN approach was able to avoid obstacles while aiming for a target location. As a result, relatively smooth obstacle avoiding trajectories were generated by the active inference process. Clearly, the paths are not as smooth as one might have expected. This is the case because the development of the sensory signals is not predicted during the active inference process. While the trajectories of the vehicle are predicted, thus allowing the optimization of the motor commands to pursue goal locations while avoiding local obstacle signals, trajectories around obstacles currently emerge in a rather reactive manner. Thus, we are currently working on integrating sensory distance predictions.

Another huge challenge for such models, however, is to reach true planning and motor decision making versatility on multiple levels of abstraction. Our human minds seem to be very good in abstracting, clustering, and generalizing sensorimotor structures and other environmental experiences into conceptual event structures and hierarchies thereof. Our recent work on the REPRISE system shows that such structures might emerge from exploiting temporal stabilities over time [4], that is, learning hidden dynamically more stable contextual states that modify the lower-level sensorimotor dynamics to the current system dynamics. When such structures can develop into loosely hierarchically organized conceptual and event taxonomies, it will be possible to unfold hierarchical, model-based reinforcement learning [1,2] mechanisms on deeper conceptual event-predictive levels [3]. As a result, deeper foresight, planning and reasoning on conceptual cognitive levels may become possible.

References

1. Botvinick, M., Niv, Y., Barto, A.C.: Hierarchically organized behavior and its neural foundations: a reinforcement learning perspective. Cognition **113**(3), 262–280 (2009). https://doi.org/10.1016/j.cognition.2008.08.011

2. Botvinick, M., Weinstein, A.: Model-based hierarchical reinforcement learning and human action control. Philos. Trans. Roy. Soc. London B: Biol. Sci. **369**(1655) (2014). https://doi.org/10.1098/rstb.2013.0480

3. Butz, M.V.: Towards a unified sub-symbolic computational theory of cognition. Front. Psychol. **7**(925) (2016). https://doi.org/10.3389/fpsyg.2016.00925

4. Butz, M.V., Bilkey, D., Humaidan, D., Knott, A., Otte, S.: Learning, planning, and control in a monolithic neural event inference architecture. Neural Networks (2019). https://doi.org/10.1016/j.neunet.2019.05.001

5. Butz, M.V., Bilkey, D., Knott, A., Otte, S.: Reprise: a retrospective and prospective inference scheme. In: Proceedings of the 40th Annual Meeting of the Cognitive Science Society, pp. 1427–1432 (2018)

6. Butz, M.V., Kutter, E.F.: How the Mind Comes Into Being: Introducing Cognitive Science from a Functional and Computational Perspective. Oxford University Press, Oxford (2017)

7. Camacho, E.F., Bordons, C.: Model Predictive Control. Springer, London (1999). https://doi.org/10.1007/978-1-4471-3398-8

8. Friston, K.: The free-energy principle: a rough guide to the brain? Trends Cogn. Sci. **13**(7), 293–301 (2009)

9. Friston, K., FitzGerald, T., Rigoli, F., Schwartenbeck, P., Pezzulo, G.: Active inference: a process theory. Neural Comput. **29**(1), 1–49 (2016)

10. Hochreiter, S., Schmidhuber, J.: Long short-term memory. Neural Comput. **9**(8), 1735–1780 (1997). https://doi.org/10.1162/neco.1997.9.8.1735

11. Kingma, D.P., Ba, J.L.: Adam: A method for stochastic optimization. In: 3rd International Conference for Learning Representations, abs/1412.6980 (2015)

12. Lake, B.M., Ullman, T.D., Tenenbaum, J.B., Gershman, S.J.: Building machines that learn and think like people. Behav. Brain Sci. **40**, e253 (2017). https://doi.org/10.1017/S0140525X16001837

13. Mnih, V., et al.: Human-level control through deep reinforcement learning. Nature **518**(7540), 529–533 (2015). https://doi.org/10.1038/nature14236

14. Otte, S., Hofmaier, L., Butz, M.V.: Integrative collision avoidance within RNN-driven many-joint robot arms. In: Kůrková, V., Manolopoulos, Y., Hammer, B., Iliadis, L., Maglogiannis, I. (eds.) ICANN 2018. LNCS, vol. 11141, pp. 748–758. Springer, Cham (2018). https://doi.org/10.1007/978-3-030-01424-7_73

15. Otte, S., Schmitt, T., Friston, K., Butz, M.V.: Inferring adaptive goal-directed behavior within recurrent neural networks. In: Lintas, A., Rovetta, S., Verschure, P.F.M.J., Villa, A.E.P. (eds.) ICANN 2017. LNCS, vol. 10613, pp. 227–235. Springer, Cham (2017). https://doi.org/10.1007/978-3-319-68600-4_27

16. Otte, S., Zwiener, A., Butz, M.V.: Inherently constraint-aware control of many-joint robot arms with inverse recurrent models. In: Lintas, A., Rovetta, S., Verschure, P.F.M.J., Villa, A.E.P. (eds.) ICANN 2017. LNCS, vol. 10613, pp. 262–270. Springer, Cham (2017). https://doi.org/10.1007/978-3-319-68600-4_31

17. Otte, S., Zwiener, A., Hanten, R., Zell, A.: Inverse recurrent models – an application scenario for many-joint robot arm control. In: Villa, A.E.P., Masulli, P., Pons Rivero, A.J. (eds.) ICANN 2016. LNCS, vol. 9886, pp. 149–157. Springer, Cham (2016). https://doi.org/10.1007/978-3-319-44778-0_18
18. Sutton, R.S., Barto, A.G.: Reinforcement learning: An introduction (1998)
19. Werbos, P.: Backpropagation through time: what it does and how to do it. Proc. IEEE **78**(10), 1550–1560 (1990). https://doi.org/10.1109/5.58337

Quality of Prediction of Daily Relativistic Electrons Flux at Geostationary Orbit by Machine Learning Methods

Irina Myagkova$^{(\boxtimes)}$, Alexander Efitorov , Vladimir Shiroky,
and Sergey Dolenko$^{(\boxtimes)}$

D.V. Skobeltsyn Institute of Nuclear Physics,
M.V. Lomonosov Moscow State University, Moscow 119991, Russia
{irina,a.efitorov,shiroky,dolenko}@sinp.msu.ru

Abstract. This study presents the results of prediction 1–3 days ahead for the daily maximum of hourly average values of relativistic electrons flux (E > 2 MeV) in the outer radiation belt of the Earth. The input physical variables were geomagnetic indexes, interplanetary magnetic field, solar wind velocity and proton density, special ultra-low frequency (ULF) indexes and hourly average values of relativistic electron flux. The phase-space for each physical component was reconstructed by time delay vectors with their own different embedding dimensions, and all of these vectors were concatenated. Next, various adaptive models were trained on this multivariate dataset. The following models were used for prediction: multi-dimensional autoregressive model, ensembles of decision trees within bagging approach, artificial neural networks of multi-layer perceptron type. The obtained results are analyzed and compared to the results of similar predictions by other authors. The best prediction quality was demonstrated by ensembles of decision trees. Also it has been demonstrated that using embedding depth based on autocorrelation function significantly improves prediction quality for one day prediction horizon.

Keywords: Prediction · Multi-layer perceptron · Auto-regression ·
Decision trees · Earth's outer radiation belt · Geomagnetic disturbances ·
Solar wind

1 Introduction

The outer radiation belt of the Earth (ERB) is a part of inner Earth's magnetosphere, in which the charged particles - electrons, protons, alpha particles - are held by the geomagnetic field (which is close to dipolar). As a first approximation, ERB is a toroid in which it is possible to distinguish two areas - inner and outer radiation belts with a gap between them. These are two distinct belts, with energetic electrons forming the outer belt and a combination of protons and electrons forming the inner belt. Spatial and temporal dynamics of inner and outer ERBs is also different. Both localization and particle flux of the inner ERB are stable, considered within temporary scales less than several months.

© Springer Nature Switzerland AG 2019
I. V. Tetko et al. (Eds.): ICANN 2019, LNCS 11730, pp. 556–565, 2019.
https://doi.org/10.1007/978-3-030-30490-4_45

For a long time it is well known that strong (more than two orders of magnitude) and abrupt changes of relativistic and sub-relativistic electron flux intensity in the outer ERB occur during magnetic disturbances due to arrival of both coronal ejections and high-speed solar wind streams to the Earth's orbit (e.g. [1]). The intensity of the flux of relativistic electrons (RE) with the energy > 2 MeV in the outer ERB is subject to the influence of solar wind (SW) and interplanetary magnetic field (IMF) parameters, which change during geomagnetic storms (e.g. [2]).

The radiation environment at geosynchronous orbit (about 35 thousand km altitude – the outer boundary of the radiation belts) is of particular interest due to the large number of satellites populating this region. Relativistic electrons (RE) of the outer ERB are called "killer electrons" since the electronic components of spacecraft can be damaged, resulting in temporary or even complete loss of spacecraft [3]. Acceleration and losses of relativistic electrons of ERB in the Earth's magnetosphere is an important fundamental problem in space physics (e.g. [2, 4]), so the main goal of our research from the point of view of the subject area is to improve understanding of the Earth's magnetosphere dynamics. From the other hand, relativistic electrons may cause dangerous malfunction of the electronics onboard spacecraft, and therefore they are called killer electrons [3, 5]. So forecast of relativistic electron flux in outer ERB is an important practical task, and the second goal of this study is to improve forecast.

In [6], it has been found that total integral day values of the fluxes – daily fluences of electrons with energy > 2 MeV, measured at geosynchronous orbit, could be predicted one day ahead, using a linear filter with solar wind speed at the input. Later on, during elaboration of REFM (Relativistic Electron Forecast Model), this method was developed further for the purpose of increasing prediction quality and horizon. Prediction carried out with the help of REFM is presented at the portal (Space Weather Prediction Center, https://www.swpc.noaa.gov/products/relativistic-electron-forecast-model). Experimental values of electron fluence, which the prediction is compared to, are obtained in the experiment at spacecraft of GOES (Geostationary Operational Environmental Satellite) series (https://www.nasa.gov/content/goes), which were designed for monitoring of the environment by US National Oceanic and Atmospheric Administration (http://www.noaa.gov).

In [24], a new model called PreMevE is used to predict storm time distributions of relativistic electrons within outer ERB, using additional data from spacecraft at low-Earth orbits, taking advantage of newly identified coherence caused by wave-electron resonance.

An alternative approach to prediction of relativistic electron fluence in the outer ERB is based on use of artificial neural networks (ANN). This approach is used in the models presented in [7–9] to predict RE fluence at geostationary orbit. The authors of this study also have experience on predicting electron flux at geostationary orbit, for hourly flux values [10–13].

The purpose of this work is to compare the quality of forecast of daily maximum of hourly average values of relativistic electrons flux at geostationary orbit with a horizon of 1 and 3 days using the following three machine learning methods: a multidimensional auto-regression model, ensembles of decision trees within the bagging approach, and artificial neural networks (multilayer perceptron).

2   Data Sources and Preparation

As input data for making predictions of daily maximum of hourly average values of relativistic (E > 2 MeV) electrons flux at geostationary orbit we used time series of daily aggregated values of the following physical quantities:

- SW parameters in Lagrange point L1 between the Earth and the Sun: Vx – x-component of SW (measured in km/s), protons density N_p (measured in cm^{-3}).
- IMF vector parameters in the same point L1 (measured in nT): Bz (IMF in GSM system) and B amplitude (IMF modulus).
- Geomagnetic indexes: equatorial index Dst (measured in nT) and global geomagnetic index Kp (dimensionless), AE index (measured in nT).
- ULF wave activity index (dimensionless).
- Average hourly fluences of relativistic electrons with energies > 2 MeV and of sub-relativistic electrons with energies > 600 keV at geostationary orbit (measured in $(cm^2 \cdot s \cdot sr)^{-1}$).

The source of the data on the SW and IMF parameters were the measurements performed continuously onboard the Advanced Composition Explorer (ACE) spacecraft (ACE Project Team) [14]. Geomagnetic indexes were obtained from World Data Center for Geomagnetism [15], which provides official data for the values of geomagnetic indices, used worldwide for scientific research and practical applications. The relativistic electron flux data was obtained from GOES-8 spacecraft of the GOES project (NOAA National Centers for Environmental Information) [16]. Electron fluences have a wide dynamical range (more than 6 orders of magnitude), so instead of the real values of these variables, their logarithmic values were used.

These physical quantities were used to build adaptive models. The resulting models are not based on any equations describing physics of the object under study. They are the results of mathematical modeling of the properties of functional mappings with adaptive (depending on available data) selection of model parameters. After eliminating all the gaps in the data, the remaining array consisted of about 2,530 days.

3   Methods of Forecast

Various adaptive models were built to predict the values of daily maxima of the fluxes of RE with energies > 2 MeV. The adaptive models used to solve the problem were based on the following algorithms: a multidimensional auto-regression model (ARM) [17]; ensembles of decision trees (EDT) [18]) within the framework of the bagging approach [19] and the ANN architecture of a multilayer perceptron [20]. The best values of hyper-parameters of each method were determined by grid search.

Since the data studied is a time series (TS), the classic approach to predict its future values is to use delay embedding, i.e. to take into account the previous values of the time series. Naturally, this involves the question about how long should be the time interval in the past that should be used, i.e. the embedding depth. There are different methods to evaluate this value. One of the most simple but effective methods for determining the optimal embedding depth for each component of the multi-dimensional time series is the calculation of the autocorrelation function (ACF) between the points of the TS separated by a specified time interval, along the entire TS. In this study, we used as the cut-off threshold the maximum value of the delay at which the ACF decreases e fold. After applying this procedure, the following number of hours preceding the observation point was selected for various input variables: AE – 9, Vx – 54, IMF Bz – 5, Kp – 20, N_p – 14, Dst – 44, the flux of sub-relativistic electrons (> 0.6 MeV) – 40, RE flux (> 2 MeV) – 44 (Fig. 1). Thus, we obtained total 238 input features.

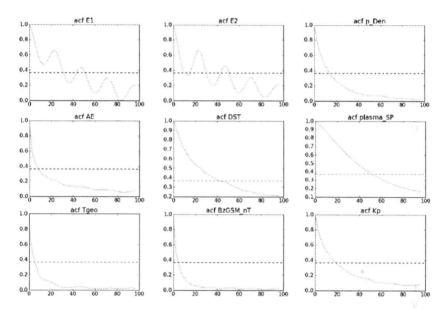

Fig. 1. Auto-correlation functions of various input variables: correlation *vs* time delay in hours.

The results obtained were compared with the results of [21], in which the forecast of the RE flux in the outer ERB was carried out with the help of ARM, with the difference that the authors of [21] included in the input data features the time series of Ultra Low Frequency (ULF) and Very Low Frequency (VLF) indices. According to [21], the use of these indices, especially ULF, should significantly improve the quality of forecasting, since they characterize «wave-particle» interaction, which largely determines the acceleration and scattering of electrons.

For completeness, we also obtained predictions by the models the input data of which were the average (and maximum, in the case of electrons) values for several previous days of all the above physical variables. All the models were formed based on data from 1996 till 2001. To compare the quality of the models, we used the value of the correlation coefficient between real values and values predicted by the model, on the test set. As the test set, i.e. the independent set not participating in the formation of the adaptive model, we used all the available observations for the years 2002–2003. The time range of the data used was determined by free data availability in the Internet and by maximum coincidence with that of [21] to compare the results.

4 Results

Table 1 compares the capabilities of the algorithms used; the data preparation procedure, delay embedding depth and horizons of predictions are fully consistent with those specified in the article [21]. From Table 1 it can be seen that in the case of building a forecast for 3 days ahead, EDT demonstrate greater accuracy than other algorithms, and even surpass the results obtained in [21], despite absence of ULF-index in our models in their first variants [22] (in agreement with [21], VLF is not very important for RE flux forecast). The explanation for this may be weak link between the data on such a long horizon of the forecast, as noted in [21]. EDT have a high degree of nonlinearity, which allows them to better describe the desired nonlinear dependence.

The main disadvantage of the EDT is "overtraining" - i.e., too good approximation of the training data set at the expense of their generalization and subsequent work on independent data, - is overcome in this case by using the bagging approach: repeated construction of similar models on various subsets of the existing set of data, with subsequent averaging of the answers [19].

Table 1. The correlation coefficient between the predicted and real data for 2002–2003, for models built on averaged daily data with delay embedding for one day.

Prediction horizon	Multi-dimensional auto-regressive model (ARM)	Artificial neural networks (ANN), MLP	Ensembles of decision trees within bagging approach (EDT)	Results of Simms et al. [21]
1 day	0.61	0.62	0.60	**0.76**
3 days	0.44	0.42	**0.51**	0.46

Table 2 presents the forecast results based on hourly average data with the choice of delay embedding depth based on autocorrelation functions, without ULF-index (because no real-time ULF-index data is available at present time).

Table 3 presents the forecast results based on hourly average data with the choice of delay embedding depth based on autocorrelation functions, using ULF-index obtained from [23]. Table 3 shows that application of EDT taking into account ULF data gives the best result of forecast.

Table 2. The correlation coefficient between the predicted and real data on the test set for 2002–2003 for models based on hourly average data with delay embedding selected on the basis of calculation of the decay of the autocorrelation function (without ULF-index).

Prediction horizon	Multi-dimensional auto-regressive model (ARM)	Artificial neural networks (ANN), MLP	Ensembles of decision trees within bagging approach (EDT)	Results of Simms et al. [21]
1 day	0.70	0.71	**0.76**	**0.76**
3 days	0.34	0.36	0.47	0.46

Table 3. The correlation coefficient between the predicted and real data on the test set for 2002–2003 for models based on hourly average data with delay embedding selected on the basis of calculation of the decay of the autocorrelation function (using ULF-index).

Prediction horizon	Multi-dimensional auto-regressive model (ARM)	Artificial neural networks ANN (MLP)	Ensembles of decision trees within bagging approach (EDT)	Results of Simms et al. [21]
1 day	0.80	0.82	**0.86**	0.76
3 days	0.46	0.48	**0.56**	0.46

The observed limitation on the correlation coefficient is due to unpredictable nature of the target time series, as the structure used was of optimal complexity (simpler models gave worse results, more complex ones overtrained).

In Fig. 2 as an example, prediction results for the logarithm of RE of outer ERB fluxes time series one day ahead by the EDT method (red curve) are compared with observational data (blue curve) from 08.25.2002 to 04.04.2003. From Fig. 2, it can be seen that the daily maximum of average hourly values predicted one day ahead in most cases of rise are in good agreement with observations.

Comparison of the values for the period 2002–2003, observed and predicted one day ahead, is presented in Fig. 3 as a scatter plot. We can see a good agreement.

Figure 4 shows prediction results for the logarithm of RE of outer ERB fluxes time series one day ahead by the EDT method (red curve) compared with observational data (blue curve) from 08.25.2002 to 04.04.2003. The forecast of the daily maximum of average hourly values 3 days ahead is worse than the forecast 1 day ahead presented in Fig. 2, but in most cases of rise it also adequately shows the real situation.

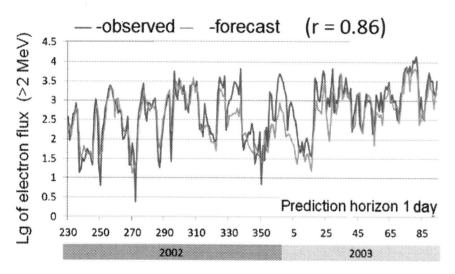

Fig. 2. Time series of daily maximum average values of hourly flux of relativistic electrons in the outer ERB: observed (blue) and predicted one day ahead by ensembles of decision trees within bagging approach (red). (Color figure online)

The same conclusion follows from the comparison of the scatter-plots in Fig. 3 (forecast 1 day ahead) and Fig. 5 (forecast 3 days ahead). The quality of the forecast one day ahead is much better, but the forecast three days ahead remains adequate.

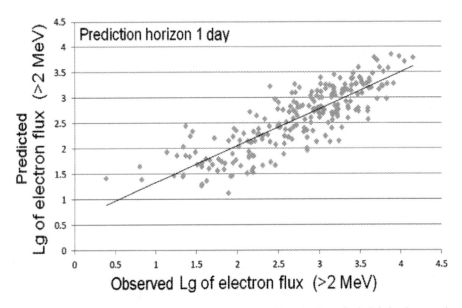

Fig. 3. Scatter plot of daily maximum average values of hourly flux of relativistic electrons in the outer ERB: observed and predicted one day ahead by ensembles of decision trees within bagging approach.

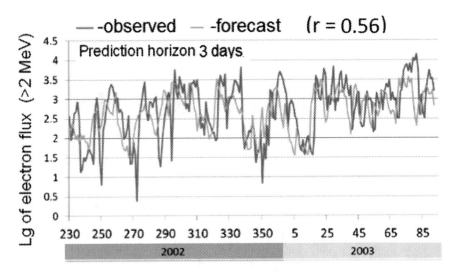

Fig. 4. Time series of daily maximum average values of hourly flux of relativistic electrons in the outer ERB: observed (blue) and predicted 3 days ahead by ensembles of decision trees within bagging approach (red). (Color figure online)

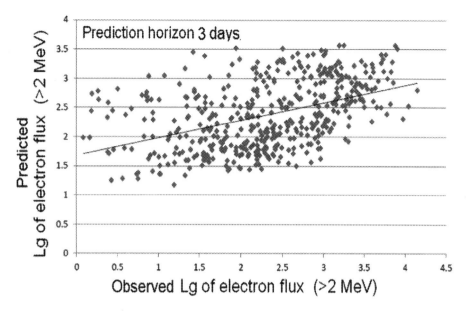

Fig. 5. Scatter plot of daily maximum average values of hourly flux of relativistic electrons in the outer ERB: observed and predicted 3 days ahead by ensembles of decision trees within bagging approach.

5   Conclusions

In the presented paper, we compared the quality of forecast of daily maximum of hourly average values of relativistic electrons flux in the outer ERB at geostationary orbit with a horizon of 1 and 3 days, based on hourly values of the input variables, using three machine learning methods: a multidimensional auto-regression model, ensembles of decision trees within the bagging approach, and artificial neural networks (multilayer perceptron).

The best quality of forecast one day ahead was demonstrated by decision tree ensembles. It is also shown that the use of delay embedding based on the calculation of the decay of the autocorrelation function significantly improves forecast quality at the forecast horizon of one day. We also compared the obtained results with the results of the prediction of daily maximum of hourly average flux values of relativistic electrons in the outer ERB at geostationary orbit with a horizon of 1 and 3 days from [21] for similar input and output data sets (daily values).

Using a more advanced nonlinear adaptive method (ensembles of decision trees within bagging approach, EDT) and hourly input values with selection of the optimal delay embedding, we have achieved the best prediction results without using the ULF wave indexes. Adding them to the number of input features significantly improved the quality of forecast.

Acknowledgements. This study has been conducted at the expense of Russian Science Foundation, grant no. 16-17-00098.

References

1. Kataoka, R., Miyoshi, Y.: Average profiles of the solar wind and outer radiation belt during the extreme flux enhancement of relativistic electrons at geosynchronous orbit. Ann. Geophys. **26**, 1335–1339 (2008). https://doi.org/10.1029/2010SW000571
2. Reeves, G.D., McAdams, K.L., Friedel, R.H.W., O'Brien, T.P.: Acceleration and loss of relativistic electrons during geomagnetic storms. Geophys. Res. Lett. **30**, 1529–1561 (2003). https://doi.org/10.1029/2002GL016513
3. Dorman, L., Iucci, N., Belov, A.: Space weather and space-crafts anomalies. Annales Geophys. **23**(9), 3009–3018 (2005). https://doi.org/10.5194/angeo-23-3009-2005
4. Friedel, R.H., Reeves, W.G.P., Obara, T.: Relativistic electron dynamics in the inner magnetosphere – a review. J. Atmos. Sol.-Terr. Phys. **64**(2), 265–283 (2002). https://doi.org/10.1016/S1364-6826(01)00088-8
5. Iucci, N., Levitin, A., Belov, A.: Space weather conditions and spacecraft anomalies in different orbits. Space Weather **3**(1), S01001 (2005). https://doi.org/10.1029/2003SW000056
6. Baker, D.N., McPherron, R.L., Cayton, T.E., Kebesadel, R.W.: Linear prediction filter analysis of relativistic electron properties at 6.6 RE. J. Geophys. Res. **95**(A9), 15133–15140 (1990)
7. Koons, H., Gorney, D.: A neural network model of the relativistic electron flux at geosynchronous orbit. J. Geophys. Res. **96**, 5549–5556 (1990). https://doi.org/10.1029/90JA02380
8. Fukata, M., Taguchi, S., Okuzawa, T., Obara, T.: Neural network prediction of relativistic electrons at geosynchronous orbit during the storm recovery phase: effects of recurring substorms. Ann. Geophys. **20**(7), 947–951 (2002). https://doi.org/10.5194/angeo-20-947-2002
9. Ling, A., Ginet, G., Hilmer, R., Perry, K.: A neural network-based geosynchronous relativistic electron flux forecasting model. Adv. Space Res. (Space Weather) **8**(9), S09003 (2010). https://doi.org/10.1029/2010SW000576
10. Myagkova, I., Dolenko, S., Shiroky, V., Sentemova, N., Persiantsev, I.: Horizon of neural network prediction of relativistic electrons flux in the outer radiation belt of the earth. In: ACM Proceedings, EANN 2015 Proceedings of the 16th International Conference on Engineering Applications of Neural Networks, article no. 9 (2015). https://doi.org/10.1145/2797143.2797169
11. Myagkova, I., Shiroky, V., Dolenko, S.: Effect of simultaneous time series prediction with various horizons on prediction quality at the example of electron flux in the outer radiation belt of the earth. In: Villa, Alessandro E.P., Masulli, P., Pons Rivero, A.J. (eds.) ICANN 2016. LNCS, vol. 9887, pp. 317–325. Springer, Cham (2016). https://doi.org/10.1007/978-3-319-44781-0_38
12. Myagkova, I.N., Dolenko, S.A., Efitorov, A.O., Shiroky, V.R., Sentemova, N.S.: Prediction of relativistic electron flux in the Earth's outer radiation belt at geostationary orbit by adaptive methods. Geomag. Aeron. **57**(1), 8–15 (2017). https://doi.org/10.1134/S0016793217010108
13. Efitorov, A., Myagkova, I., Sentemova, N., Shiroky, V., Dolenko, S.: Prediction of relativistic electrons flux in the outer radiation belt of the earth using adaptive methods. In: Samsonovich, A.V., Klimov, V.V., Rybina, G.V. (eds.) Biologically Inspired Cognitive Architectures (BICA) for Young Scientists. AISC, vol. 449, pp. 281–287. Springer, Cham (2016). https://doi.org/10.1007/978-3-319-32554-5_36

14. ACE Project Team. Advanced Composition Explorer (ACE) Home Page. http://www.srl. caltech.edu/ACE/

15. World Data Center for Geomagnetism. Geomagnetic Data Service in Kyoto. http://wdc.kugi. kyoto-u.ac.jp/wdc/Sec3.html

16. GOES Space Environment Monitor - Data Access. https://www.ngdc.noaa.gov/stp/satellite/ goes/dataaccess.html

17. Hyndman, R.J., Athanasopoulos, G.: Forecasting: principles and practice. Otexts (2012). https://www.otexts.org/book/fpp

18. Breiman, L.: Random forests. Mach. Learn. **45**(1), 5–32 (2001). https://doi.org/10.1023/A: 1010933404324

19. Breiman, L.: Bagging predictors. Mach. Learn. **24**(2), 123–140 (1996). https://doi.org/10. 1023/A:1018054314350

20. Haykin, S.O.: Neural Networks and Learning Machines, 3rd edn. Pearson, London (2008)

21. Simms, L.E., Engebretson, M.J., Pilipenko, V., Reeves, G.D., Clilverd, M.: Empirical predictive models of daily relativistic electron flux at geostationary orbit: multiple regression analysis. J. Geophys. Res. Space Phys, **121**, 3181–3197 (2016). https://doi.org/10.1002/ 2016JA022414

22. Efitorov, A.O., Myagkova, I.N., Dolenko, S.A.: Prediction of maximum daily relativistic electron flux at geostationary orbit by adaptive methods. In: Proceedings of 11th Intl School and Conference "Problems of Geocosmos", St. Petersburg, Russia, pp. 206–212, 03–07 October 2016. http://geo.phys.spbu.ru/materials_of_a_conference_2016/STP/27_Efitorov. pdf

23. Geophysical Center of Russian Academy of Sciences. ULF Data Access. http://ulf.gcras.ru/ index.html

24. Chen, Y., Reeves, G.D., Fu, X., Henderson, M.: PreMevE: new predictive model for megaelectron-volt electrons inside Earth's outer radiation belt. Space Weather **17**, 438–454 (2019). https://doi.org/10.1029/2018SW002095

Clustering

Soft Subspace Growing Neural Gas for Data Stream Clustering

Mohammed Oualid Attaoui[1,2](✉) [iD], Mustapha Lebbah[1], Nabil Keskes[2],
Hanene Azzag[1], and Mohammed Ghesmoune[1]

[1] University of Paris 13, Sorbonne Paris City LIPN-UMR 7030 - CNRS,
99, av. J-B Clément, 93430 Villetaneuse, France
`attaoui@lipn.univ-paris13.fr`
[2] LabRI Laboratory, Higher School of Computer Science (ESI-SBA),
Sidi Bel-Abbes, Algeria

Abstract. Subspace clustering aims at discovering the clusters embedded in multiple, overlapping subspaces of high dimensional data. It has been successfully applied in many domains such as financial transactions, telephone records, sensor network monitoring, website analysis, weather monitoring, etc. Data stream are ordered and potentially unbounded sequences of data points created by a typically non-stationary data generating process. Clustering this type of data requires both time and memory restrictions. In this paper, we propose S2G-Stream based on growing neural gas and soft subspace clustering. We introduce two types of entropy weighting for both features and subspaces. Experiments on public datasets showed the ability of S2G-Stream to: (1) detect relevant features and subspaces; (2) detect clusters of arbitrary shape; (3) enhance the clustering results.

Keywords: Soft subspace clustering · Growing Neural Gas ·
Data stream · Entropy weighting system

1 Introduction

As opposed to traditional data forms which are unchanging and static, a data stream has its own characteristics: (1) it consists of a flow of infinite data. (2) it is rapidly evolving data that occurs in real time with quick response requirements. (3) only one (or few) pass is possible through the data. (4) storage of the data stream is restricted, thus only a synopsis of the data can be saved. Data stream clustering is a technique that performs cluster analysis on data stream and is able to produce results in real time. The ability to process data through a single pass and summarize it, while using limited memory, is crucial to stream clustering. Subspace clustering is an extension of feature selection which tries to identify clusters in different subspaces of the same dataset. As feature selection, subspace clustering needs both a search method and an evaluation criterion. In addition, subspace clustering must somehow restrict the scope of the evaluation criterion so as to consider different subspaces for each different cluster.

© Springer Nature Switzerland AG 2019
I. V. Tetko et al. (Eds.): ICANN 2019, LNCS 11730, pp. 569–580, 2019.
https://doi.org/10.1007/978-3-030-30490-4_46

In the previous work [1], authors consider all features equally important to the clustering task. Our main contribution in this paper is to introduce a double weight system for features and subspaces in order to make relevant features and subspaces contribute more to the clustering. The rest of the paper is organized as follows: In Sect. 2, we present related literature. In Sect. 3, we explain our algorithm called Soft Subspace Neural Gas for Data Stream Clustering (S2G-Stream) and evaluate its performance in Sect. 4. Finally, we conclude this paper in Sect. 5.

2   Related Works

2.1   Data Stream

Several algorithms and methods have been proposed to deal with clustering data stream constraints. A large number of algorithms relies on two phases. An online phase processes data stream points and produces summary statistics. Then an offline component phase uses the summary data to generate the clusters [2–4]. Alternative solutions also propose to generate final clusters without using an offline phase [5,6]. Table 1 lists the differences between some methods of clustering data stream.

Table 1. Comparison between stream data clustering algorithms

Algorithm	Method	Scalability	HDD[a]	Data Type	ABS[b]
HDDStream	Density	✓	✓	Numerical	✓
SDStream	Density	✓	✗	Numerical	✓
Stream Optics	Density	✓	✗	Numerical	✗
DENGRIS-Stream	Density	✓	✗	Numerical	✓
DCU-Stream	Density	✓	✗	Numerical	✓
ExCC	Density	✓	✓	Mixed	✓
BIRCH	Hierarchical	✓	✗	Numerical	✓
ODAC	Hierarchical	✓	✓	Time Series	✓
E-Stream	Hierarchical	✓	✓	Numerical	✓
HUE-Stream	Hierarchical	✓	✓	Mixed	✓
CluStream	Partitionning	✓	✗	Numerical	✗
HP-Stream	Partitionning	✓	✗	Numerical	✗
SWClustering	Partitionning	N/A	N/A	Numerical	✗
Stream KM++	Partitionning	N/A	✓	Numerical	✗
GCHDS	Grid	N/A	✓	N/A	N/A
DGClust	Grid	✓	✓	N/A	N/A
IDEStream	Ensemble	✓	✓	Time series	✓

[a] High Dimensional Data
[b] Arbitrary Shaped clusters
* N/A: not available

2.2 Subspace Clustering

Based on the way cluster subspaces are determined, subspace clustering can be classified into two main categories: Hard Subspace Clustering (HSC) and Soft Subspace Clustering (SSC). SSC algorithms perform clustering in high dimensional spaces by assigning a weight to each dimension to measure the contribution of individual dimensions to the formation of a particular cluster [7]. SSC methods can be classified into three categories. CSSC (Conventional Subspace Clustering) uses a feature weighting process in a two steps clustering process. First, it uses some weighting strategies to find subspaces. Then, clustering is performed on the subspace that was obtained. This is referred to as separated feature weighting. Clustering can also be obtained by performing the two processes simultaneously, this is known as coupled feature weighting. ISSC(Independent Subspace Clustering) associates with each cluster its own weight vector so that every cluster forms its own subspace. XSSC(Extended Subspace Clustering) has been proposed to enhance the performance of both CSSC and ISSC.

In HSC a feature in a subspace equally contributes to the clustering process. HSC algorithms can be divided into bottom-up and top-down subspace search methods [8]. Top-down algorithms find an initial clustering in the full set of dimensions and evaluate the subspaces of each cluster. Bottom-Up approaches define an histogram to each dimension, a range with a density higher than a fixed threshold represent a cluster. Table 2 presents a comparison between some subspace clustering methods.

Table 2. Comparison between subspace clustering algorithms

Method	Category	Search method	Weighting method	Overlap of dimensions	Data type
CLIQUE	Hard	Bottom-Up	–	Yes	Mixed
MAFIA	Hard	Bottom-Up	–	Yes	Numerical
PROCLUS	Hard	Top-Down	Cluster weighting	Non	Numerical
FINDIT	Hard	Top-Down	Cluster weighting	Non	Numerical
C-k-means	Soft	CSSC	Separated feature weighting	Yes	Mixed
W-k-means	Soft	CSSC	Coupled feature weighting	N/A	Mixed
FWKM	Soft	ISSC	Fuzzy weighting	Yes	Mixed
AWFCM	Soft	ISSC	Fuzzy weighting	N/A	Numerical
IEWKM	Soft	XSSC	Entropy weighting	N/A	Mixed
SSC	Soft	XSSC	CFW[a]	Non	Numerical
Ensemble learning	Soft	XSSC	–	Non	Numerical
Imbalanced Cluster	Soft	XSSC	–	N/A	Mixed

[a] Coevolutionary Feature Weighting

* N/A: not available

3   Model Proposition

In this section we introduce soft subspace clustering (S2G-Stream) based on the Growing Neural Gas (GNG) model. Which is an incremental self-organizing approach that belongs to the family of topological maps such as Self-Organizing Maps (SOM) [9]. We assume that the data stream consists in a sequence $\mathcal{X} = \{\mathbf{x}_1, \mathbf{x}_2, ..., \mathbf{x}_n\}$ of n (potentially infinite) elements arriving at times $t_1, t_2, ..., t_n$, where $\mathbf{x}_i = (x_i^1, x_i^2, ..., x_i^d)$. At each time, S2G-Stream is represented by a graph $\mathcal{C}$, where each node represents a cluster. Each node $c \in \mathcal{C}$ is associated with: (1) a prototype $\mathbf{w}_c = (w_c^1, w_c^2, ..., w_c^d)$ representing its position (2) a weight π_c (3) an error variable $error(c)$ representing the distance between this node and the assigned data points. For each pair of nodes (r, c), we denote the shortest path between r and c on the graph by $\delta(c, r)$. Finally we denote by $\mathcal{K}^T(\delta) = \mathcal{K}(\delta/T)$ the neighborhood function, T controls the width of $\mathcal{K}$.

In our previous work [1], we consider all features equally important to the clustering task. However, in most applications some variables may be irrelevant and, among the relevant ones, some may be more or less relevant than others. Therefore, and based on [10,11], we introduce a double weight system for both features, denoted by β, and subspaces, denoted by α, in order to make relevant features and subspaces contribute more to the clustering. Figure 1 illustrates the representation of the weights and prototypes. The features $\mathcal{F}$ are divided into P subspaces $\mathcal{F} = \cup_{b=1}^{P} \mathcal{F}_b$ where $\mathcal{F}_b = \{x^j, j = 1, ..., d_b\}$ is the feature set where $d_1 + ... + d_b + ... + d_P = d$. Thus, α can be represented as a $K \times P$ matrix where α_c^b is the weight of the subspace b in the node c. β is a $K \times d$ matrix where β_b is a $K \times d_b$ matrix, where $\beta_{cb}^j(j = 1, ..., d_b)$ is the weight of the jth feature in the subspace b for the node c with $\sum_{j=1}^{d_b} \beta_{cb}^j = 1$ and $\sum_{b=1}^{P} \alpha_c^b = 1, \forall c \in \mathcal{C}$. Cluster subspaces can be retrieved from both weight matrices.

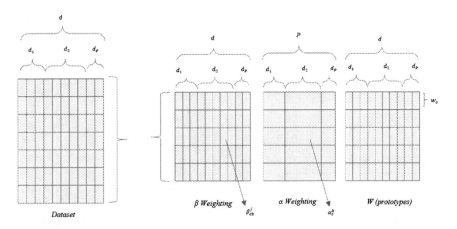

Fig. 1. Representation of α and β. α_c^b is the weight of the subspace b in the node c and $\beta_{cb}^j(j = 1, ..., d_b)$ is the weight of the jth feature in the subspace b for the node c. w_c is the prototype of node c.

Based on [1], we propose to minimize the new cost function defined below for data batch $\mathcal{X}^{(t+1)} = \{\mathbf{X}_1, \mathbf{X}_2, ..., \mathbf{X}_{t+1}\}$:

$$J^{(t+1)}(\phi, \mathcal{W}, \alpha, \beta) = \sum_{c \in C} \sum_{b=1}^{P} \sum_{\mathbf{x}_i \in \mathcal{X}^{(t+1)}} \mathcal{K}^T \left(\delta(c, \phi(\mathbf{x}_i)) \right) \alpha_c^b \mathcal{D}_{\beta_{cb}} + J_{cb} + I_c \quad (1)$$

where $\mathcal{D}_{\beta_{cb}} = \sum_{j=1}^{d_b} \beta_{cb}^j (x_i^j - \omega_c^j)^2$. $I_c = \lambda \sum_{b=1}^{P} \alpha_c^b \log(\alpha_c^b)$ and $J_{cb} = \eta \sum_{j=1}^{d_b} \beta_{cb}^j \log(\beta_{cb}^j)$ represent respectively the weighted negative entropies associated with the subspaces weight vectors and the features weight vectors. The parameters λ and η are used to adjust the relative contributions made by the features and subspaces to the clustering.

3.1 Optimization Algorithm

The optimization of the cost function is performed alternately for each batch $\mathcal{X}^{(t+1)}$ through four steps corresponding to the four parameters $\mathcal{W}, \phi, \alpha$ and β:

1. **Assignment function:** For a fixed $\mathcal{W}, \alpha$ and β, the assignment function $\phi(\mathbf{x}_i)$ is described in Eq. (2). In order to reduce the computational time, neighborhood nodes are not considered in the assignment.

$$\phi(\mathbf{x}_i) = \arg \min_{c \in \mathcal{C}} \left(\sum_{b=1}^{P} \alpha_c^b \sum_{j=1}^{d_b} \beta_{cb}^j \left(x_i^j - \omega_c^j \right)^2 \right) \quad (2)$$

2. **Update prototypes $\mathcal{W}$:** For a fixed ϕ, α and β, $\mathbf{w}_c$ prototypes are updated for every batch of data following the equation defined below.

$$\mathbf{w}_c^{(t+1)} = \frac{\mathbf{w}_c^{(t)} n_c^{(t)} \gamma + \sum_{r \in C} \mathcal{K}^T (\delta(r, c)) \mathbf{w}_r^{(t)} m_r^{(t)}}{n_c^{(t)} \gamma + \sum_{r \in C} \mathcal{K}^T (\delta(r, c)) m_r^{(t)}} \quad (3)$$

where $\mathbf{w}_c^{(t)}$ is the previous prototype, $n_c^{(t)}$ is the number of points assigned to the cluster, $\mathbf{w}_r^{(t)}$ is the previous prototype for the cluster r (which is a neighbor of c) and $m_r^{(t)}$ is the number of points added to the cluster r in the current batch: $n_c^{(t+1)} = n_c^{(t)} + m_c^{(t)}$.

3. **Update weights α:** for a fixed $\phi, \mathcal{W}$ and β, we minimize the objective function 1 with respect to α_c^b the weight of the subspace b in c-th cluster. Since there exist a constraint $\sum_{b=1}^{P} \alpha_c^b = 1$, we form the Lagrangian by isolating the terms which contain α then adding Lagrangian multipliers μ as follows:

$$\mathcal{L}(\alpha, \lambda) = J^{(t+1)}(\phi, \mathcal{W}, \alpha, \beta) - \sum_{b \in P} \mu_c \left(\sum_{b=1}^{P} \alpha_{cb} - 1 \right) \quad (4)$$

Taking the derivative with respect to α_c^b and setting it to zero yields a minimum of α_c^b at:

$$\alpha_c^b = \frac{e^{\frac{-D_{cb}}{\lambda}}}{\sum_{s=1}^{P} e^{\frac{-D_{cs}}{\lambda}}} \tag{5}$$

with $D_{cb} = \sum_{\mathbf{x}_i \in \mathcal{X}^{(t)}} \mathcal{K}^T(\delta(\phi(\mathbf{x}_i), c)) \sum_{j=1}^{d_b} \beta_{cb}^j \left(\mathbf{x}_i^j - w_c^j\right)^2$

4. **Update weights** β: for a fixed ϕ, $\mathcal{W}$ and β, we minimize the objective function 1 with respect to β_{cb}^j the weight of the feature j of subspace b in c-th cluster. Since there exist a constraint $\sum_{j=1}^{d_b} \beta_{cb}^j = 1$, we form the Lagrangian by isolating the terms which contain β then adding Lagrangian multipliers μ as follows:

$$\mathcal{L}(\alpha, \lambda) = \jmath^{(t+1)}(\phi, \mathcal{W}, \alpha, \beta) - \sum_{c \in C} \mu_{cb} \left(\sum_{j=1}^{d_b} \beta_{cb}^j - 1\right) \tag{6}$$

Taking the derivative with respect to β_{cb}^j and setting it to zero yields a minimum of β_{cb}^j at:

$$\beta_{cb}^j = \frac{e^{\frac{-E_{cb}^j}{\eta}}}{\sum_{h \in \mathcal{F}_{P_j}} e^{\frac{-E_{ch}}{\eta}}} \tag{7}$$

with $E_{cb}^j = \sum_{\mathbf{x}_i \in \mathcal{X}^{(t)}} \alpha_c^{P_j} \mathcal{K}^T(\delta(\phi(\mathbf{x}_i), c)) \left(\mathbf{x}_i^j - w_c^j\right)^2$, where P_j is the subspace the jth feature belongs to.

3.2   S2G-Stream Algorithm

S2G-Stream aims at extending the G-Stream algorithm [12] to subspace clustering by introducing subspace and feature entropy weighting. Starting with two nodes, and whenever a new data point is available, we link the nearest and the second-nearest nodes by an edge. The nearest node and its topological neighbors are moved towards the data point. We present the main functions for the S2G-Stream algorithm below.

Fading Function. Most data stream algorithms consider most recent data as more important and reflect better the changes in the data distribution. For that, the notion of time windows is used. There are three window models commonly studied: landmark, sliding and damped [13]. We consider in this paper the damped window model, in which the weight of each node decreases exponentially with time via a *fading* function by introducing a decay factor parameter $0 < \gamma < 1$.

$$\pi_c^{(t+1)} = \pi_c^{(t)} \gamma \tag{8}$$

If the weight of a node is below a threshold value, this node is considered outdated and removed (along with its links).

Edge Management. An edge linking two nodes can be either strengthened or removed. Its age grows with the exponential function $2^{\tau_{age}^{(t-t_0)}}$, where $\tau_{age} > 0$ defines age growth rate over time, t denotes the current time and t_0 is the edge creation time. A new edge can be added to connect two nodes and can be removed if it exceeds a maximum age.

Algorithm 1: Edge Management

    -Increment the age of all edges emanating from bmu and weight them;
    -Remove the edges whose age is greater than age_{max};
    -Remove nodes with emanating edges;

Node Insertion. Nodes can be inserted into the graph between the two nodes having the highest error value. If the weight of a node is lower than a threshold value then this node is considered as outdated and removed (along with its links).

Algorithm 2: Node Insertion

    -Find the node q with the largest error and its neighbor f with the largest accumulated error;
    -Add the new node r between nodes q and f: $\mathbf{w}_r = 0.5(\mathbf{w}_q + \mathbf{w}_f)$;
    -Decrease the error variables of q and f by multiplying them by a constant v where $0 < v < 1$ and assign to r the error value of q ;
    -Decrease the error of all nodes by multiplying them by a constant s, and remove isolated nodes ;

The complete description of the S2G-Stream algorithm can be found in Algorithm 3.

Algorithm 3: S2G-Stream

input : $\mathcal{X} = \{\mathbf{x}_1, \mathbf{x}_2, ..., \mathbf{x}_n\}, \pi_{min}, \tau_{age}, age_{max}, d, \eta, \lambda, \mu, \gamma, b$
output: prototypes :$W = w_1, w_2, .., w_n$ feature weights matrix β and subspace
        weights matrix α
Initialize the graph with two nodes, initialize α and β weights randomly;
while *there is a micro-batch to proceed* **do**
    -Get the micro-batch of data points arrived at time interval t ;
    1. **Assignment Step**
        -Find the nearest and the second nearest node bmu_1 and bmu_2 following (2) and create an edge between them. If it already exists: set the age to zero;
        -Assign each point to the closest center following (2);
    2. **Update Step**
        -Update the new centroid as described in (3) ;
    3. **Edge Management following Algorithm 1**
        -Update the *error* of each node: $error(bmu_1) = error(bmu_1) + ||x_i - bmu_1||^2$;
    4. *Fading Function*: apply fading following (8) and delete isolated nodes
    5. **Add Nodes following Algorithm 2**
    6. **Update weights**
        -Update feature weights following (5) and subspace weights following (7);

---

4   Experimental Results

4.1   Clustering Evaluation

The S2G-Stream method described in this article was implemented in Spark/Scala and will be available on Clustering4Ever github repository[1]. We evaluated clustering quality of S2G-Stream on real datasets from the UCI repository [14] described in Table 4. For the quality measures, we used Normalized Mutual Information (NMI) and Adjusted Rand index (ARAND).

Assuming large high-dimensional data arrives as a continually, S2G-Stream divides the streaming data into batches and processes each batch continuously. The batch size depends on the available memory and the size of the original dataset. We set the time interval between two batches to 1 s. We repeated our experiments with different initialization and have chosen those giving the best results. We set $\mu = 3$, $\gamma = 0.99$ and $age_{max} = 250$. λ and η and the batch size for each dataset are described in Table 3. The weights α and β are initialized randomly under the two constraints $\sum_{j=1}^{d_b} \beta_{cb}^j = 1$ and $\sum_{b=1}^{P} \alpha_c^b = 1$, $\forall c \in \mathcal{C}$.

Table 3. Initialization of λ, η and batch size parameters for each dataset

Datasets	λ	η	$|Batch|$
Waveform	5	15	100
IS	3	31	100
CDT	7	11	100
Pendigits	3	17	1000

To show the effectiveness of our method, we compare it to four algorithms: Growing Neural Gas (GNG) from the Scala Smile repository[2], *CluStream* and *DStream* from R package streamMOA[3]. The results are reported in Table 4. It is noticeable that S2G-Stream gives better results than the other methods except for DStream on *CTG* and *waveform* with NMI metric, and on *CTG* with ARAND metric. These results are due to the fact that S2G-Stream detects relevant features and subspaces, and allow those subspaces to contribute more to clustering. This is also due to the notion of fading which reduces the impact of non-significant data.

Figure 2 shows an example of evolution of the graph S2G-Stream on *waveform* dataset (using Sammon's nonlinear mapping), as the data flows (colored points represent labelled data points and black points represent nodes of the graph with edges in black lines). We can clearly see that S2G-Stream, beginning with two randomly chosen nodes (Fig. 2(a)), is able to recognize gradually the structure

---

[1]   https://github.com/Clustering4Ever/Clustering4Ever.
[2]   http://haifengl.github.io/smile/.
[3]   https://github.com/mhahsler/streamMOA.

Table 4. Comparing S2G-stream with different algorithms. The value after ± correspond to standard deviation.

Dataset	Metrics	S2G-Stream	GNG	CluStream	DStream
Waveform 20 features 2 subspaces (10, 10) 5000 observations	NMI	0.397 ± 0.002	0.306 ± 0.078	0.393 ± 0.065	**0.434 ± 0.003**
	ARAND	**0.137 ± 0.007**	0.006 ± 0.103	0.010 ± 0.001	0.040 ± 0.001
IS 19 features 2 subspaces (9, 10) 2310 observations	NMI	**0.550 ± 0.05**	0.542 ± 0.010	0.506 ± 0.065	0.435 ± 0.07
	ARAND	**0.418 ± 0.04**	0.102 ± 0.051	0.098 ± 0.010	0.134 ± 0.002
CTG 21 features 3 subspaces (7, 4, 10) 2126 observations	NMI	0.270 ± 0.009	0.375 ± 0.004	0.086 ± 0.06	**0.471 ± 0.170**
	ARAND	0.124 ± 0.005	0.030 ± 0.011	0.019 ± 0.008	**0.209 ± 0.002**
Pendigits 17 features 2 subspaces (10, 7) 10992 observations	NMI	**0.672 ± 0,038**	0.585 ± 0.019	0.285 ± 0.099	0.554 ± 0.15
	ARAND	**0.408 ± 0.060**	0.027 ± 0.085	0.011 ± 0.006	0.016 ± 0.011

of the data stream (Fig. 2(b, c)). At the end of the training we can observe that the topology recover all the data structure (Fig. 2(d)). It is noticeable that our method manages to recognize the structures of the data stream and can separate these structures with the best visualization. It can also detect clusters of arbitrary shapes.

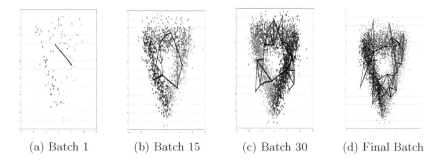

(a) Batch 1   (b) Batch 15   (c) Batch 30   (d) Final Batch

Fig. 2. Evolution of graph creation of S2G-Stream on waveform dataset (colored points represent labelled data points and black points represents nodes of the graph with edges in black lines) (Color figure online)

4.2   Subspace and Feature Weighting Analysis

For this section, we focus on CTG dataset due to space limitation. CTG dataset describes fetal cardiotocograms and is composed of 3 subspaces, subspace 1 contains 7 variables related to the heart rate of a fetus. Subspace 2 contains four variables describing heart rate variability. Subspace 3 is composed of 10 variables defining histograms of fetal cardiography.

Figure 3 represents prototypes $\mathcal{W}$, β weights and α weights for the final batch of CTG dataset. We observe in Fig. 3(b) that weights of features (8, 9, 10, 11) which are respectively ASTV(percentage of time with abnormal short term variability), MSTV(mean value of short term variability), ALTV(percentage of time with abnormal long term variability) and MLTV(mean value of long term variability) are higher than the weights of the other features for most clusters. We observe that this 4 features influence better the clustering process and are more important than the other features for most clusters. In Fig. 3(c) we observe that the α weight of the second subspace that contains this four features is also higher than the weights of the other two subspaces. We conclude from this experiment that heart rate variability influences better the fetal cardiotocograms clustering.

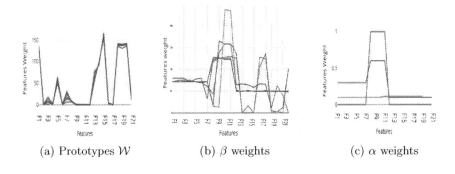

(a) Prototypes $\mathcal{W}$ (b) β weights   (c) α weights

Fig. 3. Results of weights α and β, and prototypes $\mathcal{W}$ for the final batch for CTG dataset. Each color represent a node. (Color figure online)

Based on the previous experiments, we performed S2G-Stream on only the reduced dataset i.e. only the relevant subspaces from the dataset based on the average of subspace weights α. We present the NMI and ARAND results compared with the results on the whole dataset in Fig. 4. For CTG dataset, both NMI and ARAND results on the reduced dataset are better than the results using all features and subspaces. The subspace 1 with subspace 2 provide a lower ARAND value. We conclude that subspace 1 gives better results compared to other subspaces, which confirms previous results. $Waveform$ dataset contains two subspaces of 20 features each, the second subspace being composed of only noisy features. NMI and ARAND measured on the reduced dataset (subspace 1) are higher than the whole dataset since the noisy features on the whole dataset affect the results. The same results are observed on the IS dataset. For $pendigits$ dataset the results of NMI and ARAND on the reduced dataset are lower, since both subspaces contain features that are required for the pen-based recognition.

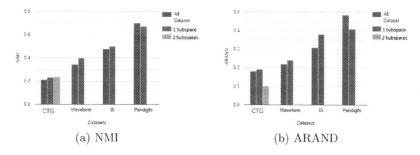

| (a) NMI | (b) ARAND |

Fig. 4. NMI and ARAND for all real datasets comparing to results on reduced datasets.

5   Conclusion

In this paper, we have proposed S2G-Stream, an efficient method for subspace clustering of an evolving data stream in an online manner. Unlike the previous works that consider all subspaces equally important to the clustering task, our method introduces a double weighting system for both features and subspaces. Thus, the proposed algorithm is able to select the most important features for the clustering task. We also introduced the notion of fading to delete outdated nodes. Experimental evaluation and comparison with well-known clustering methods demonstrates the effectiveness and efficiency of S2G-Stream in clustering results, discovering clusters of arbitrary shape and also detecting relevant features and subspaces. Future works include several experiments by varying the data ordering and also generalize our method to deal with different types of data. We plan also to visualise our results based on the topology of GNG.

References

1. Ghesmoune, M., Lebbah, M., Azzag, H.: Micro-batching growing neural gas for clustering data streams using spark streaming. Procedia Comput. Sci. **53**, 158–166 (2015)
2. Ntoutsi, I., Zimek, A., Palpanas, T., Kröger, P., Kriegel, H.P.: Density-based projected clustering over high dimensional data streams. In: Proceedings of the 2012 SIAM International Conference on Data Mining, SIAM, pp. 987–998 (2012)
3. Ren, J., Ma, R.: Density-based data streams clustering over sliding windows. In: Sixth International Conference on Fuzzy Systems and Knowledge Discovery, FSKD 2009, vol. 5, pp. 248–252. IEEE (2009)
4. Shukla, M., Kosta, Y.P., Jayswal, M.: A modified approach of optics algorithm for data streams. Eng. Technol. Appl. Sci. Res. **7**(2), 1478–1481 (2017)
5. Lu, Y., Sun, Y., Xu, G., Liu, G.: A grid-based clustering algorithm for high-dimensional data streams. In: Li, X., Wang, S., Dong, Z.Y. (eds.) ADMA 2005. LNCS (LNAI), vol. 3584, pp. 824–831. Springer, Heidelberg (2005). https://doi.org/10.1007/11527503_97
6. Khan, I., Huang, J.Z., Ivanov, K.: Incremental density-based ensemble clustering over evolving data streams. Neurocomputing **191**, 34–43 (2016)

7. Deng, Z., Choi, K.-S., Jiang, Y., Wang, J., Wang, S.: A survey on soft subspace clustering. Inf. Sci. **348**, 84–106 (2016)
8. Friedman, J.H., Meulman, J.J.: Clustering objects on subsets of attributes (with discussion). J. R. Stat. Soc.: Ser. B (Stat. Methodol.) **66**(4), 815–849 (2004)
9. Kohonen, T.: The self-organizing map. Neurocomputing **21**(1–3), 1–6 (1998)
10. Ouattara, M., Keita, N.N., Badran, F., Mandin, C.: Soft subpace clustering pour données multiblocs basée sur les cartes topologiques auto-organisées som: 2s-som. In: SFDS 2013 (2013)
11. Chen, X., Ye, Y., Xu, X., Huang, J.Z.: A feature group weighting method for subspace clustering of high-dimensional data. Pattern Recogn. **45**(1), 434–446 (2012)
12. Ghesmoune, M., Lebbah, M., Azzag, H.: A new growing neural gas for clustering data streams. Neural Netw. **78**, 36–50 (2016)
13. Zhu, Y., Shasha, D.: Statstream: statistical monitoring of thousands of data streams in real time. In VLDB 2002: Proceedings of the 28th International Conference on Very Large Databases, pp. 358–369. Elsevier (2002). Work supported in part by US NSF grants IIS-9988345 and N2010: 0115586
14. Frank, A., Asuncion, A.: UCI machine learning repository. School of Information and Computer Science, University of California, Irvine, CA, p. 213 (2010). http://archive.ics.uci.edu/ml

Region Prediction from Hungarian Folk Music Using Convolutional Neural Networks

Anna Kiss$^{(\boxtimes)}$ ⓘ, Csaba Sulyok ⓘ, and Zalán Bodó ⓘ

Faculty of Mathematics and Computer Science, Babeş–Bolyai University,
street M. Kogălniceanu nr. 1, 400084 Cluj-Napoca, Romania
annacs94@gmail.com, {sulyok.csaba,zbodo}@cs.ubbluj.ro

Abstract. Early 20th century research on folk music and its connection to regional cultures has revealed potential clues for understanding the dynamics and organization of communities over history. Therefore, significant effort has been allocated to collecting and organizing folk music into databases both in written and recorded form. Recent years have provided great advances in the fields of data analysis and machine learning, prompting musicologists to apply these advanced statistical methods to analyze the musical remnants.

The present work studies how supervised machine learning methods can be applied to analyze folk music: we train different convolutional neural network classifiers—time-content, frequency-content, black-box, convolutional recurrent neural network and time-frequency architectures—to predict folkloric regions. Results suggest that Transylvanian folkloric regions are distinguishable by the rhythmic content of their music, and while nearby villages have a higher probability of having their predicted labels swapped, the two most often confused regions are geographically remote areas having historically motivated similarity.

Keywords: Convolutional neural networks ·
Recurrent neural networks · Music classification ·
Music information retrieval · Folk music

1 Introduction

Béla Bartók, one of the pioneers of folk music research in Hungary, states that folk music research should have two main objectives: (1) to create a large, well-organized collection of folk music, and (2) to study the collected data, compare music of neighboring regions, determine musical styles and reveal their origin [1]. He furthermore underlines that this could help to understand how ordinary people lived and interacted over the course of history, what influenced them, how they experienced big historical events. The mentality of a community can be described by the types of melodies they sang in their respective era: older

© Springer Nature Switzerland AG 2019
I. V. Tetko et al. (Eds.): ICANN 2019, LNCS 11730, pp. 581–594, 2019.
https://doi.org/10.1007/978-3-030-30490-4_47

melodies may refer to a conservative community, whereas new melodies point to a progressive one.

Bartók [1] found that Hungarian-speaking areas in the Carpathian basin can be divided into four main regions based on their musical dialect: Transdanubium, Upper Hungary, the region of the Great Hungarian Plain and Transylvania. In our work, we focus on Transylvania, having a unique folklore, attributed mainly to its history: a lot of nations traversed this land on their way from East to West or in the opposite direction, bringing their habits, religion, language and rituals [16]. Due to its geographical, ethnic and religious diversity and its enclosed nature, rich archaic layers of folklore have been preserved here. The Transylvanian region has always been popular among folk music researchers, but as Pávai [20] states, a larger effort would be necessary to collect, describe and analyze the folkloric values before these fade away.

In this study we present how data analysis and machine learning could help examine folk music. More precisely, we aim to train convolutional neural network (CNN) classifiers to learn folkloric regions from the musical data presented to them. The dataset used in the experiments contains recordings collected mainly by Zoltán Kallós[1] in Transylvania, published and maintained by the Hungarian Academy of Sciences.

The motivation behind building machine learning models to classify folk music is on the one hand to aid folklore researchers in categorizing unlabeled recordings, and on the other hand to examine the performance of the models and see whether they underline aspects of musical data that were unknown beforehand.

The remainder of the paper is organized as follows: Sect. 2 gives an overview of the related music information retrieval (MIR) literature, Sect. 3 presents the dataset, its characteristics and distribution, Sect. 4 enumerates the preprocessing steps applied to the data, Sect. 5 describes the different convolutional neural network models used in the experiments. In Sect. 6, the experiments and the obtained results are presented, while Sect. 7 discusses the results and draws the appropriate conclusions.

2   Related Work

Music information retrieval is a field concerned with audio structure analysis, music recommendation through genre/author/mood recognition, as well as legitimacy checking. Many of its use cases involve detailed spectral analysis of audio signals [17].

Extracting spectral features from sound is most often performed using standard digital signal processing methods. These are mostly modified versions of the Discrete Fourier Transform (DFT) [22], a basis shift procedure measuring audio signal energy at different frequencies. To mitigate the loss of all temporal

---

[1] Zoltán Kallós (1926–2018) was a renowned Transylvanian ethnographer and folk music collector. He registered more than 15 000 melodies and released 26 casettes/CDs.

information, the Short Time Fourier Transform (STFT) takes DFTs of short, neighboring, partially overlapping segments. The output may be used as is, or mapped to a different frequency scale, such as the non-linear, perceptually motivated Mel scale [30]—a distribution of pitches judged by listeners to be equally spaced. The latter produces the mel-frequency cepstrum (MFC) described by mel-frequency cepstral coefficients (MFCCs) [19].

Cornelis et al. [5] note that MIR research based on ethnic music focuses mainly on describing and analyzing the pitch content and temporal structuring. In [14] the contour of Hungarian folk music from the Gyimes region is analyzed by building a mathematical model that relates multidimensional points to melodies. The author formulates a scalar measure for musical distance, based on which similar melodies could be queried and clusters could be analyzed. In another study, Juhász [15] introduces a memory-based maximum entropy model to find frequent and characteristic motifs of 2–6 notes.

At the time of writing no study was found by the authors aiming to determine the folkloric region for ethnic music; however we consider that the concept of a folkloric region bares resemblance to the concept of musical genres. The Cambridge Dictionary defines genre as "a style, especially in the arts, that involves a particular set of characteristics" [23]. In folk music each region has its unique and distinctive melodies, rhythm patterns and instruments, and familiar listeners can identify the regions easily after listening to the song for a few seconds. Thus, we focus on analyzing the MIR literature related to genre recognition.

Most of the articles in the field cite the work of Tzanetakis and Cook [31] as the one that introduced the problem of musical genre recognition as a pattern classification task. For automatic classification of audio signals, they propose three sets of features for representing timbral texture, rhythmic content and pitch content. After calculating the features on small windows, these are averaged, weighted and feature vectors are built by concatenation, thus forming the input for standard classifiers. Further works in the 2000s follow this approach to manually build features. However, as pointed out in [18], it is typically difficult to handcraft musical pattern knowledge into feature extractors: it is hard to determine which feature will be relevant for a given MIR task [11].

Many recent studies apply neural networks to automatically extract relevant features using the following feature extraction and learning pipeline: first, a mid-level representation of the audio data is extracted—usually STFTs or MFCCs, as seen above.

Then, providing the song labels, supervised learning is performed on the dataset. After convergence, the learned values in the layers of the neural network will define the pattern extractor, which can be used later to retrieve features from audio sequences, serving as input for supervised learning methods.

One of the earlier studies in neural network-aided feature extraction [18] proposes an approach based on convolutional neural networks. In [28], a deep four-layered neural network is introduced for genre classification. The authors argue that for large datasets a deep architecture is necessary to learn representative features. To overcome the obstacles of vanishing/exploding gradient, long training time and overfitting, they apply batch normalization, use a ReLU activation function and dropout.

Other works studying genre recognition experiment with deep belief networks (DBN) [11], multiscale architectures [7] and convolutional DBNs [6]. Dieleman et al. [8] investigate whether it is possible to apply feature learning directly to raw audio data, an approach that would lead to an end-to-end learning model. The authors find that the spectrogram representations outperform the raw audio data. This might happen because the network architecture for raw audio input is not sufficiently expressive to perform an operation similar to spectrogram extraction. In [9,27], the limits of the end-to-end approach are analyzed studying different experiments, arriving to similar conclusions in general. Pons et al. [21] present architectural choices that are musically motivated in order to ascertain what the chosen networks are learning. They aim to build CNNs that can learn generalizable musical concepts. In [4], a four-layered convolutional recurrent neural network (CRNN) is introduced for music tagging. According to the authors, such an architecture deploys the CNN in the role of the feature extractor, while the RNN acts like a temporal summarizer.

3   The Dataset

To train and test our model, we use data from two folk music databases maintained by the Institute for Musicology, Research Centre for the Humanities and the Hungarian Academy of Sciences[2].

The first database consists of the collections of Zoltán Kallós, containing 3664 digitalized audio recordings collected in Transylvania between 1929 and 1994. Each recording is labeled with metadata about the place and time of recording as well as details about the performers and collectors. The name of the village provides sufficient information to assign a folkloric region to each recording. During this categorization, we follow the structuring of Transylvanian folkloric regions as described in [20]. Researchers from various fields have been debating about the extent and boundaries of these regions for many years. Among these, the Mezőség has been one of the most ambiguous, the work of Pávai being the first to describe its inner structuring [32]. When developing his system, Pávai took geographical, historical and social aspects into consideration, and followed the methodology of folk dance/folk music research.

The second dataset we use is *The Database of Published folk music recordings*, which contains 6000 recordings from all Hungarian-speaking territories of the Carpathian basin. The audio files recorded in Transylvania are used to supplement the regions that contain too few samples, including: Székelyföld, Gyimes, Szilágyság, Bukovina. Data examination reveals that 0.44% of the audio files (the ones annotated with the *Prose* tag) contain only speech (poems, tales, etc.), therefore these are discarded.

---

[2] http://www.zti.hu.

4 Data Preprocessing

The preprocessing pipeline is shown in Fig. 1. First, the audio time series data is segmented and zero-padded [10] in case it is shorter than the required 30 s— segment length generally chosen in the literature [4,11,21,31]. After segmentation, the power spectrogram of the signal is calculated using STFT, after which the mel spectrogram is computed. Each file is randomly assigned to either the training or the test set; all segmented pieces of a single file are added to the same set to avoid overly similar segments in the disjoint sets. Figure 2 shows a mel spectrogram obtained from the preprocessing steps.

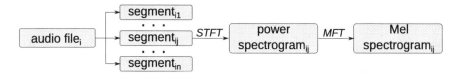

Fig. 1. Data preprocessing steps

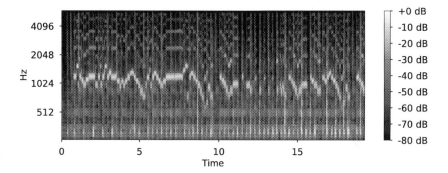

Fig. 2. Mel spectrogram extracted from an audio file containing music performed with flute and gardon in the *Gyimes* region.

Our dataset is highly imbalanced: classes range from a mere 100 min of audio up to over 30 h. A classifier trained with such data would tend to predict overrepresented classes more often, thus, imbalanced training data can have significant detrimental effect on the classification performance [12]. Data-level approaches include different sampling techniques (e.g. over - and undersampling), while classifier-level methods modify the training algorithm to handle class imbalance by defining a misclassification cost matrix or adjusting the decision threshold of the classifier [2,13]. In [2], oversampling was found to be one of the best performing methods in CNNs, while SMOTE (Synthetic Minority Over-sampling TEchnique) was shown to outperform oversampling in certain situations [3]. In a recent study [33], however, it was shown empirically that—at least for convolutional approaches—applying application-specific data augmentation techniques (using label-preserving transformations) yields better performance than using the feature-space augmentation method of SMOTE. Hence, to address the issue of class imbalance, we propose dataset balancing through domain-specific data augmentation. In the context of computer vision, data augmentation consists of rotating, scaling, translating, adding noise, brightening/darkening images to supplement the training data. If a power/mel spectrogram is regarded as an image, the analogous operations would be: pitch shifting, tempo changing, dynamic range compression (changing the volume), background noise addition—all label-preserving transformations. These techniques have been used in the MIR field, e.g. Salamon and Bello [25] apply them to augment audio for environmental sound classification. We apply pitch shifting and tempo changing by the same factors used in their research: pitch shifting of $\{-2, -1, 1, 2\}$ semitones and time scaling by a factor of $\{0.81, 0.93, 1.07, 1.23\}$. The data is augmented only if the number of segments is less than a predefined threshold. Overrepresented classes are also reduced by discarding a necessary amount of randomly selected samples.

5   CNN Architectures

This section presents the neural architectures used in our experiments. They are derived from earlier works of musically motivated CNNs. The first four are based on the work of Choi et al. [4]. We extend these approaches with a combination of time and frequency architecture derived from Pons et al. [21]. Hence, the five architectures are:

TCA (Time-Content Architecture). The kernels are one-dimensional (1 × 4), meaning that the convolution is performed along the time axis. After each convolutional layer, max-pooling is performed in the time dimension. The last feature map is a column vector, encoding a feature for each mel band. This vector is fed to fully connected layers.

FCA (Frequency-Content Architecture). Choi et al. [4] compress the frequency content in one band in the first convolutional layer with $nr\_mel\_bands \times 4$-shaped kernels. After this, convolution and max-pooling along the time axis is performed. The output is flattened and input to fully connected layers.

BBA (Black-Box architecture). Convolutional layers with 3 × 3 kernels and max-pooling layers alternate here.

CRNN (Convolutional Recurrent Neural Network). CNN layers with 3 × 3 kernels alternate with max-pooling layers that shrink the dimensions of feature maps until the frequency content is compressed into one band. This output vector is aggregated by a recurrent neural network. Choi et al. explain this choice of design by the fact that RNN architectures are better at aggregating temporal patterns, while relying on CNNs for local feature extraction.

TFA (Time-Frequency Architecture). The flattened output of a model that does convolutions along the time axis, and a model performing convolutions along the frequency axis are combined in a feedforward layer, followed by more fully-connected layers.

In case of each model, all layers except the output layer apply a ReLU activation function to their input. On the output layers, we use the softmax activation function. We apply batch normalization to all layers in the models. The success of batch normalization depends on the mini-batch size applied at training, but the computational resources allowed us to use only mini-batch sizes of 64; with greater batches the effect of batch normalization could be more beneficial.

When a layer performs convolution, its 2D input has to be padded not to lose the information in the corners and on the margins. The choice of padding value is important, because it could influence the learned features in the upper layers. Reflection padding is applied, ensuring that the marginal values of the output are similar to their neighbors [10]. For the value of the stride we choose 1 on each layer.

We apply mini-batch gradient descent with early stopping and categorical cross entropy as loss function. Adam is chosen as an optimization algorithm for its general purpose use [24]: it computes adaptive learning rates for each parameter by performing smaller updates on parameters that are associated with frequently occurring features, and larger updates for parameters associated with infrequent ones.

To enhance the training process we apply a novel approach introduced in [29]. Smith et al. propose to set the learning rate by cyclically varying it between two boundary values. The success of the technique can be attributed to traversing the saddle points in the loss function more rapidly, thus speeding up convergence and increasing accuracy. Smith also states that a cyclical learning rate can be successfully combined with adaptive methods.

Table 1. Architecture of the models that perform best on the validation data. A convolutional layer described as: $k \times conv\ m \times n\text{-}p$ performs convolution k times with a shape of $m \times n$ and a width of p. A max-pooling layer described as $mp\ m \times n$ performs max-pooling with a shape of $m \times n$. A fully connected layer described as $fc\ p$ has p units. The validation accuracy is reported on a subset of data containing files from the classes *Mezőség, Székelyföld and Moldva.*

TCA	FCA	BBA	CRNN	TFA	
conv 1×16 − 33	conv 96×4 − 43	2×conv 3×3 − 20	2×conv 3×3 − 30	TCA	2×conv 3×1 − 33
mp 1×4	2×conv 1×4 − 43	mp 2×4	mp 2×2		mp 4×2
conv 1×16 − 33	mp 1×4	2×conv 3×3 − 41	2×conv 3×3 − 60		2×conv 3×1 − 33
mp 1×5	2×conv 1×4 − 43	mp 2×4	mp 3×3		mp 4×2
conv 1×4 − 66	mp 1×5	2×conv 3×3 − 41	2×conv 3×3 − 60		2×conv 3×1 − 66
mp 1×8	2×conv 1×4 − 87	mp 2×4	mp 4×4		mp 1×4
conv 1×4 − 66	mp 1×4	2×conv 3×3 − 62	2×conv 3×3 − 60		fc 400
mp 1×8	2×conv 1×4 − 87	mp 3×5	mp 4×4		fc 400
fc 400	mp 1×5	2×conv 3×3 − 82	LSTM−60	fc 400	
fc 500	fc 400	mp 4×4	LSTM−60	fc 400	
	fc 400	fc 400			
		fc 400			
acc: 0.6982	acc: 0.5904	acc: 0.6031	acc: 0.6713	acc: 0.6885	

6   Experiments and Results

During the experiments, we focus on the design of the CNN models and the application of deep learning techniques—the refinement of the audio preprocessing pipeline is not our objective. Therefore, we choose to set the values of parameters for audio processing after [4]: the audio is downsampled to 12 kHz, a Hann window of length 512 is used with a hop length of 256 samples. The signal is segmented into 30 s long pieces (1366 samples), the number of mel bands is 96.

We tune the models on a subset of the data, which contains recordings from the three most populated classes: *Mezőség, Székelyföld* and *Moldva*. We reduce/augment the data where necessary to obtain ≈ 1800 training samples and ≈ 600 validation samples. As starting point, we take the architectures presented in [4], modifying the filter shapes, increasing the number of layers, adding more units and applying double convolution to reach higher classification accuracy. As described in Sect. 5, batch normalization is applied before each convolution,

Table 2. Segment and file level precision, recall, F_1 score of the models with 5-fold cross validation.

Model	Segments			Files		
	Precision	Recall	F_1 score	Precision	Recall	F_1 score
TCA	0.63	0.62	0.62	0.65	0.63	0.63
FCA	0.45	0.44	0.43	0.50	0.48	0.48
BBA	0.55	0.54	0.53	0.56	0.54	0.54
CRNN	0.58	0.57	0.56	0.61	0.59	0.59
TFA	0.57	0.57	0.56	0.58	0.57	0.57

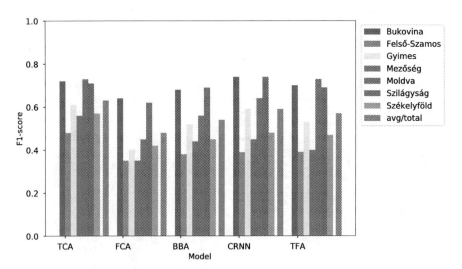

Fig. 3. F_1 score results with 5-fold cross validation.

reflection padding is used with a stride of 1 and a dropout of 0.5 is added to the fully-connected layers. We observe that after introducing the cyclical learning rate, classification accuracy increases significantly and convergence becomes faster. After finding the best model for each architecture type, a 5-fold cross-validation is performed on the entire dataset. Since a file is made up of multiple segments, the independent class label predictions are summed up for the whole musical piece using majority voting.

The results of the best architectures are reported in Tables 1, 2 and Fig. 3, and interpreted as follows:

TCA. The validation accuracy of the baseline TCA model is 67%. Its performance is improved by (1) adding more units to the fully connected layers (+1.7%), (2) applying double convolution (+2.5%), (3) adding one further convolutional layer by reducing the max-pooling window size at the last layer (+2%), (4) increasing the filter shape in the first two convolutional layers from 1×4 to 1×16 (+2.8%). The fact that a time-content architecture reaches an F_1 score of 0.62 on the segments and 0.63 on files leads to the conclusion that regions are distinguishable by the rhythmic content of their music. It is noticeable that the model performs better on the regions of Bukovina, Moldva, Szilágyság, whereas it performs worse on Felső-Szamos-vidék and Székelyföld. Bukovina, Moldva and Szilágyság are more isolated regions (see Fig. 4)—as a consequence, the folk music of other regions did not influence the population of this area as much. They have characteristic instruments, melodies and beats. This may be one of the reasons the model learns to distinguish them so well. Analyze the misclassifications between regions, we find neighboring regions are often swapped, e.g. Felső-Szamos-vidék and Mezőség. However, the most errors happen between two regions that are not neighbors: Bukovina and Székelyföld. A historical reason may explain the anomaly: the recordings from Bukovina are from villages mostly populated by Szeklers, who fled Székelyföld after the *Siculicidium*[3] [26].

FCA. The baseline FCA model yields validation accuracy of 57%. Its performance is increased by applying double convolution (+2.1%), however varying the filter shapes yields no beneficial results: neither 96×8 shaped filters on the first layer (−3.4%), nor wider, 1×16 shaped filters in the upper layers increase accuracy (−3.1%). The model reaches an F_1 score of 0.40 on the segments, which means it can not learn to distinguish the regions based on the frequency content of the music. One of the reasons behind this could be the similarity of the instrumentation—though there are region-specific instruments, the majority of them is used in every region (e.g. violin). Furthermore, as stated in [1], the melodic material of Transylvanian folk music is uniform.

---

[3] Siculicidium was a mass murder committed by the Habsburg army in 1764 as a response to the Szeklers' revolt against military service. The Szeklers from Madéfalva found refugee among the Csángós, who have been living in the Moldva region for centuries. A few years later, in 1774, the Habsburgs pardoned them and settled them down in the Bukovina region.

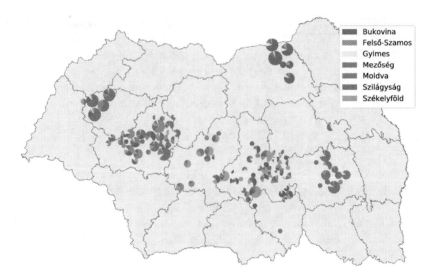

Fig. 4. Predictions of TCA displayed on the map of North-Romania. Every pie chart corresponds to a village, its size is proportional to the length of audio recorded at the settlement. Results are obtained by aggregating file-level predictions on the 5 respective test folds.

BBA. The initial performance of BBA (57%) is improved by adding fully connected layers after the convolutional layers (+1.5%), and applying double convolution (+2.8%). Using 4×4 convolutional filters or modifying the shape of max-pooling layers did not improve the categorical accuracy significantly (+1%). This model performs better than the FCA, but worse than the TCA model. Due to its design, we can not deduce what aspects of music it learns in its upper layers, and we can not provide any reasonable explanation why it learns the Bukovina region better than other regions. The inaccuracy of the BBA model underlines the need for musically motivated designs, while also pointing out that rectangular filters—despite their wide usage in image processing—are not always the best choice for MIR.

CRNN. The CRNN presented in [4] yields validation accuracy of 58%. Its performance is improved by (1) adding more units to the layers of RNN (+2.5%), (2) using LSTMs instead of GRUs to aggregate temporal patterns (+3.6%) (3) applying double convolution (+4.8%), (4) adding weak dropout of 0.1 to the layers of RNN (larger dropout produces worse results) (+8.5%). With F_1 scores of 0.56 on segments and 0.59 on files, CRNN is among the best performing classifiers. TCA and CRNN have good performances on the same classes, and their incorrect predictions are analogous as well: they mix up the same classes. The fact that two models designed for time-dependent features reach similar results validates the finding that folkloric regions are distinguishable by the rhythmic content of their music. As shown in Table 1, the long short-term memory (LSTM) layers in the CRNN model have 60 units or 60 hidden states, i.e. they have a memory of 60 time steps. It is very likely that the model could learn and perform better having more units, because LSTM is capable of processing long time series data.

TFA. In the TFA model we use the best TCA as time architecture, and we experiment with the design of the frequency architecture. The initial architecture has validation accuracy of 67%. As with other models, applying double convolution increases the accuracy (+1.7%). However, our expectation that TFA will have better performance than TCA is not met; in fact it produces more poorly for the entire dataset. The frequency architecture is not able to learn relevant features that supplement the ones extracted by TCA. This verifies our previous observations that regions are identified better by time-content features, and that frequency content might not be as relevant for the classification, because of the uniformity of the melodic material.

In case of each model we achieve better results by increasing the number of units in the fully-connected layers and by adding a dropout with a rate of 0.5.

7   Conclusions

Folk music research reveals important aspects of the dynamics and organization of communities over history. Data analysis and machine learning techniques could help musicologists better organize existing datasets and find novel ethnographic characteristics. In this study, we have described how convolutional neural network classifiers were trained to learn ethnographic regions of Transylvania from their folk music. We chose CNNs because the surveyed MIR literature shows their successful application to audio classification problems in recent years.

To train the models, we used a dataset of Transylvanian folk songs that contains the collections of Zoltán Kallós. The highly imbalanced dataset was augmented by additional pieces generated by pitch shifting and changing the tempo. As input to the models, we used mel spectrograms extracted from 30 s long audio segments.

Experiments have been performed using five types of models: time-content, frequency-content, black-box, convolutional recurrent neural network and time-frequency architectures. The time-content architecture performed best, reaching an F_1 score of 0.63. The second best classifier was the convolutional recurrent neural network with 0.59 F_1 score. These results suggest that Transylvanian folkloric regions are distinguishable mainly by the rhythmic content of their music.

Models had better accuracy on isolated regions: the time-content architecture reached an F_1 score of 0.73 on Moldva, 0.71 on Szilágyság and 0.72 on Bukovina. Regions that are closer to each other were not distinguished as well: the worst result for the time-content architecture was Felső-Szamos (in the center of Transylvania) with a score of 0.48. Classifiers swapped other neighboring regions as well, for example Felső-Szamos-vidék was often confused with Mezőség and Szilágyság. An interesting point is that Székelyföld was mistaken in many cases for a non-neighbor, Bukovina—a confusion possibly attributed to historical reasons.

Based on our findings, we conclude that convolutional neural networks are able to learn important features from folk music. Furthermore, the results achieved could be interpreted by ethnographers and musicologists to find previously unknown aspects, to check presumptions and to draw relevant conclusions.

As mentioned in Sect. 5, the success of batch normalization and training is highly affected by the choice of the mini-batch size. We therefore propose future experiments with greater mini-batch sizes. Furthermore, as described in Sect. 6, we would add more hidden states to the CRNN model in order for it to remember more time steps and to recognize motives that spread longer in time.

As classification is a supervised machine learning method, our plans for further research include experimenting with unsupervised techniques to find out if the clusters of music reflect the folkloric regions. We would also like to evaluate our models on the folk music of other nations. Furthermore, we plan to extend the dataset to Europe to see if the models perform better if countries are to be predicted.

References

1. Bartók, B.: The Hungarian Folk Song. State University of New York Press, Albany (1981)
2. Buda, M., Maki, A., Mazurowski, M.A.: A systematic study of the class imbalance problem in convolutional neural networks. Neural Netw. **106**, 249–259 (2018). https://doi.org/10.1016/j.neunet.2018.07.011
3. Chawla, N.V., Bowyer, K.W., Hall, L.O., Kegelmeyer, W.P.: SMOTE: Synthetic Minority Over-sampling Technique. J. Artif. Intell. Res. **16**, 321–357 (2002). https://doi.org/10.1613/jair.953
4. Choi, K., Fazekas, G., Sandler, M., Cho, K.: Convolutional recurrent neural networks for music classification. In: Proceedings of the International Conference on Acoustics, Speech and Signal Processing, New Orleans, LA, USA, pp. 2392–2396. IEEE (2017). https://doi.org/10.1109/icassp.2017.7952585
5. Cornelis, O., Lesaffre, M., Moelants, D., Leman, M.: Access to ethnic music: advances and perspectives in content-based music information retrieval. Signal Process. **90**(4), 1008–1031 (2010). https://doi.org/10.1016/j.sigpro.2009.06.020
6. Dieleman, S., Brakel, P., Schrauwen, B.: Audio-based music classification with a pretrained convolutional network. In: Proceedings of the 12th International Society for Music Information Retrieval Conference, University of Miami, Miami, Florida, USA, pp. 669–674 (2011). https://doi.org/10.1016/j.knosys.2018.07.033
7. Dieleman, S., Schrauwen, B.: Multiscale approaches to music audio feature learning. In: Proceedings of the 14th International Society for Music Information Retrieval Conference, Curitiba, Brazil, pp. 116–121 (2013)
8. Dieleman, S., Schrauwen, B.: End-to-end learning for music audio. In: Proceedings of the International Conference on Acoustics, Speech and Signal Processing, Florence, Italy, pp. 6964–6968. IEEE (2014). https://doi.org/10.1109/icassp.2014.6854950
9. Glasmachers, T.: Limits of end-to-end learning. In: Proceedings of the 9th Asian Conference on Machine Learning, PMLR, Seol, Korea, pp. 17–32 (2017)

10. Gonzalez, R.C., Woods, R.E.: Digital Image Processing, 4th edn. Pearson (2018)
11. Hamel, P., Eck, D.: Learning features from music audio with deep belief networks. In: Proceedings of the 11th International Society for Music Information Retrieval Conference,International Society for Music Information Retrieval, Utrecht, vol. 10, pp. 339–344 (2010). https://doi.org/10.1109/icalip.2014.7009771
12. Japkowicz, N., Stephen, S.: The class imbalance problem: a systematic study. Intell. Data Anal. **6**(5), 429–449 (2002). https://doi.org/10.3233/ida-2002-6504
13. Johnson, J.M., Khoshgoftaar, T.M.: Survey on deep learning with classimbalance. J. Big Data **6**(1), 27 (2019). https://doi.org/10.1186/s40537-019-0192-5
14. Juhász, Z.: Contour analysis of Hungarian folk music in a multidimensional metricspace. J. New Music Res. **29**(1), 71–83 (2000). https://doi.org/10.1076/0929-8215(200003)29:01;1-p;ft071
15. Juhász, Z.: Segmentation of Hungarian folk songs using an entropy-based learning system. J. New Music Res. **33**(1), 5–15 (2004). https://doi.org/10.1076/jnmr.33.1.5.35395
16. Kós, K.: Erdély. Kultúrtörténeti vázlat., Genius, Budapest (1929)
17. Li, T., Ogihara, M., Tzanetakis, G.: Music Data Mining. CRC Press, Boca Raton (2011). https://doi.org/10.1201/b11041-3
18. Li, T.L.H., Chan, A.B., Chun, A.: Automatic musical pattern feature extraction using convolutional neural network. In: Proceedings of the International MultiConference of Engineers and Computer Scientists, pp. 546–550. Newswood Limited, Hong Kong (2010)
19. Logan, B.: Mel frequency cepstral coefficients for music modeling. In: Proceedings of the 1st International Symposium on Music Information Retrieval, Plymouth, Massachusetts, USA, vol. 270, pp. 1–11 (2000)
20. Pávai, I.: Az erdélyi nagytáj a néprajz-, népzene- és néptánckutatás szemléletében. In: Kriza János Néprajzi Társaság Évkönyve 13, pp. 15–47. Kriza János Néprajzi Társaság, Kolozsvár (2005)
21. Pons, J., Lidy, T., Serra, X.: Experimenting with musically motivated convolutional neural networks. In: Proceedings of the 14th International Workshop on Content-Based Multimedia Indexing, Bucharest, Romania, pp. 1–6. IEEE (2016)
22. Proakis, J.G.: Digital Signal Processing: Principles Algorithms and Applications. Pearson Education India (2001)
23. Procter, P.: Cambridge International Dictionary of English. Cambridge University Press, Cambridge (1995)
24. Ruder, S.: An overview of gradient descent optimization algorithms (2016)
25. Salamon, J., Bello, J.P.: Deep convolutional neural networks and data augmentation for environmental sound classification. IEEE Signal Process. Lett. **24**(3), 279–283 (2017). https://doi.org/10.1109/lsp.2017.2657381
26. Sebestyén, Á.: A bukovinai székelység tegnap és ma. Ad Librum Kiadó, Budapest (2009)
27. Shalev-Shwartz, S., Shamir, O., Shammah, S.: Failures of gradient-based deep learning. In: Proceedings of the 34th International Conference on Machine Learning, PMLR, Sydney, NSW, Australia, pp. 3067–3075 (2017)
28. Sigtia, S., Dixon, S.: Improved music feature learning with deep neural networks. In: Proceedings of the International Conference on Acoustics, Speech and Signal Processing, Florence, Italy, pp. 6959–6963. IEEE (2014). https://doi.org/10.1109/icassp.2014.6854949
29. Smith, L.N.: Cyclical learning rates for training neural networks. In: Proceedings of the Winter Conference on Applications of Computer Vision, Santa Rosa, CA, USA, pp. 464–472. IEEE (2017)

30. Stevens, S.S., Volkmann, J., Newman, E.B.: A scale for the measurement of the psychological magnitude pitch. J. Acoust. Soc. Am. **8**(3), 185–190 (1937). https://doi.org/10.1121/1.1915893
31. Tzanetakis, G., Cook, P.: Musical genre classification of audio signals. IEEE Trans. Speech Audio Process. **10**(5), 293–302 (2002). https://doi.org/10.1109/TSA.2002. 800560
32. Varga, S.: Változások egy mezőségi falu XX. századi tánckultúrájában. Ph.d. thesis, Eötvös Loránd Tudományegyetem (2011)
33. Wong, S.C., Gatt, A., Stamatescu, V., McDonnell, M.D.: Understanding data augmentation for classification: when to warp? In: 18th International Conference on Digital Image Computing: Techniques and Applications, pp. 1–6. IEEE (2016). https://doi.org/10.1109/dicta.2016.7797091

Merging DBSCAN and Density Peak for Robust Clustering

Jian Hou[1]([✉])[ID], Chengcong Lv[1], Aihua Zhang[1], and Xu E[2]

[1] College of Engineering, Bohai University, Jinzhou 121013, China
dr.houjian@gmail.com
[2] College of Information Sciences, Bohai University, Jinzhou 121013, China

Abstract. In data clustering, density based algorithms are well known for the ability of detecting clusters of arbitrary shapes. DBSCAN is a widely used density based clustering approach, and the recently proposed density peak algorithm has shown significant potential in experiments. However, the DBSCAN algorithm may misclassify border data points of small density as noises and does not work well with large density variance across clusters, and the density peak algorithm has a large dependence on the detected cluster centers. To circumvent these problems, we make a study of these two algorithms and find that they have some complementary properties. We then propose to combine these two algorithms to overcome their problems. Specifically, we use the DP algorithm to detect cluster centers and then determine the parameters for DBSCAN adaptively. After DBSCAN clustering, we further use the DP algorithm to include border data points of small density into clusters. By combining the complementary properties of these two algorithms, we manage to relieve the problems of DBSCAN and avoid the drawbacks of the density peak algorithm in the meanwhile. Our algorithm is tested with synthetic and real datasets, and is demonstrated to perform better than DBSCAN and density peak algorithms, as well as some other clustering algorithms.

Keywords: Clustering · DBSCAN · Density peak

1 Introduction

Data clustering has important applications in many fields [19], and a huge amount of clustering algorithms have been proposed in the last decades. In addition to the well-known k-means algorithm, DBSCAN [12] and normalized cuts (NCuts) [35] algorithms are also widely adopted baselines in data clustering, and many variants have been proposed [2,8,9]. Traditional clustering algorithms also include hierarchical clustering [42] and distribution based algorithms [39]. In recent developments, SPRG [43] as one type of spectral clustering [29,31] is shown to perform well by constructing a special affinity matrix. The affinity propagation (AP) algorithm [5] uses the pairwise data similarity matrix as the input, and passes the affinity message among data points iteratively to identify clusters gradually. Different from many partitioning based algorithms, the

© Springer Nature Switzerland AG 2019
I. V. Tetko et al. (Eds.): ICANN 2019, LNCS 11730, pp. 595–610, 2019.
https://doi.org/10.1007/978-3-030-30490-4_48

dominant sets (DSets) algorithm [20–22,30,32,36,37] is proposed by defining dominant set as a cluster concept. It uses the pairwise similarity matrix and input and extracts clusters sequentially, without dependence on any parameters. The well-studied clustering algorithms also include subspace clustering [15,25], multi-view clustering [26] and others [4,11,13,27,33,41].

Density based clustering has an attractive property of detecting clusters of arbitrary shapes. One typical example of this type is the DBSCAN algorithm [12], which defines a density threshold with parameters Eps and $MinPts$ to differentiate between cluster members and noises. The OPTICS [2] algorithm is a generalization of the DBSCAN algorithm, which generates a hierarchical clustering result. The DeLi-Clu [1] algorithm further combines the OPTICS algorithm with single-linkage clustering, thereby removing the parameter Eps completely. Some other works related to DBSCAN also include [7,17,24]. The density peak (DP) algorithm [34] adopts a different idea from DBSCAN. This algorithm treats local density peaks as the candidates of cluster centers, and makes use of the density relationship of neighboring data points to group data points into clusters. While being simple, this algorithm has shown significant potential in many experiments. Some recent works related to the DP algorithm include [3,28].

In the DBSCAN algorithm, a density threshold is defined by the minimum number $MinPts$ of points in the neighborhood of radius Eps. After that, the core points with density above the threshold and those in the neighborhood of core points are grouped into clusters, and the other points are treated as noise. While this practice does help detect noises, the small-density data points in the border of clusters may be treated as noises by mistake. In the case that different clusters have significantly different densities, one small-density cluster may be treated as noises as a whole. With the DP algorithm, cluster centers are detected firstly, and the other data points are then grouped into clusters around the cluster centers. While the clustering results have a significant dependence on cluster center detection results, a reliable method to detect cluster centers is still not available. Consequently, it is not guaranteed to obtain good clustering results with the DP algorithm.

Noticing the nice properties and problems of the DBSCAN and DP algorithms, we study these two algorithms and find that their properties are complementary to some extent. This observation motivates us to merge both algorithms to overcome their problems. Our algorithm can be described informally as follows. The DP clustering process is divided into two steps, namely cluster center identification and grouping of non-center data. The DBSCAN clustering is inserted between these two steps, and we obtain a three-step clustering algorithm. Specifically, we detect cluster centers following the DP algorithm in the first step. After that, we do DBSCAN clustering with the cluster centers as seeds. Finally, the remaining unclustered data points are clustered following the DP algorithm. Both synthetic and real datasets are adopted in experiments, and experimental results show that our algorithm is able to overcome the problems of DBSCAN and DP and improve the clustering results evidently. Our algorithm also compares favorably with other commonly used clustering algorithms, including k-means, NCuts, DBSCAN, AP and DSets algorithms.

In Sect. 2 the DBSCAN and DP algorithms are introduced briefly and their properties are discussed. Section 3 provides the details on how DBSCAN and DP are merged to overcome their drawbacks and improve the clustering results. Our algorithm is validated with experiments and compared with other algorithms in Sect. 4. Finally, 5 summarizes the conclusions.

2   Algorithm Basis

As we plan to combine the DBSCAN and DP algorithms to overcome their drawbacks, we firstly introduce these two algorithms and discuss their properties in brief.

2.1   DBSCAN

As one popular density based clustering algorithm, DBSCAN detects clusters sequentially based on the so-called density-reachable cluster model. With the parameter Eps denoting a neighborhood radius and $MinPts$ denoting the minimum count of data points in this neighborhood, this algorithm defines a density threshold and groups data points into clusters based on the threshold. Specifically, the core points whose densities are above the threshold and those in the neighborhood of core points are grouped into clusters, and the others are regarded as noises. In implementation, we begin with any data point p and calculate its density, namely the number of data points in its Eps neighborhood. If the density is smaller than the threshold, we move to the next point. Otherwise, p is identified as a core point and its neighbors in the Eps neighborhood are included into the cluster. Then for each cluster member, we continue to check if it is a core point and add the neighbors of a core point into the cluster. After all the cluster members are traversed, we obtain the first cluster. By repeating the same procedures in the unclustered data, we are able to obtain the other clusters.

In addition to the ability to extract clusters of arbitrary shapes, DBSCAN has some other special properties. Different from many algorithms obtaining clusters simultaneously from a partitioning process, DBSCAN detects clusters one by one. In detecting each cluster, core points with large density and the neighbors of core points are included into clusters.

2.2   DP

The DP algorithm uses a different idea from DBSCAN to do density based clustering. This algorithm firstly defines two key parameters ρ and δ. With the cutoff kernel, the local density ρ_i of one data point i is calculated as the number of data points in a d_c-radius neighborhood of i, i.e.,

$$\rho_i = \sum_{j \in S, j \neq i} \chi(d_c - d_{ij}). \tag{1}$$

Here S denotes the set of data, d_{ij} means the distance between data points i and j, and d_c refers to the cutoff distance specified by user. The parameter δ is the distance between one data point and its nearest larger-density neighbor, i.e.,

$$\delta_i = \min_{j \in S, \rho_j > \rho_i} d_{ij}. \tag{2}$$

The clustering with DP is built on two assumptions, i.e., cluster centers are local density peaks distant from each other, and one data point is in the same cluster as the nearest neighbor of higher density. With the first assumption, we see that cluster centers have large ρ and large δ. Noticing that the non-center data points usually have no such a property, this property is used to detect the cluster centers. Then the clustering of non-center data points is accomplished based on the second assumption. We sort the non-center data points in decreasing order according to local density, and then group each data point to the same cluster as its nearest neighbor of higher density. As the labels of cluster centers (density peaks) are already known, this process can be accomplished efficiently.

In this algorithm, local density peaks are firstly detected and used as cluster centers, and then the second assumption is used to group the non-center data points into clusters. In other words, large-density data points are firstly grouped into clusters, and then the smaller-density ones are included. In this way, the clusters are obtained in a cluster expansion mode, and the data points are included into clusters according to the decreasing order of local density.

3   Our Algorithm

By investigating the DBSCAN and DP algorithms, we identify some major drawbacks of these two algorithms. Furthermore, we find that these two algorithms have some complementary properties. We then propose to merge the merits of these two algorithms to overcome their drawbacks. The details of our algorithm are presented below.

The DBSCAN algorithm defines core points as those data points with density above a density threshold. In clustering, only the core points and their neighbors in the Eps neighborhood are grouped into clusters, and the small-density data points distant from large-density ones are treated as noises. In other words, only the large-density data points and their neighbors in the Eps neighborhood can be grouped into clusters. While this practice is helpful to find out noises, it may classify some small-density data points as noises by mistake. Taking a cluster of Gaussian distribution illustrated in Fig. 1(a) for example, we observe that the border data points are with evidently smaller density than central data. In this case, the small-density border data points may be misclassified as noises if they are not close enough to the large-density ones. To this problem, we have a look at the DP algorithm. After cluster center identification, the DP algorithm groups the other data points into clusters with the assumption that one data point is in the same cluster as its nearest neighbor of higher density. Based on this assumption, one data point can be included into a cluster only if its nearest

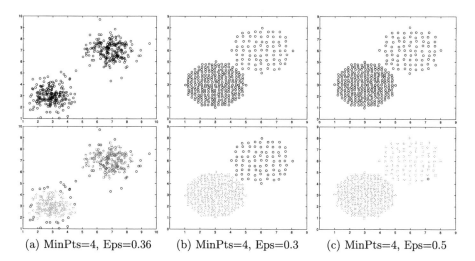

(a) MinPts=4, Eps=0.36   (b) MinPts=4, Eps=0.3   (c) MinPts=4, Eps=0.5

Fig. 1. Three cases difficult for the DBSCAN algorithm. The top row shows the original datasets, and the bottom row shows the DBSCAN clustering results. In the bottom row, the black circles indicate the detected noises by the DBSCAN algorithm. In the leftmost case, the border data points of small density are not grouped into clusters. In the middle case, the whole small-density cluster are detected as noises by a large density threshold. In the rightmost case, two clusters are detected as one by a small density threshold.

neighbor of higher density are already in the cluster. Consequently, in extracting each cluster, the large-density data points are firstly included, followed by the small-density ones. In other words, with the DP algorithm clusters are generated in a cluster-expansion manner, and the expansion is from large-density data points to small-density ones.

Based on the above discussion, we present the following method to solve the problem of DBSCAN using DP. With DBSCAN we extract a cluster by including core points and their neighbors in the *Eps* neighborhood. Instead of extracting the next cluster immediately, we do a cluster expansion step with the DP algorithm. The first step is to sort the unclustered data points in the increasing order according to the average distance to the cluster. For each unclustered data point i, we add it into the cluster if its nearest neighbor of higher density has already been included into the cluster. Otherwise, we leave i unclustered. By introducing cluster expansion with DP, we are able to include the small-density data points into clusters, no matter how far they are from large-density data. Furthermore, as we add small-density data points into the cluster based on DP, the cluster expansion is unlikely to include data points in other clusters and merge neighboring clusters into one. We still use Fig. 1(a) as the example to explain this effect. In the boundary between the two clusters, each data point is assigned the same label as its nearest neighbor of higher density. This means that the cluster expansion will not cross the density valley and include the data points in the other cluster. By dividing clusters with density valley, the cluster expansion matches the idea of density based clustering perfectly.

With the DP-based cluster expansion, we are able to group the small-density data points in the border area into clusters, on condition that each cluster from DBSCAN is a subset of one real cluster. However, with the original DBSCAN algorithm the density threshold is fixed, and the generated clusters may not be able to satisfy the condition, especially in the case that there exists a large density variance across clusters. With a large density threshold, the large-density clusters can be detected, whereas the whole small-density clusters may be treated as noises (Fig. 1(b)). This problem cannot be solved with DP-based expansion which terminates at the boundary between clusters. In contrast, with a small density threshold, the data points in the boundary area between clusters may be treated as core points. In this case, it is likely that two or more neighboring clusters are merged into one (Fig. 1(c)). This problem cannot be solved with DP-based expansion either.

Since the DBSCAN algorithm cannot deal with datasets with large density variance with a fixed density threshold, we propose to determine the density threshold for each cluster adaptively. For this purpose, our approach is to find some seeds in a cluster and infer the density threshold based on the seeds. In the DBSCAN algorithm, only core points with large density and their nearest neighbors can be included into clusters. Therefore the seeds must not be with too small density. In the DP algorithm, the first step is to detect the cluster center, which is the local density peak. Therefore the detected cluster centers have the largest density in the clusters and are most suitable to be used as seeds. Consequently, we can use the density of one cluster center to calculate the density threshold of the cluster. Considering that cluster centers are local density peaks, and have the largest density in the cluster, we determine the parameter Eps and $MinPts$ as follows. The $MinPts$ is set as 4, which is selected based on the experiments presented in Sect. 4. Then we set Eps as the distance between a cluster center and its $2 * MinPts$-th nearest neighbor. In this way we set a density threshold which is smaller than the density of the cluster center, allowing the neighboring data points of smaller density to be clustered. As we have a DP-based cluster expansion step to include small-density data points into clusters after DBSCAN clustering, the density threshold determined here, if large, will not be a big problem.

The whole process of our algorithm is described as follows. The first step is to calculate the pairwise distance matrix D, based on which the local density ρ and distance δ of each data point are obtained. Then the data points with the largest $\gamma = \rho\delta$ are selected as cluster centers. Starting from each cluster center, we determine Eps and $MinPts$ and do DBSCAN clustering to obtain an initial cluster. Then the DP algorithm is used to expand the initial cluster to include border data points of small density, yielding the final cluster. The other clusters are obtained in a similar way. The detailed procedures of our algorithm are presented formally in Algorithm 1.

Algorithm 1. Our algorithm.

Input:

     the set of data $X = \{x_i\}$, $i = 1, \cdots, n$

     number of clusters N_c

Output:

     labels of data $L = \{l_i\}$, $i = 1, \cdots, n$

1: $D = \{d_{ij}\}$, $d_{ij} = d(x_i, x_j), i, j = 1, \cdots, n$

2: $\varrho = \{\rho_i\}$, $\rho_i = rho(x_i, D), i = 1, \cdots, n$

3: $\delta_i = delta(x_i, \varrho, D), i = 1, \cdots, n$

4: $\Gamma = \{\gamma_i\}$, $\gamma_i = \rho_i * \delta_i, i = 1, \cdots, n$

5: $c_k = center(\Gamma), k = 1, \cdots, N_c$ // cluster centers

6: **for** $k = 1, \cdots, N_c$ **do**

7:     $S_0 = dbscan(X, c_k)$ // the cluster containing c_k

8:     $S = dp(X, S_0)$ // expand S_0 to S

9:     **for** $x_i \in S$ **do**

10:       $l_i = k$

11:     **end for**

12: **end for**

By merging the merits of DBSCAN and DP, our algorithm has the following properties. First, by using cluster centers as the seeds of DBSCAN clustering, we are able to determine the DBSCAN parameters for each cluster adaptively. This improves the clustering results in the case that there is a large density variance across clusters. Second, with DP-based cluster expansion, the border data points of small density are grouped into clusters, and the expansion does not cross the boundary between clusters. This helps to deal with the clusters where border data points are with significantly smaller density than central data. Third, by combining DBSCAN with DP, our algorithm solves the problems of the DBSCAN algorithm and avoids the drawbacks of the DP algorithm in the meanwhile. With the DP algorithm, one cluster center is a local density peak and has the largest density in a cluster, and all the other cluster members have smaller density. In other words, after one cluster center is identified, only data points of smaller density have the opportunity to be included into the cluster. Consequently, cluster center identification results influence the clustering results significantly. Due to the complexity of data distribution and the imperfect identification method, the identified cluster centers are not guaranteed to be the density peaks in their respective clusters. The inaccurate cluster centers definitely degrade the clustering results. In our algorithm, DBSCAN is used to generate initial clusters containing the detected cluster centers, and then DP is used to expand initial clusters to final clusters. Since DBSCAN clustering groups data points with sufficient large density into clusters, the real cluster centers with the largest density will be included in the initial clusters. Consequently, our algorithm is less influenced by the inaccuracy in cluster center identification.

It is worth noticing that both DBSCAN and DP are able to detect noises. However, as we discussed above, with DBSCAN the noises are detected based on a density threshold and an inappropriate threshold may misclassify small-density data points as noises. Instead, the DP algorithm defines a border region, and data points in that region with density smaller than an adaptive threshold are considered as noises. Therefore we adopt the method of DP to detect noises.

4   Experiments

4.1   Comparison with DBSCAN and DP

As our algorithm is proposed to combine the DBSCAN and DP algorithms for better performance, we firstly make a comparison with these two algorithms to observe if improvements are obtained. With the DBSCAN algorithm, the parameter Eps is calculated based on $MinPts$ following [10], and $MinPts$ is selected from 2, 3, $\cdots$, 10. For the DP algorithm, we implement two versions with the cutoff and Gaussian kernels and denote them by DP-cutoff and DP-Gaussian, respectively. With both versions, the parameter d_c is calculated by including a percentage of data points in the d_c-radius neighborhood, and the percentage is selected from 1.0%, 1.1%, $\cdots$, 2.0%.

The experiments are conducted on eight synthetic and seven real datasets. The eight synthetic datasets include Aggregation [16], Compound [40], D31 [38], Flame [14], Jain [23], Pathbased [6], R15 [38] and Spiral [6]. All these datasets are composed of 2D points of specially designed shapes. From UCI machine learning repository we take seven real datasets, including Breast, Glass, Iris, Thyroid, Wdbc, Wine and Yeast. In these datasets, Wdbc and Breast datasets are composed of data used for breast cancer diagnosis, and the Thyroid dataset is for thyroid disease diagnosis. The Wine, Iris and Glass datasets are composed of the features taken from different kinds of wine, iris flows and glass, respectively. The Yeast dataset is designed to classify the cellular localization sites of proteins. All these datasets have ground truth clustering results, and we use NMI to evaluate the clustering results. The clustering results comparison of our algorithm with DBSCAN, DP-cutoff and DP-Gaussian are shown in Fig. 2.

In comparison with DBSCAN, DP-cutoff and DP-Gaussian, Fig. 2(a) shows that our algorithm generates the best results on 12 datasets in all the 15 datasets. In the remaining three datasets, the best results on Aggregation and Flame datasets are very close to ground truth, and our results are close to the best ones. Only with the Spiral dataset our algorithm is outperformed by DBSCAN and DP-Gaussian evidently. Especially, the Jain dataset is composed of two clusters of significantly different densities. Our algorithm generate nearly perfect result on this dataset, showing evident advantage over DBSCAN and DP algorithms in dealing with density variance across clusters. We believe these observations show that our algorithm does merge the merits of DBSCAN and DP algorithms and obtain improvements with respect to these two algorithms.

In experiments, our algorithm does not improve the clustering results with respect to DBSCAN and DP on three datasets, namely, Aggregation, Flame and Spiral. We discuss the reason as follows. As shown in Fig. 3(a), (b) and (c), in all these three datasets the data points in each cluster are distributed

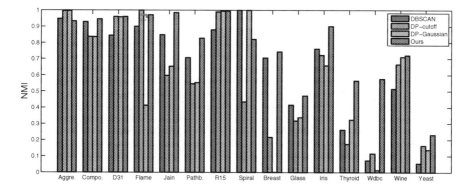

Fig. 2. Clustering results comparison of DBSCAN, DP-cutoff, DP-Gaussian and our algorithm.

rather evenly, and there is no large density difference among different clusters. This kind of datasets are easy for DBSCAN and DP algorithms, and some of them generate perfect results on these datasets, i.e., DP-cutoff and DP-Gaussian on Aggregation, DP-Gaussian on Flame, and DBSCAN and DP-Gaussian on Spiral. In this case, there is little room for improvement, and our combination of two algorithms is outperformed by the parameter tuning of two algorithms individually.

4.2   Comparison with Other Algorithms

In the comparison with other algorithms, we adopt the k-means, NCuts, DSets, AP, SPRG [43] algorithms and the one proposed in [18]. With k-means, NCuts and SPRG algorithms, we set the number of clusters as ground truth, and report the average results of five runs. With the DSets algorithm, we build the similarity matrix with $s(x, y) = exp(-d(x, y)/\sigma)$, where $\sigma = k\overline{d}$, $\overline{d}$ is the mean of pairwise distances, and k is selected from $1, 2, 5, 10, 20, \cdots, 100$. The input parameter of the AP algorithm is the preference value p, and the authors of [5] published the code to calculate the range $[p_{min}, p_{max}]$. We set this parameter as $p_{min} + m\lambda$, where $\lambda = (p_{max} - p_{min})/10$ and m is selected from $1, 2, \cdots, 9, 9.1, 9.2, \cdots, 9.9$. The algorithm proposed in [18] involves no parameters. The results comparison is reported in Table 1 with NMI as the evaluation criterion.

In the following we discuss the results shown in Table 1. Our algorithm performs the best on seven datasets (Compound, Flame, Glass, Iris, Jain, R15, Spiral), and near-best on six datasets (Aggregation, Breast, D31, Pathbased, Wdbc, Yeast). Only on two datasets (Thyroid and Wine) our algorithm are outperformed by the SPRG algorithm evidently. Our algorithm also generates the best average result (18% over the second best one) and the second smallest standard deviation. This comparison demonstrates the advantage of our algorithm in clustering accuracy. As to the observation that the SPRG algorithm performs better than our algorithm evidently on Thyroid and Wine datasets, we discuss

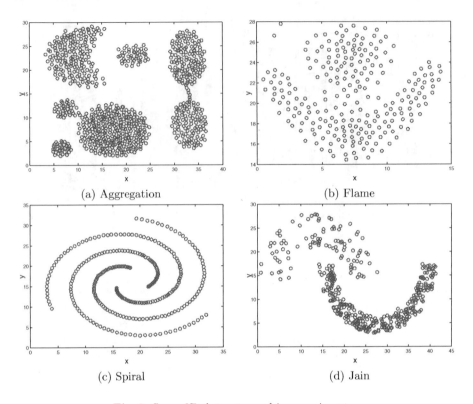

(a) Aggregation

(b) Flame

(c) Spiral

(d) Jain

Fig. 3. Some 2D datasets used in experiments.

the reason as follows. The SPRG algorithm belongs to spectral clustering, and its contribution lies in building a robust affinity graph for clustering. Noticing that NCuts as a spectral clustering algorithm performs much worse than SPRG on these two datasets, the good results of SPRG should be attributed to the specially designed affinity graph.

4.3   Discussions

Similar to many existing clustering algorithms, our algorithm involves some parameters, including the number of clusters, $MinPts$ and Eps, which are inherited from the DBSCAN and DP algorithms. In this paper we assume that the number of clusters are pre-determined by user, and we discuss the other two parameters as follows. We haven't been able to find a method to determine the optimal values for $MinPts$ and Eps automatically, and these two parameters must be tuned in experiments. Intuitively, tuning these two parameters separately for each dataset is able to generate better results than those reported in our experiments. However, in order to reduce the cost of tuning, we have tried to find a fixed $MinPts$ and a fixed Eps for *all* datasets. These fixed parameters may not be optimal for each individual dataset, but they generate the best

Table 1. Comparison of clustering results (NMI).

	k-means	DSets	NCuts	AP	SPRG	[18]	Ours
Aggregation	0.83	0.92	**0.98**	0.87	0.68	0.89	0.93
Compound	0.69	0.82	0.76	0.81	0.62	0.92	**0.94**
D31	0.91	0.92	**0.97**	0.86	0.90	0.67	0.96
Flame	0.42	0.60	0.93	0.58	0.23	0.90	**0.97**
Jain	0.36	0.52	0.22	0.51	0.46	0.87	**0.98**
Pathbased	0.55	0.76	**0.88**	0.60	0.30	0.82	0.83
R15	0.93	0.97	**0.99**	0.99	0.96	0.91	0.99
Spiral	0.00	0.56	0.23	0.53	0.00	0.66	**0.82**
Breast	0.74	0.73	0.19	**0.78**	**0.78**	0.54	0.74
Glass	0.36	0.23	0.22	0.45	0.38	0.37	**0.47**
Iris	0.71	0.76	0.61	**0.90**	0.72	0.60	**0.90**
Thyroid	0.41	0.44	0.23	0.42	**0.84**	0.42	0.56
Wdbc	**0.62**	0.37	0.38	0.57	0.55	0.44	0.58
Wine	0.82	0.68	0.46	0.79	**0.87**	0.37	0.72
Yeast	0.27	**0.29**	0.15	0.26	0.21	0.08	0.23
mean	0.58	0.64	0.55	0.66	0.57	0.63	0.78
std	0.27	0.23	0.34	0.21	0.29	0.26	0.23

overall results. We further determine Eps as the distance between a cluster center and its $2 * MinPts$-th nearest neighbor, so that a medium number of data points are used in density estimation. Therefore we are left only one parameter $MinPts$. With the 15 datasets introduced above, we test different values of $MinPts$ from 2 to 10, and obtain the clustering results shown in Fig. 4(a) and (b). Here we show the results in two subfigures to differentiate between different datasets more clearly.

From Fig. 4(a) and (b) we observe that in the range [3, 6], the variance of $MinPts$ has small influence on clustering results with most of datasets, except for Jain and Spiral datasets, and larger values of $MinPts$ rarely improve the clustering results further. On Wine and Wdbc datasets there is a slight performance improvement from $MinPts = 3$ to $MinPts = 4$, and on Wine, Thyroid and Flame datasets we observe an evident decrease in clustering quality from $MinPts = 4$ to larger values. While $MinPts = 4$ generates the worst result on Spiral, it also performs the best on Jain. All these observations together indicate that $MinPts = 4$ is a suitable option for a fixed value of this parameter. In fact, Fig. 4(c) shows that the average result on the 15 datasets reaches the peak at $MinPts = 4$, and this value is also the same as the recommended one in the original DBSCAN paper [12]. Therefore in our algorithm we fix $MinPts$ to be 4 to avoid parameter tuning. As to why the variance of $MinPts$ has a large influence on results on Spiral, Jain and Flame datasets, our opinion is that this is resulted

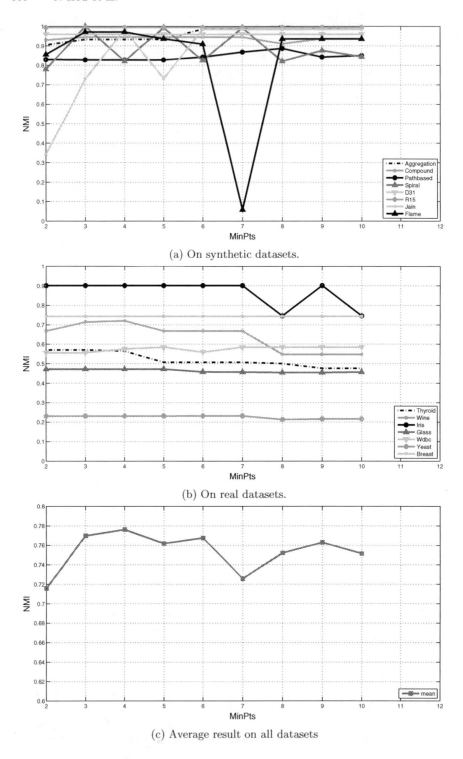

(a) On synthetic datasets.

(b) On real datasets.

(c) Average result on all datasets

Fig. 4. Influence of the *MinPts* parameter on our algorithm.

by the special structure of these datasets shown in Fig. 3(b), (c) and (d). The Spiral and Jain datasets have very special and non-spherical shapes, which make the density estimation sensitive to the number of used data points. With respect to the Flame dataset, its two clusters are composed to even-distributed data and the border between two clusters are not distinct. This may be one reason that this dataset experiences a drastic performance degradation at $MinPts = 7$.

In this paper we propose to combine the merits of DBSCAN and DP to achieve better clustering results, and experimental results do show that our algorithm is able to improve the clustering results. However, the combination of two algorithms leads to larger computation load, as in extracting each cluster we run both DBSCAN and DP clustering steps. In future work, our plan is to make full use of existing calculation results to reduce the computation load. As both DBSCAN and DP involves a large amount of distance calculation, density calculation and finding of nearest neighbors, it is possible to do these calculations only once and therefore avoid repetitive calculation.

Finally, we notice that in our experiments most of synthetic datasets are composed of clusters of even density and are suitable to be clustered by density based algorithms. Therefore our algorithm is favored in clustering with these datasets. However, with the 7 real datasets which are not constructed for density based algorithms, our algorithm performs the best on 2 datasets (Glass and Iris) and second-best on 3 datasets (Breast, Thyroid and Wdbc). Even on the remaining 2 datasets (Wine and Yeast), the differences between our results and the best ones are not large. We believe these comparisons show that our algorithm works well for not only even-density clusters, but also clusters of other types. In our opinion, the reason of the good performance of our algorithm is as follows. Our algorithm is proposed to combine the merits of DBSCAN and DP. The DBSCAN is a typical density based clustering algorithm, and it is effective in clustering datasets where the clusters are composed of evenly distributed data points. The DP algorithm groups data points into clusters following a large-density-first order, and it is suitable to cluster datasets where clusters are of Gaussian-like distribution. Consequently, our algorithm is effective for both even-density and Gaussian-distribution clusters. Considering that in many datasets the cluster distribution belongs to one of these two types or the mixture of two types, it is no strange that our algorithm performs well in clustering these datasets.

5   Conclusions

Motivated by the complementary properties of the DBSCAN and density peak algorithms, we present a robust clustering algorithm by combining these two algorithms. In the first step cluster centers are detected with the density peak algorithm. We then use the cluster centers as the seeds of DBSCAN clustering and determine the parameters of DBSCAN for each cluster adaptively. Finally, the clusters from DBSCAN are expanded with the DP algorithm, where the border data points of small density are included into clusters. By making use of the merits of the density peak algorithm, our algorithm is able to solve two major problems of DBSCAN, i.e., one set of fixed parameters do not work well with clusters of varied densities, and border data points of small density may be treated as noises. In the meanwhile, by adding DBSCAN clustering between the two steps of DP algorithm, our algorithm is less influenced by the inaccuracy of cluster center identification. In experiments, our algorithm outperforms DBSCAN and density peak algorithm on most of adopted datasets, and it also compares favorably to several commonly used clustering algorithms. These results show that our algorithm is effective in improving the clustering results.

Our algorithm depends on the DP algorithm to detect cluster centers, which are then used to determine the parameters of DBSCAN. However, we have found that the cluster centers detected by DP are not accurate in some cases. As a result, the DBSCAN parameters and then the clustering results are influenced. In the future work, we plan to explore better methods to detect large-density regions as seeds for DBSCAN.

Acknowledgement. This work is supported in part by the National Natural Science Foundation of China under Grant No. 61473045, and by the Natural Science Foundation of Liaoning Province under Grant No. 20170540013.

References

1. Achtert, E., Bohm, C., Kroger, P.: Deli-clu: boosting robustness, completeness, usability, and efficiency of hierarchical clustering by a closest pair ranking. In: International Conference on Knowledge Discovery and Data Mining, pp. 119–128 (2006)
2. Ankerst, M., Breunig, M.M., Kriegel, H.P., Sander, J.: Optics: Ordering points to identify the clustering structure. In: ACM SIGMOD International Conference on Management of Data, pp. 49–60 (1999). https://doi.org/10.1145/304182.304187
3. Bai, L., Cheng, X., Liang, J., Shen, H., Guo, Y.: Fast density clustering strategies based on the k-means algorithm. Pattern Recogn. **71**, 375–386 (2017). https://doi.org/10.1016/j.patcog.2017.06.023
4. Bansal, N., Blum, A., Chawla, S.: Correlation clustering. Mach. Learn. **56**(1–3), 89–113 (2004). https://doi.org/10.1023/B:MACH.0000033116.57574.95
5. Brendan, J.F., Delbert, D.: Clustering by passing messages between data points. Science **315**, 972–976 (2007). https://doi.org/10.1126/science.1136800
6. Chang, H., Yeung, D.Y.: Robust path-based spectral clustering. Pattern Recogn. **41**(1), 191–203 (2008). https://doi.org/10.1016/j.patcog.2007.04.010
7. Chen, Y., Tang, S., Bouguil, N., Wang, C., Du, J., Li, H.: A fast clustering algorithm based on pruning unnecessary distance computations in dbscan for high-dimensional data. Pattern Recogn. **83**, 375–387 (2018). https://doi.org/10.1016/j.patcog.2018.05.030
8. Cheng, Y.: Mean shift, mode seeking, and clustering. IEEE Trans. Pattern Anal. Mach. Intell. **17**(8), 790–799 (1995). https://doi.org/10.1109/34.400568
9. Comaniciu, D., Peter, M.: Mean shift: a robust approach toward feature space analysis. IEEE Trans. Pattern Anal. Mach. Intell. **24**(5), 603–619 (2002). https://doi.org/10.1109/34.1000236
10. Daszykowski, M., Walczak, B., Massart, D.L.: Looking for natural patterns in data: Part 1. density-based approach. Chemometr. Intell. Lab. Syst. **56**(2), 83–92 (2001). https://doi.org/10.1016/s0169-7439(01)00111-3

11. Dong, S., Liu, J., Liu, Y., Zeng, L., Xu, C., Zhou, T.: Clustering based on grid and local density with priority-based expansion for multi-density data. Inf. Sci. **468**, 103–116 (2018). https://doi.org/10.1016/j.ins.2018.08.018

12. Ester, M., Kriegel, H.P., Sander, J., Xu, X.W.: A density-based algorithm for discovering clusters in large spatial databases with noise. In: International Conference on Knowledge Discovery and Data Mining, pp. 226–231 (1996)

13. Ferone, A., Maratea, A.: Integrating rough set principles in the graded possibilistic clustering. Inf. Sci. **477**, 148–160 (2019). https://doi.org/10.1016/j.ins.2018.10.038

14. Fu, L., Medico, E.: Flame, a novel fuzzy clustering method for the analysis of dna microarray data. BMC Bioinform. **8**(1), 1–17 (2007). https://doi.org/10.1186/1471-2105-8-3

15. Gao, H., Nie, F., Li, X., Huang, H.: Multi-view subspace clustering. In: IEEE International Conference on Computer Vision, pp. 4238–4246 (2015). https://doi.org/10.1109/ICCV.2015.482

16. Gionis, A., Mannila, H., Tsaparas, P.: Clustering aggregation. ACM Trans. Knowl. Discov. Data **1**(1), 1–30 (2007). https://doi.org/10.1145/1217299.1217303

17. Hinnerberg, A., Keim, D.: An efficient approach to clustering large multimedia databases with noise. In: International Conference on Knowledge Discovery and Data Mining, pp. 58–65 (1998)

18. Hou, J., Gao, H., Li, X.: DSets-DBSCAN: a parameter-free clustering algorithm. IEEE Trans. Image Process. **25**(7), 3182–3193 (2016). https://doi.org/10.1109/TIP.2016.2559803

19. Hou, J., Gao, H., Li, X.: Feature combination via clustering. IEEE Trans. Neural Networks Learn. Syst. **29**(4), 896–907 (2018). https://doi.org/10.1109/TNNLS.2016.2645883

20. Hou, J., Liu, W.: Clustering based on dominant set and cluster expansion. In: Pacific-Asia Conference on Knowledge Discovery and Data Mining, pp. 76–87 (2017)

21. Hou, J., Liu, W.: Parameter independent clustering based on dominant sets and cluster merging. Inf. Sci. **405**, 1–17 (2017). https://doi.org/10.1016/j.ins.2017.04.006

22. Hou, J., Liu, W.: A parameter independent clustering framework. IEEE Trans. Industr. Inf. **13**(4), 1825–1832 (2017). https://doi.org/10.1109/TII.2017.2656909

23. Jain, A.K., Law, M.H.C.: Data clustering: a user's dilemma. In: International Conference on Pattern Recognition and Machine Intelligence, pp. 1–10 (2005)

24. Kumar, K.M., Reddy, A.R.M.: A fast dbscan clustering algorithm by accelerating neighbor searching using groups method. Pattern Recogn. **58**, 39–48 (2016). https://doi.org/10.1016/j.patcog.2016.03.008

25. Li, C., You, C., Vidal, R.: Structured sparse subspace clustering: a joint affinity learning and subspace clustering framework. IEEE Trans. Image Process. **26**(6), 2988–3001 (2017). https://doi.org/10.1109/TIP.2017.2691557

26. Li, J., Wang, C., Li, P., Lai, J.: Discriminative metric learning for multi-view graph partitioning. Pattern Recogn. **75**, 199–213 (2018). https://doi.org/10.1016/j.patcog.2017.06.012

27. Li, Q., Liu, W., Li, L.: Affinity learning via a diffusion process for subspace clustering. Pattern Recogn. **84**, 39–50 (2018). https://doi.org/10.1016/j.patcog.2018.07.002

28. Liu, R., Wang, H., Yu, X.: Shared-nearest-neighbor-based clustering by fast search and find of density peaks. Inf. Sci. **450**, 200–226 (2018). https://doi.org/10.1016/j.ins.2018.03.031

29. von Luxburg, U.: A tutorial on spectral clustering. Stat. Comput. **17**(4), 395–416 (2007). https://doi.org/10.1007/s11222-007-9033-z

30. Mequanint, E.Z., Pelillo, M.: Interactive image segmentation using constrained dominant sets. In: European Conference on Computer Vision, pp. 278–294 (2016)

31. Ng, A., Jordan, M., Weiss, Y.: On spectral clustering: analysis and an algorithm. In: Advances in Neural Information Processing Systems, pp. 849–856 (2002)

32. Pavan, M., Pelillo, M.: Dominant sets and pairwise clustering. IEEE Trans. Pattern Anal. Mach. Intell. **29**(1), 167–172 (2007). https://doi.org/10.1109/TPAMI.2007.250608

33. Qiu, T., Li, C., Li, Y.: D-NND: a hierarchical density clustering method via nearest neighbor descent. In: International Conference on Pattern Recognition, pp. 1414–1419 (2018). https://doi.org/10.1109/ICPR.2018.8545142

34. Rodriguez, A., Laio, A.: Clustering by fast search and find of density peaks. Science **344**, 1492–1496 (2014). https://doi.org/10.1126/science.1242072

35. Shi, J., Malik, J.: Normalized cuts and image segmentation. IEEE Trans. Pattern Anal. Mach. Intell. **22**(8), 167–172 (2000). https://doi.org/10.1109/34.868688

36. Tripodi, R., Pelillo, M.: A game-theoretic approach to word sense disambiguation. Comput. Linguist. **43**(1), 31–70 (2017)

37. Vascon, S., Mequanint, E.Z., Cristani, M., Hung, H., Pelillo, M., Murino, V.: Detecting conversational groups in images and sequences: a robust game-theoretic approach. Comput. Vis. Image Underst. **143**, 11–24 (2016). https://doi.org/10.1016/j.cviu.2015.09.012

38. Veenman, C.J., Reinders, M., Backer, E.: A maximum variance cluster algorithm. IEEE Trans. Pattern Anal. Mach. Intell. **24**(9), 1273–1280 (2002). https://doi.org/A maximum variance cluster algorithm

39. Yu, J., Chaomurilige, C., Yang, M.S.: On convergence and parameter selection of the EM and DA-EM algorithms for gaussian mixtures. Pattern Recogn. **77**, 188–203 (2018). https://doi.org/10.1016/j.patcog.2017.12.014

40. Zahn, C.T.: Graph-theoretical methods for detecting and describing gestalt clusters. IEEE Trans. Comput. **20**(1), 68–86 (1971). https://doi.org/10.1109/t-c.1971.223083

41. Zhang, H., Ren, P.: Game theoretic hypergraph matching for multi-source image correspondences. Pattern Recogn. Lett. (2016). https://doi.org/10.1016/j.patrec.2016.07.011

42. Zhong, C., Miao, D., Fránti, P.: Minimum spanning tree based split-and-merge: a hierarchical clustering method. Inf. Sci. **181**(16), 3397–3410 (2011). https://doi.org/10.1016/j.ins.2011.04.013

43. Zhu, X., Loy, C.C., Gong, S.: Constructing robust affinity graphs for spectral clustering. In: IEEE International Conference on Computer Vision and Pattern Recognition, pp. 1450–1457 (2014). https://doi.org/10.1109/cvpr.2014.188

Market Basket Analysis Using Boltzmann Machines

Mauricio A. Valle[1]([✉]) [iD] and Gonzalo A. Ruz[2] [iD]

[1] Facultad de Economía y Negocios, Universidad Finis Terrae, Santiago, Chile
mvalle@uft.cl
[2] Facultad de Ingeniería y Ciencias, Universidad Adolfo Ibáñez, Santiago, Chile

Abstract. In this paper we present a proposal to analyze market baskets using minimum spanning trees, based on couplings between products. The couplings are the result of a learning process with Boltzmann machines from transactional databases, in which the interaction between the different offers of the market are modeled as a network composed by magnetic dipoles of spins that can be in two states ($+1$ or -1). The results offer a systematic way to explore potential courses of action to determine promotions and offers for the retail manager.

Keywords: Boltzmann learning · Market basket · Ising model · Minimum spanning tree

1 Introduction

The Market Basket Analysis (MBA) is the examination and discovery of combinations of products and services that customers buy most frequently [1]. The idea is to find associations between different market offerings from the hundreds or thousands of transactions that buyers make in a given time. For example, typically in a grocery store, the manager would want to know if a particular product tends to be sold with something else. This type of knowledge is useful for establishing promotion and product bundle strategies.

The discovery of these kinds of associations has been limited to the use of *associations rules* which are generated from the Apriori Algorithm [8] and other more modern variants (see for example: [2–6]) that overcome the problem of the large number of rules that the algorithm generates, and that reduce the computational cost of rules mining by: avoiding scanning the database repeatedly, adding additional restrictions to the rule pattern structure, and through parallelization methods [7].

The popularity of the association rules may be due to the ease of their interpretation at a micro level, but they do not deliver as a result a comprehensive

The authors would like to thank CONICYT-Chile under grant Fondecyt 11160072 (M.A.V.) and Basal (CONICYT)-CMM, Fondecyt 1180706 (G.A.R.) for financially supporting this research.

I. V. Tetko et al. (Eds.): ICANN 2019, LNCS 11730, pp. 611–623, 2019.
https://doi.org/10.1007/978-3-030-30490-4_49

or global model of all inter-relationships of all the available market offer. In this sense, a network approach seems to be useful if the analyst wants to have a more systemic view of the purchasing behavior based on the relationships between the elements that make up this interconnected network. For example, using a network graph mining is an alternative to display large volumes of information by applying filters with different levels of thresholds to intuitively understand the relationships between products [10]. Using a network approach, it has also been possible to establish a methodology that simplifies the search for product sets that have a high level of co-occurrence among consumers, using minimum spanning trees to reveal the interconnectivity of products with the highest level of co-occurrence [11].

Motivated by this last line of research, we also use a network approach, but we take a step further, not only in analyzing the properties of a network of products but also in using a Boltzmann machine that allows us to learn from the relationships between different market offerings. We assume that each element of the market offer is part of a complex system with intricate interrelationships, which are determined by the revealed preferences of the buyers. Thus, transaction data from many customers is taken as input to initiate a learning process resulting in a network of couplings. The network of couplings contains all the information that determines how a certain product relates to any other product that is part of the market offer. This network is equivalent to a complete network where the magnitude of the weights of each edge quantifies the level and sign of the node-node interaction.

The strongest links carry a particular significance in the network of couplings. For example, a large magnitude positive coupling between two products in our model implies a high probability of activation of those two products simultaneously. Conversely, a large negative coupling implies a high probability that while one product is active, the other is not. In this way, the strongest links tell us a lot about the purchasing behavior of consumers. It should be noted that this is not the same as computing the correlation or the probability that pair of products will be carried at the same time in a market basket. Our approach considers the discovery of the joint probability distribution of the states of a system, i.e., the probability that a particular market basket will occur. In this process, the model is able to estimate these coupling parameters that are part of the network of couplings.

To reveal the role of the strongest links in the system, we use a minimum spanning tree (MST) over the network of couplings. By avoiding weak or negative links, the MST determines a particular cluster of edges that represent the backbone of the coupling network. In this way, we can propose a simple iterative approach of product clustering that ensures us sets of high-frequency purchase products, than could serve as a recommendation system for promotion activities.

2 Ising Model and Minimum Spanning Tree

One problem with the MBA is that the possible number of combinations of items conforming a market basket is very large. For example, a convenience grocery store would carry 2000 stock keeping units (SKUs). If on average a customer buys 10 SKUs, the total number of possible baskets with 10 products would be approximately 2.76^{26}. From this set of baskets, finding which are the most attractive for buyers is already a difficult task, even more so if from these baskets, we try to discover the strongest association relationships between products.

To deal with this problem, we model the MBA as a collective purchasing system resembling the Ising magnetic system [18]. Each part of this system is composed of microscopic variables or spins s_i that have a certain probability of interacting with other spins. Spins can take values of -1 or 1. To be more precise we describe a market basket as a vector $\mathbf{s} = (s_1, ..., s_N)$ where N is the number of spins or elements of the market offer (e.g., SKUs, or aggregated levels of categories or types of products).

The energy $H = H(\mathbf{s})$ describes the system in a configuration $\mathbf{s}$. In other words, the macroscopic state of the system is defined by the values of the local spin magnetizations. This energy of the system as a function of the spins is:

$$H = -\sum_{\{i,k\}} J_{ik} s_i s_k - \sum h_i s_i \tag{1}$$

For MBA purposes, energy H is a proxy of the utility function $U(\mathbf{s})$ [9], in which $U(\mathbf{s}) = -H(\mathbf{s})$ with pairwise and idiosyncratic parts. The expression $\{i, k\}$ indicates that the summation is made on the nearby neighbors. J_{ik} are the values of the interactions between spins and h_i is the external magnetic field. When $J_{ik} > 0$, there is a ferromagnetic interaction, which causes the spin i and k stores to be oriented in the same direction. When $J_{ik} < 0$, then one gets antiferromagnetic orientation, that is, two spins i and k tend to be in opposite orientations.

Unlike the spin glass studied in statistical physics where the connections are based on regular lattices, the collective purchasing system is equivalent to a complete network, or a *network of couplings*, that is, each spin is connected to the rest of the $N - 1$ spins through the parameters J_{ik}, resembling the infinite-ranged version of the Edwards-Anderson model [19] of the spin glass proposed by Sherrigton and Kirkpatrick [20].

We would like to know the probability $P(\mathbf{s})$ that a particular configuration $\mathbf{s}$ is found in the system. This probability can be written in the form of the Ising distribution:

$$P(\mathbf{s}) = \frac{1}{Z} e^{-H(\mathbf{s})} \tag{2}$$

where Z is the partition function,

$$Z = \sum_{\{s_i\}} e^{-H(\mathbf{s})} \tag{3}$$

and the summation is running over the 2^N points of phase space.

The problem of finding $P(\mathbf{s})$ is hard in general and it corresponds to the inverse problem of inferring the model parameters J_{ik}. For N spins, the number of parameters to infer will be $N(N - 1)/2$.

To find the parameters, we use Boltzmann learning algorithm [12], following the same procedure for transactional datasets [13]. The algorithm is initialized with an initial guess of the parameters, and then in the negative learning phase, the averages and pair correlations are calculated. The parameters are then recalculated according to the contrastive divergence formula [16]. The averages and pair correlations are calculated according to a Metropolis-hasting simulation process under the Ising distribution.

Once the coupling parameters have been found, we have the matrix of couplings, which can be represented as a complete network of interactions among spins, that we call coupling network. This information is useful to understand the behavior of the system, similar to what would be a magnetic lattice system, with the difference that the network is not regular. Similar to a spin glass, we have a kind of a disordered system in which the elements can interact in a ferromagnetic or antiferromagnetic way with a certain probability.

To describe a disordered physical system, it would be necessary to study the physical quantities or critical exponents that depend on some general features of the system. This is beyond the scope of this paper, however, it has been found that minimum spanning trees (MST) is a universal property of the system since their geometry is not altered by the level of existing disorder [14].

The MST of a graph G with vertex V, edges E and with a cost l_e, is assigned to each edge $e \in E$. In our case, we find the MST over the network of couplings, which is equivalent to a subset of G edges that connects all the vertices with no cycles. Such a tree exists because the network is connected. So the MST T is a spanning tree such that the sum of all the costs of its edges, $l(T)$:

$$l(T) = \sum_{e \in T} l_e \tag{4}$$

is minimized over the set of all spanning trees on G. In disordered systems, the path of an MST is equivalent to the path in which the energy barriers are the smallest [14,15]. In this way, we can take advantage of this interpretation to say that the edges of the MST over the coupling network have an energy e_{ik}. Thus, the total energy is the sum of all the bonds that shape the MST:

$$E^{mst} = \sum_{ik \in T} e_{ik} \tag{5}$$

This value is unique to each system. Since the paths in the MST are those in which energy barriers are minimal, we can say that the MST offers us a way in which different elements of the system can be accessed at minimal cost. For example, given the MST T, if we want the energy barrier to access a set of vertex $v \in V$, say, E_v^{mst}, it would simply be:

$$E_v^{mst} = \sum_{i,k \in v} e_{ik} \tag{6}$$

3   Model

The probability of a given state **s**, $P(\mathbf{s})$ depends on energy H. Since we are interested in the interaction between the spins of the system, we define the energy of couplings as the energetic contribution of energy due to that interaction as between the spins that are at v:

$$E_v^c(\mathbf{s}) = - \sum_{\{i,k\}} J_{ik} s_i s_k \tag{7}$$

Thus, low level coupling energies E_v^c indicate stable system configurations (or ground states). This gives us information on those system states that are most likely, or most useful to the consumer. If we combine this information $E_v^c(\mathbf{s})$ with the minimum energy barriers E_v^{mst}, it would be possible to discern what changes can be made to a particular system configuration (e.g. a minimum energy one) that will lead to a more likely state. A transition from one configuration to another occurs in such a way that the energy involved is minimal.

Associated to an initial configuration $\mathbf{s}^i$ with a set v of active nodes and with cardinality $n(v) = K$, we have the energy of coupling $E_{\mathbf{s}^i}^c$ and the energy barrier $E_{\mathbf{s}^i}^{mst}$. We want to find a configuration $\mathbf{s}$ with a set v' of active spins in which $v \subset v'$, with cardinality $n(v') = K+1$, with coupling energy and energy barrier $E_{\mathbf{s}}^c$ and $E_{\mathbf{s}}^{mst}$ respectively, such that $E_{\mathbf{s}}^c + E_{\mathbf{s}}^{mst}$ is minimum.

This process of minimization is equivalent to the search for configurations that increase the size of market baskets from an initial basket to a final one, sacrificing utility to the minimum, but whose transition from one to the other is the least costly in terms of energy. The possible universe of solutions of $\mathbf{s}$ to minimize E is huge, however, given that the MST is the path of minimum energetic barriers, the spectrum of possible solutions is reduced considerably to only testing those solutions $\mathbf{s}$ in which $v' \in T$.

The MST offers the possibility of aggregating products to the cluster at the minimum energy cost, however, this does not ensures that the cluster is at the same time a basket of minimum coupling energy. It can happen that the cluster with $K - 1$ products is one of minimum energy, but the aggregation of a new product will make that the cluster with K products is not minimal basket in terms of energy, which could lead to a violation of transitivity. For example, the combination of products A and B represent a cluster of minimum energy, as well as the combination of product B and C, but the cluster with the combination of the three products will not necessarily be of minimum energy. To deal with this problem, a simple solution is to minimize $\alpha E_{\mathbf{s}}^c + (1 - \alpha)E_{\mathbf{s}}^{mst}$. So, when $\alpha = 1$, we give priority to finding clusters of minimum energy (but not at minimum costs), and if $\alpha = 0$ we find clusters of lower energy cost (but not at minimum coupling energy).

4   Method

4.1   Data

To show an application of the proposed model, we take a real database of a national supermarket chain. The data contains 42077 transactions of a branch located in Santiago, Chile. The records indicate the customer's id, and the shopping basket, that is, the set of products that the customer bought during their visit to the supermarket. To simplify the analysis, we took the twenty-five subcategories of products with the highest level of turnover. In this way, a market basket of each purchase is represented by a vector s of length 25, with values 1 or -1 indicating whether the subcategory is present or not respectively its the basket.

4.2   Learning

We inferred the couplings parameters of the Ising model using 400 steps of the Boltzmann learning with a decreasing learning rate of $\nu = 0.8$ and a decay of 0.0001. In each step, the means and pair correlations were obtained from a Metropolis-Hasting process using 40000 steps. With this number of steps of the Boltzmann machine we have empirically ensured a convergence of the parameters with an RMSE of less than 10^{-3}.

5   Results

5.1   Distribution of the Couplings

It is worth mentioning that the mean of the inferred couplings is negative equal to 0.006. Figure 1 shows the histogram of the couplings. A proportion close to 39% of the couplings are negative and the remaining 61% are positive ones. This shows that the system is disordered, with a tendency to have most pairwise relationships anti-ferromagnetic, i.e., pairs of products tend not to be present simultaneously in the same shopping basket.

5.2   Consistency

First, it is necessary to test that the Equation model 2 correctly reproduces empirical data. For this, we compare the means and pairwise correlations of the real data with the data sampled with Metropolis-Hasting using the inferred magnetizations and couplings.

As shown in Fig. 2, the recovery of the spins orientation $\langle s_i \rangle$ (which correspond to the frequency of purchase of the products) has been satisfactory, also, the pairwise connections $\langle s_i s_j \rangle$ and the two-body averages (equivalent to the correlation between products) C_{ij}. The root mean square error (RMSE) for two-body connections, pairwise connections and one-body averages were: 0.000939 ($\rho = 0.999$), 0.0.00062 ($\rho = 0.998$) and 0.00058 ($\rho = 0.996$) respectively.

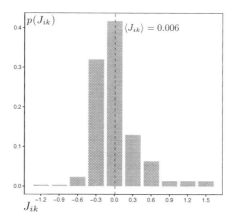

Fig. 1. Histogram of the couplings inferred by Boltzmann's machine. The mean of the couplings is $\langle J_{ik} \rangle = 0.006$

5.3   Network of Couplings and MST

Figure 3**A** shows the array of couplings J_{ik} found by the Boltzmann learning using the real dataset. It is clear that most interactions between subcategories are negative while a few are positive, which means a frustrated interaction system [17], similar to what happens in physical spin glass [18]. Although this information is interesting because it describes the behavior of the collective purchasing system, it is not useful to find combinations of products that are susceptible to promotion strategies or incentives.

The next step is to find the MST over the network of couplings. However, to find the MST, it is necessary to take into consideration that a positive coupling implies a complementary relationship between products (if product i is in the basket, then the product k will also tend to be present), while a negative sign coupling implies a substitution relationship between products (if the product i is in the basket, then the product k will tend not to be present). To accomplish this, it is necessary to carry out a proper transformation of the couplings in such a way that the original order of the couplings is preserved. This transformation converts the values of the couplings into positive magnitudes, representing a proxy of distance between vertices, in such a way that with these values they serve as input to the Prim's algorithm to find the MST.

Figure 3**B** shows the MST found. It is easy to see that some of the strongest links between nodes are those that join subcategory 80 (vitaminized noodles) with subcategory 11 (rice grade 2), 78 (flavored noodles) and 7 (vegetable oil), etc. In the next section, we see how to look for interesting market baskets according to the information of minimum distance links and coupling energies.

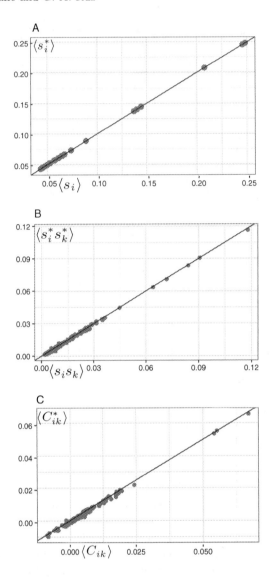

Fig. 2. Scatterplots of the following observables: **A**- one-body averages $\langle s_i s_j \rangle$, **B**- pairwise connections $\langle s_i s_j \rangle$ and, **C**- two-body connections $C_{ij} = \langle s_i s_j \rangle - \langle s_i \rangle \langle s_j \rangle$. Empirical and estimated values on x and y-axes respectively. $\{\bullet^*\}$ are the estimated observables computed from the Metropolis-Hasting sampling.

5.4   Looking for Interesting Market Baskets

To exemplify the usefulness of the methodology, let us begin by choosing an initial state $\mathbf{s}^i$. We could use any state as a starting point, however, to describe the growth process of the cluster, we start with only one active product $(n(v) = 1)$.

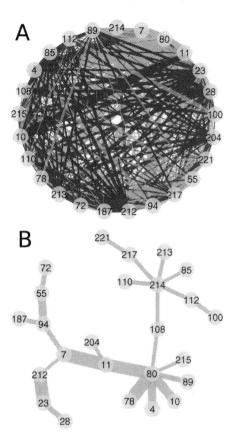

Fig. 3. Graph networks of couplings found. Blue and orange colors of the edges correspond to negative and positive interaction strengths respectively. In **A** the network of couplings. In **B** the minimum spanning tree. In this figure we draw the weight (greater thickness, greater magnitude) and signs of the original edges (blue is negative and orange is positive). (Color figure online)

To select this product we select the one with the highest purchase frequency at the supermarket that corresponds to vitaminized noodles, so, $s^i = \{80\}$. From this vertex, we look for another one. The next vector v' of active vertices provides the minimum increase of energy and at the same time go through the lowest level of energy barrier that must be overcome to cross the MST of v to v'. The result will be to increase the cardinality of the vector achieving $s = \{80, 78\}$. That is to say, the easiest way to begin to cross the MST from 80, is to go to 78 (flavored noodles). At the same time, this state is the lowest possible energy configuration so it ensures a high purchase frequency.

We can repeat this same process several times. The order in which the products appear is important because it defines the way in which they are related. In Fig. 4 we can see the path by several vertices of the MST in the plane E_v^c-E_v^{mst}.

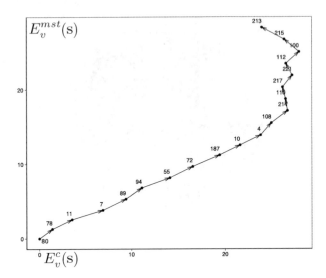

Fig. 4. The path of energies on the plane $E_v^c; E_v^{mst}$ starting from vertex 80 and using $\alpha = 0.5$.

This path describes the best aggregation of products from one initial state to the next, in terms of coupling energy and energy barriers on the MST. For example, if the retail manager wanted to design a special bundle promotion package with product 80, the best way to do it is through product 78. And if he wanted to extend the size of the promotion, the next product to include would be product 11, and so on.

It is interesting to note first, that as the number of products added to the cluster grows, the coupling energy decreases, which means that the probability of activation of the indicated spins increases. However, energy barriers are increasing due to the greater distance needed to cover more products. However, the cluster represents the most likely market basket with K products beginning the process from product 80.

Second, the energy gradient from vertex 80 to 214 (beaten yogurt) is constant. However, from this last vertex to 100 (natural milk 1L) the coupling energy does not vary too much, and only increases the energy barrier. This means that the probability of those states does not change too much, but the cost of adding more products does. Observing the MST, this behavior is related to the structure of the graph in which the vertex 108 seems to operate as a link between two large sub-trees of the MST.

Figure 5 shows three paths for different starting vertices. The black line is the original starting from node 80. If the starting point is now 72 (machine detergent powder) which is a leaf on the MST, it is possible to observe that the path at the beginning is totally different from the original (dark gold color line), however at iteration number 9, both paths become identical. This means that from this point on, promotion strategies should be the same. When starting

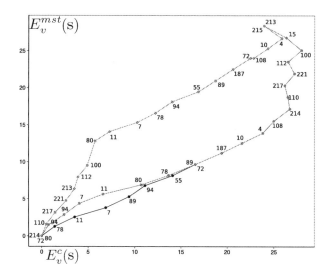

Fig. 5. Paths of energies starting from different vertexs using $\alpha = 0.5$. (Color figure online)

from vertex 214 (beaten yogurt) which is located on other sub-tree of the MST, we observe (dark orange line color) a totally different behavior, that seems to be more difficult to implement compared with the other because of the fast increase of barrier energies. This means that these products are weakly related to each other.

6 Conclusions

The spin glasses view of the purchase system considered in this study, is an approach completely different from the traditional task of finding association rules. In this proposal, we are able to find information about the conjoint probability distribution of all possible states of the system, ie., the market baskets.

The distribution of the inferred couplings indicates us that the collective system of purchases has similarities with spin glasses, a kind on material studied in condensed matter physics, in which particles can be related in a ferromagnetic or antiferromagnetic way. In the first case, the alignment of the moments of the particles occurs in the same direction, while in the second, the moments are aligned in opposite directions. Since many particles co-exist with both types of interactions, we are in the presence of a *disordered system*. This characteristic has important practical implications. In economic terms, it implies that certain products are complementary capacity, while others have substitute capacity. In the first case, the presence of one product in the market basket encourages the presence of another product, while in the second case, the presence of one product discourages the presence of another.

To find those complementary relationships between products in this disordered system, we use the universal property of MSTs to describe the complex inter-relationships. The MSTs are unique to each system and show the path that links each particle of the system with minimum energy, or in other words, show the path through each product at minimum cost.

In this paper, we have shown that the information of the coupling energy of a particular system state, and the link energy of the MST, offers us a guide to finding interesting market baskets, which describe a high probability of occurrence but also have low intervention cost. This approach is quite different from the traditional approach, which typically resorts to the well-known association rules as a classic tool of market basket analysis and whose disadvantage lies mainly in the high number of rules that the analyst must investigate, and the difficulty in observing the inter-relationships between different products in the absence of a systemic view. On the other hand, our approach allows us a more unified understanding of the inter-relationships between different products and a successive approximation of how attractive market baskets can be generated.

Acknowledgements. The authors would like to thank CONICYT-Chile under grant Fondecyt 11160072 (M.A.V.) and Basal (CONICYT)-CMM, Fondecyt 1180706 (G.A.R.) for financially supporting this research. We thank Professor Sergio Rica for his early participation and help provided in this work.

References

1. Linoff, G.S., Berry, M.J.: Data Mining Techniques: For Marketing, Sales, and Customer Relationship Management, and Customer Relationship Management, 3rd edn. Wiley, New York (2011)
2. Yuan, X. An improved Apriori algorithm for mining association rules. In: AIP Conference Proceedings, vol. 1820, no. 1, pp. 1–6. AIP Publishing (2017). https://doi.org/10.1063/1.4977361
3. Sahoo, J., Das, A.K., Goswami, A.: An efficient approach for mining association rules from high utility itemsets. Expert Syst. Appl. **42**(13), 5754–5778 (2015). https://doi.org/10.1016/j.eswa.2015.02.051
4. Lin, K.C., Liao, I.E., Chen, Z.S.: An improved frequent pattern growth method for mining association rules. Expert Syst. Appl. **38**(5), 5154–5161 (2011). https://doi.org/10.1016/j.eswa.2010.10.047
5. Narvekar, M., Syed, S.F.: An optimized algorithm for association rule mining using FP tree. Procedia Comput. Sci. **45**, 101–110 (2015). https://doi.org/10.1016/j.procs.2015.03.097
6. Chiclana, F., Kumar, R., Mittal, M., Khari, M., Chatterjee, J.M., Baik, S.W.: ARM-AMO: an efficient association rule mining algorithm based on animal migration optimization. Knowl.-Based Syst. **154**, 68–80 (2018). https://doi.org/10.1016/j.knosys.2018.04.038
7. Kotsiantis, S., Kanellopoulos, D.: Association rules mining: a recent overview. GESTS Int. Trans. Comput. Sci. Eng. **32**(1), 71–82 (2006)
8. Agarwal, R., and Srikant, R.: Fast algorithms for mining association rules. In: Proceedings of the 20th International Conference of Very Large Data Bases, vol. 1225, pp. 487–499, Santiago (1994)

9. Bury, T.: Market structure explained by pairwise interactions. Physica A **392**(6), 1375–1385 (2013). https://doi.org/10.1016/j.physa.2012.10.046

10. Videla-Cavieres, I.F., Ríos, S.A.: Extending market basket analysis with graph mining techniques: a real case. Expert Syst. Appl. **41**(4), 1928–1936 (2014). https://doi.org/10.1016/j.eswa.2013.08.088

11. Valle, M.A., Ruz, G.A., Morrás, R.: Market basket analysis: complementing association rules with minimum spanning trees. Expert Syst. Appl. **97**, 146–162 (2018). https://doi.org/10.1016/j.eswa.2017.12.028

12. Ackley, D.H., Hinton, G.E., Sejnowski, T.J.: A learning algorithm for Boltzmann machines. Cogn. Sci. **9**(1), 147–169 (1985). https://doi.org/10.1016/S0364-0213(85)80012-4

13. Valle, M.A., Ruz, G.A., Rica, S.: Market basket analysis by solving the inverse Ising problem: discovering pairwise interaction strengths among products. Physica A **524**, 36–44 (2019). https://doi.org/10.1016/j.physa.2019.03.001

14. Dobrin, R., Duxbury, P.M.: Minimum spanning trees on random networks. Phys. Rev. Lett. **86**(22), 5076–5079 (2001). https://doi.org/10.1103/PhysRevLett.86.5076

15. Cieplak, M., Maritan, A., Banavar, J.R.: Invasion percolation and Eden growth: geometry and universality. Phys. Rev. Lett. **76**(20), 3754–3757 (1996). https://doi.org/10.1103/PhysRevLett.76.3754

16. Hinton, G.E.: Training products of experts by minimizing contrastive divergence. Neural Comput. **14**(8), 1771–1800 (2002). https://doi.org/10.1162/089976602760128018

17. Dotsenko, V.: An Introduction to the Theory of Spin Glasses and Neural Networks, 1st edn. World Scientific, Singapore (1995)

18. Stein, D. L.: Spin glasses: old and new complexity. In: AIP Conference Proceedings, vol. 1389, no. 1, pp. 965–968. AIP. Geneva, Switzerland (2011). https://doi.org/10.1063/1.3637770

19. Edwards, S.F., Anderson, P.W.: Theory of spin glasses. J. Phys. F: Metal Phys. **5**(5), 965–974 (1975). https://doi.org/10.1088/0305-4608/5/5/017

20. Sherrington, D., Kirkpatrick, S.: Solvable model of a spin-glass. Phys. Rev. Lett. **35**(26), 1792–1796 (1975). https://doi.org/10.1103/PhysRevLett.35.1792

Dimensionality Reduction for Clustering and Cluster Tracking of Cytometry Data

Givanna H. Putri[1]([✉]), Mark N. Read[2,3,4], Irena Koprinska[1],
Thomas M. Ashhurst[4,5], and Nicholas J. C. King[4,5]

[1] School of Computer Science, University of Sydney, Sydney, NSW 2006, Australia
{ghar1821,irena.koprinska}@sydney.edu.au
[2] Centre for Excellence in Advanced Food Enginomics, University of Sydney,
Sydney, NSW 2006, Australia
mark.read@sydney.edu.au
[3] School of Chemical and Biomolecular Engineering, University of Sydney,
Sydney, NSW 2006, Australia
[4] The Charles Perkins Centre, University of Sydney,
Sydney, NSW 2006, Australia
{thomas.ashhurst,nicholas.king}@sydney.edu.au
[5] Sydney Cytometry Facility and Discipline of Pathology, University of Sydney,
Sydney, NSW 2006, Australia

Abstract. Mass cytometry is a new high-throughput technology that is becoming a cornerstone in immunology and cell biology research. With technological advancement, the number of cellular characteristics cytometry can simultaneously quantify grows, making analysis increasingly computationally onerous. In this paper, we investigate the potential of dimensionality reduction techniques to ease computational burden in clustering cytometry data whilst minimally diminishing clustering performance. We explore 3 such techniques: Principal Component Analysis (PCA), Autoencoders (AE) and Uniform Manifold Approximation and Projection (UMAP). Thereafter we employ a recent clustering algorithm, *ChronoClust*, which clusters data at each time-point into cell populations and explicitly tracks them over time. We evaluate this approach through a 14-dimensional cytometry dataset describing the immune response to West Nile Virus over 8 days in mice. To obtain a broad sample of clustering performance, each of the four datasets (unreduced, PCA-, AE- and UMAP-reduced) is independently clustered 400 times, using 400 unique ChronoClust parameter value sets. We find that PCA and AE can reduce the computational expense whilst incurring a minimal degradation in clustering and cluster tracking performance.

Keywords: Autoencoder · Clustering · Cytometry ·
Dimensionality reduction · PCA · UMAP

© Springer Nature Switzerland AG 2019
I. V. Tetko et al. (Eds.): ICANN 2019, LNCS 11730, pp. 624–640, 2019.
https://doi.org/10.1007/978-3-030-30490-4_50

1   Introduction

Mass cytometry is a high-throughput technology that can simultaneously quantify over 45 distinct characteristics in each cell in a sample of millions, such as taken from the bone marrow or blood [4]. It is revolutionising cell biology and immunology, enabling study of how the immune response develops in combating disease. Such study is crucial for developing effective treatments.

Mass cytometry generates a large high-dimensional dataset for each biological sample processed, each typically corresponding to a single snapshot in time. Critical in cytometry analysis is the identification of (immune) cell populations in these snapshots and tracking their development over time. This task has traditionally been performed manually, through a process termed *gating*, wherein an expert examines numerous 2-dimensional density scatter plots of the data to find boundaries (gates) defining distinct cell populations [1]. This process is extremely subjective, time-consuming, and labour-intensive.

Various automated alternatives to manual gating, based on clustering, have been proposed [1]. Such methods proved sufficiently reliable and accurate for practical use, but none could track the temporal evolution of cell populations across time-points. Thus, we proposed *ChronoClust*, an integrated clustering and cluster tracking algorithm [19]. The high-dimensional nature of cytometry data can prove cumbersome for many clustering algorithms, even on high-performance computing platforms. One potential solution is to employ dimensionality reduction techniques and transform the high-dimensional data to a lower-dimensional representation that preserves its key characteristics [25]. In addition to alleviating computational burden, these techniques might also overcome other challenges in analysing high-dimensional data such as the curse of dimensionality or difficulties in visualisation and interpretation.

In this paper we investigate this strategy, using three dimensionality reduction methods: Principal Component Analysis (PCA), Autoencoder (AE) and Uniform Manifold Approximation and Projection (UMAP). PCA was selected as a well-studied, linear method. AE and UMAP are newer and promising non-linear methods, and we envisage they may hold advantages for complex real-world biological datasets, which are also more likely to be non-linear [25]. For our investigation we employ a real-world cytometry dataset that captures the immune response to West Nile Virus infection over 8 days in mice.

The contributions of this paper are as follows:

1. We highlight the computational bottleneck posed by high-throughput cytometry data for cluster and cluster tracking analysis, and propose dimensionality reduction techniques as a solution.
2. We outline a comprehensive evaluation framework to gauge the trade-off between reduced computational load and diminishing clustering performance, using 6 distinct performance metrics and the Latin Hypercube sampling scheme.

3. We assess the ability of 3 dimensionality reduction algorithms, the linear PCA and nonlinear AE and UMAP, to overcome the computational bottleneck, using a real-world cytometry dataset representing the immune response to a viral infection over 8 days. As a clustering algorithm we employ the recently proposed ChronoClust, which clusters the data from each time-point into cell populations, and tracks them over time. To ensure a broad capture of performance, we conduct the clustering 400 times using different parameter value sets. We find that PCA and AE can considerably reduce computational requirements, with minimal degradation in clustering and cluster tracking performance.

2   ChronoClust

ChronoClust is a density-based clustering and cluster tracking algorithm developed to quantify the development of the immune response [19]. It clusters each of a time-series of discrete datasets and tracks the clusters' developments over time. We provide a brief summary of its operation here, for further details see [19] and its open source implementation https://ghar1821.github.io/Chronoclust/.

ChronoClust comprises three phases of operation performed at each time-point in the time-series: first, data-points are summarised as MicroClusters (MCs); thereafter, MCs are collected into arbitrarily shaped clusters; finally clusters in the present time-point are related to those preceding them.

MCs are classified into three categories, *core*, *potential-core* (pcore), and *outlier* based on their *weight*. MCs can persist across time-points, and their weight represents a decaying count of data-points they have captured. MC categorisation is governed by parameters β and μ, both expressed in terms of the proportion of number of data-points in the time-point being processed. MCs are classified as *core-MC*, *pcore-MC* and *outlier-MC*, if their weights are $\geq \mu$, $\geq \beta\mu$ or $< \beta\mu$, respectively. At the beginning of each time-point, duration t since the preceding time-point, MC weights are reduced through multiplication by factor $d = 2^{-\lambda t}$, and may be re-classified. *Outlier-MCs* with weights $< o$ are deleted.

MCs assume either spherical or ellipsoid shape with maximum radius ϵ. This represents ChronoClust's subspace clustering functionality, wherein MCs retain narrower distributions of data in certain *preferred* dimensions. A dimension exhibits a narrow distribution if the amount of data variance in it is $\leq \delta$, and is given a preference weighting of κ instead of 1. The number of preferred dimensions allowed is restricted by parameter π.

The summarising of data-points as MCs is followed by clustering of MCs, wherein *core-* and *pcore-MCs* that are within distance of $\leq \upsilon$ are "daisy chained" to form clusters of arbitrary shape through the PreDeCon algorithm [7]. Clusters' temporal developments are then determined through two strategies: (1) their sharing of constituent MCs over time (tracking by 'lineage determination') and (2) spatial proximity of (potentially different) MCs over time (tracking by 'historical proximity').

3 Dimensionality Reduction Techniques

3.1 PCA

PCA is widely used for dimensionality reduction. It maximally captures the variance in a dataset with a minimal number of dimensions. This is done by identifying the directions in which the dataset expresses the greatest amount of variance. These directions (called principal components) are linear combinations of the original dimensions and form the axes of the reduced dimensionality space into which the data-points are projected [12]. The principal components are ordered by decreasing capture of variance, and dimensionality reduction stems from using only the first few.

PCA has been applied in numerous fields demonstrating its effectiveness in studying high-dimensional data. For instance, PCA was used to categorise and visualise gene expressions of breast tumour samples [20], analyse the phenotypic progression of Cytotoxic CD8+ T cells [18] and B cells [5], and investigate the importance of T helper 2 cytokines against gut helminthiases in humans [23].

While PCA has been widely used in analysing high dimensional data, its potential in facilitating clustering algorithms has not been fully investigated as yet. A study comparing the quality of the clustering of a PCA-reduced dataset against the full dataset was conducted by Yeung and Ruzzo [26]. They concluded that clustering the reduced dataset using k-means (with average-link initialisation [14]) and hierarchical average-link clustering algorithms may culminate in similar or higher quality clusters.

3.2 AE

An AE is a feed-forward neural network with an odd number of hidden layers [13,25]; for simplicity we describe AE with one hidden layer. The input and output layers have the same number of nodes, corresponding to the dimensionality of the original data. The hidden layer has a smaller number of nodes, corresponding to the reduced dimensionality. An AE network is trained to auto-associate, i.e. to minimise the error between the same input and output vector, typically with the stochastic gradient descent algorithm. The output activation of the hidden layer for a given input vector can be seen as a compressed representation of this input vector. If the activation functions are non-linear, the resulting mapping from the higher to lower dimensional space is also non-linear. The weights between the hidden and output layer can be used for producing an approximate representation of the compressed input.

AEs are popular techniques for image compression and reconstruction. Recently they have been successfully applied to other domains, e.g. for HIV prediction and classification [6], prediction of unknown gene functions [8], summarising and extracting knowledge from gene expression data [21], and identification of diabetic retinopathy and macular edema in medical images [11]. For further review of application of AEs in biology and medicine, please see [9].

Van der Maaten *et al.* [25] compared the performance of an AE with PCA for reducing the dimensionality of artificial and real datasets. They concluded that while the AE was not able to consistently outperform PCA, it nevertheless was able to produce representations with low generalisation error.

3.3   UMAP

UMAP is a recently proposed non-linear dimensionality reduction technique [16]. Its theoretical foundations lie in manifold theory and topological data analysis. The main concept is to use local manifold approximations to construct a topological representation of the high and low dimensional data, and thereafter optimise the low dimensional representation by minimising the cross-entropy between the two topological representations. UMAP has been shown to be competitive with t-SNE [24], another non-linear dimensionality reduction algorithm popular in cytometry, while better preserving the global data structure and providing a faster run time [16]. It is gaining popularity for cytometry data analysis with recent research confirming its effectiveness [3].

In summary, these previous studies highlight the relevance of PCA, AE and UMAP for modelling and analysing complex high-dimensional data. However, their application in clustering of cytometry data is under-explored. In the next section, we present our findings on the impact of PCA, AE and UMAP on ChronoClust's performance for clustering and cluster tracking of cytometry data.

4   Clustering Evaluation Methodology

4.1   West Nile Virus Dataset

The cytometry data used in our study describes the immune response of mice infected with the West Nile Virus (WNV) over 8 days: from day 0 (no infection), through days 1 (mice infected) to 7. For each day, immune cells are procured from the bone marrows of four mice and quantified through flow cytometry, as described in [2]. There are 190,000 cells from each day, showing 14 measurements per cell (cell marker/antibodies) Thus, from a data mining perspective, the dataset contains 190,000 data-points described with 14 features, over 8 days.

4.2   Ground Truth for Evaluating ChronoClust's Clusters

To evaluate clustering quality, we a need *ground truth*, the true immune cell label of each data-point in the dataset. With this, we can evaluate a clustering result's recovery of available cell populations, the validity of clustered cell population developments over time (as this is biologically known), the homogeneity of the clusters produced, and its treatment of cells deemed to be noise or irrelevant. A domain expert, author Ashhurst, labelled our dataset through manual gating (see Sect. 1). In total 16 cell populations were identified, comprising both *un-activated* and *activated* states of B cells, Eosinophils, Monoblasts, Monocytes,

Neutrophils, Plasmacytoid Dendritic Cells (PDC), Stem and Progenitor cells, and T-NK cells. T-NK cells constitute T- and Natural Killer (NK-) cells, which are indistinguishable given the cell markers in the dataset. All 16 populations are detected in each of the 8 days in our dataset. Data-points in all reduced datasets adopt the ground truth labels of their unreduced counterparts.

4.3 Performance Measures

Six quantitative measures were used: clustering time, population count, F1-score, entropy, noise accuracy, and tracking accuracy. No single metric can fully capture all aspects of clustering quality. Hence, these complementary metrics serve to make our evaluation more robust.

Clustering time captures the time duration ChronoClust requires to cluster each time-point in our dataset; each clustering execution will produce a value for each of the 8 days in the dataset. It is expressed in hours.

Population count represents the number of distinct cell populations found by ChronoClust. There are 16 cell populations identified by manual gating per day. A good clustering should identify them all.

F1-score is an established metric combining precision and recall [22], quantifying the accuracy of ChronoClust in reproducing manual gating. It takes values $[0, 1]$, with 1 indicating a perfect score.

Entropy measures cluster homogeneity in terms of true class labels [22]. It is calculated per cluster, per day. Entropy per day is the sum of the entropy of each cluster, weighed by the proportion of data-points in each cluster. A value of 0 indicates high-quality clustering.

Noise accuracy quantifies ChronoClust's agreement with manual gating in labelling data-points (cells) as noise; these cells are not assigned a label. It is the percentage of cells for which manual gating assigns no label that ChronoClust also assigns no label to.

Tracking accuracy quantifies cluster tracking quality as a proportion of transitions that are biologically plausible, Fig. 1.

The last five metrics require comparison between ChronoClust-predicted cell population labels and the actual (manually gated) labels. To facilitate this, ChronoClust clusters are assigned the cell population label of their nearest manually-defined gates, through preferred dimension-weighted Euclidean distance (as described in Sect. 4.4 of [19]).

4.4 Experimental Setup

We applied PCA to the WNV dataset. Figure 2 quantifies the proportion of total variance captured by each principal component. The 'elbow' in the graph indicates a strongly diminishing capture of additional variance per component beyond the 5th; there is relatively little value in employing more than 5 principal components. These first 5 components together capture a considerable amount of the total variance, 82%. Based on these results, we chose five as the dimensionality of the reduced dataset for PCA.

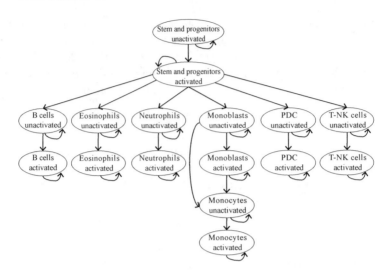

Fig. 1. Biologically plausible transitions for immune cell populations. Adapted from [19].

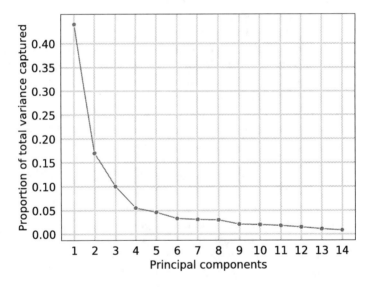

Fig. 2. The proportion of data variance captured by each principal component when applying PCA to the WNV dataset.

To ensure a fair comparison, we set AE to also produce a five dimensional representation. The AE's input, encoding and decoding layers thus contain 14, 5 and 14 nodes respectively. We used a ReLU activation function for the encoding layer and sigmoid for the decoding. The AE was trained on the entire 8 days WNV data for 3000 epochs, minimising the mean squared error through the

Adam optimisation algorithm [15], which is an extension of the stochastic gradient descent algorithm, with a learning rate of $1e^{-6}$. To assess the influence of AE's stochastic operation, we repeatedly trained the AE 60 times. The minimum mean squared error (loss value) of the trained AEs ranged from 0.0041 to 0.0090. The dataset with minimum loss value was then selected for subsequent clustering experiments.

Similarly, we applied UMAP to compress our WNV dataset to 5 dimensions. We employed a Euclidean distance metric and a learning rate of 1.0. To aid clustering, UMAP's minimum distance between each reduced point is set to 0.1, resulting in similar points being placed relatively close to one another. Lastly, UMAP assigned its initial embedding in random manner.

All three dimensionality reduction techniques processed the full 8 days dataset in a single pass. This ensures a consistent spatial encoding across days; a given cell population will always be located in the same region of dimensionality-reduced space across days.

Each feature of the unreduced dataset was scaled to the range $[0, 1]$ based on its minimum and maximum value observed across all time-points. This normalisation procedure was repeated following dimensionality reduction, ensuring compressed data also spans the range $[0, 1]$.

We performed clustering on each dataset using 400 distinct parameter value combinations. This provides a broad perspective of clustering performance across each dataset, and mitigates the chance that a given parameter value combination proved superior for one dataset, but not another. The 400 samples of ChronoClust parameter space were generated using a Latin Hypercube Sampling scheme [17]. The same 400 parameter value samples were used to cluster all four datasets. Clustering executions were performed on a high-performance computing facility. Those that failed to complete within 168 h of run-time were terminated and excluded from subsequent analysis.

ChronoClust executions for all 400 parameter value combinations were successfully completed for the PCA-, AE- and UMAP- reduced datasets (100% completion). However, only 214/400 (53.5%) executions on the unreduced dataset did so.

5   Results and Discussion

5.1   Comparison of Overall Clustering Performance

To evaluate the effect of dimensionality reduction, we cluster the unreduced 14-dimensional and the three reduced 5-dimensional datasets using the 400 distinct ChronoClust parameter value samples, and contrast their performance in terms of the aforementioned six metrics. With the exception of clustering time, each metric is reported as the median across the 8 days comprising the dataset.

Clustering Time. To compare ChronoClust's clustering time for the reduced and 14-dimensional datasets, we measure the amount of time taken to cluster the data for each day, for all parameter combinations. The results are summarised in Figs. 3 and 4 reports the 50th percentiles of these distributions.

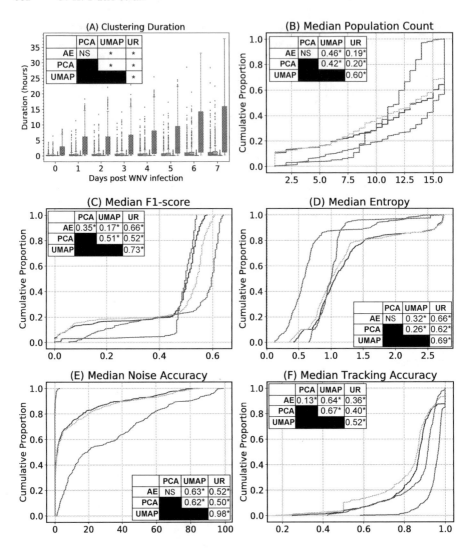

Fig. 3. ChronoClust performance on unreduced WNV dataset and all reduced datasets (median across the 8 days). Data comprise executions on 400 samples of ChronoClust parameter space. Figure A's boxplots capture the median and interquartile range (IQR) of clustering duration. Whiskers extend to the most extreme datapoints, or to 1.5 times IQR from the 1st and 3rd quartiles if outlier data exist beyond these points. Figures B–F represent cumulative distribution plots. All statistical comparisons are through the Kolmogorov-Smirnov (KS) test; * signifies p < 0.005; NS denotes not significant. In Figure A, * indicates statistically significant differences found in all days; NS, no statistical significance in any day. KS D-values are reported as a measure of effect magnitude between datasets for Figures B–F.

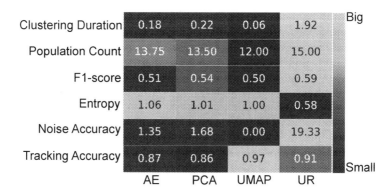

Fig. 4. Median values (50th percentiles) of the distributions reported in Fig. 3: clustering performance of AE-, PCA- and UMAP-reduced and unreduced (UR) datasets

ChronoClust execution completion was substantially faster for the reduced datasets (nearly all $\leq$2 h) than for the unreduced dataset ($\geq$3 h are very common). We note that the execution times for the 14-dimensional data are an underestimate, as the 186 parameter combinations that failed to complete within 168 h are not included in this analysis. Clustering duration for each day of the PCA- and AE-reduced datasets are not statistically distinguishable, suggesting both reduced datasets to be of comparable complexity, and thus requiring similar effort to cluster. However, we found clusterings of the UMAP-reduced dataset to be significantly faster than for the PCA- and AE-reduced datasets.

Population Count. As defined by manual gating, the maximum number of distinct cell populations to be found in the dataset is 16. All 16 are present in each day, and thus, ideally, the median reported number of cell populations detected should be 16. The actual values obtained are reported in Fig. 3B. Of the 400 ChronoClust executions that successfully completed for PCA-, AE- and UMAP-reduced datasets, 31%, 36% and 0.25% identify a median 16 cell populations across all days, respectively. Conversely, 44% of the 214 successful ChronoClust executions for the unreduced dataset identify a median of 16 cell populations. The 50th percentile values for these distributions are reported in the second row of Fig. 4. The unreduced dataset reports a 50th percentiles of 15 populations across the 8 days. PCA and AE lag only marginally behind, 13.5–13.75 populations identified, with distributions closely tracking that of the unreduced dataset. UMAP does not fare as well, and reports a 50th percentile of 12 cell populations identified.

F1-score and Entropy. The distribution for these metrics are depicted on Figs. 3C and D respectively. The unreduced dataset was the best performer in terms of both metrics. For F1-score, PCA most closely aligns with the unreduced dataset, then AE and UMAP which prove relatively comparable to one another. For entropy, the dimensionality reduced datasets offer fairly equivalent performance with one another.

Noise Accuracy. As shown in Fig. 3E, of the cells deemed noise through manual gating, far fewer are labelled as noise on the reduced datasets than on the unreduced datasets. The 50th percentile noise accuracy values from Fig. 4 show 19.3% for the unreduced data, 1.7% for PCA data, 1.3% for AE data, and 0% for UMAP data. A value of 100% would indicate that all cells our expert labelled as noise were recognised as such through ChronoClust. Whilst 73.4% of unreduced dataset clusterings reported a noise accuracy of $\leq 50\%$ (Fig. 3E), values of 100% were obtained by some. Conversely, no reduced dataset clustering reported a noise accuracy of 100%.

Tracking Accuracy. As shown in Fig. 3F, a majority of ChronoClust clustering on the unreduced datasets perform better than the AE- and PCA-reduced datasets. Curiously, the UMAP-reduced is the best performing dataset on this metric. The 50th percentile tracking accuracies were 0.91 (unreduced), 0.86 (PCA), 0.87 (AE) and 0.97 (UMAP), Fig. 4. This metric's maximum value is 1, when all transitions are biologically plausible. Attaining this maximum value are 15.5% of UMAP results, 12.5% of AE, 6.8% of PCA and a mere 1.9% of unreduced dataset results. We believe that these strong results for the reduced datasets are related to the reduced datasets capturing fewer cell populations (Fig. 3A): self-transitions over time are always deemed biologically plausible (Fig. 1), and with fewer possible inter-cluster transitions the tracking accuracy will likely increase.

Overall, in the general case, these results highlight a noticeable sacrifice in clustering performance when reducing the full 14-dimensional dataset to a mere 5. This presented most prominently on noise accuracy and entropy measures. For the other metrics (population count, F1-score, and tracking accuracy), the differences between the reduced and unreduced dataset results were more minor. Contrasting the dimensionality reduction techniques, we found that AE and PCA exhibited significant differences in F1-score and tracking accuracy only. In contrast, the UMAP performance was significantly different from PCA and AE in all metrics. For clustering duration and tracking accuracy it proved superior, for noise accuracy, worse. Elsewhere, the distribution was different but we could not universally judge UMAP results either worse or better than AE or PCA. We note that for each metric independently, the best performing PCA and AE clusterings could closely approach, and in some cases match, the best performance using the unreduced dataset. However, the present data do not indicate whether this is for the *same* parameter value combination. This we investigate in the next section.

5.2   Comparison of the Best-Performing Results for Each Dataset

From our previous sampling of 400 ChronoClust parameter value combinations, we selected the top five that yield the highest mean F1-score, and the lowest mean entropy in the event of a tie, for each dataset. We evaluated Chrono-Clust's performance in terms of the metrics discussed in Sect. 4.3. For visual

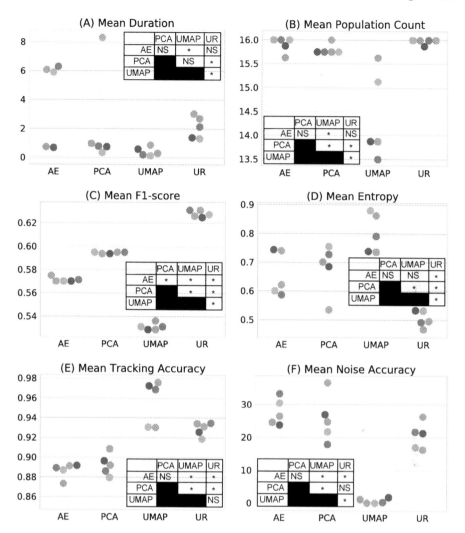

Fig. 5. Clustering performances of the top five ChronoClust parameter value combinations, according to F1-scores, for each dataset. To track the performance of individual results across the six metrics, the same colour within a dataset represents the same result. Note that colours are repeated across the datasets; these are not the same results. Colours are ordered pink (best F1 score), blue, green, orange, and brown (5th). All statistical comparisons are through the Kolmogorov-Smirnov statistic (KS) test. * indicates p-value < 0.05; NS signifies not significant. (Color figure online)

ease of comparison between datasets, these data are reported as swarm plots in Fig. 5; the exact values are tabulated as heatmaps in Fig. 6. The values reported represent the given clustering's mean value across the 8 days comprising our dataset.

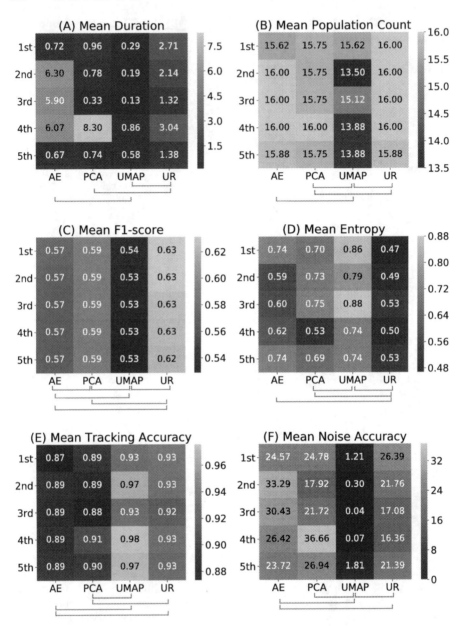

Fig. 6. Exact values of the swarm plots in Fig. 5: top five clustering performances for unreduced (UR), PCA-, AE- and UMAP-reduced datasets. All statistical comparisons are through the Kolmogorov-Smirnov statistic (KS) test. Dendograms beneath each graph indicate p-value < 0.05.

Clustering Duration. The UMAP-reduced datasets required the lowest time duration to complete, with all top-five clusterings completing faster than those of the unreduced dataset. PCA also offered a significant reduction in computational time over the unreduced dataset, however, the differences between AE and the unreduced dataset were not statistically significant. Contrasting the dimensionality reduction techniques, UMAP proved faster than AE but statistically indistinguishable from PCA.

Population Count. Amongst these top-five performing results, all datasets except UMAP identified all 16 cell populations in all days at least once. Clusterings identifying all 16 populations in *all* 8 days (mean population count = 16) are more prevalent for the unreduced dataset (4/5) than either PCA- (1/5). We note, however, that all solutions for these three datasets yielded values very close to 16, all above 15.5. UMAP was the poorest performing dataset for this metric.

F1-score and Entropy. We observed higher F1-scores for the clustering of the unreduced dataset ($\approx$0.63) than that of the PCA- ($\approx$0.59), AE- ($\approx$0.57) or UMAP- ($\approx$0.53) reduced datasets. We note that, in cytometry terms, all these F1-scores should constitute acceptable performance: discounting noise, they represent mean cell population misclassification rates 5.7% (unreduced), 9.5% (UMAP) and 17.2% (PCA and AE) - they are sufficient for non-obscure cell populations to be identifiable. For entropy, the unreduced dataset was superior to the reduced datasets. Closest to unreduced dataset performance was AE, closely followed by PCA, and lastly UMAP. We note that for the PCA-reduced dataset there was a parameter combination (case 4) where the entropy value (0.57) was within the range of the entropy values for the unreduced data (0.47–0.53), highlighting PCA's capacity to produce clusters with similar homogeneity. In summary, we found that dimensionality reduction did diminish clustering performance, but that we believe this to be relatively minor in use-case terms.

Tracking Accuracy. Clustering performance in terms of producing biologically plausible transitions in immune cell developmental states on the unreduced dataset was $\approx$0.93 (93%). Relative to this, UMAP proved superior, achieving 93–98%. Whilst impressive, this superiority may be explained in part by the slightly lower population count in UMAP's results, leading to narrower scope for biologically-implausible transitions. The AE- and PCA-reduced datasets also performed very well obtaining $\approx$0.89 (89%) accuracy. In summary, all datasets produced high tracking accuracy, with the UMAP-reduced dataset outperforming the others.

Noise Accuracy. We found that the AE-reduced dataset outperformed the unreduced dataset in capture of noise. The performance of the PCA-reduced and unreduced datasets is statistically equivalent. These results are encouraging. The UMAP-reduced dataset performed the worst, obtaining accuracies of <2%.

Whilst none of the top-five performers explored here (as defined through F1-score) exceeded 40% noise accuracy, we note that closer alignments with manual gating were attainable. Values of $>90\%$ were reported for the unreduced dataset (Fig. 3E), and the absence here of such scores serves to highlight the trade-offs that exist across performance metrics: the best performance in terms of F1-scores comes at the cost of poor performance in terms of noise accuracy.

6   Conclusion

In this study, we assessed the merit of performing dimensionality reduction prior to clustering and cluster tracking of real-world cytometry data, aiming to ease computational burden while maintaining high-quality clustering performance.

As our test-bed, we used a recently proposed clustering algorithm, ChronoClust, to cluster and track a cytometry dataset that quantifies the immune response to West Nile Virus infection over 8 days in mice. We reduced the dimensionality of the dataset from its original 14 to 5 dimensions using PCA, AE and UMAP. We repeatedly clustered the resultant four datasets with 400 independently sampled ChronoClust parameter value combinations. This mitigates the risk of selecting parameter values that perform better for some dimensionality reduction techniques than others. Thereafter, we compared the clustering results of all four datasets using six complementary metrics. This constituted a more robust analysis as no single metric can capture, without bias, all aspects of clustering, and trade-offs in performance often exist.

In the general case, across all 400 ChronoClust parameter value combinations, dimensionality reduction confers a substantial reduction in clustering time, but at the detriment of clustering performance, mainly in entropy and correct capture of noise. Focusing on only the top-five performing ChronoClust clusterings for each dataset, the benefit of a pre-clustering dimensionality reduction was a potential halving of computational expense, though a few results gained computational time. Compared to the unreduced dataset, the top-five results under AE and PCA showed minor deterioration in F1-score and entropy, similar population count and tracking accuracy and (for AE) better noise accuracy. For UMAP the trade-off was more variable: UMAP offered the greatest computational gain and actually improved tracking accuracy, but it produced inferior performance in population count, F1-score, entropy and noise accuracy.

Overall, we conclude that for large unwieldy datasets, either in terms of dimensionality or constituent time-points, dimensionality reduction can prove advantageous and is worthy of consideration if the computational expense is otherwise excessive or prohibitive.

Further work could investigate the trade-off between performance (clustering and cluster tracking) and computational expense for even higher-dimensional datasets, and also for other dimensionality reduction algorithms such as diffusion maps [10]. Investigating the extent to which our present findings hold over other datasets, or if these results hold for data labelled by other experts, is also worthy of consideration.

Acknowledgements. WNV data generation was supported by the Australian Research Council (grants LE140100149, DP160102063) and the Australian National Health and Medical Research Council (grant 1088242). All procedures involving mice were reviewed and approved by the University of Sydney AEC. We thank the Sydney Informatics Hub at the University of Sydney for access to their High-Performance Computing facility.

References

1. Aghaeepour, N., et al.: Critical assessment of automated flow cytometry data analysis techniques. Nat. Meth. **10**(3), 228 (2013). https://doi.org/10.1038/nmeth.2365
2. Ashhurst, T.M., Smith, A.L., King, N.J.C.: High-dimensional fluorescence cytometry. Curr. Protoc. Immunol. **119**(1), 5–8 (2017). https://doi.org/10.1002/cpim.37
3. Becht, E., et al.: Dimensionality reduction for visualizing single-cell data using UMAP. Nat. Biotechnol. **37**(1), 38–44 (2019). https://doi.org/10.1038/nbt.4314
4. Bendall, S.C., Nolan, G.P., Roederer, M., Chattopadhyay, P.K.: A deep profiler's guide to cytometry. Trends Immunol. **33**(7), 323–332 (2012). https://doi.org/10.1016/j.it.2012.02.010
5. Bendall, S.C., et al.: Single-cell mass cytometry of differential immune and drug responses across a human hematopoietic continuum. Science **332**(6030), 687–696 (2011). https://doi.org/10.1126/science.1198704
6. Betechuoh, B.L., Marwala, T., Tettey, T.: Autoencoder networks for HIV classification. Curr. Sci. **91**(11), 1467–1473 (2006)
7. Bohm, C., Railing, K., Kriegel, H.P., Kroger, P.: Density connected clustering with local subspace preferences. In: Proceedings of the 4th International Conference on Data Mining, pp. 27–34 (2004). https://doi.org/10.1109/icdm.2004.10087
8. Chicco, D., Sadowski, P., Baldi, P.: Deep autoencoder neural networks for gene ontology annotation predictions. In: Proceedings of the 5th ACM Conference on Bioinformatics, Computational Biology, and Health Informatics (2014). https://doi.org/10.1145/2649387.2649442
9. Ching, T., et al.: Opportunities and obstacles for deep learning in biology and medicine. J. R. Soc. Interface **15**(141), 20170387 (2018). https://doi.org/10.1098/rsif.2017.0387
10. Coifman, R.R., Lafon, S.: Diffusion maps. Appl. Comput. Harmonic Anal. **21**(1), 5–30 (2006). https://doi.org/10.1016/j.acha.2006.04.006
11. Gulshan, V., Peng, L., Coram, M., Stumpe, M.C., Wu, D., Narayanaswamy, A., Venugopalan, S., Widner, K., Madams, T., Cuadros, J., et al.: Development and validation of a deep learning algorithm for detection of diabetic retinopathy in retinal fundus photographs. J. Am. Med. Assoc. **316**(22), 2402–2410 (2016). https://doi.org/10.1001/jama.2016.17216
12. Hinton, G.E., Salakhutdinov, R.R.: Reducing the dimensionality of data with neural networks. Science **313**(5786), 504–507 (2006). https://doi.org/10.1126/science.1127647
13. Hinton, G.E., Zemel, R.S.: Autoencoders, minimum description length and helmholtz free energy. In: Advances in Neural Information Processing Systems (1994)
14. Jain, A.K., Dubes, R.C., et al.: Algorithms for Clustering Data, vol. 6. Prentice Hall, Englewood Cliffs (1988)

15. Kingma, D.P., Ba, J.: Adam: a method for stochastic optimization. arXiv preprint arXiv:1412.6980 (2014)
16. McInnes, L., Healy, J., Melville, J.: Umap: uniform manifold approximation and projection for dimension reduction. arXiv preprint arXiv:1802.03426 (2018)
17. McKay, M., Beckman, R., Canover, W.: A comparison of three methods for selecting values of input variables in the analysis of output from a a computer code. Technometrics **21**(2), 239–245 (1979). https://doi.org/10.1080/00401706. 1979.10489755
18. Newell, E.W., Sigal, N., Bendall, S.C., Nolan, G.P., Davis, M.M.: Cytometry by time-of-flight shows combinatorial cytokine expression and virus-specific cell niches within a continuum of cd8+ t cell phenotypes. Immunity **36**(1), 142–152 (2012). https://doi.org/10.1016/j.immuni.2012.12.002
19. Putri, G.H., et al.: Chronoclust: density-based clustering and cluster tracking in high-dimensional time-series data. Knowl.-Based Syst. **174**, 9–26 (2019). https:// doi.org/10.1016/j.knosys.2019.02.018
20. Ringnér, M.: What is principal component analysis? Nat. Biotechnol. **26**(3), 303 (2008). https://doi.org/10.1038/nbt0308-303
21. Tan, J., Ung, M., Cheng, C., Greene, C.S.: Unsupervised feature construction and knowledge extraction from genome-wide assays of breast cancer with denoising autoencoders. In: Pacific Symposium on Biocomputing, pp. 132–143 (2014). https://doi.org/10.1142/9789814644730_0014
22. Tan, P., Steinbach, M., Kumar, V.: Cluster analysis: basic concepts and algorithms. In: Introduction to Data Mining, Chap. 11, pp. 487–568. Addison Wesley (2005)
23. Turner, J.D., et al.: Th2 cytokines are associated with reduced worm burdens in a human intestinal helminth infection. J. Infect. Dis. **188**(11), 1768–1775 (2003). https://doi.org/10.1086/379370
24. Van Der Maaten, L., Hinton, G.: Visualizing data using t-sne. J. Mach. Learn. Res. **9**(Nov), 2579–2605 (2008)
25. Van Der Maaten, L., Postma, E., Van den Herik, J.: Dimensionality reduction: a comparative review. J. Mach. Learn. Res. **10**, 66–71 (2009)
26. Yeung, K.Y., Ruzzo, W.L.: Principal component analysis for clustering gene expression data. Bioinformatics **17**(9), 763–774 (2001). https://doi.org/10.1093/ bioinformatics/17.9.763

Improving Deep Image Clustering with Spatial Transformer Layers

Thiago V. M. Souza and Cleber Zanchettin(✉)

Centro de Informática, Universidade Federal de Pernambuco, Recife, Brazil
{tvms,cz}@cin.ufpe.br

Abstract. Image clustering is an important but challenging task in machine learning. As in most image processing areas, the latest improvements came from models based on the deep learning approach. However, classical deep learning methods have problems to deal with spatial image transformations like scale and rotation. In this paper, we propose the use of visual attention techniques to reduce this problem in image clustering methods. We evaluate the combination of a deep image clustering model called Deep Adaptive Clustering (DAC) with the Spatial Transformer Networks (STN). The proposed model is evaluated in the datasets MNIST and FashionMNIST and outperformed the baseline model.

Keywords: Image clustering · Deep neural networks ·
Visual attention · Spatial Transformer Networks · Adaptive Clustering

1 Introduction

The clustering task consists of dividing a set of data into subgroups where elements belonging to the same group are similar to each other and different from the elements of the other groups. Clustering is a method of unsupervised learning and is a common technique for statistical data analysis.

In some cases, clustering is even important to supervised learning. In many real applications of large-scale image classification, the labeled data is not available or is not enough to train supervised models, since the tedious manual labeling process requires a lot of time and labor. A widely used strategy is to applying clustering to the unlabeled training data to group in similar instances and then use minimal human effort to label annotation based in the group elements.

Image clustering is a challenging task due to the image intra-class variability. For a long time, classic techniques such as K-means were the best option to image clustering [13,14]. In recent years, deep neural networks have proved to be very effective in several image processing areas and deep clustering approaches reached the state-of-the-art in manifold image benchmarks using methods such as Deep Clustering Network (DCN) [17], Joint Unsupervised Learning (JULE) [18], Deep Embedded Cluster (DEC) [16], Deep Embbeded Cluster with Data Augmentation (DEC-DA) [4] and Deep Adaptive Clustering (DAC) [1].

I. V. Tetko et al. (Eds.): ICANN 2019, LNCS 11730, pp. 641–654, 2019.
https://doi.org/10.1007/978-3-030-30490-4_51

The deep neural networks are extremely powerful. However, it has some problems with spatial image transformations like scale and rotation. The majority of Convolutional Neural Networks (CNN) typically employ max-pooling layers using small pooling regions (e.g., 2×2 or 3×3 pixels) to deal with image transformations. The max-pooling approach provides a spatial invariance of up to only a small region, and the intermediate feature maps in the CNN is not invariant to intra-class differences of the input data.

Advanced techniques have been proposed to deal with this problem, such the visual attention solutions as Spatial Transformer Networks (STN) [5]. This modules can be inserted into the CNN as a layer and provides the ability to learn invariance to scale, rotation and the more general image deformations. We refer to these mechanisms as Spatial Transformer layers (ST layer).

In this paper, we investigate the use of a visual attention technique in deep clustering models to making the network more invariant to intra-class differences of the input data. To evaluate this approach, we added ST layers into the Deep Adaptive Clustering (DAC) [1] model. We have not found in the literature deep image clustering models that use ST layers in their composition to deal with intra-class variance.

We evaluate our approach performing experiments with the MNIST [8] and FashionMNIST [15] datasets. The next section reviews the related work, specifically on deep image clustering. In Sect. 3, we detail the background of the combined methods. Section 4 details the proposed approach Spatial Transformer - Deep Adaptive Clustering (ST-DAC). In Sect. 5, we present the experiments and Sect. 7 presents the final remarks.

2 Related Works

Many works in deep image clustering have achieved remarkable results or have become important approaches in how to handle the clustering problem [9]. All of these methods are directly related to our proposal. Among these works, we highlight the Deep Clustering Network (DCN) [17], which combines a pretrained Autoencoder (AE) network with the k-means algorithm. The Joint Unsupervised Learning (JULE) [18] which uses a hierarchical clustering module and a CNN to generate the representations of the images; each previous method joint optimize deep representations generation and the function to build image clusters. Other interesting models are based on Generative Adversarial Networks (GAN)[3] and Variational Autoencoder (VAE) [7] as Categorical Generative Adversarial Networks [11] and Variational Deep Embedding [6]. The models generate new images related to the learned image groups, besides performing clustering of these images.

The Deep Adaptive Clustering (DAC) [1] is historically one of the most representative methods in this category. Another method that brings much attention to the deep image clustering literature is the Deep Embbeded Clustering (DEC) [16]. The method performs a pretraining on a Stacked Autoencoder, then arranges the layers of the architecture to form a Deep-Autoencoder, in which the fine-tuning is performed. Then the part of the decoder is removed of the network, and the output of the encoder serves as the feature extractor for the clustering module. The network is optimized using the hardness-loss clustering method to assign the labels to the samples iteratively. This model is a reference for the evaluation of new models and experiments with deep image clustering.

All these models can achieve interesting results proposing modifications in the clustering functions, autoencoder, as well as in the network optimization. However, these works do not focus on problems already known in the deep learning approaches, such the difficult to deal with input spatial transformations variance.

The model Deep Embedded Cluster with Data Augmentation (DEC-DA) [4] follow a different approach and seeks to improve the generalization capacity of the network. In this model, the authors first train an AE in which the inputs are images with data augmentation. With the network trained and able to generate representative features, the clustering cost function and the reconstruction function of the features of the combined AE are employed in training. In this process, the decoder generates the data augmentation images features. The centroids are calculated from the representations generated by the same decoder; however, in this step, the decoder receives the original images without transformations. The whole network is optimized together. The use of data augmentation to build the AE proved to be quite efficient and reached state-of-the-art results in several datasets. Data augmentation is a technique capable of improving the generalization of the networks, however, the models still encounter difficulties when dealing with images transformations beyond those found in the augmented samples.

3 Preliminaries

3.1 Deep Adaptive Clustering - DAC

DAC [1] is a model of deep image clustering, based on a single-stage CNN, i.e. to perform the clustering of the images it is not necessary pretraining stages, nor additional stages of sequential independent clustering modules.

The model presents a somewhat innovative approach when dealing with the clustering problem, dealing with the problem differently of the other deep image clustering models. Usually, the methods use more specific clustering techniques such as hierarchical clustering or K-means. DAC proposes to attend the clustering task as a pair binary classification. In this way, the pairs of images are considered as belonging to the same cluster, or different clusters, depending on their similarities.

In a classification approach, we need the labels of the classes to train the model. In order to overcome this situation in a clustering approach, the method obtains the labels from the CNN extracted features. The technique employs some constraint on the output of the model and thus manages to generate features suitable for clustering, making the learned feature labels tending to one-hot vectors. Moreover, it uses an adaptive learning algorithm for tuning the model. Figure 1 presents all steps of the adaptive training method.

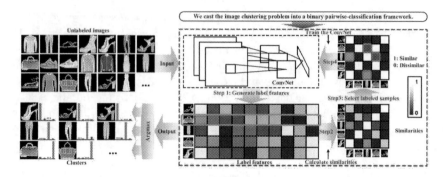

Fig. 1. Diagram of the Deep Adaptive Clustering solution. Image adapted from [1]

The CNN in the early stages of the training process is still not able to distinguish very well the similarity between images with high intra-class variance. In this way, it is necessary to employ an adaptive method for selecting the training examples, choosing samples with a high level of confidence in the predictions. This method consists of firstly select training labels from the pairs of images that show similarities or dissimilarities verified by the network during the first training iterations. These similarities correspond with a higher probability that the result of the classification between the pair is correct. As the training progresses, the network becomes more robust, so samples of training pairs with a higher level of uncertainty are presented gradually. Thus the network learns more refined clustering patterns. Based on the similarity between the pairs, the training labels are generated as show Eq. 1.

$$r_{ij} = \begin{cases} 1, & if \ f(\mathbf{x}_i; \mathbf{w}) \cdot f(\mathbf{x}_j; \mathbf{w}) \geq u(\lambda) \\ 0, & if \ f(\mathbf{x}_i; \mathbf{w}) \cdot f(\mathbf{x}_j; \mathbf{w}) < l(\lambda), \quad i, j = 1, \cdots, n, \\ Nothing, & in \ other \ case \end{cases} \quad (1)$$

Given $\mathcal{X} = \{\mathbf{x}_i\}_{i=1}^{n}$ as the set of non-labeled images presented to the cluster where the variable x_i is the i-th image of the data set. x_i and x_j are different unlabeled input images and r_{ij} is an unknown binary output variable that receive the training label generated, where if $r_{ij} = 1$ the images x_i and x_j belong to the same group, in other case, if $r_{ij} = 0$, the images belong to different groups. w are the actual parameters from the network; f is a mapping function that maps input images to label features and $f(\mathbf{x}_i; \mathbf{w}) \cdot f(\mathbf{x}_j; \mathbf{w})$ represents the dot product between two label features. λ is a adaptive parameter that controls the selection of samples presented for training, $u(\lambda)$ is the threshold for selecting samples of similar pairs, $l(\lambda)$ is a threshold used to select samples of dissimilar pairs and "Nothing" means that the sample (xi, xj, r_{ij}) is not presented for the training process.

DAC stops with the use of all training instances, and the objective cannot be improved. The DAC optimization function is defined as in the Eq. 2.

$$\min_{\mathbf{w}} \mathbf{E}(\mathbf{w}) = \sum_{i,j} v_{ij} L\left(r_{ij}, f\left(\mathbf{x}_i; \mathbf{w}\right) \cdot f\left(\mathbf{x}_j; \mathbf{w}\right)\right) \tag{2}$$

In Eq. 2 v is an indicator coefficient where $v_{ij} = 1$ indicates that the sample is selected for training, and $v_{ij} = 0$ otherwise, L is the function loss defined in Eq. 3 where $g\left(\mathbf{x}_i, \mathbf{x}_j; \mathbf{w}\right) = f\left(\mathbf{x}_i; \mathbf{w}\right) \cdot f\left(\mathbf{x}_j; \mathbf{w}\right)$.

$$L\left(r_{ij}, g\left(\mathbf{x}_i, \mathbf{x}_j; \mathbf{w}\right)\right) = -r_{ij} \log\left(g\left(\mathbf{x}_i, \mathbf{x}_j; \mathbf{w}\right)\right)\left(1 - r_{ij}\right) \log\left(1 - g\left(\mathbf{x}_i, \mathbf{x}_j; \mathbf{w}\right)\right) \tag{3}$$

Finally, the model cluster the images according to the most significant label features. The DAC reached the state-of-the-art in several public datasets [1].

3.2 Spatial Transformer Networks - STN

The Spatial Transformer Networks (STN)[5] is a visual attention mechanism consisting of differentiable modules, which can be trained using the backpropagation algorithm. The model can learn to perform spatial transformations conditioned to the input data mapping.

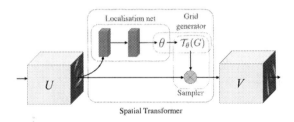

Fig. 2. Spatial transformer network. Source: [5]

The STN modules can be inserted as layers of a CNN and are composed of three distinct parts, as we can see in Figure 2, the localization network, the grid generator, and the sampler. The network receive the input data map $U \in \Re^{H \times W \times C}$ with W, H, C are the width, height, and channels, respectively. The input information can be the input image or the features map extracted by the inner layers of a CNN.

The θ transformation parameters are predicted by the localization network, which can be any CNN or Multi-Layer Perceptron with a regression layer at the output. The size of θ may vary according to the desired transformation type.

The transformation parameters are then used to generate a transformation matrix τ_θ. This matrix is applied in a sampling grid G produced by the grid generator. The sampling grid is composed of normalized coordinates that map the access to each input feature map values. Finally, the sample kernel uses the grid and the mapped features to generates the output map U.

Through these mechanisms, convolutional networks can become more robust and invariant to the transformations or variability inherent in the input images and with a low computational cost.

4   Proposed Pipeline

The method proposed in this work aims to create a new approach by adding to the DAC model some ST layers for deep image clustering. We call this new model Spatial Transformer - Deep Adaptive Clustering (ST-DAC).

To evaluate our hypothesis, we use the DAC* model, a more simple DAC version also presented in the original DAC paper [1]. In the DAC* the upper and lower sampler selection thresholds are set by the parameter λ that is added linearly at each epoch. In this method, at each iteration, all examples are also selected for training.

The CNN that composes the architecture present in the original paper is an AllConvNet [12]. However, in several experiments, we had difficulties in training the model using the ST layers. In these cases, the ST layers performed strange transformations in the images, distancing the object and making the input image noisily after some epochs and impairing the results. This behavior led us to believe that the problem could be due to the vanishing gradient. Another option could be to find an appropriate learning rate that attended the training of the CNN and STN layers at the same time.

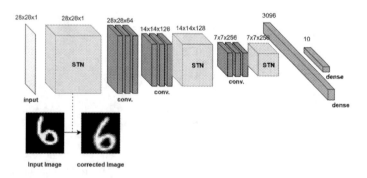

Fig. 3. The proposed convolutional architecture has three spatial transformer layers. The first one is inserted after the input layer and performs transformations in the initial image. The other ST layers are applied in the feature maps after the second and third block of convolutional layers.

To minimize this problem, we replace the standard CNN for a smaller model based on the VGG network [10]. The new model has similar results to the original approach presented in DAC. In Table 1 are presented the parameters of the proposed CNN. We verify different arrangements of ST layers, we inserted the layer after the input image and also after the convolutional layers. Finally, we used 3 ST layers, and Fig. 3 shows the complete network architecture.

We inserted one ST layer after each block of convolutional layers, applying corrections to the original input data, like in [5], and we perform transformations in the extracted features when it suffers a significant spatial transformation as after max-pooling downsampler. This structure immediately corrects the image transformation experienced by the input data, as we can see in the Fig. 3. The model does not use an ST layer after the first convolutional layers block, to reduce the computational cost, because this block does not perform resolution changes. The structure of the localization network in the spatial layers is the same proposed in [2] and detailed in Table 2. Usually, the localization network structures use the Relu activation function between the layers and leave the last layer without activation [5]. Unconventionally, [2] uses tanh activation function after all the convolutional and dense layers. In the initial experiments, it showed better results with the ST layers than the conventional structures.

Table 1. The architecture of the VGG based used in ST-DAC.

Model VGG Based
Input 28 × 28 monochrome image
3 × 3 conv. 64 BN ReLU
2 × 2 Maxpooling BN
3 × 3 conv. 128 BN ReLU
2 × 2 Maxpooling BN
3 × 3 conv. 256 BN ReLU
2 × 2 Maxpooling BN
3096 dense BN ReLU
10 dense BN ReLU SoftMax

Table 2. The architecture of the Localization Network utilized in ST Layers.

Localization Network
[a]Input N × N × M monochrome image
2 × 2 Maxpooling
5 × 5 conv. 20 Tanh
2 × 2 Maxpooling
5 × 5 conv. 20 Tanh
50 dense Tanh
6 dense Tanh
[a]At the input N × N × M corresponds the output dimensions of the anterior layers to ST module

5   Experiments

The experiments were conducted with two well-used datasets to evaluate computer vision problems: the MNIST [8] handwritten digits and the Fashion MNIST [15] based on clothing images.

The metrics used to evaluate the methods are the Adjusted Rand Index (ARI), Normalized Mutual Information (NMI), and Clustering Accuracy (ACC). These measures return results between a range [0,1], values close to 1 represent more precise results in clustering.

5.1   Experimental Settings

To evaluate the performance of the proposed ST-DAC model we perform experiments comparing the proposed approach with DEC [16], DCN [17], VADE [6], JULE [18], DEC-DA [4]. The most outstanding approach in the literature is ConvDEC-DA [4], we also compare our results with this method. Besides, we also compare the proposed model with the DAC [1] and its original version DAC*. These models present the best literature results in the two evaluated datasets.

In order to verify the importance of the ST layers to the proposed model performance, we evaluate our approach with four experiments: (1) with all the ST layers activated (ST-DAC + 3 ST Layers); (2) with the last layer off (ST-DAC + 2 ST Layers); (3) with the first layer activated (ST-DAC + 1 ST Layers); and (4) with no ST layers (ST-DAC without ST Layers). The idea is to quantify the contribution of the ST layers in the model's accuracy.

The original DAC [1] paper does not perform experiments in the Fashion MNIST dataset. For comparison purposes, we run the DAC* version in the Fashion MNIST and MNIST datasets using the same parameters suggested in the original paper. We also used the same data augmentation parameters proposed in the original DAC paper in both datasets. We only modified the initial lower and upper selection thresholds to the range [0.9 0.99] for the MNIST dataset and [0.8 0.99] for the Fashion MNIST dataset. We used Adam optimizer in our model with a learning rate of 0.0001, as suggested in [2]. We run each experiment 10 times and calculate the average of the results, which is used for comparison with the other methods.

Table 3 presents the experiments. The results taken from literature, are marked with the symbol †, the references are next to the name of the method. Results tagged with - are not available. We evaluated the behavior of STNs during the whole training phase in order to verify its contribution to the effectiveness of the model. For this purpose, the results obtained by the ST-DAC during the training were sampled, and the images of the first STN layer were extracted from the model to verify the quality of the spatial transformations applied in the input image during the training steps.

The source code of the experiments is available at a public repository[1].

6   Results

The results of the experiments with the evaluated methods are presented in Table 3. The proposed model ST-DAC without the ST layers presented inferior performance to those obtained by the DAC model. This is a familiar scenario because, compared to the original DAC model, the ST-DAC model uses a shallow convolutional network to extract the image representations. However, we can observe the ST-DAC model trained with and without ST layers was executed on the same configuration parameters. Thus, it suggests that the gain in

---

[1] https://github.com/tvmsouza/ST-DAC.

performance and results of the model resulted from the use of the ST layers in its convolutional network.

Using only one ST layer after the input layer of the proposed model, we obtain a superior result in almost all metrics in the two datasets, compared to the best results previously obtained by DCN, JULE, VADE, DEC, DAC* and DAC.

Adding one ST layer before the input layer and one ST layer after the extracted features of the second block of convolutional layers, we were able to surpass the previous best results of DCN, JULE, VADE, DEC, DAC * and DAC in both datasets and surpassing the ConvDEC-DA and DEC in Fashion MNIST by a large margin of accuracy.

Table 3. Clustering performance of DAC* and the proposed ST-DAC method, obtained from our experiments and compared methods results taken from the literature marked with †, considering Clustering Accuracy (ACC), Normalized Mutual Information (NMI) e Adjusted Rand Index (ARI).

Model	Datasets					
	MNIST			Fashion MNIST		
	ACC	NMI	ARI	ACC	NMI	ARI
DCN [4]†	0.830	0.810	-	0.501	0.558	-
VADE [4]†	0.945	0.876	-	0.578	0.630	-
JULE [4]†	0.964	0.913	-	0.563	0.608	-
DEC [4]†	0.863	0.834	-	0.518	0.546	-
ConvDEC-DA [4]†	**0.985**	**0.962**	-	**0.586**	**0.636**	-
DAC [1]†	0.977	0.935	0.948	-	-	-
DAC*[1]†	0.966	0.924	0.940	-	-	-
DAC*	0.974	0.944	0.9458	0.628	0.589	0.483
ST-DAC without ST Layers	0.957	0.932	0.923	0.612	0.591	0.460
ST-DAC + 1 ST Layer	0.978	0.950	0.953	0.649	0.650	0.520
ST-DAC + 2 ST Layers	**0.980**	**0.953**	**0.956**	0.656	0.658	0.533
ST-DAC + 3 ST Layers	0.961	0.936	0.927	**0.664**	**0.668**	**0.541**

It is notable that with the addition of more ST layers, the model can get better results. However, the idea of using more layers to improve results cannot be applied in all contexts. Using three ST layers in the Fashion MNIST experiments, we get the best result in this data set. However, in the MNIST experiments, the use of a third ST layer in some way compromised the data, reducing its final result compared to the network with two ST layers.

Figure 4 show some qualitative results, we can observe the extracted images from the output of the first transformation layer during different training epochs.

We observe that the STNs presented the same behavior as the most STN literature works. The network initially applies a powerful zoom in the image and then reduces this zoom to fit the object in a region where it can better frame all the details of the area of interest, normalizing the objects, correcting distortions and rotation during the network training. In the training phase, we used data augmentation, and the ST layers learned how to correct various transformations of rotation, scale, and translation. With this knowledge, the ST layers rotate the objects to a standard angle in which it is possible to enlarge and fill a larger area of the entire image without losing relevant information of the target object. The output images of the ST layers also have a blurred aspect and lose some details, but this loss is offset by the transformation corrections defined above.

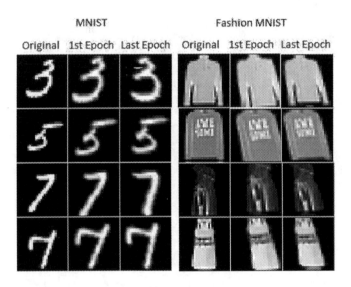

Fig. 4. Comparison between some original images and their respective output from the first ST layer. In the left column is the original image, in the center the output of the first ST layer after the first training epoch and in the right column the output of this same layer after the training.

In Figure 5 are exhibit the average, standard deviations, and variances between all images of the same class, from the original images and the processed images by the first ST layer of the ST-DAC models. All images were obtained after the training phase. It is possible to observe, in the averages results from MNIST, that the ST layers moved the image to a common region, which is evidenced by the high-density level values of the digits in the images. This normalization allows a better comparison between the elements. In addition, the STNs, as seen in previous images, applied a reliable approximation of the digits, which may have improved the capture of details and consequently, improved the results. Analyzing the standard deviation and the variance, it is possible to verify the thickness of the edges of the digits. We observed in the most cases that in the use of ST layers these thicknesses decreased, which indicates a more significant normalization between the positions and transformations of the objects from the same class. Besides, the internal gaps was a high density of variance, and the standard deviation decreased.

We verify a similar behavior in experiments with the Fashion MNIST dataset. During training, the network learns from all these transformations variations, increasing its generalization as if the training is performing a data augmentation in a controlled way.

Figure 6 presents the comparison of the performance curves of the models with and without ST layers obtained during the training. Through these curves, we realized that STNs benefited greatly from the adaptive method of sample selection. From the first epoch, it is notable that the ST layers work with the convolutional network, not causing performance losses.

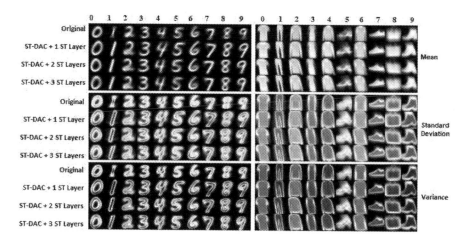

Fig. 5. Average, standard deviations and variances from original and extracted images from the first ST layers inserted in ST-DAC models.

After a few first epochs, the results are better in ST-DAC with ST layers. It is possible to notice that, even before converging, the networks also benefit from the intermediate representations obtained by the ST layers during the training. The curves remained stable in the MNIST data set following the same growth pattern without significant declines in performance over time.

Analyzing the results of the Fashion MNIST dataset, we see that ST-DAC + 3 ST layers lose performance at some points between epochs two and six and then stabilize and continue to increase. Among the combinations of layers, the growth of the ST-DAC + 2 ST layers remained more stable in comparison to the others configurations during all the training periods, despite being overcome in the final result by the network with 3 ST layers. From all these results, it is noticeable that visual attention techniques allow models using simpler convolutional networks to obtain superior results to other methods of deep image clustering.

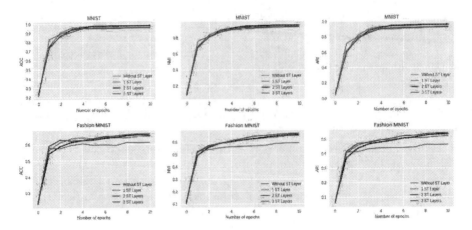

Fig. 6. Comparison of clustering performance between models with diferent numbers of ST Layers during training epochs on MNIST(Top) and Fashion MNIST(Bottom).

7 Conclusion

In this work, we propose a new approach to Deep Adaptive Clustering, replacing the original convolutional feature extraction of the DAC network with a new simpler model based on Spatial Transformer layers. We evaluated our approach by conducting experiments on two public datasets and compared it with other promissory literature methods to the problem.

We also conducted experiments by varying the amount of ST layers in the proposed convolutional model, to evaluate if, with the addition of new ST layers, using the spatial transformation correction over the internal extracted features, the model performance grow proportionally. The experiments showed that our approach was able to outperform other methods in the two evaluated datasets, achieving state-of-art results in both datasets.

Finally, we show that with the use of visual attention techniques, such as ST Layers, the deep image clustering method can obtain performance improvements. The use of ST layers has shown promising results to improve the performance of the DAC model. However, the area of visual attention continues to advance and several new approaches were proposed that extend the capacity of standard ST layers. We suggest for future work verify the performance of these new methods to improve deep image clustering models.

Acknowledgment. This work was supported by CNPq (Brazilian research agency). We gratefully acknowledge the support of NVIDIA Corporation with the donation of the Titan XP GPU used for this research.

References

1. Chang, J., Wang, L., Meng, G., Xiang, S., Pan, C.: Deep adaptive image clustering. In: 2017 IEEE International Conference on Computer Vision (ICCV), pp. 5880–5888. October 2017. https://doi.org/10.1109/ICCV.2017.626
2. Detlefsen, N.S., Freifeld, O., Hauberg, S.: Deep diffeomorphic transformer networks. In: 2018 IEEE/CVF Conference on Computer Vision and Pattern Recognition, pp. 4403–4412. June 2018. https://doi.org/10.1109/CVPR.2018.00463
3. Goodfellow, I., et al.: Generative adversarial nets. In: Ghahramani, Z., Welling, M., Cortes, C., Lawrence, N.D., Weinberger, K.Q. (eds.) Advances in Neural Information Processing Systems 27, pp. 2672–2680 (2014)
4. Guo, X., Zhu, E., Liu, X., Yin, J.: Deep embedded clustering with data augmentation. In: The 10th Asian Conference on Machine Learning (ACML) November 2018
5. Jaderberg, M., Simonyan, K., Zisserman, A., kavukcuoglu, k.: Spatial transformer networks. In: Cortes, C., Lawrence, N.D., Lee, D.D., Sugiyama, M., Garnett, R. (eds.) Advances in Neural Information Processing Systems 28, pp. 2017–2025 (2015)
6. Jiang, Z., Zheng, Y., Tan, H., Tang, B., Zhou, H.: Variational deep embedding: an unsupervised and generative approach to clustering. In: Proceedings of the 26th International Joint Conference on Artificial Intelligence. pp. 1965–1972. IJCAI 2017 (2017)
7. Kingma, D.P., Welling, M.: Auto-encoding variational bayes (2013). https://arxiv.org/pdf/1312.6114v10.pdf
8. Lecun, Y., Bottou, L., Bengio, Y., Haffner, P.: Gradient-based learning applied to document recognition. Proc. IEEE **86**(11), 2278–2324 (1998). https://doi.org/10.1109/5.726791
9. Min, E., Guo, X., Liu, Q., Zhang, G., Cui, J., Long, J.: A survey of clustering with deep learning: from the perspective of network architecture. IEEE Access **6**, 39501–39514 (2018). https://doi.org/10.1109/ACCESS.2018.2855437
10. Simonyan, K., Zisserman, A.: Very deep convolutional networks for large-scale image recognition (2014). https://arxiv.org/pdf/1409.1556.pdf
11. Springenberg, J.T.: Unsupervised and semi-supervised learning with categorical generative adversarial networks (2015). https://arxiv.org/pdf/1511.06390.pdf
12. Springenberg, J.T., Dosovitskiy, A., Brox, T., Riedmiller, M.: Striving for simplicity: The all convolutional net (2014). https://arxiv.org/pdf/1412.6806.pdf
13. Wang, J., Wang, J., Ke, Q., Zeng, G., Li, S.: Fast approximate k-means via cluster closures. In: 2012 IEEE Conference on Computer Vision and Pattern Recognition, pp. 3037–3044. June 2012. https://doi.org/10.1109/CVPR.2012.6248034
14. Wang, J., Wang, J., Song, J., Xu, X., Shen, H.T., Li, S.: Optimized cartesian k-means. IEEE Trans. Knowl. Data Eng. **27**(1), 180–192 (2015). https://doi.org/10.1109/TKDE.2014.2324592
15. Xiao, H., Rasul, K., Vollgraf, R.: Fashion-mnist: a novel image dataset for benchmarking machine learning algorithms (2017)
16. Xie, J., Girshick, R., Farhadi, A.: Unsupervised deep embedding for clustering analysis. In: Proceedings of the 33rd International Conference on International Conference on Machine Learning, vol. 48, pp. 478–487. ICML 2016 (2016)

17. Yang, B., Fu, X., Sidiropoulos, N.D., Hong, M.: Towards k-means-friendly spaces: simultaneous deep learning and clustering (2016). http://arxiv.org/abs/1610.04794
18. Yang, J., Parikh, D., Batra, D.: Joint unsupervised learning of deep representations and image clusters. In: 2016 IEEE Conference on Computer Vision and Pattern Recognition (CVPR), pp. 5147–5156. June 2016. https://doi.org/10.1109/CVPR.2016.556

Collaborative Non-negative Matrix Factorization

Kaoutar Benlamine[(✉)], Nistor Grozavu, Younès Bennani, and Basarab Matei

Université Paris 13, Sorbonne Paris Cité, LIPN UMR CNRS 7030,
99 av. J-B Cl ément, 93430 Villetaneuse, France
{kaoutar.benlamine,nistor.grozavu,younes.bennani,
basarab.matei}@lipn.univ-paris13.fr

Abstract. Non-negative matrix factorization is a machine learning technique that is used to decompose large data matrices imposing the non-negativity constraints on the factors. This technique has received a significant amount of attention as an important problem with many applications in different areas such as language modeling, text mining, clustering, music transcription, and neurobiology (gene separation). In this paper, we propose a new approach called Collaborative Non-negative Matrix Factorization (NMF_{Collab}) which is based on the collaboration between several NMF (Non-negative Matrix Factorization) models. Our approach NMF_{Collab} was validated on variant datasets and the experimental results show the effectiveness of the proposed approach.

1 Introduction

Clustering is an unsupervised learning method that aims to discover the intrinsic structures in a set of objects by forming clusters of similar units. While clustering has been emerged over years and has received a lot of attention as an important problem with many applications, the collaborative clustering still have only some works reported in the literature, see: [6] and [5]. The goal of collaborative clustering [13] is to make different clustering methods collaborate, in order to reach an agreement on the partitioning of a common dataset. The hope is that by collaborating various clustering solutions, each with its own biases and imperfections, we will get a better overall solution.

Collaborative clustering is a recent paradigm of machine learning in which a number of unsupervised algorithms work together for mutual improvement to tackle and find the underlying structures in difficult data sets [2]. It has a lot of applications such as spectral mining, the clustering of distributed and heterogeneous data, and multi-view clustering.

There are three main types of collaboration: horizontal, vertical and hybrid collaboration. Horizontal collaborative clustering: all datasets describe the same observations, so all the collaborative datasets have the same number of observations but a different number of variables. Vertical collaborative clustering: all datasets have the same variables but with different objects. Hybrid collaborative

© Springer Nature Switzerland AG 2019
I. V. Tetko et al. (Eds.): ICANN 2019, LNCS 11730, pp. 655–666, 2019.
https://doi.org/10.1007/978-3-030-30490-4_52

clustering: when both vertical and horizontal collaborative clustering approaches are used at the same time.

Recent attention has been given to NMF for clustering of non-negative data [1,16], it has been applied in different areas such as dimensionality reduction, feature extraction, clustering and text mining. NMF [11] is an unsupervised algorithm for clustering where a data matrix is factorized into (usually) two matrices with the property that all the matrices have no negative elements. This non-negativity makes the resulting matrices easier to interpret. We consider one of the matrices as a matrix containing the centroids of a data set and the other one as a data partition matrix.

Matrix factorization is used in a lot of important applications. The analyzed datasets are often non-negative, and sometimes they also have a sparse representation. Ding et al. [4] showed the equivalence between the orthogonal NMF and k-means hard clustering. Kim and Park [8] discussed this equivalence and proposed sparse NMF algorithm for data clustering. Their algorithm surpasses the k-means and NMF in terms of the consistency of the results.

In this paper, we propose a new approach which is Collaborative Non-negative Matrix Factorization where we study the collaboration between several Non-negative Matrix Factorization (NMF) models.

The remainder of this paper is organized as follows: in Sect. 2, we recall the Non-negative Matrix Factorization principle. In Sect. 3, we present the proposed method derived from the NMF algorithm in a collaborative setting. In Sect. 4, some numerical experiences are proposed and analyzed. The conclusion gives some hints about future researches.

2   Classical NMF and K-means

Let $X = (\mathbf{x}_1, \mathbf{x}_2, \ldots, \mathbf{x}_N) \in \mathbb{R}_+^{M \times N}$, be a non-negative data matrix, and K be a fixed input parameter. The NMF provides a low-rank approximation of X by the product of two non-negative matrices FG^T where T denotes the transpose operator and the factors are $F = (\mathbf{f}_1, \mathbf{f}_2, \ldots, \mathbf{f}_K) \in \mathbb{R}_+^{M \times K}$, $G = (\mathbf{g}_1, \mathbf{g}_2, \ldots, \mathbf{g}_K) \in \mathbb{R}_+^{N \times K}$. By approximating the input matrix X by the product FG^T, allows to write the column vector $\mathbf{x}_n \in \mathbb{R}_+^{M \times 1}$ as a linear combination of columns F with corresponding coefficients from G:

$$\mathbf{x}_n = \sum_{k=1}^{K} g_{nk} \mathbf{f}_k \tag{1}$$

The factors (F, G) in NMF are the solution of the following constrained optimization problem:

$$(F, G) = \operatorname*{argmin}_{F, G \geq 0} \|X - FG^T\|^2 \tag{2}$$

The constraints $F, G \geq 0$ mean that all the components of F, G are non-negative. The functional $\mathcal{J}_{NMF} = \|X - FG^T\|^2$ represents the Frobenius norm of $X - FG^T$. Several families of algorithms proposed to solve this matrix approximation

Algorithm 1. Alternate Least Square NMF

Input: data set X, number of clusters K
Initialization: randomly define F
Output: centroids and partition matrix F, G and cluster labels C
for $t = 1$ **to** *Iter* **do**
  solve in G the matrix Equation $GF^T F = X^T F$
  set to 0 the negative values of G
  solve in F the matrix Equation $FG^T G = XG$
  set to 0 the negative values of F
end
Clustering step:
for $n = 1$ **to** N **do**
  each $\mathbf{x}_n$ is assigned to the kth cluster, according to:

$$k = \underset{c}{\operatorname{argmax}}\{g_{nc}; c = 1, \ldots, K\}.$$

end
Return matrix F, G and C.

---

problem are proposed [11,17]. The initial approach proposed by Lee and Seung [9] uses multiplicative update formula. Another solution is to use *alternate least squares* strategy [7].

We have (as in [4]) that $\mathcal{J}_{NMF}$ is well approximated by the following functional:

$$\sum_{n=1}^{N} \sum_{k=1}^{K} g_{nk}^2 \|\mathbf{x}_n - \mathbf{f}_k\|^2 \tag{3}$$

The work of Lee and Seung [9] revealing that NMF has an inherent clustering property of the columns of X, since in Equation (1) the factor $(\mathbf{f}_1, \mathbf{f}_2, \ldots, \mathbf{f}_K)$ could be considered as cluster centroids, while the factor $(\mathbf{g}_1, \mathbf{g}_2, \ldots, \mathbf{g}_K)$ could be considered as cluster indicator. More precisely $g_{nk} > 0$ indicates that input data column $\mathbf{x}_n \in \mathbb{R}_+^{M \times 1}$ belongs to the kth cluster having the centroid $\mathbf{f}_k \in \mathbb{R}_+^{M \times 1}$ the kth column of F. Therefore G induce the partition of the set of columns $J = \{1, \ldots, N\}$ into K clusters $C = \{C_1, \ldots, C_K\}$ and $F \in \mathbb{R}_+^{M \times K}$ specifies the reduced cluster representation of X. We can notice the similarity between the functional in Eq. (3) and the functional associated to the K-means clustering algorithm.

The K-means clustering is one of the most used clustering methods early developed by Lloyd [10]. The K-means clustering allows to divide the set of columns $\{1, \ldots, N\}$ into K clusters $C = \{C_1, \ldots, C_K\}$ by minimizing the objective function defined by the following sum of squared errors:

$$\mathcal{J}_K = \sum_{k=1}^{K} \sum_{n \in C_k} \|\mathbf{x}_n - \mathbf{f}_k\|^2 \tag{4}$$

Let $G \in \mathbb{R}_+^{N \times K}$ be the binary classification matrix defined by $\mathbf{g}_{nk} = 1$, if the column $\mathbf{x}_n \in C_k$, and 0 otherwise. Thus, the functional in Eq. (4) writes:

$$\mathcal{J}_K = \sum_{k=1}^{K} \sum_{n=1}^{N} g_{nk} \left\| \mathbf{x}_n - \mathbf{f}_k \right\|^2 \tag{5}$$

For a fixed partition $C = \{C_1, \ldots, C_K\}$ we consider $n_k = |C_k|$ the number of elements within the cluster k. Then the cluster centroids $F = (\mathbf{f}_1, \mathbf{f}_2, \ldots, \mathbf{f}_K)$ are:

$$\mathbf{f}_k = \frac{1}{n_k} X \cdot \mathbf{g}_k, \quad k = 1, \ldots, K \tag{6}$$

and the indicator clustering matrix $(\mathbf{g}_1, \mathbf{g}_2, \ldots, \mathbf{g}_K) \in \mathbb{R}_+^{N \times K}$ are given by:

$$\mathbf{g}_k = \frac{1}{\sqrt{n_k}} (0, \ldots, 0, \underbrace{1, \ldots, 1}_{n_k}, 0, \ldots, 0)^T \in \mathbb{R}_+^{N \times 1}$$

Ding et al. [4] showed that the K-means clustering problem can be formulated as a matrix approximation problem where the clustering aim is to minimize the approximation error between the original data X and the reconstructed matrix based on the cluster structures:

$$\min_{F, G \geq 0, G^T G = I} \| X - FG^T \|^2 \tag{7}$$

In other words, the factorization FG^T characterizes the information of X that can be described by the cluster structures contained in F with the indicators contained in G. This formulation of the K-means objective function highlights some good properties of the matrices F and G [14]. These interesting properties are rich in opportunities, in fact, the consideration of these constraints on G allows us to develop different variants of NMF algorithms.

3   NMF Collaborative Clustering

Non-negative matrix factorizations are more and more used as tools for unsupervised classification and visualization of multidimensional datasets, as they allow for the projection of these large data onto small, generally two-dimensional spaces. In this work, we study the collaboration between several clustering results, in particular the collaboration between several models of Non-negative Matrix Factorization (NMF). Each dataset is clustered through an NMF-based clustering approach. We are interested in horizontal collaboration that is very close to multi-view clustering because the data to be collaborated is the same but described by different variables.

3.1   General Principle

In the context of horizontal collaborative learning, we consider a finite number of L clustering views $\mathcal{A}^{(1)}, ..., \mathcal{A}^{(L)}$ working on different attributes of a data set made of M numerical attributes $X = \{\mathbf{x}_1, ..., \mathbf{x}_N\}$ with $\mathbf{x}_n \in \mathbb{R}^{M \times 1}$. We note $X^{(l)} = \{\mathbf{x}_1^{(l)}, ..., \mathbf{x}_N^{(l)}\}, \mathbf{x}_n^{(l)} \subseteq \mathbf{x}_n$ the subset of attributes processed by a given view $\mathcal{A}^{(l)}$. We are in the discrete case and each observation $\mathbf{x}_n^{(l)}$ is a vector belonging to a M_l-dimensional euclidean feature space $\mathbb{R}^{M_l \times 1}$. Each clustering view $\mathcal{A}^{(l)}$ uses a NMF factorization. Therefore the corresponding functional for the $\mathcal{A}^{(l)}$ algorithm writes:

$$\mathcal{J}_{NMF}^{(l)}(F^{(l)}, G^{(l)}) = \|X^{(l)} - F^{(l)}(G^{(l)})^T\|^2 \tag{8}$$

Here $F^{(l)} = (\mathbf{f}_1^{(l)}, \mathbf{f}_2^{(l)}, ..., \mathbf{f}_K^{(l)}) \in \mathbb{R}_+^{M_l \times K}$ represents the matrix of cluster centroids and $G^{(l)} = (\mathbf{g}_1^{(l)}, \mathbf{g}_2^{(l)}, ..., \mathbf{g}_K^{(l)}) \in \mathbb{R}_+^{N \times K}$ represents the matrix clusters indicators obtained by the $\mathcal{A}^{(l)}$.

From there, in the collaborative NMF algorithm, when a data unit is presented from the view l, the optimization is done to minimize the distance between that unit and the centroids of each local NMF view $l' \neq l$. We would like that after the collaboration: if an observation of the $X^{(l)}$-th data set is projected onto the k-th centroid of the l-th NMF view, then the same observation viewed as an observation in the $X^{(l')}$-th data set is projected on the same unit k centroid. Therefore the pairwise collaborative $C_{l,l'}$ term between the NMF views l and l' writes:

$$C_{l,l'}(F^{(l)}, G^{(l)}) = \sum_{n=1}^{N} \sum_{k=1}^{K} \left(g_{nk}^{(l)} - g_{nk}^{(l')}\right)^2 \left\|\mathbf{x}_n^{(l)} - \mathbf{f}_k^{(l)}\right\|^2 \tag{9}$$

The idea of collaboration is to add a collaborative matching term to constraint the similarity between clustering elements of different databases, has obviously showed its ability to produce improved clustering solutions. To exchange the clustering information, all local solutions in the collaboration process share common structures see [12]. Therefore the set of centroids $F^{(l)}$ is estimated iteratively by minimizing the objective function:

$$\mathcal{C}(F^{(l)}, G^{(l)}) = \mathcal{J}_{NMF}^{(l)}(F^{(l)}, G^{(l)}) + \sum_{l' \neq l} \beta_{l,l'} \cdot C_{l,l'}(F^{(l)}, G^{(l)}) \tag{10}$$

Here $\mathcal{J}_{NMF}^{(l)}$ is the lth local term defined in Equation (8), $\beta = (\beta_{l,l'})_{l,l'}$ is the weight of the collaboration fixed by the user satisfying $\sum_{l' \neq l} \beta_{l,l'} = 1$. We could also define a global functional as follows:

$$\mathcal{C}(F, G) = \sum_{l=1}^{L} \left(\mathcal{J}_{NMF}^{(l)}(F^{(l)}, G^{(l)}) + \sum_{l' \neq l} \beta_{l,l'} \cdot C_{l,l'}(F^{(l)}, G^{(l)}) \right) \tag{11}$$

We use the notations $F = (F^{(l)})_l, G = (G^{(l)})_l, l = 1, ..., L$. Let us first remark that the cost function defined in Eq. (11) is continuously first differentiable in all variables. Therefore a minimum always exists and could be found by nonlinear programming. The minimization of the global functional should satisfy the constraints: $(G^{(l)})^T G^{(l)} = I$ for all $l \in \{1, \dots, L\}$ since $G^{(l)}$ is a partition matrix. By using Lagrange multipliers straightforward computations of the derivatives give the following update rules for $G^{(l)}$ and $F^{(l)}$:

$$g_{nk}^{(l)} = \frac{1}{2} \left(\sum_{l'=1, l' \neq l}^{L} \beta_{l,l'} g_{nk}^{(l')} \right) + w_{nk}^{(l)} \left(1 - \frac{1}{2} \left(\sum_{c=1}^{K} \sum_{l'=1, l' \neq l}^{L} \beta_{l,l'} g_{nc}^{(l')} \right) \right) \quad (12)$$

where

$$w_{nk}^{(l)} = \left(\sum_{c=1}^{K} \frac{\|\mathbf{x}_n^{(l)} - \mathbf{f}_k^{(l)}\|^2}{\|\mathbf{x}_n^{(l)} - \mathbf{f}_c^{(l)}\|^2} \right)^{-1}$$

For $m = 1, \dots, M_l$ and $k = 1, \dots, K$, the update rule for centroids is:

$$f_{mk}^{(l)} = \frac{\sum_{n=1}^{N} \left(g_{nk}^{(l)} \right)^2 x_{mn}^{(l)} + \sum_{l'=1, l' \neq l}^{L} \sum_{n=1}^{N} \beta_{l,l'} \left(g_{nk}^{(l)} - g_{nk}^{(l')} \right)^2 x_{mn}^{(l)}}{\sum_{n=1}^{N} \left(g_{nk}^{(l)} \right)^2 + \sum_{l'=1, l' \neq l}^{L} \sum_{n=1}^{N} \beta_{l,l'} \left(g_{nk}^{(l)} - g_{nk}^{(l')} \right)^2}, \quad (13)$$

Here all the database share the same units but described by different attributes. In this case, the number and the size of centroid vectors for all the NMF factorizations will be the same. That's why the objective function of the classical NMF has been modified in order to introduce this constraint on the different factorizations during the collaboration step. The collaborative term is expressed by $C_{l,l'}(F)$ which guaranty that the structure of other databases matches with the current database. Our modified version of the NMF algorithm for horizontal collaboration is shown in Algorithm 2 below.

Algorithm 2. NMF horizontal collaboration Algorithm

Initialization: Initialize all the centroids sets F randomly and β.
Local step:
forall *algorithms* $\mathcal{A}^{(l)}$ **do**
| Minimize the objective function of the NMF (7).
end
Collaborative step:
forall *algorithms* $\mathcal{A}^{(l)}$ **do**
| Update the partitions matrix of all algorithms (12).
| Update the centroids of all algorithms (13).
end

---

4   Experimental Results

Several datasets of different size and complexity are used in order to evaluate our proposed collaborative approach. To illustrate the principle of the proposed approach, more details will be given on the waveform dataset. The used datasets are the following: waveform, SpamBase, NG5, Classic30, Classic 300. As criteria to validate our approach, we used the silhouette index and the calinski-harabasz as the label is available for all dataset.

4.1   Calinski-Harabasz Index

Motivated by the clustering objectives used in well-known partitional algorithms, a number of internal indices have been proposed which assess cluster quality by considering the squared distances between data objects and cluster representatives. Formally, the within-cluster sum of squares is the total of the squared distances between each object x_i and the centroid of the cluster C_c to which it has been assigned:

$$W(C) = \sum_{c=1}^{K} \sum_{x_i \in |C_c|} d(x_i, \mu_c)^2 \tag{14}$$

When employing Euclidean distance, this is equivalent to the objective function of K-means algorithm. The between-cluster sum of squares is the total of the squares of the distances between the each cluster centroid and the centroid of the entire dataset, denoted μ' :

$$B(C) = \sum_{c=1}^{K} |C_c| \, d(\mu_c, \mu')^2, \quad \text{where} \quad \mu' = \frac{1}{n} \sum_{i=1}^{n} x_i \tag{15}$$

The statistics $W(C)$ and $B(C)$ have been combined in a number ways by different authors for the purposes of validation. Calinski-Harabasz index involves computing the normalized ratio of within-cluster relative to inter-cluster scatter:

$$CHC(C) = \frac{B(C)/k - 1}{W(C)/n - k} \tag{16}$$

This index has been frequently used as a mean of automatically selecting the number of clusters in data. A larger value is indicative of greater internal cohesion and a large degree of separation between the clusters in C.

4.2   Silhouette Validation Method

The Silhouette validation technique (Rousseeuw, 1987 [15]) calculates the width of the silhouette for each sample, the average silhouette width for each cluster and overall average silhouette width for a total dataset. Using this approach each cluster could be represented by a silhouette, based on the comparison of its tightness and separation. The average silhouette width could be used to assess the validity of clustering and could also be used to decide on the quality of the number of selected clusters. To construct the silhouettes $S(i)$ the following formula is used:

$$S(i) = \frac{(b(i) - a(i))}{\max \{a(i), b(i)\}} \tag{17}$$

where $a(i)$ is the average dissimilarity of the ith object to all other objects in the same cluster, $b(i)$ is the minimum of average dissimilarity of the ith object to all objects in other clusters (in the closest cluster), and $-1 \le s(i) \le 1$. If the silhouette value is close to 1, it means that sample is "well-clustered" and it was assigned to a very appropriate cluster. If the silhouette value is about zero, it means that the sample could be assigned to another closest cluster as well, and the sample lies equally far away from both clusters. If the silhouette value is close to -1, it means that sample is "misclassified" and is merely somewhere in between the clusters.

4.3 Datasets

– *waveform dataset* - This dataset is composed from 5000 instances divided into 3 classes. The original base included 40 variables, 19 are all noise attributes with mean 0 and variance 1. Each class is generated from a combination of 2 of 3 "base" waves.
– *Spam Base* - The SpamBase data set consists of 4601 observations described by 57 variables. Each variable describes an e-mail and its category: spam or not-spam. Most attributes indicate whether a particular word or character appears frequently in the e-mail. The run-length attributes (55–57) measure the length of sequences of consecutive capital letters.
– *Classic30 and Classic300* - are an extract of Classic3 [3] which contains three classes denoted Medline, Cisi, Cranfield as their original database source. Classic30 consists of 30 random documents described by 1000 words and Classic300 consists of 300 random documents described by 3625 words.
– *NG5: 20-Newsgroup* - NG5 (5 classes) is a subset of 20-Newsgroup data NG20 and composed by 500 documents described by 2000 words, concerning talk.politics.mideast and talk.politics.misc.

4.4 Interpretation of the Approach on the Waveform Dataset

In this example, we assume a scenario of a collaboration between two sites, in order to simplify the interpretation of the collaboration principle. We divided the basic waveform dataset size 5000×40 in two datasets: the first dataset 5000×20 which correspond to all the relevant variables and the second dataset 5000×20 containing the noisy set of variables.

We use these two datasets to show the whole process that would collaborate these data in an horizontal manner. Figure 1 represents the projection of the

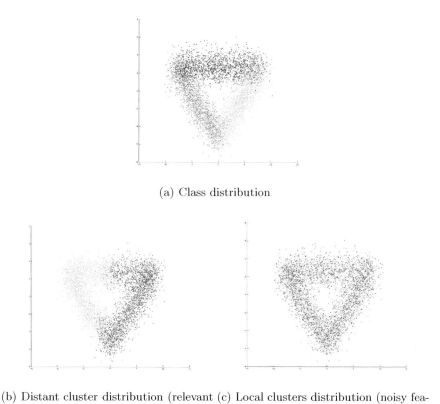

(a) Class distribution

(b) Distant cluster distribution (relevant (c) Local clusters distribution (noisy fea-
features) NMF1   tures) NMF2

Fig. 1. Visualization of the clustering results on the both relevant and noisy subsets before the collaboration

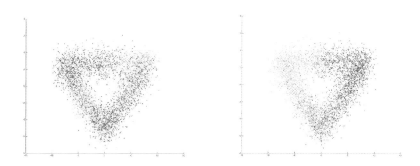

(a) Clusters distribution after the collab- (b) Clusters distribution after the collaboration (from NMF2 to NMF1)   oration (from NMF1 to NMF2)

Fig. 2. Visualization of the clustering results on the both relevant and noisy subsets after the collaboration

data in 2-dimensions using the PCA (Principal Component Analysis) and the color is the corresponding cluster of each object. Figure 1(a) represents the initial dataset using the real label. Figure 1(b) corresponds to the clustering obtained using the NMF before the collaboration on the subset containing only relevant variables. The obtained Calinski-Harabasz index is 2163. Contrarily, Fig. 1(c) corresponds to the clustering result on the noisy subset using the same NMF model. The obtained Calinski-Harabasz index is 132, and visually we can note that this distribution is noisy. Thereafter, we applied the second step of the proposed algorithm (principle of the collaboration) to exchange the clustering information between all both NMF clustering results without using the original data. Figures 2(a) and (b) illustrate an example of the collaboration between the 1st and 2nd subset (relevant vs noisy). After the collaboration of the first dataset with the irrelevant NMF2, the Calinski-Harabasz index decreased to 1548 because the NMF1 results (2163) has used the information from a noisy partition (NMF2) with a very low Calinski-Harabasz index (132). Contrarily, by applying the collaboration step in the opposite direction, the Calinski-Harabasz index of the $NMF_{2 \rightarrow 1}$ clustering increased to 1832 due to the collaboration with the relevant NMF1 clustering result. We computed also the Silhouette index in order to evaluate the clustering structure of the data and we obtained a Silhouette index of 0.39 for the first relevant subset and 0.042 for the second noisy subset. After the collaboration $NMF_{1 \rightarrow 2}$, the Silhouette index increase to 0.058 and in the case of the collaboration $NMF_{2 \rightarrow 1}$ the Silhouette index decrease from 0.39 to 0.26.

4.5   Validation on Other Datasets

Table 1. Experimental results of the horizontal collaborative approach on different datasets

Dataset	NMF	Horizontal collaboration	
		Calinski-Harabasz index	Silhouette index
SpamBase	NMF	29.08	0.52
	NMF_1	25.77	0.46
	NMF_2	29.62	0.59
	$NMF_{1 \rightarrow 2}$	27.27	0.48
	$NMF_{2 \rightarrow 1}$	28.06	0.57
NG5	NMF	11.54	0.39
	NMF_1	10.66	0.34
	NMF_2	12.04	0.39
	$NMF_{1 \rightarrow 2}$	11.89	0.35
	$NMF_{2 \rightarrow 1}$	11.68	0.38

(continued)

Table 1. (*continued*)

Dataset	NMF	Horizontal collaboration	
		Calinski-Harabasz index	Silhouette index
Classic30	NMF	2.29	0.72
	NMF_1	2.47	0.74
	NMF_2	2.07	0.68
	$NMF_{1 \to 2}$	2.37	0.68
	$NMF_{2 \to 1}$	2.30	0.76
Classic300	NMF	3.88	0.81
	NMF_1	3.74	0.78
	NMF_2	3.79	0.81
	$NMF_{1 \to 2}$	3.86	0.8
	$NMF_{2 \to 1}$	3.79	0.79

In this section, we applied the NMF_{Collab} between 2 views of different datasets and computed the Calinski-Harabasz and Silhouette index before and after the collaboration. From the Table 1, we can notice that the impact on the Silhouette index is very small after the collaboration for all the datasets, because the dataset structure doesn't change after the collaboration.

5   Conclusion

In this paper, we proposed a new approach by collaborating several Non-negative Matrix Factorization (NMF_{Collab}). This collaboration allows the interaction between several NMF in aim to reveal (to detect) the underlying structures and the regularities from the datasets.

We started by presenting the classical NMF approach, and we showed that it is equivalent to K-means. Afterwards, we explained in details our proposed horizontal learning approach which is adapted for collaboration between datasets that describe the same observations but with different variables.

The proposed approach is illustrated on various databases and the experimental results have shown very promising performance. As future work, we intend to make the vertical collaborative approach, then combine it with the horizontal one in order to get the hybrid approach.

References

1. Cichocki, A., Zdunek, R., Phan, A.H., Amari, S.i.: Nonnegative matrix and tensor factorizations: applications to exploratory multi-way data analysis and blind source separation. John Wiley & Sons, New Jersey (2009). https://doi.org/10.1002/9780470747278

2. Cornuejols, A., Wemmert, C., Gançarski, P., Bennani, Y.: Collaborative clustering: why, when, what and how. Inf. Fusion **39**, 81–95 (2018). https://doi.org/10.1016/j.inffus.2017.04.008
3. Dhillon, I.: Co-clustering documents and words using bipartite spectral graph partitioning. In: Proceedings of the International Conference ACM SIGKDD. pp. 269–274. San Francisco, USA (2001). https://doi.org/10.1145/502512.502550
4. Ding, C., He, X., Simon, H.D.: On the equivalence of nonnegative matrix factorization and spectral clustering. In: Proceedings of the 2005 SIAM International Conference on Data Mining, pp. 606–610. SIAM (2005). https://doi.org/10.1137/1.9781611972757.70
5. Forestier, G., Wemmert, C., Gancarski, P.: Collaborative multi-strategical classification for object-oriented image analysis. In: Workshop on Supervised and Unsupervised Ensemble Methods and Their Applications in Conjunction with IbPRIA, pp. 80–90. June 2007. https://doi.org/10.1007/978-3-540-78981-9-4
6. Forestier, G., Gancarski, P., Wemmert, C.: Collaborative clustering with background knowledge. Data Knowl. Eng. **69**(2), 211–228 (2010). https://doi.org/10.1016/j.datak.2009.10.004
7. Kim, H., Park, H.: Nonnegative matrix factorization based on alternating nonnegativity constrained least squares and active set method. SIAM J. Matrix Anal. Appl. **30**(2), 713–730 (2008). https://doi.org/10.1137/07069239X
8. Kim, J., Park, H.: Sparse nonnegative matrix factorization for clustering. Technical report, Georgia Institute of Technology (2008). https://doi.org/10.1137/07069239X
9. Lee, D.D., Seung, H.S.: Algorithms for non-negative matrix factorization. In: Proceedings of the 13th International Conference on Neural Information Processing Systems, pp. 535–541. NIPS 2000, MIT Press, Cambridge, MA, USA (2000). 3008751.3008829, http://dl.acm.org/citation.cfm?id=3008751.3008829
10. Lloyd, S.: Least squares quantization in PCM, special issue on quantization. IEEE Trans. Inf. Theor. **28**(2), 129–137 (1982). https://doi.org/10.1109/TIT.1982.1056489
11. Paatero, P., Tapper, U.: Positive matrix factorization: a non-negative factor model with optimal utilization of error estimates of data values. Environmetrics **5**(2), 111–126 (1994). https://doi.org/10.1002/env.3170050203
12. Pedrycz, W.: Collaborative fuzzy clustering. Pattern Recogn. Lett. **23**(14), 1675–1686 (2002). https://doi.org/10.1016/S0167-8655(02)00130-7
13. Pedrycz, W.: Knowledge-based clustering: from data to information granules. John Wiley & Sons, New Jersey (2005). https://doi.org/10.1002/0471708607
14. Rogovschi, N., Labiod, L., Nadif, M.: A topographical nonnegative matrix factorization algorithm. In: The 2013 International Joint Conference on Neural Networks, IJCNN 2013, Dallas, TX, USA, 4–9 August 2013, pp. 1–6 (2013). https://doi.org/10.1109/IJCNN.2013.6706849
15. Rousseeuw, R.: Silhouettes: a graphical aid to the interpretation and validation of cluster analysis. J. Computat. Appl. Math. **20**, 53–65 (1987). https://doi.org/10.1016/0377-0427(87)90125-7
16. Shahnaz, F., Berry, M.W., Pauca, V.P., Plemmons, R.J.: Document clustering using nonnegative matrix factorization. Inf. Process. Manag. **42**(2), 373–386 (2006). https://doi.org/10.1016/j.ipm.2004.11.005
17. Xie, Y.L., Hopke, P., Paatero, P.: Positive matrix factorization applied to a curve resolution problem. J. Chemom. **12**(6), 357–364 (1999). https://doi.org/10.1002/(SICI)1099-128X(199811/12)12:6

Anomaly Detection of Sequential Data

Cosine Similarity Drift Detector

Juan Isidro González Hidalgo⬚, Laura Maria Palomino Mariño⬚,
and Roberto Souto Maior de Barros(✉)⬚

Centro de Informática, Universidade Federal de Pernambuco, Recife, Brazil
{jigh,lmpm,roberto}@cin.ufpe.br

Abstract. Concept drift detection algorithms have several applications.
For example, nowadays many systems are interconnected by computer
networks and generate a lot of data constantly over time (data stream).
Thus, it is essential to detect when this data flow presents an abnormal
behavior as this might be an attack on the security of the network. This
paper proposes CSDD, a new method that uses the Cosine similarity
and windowing techniques to compare recent and older data and detect
concept drifts. To validate it, experiments were run with both synthetic
and real-world datasets and using Naive Bayes and Hoeffding Tree as
base learners. The accuracy results were evaluated using a variation of
the Friedman test and the Bonferroni-Dunn post-hoc test, whereas the
detections were evaluated using several metrics including the mean distance (μD), False Positives (FP), false Negatives (FN), precision, recall,
and Matthews Correlation Coefficient (MCC). The experimental results
show the effectiveness of CSDD in scenarios with abrupt and gradual
changes as it delivered the best results in nearly all artificial datasets.

Keywords: Concept drift detection · Online learning · Data streams

1 Introduction

In the information age, large amounts of data are constantly generated over time,
which are known as data streams. At the same time, the number of cyber attacks
dramatically increases each year. Thus, monitoring and controlling these data to
detect anomalous activities and behaviors are specially relevant. Some proposed
solutions aim to collect and analyse security events to assess the risk they bring
and inform the administrator, in order to take appropriate decisions [22].

For instance, consider a computer network that is protected and monitored
by a Security Information and Event Management System (SIEM). Suppose one
of its sensors shows an abnormal behavior reporting alarms that might indicate
a violation of network security. Such circumstance is often formulated as a detection task, where the point that showed the suspicious activity must be signaled.
In machine learning similar problems are commonly studied as concept drift [4].

In general, approaches to cope with concept drift can be classified in two
groups: (i) approaches that adapt a learner at regular intervals disregarding

Supported by Coord. de Aperfeiçoamento de Pessoal de Nível Superior (CAPES).

© Springer Nature Switzerland AG 2019
I. V. Tetko et al. (Eds.): ICANN 2019, LNCS 11730, pp. 669–685, 2019.
https://doi.org/10.1007/978-3-030-30490-4_53

whether changes have really occurred; and (ii) approaches that detect concept changes, and then, the learner is adapted to these changes [18]. The latter, known as informed methods, is the most interesting, as they explicitly detect drifts [4,21] using triggering mechanisms (drift detection) in the aforementioned situations.

Windowing methods have been widely used for handling drift detection. They consider that the most recent observations are the most informative, and estimate changes using either a time or a data window. A window is a short memory data structure which can store informative data or summarize some statistics concerning the model behavior or the data distribution in order to characterize the current concept. The specificity, nature, size and positioning strategy are the main characteristics that describe windows [26].

This paper proposes Cosine Similarity Drift Detector (CSDD), a new method for detecting concept drifts based on the computation of the Cosine similarity measure between vectors, a strategy that was previously adopted for treating imbalanced data streams using all its examples [2], and on sliding windows, similarly to the strategy of Wilcoxon Rank Sum Test Drift Detector (WSTD) [5]. CSDD proposes to detect drifts based on these strategies using the Positive Predictive Value (PPV) and False Discovery (FDR) rates of the stream.

The paper is organized as follows. Section 2 describes related work. Problem setting is introduced in Sect. 3. In Sect. 4, we present the main conceptual arguments for the Cosine similarity measure and explain the proposed method in detail. Section 5 shows the chosen synthetic and real-world datasets and presents the setup of our experiments. Section 6 evaluates the performance of the proposed method against other recent approaches, discusses the results, and presents the main findings that were obtained. Section 7 concludes this paper.

2   Related Work

Many concept drift detectors have been previously proposed. Some of these are described below, with emphasis on newer methods.

Drift Detection Method (DDM) [17], possibly the most well-known drift detector, detects changes in a distribution by analyzing the error rate of the base classifier and its corresponding standard deviation. Based on the Probably Approximately Correct (PAC) [30] learning model, its authors argue the error rate p_i will decrease when the number of examples i increases, if the distribution of the examples is stationary. Accordingly, an increase in the error rate suggests there was a change in the data distribution and the current base learner needs to be substituted.

Hoeffding-based Drift Detection Method (HDDM) [15] monitors the performance of the base learner by applying "some probability inequalities that assume only independent, uni-variate and bounded random variables to obtain theoretical guarantees for the detection of such distributional changes". The authors claim its first variation, Hoeffding-based Drift Detection Method A-test ($HDDM_A$), "involves moving averages and is more suitable to detect abrupt changes" whereas HDDM W-test ($HDDM_W$) "follows a widespread intuitive idea to deal with gradual changes using weighted moving averages".

Fast Hoeffding Drift Detection Method (FHDDM) is based on the idea that the accuracy of classification models should stay steady, or increase, as more instances are processed; the degradation in accuracy may indicate that the concept is changing. The FHDDM algorithm uses Hoeffding's inequality [24] to detect drifts in evolving data streams. It calculates and compares the maximum probability of correct predictions observed so far with the most recent probability of correct predictions for the purpose of drift detection.

Reactive Drift Detection Method (RDDM) [3] is a detector inspired on DDM [17]. Among other heuristic modifications, it proposes to discard older instances of very long concepts aiming to detect drifts earlier, improving the precision of its detections and especially the final accuracy, since DDM usually faces performance loss due to lack of sensitivity when the concepts become too long. These improvements in the accuracy results are especially substantial when the sizes of the concepts are many thousand instances long and in datasets with gradual concept drifts.

Fisher Test Drift Detector (FTDD) is one of three sibling concept drift detectors [9] based on an efficient implementation of Fisher's Exact test [14,40]. It draws on Statistical Test of Equal Proportions (STEPD) [31] and on the deficiency of its statistical test of equal proportions in situations where the data samples are small or imbalanced. FTDD detects drifts using Fisher's Exact test instead of the test of equal proportions in all situations.

Wilcoxon Rank Sum Test Drift Detector (WSTD) [5] is another detector inspired on STEPD [31]. It provides an efficient implementation of the Wilcoxon rank-sum statistical test [39] and applies it to detect concept drifts, improving the detections of STEPD and its accuracy in most scenarios. Although WSTD delivers strong all-round performance, its accuracy improvements are usually larger in datasets with abrupt concept drifts and its main strength is the precision of its detections of concept drifts.

3 Problem Setting

In statistical analysis, a confusion (or error) matrix is a table that typically permits the visualization of the performance of supervised learning algorithms. In classification, the formulation of a 2×2 confusion matrix provides a binary association between the predicted values of the classification and the actual values of the labeled class to calculate the values of True Positives (TP), True Negatives (TN), False Positives (FP) and false Negatives (FN).

Previous works in the area use these four rates and statistical methods to find out whether the distributions between the data samples are the same or not. Distance and similarity metrics between distributions are often calculated with the fundamental objective of detecting concept drifts and usually associate a significant change in some of these rates to detect the drifts [38]. Other proposals use vector spaces to calculate the similarity between vectors [2]. Most of these approaches are used in imbalanced datasets and do *not* use sliding windows.

Definition 1. *Given labeled datasets X_a and X_b are converted into a vector space such that $V_a = (TP_a, FP_a, TN_a, FN_a)$ and $V_b = (TP_b, FP_b, TN_b, FN_b)$. In this case, the distribution of $X_a(y)$ is said to be similar to $X_b(y)$, if the measured similarity $S(V_a, V_b) > T$ where T is a predefined threshold.*

Taking into account Definition 1, our problem can be formulated as follows. Given that V_1 and V_2 are vectors created from two error estimates or confusion matrices of two datasets, using the false and true predictions of the classification algorithms, which are stored in sliding windows, the PPV and FDR rates are going to be used. These can be computed as follows: $PPV_r = TP/(TP + FP)$ and $FDR_r = FP/(FP + TP)$.

Observe that the computation of similarity (or distance) between the two confusion matrices will determine whether the two datasets are sampled from the same distribution or not and therefore detect the presence or absence of concept drift.

4   Cosine Similarity and the Proposed Methods

Cosine similarity or distance [2,37] measures the angular distance between the coordinates of two data points (x_i and x_j). Mathematically it represents the cosine angle between the unit vectors in the direction of two standard vectors. The resulting values are between -1 and 1 as the cosine angle range. Although the angles are those that are measured, it is intended to provide the linear distance between the data points. A higher value of this function denotes that the data objects are very similar to one another.

Definition 2. *The cosine of two vectors, a and b can be derived using the Euclidean dot product formula: $a.b = \|a\| \|b\| \cos \theta$.*

Given two vectors of attributes A and B, the cosine similarity (θ) is represented using a dot product and magnitude as:

$$Similarity(S) = \cos \theta = \frac{A.B}{\|a\| \|b\|} = \frac{\sum_{i=1}^{n} A_i \times B_i}{\sqrt{\sum_{i=1}^{n}(A_i)^2} \times \sqrt{\sum_{i=1}^{n}(B_i)^2}} \quad (1)$$

where $S \in \{-1, 1\}$ such that -1 implies exactly the opposite, 1 implies exactly the same and 0 indicates orthogonality or decorrelation.

The cosine similarity can be seen as a method for normalizing the length of the document during the comparison. In the information retrieval area, the cosine similarity of two documents usually varies from 0 to 1. Thus, its applicability in the area of text mining is remarkable. In the field data mining, it is also used to measure cohesion within clusters. In addition to the properties described above, the cosine similarity is invariant to scale, so different units do *not* affect the result and it also considers the relative distance between objects at a fixed point [25].

In the process of learning from data streams with concept drift, the Cosine similarity has proved to be an excellent metric in assessments with imbalanced datasets, producing high-quality results when comparing the coefficient of similarity with a threshold to detect the drifts [2]. Our main motivation is the fact that this measure has not yet been evaluated as a tool to compare the similarity between data distributions using sliding windows aiming to detect drifts.

Next section describes the proposed method using as main motivation the use of the calculation of the cosine similarity metric between vectors, previously explained, together with the strategy of sliding windows.

4.1   CSDD

Cosine Similarity Drift Detector (CSDD) works very similarly to the Wilcoxon Rank Sum Test Drift Detector (WSTD) method [5]: it monitors predictions from the base classifier using two windows, named as recent and old, and their sizes in instances are w and w_2, respectively.

Note that the number of examples of the older window of data is also limited, as in WSTD, instead of the unlimited older window adopted by Statistical Test of Equal Proportions (STEPD). As most other concept drift detectors, CSDD also has parameters to set the limits for detecting drifts (α_d) and signaling warnings (α_w), affecting the similarity calculations implemented in the method.

The abstract pseudo-code of CSDD is illustrated in Algorithm 1. It receives as inputs a data stream and the aforementioned parameters. In lines **1**–**5** CSDD initializes its local variables, including vectors A and B used in the calculation of the cosine similarity.

After a concept drift is detected by CSDD (line **8**), the necessary adjustments in the two windows, two vectors and the other local variables are implemented (lines **9**–**12**). Lines **13** and **14** abstract the required updates on both windows and in the statistics of these windows, respectively, every time a new instance of the data stream is processed. It is worth pointing out that line **16** ensures that the detections of drifts and warnings only occur after the older window has at least the same size of the recent window, i.e. w instances.

Lines **17**–**20** simulate the computation of the PPV and FDR rates of the two windows by associating them to the values of the correct (ro, rr) and wrong (wo, wr) predictions of the classifier to determine the rate calculations that are quantified in both windows.

To permit the calculations, we associated ro and rr to TP whereas wo and wr were associated to FP. This was done with the focus of developing the above mentioned rates in coordination with the requirements of the 2×2 confusion matrix and following on the ideas presented in [2], which used TP and FP to calculate the measure of similarity. The main difference is that our method uses the more general and meaningful PPV and FDR rates instead of TP and FP.

Lines **21** and **22** store the computed rates in vectors A and B, respectively. The calculation of the Cosine similarity between the vectors is implemented in lines **23**–**26**. Finally the tests used to decide the signals of drifts and warnings are represented in lines **27**–**32**.

Algorithm 1. Cosine Similarity Drift Detector

Input: Data stream s, Recent window size w, Drift level α_d, Warning level α_w,
       Older window size w_2

1 $storedPreds \leftarrow$ **new byte** $[w]$
2 $storedPreds_2 \leftarrow$ **new byte** $[w_2]$
3 $vector_A \leftarrow$ **new double** $[2]$
4 $vector_B \leftarrow$ **new double** $[2]$
5 $n_o \leftarrow n_r \leftarrow w_o \leftarrow w_r \leftarrow r_o \leftarrow r_r \leftarrow 0$
6 $changeDetected \leftarrow$ **false**
7 **foreach** $instance$ **in** s **do**
8   **if** $changeDetected$ **then**
9   **reset** $storedPreds, storedPreds_2$
10         $n_o \leftarrow n_r \leftarrow w_o \leftarrow w_r \leftarrow r_o \leftarrow r_r \leftarrow 0$
11         $changeDetected \leftarrow$ **false**
12   **end**
13   Updates predictions in $older$ and $recent$ windows
14   Updates stats of both windows: $n_o, n_r, w_o, w_r, r_o, r_r$
15     $isWarningZone \leftarrow$ **false**
16   **if** $n_o \geq w$ **then**
17         $rateppv_o \leftarrow r_o \;/\; (r_o + w_o)$
18         $ratefdr_o \leftarrow w_o \;/\; (w_o + r_o)$
19         $rateppv_r \leftarrow r_r \;/\; (r_r + w_r)$
20         $ratefdr_r \leftarrow w_r \;/\; (w_r + r_r)$
21         $vector_A \leftarrow [rateppv_o, ratefdr_o]$
22         $vector_B \leftarrow [rateppv_r, ratefdr_r]$
23         $sp \leftarrow$ **scalarProduct** $(|vector_A, vector_B|)$
24         $sqva \leftarrow$ **squareVector** $(|vector_A|)$
25         $sqvb \leftarrow$ **squareVector** $(|vector_B|)$
26         $S \leftarrow sp \;/\; ($**sqrt** $(sqva) \times$ **sqrt** $(sqvb))$
27   **if** $S < \alpha_d$ **then**
28             $changeDetected \leftarrow$ **true**
29   **end**
30   **else if** $S < \alpha_w$ **then**
31             $isWarningZone \leftarrow$ **true**
32   **end**
33   **end**
34 **end**

---

5   Experimental Settings

This section describes the experiments designed to test CSDD. It was compared to other methods suitable for detecting concept drifts in data streams, namely: DDM, FHDDM, FTDD, $HDDM_A$, RDDM and WSTD.

Naive Bayes (NB) and Hoeffding Tree (HT) were chosen to be used as base learners in the experiments because they are the most commonly used classifiers in the data stream area and their implementations are freely available in the Massive Online Analysis (MOA) framework [8].

The accuracy of the tested methods were measured using the Prequential methodology [11] with a sliding window of size 1000 as its forgetting mechanism [23]. With this arrangement, each instance is used for testing before it is used for training, and thus the accuracy is updated incrementally. This guarantees that every instance is used both for testing and training and no training happens before testing on any instance.

Since all the executed methods do not use much execution time or memory, they were only compared in terms of accuracy and detections.

5.1 Datasets

To carry out the tests, we selected five synthetic dataset generators and built abrupt and gradual concept drift datasets with 10,000 instances and concept changes in instances 2000, 4000, 6000, and 8000. The selected synthetic datasets are: *Agrawal* [1,28], *LED* [34], *Mixed* [7], *Sine* [17,36], and *Waveform* [6,20].

In all the gradual datasets, the length of the concept drifts was set to 500 instances. In particular, the Agrawal datasets were set with 1% of noise in each of its six numeric attributes. To compute the final accuracy of the tested methods, the experiments were executed 30 times and the mean results were calculated together with the 95% confidence intervals.

Also, we selected some real-world datasets with very different number of instances and complexity, that were used in previous works in the area. In these datasets, the number and position of the concept drifts are unknown. They are: *Airlines* [35], *NslKdd99(KDD)* [32,33], *Rialto* [27], *Usenet2* [15,19], and *WhiteWine* [10].

Table 1 presents the main features of the synthetic and real-world datasets used in the experiments of this work.

Table 1. Features of synthetic and real-world datasets.

Type	Dataset	Size	#Atributes	#Classes
Synthetic	Agrawal	10,000	9	2
	Led	10,000	24	10
	Mixed	10,000	4	2
	Sine	10,000	2	2
	Waveform	10,000	40	3
Real	Airlines	45,312	8	2
	KDD	148,517	42	2
	Rialto	82,250	27	10
	Usenet2	1,500	100	2
	WhiteWine	4,898	12	9

5.2 Parametrization of the Methods

All the methods have been tested using their default parameters as proposed by their respective authors. Table 2 summarizes the default and range of all the parameters of the tested methods, also including CSDD.

Table 2. Default parameters of the methods.

Method	Parameters with defaults and [ranges]			
CSDD	n=1000 [0, 10K]	$\alpha_d = 0.99989$ [0, 1]	$\alpha_w = 1.0$ [0, 1]	w2 = 1000 [1K, 10K]
DDM	n = 30 [0, ∞]	$\alpha_w = 2.0$ [1, 4]	$\alpha_d = 3.0$ [1, 5]	
FHDDM	n = 25 [0, ∞]	$\delta = 0.000001$ [0, 1]		
FTDD	r = 30 [0, 1000]	$\alpha_d = 0.003$ [0, 1]	$\alpha_w = 0.005$ [0, 1]	
HDDMA	d = 0.001 [0, 1]	w = 0.005 [0, 1]	t = 1 [0, 1]	
RDDM	n = 129 [0, ∞]	$\alpha_w = 1.773$ [1, 4]	$\alpha_d = 2.258$ [1, 5]	max = 40K [1, ∞]
			min = 7K [1, 20K]	wLim = 1400 [1, 20K]
WSTD	n = 30 [0, 1000]	$\alpha_d = 0.003$ [0, 1]	$\alpha_w = 0.05$ [0, 1]	w2 = 4000 [30, 10K]

6 Analysis of the Experimental Results

This section discusses the results of the experiments and includes the analyses of the accuracy and drift detections of the methods.

Tables 3 and 4 present the accuracy results with 95% confidence intervals of all tested methods in the selected datasets using NB and HT, respectively. In each dataset, the best result is written in **bold**.

Table 3. Mean accuracies in percentage using NB, with 95% confidence intervals in scenarios of abrupt and gradual concept drifts with artificial and real datasets.

Type	Dataset	DDM	FHDDM	FTDD	HDDMA	RDDM	WSTD	CSDD
Abr	Agraw	61.56 ± 0.54	63.33 ± 0.30	60.85 ± 0.30	63.17 ± 0.33	63.56 ± 0.28	62.07 ± 0.38	**64.37 ± 0.27**
	LED	69.57 ± 0.31	69.32 ± 0.78	67.20 ± 0.38	69.72 ± 0.31	69.80 ± 0.30	67.60 ± 0.83	**70.02 ± 0.32**
	Mixed	89.74 ± 0.30	90.20 ± 0.23	90.39 ± 0.22	90.39 ± 0.22	90.22 ± 0.24	90.41 ± 0.23	**90.44 ± 0.24**
	Sine	85.10 ± 0.72	86.67 ± 0.24	86.75 ± 0.23	86.62 ± 0.21	86.58 ± 0.25	86.76 ± 0.23	**86.81 ± 0.22**
	Wavef	78.49 ± 0.47	79.02 ± 0.63	78.06 ± 0.48	78.73 ± 0.51	79.12 ± 0.49	78.79 ± 0.54	**79.41 ± 0.47**
Grad	Agraw	60.56 ± 0.39	61.53 ± 0.55	59.27 ± 0.31	61.25 ± 0.36	62.05 ± 0.29	60.80 ± 0.31	**62.51 ± 0.22**
	LED	67.78 ± 0.41	66.91 ± 0.94	63.11 ± 0.36	67.65 ± 0.32	**67.85 ± 0.30**	64.40 ± 0.75	67.49 ± 0.31
	Mixed	83.65 ± 0.29	84.13 ± 0.25	83.74 ± 0.28	83.61 ± 0.28	83.89 ± 0.30	83.42 ± 0.28	**84.41 ± 0.26**
	Sine	81.32 ± 0.28	82.01 ± 0.20	81.26 ± 0.19	81.51 ± 0.21	81.85 ± 0.19	81.32 ± 0.22	**82.21 ± 0.20**
	Wavef	77.99 ± 0.45	77.78 ± 0.48	76.65 ± 0.42	77.82 ± 0.51	78.46 ± 0.38	77.54 ± 0.56	**78.69 ± 0.39**
Real	Airlines	65.35	65.82	66.76	67.23	**67.50**	66.68	66.15
	KDD	88.77	88.80	88.19	88.85	**89.41**	88.19	89.26
	Rialto	36.63	41.24	27.52	43.30	**44.88**	30.48	41.39
	Usenet2	69.87	69.38	67.17	68.37	**69.93**	67.75	68.67
	WhiteWine	42.82	**46.53**	44.88	43.16	43.41	46.39	46.41
Rank	Artificial	5.1500	3.8000	5.9500	4.1500	2.8000	4.8500	**1.3000**
	Real	5.2000	3.6000	5.5000	3.6000	**1.8000**	5.1000	3.2000
	All	5.1667	3.7333	5.8000	3.9667	2.4667	4.9333	**1.9333**

Table 4. Mean accuracies in percentage using HT, with 95% confidence intervals in scenarios of abrupt and gradual concept drifts with artificial and real datasets.

Type	Dataset	DDM	FHDDM	FTDD	HDDMA	RDDM	WSTD	CSDD
Abr	Agraw	63.13 ± 0.59	64.48 ± 0.40	62.64 ± 0.40	64.47 ± 0.36	64.69 ± 0.32	63.44 ± 0.45	$\mathbf{65.58 \pm 0.44}$
	LED	69.56 ± 0.31	69.29 ± 0.77	67.01 ± 0.39	69.68 ± 0.31	69.78 ± 0.31	67.08 ± 1.05	$\mathbf{69.98 \pm 0.32}$
	Mixed	89.70 ± 0.30	90.14 ± 0.23	90.33 ± 0.22	90.32 ± 0.24	90.17 ± 0.25	90.36 ± 0.23	$\mathbf{90.39 \pm 0.24}$
	Sine	87.01 ± 0.76	88.29 ± 0.17	88.37 ± 0.16	88.39 ± 0.17	87.98 ± 0.21	88.38 ± 0.15	$\mathbf{88.44 \pm 0.21}$
	Wavef	78.45 ± 0.48	78.99 ± 0.61	78.07 ± 0.47	78.69 ± 0.51	79.09 ± 0.49	78.77 ± 0.53	$\mathbf{79.38 \pm 0.47}$
Grad	Agraw	61.57 ± 0.49	62.56 ± 0.31	61.33 ± 0.25	62.27 ± 0.38	62.92 ± 0.28	61.77 ± 0.40	$\mathbf{63.18 \pm 0.22}$
	LED	67.76 ± 0.44	66.86 ± 0.93	62.88 ± 0.37	67.58 ± 0.32	$\mathbf{67.81 \pm 0.30}$	63.99 ± 0.84	67.45 ± 0.31
	Mixed	83.49 ± 0.29	83.98 ± 0.24	83.50 ± 0.29	83.39 ± 0.28	83.70 ± 0.32	83.26 ± 0.29	$\mathbf{84.25 \pm 0.27}$
	Sine	82.43 ± 0.30	82.95 ± 0.25	82.28 ± 0.22	82.41 ± 0.28	82.66 ± 0.20	82.14 ± 0.23	$\mathbf{83.21 \pm 0.21}$
	Wavef	77.97 ± 0.45	77.77 ± 0.45	76.68 ± 0.41	77.82 ± 0.49	78.42 ± 0.38	77.57 ± 0.53	$\mathbf{78.66 \pm 0.39}$
Real	Airlines	65.30	65.37	64.75	65.00	**66.01**	65.15	65.87
	KDD	97.78	97.71	97.71	**97.85**	97.36	97.71	89.73
	Rialto	36.88	42.73	30.83	45.70	**48.17**	37.38	43.07
	Usenet2	68.29	68.48	**69.10**	68.61	68.58	68.48	**69.10**
	WhiteWine	43.33	46.09	43.32	43.31	43.84	45.27	**46.11**
Rank	Artificial	5.0000	3.9000	5.9000	4.0000	2.8000	5.1000	**1.3000**
	Real	4.8000	3.7000	5.1000	3.8000	3.2000	4.5000	**2.9000**
	All	4.9333	3.8333	5.6333	3.9333	2.9333	4.9000	**1.8333**

After a vertical evaluation of the results in these two tables, we observed that the proposed method delivered the very best results with both NB and HT as base learner in nearly all synthetic datasets. The only artificial dataset where CSDD did not deliver the top result was the LED dataset configured with gradual changes, where it presented values 67.49 and 67.45 with NB and HT, respectively. Even so, CSDD was second and reasonably close to the best result in both cases. In other words, from the total of 20 synthetic evaluated scenarios, including abrupt and gradual datasets with both NB and HT, CSDD achieved the highest accuracy in 90% of them.

Observing the results of the experimentation with real datasets, it is obvious that CSDD was comparatively less effective, especially using NB. In these tests, CSDD was the second best method in KDD and WhiteWhine, reasonably close to the best result, and was third best in Rialto.

With HT, CSDD obtained the highest accuracy in Usenet2 and WhiteWine, tied with FTDD in the former, was the second best in Airlines, and again third best in Rialto. Its worst result was in the KDD dataset, where its accuracy value (89.73) was much lower than those of all the other methods.

A more detailed view of the performance of CSDD throughout the Usenet2 and WhiteWine datasets is shown in Fig. 1. It can be seen that the behavior of the method was more stable in Usenet2 (Fig. 1(a)) than in WhineWine (Fig. 1(b)). In the latter, CSDD was competitive at the start of the dataset, until instance 600, approximately, then lost performance dramatically when compared to the other methods, being competitive again around instance 2300, and becoming the best method after instance 4000.

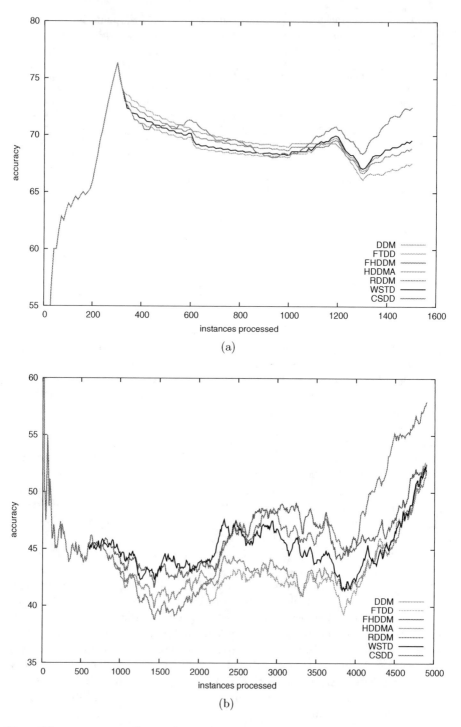

Fig. 1. Comparison of the methods using mean accuracies using HT with the real datasets: (*a*) Usenet2 and (*b*) WhiteWine.

In addition, it can be appreciated that RDDM was the best method in the real-world datasets, delivering the best result in 6 out of 10 scenarios, with results close to those of the best methods in most of the other datasets.

To conclude the analysis of the tests using real-world datasets, it is worth saying the performance of CSDD depends on the width of its two windows and the size of the concepts in the datasets: in some datasets, this probably affected the performance of the algorithm. Other possible causes include (a) some of these datasets might not have any concept drifts and (b) they might have temporary dependencies on the class label and/or imbalanced data.

To deepen the analysis of the previous results, we used a variation of the *Friedman* test [16] to verify the existence of significant differences between the evaluated methods and identify which obtained better accuracy results. The tests were used with a significance level of 5%.

Note that the numeric values of the ranks were also included in tables 3 and 4, separated by type of dataset and also with all the datasets together. Based on the aggregated ranks (All), we can say the performance of CSDD was the best in most of the designed scenarios, being the best ranked method with both classifiers, followed by RDDM, FHDDM and $HDDM_A$. The worst ranks were those of WSTD, DDM, and FTDD. Similar results are seen in the ranks using only the artificial datasets. Finally, in the real-world datasets, the ranks show CSDD as the best method with HT and second best with NB.

In addition, as the rejection of the null hypothesis of the statistical test indicates significant differences but does not define which methods are statistically different [12], the *Bonferroni-Dunn* post-hoc test [13] was applied using CSDD as the base method. Figure 2 captures the results of this comparison of the methods. We present the aggregated rank results using a graphical representation where the critical difference (CD = 2.08088) is illustrated by a bar and methods that are connected to CSDD by this bar are not statistically different.

The graphics show that, despite being ranked as the best method with both base learners, CSDD was statistically superior to FTDD, DDM, and WSTD, without significant difference to RDDM, FHDDM and $HDDM_A$ in both cases.

Even though the graphics are not presented, it is worthwhile adding that, in the evaluation with only the artificial datasets, CSDD was also statistically better than $HDDM_A$ with both base classifiers and better than FHDDM in the tests using HT. In the case of the real-world datasets, only FTDD was inferior to CSDD with NB and there were no statistical differences with HT.

Another alternative to evaluate the performance of concept drift detectors is analyzing their identifications of drifts. For this purpose, several metrics can be computed to assess how effective the methods are concerning the detection of the points where the changes occur [4]. These metrics are drift mean distance, the number of false Negatives (FN) and False Positives (FP), precision, recall, and Matthews Correlation Coefficient (MCC) [29].

Table 5 presents the results of the drift identifications of the methods in the abrupt datasets using NB and HT: the best results are shown in **bold**.

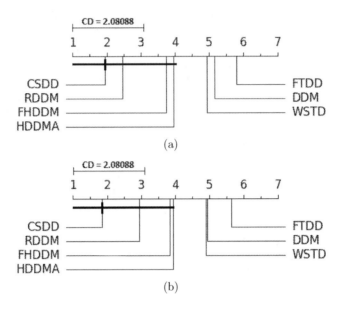

Fig. 2. Accuracy statistical comparison of the methods using the Friedman test and the Bonferroni-Dunn post-hoc test on all tested datasets with the classifiers: (*a*) Naive Bayes and (*b*) Hoeffding Tree.

These results showed the excellent performance of CSDD when compared to those of the other methods in identifying the drifts in most datasets. Specifically, in Agrawal, LED, and Waveform, CSDD was better than the other methods in most of the metrics evaluated. Considering the mean results of the methods in all datasets, we can say that, in general, CSDD was the best method in the identification of concept drifts.

Note the best values of the methods concerning mean distance (μD), FN, and FP are the ones with the lowest values whereas in precision, recall, and MCC the best results are the highest values. The final part of the table shows the calculation of the mean determined from the results of the detectors in all the datasets and gives an overview of the general behavior of the methods.

Moreover, it is worthwhile pointing out that the results of the MCC metric consist in computing a correlation coefficient between the observed and predicted classifications; it returns values between -1 and $+1$. The value $+1$ represents a perfect prediction, 0 no better than random prediction, and -1 indicates total disagreement between prediction and observation [29].

The illustrations in Fig. 3 show the performance of the tested methods in the artificial datasets according to this criterion, using NB and HT, respectively. Notice that the remarkable superiority of CSDD to the other methods in the Agrawal, LED, and Waveform datasets are clearly captured.

Table 5. Concept drift identifications of the methods in the abrupt datasets using NB and HT as base classifiers.

Detect	NB						DS	HT					
	μD	FN	FP	Prec	Rec	MCC		μD	FN	FP	Prec	Rec	MCC
DDM	NA	120	92	0.000	0.000	-0.010		NA	120	85	0.000	0.000	-0.009
FHDDM	24.9	85	140	0.215	0.292	0.249	A	25.9	77	138	0.250	0.358	0.296
FTDD	32.0	118	37	0.067	0.017	0.033	G	31.4	115	50	0.094	0.042	0.061
HDDMA	30.0	112	112	0.065	0.067	0.065	R	24.2	110	107	0.089	0.083	0.085
RDDM	32.5	118	125	0.015	0.017	0.015	A	33.0	115	140	0.034	0.042	0.037
WSTD	30.8	101	88	0.183	0.158	0.165	W	29.5	96	83	0.222	0.200	0.208
CSDD	**2.2**	**11**	**20**	**0.848**	**0.908**	**0.877**		**9.0**	**9**	**20**	**0.852**	**0.925**	**0.886**
DDM	NA	120	93	0.000	0.000	-0.011		NA	120	93	0.000	0.000	-0.011
FHDDM	17.9	40	50	0.687	0.667	0.671		17.9	40	50	0.687	0.667	0.671
FTDD	23.5	80	77	0.403	0.333	0.356	L	23.5	80	90	0.368	0.333	0.340
HDDMA	22.3	67	44	0.550	0.442	0.492	E	22.4	67	44	0.550	0.442	0.492
RDDM	33.6	112	95	0.081	0.067	0.073	D	33.6	112	95	0.081	0.067	0.073
WSTD	22.0	53	197	0.358	0.558	0.430		22.0	53	243	0.315	0.558	0.403
CSDD	**0.0**	**0**	30	**0.800**	**1.000**	**0.894**		**0.0**	**0**	30	**0.800**	**1.000**	**0.894**
DDM	29.1	1	2	0.985	0.992	0.988		29.2	2	4	0.972	0.983	0.977
FHDDM	14.2	0	0	1.000	1.000	1.000	M	14.2	0	0	1.000	1.000	1.000
FTDD	13.0	0	2	0.987	1.000	0.993	I	13.0	0	7	0.958	1.000	0.977
HDDMA	10.8	0	0	1.000	1.000	1.000	X	10.5	0	0	1.000	1.000	1.000
RDDM	18.2	0	1	0.993	1.000	0.997	E	18.3	0	2	0.987	1.000	0.993
WSTD	12.4	0	0	1.000	1.000	1.000	D	12.4	0	0	1.000	1.000	1.000
CSDD	**7.4**	0	17	0.887	1.000	0.940		**7.3**	0	18	0.880	1.000	0.937
DDM	25.6	54	94	0.435	0.550	0.485		26.4	43	124	0.445	0.642	0.525
FHDDM	14.7	0	0	1.000	1.000	1.000	S	15.5	0	0	1.000	1.000	1.000
FTDD	14.3	0	3	0.980	1.000	0.989	I	14.7	0	4	0.973	1.000	0.986
HDDMA	13.8	8	11	0.916	0.933	0.924	N	12.8	4	5	0.960	0.967	0.963
RDDM	19.5	5	40	0.788	0.958	0.862	E	19.3	4	75	0.686	0.967	0.804
WSTD	13.3	0	1	0.993	1.000	0.997		13.5	0	0	1.000	1.000	1.000
CSDD	**10.8**	3	11	0.922	0.975	0.947		**5.3**	11	28	0.795	0.908	0.848
DDM	NA	120	48	0.000	0.000	-0.007		NA	120	45	0.000	0.000	-0.007
FHDDM	23.2	101	25	0.400	0.158	0.248	W	23.2	101	25	0.400	0.158	0.248
FTDD	27.8	109	**21**	0.258	0.092	0.151	A	27.8	109	**24**	0.258	0.092	0.150
HDDMA	27.9	113	37	0.133	0.058	0.087	V	27.9	113	38	0.133	0.058	0.087
RDDM	30.7	117	56	0.044	0.025	0.033	E	18.8	116	60	0.036	0.033	0.034
WSTD	23.5	104	27	0.328	0.133	0.206	F	23.5	104	29	0.328	0.133	0.206
CSDD	**5.8**	21	34	**0.738**	**0.825**	**0.779**		**5.9**	19	32	**0.755**	**0.842**	**0.796**
DDM	27.3	83.0	65.8	0.284	0.308	0.289		27.8	81.0	70.2	0.283	0.325	0.295
FHDDM	19.0	45.2	43.0	0.660	0.623	0.634	M	19.3	43.6	42.6	0.667	0.637	0.643
FTDD	22.1	61.4	28.0	0.539	0.488	0.504	E	22.1	60.8	35.0	0.530	0.493	0.503
HDDMA	20.9	60.0	40.8	0.533	0.500	0.514	A	19.6	58.8	38.8	0.547	0.510	0.525
RDDM	26.9	70.4	63.4	0.384	0.413	0.396	N	24.6	69.4	74.4	0.365	0.422	0.388
WSTD	20.4	51.6	62.6	0.572	0.570	0.559		20.2	50.6	71.0	0.573	0.578	0.563
CSDD	**5.2**	**7.0**	**22.4**	**0.839**	**0.942**	**0.887**		**5.5**	**7.8**	**25.6**	**0.816**	**0.935**	**0.872**

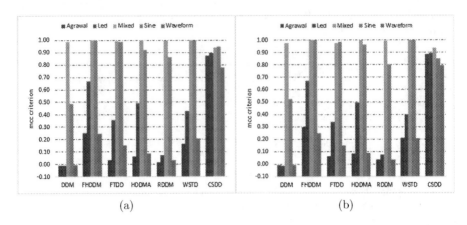

(a)   (b)

Fig. 3. Comparison of the methods using the MCC criterion on abrupt datasets with the classifiers: (a) Naive Bayes and (b) Hoeffding Tree.

7   Conclusion

This paper proposes Cosine Similarity Drift Detector (CSDD), a new concept drift detector which monitors the predictions of a base classifier and uses two sliding windows of data, named *recent* and *old*, and the Cosine similarity measure to detect the drifts based on the performance of the method in the instances of these two windows according to the Positive Predictive Value (PPV) and False Discovery (FDR) rates simulated using the right and wrong predictions of the classifier in the two windows considered.

In order to test the effectiveness of the method, experiments were run to compare it against six other published detectors. The experimentation was made with 10 synthetic and five real-world datasets and using both Naive Bayes (NB) and Hoeffding Tree (HT) as base learners. The results obtained demonstrated the superiority of CSDD against the other tested methods on both abrupt and gradual datasets in terms of accuracy and of the detections of the drifts. However, with real-world datasets the results were not as strong.

The results of the experiments were also evaluated statistically using a variation of the *Friedman* test in combination with the *Bonferroni-Dunn* post-hoc test. This evaluation confirmed the superiority of CSDD to the other tested approaches as it was ranked first in the tests performed with both base learners. Similar findings were obtained in the evaluation using with the Matthews Correlation Coefficient (MCC) criterion which confirmed that CSDD was also the best method in the detections of concept drifts. Thus, we claim that CSDD surpassed the current state of art detectors, showing that the Cosine similarity together with sliding windows and PPV and FDR rates can also produce excellent results in the detection of concept drifts.

As future work we plan to make further experimentation and evaluations of the proposed method in order to improve its performance and make it more competitive in the real-world datasets. Finally, CSDD should also be evaluated using imbalanced datasets.

Acknowledgment. Juan Hidalgo and Laura Mariño are, respectively, Ph.D. and M.Sc. students, supported by CAPES postgraduate grants. The authors thank Bruno Maciel for his MOA script generator and results extraction tool, which greatly helped speed up the scripts generation and analyze the results of the experiments. This open-source tool is available at https://github.com/brunom4ciel/moamanager.

References

1. Agrawal, R., Imielinski, T., Swami, A.: Database mining: a performance perspective. IEEE Trans. Knowl. Data Eng. **5**(6), 914–925 (1993). https://doi.org/10.1109/69.250074

2. Antwi, D.K., Viktor, H.L., Japkowicz, N.: The PerfSim algorithm for concept drift detection in imbalanced data. In: 2012 IEEE 12th International Conference on Data Mining Workshops, pp. 619–628. IEEE (2012). https://doi.org/10.1109/ICDMW.2012.122

3. Barros, R.S.M., Cabral, D.R.L., Gonçalves Jr., P.M., Santos, S.G.T.C.: RDDM: reactive drift detection method. Expert Syst. Appl. **90**, 344–355 (2017). https://doi.org/10.1016/j.eswa.2017.08.023

4. Barros, R.S.M., Santos, S.G.T.C.: A large-scale comparison of concept drift detectors. Inform. Sci. **451–452**(C), 348–370 (2018). https://doi.org/10.1016/j.ins.2018.04.014

5. Barros, R.S.M., Hidalgo, J.I.G., Cabral, D.R.L.: Wilcoxon rank sum test drift detector. Neurocomputing **275**, 1954–1963 (2018). https://doi.org/10.1016/j.neucom.2017.10.051

6. Barros, R.S.M., Santos, S.G.T.C.: An overview and comprehensive comparison of ensembles for concept drift. Inf. Fusion **52**(C), 213–244 (2019). https://doi.org/10.1016/j.inffus.2019.03.006

7. Barros, R.S.M., Santos, S.G.T.C., Gonçalves, Jr., P.M.: A boosting-like online learning ensemble. In: Proceedings of IEEE International Joint Conference on Neural Networks (IJCNN), pp. 1871–1878. Vancouver, Canada (2016). https://doi.org/10.1109/IJCNN.2016.7727427

8. Bifet, A., Holmes, G., Kirkby, R., Pfahringer, B.: MOA: massive online analysis. J. Mach. Learn. Res. **11**, 1601–1604 (2010)

9. Cabral, D.R.L., Barros, R.S.M.: Concept drift detection based on Fisher's Exact test. Inf. Sci. **442**, 220–234 (2018). https://doi.org/10.1016/j.ins.2018.02.054

10. Coetzee, P., Van Jaarsveld, F., Vanhaecke, F.: Intraregional classification of wine via ICP-MS elemental fingerprinting. Food Chem. **164**, 485–492 (2014). https://doi.org/10.1016/j.foodchem.2014.05.027

11. Dawid, A.P.: Present position and potential developments: some personal views: statistical theory: the prequential approach. J. Roy. Stat. Soc. Ser. A (General), 278–292 (1984). https://doi.org/10.2307/2981683

12. Demšar, J.: Statistical comparisons of classifiers over multiple data sets. J. Mach. Learn. Res. **7**, 1–30 (2006)

13. Dunn, O.J.: Multiple comparisons among means. J. Am. Stat. Assoc. **56**(293), 52–64 (1961). https://doi.org/10.1080/01621459.1961.10482090

14. Fisher, R.: Statistical Methods for Research Workers. Biological Monographs and Manuals, Oliver and Boyd, London, England (1934). http://www.haghish.com/resources/materials/Statistical_Methods_for_Research_Workers.pdf

15. Frías-Blanco, I., del Campo-Ávila, J., Ramos-Jiménez, G., Morales-Bueno, R., Ortiz-Díaz, A., Caballero-Mota, Y.: Online and non-parametric drift detection methods based on hoeffding's bounds. IEEE Trans. Knowl. Data Eng. **27**(3), 810–823 (2015). https://doi.org/10.1109/TKDE.2014.2345382

16. Friedman, M.: The use of ranks to avoid the assumption of normality implicit in the analysis of variance. J. Am. Stat. Assoc. **32**(200), 675–701 (1937). https://doi.org/10.1080/01621459.1937.10503522

17. Gama, J., Medas, P., Castillo, G., Rodrigues, P.: Learning with drift detection. In: Bazzan, A.L.C., Labidi, S. (eds.) SBIA 2004. LNCS (LNAI), vol. 3171, pp. 286–295. Springer, Heidelberg (2004). https://doi.org/10.1007/978-3-540-28645-5_29

18. Gama, J., Zliobaitė, I., Bifet, A., Pechenizkiy, M., Bouchachia, A.: A survey on concept drift adaptation. ACM Comput. Surv. **46**(4), 44:1–44:37 (2014). https://doi.org/10.1145/2523813

19. Gama, J., Kosina, P.: Recurrent concepts in data streams classification. Knowl. Inf. Syst. **40**(3), 489–507 (2014). https://doi.org/10.1007/s10115-013-0654-6

20. Gonçalves Jr., P.M., Barros, R.S.M.: RCD: a recurring concept drift framework. Pattern Recog. Letters **34**(9), 1018–1025 (2013). https://doi.org/10.1016/j.patrec.2013.02.005

21. Gonçalves Jr., P.M., Santos, S.G.T.C., Barros, R.S.M., Vieira, D.C.L.: A comparative study on concept drift detectors. Expert Syst. Appl. **41**(18), 8144–8156 (2014). https://doi.org/10.1016/j.eswa.2014.07.019

22. Hermanowski, D.: Open source security information management system supporting it security audit. In: 2015 IEEE 2nd International Conference on Cybernetics (CYBCONF), pp. 336–341. IEEE (2015). https://doi.org/10.1109/CYBConf.2015.7175956

23. Hidalgo, J.I.G., Maciel, B.I.F., Barros, R.S.M.: Experimenting with prequential variations for data stream learning evaluation. Comput. Intell. (2019). https://doi.org/10.1111/coin.12208

24. Hoeffding, W.: Probability inequalities for sums of bounded random variables. J. Am. Stat. Assoc. **58**, 13–30 (1963). https://doi.org/10.1080/01621459.1963.10500830

25. Jo, T., Japkowicz, N.: Class imbalances versus small disjuncts. ACM SIGKDD Explor. Newsl. **6**(1), 40–49 (2004). https://doi.org/10.1145/1007730.1007737

26. Khamassi, I., Sayed-Mouchaweh, M., Hammami, M., Ghédira, K.: Discussion and review on evolving data streams and concept drift adapting. Evolving Syst. **9**(1), 1–23 (2018). https://doi.org/10.1007/s12530-016-9168-2

27. Losing, V., Hammer, B., Wersing, H.: KNN classifier with self adjusting memory for heterogeneous concept drift. In: IEEE 16th International Conference on Data Mining (ICDM), pp. 291–300 (2016). https://doi.org/10.1109/ICDM.2016.0040

28. Maciel, B.I.F., Santos, S.G.T.C., Barros, R.S.M.: A lightweight concept drift detection ensemble. In: Proceedings of the 27th IEEE Internaional Conference on Tools with Artificial Intelligence, ICTAI 2015, pp. 1061–1068. Vietri sul Mare, Italy (2015) https://doi.org/10.1109/ICTAI.2015.151

29. Matthews, B.W.: Comparison of the predicted and observed secondary structure of t4 phage lysozyme. Biochimica et Biophysica Acta (BBA) Protein Structure **405**(2), 442–451 (1975). https://doi.org/10.1016/0005-2795(75)90109-9

30. Mitchell, T.: Machine Learning. McGraw-Hill, New York (1997). 10.1002/(SICI)1099-1689(199909)9:3%3C191::AID-STVR184%3E3.0.CO;2-E

31. Nishida, K., Yamauchi, K.: Detecting concept drift using statistical testing. In: Corruble, V., Takeda, M., Suzuki, E. (eds.) DS 2007. LNCS (LNAI), vol. 4755, pp. 264–269. Springer, Heidelberg (2007). https://doi.org/10.1007/978-3-540-75488-6_27

32. Revathi, S., Malathi, A.: A detailed analysis on NSL-KDD dataset using various machine learning techniques for intrusion detection. Int. J. Eng. Res. Technol. (IJERT) **2**(12), 1848–1853 (2013). http://citeseerx.ist.psu.edu/viewdoc/summary?doi=10.1.1.680.6760

33. Santos, S.G.T.C., Barros, R.S.M.: Online adaboost-based methods for multiclass problems. Artif. Intell. Rev.(2019). https://doi.org/10.1007/s10462-019-09696-6

34. Santos, S.G.T.C., Gonçalves Júnior, P.M., Silva, G.D.S., de Barros, R.S.M.: Speeding up recovery from concept drifts. In: Calders, T., Esposito, F., Hüllermeier, E., Meo, R. (eds.) ECML PKDD 2014. LNCS (LNAI), vol. 8726, pp. 179–194. Springer, Heidelberg (2014). https://doi.org/10.1007/978-3-662-44845-8_12

35. Santos, S.G.T.C., Barros, R.S.M., Gonçalves Jr., P.M.: Optimizing the parameters of drift detection methods using a genetic algorithm. In: Proceedings of the 27th IEEE International Conference on Tools with Artificial Intelligence. ICTAI 2015, pp. 1077–1084. Vietri sul Mare, Italy (2015). https://doi.org/10.1109/ICTAI.2015.153

36. Santos, S.G., Barros, R.S., Gonçalves Jr., P.M.: A differential evolution based method for tuning concept drift detectors in data streams. Inf. Sci. **485**, 376–393 (2019). https://doi.org/10.1016/j.ins.2019.02.031

37. Teknomo, K.: Similarity measurement (2015). https://people.revoledu.com/kardi/tutorial/Similarity

38. Wang, H., Abraham, Z.: Concept drift detection for streaming data. In: IEEE International Joint Conference on Neural Networks (IJCNN), pp. 1–9 (2015). https://doi.org/10.1109/IJCNN.2015.7280398

39. Wilcoxon, F.: Individual comparisons by ranking methods. Biometrics Bull. **1**(6), 80–83 (1945). https://doi.org/10.2307/3001968

40. Yates, F.: Contingency tables involving small numbers and the χ 2 test. Suppl. J. Roy. Stat. Soc. **1**(2), 217–235 (1934). https://doi.org/10.2307/2983604

Unsupervised Anomaly Detection Using Optimal Transport for Predictive Maintenance

Amina Alaoui-Belghiti[1,2(✉)], Sylvain Chevallier[2,3], and Eric Monacelli[2,3]

[1] Nexeya, Massy, France
amina.alaouibelghiti@nexeya.com
[2] UVSQ, Universite Paris-Saclay, Versailles, France
{sylvain.chevallier,eric.monacelli}@uvsq.fr
[3] LISV, Universite Paris-Saclay, Vélizy, France

Abstract. Anomaly detection is of crucial importance in industrial environment, especially in the context of predictive maintenance. As it is very costly to add an extra monitoring layer on production machines, non-invasive solutions are favored to watch for precursory clue indicating the possible need for a maintenance operation. Those clues are to be detected in evolving and highly variable working environment, calling for online and unsupervised methods. This contribution proposes a framework grounded in optimal transport, for the specific characterization of a system and the automatic detection of abnormal events. This method is evaluated on acoustic dataset and demonstrate the superiority of metrics derived from optimal transport on the Euclidean ones. The proposed method is shown to outperform one-class SVM on real datasets, which is the state-of-the-art method for anomaly detection.

Keywords: Predictive maintenance · Optimal transport ·
Anomaly detection · Unsupervised learning

1 Introduction

In the industrial field, the equipment operational readiness is a central and unavoidable challenge. This is a key parameter in the production budgeting or in the solution development projects [4]. The concept of operational readiness mainly covers the preventive maintenance which corresponds to systematic or periodic operations defined for each type of equipment, and/or the corrective maintenance which concerns operations to remedy the damage that has occurred during operation. But with these two kinds of maintenance, some unnecessary actions are performed or the equipment breaks down unexpectedly, moreover, these two kinds of maintenance do not take into account the specific characteristics of real operating conditions [6].

The predictive maintenance anticipates the needs and remedies its weaknesses by reducing prevention costs and avoiding unplanned downtime [16]. It becomes

© Springer Nature Switzerland AG 2019
I. V. Tetko et al. (Eds.): ICANN 2019, LNCS 11730, pp. 686–697, 2019.
https://doi.org/10.1007/978-3-030-30490-4_54

increasingly important in recent years, and is linked to terms such as the Internet of Things(IOT), big data and industry 4.0.

Predictive maintenance requires continuous monitoring of the components directly on the machine or on the installation, such as for wind turbines [9], or for aircraft engines [1], power plants, solar fields, etc. This is achieved by sensors that report information about the periphery and environmental characteristics such as temperature, vibration, noise or humidity, but also by looking at the historical and conceptual data of the equipment. These data are then recorded and evaluated by correlations, compared with models through well-targeted algorithms. In particular, anomaly detection aims to identify failing components and replace them before the occurrence of a failure.

A crucial step in predictive maintenance is the anomaly detection. It is a major challenge in industrial applications, especially for the identification of manufacturing defects or component failure. Whichever method is used, an anomaly is always defined, either implicitly or explicitly with respect to a model. The choice of the method and of the model depends entirely on the context, the objective, the available data, and their properties.

Theoretically, an observation is considered as abnormal or atypical compared to a given model, this model can be parametric, assuming a specific statistical law distribution, or non-parametric defined directly from the data. Without any assumption on the law governing the data, the model can be chosen in relation with the presence of a target variable to explain, to model, or to predict by regression or discrimination. In the opposite case, it can be related to presence of the probability density or multidimensional distribution of variables.

In the parametric cases, the law of the explanatory variables, or that of the residuals, is usually supposed to be Gaussian multidimensional. Relative to a target variable model, when considering a Gaussian linear model, the atypical or poorly adjusted observations are those diverging from the estimated variance [2]. Nevertheless, the detection of atypical observations is more similar to that of influential observations, for example using Cook's distance, well known in simple linear regression [3].

Without target variable to model, the abnormality at a multidimensional density can be characterized by the Mahalanobis distance, as used in [1] for the detection of anomalies in an aircraft engine. This distance is estimated from the inverse of the empirical covariance of the distribution.

In the non-parametric cases, there is no assumption about the multidimensional distribution of variables, it is estimated locally in different ways. Relative to a target variable model, Random forest [18] includes an original solution adapted to the taking into account of mixed variables.

Without target variable to model, this is the case with the most extensive literature with many proposed methods. A comprehensive review is proposed in [11], most notable methods are Local Outlier Factor [5] and Isolation Forest [12]. Nonetheless, these methods are applicable in situations where abnormal observations are frequent and where all data are corrupted with a low density noise. Here, the situation is different as the monitored components are first assumed to operate correctly. The abnormal events could be identified as a novelty, a sensible variation from the clean reference data. The most know algorithm in novelty detection is the One-Class SVM [13,14], which is the current state of the art.

The shift in the observed distribution could be quantified, calling for metrics and topological spaces for handling probability measures [17]. These metrics follow from the Kantorovitch problem, that define a transport plan (couplings) which is the solution of transportation problem defined by a cost matrix. Common applications are image processing, shape interpolation, similar terms in text documents [15]. The computation of this transport plan often requires a large amount of computational resources and is not feasible in high dimensions.

Recent advances yield new algorithms for fast computation of transportation distance, such as the Sinkhorn distance [7]. Adding entropic regularization to transportation distance, the Sinkhorn distance has several interesting properties as it is a scale free, non-Euclidean formulation which is less subject to the curse of dimensionality. Also, clever implementation that makes use of parallelization and GPU computation are available [10].

In this contribution, we propose to formulate a straightforward algorithm for anomaly detection in a predictive maintenance context. We consider the case of a system to monitor with non-invasive sensors, where a large amount of data from a normal behavior is available. This algorithm should be able to identify novel behavior or abnormal samples, that will be eventually process to determine if a predictive maintenance is required. Drawing on optimal transport framework, our contributions are the following:

- A novel unsupervised method for anomaly detection
- Evaluation with Euclidean methods on toy data set
- Application to real data, comparison with state-of-the-art
- Possible extension for online implementation.

The rest of this paper is organized as follows. Section 2 describes the proposed model and provides a formal description of the system. In Sect. 3, the model is evaluated on a toy data set and on real acoustic data set and compared with Euclidean methods and one-class SVM. The Sect. 4 concludes this paper.

2   Optimal Transport for Anomaly Detection

This section first provides some insight on transport algorithms, with details on the Sinkhorn algorithm. The rest of the section goes through the explanation on the proposed algorithm.

2.1   Optimal Transport with Entropic Regularization

We consider two metric spaces $\mathcal{X}$ and $\mathcal{Y}$, and $\mathcal{M}(X)$ is the set of Radon probability measures on $\mathcal{X}$. Whereas we focus on discrete measures, the proposed

OT matrix Sinkhorn

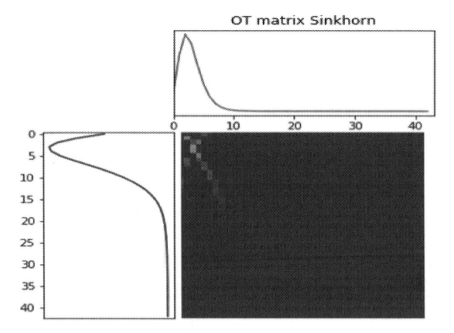

Fig. 1. Illustration of a coupling P solving the optimal transport from measures a on left to measures b on top.

approach could be extended to the continuous case without any specific problem. With discrete measure α with weight a defined on $\mathcal{X}$ in n locations and β with weight b defined on $\mathcal{Y}$ in m locations, we could consider the set of coupling matrices defined by:

$$U(a,b) = \left\{ P \in \mathbb{R}_+^{n \times m} : P\mathbf{1}_m = a \text{ and } P^T\mathbf{1}_n = b \right\} \tag{1}$$

where $\mathbf{1}_n$ is the vector of ones with n dimensions.

If we consider a cost matrix $C \in \mathbb{R}^{n \times m}$, the cost of the mapping from a to b using a transport matrix P is $\langle P, C \rangle$, with $\langle \cdot, \cdot \rangle$ is the Euclidean dot product.

$$d_C(a,b) = \min_{P \in U(a,b)} \langle P, C \rangle, \tag{2}$$

is called the optimal transport problem between a and b given cost C.

Defining the entropy of the coupling matrix as

$$H(P) = -\sum_{i,j} P_{i,j}(\log(P_{i,j}) - 1), \tag{3}$$

it is possible to add an entropic regularization term to the optimal transport problem (2):

$$d_C^\epsilon(a,b) = \min_{P \in U(a,b)} \langle P, C \rangle - \epsilon H(P). \tag{4}$$

Algorithm 1. Anomaly detection with OT

    Input: set of reference signals $\mathbf{X}$, signal to evaluate $\hat{X}$
    Output: binary classification, 1 if normal signal, -1 if abnormal
1: **procedure** PREDICT ANOMALY($\mathbf{X}, \hat{X}$)
2:     $F(\bar{\mathbf{X}}) \leftarrow \frac{1}{k} \sum_k F(X_k)$
3:     **for** i in 1 .. k **do**
4:         $d_i \leftarrow d_C^\epsilon(F(\bar{\mathbf{X}}), F(X_i))$
5:     Set threshold ϑ from LogNormal fit on $\{d_i\}_{i=1\ldots k}$
6:     $\hat{d} \leftarrow d_C^\epsilon(F(\bar{\mathbf{X}}), F(\hat{X}))$
7:     **if** $\hat{d} > \vartheta$ **then**
8:         **return** -1 ▷ Anomaly
9:     **else**
10:         **return** 1   ▷ Normal

This problem admit a unique solution of the form $P_{i,j} = u_i K_{i,j} v_j$, with scaling variables u_i and v_j belonging respectively to $\mathbb{R}^n_+$ and $\mathbb{R}^m_+$. When conforming to mass conservation, the solution of (4) could be written as:

$$u * (Kv) = a \text{ and } v * (K^T u) = b \tag{5}$$

where $*$ is the element-wise vector multiplication. By alternatively solving the following update, an iteration l of the Sinkhorn algorithm is:

$$u^{(l+1)} = \frac{a}{Kv^{(l)}} \text{ and } v^{(l+1)} = \frac{b}{K^T v^{(l)}}, \tag{6}$$

starting with an arbitrary initialization.

An illustration of the obtained coupling when solving Problem 4 is shown on Fig. 1

2.2 Anomaly Detection with Optimal Transport

The proposed detection algorithm is designed to model normal behaviors and identify abnormal behavior. We focus in this contribution on acoustic signals or vibration, as it is easy to embed such sensors in a non-invasion monitoring system. Nonetheless, the described approach could be adapted to various problems, as any sample distribution could act as an input feature. An abnormal signal can be defined by the distance between its own representation and the representation of another signal defined as a reference. Noisy signals show the highest distance from the reference representation.

Assuming a set of initial signals $\mathbf{X} = \{X_i\}_{i=1\ldots k}, X \in \mathbb{R}^t$, and a signal containing abnormal events, denoted $\tilde{X} = X + \eta N$, where N is the abnormal component and η is the component level. The signals are considered in the frequency domain, by estimating the power spectral density. For each signal, the power spectral density is evaluated with the Welch estimator $F(\cdot)$, that is the signals are split into several partially overlapping segments, a windowing function is applied (here Hamming) before computing their Fourier transform, and averaging the results for each segment. The resulting signals are $F(X) \in \mathbb{R}^n$.

The initial signals are then averaged, using a Euclidean mean, to obtain a barycenter acting as reference $F(\bar{\mathbf{X}}) = \frac{1}{k}\sum_k F(X_k)$. During preliminary tests, we have evaluated the opportunity to use Wasserstein barycenter [8] but it turned out that it yield poorer results. The distances from individual PSD $F(X_k)$ and the reference barycenter $F(\bar{\mathbf{X}})$ is computed with the Sinkhorn distance $d_C^\epsilon(F(\bar{\mathbf{X}}), F(X_k))$, using a Chebyshev cost function. The same is done for signals with anomalies $d_C^\epsilon(F(\bar{\mathbf{X}}), F(\tilde{X}))$.

A distribution following a Log-Normal distribution is then obtained from the histogram of distances. This distribution allowed us to set a distance threshold which was used to design a classifier in order to predict the tested signal as strict less than normal or abnormal. The different steps of the algorithm are shown in Algorithm 1.

The evaluation of the method by two performance metrics and its comparison with an Euclidean baseline and the one-class SVM is detailed in the following section.

3   Experimental Analysis

3.1   Datasets Description

This study is a part of a ongoing project aiming to implement a predictive maintenance solution based on the test bench monitoring of an electro-mechanical aircraft actuator. Unfortunately experiments related to this test bench are confidential and dataset from this experiment could not be shared.

To ensure the reproducibility of this study, we decided to apply our approach on public data. A first batch of data is chosen to demonstrate the robustness of the method. It also offers the possibility to compare with a Euclidean approach, to verify that the optimal transport distance has a real positive influence. We selected a sound recording of a working day in an open space[1] as reference data and different levels of pink noise are blended to simulate noisy data in a controlled way.

To further test our approach on realistic data, we also evaluated the method on a dataset similar to the private, industrial data. We selected a recording of the rotating industrial machine sound for the reference acoustic signal, which is close to the one encountered in the industrial situation. We also selected some recordings of some abnormal event sounds to represent the anomalies that are also similar to those occurring on test bench[2]. The results of these experiments are presented in the following subsections.

---

[1] The selected sound recordings are available upon request.
[2] All of these recordings are available as well upon request.

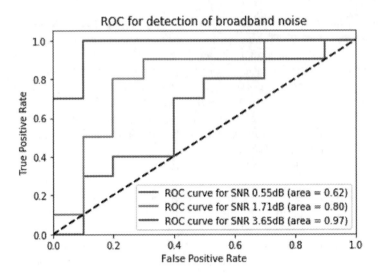

Fig. 2. ROC estimation for detecting peak noise

3.2   Robustness and Comparison with Euclidean Metrics

To test the robustness of the anomaly detection method, it is evaluated on a monoraul track recording encoded at 44100 Hz of office open space sounds. The recording is 15 min long. The reference is computed on the first 7 min, the remaining audio is either left as it or corrupted with pink noise. Two different types of abnormal noise are considered: a large broadband noise is added to the signal or a sharp peak noise.

The algorithm of Algorithm 1 is evaluated with various thresholds to compute a ROC estimation. As it is shown on Fig. 2, when the power of the noise signal is strong (SNR 3.65 dB), the algorithm easily detect the anomaly in the signal. As expected, the detection is harder when the noise peak is weaker, with a SNR of 0.55, the Area Under Curve (AUC) is 0.62 which is above chance level (here 0.5) but of limited precision.

The second experiment rely on the same kind of experiment, but with a broadband noise. The Fig. 3 show that with equivalent SNR, the proposed algorithm is able to detect anomalous event with more easiliy than in the case of the peak noise. This reflects on the AUC values which are of 0.72 for a low SNR of 0.55 dB, 0.79 for SNR of 1.71 dB and 0.88 for 3.65 dB.

This experiment on a toy dataset demonstrates the feasibility of anomaly detection with optimal transport metrics. These results show that it is possible to detect a noise when the algorithm is calibrated with real sound. The proposed algorithm shows a limited sensitivity to anomalies concentrated on a narrow frequency peak but performed well with broadband change, even if the modifications are subtle.

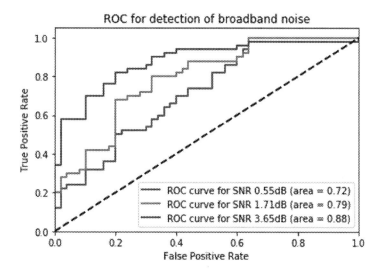

Fig. 3. Detection of broadband noise, SNR values are matching those of the peak noise experiment.

3.3   Evaluation on Real Dataset

In these experiments,a reference signal similar to the noise of an industrial bench test is chosen. The signal is recorded in monaural, at 44100 Hz for 15 min long. Two qualitatively different kinds of faulty mechanical parts are considered: the sound of a light, high pitched whistling (dataset 1) and a cyclical low-pitched sound, similar to a faulty ball bearing (dataset 2). These two datasets are also 15 min long of 44100 Hz monaural recording.

The algorithm described in Algorithm 1 is compared to a Euclidean baseline. In this baseline, this is the same algorithm but the Sinkhorn metrics are replaced with a Euclidean one on lines 4 and 6.

The state-of-the-art algorithm, one-class SVM, for novelty detection is benchmarked against the proposed algorithm. The one-class SVM relies on a Radial Basis Function (RBF) kernel and the ν value is set to reflect the ratio of anomalies.

The datasets are separated in training (500 samples) and test data (500 samples) using a repeated k-fold split, the training data are used toc train the SVM and the compute the reference signal $F(\bar{\mathbf{X}})$. The algorithms (SVM, OT and Euclidean) are then evaluated on test data: half of the test data are mixed with the faulty mechanisms sound of dataset 1 and 2.

To illustrate the input features of the algorithm, the Fig. 4 shows the PSD of the 500 training signal on the top plot. The reference computed on these training signal is shown as a thick black line. On the bottom plot, one could see the mix of the 250 test signal unmodified and of the 250 test signal mixed with the anomalous sound of dataset 1. The reference indicated in black is the same as the one on the top plot.

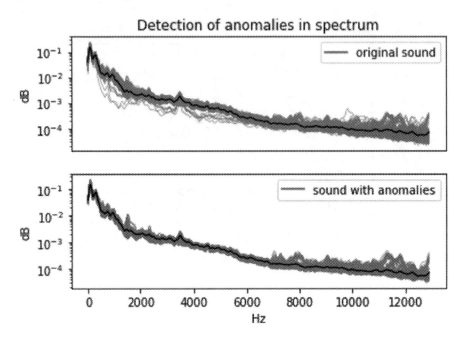

Fig. 4. Spectrum of the reference dataset is on the top plot. The PSD of the combined reference and anomalous sound is shown on the bottom.

The results are shown on Fig. 5, for the datasets 1 with light, high pitched whistling anomalies. As the results are qualitatively similar for dataset 2, the results for the dataset 1 and 2 are summarized in the Table 1. The left part

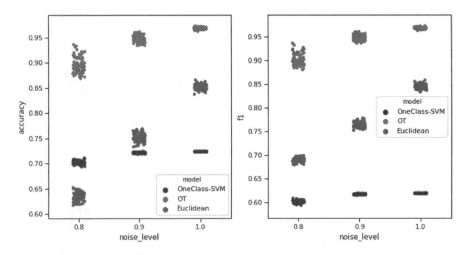

Fig. 5. Accuracy and F1-measure estimated on the first dataset for different noise levels. One-class SVM, Optimal Transport (OT) and Euclidean baseline are evaluated on this dataset.

Table 1. Accuracy and F1-measure for two datasets of acoustic recording, corrupted by faulty mechanical sounds.

	Noise level	Accuracy			F1		
		OT	OCSVM	Baseline	OT	OCSVM	Baseline
Dataset 1	0.8	**0.89**	0.70	0.63	**0.90**	0.60	0.69
	0.9	**0.95**	0.72	0.75	**0.95**	0.62	0.76
	1.0	**0.97**	0.72	0.85	**0.97**	0.62	0.84
Dataset 2	1.0	**0.54**	0.5	0.5	**0.90**	0.60	0.62
	1.5	**0.64**	0.5	0.5	**0.94**	0.61	0.62
	2.0	**0.84**	0.5	0.5	**0.97**	0.62	0.62

of Fig. 5 shows the accuracy for 3 different noise levels. The one-class SVM (OCSVM) achieves good results but misses several anomalies lowering its score around 70–75%. The Euclidean method demonstrates lower performance than OCSVM for low SNR but outperforms OCSVM for high SNR. The optimal transport algorithm yields the higher results, with 90–98% accuracy.

We also evaluated the F1-score to take into account the precision and the recall for the anomaly. These scores are shown on the right part and one could see that the optimal transport outperforms all the methods.

4   Discussion and Conclusion

Anomaly detection is a complex problem with no uniformly better solution because the choice of which method to use depends largely on the context, the properties of the variables and data observed, and also on the objective pursued. This paper focuses on a new method of anomaly detection in acoustic signals by comparing them with reference signals through the calculation of Sinkhorn distances in optimal transport. The choice fell on an unsupervised detection method, because there are no anomalies a priori defined, common in industrial equipment operating mode. This allows us an online implementation in order to an industrial deployment.

In the experimental analysis section, the robustness of the OT method has been demonstrated by observing the ROC estimation. It distinguished itself from the One Class-SVM and Euclidean methods by showing a high level of accuracy for different datasets through its evaluation by two performance metrics, accuracy and F1 measures.

As already discussed before, this study is part of a larger PhD position project that is the predictive and automated maintenance of an industrial equipment. The overall architecture of the project is divided into several parts starting with the monitoring of the equipment until the alarms propagation and the proposal of the maintenance actions to be carried out, while passing through the anomaly detection and the fault identification.

The contribution of this paper has been devoted mainly to acoustic data, but we want to broaden the study of anomaly detection in future work on other perception mechanisms set up for maintenance, such as vibratory and thermographic measurements with well-defined specifications, while integrating the confidence interval questions for each type of measurement.

References

1. Abdel-Sayed, M., Duclos, D., Faÿ, G., Lacaille, J., Mougeot, M.: Dictionary comparison for anomaly detection on aircraft engine spectrograms. Machine Learning and Data Mining in Pattern Recognition. LNCS (LNAI), vol. 9729, pp. 362–376. Springer, Cham (2016). https://doi.org/10.1007/978-3-319-41920-6_28
2. Aguinis, H., Gottfredson, R.K., Joo, H.: Best-practice recommendations for defining, identifying, and handling outliers. Organ. Res. Meth. **16**(2), 270–301 (2013)
3. Atkinson, A., Riani, M.: Robust Diagnostic Regression Analysis. Springer Science & Business Media, Berlin (2012)
4. Baptista, M., Sankararaman, S., de Medeiros, I.P., Nascimento Jr., C., Prendinger, H., Henriques, E.M.: Forecasting fault events for predictive maintenance using data-driven techniques and arma modeling. Comput. Ind. Eng. **115**, 41–53 (2018)
5. Breunig, M.M., Kriegel, H.P., Ng, R.T., Sander, J.: Lof: identifying density-based local outliers. In: ACM Sigmod Record. vol. 29, pp. 93–104. ACM (2000)
6. Camci, F.: System maintenance scheduling with prognostics information using genetic algorithm. IEEE Trans. Reliab. **58**(3), 539–552 (2009)
7. Cuturi, M.: Sinkhorn distances: Lightspeed computation of optimal transport. In: Advances in Neural Information Processing Systems. pp. 2292–2300 (2013)
8. Cuturi, M., Doucet, A.: Fast computation of wasserstein barycenters. In: International Conference on Machine Learning, pp. 685–693 (2014)
9. Garcia, M.C., Sanz-Bobi, M.A., del Pico, J.: Simap: Intelligent system for predictive maintenance: application to the health condition monitoring of a windturbine gearbox. Comput. Ind. **57**(6), 552–568 (2006)
10. Genevay, A., Cuturi, M., Peyré, G., Bach, F.: Stochastic optimization for large-scale optimal transport. In: Advances in Neural Information Processing Systems, pp. 3440–3448 (2016)
11. Goldstein, M., Uchida, S.: A comparative evaluation of unsupervised anomaly detection algorithms for multivariate data. PloS One **11**(4), e0152173 (2016)
12. Liu, F.T., Ting, K.M., Zhou, Z.H.: Isolation forest. In: 2008 Eighth IEEE International Conference on Data Mining, pp. 413–422. IEEE (2008)
13. Ma, J., Perkins, S.: Time-series novelty detection using one-class support vector machines. In: 2003 Proceedings of the International Joint Conference on Neural Networks, vol. 3, pp. 1741–1745. IEEE (2003)
14. Manevitz, L.M., Yousef, M.: One-class svms for document classification. J. Mach. Learn. Res. **2**, 139–154 (2001)
15. Peyré, G., Cuturi, M., et al.: Computational optimal transport. Technical report (2017)

16. Susto, G.A., Schirru, A., Pampuri, S., McLoone, S., Beghi, A.: Machine learning for predictive maintenance: a multiple classifier approach. IEEE Trans. Ind. Inform. **11**(3), 812–820 (2015)
17. Villani, C.: Optimal transport: Old and New, vol. 338. Springer Science & Business Media, Berlin (2008)
18. Zhang, J., Zulkernine, M., Haque, A.: Random-forests-based network intrusion detection systems. IEEE Trans. Syst., Man, Cybern. Part C (Appl. Rev.) **38**(5), 649–659 (2008)

Robust Gait Authentication Using Autoencoder and Decision Tree

Mitsuhiro Ogihara and Hideyuki Mizuno$^{(\boxtimes)}$ ⓘ

Suwa University of Science, Toyohira, Chino, Nagano 5000-1, Japan
h_mizuno@rs.sus.ac.jp

Abstract. Various biometric authentication technologies have been developed for protecting smartphones against unauthorized access. Most authentication methods provide highly accurate authentication; however, an unlocked device can be used freely until it is re-locked. This study proposes a robust gait-based authentication method that identifies various walking styles using only a smartphone accelerometer. However, walking motion is dependent on individuals and their walking style. Based on features extracted from acceleration data, the proposed method first introduces a decision tree for classifying walking style prior to verifying identity. Then, identification is performed using the reconstruction error of the autoencoder for a specified walking style. Results confirm the effectiveness of the proposed method, which utilizes the novel approach of combining two simple methods to achieve superior performance.

Keywords: Authentication · Autoencoder · Decision tree

1 Introduction

Biometric authentication methods are based on biological features, such as fingerprints and facial features, and on behavioral features such as gestures and signatures. However, these methods require special sensors for sensing biological features and low-end or small devices, such as smartwatches, with such sensors is impractical. Moreover, a device that has been unlocked can be only accessed until it is re-locked. Thus, if the device is stolen soon after authentication, personal information can be accessed. Keeping a mobile device secure at all times without special hardware is thus a critical task.

Gait-based continuous authentication utilizes unique characteristics of an individual's walking behavior. Because walking is a natural human activity, a gait-based approach does not require special cooperation from users. In addition, the risk of impersonation is as low as for other biometric authentication methods. To examine gait-based continuous authentication, smartphones' built-in accelerometers are used. Using statistical features extracted from an accelerometer enhances identification and authentication performance [1]. A pace-independent gait identification system using wavelet features [2] demonstrates highly accurate authentication in certain cases.

Deep learning has also been applied to authentication. Neural networks and support vector machines are combined to achieve low levels of misclassification [3]. However, gait-based authentication has higher error rate than other biometric authentication

© Springer Nature Switzerland AG 2019
I. V. Tetko et al. (Eds.): ICANN 2019, LNCS 11730, pp. 698–702, 2019.
https://doi.org/10.1007/978-3-030-30490-4_55

technologies such as fingerprint recognition, resulting in a false acceptance rate (FAR) of less than 0.0001%. Performing accurate identification on different walking styles is difficult. Therefore, this study proposes a gait-based authentication method that can be used during regular walking and can achieve comparable performance to other biometric authentication methods. The proposed method uses a decision tree for classifying a walking style and an autoencoder for recognizing a genuine user.

2 Authentication by Combining Decision Tree and Autoencoder

2.1 Outline

Figure 1 outlines the proposed method. Statistical features are first extracted with a fixed window length from the acceleration data obtained from a smartphone accelerometer. Features, mean, standard deviation, mean absolute deviation, time interval between peaks, and bin distribution are used based on the method outlined in [1]. A decision tree then determines the walking style. Walking motions patterns change according to walking styles, resulting in feature variations.

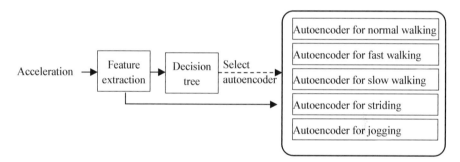

Fig. 1. Outline of proposed method.

Five walking styles are examined herein: normal walking, fast walking, slow walking, striding, and jogging. Differences in walking style, not in walking pace, are addressed. Two individuals of different heights having similar walking styles may have different walking speeds. To classify the walking style, a decision tree is trained using the features extracted from the acceleration data on the walking motion patterns. Then, an autoencoder is used for each walking style to determine whether that individual is the target user.

Five autoencoders, each trained for a specific walking style, are provided for the target user. Features automatically classified by the decision tree are used for training the autoencoder for each walking style because autoencoder performs authentication when the walking style is incorrectly determined.

2.2   Authentication Procedure Using Autoencoder

Reconstruction error of an autoencoder is used for authentication. The autoencoder is generally used for obtaining an appropriate data expression and automatically acquire features of the input data; therefore, the reconstructed output must be almost identical to the input. The reconstruction error is defined as $|x - x'|$, where x' is obtained by propagating the input data x to the final layer. Authentication can be processed by considering bogus data as an anomaly similar to anomaly detection, which uses several autoencoder-based methods [4]. Herein, the average value and variance of the reconstruction error are used for authentication. Although these values are dependent on the user, their distribution shapes can be similar for different users. Assuming that the distribution is a normal distribution, an outlier can be determined via Hotelling's T-squared statistic calculated using the mean value and variance of the reconstruction error. Because this statistic is one-dimensional, it can be simply expressed as

$$T = \frac{x - m}{s}, \tag{1}$$

where m and s are the average reconstruction error and standard deviation, respectively. When statistic T (obtained from input x) $\leq T_{th}$ (a given threshold), the input originates from the genuine user. When $T > T_{th}$, the authentication fails.

3   Experiment

3.1   Experimental Data

Acceleration data were collected from 10 male participants (20-year-old males) holding a ZenFone 5 parallel to the floor. Participants were instructed to walk 36 m in five different walking styles: normal walking, fast walking, slow walking, striding, and jogging. The average speed and elapsed time for each walking style are as follows: normal walking, 4.3 km/h (30.9 s); fast walking, 5.4 km/h (24.3 s); slow walking, 2.9 km/h (46.0 s); striding, 4.2 km/h (32.7 s); and jogging, 7.9 km/h (16.9 s).

3.2   Experiment Results

We then performed authentication experiments. For feature extraction, the frame length and frame shift were 10 s and 10 ms, respectively. The total number of data points was 225,354. A total of 54 features were extracted from the acceleration data on the x-, y-, and z-axes, and their norm was used. The classification and regression tree (CART) was used as the decision tree with a total of 45 leaf nodes. Table 1 presents the autoencoder properties. Ninety percent of the randomly selected data was used for training and the remaining 10% was used for testing dependently of person. Table 2 shows the experimental results. Figure 2 illustrates the relation between FAR and false rejection rate (FRR) and threshold T_{th} for (a) fast walking, (b) normal walking, and (c) slow walking. Results confirm that FRR can be < 0.053% when FAR is restricted to 0% and T_{th} is 5.0.

Table 1. Autoencoder properties.

Number of layers	7 (Encoder:3, Decoder:3)
Number of units for each layer	54/512/256/32/256/512/54
Drop out	0.2
Activation function for hidden layers	ReLU

Table 2. Experimental results.

Walking style	Fast	Normal	Slow	Stride	Jog
FAR [%]	0	0	0	0	0
Maximum of FRR [%]	0	0	0	0.053	0

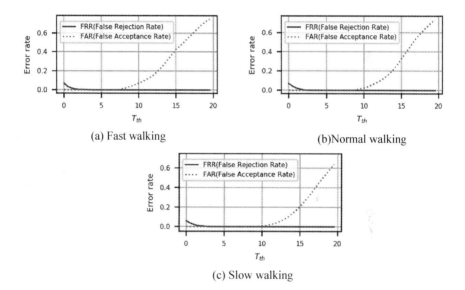

(a) Fast walking

(b) Normal walking

(c) Slow walking

Fig. 2. FAR and FRR for various thresholds T_{th}.

4 Conclusion

We developed a personal authentication method that supports various walking styles. Experimental results confirm that personal authentication can be achieved with very high accuracy by combining a decision tree and multiple autoencoders.

References

1. Kwapisz, J.R., Weiss, G.M., Moore, S.A.: Cell phone-based biometric identification. In: 2010 Fourth IEEE International Conference on Biometrics: Theory, Applications and Systems (BTAS), pp. 1–7. IEEE Press, Washington (2010). https://doi.org/10.1109/btas.2010.5634532
2. Juefei-Xu, F., Bhagavatula, C., Jaech, A., Prasad, U., Savvides, M.: Gait-id on the move: pace independent human identification using cell phone accelerometer dynamics. In: 2012 IEEE Fifth International Conference on Biometrics: Theory, Applications and Systems (BTAS), pp. 8–15. IEEE Press, Arlington (2012). https://doi.org/10.1109/btas.2012.6374552
3. Gadaleta, M., Rossi, M.: Idnet: smartphone-based gait recognition with convolutional neural networks. Pattern Recogn. **74**, 25–37 (2018). https://doi.org/10.1016/j.patcog.2017.09.005
4. Sakurada, M., Yairi, T.: Anomaly detection using autoencoders with nonlinear dimensionality reduction. In: Proceedings of the MLSDA 2014 2nd Workshop on Machine Learning for Sensory Data Analysis (MLSDA 2014), p. 4. ACM, Gold Coast (2014). https://doi.org/10.1145/2689746.2689747

MAD-GAN: Multivariate Anomaly Detection for Time Series Data with Generative Adversarial Networks

Dan Li[1(✉)] , Dacheng Chen[1] , Baihong Jin[2] , Lei Shi[1], Jonathan Goh[3], and See-Kiong Ng[1]

[1] Institute of Data Science, National University of Singapore, 3 Research Link, Singapore 117602, Singapore
{idsld,idscd,shilei,seekiong}@nus.edu.sg
[2] Department of Electrical Engineering and Computer Sciences, University of California, Berkeley, CA 94720, USA
bjin@berkeley.edu
[3] ST Electronics (Info Security) Pte Ltd., 100 Jurong East Street 21, Singapore 609602, Singapore
goh.whyewei.jonathan@stee.stengg.com

Abstract. Many real-world cyber-physical systems (CPSs) are engineered for mission-critical tasks and usually are prime targets for cyber-attacks. The rich sensor data in CPSs can be continuously monitored for intrusion events through anomaly detection. On one hand, conventional supervised anomaly detection methods are unable to exploit the large amounts of data due to the lack of labelled data. On the other hand, current unsupervised machine learning approaches have not fully exploited the spatial-temporal correlation and other dependencies amongst the multiple variables (sensors/actuators) in the system when detecting anomalies. In this work, we propose an unsupervised multivariate anomaly detection method based on Generative Adversarial Networks (GANs), using the Long-Short-Term-Memory Recurrent Neural Networks (LSTM-RNN) as the base models (namely, the generator and discriminator) in the GAN framework to capture the temporal correlation of time series distributions. Instead of treating each data stream independently, our proposed Multivariate Anomaly Detection with GAN (MAD-GAN) framework considers the entire variable set concurrently to capture the latent interactions amongst the variables. We also fully exploit both the generator and discriminator produced by the GAN, using a novel anomaly score called DR-score to detect anomalies through discrimination and reconstruction. We have tested our proposed MAD-GAN using two recent datasets collected from real-world CPSs: the Secure Water Treatment (SWaT) and the Water Distribution (WADI) datasets. Our experimental results show that the proposed MAD-GAN is

This work was supported by the Singapore National Research Foundation and the Cyber-security R&D Consortium Grant Office under Seed Grant Award No. CRDCG2017-S05.

I. V. Tetko et al. (Eds.): ICANN 2019, LNCS 11730, pp. 703–716, 2019.
https://doi.org/10.1007/978-3-030-30490-4_56

effective in reporting anomalies caused by various cyber-attacks inserted in these complex real-world systems.

Keywords: Anomaly detection · Cyber-physical system · Generative Adversarial Networks · Multivariate time series

1 Introduction

A significant volume of real-world data is multivariate time series in nature, e.g., sequences collected in equipment logs and data streams generated by sensors deployed in Cyber-Physical Systems (CPSs) [10]. Anomaly detection for multivariate time series has been attracting tremendous attention nowadays due to its importance in monitoring the system's working conditions and alarming in time to avoid serious financial losses. Application cases include event detection [25], fault detection [11], and intrusion detection [22], which are throughout numerous industries such as energy, information technology, security, etc.

The basic task of anomaly detection for time series is to identify whether the testing data is conform to the normal data distributions, and the non-conforming points are called anomalies, outliers, intrusions, failures or contaminants in various application domains [5]. Traditionally, Statistical Process Control (SPC) methods such as CUSUM, EWMA and Shewhart charts were popular solutions for monitoring quality of industrial processes to find out working states that are out of range [17]. These conventional detection techniques fall short difficult to handle the multivariate data streams generated by the increasingly dynamic and complex nature of modern CPSs. As such, researchers have moved beyond specification or signature-based techniques and begun to exploit machine learning techniques to exploit the large amounts of data generated by the systems [5]. Due to the inherent lack of labelled data, anomaly detection is typically treated as an unsupervised machine learning task. However, most existing unsupervised methods are built through linear projection and transformation that is unable to handle non-linearity in the hidden inherent correlations of the multivariate time series [7,12]. Also, most of the current techniques employ simple comparisons between the present states and the predicted normal ranges to detect anomalies, which can be inadequate given the highly dynamic nature of the systems [20].

In this work, we propose a novel Multivariate Anomaly Detection strategy with GAN (MAD-GAN) to model the complex multivariate correlations among the multiple data streams to detect anomalies using both the GAN-trained generator and discriminator. Unlike traditional supervised classification methods, the GAN-trained discriminator learns to detect fake data in an unsupervised fashion, making it an attractive unsupervised machine learning technique for anomaly detection [4,23]. Inspired by [16] and [19] that update a mapping from the real-time space to a certain latent space to enhance the training of generator and discriminator, researchers have recently proposed to train a latent space understandable GAN and apply it for unsupervised learning of rich feature representations for arbitrary data distributions [3,6,21]. Specifically, [18]

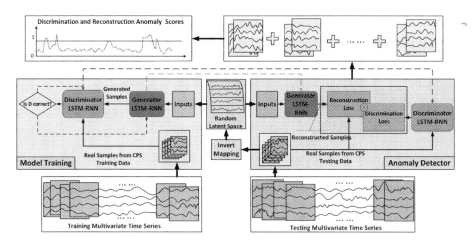

Fig. 1. MAD-GAN: Unsupervised GAN-based anomaly detection. On the left is a GAN framework in which the generator and discriminator are obtained with iterative adversarial training. On the right is the anomaly detection process where both the GAN-trained discriminator and generator are applied to compute a combined anomaly score based on discrimination and reconstruction.

and [8] showed the possibility of recognizing anomalies with reconstructed test samples from latent space, and successfully applied the proposed GAN-based detection strategy to discover unexpected markers for images. We have leveraged on these previous works (as mentioned in Sect. 3.2, the anomaly detection loss function Eq. (5) is taken from the formulation of [18]) to make use of both the GAN-trained generator and discriminator to detect anomalies based on both reconstruction and discrimination losses.

The rest of this paper is organized as follows. In Sect. 2, we introduce the proposed MAD-GAN framework. Section 3 introduces how to conduct anomaly detection with GAN. In Sect. 4, we show the experimental results of our proposed MAD-GAN on two real-world CPS datasets and compare it with state-of-the-art methods. Finally, Sect. 5 summarizes the paper and suggests possible future work.

2   MAD-GAN Architecture

First, to handle the time-series data, we construct the GAN's generator and discriminator as two Long-Short-Term Recurrent Neural Networks (LSTM-RNN), as shown in the left middle part of Fig. 1. Following a typical GAN framework, the generator (G) generates fake time series with sequences from a random latent space as its inputs, and passes the generated sequence samples to the discriminator (D), which will try to distinguish the generated (i.e. "fake") data sequences from the actual (i.e. "real") normal training data sequences.

Instead of treating each data stream independently, the MAD-GAN framework considers the entire variable set concurrently in order to capture the latent interactions amongst the variables into the models. We divide the multivariate time series into sub-sequences with a sliding window before discrimination. To empirically determine an optimal window length for sub-sequences representation, we used different window sizes to capture the system status at different resolutions, namely $s_w = 30 \times i, i = 1, 2, ..., 10$.

In the training stage, the parameters of D and G are updated based on the outputs of D, so that the discriminator can be trained to be as sensitive as possible to assign correct labels to both real and fake sequences, while the generator will be trained to be as smart as possible to fool the discriminator (i.e. to mislead D to assign real labels to fake sequences) after sufficient rounds of iterations. By being able to generate realistic samples, the generator G will have captured the hidden multivariate distributions of the training sequences and can be viewed as an implicit model of the system at normal status. At the same time, the resulting discriminator D has also been trained to be able to distinguish fake (i.e. abnormal) data from real (i.e. normal) data with high sensitivity.

In this work, we propose to exploit both G and D for the anomaly detection task by (i) reconstruction: exploiting the residuals between real-time testing samples and reconstructed samples by G based on the mapping from real-time space to the GAN latent space; and (ii) discrimination: using the discriminator D to classify the time series. This is depicted in the right middle part of Fig. 1. As shown, the testing samples are mapped back into the latent space to calculate the corresponding reconstruction loss based on the difference between the reconstructed testing samples (by the generator G) and the actual testing samples. At the same time, the testing samples are also fed to the trained discriminator D to compute the discrimination loss. Note that the testing multivariate time series are similarly divided into a set of sub-sequences by sliding window and before being fed into the detection model. We use a novel Discrimination and Reconstruction Anomaly Score (DR-Score) to combine the two losses to detect potential anomalies in the data (more details are described in Sect. 3.2).

3   Anomaly Detection with Generative Adversarial Training

3.1   GAN-Based Anomaly Detection

Let us now formulate the anomaly detection problem using GAN. Given a training dataset $\mathcal{X} \subseteq \mathcal{R}^{M \times T}$ with T streams and M measurements for each stream, and a test dataset $\mathcal{X}^{test} \subseteq \mathcal{R}^{N \times T}$ with T streams and N measurements for each stream, the task is to assign binary (0 for normal and 1 for anomalous) labels to the measurements of test dataset. Note that we assume here that all the points in the training dataset are normal.

We apply a sliding window with window size s_w and step size s_s to divide the multivariate time series into a set of multivariate sub-sequences $X = \{x_i, i = 1, 2, ..., m\} \subseteq \mathcal{R}^{s_w \times T}$ (as shown in the left bottom of Fig. 1), where $m = \frac{(M - s_w)}{s_s}$ is the number of sub-sequences. Similarly, $Z = \{z_i, i = 1, 2, ..., m\}$ is a set of multivariate sub-sequences taken from a random space. By feeding X and Z to the GAN model, we train the generator and discriminator with the following two-player minimax game:

$$\min_{G} \max_{D} V(D,G) = \mathcal{E}_{x \sim p_{data}(X)} \left[\log D(x) \right] + \mathcal{E}_{z \sim p_z(Z)} \left[\log(1 - D(G(z))) \right] \quad (1)$$

In this work, both the generator (G) and the discriminator (D) of GAN are Long Short Term-Recurrent Neural Networks (LSTM-RNN) [13]. After sufficient rounds of training iterations, the trained discriminator D and the generator G can then be employed to detect anomalies in $\mathcal{X}^{test}$ using a combined Discrimination and Reconstruction Anomaly Score (DR-Score, shown in Eq. (6)), which will be introduced in Sect. 3.2.

During test, the test dataset $\mathcal{X}^{test} \subseteq \mathcal{R}^{N \times T}$ is similarly divided into multivariate sub-sequences $X^{tes} = \{x_j^{tes}, j = 1, 2, ..., n\}$ with a sliding window (shown in the right bottom of Fig. 1), where $n = \frac{(N - s_w)}{s_s}$. Using the computed DR-Scores (DRS) to be introduced in the next part, we label each of the sub-sequences in the test dataset as follows:

$$A_t^{tes} = \begin{cases} 1, & if \; \mathcal{H}\left(DRAS_t, 1\right) > \tau \\ 0, & else \end{cases} \quad (2)$$

where $A_t^{tes} \in \mathcal{R}^N$ is a label vector for the test dataset, where non-zero values indicate an anomaly is detected. Note that the DR-Score is normalized to $[0,1]$ interval, where the high score values indicate anomalies and the corresponding points are thus assigned as "label=1".

3.2 DR-Score: Anomaly Detection Using both Discrimination and Reconstruction

An advantage of using GAN is that we will have a discriminator and a generator trained simultaneously. We propose to exploit both the discriminator and generator that have been jointly trained to represent the normal anatomical variability for identifying anomalies. Following the formulation in [18], the GAN-based anomaly detection consists of the following two parts:

1. **Discrimination-based Anomaly Detection**
   Given that the trained discriminator D can distinguish fake data (i.e. anomalies) from real data with high sensitivity, it serves as a direct tool for anomaly detection.
2. **Reconstruction-based Anomaly Detection**
   The trained generator G, which is capable of generating realistic samples, is actually a mapping from the latent space to real data space: $G(Z) : Z \rightarrow X$, and can be viewed as an implicit system model that reflects the normal data's distribution. Due to the smooth transitions of latent space mentioned in [2], the generator outputs similar samples if the inputs in the latent space are close. Thus, if it is possible to find the corresponding Z^{tes} in the latent space

for the test data X^{tes}, the similarity between X^{tes} and $G(Z^{tes})$ (which is the reconstructed test samples) could explain to which extent is X^{tes} follows the distribution reflected by G. In other words, we can also use the residuals between X^{tes} and $G(Z^{tes})$ for identifying anomalies in test data.

To find the optimal Z^{tes} that corresponds to the test samples, we first sample a random set Z^1 (with the same size of test samples) from the latent space and obtain reconstructed raw samples $G(Z^1)$ by feeding it to the generator (as shown in the right part of Fig. 1). Then, we update the samples from the latent space with the gradients obtained from the error function defined with X^{tes} and $G(Z^{tes})$.

$$\min_{Z^{tes}} Er(X^{tes}, G_{rnn}(Z^{tes}))$$
$$= \min_{Z^{tes}}\{1 - Simi(X^{tes}, G_{rnn}(Z^{tes}))\} \tag{3}$$

where the similarity between sequences $Simi(.,.)$ could be defined as co-variance for simplicity.

With enough iteration rounds (e.g., the $k - th$ rounds) such that the error is small enough, the samples Z^k is recorded as the corresponding best mapping in the latent space for the test samples. The residual at time t for the $j - th$ test sample is calculated as

$$Res(X_{j,t}^{tes}) = \sum_{i=1}^{T} \mid x_{j,t}^{tes,i} - G_{rnn}(Z_{j,t}^{k,i}) \mid \tag{4}$$

where $X_{j,t}^{tes} \subseteq \mathcal{R}^T$ is the measurements at time step t for the $j - th$ test sample with T variables. Then, the the anomaly detection loss is

$$L_{j,t}^{tes} = \lambda Res(X_{j,t}^{tes}) + (1 - \lambda)\mathcal{H}(D_{rnn}(X_{j,t}^{tes}), 1) \tag{5}$$

Note that higher residuals (reconstruction error) indicate potential anomalies, while higher discrimination outputs indicate that the test samples are assigned with real labels (be recognized as normal). Thus, to be consistent with the reconstruction error, the discrimination error is calculated as the the cross entropy error $\mathcal{H}(D_{rnn}(X_{j,t}^{tes}), 1)$, and thus higher error indicates larger possibility of anomaly. The parameter $\lambda \in [0, 1]$ which weight the two losses should be jointly validated based on the best detection performance.

Based on the above descriptions, the GAN-trained discriminator and generator will output a set of anomaly detection losses $L = \{L_{j,t}, j = 1, 2, ..., n; t = 1, 2, ..., s_w\} \subseteq \mathcal{R}^{n \times s_w}$ for each test data sub-sequence. We compute a combined discrimination-cum-reconstruction anomaly score called the DR-Score (DRS) by mapping the anomaly detection loss of sub-sequences back to the original time series (shown in the top part of Fig. 1).

$$DRS_k = \frac{\sum\limits_{j,t \in \{j+t=k\}} L_{j,t}}{lc_t} \tag{6}$$
$$lc_t = count(j, t \in \{j + t = k\})$$

where $k \in \{1, 2, ..., N\}$, $j \in \{1, 2, ..., n\}$, and $t \in \{1, 2, ..., s_w\}$.

4   Experiments

4.1   CPSs: Water Treatment and Distribution Systems

SWaT. The Secure Water Treatment (SWaT) system is an operational test-bed for water treatment that represents a small-scale version of a large modern water treatment plant found in large cities [15]. The water purification process in SWaT is composed of six sub-processes referred to as $P1$ through $P6$ [9]. The first process ($P1$) is for raw water supply and storage, and $P2$ is for pre-treatment where the water quality is assessed. Undesired materials are them removed by ultra-filtration (UF) backwash in $P3$. The remaining chlorine is destroyed in the Dechlorination process ($P4$). Subsequently, the water from $P4$ is pumped into the Reverse Osmosis (RO) system ($P5$) to reduce inorganic impurities. Finally, $P6$ stores the water ready for distribution. 36 attacks were launched on the testbed with different intents and diverse lasting durations (from a few minutes to an hour) in the final four days. Please refer to the SWat website[1] for more details about the SWaT dataset.

WADI. The Water Distribution (WADI) test-bed is an extension of the SWaT system, which is similarly equipped with chemical dosing systems, booster pumps and valves, instrumentation and analyzers [1]. There are three control processes in the water distribution system. The first process is to intake the raw water from SWaT, Public Utility Board (PUB) inlet or the return water in WADI, and store the raw water in two tanks. $P2$ distributes water from two elevated reservoir tanks and six consumer tanks based on a pre-set demand pattern. Water is recycled and sent back to $P1$ at the third process. A total of 15 attacks were launched in WADI system. Please refer to the WADI website[2] for more details about the WADI dataset.

4.2   Data Preparation and System Architecture

In the SWaT dataset, $496,800$ samples for 51 variables were collected under normal working conditions, and $449,919$ samples were collected when various cyber-attacks were inserted to the system subsequently. Similarly, for the WADI dataset, $789,371$ samples for 118 variables were collected under normal working conditions, and $172,801$ samples were collected when various cyber-attacks were inserted to the system. For both of these datasets, the first $21,600$ samples were removed from the training data (normal data) in consideration of the system's stabilization time [9]. Note that in the original test data file, only points on the attacking period are labelled as "1" (means anomalous), while the system needs some time to recover from abnormal to normal after each attack revocation. In our testing scenario, we assumed that it takes 2 h for the system to recover after an attack, where points were also labelled as "1" in the ground truth file during.

---

[1] https://itrust.sutd.edu.sg/testbeds/secure-water-treatment-swat/.

[2] https://itrust.sutd.edu.sg/testbeds/water-distribution-wadi/.

In the anomaly detection process, we subdivided the original long multiple sequences into smaller time series by taking a sliding window across raw streams. Since it is an important topic in time series study to decide the optimal window length for sub-sequences representation, we tried out a set of different window sizes to capture the system status at different resolutions, namely $s_w = 30 \times i, i = 1, 2, ..., 10$. To capture the relevant dynamics, the window is applied to the training and test datasets with shift length $s_s = 10$. For the generator, we used a stacked LSTM network with depth 3 and 100 hidden (internal) units. The discriminator is a relatively simpler LSTM network with depth 1 and 100 hidden units.

4.3   Evaluation Metrics

We use the standard metrics, namely Precision (Pre), Recall (Rec), and F_1 scores, to evaluate the anomaly detection performance of MAD-GAN:

$$Pre = \frac{TP}{TP + FP} \tag{7}$$

$$Rec = \frac{TP}{TP + FN} \tag{8}$$

$$F_1 = 2 \times \frac{Pre \times Rec}{Pre + Rec} \tag{9}$$

where TP is the correctly detected anomaly (True Positives: $A_t = 1$ while real label $L_t = 1$), FP is the falsely detected anomaly (False Positives: $A_t = 1$ while real label $L_t = 0$), TN is the correctly assigned normal (True Negatives: $A_t = 0$ while real label $L_t = 0$), and FN is the falsely assigned normal (False Negatives: $A_t = 0$ while real label $L_t = 1$).

The accuracy metric is usually used to measure how many labels are assigned correctly by the detector/classifier. However, for unbalanced data (with large percentage of actual negatives, such as the SWaT and WADI datasets), accuracy is not a efficient metric since it can be largely contributed by a large number of true negatives while detection of positives is not well reflected. Thus, the precision, recall and F_1 score can better evaluate the anomaly detection performance of unbalanced data by measuring the true positives [14]. Moreover, as shown by Eq. (7), the precision measures how many predicted positives are actual positives, thus the precision is a good measure when false positive cost is expensive. On the other hand, as shown in Eq. (8), the recall measures how many actual positives are reported by the detector/classifier, and it is a good metric if the cost of false negatives is high.

4.4   Results

We evaluated the anomaly detection performance of MAD-GAN on the aforementioned SWaT and WADI. For comparison on the anomaly detection performance, we applied PCA, One-Class SVM (OCSVM), K-Nearest Neighbour

(KNN), Feature Bagging (FB), and Auto-Encoder (AE) that are popular unsupervised anomaly detection methods[3] on the datasets. To compare with a GAN-based method, we also tested both datasetds with the Efficient GAN-based (EGAN) method of [8] whose discriminator and generator were implemented as fully connected neural networks.

Anomaly Detection Performance. In this work, we used Precision (Pre), Recall (Rec) and F_1 values are the metrics to evaluate the anomaly detection results. In Table 1, the best performance by the popular unsupervised methods (PCA, OCSVM, KNN, FB and AE) was marked with underlines, and the overall best performance was marked in bold. As mentioned in Sect. 4.2, MAD-GAN was tested with multiple sub-sequence resolutions. The metrics along different resolutions were reported in terms of best F_1[4].

From Table 1, we observe the following:

- For the SWaT dataset, MAD-GAN outperformed the best performance by four popular conventional methods (OCSVM) by 17.58% and 42.94% for precision and recall, respectively. In fact, MAD-GAN achieved high recall (95.40%) with a relatively high precision (70.00%), and thus achieving the highest F_1 score (0.81).
- For the WADI dataset, MAD-GAN also outperformed the best results by popular methods by 1.78% and 22.95% for precision and recall, respectively.
- Although the precision values by MAD-GAN for both datasets were not obviously high (70.00% and 53.75%, respectively), they were better than that by other methods. The relatively low precision (but still better than that by state-of-the-art methods) was caused by the false positives reported for the unbalanced data (i.e., there were more true negatives than true positives in the test data). Given that our application in this work is to detect intrusions (cyber-attack) which are rare, it is important for the system to detect all the attacks even if it requires tolerating a few false alarms.
- It can also been seen that MAD-GAN performed better than EGAN for both SWaT and WADI datasets. This is because LSTM-RNN, which is used in MAD-GAN, is capable of learning complex time series better than the CNNs used in EGAN. In fact, looking at the relative performance of EGAN with other non-GAN methods, we can see that GAN-based anomaly detection is unable to compete other traditional methods if we do not model temporal correlation appropriately.

Overall, MAD-GAN consistently outperformed the tested state-of-the-art unsupervised detection methods. One drawback is that it takes LSTM-RNN more time to deal with longer sub-sequences (to be specific, the model becomes slow when the sub-sequence length s_w is larger than 200). It will be worthwhile

---

[3] Note that codes of OCSVM, KNN, FB and AE are taken from PyOD [24].

[4] The best F_1 for the SWaT dataset is obtained with sub-sequence length equals to 150 at the 9th iteration (100 iterations in total). Also, the best F_1 for the WADI dataset is obtained with $s_w = 240$ at the 43th iteration (100 iterations in total).

Table 1. Anomaly detection performance of different methods

Datasets	Methods	Pre	Rec	F_1
SWaT	PCA	46.29	59.10	0.51
	OCSVM	52.46	52.46	0.52
	KNN	34.79	34.79	0.35
	FB	35.79	35.79	0.36
	AE	51.61	51.61	0.52
	EGAN	40.57	67.73	0.51
	MAD-GAN	**70.00**	**95.40**	**0.81**
WAD	PCA	50.35	16.62	0.25
	OCSVM	51.17	51.17	0.51
	KNN	29.92	29.92	0.30
	FB	33.64	33.64	0.34
	AE	51.97	51.97	0.52
	EGAN	34.45	34.45	0.34
	MAD-GAN	**53.75**	**74.92**	**0.62**

to explore using other learning models to capture the temporal correlation and explore how to choose the sub-sequence length with theoretical guarantee for future work. In this work, we will discuss the results in terms of sub-sequence resolutions in the following part.

Sub-sequence Resolution. Selecting a suitable sub-sequence resolution (ie. sub-sequence length) is critical for RNN and time series related studies. In this work, we empirically determined the optimal sub-sequence resolution by trying a series of different sub-sequence lengths (i.e. window sizes, $s_w = \{30 \times i, i = 1, 2, ..., 10\}$). For each sub-sequence length, the GAN model was trained recursively for 100 iterations (i.e. epochs). We depict the box-plots of the recall and evaluation metrics (precision, recall and F_1) of MAD-GAN at each of the training iterations over different sub-sequence lengths in Fig. 2.

From Fig. 2, we can observe the following differences:

- It can be observed that MAD-GAN achieved better recall at sub-sequence length $s_w = \{60, 150, 180, 270\}$ for SWaT, and the precision values presented slightly similar trends at the same sub-sequence lengths. Also, it is seen that MAD-GAN achieved better recall at sub-sequence length $s_w = \{30, 210, 240, 300\}$ for WADI, while the overall precision values presented no big difference along different sub-sequence lengths. This indicates that the MAD-GAN is generally not sensitive to the sub-sequence length (i.e., window size) when identifying anomalous points for long time series CPS data.
- Between the two datasets, MAD-GAN generated better precision values for SWaT while the average recall values for WADI were slightly better; however,

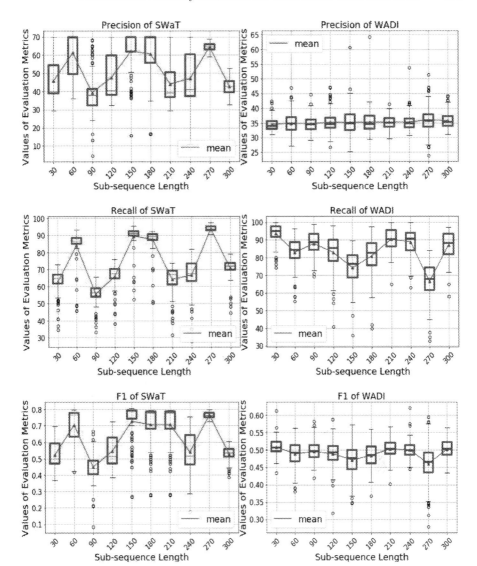

Fig. 2. Values of evaluation metrics (precision, recall and F_1) as a function of sub-sequence lengths for SWaT and WADI. The boxes show the MAD-GAN performance at fixed 100 training iterations. The green lines in all the boxes are the median values. The mean values of each box are shown as green triangles and they are linked together with a red line. (Color figure online)

SWaT's overall F_1 scores were better than these of WADI. This is because WADI is more unbalanced than SWaT (i.e. WADI has less actual positives and more actual negatives), which leads to higher true positive rate with more false positives. In addition, the WADI dataset has a larger feature dimension with higher actuator rate than SWaT. Since actuators just record ON/OFF signals, they recover relatively less system behaviour patterns than sensor variables do.

- While there were fluctuations in performance (in particular recall) and no convergence along the range of tested sub-sequence lengths for both datasets, we can see that the average recall values were roughly oscillating within relatively acceptable bounds (50–100%) for both datasets. Since there is no rule of thumb for deciding LSTM-RNN's sequence length but depends on the nature of data, a relatively small sub-sequence length (such as $s_w = 60$ for SWaT and $s_w = 30$ for WADI) could be a safe choice for CPS datasets like SWaT and WADI. This choice of small sub-sequence length can save lots of time[5] while the performance can be guaranteed. It would be a worthy further work for us to investigate and develop a principled approach to determine the optimal sub-sequence resolution for time-series analysis using GAN.

5   Conclusions

In this paper, we have explored the use of GAN for multivariate anomaly detection on the time series data generated by the CPSs. We proposed a novel MAD-GAN framework to train LSTM-RNNs on the multivariate time-series data and then utilize both the discriminator and the generator to detect anomalies using a novel DR-Score. We tested MAD-GAN on two complex cyber-attack CPS datasets collected form the Secure Water Treatment Testbed (SWaT) and Water Distribution System (WADI), and showed superior performance over existing unsupervised detection methods, including a GAN-based approach.

Given that this is an early attempt on multivariate anomaly detection on time series data using GAN, there are interesting issues that await further investigations. For example, we have noted the need of determining the optimal sub-sequence length. For future work, we plan to conduct further research on feature selection and sub-sequence decision for multivariate anomaly detection.

References

1. Ahmed Chuadhry Mujeeb, V.R.P., Mathur, A.P.: Wadi: a water distribution testbed for research in the design of secure cyber physical systems. In: In Proceedings of the 3rd International Workshop on Cyber-Physical Systems for Smart Water Networks, pp. 25–28. ACM (2017). https://doi.org/10.1145/3055366.3055375
2. Alec, R., Metz, L., Chintala, S.: Unsupervised representation learning with deep convolutional generative adversarial networks. arXiv preprint arXiv 1511(06434) (2015)

---

[5] For SWaT, With a GeForce GTX 1080 Ti, the 100-epoch training-testing round took 6.15 h when $s_w = 60$, while it took 23.34 h when $s_w = 300$. For WADI, the 100-epoch training-testing round took 1.79 h when $s_w = 30$, while it took 6.68 h when $s_w = 300$. Note that WADI took less computation burden since most of its variables are actuator signals (ON/OFF).

3. Budhraja, K.K., Oates, T.: Adversarial feature selection. In: IEEE International Conference on Data Mining Workshop (ICDMW), pp. 288–294. IEEE (2015). https://doi.org/10.1109/icdmw.2015.59
4. Chun-Liang, L., Chang, W.C., Cheng, Y., Yang, Y., Póczos, B.: MMD GAN: towards deeper understanding of moment matching network. In: In Advances in Neural Information Processing Systems, pp. 2203–2213 (2017)
5. Donghwoon, K., Kim, H., Kim, J., Suh, S.C., Kim, I., Kim, K.J.: A survey of deep learning-based network anomaly detection. Cluster Comput. 1–139 (2017). https://doi.org/10.1007/s10586-017-1117-8
6. Fei, Z., Chan, P.P., Biggio, B., Yeung, D.S., Roli, F.: Adversarial feature selection against evasion attacks. IEEE Trans. Cybern. **46**(3), 766–777 (2016). https://doi.org/10.1109/tcyb.2015.2415032
7. Harrou, F., Nounou, M.N., Nounou, H.N., Madakyaru, M.: Pls-based EWMA fault detection strategy for process monitoring. J. Loss Prev. Process Ind. **36**, 108–119 (2015). https://doi.org/10.1016/j.jlp.2015.05.017
8. Houssam, Z., Foo, C.S., Lecouat, B., Manek, G., Chandrasekhar, V.R.: Efficient GAN-based anomaly detection. arXiv preprint arXiv 1802(06222) (2018)
9. Jonathan, G., Adepu, S., Junejo, K.N., Mathur, A.: A dataset to support research in the design of secure water treatment systems. In: International Conference on Critical Information Infrastructures Security, pp. 88–99 (2016). https://doi.org/10.1007/978-3-319-71368-7_8
10. Jonathan, G., Adepu, S., Tan, M., Lee, Z.S.: Anomaly detection in cyber physical systems using recurrent neural networks. In: In IEEE 18th International Symposium on High Assurance Systems Engineering (HASE), pp. 140–145. IEEE (2017). https://doi.org/10.1109/HASE.2017.36
11. Li, D., Hu, G., Spanos, C.J.: A data-driven strategy for detection and diagnosis of building chiller faults using linear discriminant analysis. Energy Build. **128**, 519–529 (2016). https://doi.org/10.1016/j.enbuild.2016.07.014
12. Li, S., Wen, J.: A model-based fault detection and diagnostic methodology based on pca method and wavelet transform. Energy Build. **68**, 63–71 (2014). https://doi.org/10.1016/j.enbuild.2013.08.044
13. Lipton Zachary C., J.B., Elkan, C.: A critical review of recurrent neural networks for sequence learning. In: arXiv preprint arXiv:1506.00019 (2015)
14. Martin, P.D.: Evaluation: from precision, recall and f-measure to roc, informedness, markedness and correlation. J. Mach. Learn. Technol. **2**(1) (2011)
15. Mathur, A.P., Tippenhauer, N.O.: Swat: a water treatment testbed for research and training on ICS security. In: International Workshop on Cyber-physical Systems for Smart Water Networks (CySWater), pp. 31–36. IEEE (2016). https://doi.org/10.1109/cyswater.2016.7469060
16. Raymond, Y., Chen, C., Lim, T.Y., Hasegawa-Johnson, M., Do, M.N.: Semantic image inpainting with perceptual and contextual losses. arXiv preprint arXiv 1607(07539) (2016)
17. Sun, B., Luh, P.B., Jia, Q.S., O'Neill, Z., Song, F.: Building energy doctors: an SPC and Kalman filter-based method for system-level fault detection in HVAC systems. IEEE Trans. Autom. Sci. Eng. **11**(1), 215–229 (2014). https://doi.org/10.1109/tase.2012.2226155
18. Thomas, S., Seeböck, P., Waldstein, S.M., Schmidt-Erfurth, U., Langs, G.: Unsupervised anomaly detection with generative adversarial networks to guide marker discovery, pp. 146–157 (2017). https://doi.org/10.1007/978-3-319-59050-9_12

19. Tim, S., Goodfellow, I., Zaremba, W., Cheung, V., Radford, A., Chen, X.: Improved techniques for training GANS. In: Advances in Neural Information Processing Systems, pp. 2234–2242 (2016)

20. Xuewu, D., Gao, Z.: From model, signal to knowledge: a data-driven perspective of fault detection and diagnosis. IEEE Trans. Industr. Inf. **9**(4), 2226–2238 (2013). https://doi.org/10.1109/tii.2013.2243743

21. Yongjie, L., Wang, Q., Gu, Y., Kamijo, S.: A latent space understandable generative adversarial network: selfexgan. In: International Conference on Digital Image Computing: Techniques and Applications (DICTA), pp. 1–8. IEEE (2017). https://doi.org/10.1109/dicta.2017.8227390

22. Yu, W., Cheng, W., Aggarwal, C.C., Zhang, K., Chen, H., Wang, W. : Netwalk: a flexible deep embedding approach for anomaly detection in dynamic networks. In: Proceedings of the 24th ACM SIGKDD International Conference on Knowledge Discovery & Data Mining, pp. 2672–2681. ACM (2018). https://doi.org/10.1145/3219819.3220024

23. Yuan, X., Xu, T., Zhang, H., Long, R., Huang, X.: SEGAN: adversarial network with multi-scale l1 loss for medical image segmentation. arXiv preprint arXiv **1706**(01805) (2017). https://doi.org/10.1007/s12021-018-9377-x

24. Zhao, Y., Nasrullah, Z., Li, Z.: Pyod: a python toolbox for scalable outlier detection. J. Mach. Learn. Res. **20**, 1–7 (2019). http://jmlr.org/papers/v20/19-011.html

25. Zhou, Y., Arghandeh, R., Konstantakopoulos, I., Abdullah, S., Spanos, C.J.: Data-driven event detection with partial knowledge: a hidden structure semi-supervised learning method. In: In American Control Conference (ACC), pp. 5962–5968. IEEE (2016). https://doi.org/10.1109/acc.2016.7526605

Intrusion Detection via
Wide and Deep Model

Zhipeng Li, Zheng Qin$^{(\boxtimes)}$, and Pengbo Shen

School of Software, Tsinghua University, Beijing 100084, China
{lizp14,spb17}@mails.tsinghua.edu.cn, qingzh@mail.tsinghua.edu.cn

Abstract. Intrusion detection system is designed to detect threats and attacks, which are especially important in nowadays' constantly emerging information security incidents. There has been a lot of work devoted to realizing anomaly detection mode of intrusion detection via deep learning, since deep learning becomes a research hot spot. However, there is rarely work that uses different deep learning networks as hybrid architecture to benefit the advantages of each special part. In this paper, we are inspired by the Google's Wide & Deep model which is proposed to combine memorization with generalization via different networks. We propose a framework to use Wide & Deep model for intrusion detection. To get comprehensive categorical representations of continuous features, we use a density-based clustering (DBSCAN) to convert the KDD'99\NSL_KDD format features into sparse categorical feature representations. A widely used and popular NSL_KDD dataset is used for evaluating the proposed model. A comprehensive empirical evaluation with hypothesis testing demonstrates that the revised Wide & Deep framework outperforms the separated part alone. Compared with other machine learning base line methods and advanced deep learning methods, the proposed model outperforms the baseline results and achieves a steady and promising performance in tests with different levels.

Keywords: Intrusion detection · DBSCAN · Wide & Deep model · NSL_KDD

1 Introduction

With the rapid growth of IoT, Big Data and AI, more and more facilities are exposed on the Internet, attacks from Internet treat everyone in modern society. Intrusion detection is an important information security protection facility. Intrusion Detection System (IDS) is designed to recognize potential treats and attacks, IDS can rise alarms to system or operator. Some IDS even developed to have the defense ability, and so-called Intrusion Prevention System (IPS). How to protect Internet information system via intrusion detection has been a research focus for a long time.

© Springer Nature Switzerland AG 2019
I. V. Tetko et al. (Eds.): ICANN 2019, LNCS 11730, pp. 717–730, 2019.
https://doi.org/10.1007/978-3-030-30490-4_57

Intrusion detection system is proposed as a theoretical concept with a definite frame work in 1978 by Denning [2]. There can be host-based mode or network-based mode or hybrid (both network and host system) as the deployment taxonomy. UCDavis first developed Network Security Monitor (NSM) as the first network IDS and Stanford research institute had realized the first real time prototype. Snort [13] is an open source software, which enjoys great reputation. Intrusion detection system also can be divided into misuse detection mode and anomaly detection mode according IDS work mode. The misuse detection is a traditional work mode, it uses signatures of attack definitions to detect potential attacks. It is a fundamental prototype of IDS. An advantage of misuse detection is that detection procedure is relatively accurate. The false positive rate of the results is low. The shortcoming is that misuse detection cannot detect unknown novel attack forms. The detection rules must be defined by human expert which is complicated to maintain. The anomaly detection method is based on physical statics, AI algorithms or machine learning methods and so on. Anomaly detection can detect novel attack forms to a certain extent, which is crucial in nowadays rapid IT developments. The bad aspect is: anomaly detection bears false alarm rate (false positive rate) as a side effect of automatic attack recognition.

Deep learning is a research hot spot in recent years. With the rapid growth of hardware computing ability, especially benefits from the parallel computing application of graphic process unit, neural networks is getting deeper and deeper. The deeper networks gets more accurate results in many areas, and some amazing achievements have been made in image processing, audio processing, and natural language processing. Various variant designs and applications have been proposed in various application scenarios. Generative Adversarial Networks and reinforcement learning even have reached a level beyond the human limits. Scholars have made efforts to realize anomaly detection via machine learning. And various deep learning methods have been proposed since the deep learning becomes a main approach to achieve AI. [3,6,16] use deep neural networks to learn the feature representation. [15] uses deep auto encoder for unsupervised feature learning. [9,20] use recursive neural networks to treat the issue as a sequence to label problem. [10,18] use convolutional neural networks to recognize the abstract network data information. [14] use deep learning for feature representation and a SVM classifier to form a hybrid model.

Among the literal works, deep learning method is the most commonly used method in feature extraction. Academics use certain specific frameworks alone to solve the intrusion detection issue. Convolutional neural networks and recursive neural networks are used to get the relative sequence information or relative spacial information of atomic data feature. To the best of our knowledge, there is no work considering the combination of deep feature extraction ability with some specific deep models. Inspired by the wide & deep model for recommender system [1], we propose a framework to use the wide & deep model for intrusion detection. In this paper, a hybrid model which combines memorization wide model and generalization deep model is proposed. An unsupervised clustering process is used for feature conversion. Dense features are processed to retain the data information. Jointly training generalized linear model with cross-product feature transformations and neural networks with dense embedding is given in detail. The model is evaluated on a popular NSL_KDD dataset. Comparative experiments are taken to verify the rationality of proposed architecture.

The rest of the paper is organized as follows. Section 2 provides some related work and background information. Section 3 gives a detailed information of proposed method. Section 4 shows the experiments and experiment results analysis. Section 5 gives the conclusion and future work.

2 Related Works

Anomaly detection is thought to be a feasible method to achieve novel attacks recognition. Lots of literature works tries to find ways to combine misuse detection with anomaly detection. Hybrid architectures are proposed to take advantage of both of them [4, 7, 21]. Some works uses AI algorithms or machine learning methods to do feature engineering [8, 14]. To the best of our knowledge, there is no work using a hybrid deep learning model by jointly training each learning part.

Wide & Deep model was proposed by Google Inc. for recommender systems. The wide part can memorize more relationship among user-item pair by cross-product transformation. The deep part can generalize to more universal scene by using deep learning to represent features. The need for memorizing and generalizing is pervasive in many applications. [11] uses a deep sequence model for traffic prediction. [22] uses a deep and shallow model for insurance churn prediction service. [19] proposes a Deep & Cross network for advertisement click predictions.

Inspired by the Wide & Deep model and the extension applications, in this paper we propose a method to apply the wide & Deep model to intrusion detection. A common data processing process is proposed to fit each input part. We use clustering method to convert the continuous feature type, in which the conversion can maintain information for memorizing. We jointly train the model to optimize the benefits of memorization and generalization.

3 Proposed Methods

As a combination of wide models and deep models, the model uses both network structure to get memorization and generalization. The raw network data can be abstract as the KDD'99 dataset datatype. The abstract datatype is abstracted by domain experts. The NSL_KDD dataset remains the same datatype. As there are different types of data, we use clustering method to convert the continuous feature into categorical feature representation, for the need to memory the specific relationship of feature representation. And the transformation also can be used in the deep part, which can find more complicated representation of features. The general illustration of our proposed method is shown in Fig. 1.

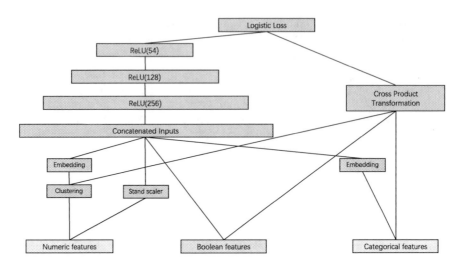

Fig. 1. Overview of Deep & Shallow model for intrusion detection

3.1   Data Processing

As illustrated in Fig. 1, the deep part is a deep feed-forward neural network. There are different kinds of data types in KDD'99\NSL_KDD dataset. For sparse categorical features (e.g. protocol_type, flag, etc), these features can be converted into a dense embedding vector through dense embedding. Some numeric features (e.g. src_bytes, same_srv_rate, etc), need to be converted into sparse categorical features. Yet the categorical conversion of numeric features can make the deep network find more complicated transformation between features, and what is more important is that the wide part of network need the categorical representation of features. Only the discrete representation of features can get a more specific memorization by cross-product transformation.

There are many clustering methods which can discover useful intrinsic clustering information, e.g. K-MEANS (distance partitioning methods), BIRCH (hierarchical methods), Fuzzy c-means [12] (fuzzy mathematical methods), DBSCAN (density partitioning methods), etc. The clustering performance can be measured using F1 score (with classification results) or $MaxDist$ and Function J (without classification results). $MaxDist$ stands for the longest distance between the clustering center and the cluster inner point. Function J is defined as:

$$J = \sum_{j=1}^{n} J_i = \sum_{j=1}^{n} \left(\sum_{k, x_k \in C_j} \left\| x_k - C_{c_j} \right\| \right) \tag{1}$$

where C_{c_j} stands for the center of clusters and x_k stands for cluster C_j inner point. However, according to the specific application in this paper, we just need a meticulous detailed categorical transformation representation of each specific feature. So the clustering algorithm should be unsupervised and can find the intrinsic feature structure without given the number of clusters. And considering the scale of the data set, the chosen clustering algorithm should be efficient and low memory consumption.

To convert the continuous features into categorical features, we use a clustering method. There is some works using fixed-distance bucket numbering method to discrete the numeric data types. But we think the abstracted KDD'99\NSL_KDD numeric features have specific physical meanings and need a more appropriate transformation to maintain the internal data structure. Firstly, we need an unsupervised clustering method without given clustering numbers, and secondly considering the complexity and rationality, we use DBSCAN as our clustering method. DBSCAN clustering method is shown in Algorithm 1:

Algorithm 1. DBSCAN Clustering Algorithm

Input:
    D: The set include n samples
    ϵ: The neighborhood distance threshold of a sample
    $MinPts$: The threshold of sample numbers in distant of ϵ
Output:
    Density-based clusters
 1: Label all samples be unvisited;
 2: **repeat**
 3:    Random choose a sample p;
 4:    Mark p visited;
 5:    **if** there are at least $Minpts$ samples in the ϵ neighborhood **then**
 6:      Create a new cluster C, add p into C;
 7:      Make N to be the sample set which is ϵ-neighborhood of p;
 8:      **for** Every sample p' in N **do**
 9:        **if** p' is unvisited; **then**
10:          Mark p' is visited;
11:          **if** there are at least $Minpts$ samples in ϵ neighborhood of p' **then**
12:            Add these samples to N;
13:          **end if**
14:          **if** p' is still not a memeber of any cluster **then**
15:            Add p' into C;
16:          **end if**
17:        **end if**
18:      **end for**
19:      Output C;
20:    **else**
21:      Mark p as noise;
22:    **end if**
23: **until** There is no marked as unvisited sample;

3.2 The Deep Part

As deep part of the model shown in the left part of Fig. 1, the deep part is a feed-forward neural networks. The categorical features (e.g. protocol_type, service, flag) are converted into dense embedding vectors via an embedding function. The numeric features are first clustered to sparse categorical representation, and then converted into a dense embedding representation of the categorical features. These dense embedding vectors and the raw input after stand-scale are fed into the input layer. By using forward pass algorithm, each hidden layer computes:

$$a^{(l+1)} = f(W^{(l)}a^{(l)} + b^{(l)}) \tag{2}$$

where f stands for the rectified linear units (ReLUs) activation function and l stands for layer number. $a^{(l)}, b^{(l)}$ are the activations and bias. $W^{(l)}$ is the l-layer weights of the network.

3.3 The Wide Part

The wide part is used for memorizing a specific combination of features, which is shown in the right part in Fig. 1. In recommend systems, some general linear models are widely used, e.g. Logistic Regression (LR). For feature A the coding bitA $= 1$, stands for having the feature A, and bitB $= 1$ stands for having the feature B. Cross-product features can represent having feature A and B. Wide model can use cross-product to realize memorizing features for recommend purpose. We need the comprehensive representation of features, and we make the continuous features a categorical representation via DBSCAN clustering. The numeric inputs are clustered to categorical representations for memorizing the unique feature element with others. The most important function operator is the cross-product transformation, which is defined as:

$$\phi_k(x) = \prod_{i=1}^{d} x_i^{c_{ki}} \qquad c_{ki} \in 0, 1 \tag{3}$$

where c_{ki} has boolean value, that 1 (true) means the i-th feature or the corresponding categorical feature ingredient is in the k-th transformation ϕ_k, and 0 means not. For categorical features and the categorical continuous features, the cross-product transformation (e.g., after clustering 'same_srv_rate' has '1' as a discrete value which means the rate is in section [0.07, 0.09], AND (service = 'ftp_data', same_srv_rate = '1')) is 1 and only if the corresponding features (service = 'ftp_data' and same_srv_rate = '1') are all 1, and 0 otherwise. This wide part can memorize the interactions between the categorical features and the continuous features after clustering discretion. The logical AND operator creates non-linearity to the model.

3.4 Joint Training

In the Wide & Deep model, the two parts (wide part and deep part) are combined by a weighed sum of their output log odds, which form one common logistic loss function inputs. The joint training logistic regression can be written as below:

$$P(Y = 1|x) = \sigma(w_{wide}^T[x, \phi(x)] + w_{deep}^T a^{l_f} + b) \qquad (4)$$

where Y is the predicted output label, $\phi(\cdot)$ stands for sigmoid function, $\phi(x)$ is the cross-product transformation of inputs feature representations, and b is the bias term. w_{wide} and w_{deep} are weights of each part. The model can be jointly trained by using Follow The-Regularized-Leader (FTRL) algorithm with $L1$ regularization as the optimizer for the wide part, and AdaGrad for the deep [1].

4   Experiment and Analysis

In this section, we conduct experiments to evaluate the efficacy of our revised model for intrusion detection. Firstly, we use a popular NSL_KDD dataset to show the continuous feature to categorical representation processing procedure. Then, comprehensive experiments with hypothesis testing are conducted to test the performance of each individual part and joint together as a whole unit. Finally, we compare the results of binary classification with other work, which proves that this Wide & Deep method achieves performance improvement and make a promising performance on different test dataset.

4.1   NSL_KDD Dataset and Feature Conversion

DARPA (Defense Advanced Research Projects Agency) raised an intrusion detection evaluation program which was conducted by MIT Lincoln Laboratory in 1998. The program used network traffic and audit logs which were collected on a simulation network. The simulation collected 7-week raw network data for training and 2-week for testing which kept famous and authoritative in intrusion detection area for a long time. In 1999, KDD-Cup (Data Mining and Knowledge Discovery) chose the topic 'Computer Network Intrusion Detection' and used the DARPA 1998 dataset as the prototype dataset for competition. KDD CUP extracted 4 main categories, 41 specific features from the raw dataset and formed a new KDD'99 dataset. With lots of works focused on experimenting with KDD'99, there have been some deficiencies exposed in KDD'99, such as imbalance between data categories, data redundancy and so on. NSL_KDD is a successor improved version of KDD'99 [17]. NSL_KDD is proposed for overcoming the disadvantages of KDD'99 while keeping the same abstract features to KDD'99.

NSL_KDD data set is the most popular dataset in intrusion detection for the authority (successor of DARPA'98) and the rationality (no redundant). Aiming to get an exquisite description of continuous features, we use extreme parameters to make each feature to form more clusters. We use $\epsilon = 0.01$ for float features, $\epsilon = 1$ for int features as the minimum interval, and $MinPts = 50$ as the minimum cluster data point numbers. And there are 125973 data points in train data set, $MinPts = 50$ is a very small number comparing to the samples number in train data set. We use DBSCAN clustering for these float rate features ($\epsilon = 0.01, MinPts = 50$) and integer features ($\epsilon = 1, MinPts = 50$). The clustering intervals are used for representing categorical information. The detail of category representation of NSL_KDD features is shown in Table 1.

Table 1. Features & categorical representation conversion

Feature name	Category conversion & data types
same_srv_rate	[0.0,0.03] 0.04 [0.05, 0.06] [0.07, 0.09] [0.1, 0.12] [0.14, 0.15] [0.17,0.18] 0.5 [0.13, 0.99]
duration	[0,5] [6,42908]
protocol_type	tcp udp icmp
service	ftp_data other private http remote_job name netbios_ns eco_i mtp telnet finger domain_u supdup uucp_path Z39_50 smtp csnet_ns uucp netbios_dgm urp_i auth domain ftp bgp ldap ecr_i gopher vmnet systat http_443 efs whois imap4 iso_tsap echo klogin link sunrpc login kshell sql_net time hostnames exec ntp_u discard nntp courier ctf ssh daytime shell netstat pop_3 nnsp IRC pop_2 printer tim_i pm_dump red_i netbios_ssn rje X11 urh_i http_8001 aol http_2784 tftp_u harves
flag	SF S0 REJ RSTR SH RSTO S1 RSTOS0 S3 S2 OTH
src_bytes	[0, 1] [6, 10] [28, 30] [41, 46] [145, 148] [205, 209] [218, 222] noises
dst_bytes	[0, 1] [44, 46] [105, 107] [327, 334] noises
land	0 1
wrong_fragment	0 1 3
urgent	0 1 2 3
hot	0 1 2 3 4 5 6 7 11 15 18 19 22 24 28 30
num_failed_logins	0 1 2 3 4 5
logged_in	0 1
num_compromised	0 1 2 3 4 5
root_shell	0 1
su_attempted	0 1 2
num_root	0 1 2 5 6 9
num_file_creations	0 1 2 3 4 5 6 7 8 10 11 12 14 15 17 18 20 25 26 40
num_shells	0 1 2
num_access_files	0 1 2 3 4 5 6 8
num_outbound_cmds	0
is_host_login	0 1
is_guest_login	0 1
count	[0,29] [509,511] noises
srv_count	[0,29] [509,511] noises
serror_rate	[0.0, 0.02] [0.03, 0.99] 1
srv_serror_rate	[0.0, 0.02] [0.03, 0.99] 1
rerror_rate	[0.0, 0.02] [0.03, 0.99] 1
srv_rerror_rate	0, [0.02,0.96] 1
same_srv_rate	[0.0,03] 0.04 [0.05,0.06] [0.07,0.09] [0.1,0.12] 0.13 [0.14,0.15] [0.17,0.18] 0.5 1 noises
diff_srv_rate	[0.0,0.03] [0.05,0.06] [0.07,0.09] [0.1,0.12] [0.04,0.99]

(continued)

Table 1. (*continued*)

Feature name	Category conversion & data types
srv_diff_host_rate	[0.0,0.03] [0.07,0.09] [0.1,0.12] [0.14,0.15] [0.04,0.83]
dst_host_count	[1:255]
dst_host_srv_count	[1:255]
dst_host_same_srv_rate	[0.0,0.03] 0.04 [0.05,0.06] [0.07,0.09] [0.1,0.12] [0.13,0.099] noises
dst_host_diff_srv_rate	[0.0,0.03] 0.04 [0.05,0.06] [0.07,0.09] [0.1,0.12] [0.13,0.99] noises
dst_host_same_src_port_rate	[0.0,0.03] 0.04 [0.05,0.06] [0.07,0.09] [0.1,0.12] [0.13,0.99] 1
dst_host_srv_diff_host_rate	[0.0,0.03] 0.04 [0.05,0.06] [0.07,0.09] noises
dst_host_serror_rate	[0.0,0.03] [0.07,0.09] [0.04,0.99] 1
dst_host_srv_serror_rate	[0.0,0.03] [0.04,0.98] 1
dst_host_rerror_rate	[0.0,0.03] [0.04,0.99] 1
dst_host_srv_rerror_rate	[0,0.03] [0.04,0.99] 1

4.2 Implementation Details and Model Performance

We separately test each divided part of the Wide & Deep networks to get the performance of memorization and generalization model. The wide part and deep part keep the same structure as the unit networks for a fair comparison. All of the networks are implemented via TensorFlow, which is a deep learning software framework. We set a mini-batch size 256 as data input batch size for training (mini-batch size = 128, 256, 512 are tested, mini-batch size = 256 gets the best performance). A TITAN X Pascal GPU is used to accelerate computing.

We test the three models for comparison, the wide part network, the deep part network and the Wide & Deep model on two test datasets. NSL_KDD dataset contains one train dataset and two test datasets of different difficulty level. There are new attack forms that have never been included in training dataset, which makes the test task more realistic and challenging. Test data were randomly selected from KDD'99 to form a test dataset Test$^+$. Data misclassified by 21 pretrained model forms a Test^{-21} test dataset.

As shown in Table 2, the Wide & Deep model achieves the best results among the Wide model, Deep model and Wide & Deep model in accuracy, precision and F1 score. The confusion matrix of Deep & Wide model binary test on Test$^+$ and Test^{-21} are shown in Fig. 2. To verify reliability of our results and avoid effect of random error, we take the hypothesis testing for our test. We use Gaussian distribution to initialize parameters in our model. After 10 repeated experiments, the hypothesis testing shows the P-value is 0.1102 for Test$^+$ dataset and 0.1272 for Test^{-21} dataset, which are both obviously greater than 0.05. Besides, the P-value is not too big to doubt whether the model has been overfitted. Results show that the Wide & Deep model can benefit from both the Wide part's memorization and the Deep part's generalization. The performance is limited by the difficulty of the test task. When the test dataset has more novel data the performance is starting to suffer.

Table 2. Binary classification metrics of different models

	Accuracy	Precision	Recall	F1 score
Wide model on Test$^+$	76.12%	80.42%	**75.09%**	77.66%
Deep model on Test$^+$	77.68%	81.47%	60.31%	69.31%
Wide & Deep model on Test$^+$	**82.79%**	**92.16%**	74.43%	**82.34%**
Wide model on Test^{-21}	66.74%	67.13%	**86.74%**	75.69%
Deep model on Test^{-21}	67.23%	67.77%	75.56%	71.45%
Wide & Deep on Test^{-21}	**69.17%**	**69.32%**	85.34%	**76.50%**

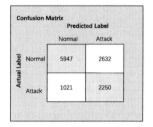

(a) NSL_KDD Test$^+$ (b) NSL_KDD Test^{-21}

Fig. 2. Confusion matrix of binary test

The NSL_KDD dataset is created by Tavallaee, in [17] the intrusion detection is treated as a binary classification problem and the dataset is tested by 7 machine learning methods which are considered the baseline of this dataset. With the study development of deep learning in intrusion detection, many deep models advance the state of the art [5,9,10,20]. There are also many other works which treat the problem as a 5-classification problem and even n-classification problem. Some work uses feature engineering to improve performance and some uses the cross-validation test with training data set, instead of test dataset (Test$^+$ or Test^{-21}), to measure the performance. One of main advantages of deep learning is no need of feature engineering. And it is a serious mistake not to use test data set in intrusion detection, for there are many novel attacks in test dataset which make the task more realistic and difficult. For a fair comparison, we list the results of different models using NSL_KDD test dataset focused on binary classification as shown in Table 3.

As shown in Table 3 and Fig. 3, compared with other models [17], in Test$^+$, our proposed method gets the better accuracy performance (82.79%) than CNN based model (GoogLeNet 77.04%) which gets the best performance in Test^{-21} and almost has the similar performance as RNN (83.28%). For the intrusion detection data, we think the data structure has important sequence information

Table 3. Accuracy comparison of different models

Model	KDD Test$^+$	KDD Test^{-21}
J48 [17]	81.05%	63.97%
Naive Bayes [17]	76.56%	55.77%
NB Tree [17]	82.02%	66.16%
Random Forest [17]	80.67%	63.26%
Random Tree [17]	81.59%	58.51%
Muti-layer Perceptron [17]	77.41%	57.34%
SVM [17]	69.52%	42.29%
RNN [20]	**83.28%**	**68.55%**
Semantic LSTM [9]	82.21%	66.10%
CNN (ResNet50) [10]	79.14%	81.57%
CNN (GoogLeNet) [10]	**77.04%**	**81.84%**
Wide & Deep	**82.79%**	**69.17%**

which causes RNN to make the best performance. Our model has the deep part which generalizes well in the relative simpler test dataset (Test$^+$ has fewer novel attacks than Test^{-21}) and take a relatively good performance. And in Test^{-21}, CNN gets the best performance due to its sensitive image memory ability but our model (69.17%) shows better performance than RNN (68.55%). We think the wide part of our model gives the model better memory ability. Our model is less deep than CNN, which have fewer parameters to train and take fewer

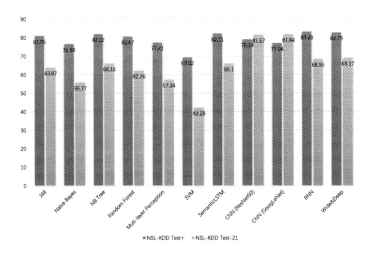

Fig. 3. Accuracy comparison of different method

time to train. In conclusion, our model is better than CNN on Test$^+$ and a little weaker than RNN. For a more difficult Test^{-21}, our model is better than RNN, but weaker than CNN. These comparisons show that our model has better outperform than machine learning baseline method, and is promising compared to other current deep learning based methods.

5   Conclusion and Future Work

We proposed a method to use Wide & Deep model for intrusion detection. To get a comprehensive categorical feature representation, a common data processing framework is proposed to convert a raw datatype into categorical representation of features. The DBSCAN clustering transformation for categorical representation is given in detail. By jointly training the both networks, the model benefits from both the memorization and generalization. A comprehensive empirical evaluation with hypothesis testing is taken on a popular NSL_KDD dataset. Results show that the revised Wide & Deep framework outperforms the separated part alone. Compared with other machine learning methods and deep learning models, the proposed model outperforms the baseline results and achieves a steady and promising performance in tests with different levels.

In the future, we consider using sequence model instead of the wide part or working as a new side input to get the temporal sequence information. Furthermore, more special attack form dataset is also an option.

References

1. Cheng, H.T., et al.: Wide & deep learning for recommender systems. In: Proceedings of the 1st Workshop on Deep Learning for Recommender Systems, pp. 7–10. ACM (2016). https://doi.org/10.1145/2988450.2988454
2. Denning, D.E.: An intrusion-detection model. IEEE Trans. Software Eng. **2**, 222–232 (1987). https://doi.org/10.1109/TSE.1987.232894
3. Gao, N., Gao, L., Gao, Q., Wang, H.: An intrusion detection model based on deep belief networks. In: 2014 Second International Conference on Advanced Cloud and Big Data, pp. 247–252. IEEE (2014). https://doi.org/10.1109/cbd.2014.41
4. Hwang, K., Cai, M., Chen, Y., Qin, M.: Hybrid intrusion detection with weighted signature generation over anomalous internet episodes. IEEE Trans. Dependable Secure Comput. **4**(1), 41–55 (2007). https://doi.org/10.1109/TDSC.2007.9
5. Ieracitano, C., et al.: Statistical analysis driven optimized deep learning system for intrusion detection. In: Ren, J., et al. (eds.) BICS 2018. LNCS (LNAI), vol. 10989, pp. 759–769. Springer, Cham (2018). https://doi.org/10.1007/978-3-030-00563-4_74
6. Javaid, A., Niyaz, Q., Sun, W., Alam, M.: A deep learning approach for network intrusion detection system. In: Proceedings of the 9th EAI International Conference on Bio-inspired Information and Communications Technologies (formerly BIONETICS), pp. 21–26. ICST (Institute for Computer Sciences, Social-Informatics and ... (2016). https://doi.org/10.4108/eai.3-12-2015.2262516

7. Kim, G., Lee, S., Kim, S.: A novel hybrid intrusion detection method integrating anomaly detection with misuse detection. Expert Syst. Appl. **41**(4), 1690–1700 (2014). https://doi.org/10.1016/j.eswa.2013.08.066

8. Kuang, F., Xu, W., Zhang, S.: A novel hybrid KPCA and SVM with GA model for intrusion detection. Appl. Soft Comput. **18**, 178–184 (2014). https://doi.org/10.1016/j.asoc.2014.01.028

9. Li, Z., Qin, Z.: A semantic parsing based LSTM model for intrusion detection. In: Cheng, L., Leung, A.C.S., Ozawa, S. (eds.) ICONIP 2018. LNCS, vol. 11304, pp. 600–609. Springer, Cham (2018). https://doi.org/10.1007/978-3-030-04212-7_53

10. Li, Z., Qin, Z., Huang, K., Yang, X., Ye, S.: Intrusion detection using convolutional neural networks for representation learning. In: Liu, D., Xie, S., Li, Y., Zhao, D., El-Alfy, E.-S.M. (eds.) ICONIP 2017. LNCS, vol. 10638, pp. 858–866. Springer, Cham (2017). https://doi.org/10.1007/978-3-319-70139-4_87

11. Liao, B., et al.: Deep sequence learning with auxiliary information for traffic prediction. In: Proceedings of the 24th ACM SIGKDD International Conference on Knowledge Discovery & Data Mining, pp. 537–546. ACM (2018). https://doi.org/10.1145/3219819.3219895

12. Opresnik, D., Fiasché, M., Taisch, M., Hirsch, M.: An evolving fuzzy inference system for extraction of rule set for planning a product-service strategy. Inf. Technol. Manag. **18**(2), 131–147 (2017). https://doi.org/10.1007/s10799-015-0242-4

13. Roesch, M., et al.: Snort: lightweight intrusion detection for networks. In: Lisa, 99, pp. 229–238 (1999)

14. Salama, M.A., Eid, H.F., Ramadan, R.A., Darwish, A., Hassanien, A.E.: Hybrid intelligent intrusion detection scheme. In: Gaspar-Cunha, A., Takahashi, R., Schaefer, G., Costa, L. (eds.) Soft Computing in Industrial Applications, pp. 293–303. Springer, Heidelberg (2011). https://doi.org/10.1007/978-3-642-20505-7-26

15. Shone, N., Ngoc, T.N., Phai, V.D., Shi, Q.: A deep learning approach to network intrusion detection. IEEE Trans. Emerg. Top. Comput. Intell. **2**(1), 41–50 (2018). https://doi.org/10.1109/TETCI.2017.2772792

16. Tang, T.A., Mhamdi, L., McLernon, D., Zaidi, S.A.R., Ghogho, M.: Deep learning approach for network intrusion detection in software defined networking. In: 2016 International Conference on Wireless Networks and Mobile Communications (WINCOM), pp. 258–263. IEEE (2016). https://doi.org/10.1109/wincom.2016.7777224

17. Tavallaee, M., Bagheri, E., Lu, W., Ghorbani, A.A.: A detailed analysis of the KDD cup 99 data set. In: 2009 IEEE Symposium on Computational Intelligence for Security and Defense Applications, pp. 1–6. IEEE (2009). https://doi.org/10.1109/cisda.2009.5356528

18. Vinayakumar, R., Soman, K., Poornachandran, P.: Applying convolutional neural network for network intrusion detection. In: 2017 International Conference on Advances in Computing, Communications and Informatics (ICACCI). pp. 1222–1228. IEEE (2017). https://doi.org/10.1109/icacci.2017.8126009

19. Wang, R., Fu, B., Fu, G., Wang, M.: Deep & cross network for ad click predictions. In: Proceedings of the ADKDD 2017, p. 12. ACM (2017). https://doi.org/10.1145/3124749.3124754

20. Yin, C., Zhu, Y., Fei, J., He, X.: A deep learning approach for intrusion detection using recurrent neural networks. IEEE Access **5**, 21954–21961 (2017). https://doi.org/10.1109/access.2017.2762418

21. Zhang, J., Zulkernine, M.: A hybrid network intrusion detection technique using random forests. In: First International Conference on Availability, Reliability and Security. ARES 2006, p. 8-pp. IEEE (2006). https://doi.org/10.1109/ARES. 2006.7
22. Zhang, R., Li, W., Tan, W., Mo, T.: Deep and shallow model for insurance churn prediction service. In: 2017 IEEE International Conference on Services Computing (SCC), pp. 346–353. IEEE (2017). https://doi.org/10.1109/scc.2017.51

Towards Attention Based Vulnerability Discovery Using Source Code Representation

Junae Kim$^{(\boxtimes)}$ ⬵, David Hubczenko, and Paul Montague

Defence Science and Technology, Edinburgh, Australia
{junae.kim,david.hubczenko,paul.montague}@dst.defence.gov.au

Abstract. Vulnerability discovery in software is an important task in the field of computer security. As vulnerabilities can be abused to enable cyber criminals and other malicious actors to exploit systems, it is crucial to keep software as free from vulnerabilities as is possible. Traditional approaches often comprise code scanning tasks to find specific and already-known classes of cyber vulnerabilities. However these approaches do not in general discover new classes of vulnerabilities. In this paper, we leverage a machine learning approach to model source code representation using syntax, semantics and control flow of source code and to infer vulnerable code patterns to tackle large code bases and identify potential vulnerabilities that missed by any existing static software analysis tools. In addition, our attention-based bidirectional long short-term memory framework adaptively localise regions of code illustrating where the possible vulnerable code fragment exists. The highlighted region may provide informative guidance to human developers or security experts. The experimental results demonstrate the feasibility of the proposed approach in the problem of software vulnerability discovery.

Keywords: Vulnerability discovery · Software analysis · Deep learning

1 Introduction

Vulnerability discovery is the problem of finding defects or bugs in applications which may enable cyber attackers to exploit the systems. The number of reported cyber security incidents has increased rapidly and the types of software vulnerabilities have expanded [24,34]. The cyber domain cannot be reliably and effectively defended solely by the limited number of security experts. Traditional approaches for discovering vulnerabilities, such as symbolic execution [2,5,14,19], are often code scanning tasks for discovery of specific and already-reported cases of cyber vulnerabilities which do not cover potential vulnerabilities or zero-day problems. Approaches such as fuzzing [11,32] are, on the other hand, agnostic to the class of vulnerability, though such techniques have drawbacks and are limited in the types of vulnerabilities which can be found.

© Crown 2019
I. V. Tetko et al. (Eds.): ICANN 2019, LNCS 11730, pp. 731–746, 2019.
https://doi.org/10.1007/978-3-030-30490-4_58

Machine learning approaches are capable of analysing code patterns of similar vulnerabilities which can lead to identification of potential vulnerabilities. In this work, we leverage a machine learning approach to model syntax, semantics and control flow of source code and infer vulnerable code patterns to tackle large code bases, then eventually identify potential vulnerable patterns.

The vulnerability discovery task generally consists of two parts: source code representation in embedding space and a machine learning approach to classify vulnerable source code. Most machine learning approaches can detect numerical features while program code is of course character-based tokenised strings. To bridge this gap, we have to learn numerical representations to best describe the features in software.

Hindle et al. [9] show that programming languages have repetitive and predictable statistical properties, which allow them to be captured in statistical language models. Thus, in software analysis, the source code including comments as well as meta-comments in commit history has been analysed using natural language processing (NLP) techniques such as Bag-of-words [25,30], N-grams [28,33] and so on. But these approaches are not able to catch informative relation between code tokens to represent proper numerical vectors representing the programming language.

Over the past year, deep learning has achieved huge success in various domains and much work with deep learning models has involved learning word vector representations [13,20,27]. These machine learning techniques such as Word2Vec [20] or Glo2Vec [27] have been used for generating numerical features for measuring similarity and identifying/classifying features extracted from text. However the successful deployment of those approaches is limited to the natural language domain. Programming languages differs from natural languages, for example, programming languages have syntactic structures and complicated flow paths to be traversed through a program while natural languages flow in one direction with a flatter structure.

In this paper, we test the hypothesis that better representations can be obtained by incorporating knowledge of semantics/syntax and control flow from abstract syntax trees (ASTs) and control flow graphs (CFGs) respectively. We leverage a machine learning approach to model source code representation using ASTs and CFGs. The representation feeds into deep learning frameworks in order to predict the label in vulnerability discovery.

Deep learning approaches have shown remarkable results in many applications such as machine translation, speech recognition, hand written letter recognition, image captioning, visual question answering and so on [3,8,18,22,35]. However there haven't been much work in applying deep learning methods in software vulnerability discovery. We design a deep learning framework using attention-based bidirectional long short-term memory (Bi-LSTM) for source code vulnerability discovery to infer vulnerable code patterns to tackle large code bases and identify potential vulnerabilities that missed by any existing static analysis tools. The adaptively localised regions of code highlighted by attention illustrate where the possible vulnerable code fragment exists, which may provide informative guidance to human developers or security experts.

Our objective is to make this work applicable in vulnerability discovery problems where there are challenges particularly (i) the length of source code functions can be very long, (ii) the syntactic structure of the functions can be complicated and (iii) important information relevant to the vulnerability can appear at any position in the source code "sentence". We evaluate our model on publicly available code projects, where it learns vulnerable patterns without explicit information of where the vulnerability exists.

The main contributions of this paper can be summarised as follows:

- Our software program representation maps function source code to numerical feature vectors, such that vulnerabilities in not only semantics/syntax, but also control flow information of source code are capable of being detected.
- We utilise an attention-based Bi-LSTM framework in vulnerability discovery problems that is able to adaptively select regions of code in long sequenced function input where vulnerabilities possibly exist.
- Our approach is capable of discovering vulnerabilities on datasets with not only existing vulnerable patterns but also potential vulnerable patterns appearing in the test dataset.

2   Related Work

Software analysis has been studied by the machine learning community to discover flaws, bugs or vulnerabilities. Raychev et al. [28] introduce a probabilistic approach to fill holes in synthesized programs. They predict names of identifiers and type annotations of variables learned from existing data. Wang et al. [33] detect a software bug based on n-gram language models. Yamaguchi et al. [36] propose an automatic pattern searching system to detect taint-style vulnerabilities in software source code. They define the anomaly score for a function based on the information from similar functions. The similarity is calculated using embeddings of functions from a bag-of-words model.

These works focus mostly on one-dimensional sequential feature representations of language such as n-grams and bag-of-words. While these models are well suited to capture semantics of languages, they are designed for natural language processing and thus cannot model other characteristics that become apparent in programming languages. In addition, those works do not adapt deep learning approaches which have the advantage of an ability to classify highly complicated features. Software can have long implementations which leads to an issue of long-range dependencies on complicated features.

Russell et al. [29] propose deep learning based program representation to detect vulnerabilities in source code. However they process source code sequences the same as natural language sequences and ignore the characteristics of programming languages such as control flows or the abstract syntactic structure. Peng et al. introduce a program representation based on ASTs extracted from source code [26]. As following work, Mou et al. [23] propose a tree structure-based convolutional neural network (TBCNN) using tree structural information of the source code. ASTs capture characteristics of programming languages but these works [23,26] extract ASTs' structural information only and ignore the semantics of programs. Semantics of program codes are able to play an important role in vulnerability discovery. Caliskan-Islam et al. [6] proposed a method to reveal the developers who implemented the program by analysing coding style found in source code. The approach generates features from ASTs but they use a traditional machine learning approach – random forest, not deep learning approaches. Hu et al. [12] propose a code summary model adopting an attention-based Seq2Seq model. They generate sequential embeddings using ASTs and a structure-based tree traversal method. However the problem is different from vulnerability discovery. Allamanis et al. [1] build program representations by applying Gated Graph Neural Networks [15] to ASTs and data flow edges of source code. The paper describes an application of ML to predict a specific vulnerability type related to a correct variable usage in code, but not general vulnerabilities.

The most relevant works are [16,17] which adopt a bi-directional Long-Short Term Memory (LSTM) framework for vulnerable function discovery. Those works predict vulnerabilities of source code given the representation generated from ASTs. However they do not cover control flow information of programming languages which is able to play an important role in analysing source code. In addition, they are not able to find where the possible vulnerabilities exist in functions. It is hard to verify the results since functions in source code can have a very large number of code lines.

In this paper, we formulate the vulnerability discovery task as a combination of (i) a program vector representation task that embeds source code into a numerical feature space and (ii) a classification problem that classifies vulnerable functions based on an attention network in a supervised fashion. We firstly propose source code representations obtained from ASTs and CFGs to capture knowledge of the semantics/syntax and control flow respectively. We also adopt an attention-based LSTM model that is capable of extracting information from a sequence of source code by adaptively selecting regions of code. The presented model is able to discover/localise vulnerabilities of code in various length functions including long-sequenced ones.

3   Vulnerability Discovery by Bi-LSTM with Attention

The problem of vulnerability discovery can be formulated as an optimisation problem over $P(y_i|X_i)$, where $X_i = \{x_{ij}\}, j = 1, \ldots, n$ are the nodes/edges from the AST or CFG of the i-th function[1] and y_i is the vulnerability label of the function.

3.1   Program Vector Representation

In this section, we first design a module to build up representations for each function based on ASTs and CFGs to encode the X_i of the i-th function into

---

[1] We do not distinguish a node in the AST and an edge in the CFG in the notation because we process them in the same way.

$V_i = \{v_{ij}\}, j = 1, \ldots, n$, where v_{ij} is the result of applying our embedding to X_{ij}. Here $v_{ij} \in \mathbb{R}^d$ is a 1-D vector standing for a representation in d-dimensional space corresponding to a node of the AST or an edge of the CFG from the i-th function. The whole AST/CFG is represented by V_i. V_i is thus represented as a 2-D matrix $V_i \in \mathbb{R}^{d \times n}$ and used as features for vulnerability discovery tasks.

In order to keep the link between a program vector representation V_i and the source code of the i-th function, we allocate a unique id i to each function. This allows us to interpret the prediction result and analyse software to find vulnerable code lines in functions.

ASTs and CFGs in Source Code. We employ a vulnerability discovery system based on source code written in C^2. Text-based source code is based on sequences of characters similar to natural language. We use Word2Vec [20] in order to generate $v_{ij} \in V_i$. Word2Vec is one of the most popular embedding models in Natural Language Processing (NLP). The dictionary of function embeddings used here is trained by Word2Vec with the Continuous Bag-of-Words (CBOW) model. The CBOW model is able to apply over the whole function code similar to text in NLP, but natural language and programming languages are compositional in very different ways.

Source code implemented in a specific programming language can be regarded as a structured document. Even though two functions in source code consist of the same words, it is possible to have different semantics due to different structures. For example FUNCTION1 in Fig. 1(a) works differently to FUNCTION2 in Fig. 1(b) even though they consist of the same text and the same parameter value n. ASTs represent the abstract syntactic structure of source code and are able to capture the difference in the semantics of FUNCTION1 and FUNCTION2. Thus ASTs are capable of being used for analysis of syntax as well as semantics. Figures 2 and 3 show the ASTs of FUNCTION1 and FUNCTION2 respectively with the differences highlighted.

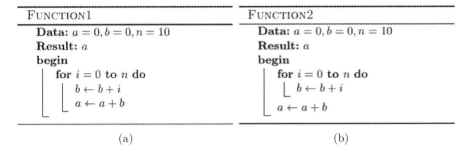

Fig. 1. (a) Function1 and (b) Function2

---

[2] C was chosen because of its ubiquity and the abundance of datasets. We believe that our technique would be applicable to other programming languages.

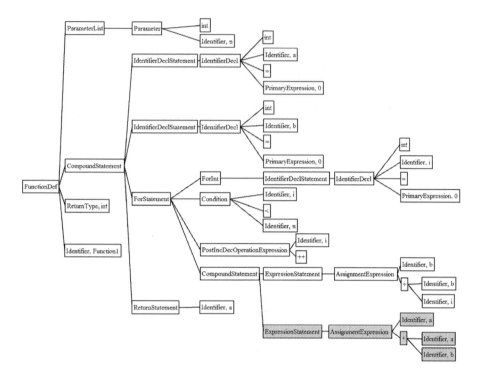

Fig. 2. AST of FUNCTION1

In addition, the flow of source code in programming language differs from the flow of text in natural language. A text document in natural language is supposed to be read in one direction, i.e. one word is processed followed by the next word to analyse the semantics. The source code in a programming language has a work-flow which has steps of processing. The order of those steps does not go solely in one direction, but can have multiple possible directions such as conditional branches, loops, function calls, multiple classes and/or files and so on. It is often required to follow the flow of source code in programming language to understand, analyse, design or manage the program. We hypothesize that vulnerabilities are able to be detected with the semantics and/or control flow of programs.

To represent syntax, semantics and control flow of source code written in a programming language, we (i) build up ASTs of program source code at the function level to represent the syntax and semantics of the code, where each node indicates source code information such as type of code token, keywords, operators, etc., and (ii) construct CFGs where edges represent possible control flows from one node to another node of the function code.

Machine learning approaches generally classify data samples based on similarity of features. Since software is built by human developers, there are unique, project-specific styles in source codes. This sometimes prevent machine learning

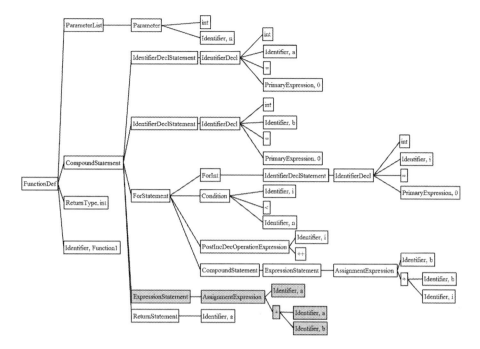

Fig. 3. AST of FUNCTION2

approaches from learning patterns of vulnerabilities properly. To build our program representations meaningfully, we remove words in code which are related to the ways a piece of code can be written by individual developers, e.g. variable names, function declaration names, values of variables and so on. In our case, we do not use the value of 'Identifier' and 'PrimaryExpression' in ASTs or CFGs. Comments are not included either. This preprocessing helps the machine learning system use features in high frequency and results in decreasing the size of the vocabulary and increasing training efficiency.

Both ASTs and CFGs form tree structures. To feed data into machine learning approaches, we serialise ASTs and CFGs by Depth First Traversal (DFT). When DFT is applied in ASTs, it is possible that the traversed output misses some information, for example, the difference between the serialised ASTs of FUNCTION1 and FUNCTION2. In this case, CFGs are capable of grasping the difference as shown in Fig. 4. Since edges of CFGs represent the control flow, we map a CFG into a 1D vector using edge information between two nodes.

To combine ASTs and CFGs, we construct an ensemble learning framework with ASTs and CFGs which receives pairwise probabilities of vulnerability $(P(y_i^{AST}|X_i), P(y_i^{CFG}|X_i))$ for the i-th function and returns an ensemble score defined by $P(y_i|X_i) = f(P(y_i^{AST}|X_i), P(y_i^{CFG}|X_i))$. y_i^{AST} and y_i^{CFG} are y_i from ASTs and CFGs respectively. In our experiment, computing its probability $f(P(y_i^{AST}|X_i), P(y_i^{CFG}|X_i))$ involves simple summation.

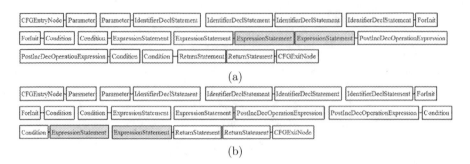

Fig. 4. Serialised CFGs of (a) FUNCTION1 and (b) FUNCTION2 by DFT

3.2 Attention Based Bi-directional LSTM

A function written in a programming language may be coded in very large number of lines which results in a large AST and a long CFG. That is, our deep learning framework using function representation can have long-range sequenced input V_i. Recurrent Neural Networks (RNNs) are deep learning approaches for sequence data, processing sequential data one element at a time. One of RNN's strengths is its ability to model sequential dependencies. This "temporal" information from source code is useful to perform the semantic information extraction. However, RNNs are known to have problems dealing with long range dependencies which exist in our case. In theory, Long Short Term Memory (LSTM) [10] should be able to deal with the issue, but it is still problematic in practice [4]. In addition, LSTM processes sequences in forward temporal order only and ignores the context which is obtained from backward temporal order.

To overcome this limitation, we apply a Bi-directional LSTM (Bi-LSTM) to process the sequence V_i. Bi-LSTM extends LSTM by introducing an additional layer, where the hidden to hidden connections flow in backward temporal order. Thus Bi-LSTM is able to better capture feature semantics which are obtained by access to right context as well as left context in bi-directional temporal information from source code. In consequence, Bi-LSTM has more capability of long-term memorizing, e.g., the first part v_{i1} of a long input vector V_i can be preserved via the backward LSTM while the forward LSTM might lose some degree of information about v_{i1}. The hidden states h_t where $t = 1, \ldots, m$ are created both from the forward LSTM $\overleftarrow{h_t}$ and from the backward LSTM $\overrightarrow{h_t}$ as $h_t = [\overleftarrow{h_t}; \overrightarrow{h_t}]$.

Another way to address the limitation is an attention model which is able to selectively focus on important semantic/syntax information from long sequence input features. Not all features contribute equally to the representation of the function in vulnerability discovery. Hence we utilise an attention mechanism to extract such features that are important to the degree of vulnerability of the function and aggregate the representation of those informative features to form a vector sequence. To reward vectors that are clues to correctly classifying a function, we use the soft attention mechanism [7, 35].

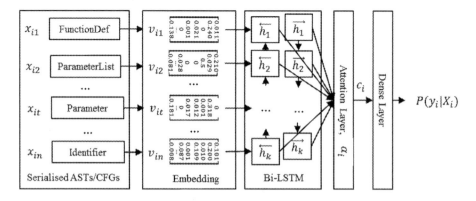

Fig. 5. The proposed deep learning framework for vulnerability discovery.

Figure 5 illustrates our attention mechanism with Bi-LSTM. The attention mechanism takes the whole Bi-LSTM hidden states h_t as input, and outputs a vector of weights α as $\alpha_{it} = \text{softmax}(e_{it})$ where $e_{it} = g(h_t)$. The function g is a linear transformation that takes different forms depending on simple neural networks with multiple dense layers. We use one dense layer in our experiments. $\alpha_{it} \in \mathcal{R}$ measures the importance of the features and is used to compute the context vector $c_i = \sum_t \alpha_{it} h_t$. The context vector c_i provides a summary of the input sequences and is used for predicting the output y_i. The output score $P(y_i|X_i)$ is a weighted sum of the hidden states of a final dense layer.

3.3 Discovery of Potential Vulnerable Patterns

To discover potential patterns for vulnerabilities in source code, we exploit the '1-vs-Rest Layer' [31] to adopt the concept of open-class classification where the set of labels is not defined during training. The '1-vs-Rest Layer' allows the model to refuse to classify samples of which patterns have not appeared in training. It tightens the decision boundaries of sigmoid functions with Gaussian fitting in the final layer and rejects the sample if it does not fit inside of the tightened decision boundary. In our experiments, we set two initial classes $y_i = \{0, 1\}$ where 0 indicates a secure class and 1 is a vulnerable function class. When a new sample X_i is rejected at each decision boundary $y_i = 0$ and $y_i = 1$ in the 1-vs-Rest Layer, it is classified as a potential 'new' class sample.

4 Experiments

In this section, we test the Bi-LSTM with attention model on vulnerability discovery tasks.

Experiments are conducted on three datasets, FFmpeg, LibPNG and LibTiff from [17][3]. They collected functions from open-source projects and acquired the

---

[3] The datasets are publicly available on Github, https://github.com/DanielLin1986/
TransferRepresentationLearning.

vulnerability data from the National Vulnerability Database (NVD) and the Common Vulnerability and Exposures (CVE).

We randomly select 70% for training and 30% for testing. 10% of training is for validation. The C/C++ parser 'Joern' is employed, which is able to produce ASTs and CFGs for full code or just code fragments. Summary statistics of the datasets are in Table 1.

Table 1. Datasets used in the experiments

	N_{trn}		N_{tst}	
	Secure	Vulnerable	Secure	Vulnerable
FFMpeg	3,681	127	1,990	61
LibPNG	374	28	202	15
LibTiff	474	57	252	35

The library of word embeddings used here is Gensim which is a NLP tool for vector space modelling and topic modelling from text. The dimensionality of the embedding vector $v_{ij} \in \mathbb{R}^d$ is $d = 128$. The Bi-LSTM with attention is implemented by Keras with a TensorFlow backend.

We generally feed data into the neural networks in small batches. However, we truncate the embedding vector V_i to handle memory allocation issues. To avoid consequent performance degradation, the truncation length is tailored to cover 99% of the data features.

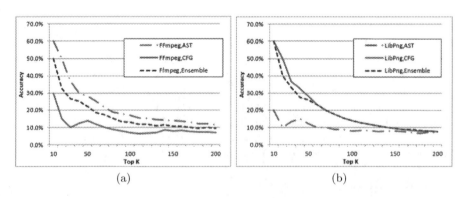

(a)　　　　　　　　　　　　　　　　(b)

Fig. 6. Comparison of the performance between representations using ASTs, CFGs and an ensemble of ASTs and CFGS on (a) FFmpeg and (b) LibPNG

We induce a linear ordering of $P(y_i|X_i)$ and count the number of vulnerable functions. For example, the accuracy becomes 50% when there exist 5 vulnerable functions in the top 10 scored functions. The x axis thus shows the top k values

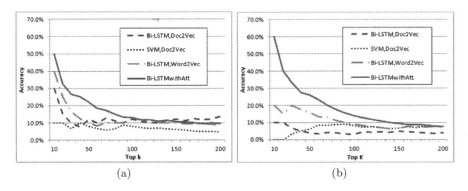

Fig. 7. Comparison of the performance between our Bi-LSTM using Doc2Vec, SVM using Doc2Vec, Bi-LSTM using Word2Vec and our Bi-LSTMwithAtt on (a) FFmpeg and (b) LibPNG

in Figs. 6, 7 and 8. The y axis presents the classification accuracy based on the top k values of the scoring function $P(y|X)$.

These experiments demonstrate the effectiveness of program representations using ASTs, CFGs and an ensemble of them. As shown in Fig. 6, the vulnerable function patterns are able to be largely characterised by ASTs in some cases like FFmpeg rather than CFGs, while it is possible that the vulnerability patterns are hidden in CFG representations rather than ASTs in other cases like LibPNG. Even though the ensemble does not boost the performance, it is a reasonable compromise as it discovers vulnerabilities existing in either ASTs or CFGs.

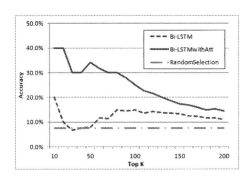

Fig. 8. Comparison between our Bi-LSTMwithAtt, Bi-LSTM and random selection on FFmpeg+LibPNG for training and LibTiff for testing

Also, we compare our Bi-LSTM with attention model 'Bi-LSTMwithAtt' with Bi-LSTM without attention 'Bi-LSTM' to analyse the efficacy of attention. In addition, we compare the performance with a traditional machine learning technique, Support Vector Machines (SVMs). Since Word2Vec generates 2-D embedding data V_i, we made a 1-D vector input using Doc2Vec, PV-DM [21] for SVMs. Doc2Vec produces a fixed-length numeric representation from a variable-length document by using the Word2Vec model and adding another vector, paragraph ID. Bi-LSTM with Doc2Vec 'Bi-LSTM,Doc2Vec' is also evaluated in order

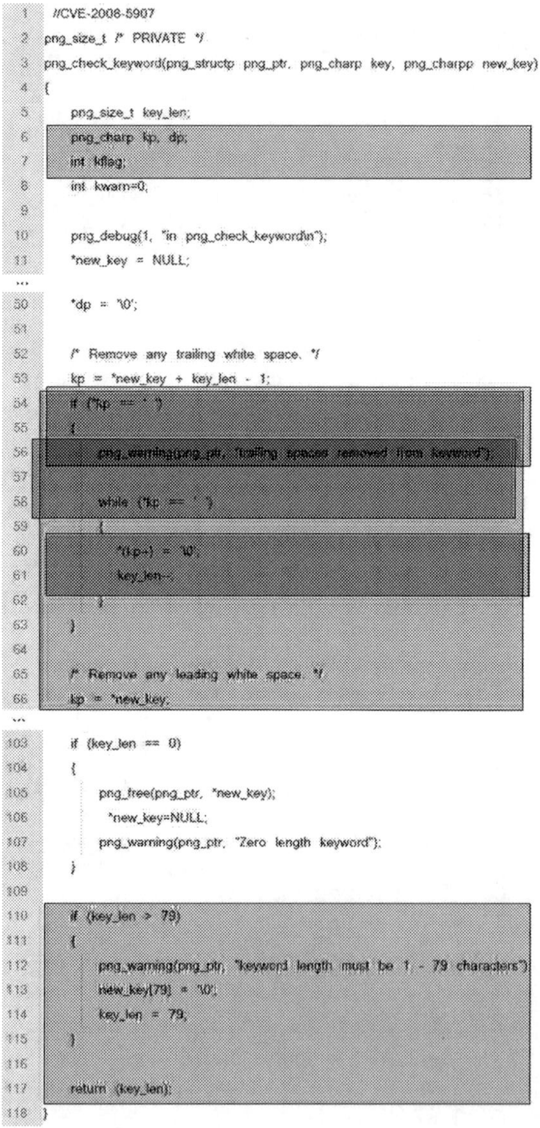

Fig. 9. Adaptively selecting regions of code by the attention model, using the CFG from CVE-2008-5907, LibPNG. The rectangular areas indicate code fragments which have high attention weights.

to compare the embedding performance. We exclude the case of Bi-LSTM with attention using the representation from Doc2Vec since it is hard to inverse-match from the results to code using attention in that case.

Figure 7 compares the accuracy of our Bi-LSTMwithAtt with Bi-LSTM and SVM over the top $k = 10, 20, \ldots, 200$ scored samples. It shows that our Bi-LSTM with attention ourperforms than classical Bi-LSTM and traditional SVMs. In addition the representation with Word2Vec is better than the representation with Doc2Vec.

We evaluate our framework for the scenario of discovery of potential vulnerabilities by combining FFmpeg and LibPNG for training and LibTiff for testing. When we apply the '1-vs-Rest Layer' to reject unseen class samples in this experimental case, it rejects 226 samples out of 474 test samples in LibTiff. That is, since LibTiff is collected from a different project from FFmpeg and LibPNG, LibTiff has distinguishable patterns in both secure and vulnerable classes compared to FFmpeg and LibPNG. Thus it is hard to discover the data patterns in LibTiff using the data information from FFmpeg and LibPNG. However our Bi-LSTMwithAtt without 1-vs-Rest Layer is able to classify some potential vulnerable patterns even though they differ from existing vulnerable patterns as shown in Fig. 8.

The attention model is validated by localising the possible vulnerable code region in Fig. 9. The rectangular regions indicate the code fragments to which the model roughly attends. The attention has high weights in edges of the control flows from lines 6 to 7, 54 to 56, 54 to 66, 56 to 58, 60 to 61 and 110 to 117 in CVE-2008-5907, LibPNG. We draw squares since a flow in CFG does not match to single line of code. It has been reported that there is a vulnerability at $new\_key[79] = '\backslash0';$ in line 113[4].

5 Conclusion and Future Work

In this work, we have presented a machine learning-based representation and framework for discovering vulnerabilities in software source code which exist in significantly long or complicated functions. We demonstrate the advantages of our program representations obtained by incorporating knowledge of semantics/syntax and control flow. We also show the feasibility of our attention based Bi-LSTM framework in software vulnerability discovery by comparing the classic LSTM-based model and support vector machines, although its evaluation is still at an early stage. The possible vulnerable code fragments are localised by attention, which may provide informative guidance to human developers or security experts. Security applications including static analysis tools generally suffer from the issue of high false positive rates. By guiding human auditors or tools to focus on particular code fragments, our approach is capable of empowering existing static analysis tools to have the better capability of discovering vulnerabilities with lower false positive rates.

---

[4] The description of the vulnerability can be found at https://cve.mitre.org/cgi-bin/cvename.cgi?name=CVE-2008-5907.

Future work will collect more open source code to improve the quality of source code representation in the embedding space. We will also explore more explicit features of hyper-parameters in our framework to enhance its performance, and further test the effectiveness of it on collected source code.

References

1. Allamanis, M., Brockschmidt, M., Khademi, M.: Learning to represent programs with graphs. In: International Conference on Learning Representations (2018)
2. Avancini, A., Ceccato, M.: Comparison and integration of genetic algorithms and dynamic symbolic execution for security testing of cross-site scripting vulnerabilities. Inf. Softw. Technol. **55**(12), 2209–2222 (2013)
3. Ba, J., Mnih, V., Kavukcuoglu, K.: Multiple object recognition with visual attention. arXiv preprint arXiv:1412.7755 (2014)
4. Brownlee, J.: How to handle very long sequences with long short-term memory recurrent neural networks. Machine Learning Mastery, June 2017, https://machinelearningmastery.com/handle-long-sequences-long-short-term-memory-recurrent-neural-networks/
5. Cadar, C., Dunbar, D., Engler, D.: KLEE: unassisted and automatic generation of high-coverage tests for complex systems programs. In: Proceedings of the 8th USENIX Conference on Operating Systems Design and Implementation, pp. 209–224. USENIX Association, San Diego (2008)
6. Caliskan-Islam, A., et al.: De-anonymizing programmers via code stylometry. In: Proceedings of the 24th USENIX Conference on Security Symposium. pp. 255–270. USENIX Association, Berkeley (2015)
7. Gregor, K., Danihelka, I., Graves, A., Rezende, D.J., Wierstra, D.: Draw: a recurrent neural network for image generation. arXiv preprint arXiv:1502.04623 (2015)
8. Hermann, K.M., et al.: Teaching machines to read and comprehend. In: Advances in Neural Information Processing Systems, pp. 1693–1701 (2015)
9. Hindle, A., Barr, E.T., Su, Z., Gabel, M., Devanbu, P.: On the naturalness of software. In: Proceedings of the 34th International Conference on Software Engineering, pp. 837–847. IEEE, Zurich, June 2012
10. Hochreiter, S., Schmidhuber, J.: Long short-term memory. Neural Comput. **9**(8), 1735–1780 (1997)
11. Höschele, M., Zeller, A.: Mining input grammars from dynamic taints. In: Proceedings of the 31st IEEE/ACM International Conference on Automated Software Engineering, pp. 720–725. ACM, Singapore (2016)
12. Hu, X., Wei, Y., Li, G., Jin, Z.: CodeSum: translate program language to natural language. arXiv preprint arXiv:1708.01837 (2017)
13. Le, Q., Mikolov, T.: Distributed representations of sentences and documents. In: International Conference on Machine Learning, pp. 1188–1196 (2014)
14. Li, Y., Su, Z., Wang, L., Li, X.: Steering symbolic execution to less traveled paths. In: Proceedings of the 2013 ACM SIGPLAN International Conference on Object Oriented Programming Systems Languages & Applications, pp. 19–32. ACM, New York (2013)
15. Li, Y., Tarlow, D., Brockschmidt, M., Zemel, R.: Gated graph sequence neural networks. In: International Conference on Learning Representations (2015)

16. Lin, G., Zhang, J., Luo, W., Pan, L., Xiang, Y.: Poster: vulnerability discovery with function representation learning from unlabeled projects. In: Proceedings of the 2017 ACM SIGSAC Conference on Computer and Communications Security, pp. 2539–2541. ACM (2017)
17. Lin, G., et al.: Cross-project transfer representation learning for vulnerable function discovery. IEEE Trans. Industr. Inf. **14**(7), 3289–3297 (2018)
18. Luong, M.T., Pham, H., Manning, C.D.: Effective approaches to attention-based neural machine translation. arXiv preprint arXiv:1508.04025 (2015)
19. Meng, Q., Wen, S., Zhang, B., Tang, C.: Automatically discover vulnerability through similar functions. In: Proceedings of the 2016 Progress in Electromagnetic Research Symposium, pp. 3657–3661. IEEE, Shanghai, August 2016
20. Mikolov, T., Chen, K., Corrado, G., Dean, J.: Efficient estimation of word representations in vector space. arXiv preprint arXiv:1301.3781 (2013)
21. Mikolov, T., Sutskever, I., Chen, K., Corrado, G.S., Dean, J.: Distributed representations of words and phrases and their compositionality. In: Advances in Neural Information Processing Systems, pp. 3111–3119 (2013)
22. Mnih, V., Heess, N., Graves, A.: Recurrent models of visual attention. In: Advances in Neural Information Processing Systems, pp. 2204–2212 (2014)
23. Mou, L., Li, G., Zhang, L., Wang, T., Jin, Z.: Convolutional neural networks over tree structures for programming language processing. In: AAAI Conference on Artificial Intelligence, pp. 1287–1293 (2016)
24. Ozkan, S.: CVEdetails.com - Security vulnerability database. Security Vulnerabilities, exploits, references and more (2018). https://www.cvedetails.com/
25. Pang, Y., Xue, X., Namin, A.S.: Predicting vulnerable software components through N-Gram analysis and statistical feature selection. In: Proceedings of the 14th IEEE International Conference on Machine Learning and Applications, pp. 543–548. IEEE, Miami, December 2015
26. Peng, H., Mou, L., Li, G., Liu, Y., Zhang, L., Jin, Z.: Building program vector representations for deep learning. In: Zhang, S., Wirsing, M., Zhang, Z. (eds.) KSEM 2015. LNCS (LNAI), vol. 9403, pp. 547–553. Springer, Cham (2015). https://doi.org/10.1007/978-3-319-25159-2_49
27. Pennington, J., Socher, R., Manning, C.D.: Glove: global vectors for word representation. In: EMNLP, vol. 14, pp. 1532–1543 (2014)
28. Raychev, V., Vechev, M., Krause, A.: Predicting program properties from "Big Code". In: Proceedings of the ACM SIGPLAN-SIGACT Symposium on Principles of Programming Languages, pp. 111–124. ACM, New York (2015)
29. Russell, R., et al.: Automated vulnerability detection in source code using deep representation learning. In: 17th IEEE International Conference on Machine Learning and Application, pp. 757–762 (2018)
30. Scandariato, R., Walden, J., Hovsepyan, A., Joosen, W.: Predicting vulnerable software components via text mining. IEEE Trans. Software Eng. **40**(10), 993–1006 (2014)
31. Shu, L., Xu, H., Liu, B.: Doc: Deep open classification of text documents. In: EMNLP, pp. 2911–2916 (2017)
32. Sutton, M., Greene, A., Amini, P.: Fuzzing: Brute Force Vulnerability Discovery. Addison-Wesley Professional, Reading (2007)
33. Wang, S., Chollak, D., Movshovitz-Attias, D., Tan, L.: Bugram: bug detection with n-gram language models. In: Proceedings of the 31st IEEE/ACM International Conference on Automated Software Engineering, pp. 708–719. ACM (2016)

34. Wilshusen, G.C.: Cybersecurity: recent data breaches illustrate need for strong controls across federal agencies. In: Technical Report, GAO-15-725T. U.S. Government Accountability Office (GAO) (2015)
35. Xu, K., et al.: Show, attend and tell: neural image caption generation with visual attention. In: International Conference on Machine Learning, pp. 2048–2057 (2015)
36. Yamaguchi, F., Wressnegger, C., Gascon, H., Rieck, K.: Chucky: exposing missing checks in source code for vulnerability discovery. In: Proceedings of the SIGSAC Conference on Computer & Communications Security, pp. 499–510. ACM (2013)

Convolutional Recurrent Neural Networks for Computer Network Analysis

Jakub Nowak⊙, Marcin Korytkowski⊙, and Rafał Scherer(✉)⊙

Computer Vision and Data Mining Lab, Institute of Computational Intelligence,
Częstochowa University of Technology, Al. Armii Krajowej 36,
42-200 Częstochowa, Poland
{jakub.nowak,marcin.korytkowski,rafal.scherer}@iisi.pcz.pl
http://iisi.pcz.pl

Abstract. The paper proposes a method of computer network user detection with recurrent neural networks. We use long short-term memory and gated recurrent unit neural networks. To present URLs from computer network sessions to the neural networks, we add convolutional input layers. Moreover, we transform requested URLs by one-hot character-level encoding. We show detailed analysis and comparison of the experiments with the aforementioned neural networks. The system was checked on real network data collected in a local municipal network. It can classify network users; hence, it can also detect anomalies and security compromises.

Keywords: Computer networks · Security · Recurrent neural networks

1 Introduction

Collecting massive data concerning computer network traffic is relatively simple nowadays. We can use such data, e.g. to profile the users or to detect intrusions. Users generate traffic that is his or her biometric signature. Analysis of such large datasets is not trivial. Usually, features have to be preprocessed to enable machine learning algorithms to handle such data. In [16], compacted data sequences from the NetFlow protocol are used by the hidden Markov model to model and recognise user-generated traffic. Wireless traffic is analysed in [7] to detect infected users using the information about the traffic such as session length, numbers of packets, the number of unique source IP addresses or ports. These features are preprocessed to reduce dimensionality and then clustered. Anomalous user behaviour can mean security breach or bot activity but can also inform of spreading rumours or diseases outbreak. In [2], recurrent neural networks and autoencoders are combined to detect rumours on microblogs by analysing users behaviour by unsupervised learning. Intrusion detection system with an ensemble of neural networks is presented in [12]. Computer networks can be analysed even to diagnose not direct phenomena such as rainfall classification in [1].

© Springer Nature Switzerland AG 2019
I. V. Tetko et al. (Eds.): ICANN 2019, LNCS 11730, pp. 747–757, 2019.
https://doi.org/10.1007/978-3-030-30490-4_59

The method proposed in this paper uses URLs generated by the users of a medium-size municipal local computer network to classify them and detect any anomalies. We do not use any data dimensionality reduction mechanisms thanks to the application of deep learning techniques, namely recurrent neural networks (RNNs) with convolutional layers.

Multilayer perceptrons (fully-connected networks) and convolutional neural networks work on information that is presented in a complete set for a given object. Thus, we must assume how much data is provided, e.g. how many URLs are fed in one sequence. If we do not have enough URLs, the input vector must be filled with, for example, empty spaces, zeros or -1's. In RNNs, a different approach to data processing is used. Recurrent neural networks such as long short-term memory (LSTM) [6,9] or gated recurrent units (GRU) are a special variant of artificial neural networks. Their basic element is a recurrent cell with an appropriate gate to remember important information (gating information). A comparison of both cell types can be found in [4]. Both GRUs and LSTMs use similar mechanisms; however, GRUs are less computationally complex and are therefore more efficient to use. Recurrent neural networks are useful tools for prediction, classification and content creation, especially when the input vector lengths are variable. LSTM networks are currently the most used tools for learning sequential data. They address the problem of vanishing gradient existing in recurrent neural networks. LSTMs can be trained with very large lag between an input event and the target data. The basic LSTM unit is a memory block with memory cell or cells and gate units. Gated recurrent unit (GRU) networks were proposed by Cho et al. [3] and turned out to yield excellent results in capturing long-term dependencies.

We checked also bidirectional LSTMs and GRUs [8,17], denoted, respectively, BiLSTM and BiGRU. In this case, we use two LSTM/GRU cells for one network, for the first one data is fed from the first to the last, and in the second cell from the last to the first. The outputs from both cells are transferred additionally to the fully connected network [10] for the final classification. A general model of bidirectional network used in the paper is presented in Fig. 2.

In the paper, recurrent networks are used for classification, therefore we are interested in the cell state only after providing all input data, colloquially this variant is called many-to-one (Figs. 1 and 2). Multiple input data (multiple URLs) are used to obtain one output (n users encoded in a one-hot vector).

RNNs require proper encoding of input data. The choice of the input text coding method is a crucial thing in NLP processing. In the case of text, one of the possible approaches is to create an n-element dictionary, and each word is fed to the network in a one-hot encoding format. The first satisfactory results were obtained by solutions based on one-hot encoding in [19]. Of course, a dictionary with more elements than exist in the training data is inefficient. Moreover, we do not know what "words" can appear in a computer network as URLs are not made entirely of natural language components. Another method that is used in natural language processing [21] is the word2vec model family for word embedding [13, 14]. In our case, the initial experiments showed that the word2vec model yielded much worse results compared to our method, as URL addresses have a specific construction. In the case of word-level dictionaries and word2vec models, the first neural network layer had a considerable size what caused substantial hardware requirements.

In the case of URL stream classification, the idea of using recurrent networks should work better than other architectures. We found out empirically that standard recurrent networks are not very friendly to the URL strings. In this article, we use recurrent networks with convolutional layers. Such neural networks obtained good results in generating image descriptions in [5], where the authors used so-called many-to-many structure. That is, words describing the image are gradually generated from many inputs. In our experiment, we classify rather than generate; thus we use many-to-one model (Figs. 1 and 2). The input data is a stream of character level-encoded one-hot vectors [20]. The one-hot vectors are processed by a three-layer convolutional neural network, marked in the figures as "Convolution". Afterwards, the signal is passed to LSTM or GRU cells. Then, the signal is transferred to the fully-connected layer to output the final result from the network.

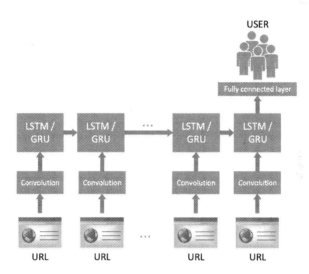

Fig. 1. LSTM and GRU many-to-one model used in the paper. The "Convolution" block is a multilayer convolutional neural network.

Through this research, we highlight the following features and contributions of the proposed model.

- We present a novel efficient way to profile users in a local network based on HTTP requests in a local computer network.
- Our work provides new insights, showing that one-hot character level encoding of URLs provides better results than word-level approaches.

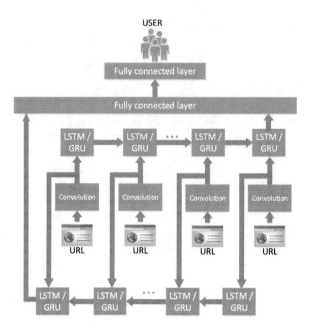

Fig. 2. BiLSTM and BiGRU many-to-one model used in the paper. The "Convolution" block is a multilayer convolutional neural network.

– We showed that recurrent neural networks are a good alternative to feedforward networks as the accuracy increases with new incoming data. We do not have to assume the length of the sequence analyzed in advance.
– The proposed system is fast and can be applied in computer network security solutions.

The remainder of the paper is organised as follows. Section 2 describes the computer network log data used in the paper. Experiments are presented in Sect. 3. The last section concludes the paper.

2   Network Data

We used data from a cluster of PaloAlto devices working in an active-active mode securing edge traffic in a large LAN network. The network is routed by the Open Shortest Path First (OSPF) algorithm with virtual routing and forwarding (VRF). The network uses four CISCO core switches, and its users are authenticated using the accounts in Active Directory services. A RADIUS service is configured for users using the wireless network. PaloAlto devices are integrated with the list of accounts contained in domain controllers, thanks to which each user's network traffic is logged using its Active Directory name. The data had the form of logs from the MS SQL database originally. We sorted the logs by usernames, by the dates when they were recorded, and by the name of the URL address. Sorting by date was meant to reflect the order of websites that were visited. We do not use exact dates. Throughout the earlier experiments, we found out the best maximal size of a single URL to be 45 characters. Thus, we truncated longer URLs as further characters were not meaningful for the user identification purposes. The session consists of 8 to 100 URLs sorted by the time the user requested them. The session was interrupted earlier if the time between requests was greater than 30 min. This time was chosen empirically; our intention was to analyse users in a short time. We assumed that if the user was inactive by 30 min, he or she started to search for something else. Our findings turned out to be coincident with e-commerce analysis findings [15].

In the case of RNNs, the input data is a sequence fed in smaller portions, which modify the state of the recurrent cells. In our case, we modify the state of the LSTM or GRU cells by providing next incoming URLs. We do not assume how long the sequence is. We only assume that the sequence (session) cannot be longer than 100 URLs not to use all the data for one training example. Hence, the RNN cells are modified by at most 100 URLs (randomly from 8 to 100).

The training data consisted of 87,903 training vectors (278 GB of data) and 21,946 test vectors (69 GB of data). Test data constitute 20% of all the network logs. The condition for dividing our data into test and training sets was the time of registering the URL. The system is supposed to work on data recorded from the past; therefore we tended not to divide the session randomly into training/test sets. The data had to be properly distributed in time to the training sessions recorded earlier and test records registered later.

3 Experiments

We used four types of recurrent neural networks: LSTM, BiLSTM, GRU and BiGRU with convolutional input layers. The input data to the networks was a 70×45-pixel image with character-level one-hot encoding, as we have 70 possible characters:
```
abcdefghijklmnopqrstuvwxvyz_0123456789
-;.!?:/\|#$%&'+=<>()[],"'|^
```
and up to 45 characters for one URL. The convolutional layer in all RNNs had two versions:
Version 1:

- Input $45 \times 70 \times 1$
- Embedding 32 ($45 \times 32 \times 1$)
- Convolution 128 feature maps, filter 1D size 5 stride 1
- Convolution 256 feature maps, filter 1D size 3 stride 1
- Convolution 512 feature maps, filter 1D size 2 stride 1
- MaxPooling 6
- $512 \times 7 = 3584$ (input to LSTM)

Version 2:

- Input $45 \times 70 \times 1$

- Embedding 32 (45 × 32 × 1)
- Convolution 64 feature maps, filter 1D size 5 stride 1
- Convolution 128 feature maps, filter 1D size 3 stride 1
- Convolution 256 feature maps, filter 1D size 2 stride 1
- MaxPooling 6
- 56 × 7 = 1792 (input to LSTM)

Table 1. Training rate (η) values used in the experiments.

η for BiGRU & GRU	η for BiLSTM & LSTM	Epochs
0.00300	0.0010	2
0.00150	0.0003	5
0.00088	0.0002	20
0.00088	0.0001	Till the end

We obtained the best results for LSTM and GRU internal size 330; thus we kept this value during the experiments. We used CNTK FsAdaGrad optimizer (https://cntk.ai/) [11, 18]. The training rate change through epochs is presented in Table 1. We kept the parameters of both LSTM and GRU networks and their training parameters as close as possible. LSTM required much smaller training rate than GRU. Cross-Entropy with Softmax was used as a loss function. Momentum has been fixed at a constant level of 0.9 throughout the training. In the case of training, we paid special attention not only to the final result but also to the time in which the network is trained. All the networks were trained by 150 epochs. CNTK every one epoch saves the network state; thus, we enlarged the epoch size randomly to 7.100 examples per epoch to save disk space and time. All the networks where two BiLSTM and BiGRU recurrent cells are used had to be trained much longer, i.e. about 283 s per epoch. In the case of LSTM and GRU with one cell, an average per epoch is 140 s (Table 2). All the experiments were performed on the nVidia 1080Ti GPU. As we can see in Table 2, GRU networks converge the fastest. More importantly, the training convergence also speaks in favour of GRU. As we can see in Figs. 3 and 4, the error on the training data decreases slower with LSTM.

Table 2. Training times per one epoch for all the neural networks with two variants of input convolutional layers.

RCNN type	Time [s/epoch]	
	Version 1	Version 2
LSTM	161	203
BiLSTM	289	352
GRU	140	191
BiGRU	279	290

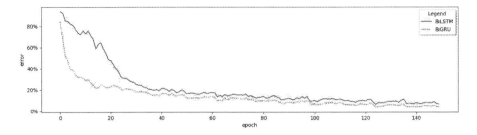

Fig. 3. BiLSTM and BiGRU training error.

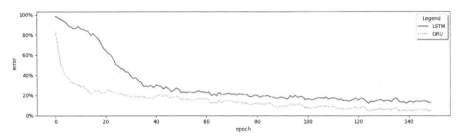

Fig. 4. LSTM and GRU training error.

Table 3. Testing error for all the neural networks with two variants of input convolutional layers. The networks were tested on future data not used during training.

Network	Error %	
	Version 1	Version 2
LSTM	28.90%	27.10%
BiLSTM	28.00%	28.20%
GRU	26.58%	26.60%
BiGRU	25.40%	26.20%

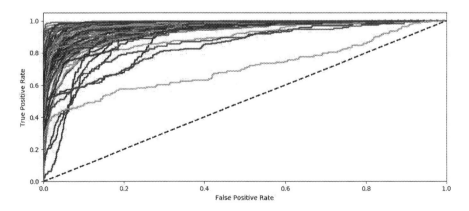

Fig. 5. ROC curves for all users for the BiGRU network (Table 3).

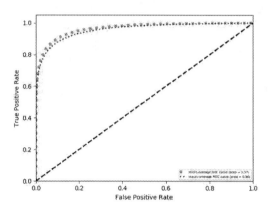

Fig. 6. Average ROC curve for all the users for the BiGRU network (Table 3).

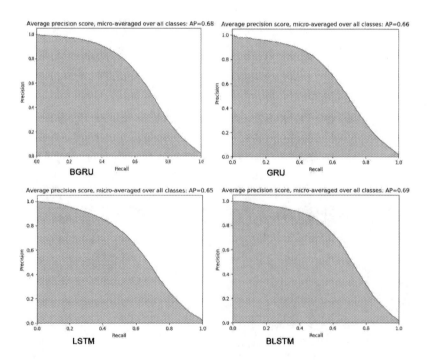

Fig. 7. Average precision-recall curves for all the users for all the four neural networks (Table 3).

Table 4. Precision and recall values for all the users for all four neural networks.

User	LSTM		GRU		BiLSTM		BiGRU		User	LSTM		GRU		BiLSTM		BiGRU	
	pr.	rec.	pr.	rec.	pr.	rec.	pr.	rec.		pr.	rec.	pr.	rec.	pr.	rec.	pr.	rec.
U1	0.83	0.86	0.88	0.71	0.87	0.83	0.85	0.83	U33	0.94	0.58	0.90	0.69	0.93	0.60	0.85	0.66
U2	0.72	0.66	0.65	0.73	0.64	0.75	0.66	0.72	U34	0.97	0.75	0.86	0.67	0.91	0.72	0.86	0.60
U3	0.86	0.73	0.83	0.78	0.80	0.79	0.82	0.76	U35	0.83	0.87	0.81	0.90	0.70	0.87	0.88	0.88
U4	0.97	0.94	0.98	0.97	0.98	0.95	0.98	0.97	U36	0.58	0.56	0.60	0.51	0.60	0.55	0.62	0.65
U5	0.50	0.67	0.59	0.63	0.56	0.55	0.59	0.65	U37	0.75	0.60	0.69	0.68	0.71	0.66	0.64	0.72
U6	0.90	0.68	0.89	0.81	0.97	0.71	0.90	0.75	U38	0.64	0.89	0.72	0.86	0.71	0.88	0.64	0.92
U7	0.70	0.85	0.82	0.81	0.61	0.90	0.74	0.86	U39	0.69	0.65	0.59	0.72	0.60	0.76	0.60	0.68
U8	0.97	0.88	0.97	0.93	0.95	0.90	0.97	0.96	U40	0.49	0.23	0.37	0.29	0.54	0.23	0.48	0.30
U9	0.94	0.92	0.86	0.91	0.94	0.94	0.94	0.89	U41	0.39	0.80	0.53	0.88	0.54	0.86	0.60	0.86
U10	0.70	0.68	0.64	0.66	0.72	0.71	0.69	0.70	U42	0.53	0.52	0.45	0.66	0.50	0.57	0.49	0.67
U11	0.36	0.51	0.40	0.52	0.40	0.51	0.37	0.50	U43	0.94	0.93	0.92	0.90	0.94	0.92	0.90	0.95
U12	0.87	0.96	0.95	0.96	0.89	0.95	0.96	0.97	U44	0.56	0.75	0.72	0.81	0.60	0.84	0.62	0.79
U13	0.66	0.67	0.65	0.72	0.76	0.50	0.69	0.61	U45	0.68	0.64	0.64	0.71	0.57	0.69	0.67	0.73
U14	0.63	0.92	0.80	0.90	0.76	0.91	0.73	0.92	U46	0.96	0.67	0.94	0.71	0.90	0.67	0.89	0.68
U15	0.89	0.93	0.93	0.91	0.97	0.85	0.95	0.90	U47	0.19	0.10	0.15	0.11	0.17	0.11	0.15	0.11
U16	0.74	0.82	0.81	0.83	0.79	0.88	0.84	0.82	U48	0.61	0.74	0.72	0.66	0.68	0.68	0.81	0.71
U17	0.56	0.54	0.56	0.67	0.66	0.55	0.54	0.57	U49	0.83	0.89	0.86	0.98	0.75	0.93	0.86	0.98
U18	0.89	0.57	0.80	0.64	0.96	0.52	0.80	0.66	U50	0.60	0.74	0.83	0.69	0.76	0.73	0.66	0.73
U19	0.80	0.68	0.83	0.69	0.83	0.69	0.83	0.66	U51	0.80	0.58	0.78	0.59	0.76	0.70	0.63	0.71
U20	0.71	0.83	0.51	0.87	0.64	0.86	0.67	0.82	U52	0.45	0.68	0.66	0.75	0.58	0.83	0.72	0.72
U21	0.84	0.62	0.82	0.61	0.79	0.66	0.73	0.62	U53	0.19	0.63	0.36	0.53	0.31	0.58	0.39	0.47
U22	0.07	0.04	0.26	0.37	0.15	0.08	0.27	0.32	U54	0.98	0.40	0.78	0.58	0.88	0.61	0.80	0.47
U23	0.82	0.81	0.79	0.90	0.89	0.87	0.84	0.89	U55	0.19	0.34	0.44	0.45	0.29	0.47	0.24	0.44
U24	0.85	0.51	0.78	0.58	0.83	0.60	0.79	0.54	U56	0.57	0.55	0.53	0.55	0.66	0.53	0.65	0.49
U25	0.85	0.54	0.61	0.80	0.75	0.71	0.73	0.77	U57	0.27	0.53	0.40	0.54	0.33	0.55	0.36	0.54
U26	0.74	0.49	0.73	0.34	0.57	0.42	0.70	0.37	U58	0.70	0.49	0.71	0.66	0.80	0.77	0.79	0.50
U27	0.60	0.81	0.80	0.77	0.64	0.80	0.71	0.78	U59	0.68	0.71	0.74	0.71	0.68	0.62	0.69	0.57
U28	0.88	0.68	0.82	0.56	0.82	0.70	0.75	0.66	U60	0.62	0.07	0.37	0.10	0.62	0.07	0.56	0.16
U29	0.76	0.91	0.81	0.93	0.82	0.94	0.80	0.93	U61	0.84	0.70	0.87	0.81	0.80	0.79	0.86	0.74
U30	0.61	0.77	0.68	0.74	0.53	0.87	0.59	0.81	U62	0.52	0.36	0.60	0.36	0.75	0.35	0.57	0.35
U31	0.95	0.44	0.84	0.51	0.93	0.53	0.91	0.53	U63	0.70	0.49	0.71	0.66	0.80	0.77	0.79	0.50
U32	0.90	0.67	0.78	0.76	0.84	0.71	0.81	0.74									

It is relatively easy to choose the training meta-parameters in the first training stages (epochs). The problem arises when the training error drops below 40%. Then, the training visibly slows down. If we try to apply faster meta-parameters, the problem arises at the end, when the training falls into a local minimum, and the final error cannot drop below 15%. The results from the best-trained networks have been collected in Table 3. These errors are computed on logs registered after those from the training data. By analyzing the ROC plot (Fig. 5) for the best BiGRU network with 25.4% error, it can be seen that only one user is poorly recognized. About four of them are detected not very accurately, but the others are recognised with satisfactory accuracy. The plot is not easily readable for such a large number of classes, and we provide the average ROC in Fig. 6. Figure 7 presents precision-recall curves averaged for all the users for all the four neural networks (Table 4).

4   Conclusion

We showed that LSTM and GRU networks with input convolutional layers are suitable for identifying network users based on URLs they requesting. The convolutional layers and one-hot encoding on the character level we applied, entirely replace the use of a dictionary or other ways of feeding text to recurrent networks. Such an approach is especially useful in the case of URLs which often do not use regular English (or any other language) words. Initially, we checked word-based and word2vec solutions with much worse results. The proposed solution can be used to make network user profiles and to detect anomalies in the traffic. Adding more parameters and statistics concerning the network traffic would further improve the reliability of the method.

Acknowledgements. The project financed under the program of the Minister of Science and Higher Education under the name "Regional Initiative of Excellence" in the years 2019–2022 project number 020/RID/2018/19, the amount of financing 12,000,000 PLN.

References

1. Beritelli, F., Capizzi, G., Lo Sciuto, G., Scaglione, F., Połap, D., Woźniak, M.: A neural network pattern recognition approach to automatic rainfall classification by using signal strength in LTE/4G networks. In: Polkowski, L., et al. (eds.) IJCRS 2017. LNCS (LNAI), vol. 10314, pp. 505–512. Springer, Cham (2017). https://doi.org/10.1007/978-3-319-60840-2_36
2. Chen, W., Zhang, Y., Yeo, C.K., Lau, C.T., Lee, B.S.: Unsupervised rumor detection based on users' behaviors using neural networks. Pattern Recogn. Lett. **105**, 226–233 (2018)
3. Cho, K., et al.: Learning phrase representations using RNN encoder-decoder for statistical machine translation. arXiv preprint arXiv:1406.1078 (2014)
4. Chung, J., Gülçehre, Ç., Cho, K., Bengio, Y.: Empirical evaluation of gated recurrent neural networks on sequence modeling. CoRR abs/1412.3555 (2014)

5. Donahue, J., et al.: Long-term recurrent convolutional networks for visual recognition and description. In: Proceedings of the IEEE Conference on Computer Vision and Pattern Recognition, pp. 2625–2634 (2015)
6. Gers, F.A., Schmidhuber, J., Cummins, F.: Learning to forget: continual prediction with LSTM. In: 1999 Ninth International Conference on Artificial Neural Networks, ICANN 1999 (Conf. Publ. No. 470), vol. 2, pp. 850–855, September 1999
7. Gratian, M., Bhansali, D., Cukier, M., Dykstra, J.: Identifying infected users via network traffic. Comput. Secur. **80**, 306–316 (2019)
8. Graves, A., Schmidhuber, J.: Framewise phoneme classification with bidirectional lstm and other neural network architectures. Neural Netw. **18**(5–6), 602–610 (2005)
9. Greff, K., Srivastava, R.K., Koutník, J., Steunebrink, B.R., Schmidhuber, J.: LSTM: a search space Odyssey. IEEE Trans. Neural Netw. Learn. Syst. **28**(10), 2222–2232 (2017)
10. Kamimura, R.: Supposed maximum mutual information for improving generalization and interpretation of multi-layered neural networks. J. Artif. Intell. Soft Comput. Res. **9**(2), 123–147 (2019)
11. Kinga, D., Adam, J.B.: A method for stochastic optimization. In: International Conference on Learning Representations (ICLR), vol. 5 (2015)
12. Ludwig, S.A.: Applying a neural network ensemble to intrusion detection. J. Artif. Intell. Soft Comput. Res. **9**(3), 177–188 (2019)
13. Mikolov, T., Chen, K., Corrado, G., Dean, J.: Efficient estimation of word representations in vector space. arXiv preprint arXiv:1301.3781 (2013)
14. Mikolov, T., Sutskever, I., Chen, K., Corrado, G.S., Dean, J.: Distributed representations of words and phrases and their compositionality. In: Advances in Neural Information Processing Systems, pp. 3111–3119 (2013)
15. Molina, L.E., Bhulai, S., Reader, V.S., de Jeu, R., Tjepkema, J.: Understanding user behavior in e-commerce with long short-term memory (LSTM) and autoencoders. Masters thesis, Vrije Universiteit Amsterdam (2018)
16. Verde, N.V., Ateniese, G., Gabrielli, E., Mancini, L.V., Spognardi, A.: No NAT'd user left behind: fingerprinting users behind NAT from NetFlow records alone. In: 2014 IEEE 34th International Conference on Distributed Computing Systems, pp. 218–227, June 2014
17. Wu, Z., King, S.: Investigating gated recurrent networks for speech synthesis. In: 2016 IEEE International Conference on Acoustics, Speech and Signal Processing (ICASSP), pp. 5140–5144, March 2016
18. Xiong, W., Wu, L., Alleva, F., Droppo, J., Huang, X., Stolcke, A.: The Microsoft 2017 conversational speech recognition system. In: 2018 IEEE International Conference on Acoustics, Speech and Signal Processing (ICASSP), pp. 5934–5938. IEEE (2018)
19. Yao, K., Zweig, G., Hwang, M.Y., Shi, Y., Yu, D.: Recurrent neural networks for language understanding. In: Interspeech, pp. 2524–2528 (2013)
20. Zhang, X., Zhao, J., LeCun, Y.: Character-level convolutional networks for text classification. In: Advances in Neural Information Processing Systems, pp. 649–657 (2015)
21. Zhou, C., Sun, C., Liu, Z., Lau, F.: A C-LSTM neural network for text classification. arXiv preprint arXiv:1511.08630 (2015)

Author Index

Printed in the United States
By Bookmasters